THE

WAR OF THE REBELLION:

A COMPILATION OF THE

OFFICIAL RECORDS

OF THE

UNION AND CONFEDERATE ARMIES.

PUBLISHED UNDER THE DIRECTION OF

The Hon. DANIEL S. LAMONT, Secretary of War,

BY

MAJ. GEORGE B. DAVIS, U. S. A.,
MR. LESLIE J. PERRY,
MR. JOSEPH W. KIRKLEY,
Board of Publication.

SERIES I—VOLUME XLV—IN TWO PARTS.
PART II—CORRESPONDENCE, ETC.

WASHINGTON:
GOVERNMENT PRINTING OFFICE.
1894.

PART II.–VOL. XLV.

CORRESPONDENCE, ORDERS, AND RETURNS RELATING TO OPERATIONS IN KENTUCKY, SOUTHWEST VIRGINIA, TENNESSEE, MISSISSIPPI, ALABAMA, AND NORTH GEORGIA, FROM DECEMBER 1, 1864, TO JANUARY 23, 1865.*

UNION CORRESPONDENCE, ETC.

NASHVILLE, *December 1, 1864—8 a. m.*
(Received 12 m.)

Lieutenant-General GRANT,
City Point:

I sent your dispatch of 11.30 a. m. yesterday† to Major-General Stoneman, at Knoxville; he telegraphs in reply that he cannot learn from any source that Breckinridge has more than 3,000 or 4,000 men. He also reports that a woman who has come through the enemy's lines says that she was told by one of Breckinridge's officers that Lee was evacuating Richmond, and that his advance was at Dublin Station or New River. I have no further news from General Schofield, but feel sure everything goes well.

GEO. H. THOMAS,
Major-General, U. S. Volunteers, Commanding.

———

NASHVILLE, TENN., *December 1, 1864—9.30 p. m.*

Maj. Gen. H. W. HALLECK,
Washington, D. C.:

After General Schofield's fight of yesterday, feeling convinced that the enemy very far outnumbered him, both in infantry and cavalry, I determined to retire to the fortifications around Nashville, until General Wilson can get his cavalry equipped. He has now but about one-fourth the number of the enemy, and consequently is no match for him. I have two iron-clads here, with several gun-boats, and Commander Fitch assures me that Hood can neither cross the Cumberland nor blockade it. I therefore think it best to wait here until Wilson can equip all his cavalry. If Hood attacks me here, he will be more seriously damaged than he was yesterday; if he remains until Wilson gets equipped, I can whip him and will move against him at once. I have Murfreesborough strongly held, and therefore feel easy in regard to its safety. Chattanooga, Bridgeport, Stevenson, and Elk River bridge also have strong garrisons.

GEO. H. THOMAS,
Major-General, U. S. Volunteers, Commanding.

---

*For Correspondence, etc., from November 14, 1864, to November 30, 1864, see Part I, p. 876, *et. seq.*
†See Part I, p. 1166.

(3)

MOUND CITY, *December 1, 1864—1 p. m.*
Major-General THOMAS:

Your dispatch of yesterday received.* I have ordered the iron-clads to return to the Cumberland River and convoy your transports up and down that river. I send also a similar order, by dispatch-boat, to Paducah. On Sunday I will have another iron-clad ready, and will send it to Smithland to operate on either river, and expect to go there myself.

S. P. LEE,
Rear-Admiral.

NASHVILLE, *December 1, 1864—9.20 p. m.*
Admiral S. P. LEE,
Mound City:

Your communication by Commander Fitch and telegram of 1 p. m. this date are received, and I am much indebted to you for having changed the destination of the iron-clads. Commander Fitch thinks if the iron-clads you expect at Smithland were stationed at Clarksville the river could then be made perfectly safe. Will you please order it to Clarksville.

GEO. H. THOMAS,
Major-General, U. S. Volunteers, Commanding.

NASHVILLE, TENN., *December 1, 1864—7 p. m.*
Major ECKERT:

Attack at Franklin last night was a severe battle, the enemy acting with all his forces, and suffering heavily in killed, wounded, and prisoners; of the latter, 1,000 have been brought in, and the former is estimated at not less than 3,000, while our entire list of casualties will not reach 1,000. After caring for our part, we fell back, leaving Franklin at 3 a. m., and now confront Hood from the fortifications of Nashville. General Steedman has arrived with part of his troops. Our cavalry, under Wilson, gave Forrest a good fight on the Hillsborough road, and came in all right. Rebel infantry appeared on our front at 4.30 p. m. Things look like work here to-morrow. No telegraphs out of Nashville, except toward the north.

J. C. VAN DUZER.

DUNCAN'S HOUSE, *Franklin Pike,* [*December 1, 1864*]—*7 p. m.*
Major-General THOMAS:

An officer who came in at 5 p. m. reports that a column of rebel cavalry followed him in to within two miles of this place; a small squad of Hatch's men, going out after dark, were fired on a mile from this and came back. The pack train with ammunition for Croxton has just arrived here; I informed the officer in charge of it of the facts, and ordered him to report to you to ascertain how he could communicate with his command. The enemy undoubtedly reached Brentwood before Wilson, and have thrown him off toward Nolensville. I have taken

---

* See Part I, p. 1167.

the precaution of strengthening the pickets by two regiments on this pike. About half a mile in front of my pickets is a squad of six soldiers guarding some provisions; they might be hauled in to-night without risk.

D. S. STANLEY,
Major-General.

HEADQUARTERS RIGHT WING, SIXTEENTH ARMY CORPS,
Nashville, Tenn., December 1, 1864.
Brig. Gen. J. McARTHUR,
Commanding First Division, Sixteenth Army Corps:

GENERAL: I am directed by the major-general commanding to say that you will have your effective force in readiness to move at ten minutes' notice.

I am, very respectfully, your obedient servant,
J. HOUGH,
Major and Assistant Adjutant-General.

HDQRS. CAVALRY CORPS, MIL. DIV. OF THE MISSISSIPPI,
Near Franklin, Tenn., December [1], 1864—2 a. m.
Maj. J. A. CAMPBELL,
Assistant Adjutant-General:

MAJOR: Stewart's brigade is just in from Nolensville, and Hammond writes from Triune (now at Wilson's Mill, on Brentwood road) no enemy in that quarter. Very clear that the rebel cavalry has not passed in this quarter; you had better look for it west. No enemy of any kind on this flank north of the Harpeth.

Very respectfully,
J. H. WILSON,
Brevet Major-General.

HEADQUARTERS ARMY OF THE OHIO,
Brentwood, December 1, 1864.
Major-General WILSON,
Commanding Cavalry:

GENERAL: I am directed by the major-general commanding to inform you that he will not make a stand here, but will push on to Nashville at once, and desires you to conform to the movement. If the enemy press heavily he wishes you to act stubbornly on the defensive.

Respectfully,
WM. M. WHERRY,
Major and Aide-de-Camp.

HEADQUARTERS CAVALRY CORPS,
Brentwood, December 1, 1864—9 a. m.
Maj. J. A. CAMPBELL,
Assistant Adjutant-General:

The general commanding directs me to inform you that there is no appearance of the enemy in our rear.

I am, very respectfully, your obedient servant,
JOHN N. ANDREWS,
Captain and Acting Assistant Adjutant-General.

HDQRS. CAVALRY CORPS, MIL. DIV. OF THE MISSISSIPPI,
In Front of Brentwood, December 1, 1864—12 m.
Major-General SCHOFIELD:

Since my last the enemy has begun skirmishing with my rear near Wilson's Mill. Your order is received; I shall obey it as follows: Hatch moves by road north of Brentwood to Thompson's Chapel; Johnson by road south of Brentwood to Winsted pike and Thompson's Chapel; Hammond to same place, moving on Johnson's right; all having out strong rear guards.

J. H. WILSON,
Brevet Major-General.

A prisoner from the rebel infantry, just brought in, says the rebels crossed Harpeth early this morning and are marching on.

J. H. W.

HDQRS. CAV. CORPS, MIL. DIV. OF THE MISSISSIPPI,
Five Miles from Nashville, on Nolensville Pike,
December 1, 1864—3.20 p. m.
Maj. Gen. G. H. THOMAS,
Commanding Department of the Cumberland:

GENERAL: I occupy a most excellent position. Colonel Wharton will explain fully my views. If you can protect my right flank by infantry we can beat Forrest's whole force. We need rations, medical officers, and all the mounted and dismounted men belonging to the regiments now with me. Send out Hatch's and Croxton's men first. No enemy in my front yet. I will picket well out and well around to the eastward.

Very respectfully, your obedient servant,
J. H. WILSON,
Brevet Major-General.

HDQRS. CAVALRY CORPS, MIL. DIV. OF THE MISSISSIPPI,
Near Brentwood, December 1, 1864.
Maj. J. A. CAMPBELL,
Assistant Adjutant-General, Army of the Ohio:

MAJOR: I am directed by General Wilson to inform you that the cavalry sent out on the Franklin pike discovered a column of infantry advancing up toward Nashville.

Very respectfully,
JOHN N. ANDREWS,
Captain and Acting Assistant Adjutant-General.

HDQRS. CAVALRY CORPS, MIL. DIV. OF THE MISSISSIPPI,
Brentwood, December 1, 1864.
Maj. E. B. BEAUMONT,
Assistant Adjutant-General:

The general commanding directs that you send the Fourth U. S. Cavalry out on the Nolensville pike, to join us at Thompson's Chapel.

Instruct them to drive all cavalrymen back out of town to the corps. Send out ammunition—Sharps, Burnside, and Spencer—immediately; have it consigned to division ordnance officer.

Very respectfully,

JOHN N. ANDREWS,
Captain and Acting Assistant Adjutant-General.

HDQRS. CAVALRY CORPS, MIL. DIV. OF THE MISSISSIPPI,
Five Miles south of Nashville, December 1, 1864.

Maj. E. B. BEAUMONT,
Assistant Adjutant-General:

See General Thomas and make arrangements to send four batteries to me in the morning. I would like McCook's battery and the two regular batteries, if they can be got ready. My position is splendid. No enemy yet in front. Had pretty sharp skirmish at Brentwood all night. I have directed all the roads from the Franklin pike to the Lebanon to be picketed. Show this to General Thomas.

Respectfully,

J. H. WILSON,
Brevet Major-General.

HDQRS. CAVALRY CORPS, MIL. DIV. OF THE MISSISSIPPI,
December 1, 1864.

Maj. E. B. BEAUMONT,
Assistant Adjutant-General:

The general commanding directs that you send to him immediately a morning report of Camp Webster, and order all the officers at our headquarters to report to him.

Very respectfully,

JOHN N. ANDREWS,
Captain and Acting Assistant Adjutant-General.

HDQRS. CAVALRY CORPS, MIL. DIV. OF THE MISSISSIPPI,
Nashville, December 1, 1864.

[Brevet Major-General WILSON:]

GENERAL: I send the morning report* called for, and have ordered the officers out. It is impossible to let Carling go, as his presence is of the utmost importance here to take charge of the large number of wagons now here. All the men in Camp Webster have been armed and equipped, and are in position stretching from the river to the Murfreesborough pike. General Watkins is in command, by direction of General Thomas. We have two batteries, Eighteenth Indiana and First Illinois Artillery, eight guns in all. Watkins' brigade is expected to-night. I have ordered the Fourth, what there is mounted, to march, escort the ammunition train, and take out stragglers. You did not specify how many rounds of ammunition you wanted, and I had to

---

* Not found.

guess—100,000 Sharps, 100,000 Burnside, and 60,000 Spencer; if you need more it can be sent. The Fifth Iowa will march out to report to you to-night, and 300 men of the Thirteenth Indiana. I have ordered Major Carland, Ninth Indiana, to take command of all the detachments that came in as guard to the train, to collect all stragglers, and send them to you as rapidly as possible. We have no mounted men except the detachment that General Thomas ordered to be mounted for courier duty. These are now on picket and patrolling the Lebanon, Murfreesborough, and other pikes. Our cavalry line stretches from in front of Camp Webster obliquely toward the city, and is expected to fall back across the bridge on the Lebanon pike to the rising ground just this side the creek and join General Miller's line. All the dismounted men we could get hold of have been armed with infantry musket, and the force you see on paper has been organized into companies of fifties and battalions of 300 and 400 men. I have been, of course, unable to communicate with you, for General Thomas could not tell where you would be.

I am, general, &c.,

E. B. BEAUMONT,
Major and Assistant Adjutant-General.

CIRCULAR.] HDQRS. CAVALRY CORPS, MIL. DIV. OF THE MISS.,
Brentwood, December 1, 1864—11.30 a. m.

The command will march in the following order:

1. Fifth Division by the road north of Brentwood to Thompson's Chapel, forming behind the little stream at that place and on the right of the pike, facing south.

2. The Sixth Division and Croxton's brigade by the road in front of Brentwood to same place, forming across the pike.

3. General Hammond's brigade by road parallel with Winsted pike to Thompson's Chapel, forming on left of the pike, facing south.

All division commanders will keep out strong rear guards and watch the movements of the enemy, reporting promptly all information gained.

By command of Brevet Major-General Wilson:

JOHN N. ANDREWS,
Captain and Acting Assistant Adjutant-General.

HDQRS. CAVALRY CORPS, MIL. DIV. OF THE MISSISSIPPI,
Five Miles from Nashville, December 1, 1864—7.30 p. m.

The Cavalry Corps will retire in the morning at 6 o'clock in the following order: Fifth Division by the right flank of brigade parallel with the pike; Sixth Division by the right flank on the pike, Croxton's brigade covering the rear; Seventh Division (Hammond's brigade) by the left flank parallel with the pike. The pickets will be withdrawn in time to begin the movement with their commands, and will be deployed as skirmishers to cover the movement.

By command of Brevet Major-General Wilson:

JOHN N. ANDREWS,
Captain and Acting Assistant Adjutant-General.

HEADQUARTERS FOURTH DIVISION, CAVALRY CORPS,
MILITARY DIVISION OF THE MISSISSIPPI,
Memphis, Tenn., December 1, 1864.

Bvt. Maj. Gen. J. H. WILSON,
   Comdg. Cavalry Corps, Military Division of the Mississippi:

GENERAL: Yours of November 20, by Lieutenant Noyes, has just reached me by mail at this place.* Since Captain Woodward reached me with your orders I have twice written you, neither of which letters you appear to have received. I shall send this by special messenger, that you may be more certain of receiving it. That your orders and those of Major-General Thomas concerning the cavalry have not been carried out is certainly no fault of mine. Half the command were in Missouri or Arkansas, where they could not be reached, and were acting under the orders of officers far above me in authority. The other half were at Memphis, and could not be taken away from there, because Major-General Washburn would not permit it, neither would he now, until General Dana arrives. He is expected on Saturday next. The cavalry which first arrived at Saint Louis, and which were ordered to Memphis by General Rosecrans upon Captain Woodward's suggestion, were a detachment of 400 men consisting of from one to ten men from every company in seven different regiments. These men had been absent from their commands seventy-five days, without clothing, &c., and had not been paid for six months; neither could they receive pay until the descriptive rolls of each one were furnished to the officer commanding them. Moreover, they all belonged to regiments which General Washburn and Lieutenant Noyes have arranged to leave here. When Captain Woodward arrived in Saint Louis after leaving you he found that with the exception of this mixed detachment all the rest of Winslow's command had proceeded back through Missouri and Arkansas, and he even received intelligence from officers returning from that command that they had already been detached from General Curtis' command and sent overland to Memphis. He told General Rosecrans that it was your wish to have the command concentrated at some convenient point as quickly as possible and sent to Nashville. General Rosecrans stated that it was adverse to his orders to do so, but agreed with Captain Woodward that as at that time it was more than probable that the majority of Colonel Winslow's command would come out at Memphis, it would be best for that detachment to be sent to their companies in Memphis to refit. In doing this Captain Woodward also acted in obedience to my directions, as Memphis would certainly have been the best point to have concentrated had Winslow's command come there, as was expected at that time. Besides, could I have concentrated Winslow's and the Vicksburg cavalry at Memphis immediately upon the receipt of your order, as was undoubtedly your intention, I would have had force sufficient to have marched overland via Fort Henry to Nashville, which would have been the most expeditious route. But, as you will see, I was powerless, my command being scattered from Kansas to Middle Tennessee by orders from superior authority. I certainly understood your instructions, and every move which I have made was with the intention of carrying them out with the least possible delay. In answer to your inquiry as to why I was absent from Saint Louis or Memphis, I have the honor to state that it was by virtue of extract 7, Special Orders, No. 183, from headquarters District of West Tennessee, by which order I was sent to Missouri and

---

* See Part I, p. 954.

Illinois on military business connected with my command. While in Saint Louis I applied to Washington for an entire remount for Winslow's command, which I obtained, and had the horses (2,000 in number) shod in readiness for them. My leaving here, in the first place, was for the purpose of getting together all the troops I possibly could, in pursuance of instructions from Major-General Howard and yourself, in order that I might be able to make the expedition first indicated by you and which was afterward abandoned.

Hoping this explanation of the cause of delay may prove satisfactory,

I am, sir, very respectfully, your obedient servant,

B. H. GRIERSON,
Brigadier-General.

HEADQUARTERS FIFTH IOWA CAVALRY,
Nashville, December 1, 1864—5 p. m.

Captain ANDREWS,
Acting Assistant Adjutant-General:

I have the honor to report that, by direction of Major-General Schofield, I covered the west flank of the army into Nashville by way of the Granny White pike, and find myself separated from the general commanding. By direction of Major Beaumont, I am drawing ammunition, horseshoes, &c., and expect to start my command to rejoin you by 8 p. m. Having completed the duty assigned me by Major-General Schofield, I trust upon your relieving me without having first to report to him to be relieved, as he is upon another road, and I might lose much time thereby. The duty assigned my regiment by General Schofield last evening I believe was performed satisfactorily, having patrolled as far down as the Hillsborough pike and retired from the front the last of all the troops.

I am, very respectfully, your most obedient servant,

J. MORRIS YOUNG,
Major, Commanding Regiment.

HEADQUARTERS THIRTEENTH INDIANA CAVALRY,
La Vergne, December 1, 1864.

Major BEAUMONT,
Assistant Adjutant-General, Cavalry Corps:

SIR: I have the honor to report having just returned from a scout to Nolensville; met no enemy in force; gave unsuccessful chase to small squads. The command of Colonel Stewart passed through there last evening in the direction of Triune. I gathered up several stragglers of the Eleventh Indiana Cavalry. They state they have been severely dealt with and routed on the Wilson pike about eight miles from Nolensville. Nolensville pike is now clear; the indications are, however, that it will be heavily scouted by the enemy to-morrow. The force engaging Stewart used artillery. Major Hannum, of the Eleventh Indiana Cavalry, in charge of two companies of the routed men, passed one of my scouting parties and went in the direction of Nashville. I was three miles distant. He sent me verbal information relative to it, but did not wait to see me; whether he reached Nashville or not I cannot state. My rations expire to-morrow night. If you have no additional orders for me, please order my regimental commissary subsistence and regimental quartermaster to forward rations and forage per railroad.

I am, sir, your obedient servant,

G. M. L. JOHNSON,
Colonel Thirteenth Indiana Cavalry.

P. S.—One squadron of Ninth Indiana Cavalry, General Hammond's brigade, has just arrived at this point. They report to me that they were cut off from their command at Wilson's pike to-day. They intend going to Nashville in the morning. If any orders for me, send per bearer.

G. M. L. JOHNSON,
Colonel Thirteenth Indiana Cavalry.

———

HDQRS. CAVALRY CORPS, MIL. DIV. OF THE MISSISSIPPI,
Nashville, Tenn., December 1, 1864.
Col. G. G. MINER,
Commanding Camp Webster:

COLONEL: The batteries will not move out in the morning to report to General Wilson; the order is countermanded. Let the battery commanders be ready to report to General Wilson to-morrow morning very early. He will be on the Lebanon pike between the city and your headquarters.

By command of Brevet Major-General Wilson:

E. B. BEAUMONT,
Major and Assistant Adjutant-General.

———

HDQRS. CAVALRY CORPS, MIL. DIV. OF THE MISSISSIPPI,
Nashville, Tenn., December 1, 1864.
Maj. P. CARLAND,
Ninth Indiana Cavalry:

You will take command of the detachments acting as escort to the cavalry trains coming from the front; collect all the stragglers from the cavalry, and as soon as a considerable party is collected take measures to send them back to their commands. Communicate with these headquarters to know where such stragglers are to be sent. Send parties out on the Franklin pike and the different roads upon which the stragglers might be expected.

By command of Brevet Major-General Wilson:

E. B. BEAUMONT,
Major and Assistant Adjutant-General.

———

MURFREESBOROUGH, *December 1, 1864.*
Major-General THOMAS:

I am sending out a small construction train, and also telegraph repairers, to see what detains General Steedman, and to aid in repairing the road, if it may be broken. I have two trains here, and if the

track in the road cannot well be repaired, will use these trains to bring
Steedman's troops on up from the gap.   General Milroy stayed at Wartrace last night; his troops three miles beyond.   All right here.

> LOVELL H. ROUSSEAU,
> *Major-General.*

MURFREESBOROUGH, *December 1, 1864—2.15 p. m.*
Major-General THOMAS:

I shall be ready to send back block-house garrisons as far as Duck
River so soon as General Steedman's troops shall all pass here.   Shall I
not do this?   They have all been brought off.   If I do not hear from
you when General Steedman passes, I shall send the garrisons back, as
I fear delay may result in the loss of the bridges.   Hope you will
approve; I can recall if you direct it.

> L. H. ROUSSEAU,
> *Major-General.*

NASHVILLE, *December 1, 1864.*
Major-General ROUSSEAU,
    Murfreesborough:

Your dispatch of 2.15 p. m. is received.   Send back the garrisons to
reoccupy the block-houses up to and including Duck River bridge, as
you have arranged for.

> GEO. H. THOMAS,
> *Major-General, U. S. Volunteers, Commanding.*

MURFREESBOROUGH, *December 1, 1864—2.45 p. m.*
Major-General THOMAS:

Train and garrison ready to start to occupy the block-houses to and
including Duck River bridge.   Shall I send them?   I suppose General
Steedman's coming might prompt a change in your orders as to these
garrisons.

> LOVELL H. ROUSSEAU,
> *Major-General.*

NASHVILLE, *[December 1,] 1864.*
Major-General ROUSSEAU,
    Murfreesborough:

Yours received.   Send back the block-house garrisons as far as Duck
River when General Steedman's troops have passed.

> WM. D. WHIPPLE,
> *Brigadier-General and Assistant Adjutant-General.*

MURFREESBOROUGH, *December 1, 1864—12.25 p. m.*
Major-General THOMAS:

I have just arrived with the advance trains of my command; the
balance of the trains are following closely.   I await orders here.

> J. B. STEEDMAN,
> *Major-General.*

[Indorsement.]

Answered. I told him to come on and disembark at junction of North Alabama railroad, the railroad yard being full.

W. D. W.

MURFREESBOROUGH, TENN., *December 1, 1864.*

Maj. Gen. G. H. THOMAS:

I am detained here on account of the train dispatcher at Nashville being absent from the office, said to be eating dinner.

J. B. STEEDMAN,
Major-General.

NASHVILLE, *December 1, 1864.*

Maj. Gen. J. B. STEEDMAN,
Murfreesborough :

Come on to this place with your command.

WM. D. WHIPPLE,
Brigadier-General.

KNOXVILLE, *December 1, 1864.*

General STEEDMAN:

All quiet in this region. Rumors that enemy is coming down the railroad from Lynchburg not reliable. Telegraph working through by Cumberland Gap. Report is that enemy is on the road between you and Nashville. Which way is he going? What is the news?

STONEMAN,
Major-General.

WARTRACE, *December 1, 1864.*

Major-General STEEDMAN:

I have near 3,000 men camped to-night two miles this side of the bridge, and if you are coming up with a train I will send back a guard of fifty men to the bridge; a less number than that would not be prudent. My men will march at 5 a. m. What time will your train arrive at the bridge?

R. H. MILROY,
Major-General.

WHITESIDE'S, *December 1, 1864.*

Maj. S. B. MOE,
Assistant Adjutant-General, District of the Etowah :

Guerrillas, about seventy-five in number, robbed Mr. Thompson, Government employé, three miles from here, between this place and Shellmound, last night. They started down Sand Mountain. I sent scouts after them this morning; also down the valley to Trenton.

O. C. JOHNSON,
Lieutenant-Colonel, Commanding Post.

DALTON, *December 1, 1864.*
Capt. H. A. FORD,
    Acting Assistant Adjutant-General:
There is about 300 rebel cavalry and guerrillas hanging around my lines, frequently firing on my pickets. It is also reported that a large force is crossing in from the direction of Rome. I have only five scouts, and they cannot render me much service. I want you to send me some horses or mounted men; my position demands it. My pickets are assaulted by the enemy with impunity, for they know I cannot pursue them. I do not know how much credit to give the report that a force is coming from Rome. If I had some cavalry I could soon inform myself.

J. B. CULVER,
Colonel, Commanding.

KINGSTON SPRINGS, *December 1, 1864.*
Major-General THOMAS:
Dispatch received.* There was no communication either way last night, and the trains due were so far behind that I thought them captured. Concentrated my regiment this morning at this point. One train is here now; the other will probably be here soon. The One hundredth [U. S. Colored] left Sneedsville, as per orders, this a. m., after trains passed.

W. R. SELLON,
Lieutenant-Colonel, Commanding Twelfth U. S. Colored.

NASHVILLE, *December 1, 1864.*
Major-General STONEMAN,
        Knoxville:
Your letter of November 26 received.† The major-general commanding approves your suggestions as contained therein.
WM. D. WHIPPLE,
Brigadier-General and Assistant Adjutant-General.

KNOXVILLE, TENN., *December 1, 1864.*
(Via Cumberland Gap.)
Major-General BURBRIDGE:
Your two telegrams of 30th instant [ultimo] received. I sent you a long telegram last night containing one from U. S. Grant; have you received it? My instructions therein contained were based upon the supposition that you would be at Bean's Station. If the Clinch is not easily forded you had better leave your incumbrances on the other side of the Clinch until you have thoroughly scouted the country toward Kingsport and between the Clinch and the Holston. A demonstration in that direction will almost certainly cause the enemy to fall back to Bristol. Get all the information you can as to what the enemy is doing

---

* See Part I, 7.30 p. m., p. 1195.
† See Part I, p. 1073.

at Bristol and beyond. From all I can learn there are not more than 100 of the enemy between the Holston and Clinch. Do not draw any supplies from Cumberland Gap if you can possibly avoid it. Enemy is on the road between Nashville and Chattanooga. Be sure and keep the telegraph line open from Cumberland Gap to Lexington, and look out for the enemy coming down the railroad from Lynchburg; the report is they are coming.

GEORGE STONEMAN,
Major-General, Commanding.

CLINCH MOUNTAIN, *December 1, 1864.*

Capt. J. BATES DICKSON:

Two brigades have crossed the Clinch to-day, and my third and last is crossing to-night. The river is very rapid and difficult, but we crossed the men and saddles on rafts, and swam the horses. The enemy skirmished with us at Clinch Mountain, but we forced the gap, and occupied Bean's Station this evening. Scouts report Breckinridge at Morristown with 3,000 infantry, and his cavalry at Mossy Creek; others say Breckinridge's infantry has gone to Bristol. We go in the morning to Bean's Station, and will reconnoiter toward Morristown. All well. Plenty of forage here. Command in fine condition, and all in the best of spirits.

JAMES S. BRISBIN,
Colonel.

STANFORD, *December 1, 1864.*

Brigadier-General McLEAN:

I have just returned from scouting the counties of Henry, Shelby, Nelson, and Washington. Colonel Jessee has from 75 to 150 men; he is stealing horses to mount new recruits upon, and will doubtless endeavor to get through, either by way of Eastern Kentucky or via Burkesville or the Cumberland River.

J. H. BRIDGEWATER,
Captain State Troops.

MEMPHIS, TENN., *December 1, 1864.*

Col. J. W. NOBLE,
Commanding Second Brigade:

It is reported that there were 1,000 rebels at White's Station this afternoon; keep a sharp lookout in that direction.

B. H. GRIERSON,
Brigadier-General.

WAR DEPARTMENT,
Washington, December 2, 1864—10.30 a. m.

Lieutenant-General GRANT,
City Point:

The President feels solicitous about the disposition of General Thomas to lay in fortifications for an indefinite period "until Wilson gets equipments." This looks like the McClellan and Rosecrans strategy of do nothing and let the rebels raid the country. The President wishes you to consider the matter.

E. M. STANTON,
Secretary of War.

CITY POINT, VA., *December 2, 1864—1 p. m.*

Hon. E. M. STANTON,
Secretary of War, Washington:

Immediately on receipt of Thomas' dispatch I sent him a dispatch, which no doubt you read as it passed through the office.*

U. S. GRANT,
Lieutenant-General.

CITY POINT, VA., *December 2, 1864—7.30 p. m.*

Hon. E. M. STANTON,
Secretary of War:

Do you not think it advisable to authorize Wilson to press horses and mares in Kentucky to mount his cavalry, giving owners receipts so they can get their pay? It looks as if Forrest will flank around Thomas until Thomas is equal to him in cavalry.

U. S. GRANT,
Lieutenant-General.

WAR DEPARTMENT,
December 2, 1864—9 p. m.

Lieutenant-General GRANT:

General Thomas ought to seize horses and everything else he needs. It has been [done] heretofore, and he surely cannot be hesitating about it. The officer in command at Louisville should also seize or Thomas send some one to do so for him.

EDWIN M. STANTON,
Secretary of War.

CITY POINT, VA., *December 2, 1864—9.30 p. m.*

Hon. EDWIN M. STANTON,
Secretary of War:

If you agree with me I would like that Thomas be directed to assign Couch to the command of Kentucky. The reports from there show conclusively that Burbridge should not be retained.

U. S. GRANT,
Lieutenant-General.

CITY POINT, VA., *December 2, 1864—10 p. m.*
(Received 10.45 p. m.)

Maj. Gen. H. W. HALLECK,
Washington, D. C.:

Is it not possible now to send re-enforcements to Thomas from Hooker's department? If there are new troops, organized State

---

*For remainder of dispatch, relating to General Rosecrans, see Vol. XLI, Part IV, p. 742.

militia, or anything that can go, now is the time to annihilate Hood's army. Governor Bramlette might put from 5,000 to 10,000 horsemen into the field to serve only to the end of the campaign. I believe if he was asked, he would do so.

U. S. GRANT,
Lieutenant-General.

CITY POINT, VA., *December 2, 1864—11 a. m.*
Major-General THOMAS,
Nashville, Tenn.:

If Hood is permitted to remain quietly about Nashville, you will lose all the road back to Chattanooga, and possibly have to abandon the line of the Tennessee. Should he attack you it is all well, but if he does not you should attack him before he fortifies. Arm and put in the trenches your quartermaster employés, citizens, &c.

U. S. GRANT,
Lieutenant-General.

CITY POINT, VA., *December 2, 1864—1.30 p. m.*
Major-General THOMAS,
Nashville, Tenn.:

With your citizen employés armed, you can move out of Nashville with all your army and force the enemy to retire or fight upon ground of your own choosing. After the repulse of Hood at Franklin, it looks to me that instead of falling back to Nashville, we should have taken the offensive against the enemy where he was. At this distance, however, I may err as to the best method of dealing with the enemy. You will now suffer incalculable injury upon your railroads, if Hood is not speedily disposed of. Put forth, therefore, every possible exertion to attain this end. Should you get him to retreating, give him no peace.

U. S. GRANT,
Lieutenant-General.

NASHVILLE, *December 2, 1864—10 p. m.*
(Received 1.15 a. m. 3d.)
Lieut. Gen. U. S. GRANT,
City Point:

Your two telegrams of 11 a. m. and 1.30 p. m. to-day are received. At the time that Hood was whipped at Franklin, I had at this place but about 5,000 men of General Smith's command, which added to the force under General Schofield would not have given me more than 25,000 men; besides, General Schofield felt convinced that he could not hold the enemy at Franklin until the 5,000 could reach him. As General Wilson's cavalry force also numbered only about one-fourth that of Forrest's, I thought it best to draw the troops back to Nashville and wait the arrival of the remainder of General Smith's force, and also a force of about 5,000 commanded by Major-General Steedman, which I had ordered up from Chattanooga. The division of General Smith arrived yesterday morning, and General Steedman's troops arrived last night. I now have infantry enough to assume the offensive, if I had more cavalry, and will take the field anyhow as soon as the remainder of General McCook's division of cavalry reaches here, which

I hope it will do in two or three days. We can neither get re-enforcements or equipments at this great distance from the North very easily;
and it must be remembered that my command was made up of the two
weakest corps of General Sherman's army and all the dismounted cavalry except one brigade, and the task of reorganizing and equipping
has met with many delays, which have enabled Hood to take advantage of my crippled condition. I earnestly hope, however, that in a few
more days I shall be able to give him a fight.

GEO. H. THOMAS,
Major-General, U. S. Volunteers, Commanding.

NASHVILLE, December 2, 1864—10 p. m.

Maj. Gen. H. W. HALLECK,
  Washington, D. C.:

I have succeeded in concentrating a force of infantry about equal to
that of the enemy's, and as soon as I can get the remaining brigade of
General McCook's division of cavalry here I will move against the
enemy, although my cavalry force will not be more than half of that of the
enemy. I have labored under many disadvantages since assuming the
direction of affairs here, not the least of which was the reorganizing,
remounting, and equipping of a cavalry force sufficient to contend with
Forrest. The signal officers and reconnoitering parties report this
afternoon that the enemy are moving to our right and going into
position southwest of the city, or below. That would be by far the
most advantageous position he could take for us, as his line of communication would be more exposed with him in that position than in
any other. The iron-clads and gun-boats are so disposed as to prevent
Hood from crossing the river, and Captain Fitch assures me that he
can safely convoy steamers up and down the river. I have also taken
measures to have the river patrolled as high up as Carthage.

GEO. H. THOMAS,
Major-General, U. S. Volunteers, Commanding.

WAR DEPARTMENT,
December 1 [2?], 1864—9.30 p. m.

Major-General THOMAS,
  Nashville:

You are authorized to seize and impress horses and every other
species of property needed for the military service in your command.
You should not hesitate an hour about exercising this power at Nashville and Louisville, and wherever property can be had. Horses and
equipments enough for Wilson might thus be procured immediately.
Receipts may be given for the property by the seizing officer, designating the property and its value.

EDWIN M. STANTON,
Secretary of War.

MOUND CITY, ILL., December 2, 1864.
(Received 8.40 p. m.)

Major-General THOMAS:

Your confidential telegram of 1st received to-day, this afternoon. I
will do as you wish as soon as the iron-clad is repaired, which will take

several days. The aide who probably penned your dispatch of 30th communicated an order instead of a request. Please accept my sincere congratulations on your success at Franklin, and when practicable and convenient inform me of the military situation.

S. P. LEE,
Rear-Admiral, Commanding Mississippi Squadron.

NASHVILLE, TENN., *December 2, 1864—8.30 p. m.*

Maj. T. T. ECKERT:

Enemy shows more force on right of our position; seems massing out of reach of guns of forts, on level, open fields, directly west from State House, which is the weakest part of our line. Spies report large force twenty miles down the river, toward Harpeth Shoals, and say rebels propose to cross the Cumberland there as soon as it can be forded or is too low for gun-boats, which will be soon, unless rain falls. General Wood took command of Fourth Corps to-day, in the absence of General Stanley.

J. C. VAN DUZER.

CHATTANOOGA, TENN., *December 2, 1864.*

Major-General THOMAS:

Colonel Palmer, Fifteenth Pennsylvania Cavalry, desires me to telegraph you the following, viz:

I did not get General Steedman's order to return from Bridgeport to Wauhatchie until reaching here [Cowan]. That I have over 500 cavalry, and wish to know what I shall do under the altered circumstances.

SOUTHARD HOFFMAN,
Assistant Adjutant-General.

CARLINVILLE, ILL., *December 2, 1864.*

Maj. Gen. G. H. THOMAS:

Can I be of any service to you? If so, I will report to you at once.

JNO. M. PALMER,
Major-General.

NASHVILLE, *December 2, 1864.*

Maj. Gen. JOHN M. PALMER,
Carlinville, Ill.:

Your dispatch of this day is received. Much obliged for your kind tender of services, but I have no suitable command to assign you to.

GEO. H. THOMAS,
Major-General, U. S. Volunteers, Commanding.

COWAN, *December 2, 1864.*

Major HOFFMAN:

I am here entirely in the dark. Please send me the latest you know from Nashville; it might enable me to do something on the flanks.

WM. J. PALMER,
Colonel Fifteenth Pennsylvania Cavalry.

CHATTANOOGA, *December 2, 1864.*

Col. WILLIAM J. PALMER,
    Fifteenth Pennsylvania Cavalry, Cowan, Tenn.:

There is nothing in the way of news here, except the fight at Franklin, Tenn. Hood was whipped, with a loss of 6,000.

SOUTHARD HOFFMAN,
Assistant Adjutant-General.

———

QUARTERMASTER-GENERAL'S OFFICE,
Washington, D. C., December 2, 1864.

Brig. Gen. R. ALLEN,
    Chief Quartermaster, Louisville, Ky. :

GENERAL: The following is a copy of a telegram sent to your address yesterday:

Report is made that cavalry horses at Nashville are suffering and breaking down from want of long forage (hay), and that the cavalry inspectors report that the means of transportation are ample. Report the cause and the possible remedy.

CHS. THOMAS,
Assistant Quartermaster-General.

Very respectfully, your obedient servant,

CHS. THOMAS,
Assistant Quartermaster-General.

———

LOUISVILLE, *December 2, 1864.*
(Received 9.15 p. m.)

Maj. Gen. M. C. MEIGS,
    Quartermaster-General :

There was no scarcity of hay at Nashville until after the burning of Johnsonville, since which time it has simply been impossible to keep up the supply. We should be congratulated that in the face of this terrible disaster we have met other wants. Horses for a few weeks will not suffer on a full ration of grain, if properly taken care of. Officers shamefully abuse their horses and charge it to hay. Inspecting officers know nothing about the difficulty of procuring hay, and less about the transporting of it. All that was possible to ship has been sent, and no one who understands the circumstances will complain General Thomas is satisfied.

ROBT. ALLEN,
Brigadier-General and Chief Quartermaster.

———

DECEMBER 2, 1864.

Major-General THOMAS:

SIR: General Wood directed me to inform you that the officer he sent to General Kimball had returned, and that he reports that he himself saw what he supposed to be three regiments of infantry pass to our right. At the time he saw them they were moving to the right of the Franklin pike, about half a mile in advance of our picket-line, and that when he left they were still moving.

Most respectfully, your most obedient servant,

GEORGE SHAFFER,
Lieutenant, Staff of General Wood.

SPECIAL FIELD ORDERS, ⎱ HDQRS. DEPT. OF THE CUMBERLAND,
    No. 330. ⎰   *Nashville, Tenn., December 2, 1864*

*   *   *   *   *   *   *

VI. Brig. Gen. W. L. Elliott, U. S. Volunteers, is hereby assigned to the command of the Second Division, Fourth Army Corps.

By command of Major-General Thomas:

HENRY M. CIST,
Captain and Assistant Adjutant-General.

GENERAL ORDERS, ⎱ HDQRS. 2D DIVISION, 4TH ARMY CORPS,
    No. 25. ⎰   *Nashville, Tenn., December 2, 1864.*

I. Capt. E. G. Whitesides, One hundred and twenty-fifth Ohio Volunteer Infantry, is hereby announced as acting assistant adjutant general of this division. He will be obeyed and respected accordingly.

II. Capt. George Lee, assistant adjutant-general of volunteers, is hereby relieved from duty at these headquarters and will report to the commanding general Middle Military Division for assignment to duty in accordance with Special Orders, No. 411, War Department, November 22, 1864.

*   *   *   *   *   *   *

By order of Brig. Gen. G. D. Wagner:

E. G. WHITESIDES,
Captain and Acting Assistant Adjutant-General.

ORDERS.]   HDQRS. THIRD DIVISION, FOURTH ARMY CORPS,

Nashville, Tenn., December 2, 1864.

The undersigned hereby assumes command of the Third Division.

SAML. BEATTY,
Brigadier-General of Volunteers.

HEADQUARTERS ARMY OF THE OHIO,
Nashville, Tenn., December 2, 1864.

Major-General THOMAS,
    Commanding Department of the Cumberland:

GENERAL: I inclose herewith a copy of a dispatch* from the Adjutant-General of the Army directing me to relieve Major-General Stoneman from duty in my department; also a copy of my reply. I have no competent officer whom I can spare from other service to take command in East Tennessee at this critical period; therefore, refer the matter to you for such action as you may think proper.

    Very respectfully,

J. M. SCHOFIELD,
Major-General.

See Part I, p. 1109.

NASHVILLE, TENN., *December 2, 1864.*

Col. E. D. TOWNSEND,
  Assistant Adjutant-General, Washington, D. C.:

I have received your dispatch of November 28.* General Burbridge is wrong in saying I had " relieved him from the command assigned by the President." He still commands the District of Kentucky, to which he was assigned according to his brevet rank. He was also authorized, under my direction, to exercise the powers of department commander. I have simply informed him that I do not direct him to exercise any such powers, because I have selected another officer to represent me in my absence. I respectfully submit, that as department commander I have clearly a right so to do. If this is not so, then Brevet Major-General Burbridge is independent of me, and I am only nominally in command of the Department of the Ohio. I shall, of course, obey the honorable Secretary's order at once, although I believe it greatly injurious to the service at this critical time.

J. M. SCHOFIELD,
  Major-General.

SPECIAL FIELD ORDERS, }   HDQRS. ARMY OF THE OHIO,
       No. 168.   }   *Nashville, Tenn., December 2, 1864.*

First Lieut. L. M. Palmer, Battery D, First Ohio Light Artillery, is hereby appointed acting ordnance officer of the army in the field. He will be obeyed and respected accordingly.

By command of Major-General Schofield:
J. A. CAMPBELL,
  Major and Assistant Adjutant-General.

HDQRS. THIRD DIVISION, TWENTY-THIRD ARMY CORPS,
         Block-house, Casino, December 2, 1864.

Maj. J. A. CAMPBELL,
  Assistant Adjutant-General, Army of the Ohio:

MAJOR: The display of the enemy's force on the south front is such, as reported by the signal officers, that I am extremely anxious to know whether any final determination has been reached as to my position. The brigade commanders of the Fourth Corps near me say no position has as yet been assigned them, and I fear there has been some delay in the transmittal of orders which may embarrass us if the enemy push in rapidly.

Very respectfully, your obedient servant,
J. D. COX,
  Brigadier-General, Commanding.

HEADQUARTERS RIGHT WING, SIXTEENTH ARMY CORPS,
        Nashville, Tenn., December 2, 1864.

Brig. Gen. J. MCARTHUR,
  Commanding First Division, Sixteenth Army Corps:

GENERAL: I am directed by the major-general commanding to say that the enemy having made his appearance in our front, it is desirable

---

that you have strong pickets in your front and your whole line in readiness to take arms at a moment's warning. The fires at the picket stations and on the tops of the hills must be discontinued entirely, and fires for cooking only allowed in the main line, which must be put out as soon as the cooking is done.

I am, general, very respectfully, your obedient servant,

J. HOUGH,
Major and Assistant Adjutant-General.

HDQRS. CAV. CORPS, MIL. DIV. OF THE MISSISSIPPI,
Five Miles from Nashville, on Nolensville Pike,
December 2, 1864—2 a. m.

Major-General THOMAS,
Commanding Department of the Cumberland:

General Hatch reports it's his impression from observations that the enemy is moving into position toward the western and southwestern defenses of Nashville. A large force of the enemy, supposed to be cavalry, has been crossing from the Nolensville and Winsted pikes to the Franklin pike. This movement has been constant since 9 o'clock. A considerable force has been camped on the Winsted pike since just after dark. I have made my arrangements to retire to the position assigned me nearer Nashville at 5 a. m. Will report promptly any further information.

J. H. WILSON,
Brevet Major-General.

HDQRS. CAVALRY CORPS, MIL. DIV. OF THE MISSISSIPPI,
Nashville, Tenn., December 2, 1864.

ADJUTANT-GENERAL U. S. ARMY,
Washington, D. C.:

SIR: I have the honor to request that Bvt. Brig. Gen. L. D. Watkins, colonel of the Sixth Regiment Kentucky Cavalry, now commanding the Second [Third] Brigade of the First Division, Cavalry Corps, Military Division of the Mississippi, be assigned to duty according to his brevet rank. General Watkins is a meritorious and competent officer, entitled by continuous and honorable service to this promotion. It is thought that by bestowing such substantial commendation upon officers of acknowledged merit the best interests of the public service may be advanced. The cavalry officers of this military division have not heretofore received the proper reward for their good conduct.

Very respectfully, your obedient servant,

J. H. WILSON,
Brevet Major-General.

SPECIAL   HEADQUARTERS CAVALRY CORPS,
FIELD ORDERS,   MILITARY DIVISION OF THE MISSISSIPPI,
No. 3.   *Nashville, Tenn., December 2, 1864.*

*   *   *   *   *   *   *

III. The Board of Trade Battery, Captain Robinson, will report for temporary duty to Brigadier-General Croxton, commanding First Brigade, First Division, Cavalry Corps.

IV. The Fourth Ohio Volunteer Cavalry will, without delay, report to Brigadier-General Croxton, commanding First Brigade, First Division Cavalry, for temporary duty with his brigade.

By command of Brevet Major-General Wilson:

E. B. BEAUMONT,
Major and Assistant Adjutant-General.

CIRCULAR.]   HDQRS. CAV. CORPS, MIL. DIV. OF THE MISS.,
Nashville, Tenn., December 2, 1864—9.15 a. m.

The Cavalry Corps will move to the north bank of the Cumberland, by the railroad bridge, to a camp to be selected by Brigadier-General Johnson. Order of march: First, Sixth Division and Croxton's brigade, of the First Division; second, Fifth Division.

Requisitions for clothing, &c., will be sent in at once, extra shoes fitted, horses will be shod, and all means necessary will be taken for rendering the command efficient.

By command of Brevet Major-General Wilson:

E. B. BEAUMONT,
Major and Assistant Adjutant-General.

NASHVILLE, TENN., *December 2, 1864.*

Major-General WILSON, or
ASSISTANT ADJUTANT-GENERAL, CAVALRY CORPS:

GENERAL: I respectfully request permission to move my brigade to Edgefield, or where there is ground suitable for camping. If allowed the opportunity, I can, even in forty-eight hours, do much to improve the condition of my command, which has become shattered by long and severe service. I desire also to have two regiments paid that have drawn no pay for twelve months. For more than three months my command has been upon the most arduous service, separated from its transportation and baggage, and needs rest, and must have it. I ask it at this time because I believe it can be granted with less inconvenience than hereafter. In the event you do not feel authorized to grant my request, I ask that you forward this with your approval to General Thomas by special courier.

I am, general, very respectfully, your obedient servant,

JOHN T. CROXTON,
Brigadier-General of Volunteers.

GENERAL ORDERS, ⎱ HDQRS. 2D BRIG., 1st DIV., CAV. CORPS,
⎰   MILITARY DIVISION OF THE MISSISSIPPI,
No. 5.   ⎰   *Near Louisville, Ky., December 2, 1864.*

This command will march at 8 a. m. on Saturday, the 3d instant. Three days' rations will be carried in the haversacks. The cartridge-boxes will be filled. No straggling will be permitted. Orderlies who may be necessitated to fall out of ranks will be furnished with permanent passes, approved at these headquarters before marching. No officer will lodge in a house, except by order of regimental surgeons, approved at these headquarters. Only the amount of baggage allowed by regulations to cavalry in the field will be carried, and the inspector will be ordered to see that any excess is destroyed. Any enlisted man found riding his horse faster than a walk without proper authority will be dismounted and compelled to make the march on foot. Any soldier found attempting to run the guard or absenting himself from camp without proper authority will be tied behind the wagons for the entire march. This order will be read to each company at retreat this evening and at reveille to-morrow morning.

By order of Col. O. H. La Grange:

DAN. S. MOULTON,
Lieutenant and Acting Assistant Adjutant-General.

HDQRS. CAVALRY CORPS, MIL. DIV. OF THE MISSISSIPPI,
Nashville, Tenn., December 2, 1864.

Brig. Gen. R. W. JOHNSON,
Commanding Sixth Division, Cavalry Corps:

Send the regiment of your command which is in the most effective condition ten miles down the river, with directions to picket the right flank. The regiment will take post about ten miles down, picketing the river above and below. It is not expected to defend the crossing of the river, if the enemy attempt it in force, but merely to observe his movements.

By command of Brevet Major-General Wilson:

E. B. BEAUMONT,
Major and Assistant Adjutant-General.

GENERAL ORDERS, }   HDQRS. SIXTH DIVISION, CAV. CORPS,
                {   MILITARY DIVISION OF THE MISSISSIPPI,
No. 2.   }   *Franklin, Tenn., December 2, 1864.*

The Fifth Iowa Cavalry, Maj. J. Morris Young commanding, and the Seventh Ohio Cavalry, Colonel Garrard commanding, are hereby temporarily assigned to the First Brigade, and until further orders will report and do duty accordingly.

By command of Brigadier-General Johnson:

E. T. WELLS,
Assistant Adjutant-General.

HDQRS. CAVALRY CORPS, MIL. DIV. OF THE MISSISSIPPI,
Nashville, Tenn., December 2, 1864.

Brig. Gen. J. H. HAMMOND:

You will move your command, with as little delay as possible, to the vicinity of Gallatin Ford, select a good camp in that vicinity, cover the ford, and watch the river above and below it. Rest your command, and put it in the best possible condition for service. You are not expected to defend the crossing of the river; should the enemy attempt it in force, give timely notice of his movements.

By command of Brevet Major-General Wilson:

E. B. BEAUMONT,
Major and Assistant Adjutant-General.

HEADQUARTERS FIRST BRIGADE, SEVENTH DIVISION,
Edgefield, December 2, 1864.

Major-General WILSON,
    Commanding Corps:

GENERAL: Your order to march was received a few minutes since. I suppose, of course, you want me to get there as soon as possible. Our horses are very much tired, and have had nothing to eat since yesterday evening. It is now 12 m., and I think that by the time the horses and men are fed and the horses well cleaned and rested, it will be near night. Every exertion is being made to prepare, but men and officers are tired and sluggish. Gallatin Ford is, I suppose, Gallatin Ferry, as a boat is used in crossing at all times of the year. Shall I destroy all boats in reach? I require fifty horses very much, and will feel obliged if you will order them to be given me. The quartermaster will do all he can to give them to me. I can fit out, I suppose, as well at Gallatin as here. My command requires more carbines, ammunition, and boots; these things, a day's rest, and some shoeing will make me all right. While I am writing the teams come in sight with forage and rations; I can, therefore, get away before dark.

Very respectfully, your obedient servant,
                        J. H. HAMMOND,
                            Brigadier-General.

P. S.—Will you please return answer by bearer as to whether I am mistaken as to the crossing, *i. e.*, the crossing two miles and a half from Gallatin, on the Cumberland River. Blacksmiths are at work.
                        J. H. HAMMOND,
                            Brigadier-General.

CHATTANOOGA, *December 2, 1864.*

Brigadier-General WHIPPLE:
    Have you any news from Hood to-day?
                        J. M. BRANNAN,
                            Brigadier-General of Volunteers.

NASHVILLE, *December 2, 1864.*

Brig. Gen. J. M. BRANNAN,
    Chattanooga:

The enemy has developed his lines a little more to-day, and advanced his skirmish lines about 500 yards. Some skirmishing has taken place and artillery firing on our side. Rebel battery at Harpeth Shoals stops boats. General Elliott assigned to command of Second Division, Fourth Corps.

                        WM. D. WHIPPLE,
                            Brigadier-General.

CHATTANOOGA, *December 2, 1864.*

Brigadier-General WHIPPLE:
    Your dispatch received. Send me some more news.
                        J. M. BRANNAN,
                            Brigadier-General.

HEADQUARTERS POST OF MURFREESBOROUGH,
Murfreesborough, Tenn., December 2, 1864.

Lieut. JOHN DEUBLE,
   115th Ohio Volunteers:

SIR: Major-General Rousseau directs that you take up the garrisons at Christiana and Fosterville, and move with them to garrison Normandy and Duck Creek trestle block-houses; the latter beyond Tullahoma. You will take with you your supplies of rations and ammunition, and the telegraph operator at Fosterville or Christiana, who will remain at your headquarters. Move down to the places indicated, on the train, taking this dispatch, as promptly as possible, and after getting located send the train to this place. If the block-houses are unfinished, put them in as good shape as possible.

Very respectfully, your obedient servant,

E. A. OTIS,
Assistant Adjutant-General.

CLARKSVILLE, *December 2, 1864.*

Brig. Gen. W. D. WHIPPLE,
   Assistant Adjutant-General:

A transport with troops passed up last night.

A. A. SMITH,
Colonel, Commanding.

CLARKSVILLE, *December 2, 1864.*
(Received 3 p. m.)

Brigadier-General WHIPPLE,
   Assistant Adjutant-General.

Two transports have just passed up with troops.

A. A. SMITH,
Colonel, Commanding.

KNOXVILLE, *December 2, 1864.*

General WHIPPLE:

Please inform me of the condition of things. A thousand rumors are afloat, and I hardly know how to act. The operator says he has news, but is contraband. Your telegram of yesterday is received. All quiet about here.

GEORGE STONEMAN,
Major-General.

NASHVILLE, *December 2, 1864.*
(Received 10.15 p. m.)

Major-General STONEMAN,
   Knoxville, Tenn.:

The enemy attacked our forces at Franklin with two corps about 4 o'clock on the 30th ultimo. The attack was most persistent and the fighting on both sides desperate. Rebels were repulsed with heavy loss, 4,000. We captured about 600 prisoners and a large number of flags. Our forces then came into Nashville, and are now in line of battle with rebel army confronting them; battle will come off as soon as Hood wishes.

WM. D. WHIPPLE,
Brigadier-General.

LEXINGTON, KY., *December 2, 1864.*
(Received 5 p. m.)

Maj. THOMAS T. ECKERT,
Washington, D. C.:

We have news from Burbridge this morning. Our forces at Clinch Mountain. Slight skirmish with enemy yesterday. Scout reports Breckinridge at Morristown with 3,000 infantry; his cavalry at Bristol. Our forces expected to be at Bean's Station to-day. Shall I report daily?

CAREY,
Cipher Operator.

CAMP NELSON, *December 2, 1864.*

Capt. J. S. BUTLER,
Assistant Adjutant-General:

I have just received a letter from a most reliable Union man in Washington County, giving an account of the most horrid outrages committed by a gang of guerrillas upon the people in that county. They have killed in a few days past some fourteen quiet, inoffensive citizens, among them one discharged soldier. I have now 150 of the Thirteenth Kentucky Cavalry, sent back by General Burbridge. If there [are] no orders for them to move, I respectfully request that I be allowed to send a portion of them in that region to catch these scoundrels, and then afford these people (the most of whom I know to be loyal) some relief.

S. S. FRY,
Brigadier-General.

WAR DEPARTMENT,
December 3, 1864—10 a. m.

Lieutenant-General GRANT:

Couch is not a good administrative officer for Kentucky; I would prefer Stoneman to him. The President would like to see the reports about Burbridge to which you refer. There is no disposition to retain him if there be any well-grounded complaints, but if the military authority is surrendered to a sympathizer with Bramlette, Doctor Breckinridge says it will be necessary to conquer Kentucky.

EDWIN M. STANTON,
Secretary of War.

WASHINGTON, *December 3, 1864—2 p. m.*

Lieutenant-General GRANT,
City Point, Va.:

Every available man from Hooker's and other western departments have been sent to General Thomas. Hooker is already calling for more troops to be sent to him, to guard his prisoners, and General Fry is getting all he can from the hospitals.   Thomas was authorized some time ago to call on the Governors of any Western State for militia, if he wanted them.   He himself says that no more troops should be sent from Kentucky.   Loyal Kentuckians say that if Bramlette's militia are armed, a large portion of them will join the rebels.   All cavalry horses that could be procured in the Western States have been sent to Nashville, to the entire neglect of other departments.   I believe that every possible effort has been made to supply General Thomas' demands and wants, so far as the means at the disposition of the Government permitted.   General A. J. Smith's command was thirty-one days, after General Rosecrans received the orders, in reaching Nashville.

H. W. HALLECK,
Major-General and Chief of Staff.

DECEMBER 3, 1864.—For Grant to Sherman, referring to operations of Thomas' and Hood's armies, see Vol. XLIV, p. 611.

HEADQUARTERS DEPARTMENT OF THE CUMBERLAND,
Nashville, December 3, 1864.

Hon. EDWIN M. STANTON,
    Secretary of War, Washington, D. C.:

I have the honor to respectfully forward the following recommendation for the promotion of Col. Thomas J. Harrison to brigadier-general by brevet, warmly approving the same and recommending his immediate appointment, for previous gallant and honorable service in this army:

NASHVILLE, TENN., *December 2, 1864.*

Major-General THOMAS:

Please ask the appointment by brevet of Col. Thomas J. Harrison, Eighth Indiana Cavalry.   He is worthy and highly merits the promotion.
    Yours, respectfully,

R. W. JOHNSON,
Brigadier-General.
TH. J. WOOD,
Brigadier-General.

GEO. H. THOMAS,
Major-General, U. S. Volunteers, Commanding.

NASHVILLE, TENN., *December 3, 1864—9.30 p. m.*

Maj. Gen. H. W. HALLECK,
        Chief of Staff:

The enemy made no demonstration to-day, except to advance his pickets about 500 yards on the Nolensville, Franklin, and Hillsborough pikes.   I have a good intrenched line on the hills around Nashville, and hope to be able to report 10,000 cavalry mounted and equipped in less than a week, when I shall feel able to march against Hood.   I gave the order for the impressment of horses last night, and received the authority of the Secretary of War this morning.

GEO. H. THOMAS,
Major-General, U. S. Volunteers, Commanding.

NASHVILLE, *December 3, 1864.*

Admiral S. P. LEE,
        Mound City:

Your telegram of yesterday received last night. My force of cavalry and infantry at Franklin being so much less than that of the enemy, I determined to fall back to this place to concentrate my infantry and give time to General Wilson to arm and equip sufficient cavalry to meet Forrest. I have here now nearly as much infantry as Hood, and in a few days hope to have cavalry enough to enable me to assume the offensive. In the meantime Captain Fitch has cheerfully complied with my request to patrol the river above and below the city. I am, therefore, in hopes we shall in a few days be able to take the offensive on pretty even terms with the enemy. I regret much that my telegram of the 30th implied an order to you, which was not intended.

With many thanks for your previous prompt co-operation, I am, yours, truly,

GEO. H. THOMAS,
Major-General, U. S. Volunteers, Commanding.

NASHVILLE, TENN., *December 3, 1864.*

Maj. SOUTHARD HOFFMAN,
        Assistant Adjutant-General:

Your dispatch concerning Colonel Palmer is received. You can inform Colonel Palmer that he will return to Wauhatchie.

GEO. H. THOMAS,
Major-General, U. S. Volunteers, Commanding.

HEADQUARTERS DEPARTMENT OF THE CUMBERLAND,
        Nashville, Tenn., December 3, 1864.

Brig. Gen. JOHN F. MILLER,
        Post Commandant, Nashville, Tenn.:

GENERAL: The major-general commanding directs that you form the recruits, drafted men, and soldiers returning from furlough now in barracks, belonging to commands absent with Major-General Sherman, into battalion organization, under officers who will be ordered to report to you for this duty, of such strength as most desirable for efficient service in the garrison of this post. All soldiers belonging to the classes above mentioned reporting at this post will be placed in these organizations.

Very respectfully, your obedient servant,

HENRY M. CIST,
Assistant Adjutant-General.

HEADQUARTERS DEPARTMENT OF THE CUMBERLAND,
        Nashville, Tenn., December 3, 1864.

Brig. Gen. JOHN F. MILLER,
        Post Commandant, Nashville:

GENERAL: The major-general commanding directs that all officers in this city who are not on duty here under proper orders, and those whose commands are absent with Major-General Sherman, be ordered to report to you for assignment to duty in the battalions of recruits, &c., ordered to be formed at this place under your orders. All officers coming to this place who cannot rejoin their commands for duty will be ordered to report to you for like assignment.

Very respectfully, your obedient servant,

HENRY M. CIST,
Assistant Adjutant-General.

HEADQUARTERS DEPARTMENT OF THE CUMBERLAND,
Nashville, Tenn., December 3, 1864.

Capt. LE ROY FITCH,
Commanding Squadron, Nashville, Tenn.:

CAPTAIN: The major-general commanding directs me to say that inasmuch as the enemy has made no attack to-day, and great uncertainty attends his movements, he thinks it unsafe to trust the courier-line between Gallatin and Carthage to bring us information of any attempt which might be made by the rebels to cross the river above here, and is of the opinion that to render us secure, you had better patrol the river as far as Carthage with at least one iron-clad and two gun-boats, if you think there is sufficient water in the channel to enable you to do it.

Very respectfully, your obedient servant,

WM. D. WHIPPLE,
Assistant Adjutant-General.

LOUISVILLE, *December 3, 1864—11 a. m.*

Brigadier-General WHIPPLE,
Chief of Staff:

I am here, and there shall be no delay in reporting in person to the general.

D. N. COUCH,
Major-General.

HEADQUARTERS DEPARTMENT OF THE CUMBERLAND,
Nashville, Tenn., December 3, 1864.

Capt. J. F. RUSLING,
Acting Chief Quartermaster, Department of the Cumberland:

CAPTAIN: The major-general commanding directs me to say that the garrison in block-houses from Edgefield Junction to Clarksville, reporting to Col. T. J. Downey, Fifteenth Regiment U. S. Colored Troops, remain in their present position, guarding the line of the railroad and the property of the United States along it, until further orders. Colonel Downey will keep himself well advised of the movements of the enemy, and give timely notice of their approach, so that orders for his withdrawal may be issued from these headquarters.

I have the honor to be, captain, very respectfully, your obedient servant,

ROBT. H. RAMSEY,
Assistant Adjutant-General.

NASHVILLE, TENN., *December 3, 1864—10.30 p. m.*

Maj. T. T. ECKERT:

General Thomas has made every preparation for receiving and repelling an attack early to-morrow. Our earth-works reach from the Cumberland on the right to the Cumberland on the left, distant about two miles from Capitol, average distance, forming nearly half circle, with second line in weak places; it is a very strong line and strongly held— the Sixteenth Corps on right, Twenty-third in center, and Fourth on left. Some skirmishing has occurred to-day, and, upon a rebel column showing in the fields, near Franklin road, our artillery opened with shell and sent them to cover. Nothing heard from Forrest, but General Wilson is looking after him, and no apprehension is felt. No telegraph south from Nashville, of course; but we communicate with Chattanooga by the way of Cumberland Gap and Knoxville. All quiet there.

J. C. VAN DUZER.

SPECIAL FIELD ORDERS, ｝ HDQRS. DEPT. OF THE CUMBERLAND,
    No. 331.   ｝   *Nashville, Tenn., December 3, 1864.*

*   *   *   *   *   *   *

III. So much of special field orders of November 27, 1864, from these headquarters, as assigns the following named regiments to the Fourth and Twenty-third Army Corps is hereby revoked, and the commanding officers of the respective regiments will report without delay for duty to Maj. Gen. A. J. Smith: Fortieth Missouri Volunteer Infantry and Tenth Kansas Volunteer Infantry, to Fourth Army Corps. Forty-fourth and Forty-second Missouri Volunteer Infantry, Twenty-third Army Corps.

*   *   *   *   *   *   *

V. The One hundred and eighty-second Ohio Volunteers is hereby assigned to the Second Brigade, Fourth Division, Twentieth Army Corps, and will relieve the One hundred and seventy-third Ohio Volunteers from duty with Second Brigade, Fourth Division, Twentieth Army Corps. Upon being relieved, the One hundred and seventy-third Ohio Infantry will report to Major-General Rousseau for assignment to duty in that division.

*   *   *   *   *   *   *

By command of Major-General Thomas:

HENRY M. CIST,
Assistant Adjutant-General.

ORDERS.]   HEADQUARTERS FOURTH ARMY CORPS,
              Nashville, Tenn., December 3, 1864.

The undersigned hereby assumes command of the Fourth Corps.

TH. J. WOOD,
Brigadier-General of Volunteers.

HEADQUARTERS FOURTH ARMY CORPS,
Near Nashville, Tenn., December 3, 1864.

Brig. Gen. W. D. WHIPPLE,
Chief of Staff and Assistant Adjutant-General:

GENERAL: I have the honor to report for the information of the commanding general of the forces that I have examined the entire line of defense occupied by my command, and can report it in a very defensible state now, and in a few hours more I think it will be impregnable. I will keep the men employed till the work is completed.

I am, very respectfully, your obedient servant,
TH. J. WOOD,
Brigadier-General of Volunteers, Commanding.

———

CIRCULAR, }   HEADQUARTERS FOURTH ARMY CORPS,
No. 22.   }   *Nashville, December 3, 1864—6 p. m.*

Division commanders will have reveille at 4.30 a. m. to-morrow. At the earliest appearance of daylight the troops must be under arms; at 5.30 a. m. division officers of the day and picket officers must be on the line to see that all is right. Division commanders will promptly report any movement of the enemy that may be discerned to-morrow morning.

By command of Brigadier-General Wood:
J. S. FULLERTON,
Lieutenant-Colonel and Assistant Adjutant-General.

———

HEADQUARTERS FOURTH ARMY CORPS,
Nashville, Tenn., December 3, 1864—10 p. m.

Brigadier-General BEATTY,
Commanding Third Division:

The general commanding directs that you relieve the Fortieth Regiment Missouri Infantry and Tenth Kansas Infantry, at daylight to-morrow morning, from duty with your division, and order them to report to Maj. Gen. A. J. Smith. This in accordance with orders received from headquarters Department of the Cumberland.

Very respectfully, your obedient servant,
W. H. SINCLAIR,
Assistant Adjutant-General.

———

HDQRS. FIRST BRIGADE, THIRD DIVISION, 23D ARMY CORPS,
Nashville, Tenn., December 3, 1864.

Capt. THEO. COX,
Asst. Adjt. Gen., Third Division, Twenty-third Army Corps:

CAPTAIN: In compliance with instructions, I would respectfully state that there was no estimate of the prisoners taken on the 30th ultimo; they were ordered to the rear as soon as received in our lines. There were no arms captured, all being left on the field.

Very respectfully, your obedient servant,
J. W. REILLY,
Brigadier-General, Commanding.

HEADQUARTERS DEPARTMENT OF THE CUMBERLAND,
Nashville, December 3, 1864.

Maj. Gen. A. J. SMITH,
Commanding Detachment Army of the Tennessee:

GENERAL: The front occupied by General Wood's corps is quite long and as much extended as the number of his troops will admit. The withdrawal of the Fortieth Missouri and Tenth Kansas Regiments, already in line, will leave a gap which he has not the power to fill, except by contracting his line, without causing it to become much attenuated. In consequence of this state of things, the major-general commanding directs that you occupy a portion of General Wood's line equal to the front of two regiments, as being the only method which occurs to him of remedying the difficulty.

Very respectfully, your obedient servant,
WM. D. WHIPPLE,
Brigadier-General and Chief of Staff.

HDQRS. CAVALRY CORPS, MIL. DIV. OF THE MISSISSIPPI,
Nashville, Tenn., December 3, 1864.

Maj. W. P. CHAMBLISS,
Special Inspector of Cavalry:

MAJOR: I send Captain Van Antwerp, aide-de-camp, with the orders directing the seizure of every species of property necessary to put the cavalry forces of this division into efficient condition. You will perceive that the authority is ample; use it without stint for seizure both of equipments and horses. You may send Captain Van Antwerp to hunt for arms and other property consigned to you. With the authority in his hands I think he can do good service. I leave many of the details to you, in pursuance of General Thomas' general instructions, confident that you will do all in your power to push matters to the utmost. Spare nothing which is necessary, but have everything done in an orderly manner.

Very respectfully, your obedient servant,
J. H. WILSON,
Brevet Major-General.

SPECIAL ORDERS, }   HEADQUARTERS CAVALRY CORPS,
                           MILITARY DIVISION OF THE MISSISSIPPI,
No. 27.   }   *Nashville, Tenn., December 3, 1864.*

*   *   *   *   *   *   *

II. Brig. Gen. L. D. Watkins, temporarily assigned to the command of the mounted and dismounted men of Cavalry Corps, Military Division of the Mississippi, at Nashville, per paragraph III, Special Orders, No. 23, from these headquarters, of date November 29, 1864, is hereby relieved from this duty, and will assume command of his brigade.

*   *   *   *   *   *   *

By command of Brevet Major-General Wilson:
E. B. BEAUMONT,
Major and Assistant Adjutant-General.

GENERAL ORDERS, ⎰ HEADQUARTERS CAVALRY CORPS,
　　　　　　　　 ⎱ MILITARY DIVISION OF THE MISSISSIPPI,
　　No. 5.　　　　　　　　 *Nashville, Tenn., December 3, 1864.*

I. By authority of the Secretary of War, sufficient serviceable cavalry horses will be immediately seized to mount all dismounted men of the Cavalry Corps.

II. Division commanders will make the necessary details to carry this order into effect. They are authorized to send detachments to any part of Tennessee and Kentucky, under the command of trustworthy and competent officers, who will give memorandum receipts for all horses taken. Upon the presentation of the memorandum receipts to the division or corps quartermaster, the proper vouchers will be issued. The price allowed will be that fixed by the Cavalry Bureau. Horses and mares will be taken. The names of the officers detailed must be sent at once to these headquarters.

By command of Brevet Major-General Wilson:

　　　　　　　　　　　E. B. BEAUMONT,
　　　　　　　Major and Assistant Adjutant-General.

CIRCULAR.]   HDQRS. CAV. CORPS, MIL. DIV. OF THE MISS.,
　　　　　　　　　　 Edgefield, Tenn., December 3, 1864.

In order to facilitate the pressing of horses, and that there may be no collision between the details organized under General Orders, No. 5, from these headquarters, division commanders will instruct the officers sent in command of the details from their respective divisions to confine their operations strictly to the districts of country assigned them below, viz: The Sixth Division, Brigadier-General Johnson commanding, will have that portion of country lying west of the Springfield and Russellville turnpike, and will send as far north as Hopkinsville, Ky.; the First Division, Brigadier-General Croxton commanding, will have that portion of the country lying east of the Russellville turnpike and west of the Bowling Green turnpike, and will send as for north as the railroad from Bowling Green to Russellville; the Seventh Division, Brigadier-General Knipe commanding, will have that portion of the country lying between the Bowling Green and Glasgow roads, sending as far north as the road from Bowling Green to Glasgow; the Fifth Division, Brigadier-General Hatch commanding, will have all the country lying east of the Glasgow road, sending as far as Tompkinsville.

By command of Brevet Major-General Wilson:

　　　　　　　　　　　A. J. ALEXANDER,
　　　　　　Lieutenant-Colonel and Acting Chief of Staff.

　　HDQRS. CAVALRY CORPS, MIL. DIV. OF THE MISSISSIPPI,
　　　　　　　　　　 Nashville, Tenn., December 3, 1864.
Brig. Gen. J. T. CROXTON,
　　Comdg. First and Second Brigades, First Cavalry Division:

GENERAL: You will please send one regiment out on the Franklin pike to-day at 10 a. m. to make a reconnaissance; having accomplished this duty, you will return to camp.

By command of Brevet Major-General Wilson:

　　　　　　　　　　　E. B. BEAUMONT,
　　　　　　Major and Assistant Adjutant-General.

GENERAL ORDERS, ⎱ HDQRS. 2D BRIG., 1ST DIV., CAV. CORPS,
                ⎰   MILITARY DIVISION OF THE MISSISSIPPI,
    No. 7.   ⎰   *Louisville, Ky., December 3, 1864.*

This command will march at 8 a. m. to-morrow on the Shepherdsville pike, in the following order: First Wisconsin Cavalry, Second Indiana Cavalry, Fourth Indiana Cavalry. No passes will be given in the morning, and the men must be kept in camp. The orders issued yesterday will be enforced.

By command of Col. O. H. La Grange:

DAN. S. MOULTON,
Lieutenant and Acting Assistant Adjutant-General.

HDQRS. CAVALRY CORPS, MIL. DIV. OF THE MISSISSIPPI,
Nashville, Tenn., December 3, 1864.

Brig. Gen. ELI LONG,
    Comdg. Second Div., Cav. Corps, Mil. Div. of the Mississippi:

GENERAL: This and an order for the seizure of every species of property necessary to put your command in an efficient condition will be handed you by Captain Van Antwerp, aide de-camp. In executing this order, confer freely with Major Chambliss, to whom ample instructions have been sent. In sending out details, select good judges of horses, and require them to use the form of receipt herewith inclosed;* have them printed, and send the bill to Captain Carling, chief quartermaster Cavalry Corps. I cannot impress it too strongly upon you to use your utmost exertions in carrying out this order. If you should not be able to procure arms enough for your entire command by the time horses and equipments are seized, leave the unarmed portion, under command of proper officers, to come forward as soon as arms are supplied. Report to me at once and from time to time when you can be here.

I am, general, your obedient servant,

J. H. WILSON,
Brevet Major-General.

SAINT LOUIS, MO., *December 3, 1864.*

Major-General WILSON:

Cannot leave Saint Louis before 7th instant; have marched 1,800 miles; command was broken down; did not get a horse to Saint Louis; obtained 1,100 horses here, and other equipments. Colonel Winslow's detachment will leave Memphis on 6th instant.

F. W. BENTEEN,
Colonel.

HEADQUARTERS SEVENTH OHIO VOLUNTEER CAVALRY,
Near Hyde's Ferry, December 3, 1864—12 m.

Capt. W. B. SMITH,
    Actg. Asst. Adjt. Gen., First Brig., Sixth Div., Cavalry Corps:

CAPTAIN: I have the honor to report that I stopped the ferry-boat communications at Buena Vista and Hyde's Ferries, by detaching the

---

* Omitted.

boats from the floats and tying up the boats, under guard, on this bank. Two companies are on duty scouting and picketing in rear of each of the ferries, and the remainder of the companies near the ferries. Scouts are being made down the country, out on the road leading back from Hyde's Ferry. Their reports will be forwarded.

Very respectfully,

ISRAEL GARRARD,
Colonel Seventh Ohio Volunteer Cavalry.

HEADQUARTERS SEVENTH OHIO VOLUNTEER CAVALRY,
Hyde's Ferry, December 3, 1864—8 p. m.

Capt. W. B. SMITH,
Actg. Asst. Adjt. Gen., First Brig., Sixth Div., Cavalry Corps:

CAPTAIN: I have the honor to report that the scout made down to the point below Bell's Mill, where the bend of the river comes back near the turnpike, as shown on the map given me, reports a few rebel cavalrymen on this side of the river, having swum their horses over; none were seen. The naval supply steam-boat was fired into from the bluffs between here and Bell's Mill, struck several times, but ran past that battery, but finding another battery below, ran into this shore and tied up. The captain of the boat has come up here to get the gun-boat lying here to assist him, and has reported these facts. The boat lies about eight miles from here. I have had no instructions or orders but to stop the ferries and tie up the boats on this side of the river. I would like to have such instructions as would guide me in the nature and extent of the scouting to be done by me. Up to this time the gun-boat has not gone down to render assistance to the naval supply boat, and is, I understand, waiting for orders. The crew of the boat are with it.

Very respectfully, your obedient servant,

ISRAEL GARRARD,
Colonel Seventh Ohio Volunteer Cavalry.

GALLATIN ROAD, NEAR CUMBERLAND RIVER,
December 3, 1864.

Maj. E. B. BEAUMONT,
Assistant Adjutant-General, Cavalry Corps, Nashville, Tenn.:

MAJOR: Am here in good shape. Just before leaving Edgefield, at 4 p. m. of the 2d, the battalion which was at Petersburg [was] chased to within three miles of Nashville on the Murfreesborough pike. I would like to furnish my command and fit it for field service here, where there are good facilities for it. I can get horses, forage, and, indeed, everything save arms and ammunition. There are some 2,000 convalescent horses around the town; the guerrillas steal large numbers of them. They seem to be concentrating hereabout, as several bodies of 75 and 100 are known to exist. I will try to disperse some of them. I find that I cannot send less than fifty men three miles from camp. A large drove of beeves was scattered yesterday at the tunnel, and day before 200 horses taken from a corral. I believe that these small bodies are preparing to join Forrest for some move, sure. A crying evil exists in the fact that almost every citizen, without reference to politics, has protection from some general or other for his horses, mules, forage, stock, &c.; without trespassing on these, it will puzzle any one to subsist his command. Please call attention to this. General Wilson can probably get an order overriding the whole concern; should be done if possible. General Schofield's train is at Franklin, [Ky.]; I have sent to hurry it, and will do all I can to help it. I have detailed some good men to dress in citizens' clothes and scout on the other side of the Cumberland. Two skiffs for these will be kept; all others for forty miles up and ten down I will destroy. Main roads will picket. Will communicate when anything turns up. The force here—Eleventh Minnesota and some negroes, total, 500—should be at the tunnel, seven miles up the railroad. Forrest, if he does get up the r[iver], could render the railroad useless there in an hour or two for six months. Enough forage for us and the enemy all over the country. My force will be shod completely in two days. Please order every man fit for duty from Camp Webster to this place, and let me have about 400 carbines and enough ammunition to run my supplies to 200 rounds. This is a good location to put everything in trim for a campaign.

Very respectfully, your obedient servant,

J. H. HAMMOND,
Brevet Brigadier-General.

GALLATIN, *December 3, 1864.*

Maj. E. B. BEAUMONT,
Assistant Adjutant-General, Cavalry Corps:

This town amounts to nothing, but the railroad tunnel, some seven miles north of this, should be defended. If Forrest crosses the river he could in two hours destroy communication for three months.

J. H. HAMMOND,
Brigadier-General.

GALLATIN, TENN., *December 3, 1864.*

Maj. E. B. BEAUMONT,
Assistant Adjutant-General, Cavalry Corps:

Eight companies Twenty-eighth Michigan Infantry with the wagon train; have sent to hasten it, and will help it all I can My command in camp one mile from Cumberland River on Gallatin road. There are plenty of crossings above and below there; principal ones at Huntsville, six miles by pike, Carthage, thirty-six. I will secure or destroy all boats on the river to these points and twenty miles below. I have detailed twenty men to act as scouts on the other side of the river, and will guard besides. Enough forage in the country. This is a better place to organize than Nashville; can get all I want here except ammunition and carbines. Blacksmiths at work, and have pressed and receipted for enough horses to complete the mounting of my command. About 2,000 convalescent horses feeding here, and the guerrillas stealing them as fast as they are good. Bodies of guerrillas (as many as seventy-five together) are through the country.

J. H. HAMMOND,
Brigadier-General.

GALLATIN, *December 3, 1864.*

Major-General WILSON:

Your order to take horses received. Will take all I can find and push the matter with vigor and watch the river well. General Schofield's train left Franklin [Ky.] this evening with 400 guards.

J. H. HAMMOND,
Brevet Brigadier-General.

———

HDQRS. CAVALRY CORPS, MIL. DIV. OF THE MISSISSIPPI,
Nashville, Tenn., December 3, 1864.

Col. G. G. MINER,
Commanding Camp Webster:

COLONEL: You will at once take measures to move all the property of Camp Webster inside the line of fortifications; direct Captain Wilson to procure the necessary transportation. Order at once to their regiments across the river all the men that are fit for active service. Steps are being taken to mount all the cavalry in the command. The Secretary of War has ordered the seizure of all horses for this purpose. The defense of the city is left to the infantry. The infantry arms are to be returned to the arsenal. The Fifth and Sixth Cavalry Divisions, General Croxton's and General Watkins' brigades, of the First Division, are across the river.

By command of Brevet Major-General Wilson:

E. B. BEAUMONT,
Major and Assistant Adjutant-General.

———

GENERAL AND   } HDQRS. DISTRICT OF THE ETOWAH,
SPECIAL ORDERS, No. 1. }   *Chattanooga, December 3, 1864.*

I. The general commanding the district, considering it highly advisable to have this post and its several defenses as strongly held as possible, hereby orders that all civilians within the lines of the post be enrolled and organized into a military force.

II. With the view of having the force enrolled and effectually organized, the general orders and authorizes Col. Edwin S. McCook to take the business in hand at once, and orders him to the command of the force he shall so enroll and organize.

III. All civilians, therefore, within the lines of this post, who are not in the actual employment and pay of the United States Goverement at this post, will proceed instantly, on the publication of these orders, to the rear office of the post guard, there report to Colonel McCook, register their names and residences, have themselves properly enrolled and assigned for military duty, and having been enrolled, hold themselves subject to his orders.

IV. The military duty indicated in these orders will not take the civilians enrolled and organized by Colonel McCook beyond the exterior lines of defense.

V. Colonel McCook has full power to organize the force contemplated in these orders as his experience and judgment best dictate, and he will appoint and order such officers and other assistants to act under him as he thinks best qualified for command, or any other work or duties in connection with the force contemplated.

VI. The force commanded by Colonel McCook will be known as the Civic Guard of Chattanooga.

VII. This order of enrollment and organization comprehends not only all the civilians who may be permanently resident at this post, but all civilians who may be temporarily detained here, whether on business or pleasure, or owing to obstructions on the road.

VIII. Colonel McCook will have every facility afforded him for the proper arming and equipment of the Civic Guard, and will determine, subject to the approval of the general commanding, the signal for the assembling of his command on any sudden emergency.

IX. Every civilian enrolled in the Civic Guard of Chattanooga will be furnished by Colonel McCook with a printed certificate of enrollment. The post provost guards on and after Tuesday, the 6th day of December, will demand, in addition to the usual city pass, the said certificate of enrollment.

X. Any civilian hereby ordered to register and enroll himself in the Civic Guard failing to procure, or to produce on proper demand, the said certificate of enrollment, will be arrested on the spot and handed over to the provost-marshal.

XI. Should the party or parties so arrested fail satisfactorily to explain the circumstances of their not having, or their not producing, the said certificate of enrollment, said party or parties will immediately be sent by the post provost-marshal to work for thirty days on the streets or fortifications.

By order of Brigadier-General Meagher:

H. A. FORD,
Captain and Acting Assistant Adjutant-General.

CLEVELAND, TENN., *December 3, 1864.*

Capt. H. A. FORD,
   Acting Assistant Adjutant-General:

I have sent reconnoitering parties on three of the most important approaches from the south and west, and taken all possible precaution toward the protection of this place. At Tyner's Station I have 200 men and two pieces of artillery; they have a good earth-work, and can without doubt hold it.

H. BOUGHTON,
Colonel.

CLEVELAND, *December 3, 1864.*

Capt. H. A. FORD,
   Acting Assistant Adjutant-General:

One of the patrols I sent out this afternoon has just returned, and reports that a party of rebel cavalry, about eighty strong, crossed the Cleveland and Dalton Railroad at Red Clay before daylight this morning, going in the direction of Ooltewah. Shortly after daylight they returned, recrossed at Red Clay, and passed south. Nothing has been heard of them since that time.

HORACE BOUGHTON,
Colonel, Commanding.

DALTON, *December 3, 1864.*

Capt. H. A. FORD,
    Acting Assistant Adjutant-General:
My picket-lines are attacked. The enemy has sent in a flag of truce.
I will not surrender.

J. B. CULVER,
Colonel, Commanding.

CLARKSVILLE, *December 3, 1864.*

Brig. Gen. WILLIAM D. WHIPPLE,
    Assistant Adjutant-General:
The steamer Kentucky, with three companies of Nineteenth Pennsylvania Cavalry and 170 infantry, has returned, not being able to pass a battery near Harpeth Shoals. A courier has just arrived with dispatches from Colonel Thompson, from Johnsonville, that his force will reach here to-morrow afternoon. A courier says that he could not reach General Cooper, at Centerville.

A. A. SMITH,
Colonel, Commanding.

DANVILLE, *December 3, 1864.*

Brig. Gen. S. S. FRY:
Mr. John Ferry has just reached here direct from his home, three miles east of Perryville; he met a party of twenty-five or thirty guerrillas near his house, was pursued and fired upon by them, but escaped. The guerrillas were moving toward Harrodsburg on the pike between Perryville and that place. Can you send a squad of fifteen or twenty mounted men here to-night? Telegraph line has just been [cut] between here and Lebanon. Please reply.

W. L. GROSS,
Captain and Assistant Superintendent.

HEADQUARTERS DISTRICT OF ILLINOIS,
    Springfield, Ill., December 3, 1864.

Capt. C. H. POTTER,
    Assistant Adjutant-General, Northern Department:
CAPTAIN: I have the honor to transmit herewith the report* of Col. B. J. Sweet, Eighth Regiment Veteran Reserve Corps, commanding post of Chicago, in regard to the late attempted insurrection at that place and the release of the prisoners of war at Camp Douglas by rebel officers and the treasonable order known as the Sons of Liberty. That it was their plan to release all the prisoners of war in this State and Indiana and burn and pillage the country (if successful at Chicago), there is no room for doubt. This order of Sons of Liberty exists in

---

* See November 23, Part I, p. 1077.

nearly every county in this State and Indiana, and robberies and murders are constantly being committed by its members, as I verily believe, assisted to some extent by refugees and guerrillas from the rebel army. The small force at my disposal, outside of the respective garrisons in the district, and most of which has been turned over to the district provost-marshal for the enforcement of the draft, precludes me from suppressing these unlawful acts. Another obstacle is that all the force in this State are infantry. I would recommend that a regiment of cavalry or mounted infantry be sent to this State. If this were done the garrisons of Rock Island and Chicago could be strengthened (which is very much needed) from the One hundred and forty-sixth Illinois and Forty-second Wisconsin, now scattered over the State, and the mounted troops could operate to some purpose against guerrillas. I would respectfully call the attention of the major-general commanding to the very efficient services rendered by Colonel Sweet in the late trouble in Chicago. I can cheerfully recommend Colonel Sweet as an able officer and worthy of promotion.

I have the honor to be, very respectfully, your obedient servant,

JOHN COOK,
Brigadier-General, Commanding.

CHICAGO, *December 3, 1864.*

Major-General HOOKER:

They talk of habeas corpus to release the Sons of Liberty arrested. I ought to have authority from the President to hold them, one and all.

B. J. SWEET,
Colonel, Commanding Post.

HEADQUARTERS NORTHERN DEPARTMENT,
Cincinnati, Ohio, December 3, 1864.

His Excellency Governor BROUGH,
Governor of Ohio:

GOVERNOR: I learned yesterday, through sources I cannot disregard, that unusual activity prevails among Confederate refugees in Canada, and that they have it in mind to make an early descent on Cleveland or Detroit, for purposes of plunder and incendiarism. I learn this from one of our detectives, who is, in fact, one of their own number. For this reason I think that it would be advisable to retain in service the Ohio battery now at Cleveland, if you know of no objection to it, and until further orders keep it where it now is. Should an effort be made to enter the harbor of Cleveland by water, the battery would be of great service at that point. My means of obtaining information are so well perfected that in case that any raid should be projected along the Canada line in my department I expect to have the news in season to anticipate it. I need not tell you, Governor, that if anything of this sort is attempted I intend that somebody shall be hurt before it is over, if I have to go into Canada to do it. If the Canadian authorities allow our enemies to enter the territory to organize for hostile purposes, I shall exercise the same right, and if exception is taken it can be arranged

afterward by negotiation. I am determined that security and tran-
quillity shall prevail along the border while I exercise command of this
department.

Very respectfully, your obedient servant,

JOSEPH HOOKER,
Major-General, Commanding.

WAR DEPARTMENT,
Washington City, December 3, 1864.

Major LUDINGTON,
Lexington:
Your plan approved.*

EDWIN M. STANTON,
Secretary of War.

NASHVILLE, *December 4, 1864—10 p. m.*

Maj. Gen. H. W. HALLECK,
Washington, D. C.:
Last night the enemy planted a battery on the river at Bell's Landing and succeeded in capturing two boats on their way down. As
soon as it was reported, at my request, Commander Fitch, U. S. Navy,
went down with an iron-clad and two or three gun-boats and soon drove
the battery away, recapturing the two steamers. He will make a
reconnaissance in force down the river to-morrow. The enemy remains
in the same position to-day as yesterday. I have also heard from Tullahoma, via Knoxville, to-day; the railroad is uninjured that far, and
no signs of the enemy in that neighborhood; I have heard no firing in
the direction of Murfreesborough, and therefore infer that the enemy has
made no move in that direction yet, but is now turning his attention to
crossing the river below; for any such attempt I am prepared to meet.

GEO. H. THOMAS,
Major-General, U. S. Volunteers, Commanding.

HEADQUARTERS DEPARTMENT OF THE CUMBERLAND,
Nashville, December 4, 1864.

Bvt. Brig. Gen. E. D. TOWNSEND:
Major-General Schofield informs me that Major-General Stoneman
has, by order of the Secretary of War, been relieved from duty in the
Department of the Ohio. I respectfully request that the order may be
countermanded, as General Schofield has no other general officer to
whom he can intrust the affairs of East Tennessee with as much safety
as General Stoneman.

GEO. H. THOMAS.
Major-General, U. S. Volunteers, Commanding.

---

* See November 29, Part I, p. 1165.

MOUND CITY, ILL., *December 3 [4?], 1864—5 p. m.*
Major-General THOMAS:

Your confidential dispatch of 11 o'clock yesterday just received.
Accept my heartiest thanks for the information given and correction
made. I have had night and Sunday work done to get another good
iron-clad ready. Hope to see you in a few days. Please instruct operators always to hand you a copy of my dispatches to my officers operating
near you. Wishing you the fullest success,

Faithfully, yours,

S. P. LEE.

U. S. STEAMER MOOSE,
Off Nashville, Tenn., December 4, 1864.
Major-General THOMAS,
Comdg. *Army of the Cumberland, Nashville, Tenn.:*

GENERAL: The enemy has heavy batteries on the river at Bell's
Mills. I went down last night and engaged them, and had them
silenced for a time. Two of my boats passed below them, and are still
down the river. It was too dark for us to continue the engagement
successfully, there being danger of getting our boats foul and unman-
ageable. I am going with the other iron-clad to make a reconnaissance
in force this morning. From the force that we found last night, the
appearance of the batteries, the great number of camp-fires, &c., I am
led to believe that Hood's left rests on the river at that point, and that
Forrest commands them. Will you please telegraph to Clarksville for-
bidding steamers coming above that place, and also allow none to leave
Nashville for down the river until the batteries are removed. The
enemy seems to have a heavy force at this end of his line.

Very respectfully, your obedient servant,

LE ROY FITCH,
Lieut. Commander, Comdg. 9th and 10th Dists., Miss. Squadron.

U. S. STEAMER MOOSE,
Cumberland River, December 4, 1864.
Major-General THOMAS,
Comdg. *Army of the Cumberland, Nashville, Tenn.:*

GENERAL: I have cleaned out the rebel battery and recaptured the
two steamers captured by the enemy last night, and driven their left
flank back from the river at that point, though I do not think it safe
for transports to run yet from Clarksville up. I think Forrest commands the left of Hood's army, as General Buford's brigade engaged
us last night.

Very respectfully, your obedient servant,

LE ROY FITCH,
Lieut. Commander, Comdg. 9th and 10th Dists., Miss. Squadron.

U. S. STEAMER MOOSE,
Off Nashville, December 4, 1864.
Maj. Gen. GEORGE H. THOMAS,
Comdg. *the Army of the Cumberland, Nashville, Tenn.:*

GENERAL: Your kind note* of this evening is received. I perceive
you are under a slight error in regard to the position of the battery

------

* Not found.

which we engaged. The battery we engaged last night was not at Harpeth Shoals, but at Bell's Mills. It is about thirty-five miles from here to Harpeth, while it is only four miles to Bell's Mills—that is, four miles by land, but eighteen by river. The river makes a large bend and comes nearly back to the city. Bell's Landing is in this bend, at the nearest point to the city. I would have gone down to Harpeth to-day, but I heard firing in this direction and thought, perhaps, there would be a general attack, and that my boats might be able to assist you on the right. The heavy boats are so slow that I would not have been able to reach here again until to-morrow afternoon. I will make a thorough reconnaissance down there as soon as possible, and will inform you just as soon as I know the river to be clear. I will then try to arrange regular convoys, but at present, owing to the position of the enemy's left and the crookedness of the river, it would be best for us not to give the rebels the least chance to disable or capture any more of our boats.

Very respectfully, your obedient servant,
LE ROY FITCH,
Lieut. Commander, Comdg. 9th and 10th Dists., Miss. Squadron.

NASHVILLE, TENN., *December 4, 1864.*

Brig. Gen. W. D. WHIPPLE,
Chief of Staff:

GENERAL: The following copy of a telegram just received is respectfully furnished you for the information of the major-general commanding:

CLARKSVILLE, *December 3, 1864.*

Courier just arrived reports that Colonel Thompson, in command of forces from Northwestern Railroad, will arrive to-morrow.
I. P. WILLIAMS,
Captain and Assistant Quartermaster.

Very respectfully, your obedient servant,
JAS. F. RUSLING,
Captain and Assistant Quartermaster,
Acting Chief Quartermaster, Department of the Cumberland.

NASHVILLE, TENN., *December 4, 1864—10 p. m.*

Maj. T. T. ECKERT:

Nothing of special importance since last report. The enemy has extended his lines and thrown up works. Our artillery has been used quite freely to impede his movements, and the replies have been feeble and quickly silenced. At nearest point the rebel skirmish line is about 400 yards from our main works. Citizens and negroes have been impressed to complete the intrenchments, which are now very strong. River falling slowly. Large number of tin-clads and one heavy iron-plated gun-boat here. All quiet at Chattanooga, Dalton, and Tullahoma. No news of Forrest.

J. C. VAN DUZER.

SPECIAL ORDERS, } HDQRS. DEPT. AND ARMY OF THE TENN.,
    No. 273.   }   *Louisville, Ky., December 4, 1864.*

I. Maj. Gen. John A. Logan, commanding Fifteenth Army Corps, having reported to these headquarters on expiration of his leave of absence, and being unable to join his command on account of the present movement of the army, has permission, at his own request, to visit City Point, Va.

By order of Maj. Gen. O. O. Howard:

WM. T. CLARK,
Assistant Adjutant-General.

HEADQUARTERS ARMY OF THE OHIO,
Nashville, Tenn., December 4, 1864.

Colonel MAXWELL,
    Comdg. Twenty-sixth Kentucky Infty., Bowling Green, Ky.:

Come forward at once with your regiment, by rail, to this city and report at these headquarters. The quartermaster's department will furnish transportation.

By order of Major-General Schofield:

J. A. CAMPBELL,
Major and Assistant Adjutant-General.

BOWLING GREEN, *December 4, 1864.*

General SCHOFIELD:

The Twenty-sixth Kentucky is ordered from this post to Nashville, which leaves this post almost without troops. Can the Twenty-sixth Kentucky remain here?

J. H. GRIDER,
Colonel, Commanding.

HDQRS. CAVALRY CORPS, MIL. DIV. OF THE MISSISSIPPI,
Edgefield, December 4, 1864—10 p. m.

Major-General THOMAS:

General Hammond reports a force of rebel cavalry at Lebanon, but no evidence of an intention to move to Gallatin further than that indicated by their position.

Very respectfully, your obedient servant,

J. H. WILSON,
Brevet Major-General.

HDQRS. CAVALRY CORPS, MIL. DIV. OF THE MISSISSIPPI,
Nashville, Tenn., December 4, 1864.

ADJUTANT-GENERAL U. S. ARMY,
    Washington, D. C.:

SIR: I have the honor to recommend and request the appointment of the following officers upon the staff of the Cavalry Corps, Military Division of the Mississippi:

Maj. E. B. Beaumont, assistant adjutant-general, to be assistant adjutant-general, with the rank of lieutenant-colonel; First Lieut.

Henry E. Noyes, Second U. S. Cavalry, to be assistant inspector-general, with the rank of lieutenant-colonel; Capt. Elias B. Carling, assistant quartermaster, to be chief quartermaster, with the rank of lieutenant-colonel; Capt. J. C. Read, commissary of subsistence of volunteers, to be chief commissary of subsistence, with the rank of lieutenant-colonel, to date from December 4, 1864. These appointments, with the exception of the last, should be made to date from the 24th of October, 1864, the officers having performed their duties since that time.

I have also to request that First Lieut. John N. Andrews, Eighth U. S. Infantry, may be appointed as an aide-de-camp on my personal staff, with the rank of major, to date from October 5, the date of my appointment to duty as a major-general by brevet. I hope the full staff may be allowed, as my command is extensive and demands all the activity and zeal the officers are capable of giving.

Very respectfully, your obedient servant,

J. H. WILSON,
Brevet Major-General.

HDQRS. CAVALRY CORPS, MIL. DIV. OF THE MISSISSIPPI,
Nashville, Tenn., December 4, 1864.

Lieut. JOSEPH HEDGES,
Commanding Fourth U. S. Cavalry:

LIEUTENANT: General Wilson directs that you report to him with the Fourth U. S. Cavalry, at an early hour to-morrow, at his headquarters in Edgefield.

By command of Brevet Major-General Wilson:

E. B. BEAUMONT,
Major and Assistant Adjutant-General.

LOUISVILLE, *December 4, 1864.*

Captain BEAUMONT,
Assistant Adjutant-General:

The Second Brigade, First Cavalry Division, marches for Nashville this morning.

O. H. LA GRANGE,
Colonel, Commanding.

HEADQUARTERS SECOND DIVISION, CAVALRY CORPS,
MILITARY DIVISION OF THE MISSISSIPPI,
Camp near Louisville, Ky., December 4, 1864.

Bvt. Maj. Gen. J. H. WILSON,
Chief of Cavalry, Military Division of the Mississippi:

I have received your two dispatches of this date. Will consult with Major Chambliss, who will be in town to-morrow, and will probably be able to secure the most of the horses in Louisville on the 7th and 8th. You have a statement of how the command is armed. Shall I arm them with muskets or anything I can get? They have now on hand here nearly enough, and before I get the requisite number of horses will probably have quite enough horse equipments to fit out the command. I will get my headquarters and the cavalry brigade off as soon as I possibly can after receiving an answer to this from you, and will leave Miller to come along with his brigade as soon as he can. There are 1,400 horses here for issue in the Government stables, and the Fourth Michigan takes 800 of them to-morrow. While I individually am disposed to do all that I can to get the division in the field, and to the assistance of the command at Nashville as soon as possible, and have no desire to keep it here, as it is doing no earthly good to itself or any one else here, still I think that although we might assist in relieving the temporary pressure by hurrying into the field poorly armed and equipped (though probably not sufficiently to affect the ultimate result), that the material and permanent interests of the service would not be as beneficially affected as if we were allowed to remain here and get into proper shape before entering the field.

I am, very respectfully, your obedient servant,

ELI LONG,
Brigadier-General, U. S. Vols., Comdg. Second Cavalry Division.

HDQRS. CAVALRY CORPS, MIL. DIV. OF THE MISSISSIPPI,
Edgefield, Tenn., December 4, 1864.

Brig. Gen. EDWARD HATCH,
Commanding Fifth Division, Cavalry Corps:

GENERAL: The brevet major-general commanding directs me to say that he has used every exertion to stop the straggling, plundering, and stealing from the citizens in this vicinity by the soldiers of this command; as yet, however, it has been unavailing. He therefore directs that you order a detail of 300 men, under an efficient field officer, to report at once at these headquarters, for the purpose of establishing a line of sentinels in front of this camp. He desires you to have a roll-call at once, and punish severely all men absent without proper authority.

I am, general, very respectfully, your obedient servant,

A. J. ALEXANDER,
Lieutenant-Colonel and Acting Chief of Staff.

(Same to Brig. Gen. R. W. Johnson, commanding Sixth Division, and Brig. Gen. J. F. Knipe, commanding Seventh Division.)

HEADQUARTERS SIXTH DIVISION, CAVALRY CORPS,
MILITARY DIVISION OF THE MISSISSIPPI,
Edgefield, Tenn., December 4, 1864.

Maj. E. B. BEAUMONT,
Assistant Adjutant-General, Cavalry Corps:

MAJOR: The officer who commanded the reconnaissance sent to investigate the reported crossing of the enemy at Bell's Mills, reports that he has visited the place of the alleged crossing, and finds no enemy there; that they captured two boats there, or near there, last evening and commenced unloading them; that our gun-boats coming up shelled the enemy, drove them off, reloaded the boats, and brought them away.

The enemy's pickets are visible on the opposite side of the [river], but no considerable force has been seen by the citizens in the vicinity, and there is nothing to indicate the presence of any.

Very respectfully, your obedient servant,

R. W. JOHNSON,
Brigadier-General of Volunteers.

GENERAL ORDERS, ⎱ HDQRS. SIXTH DIVISION, CAV. CORPS,
　　　　　　　　⎰ MILITARY DIVISION OF THE MISS.,
No. 3.　　　　　　　*Edgefield, Tenn., December 4, 1864.*

The following officers are announced as the staff of this division: Capt. E. T. Wells, assistant adjutant-general; Surg. Isaac Train, Seventh Ohio Cavalry, chief surgeon; First Lieut. L. T. Morris, Nineteenth U. S. Infantry, aide-de-camp; First Lieut. W. R. Lowe, Nineteenth U. S. Infantry, aide-de-camp; Capt. T. F. Allen, Seventh Ohio Cavalry, inspector; Capt. E. D. Baker, assistant quartermaster; Capt. Samuel C. Glover, commissary of subsistence; Capt. John J. Kessler, Forty-ninth Ohio Volunteers, provost-marshal; First Lieut. D. W. Fisher, Seventh Ohio Cavalry, ambulance director; First Lieut. R. A. McKee, Fifth Iowa Cavalry, ordnance officer. Those of the officers above-named not now upon duty will report in person without delay.

R. W. JOHNSON,
Brigadier-General of Volunteers.

HEADQUARTERS FIRST BRIGADE, SEVENTH DIVISION,
Gallatin Road, December 4, 1864.
Maj. E. B. BEAUMONT,
Assistant Adjutant-General, Cavalry Corps:

MAJOR: I learn that there is a heavy force of the enemy's cavalry in Lebanon; they came there last night. I have all the crossings picketed to Hartsville up and Bender's Ferry below this. My scouts cross the river to-night regularly organized, and with the means of communicating with me. I have 375 men out, in three parties, pressing horses.

Very respectfully, your obedient servant,

J. H. HAMMOND,
Brevet Brigadier-General.

GALLATIN. *December 4, 1864.*
Maj. E. B. BEAUMONT,
Assistant Adjutant-General, Cavalry Corps:

There is a heavy force of the enemy at Lebanon, Tenn., ten miles from the Cole's Ferry crossing, twelve from Gallatin crossing. I have pickets at all the crossings for twelve miles up the river. Please order all my men at Nashville and Camp Webster, with officers, fit for duty to report to me here at once. General Schofield's train is mostly in, and will be pushed forward at once.

J. H. HAMMOND,
Brevet Brigadier-General.

BUCK LODGE, TENN., *December 4, 1864.*

Lieut. H. D. BROWN,
    Acting Assistant Adjutant-General, Gallatin, Tenn.:

SIR: I have the honor to report to you that yesterday at 4 p. m. it was reported to me by a citizen that about twenty guerrillas had crossed the railroad between Buck Lodge and South Tunnel, and that perhaps the railroad was damaged. I sent immediately a patrol toward South Tunnel, and found that at a point one mile south of Buck Lodge, and half a mile north of the bridge picket, four rails had been removed from the track and the telegraph cut. I ordered my men to repair the track, and the same time stopped the passenger train which was just coming down. The telegraph was repaired by the engineer. You will allow me to say that the act was done in full sight of the bridge picket, and that it could not have been done if the workmen on the railroad had made application for a guard instead of working without. I was with my company at skirmish drill at the same time, not more than half a mile from that place, and heard the hammering, but as I knew the workmen were there I had no suspicion.

I remain, sir, very respectfully, your obedient servant,

ADAM BUCK,
Captain Company A, Commanding Post.

TANTALON, *December 4, 1864.*

Major HOFFMAN:

I have just returned from Elk River bridge; there has been no enemy heard of in that vicinity, and neither the road nor telegraph has been disturbed to Murfreesborough. Breckinridge is reported at McMinnville. The officers at Elk River bridge say they have heard cannonading all day in the direction of Nashville.

WM. J. PALMER,
Colonel Fifteenth Pennsylvania Cavalry.

MURFREESBOROUGH, *December 4, 1864.*

COMMANDING OFFICER,
    Chattanooga:

Hood is now front of Nashville. No communication between this and that place. Heavy firing heard in that direction between 10 and 12 o'clock last night. It may be an effort was made to take some block-houses, or perhaps a fight at Nashville. A. J. Smith and force was at Nashville on the 30th with two corps and a piece. General Steedman was recalled on the 1st instant, though I fear two of his trains were captured; one of them got off the track, and both were delayed till the 2d instant. It is reported the trains were captured, but not the troops. A heavy battle was fought at Franklin on the evening of the 30th. The rebels charged and took two lines of intrenched rifle-pits, so they say, and wanted to take the third. Have Captain Leadenbetter prisoner here, who was at the fight. He says the rebels lost nine generals, five killed and four wounded, and between 5,000 and 8,000 killed and wounded. The battle began about one hour by sun and lasted until 11 or 11.30 o'clock. They made repeated efforts to take by assault our third line, but failed. I believe Schofield and Stanley only were in the battle. After the fight they withdrew toward Nashville. Captain Leadenbetter says all right here, and able to flog Hood, if he will come. Block-houses on road south of here garrisoned and all right, also up to and beyond La Vergne.

LOVELL H. ROUSSEAU,
Major-General.

ORDERS.]   HEADQUARTERS DISTRICT OF THE ETOWAH,
Nashville, December 4, 1864.

I. Captain Hotchkiss, acting chief of artillery, District of the Etowah, is relieved from further duty in that capacity, and will rejoin his company as soon as practicable.

II. Captain Aleshire, Eighteenth Ohio Battery, senior artillery officer with this command, will act as chief of artillery during the present campaign. He will be respected accordingly.

By command of Major-General Steedman:

S. B. MOE,
Major and Assistant Adjutant-General.

HEADQUARTERS DEPARTMENT OF THE CUMBERLAND,
Nashville, December 4, 1864—9 a. m.

Col. A. A. SMITH,
Clarksville:

Do not allow any more transport steamers to come up the river until further orders. Get Colonel Thompson and command across the river as soon as possible.

GEO. H. THOMAS,
Major-General, U. S. Volunteers, Commanding.

NASHVILLE, *December 4, 1864.*

Col. A. A. SMITH,
Clarksville:

Captain Fitch has cleaned out the rebel battery down the river and recaptured the two steamers captured last night. He does not think it safe for transports to run up from Clarksville yet.

WM. D. WHIPPLE,
Brigadier-General.

CLARKSVILLE, *December 4, 1864—1.30 p. m.*

Brig. Gen. W. D. WHIPPLE:

Just arrived; the head of my column is opposite; will be ready to cross in three hours; will bring teams first. It will probably take us all night to cross, as there are nearly 200 wagons. Have you any further orders? The command is in good condition; all we need is provisions.

C. R. THOMPSON,
Colonel, Commanding.

NASHVILLE, *December 4, 1864.*

Col. C. R. THOMPSON,
    Clarksville :

Come to this place with your command, unless Colonel Smith desires another regiment, in which case leave one and come with the rest.

WM. D. WHIPPLE,
Brigadier-General, &c.

———

ACTING ASSISTANT QUARTERMASTER'S OFFICE,
RIVER AND DEPOT TRANSPORTATION,
Nashville, Tenn., December 4, 1864.

Bvt. Brig. Gen. J. L. DONALDSON,
    Chief Quartermaster, Department of the Cumberland :

GENERAL: I have the honor to report that, agreeable to my orders of the 3d instant, the U. S. tow-boat N. J. Bigley, under convoy of the U. S. gun-boat Newsboy, proceeded up the river to Young's Point, near Hartsville, 100 miles above this place, for the purpose of bringing to this post detachments from different batteries cutting timber at that point, arriving there at 11 a. m., leaving at 12.30 p. m. to-day, and reaching this post at 7 o'clock this evening with the troops on board. No enemy seen, or any evidence that he had been upon the river.

I am, general, very respectfully, your obedient servant,

S. H. STEVENS,
First Lieut., Chicago Board of Trade Battery, Illinois Vols., and Acting Assistant Quartermaster, U. S. Volunteers.

———

HEADQUARTERS DEPARTMENT OF THE OHIO,
Louisville, Ky., December 4, 1864.

Major-General STONEMAN,
    Knoxville, Tenn. :

I received a few days ago a telegram to General Schofield, from the War Department, directing him to relieve you from duty in this department and order you to Cincinnati to await orders. I sent it forward to him, and have heard nothing from it since.

G. M. BASCOM,
Lieutenant-Colonel and Assistant Adjutant-General.

———

HEADQUARTERS DEPARTMENT OF THE OHIO,
Louisville, Ky., December 4, 1864.

Maj. Gen. GEORGE STONEMAN,
    Knoxville, Tenn.:

Richmond papers admit that Sherman will reach the sea-coast; he crossed the Oconee River some days ago. Great fears are expressed for the safety of Savannah. It is reported that Sherman captured Millen, on the Georgia Central Railroad, on the 29th ultimo. All quiet around Richmond. No heavy fighting near Nashville since the battle at Franklin. There are rumors that Hood is trying to cross the Cumberland River.

G. M. BASCOM,
Lieutenant-Colonel and Assistant Adjutant-General.

LEXINGTON, KY., *December 4, 1864.*

Major WEST,
    Eleventh Michigan Cavalry, Mount Sterling, Ky. :
Send scouts to the front, toward Pound and Stony Gaps, and Hazard, to learn all they can about a force reported coming in that way; direct them to go as far as possible. Report the receipt of this order and what they learn. Press horses, if necessary, to mount men, and report how many men you can mount armed.
    By order of Brigadier-General McLean:
                                        J. S. BUTLER,
                                Assistant Adjutant-General.

———

MOUNT STERLING, *December 4, 1864.*

Capt. J. S. BUTLER,
    Assistant Adjutant-General :
SIR: I will send the scout immediately. Can mount seventy-five men in the Eleventh Michigan; have only thirteen carbines for them. I sent you a report last week that will show you how we stand.
    Respectfully, yours,
                                        GEO. J. WEST,
                                Major, Commanding Post.

———

LEXINGTON, KY., *December 4, 1864.*

Col. GEORGE W. GALLUP,
    Louisa, Ky. :
Send scouts immediately from Louisa to Pound and Stony Gaps and Louisa Fork, and direct them to go as far as possible and learn all about a force coming in that way. Report the receipt of these orders and anything you learn. If necessary, press horses to mount men.
    By order of Brigadier-General McLean:
                                        J. S. BUTLER,
                                Assistant Adjutant-General.

———

LEXINGTON, *December 4, 1864.*

Brig. Gen. HUGH EWING,
    Louisville, Ky. :
Dr. J. M. Bailey, Twenty-sixth Kentucky, telegraphs from Bowling Green that the Twenty-sixth leaves there to-day, and the rebels will take possession of the place as soon as the regiment leaves. No troops can be sent from General McLean's command to you at present. Is there not sufficient of the Twelfth [U. S. Colored] Heavy Artillery at Bowling Green to protect the place?
    Respectfully,
                                        J. BATES DICKSON,
                                Captain and Assistant Adjutant-General.

LEXINGTON, *December 4, 1864.*

Brig. Gen. HUGH EWING,
    Louisville, Ky. :

Keep your command well in hand and ready for any emergency; there seems to be good reason for anticipating an invasion of Eastern Kentucky. Should it occur you must spare every available man and send here, if needed, any troops en route through Louisville. Be vigilant, and if called on for troops have them in such shape they can move at once.

By order of Brevet Major-General Burbridge:
                    J. BATES DICKSON,
            Captain and Assistant Adjutant-General.

———

SMITHLAND, *December 4, 1864.*

Brigadier-General MEREDITH:

SIR: Steamer Mars reports being fired into by both artillery and musketry eighteen miles this side of Nashville, Tenn.
                    HENRY P. REED,
                Captain, Commanding Post.

———

WAR DEPARTMENT,
                December 5, 1864—11.55 a. m.

Lieutenant-General GRANT:

It appears from an order of Schofield's that he had assigned Stoneman to duty as second in command of the Department of the Ohio. Generals Thomas and Schofield both wish him to hold that position. If you approve of his so doing I am content, although I think him one of the most worthless officers in the service and who has failed in everything intrusted to him. Please say whether he had better be restored to the command given by Schofield, or whether Ammen should not be the chief in command in Schofield's absence. If so, send the order to Adjutant-General Townsend.
                    .EDWIN M. STANTON.

———

CITY POINT, VA., *December 5, 1864—1 p. m.*

Hon. E. M. STANTON,
        Washington :

I am not in favor of using officers who have signally failed when intrusted with commands in important places. Again, as a general rule, when an officer is intrusted with the command of a department, he ought to be allowed to use the material given him in his own way. I would simply suggest the transmission of this dispatch to General Schofield, and leave it discretionary then with him to employ General Stoneman, or relieve him from duty, as he deems best.
                    U. S. GRANT,
                    Lieutenant-General.

WASHINGTON, *December 5, 1864—3.30 p. m.*

Lieutenant-General GRANT,
  City Point, Va.:

The records show that there have been issued at Louisville, Lexington, and Nashville since September 20, 22,000 cavalry horses. This number is exclusive of the cavalry horses previously issued and brought into the department by Grierson and others, and the commands of Burbridge and Garrard, and those sent to Sherman. If this number, without any campaign, is already reduced to 10,000 mounted men, as reported by General Wilson, it may be safely assumed that the cavalry of that army will never be mounted, for the destruction of horses in the last two months has there alone been equal to the remounts obtained from the entire West. None are issued to Rosecrans, Steele, or Canby.

        H. W. HALLECK,
      Major-General and Chief of Staff.

CITY POINT, *December 5, 1864—8 p. m.*

Major-General THOMAS,
  Nashville, Tenn.:

Is there not danger of Forrest moving down the Cumberland* to where he can cross it? It seems to me whilst you should be getting up your cavalry as rapidly as possible to look after Forrest, Hood should be attacked where he is. Time strengthens him, in all probability, as much as it does you.

        U. S. GRANT,
        Lieutenant-General.

NASHVILLE, TENN., *December 5, 1864—10 p. m.*

Maj. Gen. H. W. HALLECK,
  Washington, D. C.:

I have been along my entire line to-day. The enemy has not advanced at all since the 3d instant. If I can perfect my arrangements I shall move against the advanced position of the enemy on the 7th instant. I have heard from Chattanooga this evening that the wires were working north as far as Murfreesborough, though I have not heard anything from General Rousseau. Prisoners we have taken yesterday and to-day report that Hood has to draw his supplies from the Memphis and Charleston Railroad, wagoning from Cherokee Station. If an expedition could be started from Memphis against the Mobile and Ohio Railroad, and thus cut off Hood's means of supply, he will run the risk of losing his whole army, if I am successful in pushing him back.

        GEO. H. THOMAS,
    Major-General, U. S. Volunteers, Commanding.

---

*As recorded in Thomas' telegrams-received book it reads—Tennessee River.

HEADQUARTERS DEPARTMENT OF THE CUMBERLAND,
Nashville, Tenn., December 5, 1864.

Brig. Gen. RICHARD DELAFIELD,
Chief Engineer U. S. Army, Washington, D. C.:

GENERAL: I have the honor to acknowledge the receipt of your communication of the 21st ultimo, and in reply thereto to recommend the following-named officers of the Corps of Engineers for promotion to brevet rank for meritorious services rendered in the discharge of their appropriate duties since they have been assigned to duty in this department: Capt. William E. Merrill, U. S. Engineers, to the brevet rank of major; First Lieut. H. C. Wharton, to the brevet rank of captain.

Very respectfully, your obedient servant,
GEO. H. THOMAS,
Major-General, Commanding.

SAINT LOUIS, MO., *December 5, 1864—3 p. m.*

Major-General THOMAS,
Nashville, Tenn.:

Regret the delay in forwarding Winslow's cavalry for want of horses. Hope they will be supplied in two or three days. Merrill's Horse has large detachments waiting to go; remainder with Steele. He would much like to be with you.

W. S. ROSECRANS,
Major-General.

NASHVILLE, TENN., *December 5, 1864—7.30 p. m.*

Maj. Gen. W. S. ROSECRANS,
Saint Louis, Mo.:

Your telegram of this date just received. Am much obliged for your offer of Merrill's Horse. I hardly suppose any order separating him so far from his proper command would meet the approval of the Department at Washington. I hope you may be able to forward Winslow's cavalry in two or three days, and shall be very much obliged if you will hurry them forward as rapidly as possible.

GEO. H. THOMAS,
Major-General, U. S. Volunteers, Commanding.

HEADQUARTERS DEPARTMENT OF THE CUMBERLAND,
Nashville, Tenn., December 5, 1864.

General J. B. HOOD,
Commanding Confederate Forces, on Franklin Road:

GENERAL: I have the honor to acknowledge the receipt of your communication* of this date, making proposition for the exchange of the

---
* Not found.

prisoners of the Army of the United States now in your possession for a like number of Confederate prisoners belonging to your army in my hands. In reply, I have to state that, although I have had quite a large number of prisoners from your army, they have all been sent North, and consequently are now beyond my control. I am therefore unable to make the exchange proposed by you.

Very respectfully, yours, &c.,

GEO. H. THOMAS,
Major-General, U. S. Volunteers, Commanding.

NASHVILLE, TENN., *December 5, 1864—10 a. m.*

Brig. Gen. D. C. McCALLUM:

Only one of the floating divisions of the construction corps is here; the others are at Chattanooga, and all communication with them is cut off. Owing to the close proximity of the rebel army to this place, and the almost certainty that they will do much damage to our roads, General Thomas thinks it would not be advisable to send away this division now.

W. W. WRIGHT,
Chief Engineer.

ALBANY, KY., *December 5, 1864.*
(Via Burkesville 8th.)

Major-General THOMAS:

Four men are just in from the Cumberland Gap. They came alone through by the Pine Knot Tavern, and report no rebels along the route. Beatty knows of none in Fentress. There are none in Overton, and [from] what I can hear, none about here.

J. D. HALE.

NASHVILLE, TENN., *December 5, 1864—9.30 p. m.*
(Received 11.30 p. m.)

Maj. THOMAS T. ECKERT,
Washington, D. C.:

Reconnaissance to-day from right center found rebel lines there and no earth-works, or only slight affairs. On left center and left they are strong and intrenched. The usual artillery firing had been done by our batteries, but without getting reply. General Thomas works on hypothesis that Hood is here with whole force. Telegraph working from south to Murfreesborourgh, from which place we have report that Bate's rebel division, with two batteries, attacked block-houses seven and ten miles north of Murfreesborough yesterday 2 p. m., but were defeated by re-enforcements under command of General Milroy, losing six guns, some prisoners, and failing to carry either stockade. River still falling.

J. C. VAN DUZER,
Captain, &c.

SPECIAL FIELD ORDERS, ⎰ HDQRS. DEPT. OF THE CUMBERLAND,
      No. 333.   ⎱   Nashville, Tenn., December 5, 1864.

I. Maj. Gen. D. N. Couch, U. S. Volunteers, having reported at these headquarters in obedience to orders of the War Department, is assigned to duty with the Fourth Army Corps, and will report to Maj. Gen. D. S. Stanley, commanding.

*   *   *   *   *   *   *

By command of Major-General Thomas:

HENRY M. CIST,
Captain and Assistant Adjutant-General.

HEADQUARTERS FOURTH ARMY CORPS,
Near Nashville, Tenn., December 5, 1864.

Brig. Gen. W. D. WHIPPLE,
Assistant Adjutant-General and Chief of Staff:

GENERAL: I have the honor to report for the information of the commanding general of the forces that, so far as can be observed this morning, in the intense haze and smoke, no change occurred in the enemy's position in front of this corps during the night.

Very respectfully, your obedient servant,

TH. J. WOOD,
Brigadier-General of Volunteers, Commanding.

HEADQUARTERS 125TH OHIO VOLUNTEER INFANTRY,
Nashville, Tenn., December 5, 1864.

Capt. E. G. WHITESIDES,
Acting Assistant Adjutant-General:

CAPTAIN: The officers in charge of picket stations to each brigade of the division report the moving of trains to the left from 1 to 3 this a. m., also some to the right; did not think it to be artillery. No other demonstrations were made.

Very respectfully, your obedient servant,

EDWD. P. BATES,
Captain, 125th Ohio Volunteer Infantry, and Officer of the Day.

WAR DEPARTMENT,
December 5, 1864.

Major-General SCHOFIELD,
Nashville:

The Secretary of War directs me to inform you that General Stoneman was, in the first instance, relieved by an order of General Grant, which was temporarily suspended by the Secretary. It was afterward renewed by the Secretary. Upon receipt of your telegram to me to-day the matter was referred to General Grant for such action as he deemed proper. General Grant has in reply sent the following telegram.* The Secretary of War directs that if, on consideration, you think it expedient to intrust General Stoneman with the important command of

---

* See Grant to Stanton, 1 p. m., p. 54.

your department, you are authorized to do so, or to assign the command as you please, you being responsible for the exercise of proper discretion. You will immediately notify this Department of your determination.

E. D. TOWNSEND,
Assistant Adjutant-General.

NASHVILLE, TENN., *December 5, 1864—11 p. m.*

Col. E. D. TOWNSEND,
Assistant Adjutant-General:

I have received your dispatch of this date. While I fully approve the correctness of the rule stated by Lieutenant-General Grant, I am certain the best I can do for the present is to retain General Stoneman in his present command. He was assigned after consultation with General Sherman, and with his approval. I will therefore avail myself of the authority contained in your dispatch to do so. General Stoneman is now in East Tennessee, preparing to carry out General Grant's instructions. If the general can send there an officer in whom he has more confidence, I shall be much gratified to have him do so.

J. M. SCHOFIELD,
Major-General.

SPECIAL FIELD ORDERS, } HEADQUARTERS ARMY OF THE OHIO,
No. 171. } *Nashville, Tenn., December 5, 1864.*

*   *   *   *   *   *   *

II. By direction of the Secretary of War, Maj. Gen. George Stoneman is relieved from duty in the Department of the Ohio, and will repair to Cincinnati, Ohio, report his arrival there by letter to the Adjutant-General of the Army, and await further orders.

*   *   *   *   *   *   *

By command of Major-General Schofield:

J. A. CAMPBELL,
Major and Assistant Adjutant-General.

CLARKSVILLE, *December 5, 1864.*

Brigadier-General WHIPPLE,
Assistant Adjutant-General:

I have just arrived with my command all safe, with a loss of only two wagons. The feet of my men are very sore, many of them barefoot. I was within eight miles of Nashville on the night of the 2d instant, and found, by information received from prisoners, that the way was not open, so, without orders, I returned to this place, and now await further orders.

Respectfully,

J. A. COOPER,
Brigadier-General.

NASHVILLE, *December 5, 1864—7.30 p. m.*

Brig. Gen. J. A. COOPER,
        Clarksville:

Your dispatch of this date is received.   March with your command by road to this place on the north side of the river.

                        GEO. H. THOMAS,
            Major-General, U. S. Volunteers, Commanding.

GALLATIN, *December 5, 1864.*

Major-General WILSON,
        Commanding Cavalry:

I have fourteen men since 12 last night in the enemy's country. There is reason to believe that the citizens are building pontoons in their houses.   Could you send me a transport or a steam ferry to-night at 7 o'clock to Gallatin Landing if my suspicions are confirmed? Answer.

                            J. H. HAMMOND,
                                Brigadier-General.

HDQRS. CAVALRY CORPS, MIL. DIV. OF THE MISSISSIPPI,
            Edgefield, Tenn., December 5, 1864.

Brig. Gen. W. D. WHIPPLE,
        Chief of Staff:

GENERAL: I have the honor to inclose for the information of the general commanding a copy of a telegram* received from Brigadier-General Hammond, commanding brigade at Gallatin.   If a gun-boat can be sent up to General Hammond to-night, please notify me, and I will telegraph him to that effect.

        Respectfully,

                        J. H. WILSON,
            Brevet Major-General, Commanding Cavalry.

HEADQUARTERS DEPARTMENT OF THE CUMBERLAND,
            Nashville, December 5, 1864.

Bvt. Maj. Gen. J. H. WILSON,
        Comdg. Cavalry Corps, Military Division of the Mississippi:

GENERAL: The major-general commanding directs me to say that, in accordance with your request, a gun-boat will be sent to Gallatin to-night, and will co-operate with General Hammond in his operations in that section.

I have the honor to be, general, very respectfully, your obedient servant,

                        ROBT. H. RAMSEY,
                            Assistant Adjutant-General.

---

* See next, *ante.*

HDQRS. CAVALRY CORPS, MIL. DIV. OF THE MISSISSIPPI,
[*December 5, 1864.*]

Maj. E. B. BEAUMONT,
    Assistant Adjutant-General, Cavalry Corps:

MAJOR: I have the honor to submit the following report of the result of my journey to Saint Louis and Memphis, made in accordance with orders, instructions, &c., from General Thomas' headquarters and from headquarters Cavalry Corps:

I left here on the morning of the 20th ultimo and arrived in Saint Louis on the 23d. The unusual length of time en route to Saint Louis was caused by an accident to the train, and by another circumstance, which I make the object of a special report. At General Rosecrans' headquarters I learned that Colonel Winslow's command would probably arrive in Saint Louis by the 1st of December. I met Colonel Winslow, and after making the necessary and most speedy arrangements for the transfer of that portion of his command to this place, we left November 24 for Memphis. Lieutenant-Colonel Benteen, Tenth Missouri Cavalry, was left in Saint Louis to superintend the transfer. General Rosecrans assured me that he should have every facility for remounting, re-equipping, &c., as quickly as possible. We arrived in Memphis Monday morning, November 28. I saw General Washburn, district commander; at first he did not seem inclined to part with Colonel Winslow's command. The next morning Colonel Winslow and I had another interview with him, when he concluded to let Colonel Winslow's old brigade (Third and Fourth Iowa and Tenth Missouri) go, retaining the following regiments: First Mississippi Mounted Rifles, Second New Jersey Cavalry, Fourth Missouri Cavalry, Seventh Indiana Cavalry. These he claimed as ordered to be left there by the brevet major-general commanding the Cavalry Corps. As far as I have been able to learn the First Mississippi Mounted Rifles amounts to but little. The Second New Jersey Cavalry is a very large regiment, but nearly half the men are one-year recruits; the regiment is very poorly disciplined. The two remaining regiments (Fourth Missouri and Seventh Indiana) constitute the real strength of what is to be left, and of these I should think the Fourth Missouri the better regiment. Colonel Winslow's letter to me, written after I had left him, will give you a good idea of the matter, and from what I saw of him I judge him to be a very efficient officer, although now unfit for field duty, having been recently wounded. He was perfectly informed on the most minute points, even concerning the condition, wants, &c., of his command, and seemed to take great pride in it. I think his opinion worthy of more than ordinary consideration. The organization of the portion of the command to be left in Memphis shows an aggregate of about 3,000; of this number not more than 1,000 or 1,200 are effective, and it appeared difficult to keep even these effective. That portion which is to leave Memphis will number about 1,400 effective; add to these the detachment from Saint Louis, say 1,300, it gives an aggregate of about 2,700. This calculation includes only the following regiments: Third and Fourth Iowa and Tenth Missouri (Winslow's old brigade). Before leaving Memphis General Washburn assured me that he would render Colonel Winslow the necessary facilities for a speedy departure; but as a portion of the command was about starting on a scout, thought they would be unable to leave before to-day (5th). The Saint Louis detachment will probably leave to-day also. In Memphis I learned that General Grierson was at his home in Jacksonville, Ill. He had been absent several weeks.

I inclose the letter* of Colonel Winslow referred to on the preceding page.

I left Memphis November 29 and arrived here this morning (December 5). Was delayed a day or two in Louisville, as the regular trains were not running.

I am, major, very respectfully, your obedient servant,

HENRY E. NOYES,
Lieutenant and Aide-de-Camp.

GENERAL ORDERS,　　HEADQUARTERS CAVALRY CORPS,
　　　　　　　　　　MILITARY DIVISION OF THE MISSISSIPPI,
　　No. 7.　　　　　　　　　*Nashville, Tenn., December 5, 1864.*

The following allowance of transportation for the Cavalry Corps has been adopted, and will be at once carried into effect under the direction of the chief quartermaster: For headquarters of the corps, four wagons for baggage and desks, and a sufficient number to carry subsistence stores for sales to officers and issues to enlisted men on duty at headquarters. For a division, thirty-five wagons, of which sixteen shall compose the ordnance train of the division, eight shall carry subsistence stores, eight, quartermaster's stores, and three shall be for the division commanders and staff. For brigade headquarters, two wagons for every 1,000 men in the brigade, thirteen wagons for subsistence stores and two wagons for quartermaster's stores. For each regiment there will be allowed five wagons, to be used as follows: One for regimental headquarters, two for baggage of officers, one for quartermaster's and commissary tools, and one, under control of the regimental commander, to carry surplus ordnance stores until they can be turned over. In addition to the above, and for operations at a distance from the supply trains, there will be allowed for division and brigade headquarters, each, one light wagon; to each regimental commander, one pack-mule, one to every two field and staff officers, one to officers of each company, and one to every twenty-five men. The allowance of ambulances and hospital wagons will be regulated by the medical director of the corps, but for present use, in case of an emergency, there will be allowed to headquarters of the corps and division two ambulances, to each brigade, one, and to each regiment, two.

By command of Brevet Major-General Wilson:

E. B. BEAUMONT,
Major and Assistant Adjutant-General.

SPECIAL ORDERS,　　HEADQUARTERS CAVALRY CORPS,
　　　　　　　　　　MILITARY DIVISION OF THE MISSISSIPPI,
　　No. 28.　　　　　　　　　*Nashville, December 5, 1864.*

*　　　*　　　*　　　*　　　*　　　*　　　*

II. Lieut. Col. A. J. Alexander, assistant adjutant-general, Seventeenth Army Corps, having reported for temporary duty in compliance with orders from Major-General Blair, commanding Seventeenth Army Corps, is assigned to duty on the staff of the brevet major-general commanding.

III. Capt. Levi T. Griffin, Fourth Michigan Volunteer Cavalry, having reported in obedience to orders, is assigned to duty as acting assistant adjutant-general and stationed at cavalry headquarters, Nashville, Tenn. This order to date from November 30, 1864.

---

* Not found as an inclosure.

IV. Capt. W. W. Van Antwerp, Fourth Michigan Volunteer Cavalry, having reported in obedience to orders, is assigned to duty as acting aide-de-camp. This order to date from November 30, 1864.

By command of Brevet Major-General Wilson:

E. B. BEAUMONT,
Major and Assistant Adjutant-General.

HDQRS. CAVALRY CORPS, MIL. DIV. OF THE MISSISSIPPI,
Edgefield, Tenn., December 5, 1864.

Brig. Gen. J. T. CROXTON,
Commanding First Division, Cavalry Corps:

GENERAL: The brevet major-general commanding directs that you replace all the men belonging to General Watkins' brigade that are on detached duty by men from your other brigade, and hold General Watkins' brigade in readiness to move at short notice.

Very respectfully, your obedient servant,

A. J. ALEXANDER,
Lieutenant-Colonel and Acting Chief of Staff.

NASHVILLE, *December* [5], *1864.*

General ELI LONG,
Commanding Second Division:

Mount all the men for whom you have horses, arms, and equipments, and report to me what articles you are short, and how many. The order of the Secretary of War contemplates and authorizes the seizure of every species of property necessary to put your command in an efficient condition. If saddles, blankets, or arms can be found you should take them at once. Answer as soon as possible.

J. H. WILSON,
Brevet Major-General.

GALLATIN, *December 5, 1864.*

Maj. E. B. BEAUMONT,
Assistant Adjutant-General:

My scouts in; chased by the rebels to the river. Breckinridge, with three brigades of 8,000 mounted men, left Lebanon this morning, and is expected to cross at Carthage to-night or to-morrow. He is to go to Kentucky, striking the railroad near Bowling Green. He arrived in Lebanon Sunday. Citizens say that Forrest will cross near Clarksville. Biffle's brigade is in Lebanon, and is thought by some to be a re-enforcement for Breckinridge; by others to remain and watch us and the rebel rear. The men went to three miles and a half of Lebanon before being suspected. I have another out alone, who expects to be in the town to-night and reach me before morning. The country south of the river is full of rebels gathering horses and clothing and receiving horses and supplies from this side. I will get all the horses in the country; there are but few. I have 400 men out in all directions pressing. Have been destroying all the boats I could find since arrival. I have started all my available force to Carthage, thirty-three miles east, as a corps of observation, besides scouts.

J. H. HAMMOND,
Brevet Brigadier-General.

GALLATIN, *December 5, 1864.*

Maj. E. B. BEAUMONT,
          Assistant Adjutant-General:

General Schofield's train, with 400 infantry and fifty of my men as advance guard, left here for Nashville at 1 o'clock this morning; 500 wagons.

J. H. HAMMOND,
Brevet Brigadier-General.

HDQRS. CAVALRY CORPS, MIL. DIV. OF THE MISSISSIPPI,
          Nashville, Tenn., December 5, 1864.

Brig. Gen. J. F. KNIPE,
          Comdg. Seventh Div., Cav. Corps, Mil. Div. of the Mississippi:

GENERAL: You will send a staff officer to Clarksville, with orders to bring the detachment of the Nineteenth Pennsylvania Cavalry from that place, also all other detachments of Winslow's or Hatch's divisions which may have arrived at that place. They will march through the country, and bring in all serviceable cavalry horses that may be obtained, bringing their baggage and equipments by wagons. Colonel Johnson, commanding colored troops, will give them all the assistance in his power. Inclosed find a quantity of blank receipts.

By command of Brevet Major-General Wilson:
LEVI T. GRIFFIN,
Captain and Acting Assistant Adjutant-General.

NASHVILLE, *December 5, 1864—8 p. m.*

Major-General ROUSSEAU,
          Murfreesborough:

It is reported to me that General Milroy has captured six pieces of artillery from the enemy, who attacked block-houses 6 and 7 yesterday p. m. If this report is correct I desire you to have pieces taken to Murfreesborough and put in position in the fortifications at that place. Make me a full report of your operations since our communication has been broken up. We are all right here, only waiting for our cavalry, which will be here in a few days.

GEO. H. THOMAS,
Major-General, U. S. Volunteers, Commanding.

MURFREESBOROUGH, TENN., *December 5, 1864.*

Maj. JAMES T. HICKEY,
          181st Ohio Volunteer Infantry:

SIR: Major-General Rousseau directs that you take command of a construction train and guard and move out, with as little delay as possible, to repair the railroad between this place and Nashville. You will take with you a telegraph operator and an instrument, and establish telegraphic communications with this place. You will communicate promptly to these headquarters all the information you can obtain of movements of the enemy. Use the utmost vigilance in guarding your train, and for this purpose the cavalry at Overall's Creek has been ordered to scout on your front and flanks.

By order of Major-General Rousseau:

E. A. OTIS,
Assistant Adjutant-General.

HEADQUARTERS DISTRICT OF THE ETOWAH,
Nashville, December 5, 1864.

Brig. Gen. W. D. WHIPPLE,
Chief of Staff:

GENERAL: I have the honor to report that this morning I sent out the Sixth Indiana (dismounted) Cavalry, Sixty-eighth Indiana Volunteer Infantry, Fourteenth and Sixteenth U. S. Colored Troops, to reconnoiter in front of my present position. They met some resistance in advancing through the woods between my works and my former position, in front of the residence of Mr. Rains, but successfully pushed their advance to the works, driving the enemy from the position. They were unable to discover any considerable force of the enemy. The reconnoitering party captured seventeen prisoners—one lieutenant and sixteen enlisted men—who were forwarded to Captain Goodwin. The prisoners belong to the division known as " Cleburne's division," commanded by General Lowrey, who, the rebel lieutenant captured this morning says, succeeded to the command after the death of General Cleburne, at Franklin. The prisoners all concur in stating that this force of the rebels is their extreme right, resting on the railroad, where they have strong rifle-pits.

Respectfully,

JAMES B. STEEDMAN,
Major-General, Commanding.

DALTON, *December 5, 1864.*

Capt. H. A. FORD,
Acting Assistant Adjutant-General:

A squad of fifty guerrillas attacked water-tank two miles and a half above here at 1 o'clock this morning. The guard, nine men, ran away. Rebels then went to the bridge one mile above and captured the guard, thirty men, cut the wire, and left. The thirty men captured belonged to the command at Tunnel Hill. No damage done the road.

J. B. CULVER,
Colonel Thirteenth Michigan, Commanding.

NASHVILLE, *December 5, 1864.*

Col. A. A. SMITH,
Clarksville:

Do not permit boats to pass up the river above Clarksville until you hear from here that the river is clear.

WM. D. WHIPPLE,
Brigadier-General and Assistant Adjutant-General.

CLARKSVILLE, *December 5, 1864.*

Brig. Gen. W. D. WHIPPLE,
        Assistant Adjutant-General:

I will detain all boats here. U. S. hospital boat is here awaiting orders. One hundred and seventy stragglers of Sixteenth Army Corps here. Shall I send by railroad? Colonel Thompson's command, except Forty-third Wisconsin, have commenced to move overland.

A. A. SMITH,
        Colonel, Commanding.

NASHVILLE, *December 5, 1864.*

Col. A. A. SMITH,
        Clarksville:

Send the stragglers of Sixteenth Army Corps either by rail or boat.

WM. D. WHIPPLE,
        Brigadier-General, &c.

NASHVILLE, TENN., *December 5, 1864.*

Col. A. A. SMITH,
        Clarksville:

Gun-boats will soon start for Clarksville. Send back under convoy such transports as may be there waiting.

WM. D. WHIPPLE,
        Brigadier-General, &c.

CLARKSVILLE, *December 5, 1864.*

Brigadier-General WHIPPLE:

Colonel Smith desires one regiment left for a short time at least. Will leave the Forty-third Wisconsin, unless I have further orders. With the command left will be in Nashville on the 7th, if no accident happens.

CHAS. R. THOMPSON,
        Colonel, Commanding.

NASHVILLE, *December 5, 1864.*

Col. C. R. THOMPSON,
        Clarksville:

You are authorized to detain the Forty-third Regiment Wisconsin Volunteers until further orders.

GEO. H. THOMAS,
        Major-General, U. S. Volunteers, Commanding.

CLARKSVILLE, *December 5, 1864.*

Brig. Gen. WILLIAM D. WHIPPLE:

General Cooper will be here to-day. The headquarters of his column is about one mile from here, on the other side of the river. Can get no particulars yet, but he has his artillery with him.

CHAS. R. THOMPSON,
        Colonel, Commanding, &c.

BRIDGEPORT, *December 5, 1864.*

Major-General THOMAS:

I have the honor to report the safe arrival of my command at Stevenson, about 250 wagons, followed by a large concourse of refugees and contrabands. Five hundred or 600 of the enemy's cavalry followed us yesterday, threatened the train, but were easily driven off. The roads were wretched, and the streams barely passable. The locomotive and two cars sent back to Huntsville were escorted by 120 men, all that could be got on. They were not captured, but lost by the carelessness of a frightened engineer, who ran the engine off the track, being fired at by a few citizens, who were all the enemy in the town.

R. S. GRANGER,
Brigadier-General.

NASHVILLE, *December 5, 1864—8 p. m.*

Major-General STONEMAN, *Knoxville, Tenn.:*

The enemy are in our front, and we are only waiting to get our cavalry up, when we will resume the offensive again. What news have you of the enemy's movements in your vicinity, or of General Sherman's in Georgia?

GEO. H. THOMAS,
Major-General, U. S. Volunteers, Commanding.

KNOXVILLE, *December 5, 1864—10.30 p. m.*

Brigadier-General WHIPPLE:

All accounts agree in locating the enemy north of the Wautaga River; I will know for certain to-morrow or next day. I am shoeing horses and collecting my party together for a sudden push in the direction indicated in my telegram; also to destroy the railroad desired by General Thomas.

GEORGE STONEMAN,
Major-General.

HEADQUARTERS ARMY OF THE OHIO,
Nashville, Tenn., December 5, 1864.

Lieutenant-Colonel BASCOM,
Assistant Adjutant-General, Louisville, Ky.:

Colonel Grider informs me that when the Twenty-sixth Kentucky leaves Bowling Green that place will be left almost without troops. Where are the four regiments I sent to relieve the Twenty-sixth? It is nearly a month since the change was ordered and the Twenty-sixth is not here yet. See to it at once.

J. M. SCHOFIELD,
Major-General.

BEAN'S STATION, *December 5, 1864.*
(Received 6th.)

Capt. J. BATES DICKSON:

I am informed that a large rebel force is concentrating for the invasion of Kentucky at Jonesborough and Bristol. I do not credit it, but if an invasion occurs they will probably go by way of Estillville, Jonesborough, and through Crank's Gap, or through Stony Gap or Pound Gap. Be vigilant. I will watch the lower gap, and you look out for Stony and Pound Gaps. Consult General McLean and General [L.] Thomas, and have him get troops ordered into Kentucky, and hold the State until I can return.

BURBRIDGE,
Major-General.

BEAN'S STATION, *December 5, 1864.*

Brigadier-General McLEAN:

I am informed that a large force of rebels is concentrating at Jonesborough and Bristol for the invasion of Kentucky. I do not credit it, but if an invasion occurs they will probably go by way of Estillville, Jonesborough, and through Crank's Gap or Pound Gap. Be vigilant. I will watch the lower gap, and [you] look out for Stony and Pound Gaps. Consult with General L. Thomas, and if danger comes get him to confer with the authorities [at] Washington, and have troops ordered into the State, and hold it until I can return.

BURBRIDGE,
Major-General.

LEXINGTON, KY., *December 5, 1864.*

Col. J. W. WEATHERFORD, *Camp Nelson, Ky.:*

Send a good officer with fifty men of your regiment to Crab Orchard, to reach there to-morrow night, with instructions to patrol the telegraph line with squads to Cumberland Gap. He must be vigilant, and use his judgment as to the places to put men.

By order of Brigadier-General McLean:

J. S. BUTLER,
Captain and Assistant Adjutant-General.

LOUISVILLE, KY., *December 5, 1864.*

Capt. J. BATES DICKSON:

The Forty-eighth, Fifty-second, and Fourteenth Kentucky Regiments and one battery Twelfth U. S. Colored Heavy Artillery are at Bowling Green. If they will do their duty they can hold the place against an ordinary force.

HUGH EWING,
Brigadier-General.

LEXINGTON, KY., *December 5, 1864.*

S. GILL,
Superintendent Louisville and Lexington Railroad:

SIR: General McLean directs me to inform you that he will order a detachment of troops now at Versailles to march to Frankfort to-morrow, to go to Bagdad and Eminence, for the protection of the railroad and telegraph offices. The detachment will number about forty men, and is ordered to be at Frankfort by 12 m. It would be well for you to have transportation ready for them. The force will be equally divided between the two stations.

Very respectfully, your obedient servant,

[GEO. T. STAGG,]
Aide-de-Camp.

WAR DEPARTMENT,
Washington City, December 5, 1864.

Maj. E. H. LUDINGTON,
Assistant Inspector-General, Capital Hotel, Frankfort, Ky.:

MAJOR: I am instructed by the Secretary of War to acknowledge the receipt of your communication of the 29th of November,* and to direct that you await the return of General Burbridge.

Very respectfully, your obedient servant,

JAS. A. HARDIE,
Colonel and Inspector-General.

——

LOUISVILLE, KY., *December 5, 1864—8.30 p. m.*

Maj. T. T. ECKERT:

Affairs in East Tennessee look unfavorable. General Burbridge, in cipher to General Stoneman, says: "Citizens reported on the 3d that Bushrod Johnson had arrived at Greeneville with two divisions of infantry, and considerable force of cavalry still foraging at Chucky Bend." Duke is at Bull's Gap to-day; Burbridge at Bean's Depot. Telegraph works by way of Knoxville and Chattanooga to Murfreesborough.

S. BRUCH,
Captain, &c.

——

ACTING ASST. PROVOST-MARSHAL-GENERAL'S OFFICE,
Detroit, Mich., December 5, 1864.

Brig. Gen. JAMES B. FRY,
Provost-Marshal-General:

SIR: I have the honor to report that I am informed that a plot is being matured in Canada for the burning of our lake cities. This information is derived partly from persons who are looked upon as being thoroughly in the confidence of the rebel agents in Canada, and is confirmed by information through other sources. My attention has of late frequently been called to the largely increased number of rebels in Canada, and I sought and obtained an interview with an East Tennesseean who resides in Canada and who was said to be a loyal man. He explained the reason why he came to Canada, and I became assured that it was from no want of loyalty to the Government that he was there. He also stated that Colonel Butler's regiment of Kentucky rebel troops had been disbanded in Kentucky, with directions to make their way through the lines and report in Canada, and that they had done so in large numbers, and that Colonel Butler himself has arrived in Canada. The information I receive is, that as soon as the ice forms in Detroit River a large force is to cross on the ice and openly attack this place. I have but a small military force here, not more than enough to guard prisoners, and I have thought it proper to call the attention of the Governor of the State and the mayor of the city to the subject, and recommend that a regiment of militia be organized and armed for local protection. I beg also to recommend that the attention of the honorable Secretary of State be called to this subject, with a view

* See Part I, p. 1165.

of presenting it to the Canadian authorities.   Unless a military force is maintained by the Canadian authorities on the frontier to keep in check the rebels congregated there, there will be frequent raids from Canada at exposed points, which will lead to retaliation by our citizens whose property may be destroyed, and lead to trouble between the two Governments, which it is so desirable should be avoided.

I am, very respectfully, your obedient servant,

B. H. HILL,
Lieut. Col., U. S. Army, Actg. Asst. Provost-Marshal-General.

CITY POINT, VA., *December 6, 1864—4 p. m.*

Maj. Gen. G. H. THOMAS,
Nashville, Tenn.:

Attack Hood at once, and wait no longer for a remount of your cavalry.   There is great danger of delay resulting in a campaign back to the Ohio River.

U. S. GRANT,
Lieutenant-General.

NASHVILLE, *December 6, 1864—8 p. m.*

Lieut. Gen. U. S. GRANT,
City Point:

Your telegram of 6.30 [8] p. m. December 5 is just received.   As soon as I can get up a respectable force of cavalry I will march against Hood. General Wilson has parties out now pressing horses, and I hope to have some 6,000 or 8,000 cavalry mounted in three days from this time. General Wilson has just left me, having received instructions to hurry the cavalry remount as rapidly as possible.   I do not think it prudent to attack Hood with less than 6,000 cavalry to cover my flanks, because he has, under Forrest, at least 12,000.   I have no doubt Forrest will attempt to cross the river, but I am in hopes the gun-boats will be able to prevent him.   The enemy has made no new developments to-day.   Breckinridge is reported at Lebanon, Tenn., with 6,000 men, but I cannot believe it possible.

GEO. H. THOMAS,
Major-General, U. S. Volunteers, Commanding.

NASHVILLE, TENN., *December 6, 1864—9 p. m.*
(Received 12.25 a. m. 7th.)

Lieut. Gen. U. S. GRANT,
City Point:

Your telegram of 4 p. m. this day is just received.   I will make the necessary dispositions and attack Hood at once, agreeably to your order, though I believe it will be hazardous with the small force of cavalry now at my service.

GEO. H. THOMAS,
Major-General, U. S. Volunteers, Commanding.

WASHINGTON, D. C., *December 6, 1864—1 p. m.*

Major-General THOMAS,
          Nashville, Tenn.:

The movements against the Mobile and Ohio Railroad were ordered by General Canby on the 25th and 26th ultimo, and the orders have been repeated. Records show that 22,000 cavalry horses have been issued at Louisville, Lexington, and Nashville since the 20th of September.

> H. W. HALLECK,
> *Major-General and Chief of Staff.*

NASHVILLE, TENN., *December 6, 1864—8 p. m.*

Maj. Gen. H. W. HALLECK,
          Washington, D. C.:

Your telegram of 1 p. m. this day is just received. I know that a great many horses have been issued to the cavalry of the Military Division of the Mississippi since September. A great many have been lost in battle, and a great many have died of glanders and distemper, and a large number of the men are still dismounted. I have seen General Wilson to-night, who encourages me to hope that he will be able to mount 6,000 or 7,000 in three days from this time. The enemy have made no new developments to-day. I will attack him as soon as General Wilson can get together a sufficient cavalry force to protect my flanks.

> GEO. H. THOMAS,
> *Major-General, U. S. Volunteers, Commanding.*

> HEADQUARTERS,
> *Saint Louis, December 6, 1864.*

Major-General THOMAS:

The Forty-seventh Illinois Infantry has reported to me under orders from the War Department, through the superintendent volunteer recruiting, State of Illinois, to General Smith. The regiment consists of 394 men, but 115 armed and equipped. Two commissioned officers here, and where shall they be sent?

> W. S. ROSECRANS,
> *Major-General.*

NASHVILLE, *December 6, 1864.*

Major-General THOMAS,
          Commanding:

The following just received from Chattanooga via Cumberland Gap:

> DECEMBER 5, 1864.

Fifty guerrillas captured the guard of thirty men this morning at Buzzard's Roost, but did not disturb the railroad.

> PATTERSON.

Respectfully,

> JOHN C. VAN DUZER,
> *Captain, &c.*

HEADQUARTERS FOURTH ARMY CORPS,
December 6, 1864.

General WHIPPLE:

The enemy's appearance in front is same as yesterday.

TH. J. WOOD,
Brigadier-General of Volunteers, Commanding.

ORDERS.]   HEADQUARTERS FOURTH ARMY CORPS,
Nashville, Tenn., December 6, 1864.

The undersigned having been ordered to duty with the Fourth Army Corps, hereby assumes temporary command of the same.

D. N. COUCH,
Major-General, U. S. Volunteers.

HEADQUARTERS DEPARTMENT OF THE CUMBERLAND,
Saint Cloud Hotel, December 6, 1864.
(Received 8.30 a. m. 7th.)

Major-General COUCH,
General Wood's Headquarters:

You can be assigned to a division in General Schofield's army if you are willing. This arrangement will enable General Kimball to retain his division in the Fourth Army Corps. Answer.

GEO. H. THOMAS,
Major-General, U. S. Volunteers, Commanding.

HEADQUARTERS FOURTH ARMY CORPS,
Nashville, Tenn., December 6, 1864.

Brigadier-General KIMBALL,
Commanding First Division, Fourth Army Corps:

GENERAL: The general commanding directs me to say that information has been received that General Hood is calling for volunteers in order to attack our lines. The general desires that extra care and watchfulness be observed by division commanders during the night, and that the picket officers of the division be upon the line frequently.

Very respectfully, your obedient servant,

H. E. STANSBURY,
Captain and Aide-de-Camp.

(Same to Brigadier-General Elliott, commanding Second Division.)

WASHINGTON, *December 6, 1864.*

General SCHOFIELD:

Your telegram of the 5th, acknowledging receipt of mine of same date, has been seen by the Secretary of War, who desires you to do as you propose.

E. D. TOWNSEND,
Assistant Adjutant-General.

SPECIAL FIELD ORDERS, }   HDQRS. ARMY OF THE OHIO,
 No. 172.   } *Nashville, Tenn., December 6, 1864.*
* * * * * * *

V. Paragraph II, of Special Field Orders, No. 171, current series, from these headquarters, relieving Major-General Stoneman from duty in the Department of the Ohio, and ordering him to repair to Cincinnati, Ohio, is hereby revoked.
* * * * * * *

By command of Major-General Schofield:
          J. A. CAMPBELL,
      Major and Assistant Adjutant-General.

HEADQUARTERS RIGHT WING, SIXTEENTH ARMY CORPS,
        December 6, 1864—8 p. m.
Major-General THOMAS,
  Commanding:

The enemy have a battery on the Charlotte pike, and developed some infantry force this evening, moving toward our right. All quiet at present.

          A. J. SMITH,
          Major-General.

SPECIAL FIELD ORDERS, }   HDQRS. DEPT. OF THE CUMBERLAND,
 No. 334.   } *Nashville, Tenn., December 6, 1864.*
* * * * * * *

IX. Inasmuch as the Sixteenth Army Corps has been discontinued, the troops which formerly composed a portion of that organization, now under command of Maj. Gen. A. J. Smith, will be known as the Detachment of the Army of the Tennessee.
* * * * * * *

By command of Major-General Thomas:
          HENRY M. CIST,
     Captain and Assistant Adjutant-General.

GENERAL STEEDMAN'S HEADQUARTERS,
         December 6, 1864.
Brig. Gen. T. J. WOOD:

What news have you of the movements of the enemy to-day?
          J. B. STEEDMAN,
          Major-General.

         DECEMBER 6, 1864.
Maj. Gen. J. B. STEEDMAN:

The enemy in our front to-day has been rather quiet. No movements of interest, but he has been quite busy in strengthening his works, which are quite near to our works. Will keep you informed.
          TH. J. WOOD,
       Brigadier-General of Volunteers.

CHIEF QUARTERMASTER'S OFFICE,
DEPARTMENT OF THE CUMBERLAND,
Nashville, Tenn., December 6, 1864.

Capt. E. B. CARLING,
Assistant Quartermaster, Cavalry Corps:

CAPTAIN: I have the honor to inform you that the quartermaster's department is engaged to-day in laying a pontoon bridge across the Cumberland, from near the end of Church street to the opposite bank of the river, for the purpose of accommodating the cavalry trains and for other purposes. It will be a double-track bridge, and the regulation will be for trains coming this way to use one track, and those going the other way, the other. I expect to have it ready for service to-night, or in the morning at the farthest. Please notify General Wilson of the arrangement, and oblige,

Very respectfully,

JAS. F. RUSLING,
Captain and Assistant Quartermaster and
Acting Chief Quartermaster, Department of the Cumberland.

SPECIAL ORDERS, }   HEADQUARTERS CAVALRY CORPS,
                         MILITARY DIVISION OF THE MISSISSIPPI,
No. 29.   }   *Nashville, December 6, 1864.*

I. Capt. J. D. Moxley, First Ohio Cavalry, is hereby detailed as acting assistant inspector-general, and will report to Lieut. Col. G. G. Miner, commanding dismounted cavalry, at Camp Webster, for duty.

*   *   *   *   *   *   *

III. Maj. J. M. Young, Fifth Iowa Cavalry, is hereby detailed as provost-marshal, Cavalry Corps, Military Division of the Mississippi, and will report to these headquarters when relieved from duty on general court-martial.

*   *   *   *   *   *   *

By command of Brevet Major-General Wilson:

E. B. BEAUMONT,
Major and Assistant Adjutant-General.

CIRCULAR, }   HDQRS. CAVALRY CORPS, MIL. DIV. OF THE MISS.,
No. 2.   }   *Edgefield, Tenn., December 6, 1864.*

Division commanders will take immediate measures to concentrate the whole of their respective commands at this point by noon of Friday, the 9th instant. They will also use every exertion to get all the horses possible by that time.

By command of Brevet Major-General Wilson:

A. J. ALEXANDER,
Lieutenant-Colonel and Chief of Staff.

HDQRS. CAVALRY CORPS, MIL. DIV. OF THE MISSISSIPPI,
Edgefield, Tenn., December 6, 1864.

Colonel LA GRANGE,
Commanding Brigade, First Division:

COLONEL: An order is in force from the Secretary of War permitting General Wilson to press a sufficient number of serviceable horses to mount his command. He has had parties out in this vicinity some days on this duty, but is still in want of several thousand horses. He therefore desires you to press all the serviceable cavalry horses and mules you may find in the vicinity of your line of march and bring them with you to this point. I send you a package of memorandum receipts, which you will cause the officers detailed for the duty to give to the persons from whom they take the animals, and say to them that these receipts will be replaced by the proper Government vouchers upon presentation to Captain Carling, chief quartermaster of this corps, at Nashville, Tenn. Should a horse be taken that is not worth the maximum price paid by the Government ($160), the officer signing the receipt will state his estimated value on the receipt. All the horses you may be able to obtain will be turned in on your arrival to Capt. W. M. Wilson, acting assistant quartermaster. It is desirable in this matter that the citizens be treated with all due consideration, and that receipts be given with every animal which is taken.

By command of Brevet Major-General Wilson:

A. J. ALEXANDER,
Lieutenant-Colonel and Chief of Staff.

HDQRS. CAVALRY CORPS, MIL. DIV. OF THE MISSISSIPPI,
Edgefield, Tenn., December 6, 1864.

Brig. Gen. J. T. CROXTON,
Commanding First Division:

The general commanding directs that you send an officer to Colonel La Grange, and urge him to reach this point by Friday night at the farthest.

Very respectfully, your obedient servant,

A. J. ALEXANDER,
Lieutenant-Colonel and Chief of Staff.

NASHVILLE, *December 6, 1864.*

General ELI LONG:

Telegram of to-day received. If the proper arms are not ready by the time you are all mounted take anything you can get, and leave an officer to receive the arms required as soon as they arrive. This is a matter of very great importance and allows of no delay. Is the Fifth Indiana all at Louisville? If Major Chambliss is not there to carry out the instructions in regard to seizures, give them to the commanders of all detachments and act for me till he arrives. As you come through from Louisville direct your division and brigade quartermasters to seize all horses fit for cavalry service and bring them through, for transfer to the chief quartermaster of the corps for issue to the dismounted men here. Communicate this order to McCook, so that he may give similar instructions to La Grange. We need 4,000 horses here.

J. H. WILSON,
Brevet Major-General.

HDQRS. CAVALRY CORPS, MIL. DIV. OF THE MISSISSIPPI,
Nashville, Tenn., December 6, 1864.

Brig. Gen. ELI LONG,
Comdg. Second Div., Cav. Corps, Mil. Div. of the Mississippi:

Your communication of December 4 has just been received. I telegraphed to-day directing you to mount all your men at once, or as soon as possible, and start as soon as you could, arming the dismounted men with whatever you could get, and leaving an officer behind to bring forward the good arms as soon as they arrive. If horse equipment and horses cannot be obtained from the bureau seize such as can be found. I fully agree with you in regard to the impolicy of hurrying into the field half prepared. It is expensive and injurious to the service, and I do not wish you to think I am any party to the necessity which impels us to do such things. I am as unwilling as you or Major Chambliss, but you must not forget we are all under the authority of others. General Thomas himself manifests every desire in the world to give us time, but Hood is very near, and the authorities in Washington are very anxious. I beg you to assure Major Chambliss that I bear ample testimony to his activity and zeal in furnishing remounts and in hurrying troops to the field. I am sure he has done everything in his power, and ought to be gratified with the result. I am sorry that arms cannot be furnished more rapidly, and that horse equipments are brought forward so slowly. I wish you to bear in mind, however, that when your command does come, I would like to have it completely equipped. After conversing with General Garrard, I am inclined to make no change in your command, except to transfer the First Ohio out of it, leaving you eight old regiments. If this one regiment is the one you wish transferred, please regard the matter settled, and make your arrangements accordingly.

Hoping that you will be able to leave Louisville very soon and with a complete outfit,

I am, general, very respectfully, your obedient servant,

J. H. WILSON,
Brevet Major-General.

HDQRS. CAVALRY CORPS, MIL. DIV. OF THE MISSISSIPPI,
Edgefield, Tenn., December 6, 1864.

Brig. Gen. EDWARD HATCH,
Commanding Fifth Division:

GENERAL: The general commanding desires you to withdraw that portion of your command which is guarding the river at such a time as will enable them to reach this point by Friday night.

Very respectfully, your obedient servant,

A. J. ALEXANDER,
Lieutenant-Colonel and Chief of Staff.

HDQRS. CAVALRY CORPS, MIL. DIV. OF THE MISSISSIPPI,
Edgefield, Tenn., December 6, 1864.

Brig. Gen. R. W. JOHNSON,
Commanding Sixth Division:

The general commanding desires you to issue such orders as will concentrate all your forces which are watching the river at this camp by Friday night.

Very respectfully, your obedient servant,

A. J. ALEXANDER,
Lieutenant-Colonel and Chief of Staff.

HEADQUARTERS SIXTH DIVISION, CAVALRY CORPS,
MILITARY DIVISION OF THE MISSISSIPPI,
Edgefield, Tenn., December 6, 1864—9.45 p. m.

Col. T. J. HARRISON,
　　Commanding Brigade:

I am just in receipt of a circular from corps headquarters requiring the whole of the cavalry force to be concentrated here by Friday night, the 9th instant. I am not inclined, in the absence of General Johnson, to give orders in the premises, but respectfully suggest to you the propriety of dispatching a messenger, with such escort as you may think necessary, to Lieutenant-Colonel Baird, commanding Fifth Iowa Cavalry, requiring him to return at once, by the best route, bringing with him what horses he may have collected, or may be able to collect on his return march. Every exertion consistent with the concentration of the command at the day named must in the meantime be used. Please notify Colonel Garrard in the morning that he must be here by Friday night.

Very respectfully, your obedient servant,

E. T. WELLS,
Assistant Adjutant-General.

GALLATIN, *December 6, 1864.*

Maj. E. B. BEAUMONT,
　　Assistant Adjutant-General, Cavalry Corps:

It does seem incredible that Breckinridge should be able to come in with so large a force, but the scouts all agreed in their accounts; another who came in later says pontoons have been building at Lebanon. Lebanon is on the Sparta route from East Tennessee. My force toward Carthage will report the moment there is anything certain, and I will use every effort to obtain information. I have not exceeding 100 serviceable horses, and they are all needed for my command, but I have three large parties out two days that should bring me 150 more to-day. Gun-boats had not arrived at 7 o'clock; expect them when I reach the landing. I move camp on Cole's Ferry road this morning.

J. H. HAMMOND,
Brevet Brigadier-General.

GALLATIN, *December 6, 1864.*

Maj. E. B. BEAUMONT,
　　Assistant Adjutant-General, Cavalry Corps:

My cavalry reached Carthage this morning; all quiet there. If Breckinridge has come through at all, he has not come by way of Sparta; no force there. Have ordered my couriers to scout from Carthage toward Lebanon as far as possible, and on return destroy all boats down until my party is met destroying up. Scouts to Lebanon failed to get in to-day. Small rebel forces of Dibrell's command picket the river in my front and pressing horses. No gun-boats have appeared. Will be able to make a return of horses day after to-morrow.

J. H. HAMMOND,
Brevet Brigadier-General.

GALLATIN, *December 6, 1864.*

Maj. E. B. BEAUMONT,
  Assistant Adjutant-General, Cavalry Corps:

One gun-boat arrived 8 p. m. and reports two more following. Will act with the commanders.

J. H. HAMMOND,
Brevet Brigadier-General.

NASHVILLE, *December 6, 1864.*

Major-General ROUSSEAU,
  Murfreesborough:

I telegraphed you yesterday p. m. asking for a report of your operations since communication has been broken; no answer received yet. The enemy is still in our front, massed between the Nolensville and Franklin pike. He has made no demonstration against the city up to this time. All right here and ready for any attack.

GEO. H. THOMAS,
Major-General, U. S. Volunteers, Commanding.

NASHVILLE, *December 6, 1864.*

Brig. Gen. R. S. GRANGER,
  Bridgeport, Ala.:

Your dispatch of 5th instant just received. You must hold the country about Stevenson and Bridgeport securely until we can open up communication from this place.

GEO. H. THOMAS,
Major-General, U. S. Volunteers, Commanding.

BRIDGEPORT, *Decembor 6, 1864.*

General T. F. MEAGHER,
  Commanding District of the Etowah:

I have the honor to report that in accordance with orders from Major-General Steedman I have returned with my regiment from Cowan, and will reach my camp at Wauhatchie to-morrow afternoon.

WM. J. PALMER,
Colonel Fifteenth Pennsylvania Cavalry.

DALTON, GA., *December 6, 1864.*

Capt. H. A. FORD,
  Acting Assistant Adjutant-General:

One of my scouts informs me that Colonel Graham, with one gun, has joined the rebel forces at Spring Place with a force of 500 men, and that they contemplate assaulting Dalton within forty-eight hours. I credit this report, and will be ready for them. Can't you send me the cavalry immediately. I expect to whip them, and want to follow up any advantage I may obtain. Please send me thirty boxes more of ammunition at once.

J. B. CULVER,
Colonel, Commanding.

DALTON, GA., *December 6, 1864.*

Capt. H. A. FORD,
　Acting Assistant Adjutant-General:

Your dispatch received.* I telegraphed, in brief, yesterday particulars of capture of thirty men of Major Hamill's command at bridge three miles south of Tunnel Hill. The garrison, commanded by Sergt. John H. Bayly, Thirtieth Illinois Infantry, consisted of thirty men, who were surprised and captured by about fifty guerrillas. Our troops made no resistance; all conscripts except Sergeant Bayly. There is no block-house or stockade at the bridge, and in my judgment Major Hamill is much to blame in this matter. He informed me yesterday that he never visited that post. On my return I directed his new guard to throw up a defense of logs and earth, and bade them stay there and fight. You are doubtless aware that neither the post nor men there are under my command.

J. B. CULVER,
Colonel Thirteenth Michigan Infantry, Commanding.

CLARKSVILLE, *December 6, 1864.*

Brigadier-General WHIPPLE:

Forty-second Missouri have just arrived on two transports. Gunboats have not arrived yet. General Cooper got safely across river; went into camp last night near city.

A. A. SMITH,
Colonel, Commanding.

CLARKSVILLE, *December 6, 1864.*

Brigadier-General WHIPPLE,
　Chief of Staff:

I have information that the rebel General Lyon was crossing the Tennessee River the 4th with 3,000 or 4,000 men at the bridge, said to be moving into Kentucky. I fear he may be going to Fort Donelson. The Forty-second Missouri are here on boats, and could be sent down, if you think best.

A. A. SMITH,
Colonel, Commanding.

CLARKSVILLE, *December 6, 1864.*

General WHIPPLE:

Your dispatch of this date, directing the return of the Forty-second Missouri Volunteers to Fort Donelson, received. Will start immediately.

By order of William Forbes, colonel Forty-second Missouri Volunteers:

JOHN M. LOUDON,
Adjutant.

---

* Not found.

KNOXVILLE, TENN., *December 6, 1864—12.30 p. m.*

Major-General THOMAS:

Your dispatch of last evening, just received, sets our minds at ease. Enemy have all fallen back into Virginia and North Carolina, with but little opposition. Rumors, not reliable, that Bushrod Johnson is on his way with a force down to Bristol. I will have the railroad destroyed in a few days, as you wish. I will hit them a lick they are not prepared for. No news from Sherman. Bristol papers say Hood has whipped Thomas badly, and that Hood is on his way into Kentucky, where he will be joined by Longstreet. Have not seen the paper myself, but am so told by a person who says he saw it. I have every available man employed in completing and strengthening the lines around Knoxville. About forty officers who escaped from Columbia, S. C., have arrived here during the past two weeks. I can issue them rations and clothing, but the paymaster here refuses to pay them. They are, of course, entirely destitute.

GEORGE STONEMAN,
Major-General, Commanding.

NASHVILLE, *December 6, 1864—8.30 p. m.*

Major-General STONEMAN, *Knoxville:*

Your dispatches of 10.30 p. m. 5th instant and 12.30 p. m. to-day are just received. If you can effectually destroy the railroad for twenty-five or thirty miles beyond the Virginia line, East Tennessee will, I think, then be perfectly secure from further invasion. After destroying the railroad and the salt-works, if you can, you had better draw your main force back to the vicinity of Knoxville for the defense of East Tennessee.

GEO. H. THOMAS,
Major-General, U. S. Volunteers, Commanding.

HEADQUARTERS ARMY OF THE OHIO,
Nashville, Tenn., December 6, 1864.

Major-General STONEMAN, *Knoxville:*

I approve of the first part of the plan proposed in your letter of November 26, viz, to push the enemy as far back as practicable into Virginia and destroy the salt-works and railroad. I cannot decide as to further operations until affairs here take a more definite shape; therefore, do not undertake the other enterprise without further orders. Inform me by telegraph when you start, and keep me advised of your progress.

J. M. SCHOFIELD,
Major-General.

LEXINGTON, KY., *December 6, 1864.*

Major-General BURBRIDGE,
Bean's Station, Tenn.:

Dispatch received. Several days ago ordered scouts from Louisa to watch Stony, Pound, and Louisa Fork Gaps, also sent scouts out from Mount Sterling on road to gaps. Will be vigilant, and in case of invasion, do all that is possible in defense.

McLEAN,
Brigadier-General, Commanding.

LEXINGTON, KY., *December 6, 1864.*

Colonel WEATHERFORD,
 Camp Nelson, Ky.:

Did you receive the order to guard telegraph line to Cumberland Gap? Have you sent the men?

        J. S. BUTLER,
        Assistant Adjutant-General.

CAMP NELSON, *December 6, 1864.*

Capt. J. S. BUTLER,
 Assistant Adjutant-General:

The men will start in time to reach Crab Orchard to-night, as ordered. Cannot forces at Cumberland Gap patrol as far as Barboursville? I can then keep men continually going back and forth from Crab Orchard to Barboursville. There is no subsistence for men between Cumberland Gap and Crab Orchard. Answer.

        J. W. WEATHERFORD,
        Colonel, &c.

LEXINGTON, KY., *December 6, 1864.*

Col. G. W. GALLUP,
 Louisa, Ky.:

Did you receive the orders to send scouts to Pound and Stony Gaps? Have you sent them? Be watchful for a force concentrating at Jonesborough and Bristol.

        J. S. BUTLER,
        Assistant Adjutant-General.

COVINGTON, *December 6, 1864.*

Capt. J. S. BUTLER,
 Assistant Adjutant-General:

A detective has reliable information that forty rebels will pass Jackstown at McCarnihan's Mill to-night. Troops from Paris could intercept them.

        P. T. SWAINE,
        Colonel, Commanding.

LEXINGTON, KY., *December 6, 1864.*

Colonel EARNEST,
 Commanding, Paris, Ky.:

A squad of forty rebels will cross the railroad from Jackstown to-night. Send a force to intercept them.

By command of Brigadier-General McLean:

        [JAS. M. WATTS,]
        Lieutenant and Aide-de-Camp.

WASHINGTON, D. C., *December 6, 1864—10 a. m.*

COMMANDING OFFICER,
    Vicksburg, Miss.:

You will make every possible exertion to destroy the Mobile and Ohio Railroad, by which Hood's army is now supplied.

H. W. HALLECK,
    Major-General and Chief of Staff.

Commanding officer at Cairo will forward this by a special messenger.

H. W. H.,
    Major-General.

WASHINGTON, D. C., *December 6, 1864—10 a. m.*

COMMANDING OFFICER,
    Memphis:

You will immediately endeavor to cut the Mobile and Ohio Railroad so that Hood's army cannot be supplied by that route. Call on General Reynolds for assistance if necessary.

H. W. HALLECK,
    Major-General and Chief of Staff.

Commanding officer at Cairo will forward this by special messenger.

H. W. H.

HEADQUARTERS NORTHERN DEPARTMENT,
    Cincinnati, Ohio, December 6, 1864.

Brig. Gen. E. D. TOWNSEND,
    Assistant Adjutant-General U. S. Army:

GENERAL: I have the honor to forward herewith a copy of a letter dated 3d instant, just received from Lieut. Col. B. H. Hill, commanding the District of Michigan, as it contains information of importance to all of our frontier bordering upon Canada. The information has been furnished by one of our most reliable detectives, and unusual confidence may be placed in it. A few days since advices of similar import were received by me. From the letter it will be seen that refugees and deserters from the rebel Confederacy are engaged in the manufacture of Greek fire at Windsor, in Canada, to facilitate their incendiary purposes. With regard to attacks from armed bodies of rebels, I feel much less apprehensive than from individual efforts to burn and plunder our cities, as my means of information are such that I hope to be able to anticipate the former. It is almost unnecessary for me to add that I have enjoined unceasing vigilance and activity on the part of the military and civil authorities throughout my command.

Very respectfully, your obedient servant,

JOSEPH HOOKER,
    Major-General, Commanding.

[Inclosure.]

HEADQUARTERS DISTRICT OF MICHIGAN,
    Detroit, Mich., December 3, 1864.

Capt. C. H. POTTER,
    Asst. Adjt. Gen., Hdqrs. Northern Dept., Cincinnati, Ohio:

SIR: I have the honor to report that from information I have received I am satisfied that very extensive preparations are being made in

Canada for burning not only cities on the lakes, but others; and it is very necessary that great precaution and vigilance should be observed everywhere. I have the assurance that Greek fire is being prepared in Windsor. Buffalo, Cleveland, and this city will be the principal cities to be burned, and there will be armed attempts to rob and plunder; Cincinnati and Louisville are also mentioned. I am also informed that by some means a large number of rebel soldiers have been introduced into Canada; some, it is said, have been furloughed, and have made their way through the lines. I have at this time very excellent means of obtaining information, and the only apprehension I have is that the persons in my employ may fail me at the last moment. In this city I have called the attention of the hotel keepers to the necessity of observing great vigilance in regard to their guests, and the hotels are daily visited by a secret agent in my employ.

I am, captain, very respectfully, your obedient servant,

B. H. HILL,
Lieut. Col. Fifth U. S Artillery, Comdg. District of Michigan.

———

CINCINNATI, OHIO, *December 6, 1864—11.45 a. m.*

Col. B. J. SWEET,
Commanding Camp Douglas, Ill.:

The writ of habeas corpus has been suspended by proclamation of the President in all cases arrested by or charged with any offense against the Government when the officer having custody of the person makes affidavit that he is so held.

C. H. POTTER,
Assistant Adjutant-General.

———

CHICAGO, ILL., *December 6, 1864.*

Major-General HOOKER:

The undersigned, having been appointed a committee with reference to public safety, would respectfully urge your presence here. Matters of the utmost importance in connection with the recent arrests seem to demand prompt and early action. Please answer in regard to your coming.

GEO. SCHNEIDER.
PETER PAGE.
S. JOHN.
J. L. HANCOCK.
C. P. J. ARCON.
CHAS. G. WICKER.

———

CINCINNATI, OHIO, *December 6, 1864—11.45 a. m.*

Lieut. Col. B. H. HILL,
Commanding District of Michigan, Detroit:

Can you learn the locality in Windsor in which the preparations you speak of in your letter of the 3d instant are being made?

J. HOOKER,
Major-General, Commanding.

DETROIT, *December 6, 1864.*

Maj. Gen. JOSEPH HOOKER:

I cannot give the place, but I am informed that some of the preparations were purchased in this city. I believe I will have a clue to whole affair.

B. H. HILL,
Lieutenant-Colonel, U. S. Army.

WAR DEPARTMENT,
Washington, December 7, 1864—10.20 a. m.

Lieutenant-General GRANT:

You remember that when Steele was relieved by Canby he was ordered to Cairo to report to this Department. What shall be done with him? The order superseding Rosecrans by Dodge has been issued. Thomas seems unwilling to attack because it is hazardous, as if all war was anything but hazardous. If he waits for Wilson to get ready, Gabriel will be blowing his last horn.

EDWIN M. STANTON.

CITY POINT, VA., *December 7, 1864—1.30 p. m.*

Hon. EDWIN M. STANTON,
Secretary of War:

You probably saw my order to Thomas to attack. If he does not do it promptly, I would recommend superseding him by Schofield, leaving Thomas subordinate. Steele is an admirable corps commander, and I would say order him to report to Canby until there is an opening to put him in command of a corps. I would have no objection [and] would like General Steele appointed to command of Ninth Corps, and General Parke ordered to report to General Canby.

U. S. GRANT,
Lieutenant-General.

CITY POINT, VA., *December 7, 1864—5 p. m.*
(Received 10 p. m.)

Major-General THOMAS:

The Richmond Sentinel of to-day has the following quotation:

Intelligence received yesterday from East Tennessee announces the advance of Burbridge from Kentucky, which was met on the part of General Breckinridge by a retrograde movement to Greeneville, in order to protect his communications with the rear.

U. S. GRANT,
Lieutenant-General.

NASHVILLE, TENN., *December 7, 1864—10 p. m.*
(Received 3.30 p. m. 8th.)

Lieut. Gen. U. S. GRANT,
City Point, Va.

Your dispatch of 5 p. m. this day is just received. Major-General Stoneman telegraphed me yesterday that Breckinridge had fallen back. I have directed Stoneman to pursue him as far as he can into Virginia, breaking and destroying twenty-five or thirty miles of railroad, and also to destroy the salt-works if possible.

GEO. H. THOMAS,
Major-General, U. S. Volunteers, Commanding.

NASHVILLE, TENN., *December 7, 1864—9 p. m.*

Maj. Gen. H. W. HALLECK,
        Washington, D. C.:

The enemy has not increased his force in our front. Have sent gun-boats up the river above Carthage; one returned to-day and reported no signs of the enemy on the river-bank from forty miles above Carthage to this place. Captain Fitch, U. S. Navy, started down the river yesterday with a convoy of transport steamers, but was unable to get them down, the enemy having planted three batteries on a bend of the river between this and Clarksville. Captain Fitch was unable to silence all three of the batteries yesterday, and will return again to-morrow morning, and, with the assistance of the Cincinnati, now at Clarksville, I am in hopes will now be able to clear them out. So far the enemy have not materially injured the Nashville and Chattanooga Railroad.

GEO. H. THOMAS,
Major-General, U. S. Volunteers, Commanding.

SAINT LOUIS, *December 7, 1864—11 a. m.*

Brig. Gen. E. D. TOWNSEND,
        Assistant Adjutant-General, Washington, D. C.:

Your dispatch of 6th instant, 12.25 p. m., duly received. Fourth Missouri Cavalry will be sent with the rest of Winslow's cavalry.

W. S. ROSECRANS,
Major-General.

NASHVILLE, TENN., *December 7, 1864.*

Major-General ROSECRANS,
        Saint Louis, Mo.:

Your dispatch of 6th instant is received. Send the Forty-seventh Regiment Illinois Volunteers to this place by boat. Please inform me how the remounting of Winslow's cavalry is progressing and when the division can start for this place; it should be here as soon as possible.

GEO. H. THOMAS,
Major-General, U. S. Volunteers, Commanding.

SAINT LOUIS, *December 7, 1864.*

Maj. Gen. GEORGE H. THOMAS:

Forty-seventh Illinois Volunteers will join immediately. Winslow's cavalry will begin to move for Nashville to-morrow, so the commanding officer says.

W. S. ROSECRANS,
Major-General.

CLARKSVILLE, *December 7, 1864.*

Major-General THOMAS:

Are coaling. Where is Fitch? Please acquaint him with my arrival. Shall ascend as far as the fast falling river allows.

S. P. LEE,
Acting Rear-Admiral, Commanding Mississippi Squadron.

NASHVILLE, *December 7, 1864—9.15 p. m.*

Admiral S. P. LEE, *Clarksville:*

Your dispatch of 8 p. m. is just received. Captain Fitch is here, and will go down the river at daylight to-morrow morning as far as Harpeth Shoals.

GEO. H. THOMAS,
Major-General, U. S. Volunteers, Commanding.

CHIEF QUARTERMASTER'S OFFICE,
DEPARTMENT OF THE CUMBERLAND,
Nashville, Tenn., December 7, 1864.

Brig. Gen. W. D. WHIPPLE,
    Chief of Staff, Headquarters Department of the Cumberland:

GENERAL: The following copy of a telegram just received is furnished you for the information of the major-general commanding:

LOUISVILLE, KY., *December 7, 1864.*

General Donaldson arrived this morning. Please inform General Thomas that he will leave for Nashville soon as possible.

ROBT. ALLEN,
Brigadier-General and Chief Quartermaster.

Very respectfully, your obedient servant,

JAMES F. RUSLING,
Capt. and Asst. Qm., Actg. Chief Qm., Dept. of the Cumberland.

SPECIAL FIELD ORDERS, } HDQRS. DEPT. OF THE CUMBERLAND,
    No. 335.   }   *Nashville, Tenn., December 7, 1864.*

*   *   *   *   *   *   *

IV. Brig. Gen. K. Garrard, U. S. Volunteers, is hereby relieved from duty with the Second Cavalry Division, and will report in person to Maj. Gen. A. J. Smith, commanding the Detachment Army of the Tennessee, for assignment to duty.

V. Paragraph I, Special Field Orders, No. 333, current series, from these headquarters, assigning Maj. Gen. D. N. Couch, U. S. Volunteers, to duty with the Fourth Army Corps, is hereby revoked. Major-General Couch will report in person to Maj. Gen. J. M. Schofield, commanding Twenty-third Army Corps, for assignment to duty.

VI. Colonel Doolittle, Eighteenth Michigan Volunteers, is hereby relieved from duty with Brigadier-General Miller, commanding post, and will report for temporary duty to Brigadier-General Cox, commanding Third Division, Twenty-third Army Corps.

*   *   *   *   *   *   *

By command of Major-General Thomas:

HENRY M. CIST,
Captain and Assistant Adjutant-General.

HEADQUARTERS FOURTH ARMY CORPS,
December 7, 1864—8.30 a. m.

Major-General THOMAS:

Your telegram of the 6th instant received this morning. I shall readily serve wherever I am ordered, but cannot, of my own election, take a position that would throw me into a lesser command.

D. N. COUCH,
Major-General.

HEADQUARTERS FOURTH ARMY CORPS,
Near Nashville, Tenn., December 7, 1864—7 p. m.

Brig. Gen. W. D. WHIPPLE,
Assistant Adjutant-General and Chief of Staff:

GENERAL: I made a thorough examination of the entire front of the Fourth Corps late this afternoon, with a view, first, to advancing the picket-line and, secondly, to developing, if possible, whether the enemy is in force in our immediate front. The examination led me to the conclusion that I could advance the picket-line on the right and left of the fortified ridge immediately in front of Colonel Streight's brigade, without much trouble or loss; but immediately in front of that ridge the skirmishers on both sides, in their intrenched holes, are only a short distance apart, and no advance, except in force, could be made with any hope of success. To take the ridge would necessarily be a much more serious affair than merely advancing the picket-line, and would probably require the movement of a considerable part of a division at least, if it is occupied with a force proportionate to the apparent strength of the works on it. It would be useless to advance the picket-line on the right and left of the ridge, beyond it, without also taking it, for the enemy remaining on the ridge could flank our advanced lines to the right and left of it. I consequently concluded, after a full examination, that it would not be judicious to make any movement of the picket-line this afternoon, and think it may not be judicious to make any movement until we are ready for final and decisive work. I rode out on the Hillsborough pike as far as our picket-line, and the examination strengthened the opinion that the enemy's intrenchments do not extend farther toward [*sic*] than the most westerly point of the ridge immediately in front of Colonel Streight's brigade. My opinion is that his works terminate on that ridge with a very short return, bearing in a southwesterly direction.

I am, general, very respectfully, your obedient servant,

TH. J. WOOD,
Brigadier-General of Volunteers, Commanding.

CIRCULAR.]   HEADQUARTERS FOURTH ARMY CORPS,
Nashville, Tenn., December 7, 1864.

Division commanders will at once have subsistence trains loaded to their utmost capacity with the following articles: Full ration of bread, sugar, coffee, salt, and salt meat, in proportion of two days in seven. Trains will be kept constantly loaded ready for an instantaneous movement. Arrangements will also be made so that, without interfering with the stores in trains, the troops may be constantly supplied with three days' rations. The remainder of the meat ration, five out of every seven days, will be carried on the hoof, and commissaries must make necessary arrangements for the cattle. Ordnance trains must be filled to their utmost capacity, and must be constantly supplied with sixty rounds in cartridge-boxes. Ten days' forage, at the rate of six pounds to the animal, will be kept constantly on hand, except for the artillery, which will take full forage. The order in regard to allowance of six pounds per animal will not apply while in camp. Animals will get full forage while the command is in camp.

By order of Brigadier-General Wood:

WM. H. SINCLAIR,
Assistant Adjutant-General.

HEADQUARTERS THIRD DIVISION, FOURTH ARMY CORPS,
December 7, 1864.

Col. A. D. STREIGHT,
First Brigade:

COLONEL: I am directed to recall the order announcing Major-General Couch as in command of the corps. If you have promulgated it to your regiments, please recall it.

By order of Brigadier-General Beatty:

M. P. BESTOW,
Assistant Adjutant-General.

SPECIAL FIELD ORDERS, }   HDQRS. ARMY OF THE OHIO,
No. 173.   }   *Nashville, Tenn., December 7, 1864.*

*   *   *   *   *   *   *

VIII. The Twenty-sixth Kentucky Infantry is hereby assigned to the First Brigade, Second Division, Twenty-third Army Corps.

IX. The Twenty-eighth Michigan Infantry is hereby assigned to the Third Division, Twenty-third Army Corps. The division commander will assign it to a brigade.

*   *   *   *   *   *   *

By command of Major-General Schofield:

J. A. CAMPBELL,
Major and Assistant Adjutant-General.

[Indorsement on General Schofield's report of December 7, 1864.*]

HEADQUARTERS DEPARTMENT OF THE CUMBERLAND,
Nashville, Tenn., December 7, 1864.

Respectfully forwarded to the Adjutant-General of the Army, cordially recommending the gallantry and skill of Major-General Schofield to the commendation of the War Department.

GEO. H. THOMAS,
Major-General, U. S. Volunteers, Commanding.

GENERAL ORDERS, }   HDQRS. FIRST BRIG., DIV. 17TH A. C.,
No. 1.   }   *Nashville, Tenn., December 7, 1864.*

In compliance with Special Orders, No. 93, headquarters Division Seventeenth Army Corps, of this date, the undersigned hereby assumes command of the First Brigade, Division Seventeenth Army Corps. The following is announced as the organization of the brigade staff: Adjt. John M. Read, Fourteenth Wisconsin Infantry, acting assistant adjutant-general; Capt. George B. Carter, Thirty-third Wisconsin Infantry, acting assistant inspector-general; First Lieut. O. R. Potter, Fourteenth Wisconsin Infantry, acting assistant quartermaster.

L. M. WARD,
Colonel Fourteenth Wisconsin Infantry.

---

* See Part I, p. 341.

HEADQUARTERS DEPARTMENT OF THE CUMBERLAND,
Nashville, Tenn., December 7, 1864.

Maj. Gen. JAMES B. STEEDMAN:

GENERAL: The major-general commanding directs that, as Colonel Thompson has reported to you with his command, the Sixth Indiana Cavalry be relieved from your command and directed to report to Brig. Gen. R. W. Johnson, or Brevet Major-General Wilson, commanding Cavalry Corps.

Very respectfully, your obedient servant,

HENRY STONE,
Assistant Adjutant-General.

HEADQUARTERS FOURTH ARMY CORPS,
Nashville, Tenn., December 7, 1864.

Maj. Gen. J. B. STEEDMAN,
Commanding:

Give me the result of your morning's operations. The enemy in my front quiet, except strengthening their works when it can be done out of effective range of artillery; seem to be making preparations for planting artillery.

Very respectfully, your obedient servant,

TH. J. WOOD,
Brigadier-General of Volunteers, Commanding.

CHIEF QUARTERMASTER'S OFFICE,
DEPARTMENT OF THE CUMBERLAND,
Nashville, Tenn., December 7, 1864.

Maj. E. B. BEAUMONT,
Assistant Adjutant-General:

MAJOR: I have the honor to state for the information of Major-General Wilson, commanding Cavalry Corps, that I have established a ferry at a point just above the railroad bridge, known as Brown's Ferry, and that the same is now ready to cross cavalry or infantry with their trains, the first-class ferry-boat Metamora having been detailed for that purpose. This in addition to the pontoon bridge, which promises to be done by to-night.

Very respectfully,

JAS. F. RUSLING,
Captain and Assistant Quartermaster, and
Acting Chief Quartermaster, Department of the Cumberland.

HDQRS. CAVALRY CORPS, MIL. DIV. OF THE MISSISSIPPI,
Nashville, Tenn., December 7, 1864.

Col. G. G. MINER,
Commanding Cavalry Depot:

COLONEL: Please inform me whether the Chicago Board of Trade Battery is equipped and ready for the field. Has it horses, &c.? If it is not direct the commanding officer to hand in his requisitions and fit out the battery at once.

By command of Brevet Major-General Wilson:

E. B. BEAUMONT,
Major and Assistant Adjutant-General.

SPECIAL ORDERS,   }   HEADQUARTERS CAVALRY CORPS,
                  MILITARY DIVISION OF THE MISSISSIPPI,
No. 30.   }   *Nashville, December 7, 1864.*

I. Lieut. F. G. Smith, commanding Battery I, Fourth Artillery, having reported in accordance with Special Field Orders, No. 333, extract II, headquarters Department of the Cumberland, December 5, 1864, is hereby assigned to duty with the Sixth Cavalry Division, Military Division of the Mississippi, and will report to Brig. Gen. R. W. Johnson, commanding.

*   *   *   *   *   *   *

By command of Brevet Major-General Wilson:
                          E. B. BEAUMONT,
                  Major and Assistant Adjutant-General.

HEADQUARTERS FOURTH DIVISION, CAVALRY CORPS,
        MILITARY DIVISION OF THE MISSISSIPPI,
               Memphis, Tenn., December 7, 1864.

Bvt. Maj. Gen. J. H. WILSON,
    Chief of Cavalry, Military Division of the Mississippi:

GENERAL: Major-General Dana has just arrived, and I have at last obtained the order for one brigade of my command to proceed to Nashville. The troops are now embarking. I have also received dispatch from Saint Louis that the detachment of the brigade at that point has been remounted and equipped and would leave there to-day. The other brigade, consisting of the Second New Jersey, Seventh Indiana, Fourth Missouri, and First Mississippi, as well as the cavalry at Vicksburg, has been retained here by General Dana's order. As soon as the troops which are to go are all under way, I will proceed to Nashville and report to you in person.

Respectfully, your obedient servant,
                          B. H. GRIERSON,
                          Brigadier-General.

DECEMBER 9, 1864.

As the above was being inclosed I received an order to suspend the embarkation of the cavalry. A few hours afterward I was ordered to continue the embarkation, and still a few hours later I received Special Orders, No. 1, from General Dana's headquarters, ordering me to remain in Memphis with my command until further orders. I think the detention is made in accordance with some orders from Washington received by General Dana. I will write you as soon as any change occurs.

Respectfully, &c.,
                          B. H. GRIERSON,
                          Brigadier-General.

HEADQUARTERS,
        Saint Louis, December 7, 1864.

Major-General WILSON,
    Commanding Cavalry Corps:

SIR: Have been delayed in getting horses; now mounted by order from Washington. Shall I proceed to join you via Louisville, or proceed to Nashville directly? Boats are here in readiness to transport us to Nashville. Please answer. Address 281 Franklin avenue.
                          F. W. BENTEEN,
                          Lieutenant-Colonel.

HDQRS. CAVALRY CORPS, MIL. DIV. OF THE MISSISSIPPI,
Edgefield, Tenn., December 7, 1864.

Brig. Gen. R. W. JOHNSON,
Commanding Sixth Division, Cavalry Corps:

GENERAL: The general commanding desires to know if Lieutenant Smith, with his battery of the Fourth Artillery, has reported to you.

Very respectfully, your obedient servant,

A. J. ALEXANDER,
Lieutenant-Colonel, &c.

Lieutenant Smith reported yesterday and brought his battery over to-day. I have instructed him to draw some more horses, so as to make the battery able to go where and when cavalry can go.

R. W. JOHNSON,
Brigadier-General.

HEADQUARTERS SIXTH DIVISION, CAVALRY CORPS,
Edgefield, Tenn., December 7, 1864.

Col. JAMES BIDDLE,
Commanding Sixth Indiana Cavalry:

General Johnson directs me to say that orders have been issued from the headquarters of Major-General Thomas some days since requiring you to report with your regiment at these headquarters. He desires you to report without delay, in order that so much as is practicable during the present delay here may be done toward refitting you.

Very respectfully, your obedient servant,

E. T. WELLS,
Assistant Adjutant-General.

GUN-BOAT BRILLIANT, No. 18,
Cairo, December 7, 1864—12 m.

Maj. E. B. BEAUMONT,
Assistant Adjutant-General, Cavalry Corps, Nashville, Tenn.:

MAJOR: I have just returned from a thorough scouring of the country, from the lower Gallatin landing back five miles and around to this place. At the same time I sent a strong party under Colonel Jackson, Ninth Indiana Cavalry, into Lebanon. The information obtained by my party and his, after sifting and allowances, amounts to the same thing, viz: Breckinridge is expected at Lebanon with a large force, and is supposed to be now somewhere about Sparta on his way; and that Biffle has been near Lebanon, but has gone, not known where certainly. The only force now in front of me is guerrilla, which pickets the river and watches me. There are a good many of them, also a number of rebel soldiers in squads of two or three. The force that chased my scouts on Sunday was citizens. The nearest large force we could hear of is one on Stone's River, supposed to be part of Cheatham's command. I heard from Sparta direct yesterday and day before; no force there then, or as far up as Livingston. I found the country all the way to Lebanon cleaned of horses; all run off to the rebel army; we only obtained eight of any account. Could find no indications of pontoons, only rumors, and only one spot yet to examine. I believe that it would be well to have a picket opposite the mouth of Stone's River; the citizens are impressed with the idea of a move there, and it will be no harm to watch. Three of my horse-pressing parties have not returned. I suppose that finding few horses they have gone clear into Kentucky, as they had orders "to bring horses." A portion of my men went out from Carthage to-day, and this, with the movement here, will probably produce the impression of a crossing in force. The aid of a gun-boat or transport at any time you may desire it will enable me to examine the country in person. I can't trust scouts at all, and the wildest rumors prevail. All means of crossing between here and Carthage is by this time destroyed. My force crossed on the gun-boat. But two prisoners brought in.

     I am, major, very respectfully, your obedient servant,

J. H. HAMMOND,
Brevet Brigadier-General.

NASHVILLE, *December 7, 1864.*

Col. A. A. SMITH,
     Clarksville:

     What news have you of matters about Clarksville? Have the gun-boats arrived at Clarksville yet, and what news have they of the enemy? Give me a full report of all that has transpired since your last dispatch.

GEO. H. THOMAS,
Major-General, U. S. Volunteers, Commanding.

CLARKSVILLE, *December 7, 1864.*

Major-General THOMAS:

     Gun-boats have not arrived. Forty-second Missouri went to Fort Donelson yesterday. Rebel General Lyon is between the rivers somewhere, with from 900 to 2,000 men—reported. I sent scouts yesterday; they did not discover his location. There are five transports here and one hospital boat. General Cooper's command moved this 5 a. m. for Nashville.

A. A. SMITH,
Colonel, Commanding.

CLARKSVILLE, *December 7, 1864—6.30 p. m.*

Brigadier-General WHIPPLE,
     Assistant Adjutant-General:

     Six transports and gun-boat Cincinnati have just arrived. There being about 350 men, detachments, will send them by rail, if not otherwise ordered.

A. A. SMITH,
Colonel, Commanding.

NASHVILLE, TENN., *December 7, 1864—9 p. m.*

Col. A. A. SMITH,
     Clarksville:

     Send the detachments referred to in your dispatch of this p. m. by rail, as proposed.

GEO. H. THOMAS,
Major-General, U. S. Volunteers, Commanding.

SWEETWATER, *December 7, 1864—7.15 p. m.*

Brigadier-General AMMEN:

Reliable man just in from near Madisonville reports between 75 and 150 rebels approaching Madisonville, and were at 4 o'clock within three miles of town. Captain Lyons, in command of the forces there, was then hurrying off his stores toward Loudon. It was reported rebels intended striking railroad at Sweetwater to-night. I have twelve men here with arms, but no ammunition. There is considerable corn stored here; also two cars on siding. Can you send some men from Loudon to-night?

G. M. LYONS,
Agent and Operator.

———

LOUISVILLE, KY., *December 7, 1864.*

Hon. E. M. STANTON,
    Secretary of War, Washington, D. C.:

SIR: A delegation of prominent citizens of Kentucky are now upon their way to Washington to urge upon you a change of policy in the military administration of their State. In view of which, I have the honor to submit the following conclusions relative to such administration at which I have arrived, after consultation with many influential citizens of different localities and of conflicting opinions:

I.——THE CONDITION OF THE STATE.

There is scarcely any security for person or property. In nearly every county guerrillas are destroying the property and taking the lives of all who have been, or now are, in the U. S. armies. The citizens are so bitterly arrayed against each other as to afford immunity, if not assistance, to these desperadoes, for each party is glad to see men of the other murdered. From this intestine hatred guerrillas have their origin and maintenance.

II.——TEMPER OF THE PEOPLE.

Kentucky remained in the Union to preserve slavery and avoid becoming the theater of war, although strongly in sympathy with the rebellious States. Being humored and favored for the first two years, many people avowed their devotion to the Union; but the moment that Government attempted to draft men or enlist negroes, the true feeling of these people was evinced. They resisted our officers, and became more violent in their denunciations of the administration than the original rebels. A large majority of Kentuckians are to-day undoubtedly disloyal.

III.——CHARACTER OF TROOPS IN KENTUCKY.

The forces consist almost entirely of regiments raised in the State for the term of one year's service within the State. They are generally distributed in very small detachments as soon as organized—never serving together as regiments. As a rule, their officers have little capacity and are entirely ignorant of their duties. There is neither drill nor discipline among the men; they are merely a uniformed mob. Serving at home with their local prejudices, they regard their own interests instead of the country's. They do little to punish guerrillas—much against personal enemies. They capture few men in arms, but show their zeal in seizing unarmed people. They plunder largely at their own discretion. As a natural result their victims, with all their friends, become exasperated against the Government, and thus the very troops it employs to serve it prove its worst enemies. Not a regiment raised in Kentucky ought to serve in the State.

IV.—CIVIL ADMINISTRATION IN KENTUCKY.

Governor Bramlette prefers union to rebellion, but he loves slavery also. He has slender capacity, great vanity, and greater ambition. He hopes to gratify his aspirations for election to U. S. Senate by yielding to the pressure bearing upon him from the slave interests in the State. He knows his people are disloyal, and so qualifies his Unionism. His advisers do not conceal their hostility to enlisting negroes. The Governor's policy is simply self first, State second, Union last. But he has not backbone enough to make a direct issue with the Administration; therefore its policy need not be affected in any way by his views.

V.—MILITARY ADMINISTRATION.

Realizing the difficulties surrounding the military administration of affairs in this State, General Burbridge has relied much upon the advice of others. Their prejudices and interests have at times led him astray, but his administration has been mainly a good one. He has shown some vascillation, attributable, no doubt, to his relying upon others. In matters purely military he appears to be somewhat lax. Everything seems to be in confusion. After making every allowance for the inefficiency of field and line officers under his command, there is evident want of capacity or energy. He is now heartily hated by a majority of people in the State, but that signifies nothing if he pursues a policy stringent and impartial. In all I have heard there is nothing to demand his removal, but the substitution of a man stronger in capacity and character would be an advantage.

VI.—SUGGESTIONS AS TO POLICY.

First. It is absolutely necessary to crush out the guerrillas in the State. This may be effected by placing in each exposed county 100 good troops from another State, mounted and well officered.

Second. All troops raised in Kentucky should be assigned to duty elsewhere. They would become efficient, and there would be no objection to the Governor's organizing and officering them, and thus one great cause of complaint upon his part would be removed. No troops should be allowed in State service.

Third. Noisy and active sympathizers with rebels and rebellion should be dealt with most rigorously. Offenses should be clearly proved, and after proof, no relenting. Every distinction should be made in favor of active and tried Union men.

Fourth. The policy of the Administration should be rigidly enforced, and Kentucky feel herself governed, as she now is not either by civil or military authorities. If the Governor should array himself against the Administration, there should be no hesitancy in superseding him.

Very respectfully submitted, and I have the honor to be, sir, your most obedient servant,

E. H. LUDINGTON,
Assistant Inspector-General.

TUNNEL HILL, *December 7, 1864.*

Brigadier-General MEAGHER:

I have just received the following telegram:

RINGGOLD, *December 7, 1864.*

I have just learned Wharton's brigade of cavalry are three miles northeast of Parker's Gap, en route for this place. The information is creditable and from good authority.

J. E. C. COVEL,
Lieutenant, Commanding.

Have you any instructions? Please answer.

M. G. HAMILL,
Major, Commanding Post.

CINCINNATI, OHIO, *December 7, 1864—11.30 a. m.*

J. L. HANCOCK, Esq.,
President Chicago Board of Trade, Chicago, Ill.:

Official engagements will prevent my leaving for Chicago before to-morrow morning; unless a pressing necessity exists I should not leave then. Answer.

J. HOOKER,
Major-General, Commanding.

CINCINNATI, OHIO, *December 7, 1864—11 a. m.*

Maj. JOHN W. SKILES,
Tod Barracks, Columbus, Ohio:

Where is the organized band that is to attempt to burn the bridges on the Little Miami Railroad, or any part of them? If there are any such men in this department the general wants to know it and where they can be found. Answer.

C. H. POTTER,
Assistant Adjutant-General.

COLUMBUS, OHIO, *December 7, 1864.*

Capt. C. H. POTTER,
Assistant Adjutant-General:

CAPTAIN: The superintendent of the Columbus and Piqua Railroad applied to me yesterday evening for a guard to send to one of their important bridges, saying that Mr. Clement, superintendent of Little Miami Railroad, had informed the railroad authorities here that this band was organized for the destruction of bridges on all the roads in Ohio; he did not give any other information. I presume Mr. Clement can give all the facts. The statement I sent by mail yesterday of what was going on here may have something to do with this.

JOHN W. SKILES,
Major and Provost Marshal, City of Columbus.

WASHINGTON, D. C., *December 8, 1864—1.20 p. m.*
Lieutenant-General GRANT, *City Point, Va.:*

Last returns from Department of Missouri exhibit a force present for duty (exclusive of A. J. Smith's forces) of about 19,000 men, of which about 6,000 were in and around Saint Louis. Requisitions have just been received for $20,000, to construct new barracks for the accommodation of troops in Saint Louis. From all the information I can get, Saint Louis is in no more danger of an insurrection than Chicago, Philadelphia, or New York, and that troops are required there only for the defense of the public stores and for prison guards. Moreover, that Missouri is not in the slightest danger of an invasion this winter. I therefore respectfully suggest that now the commanding officer has been changed, 5,000 men from that department can be sent to General Thomas at Nashville. In case of any real difficulty in Missouri they can readily be returned. As General Rawlins (your chief of staff) has recently visited Saint Louis, I submit the matter for your consideration.

H. W. HALLECK,
Major-General and Chief of Staff.

CITY POINT, VA., *December 8, 1864—4 p. m.*
(Received 5.30 p. m.)

Major-General HALLECK, *Washington:*

Please direct General Dodge to send all the troops he can spare to General Thomas. With such an order he may be relied on to send all that can properly go. They had probably better be sent to Louisville, for I fear either Hood or Breckinridge will get to the Ohio River. I will submit whether it is not advisable to call on Ohio, Indiana, and Illinois for 60,000 men for thirty days. If Thomas has not struck yet, he ought to be ordered to hand over his command to Schofield. There is no better man to repel an attack than Thomas, but I fear he is too cautious to ever take the initiative.

U. S. GRANT,
Lieutenant-General.

WASHINGTON, D. C., *December 8, 1864—9 p. m.*

Lieutenant-General GRANT, *City Point:*

If you wish General Thomas relieved from [command], give the order. No one here will, I think, interfere. The responsibility, however, will be yours, as no one here, so far as I am informed, wishes General Thomas' removal.

H. W. HALLECK,
Major-General and Chief of Staff.

CITY POINT, VA., *December 8, 1864—10 p. m.*

Major-General HALLECK, *Washington:*

Your dispatch of 9 p. m. just received. I want General Thomas reminded of the importance of immediate action. I sent him a dispatch this evening which will probably urge him on. I would not say relieve him until I hear further from him.

U. S. GRANT,
Lieutenant-General.

City Point, Va., *December 8, 1864—8.30 p. m.*

Major-General Thomas,
      Nashville, Tenn.:

Your dispatch of yesterday received. It looks to me evident the enemy are trying to cross the Cumberland River and are scattered. Why not attack at once? By all means avoid the contingency of a foot race to see which, you or Hood, can beat to the Ohio. If you think necessary, call on the Governors of States to send a force into Louisville to meet the enemy if he should cross the river. You clearly never should cross except in rear of the enemy. Now is one of the finest opportunities ever presented of destroying one of the three armies of the enemy. If destroyed, he never can replace it. Use the means at your command, and you can do this and cause a rejoicing that will resound from one end of the land to another.

U. S. GRANT,
Lieutenant-General.

———

Nashville, Tenn., *December 8, 1864—9.30 p. m.*

Maj. Gen. H. W. Halleck,
      Washington, D. C.:

No material change has been discovered in the enemy's position to-day. He attempted to advance his picket-line on the Franklin road, but was driven back. With every exertion on the part of General Wilson, he will not be able to get his force of cavalry in condition to move before Sunday. I have a report from the river as high up as Carthage; no body of the enemy can be seen or heard of. I also have information that there is no enemy between Carthage and Albany, Ky. There are two iron-clads above Harpeth Shoals, on the Cumberland River, and Admiral Lee is at Clarksville with the Cincinnati. I have requested him to patrol the river from Clarksville to Harpeth, so as to discover and effectually prevent any attempt of the enemy to cross below.

GEO. H. THOMAS,
Major-General, U. S. Volunteers, Commanding.

———

Washington, D. C., *December 8, 1864—9 p. m.*

Major-General Dodge,
      Saint Louis:

Send all the troops you can spare to General Thomas by such route as you may deem best. They can be returned to you when required. I think 5,000 men can be spared from Missouri.

H. W. HALLECK,
Major-General and Chief of Staff.

———

Nashville, Tenn., *December 8, 1864—8 p. m.*

Maj. T. T. Eckert:

No change in position since last report. Enemy still in force in front, as was found out by reconnaissance, and a large artillery force upon south bank of the Cumberland below, between here and the Shoals. One of our gun-boats came to grief in exchange of iron at Bell's

Ferry. Rebel General Lyon holds same bank below Harpeth, to Fort Donelson, but does not fight gun-boats. Re-enforcements now at Clarksville; will reach here by railroad to-morrow night. Colonel Thompson's black brigade reached here yesterday, having come from Johnsonville, via Clarksville. Deserters report Hood's headquarters seven miles out on Hillsborough pike; Forrest three miles on Granny White road, with main army on same road nearer town.

J. C. VAN DUZER.

NASHVILLE, *December 8, 1864.*

Admiral S. P. LEE,
Clarksville:

I have just received a report from Lieutenant-Commander Fitch, who says he is informed that the enemy have crossed the river below Harpeth. I will be much obliged, if the Cincinnati can get up to the Harpeth Shoals, if you patrol the river between Clarksville and Harpeth Shoals and destroy their pontoon bridge, if they have one laid down. I shall thank you if you will ascertain the truth of the report of the enemy's crossing the river.

GEO. H. THOMAS,
Major-General, U. S. Volunteers, Commanding.

CLARKSVILLE, *December 8, 1864.*

Maj. Gen. G. H. THOMAS:

Best pilots here report five feet four inches on Harpeth Shoals and river falling rapidly, especially below. My pilots urge that this heavy vessel cannot get up, and cannot get over the bars below, unless she moves down immediately. Please ascertain if there is a reasonable prospect of a rise from above. Do you wish convoy down given to transports now here, or shall they stay, irrespective of my movements, which must be governed by the stage of the river? Cincinnati must not be caught above the bars.

S. P. LEE,
Acting Rear-Admiral, Commanding Mississippi Squadron.

CLARKSVILLE, *December 8, 1864.*

Maj. Gen. GEORGE H. THOMAS:

Quartermaster Donaldson's dispatch to Captain Williams just shown me. From want of water the Cincinnati cannot remain here, and there is no other gun-boat here. Your final dispositions in regard to transports should be promptly made. I move down now.

S. P. LEE,
Acting Rear-Admiral, Commanding Mississippi Squadron.

CLARKSVILLE, *December 8, 1864.*

Maj. Gen. G. H. THOMAS:
Please reply to my offer.

S. P. LEE,
Acting Rear-Admiral.

NASHVILLE, *December 8, 1864.*

Acting Rear-Admiral S. P. LEE,
    Commanding Mississippi Squadron, Clarksville, Tenn.:

Your two dispatches just received. Under the circumstances I think it would be advisable to take the transports down with you, and will be obliged if you will convoy them.

GEO. H. THOMAS,
Major-General, Commanding.

CLARKSVILLE, TENN., *December 8, 1864—11 a. m.*

Maj. Gen. G. H. THOMAS:

Since telegraphing you I have seen the harbor master, who informed me that this vessel cannot cross Davis' Ripple, and my pilots state that, unless I go down immediately, this deep-draught vessel cannot get out of the river, and will, in all probability, have to remain all winter. I therefore now return down the river. Have seen the colonel commanding and offered to convoy what transports he may wish to send away, though General Donaldson's telegram provides for keeping them here. I will attend to General Lyon's force, which I am informed will attempt to cross the river below here. I deeply regret not having met a rise to allow a junction of my force to co-operate against the batteries which are now inaccessible to my iron-clads.

S. P. LEE,
Rear-Admiral, Commanding Mississippi Squadron.

CLARKSVILLE, *December 8, 1864—12.30 p. m.*

Major-General THOMAS:

Telegram received. I will take the convoy down as you desire, or will remain to take the chance of wintering here, if you think it justifiable.

S. P. LEE,
Acting Rear-Admiral.

CLARKSVILLE, *December 8, 1864—4.45 p. m.*

Maj. Gen. G. H. THOMAS:

Your telegram received. I will cheerfully remain here, as you desire. Please inform Lieutenant-Commander Fitch, who has not communicated with me to-day, as he proposed, of this. Can you send a cipher operator here?

S. P. LEE,
Acting Rear-Admiral.

NASHVILLE, TENN., *December 8, 1864—5.30 p. m.*

Admiral S. P. LEE,
    Clarksville:

Your three dispatches—of 11 a. m., 12.30 p. m., and a later dispatch, not timed—have just been handed me. They were taken by one of my staff officers to follow me up while on the lines, and he has just returned.

I regret not having received them sooner. As I write this your dispatch of 4.45 p. m. has just been handed me from telegraph office. Will inform Lieutenant-Commander Fitch as you request, and will send you a cipher operator if they have one here.

GEO. H. THOMAS,
Major-General, U. S. Volunteers, Commanding.

CLARKSVILLE, *December 8, 1864.*

Major-General THOMAS:

I am in telegraph office to talk with you and settle on place. I will stay here most willingly, taking chance of wintering here, if you think best or even wish it.

S. P. LEE,
Acting Rear-Admiral.

NASHVILLE, *December 8, 1864.*

Acting Rear-Admiral S. P. LEE,
Commanding Mississippi Squadron, Clarksville, Tenn.:

General Thomas is out on the lines. General Whipple has taken your dispatches to him, and will answer you soon as possible—in an hour, at outside.

Very respectfully,

HENRY STONE,
Assistant Adjutant-General.

NASHVILLE, *December 8, 1864.*

Acting Rear Admiral S. P. LEE,
Commanding Mississippi Squadron, Clarksville, Tenn.:

I have just come in, and will be happy to talk with you.

GEO. H. THOMAS,
Major-General, Commanding.

NASHVILLE, *December 8, 1864.*

Acting Rear-Admiral S. P. LEE,
Commanding Mississippi Squadron, Clarksville, Tenn.:

I was out on the lines when your dispatch came. I will be greatly obliged if you will remain until we get rid of the enemy, or until the river rises.

GEO. H. THOMAS,
Major-General, Commanding.

CLARKSVILLE, *December 8, 1864—8.45 p. m.*

Major-General THOMAS:

Your two telegrams of 5.30 and 7 p. m. just received. I am informed here that this iron-clad cannot cross Davis' Ripple, which is fifteen miles from here and considered the foot of Harpeth Shoals. My pilot says Cumberland River shoals gradually from Davis' Ripple, where there are now seven feet, rather less than we draw, to Harpeth River, and the head of Harpeth Shoals is two miles farther up, at Harpeth Island, where the shoalest water is, but it runs swiftly there. It is unfortunate that the enemy is now inaccessible to the iron-clads along an extent of seventeen miles. If I move up to Davis' Ripple this place will be left exposed, and I am told the water runs swiftly there, which would not be as favorable to crossing as some intermediate portions of the shoals with landings and with roads leading to and from it. I will, however, reconnoiter to the foot of the shoal, if desired. It is likely the enemy would cross at the landing marked Williams on the map and called Hinton's, on the lower point of Harpeth River.

S. P. LEE,
Acting Rear-Admiral, Commanding Mississippi Squadron.

NASHVILLE, December 9 [8], 1864.

Admiral S. P. LEE,
> Clarksville:

Your dispatch of 8.45 p. m. is received. It was not my intention in requesting to have the river patrolled up to Harpeth to wish the gun-boat to remain there, but simply that the position be reconnoitered, so as to ascertain whether there was any truth in the reported crossing of the enemy below Harpeth. I shall be obliged to you if you will have the river patrolled as proposed, and I will request Lieutenant-Commander Fitch to have the same done from this point down to Harpeth.

GEO. H. THOMAS,
Major-General, U. S. Volunteers, Commanding.

U. S. STEAMER NEOSHO,
Robinson's Island, December 8, 1864.

Maj. Gen. GEORGE H. THOMAS,
> Commanding Army of the Cumberland, Nashville, Tenn.:

GENERAL: There is a portion of the enemy—cavalry, I think—across the river, and I suppose foraging; the force is represented to be pretty strong. They were moving up the river to strike the Springfield pike, taking cattle and everything within reach. They crossed well down the river, below the mouth of Harpeth, I am told. The water is getting so low that I cannot get down that far with the heavy boats. I asked the admiral by telegraph this morning to let the Cincinnati come up as far as possible; she ought to get near that point. I will go down as far as possible with these boats, but fear I cannot more than reach Ashland. If I get aground the boats will be useless, as the river is falling so fast that I fear we cannot get off again before a rise. I will have to move down without the company of soldiers, as it would not now be safe for only one company to venture on the reconnaissance. I will try to get back as soon as possible, but may be detained a day or two, but, if possible, will get to where they crossed, and if there is a pontoon will destroy it. I could not stop to gather further information, as I wished to get the word to you as soon as possible.

Very respectfully, your obedient servant,
LE ROY FITCH,
Lieut. Commander, Comdg. Tenth District, Mississippi Squadron.

[First indorsement.]

HEADQUARTERS DEPARTMENT OF THE CUMBERLAND,
Nashville, Tenn., December 8, 1864.

Respectfully referred to Maj. Gen. J. H. Wilson, commanding Cavalry Corps, Military Division of the Mississippi, who will cause the within statement to be fully investigated and its truthfulness ascertained.

By command of Major-General Thomas:

ROBT. H. RAMSEY,
Assistant Adjutant-General.

[Second indorsement.]

HDQRS. CAVALRY CORPS, MIL. DIV. OF THE MISSISSIPPI,
Edgefield, Tenn., December 8, 1864.

Respectfully referred to Brig. Gen. R. W. Johnson, commanding Sixth Division, for investigation and report, to be returned with these papers.

By order of Brevet Major-General Wilson:

A. J. ALEXANDER,
Lieutenant-Colonel and Acting Chief of Staff.

[Third indorsement.]

HEADQUARTERS SIXTH DIVISION, CAVALRY CORPS,
December 8, 1864—7.20 p. m.

Copy furnished to Colonel Harrison, commanding First Brigade, with directions to send out a sufficient party, in command of a reliable officer, to investigate this report and report as soon as possible.

E. T. WELLS,
Assistant Adjutant-General.

U. S. STEAMER SILVER LAKE,
December 8, 1864.

Maj. Gen. GEORGE H. THOMAS,
Commanding Army of the Cumberland, Nashville, Tenn.:

GENERAL: The gun-boats Brilliant and Springfield have just returned from up river. There is no force on the river between this point and Carthage. Breckinridge is reported at Sparta with about 3,000 men, though with what reliability we cannot say.

Very respectfully, your obedient servant,

H. A. GLASSFORD,
Acting Volunteer Lieutenant, U. S. Navy.

HEADQUARTERS FOURTH ARMY CORPS,
December 8, 1864—10.30 a. m.

General WHIPPLE:

Dispatch* just received. Will be in immediately.

TH. J. WOOD,
Brigadier-General of Volunteers.

---

* See Ramsey to Schofield, p. 103.

HEADQUARTERS FOURTH ARMY CORPS,
December 8, 1864.

Brigadier-General WHIPPLE,
    Chief of Staff:

Major Dawson, inspector of pickets, reports that the appearance of the enemy's lines, their fires, &c., are the same this morning as on previous days, but that there is less firing, which may be accounted for by the sharp cold of the morning and from the fact that the lines have been so near each other for several days.

TH. J. WOOD,
Brigadier-General, Commanding.

HEADQUARTERS FOURTH ARMY CORPS,
December 8, 1864—6.30 p. m.

Maj. Gen. J. B. STEEDMAN:

Appearances in my front the same as when you were with me to-day.

TH. J. WOOD,
Brigadier-General of Volunteers.

HEADQUARTERS DEPARTMENT OF THE CUMBERLAND,
December 8, 1864.

Major-General SCHOFIELD:

GENERAL: I am directed by the major-general commanding to say that he desires to see you at these headquarters at 10 o'clock this morning.

Very respectfully, your obedient servant,

ROBT. H. RAMSEY.

(Same to Maj. Gen. A. J. Smith, Maj. Gen. James B. Steedman, and Brig. Gen. Thomas J. Wood.

HEADQUARTERS DEPARTMENT OF THE CUMBERLAND,
[*December 8, 1864.*]

Major-General SCHOFIELD:

The major-general commanding desires to see yourself and General Ruger at these headquarters this evening. Please notify General Ruger.

Respectfully,

ROBT. H. RAMSEY,
Assistant Adjutant-General.

SPECIAL FIELD ORDERS, ⎱ HDQRS. ARMY OF THE OHIO,
                       ⎰   *In the Field, Nashville, Tenn.,*
    No. 174.   *December 8, 1864.*

*　　　*　　　*　　　*　　　*　　　*　　　*

II. Brig. Gen. Thomas H. Ruger, U. S. Volunteers, is hereby relieved from the command of the Second Division, Twenty-third Army Corps, and assigned to the command of the First Division, Twenty-third Army Corps, which division he will proceed to organize with as little delay as practicable.

III. Maj. Gen. D. N. Couch, U. S. Volunteers, having reported at these headquarters for duty, is hereby assigned to the command of the Second Division, Twenty-third Army Corps.

By command of Major-General Schofield:

J. A. CAMPBELL,
Major and Assistant Adjutant-General.

GENERAL SMITH'S HEADQUARTERS,
December 8, 1864.

General W. D. WHIPPLE,
Assistant Adjutant-General:

Appearances on our front same as yesterday. All quiet.

A. J. SMITH,
Major-General.

GENERAL ORDERS, }   HDQRS. DETACH. ARMY OF THE TENN.,
No. 19.   }   *Nashville, Tenn., December 8, 1864.*

The Sixteenth Army Corps as a corps organization having been discontinued by orders from the War Department, the troops heretofore reported to Right Wing, Sixteenth Army Corps, will hereafter be known as "The Detachment of the Army of the Tennessee." The organization of the divisions will not be changed—First Division, Brig. Gen. J. McArthur commanding; Second Division (Third Division, Sixteenth Army Corps), Brigadier-General Garrard commanding; Third Division, Col. J. B. Moore commanding. All reports and returns will be made to these headquarters, as required by existing orders.

By order of Maj. Gen. A. J. Smith:

J. HOUGH,
Assistant Adjutant-General.

HDQRS. FIRST BRIGADE, FIRST DIVISION, 16TH ARMY CORPS,
Nashville, Tenn., December 8, 1864.

Capt. W. H. F. RANDALL,
Assistant Adjutant-General:

CAPTAIN: In compliance with instructions of the general commanding, received yesterday, I have the honor to report that during the day yesterday the enemy in front of my command maintained about the same positions and in about the same numbers as for several days past. During the night he withdrew the two pieces of artillery with which he opened on us the day before. Yesterday morning I moved one of my Rodman guns out to the skirmish line, and shelled their reserve picket-posts with evident effect, as they moved their horses to the rear. During the night everything was quiet, and no movements of the enemy have been seen or reported this morning. A report this moment received from the officer in command of the cavalry on the Charlotte pike says the enemy's pickets occupy the same position they did yesterday.

I am, captain, very respectfully, your obedient servant,

W. L. McMILLEN,
Colonel, Commanding.

HEADQUARTERS SECOND BRIGADE, FIRST DIVISION,
ARMY OF THE TENNESSEE,
Nashville, Tenn., December 8, 1864—6.30 a. m.

Capt. W. H. F. RANDALL,
Assistant Adjutant-General, First Division:

CAPTAIN: I have the honor to report as follows regarding the situation in my front during the past twenty-four hours:

There has been no body of the enemy seen except the detachment of cavalry, which seems to be upon picket duty about three miles out on the Charlottesville pike. I made an effort to throw shell among them during the forenoon yesterday, from the position occupied by the Second Iowa Battery, but was unable to effect anything. A larger number of the enemy's picket-fires were observable last night than at any time previous, owing, perhaps, to the increased severity of the weather. An unusual degree of quiet prevailed all night. My pickets report that no shots were heard after 8 o'clock yesterday evening.

Very respectfully, your obedient servant,

L. F. HUBBARD,
Colonel, Commanding.

GENERAL ORDERS, }   HEADQUARTERS SECOND DIVISION,
}   DETACHMENT ARMY OF THE TENNESSEE,
No. 25.   }   *Nashville, Tenn., December 8, 1864.*

In compliance with Special Orders, No. 151, headquarters Detachment Army of the Tennessee, the undersigned hereby assumes command of the Second Division, Detachment Army of the Tennessee, late Third Division, Sixteenth Army Corps. The staff and existing orders will remain unchanged until further orders.

K. GARRARD,
Brigadier-General, U. S. Volunteers.

HEADQUARTERS DETACHMENT ARMY OF THE TENNESSEE,
Nashville, Tenn., December 8, 1864.

Col. J. B. MOORE,
Commanding Third Division:

COLONEL: The major-general commanding directs me to state that the U. S. steamer Moose (a tin-clad) will be at the extremity of your lines on the river, and he desires that you send one large company of infantry on board, with one day's rations, as a guard for the boat. The boat will return to-day.

I am, very respectfully, your obedient servant,

J. HOUGH,
Major and Assistant Adjutant-General.

HDQRS. CAVALRY CORPS, MIL. DIV. OF THE MISSISSIPPI,
Nashville, December 8, 1864—6.30 p. m.

Brig. Gen. W. D. WHIPPLE,
Chief of Staff:

In regard to the report concerning the presence of a force of rebel cavalry on the north side of the Cumberland, an officer of General Knipe's command, in from Clarksburg to-day, says he heard very generally through the country that only a small force of scouts, not to exceed fifty men, had crossed the river. He doesn't think any more have crossed. I have, however, directed General Johnson to investigate the matter fully.

Very respectfully, your obedient servant,

J. H. WILSON,
Brevet Major-General.

HDQRS. CAVALRY CORPS, MIL. DIV. OF THE MISSISSIPPI,
Edgefield, Tenn., December 8, 1864—7 p. m.

Brig. Gen. W. D. WHIPPLE, *Chief of Staff:*

GENERAL: After conference with my division commanders, I have to state, for the information of the major-general commanding, that the cavalry forces cannot be assembled and put in a proper condition to move in a general campaign before Sunday afternoon. There are 3,000 well-mounted men absent, some of whom cannot get back [before] to-morrow night, and when they do arrive will be necessarily considerably jaded. The horses they bring will require shoeing, and some time to issue. If the parties impressing have been ordinarily successful, by waiting until Sunday our force will be materially increased, say 3,000 men. Brigadier-General Croxton informs me that it will be almost impossible for La Grange's brigade to get here before Saturday night. If, in consideration of all these facts, the major-general commanding determines to delay the movement till Monday, be good enough to inform me at your earliest convenience, in order that I may continue my efforts to make the cavalry force efficient. If he does not so decide, I shall have to begin crossing the river to-morrow at noon, and all arrangements not completed must necessarily be indefinitely postponed. I will see the major-general commanding early to-morrow morning.

I am, general, very respectfully, your obedient servant,

J. H. WILSON,
Brevet Major-General, Commanding.

HDQRS. CAVALRY CORPS, MIL. DIV. OF THE MISSISSIPPI,
Edgefield, Tenn., December 8, 1864.

Lieut. JOSEPH HEDGES, *Commanding Fourth U. S. Cavalry:*

LIEUTENANT: The brevet major-general commanding directs that you send fifty men from your command, under a competent officer, with instructions to take all the hack, omnibus, and carriage horses in Nashville that are suitable for cavalry purposes. Adams Express Company horses are exempted. These horses will be brought to these headquarters.

Very respectfully, your obedient servant,

A. J. ALEXANDER,
Lieutenant-Colonel and Chief of Staff.

HEADQUARTERS DEPARTMENT OF THE MISSISSIPPI,
Memphis, Tenn., December 8, 1864.

Col. E. F. WINSLOW,
Fourth Iowa Cavalry, Memphis, Tenn.:

SIR: You will proceed, on City of Cairo, this evening, to Cairo, Ill., and from thence forward, by telegraph, the dispatch* handed you for

---

* See Vol. XLI, Part IV, p. 799.

Major-General Halleck, Chief of Staff of the Army, Washington, and will await an answer, proceeding, however, to Saint Louis, Louisville, or elsewhere, if found necessary, to accomplish the objects of your mission. Should the detachments of Fourth Missouri and Seventh Indiana Cavalry, now in Missouri, arrive at Cairo, you will cause them to be immediately embarked for Memphis. If the portions of the Fourth Iowa, Third Iowa, and Tenth Missouri Cavalry, now supposed to be en route from Saint Louis, should arrive at Cairo, you will cause their detention at Cairo until orders are received from Washington in regard to them; should they have already passed Cairo for Louisville, you will telegraph the fact to Major-General Halleck. The commanding officer at Cairo will afford all necessary assistance and give necessary orders for securing transportation, &c. You will report proceedings by letter from day to day, and in person when this duty is accomplished, to these headquarters.

By order of Major-General Dana:

T. H. HARRIS,
Lieutenant-Colonel and Assistant Adjutant-General.

HEADQUARTERS SIXTH DIVISION, CAVALRY CORPS,
Edgefield, Tenn., December 8, 1864.

Lieut. Col. A. J. ALEXANDER,
Chief of Staff, Cavalry Corps:

COLONEL: I have just received a dispatch from Lieutenant-Colonel Baird, commanding Fifth Iowa Cavalry, dated Hopkinsville, Ky., yesterday, as follows:

I have just arrived here. I have three companies yet out, but am expecting them in to-night. I cannot reach Nashville earlier than Saturday evening.

I have telegraphed him to use all possible expedition to be here by to-morrow noon.

Very respectfully, your obedient servant,

R. W. JOHNSON,
Brigadier-General of Volunteers.

HDQRS. FIRST BRIG., SEVENTH DIV., CAVALRY CORPS,
Cole's Ferry Road, Gallatin, December 8, 1864.

Maj. E. B. BEAUMONT:

My command, all that I can reach, will be well out on the Nashville pike to-day; will concentrate at Edgefield to-morrow evening.

J. H. HAMMOND,
Brevet Brigadier-General.

GALLATIN, *December 8, 1864.*

Maj. E. B. BEAUMONT,
Assistant Adjutant-General, Cavalry Corps:

Have been into Lebanon. Breckinridge expected and supposed to be somewhere near Sparta, now doubtful. Biffle gone from Lebanon; not known where. No reliable information from Murfreesborough. Part of Cheatham's division supposed to be there and along Stone's River. No pontoons. Guerrilla forces picket in my front.

J. H. HAMMOND,
Brevet Brigadier-General.

STEVENSON, *December 8, 1864.*

Capt. HENRY A. FORD,
       Acting Assistant Adjutant-General:

General Granger desires to inform General Meagher that he has assumed no control over the telegraph office at this post. Colonel Krzyzanowski is in command of the post, and the general's communication has been referred to him. Stevenson has been placed within the command of Northern Alabama, by command of General Thomas, and I have continued Colonel Krzyzanowski in command of post. I presume that he, no more than myself, is aware that the wires have been used to convey the impertinent message referred to in the general's communication.

R. S. GRANGER,
Brigadier-General.

SPECIAL ORDERS, }   HDQRS. DISTRICT OF THE ETOWAH,
   No. 59.   }   *Chattanooga, December 8, 1864.*

*   *   *   *   *   *   *

II. The signal for the assembling of the Civic Guard of Chattanooga, organized in accordance with Special and General Orders, No. 1, from these headquarters, is hereby fixed, and ordered to be three guns, fired at intervals of one minute, from the headquarters of the district.

*   *   *   *   *   *   *

By order of Brigadier-General Meagher:

H. A. FORD,
Captain and Acting Assistant Adjutant-General.

CLARKSVILLE, *December 8, 1864—11.30 a. m.*

Brigadier-General WHIPPLE,
       Assistant Adjutant-General:

If there is a probability of the enemy planting a battery on the south side of the river to destroy transports, I would suggest that they drop back to Fort Donelson, where, under the bluff, they would be comparatively safe. Admiral Lee is compelled to leave here for want of water. I have no news of an enemy in this vicinity.

A. A. SMITH,
Colonel, Commanding Post.

NASHVILLE, TENN., *December 8, 1864.*

Col. A. A. SMITH,
       Clarksville:

How long will it take to unload stores from transports at Clarksville, and how many car-loads do you suppose there will be in all?

GEO. H. THOMAS,
Major-General, U. S. Volunteers, Commanding.

KNOXVILLE, *December 8, 1864.*

General SCHOFIELD:

The beef-cattle arrived from Chattanooga day before yesterday. The First and Second [Ohio] Artillery moved up to the Plains yesterday.

The supply train and cattle go up to-day. I am making use of all the old horse equipments in store-house to fit out General Gillem's command, and hope to get them off to-morrow; if so, shall leave myself with them and join Burbridge at Bean's Station, and immediately push for Bristol and endeavor to intercept any force which may be this side of State line. Have no news from Richmond or from this side. River very low and roads passable. Have you any information that would interest or affect us? Is there any chance of Hood's coming this way? Where is General Sherman? Will keep you advised daily, if I can.

GEO. STONEMAN,
Major-General.

HEADQUARTERS ARMY OF THE OHIO,
Nashville, Tenn., December 8, 1864.

Major-General STONEMAN, *Knoxville, Tenn.:*

Dispatch received. Have no definite news from Sherman. No danger of Hood going that way, for some time at least; but your work should be done soon, so that you may be ready for anything. Your force may be wanted about Chattanooga after a while.

J. M. SCHOFIELD,
Major-General.

PRIVATE.]   HEADQUARTERS NORTHERN DEPARTMENT,
Cincinnati, Ohio, December 8, 1864.

Hon. HENRY WILSON, *United States Senate:*

Since my connection with the rebellion friends high in position have kindly tendered me their offices in securing my preferment or assignment to important command, but, with the single exception of the aid that was rendered me on the occasion of my return to the army, I have uniformly declined them, believing that if health and strength were given me, I could accomplish my advancement with my sword, and that it would come to me when I had earned it. It was with this feeling that I assured you at the asylum that the command of the Army of the Potomac would fall to me soon enough, without the effort of my friends to hasten it. It did come, and I exercised it as long as I could with advantage to the cause and with a becoming regard for my honor and self-respect. I trust that an opportunity will be afforded me by the present Congress to lay before the public the facts connected with this part of my military history, which has hitherto been denied me, after having made the most strenuous efforts to have it placed on record and spread before the world. It is sufficient to say that now it is not understood. I am, and have been, censured for that which I consider as the most meritorious of my military services. Time will tell whether I am in error, or those who have succeeded thus far in concealing that part of the history of the rebellion from the public mind. Be that as it may, in the public estimation I was considered with less favor until I was transferred to the West, when my star rose again higher than ever, until now, when I would not exchange the consideration I enjoy in the army for services rendered with any officer who has participated in the war.

It is a fact you may not be aware of, that we have no army in the field that would not welcome my return to it with demonstrations bordering on enthusiasm. Officers in command of these armies know this, and the highest civil authorities of the land know it, if they know anything. Every letter that I receive, every step that I take among the friends and relatives of the troops, furnish abundant evidence of the truthfulness of what I state. Still I have no active command. Why is it? I am informed that I enjoy the unshaken confidence of His Excellency the President and of the Secretary of War, and yet I am laid on the shelf, nay, more, I am not only deprived of the command I have earned with my saber, but whenever a vacancy is to be filled in the list of major-generals in the regular army my juniors are placed in nomination for promotion over my head, when I have encountered more fire and gained more successes in the estimation of the soldiers of the army than any ten of them; and this will be the verdict of the people when placed in possession of all the facts.

Of my campaigns in the West last fall and the present year but little is known, except by those actually present, for the reason that a studied effort has been made by Generals Grant and Sherman to keep me in the background. I understand that I incurred the displeasure of the lieutenant-general in my assault of Lookout Mountain, and although it was made with strict conformity to his orders, that I cannot have his forgiveness. It was too successful; I carried away the honors, when he intended that I should be a spectator to Sherman's operations. In the campaign of this summer under Sherman it was the fortune of the Twentieth Corps, which I commanded, to do the heavy work, and it was accomplished in a manner that extorted the applause of all the armies. They became so partial to me that Sherman offered me a professional and personal indignity, which he knew would drive me from the army, and it was permitted to be done by the President of the United States. When McPherson fell, Sherman took Howard, my junior, an officer who cannot make himself felt on the field of battle, and assigned him to the command of that army, when the rumor that I was to have it was received with expressions of great joy from one end of the line to the other. The dissatisfaction of the troops at this continues to this day.

On going to the West with the Eleventh and Twelfth Corps, I had to encounter the prejudice, which expressed itself at all times and on all occasions, of a fancied superiority of Western troops over those from the East, but that disappeared at the first encounter I had with the enemy, and in the following campaign, this summer, my corps became in the minds of all the grandest corps of the war. It fought its way to the very hearts of our companions, notwithstanding an insult was offered, to have countenanced which for one moment would have made me lose caste with all soldiers, and, what is more, I would have lost caste with myself. For the private part of the indignity, it would have given me the greatest satisfaction to have broken my saber over the head of Sherman; for the professional part, I could but make application to be removed from that army. Every one understood the cause, and every one appreciated and approved of my withdrawal. During that entire campaign, Schofield, an officer unknown to the war, was in command of the Army of the Ohio, and McPherson, another of my juniors, exercised the command of the Army of the Tennessee. Such was my feeling of degradation, or humiliation, that I saw no day on that campaign that I would not have withdrawn from the service in disgust, could I have done so with justice to myself and the cause in which I was engaged. I could die, but I could not commit suicide. On coming East a new command was just about to be sent up the Potomac River, and it was given to Sheridan, a new man; but it was thought better to experiment with him, than give it to one who had won and sustained the character of "Fighting Joe" in all the armies. Sheridan was first made a brigadier-general for comparatively nothing, and now for his fight at Cedar Run they are attempting to push him forward in an unprecedented manner, over my head, to a major-generalcy. Understand me, I do not wish to underestimate his conduct in his last battle; but who will say, as a feat of arms, that it was to be compared with Lookout Mountain, or Peach Tree Creek, the 20th of July last? In this last fight my adversary outnumbered me two to one; in his the disparity of forces was the same, but in his favor.

Every word I write you is true. Then let me ask again, why is all this? To avoid the trouble and responsibilities of the war, does the President surrender everything to General Grant? Is he willing, in his desire to have an easy time, that injustice of the most monstrous character should be visited upon subordinates? My blood curdles to think of it. You probably have taken the measure of General Grant before this; if you have not, you will soon have an opportunity.

As for Sherman, no man occupying his position has been more unfortunate. His attack on Vicksburg in 1861 [1862] was a failure; his attack on Mission Ridge was a terrible repulse; his campaign to Meridian early this year was worse than a failure; and in his campaign of Atlanta (considering his men, means, and field of operations, the most splendid opportunity for the display of generalship the rebellion has presented) he succeeded in pushing back the enemy, inferior to him as one to three, and even that advantage he abandoned in cutting loose from Atlanta to run away from his adversary, instead of toward him. Now Hood is investing Nashville, occupying a position he held two years ago, after two years of campaigning to drive him into the interior. You and I know that the rebellion is dead when its military power is destroyed, and not until then; it is to be killed by blows, not marches; and, after an experience of four years, it does seem as if we ought to know this fact. Had Sherman marched against Hood, there was no earthly reason why he should escape; I hope that he will not now. Sherman is crazy; he has no more judgment than a child; and yet it is with such men that the high places of the army are being filled. Grant is determined to have no officer of ability near him in rank. Unless the Senate should interpose, our armies will be more and more feebly commanded as the war progresses. The absolute want of a just standard by which to award the rewards and punishments of service has tended more than any other one fact to prevent the army from arriving at that excellence in discipline and that success in battle we had the right and reason to expect. With a proper appreciation of merit on the part of the civil and military authorities in rebeldom, they have made an army inferior in number and inferior in character equal to if not superior to our own.

Excuse my long letter, though I have not written you half as much as I desire to. I have only time to touch some of the most prominent points.

With regard to myself, I can only state, that if my services have not been such as to merit reward, they should shield me from punishment. It has been my wish to continue in service until the rebellion is dead and buried, but unless I can be protected from indignity, the sooner I quit the better.

Will write you again shortly.

Very respectfully, &c.,

JOSEPH HOOKER,
Major-General, Commanding.

PRIVATE.]   HEADQUARTERS NORTHERN DEPARTMENT,
                                Cincinnati, Ohio, December 8, 1864.

Hon. BENJ. F. WADE,
        United States Senate:

Now that the election is over, I trust that no objection will be made to my appearing before the Committee on the Conduct of the War, to render an account of my stewardship while in command of the Army of the Potomac. I feel, and know, that great injustice has been done me by those who have professed to be my friends in not permitting me to make my disclosure at an earlier period, as it is the only way in which I can have it spread before the public, so long as General Halleck exercises the influence he now does over the highest national authorities. The issues involved in my case mainly rest between myself and that officer, so far as I know, and it is for his interest to delay their publicity to the last practicable moment. This is my impression; of its accuracy, you will be able to determine as soon as an opportunity presents itself for you to become acquainted with the facts. I know of no public duties connected with my present command that can be urged as an objection to my absence for a few days early in the coming month, should the Committee deem it expedient to summon me before them. Allow me to request that you will inform me at your earliest convenience if I may look for this privilege to be extended to me. A refusal will be deeply injurious to me. I have already suffered severely, as you well know, from the ignorance of the public in regard to the events to which I refer, although my subsequent services have done much to obliterate the recollection and quiet the censures of my enemies. It is only with the authorities that I am prejudiced now. Every step that I take among the people satisfies me that I am right with them, and I know that we have no army in the field that would not welcome my return to it with enthusiasm. Yet I cannot have an active command given me, and an effort is being made to degrade me by promoting juniors over my head.

Generals Sherman and Sheridan, I am informed, have been nominated to the Senate for commissions of major-general in the regular army, while I am their senior as a brigadier. This is an outrage to me, and would be so pronounced by nine-tenths of the army were they allowed a free expression of their opinion. No matter what the newspapers may say to the contrary, no officer high in command has been more unfortunate than Sherman, and this moment he is engaged in a raid which will tend to prolong the war, when he had it in his power to have utterly destroyed Hood's army. At the time he cut loose from Atlanta, Hood was on the north side of the Tennessee River, but instead of marching for him, he chose to march from him. Blows, not marches, are to kill the rebellion. It is our duty to look after the rebel armies, and not territory, for that will come when the military power of the rebels is broken. Sherman's present raid will be likely to resemble in its results that of last winter to Meridian, in which he suffered much more than his adversary. We will, however, hope for the best. Whatever was gained by the campaign of Atlanta, all will admit was abandoned when he quit Atlanta, undoing at the close of the year what he had gained at the beginning. As regards the campaign of Atlanta, considering the relative strength of the forces and the means of each, taken in connection with the field of operations, the rebellion has presented no such opportunity for the display of generalship, and yet how badly improved. We merely crowded back an enemy inferior to us as one to three, instead of annihilating him, as we had many opportunities to do. No campaign of ours is open to more severe criticism, and if it has hitherto escaped, it has been for the reason that the political condition of the country did not justify it; it was barren of fruit, but prolific in deeds of the noblest heroism on the part of the troops. Sherman is active and intelligent, but so devoid of judgment that it is actually unsafe to trust an army to his command. I know of what I am writing. If he is not flighty, I never saw a flighty man.

Sheridan has just been made a brigadier, and now I hear he is named for a major-generalcy for Cedar Run. I have no disposition to disparage his conduct on this field, but how many times would I have been advanced had my conduct been regarded with equal favor? I have no objection to his being rewarded, but not at my expense, when I have had ten fields to his one, and acknowledged by my companions to have been a fighting general on all of them. What does it mean, then, Senator, that these indignities are crowded upon me? I am informed that Grant will never forgive me for taking Lookout Mountain, although assaulted in obedience to his orders; but the trouble was, I was too successful. But can it be possible that the President of the United States will adopt the opinions of the lieutenant-general in regard to men and war as his standard, by which he shall award the rewards and punishments of service? Is it possible that he should not be fully understood after the operations of this summer? If not, be assured, Senator, after four years of war all the high places of the army will be filled with men of medium ability, unless the Senate should interpose to prevent it. Every day one is made to blush at the ignorance which prevails in regard to the war, and this will continue to be the case until we can have a national organ, controlled by the highest intelligence of the land, to enunciate the truth in regard to passing events. Our people read newspapers to avoid thinking, and hence it is not surprising that they should often appear to great disadvantage. But I am wandering from my subject.

My object in writing was to be summoned before your Committee; this I especially desire. I need not tell you that I wish to be in a state of readiness to quit the service, in case I should be compelled to from the outrages done me.

Hoping that I may soon hear from you, and wishing you well, I remain
  Your friend and servant,
          JOSEPH HOOKER,
         Major-General, Commanding.

    HEADQUARTERS NORTHERN DEPARTMENT,
     Cincinnati, Ohio, December 8, 1864—11.35 a. m.
COMMANDING OFFICER,
   Louisville, Ky.:

The captain of the steamer Bostona, No. 1, Madison packet, [reports that he] was fired into at Carrollton, at the mouth of Kentucky River, yesterday, and the citizens reported that the force was Jessee's rebel cavalry, and numbered about 150. I request that a force be sent to capture this band of guerrillas, if possible. I have no men to send; all of my troops are now guarding prisoners. Please answer.
          JOSEPH HOOKER,
         Major-General, Commanding.

GENERAL ORDERS, ⎱ WAR DEPT., ADJT. GENERAL'S OFFICE,
    No. —.   ⎰   *Washington, D. C., December 9, 1864.*

In accordance with the following dispatch from Lieutenant-General Grant, viz—

Please telegraph order relieving him (General Thomas) at once and placing Schofield in command. Thomas should be directed to turn over all dispatches received since the battle of Franklin to Schofield.

U. S. GRANT,
Lieutenant-General.

The President orders:

I. That Maj. Gen. J. M. Schofield assume command of all troops in the Departments of the Cumberland, the Ohio, and the Tennessee.

II. That Maj. Gen. George H. Thomas report to General Schofield for duty and turn over to him all orders and dispatches received by him, as specified above.

By order of the Secretary of War:

——— ———.

WASHINGTON, D. C.,
December 9, 1864—10.30 a. m.

Major-General THOMAS,
    Nashville, Tenn.:

General Grant expresses much dissatisfaction at your delay in attacking the enemy. If you wait till General Wilson mounts all his cavalry, you will wait till doomsday, for the waste equals the supply. Moreover, you will soon be in same condition that Rosecrans was last year—with so many animals that you cannot feed them. Reports already come in of a scarcity of forage.

H. W. HALLECK,
Major-General and Chief of Staff.

NASHVILLE, TENN., *December 9, 1864—2 p. m.*
Maj. Gen. H. W. HALLECK,
    Washington D. C.:

Your dispatch of 10.30 a. m. this date is received. I regret that General Grant should feel dissatisfaction at my delay in attacking the enemy. I feel conscious that I have done everything in my power to prepare, and that the troops could not have been gotten ready before this, and if he should order me to be relieved I will submit without a murmur. A terrible storm of freezing rain has come on since daylight, which will render an attack impossible until it breaks.

GEO. H. THOMAS,
Major-General, U. S. Volunteers, Commanding.

NASHVILLE, TENN., *December 9, 1864—9.30 p. m.*
Maj. Gen. H. W. HALLECK,
    Washington, D. C.:

There is no perceptible change in the appearance of the enemy's lines to-day. Have heard from Cumberland River, between Harpeth and Clarksville, and there are no indications of any preparations on the part of the enemy to cross. The storm still continues.

GEO. H. THOMAS,
Major-General, U. S. Volunteers, Commanding.

NASHVILLE, *December 9, 1864—1 p. m.*

Lieut. Gen. U. S. GRANT, *City Point, Va.:*

Your dispatch of 8.30 p. m. of the 8th is just received. I had nearly completed my preparations to attack the enemy to-morrow morning, but a terrible storm of freezing rain has come on to-day, which will make it impossible for our men to fight to any advantage. I am, therefore, compelled to wait for the storm to break and make the attack immediately after. Admiral Lee is patrolling the river above and below the city, and I believe will be able to prevent the enemy from crossing. There is no doubt but that Hood's forces are considerably scattered along the river with the view of attempting a crossing, but it has been impossible for me to organize and equip the troops for an attack at an earlier time. Major-General Halleck informs me that you are very much dissatisfied with my delay in attacking. I can only say I have done all in my power to prepare, and if you should deem it necessary to relieve me I shall submit without a murmur.

> GEO. H. THOMAS,
> *Major-General, U. S. Volunteers, Commanding.*

CITY POINT, VA., *December 9, 1864—7.30 p. m.*

Major-General THOMAS,
> *Nashville, Tenn.:*

Your dispatch of 1 p. m. received. I have as much confidence in your conducting a battle rightly as I have in any other officer; but it has seemed to me that you have been slow, and I have had no explanation of affairs to convince me otherwise. Receiving your dispatch of 2 p. m. from General Halleck, before I did the one to me, I telegraphed to suspend the order relieving you until we should hear further. I hope most sincerely that there will be no necessity of repeating the orders, and that the facts will show that you have been right all the time.

> U. S. GRANT,
> *Lieutenant-General.*

NASHVILLE, *December 9, 1864—11.30 p. m.*
> (Received 10th.)

Lieut. Gen. U. S. GRANT, *City Point, Va.:*

Your dispatch 7.30 p. m. is just received. I can only say in further explanation why I have not attacked Hood that I could not concentrate my troops and get their transportation in order in shorter time than it has been done, and am satisfied I have made every effort that was possible to complete the task.

> GEO. H. THOMAS,
> *Major-General, U. S. Volunteers, Commanding.*

CITY POINT, VA., *December 9, 1864—11 a. m.*
> (Received 1.45 p. m.)

Major-General HALLECK,
> *Washington, D. C.:*

Dispatch of 8 p. m. last evening from Nashville shows the enemy scattered for more than seventy miles down the river, and no attack yet made by Thomas. Please telegraph orders relieving him at once and placing Schofield in command. Thomas should be directed to turn over all orders and dispatches received since the battle of Franklin to Schofield.

U. S. GRANT,
Lieutenant-General.

WASHINGTON, *December 9, 1864—4.10 p. m.*

Lieutenant-General GRANT,
City Point, Va.:

Orders relieving General Thomas had been made out when his telegram of this p. m. was received. If you still wish these orders telegraphed to Nashville they will be forwarded.

H. W. HALLECK,
Major-General and Chief of Staff.

CITY POINT, VA., *December 9, 1864—5.30 p. m.*
(Received 6 p. m.)

Major-General HALLECK,
Washington:

General Thomas has been urged in every way possible to attack the enemy, even to the giving the positive order. He did say he thought he would be able to attack on the 7th, but didn't do so, nor has he given a reason for not doing it. I am very unwilling to do injustice to an officer who has done as much good service as General Thomas has, however, and will, therefore, suspend the order relieving him until it is seen whether he will do anything.

U. S. GRANT,
Lieutenant-General.

CLARKSVILLE, *December 9, 1864.*

Maj. Gen. G. H. THOMAS:

I reconnoitered the river to-day as far as the best pilots thought practicable, but saw nor heard nothing of interest.

S. P. LEE,
Acting Rear-Admiral, Commanding Mississippi Squadron.

NASHVILLE, *December 9, 1864—8.30 p. m.*

Admiral S. P. LEE,
Clarksville:

Your dispatch of this date is just received. If you have any gunboats at Clarksville with you, I will be obliged if you will send as many as you can spare to Smithland, to convoy transports with cavalry on board as far up the river as Clarksville. I have not heard from Captain Fitch since he started down the river this morning.

GEO. H. THOMAS,
Major-General, U. S. Volunteers, Commanding.

CLARKSVILLE, *December 9, 1864—10 p. m.*
Maj. Gen. G. H. THOMAS:

Telegram received. Unfortunately, all the gun-boats of this division are above the Shoals; none here. I expect two at Smithland to-morrow or next day; prepared to convoy.

S. P. LEE,
Acting Rear-Admiral.

SAINT LOUIS, *December 9, 1864—5.50 p. m.*
Maj. Gen. H. W. HALLECK,
Washington, D. C.:

Dispatch of the 8th received and acted upon.

G. M. DODGE,
Major-General.

SAINT LOUIS, *December 9, 1864—5.45 p. m.*
Maj. Gen. GEORGE H. THOMAS,
Nashville, Tenn.:

Colonel Benteen's brigade of cavalry left here this morning on boat for Cairo. Boats do not like to go up the Cumberland. Please send orders to Cairo how they shall proceed from that point.

G. M. DODGE,
Major-General.

NASHVILLE, *December 9, 1864—8.30 p. m.*
Colonel BENTEEN,
Cairo:

Transports can ascend Cumberland River as far as Clarksville with perfect safety. Your command can disembark at that point and march to this place on the north bank of the river. You should reach here as soon as possible.

GEO. H. THOMAS,
Major-General, U. S. Volunteers, Commanding.

NASHVILLE, TENN., *December 9, 1864—8.30 p. m.*
(Received 11.20 p. m.)
Maj. THOMAS T. ECKERT:

Storm of sleet and snow to-day prevents any movement of our force or of the enemy. Absolutely nothing to report.

J. C. VAN DUZER,
Captain, &c.

SPECIAL FIELD ORDERS, } HDQRS. DEPT. OF THE CUMBERLAND,
No. 337.   }   *Nashville, Tenn., December 9, 1864.*

*   *   *   *   *   *   *

II. Brig. Gen. George D. Wagner is, at his own request, relieved from further duty with the Army of the Cumberland, and will proceed to Indianapolis, Ind., and report by letter to the Adjutant-General of the Army for orders.

*   *   *   *   *   *   *

V. Col. W. W. Wheeler, commanding Twenty-eighth Michigan Volunteer Infantry, will report in person to Brig. Gen. John F. Miller, U. S. Volunteers, with his regiment, for temporary duty with the garrison at Nashville.

*   *   *   *   *   *   *

By command of Major-General Thomas:

HENRY M. CIST,
Captain and Assistant Adjutant-General.

HEADQUARTERS DEPARTMENT OF THE CUMBERLAND,
December 9, 1864.

Maj. Gen. JOHN M. SCHOFIELD,
Commanding Twenty-third Army Corps:

What news have you of the position this morning, and have the enemy's lines been changed or any movement on his part been discovered?

GEO. H. THOMAS,
Major-General, U. S. Volunteers, Commanding.

(Same to Maj. Gen. A. J. Smith, commanding Detachment Army of the Tennessee; Brig. Gen. Thomas J. Wood, commanding Fourth Army Corps; Maj. Gen. James B. Steedman, commanding District of the Etowah.)

HEADQUARTERS DEPARTMENT OF THE CUMBERLAND,
December 9, 1864.

Maj. Gen. JOHN M. SCHOFIELD,
Commanding Twenty-third Army Corps:

Owing to the severity of the storm raging to-day it is found necessary to postpone the operations designed for to-morrow morning until the breaking up of the storm. I desire, however, that everything be put in condition to carry out the plan contemplated as soon as the weather will permit it to be done, so that we can act instantly when the storm clears away. Acknowledge receipt.

GEO. H. THOMAS,
Major-General, U. S. Volunteers, Commanding.

(Same to Maj. Gen. A. J. Smith, commanding Detachment Army of the Tennessee; Maj. Gen. J. B. Steedman, commanding District of the Etowah; Brig. Gen. Thomas J. Wood, commanding Fourth Army Corps.)

HEADQUARTERS FOURTH ARMY CORPS,
December 9, 1864.

Brigadier-General WHIPPLE,
Chief of Staff:

Everything along the line is apparently in the same condition as yesterday; no change perceptible.

TH. J. WOOD,
Brigadier-General.

HEADQUARTERS FOURTH ARMY CORPS,
[*December 9, 1864.*]
Major-General THOMAS,
 Commanding:

Dispatched you early this morning, but probably you have not received it, the entire appearance of the enemy in front of the Fourth Army Corps, so far as could be discovered, remains unchanged, and is as yesterday. Major Dawson, inspector of pickets, was on the line just after daylight this morning, and reports no change since yesterday apparent. Colonel Fullerton is now out to examine the distant works of the enemy to our right of Hillsborough pike and in front of General Smith's left; so soon as I have his report, will send it to you.

         TH. J. WOOD,
      Brigadier-General of Volunteers.

HEADQUARTERS FOURTH ARMY CORPS,
December 9, 1864.
Major-General THOMAS,
 Commanding, &c.:

Colonel Fullerton has just returned from examining the enemy's line in front of General Smith's left, but says the atmosphere is so close it is impossible to see the enemy's line. The officer in command of the battery on the hill near General Smith's left told Colonel Fullerton that early this morning he could see the enemy's line, and did not see that it had been extended any since yesterday. I will keep you advised of any changes.

         TH. J. WOOD,
      Brigadier-General of Volunteers.

HEADQUARTERS FOURTH ARMY CORPS,
December 9, 1864.
Maj. Gen. G. H. THOMAS,
 Commanding:

Your dispatch postponing, &c., just received. Everything will be held in readiness for the movement whenever you may order it. I have had Colonel Opdycke out in person much of the morning watching and observing and reconnoitering the ground. Under cover of the storm I thought he might individually get up nearer and see what could not be seen otherwise. After receiving General Kimball's report of this morning in regard to the deserter who came in through the Twenty-third Corps front, I sent out Major Dawson to visit the entire picket-line and order the most careful watch to be kept on the enemy and report immediately any movement. Major Dawson reported he could detect no change in the appearance of the enemy's lines and camps. I am now about going out to the front, and will give you the result of my observations.

         TH. J. WOOD,
    Brigadier-General of Volunteers, Commanding.

HEADQUARTERS FOURTH ARMY CORPS,
Near Nashville, Tenn., December 9, 1864.

Brigadier-General WHIPPLE,
Chief of Staff, Department of the Cumberland:

Paragraph III, General Orders, No. 160, War Department, series of 1862, limits the allowance of tentage to company officers to one shelter-tent each. For an active campaign in pleasant weather company officers can manage to get along with this allowance and perform the duties required of them, but in inclement and winter weather it is impossible. I would therefore suggest that the quartermaster's department, if the amelioration can be allowed, be directed to issue four wall-tents for the use of the company officers of each regiment. In this number of tents the present limited number of company officers could find shelter and have the means of doing their proper work. Some additional means of transportation should also be given to them for bedding. The one wagon now allowed to a regiment barely suffices to transport the regimental and company desks, the three tents allowed to the field and staff of the regiment, a small supply of necessary arrangements and provisions, and the most limited amount of bedding and the officers' valises. In this corps there are fifty-four regimental organizations, and I cannot allow another wagon to each regiment without so weakening the supply train as to render it impossible to transport subsistence enough for any protracted operations. I would hence ask that the quartermaster's department be directed to turn over to the corps at least fifty additional wagons and teams, and if this cannot be done that each regiment be allowed six mules and pack-saddles for the use of the company officers. With this additional means of transportation the comfort, convenience, and efficiency of the company officers would be greatly enhanced, and consequently the general efficiency of the army. I would hence invite the attention of the commanding general to the matter at his earliest convenience.

I am, general, very respectfully, your obedient servant,
TH. J. WOOD,
Brigadier-General, Commanding.

HDQRS. SECOND DIVISION, FOURTH ARMY CORPS,
December 9, 1864.

General W. D. WHIPPLE:

Don't expect me to-day; too risky for smooth shod to travel.
W. L. ELLIOTT,
Brigadier-General.

HEADQUARTERS TWENTY-THIRD ARMY CORPS,
December 9, 1864.

Major-General THOMAS:

I know of no change yet; have sent out to ascertain.
J. M. SCHOFIELD,
Major-General, Commanding.

HEADQUARTERS ARMY OF THE OHIO,
In the Field, Nashville, December 9, 1864.

Major-General THOMAS,
Commanding Department of the Cumberland:

GENERAL: A rebel deserter came into our lines this a. m. and states that—

The report is Hood is trying to flank the Yankees. One division of Cheatham's corps went to Murfreesborough several days since—Bate's division—and he sent for re-enforcements, and another division sent him two days since. Rebels do not intend to attack Nashville, but expect to take Murfreesborough and winter there.

No perceptible change on my front.
Very respectfully, your obedient servant,
J. M. SCHOFIELD,
Major-General.

HEADQUARTERS ARMY OF THE OHIO,
Nashville, Tenn., December 9, 1864.

Major-General THOMAS:

I have received your dispatch postponing to-morrow's movement. I will have everything to move at a moment's warning.
J. M. SCHOFIELD,
Major-General.

HDQRS. THIRD DIVISION, TWENTY-THIRD ARMY CORPS,
Nashville, Tenn., December 9, 1864.

Maj. J. A. CAMPBELL,
Assistant Adjutant-General:

MAJOR: I have the honor to forward for the information of the commanding general the following statement of a deserter from the rebel lines who came in last evening:

Charles O'Brien, Thirteenth Louisiana Infantry, an Irishman, thirteen years in this country, lived in New Orleans before the war; his family still there, and he desires to join them; belonged to Gibson's brigade, Clayton's division, Lee's corps; was on the skirmish line yesterday, which was strengthened and supported by heavy supports, and drove in our line of pickets. At evening all were withdrawn except two men in each rifle-pit; this, taken with camp rumors, made him think the army intended moving last night, and he therefore came into our lines. He says further that it was generally understood in camp that Bate's division was sent some three days ago to take Murfreesborough, but Bate sent back that he was not strong enough, and another division was sent to him; that it was rumored in camp that the whole army would soon move to Murfreesborough. He reports the rebel loss in killed at Franklin 1,700; says there is no doubt Cleburne was killed; says the division he belongs to has from 6,000 to 7,000 men, and that the army is believed to have from 35,000 to 40,000 infantry and artillery since the battle of Franklin. The other divisions of Lee's corps are Stevenson's and Johnson's.

No change in my immediate front is perceptible this morning.
Very respectfully, your obedient servant,
J. D. COX,
Brigadier-General.

HEADQUARTERS ARMY OF THE OHIO,
In the Field, December 9, 1864.

Brigadier-General COX,
    Commanding Third Division:

GENERAL: The signal officer reports our pickets driven back from forty rods on the right to half a mile on the left. Do not permit this; strengthen your line and drive the enemy back. I will be on the line soon.

Respectfully,

J. M. SCHOFIELD,
Major-General.

HDQRS. THIRD DIVISION, TWENTY-THIRD ARMY CORPS,
Nashville, December 9, 1864.

Major-General SCHOFIELD,
    Commanding Army of the Ohio:

GENERAL: In reply to your note of this date, I have the honor to report that on yesterday I myself called on General Kimball at his headquarters in regard to the picket-line, and went with his assistant inspector-general to the line on the Franklin pike, and there agreed with him as to the proper place for it, my own line being then upon it. Subsequently my inspector, Major Dow, met General Kimball himself at the same place, and General K. expressed himself satisfied with the connection. I therefore do not understand the report to which you refer. My line was over a mile from my works, and I did not regard it necessary or best to keep it out so far, as it was at all times liable to capture, unless a far larger part of the whole command was put upon picket than is usual. I will, of course, place it at any position you may indicate, but have no report of its being driven back to-day.

Very respectfully, your obedient servant,

J. D. COX,
Brigadier-General, Commanding.

HEADQUARTERS DETACHMENT ARMY OF THE TENNESSEE,
December 9, 1864.

Major-General THOMAS:

No material change in front of the left. On center of the line a battery, regiment of infantry, and some cavalry discovered moving toward the right, near the river.

A. J. SMITH,
Major-General.

HEADQUARTERS DETACHMENT ARMY OF THE TENNESSEE,
December 9, 1864—2.40 p. m.

Major-General THOMAS:

Received telegram in relation to move.

A. J. SMITH,
Major-General.

SPECIAL ORDERS, ⎱   HDQRS. DETACH. ARMY OF THE TENN.,
No. 152.   ⎰   *Nashville, Tenn., December 9, 1864.*

*   *   *   *   *   *   *

VI. The Tenth Kansas Volunteer Infantry is hereby assigned to the Second Brigade of the Second Division, Detachment Army of the Tennessee, and will forthwith report to Col. J. I. Gilbert, commanding brigade, for orders.

By order of Maj. Gen. A. J. Smith:

J. HOUGH,
Assistant Adjutant-General.

SPECIAL ORDERS, ⎱   HEADQUARTERS FIRST DIVISION,
⎰   DETACHMENT ARMY OF THE TENNESSEE,
No. 165.   ⎰   *Near Nashville, Tenn., December 9, 1864.*

*   *   *   *   *   *   *

II. In obedience to Special Orders, No. 152, extract 7, headquarters Detachment Army of the Tennessee, dated Nashville, Tenn., December 9, 1864, the Eighth Regiment Iowa Infantry Volunteers will be dropped from the returns and rosters of the First Division. All men in this command belonging to that regiment will immediately be sent to it at Memphis, Tenn.

By command of Brig. Gen. J. McArthur:

W. H. F. RANDALL,
Assistant Adjutant-General.

GENERAL STEEDMAN'S HEADQUARTERS,
December 9, 1864.

Maj. Gen. G. H. THOMAS,
Commanding.

Your dispatch received. No news whatever this morning. The enemy's lines and position remain unchanged. He is perfectly quiet in my front.

J. B. STEEDMAN,
Major-General.

GENERAL STEEDMAN'S HEADQUARTERS,
December 9, 1864—2.45 p. m.

Maj. Gen. G. H. THOMAS:

Your dispatch received. I will carry out your instructions.

J. B. STEEDMAN,
Major-General of Volunteers.

GENERAL STEEDMAN'S HEADQUARTERS,
December 9, 1864—6 p. m.

Major-General THOMAS:

Everything quiet in my front; no change of position in camps of enemy to-day. I am constructing the dam of Brown's Creek, on the Lebanon pike; can by a succession of dams overflow my entire front.

J. B. STEEDMAN,
Major-General.

HEADQUARTERS DEPARTMENT OF THE CUMBERLAND,
Nashville, Tenn., December 9, 1864.

Maj. Gen. J. H. WILSON,
Commanding Cavalry Corps:

I have the honor, by the direction of the major-general commanding, to say that, owing to the severity of the storm raging to-day, it is found necessary to postpone the operations designed for to-morrow morning until the breaking up of the storm. He desires, however, that everything be put in condition to carry out the plan contemplated, as soon as the weather will permit it to be done, so that all can act instantly when the storm clears away. Please acknowledge receipt.

I am, general, very respectfully, your obedient servant,

ROBT. H. RAMSEY,
Assistant Adjutant-General.

HDQRS. CAVALRY CORPS, MIL. DIV. OF THE MISSISSIPPI,
Edgefield, Tenn., December 9, 1864.

Captain CIST,
Assistant Adjutant-General, Department of the Cumberland:

CAPTAIN: I have the honor to acknowledge the receipt of your communication notifying me of the intention on the part of the major-general commanding to postpone the operations designed for to-morrow, and shall govern myself accordingly, in the meantime urging with all possible dispatch the preparation of my command for active service.

I am, captain, very respectfully, your obedient servant,

J. H. WILSON,
Brevet Major-General.

HDQRS. CAVALRY CORPS, MIL. DIV. OF THE MISSISSIPPI,
Edgefield, Tenn., December 9, 1864.

Brig. Gen. J. T. CROXTON:

GENERAL: The general commanding desires to be advised of the arrival of your pressing detachments, with the number and character of the horses they bring.

I am, very respectfully, your obedient servant,

A. J. ALEXANDER,
Lieutenant-Colonel and Chief of Staff.

(Same to Brig. Gen. Edward Hatch, Brig. Gen. R. W. Johnson, Brigadier-General Knipe.)

HEADQUARTERS SIXTH DIVISION, CAVALRY CORPS,
MILITARY DIVISION OF THE MISSISSIPPI,
Edgefield, Tenn., December 9, 1864.

Lieut. Col. A. J. ALEXANDER,
Chief of Staff, Cavalry Corps:

COLONEL: In reply to your note of to-day I have the honor to say that the pressing details from my regiments have not all of them as yet reported. So far as heard from they have met with but indifferent success. The regiments here have not received twenty horses so far, all told.

The Seventh Ohio, which was stationed at Hyde's Ferry, eight miles below, scouted all the country in their rear, but I am informed by an officer (the colonel commanding has not yet reported) they procured only about one dozen horses. The Fifth Iowa not yet heard from.

Very respectfully, your obedient servant,

R. W. JOHNSON,
Brigadier-General.

GENERAL ORDERS, ⎞ HDQRS. SIXTH DIVISION, CAV. CORPS,
           ⎬   MILITARY DIVISION OF THE MISSISSIPPI,
No. 4.   ⎠   *Edgefield, Tenn., December 9, 1864.*

I. With the approval of the brevet major-general commanding the corps, the following is announced as the organization of this division: First Brigade, Col. Thomas J. Harrison commanding—Eighth Michigan Cavalry, Fourteenth Illinois Cavalry, Sixteenth Illinois Cavalry, Seventh Ohio Cavalry; Second Brigade, Col. James Biddle commanding—Fifth Indiana Cavalry; Sixth Indiana Cavalry, Fifth Iowa Cavalry, Third Tennessee Cavalry; Third Brigade (will be commanded by the senior officer present)—Fifteenth Pennsylvania Cavalry, Fifth Tennessee Cavalry.

II. The several regimental commanders will report in accordance with this assignment.

By command of Brigadier-General Johnson:

E. T. WELLS,
Assistant Adjutant-General.

HEADQUARTERS SEVENTH OHIO CAVALRY,
December 9, 1864—4 p. m.

Capt. W. B. SMITH.
Actg. Asst. Adjt. Gen., First Brig., Sixth Div., Cav. Corps:

CAPTAIN: I have the honor to report that I sent three companies, under command of Capt. R. C. Rankin, on the reconnaissance down the river ordered last night. They were ordered to proceed as far as Ashland, a point twenty miles below here, near Harpeth Shoals. Captain Rankin reports that night before last a party of fourteen dismounted men crossed the river near Bell's Mill, in Anderson's Bend, near where the boats were captured last Saturday night; that on reaching this side they pressed horses and a guide and struck out for Kentucky. They were probably deserters. He could hear of no other parties on this side of the river. He went down below Ashland one mile and a half to where some guerrillas were said to be, but could find nothing of them. The Hyde's Ferry pike strikes the river about eight or ten miles below here, and for two miles takes its course along the bank of the river under the cliff. This exposes a force traveling the road to fire at a short range from the southern shore. Captain Rankin followed this route both going and coming without attracting any fire from the opposite bank. If the enemy had crossed as stated in the communication of the officer commanding U. S. steamer Neosho, it is quite probable that I would have heard of it while scouting down within twenty miles of Clarksville for horses, and that Captain Rankin would have ascertained it by the scout of to-day. It is his opinion, as it is my own, that no cavalry force of the enemy has crossed the river.

Very respectfully, your obedient servant,

ISRAEL GARRARD,
Colonel Seventh Ohio Volunteer Cavalry.

EDGEFIELD, TENN., *December 9, 1864.*

Brig. Gen. J. F. KNIPE,
    Commanding Seventh Division, Cavalry Corps:

GENERAL: I have been directed by Major-General Wilson to make a summary of the information obtained during a recent scout to Lebanon. We found only straggling parties of the enemy, ones and twos, visiting families. Biffle's cavalry had been at Lebanon, but had ·gone, many thought, toward Carthage, but the weight of evidence was in favor of "to the south of Nashville and to Forrest." The opinion of the people was that Forrest either had gone or intended going to a point near Clarksville about eight miles above, and there crossing for a strike at our communications. This notion was very general, and Bowling Green was the point indicated. Breckinridge was expected, and every man, black and white, thought him on the way, via Sparta. I have, however, seen East Tennesseeans from beyond Livingston, and he was not anywhere there. I could hear of pontoons, but found none. I could not obtain certain information as to whether we still hold Murfreesborough, or not, but the people seemed to think (especially negroes) that we do still hold it. Two men informed me that the Thirteenth Indiana were in La Vergne, and armed with muskets only (bad ones), and that the enemy had charged in with cavalry and taken the place and the force prisoners. They had this from a third party, who said he saw it. A man named Dibble [Dibrell] was expected at Lebanon. He had recently been made a brigadier-general, but I inclined to the opinion that he was expected to conscript his command, rather than bring it. Cheatham's division, or part of it, was said to be on Stone's River, and that was the only certainty of a force that I could find. All the horses in the country seemed to have been carried off. Our scout, which extended from Gallatin, crossing out to Lebanon and around it, back to the river at Cairo crossing, a travel of forty miles, with numerous branch detachments, obtained only eight horses. The country was full of rumors, of which what I have written are the only tangible ones. All means of crossing as high up as Hartsville and all at Carthage have been destroyed by my force, and the gun-boat Post Boy had orders to destroy all found. My force under Major Stephens, Fourth Tennessee Cavalry, found everything quiet at Carthage and could hear of no enemy in that region. The country on both sides of the river had been stripped of horses completely, even to the stallions, but there is plenty of forage—plenty.

I am, general, very respectfully, your obedient servant,
                    J. H. HAMMOND,
                        Brevet Brigadier-General.

(Forwarded to Major-General Thomas by Brevet Major-General Wilson.)

NASHVILLE, TENN., *December 9, 1864—8.15 a. m.*

Colonel GILFILLAN, or
COMDG. OFFICER ELEVENTH MINNESOTA VOLUNTEERS,
                    Gallatin:

You are hereby directed to have the Second Tennessee Cavalry*
(Colonel Murphy commanding, which has been ordered to Gallatin for

---
* Mounted infantry.

duty) patrol the river from Gallatin up to Carthage and beyond, and from Gallatin to this place, keeping a sharp lookout for any attempted crossing of the enemy, and promptly making a report through you to myself if such a movement is discovered. You will be held responsible that this order is faithfully and fully carried out. Acknowledge receipt.

GEO. H. THOMAS,
Major-General, U. S. Volunteers, Commanding.

GALLATIN, TENN., *December 9, 1864.*

Maj. Gen. G. H. THOMAS:

Your order by telegraph directing me to have the Tennessee River patrolled by Second Tennessee Cavalry,* Colonel Murphy, is received.

JAMES GILFILLAN,
Colonel Eleventh Minnesota Infantry, Commanding Post.

CLARKSVILLE, *December 9, 1864.*

Maj. Gen. G. H. THOMAS:

There are 2,485 tons of Government stores, and barge of hay, and thirty-three ambulances, here. One car would carry between six and seven tons on this railroad. Quartermaster cannot state how long it will take to unload. In addition to quartermaster's force, I have detailed as many men as have room to work on levee.

A. A. SMITH,
Colonel, Commanding.

NASHVILLE, *December 9, 1864.*

Col. A. A. SMITH,
Clarksville:

Your dispatch of this a. m. is received. Unload the transports as rapidly as possible and store away, for protection against the weather, all the stores you can, until they can be brought away by rail, which will be as rapidly as possible.

GEO. H. THOMAS,
Major-General, U. S. Volunteers, Commanding.

BRIDGEPORT, *December 9, 1864.*

Brig. Gen. T. F. MEAGHER:

A scout just arrived reports detachments from the Seventh Alabama and Third Confederate Cavalry leaving Lebanon, De Kalb County, Ala., on the 7th instant for the purpose of attacking the railroad at Whiteside's, and that they camped in Will's Valley on the night of the 7th instant, a distance of about twenty miles from Whiteside's.

M. C. TAYLOR,
Commanding.

---

* Mounted infantry.

PADUCAH, *December 9, 1864.*

Brig. Gen. W. D. WHIPPLE:

GENERAL: I have just received reliable information that Lyon and Cheatham have crossed the Tennessee River at Danville bridge yesterday; their forces number from 2,000 to 2,500, with six pieces of artillery.

Respectfully,

S. MEREDITH,
Brigadier-General.

LEXINGTON, *December 9, 1864—8 p. m.*

Brevet Major-General BURBRIDGE,
Bean's Station:

General Meredith telegraphs that he has reliable information Lyon's command, 2,000 men and six pieces of artillery, are constructing boats to cross the Tennessee, twenty miles above Fort Heiman, and strike for the Green River bridge. He has sent a gun-boat to reconnoiter. I have notified General Ewing. Do not put much faith in Lyon's ability to cross the Tennessee and Cumberland. Have heard nothing from Nashville to-day.

J. BATES DICKSON,
Captain and Assistant Adjutant-General.

HDQRS. FIRST DIVISION, MILITARY DIST. OF KENTUCKY,
Lexington, Ky., December 9, 1864.

Lieutenant-Colonel FERGUSON,
Thirty-ninth Kentucky Infantry Volunteers:

You will proceed to the front and report to General Burbridge with all the men you can gather up belonging to any regiment with General Burbridge able for duty. You have full power to take all men of those regiments from Lexington and Camp Nelson (except telegraph guards), and will use your best exertions to reach the general with all the men possible.

By command of Brigadier-General McLean:

J. S. BUTLER,
Assistant Adjutant-General.

HDQRS. FIRST DIVISION, MILITARY DIST. OF KENTUCKY,
Lexington, Ky., December 9, 1864.

Adjt. Gen. D. W. LINDSEY,
Frankfort, Ky.:

I am directed by Brigadier-General McLean to inform you that fifty of the force of 100 men at Georgetown have been ordered to report to you at Frankfort. You can impress horses from the country for the temporary purpose of mounting a company or so, in order to protect the railroad and country from guerrillas, the horses to be returned to the owners as soon as the object is accomplished. Proper receipts should be given by an officer, and the horses promptly returned and the receipts taken up. If you think proper, you can mount two companies Forty-seventh Kentucky, at Frankfort, under Captain Cockrill. Inclosed I have the honor to transmit a dispatch* (copy) from Supt. S. Gill for your information.

Very respectfully, your obedient servant,

J. S. BUTLER,
Captain and Assistant Adjutant-General.

LOUISA, KY., *December 9, 1864.*

Capt. J. S. BUTLER,
Assistant Adjutant-General:

Received the order. Scouts sent out. No force this side the mountain except Prentice. Sent force after him. Scout gone to Pound Gap and head of Kentucky River.

GEORGE W. GALLUP,
Colonel, Commanding.

LEXINGTON, KY., *December 9, 1864.*

Col. GEORGE W. GALLUP,
Commanding U. S. Forces, Louisa, Ky. :

Scouts coming into Mount Sterling to-day from six miles of Jackson report 300 rebels there, 100 more at Compton, and 150 at Beaver; also that rebels are concentrating at Salyersville. Has not the scout mistaken your force for rebels? Answer immediately.

By order of Brigadier-General McLean:

J. S. BUTLER,
Captain and Assistant Adjutant-General.

MOUNT STERLING, *December 9, 1864.*

Capt. J. S. BUTLER,
Assistant Adjutant-General :

The scout sent to the mountains has returned, reporting they went within six miles of Jackson. Ben. Connell is there with 300 men; another force at Compton of about 150; a third at Beaver of 150. The scout has traveled from beyond Hazle Green since yesterday, marching all night. The lieutenant also reports a force at Salyersville, and that they are concentrating there.

JOHN J. SEWELL,
Lieutenant and Post Adjutant.

LEXINGTON, KY., *December 9, 1864.*

Maj. GEORGE J. WEST,
Mount Sterling, Ky. :

The officer in command of scout must be mistaken, for the following dispatch was received from Colonel Gallup, Louisa, Ky.:

I have two companies at Collierville (supposed to be Salyersville), three companies at Paintville, and scouts above.

---

* Not found.

Send out your scouts again and be certain there are no rebels in your front. Colonel Gallup scouts as far as possible toward gap.

By order of Brigadier-General McLean:

J. S. BUTLER,
Captain and Assistant Adjutant-General.

CITY POINT, VA., *December 10, 1864—10.30 p. m.*

Major-General HALLECK,
Washington:

I think it probably will be better to bring Winslow's cavalry to Thomas until Hood is driven out. So much seems to be awaiting the raising of a cavalry force that everything should be done to supply this want.

U. S. GRANT,
Lieutenant-General.

WASHINGTON, D. C., *December 10, 1864—1.40 p. m.*

Major-General THOMAS,
Nashville, Tenn.:

It is reported that most of the cavalry horses sent to mount Garrard's division were used for other purposes, and that 2,400 cavalry horses have been issued at Lexington during the last month to newly organized Kentucky infantry regiments. Nearly one-third of the cavalry of the entire army is now dismounted, and the mounting of infantry regiments, except in cases of great emergency, is contrary to regulations and repeated orders. It should immediately cease, and the officers who have done it without proper authority brought to account.

H. W. HALLECK,
Major-General and Chief of Staff.

NASHVILLE, TENN., *December 10, 1864—8.30 p. m.*

Maj. Gen. H. W. HALLECK,
Washington, D. C.:

Your dispatch of 2 [1.40] p. m. this date is received. I have inquired of General Wilson about the diversion of the horses sent to Louisville to mount Garrard's division to other purposes. He thinks the report a mistake. No horses have been used for mounting infantry that I know of, except those used by General Burbridge in October, before he came under my authority. I will make inquiry of Major Chambliss, and give the necessary orders to govern the case in future. There is no apparent change in the enemy's position to-day. The sleet and inclement weather still continue, rendering offensive operations extremely hazardous, if not impossible.

GEO. H. THOMAS,
Major-General, U. S. Volunteers, Commanding.

[DECEMBER 10, 1864.—For abstract from return of the U. S. forces under command of Maj. Gen. George H. Thomas, see Part I, p. 54.]

CHATTANOOGA, *December 10, 1864.*

Major-General THOMAS:

Shall I send the pontoon battalion to Nashville by way of Cumberland Gap? They can be there in two weeks.

W. E. MERRILL,
Chief Engineer.

NASHVILLE, *December 10, 1864—6 p. m.*

Col. W. E. MERRILL,
Chief Engineer, Dept. of the Cumberland, Chattanooga:

Do not send the pontoon battalion to Nashville.

GEO. H. THOMAS,
Major-General, U. S. Volunteers, Commanding.

SPECIAL ORDERS, } HDQRS. RESERVE ARTILLERY,
  ARMY OF THE TENNESSEE,
No. 21. } *Nashville, Tenn., December 10, 1864.*

*   *   *   *   *   *   *   *

V. In accordance with instructions from Major-General Thomas, commanding Department of the Cumberland, Battery I, First Illinois Artillery, is hereby transferred from the Reserve Artillery, Army of the Tennessee, to the Cavalry Corps, Military Division of the Mississippi. Lieutenant McCartney, commanding Battery I, First Illinois Artillery, [will,] without unnecessary delay, report for duty with his battery to Bvt. Maj. Gen. James H. Wilson, commanding Cavalry Corps, Military Division of the Mississippi.

VI. In accordance with instructions from Major-General Thomas, commanding Department of the Cumberland, Cogswell's Independent Battery is relieved from duty with the Reserve Artillery, Army of the Tennessee. The commanding officer of Cogswell's Independent Battery will report immediately for duty to Maj. Gen. A. J. Smith, commanding Detachment Army of the Tennessee.

*   *   *   *   *   *   *   *

By order of Maj. Fred. Welker:

ED. B. WRIGHT,
First Lieutenant and Acting Assistant Adjutant-General.

HEADQUARTERS DEPARTMENT OF THE CUMBERLAND,
December 10, 1864.

Maj. Gen. JOHN M. SCHOFIELD,
Commanding Twenty-third Army Corps:

What have you to report this morning concerning the appearance of the enemy's line? Has there been any change, or has anything of interest transpired since last report?

GEO. H. THOMAS,
Major-General, U. S. Volunteers, Commanding.

(Same to Maj. Gen. A. J. Smith, commanding Detachment Army of the Tennessee; Maj. Gen. James B. Steedman, commanding District of the Etowah; Brig. Gen. Thomas J. Wood, commanding Fourth Army Corps.)

HEADQUARTERS DEPARTMENT OF THE CUMBERLAND,
December 10, 1864.

Major-General SCHOFIELD,
    Commanding Twenty-third Army Corps:

The major-general commanding directs me to say that he desires to see you at these headquarters to-morrow (Sunday) morning at 10 o'clock.

Very respectfully, your obedient servant,
ROBT. H. RAMSEY,
Assistant Adjutant-General.

(Same to Major-General Smith, commanding Detachment Army of the Tennessee; Brig. Gen. Thomas J. Wood, commanding Fourth Army Corps.)

HEADQUARTERS FOURTH ARMY CORPS,
December 10, 1864.

Brigadier-General WHIPPLE:

Picket officers report no changes in my front this morning. But very little firing on the picket-line, probably on account of the inclemency of the weather.

TH. J. WOOD,
Brigadier-General, Commanding.

HEADQUARTERS FOURTH CORPS,
December 10, 1864.

Major-General THOMAS,
    Commanding:

Nothing new to report this morning. Can as yet detect no change in the appearance of the enemy's lines or camps. Will watch closely and report promptly everything of interest. Sent in report for this morning more than two hours ago.

TH. J. WOOD,
Brigadier-General of Volunteers, Commanding.

HEADQUARTERS DEPARTMENT OF THE CUMBERLAND,
December 10, 1864.

Brig. Gen. THOMAS J. WOOD,
    Commanding Fourth Army Corps:

What is the condition of the ground between the enemy's line and your own? Is it practicable for men to move about on it with facility? I would like your opinion about it.

GEO. H. THOMAS,
Major-General, U. S. Volunteers, Commanding.

HEADQUARTERS FOURTH ARMY CORPS,
Near Nashville, December 10, 1864—3 p. m.

Maj. Gen. GEORGE H. THOMAS,
    Commanding:

The ground between the enemy's lines and my own is covered with a heavy sleet, which would make the handling of troops very difficult, if not impracticable. I am confident troops cannot move with facility.

From the condition of the ground an offensive movement would necessarily be feeble, and feebleness of movement would almost certainly result in failure. I will send you, as soon as I can prepare it, a more full report of certain facts in writing, and will probably call at your headquarters this evening.

TH. J. WOOD,
Brigadier-General of Volunteers, Commanding.

HEADQUARTERS FOURTH CORPS,
December 10, 1864.

General WHIPPLE,
Assistant Adjutant-General:

Dispatch to come to department headquarters at 10 a. m. to-morrow received. Will be there.

TH. J. WOOD,
Brigadier-General of Volunteers, Commanding.

CIRCULAR, ?   HEADQUARTERS FOURTH ARMY CORPS,
No. 29.   }   *Nashville, Tenn., December 10, 1864.*

It has been reported that our pickets have been conversing and holding truces with the enemy's pickets. This must be at once prevented, and officers of the pickets who hereafter allow such practices, or who do not prevent the same, will be arrested and tried by court-martial for correspondence with the enemy. Division commanders will, as soon as practicable, publish this circular to their commands.

By order of Brigadier-General Wood:

J. S. FULLERTON,
Assistant Adjutant-General.

HEADQUARTERS TWENTY-THIRD ARMY CORPS,
December 10, 1864.

Major-General THOMAS:

Nothing new is reported in my front this morning. I am about starting to the front, and will examine the lines personally and report.

J. M. SCHOFIELD,
Major-General, Commanding.

WAR DEPARTMENT, ADJUTANT-GENERAL'S OFFICE,
Washington, December 10, 1864.

Maj. Gen. J. M. SCHOFIELD, U. S. Volunteers,
Commanding Department of the Ohio, Nashville, Tenn.:

SIR: In response to a communication from Col. W. M. Dunn, assistant judge-advocate-general, transmitted through the Judge-Advocate-General, the Secretary of War decides that the assignment to duty of Major-General Stoneman, under General Orders, No. 94,* headquarters

---

* See Vol. XXXIX, Part III, p. 592.

Department of the Ohio, of November 1, 1864, does not invest him with authority to exercise those powers which by law are required to be exercised by a department commander alone. The authority expressly conferred upon you by law as such commander cannot be delegated by you to a subordinate. While, therefore, you continue to be the only commander appointed by the President to the Department of the Ohio, you alone can confirm, execute, remit, or mitigate sentences of death, or of cashiering or dismissing an officer pronounced therein by military courts.

I am, sir, very respectfully, your obedient servant,

E. D. TOWNSEND,
Assistant Adjutant-General.

(Copy to Judge-Advocate-General.)

SPECIAL FIELD ORDERS, ⎰   HDQRS. ARMY OF THE OHIO,
No. 176.   ⎱   *Nashville, Tenn., December 10, 1864.*

*   *   *   *   *   *   *

II. General Orders, No. 60, current series, headquarters Department of the Ohio, is hereby amended to read as follows: The allowance of transportation for the headquarters of a division during the winter campaign will be, for baggage, camp equipage, desks, &c., three wagons; for forage, one wagon; for mechanics' tools and materials, one wagon; for shoes for the men, one wagon; for subsistence stores for sale to officers, one wagon; for a division ammunition train, a sufficient number of wagons to carry sixty rounds of ammunition for each enlisted man present in the infantry regiments in the division; one wagon for artillery ammunition for each battery in the division; one wagon for intrenching tools; one wagon for intrenching tools will also be allowed each brigade headquarters.

III. Capt. J. B. Campbell, assistant quartermaster, is hereby relieved from duty as quartermaster Third Division, Twenty-third Army Corps, and assigned as assistant chief quartermaster Twenty-third Army Corps.

IV. Lieut. G. A. Lyon, Twenty-third Michigan Infantry, and acting assistant quartermaster, is assigned as quartermaster of transportation of the corps, and will have charge, under the direction of the assistant chief quartermaster, of the supply train and the corps ordnance train.

V. Capt. E. B. Whitman, assistant quartermaster, is assigned as quartermaster Fourth Division, Twenty-third Army Corps, and chief quartermaster District of East Tennessee.

VI. Capt. D. W. H. Day, assistant quartermaster, is assigned as quartermaster Fifth Division, Twenty-third Army Corps, and chief quartermaster District of Kentucky.

VII. Capt. George C. Winslow, assistant quartermaster, is relieved as quartermaster Second Division, Twenty-third Army Corps, and assigned as disbursing quartermaster for the District of Kentucky, and will report for duty to Lieut. Col. J. F. Boyd, chief quartermaster Department of the Ohio, Louisville, Ky.

*   *   *   *   *   *   *

IX. Capt. Tyler P. Rood, assistant quartermaster, is assigned as quartermaster Second Division, Twenty-third Army Corps.

By command of Major-General Schofield:

J. A. CAMPBELL,
Major and Assistant Adjutant-General.

MAJOR-GENERAL STEEDMAN'S HEADQUARTERS,
December 10, 1864.

Maj. Gen. G. H. THOMAS:

Your message received. The enemy's lines and position appear to be unchanged. He is perfectly quiet. I am confident his right has not been changed since I saw you.

JAMES B. STEEDMAN,
Major-General of Volunteers.

SPECIAL ORDERS, }   HDQRS. DISTRICT OF THE ETOWAH,
No. 61.   }   *Chattanooga, December 10, 1864.*

*   *   *   *   *   *   *

II. Col. A. O. Millington, commanding Eighteenth U. S. Colored Infantry, will move his regiment, without delay, to Bridgeport, Ala., by special train, and report his arrival at that point to Col. M. C. Taylor, commanding post.

By order of Brigadier-General Meagher:

H. A. FORD,
Captain and Acting Assistant Adjutant-General.

[DECEMBER 10, 1864.—For abstract from return of the District of Tennessee, commanded by Maj. Gen. Lovell H. Rousseau, U. S. Army, see Part I, p. 58.]

[DECEMBER 10, 1864.—For abstract from return of the District of the Etowah, commanded by Maj. Gen. James B. Steedman, U. S. Army, see Part I, p. 59.]

SPECIAL ORDERS, } HDQRS. CAV. CORPS, MIL. DIV. OF THE MISS.,
No. 33.   }   *Nashville, Tenn., December 10, 1864.*

*   *   *   *   *   *   *

V. Brig. Gen. J. H. Hammond, U. S. Volunteers, having reported for duty at these headquarters, is assigned to the command of the First Brigade, Seventh Cavalry Division, Military Division of the Mississippi, Brig. Gen. J. F. Knipe commanding. This order to date from November 25, 1864.

By command of Brevet Major-General Wilson:

E. B. BEAUMONT,
Major and Assistant Adjutant-General.

CIRCULAR.] HDQRS. CAVALRY CORPS, MIL. DIV. OF THE MISS.,
Nashville, Tenn., December 10, 1864.

Division commanders will take instant measures to mount regiments complete by dismounting partially dismounted regiments. Those to be mounted will be selected from the best armed and disciplined regiments in the command. These changes will be made to-day, and division commanders will report their action to-night, with the designation and strength of the regiments in which changes have been made. Disposition will hereafter be made of the dismounted regiments.

By command of Brevet Major-General Wilson:

E. B. BEAUMONT,
Major and Assistant Adjutant-General.

HDQRS. CAVALRY CORPS, MIL. DIV. OF THE MISSISSIPPI,
Edgefield, Tenn., December 10, 1864.

Brig. Gen. L. D. WATKINS,
Commanding Third Brigade, First Division:

GENERAL: The brevet major-general commanding directs that you move at once with your entire command, by rapid marches, to Bowling Green, Ky., where you will report to General McCook. Should you, however, meet Colonel La Grange's command before reaching that point, you will operate in conjunction with him, to prevent the Confederate General Lyon from making the railroad in that vicinity. General McCook leaves by special train to-night. If the battery belonging to your division is near you you will take it with you.

Respectfully, &c.,

A. J. ALEXANDER,
Lieutenant-Colonel and Chief of Staff.

NASHVILLE, *December 10, 1864.*

Brig. Gen. ELI LONG:

Brigadier-General Meredith reports to General Thomas, from Paducah, that Lyon had crossed the Tennessee on the 8th with 2,500 men, and would probably try to cross the Cumberland and strike Green River bridge. General Thomas wishes you make arrangements to counteract any movement which may be developed in that direction. I will keep you advised as nearly as may be of what transpires looking to that.

J. H. WILSON,
Brevet Major-General.

WASHINGTON, D. C., *December 10, 1864—3 p. m.*

Colonel WINSLOW,
      Cairo:

All troops from Missouri must go to General Thomas till further orders.

H. W. HALLECK,
Major-General and Chief of Staff.

HDQRS. SECOND BRIG., FOURTH DIV., CAVALRY CORPS,
      MILITARY DIVISION OF THE MISSISSIPPI,
            Cairo, Ill., December 10, 1864.

Lieutenant-Colonel BEAUMONT,
      Assistant Adjutant-General, Cavalry Corps, Nashville, Tenn.:

COLONEL: I came here on business connected with my command. The detachments of the Third and Fourth Iowa and Tenth Missouri Regiments Cavalry are en route from Saint Louis to Clarksville, Tenn. Portions of above regiments will reach here to-night and to-morrow. I shall go to Memphis to-night, to make every effort to have the detachments there ordered and forwarded to Nashville. I had got orders once for this from Major-General Washburn, but Major-General Dana has thus far delayed movements, thinking it not unlikely that the portions in Missouri might join him at Memphis. Major-General Halleck has, however, definitely settled that matter. I have left Colonel Benteen full instructions to push for Nashville from Clarksville.

Very respectfully, your obedient servant,

E. F. WINSLOW,
Colonel Fourth Iowa Cavalry, Commanding Brigade.

HEADQUARTERS SIXTH DIVISION, CAVALRY CORPS,
MILITARY DIVISION OF THE MISSISSIPPI,
Edgefield, Tenn., December 10, 1864.

Maj. E. B. BEAUMONT,
Assistant Adjutant-General:

MAJOR: Lieutenant-Colonel Baird, commanding Fifth Iowa Cavalry, has just reported. His command will reach here in about one hour. He reports as follows: Left camp on the evening of the 3d instant; reached Hopkinsville on the night of Wednesday last, the 7th instant, having made a detour to the right to Russellville on his march thither, in order to pick up sixty horses at that place, of which he had information. The Eighth Iowa Cavalry, however, had preceded him and picked up all these horses. At Elkton, on his march up, he obtained fifteen horses (about). From Hopkinsville he detached parties over all the surrounding country. He obtained in all, he states, about 300 horses, very poorly shod; they will nearly all need reshoeing. A full report, with the record of receipts given, will speedily be forwarded. Of these horses Colonel Baird reports that he will need near 250 in his regiment, and, supposing that this would meet the approval of Major-General Wilson, I have instructed him to retain sufficient to mount all of his men. Lieutenant-Colonel Baird thinks that horses enough can still be procured in that country to mount a brigade.

Very respectfully, your obedient servant,

R. W. JOHNSON,
Brigadier-General of Volunteers.

GALLATIN, TENN., *December 10, 1864.*

Maj. Gen. G. H. THOMAS:

The Second Tennessee Cavalry,* with which I am to patrol the river, has not yet reported here.

JAMES GILFILLAN,
Colonel Eleventh Minnesota Infantry, Commanding Post.

---

* Mounted infantry.

NASHVILLE, TENN., *December 10, 1864.*

Col. JAMES GILFILLAN,
    Commanding Eleventh Minnesota Infantry, Gallatin:

The Second Regiment Tennessee Cavalry* was to start from Nashville to Gallatin to-day.

GEO. H. THOMAS,
    Major-General, U. S. Volunteers, Commanding.

DECHERD, *December 10, 1864—3 p. m.*

Major-General THOMAS:

Your telegrams of the 5th and 8th to General Rousseau just received here. Wires don't work any further north. I will send to Murfreesborough by courier, and think I can get them through and back. All quiet here. No news.

WILLARD WARNER,
    Colonel 180th Ohio Volunteer Infantry.

CLARKSVILLE, *December 10, 1864.*

Brigadier-General WHIPPLE,
    Assistant Adjutant-General:

The flag of truce sent in to Fort Donelson on the 8th by rebel General Lyon was not to demand a surrender of the place, but the surrender of one of our men, who is charged with killing a rebel after he was captured.

A. A. SMITH,
    Colonel, Commanding.

SAINT LOUIS, *December 10, 1864—10 a. m.*

Maj. Gen. GEORGE H. THOMAS, *Nashville, Tenn.:*

I am sending you four regiments of infantry, two of cavalry—infantry by rail, cavalry by water. Ordered to report to you by telegraph from Louisville and Cairo for orders.

G. M. DODGE,
    Major-General.

NASHVILLE, *December 10, 1864—3 p. m.*

Maj. Gen. G. M. DODGE, *Saint Louis, Mo.:*

Are the two regiments of cavalry mentioned in your dispatch of 10 a. m. to-day a portion of Colonel Benteen's brigade, or independent of his command?

GEO. H. THOMAS,
    Major-General, U. S. Volunteers, Commanding.

SAINT LOUIS, *December 10, 1864—2 p. m.*

Major-General THOMAS, *Nashville:*

Do you want any batteries?

G. M. DODGE,
    Major-General.

---

* Mounted infantry.

NASHVILLE, *December 10, 1864—6 p. m.*
Maj. Gen. G. M. DODGE,
  Saint Louis, Mo.:
  Your dispatch of 2 p. m. is received. I have an ample supply of batteries.

GEO. H. THOMAS,
Major-General, U. S. Volunteers, Commanding.

LOUISVILLE, KY., *December 10, 1864.*
(Received 6.10 p. m.)
Hon. E. M. STANTON:
  The general impressment of horses by the military is so oppressive here that we cannot think it meets your approbation. All horses are taken without regard to the occupation of the owner or his loyalty. Loaded country wagons with produce for market are left in the road; milk carts, drays, and butcher's wagons are left in the street, their horses seized. We know not the immediate necessities of the service, but we are certain that great wrong is being done in carrying out the order. If there be such, we pray you to look into it.

J. F. SPEED,
BLAND BALLARD.

NASHVILLE, *December 10, 1864—9.45 a. m.*
Brigadier-General MEREDITH,
  Paducah:
  Your dispatch of the 9th instant is received. If you should learn further of the movements of Lyon and Cheatham I shall be obliged if you will inform me at the earliest moment.

GEO. H. THOMAS,
Major-General, U. S. Volunteers, Commanding.

PADUCAH, *December 10, 1864.*
Brigadier-General WHIPPLE:
  GENERAL: I have just received reliable information that Lyon and Cheatham crossed the Tennessee River at Danville bridge on the 8th. They will apparently demonstrate between the Cumberland and Green Rivers. I think they will strike the Green River bridge. Their forces number some 2,000 to 2,500 men, with six guns. I have sent a steamboat to reconnoiter.

S. MEREDITH,
Brigadier-General.

NASHVILLE, TENN., *December 10, 1864.*
Brig. Gen. S. MEREDITH,
  Paducah:
  Your dispatch of this date is received. Am much obliged for your attention, and would like you to give me the first intimation of the enemy's movements.

GEO. H. THOMAS,
Major-General, U. S. Volunteers, Commanding.

HEADQUARTERS U. S. FORCES,
Fort Donelson, Tenn., December 10, 1864.

Brigadier-General MEREDITH,
Commanding at Paducah, Ky.:

SIR: I have the honor to make the following statements in regard to the status of operations in this locality: Brigadier-General Lyon, C. S. Army, on yesterday afternoon, captured transport "Thomas E. Tutt," at Cumberland City, twenty miles above us, and crossed the Cumberland River at that point with his division, numbering about 4,000 men. The crossing was completed to-day about noon. I have information which I deem reliable that they intend marching upon Hopkinsville, Ky. An attack is also anticipated at Clarksville, Tenn. I have about 700 available men at this post, and am amply able to hold it against any force they can bring to bear. I have no mounted men, however, and am not able to harass them in their march.

Very respectfully, your obedient servant,

WM. FORBES,
Colonel Forty-second Missouri Infantry, Commanding Post.

CINCINNATI, OHIO, *December 10, 1864—2.45 p. m.*

COMMANDING OFFICER, *Louisville, Ky.:*

The following has just been received and sent for your information and action:

INDIANAPOLIS, IND., *December 10, 1864.*

Capt. C. H. POTTER,
Assistant Adjutant-General:

I am informed by an officer in whom I have confidence that Maj. Walker Taylor, C. S. Army, is at Haynesville, Ky., opposite Carrollton, Ind., with 400 armed men, recruiting and conscripting for the rebel army.

A. P. HOVEY,
Brevet Major-General.

J. HOOKER,
Major-General, Commanding.

FRANKFORT, *December 10, 1864.*

Brigadier-General McLEAN:

On account of increased trouble on road below here, I have sent an additional force of thirty-five men to Pleasureville, and a sufficient mounted force with instructions to hunt down guerrillas and close the road. Have you any news from Major-General Burbridge?

D. W. LINDSEY,
Inspector-General and Adjutant-General.

CAMP NELSON, *December 10, 1864.*

Capt. J. S. BUTLER, *Assistant Adjutant-General:*

Have a light [force] at Forts Nelson, Jackson, and Taylor; no ordnance at any other. This guard consists of the thirty-five men referred to in my telegram of November 28 to you. Thirteenth Kentucky Cavalry are guarding camp and military prison, in which there are sixty-one prisoners. Some colored troops have just been armed. Will send a full report to-morrow by mail of available force in camp.

S. S. FRY,
Brigadier-General.

LEXINGTON, KY., *December 10, 1864.*

Lieutenant BLAND,
    Quartermaster Thirteenth Kentucky, Burkesville, Ky.:

There is a rumor that Forrest has crossed the Cumberland. Keep scouts out as far as possible in the direction of Nashville, and inform me immediately should the enemy come your way. Should a force approach you destroy the pontoons and fall back.

By order of Brigadier-General McLean:

J. S. BUTLER,
Assistant Adjutant-General.

CAMP NELSON, *December 10, 1864.*

Capt. J. S. BUTLER,
    Assistant Adjutant-General:

The men left at Burkesville when I came away were convalescents and dismounted men. Lieutenant Bland telegraphs me this evening that you ordered him to keep scouts out toward Nashville. If he divides what men he has there he will lose them all. The pontoon is not worth the risk, and we have nothing to amount to anything outside of it to lose.

J. W. WEATHERFORD,
Colonel Thirteenth Kentucky Cavalry.

NASHVILLE, TENN., *December 10, 1864.*

COMMANDING OFFICER,
    Smithland:

Will you please hand to Colonel Benteen, commanding brigade of cavalry, now on board transports bound for this place, the accompanying dispatch, and at the same time say to him that transports can ascend the Cumberland as far as Clarksville without danger. He will, however, await at Smithland the arrival of gun-boats to convoy him to Clarksville, where he will disembark his command and march to this place on the north bank of the river. Acknowledge receipt.

GEO. H. THOMAS,
Major-General, U. S. Volunteers, Commanding.

[Inclosure.]

NASHVILLE, *December 10, 1864.*

Colonel BENTEEN,
    Commanding Cavalry Brigade, Smithland:

Await at Smithland the arrival of gun-boats, which, Admiral Lee informs me, will be there to convoy your transports to Clarksville. As soon as they arrive you will at once proceed to Clarksville, where you will disembark and march on the north bank of the river to this place. Should you learn of the presence of any force of the enemy between the Cumberland and Tennessee Rivers when you arrive at Clarksville, move your brigade against it and drive it off, unless you are satisfied he is too strong for you, in which case you will report the fact by telegraph to me at this place.

GEO. H. THOMAS,
Major-General, U. S. Volunteers, Commanding.

HEADQUARTERS POST, CAMP DOUGLAS,
Chicago, Ill., December 10, 1864.

Col. N. P. CHIPMAN,
        Acting Aide-de-Camp, Washington, D. C.:

Judge Buckner S. Morris was arrested on the night of the 6th November, by my order, for assisting prisoners of war to escape, relieving the enemy with money, holding correspondence with the enemy, and complicity with the plot to attack Camp Douglass. For full particulars, see my report* to Brig. Gen. H. W. Wessells, Commissary-General of Prisoners, of date November 23. Judge-Advocate Burnett is now here investigating and arranging for trial.

B. J. SWEET,
Colonel, Commanding Post.

WASHINGTON, D. C., *December 10, 1864—1 p. m.*

Major-General DANA,
        Memphis:

General Grant ordered all available troops in Missouri to re-enforce General Thomas at Nashville. All cavalry horses in the West were also ordered there, to remount General Thomas' cavalry. As soon as the crisis there has passed horses will be again sent down the Mississippi River. In the meantime you must do the best you can with the means at your disposal.

H. W. HALLECK,
Major-General and Chief of Staff.

WASHINGTON, D. C., *December 10, 1864—10.30 a. m.*

Major-General DODGE,
        Saint Louis:

General Thomas has more cavalry now than he can mount, and requires all the horses to mount his own men. If you can send him infantry or artillery please do so. If the Cumberland River is closed they should go by Louisville. Whatever you can send can be returned as soon as the crisis is passed.

H. W. HALLECK,
Major-General and Chief of Staff.

SAINT LOUIS, *December 10, 1864—4 p. m.*

Maj. Gen. H. W. HALLECK,
        Washington, D. C.:

I send five regiments of infantry, all there are in the department organized subject to be sent outside of State; one regiment of cavalry well mounted, and will send batteries. They go by rail.

G. M. DODGE,
Major-General.

---

* See Part I, p. 1076.

NASHVILLE, TENN., *December 11, 1864—9.30 p. m.*
Maj. Gen. H. W. HALLECK,
    Washington, D. C.:

The position of the enemy appears the same to-day as yesterday. The weather continues very cold and the hills are covered with ice. As soon as we have a thaw, I will attack Hood. It is reported to me, from Clarksville, that the rebel General Lyon has crossed the Cumberland at Cumberland City, below Clarksville, with between 2,000 and 3,000 men and six pieces of artillery, and it is supposed he is moving on Bowling Green. I have sent two brigades of cavalry to intercept him. I have also received a dispatch from Major-General Rousseau, at Murfreesborough, dated 8th instant. He reports that Bate's division, of Cheatham's corps, threatened Murfreesborough on the 6th and 7th instant, and on the afternoon of the 7th Milroy, with six regiments of infantry and a battery of artillery, succeeded in getting on the enemy's flank and completely routed him, capturing two pieces of artillery and 207 prisoners, of whom 18 are officers. Our loss was 30 killed and 175 wounded. He does not report the enemy's killed and wounded. Just before Milroy attacked, a portion of the enemy's cavalry attacked the town, but were soon driven off by a regiment of infantry and a section of artillery, sent against them from the fort. At the time of making the report everything was quiet, and no appearance of the enemy in any direction.

GEO. H. THOMAS,
Major-General, U. S. Volunteers, Commanding.

CITY POINT, VA., *December 11, 1864—4 p. m.*

Major-General THOMAS,
    Nashville, Tenn.:

If you delay attack longer the mortifying spectacle will be witnessed of a rebel army moving for the Ohio River, and you will be forced to act, accepting such weather as you find. Let there be no further delay. Hood cannot stand even a drawn battle so far from his supplies of ordnance stores. If he retreats and you follow, he must lose his material and much of his army. I am in hopes of receiving a dispatch from you to-day announcing that you have moved. Delay no longer for weather or re-enforcements.

U. S. GRANT,
Lieutenant-General.

NASHVILLE, *December 11, 1864—10.30 p. m.*

Lieut. Gen. U. S. GRANT,
    City Point:

Your dispatch of 4 p. m. this day is just received. I will obey the order as promptly as possible, however much I may regret it, as the attack will have to be made under every disadvantage. The whole country is covered with a perfect sheet of ice and sleet, and it is with difficulty the troops are able to move about on level ground. It was my intention to attack Hood as soon as the ice melted, and would have done so yesterday had it not been for the storm.

GEO. H. THOMAS,
Major-General, U. S. Volunteers, Commanding.

NASHVILLE, *December 11, 1864—4 p. m.*

Admiral S. P. LEE,
              Clarksville:

Colonel Smith, of Clarksville, reports the capture by rebel General Lyon of two steamers, and the crossing of the river by his force on the captured boats. I have the honor to request whether you cannot send down the river and recapture the boats and destroy the enemy's force. If you can do so, I shall be much indebted to you, as it is very important service. The boats were captured at Cumberland City.

GEO. H. THOMAS,
Major-General, U. S. Volunteers, Commanding.

FLAG-SHIP CINCINNATI,
Clarksville, December 11, 1864—5 p. m.

Maj. Gen. G. H. THOMAS:

Your telegram is just brought off by the cipher operator. It is probable, from the personal reports of the steam-boat captain and pilots, that three boats have been captured and destroyed by the enemy, and that General Lyon has crossed the river. I should immediately upon hearing of the enemy's operations have gone down the river to the point of crossing, but that it is below a shoal where there is not water enough for this vessel. Colonel Smith has sent me word that the rebels were coming into the lower part of this town, and since that he believes their movement is a feint. I expect two gun-boats and two transports with ammunition for Fitch up the river to-night or to-morrow, and am further disappointed at not being able to meet and convoy them.

S. P. LEE,
Acting Rear-Admiral.

SAINT LOUIS, *December 11, 1864—12.10 p. m.*

Maj. Gen. GEORGE H. THOMAS,
              Nashville, Tenn.:

The regiments mentioned by me are not a part of Colonel Benteen's troops. All I speak of are in addition to what had been ordered before I took command. General Halleck says not send any cavalry to you, only mounted. The infantry are scattered, but will commence to leave by rail to-morrow. How about cavalry? If this weather holds it will not be safe to send them by boat, and I fear Benteen will be closed in some point.

G. M. DODGE,
Major-General.

SAINT LOUIS, *December 11, 1864—2 p. m.*

Maj. Gen. GEORGE H. THOMAS,
              Nashville, Tenn.:

I have had to unload 400 men and 300 horses, the last of Colonel Benteen's command, caught in ice, and send them by rail to Louisville, at which place please give them orders.

G. M. DODGE,
Major-General.

NASHVILLE, *December 11, 1864—4 p. m.*

Maj. Gen. G. M. DODGE,
    Saint Louis, Mo.:

Your dispatch of 12 m. to-day is received. I am of the opinion that the boats you have already started can get through, at least to Smithland, at which point I have directed all boats coming up the Cumberland to halt and report to me for orders. Send the infantry on, but hold all cavalry not actually on the way till the present cold snap is over, to avoid running risks.

GEO. H. THOMAS,
Major-General, U. S. Volunteers, Commanding.

CHIEF QUARTERMASTER'S OFFICE,
DEPARTMENT OF THE CUMBERLAND,
Nashville, Tenn., December 11, 1864.

Brig. Gen. W. D. WHIPPLE,
    Chief of Staff:

GENERAL: The following copies of telegrams just received are furnished for the information of the major-general commanding:

CLARKSVILLE, *December 11, 1864.*

Fleet empty boats left last night for down the river. The boat Ben South, some two hours in advance, it is reported, burned by General Lyon's force at Cumberland City, some twenty miles below this post.

I. P. WILLIAMS,
Captain and Assistant Quartermaster.

CLARKSVILLE, *December 11, 1864.*

Courier just in from Fort Donelson reports capture of tow-boat Echo, and destroyed; also steamer Thomas E. Tutt, loaded with grain and troops, coming up, taken and destroyed at Cumberland City.

I. P. WILLIAMS,
Captain and Assistant Quartermaster.

Very respectfully, your obedient servant,

J. L. DONALDSON,
Brevet Brigadier-General and Chief Quartermaster.

NASHVILLE, TENN., *December 11, 1864—9.30 p. m.*
(Received 10.55 p. m.)

Maj. THOMAS T. ECKERT,
    Washington:

Frost still holds everybody, except wood-cutters, idle. No movement to report either on our part or that of the enemy for the past three days.

J. C. VAN DUZER,
Captain, &c.

HEADQUARTERS FOURTH CORPS,
December 11, 1864.

Maj. Gen. GEORGE H. THOMAS,
    Commanding:

I spent a good part of the afternoon in examining the enemy's lines, and gained some information which I had not before and which I would be glad to point out to you in person, as I think it would be well for you to see the whole ground. I believe it would aid you in making your arrangements. If it will suit your convenience to come out to-morrow, and you will name an hour when you will be at my headquarters, I will be here to meet and accompany you to the different positions for observation.

TH. J. WOOD,
Brigadier-General of Volunteers, Commanding.

HEADQUARTERS DEPARTMENT OF THE CUMBERLAND,
December 11, 1864.

Brig. Gen. THOMAS J. WOOD,
  Commanding Fourth Army Corps:

Your dispatch is received. Will try to be at your headquarters at 11 a. m. or 12 m. to-morrow.

GEO. H. THOMAS,
Major-General, U. S. Volunteers, Commanding.

HEADQUARTERS FOURTH ARMY CORPS,
December 11, 1864—10.45 p. m.

Maj. Gen. G. H. THOMAS,
    Commanding :

Your dispatch of this 10 p. m. received.* Orders will be complied with.

TH. J. WOOD,
Brigadier-General of Volunteers, Commanding.

NASHVILLE, TENN., *December 11, 1864.*

TO THE OFFICERS AND MEN OF THE SECOND BRIGADE,
    SECOND DIVISION, FOURTH ARMY CORPS:

Having been relieved from duty with the department at my own request, I find it very hard to part from a command with which I have been so long associated—a command that has made itself notorious for its gallant and meritorious deeds; but wherever I may be, I shall rejoice to hear of your success, as I will, for you can say what few commands can, you never fail. Let us never forget the gallant men that have fallen with us, and if we ever meet any of their families that need our help, divide the last cent with them.

Hoping to meet you again in times of peace,
    I am, your obedient servant,

G. D. WAGNER,
Brigadier-General of Volunteers.

---

* See Thomas to Schofield, p. 147.

NASHVILLE, *December 11, 1864.*

Major-General SCHOFIELD·

Have your command put in readiness to-morrow for operations. I wish to see you at my headquarters at 3 p. m. to-morrow. Acknowledge receipt.

GEO. H. THOMAS,
Major-General, U. S. Volunteers, Commanding.

(Same to Major-General Steedman, Major-General Smith, and Brigadier-General Wood.)

HEADQUARTERS TWENTY-THIRD ARMY CORPS,
December 11, 1864—11 p. m.

[Major-General THOMAS:]

Your dispatch of this date received. I shall be ready.

J. M. SCHOFIELD,
Major-General.

SPECIAL FIELD ORDERS, ⎱   HDQRS. ARMY OF THE OHIO,
No. 177.   ⎰   *Nashville, Tenn., December 11, 1864.*

*   *   *   *   *   *   *

XVI. The Fifteenth Indiana Battery, Capt. A. D. Harvey commanding, is hereby transferred from the Third to the Second Division, Twenty-third Army Corps, and will report to Major-General Couch, commanding.

XVII. Battery F, First Michigan Light Artillery, Capt. B. D. Paddock commanding, and the Twenty-second Indiana Battery, Capt. E. W. Nicholson commanding, are hereby transferred from the Second to the First Division, and will report to Brigadier-General Ruger, commanding.

*   *   *   *   *   *   *

By command of Major-General Schofield:

J. A. CAMPBELL,
Major and Assistant Adjutant-General.

HEADQUARTERS ARMY OF THE OHIO,
Nashville, Tenn., December 11, 1864.

Maj. Gen. D. N. COUCH,
Commanding Second Division, Twenty-third Army Corps:

GENERAL: The commanding general directs you to instruct the officers in command of your pickets not to permit any intercourse or anything like a truce between our pickets and those of the enemy.

Very respectfully, your obedient servant,

J. A. CAMPBELL,
Major and Assistant Adjutant-General.

HEADQUARTERS DETACHMENT ARMY OF THE TENNESSEE,
December 11, 1864.

Brigadier-General WHIPPLE,
        Chief of Staff:

All quiet in my front; not as many picket fires on my right front; on the left everything remains the same.

A. J. SMITH,
Major-General.

GENERAL STEEDMAN'S HEADQUARTERS,
December 11, 1864.

Maj. Gen. G. H. THOMAS:

Can I defer visiting your quarters to 2 p. m.? My dam broke during the night, and I have just got the water stopped, and wish to remain to attend to it. I would also like to feel the enemy, to ascertain whether he has changed. I think he has changed, but cannot ascertain certain without feeling him.

J. B. STEEDMAN,
Major-General of Volunteers.

NASHVILLE, *December 11, 1864.*

Major-General STEEDMAN:

You can defer your visit to these headquarters until 2 o'clock, and feel the enemy as you propose.

WM. D. WHIPPLE,
Brigadier-General, &c.

HEADQUARTERS DEPARTMENT OF THE CUMBERLAND,
Nashville, December 11, 1864.

Maj. Gen. J. H. WILSON,
        Comdg. Cavalry Corps, Military Division of the Mississippi:

GENERAL: The major-general commanding directs that you commence the crossing of your command over the river to-morrow morning, as positive orders have been received by him to at once attack the enemy. They will go into position as has already been designated in your consultations with the major-general commanding.

I have the honor to be, general, very respectfully, your obedient servant,

ROBT. H. RAMSEY,
Assistant Adjutant-General.

SPECIAL ORDERS, ⎫   HEADQUARTERS CAVALRY CORPS,
                     ⎬   MILITARY DIVISION OF THE MISSISSIPPI,
No. 34.   ⎭   *Nashville, Tenn., December 11, 1864.*

I. The Fourteenth Ohio Battery, Lieutenant Myers commanding, having reported in accordance with Special Orders, No. 21, paragraph II, headquarters Artillery Reserve, Department of the Tennesseee,

December 10, 1864, is hereby assigned to duty with Seventh Division, Cavalry Corps, Military Division of the Mississippi, Brig. Gen. J. F. Knipe commanding.

*   *   *   *   *   *   *

By command of Brevet Major-General Wilson:

E. B. BEAUMONT,
Major and Assistant Adjutant-General.

SPECIAL ⎱   HEADQUARTERS CAVALRY CORPS,
FIELD ORDERS, ⎰   MILITARY DIVISION OF THE MISSISSIPPI,
No. 1.* ⎰   *Edgefield, Tenn., December 11, 1864.*

This command will move to-morrow as follows :

1. The Fifth Division, Brigadier-General Hatch commanding, will move promptly at 8.30 a. m., leaving General Johnson's command on the right, will cross the pontoon bridge, and, passing through Nashville, take the position previously indicated by the brevet major-general commanding.

2. The First Division, Brigadier-General Croxton commanding, will move promptly at 8.30 a. m. across the railroad bridge, and, passing through Nashville, take position as previously indicated.

3. The Seventh Division, Brigadier-General Knipe commanding, will move in rear of the First Division, and, crossing the railroad bridge, will take a position which will be indicated.

4. The Sixth Division, Brigadier-General Johnson commanding, will commence crossing on the pontoon bridge after the Fifth Division, and, should the railroad bridge be vacant, use both bridges, pass through Nashville, and occupy a position on the right of the First Division, as previously indicated.

5. The ordnance train and ambulances will follow the troops and will be followed by the other wagons of the command.

6. Each man will be provided with three days' rations and one day's forage, to be carried on the horses.

7. Every man, mounted or dismounted, will cross.

By order of Brevet Major-General Wilson:

A. J. ALEXANDER,
Acting Chief of Staff.

HDQRS. CAVALRY CORPS, MIL. DIV. OF THE MISSISSIPPI,
Edgefield, December 11, 1864.

Brigadier-General McCOOK:

You will proceed without delay to Bowling Green, concentrating Watkins' and La Grange's brigades, and move at once against the rebel cavalry under General Lyon. Lyon crossed the Cumberland yesterday below Clarksville, and is supposed to be moving toward Hopkinsville, Russellville, and Bowling Green; his force is estimated at 2,000 men. The greatest celerity is necessary. You may proceed direct by a special train, which Captain Carling, chief quartermaster, will have provided.

Very respectfully,

J. H. WILSON,
Brevet Major-General, Commanding.

---

* So in original, but recorded in Wilson's book of "Special Field Orders" as No. 3.

NASHVILLE, *December 11, 1864.*

Maj. Gen. J. H. WILSON:

The railroad agent informs me that it will be impossible to send any special trains through, as there are sixteen trains on the way between here and there. Captain Carling, of your staff, can inform you more explicitly as to the nature of the indorsement the agent made. I will go on the morning train at 7 o'clock, which is the first opportunity.

Very respectfully, your obedient servant,

E. M. McCOOK,
Brigadier-General.

HEADQUARTERS FIRST DIVISION, CAVALRY CORPS,
Nashville, Tenn., December 11, 1864—9 p. m.

Bvt. Maj. Gen. J. H. WILSON,
Comdg. Cavalry Corps, Military Division of the Mississippi:

GENERAL: I have the honor to inform you that it has just been stated to me by Doctor Spilman, acting division chief surgeon, that Brevet Brigadier-General Watkins was still holding his brigade and the Eighteenth Indiana Battery in readiness to start. I have therefore issued orders for him to start without further delay.

I am, general, very respectfully, your obedient servant,

EDWARD M. McCOOK,
Brigadier-General, Commanding.

HDQRS. FIRST BRIGADE, FIRST CAVALRY DIVISION,
MILITARY DIVISION OF THE MISSISSIPPI,
Edgefield, Tenn., December 11, 1864.

Lieut. Col. A. J. ALEXANDER,
Actg. Chief of Staff, Cav. Corps, Mil. Div. of the Mississippi:

COLONEL: I have the honor to report that my command is at this time all mounted, with the exception of the Fourth Kentucky Mounted Infantry, which regiment needs about 300 horses. I have still one company out, which I believe will bring in nearly a sufficient number to mount all the command.

I am, colonel, very respectfully, your obedient servant,

JOHN T. CROXTON,
Brigadier-General, Commanding.

HEADQUARTERS CAVALRY CORPS,
Edgefield, Tenn., December 11, 1864.

Brig. Gen. E. LONG:

Two brigades of McCook's division have been ordered to Bowling Green. Consequently, your orders to move to that point are revoked. I want you to use all haste, however, to get your command in readiness and move to this point.

J. H. WILSON,
Brevet Major-General.

HEADQUARTERS FIFTH DIVISION, CAVALRY CORPS,
MILITARY DIVISION OF THE MISSISSIPPI,
Edgefield, Tenn., December 11, 1864.

Lieut. Col. A. J. ALEXANDER,
Actg. Chief of Staff, Cav. Corps, Mil. Div. of the Mississippi:

I have the honor to state, for the information of the brevet major-general commanding Cavalry Corps, Military Division of the Mississippi, that I visited the ground assigned to my division on the right of Maj. Gen. A. J. Smith to-day. It is my impression that the rebels have retired their line, from personal observation.

Very respectfully, your obedient servant,

EDWARD HATCH,
Brigadier-General, Commanding.

HEADQUARTERS FIFTH DIVISION, CAVALRY CORPS,
MILITARY DIVISION OF THE MISSISSIPPI,
Edgefield, Tenn., December 11, 1864.

Maj. E. B. BEAUMONT,
Asst. Adjt. Gen., Cav. Corps, Mil. Div. of the Mississippi:

MAJOR: In compliance with circular of this date, I have the honor to state, for the information of the brevet major-general commanding, that the effective men of my command will undoubtedly be mounted to-morrow. The Sixth Illinois Cavalry is still out pressing horses, and will probably obtain a large number. The regiment is expected in to-night.

Very respectfully, your obedient servant,

EDWARD HATCH,
Brigadier-General, Commanding.

HEADQUARTERS SIXTH DIVISION, CAVALRY CORPS,
MILITARY DIVISION OF THE MISSISSIPPI,
Edgefield, December 11, 1864.

Maj. E. B. BEAUMONT:

I have the honor to report that, in obedience to your orders, I have had the Eighth Michigan and Fourteenth Illinois dismounted, and with their horses fully mounted the Sixteenth Illinois and Seventh Ohio. By this arrangement I will have about forty horses surplus, but our men are returning from hospitals, &c., every day, and I think it advisable to retain them. This arrangement will leave about 750 well mounted men in the First (Harrison's) Brigade. In the Second (Biddle's) Brigade the Fifth Iowa only is mounted, about 590 men. First Brigade, 750 men; Second Brigade, 590 men; total, 1,340 men. Their battery is fitted out with eight horses to each carriage, ten cannoneers, all mounted, and is in good condition for service. I have the following regiments dismounted: Eighth Michigan, at Edgefield; Fourteenth Illinois, at Edgefield; Fifth Indiana, at Louisville; Sixth Indiana, at Edgefield.

R. W. JOHNSON,
Brigadier-General of Volunteers.

HDQRS. 6TH DIV., CAV. CORPS, MIL. DIV. OF THE MISS.,
Edgefield, Tenn., December 11, 1864.

Col. T. J. HARRISON, *Commanding Brigade:*

COLONEL: In accordance with instructions received from Major-General Wilson, General Johnson directs that you take instant measures to mount regiments complete by dismounting partially mounted regiments. You will make this change to-day, and report your action as soon as possible after the arrangements are completed, with the designation and the strength of the regiments in which changes have been made. A report is required from General Johnson to-night.

This by direction of Brigadier-General Johnson:

E. T. WELLS,
Assistant Adjutant-General.

HEADQUARTERS DEPARTMENT OF THE CUMBERLAND,
Nashville, Tenn., December 11, 1864.

Maj. Gen. L. H. ROUSSEAU,
Commanding District of Tennessee, Murfreesborough:

GENERAL: By direction of the major-general commanding, I have the honor to acknowledge the receipt of your report* of 12 m. 8th instant, at the hands of your special messenger, just arrived. Your report has been read with a great deal of pleasure by the major-general commanding, and especially your very flattering testimonal to the good conduct and bravery of the new regiments embraced in your command. So gratifying, indeed, is your report concerning them, that it is the desire of the major-general commanding that you express to these troops and to all the troops in your command participating in operations about Murfreesborough his highest commendation and hearty thanks for their gallant conduct in so successfully and steadily repelling the attacks of the enemy and in finally driving him off. Having thus merited his confidence, he expresses the hope that they will acquit themselves as nobly in the future as in the past. You have a good supply of provisions in Murfreesborough, and the major-general commanding expects you to hold out against all attacks of the enemy until you are relieved by the forces from this place.

Since the dispatches of the 4th and 5th instant (which doubtless you have received by this time), the situation at Nashville is comparatively unchanged. Operations offensive have necessarily been deferred on account of the prevalence of a severe storm of sleet and rain, making it, by reason of the freezing weather we are having, a very difficult, if not altogether impracticable, matter to move troops. Reports received from deserters would indicate that Forrest, with three divisions of infantry, has been sent to operate against Murfreesborough, which, however, is not conclusive that such is the fact. They hope to effect a capture of the place (in which hope he trusts you will fully be able to disappoint them), when the proposition seems to be for Hood's army to fall back to M[urfreesborough] and go into winter quarters. The army here is in good condition and excellent spirits, and cavalry and infantry will give a good account of themselves when the moment for action arrives.

I have the honor to be, general, very respectfully, your obedient servant,

ROBT. H. RAMSEY,
Assistant Adjutant-General.

SMITHLAND, *December 11, 1864.*

Capt. JAMES GRAHAM, *Assistant Adjutant-General:*

SIR: Lieutenant-Colonel Buchanan, of the Seventh Missouri, who has just arrived at this post, states that the steamer Thomas E. Tutt was

---

*See Part I, p. 612.

captured, between Fort Donelson and Clarksville, on the evening of the 9th. The officers and men were paroled and the steamer was burned. General Lyon crossed the Cumberland with 3,000 men, using the T. E. Tutt to cross with. Boats were also fired into at the same point last night coming down the river.

Respectfully,

HENRY P. REED,
Captain, Commanding Post.

NASHVILLE, TENN., *December 11, 1864—4 p. m.*
COMMANDING OFFICER, *Smithland:*

You will direct all boats designing to ascend the Cumberland to halt at Smithland and report to me at this place for further orders. Colonel Benteen will also follow these instructions, as it is not advisable to move up the river at this time. Acknowledge receipt.

GEO. H. THOMAS,
Major-General, U. S. Volunteers, Commanding.

CLARKSVILLE, *December 11, 1864—10.20 a. m.*
Brigadier-General WHIPPLE, *Chief of Staff:*

Rebel General Lyon, with from 2,000 to 3,000 men, with nine pieces of artillery, captured an up boat, at Cumberland City, Friday evening, and was crossing the river yesterday. He captured the Ben South that left here yesterday. The other boats all returned except two, who ran the battery and are at Fort Donelson.

A. A. SMITH,
Colonel, Commanding.

NASHVILLE, *December 11, 1864—6 p. m.*
Col. A. A. SMITH, *Clarksville:*

It has been reported by the assistant quartermaster at Clarksville that the boats captured by the rebel General Lyon have all been burned. Will you report at once whether the statement is correct.

GEO. H. THOMAS,
Major-General, U. S. Volunteers, Commanding.

CLARKSVILLE, *December 11, 1864.*
Major-General THOMAS:

The Thomas E. Tutt and Ben South are certainly burned. Tow-boat Echo has not returned—supposed to have been burned. A courier left Donelson last night at 12 o'clock. Echo had not arrived there. The two that had run the battery had arrived.

A. A. SMITH,
Colonel, Commanding.

CLARKSVILLE, *December 11, 1864.*
Brigadier-General WHIPPLE, *Assistant Adjutant-General:*

My scouts have just been driven in by Lyon's men, but I do not think he will come here, but threaten me. I think he will go to Hopkinsville, Bowling Green, or Russellville. I am ready for him.

A. A. SMITH,
Colonel, Commanding.

CLARKSVILLE, *December 11, 1864—6.30 p. m.*

Brigadier-General WHIPPLE,
    Assistant Adjutant-General:

The trains that came in to-day have no guard. Am I expected to furnish one? Have had no order. Lyon's advance has retired. He may attack in the morning; I feel confident that I can hold the place if he does.

A. A. SMITH,
Colonel Eighty-third Illinois Volunteers, Commanding.

RUSSELLVILLE, KY., *December 11, 1864.*

Brig. Gen. HUGH EWING,
    Louisville, Ky.:

General Lyon, with his brigade, crossed the Cumberland at mouth of Yellow Creek, day before yesterday, and occupied La Fayette yesterday, eighteen miles south of Hopkinsville.

S. F. JOHNSON,
Lieutenant-Colonel, Commanding.

HEADQUARTERS DEPARTMENT OF THE CUMBERLAND,
Nashville, December 11, 1864.

Lieutenant-Colonel FAIRLEIGH, or
COMMANDING OFFICER,
    Louisville, Ky.:

Send by rail to Bowling Green, as rapidly as possible, all troops arriving at Louisville destined for this place. The rebel General Lyon has crossed the Cumberland below Clarksville, with the intention, it is said, of destroying the Green River railroad bridge, if he can. The troops are expected to defend the bridge.

GEO. H. THOMAS,
Major-General, U. S. Volunteers, Commanding.

PADUCAH, *December 11, 1864.*

Brig. Gen. W. D. WHIPPLE:

GENERAL: I have the honor to report the result of the reconnaissance of the gun-boat Peosta up the Tennessee River. They report that General Lyon crossed at Danville bridge at 4 p. m. the 9th instant, 2,000 strong, with two pieces of artillery. I received information from another source that four pieces of artillery were crossed above. Gunboat brought down four barges that have been used crossing the enemies' troops; two of them were barges not destroyed at Johnsonville, which had been cut down for the purpose. There are 1,000 men, with four pieces of artillery, in camp near the Danville crossing, building boats. Just received information from Colonel Forbes, commanding Fort Donelson, that the enemy have captured the Thomas E. Tutt at Cumberland City, with 1 lieutenant-colonel, 2 lieutenants, and 23 privates on board, and has just captured another, name not known, and two barges. From information that I consider reliable Lyon intends moving on Green River bridge.

Very respectfully,

S. MEREDITH,
Brigadier-General.

CITY POINT, VA., *December 12, 1864—11.30 p. m.*

Major-General HALLECK,
          Washington, D. C.:

There are at Springfield, Ill., a large number of recruits for Sherman's army. Please order the whole camp removed from Camp Butler to Nashville. At the latter place they will be of use whilst waiting an opportunity to join the regiments to which they belong.

U. S. GRANT,
Lieutenant-General.

NASHVILLE, TENN., *December 12, 1864—10.30 p. m.*

Maj. Gen. H. W. HALLECK,
          Washington, D. C.:

I have the troops ready to make the attack on the enemy as soon as the sleet which now covers the ground has melted sufficiently to enable the men to march. As the whole country is now covered with a sheet of ice so hard and slippery it is utterly impossible for troops to ascend the slopes, or even move over level ground in anything like order. It has taken the entire day to place my cavalry in position, and it has only been finally effected with imminent risk and many serious accidents, resulting from the number of horses falling with their riders on the roads. Under these circumstances I believe an attack at this time would only result in a useless sacrifice of life.

GEO. H. THOMAS,
Major-General, U. S. Volunteers, Commanding.

HEADQUARTERS FOURTH ARMY CORPS,
December 12, 1864.

Brigadier-General WHIPPLE,
          Assistant Adjutant-General:

No change in my front this morning.

TH. J. WOOD,
Brigadier-General, Commanding.

HEADQUARTERS FOURTH ARMY CORPS,
Nashville, Tenn., December 12, 1864.

Brigadier-General WHIPPLE,
          Chief of Staff:

I have the honor to request that you will direct Colonel Loomis, chief of artillery, District of the Tennessee, to order Battery E, First Michigan Artillery, to relieve Battery A, First Ohio Light Artillery, and the Twenty-fifth Indiana Light Battery to relieve Bridges' Battery Illinois Light Artillery, without delay. The two batteries that I desire to have relieved have served through the Chickamauga, East Tennessee, Atlanta, and the recent Franklin campaigns, and need an opportunity to refit. The two batteries asked for, Colonel Loomis informs me, are supplied with an entire new equipment, and one of them, the First Michigan battery, has been in camp at this place one year. I have the honor to request that you will direct that the above-mentioned batteries may be ordered to report to the chief of artillery of this corps to-day, in order that the horses now in possession of the batteries to be relieved may be assigned to the other batteries of the corps.*

Very respectfully, your obedient servant,

TH. J. WOOD,
Brigadier-General, Commanding.

CIRCULAR, }
No. 30.   }
　　　　　HEADQUARTERS FOURTH ARMY CORPS,
　　　　　Nashville, Tenn., December 12, 1864.

I. Division commanders will have their men fully supplied to-day with such clothing as they may need. They will instruct their inspectors to go through the camps and make a personal examination of the troops and see what articles are needed. This clothing must be drawn to-day.

II. The troops of this command must have in their haversacks three days' rations, counting from to-morrow morning, and they must be supplied this evening with sixty rounds of ammunition per man.

By order of Brigadier-General Wood:

J. S. FULLERTON,
Lieutenant-Colonel and Assistant Adjutant-General.

Weekly report of effective force of Fourth Army Corps, Brig. Gen. Thomas J. Wood, U. S. Army, commanding, for December 12, 1864.

Command.	Headquarters.			Infantry.			Cavalry.		
	Officers.	Men.	Total.	Officers.	Men.	Total.	Officers.	Men.	Total.
Headquarters Fourth Army Corps, Brig. Gen. T. J. Wood.	20	122	142	......	......	......	......	......	......
Headquarters First Division, Brig. Gen. N. Kimball.	12	80	92	......	......	......			
First Brigade, Col. I. M. Kirby.	10	25	35	85	1,507	1,592			
Second Brigade, Brig. Gen. W. C. Whitaker.	10	38	48	82	2,340	2,422			
Third Brigade, Brig. Gen. W. Grose.	9	43	52	93	2,097	2,190			
Total	41	186	227	260	5,944	6,204	......	......	......
Headquarters Second Division, Brig. Gen. W. L. Elliott.	14	45	59	......	......	......			
First Brigade, Col. E. Opdycke.	7	46	53	76	1,452	1,528			
Second Brigade, Col. J. Q. Lane.	8	52	60	80	1,399	1,479			
Third Brigade, Col. J. Conrad.	9	30	39	58	1,296	1,354			
Total	38	173	211	214	4,147	4,361	......	......	......
Headquarters Third Division, Brig. Gen. Samuel Beatty.	15	203	218	......	......	......			
First Brigade, Col. A. D. Streight.	7	44	51	75	1,602	1,677			
Second Brigade, Col. P. Sidney Post.	9	53	62	74	1,578	1,652			
Third Brigade, Col. Fred. Knefler.	7	34	41	51	832	883			
Total	38	334	372	200	4,012	4,212	......	......	......
Artillery Brigade, Capt. Lyman Bridges.	8	127	135	......	......	......			
Grand total	145	942	1,087	672	14,103	14,777	......	......	......

* The transfers herein recommended were made by paragraphs III and IV, Special Field Orders, No. 340, Department of the Cumberland, December 12, 1864.

Weekly report of effective force of Fourth Army Corps, &c.—Continued.

Command.	Artillery.			Total.				
	Officers.	Men.	Total.	Officers.	Men.	Aggregate.	Horses.	Guns.
Headquarters Fourth Army Corps, Brig. Gen. T. J. Wood.	......	....	....	20	122	142	......	......
Headquarters First Division, Brig. Gen N. Kimball.	......	....	....	12	80	92	......	......
First Brigade, Col. I. M. Kirby.	......	....	....	95	1,532	1,627	......	......
Second Brigade, Brig. Gen. W. C. Whitaker.	......	....	....	92	2,378	2,470	......	......
Third Brigade, Brig. Gen. W. Grose.	......	....	....	102	2,140	2,242	......	......
Total	......	....	....	301	6,130	6,431	......	......
Headquarters Second Division, Brig. Gen. W. L. Elliott.	......	....	....	14	45	59	......	......
First Brigade, Col. E. Opdycke.	......	....	....	83	1,498	1,581	......	......
Second Brigade, Col. J. Q. Lane.	......	....	....	88	1,451	1,539	......	......
Third Brigade, Col. J. Conrad ..	......	....	....	67	1,326	1,393	......	......
Total	......	....	....	252	4,320	4,572	......	......
Headquarters Third Division, Brig. Gen. Samuel Beatty.	......	....	....	15	203	218	......	......
First Brigade, Col. A. D. Streight.	......	....	....	82	1,646	1,728	......	......
Second Brigade, Col. P. Sidney Post.	......	....	....	83	1,631	1,714	......	......
Third Brigade, Col. Fred. Knefler.	......	....	....	58	866	924	......	......
Total	......	....	....	238	4,346	4,584	......	......
Artillery Brigade, Capt. Lyman Bridges.	25	756	781	33	883	916	587	30
Grand total.................	25	756	781	844	15,801	16,645	......	......

TH. J. WOOD,
Brigadier-General of Volunteers, Commanding.

HEADQUARTERS ARMY OF THE OHIO,
In the Field, Nashville, December 12, 1864.

Major-General THOMAS:

My signal officers report that the enemy withdrew all but a picket-line from the advance works in front of General Wood to-day, and that they are constructing a second line in rear, which they appear to occupy in force. They also report the enemy's camp-fires extending several miles up the river, and observed the movement of troops and trains in that direction to-day. The reports are rather indefinite. I have ordered a more careful examination to be made early in the morning, and will also go out early myself. I think the river should be guarded very carefully from here to Gallatin, and for a short distance above that point, though it seems hardly possible that Hood can attempt any move at this time.

J. M. SCHOFIELD,
Major-General,

SPECIAL FIELD ORDERS, ⎱ HEADQUARTERS ARMY OF THE OHIO,
        No. 178.   ⎰   *Nashville, Tenn., December 12, 1864.*

I. All preparations will be made to-day for active operations. The men will have three days' rations in haversacks this evening. Supply trains, including forage, will be loaded and ready to move to-morrow morning. Ammunition trains will be fully loaded. Artillery horses will be rough-shod, as far as practicable.

*   *   *   *   *   *   *

XIV. Lieut. Col. J. F. Boyd, chief quartermaster Department of the Ohio, will proceed to Louisville, Ky., and establish his office there.

*   *   *   *   *   *   *

By command of Major-General Schofield:
                                        J. A. CAMPBELL,
                                Major and Assistant Adjutant-General.

———

HDQRS. THIRD DIVISION, TWENTY-THIRD ARMY CORPS,
                                        December 12, 1864.

Major-General SCHOFIELD:

Colonel Hayes, One hundredth Ohio, reports that this morning large bodies of the enemy, with trains, were moving toward our left. There appears to be some movement amongst them. This p. m. a column moved from their first works back to their second line. Some shells from Fort Negley seemed to reach them, and they passed directly to the rear, out of sight. Am not certain it was to avoid the shells, or permanent movement. Would send out a reconnaissance, but it is so icy that it would be dark before they got far enough to discover anything. There was a reported movement of a skirmish advance on our right, but has not developed anything yet. I mention this to enable you to compare with reports from other parts of the lines.

                                        J. D. COX,
                                        Brigadier-General.

———

HEADQUARTERS DETACHMENT ARMY OF THE TENNESSEE,
                                Nashville, Tenn., December 12, 1864.

Maj. Gen. HENRY W. HALLECK,
                        Chief of Staff:

GENERAL: I have the honor to introduce to you hereby Col. William F. Lynch, Fifty-eighth Illinois Volunteer Infantry, who has been serving for the past eighteen months in my command as regimental and brigade commander. He entered the service in April, 1861, as a private, and afterward raised the Fifty-eighth Illinois, and was mustered into service with it December 20, 1861. Since that time he has been in the battles of Fort Donelson, Shiloh (where he was captured, after a heavy loss in officers and men), Fort De Russy, Pleasant Hill, and Yellow Bayou, La., in which last battle he was severely wounded in the leg while cheering his men to the charge. As regimental and brigade commander he has few equals in energy, decision, and tact in the service; as an officer he is cool and courageous, and as a gentleman courteous and refined. His services and ability entitle him to a higher position than the one which he now holds, and I earnestly recommend that he be appointed brigadier-general of volunteers as an act of justice and policy.

I have the honor to be, very respectfully, your obedient servant,
A. J. SMITH,
Major-General.

NASHVILLE, TENN., *December 12, 1864.*

Col. E. D. TOWNSEND,
Assistant Adjutant-General, Washington, D. C.:

I have the honor to report that I am here with my command. General Orders, No. 227, breaking up the Sixteenth Army Corps, has been received. I am now, by Special Field Orders, No. 334, dated headquarters Department of the Cumberland, Nashville, Tenn., December 6, 1864, called the Detachment Army of the Tennessee. I make this my report to show you my whereabouts.

I am, sir, very respectfully, your obedient servant,
A. J. SMITH,
Major-General.

HEADQUARTERS DETACHMENT ARMY OF THE TENNESSEE,
December 12, 1864.

Major-General THOMAS:

Received dispatch of yesterday, and will be in according to orders.
A. J. SMITH,
Major-General.

HEADQUARTERS DETACHMENT ARMY OF THE TENNESSEE,
December 12, 1864.

Major-General THOMAS:

All is quiet in our front. No change from yesterday.
A. J. SMITH,
Major-General.

HEADQUARTERS DETACHMENT ARMY OF THE TENNESSEE,
Nashville, Tenn., December 12, 1864.

Brig. Gen. J. McARTHUR,
Comdg. First Division, Detachment Army of the Tennessee:

GENERAL: The major-general commanding directs me to say that he desires the subsistence trains to be loaded as rapidly as possible with field rations, and that full rations be drawn to include the 15th instant to-day. Care should be taken that the cartridge-boxes of the men and the ammunition-chests of the batteries are full, and that each regiment has its ten additional rounds per man.

I am, very respectfully, your obedient servant,
J. HOUGH,
Major and Assistant Adjutant-General.

HEADQUARTERS DEPARTMENT OF THE CUMBERLAND,
Nashville, December 12, 1864.

Maj. Gen. J. H. WILSON,
   Comdg. Cavalry Corps, Military Division of the Mississippi:

GENERAL: The major-general commanding directs me to inform you that he desires to see you at these headquarters this afternoon at 3 o'clock.

I have the honor to be, general, very respectfully, your obedient servant,

ROBT. H. RAMSEY,
Assistant Adjutant-General.

SPECIAL ORDERS,   HEADQUARTERS CAVALRY CORPS,
                  MILITARY DIVISION OF THE MISSISSIPPI,
   No. 35   *Nashville, Tenn., December 12, 1864.*

*   *   *   *   *   *   *

II. The cavalry depot will be moved to the ground on the north side of the Cumberland River designated by Capt. John Green, special inspector cavalry, and Lieut. Col. G. G. Miner, commanding cavalry depot. Capt. W. M. Wilson, cavalry depot quartermaster, will take immediate measures for the removal of his stores and buildings to the proposed location. Stables will be erected without delay for the reception of cavalry horses.

*   *   *   *   *   *   *

By command of Brevet Major-General Wilson:

E. B. BEAUMONT,
Major and Assistant Adjutant-General.

SPECIAL   HEADQUARTERS CAVALRY CORPS,
FIELD ORDERS,   MILITARY DIVISION OF THE MISSISSIPPI,
   No. 2.*   *Nashville, Tenn., December 12, 1864.*

I. Commanders of divisions and detachments will send to these headquarters by 2 o'clock this p. m. an approximate field return of their respective commands, both mounted and dismounted. This return will show the number of men they have actually in hand.

II. Commanders of divisions and detached brigades will place strong guards around their camps and prevent the men from straggling.

III. The Chicago Board of Trade Battery, Captain Robinson, will report for temporary duty to Brigadier-General Croxton, commanding First Brigade, First Division Cavalry.

IV. The Fourth Ohio Volunteer Cavalry will, without delay, report to Brigadier-General Croxton, commanding First Brigade, First Division Cavalry, for temporary duty with his brigade.

V. The command is not expected to move to-morrow. Commanding officers will take measures to get their baggage from the other bank of the river and supply their men with fuel.

By command of Brevet Major-General Wilson:

A. J. ALEXANDER,
Lieutenant-Colonel and Acting Chief of Staff.

---

* Recorded in order book as No. 4.

SPRINGFIELD, TENN., *December 12, 1864.*

General McCOOK, *Bowling Green:*

The following dispatch has just been received from Nashville:

Your telegram received. The major-general directs that you make the best defense you can at Springfield and communicate with General McCook, who is at Bowling Green, who will move at once to intercept General Lyon. He directs that you will hold Springfield to the last. No re-enforcements can be sent from here. Do not fail to communicate with General McCook.

J. L. DONALDSON,
Chief Quartermaster.

It is reported here that General Lyon has crossed the Cumberland River above Clarksville, and has burned the water-tanks and destroyed the trestle-work at Hampton's Station, on the Memphis branch, two miles west of the State line. His force is variously estimated from 2,000 to 5,000. The telegraph operators have all been ordered in between here and the State line, and we have nothing later than 4 p. m. to-day.

T. J. DOWNEY,
Colonel, Commanding.

HEADQUARTERS U. S. FORCES,
Fort Donelson, Tenn., December 12, 1864.
(Via Clarksville 13th.)

Brig. Gen. WILLIAM D. WHIPPLE, *Assistant Adjutant-General:*

SIR: A force of rebels numbering about 4,000 mounted men, with nine pieces of artillery, commanded by Brigadier-General Lyon, C. S. Army, crossed Cumberland River at Cumberland City, on the 10th and 11th instant. While crossing they captured and burned three transports and several barges, and several prisoners, including Lieutenant-Colonel Buchanan, Seventh Missouri Infantry, all of whom they paroled. Messengers with the intelligence have been sent to Hopkinsville, Ky., and Clarksville, Tenn. The one sent to Hopkinsville has returned, having gone and returned safely. Their movements indicate that they will attempt the capture of Hopkinsville.

Very respectfully, your obedient servant,

WM. FORBES,
Colonel, Commanding.

BOWLING GREEN, *December 12, 1864.*

Maj. E. B. BEAUMONT, *Assistant Adjutant-General, Cavalry Corps:*

Lyon reported occupied La Fayette, Christian County, day before yesterday. No definite information as to his movements. Scouts will be sent from Russellville this afternoon, and I will send you first information received. I will stop Watkins at Franklin, and march there with La Grange, if I learn the enemy are coming in that direction, through Middletown or Russellville.

E. M. McCOOK,
Brigadier-General.

NASHVILLE, *December 12, 1864.*
(Received 11 p. m.)

Brigadier-General McCOOK:

Your dispatch of to-day is received. General Donaldson has just received a dispatch from Springfield, saying, "Lyon is in the vicinity of Red River, and moving in the direction of Springfield." Get your forces together as soon as possible and go for him. The commanding officer at Springfield will give you all the information he gets.

J. H. WILSON,
Brevet Major-General.

Weekly report of effective force of the troops of the Dis 'ct of Tennessee, Maj. Gen. Lovell H. Rousseau, U. S. Army, commanding, for December 12, 1864.

Command.	Headquarters.			Infantry.			Cavalry.		
	Officers.	Men.	Total.	Officers.	Men.	Total.	Officers.	Men.	Total.
District of Tennessee, Major-General Rousseau.	16	62	78	......	......	......			
First Brigade, Fourth Division, Twentieth Army Corps, Col. C. C. Doolittle.	6	2	8	46	1,075	1,121			
Second Brigade, Fourth Division, Twentieth Army Corps, Brig. Gen. John F. Miller.	3	......	3	141	3,310	3,451			
Unassigned regiments, Fourth Division, Twentieth Army Corps:									
83d Illinois Infantry, Maj. W. G. Bond.				22	472	494			
115th Ohio Infantry, Col. T. C. Boone.				29	676	705			
Detachment 59th Ohio Infantry, Capt. E. M. Sargent.				1	70	71			
58th New York Infantry, Maj. M. Esembaux.				3	125	128			
68th New York Infantry, Col. F. Prince Salm.				18	293	311			
75th Pennsylvania Infantry, Lieut. Col. A. V. Matzdorff.				12	170	182			
106th Ohio Infantry, Lieut. Col. Gustavus Tafel.				13	424	437			
6th Kentucky Infantry, Lieut. Col. R. C. Dawkins.				13	173	186			
Detachment 78th Pennsylvania Infantry, Lieut. Col. A. B. Bonnaffon.				2	173	175			
11th Minnesota Infantry, Lieut. Col. John Ball.				30	793	823			
173d Ohio Infantry, Col. J. R. Hurd.				30	872	902			
175th Ohio Infantry, Lieut. Col. D. McCoy.				32	790	822			
43d Wisconsin Infantry, Lieut. Col. Byron Paine.				27	715	742			
29th Michigan Infantry, Col. Thomas Saylor.				21	565	586			
61st Illinois Infantry *a*									
9th Ohio Battery, Capt. H. B. York.									
Total.	9	2	11	440	10,696	11,136			
Unattached troops:									
Post Nashville, Brig. Gen. John F. Miller.				58	1,803	1,861	42	908	950
183d Ohio Infantry *a*									
Garrison Artillery, Maj. John J. Ely.	2	5	7						
Springfield, Tenn., Col. T. J. Downey.				12	529	541			
Fort Donelson, Tenn., Lieut. Col. E. C. Brott.	2	2	4						
Clarksville, Tenn., Col. A. A. Smith.	2	3	5						
Gallatin, Tenn., Col. James Gilfillan.									
Nashville and Northwestern Railroad, Col. C. R. Thompson.	5	......	5	57	1,826	1,883			
Murfreesborough, Tenn., Brigadier-General Van Cleve.	8	9	17	59	1,297	1,356			

a No effective force report received.

Weekly report of effective force of the troops of the District of Tennessee, &c.—Continued.

Command.	Headquarters.			Infantry.			Cavalry.		
	Officers.	Men.	Total.	Officers.	Men.	Total	Officers.	Men.	Total.
Unattached troops—Continued.									
3d and 4th Michigan Infantry, 181st Ohio, and 140th Indiana Infantry.a	......	......	......	......	......	......	......	......	......
Nashville and Chattanooga Railroad, Major-General Milroy.	2	......	2	46	945	991	15	400	415
Bridgeport, Ala., Capt. N. A. Baldwin.	......	......	......	......	......	......	......	......	......
District of Northern Alabama, Brig. Gen. R. S. Granger.	6	27	33	......	......	......	......	......	......
Post Stevenson, Col. W. Krzyzanowski.	7	33	40	32	703	735	73	1,425	1,498
Nashville, Tenn., Brig. Gen. J. C. Starkweather.	6	18	24	9	269	278	72	2,122	2,194
Total......................	40	97	137	273	7,372	7,645	202	4,855	5,057

Command.	Artillery.			Total.		Aggregate.	Horses.	Guns.
	Officers.	Men.	Total.	Officers.	Men.			
District of Tennessee, Major-General Rousseau.	......	......	......	16	62	78	......	......
First Brigade, Fourth Division, Twentieth Army Corps, Col. C. C. Doolittle.	......	......	......	52	1,077	1,129	......	......
Second Brigade, Fourth Division, Twentieth Army Corps, Brig. Gen. John F. Miller.	......	......	......	144	3,310	3,454	......	......
Unassigned regiments, Fourth Division, Twentieth Army Corps:								
83d Illinois Infantry, Maj. W. G. Bond.	......	......	......	22	472	494	102	......
115th Ohio Infantry, Col. T. C. Boone.	......	......	......	29	676	705	......	......
Detachment 59th Ohio Infantry, Capt. E. M. Sargent.	......	......	......	1	70	71	......	......
58th New York Infantry, Maj. M. Esembaux.	......	......	......	3	125	128	......	......
68th New York Infantry, Col. F. Prince Salm.	......	......	......	18	293	311	......	......
75th Pennsylvania Infantry, Lieut. Col. A. V. Matzdorff.	......	......	......	12	170	182	......	......
106th Ohio Infantry, Lieut. Col. Gustavus Tafel.	......	......	......	13	424	437	......	......
6th Kentucky Infantry, Lieut. Col. R. C. Dawkins.	......	......	......	13	173	186	......	......
Detachment 78th Pennsylvania Infantry, Lieut. Col. A. B. Bonnaffon.	......	......	......	2	173	175	......	......
11th Minnesota Infantry, Lieut. Col. John Ball.	......	......	......	30	793	823	......	......
173d Ohio Infantry, Col. J. R. Hurd.	......	......	......	30	872	902	......	......
175th Ohio Infantry, Lieut. Col. D. McCoy.	......	......	......	32	790	822	......	......
43d Wisconsin Infantry, Lieut. Col. Byron Paine.	......	......	......	27	715	742	......	......
29th Michigan Infantry, Col. Thomas Saylor.	......	......	......	21	565	586	......	......
61st Illinois Infantry a	......	......	......	......	......	......	......	......
9th Ohio Battery, Capt. H. B. York.	3	133	136	3	133	136	53	6
Total	3	133	136	452	10,831	11,283	155	6

a No effective force report received.

Weekly report of effective force of the troops of the District of Tennessee, &c.—Continued.

Command.	Artillery.			Total.		Aggregate.	Horses.	Guns.
	Officers.	Men.	Total.	Officers.	Men.			
Unattached troops:								
Post Nashville, Brig. Gen. John F. Miller.	.....	.....	.....	100	2,711	2,811	.....	.....
183d Ohio Infantry a	.....	.....	.....	.....	.....	.....	.....	.....
Garrison Artillery, Maj. John J. Ely.	32	1,093	1,125	24	1,098	1,132	458	50
Springfield, Tenn., Col. T. J. Downey.	.....	.....	.....	12	529	541	.....	.....
Fort Donelson, Tenn., Lieut. Col. E. C. Brott.	2	109	111	4	111	115	56	6
Clarksville, Tenn., Col. A. A. Smith.	3	118	121	5	121	126	98	6
Gallatin, Tenn., Col. James Gilfillan.	4	145	149	4	145	149	.....	6
Nashville and Northwestern Railroad, Col. C. R. Thompson.	2	103	105	64	1,929	1,993	90	6
Murfreesborough, Tenn., Brigadier-General Van Cleve.	9	387	396	76	1,693	1,769		57
3d and 4th Michigan Infantry, 181st Ohio, and 140th Indiana Infantry. a	.....	.....	.....					
Nashville and Chattanooga Railroad, Major-General Milroy.	3	83	86	66	1,428	1,494	2	8
Bridgeport, Ala., Capt. N. A. Baldwin.	2	131	133	2	131	133	1	4
District of Northern Alabama, Brig. Gen. R. S. Granger.	.....	.....	.....	6	27	33	.....	
Post Stevenson, Col. W. Krzyzanowski.	13	441	454	125	2,602	2,727	187	32
Nashville, Tenn., Brig. Gen. J. C. Starkweather.	3	135	138	90	2,544	2,634	1,472	6
Total	73	2,745	2,818	588	15,069	15,657	2,364	181

a No effective force report received.

LOVELL H. ROUSSEAU,
Major-General, Commanding.

SPECIAL ORDERS, }   HDQRS. DEPT. OF THE CUMBERLAND,
No. 145.   *Chattanooga, Tenn., December 12, 1864.*

*   *   *   *   *   *   *

IV. The following is hereby announced as the armament of the permanent garrison of Chattanooga, Tenn., and the disposition of that armament will not be changed except by orders from these headquarters: Fort Creighton, eight 3-inch Rodman guns and six light 12-pounder guns; Fort Phelps, seven 3-inch Rodman guns and three light 12-pounder guns; Battery McAloon, four 12-pounder howitzers; Battery Bushnell, two 20-pounder Parrott guns and two 3-inch Rodman guns; Lunette O'Meara, two 30-pounder Parrott guns and six light 12-pounder guns; Redoubt Putnam, two 4½ inch Rodman guns and four 12-pounder howitzers; Battery Erwin, four 3-inch Rodman guns and two 12-pounder howitzers; Battery Jones, one 20-pounder Parrott gun, two 12-pounder howitzers, and three light 12-pounder guns; Fort Lytle, three 20-pounder Parrott guns and two light 12-pounder guns; Fort Crutchfield, one 4½ inch Rodman gun and two light 12-pounder guns; Fort Mihalotzy, four 4½-inch Rodman guns and four 3-inch Rodman guns; Redoubt Coolidge, two 3-inch Rodman guns and two 12-pounder howitzers; Cameron Hill, four 100-pounder Parrott guns; Redoubt Carpenter, two 100-pounder Parrott guns, two 3-inch Rodman guns, and two light 12-pounder guns.

*   *   *   *   *   *   *

By command of Major-General Thomas:

S. HOFFMAN,
Major and Assistant Adjutant-General.

TUNNEL HILL, *December 12, 1864.*

Capt. H. A. FORD:

There are thirty-three men at Graysville bridge and twenty-four at Graysville.

M. G. HAMILL,
Commanding.
By W. T. BENNETT,
Lieutenant and Acting Assistant Quartermaster.

BEAN'S STATION, *December 12, 1864.*

General SCHOFIELD:

Supply train will be up to-day. Arms and ammunition and subsistence will be issued to-night. All wagons will be left here in charge of infantry at this post. Infantry will be up early to-morrow. I leave with cavalry of Burbridge and Gillem to-morrow morning at daylight; we go via Rogersville and Kingsport, and hope to strike Bristol day after to-morrow night. Roads are quite heavy, but hope we can make it in time to cut enemy's train. Have sent a force to occupy pass into North Carolina. Hope you will hear good account of us.

GEO. STONEMAN,
Major-General.

HEADQUARTERS DEPARTMENT OF THE OHIO,
Louisville, Ky., December 12, 1864.

Major-General STONEMAN,
Knoxville, Tenn.:

Telegram from General Thomas says the rebel General Lyon has crossed the river below Clarksville and is moving on Bowling Green. He is reported at Hopkinsville, with about 2,000 men. A loyal citizen reports to Colonel Fairleigh that he was in Breckinridge's camp at Sparta, Tenn., a few days since. He says he saw about 5,000 men. Have you heard of any force being at Sparta?

G. M. BASCOM,
Lieutenant-Colonel and Assistant Adjutant-General.

LEXINGTON, *December 12, 1864.*
(Via Cumberland Gap.)

Bvt. Maj. Gen. S. G. BURBRIDGE,
Bean's Station:

An energetic post commander, who will stay at his post and attend to his duties, is needed at Camp Nelson. I would suggest that General

Fry be permanently relieved and Colonel Carpenter appointed. The report of Captain Saunders, acting assistant inspector-general, shows a condition of affairs there that demands an immediate change. General Thomas left this morning for Louisville. He will, if possible, stay in the State until you return. Guerrillas are becoming very bold, and I fear may do serious injury if the command remains absent much longer. I know nothing officially of Forrest's movements, and hear nothing further of Lyon. All well.

J. BATES DICKSON,
Captain and Assistant Adjutant-General.

LOUISA, KY., *December 12, 1864.*

Capt. J. S. BUTLER,
Assistant Adjutant-General:

My forces have been in quiet possession of Paintville and Salyersville. Up to last returns my scouts were in Butt [Knott County] and near Pound Gap. No indications of force entering in the State from that direction. Prentice did come in with about 300 men, but has not come down.

G. W. GALLUP,
Colonel, &c.

MOUNT STERLING, *December 12, 1864.*

Capt. J. S. BUTLER,
Assistant Adjutant-General:

We sent a scout toward the mountains Saturday morning, with orders to go until the position of the enemy could be ascertained. The scout consisted of a lieutenant and fifteen men, the largest we could send. They will go toward Jackson.

JOHN J. SEWELL,
Lieutenant and Acting Post Adjutant.

NASHVILLE, *December 12, 1864.*
(Received 13th.)

Brig. Gen. S. MEREDITH,
Paducah:

If you are satisfied of the correctness of the report of 1,000 rebels being at Danville bridge, on the Tennessee River, constructing boats, I desire you to send a sufficient force against them to drive them off, and destroy their work and means of crossing the river, if possible. Answer.

GEO. H. THOMAS,
Major-General, U. S. Volunteers, Commanding.

LEXINGTON, *December 12, 1864—3.45 p. m.*

Brig. Gen. S. MEREDITH,
Paducah, Ky.:

Send the battalion Fifth U. S. Colored Cavalry as soon as practicable, by boat, to Westport, on the Ohio River, with orders to disembark at that point and move thence at once to La Grange, on the Louisville and Lexington Railroad. Direct the commanding officer to report his arrival at Westport and at La Grange, both by telegraph and letter, to Brig. Gen. N. C. McLean, at this place. Acknowledge receipt, and state when the battalion will leave.

By order of Brevet Major-General Burbridge:

J. BATES DICKSON,
Captain and Assistant Adjutant-General.

HEADQUARTERS,
Louisville, December 12, 1864.

Brigadier-General WHIPPLE:

I have ordered the Ninth and Seventeenth Kentucky Regiments, here awaiting muster-out, to Bowling Green, to re-enforce the garrison, and Twenty-seventh Kentucky to Murfreesborough—all small regiments.

HUGH EWING,
Brigadier-General.

BOWLING GREEN, KY., *December 12, 1864.*

Capt. E. B. HARLAN,
Assistant Adjutant-General, Louisville, Ky.:

Brig. Gen. Ed. McCook is here from Nashville. Will have two brigades cavalry to-morrow night to watch movements of Lyon, &c.

S. P. LOVE,
Colonel, Commanding Brigade.

WASHINGTON, D. C., *December 12, 1864—4 p. m.*

Brevet Major-General HOVEY,
Indianapolis:

It is officially reported that you have twenty-eight enlisted men mounted on serviceable horses. The Secretary of War directs that these horses be immediately turned over to the quartermaster's department and sent forward to General Thomas, at Nashville. Condemned horses must be used for mounting orderlies not in the field.

H. W. HALLECK,
Major-General and Chief of Staff.

(Copy to Cavalry Bureau.)

HEADQUARTERS NORTHERN DEPARTMENT,
Cincinnati, Ohio, December 12, 1864.

His Excellency AUSTIN BLAIR,
Governor of Michigan:

GOVERNOR: Late advices from Canada, relating to the activity and designs of the Confederates with their sympathizing friends, makes me solicitous for the property of your citizens along the border. I have no apprehensions from the acts of armed bodies, of course, as my means of information are such as I hope to learn of the movements of any considerable force in season to anticipate them in any injury they may attempt to inflict. With regard to the efforts of individuals or small parties to burn and plunder, I feel less at ease. The closing of the river between you and them will afford these miscreants unusual facilities for carrying their designs into execution, and it is for this reason I require the services of the regiment you are raising for home service as early as practicable. Will you have the goodness to inform me what portion of the regiment you have for my disposal at this time and the probable time the whole regiment will be in readiness for service? Of the portion of the border intrusted to my command it is unnecessary for me to assure you that your State is the most exposed, and hence it is I desire to have it most efficiently guarded as early as practicable. Please furnish me with this information at your earliest convenience.

Very respectfully, your obedient servant,

JOSEPH HOOKER,
Major-General, Commanding.

NASHVILLE, TENN., *December 13, 1864—9 p. m.*
(Received 8 a. m. 14th.)

Maj. Gen. H. W. HALLECK,
Washington, D. C.:

There is no change in the enemy's position in my front to-day. At length there are indications of a favorable change in the weather, and as soon as there is I shall move against the enemy, as everything is ready and prepared to assume the offensive. I have heard from Clarksville to-day, the wires being in working order to that place. Two gun-boats and a transport had arrived there from below, and report that the rebel General Lyon's means of recrossing the Cumberland were destroyed. I have ample force in pursuit of him to effectually destroy him, and I have no apprehension about the Louisville and Nashville Railroad. The Cumberland River is constantly patrolled as high up as Carthage, and there is no evidence of the presence of the enemy in that direction. I am in hopes of a sufficient rise in the river to enable me to use the gun-boats in reopening the Cumberland as far as Nashville.

GEO. H. THOMAS,
Major-General, U. S. Volunteers, Commanding.

CLARKSVILLE, *December 13, 1864—4.30 p. m.*

Major-General THOMAS:

The commanding officer of gun-boat Peosta, stationed at Paducah, telegraphs, under date of 11th, 6 p. m., that he had just been ninety-three miles up the Tennessee River, where he learned that General Lyon had crossed on the evening of the 8th with 2,000 cavalry and two pieces of artillery, marching for Clarksville. The Peosta towed to Paducah two large barges and two boats in which the rebels crossed the Tennessee River. I hear there were two heavy barges left at Johnsonville after the affair of November 4. I infer that the presence of this vessel diverted the rebels from making an attack on the transports here, and induced them to take up a position below bars, which we could not cross at the present stage of water. I have no intelligence from my gun-boats, which are due here to-day.

S. P. LEE,
Acting Rear-Admiral, Mississippi Squadron.

CLARKSVILLE, *December 13, 1864—8.30 p. m.*

Major-General THOMAS:

Please see my telegram of this date to Lieutenant-Commander Fitch. Will give you convoy down to convoy transports as soon as you wish. Lieutenant Naile heard from or at Cumberland City that General Lyon had two guns at Paducah and Fort Donelson. General Lyon reported to have from five to nine guns. Naile heard along the river that Lyon had gone to Hopkinsville. Two or three transports declined convoy from Smithland. The brigade of cavalry had not arrived there. I will have three good tin-clads to convoy it up as soon as those here return.

S. P. LEE,
Rear-Admiral, Commanding Mississippi Squadron.

CLARKSVILLE, *December 13, 1864—4.30 p. m.*

Lieut. Commander LE ROY FITCH:

Your telegram of 11th instant is just received. Lieutenant Naile, with two gun-boats, convoying two naval transports loaded with 100 rounds of ammunition for your vessels and towing two coal barges, was to have left Smithland last Sunday morning for this place. I have no intelligence of him since he left Mound City Saturday morning. The Peosta returned to Paducah Sunday morning with two large barges and two boats, in which Forrest crossed the Tennessee River, near Welch Bridge, on the evening of the 8th instant.

S. P. LEE,
Acting Rear-Admiral, Mississippi Squadron.

CLARKSVILLE, *December 13, 1864—8.30 p. m.*

Lieut. Commander LE ROY FITCH:

Your two telegrams of 8th instant, sent to Mound City, just received by gun-boats Nos. 19, 33, and 15, which bring two coal barges and a full regulation supply of ammunition for you. The Benefit left Smithland 1 a. m. Sunday for Louisville with the ammunition you desired. What sort of works and guns did you engage on the 8th? Where at, and with what effect? The endurance of the Neosho is gratifying. Lieutenant Naile was delayed by searching for rebel ammunition opposite Cumberland City, where he captured nine boxes of carbine cartridges and one caisson. I will give army transports convoy from here as soon as desired.

S. P. LEE,
Acting Rear-Admiral, Mississippi Squadron.

U. S. STEAMER MOOSE,
Below Nashville, December 13, 1864.

Maj. Gen. GEORGE H. THOMAS,
Comdg. Army of the Cumberland, Nashville, Tenn.:

GENERAL: The indication of the weather is such to-day that I think we may soon look for a change, probably by morning. If you make any move in which I can be of any service, please give me timely notice, as the river is now so low that I cannot move but one of the heavy boats, and I will have to drop her down below Robinson's Island by hand; that is, by lines, which will be slow work; it is so bad there that I cannot trust to steam to take her through. If there is a change in the weather, so that the men can move on the monitor to handle her, I will commence moving in the morning early.

Very respectfully, your obedient servant,

LE ROY FITCH,
Lieut. Commander, Comdg. Tenth District, Miss. Squadron.

HEADQUARTERS DEPARTMENT OF THE CUMBERLAND,
Nashville, Tenn., December 13, 1864.

Lieut. Commander LE ROY FITCH,
Commanding Tenth District, Mississippi Squadron:

SIR: I have the honor, by direction of the major-general commanding, to acknowledge the receipt of your communication of this date, and in reply I am instructed to say that should there really be a change of weather and a rise in the river results sufficient to enable you to move your fleet with facility, it is the desire of the major-general commanding to have you co-operate in any move which may take place against the enemy, by engaging the batteries on the river below the city, and thus attracting their attention while the troops are in motion against the enemy's position. The major-general commanding returns his thanks for your cordial co-operation heretofore, as well as for the tender of your services in future movements, of which timely notice will be given you. The major-general commanding will be much indebted to you if you will have the river above the city as far up as Carthage, if you can get up as far, patrolled by one or two boats of your fleet constantly, in order that any movement on the part of the enemy in that direction may be instantly detected.

I am, very respectfully, your obedient servant,

ROBERT H. RAMSEY,
Assistant Adjutant-General.

U. S. STEAMER MOOSE,
Below Nashville, December 13, 1864.

Capt. ROBERT H. RAMSEY,
Assistant Adjutant-General, Nashville, Tenn.:

CAPTAIN: I have the honor to acknowledge the receipt of your letter of this date. I will have a patrol of the river kept up above, as requested, and do all in my power to fill all the wishes the general commanding may designate. I sincerely hope that we may before this time to-morrow be cheered by better prospects as to weather and water. If the weather and water will permit I will surely give the rebel batteries below sufficient amusement to keep them occupied, and at the same time try to induce them to bring as many guns on the river as possible.

Very respectfully, your obedient servant,

LE ROY FITCH,
Lieut. Commander, Comdg. Tenth District, Miss. Squadron.

NASHVILLE, *December 13, 1864.*

Major-General DODGE,
          Saint Louis, Mo.:

If you have any further re-enforcements to send to this place, I would like you to send three regiments of infantry or cavalry, if you can spare them, to Paducah, to report to General Meredith for special duty of driving the enemy from Danville bridge, on the Tennessee River.

GEO. H. THOMAS,
Major-General, U. S. Volunteers, Commanding.

NASHVILLE, TENN., *December 13, 1864—8 p. m.*

Maj. T. T. ECKERT:

Reconnaissance to-day showed enemy's force all around; in greatest strength on right, where some artillery opened. Thaw has begun, and to-morrow we can move without skates. Rebel General Lyon crossed the Cumberland twenty miles below Clarksville, Sunday, by capturing a transport; so we may lose use of Louisville railroad soon, and communication by telegraph, but he cannot stay long—not strong enough. Trains run from Murfreesborough to Chattanooga. All quiet in that quarter and in East Tennessee.

J. C. VAN DUZER.

SPECIAL ORDERS, ⎞ HDQRS. ARMIES OF THE UNITED STATES,
     No. 149.   ⎠   *City Point, Va., December 13, 1864.*

I. Maj. Gen. John A. Logan, U. S. Volunteers, will proceed immediately to Nashville, Tenn., reporting by telegraph to the lieutenant-general commanding his arrival at Louisville, Ky., and also his arrival at Nashville, Tenn.

 *   *   *   *   *   *   *

By command of Lieutenant-General Grant:

T. S. BOWERS,
Assistant Adjutant-General.

SPECIAL FIELD ORDERS, ⎞ HDQRS. DEPT. OF THE CUMBERLAND,
     No. 341.   ⎠   *Nashville, Tenn., December 13, 1864.*

I. Brig. Gen. E. Upton, brevet major-general of volunteers, having reported at these headquarters in obedience to orders from Headquarters of the Army, is assigned to duty with the Cavalry Corps, Military Division of the Mississippi, and will report in person to Bvt. Maj. Gen. J. H. Wilson, commanding.

 *   *   *   *   *   *   *

IX. The Sixteenth U. S. Colored Infantry is hereby ordered to report for temporary duty to Lieut. Col. H. C. Wharton, U. S. Engineers, chief topographical engineer, Department of the Cumberland.

 *   *   *   *   *   *   *

By command of Major-General Thomas:

HENRY M. CIST,
Captain and Assistant Adjutant-General.

Circular.]   Hdqrs. Department of the Cumberland,
                                  Nashville, Tenn., December 13, 1864.

Hereafter corps commanders will use the necessary means of keeping both officers and men in camp at night, and all other times, except when required by military reasons to be absent. The liability of a movement at any moment against the enemy requires that every man should be constantly at his post.

By command of Major-General Thomas:

                                     HENRY STONE,
                                  Assistant Adjutant-General.

                          Headquarters Fourth Army Corps,
                                          December 13, 1864.

Brigadier-General WHIPPLE:

No change in my front this morning.

                                     TH. J. WOOD,
                                  Brigadier-General, Commanding.

General Orders, } Headquarters Fourth Army Corps,
    No. 22.   }   *Nashville, Tenn., December 13, 1864.*

Maj. W. F. Goodspeed, First Ohio Light Artillery, having been ordered to report to these headquarters for duty, is hereby assigned to temporary duty as chief of artillery Fourth Army Corps. He will be respected accordingly.

By command of Brigadier-General Wood:

                                     WM. H. SINCLAIR,
                                  Major and Assistant Adjutant-General.

            Hdqrs. Third Division, Twenty-third Army Corps,
                                  Nashville, December 13, 1864.

Maj. J. A. CAMPBELL,
    Assistant Adjutant-General, Army of the Ohio:

MAJOR: In reply to the commanding general's note of last evening, I have the honor to report that the enemy's principal line of works on the Nolensville pike is held by them this morning with apparently the usual force, though I think a smaller and more advanced work (near the old line of trenches dug by General Steedman's command) is held only by picket reserves. Their picket-line is not so far advanced as it was in our front three days ago, and our own line has resumed the position originally taken by it when we came into position here. The smoke of camp-fires appears extended farther to our left, indicating the extension of the enemy's line in that direction, though refused. The impression is strong amongst all my officers who watched their operations yesterday that some considerable movement was made by them toward their right and rear, but I have not myself been able to reach a definite conclusion on the subject. Everything is quiet on the line this morning, and no appearance of any movement in the enemy's camp.

Very respectfully, your obedient servant,

                                     J. D. COX,
                                  Brigadier-General, Commanding.

HEADQUARTERS DETACHMENT ARMY OF THE TENNESSEE,
December 13, 1864.

Maj. Gen. G. H. THOMAS :

All quiet this morning in our front. No changes from yesterday. First Division is ordered to fire their guns at 12 m.

A. J. SMITH,
Major-General.

STEEDMAN'S HEADQUARTERS,
December 13, 1864. (Received 7.15 p. m.)

Major-General SCHOFIELD :

The reconnaissance made by a portion of my command this afternoon brought out the enemy in strong force between the Nolensville and Murfreesborough pikes beyond the residence of Mr. Rains, but not extending to the Murfreesborough pike. They seemed to be strongest just to the left of the railroad, where they have works extending as if to protect their flank. General Lowrey occupies a house about half a mile beyond Rains' house as headquarters. Citizens, rebel women, residing there informed us that General Hood rode that part of his lines yesterday, having his engineer with him, and directed the building of more works, and expressed himself confident of taking Nashville.

JAMES B. STEEDMAN,
Major-General, U. S. Volunteers.

(Same to General Thomas.)

SPECIAL ORDERS, }   HEADQUARTERS CAVALRY CORPS,
                      MILITARY DIVISION OF THE MISSISSIPPI,
No. 36.   }   *Nashville, December 13, 1864.*

*   *   *   *   *   *   *

III. Brig. Gen. B. H. Grierson is relieved from the command of the Fourth Division, Cavalry Corps, Military Division of the Mississippi.

IV. Bvt. Maj. Gen. E. Upton, U. S. Volunteers, having reported for duty in accordance with Special [Field] Orders, No. [341], from head-quarters Department of the Cumberland, is assigned to the command of the Fourth Division, Cavalry Corps, Military Division of the Mississippi.

V. Bvt. Maj. Gen. E. Upton will proceed to Louisville, Ky., Saint Louis, Mo., and Memphis, Tenn., for the purpose of collecting the men, horses, and transportation of his division and bringing it to Nashville, via Louisville, Ky. If necessary General Upton will take measures to furnish his troops with new arms and equipments.

By command of Brevet Major-General Wilson :

E. B. BEAUMONT,
Major and Assistant Adjutant-General.

HDQRS. CAVALRY CORPS, MIL. DIV. OF THE MISSISSIPPI,
Nashville, Tenn., December 13, 1864—1 a. m.

COMMANDING OFFICER FOURTH OHIO CAVALRY :

You will, without delay, take position with your regiment at some convenient point twelve or fifteen miles above here, at or near the Cumberland River, and watch all the crossings between Gallatin and this place. There are indications of movements of the enemy in some force in that direction. You will do all in your power to keep me informed of everything of importance. If practicable, get scouts to Spring Hill, Green Hill, and Lebanon.

> J. H. WILSON,
> *Brevet Major-General.*

NASHVILLE, *December 13, 1864.*

Brig. Gen. E. M. McCOOK,
 Bowling Green, Ky.:

Lyon seems to have avoided Springfield, and is probably making for Hopkinsville or Russellville. Send out scouts to ascertain his whereabouts and movements, and move against him wherever found.

By command of General Thomas:

> HENRY STONE,
> *Assistant Adjutant-General.*

BOWLING GREEN, *December 13, 1864—10 a. m.*

Maj. Gen. J. H. WILSON,
 Commanding Cavalry Corps, Nashville:

La Grange moving to Franklin to join Watkins. I will be there this afternoon. Colonel Johnson telegraphs from Russellville 1,200 rebels entered Hopkinsville at 3 o'clock yesterday. I move in accordance with your dispatch, taking for granted that Lyon's main force is moving on Springfield; I will march from Franklin there. Is this right? Colonel Downey furnishes no information from Springfield, except that it was reported Lyon had crossed and burned water-tanks near State line. It seems impossible to get accurate information from these posts. Franklin is a better point than this to move in any direction.

> E. M. McCOOK.

NASHVILLE, TENN., *December 13, 1864.*

Brigadier-General McCOOK,
 Franklin, Ky.:

Lyon was at or near Hopkinsville yesterday conscripting and roaming about the country. If you can get in upon him while in this condition you will be able to break him up entirely. Have ordered a party from Croxton's brigade after the horses at Franklin.

> J. H. WILSON,
> *Brevet Major-General.*

BOWLING GREEN, *December 13, 1864—10 a. m.*

General L. D. WATKINS,
 Commanding Cavalry Brigade, Franklin:

Remain in Franklin until I come this afternoon. La Grange is marching down to meet you there.

> E. M. McCOOK,
> *Brigadier-General.*

FRANKLIN, KY., *December 13, 1864.*

Brevet Brigadier-General WATKINS:

Send me word by these couriers when you will reach here. I wish to move on Russellville at daylight, and want you to camp near here to-night. Write me where you are when this meets you. La Grange will be here to-night.

E. M. McCOOK,
Brigadier-General, Commanding.

———

BOWLING GREEN, *December 13, 1864—11 a. m.*

Col. O. H. LA GRANGE,
  Commanding Second Brigade:

Lyon is reported to be moving on Springfield, and it is necessary that you reach Franklin to-night if possible. You will march immediately, and camp near the place. I will go there this p. m. You will report to me on your arrival and let me know the whereabouts of your brigade.

E. M. McCOOK,
Brigadier-General, Commanding.

———

BOWLING GREEN, *December 13, 1864.*
(Received 3.50 p. m.)

Brigadier-General McCOOK,
  Franklin:

Colonel Johnson, at Russellville, just telegraphed that the enemy, 1,500 or 2,000 strong, are advancing on Russellville; are at Elkton. Their advance is skirmishing with his men. They have four pieces artillery. Will you go to his help? If not, he will, as he says, have to fall back. Answer.

S. P. LOVE,
Colonel, Commanding.

———

FRANKLIN, *December 13, 1864—4 p. m.*

Col. S. P. LOVE,
  Bowling Green:

Telegraph Colonel Johnson I have sent a courier to him that a brigade will start to him at daylight, and to have his scouts to watch the rebel movements, that we will get on the right track at once.

E. M. McCOOK,
Brigadier-General.

———

HEADQUARTERS U. S. FORCES,
  Russellville, Ky., December 13, 1864.

General McCOOK:

SIR: I was ordered by the commanding officer at Bowling Green to report to you the position of the enemy below. The commander at Fort Donelson reported on Sunday that General Lyon, with from 3,000 to 4,000 men, crossed the Cumberland fifteen miles above the fort, moving in the direction of Hopkinsville, Ky. I have not been able yet to ascertain the strength of the rebels, but think it is not over

1,200, if that strong. They burned the trestle-work on the Memphis branch road ten miles this side of Clarksville. They were at Hopkinsville last night. I have 400 mounted men here ready to move at once. If another regiment could be sent to co-operate with us, and move from this point on the enemy, I think the command could be broken up. I will wait to hear from you.

Your obedient servant,

S. F. JOHNSON,
Lieutenant-Colonel Fifty-second Kentucky Vols., Commanding.

FRANKLIN, KY., *December 13, 1864—3.30 p. m.*

Colonel JOHNSON:

I will start a brigade to Russellville at daylight in the morning. Keep your scouts out and gain definite information as to the movements of the enemy, so that no time may be lost in pursuit. Let your scouting parties follow him so closely that no mistake may be made as to the direction he marches in; I don't want to march my troops on a false trail. If you gain any information you think of importance enough to communicate to me here, send it through to-night, and let the messenger impress any horses he may find to carry it. I will leave here to join you in the morning, unless something happens that requires me to go some place else.

E. M. McCOOK,
Brigadier-General, Commanding.

P. S.—You must not let them drive you, if you can possibly help it, as I will get there as soon as possible.

RUSSELLVILLE, *December 13, 1864.*
(Received 3.50 p. m.)

General E. M. McCOOK,
Franklin, Ky.:

We have developed the rebels' strength at Hopkinsville; drove in their pickets. Had one man killed. Killed and wounded several. They were in the town 1,500 strong this morning. They are conscripting every able-bodied man.

S. F. JOHNSON,
Lieutenant-Colonel Fifty-second Kentucky, Commanding.

HEADQUARTERS SECOND DIVISION, CAVALRY CORPS,
MILITARY DIVISION OF THE MISSISSIPPI,
Louisville, December 13, 1864.

Maj. E. B. BEAUMONT,
Asst. Adjt. Gen., Cavalry Corps, Mil. Div. of the Mississippi:

MAJOR: For the information of the general commanding the corps, I hereby respectfully report the condition of the division: The Second Brigade are all mounted except the Seventh Pennsylvania Cavalry, who will draw their horses to-day. There will then probably remain in the quartermaster's corral ready for issue enough horses to mount one regiment of Colonel Miller's brigade, which regiment's requisition will be approved to-day, and they will draw their horses to-morrow. I have received 1,130 horses from the impressment in Louisville and vicinity, out of which about 100 will be rejected by the inspectors.

Very respectfully, your obedient servant,

ELI LONG,
Brigadier-General, U. S. Volunteers, Commanding Division.

NASHVILLE, *December 13, 1864.*

Col. A. A. SMITH,
Clarksville:

What news have you of Lyon's movements?

GEO. H. THOMAS,
Major-General, Commanding.

CLARKSVILLE, *December 13, 1864.*

Major-General THOMAS,
Commanding:

I sent 200 men on train last night to see damage to railroad and telegraph. They found forty feet trestle burned ten miles from here. They repaired wire to State line. Report Lyon at or near Hopkinsville with detachment of his command, roaming around country, conscripting, &c. Sent guard to-day with men to repair bridge. Also sent transport down river with guard to look after battery; have just returned. Report they met two gun-boats and one transport coming up; think river is clear. Gun-boats have not arrived. Will report further.

A. A. SMITH,
Colonel, Commanding.

NASHVILLE, *December 13, 1864.*

Col. T. J. DOWNEY,
Springfield:

What further news have you of the rebel General Lyon's movements? What is the strength of your command? You must resist all attacks, and defend the place to the last, if attacked.

GEO. H. THOMAS,
Major-General, U. S. Volunteers, Commanding.

SPRINGFIELD, *December 13, 1864.*

Maj. Gen. G. H. THOMAS:

Your dispatch of this date is received and in reply I have the honor to state that nothing further is known of the rebel General Lyon's movements, the operators between here and State line having left for Nashville. Word from Clarksville that the burning of the trestle at Hampton's Station is confirmed. We have 400 effective force at this place, with one section of artillery, and 650 including what we have along the line between Red River and Edgefield Junction. We will hold this place at all hazards until further orders. I have communicated to General McCook, at Bowling Green.

Respectfully,

T. J. DOWNEY,
Colonel, Commanding Post.

LEXINGTON, *December 13, 1864.*

Adjt. Gen. L. THOMAS, *Louisville, Ky.:*

General Burbridge advanced toward Rogersville yesterday; General Stoneman had joined him.

J. BATES DICKSON,
Captain and Assistant Adjutant-General.

PADUCAH, KY., *December 13, 1864.*

Brig. Gen. W. D. WHIPPLE, *Nashville, Tenn.:*

GENERAL: In reply to your telegram of this date,* I have the honor to state that I have not a sufficient force in my command to assume the offensive and drive the enemy from Danville bridge, on the Tennessee River. My command at Paducah consists of Thirty-fourth New Jersey Volunteers, 16 officers and 465 men; Eighth U. S. Colored Heavy Artillery, 26 officers and 954 men; Seventh Tennessee, and Third Illinois Cavalry, 171 men. After furnishing the requisite details I have about 900 men left. My force at Columbus, Ky., consists of Fourth U. S. Colored Heavy Artillery, 22 officers and 635 men, which force is wholly inadequate for the defense of this district. Had I a sufficient number of troops I could drive Lyon out of Tennessee; but, situated as I am at present, it is impossible for me to move from any of my posts, my force being so small. I am perfectly satisfied that the report of 1,000 men being at Danville bridge constructing boats was correct at the time reported. I will start a gun-boat immediately up the river on a reconnaissance and will report the result. I will make application to Major-General Dodge for re-enforcements, and if I can obtain them will assume the offensive at once.

S. MEREDITH,
Brigadier-General.

PADUCAH, KY., *December 13, 1864.*

Brig. Gen. W. D. WHIPPLE, *Nashville, Tenn.:*

GENERAL: I have not 900 effective men in my district after making the requisite details. I telegraphed to Major-General Dodge for more troops. He has none to give me; he has forwarded them to Nashville. He states that Colonel Benteen's cavalry brigade is now at Cairo and four regiments of infantry. If you telegraph orders to me to stop a sufficient force, I will take the field in person and attack Lyon in the rear. Please answer.

S. MEREDITH,
Brigadier-General.

NASHVILLE, *December 13, 1864—10.30 p. m.*

Brig. Gen. S. MEREDITH, *Paducah:*

You can make use of the four infantry regiments now at Cairo en route to Nashville for the expedition to Danville bridge, after which they will return to Paducah and come to this place by the first opportunity.

GEO. H. THOMAS,
Major-General, U. S. Volunteers, Commanding.

---

* See 12th (received 13th), p. 166.

PADUCAH, KY., *December 13, 1864—2 p. m.*

Maj. Gen. G. M. DODGE:

GENERAL: I have just received a telegram from General Thomas, at Nashville, ordering me, if I had sufficient force, to move upon Lyon at Danville bridge, where he was constructing boats on the 8th instant. I respectfully request that you send me two or three regiments of infantry and some cavalry and artillery, so that I may comply with this order and enable me to drive Lyon from Danville, which force you can withdraw from this point as soon as this object is accomplished, as, circumstanced as I am at present, it is impossible for me to move from any post in my district, as I cannot muster 1,000 effective men after furnishing the requisite details. Please answer.

S. MEREDITH,
Brigadier-General.

SAINT LOUIS, *December 13, 1864—3.20 p. m.*

Brigadier-General MEREDITH,
Paducah, Ky.:

I have no troops; have just sent the last to Thomas. Colonel Benteen's cavalry brigade are now on their way to Thomas, now at Cairo or Smithland, and four regiments of infantry leaving here for him via Louisville, the last in the department.

G. M. DODGE,
Major-General.

BOWLING GREEN, KY., *December 13, 1864.*

Capt. E. B. HARLAN,
Louisville, Ky.:

Following dispatch just received from Colonel Johnson, commanding at Russellville:

Twelve hundred rebels entered Hopkinsville at 3 o'clock yesterday. If you can send me 300 mounted men, I will move them across the river.

S. P. LOVE,
Colonel, Commanding Second Brigade, Second Division.

BOWLING GREEN, KY., *December 13, 1864.*

Capt. E. B. HARLAN,
Louisville, Ky.:

General McCook just received orders to go for General Lyon. He will drive him out of the State, or follow till he gets a fight out of him.

S. P. LOVE,
Colonel, Commanding, &c.

BOWLING GREEN, KY., *December 13, 1864.*

Capt. E. B. HARLAN,
Louisville, Ky.:

General McCook telegraphs me he will start re-enforcements to Colonel Johnson at daylight to-morrow. In the meantime, send a courier to find out state of affairs.

S. P. LOVE,
Colonel, Commanding.

BOWLING GREEN, KY., *December 13, 1864.*

Capt. E. B. HARLAN,
        Louisville, Ky.:

Colonel Johnson, at Russellville, says the rebels are advancing on that place. They are at Elkton, 1,500 or 2,000 strong. His men are now fighting with the enemy's advance. He calls upon me for re-enforcements of men and artillery. I have none. What shall I do? I have ordered him to hold the place as long as he can, and communicate with General McCook, at Franklin, Ky., who has 2,500 cavalry and a battery. Give me instructions at once.

S. P. LOVE,
Colonel, Commanding Second Brigade, Second Division.

LOUISVILLE, KY., *December 13, 1864.*

Col. S. P. LOVE,
        Bowling Green, Ky.:

If Johnson can hold out until re-enforced by McCook, let him do so; if in danger of capture, however, let him fall back on Bowling Green.

By command of Brig. Gen. Hugh Ewing:

E. B. HARLAN,
Captain and Assistant Adjutant-General.

WASHINGTON, D. C., *December 14, 1864—12.30 p. m.*

Major-General THOMAS,
        Nashville:

It has been seriously apprehended that while Hood, with a part of his forces, held you in check near Nashville, he would have time to operate against other important points left only partially protected. Hence, General Grant was anxious that you should attack the rebel force in your front, and expressed great dissatisfaction that his orders had not been carried out. Moreover, so long as Hood occupies a threatening position in Tennessee, General Canby is obliged to keep large forces upon the Mississippi River, to protect its navigation and to hold Memphis, Vicksburg, &c., although General Grant had directed a part of these forces to co-operate with General Sherman. Every day's delay on your part, therefore, seriously interferes with General Grant's plans.

H. W. HALLECK,
Major-General and Chief of Staff.

NASHVILLE, TENN., *December 14, 1864—8 p. m.*

Maj. Gen. H. W. HALLECK,
        Washington, D. C.:

Your telegram of 12.30 p. m. to-day is received. The ice having melted away to-day, the enemy will be attacked to-morrow morning. Much as I regret the apparent delay in attacking the enemy, it could not have been done before with any reasonable hope of success.

GEO. H. THOMAS,
Major-General, U. S. Volunteers, Commanding.

NASHVILLE, *December 14, 1864—8.30 a. m.*

Admiral S. P. LEE,
　　　Clarksville:

Your two telegrams of 4.30 p. m. and 8.30 p. m. yesterday are received. I have no doubt that the presence of your iron-clad at Clarksville prevented Lyon from moving up opposite that place and destroying the transports. General Meredith telegraphed me of the reconnaissance of your gun-boat up the Tennessee River. As I hear from all directions that Lyon has gone to Hopkinsville, I think the transports now at Clarksville could be convoyed down the river with perfect safety. Although not so stated in your dispatch, I infer from what you have said that Lyon's means of crossing the Cumberland have either been taken possession of or destroyed, and as I have a force after Lyon I have great hopes of capturing him.

　　　　　　　GEO. H. THOMAS,
　　　Major-General, U. S. Volunteers, Commanding.

———

CLARKSVILLE, *December 14, 1864—11 a. m.*

Major-General THOMAS:

I am ready to give convoy down. Please say if convoy is required up, when, whether of freight or troops.

　　　　　　　S. P. LEE,
　　Acting Rear-Admiral, Commanding Mississippi Squadron.

———

CLARKSVILLE, *December 14, 1864—1.30 p. m.*

Major-General THOMAS:

Yours received since mine of 11 a. m. Yesterday Lieutenant Naile saw the burnt wrecks of four steam-boats near Cumberland City, and captured one large barge on right bank there. Lyon has no visible means of recrossing. I cannot pronounce transports perfectly safe on a long, shoal, crooked, and narrow river, with high banks and hills, where a mounted enemy with artillery occupying the country is ready to attack them suddenly in different localities. Our rifle-proof river steam gun-boats can generally protect transports, but there is unavoidable risk in places in such convoys, especially to troops and cavalry, which ought not to be encumbered unnecessarily by the transports. The best plan is to capture the batteries, and I am glad to hear you have the means of preventing Lyon's stay or escape inland. Quartermaster here will not be ready until to-morrow afternoon.

　　　　　　　S. P. LEE.
　　Acting Rear-Admiral, Commanding Mississippi Squadron.

———

NASHVILLE, *December 14, 1864—8 p. m.*

Admiral S. P. LEE,
　　　Clarksville:

Your dispatches of 11 a. m. and 1.30 p. m. are received. I am of opinion that it would be best for the transports now at Clarksville to go down the river as soon as unloaded. Perhaps it would be well not to bring up any convoy from Smithland for the present, but let all transports remain there until Lyon is disposed of and the river is safe. I shall be obliged to you if you will continue to have the river constantly patroled and report to me any movements discovered.

GEO. H. THOMAS,
Major-General, U. S. Volunteers, Commanding.

HEADQUARTERS DEPARTMENT OF THE CUMBERLAND,
Nashville, Tenn., December 14, 1864—8 p. m.

Lieut. Commander LE ROY FITCH,
Commanding Tenth District, Mississippi Squadron:

SIR: I have the honor, by direction of the major-general commanding, to inform you that the enemy will be attacked at an early hour in the morning. If you can drop down the river and engage their batteries on the river-bank, it will be excellent co-operation, for which the major-general commanding will be much obliged. It is very probable that these river batteries of the enemy will be attacked in rear by our forces, and it is very desirable and necessary that your fire does not injure the attacking force, and to this end it is advisable you should be informed of the proposed attack.

I am, very respectfully, your obedient servant,
ROBT. H. RAMSEY,
Assistant Adjutant-General.

SAINT LOUIS, *December 14, 1864—2 p. m.*

Maj. Gen. GEORGE H. THOMAS,
Nashville, Tenn.:

We have been blocked here three days by ice. Hope to get over to-day, and have directed three regiments of infantry ordered to you to go to Paducah.

G. M. DODGE,
Major-General.

NASHVILLE, *December 14, 1864—8 p. m.*

Maj. Gen. G. M. DODGE,
Saint Louis, Mo.:

Your dispatch of 2 p. m. this day is received. Hope you will be able to get the three regiments of infantry off soon for Paducah.

GEO. H. THOMAS,
Major-General, U. S. Volunteers, Commanding.

CHATTANOOGA, *December 14, 1864.*

Major-General THOMAS:

Is there any means by which I can get a detachment of the Signal Corps to Murfreesborough from La Vergne? I can communicate with the state-house in Nashville, if it is possible to get there.

Respectfully,
J. L. HOLLOPETER,
First Lieut., Acting Chief Signal Officer, Dept. of the Cumberland.

NASHVILLE, *December 14, 1864——8 p. m.*

Lieut. J. L. HOLLOPETER,
    Actg. Chief Signal Officer, Dept. of the Cumberland, Chattanooga:

There is no way by which you can get a signal party to Murfrees-borough at present.

ROBT. H. RAMSEY,
Assistant Adjutant-General.

NASHVILLE, *December 14, 1864——10.20 p. m.*

General THOMAS:

The train which left Gallatin for north at 8 this evening has returned to that place, and reports Lyon's men at the tunnel destroying the rail-road, having driven our guard away. The telegraph line stopped working north of Gallatin at about 5 this p. m.

J. C. VAN DUZER.

[Indorsement.]

HEADQUARTERS DEPARTMENT OF THE CUMBERLAND,
Nashville, December 14, 1864——11 p. m.

Respectfully referred to Maj. Gen. J. H. Wilson, commanding Cavalry Corps, Military Division of the Mississippi, with directions to instruct the officer in command of the cavalry detachment at and near Gallatin to collect as many of his men together as possible and ascertain the truth of the within report and all the facts in the case.

By command of Major-General Thomas:

ROBT. H. RAMSEY,
Assistant Adjutant-General.

NASHVILLE, *December 14, 1864——11 p. m.*

General THOMAS:

The line between Clarksville and Bowling Green is also cut, which severs connection with Louisville entirely for to-day. I will endeavor to have the Clarksville route re-established in the morning. Nothing further from tunnel.

J. C. VAN DUZER.

SPECIAL FIELD ⎱   HDQRS. DEPT. OF THE CUMBERLAND,
ORDERS, No. 342. ⎰   *Nashville, Tenn., December 14, 1864.*

As soon as the weather will admit of offensive operations the troops will move against the enemy's position in the following order:

First. Maj. Gen. A. J. Smith, commanding Detachment of the Army of the Tennessee, after forming his troops on and near the Hardin pike, in front of his present position, will make a vigorous assault on the enemy's left.

Second. Bvt. Maj. Gen. J. H. Wilson, commanding the Cavalry Corps, Military Division of the Mississippi, with three divisions, will move on and support General Smith's right, assist as far as possible in carrying the left of the enemy's position, and be in readiness to throw his force upon the enemy the moment a favorable opportunity occurs. Major-General Wilson will also send one division on the Charlotte pike to clear that road of the enemy and observe in the direction of Bell's Landing, to protect our right rear until the enemy's position is fairly turned, when it will join the main force.

Third. Brig. Gen. Th. J. Wood, commanding Fourth Army Corps, after leaving a strong skirmish line in his works from Laurens' Hill to his extreme right, will form the remainder of the Fourth Corps on the Hillsborough pike to support General Smith's left and operate on the left and rear of the enemy's advanced position on the Montgomery Hill.

Fourth. Maj. Gen. John M. Schofield, commanding Twenty-third Army Corps, will replace Brigadier-General Kimball's division, of the Fourth Corps, with his troops, and occupy the trenches from Fort Negley to Laurens' Hill with a strong skirmish line. He will mass the remainder of his force in front of the works and co-operate with General Wood, protecting the latter's left flank against an attack by the enemy.

Fifth. Maj. Gen. James B. Steedman, commanding District of the Etowah, will occupy the interior line in rear of his present position, stretching from the reservoir on the Cumberland River to Fort Negley, with a strong skirmish line, and mass the remainder of his force in his present position, to act according to the exigencies of the service during these operations.

Sixth. Brig. Gen. J. F. Miller, with the troops forming the garrison of Nashville, will occupy the interior line from the battery on Hill 210 to the extreme right, including the inclosed work on the Hyde's Ferry road.

Seventh. The quartermaster's troops, under command of Bvt. Brig. Gen. J. L. Donaldson, will, if necessary, be posted on the interior line from Fort Morton to the battery on Hill 210.

The troops occupying the interior line will be under the direction of Major-General Steedman, who is charged with the immediate defense of Nashville during the operations around the city.

Should the weather permit the troops will be formed in time to commence operations at 6 a. m., or as soon thereafter as practicable.

By command of Major-General Thomas:

WM. D. WHIPPLE,
Assistant Adjutant-General.

CONFIDENTIAL.]   HEADQUARTERS FOURTH ARMY CORPS,
Near Nashville, Tenn., December 15 [*14?*], *1864.*

Maj. Gen. GEORGE H. THOMAS,
Commanding, &c.:

GENERAL: A close examination and study of the enemy's position in front of the Fourth Corps during the past two days has led me to the conclusion that his line is continuous to the point we observed the day before yesterday in front of the hills near to General Smith's left. This opinion is sustained by Colonel Opdycke, who has spent much time under my orders in studying the enemy's front. If my conclusion in this respect be correct, I respectfully submit that it may be necessary to make some modifications of our plans with regard to the proposed attack on the enemy's lines; and with a view to a more full understanding of the necessary modifications, I would most respectfully suggest that a meeting of Generals Schofield, Smith, Wilson, and myself be ordered at your headquarters at such time as may suit your convenience. I make this suggestion at the instance of Generals Schofield and Smith, both of whom came to see me to-day. When we strike we must win.

I am, general, very respectfully, your obedient servant and friend,

TH. J. WOOD,
Brigadier-General, U. S. Volunteers, Commanding.

HEADQUARTERS,
December 14, 1864—10.30 a. m.

Major-General SCHOFIELD:

GENERAL: The major-general commanding directs that you make your preparations for a move as per previous arrangements. It is the desire of the major-general commanding to see you at his room this afternoon at 3 o'clock.

Very respectfully, your obedient servant,

ROBT. H. RAMSEY,
Assistant Adjutant-General.

(Same to Generals Wood, Smith, Steedman, and Wilson.)

HEADQUARTERS FOURTH ARMY CORPS,
Near Nashville, Tenn., December 14, 1864.

Orders of the day for Fourth Army Corps for to-morrow, December 15, 1864:

I. Reveille will be sounded at 4 a. m. The troops will get their breakfast, break up their camps, pack up everything, and be prepared to move at 6 a. m.

II. Brigadier-General Elliott, commanding Second Division, will move out by his right, taking the small road which passes by the right of his present position, form in echelon with General A. J. Smith's left, slightly refusing his own left, and, maintaining this relative position to General Smith's troops, will advance with them. When he moves out he will leave a strong line of skirmishers in his solid works.

III. Brigadier-General Kimball, commanding First Division, on being relieved by General Steedman, will move his division to the Hillsborough pike, inside of our lines, and by it through the lines, and form in echelon to General Elliott's left, slightly refusing his own left. He will maintain this position and advance with General Elliott.

IV. As soon as General Kimball's division has passed out of the works by the Hillsborough pike, General Beatty, commanding Third Division, will take up the movement, drawing out by his left, and will form in echelon to General Kimball's left. He will maintain this position and advance with General Kimball. He will also leave a strong line of skirmishers behind the solid works along his present position.

V. The pickets on post, being strengthened when in the judgment of division commanders it becomes necessary, will advance as a line of skirmishers to cover the movement. The formation of the troops will be in two lines—the first line deployed, the second line in close column by divisions, massed opposite the intervals in the front line. Each division commander will, so far as possible, hold one brigade in reserve. Five wagon-loads of ammunition, ten ambulances, and the wagons loaded with intrenching tools, will, as nearly as possible, follow immediately after each division; all remaining ammunition wagons, ambulances, and all other wagons, will remain inside of our present lines until further orders. One rifle battery will accompany the Second Division, and one battery of light 12-pounders will accompany each of the remaining divisions. The rest of the artillery of the corps will maintain its present position in the lines.

By command of Brigadier-General Wood:

J. S. FULLERTON,
Assistant Adjutant-General.

HEADQUARTERS ARMY OF THE OHIO,
December 14, 1864.

Capt. R. H. RAMSEY,
        Assistant Adjutant-General:

I will be ready to move as directed by the major-general commanding, and will call at the headquarters at 3 p. m.

J. M. SCHOFIELD,
Major-General.

HDQRS. THIRD DIVISION, TWENTY-THIRD ARMY CORPS,
Nashville, Tenn., December 14, 1864.

Lieut. A. W. BEIGHLE,
        Ambulance Corps:

LIEUTENANT: The command is ordered to move in the morning at 6 o'clock, and all trains are ordered to be parked until further orders in the vicinity of the Hillsborough pike, but the ambulances and ordnance trains will be parked so that they can move out first. Care will be taken not to obstruct the roads from left to right, as General Steedman's command will be moving in that direction about daylight.

By command of Brigadier-General Cox:

THEO. COX,
Captain and Assistant Adjutant-General.

SPECIAL ORDERS, }   HDQRS. THIRD DIV., 23D ARMY CORPS,
        No. 141.   {   *Nashville, Tenn., December 14, 1864.*

*   *   *   *   *   *   *

IV. All the tents will be struck and the troops of this command be moved back from the trenches far enough to cover them from the enemy's view by 6 a. m. to-morrow. Brigade commanders will select positions for thus massing their troops with a view of moving them under cover to the right of the Fourth Corps, but will make no further movement until further orders. The picket-line will be relieved and new picket-line established as usual. The artillery will be parked to the right and rear of Fort Morton by the hour above named. Baggage wagons will be parked, under the direction of the division quartermaster, in the vicinity of the Hillsborough pike and await further orders.

Ambulance and ordnance trains will park in the same vicinity, but be prepared to take the road first. Care will be taken not to obstruct the passage from left to right, as troops of General Steedman's command will be moving in that direction at or before daylight through the troops of this command, to relieve a portion of the Fourth Corps.

This order does not affect the One hundred and seventy-fifth Ohio Volunteer Infantry, which will remain in the fort, as now.

V. Col. C. C. Doolittle, chief of staff, is hereby assigned to the command of the First Brigade, Third Division, Twenty-third Army Corps, during the temporary absence of Brigadier-General Reilly.

By command of Brig. Gen. J. D. Cox:

THEO. COX,
Captain and Assistant Adjutant-General.

HEADQUARTERS DETACHMENT ARMY OF THE TENNESSEE,
December 14, 1864.

Brig. Gen. W. D. WHIPPLE,
Chief of Staff, Department of the Cumberland:

Everything unchanged in my front. The rebels opened a battery, in my front, of two guns, on a foraging party for hay, in front of my center, yesterday afternoon, but did no damage. They seem to be in more force on my right, but no material change.

A. J. SMITH,
Major-General.

HEADQUARTERS DETACHMENT ARMY OF THE TENNESSEE,
December 14, 1864.

Maj. Gen. G. H. THOMAS:

I will see you at 3 p. m., as desired, and will then answer your questions.

A. J. SMITH,
Major-General.

HEADQUARTERS DETACHMENT ARMY OF THE TENNESSEE,
Nashville, Tenn., December 14, 1864.

Brig. Gen. J. McARTHUR,
Commanding First Division:

I am directed by the major-general commanding to say that he wishes the men to be supplied with three days' rations in haversacks to-night (to include the 17th instant). In moving out to-morrow the ambulances and artillery only will move with the command. Camp and garrison equipage and baggage will be packed up and loaded ready to move when sent for. The command must be in readiness to move at 6 a. m. The men will be waked up at 4 a. m. to-morrow morning without reveille, and reveille will be beaten in each regiment at camp at 5 a. m.

I am, very respectfully, your obedient servant,

J. HOUGH,
Major and Assistant Adjutant-General.

(Same to Garrard and Moore.)

HDQRS. CAVALRY CORPS, MIL. DIV. OF THE MISSISSIPPI,
Nashville, December 14, 1864—11.40 p. m.

Captain RAMSEY,
    Assistant Adjutant-General:

CAPTAIN: The two telegrams* from Gallatin are received, but as the second is strongly confirmatory of the first, and there seems to be no doubt of the presence of the enemy on the road, I hesitate to collect the Fourth Ohio and the squadron at Gallatin unless the major-general commanding still wishes it. It seems to me the force under General McCook must be able to drive off Lyon, and that he will be after him before the troops scattered between here and Gallatin can do any good. Be good enough to inform me by return messenger whether I shall send any orders to the latter.

Very respectfully, your obedient servant,
                          J. H. WILSON,
                              Brevet Major-General.

[Indorsement.]

HEADQUARTERS DEPARTMENT OF THE CUMBERLAND,
                Nashville, December 14, 1864.

Respectfully returned to Major-General Wilson, commanding Cavalry Corps.

The major-general commanding is of the opinion that the force alluded to as on the railroad is not Lyon at all, but a party of guerrillas, which can be driven off by the squadron of cavalry now at Gallatin, with the troops ordered to be sent from Gallatin.

By command of Major-General Thomas:
                          ROBT. H. RAMSEY,
                              Assistant Adjutant-General.

HDQRS. CAVALRY CORPS, MIL. DIV. OF THE MISSISSIPPI,
        Nashville, Tenn., December 14, 1864—12 m.

COMMANDING OFFICER FOURTH OHIO CAVALRY,
                Near Gallatin:

You will concentrate all the cavalry you can, and join the infantry force from Gallatin, moving on the enemy who are on the railroad. Use the utmost expedition.

By order of Brevet Major-General Wilson:
                          A. J. ALEXANDER,
                              Lieutenant-Colonel and Chief of Staff.

SPECIAL FIELD ORDERS, ┐   HEADQUARTERS CAVALRY CORPS,
        No. 3.†   ┘   *Nashville, Tenn., December 14, 1864.*

The Cavalry Corps will be prepared to move on the enemy to-morrow at 6 a. m., in the following order:

I. The Fifth Division, Brigadier-General Hatch commanding, will debouch from the fortifications at or near the Hardin pike, and move with its right flank on the Hardin pike and its left flank con-

---

* See Gilfillan to Thomas, 10 p. m. and 10.40 p. m., p. 191.
† So in original, but recorded in order book as No. 6.

necting with the infantry of Major-General Smith. As soon as the rebel advance position is carried by General Smith, and its own front cleared of the enemy, it will swing to the left, endeavoring to envelope and take in reverse the enemy's left flank.

II. Croxton's brigade, of the First Division, will debouch near the Hardin pike by the dirt road between that and the Charlotte pike, and will move with his left flank connecting with Fifth Division and his right following the line of ridge between the Charlotte and Hardin pikes. After clearing the Hardin pike of any enemy that may be upon it, and crossing Richland Creek, it will conform in its movements to that of the Fifth Division.

III. The Sixth Division, Brigadier-General Johnson commanding, will move by the Charlotte pike, and clear that road of the enemy, pushing as far as Davidson's house, covering the right and rear of the entire movement from the enemy's left, communication being kept up with General Croxton by patrols or skirmishers, as may be found most convenient. The guns of the enemy on the river at Bell's Landing and the forces with them should be captured.

IV. The Seventh Division, Brigadier-General Knipe commanding, will be held in reserve between the Charlotte and Hardin pikes, ready to move in any direction that the exigencies of the action may demand. It will not debouch from the fortifications till they have been cleared and the success of the general movement determined.

V. The object of the entire operations of the cavalry is to clear the enemy from its immediate front, cover the right of the infantry, envelope the enemy's left flank, and, if possible, reach the Franklin pike somewhere in the vicinity of Brentwood. The greatest celerity of movement is therefore necessary. No wheels will accompany the troops except the artillery. As much forage should be carried on the horses as practicable and three days' rations for the men.

VI. The supply trains will move with the general trains of the army.

VII. Corps headquarters will be on the Hardin pike until the success of the movement is fully known, after which they will be with the Fifth Division.

By order of Brevet Major-General Wilson:

A. J. ALEXANDER,
Lieutenant-Colonel and Acting Chief of Staff.

GENERAL ORDERS, }   HEADQUARTERS CAVALRY CORPS,
              }   MILITARY DIVISION OF THE MISSISSIPPI,
No. 8.   }   *Nashville, Tenn., December 14, 1864.*

Until further orders the following-named officers will constitute the staff of the brevet major-general commanding; they will be obeyed and respected accordingly: Lieut. Col. A. J. Alexander, assistant adjutant-general, acting chief of staff; Maj. E. B. Beaumont, assistant adjutant-general; Maj. J. M. Young, Fifth Iowa Cavalry, provost-marshal; Maj. Francis Salter, U. S. Volunteers, medical director; Maj. William F. Cady, U. S. Volunteers, medical inspector; Capt. Levi T. Griffin, Fourth Michigan Cavalry, acting assistant adjutant-general; Capt. J. N. Andrews, aide-de-camp; Capt. G. H. Kneeland, Fourth Indiana Cavalry, acting aide-de-camp; Capt. W. W. Van Antwerp, Fourth Michigan Cavalry, acting aide-de-camp; Capt. M. M. Pool, acting aide-de-camp; Capt. E. B. Carling, chief quartermaster; Capt. J. C. Read, commissary of subsistence; Capt. L. M. Hosea, Sixteenth

U. S. Infantry, commissary of musters; Lieut. H. E. Noyes, acting assistant inspector-general; Lieut. Joseph A. Goddard, Fourth Ohio Cavalry, acting assistant quartermaster.

By command of Brevet Major-General Wilson:

E. B. BEAUMONT,
Major and Assistant Adjutant-General.

CIRCULAR.]   HDQRS. CAV. CORPS, MIL. DIV. OF THE MISS.,
Nashville, Tenn., December 14, 1864.

Commanders of divisions and detached brigades are requested to report at these headquarters (No. 24 High street) at 3 o'clock this afternoon.

By command of Brevet Major-General Wilson:

A. J. ALEXANDER,
Lieutenant-Colonel and Acting Chief of Staff.

GENERAL ORDERS, } HDQRS. FIFTH DIV., CAVALRY CORPS,
        MILITARY DIVISION OF THE MISSISSIPPI,
No. 7.   }   *Near Nashville, Tenn., December 14, 1864.*

I. This command will be ready to move at daylight to-morrow morning, with one day's rations and 100 rounds of ammunition in cartridge-box and on person.

II. The brigades will move in columns of regiments, with space between regiments sufficient to deploy in line dismounted, with the exception of one regiment mounted in column in rear of each brigade. The led horses will follow the brigades at a distance of 500 to 1,000 yards.

III. The left of the Second Brigade will move on the right of Maj. Gen. A. J. Smith's corps, conforming to the movements of the infantry line; the First Brigade on the right of the Second, conforming to the movements of the Second Brigade.

IV. Battery I, First Illinois Light Artillery, will move, where the road will allow it, on the left and rear of the Second Brigade. The Second Brigade will support the battery.

V. Brigade commanders will attack vigorously and push the enemy home wherever the attack commences, losing no opportunity for throwing their mounted regiments in on the charge wherever the opportunity offers.

VI. It being impossible to issue rations to-night, two days' rations will be loaded into wagons, and remain in camp ready to move at a moment's notice.

By order of Brig. Gen. Edward Hatch:

HERVEY A. COLVIN,
Adjutant Twelfth Tennessee Cavalry and Actg. Asst. Adjt. Gen.

HDQRS. CAVALRY CORPS, MIL. DIV. OF THE MISSISSIPPI,
Nashville, Tenn., December 14, 1864.
Brigadier-General UPTON,
        Cairo, Ill.:

By direction of brevet major-general commanding, I have the honor to report the following regiments as belonging to the Fourth Division:

Tenth Missouri Cavalry, Third Iowa Cavalry, Fourth Iowa Cavalry, Second New Jersey Cavalry, Seventh Indiana Cavalry, Sixth Tennessee Cavalry, Nineteenth Pennsylvania Cavalry.

I am, general, very respectfully, your obedient servant,

LEVI T. GRIFFIN,
Captain and Acting Assistant Adjutant-General.

HDQRS. CAVALRY CORPS, MIL. DIV. OF THE MISSISSIPPI,
Nashville, Tenn., December 14, 1864.

Brig. Gen. R. W. JOHNSON,
Commanding Sixth Division, Cavalry Corps:

GENERAL: I am instructed to inform you that Commodore Fitch will drop down in the morning and open on the rebel battery at Bell's Landing. This battery is opposite and near Davidson's house, as was supposed, and the general commanding thinks by moving with rapidity you can capture it.

Very respectfully, your obedient servant,

A. J. ALEXANDER,
Lieutenant-Colonel and Chief of Staff.

GALLATIN, *December 14, 1864—10 p. m.*

Maj. Gen. G. H. THOMAS:

The captain in charge of a party of Fourth Tennessee Cavalry sent up the river this morning has just reported that he met two of our scouts, who told him that a force of rebels, with artillery, is opposite Hunter's Point, about twelve miles above here, and they will probably attempt to cross.

JAMES GILFILLAN,
Colonel Eleventh Minnesota Infantry.

GALLATIN, *December 14, 1864—10.40 p. m.*

Major-General THOMAS:

Captain Buck, of my regiment, stationed at Buck Lodge, on the railroad, ten miles above here, reports that a force of about 200 rebel cavalry were, about 6 o'clock this evening, at Fountain Head, one mile and a half above his station, tearing up the track and destroying the telegraph.

JAS. GILFILLAN,
Colonel Eleventh Minnesota Infantry, Commanding.

NASHVILLE, *December 14, 1864—11 p. m.*

Col. JAMES GILFILLAN,
Gallatin:

What is the real state of affairs at the tunnel? It is reported Lyon is on the road breaking it up. Send as full and accurate report as you can obtain at once.

GEO. H. THOMAS,
Major-General, U. S. Volunteers, Commanding.

NASHVILLE, *December 14, 1864—11.10 p. m.*

Col. JAMES GILFILLAN,
    Eleventh Minnesota Infantry, Gallatin:

Your dispatch of this evening just received. Re-enforce the guard at the tunnel at once and hold that place. Have the squadron of cavalry collected together and sent to the threatened point as soon as possible.

GEO. H. THOMAS,
    Major-General, U. S. Volunteers, Commanding.

GALLATIN, *December 14, 1864—12 p. m.*

Major-General THOMAS,
    Commanding:

Have nothing further from the tunnel. Captain Buck sent a man through with a message to the effect that upon learning the presence of the enemy, he sent out a party, who ascertained that they numbered about 200 and that they were destroying the road. Whose command they were of he did not learn. The trains going up have been turned back. Am sending up all my disposable infantry force.

JAMES GILFILLAN,
    Colonel, Commanding.

BRIDGEPORT, *December 14, 1864.*

Captain FORD,
    Acting Assistant Adjutant-General:

Scouts that came in to-night report a company of forty rebels twelve miles from this place, on the south side of the river. They claim to be an independent organization, and are scouting the country. The defenses of this place will require considerable labor to put them in a defensible condition, and an additional force of from 300 to 500 would be desirable for the purpose of fatigue and garrison duty.

M. C. TAYLOR,
    Colonel, Commanding.

PADUCAH, KY., *December 14, 1864.*

Brig. Gen. WILLIAM D. WHIPPLE,
    Assistant Adjutant-General:

General Lyon took possession of Princeton, Ky., last night, plundered the place, and conscripted all he could, and is reported to be moving on Eddyville, Ky. This news is received from a resident of Princeton that escaped and has just arrived at Smithland. The four regiments of infantry have not arrived yet. Could I have the cavalry when they arrive, which would enable me to pursue him? Please answer.

S. MEREDITH,
    Brigadier-General.

NASHVILLE, *December 14, 1864—8 p. m.*
(Received 17th.)
Brig. Gen. S. MEREDITH,
Paducah:

Your dispatch of this date is received. I have a force of cavalry in pursuit of Lyon sufficient to destroy or capture his command, and I have only to desire you to make use of the three regiments infantry ordered to report to you in driving away the enemy's force working at Danville bridge, on the Tennessee River, and destroy their works, if possible; the regiments will then return to Paducah and come on to this place the first opportunity.

GEO. H. THOMAS,
Major-General, U. S. Volunteers, Commanding.

PADUCAH, KY., *December 14, 1864.*

Rear-Admiral S. P. LEE,
Clarksville, Tenn.:

ADMIRAL: Can you inform me about the movements of Lyon; has he crossed the river yet? Please answer.

S. MEREDITH,
Brigadier-General.

PADUCAH, KY., *December 14, 1864.*

Rear-Admiral S. P. LEE,
Clarksville, Tenn.:

ADMIRAL: Please allow Captain Smith and gun-boat Peosta to remain here. I would like to send him up the river on a reconnaissance. I am about to take the field against Lyon at Danville, and want to find out all particulars about his movements.

Respectfully,

S. MEREDITH,
Brigadier-General.

CLARKSVILLE, *December 14, 1864—6.15 p. m.*

Brig. Gen. S. MEREDITH:

Your two telegrams of this date just received. Lyon understood to be at Hopkinsville. Have no knowledge that he has recrossed the river. I now telegraph gun-boat Peosta to make the reconnaissance you wish, as far as practicable, though she is wanted to convoy on the Cumberland. Captain Smith will always comply with your request when not incompatible with the duty assigned him by myself or his division officers.

S. P. LEE,
Rear-Admiral, Commanding.

BOWLING GREEN, KY., *December 14, 1864.*

Capt. E. B. HARLAN,
    Assistant Adjutant-General, Louisville, Ky.:

Colonel Johnson reports all quiet at Russellville. Rebel's main force at Fairview, Christian County, Ky. Citizens report that Lyon is conscripting all the men he can get and taking all the horses and supplies that he can find.

S. P. LOVE,
Colonel, Commanding Second Brigade.

LOUISVILLE, *December 14, 1864.*

Major-General THOMAS,
    Commanding Army of the Cumberland:

SIR: In accordance with instructions of Special Orders, No. 343,* headquarters Department of the Missouri, signed Major-General Dodge, I have the honor to report my command, the Forty-seventh Regiment Illinois Infantry Volunteers, 226 strong, but 78 of which are armed, at this post, subject to your instructions.

I am, sir, very respectfully, your obedient servant,

EDWARD BONHAM,
First Lieutenant, Commanding Regiment.

NASHVILLE, *December 14, 1864—8 p. m.*

First Lieut. EDWARD BONHAM,
    Comdg. Forty-seventh Regt. Illinois Vols., Louisville, Ky.:

Report your command to General Ewing, at Louisville, for temporary assignment to duty at Bowling Green, for the protection of the bridge. Draw arms for the unarmed portion of the regiment at Louisville.

GEO. H. THOMAS,
Major-General, U. S. Volunteers, Commanding.

NASHVILLE, TENN., *December 15, 1864—9 p. m.*
(Received 11.25 p. m.)

Maj. Gen. H. W. HALLECK,
    Washington, D. C.:

I attacked the enemy's left this morning and drove it from the river, below the city, very nearly to the Franklin pike, a distance about eight miles. Have captured General Chalmers' headquarters and train, and a second train of about 20 wagons, with between 800 and 1,000 prisoners and 16 pieces of artillery. The troops behaved splendidly, all taking their share in assaulting and carrying the enemy's breast-works. I shall attack the enemy again to-morrow, if he stands to fight, and, if he retreats during the night, will pursue him, throwing a heavy cavalry force in his rear, to destroy his trains, if possible.

GEO. H. THOMAS,
Major-General, U. S. Volunteers, Commanding.

---

* See Vol. XLI, Part IV, p. 830.

WAR DEPARTMENT,
Washington, December 15, 1864—12 midnight.
(Sent 12.05 a. m. 16th.)

Major-General THOMAS,
  Nashville:

I rejoice in tendering to you and the gallant officers and soldiers of your command the thanks of this Department for the brilliant achievements of this day, and hope that it is the harbinger of a decisive victory, that will crown you and your army with honor and do much toward closing the war. We shall give you a hundred guns in the morning.

     EDWIN M. STANTON,
      Secretary of War.

WASHINGTON, D. C., *December 15, 1864—11.30 p. m.*

Major-General THOMAS,
  Nashville, Tenn.:

I was just on my way to Nashville, but receiving a dispatch from Van Duzer, detailing your splendid success of to-day, I shall go no farther. Push the enemy now, and give him no rest until he is entirely destroyed. Your army will cheerfully suffer many privations to break up Hood's army and render it useless for future operations. Do not stop for trains or supplies, but take them from the country, as the enemy have done. Much is now expected.

     U. S. GRANT,
      Lieutenant-General.

WASHINGTON, D. C., *December 15, 1864—11.45 p. m.*

Major-General THOMAS,
  Nashville, Tenn.:

Your dispatch of this evening just received.* I congratulate you and the army under your command for to-day's operations, and feel a conviction that to-morrow will add more fruits to your victory.

     U. S. GRANT,
      Lieutenant-General.

WASHINGTON CITY, *December 15, 1864—11.50 p. m.*

Brig. Gen. J. A. RAWLINS,
  City Point, Va.:

I send you dispatch just received from Nashville.* I shall not now go there. Will remain absent, however, until about Monday.

     U. S. GRANT,
      Lieutenant-General.

NASHVILLE, *December 15, 1864.*

Mrs. F. L. THOMAS,
  New York Hotel, New York:

We have whipped the enemy, taken many prisoners and considerable artillery.

     GEO. H. THOMAS,
     Major-General, U. S. Volunteers, Commanding.

---

* See Thomas to Halleck, 9 p. m., p. 194.

NASHVILLE, TENN., *December 15, 1864—10.30 p. m.*

(Received 11 p. m.)

Maj. T. T. ECKERT:

Our line advanced and engaged the rebel line at 9 this a. m. The line was formed thus: Steedman on the left; T. J. Wood, with the Fourth Corps, next; A. J. Smith next; with Cox, in reserve, next; and the cavalry, under Wilson, fighting dismounted, occupying the extreme right, aided by gun-boats on the river. The artillery practice has been fine, and at times the musketry firing continuous and heavy, and, though the casualties have been light, the results are very fair. The left occupies the same ground as at morning, but right has advanced five miles, driving enemy from river, from his intrenchments, from the range of hills on which his left rested, and forced back upon his right and center. His center pushed back from one to three miles, with loss, in all, of 17 guns and about 1,500 prisoners, and his whole line of earth-works, except about a mile on his extreme right, where no serious attempt was made to dislodge him. From our new line General Thomas expects to be able to drive the enemy at daylight east of the road to Franklin, and so open communication with our forces at Murfreesborough. The whole of Hood's army is here, except the cavalry and one division, which has been detached to threaten or attack Murfreesborough. The whole action of to-day was splendidly successful. The divisions commanded by General Kimball, of the Fourth Corps, by General Garrard, of the command under General A. J. Smith, and the cavalry division under General Knipe, were under my observation, and I have never seen better work. General Kimball's division carried two fortified positions by assault, with very slight loss, capturing at one point 400 prisoners and 6 guns. No doubt the other parts of the line did as well; I only speak of what I saw.

J. C. VAN DUZER.

CLARKSVILLE, *December 15, 1864.*

General THOMAS:

I sent two gun-boats at 4 o'clock this morning, accompanied by an army transport, and twenty men furnished by Colonel Smith, which destroyed about twenty of Lyon's canoes and skiffs, and brought away two artillery barges, found near Cumberland and in the creeks. None of burnt transports interfere with channel.

S. P. LEE,
Acting Rear-Admiral, &c.

CLARKSVILLE, *December 15, 1864—5.30 p. m.*

Major-General THOMAS:

Telegram just received from commanding officer Black Hawk, at Smithland, reports force of 900 rebels, with two guns, at Eddyville. Three gun-boats convoying transports from here had got off before it was received here. I have ordered an iron-clad and heavy gun-boats, just arrived at Mound City, from there to Eddyville, thence as far up as stage of water will allow.

S. P. LEE,
Acting Rear-Admiral, Commanding Mississippi Squadron.

CLARKSVILLE, *December 15, 1864—6 p. m.*

Maj. Gen. G. H. THOMAS:

Commanding officer of Black Hawk telegraphs that transport Nauga-tuck was fired into by artillery and infantry at Kelly's crossing, twelve miles below Eddyville, by Lyon's force, and that our scouts report eight guns at Kelly's crossing.

S. P. LEE,
Acting Rear-Admiral, Commanding Mississippi Squadron.

GENERAL THOMAS' HEADQUARTERS,
December 15, 1864.

Rear-Admiral S. P. LEE,
      Clarksville :

Your two dispatches received. We have turned the enemy's left; carried three or four redoubts and enemy's main line; captured 1,000 prisoners, 16 pieces of artillery, and 14 wagons—Chalmers' head-quarters train. Our loss probably 500 killed and wounded.

WM. D. WHIPPLE,
Brigadier-General and Chief of Staff.

CLARKSVILLE, *December 15, 1864—10 p. m.*

Brig. Gen. W. D. WHIPPLE:

Please accept my hearty thanks for your telegram informing me of General Thomas' important success, and make my warm congratula-tions to the general.

S. P. LEE,
Acting Rear-Admiral, Commanding Mississippi Squadron.

U. S. STEAMER MOOSE,
Robinson's Island, Cumberland River, December 15, 1864.

Brig. Gen. WILLIAM D. WHIPPLE,
      Chief of Staff, Army of the Cumberland:

GENERAL: I have the honor to acknowledge the receipt of your favor of this date, and am happy to state in reply that things here are working well. Our forces have captured the guns in the upper rebel battery on the river. There was another battery back from the river near the landing; I think the forces on shore and the Monitor silenced it, as we did not hear from it after dark. At dark I withdrew my boats, fearing they might by accident fire into our own men. I am just above the batteries to-night; will move at early daylight.

Very respectfully, your obedient servant,
LE ROY FITCH,
Lieut. Commander, Comdg. Tenth District, Mississippi Squadron.

HEADQUARTERS DETACHMENT ARMY OF THE TENNESSEE,
December 15, 1864.

Brig. Gen. THOMAS J. WOOD:

I will move out and form, my left resting on your right.

A. J. SMITH,
Major-General.

HEADQUARTERS FOURTH ARMY CORPS,
December 15, 1864—4.40 p. m.

Major-General THOMAS:

GENERAL: We assaulted a strong wooded hill on which the enemy's main line of works is. At 4.35 Kimball's division took the hill and works by assault. We have captured two brass pieces.

TH. J. WOOD,
Brigadier-General, Commanding.

———

HEADQUARTERS FIRST DIVISION, FOURTH ARMY CORPS,
December 15, 1864—11.40 p. m.

General THOMAS, or
General WOOD:

General Grose has just ridden along and in front of the picket-line of my own and Beatty's division, and reports that there is nothing in front of my left for half a mile nor in front of the center of the Third for three quarters of a mile. The enemy have, he thinks, more fires than usual, and they were in motion. He could not tell what they were doing.

NATHAN KIMBALL,
Brigadier-General.

———

HEADQUARTERS FOURTH ARMY CORPS,
Near Nashville, Tenn., December 15, 1864—11.20 p. m.

Orders of the day for the Fourth Army Corps for to-morrow, December 16, 1864:

If the enemy is in their front at daylight to-morrow morning division commanders will advance at that time, attack, and carry whatever may be before them. If the enemy retreats to-night we will follow them. General Elliott, commanding Second Division, will cross to the east of the Franklin pike, then move southward parallel to it. He will deploy two regiments, connect with skirmishers, and the rest of his division will move by flank. General Kimball will follow, then General Beatty. The batteries attached to each division to-day will accompany them to-morrow. Ten ambulances and five ammunition wagons will follow each division.

By order of Brigadier-General Wood:

J. S. FULLERTON,
Lieutenant-Colonel and Assistant Adjutant-General.

———

NASHVILLE, *December 15, 1864.*

Major-General THOMAS:

I am ready to move. Shall I attack the enemy's right, or await your orders? My reserves are now in the inner line.

A. J. SMITH,
Major-General.

———

HEADQUARTERS FOURTH CORPS,
December 15, 1864.

Major-General STEEDMAN:

Do you observe any movements of the enemy? Have you any news? Wood has carried the hill at Montgomery's house in fine style.

GEO. H. THOMAS,
Major-General, Commanding.

STEEDMAN'S HEADQUARTERS,
December 15, 1864—2.10 p. m.

Maj. Gen. G. H. THOMAS,
   Commanding:

I have been unable to discover any movements of the enemy since about 10 o'clock, when he moved what appeared 2,000 troops in rear of his line to our right. I pressed his right strongly, getting possession of the works constructed by my troops. I found him in strong force, with artillery in position. I retired my left, but still hold the works in my front on the right of the railroad. Hope all will go well.

JAMES B. STEEDMAN,
Major-General.

STEEDMAN'S HEADQUARTERS,
December 15, 1864—7.30 p. m.

Major-General THOMAS:

That part of my command used against the enemy to-day now occupy the works on right of railroad, made by my command, and nearly all the works on left of railroad, except one square fort built by enemy, which I completely command by occupying the building of Mr. Rains, which is loopholed. My advance posts report considerable force assembled on my front to-night. My loss is nearly 250.

J. B. STEEDMAN,
Major-General.

GENERAL THOMAS' HEADQUARTERS,
December 15, 1864.

Major-General STEEDMAN:

Yours received. Keep a good lookout for the enemy in the morning. Position at dark: Two divisions Fourth Army Corps, Twenty-third Army Corps, General A. J. Smith's troops, and Hatch's cavalry to left and rear of enemy, from Granny White pike to Brentwood range of hills. We hold rebel main line; have captured a thousand prisoners, 16 pieces of artillery, 14 wagons, Chalmers' headquarters train.

WM. D. WHIPPLE,
Brigadier-General.

DECEMBER 15, 1864.

Maj. S. B. MOE,
   Assistant Adjutant-General:

The enemy seem to be massing a force about three-quarters of a mile on my right in the woods. They can be enfiladed by the guns of Fort Negley. I think a strong skirmish line should be kept on the right and left of the Nolensville pike to watch their movements.

Respectfully, &c.,

CHAS. R. THOMPSON,
Colonel, Commanding, &c.

Hdqrs. Cavalry Corps, Mil. Div. of the Mississippi,
December 15, 1864.
Brigadier-General WHIPPLE,
  Assistant Adjutant-General:

GENERAL: I have driven in the enemy's skirmish line, after a sharp skirmish, and am advancing rapidly.

Very respectfully, &c.,

J. H. WILSON,
Brevet Major-General, Commanding.

———

HEADQUARTERS DEPARTMENT OF THE CUMBERLAND,
December 15, 1864—12.20 p. m.
General WILSON,
  Commanding Cavalry:

GENERAL: Your dispatch received. The general commanding desires you to secure General Smith's right well by a strong body of cavalry, and then crowd the enemy as much as possible. Send word to General Johnson to guard our right rear well.

Very respectfully,

HENRY STONE,
Assistant Adjutant-General.

———

Hdqrs. Cavalry Corps, Mil. Div. of the Mississippi,
December 15, 1864.
Brigadier-General WHIPPLE,
  Chief of Staff:

GENERAL: General Hatch's left is at Henry Compton's house, between Hardin and Hillsborough pikes. General Hood's headquarters are at John Overton's, on the Franklin pike. General Chalmers' headquarters are at General Hardin's; General Marshall's, at Felix Compton's, between Granny White and Hillsborough pikes. Nothing but cavalry in our front. The infantry were at Felix Compton's house and to the left.

J. H. WILSON,
Brevet Major-General.

———

Hdqrs. Cavalry Corps, Mil. Div. of the Miss.,
  Hardin Pike, Four Miles from Nashville,
  December 15, 1864—1.10 p. m.
Brig. Gen. W. D. WHIPPLE,
  Chief of Staff:

A part of Hatch's division has captured a wagon train of 14 wagons and about 20 prisoners. Johnson seems to be getting along well, though the enemy were strongly posted. I have directed Hatch to move by Williams' house, on south side of Richland Creek, toward Hillsborough pike, striking it six or seven miles from the city. Our prisoners are from Chalmers' division, whose headquarters are, or were, at Hardin's house this morning.

J. H. WILSON,
Brevet Major-General.

HEADQUARTERS ARMY OF THE CUMBERLAND,
December 15, 1864—2.05 p. m.

Brevet Major-General WILSON,
    Comdg. Cavalry Corps, Military Division of the Mississippi:

If you are able to strike the Hillsborough pike, six or seven miles from the city, you will be able to turn the enemy's left completely, and, to insure that as much as possible, I have directed General Schofield to put his corps on the right of General Smith's command. Wood connects with General Smith's left, and still has a considerable force in reserve. If the Hillsborough pike can be opened, we can strike the enemy a severe blow. I am very much gratified with the success all along the line. Push as far as you can, and get possession of the Hillsborough pike, if possible, but do not run the risk of an attack in flank in the morning.

GEO. H. THOMAS,
Major-General, U. S. Volunteers, Commanding.

I can see a large wagon train of the enemy's moving to their right. If you can get possession of it at Brentwood to-morrow you will do a good thing.

GEO. H. THOMAS,
Major-General, U. S. Volunteers, Commanding.

BRAGG SIGNAL STATION, *December 15, 1864.*

General WILSON:

The infantry is driving the rebels on the left. If you need infantry I can send some. Wood has possession of the Montgomery house. I believe Johnson has carried the battery on the Charlotte pike; I have seen troops leaving there.

THOMAS.

HDQRS. CAVALRY CORPS, MIL. DIV. OF THE MISSISSIPPI,
Compton's House, December 15, 1864—7 p. m.

Brigadier-General WHIPPLE,
    Assistant Adjutant-General:

GENERAL: I have the honor to inform you, for the information of the major-general commanding, that General Hatch has just reported that he captured to-day 2 redoubts and 13 guns and 300 or 400 prisoners. He also reports that he compelled the enemy to abandon a large number of small-arms, which are now lying on the ground. He also captured about 40 wagons, principally ammunition wagons, and about 80 beef-cattle. General Hatch says the enemy were very much demoralized, and that he drove them from the large hill they occupied when the major-general commanding left the ground.

Very respectfully, your obedient servant,

J. H. WILSON,
Brevet Major-General, Commanding.

HDQRS. CAVALRY CORPS, MIL. DIV. OF THE MISSISSIPPI,
            Compton's House, December 15, 1864—7 p. m.
Brigadier-General WHIPPLE,
        Assistant Adjutant-General:

GENERAL: Prisoners just taken state that Forrest, with three divisions of cavalry and Cheatham's division of infantry, was at Murfreesborough. Chalmers' division of cavalry and one brigade of infantry were on the extreme right. I will endeavor to dispose of them to-morrow with Johnson's and Croxton's forces.

Very respectfully, your obedient servant,
                    J. H. WILSON,
                Brevet Major-General, Commanding.

HEADQUARTERS DEPARTMENT OF THE CUMBERLAND,
            Nashville, Tenn., December 15, 1864.
Maj. Gen. J. H. WILSON,
        Comdg. Cavalry Corps, Military Division of the Mississippi:

GENERAL: I am directed by the major-general commanding to say to you that you will remain in your present position until it is satisfactorily known whether the enemy will fight or retreat. In case he retreats you will move your command on the Hillsborough pike across the Harpeth, and then take the most direct road or roads to the Franklin pike, and endeavor to capture or destroy the enemy's trains in their rear.

I have the honor to be, general, very respectfully, your obedient servant,

                    ROBT. H. RAMSEY,
                Assistant Adjutant-General.

NASHVILLE, TENN., *December 15, 1864.*
Brig. Gen. E. M. McCOOK,
        Commanding Division of Cavalry, Russellville:

(To be forwarded.)
Your requisition for ammunition only reached here this evening. It will be filled and go in the morning. We have driven the enemy from all his positions on our right, captured 16 guns, 1,000 prisoners, General Chalmers' headquarters, a train of 40 wagons, large numbers of small-arms, and 80 beef-cattle. We carried every redoubt we assaulted. Push Lyon to the wall.

By command of General Thomas:
                    HENRY STONE,
                Assistant Adjutant-General.

HDQRS. CAVALRY CORPS, MIL. DIV. OF THE MISSISSIPPI,
        Near Hardin Pike, December 15, 1864—12.15 p. m.
Brig. Gen. J. T. CROXTON,
        Commanding First Brigade, First Division:

GENERAL: The brevet major-general commanding desires you, should the enemy still remain in the front of General Johnson, to swing in to the right and try to cut them off. After this is accomplished, or should the enemy have withdrawn, he desires you to push forward rapidly and connect with General Hatch on your left.

Respectfully, your obedient servant,

A. J. ALEXANDER,
Chief of Staff.

HDQRS. CAVALRY CORPS, MIL. DIV. OF THE MISSISSIPPI,
December 15, 1864.

Brigadier-General CROXTON,
Commanding First Brigade, First Division :

GENERAL: It is not absolutely necessary for you to support General Johnson. Move your command to Williams' farm and join on to General Hatch's right. Everything thus far has and is still going on handsomely. General Thomas expresses himself well satisfied with the result so far. Cross the Hardin and Hillsborough pikes and push along on the right of General Hatch as rapidly as possible.

By command of Brevet Major-General Wilson:

E. B. BEAUMONT,
Major and Assistant Adjutant-General.

HDQRS. CAVALRY CORPS, MIL. DIV. OF THE MISSISSIPPI,
December 15, 1864—5 o'clock.

Brig. Gen. J. T. CROXTON,
Commanding First Brigade, First Division Cavalry :

The general commanding desires you to camp on the Hillsborough pike to-night at the nearest point to him, and send a staff officer back with the teams to report.

Very respectfully,

A. J. ALEXANDER,
Lieutenant-Colonel and Chief of Staff.

HDQRS. CAVALRY CORPS, MIL. DIV. OF THE MISSISSIPPI,
Compton's House, December 15, 1864—7 p. m.

Brig. Gen. J. T. CROXTON,
Commanding First Brigade, First Division:

GENERAL: The brevet major-general commanding desires you to maintain your position on the Hardin pike until morning, and then attack the enemy or drive him off, if possible. If you have not force enough, call on General Johnson for re-enforcements. Ector's brigade of infantry and Chalmers' division of cavalry were all that was on the river, and should be disposed of to-morrow. General Hatch captured 2 redoubts, 13 guns, 300 prisoners, 40 wagons, 30 head of cattle, and a large number of small-arms.

Very respectfully, your obedient servant,

A. J. ALEXANDER,
Lieutenant-Colonel and Chief of Staff.

HEADQUARTERS SECOND BRIGADE, FOURTH DIVISION,
Memphis, Tenn., December 15, 1864.

Lieutenant NOYES,
Second U. S. Cavalry, Nashville, Tenn.:

LIEUTENANT: I had expected to see you before this, but circumstances over which I had no control have detained here this detachment of my command. The day on which Major-General Dana arrived here I procured, after much solicitation, an order from Major-General Washburn for the embarkation of my troops. General Dana, arriving in the evening (7th), countermanded the order. Upon my representing the condition of the command, he said we might embark; meantime one regiment would have been in Cairo. On the 8th Major-General Dana said he would telegraph General Halleck, Chief of Staff, that he could not execute orders just received from him, unless the detachments of my command in Missouri were sent here. As he then had his dispatch ready I asked to be allowed to go to Cairo and there see the other portion of my troops, while I would thus be able to learn early what the final disposition would be. General Halleck directed troops in Missouri to proceed to Nashville. I then came here to urge the immediate shipment of these parts of regiments. Major-General Dana will not allow them to leave until after the return of an expedition to the Mobile and Ohio Railroad, in which we are to take part. I do not know by what authority we are kept, but do know that my whole command is suffering very much by this long-continued separation. I sincerely hope Major-General Wilson will cause this portion to be brought to Nashville at once. I am powerless here, or anywhere, in this matter; but had my efforts here been properly seconded by Brigadier-General Grierson, I am perfectly confident that we should now be in Nashville. I am not complaining of General Grierson, or of any one, but I do not hesitate to say that if the affairs and condition of my command could be seen by others as by myself, there would have been a different result. Lieutenant-Colonel Benteen has met with a very serious accident on the Maria, and I'm afraid some of his command will be delayed by the ice in Mississippi River. I do not know the cause of his delay, not having had any communication from him since the 3d instant. I write this communication as a private one, but hold myself ready to be called upon for sustaining every sentence. Will you please have this delay of my command properly understood? Of course I am debarred from any communication direct with Major-General Wilson.

Very truly, yours,

E. F. WINSLOW,
Colonel Fourth Iowa Cavalry, Commanding.

P. S.—I take about 1,000 men on the contemplated expedition.

HEADQUARTERS FIFTH DIVISION, CAVALRY CORPS,
In the Field, December 15, 1864—4.30 o'clock.

Major-General WILSON,
Commanding Cavalry Corps:

GENERAL: I have taken three more brass rifled guns and four wagons.

Very respectfully, your obedient servant,

EDWARD HATCH,
Brigadier-General, Commanding Fifth Division.

NEAR NASHVILLE, *December 15, 1864—9.55 a. m.*
Bvt. Maj. Gen. J. H. WILSON,
 Comdg. Cavalry Corps, Military Division of the Mississippi:

GENERAL: General Johnson's forces are not engaged; it is General McArthur, with two brigades of infantry. General J. thinks he can take the position now occupied by the enemy when he is ordered to move, and will try to take the battery.

I am, very respectfully, your obedient servant,
     G. H. KNEELAND,
    Captain and Acting Aide-de-Camp.

   SIX MILES FROM NASHVILLE, *December 15, 1864.*
Major-General WILSON,
 Comdg. Cavalry Corps, Military Division of the Mississippi:

GENERAL: General Johnson's command is now six miles from N[ash-ville] on the C[harlotte] pike. They have pressed the enemy back on what seems to be a strong line, but I think Colonel Harrison will push them out in a short time (as soon as he gets his brigade in position). They did not leave their guns in the position occupied by them this morning hardly long enough for General J. to get them.

I am, very respectfully, your obedient servant,
     G. H. KNEELAND,
    Captain and Acting Aide-de-Camp.

HDQRS. CAVALRY CORPS, MIL. DIV. OF THE MISSISSIPPI,
     December 15, 1864—12 m.
Brig. Gen. R. W. JOHNSON,
 Commanding Sixth Division:

GENERAL: The major-general commanding directs that you push forward with the utmost rapidity. Hatch is far in advance, and as you will have so [much] farther to march it will take the utmost exertion to keep up. The general would like you to communicate frequently with him.

Very respectfully, your obedient servant,
     A. J. ALEXANDER,
    Lieutenant-Colonel and Chief of Staff.

     DECEMBER 15, 1864—1 p. m.
General WILSON,
 Commanding Cavalry Corps:

GENERAL: The enemy has been driven from the creek, the hills on south bank occupied, and we are driving them handsomely through the valley beyond. Prisoners taken report Chalmers' division in our front. Our advance is slow, but I think my portion of the line is as far advanced as any portion of the cavalry line at this time. We did not capture the guns for reasons which I can fully explain to you at another time.

Respectfully,
     R. W. JOHNSON,
     Brigadier-General.

DECEMBER 15, 1864—2.15 p. m.

General WILSON,
    Commanding Cavalry Corps:

At Widow Bass', one mile from Davidson's. Rebs seem to have turned to left at Davidson's. Will leave pike at that point if rebs have all gone in that direction.

        Respectfully,
                        R. W. JOHNSON,
                            Brigadier-General.

DECEMBER 15, 1864—3.15 p. m.

[General WILSON:]

GENERAL: Dispatch received. We are safe from any attack from our right or rear. My right rests on the river. The rebs have chosen a good position, which was charged by the Seventh Ohio, which met with some loss and accomplished nothing. We have two rebel guns in a pocket, and hope to secure them. My only concern is with reference to my left. Croxton does not keep up. I will push everything, and hope to come up to your expectation.

        Respectfully,
                        R. W. JOHNSON,
                            Brigadier-General.

HDQRS. CAVALRY CORPS, MIL. DIV. OF THE MISSISSIPPI,
                        December 15, 1864.

Brigadier-General JOHNSON,
    Commanding Sixth Division Cavalry:

GENERAL: Your dispatch is received. General Hatch has also met a portion of Chalmers' command, and captured his headquarters train and some prisoners. Push the enemy as vigorously as possible. Everything is going on handsomely on the left. The very moment you have reached Davidson's house and cleared the country, swing in with your mounted brigade, and as much of the dismounted brigade as possible, toward Brentwood. General Knipe will be placed on Hatch's right, and a strong effort be made for the Hillsborough and Franklin pike, so as to take the enemy in rear, if possible. I have just had a note from General Thomas expressive of great satisfaction of the result so far. General Wood has carried the Montgomery house intrenchments, and still has men in reserve. Communicate with me frequently any information of importance you may obtain, particularly with reference to whatever may indicate a movement against our right and rear. All we want is to feel safe, and then we will push ahead.

By command of Brevet Major-General Wilson:
                        E. B. BEAUMONT,
                    Major and Assistant Adjutant-General.

HDQRS. CAVALRY CORPS, MIL. DIV. OF THE MISSISSIPPI,
        Compton's House, December 15, 1864—7 p. m.

Brig. Gen. R. W. JOHNSON,
    Commanding Sixth Division:

GENERAL: I am directed to inform you that General Hatch captured to-day 2 redoubts, 13 guns, 300 prisoners, 40 wagons, 80 beef-cattle, and a large amount of small-arms. The Fifth and Seventh Divisions will move at 3 a. m. to-morrow on Franklin by the Hillsborough pike. Chalmers' division and Ector's brigade of infantry are in your vicinity, and the brevet major-general commanding desires you, in conjunction with General Croxton, to attack him early in the morning, say 3 or 4 o'clock, and drive him across the Harpeth River, protecting our right and covering the city. The general desires you to push the enemy with the utmost vigor.

I have the honor to be, very respectfully, your obedient servant,

A. J. ALEXANDER,
Chief of Staff.

HEADQUARTERS SEVENTH DIVISION, CAVALRY CORPS,
MILITARY DIVISION OF THE MISSISSIPPI,
Nashville, Tenn., December 15, 1864.

Brevet Major-General WILSON:

GENERAL: I have the honor to report that a prisoner taken by my command states that General Cheatham has moved to the left, his left resting about half a mile from the junction of this road and the Granny White pike, and further, that their wagon trains are passing back on the Franklin pike.

I am, general, very respectfully, your obedient servant,

JOS. F. KNIPE,
Brigadier-General.

(Forwarded to Major-General Thomas.)

GALLATIN, *December 15, 1864—4 a. m.*

Major-General THOMAS,
Commanding:

Lieutenant-Colonel Ball, whom I sent with re-enforcements to the tunnel, reports that Captain Buck went out and drove off the rebels, who appear not to have been so numerous as first supposed. They did but little damage, beyond breaking the telegraph and burning a pile of cordwood. I don't think they are Lyon's men. A Captain Rickman, of Forrest's command, has had for the past two or three weeks some forty or fifty soldiers scattered about through the country north of here, who occasionally get together and make a dash at the road or at a drove of cattle or horses. I think they are the men who made the attack last night. Colonel Ball says that trains can run in the morning.

JAMES GILFILLAN,
Colonel Eleventh Minnesota Infantry.

GALLATIN, *December 15, 1864.*

Capt. HENRY STONE,
Assistant Adjutant-General:

I sent the cavalry back to their original positions this morning.

JAMES GILFILLAN,
Colonel Eleventh Minnesota Infantry.

CLARKSVILLE, *December 15, 1864.*

Brigadier-General WHIPPLE:

Courier has arrived with countersign and papers. Train left this a. m. with new bridge for Hampton's Station. Lyon still at Hopkinsville.

A. A. SMITH,
Colonel, Commanding.

NASHVILLE, *December 15, 1864.*

Brig. Gen. J. M. BRANNAN,
Chattanooga:

We have turned the enemy's left; carried three or four redouts and main line; captured 1,000 prisoners, 16 guns, and 14 wagons—Chalmers' headquarters train. Our loss probably 500.

WM. D. WHIPPLE,
Brigadier-General.

NASHVILLE, *December 15, 1864.*

Brig. Gen. J. M. BRANNAN,
Chattanooga:

Colonel Cotter is on duty here with General Steedman. We carried every point held by the enemy to-day on the right; captured 30 cannon, 40 to 50 wagons, and 1,000 prisoners.

HENRY STONE,
Captain and Assistant Adjutant-General.

PADUCAH, *December 15, 1864.*

Brig. Gen. W. D. WHIPPLE:

GENERAL: The steamer Naugatuck, just arrived at Smithland, reports being fired into twelve miles this side of Eddyville, at Kelly's crossing, by artillery and musketry. Lyon is reported to have captured Princeton, Ky., and Eddyville, and commands the river at Kelly's crossing with eight pieces of artillery. The four regiments of infantry have not arrived at Cairo yet.

S. MEREDITH,
Brigadier-General, Commanding.

NASHVILLE, TENN., *December 15, 1864.*

Brig. Gen. S. MEREDITH,
Paducah:

Your dispatch of this day is received. I was under the impression that the infantry regiments were already at Cairo. You can only wait their arrival at Paducah, when you will make use of them, as heretofore directed.

GEO. H. THOMAS,
Major-General, U. S. Volunteers, Commanding.

PADUCAH, KY., *December 15, 1864.*

Capt. J. BATES DICKSON,
    Assistant Adjutant-General, Lexington, Ky.:

CAPTAIN: The steamer Naugatuck, just arrived at Smithland, reports being fired into by artillery and musketry twelve miles this side of Eddyville. Lyon has captured Princeton, Ky., and Eddyville, and commands the river at Kelly's crossing with eight pieces of artillery. I have telegraphed to General Dodge, at Saint Louis, and he has no force to assist me. I have also telegraphed to General Thomas, at Nashville. General Dodge has sent his troops to Nashville. I have no force here to take the field against Lyon, as you know. He has not touched my district yet, but if I had sufficient force I would move against him. If you can possibly render me any assistance to enable me to do so, please answer.

S. MEREDITH,
    Brigadier-General.

SMITHLAND, *December 15, 1864.*

Capt. JAMES GRAHAM,
    Assistant Adjutant-General:

Captain Lawrence, of the Seventeenth Kentucky Cavalry, has returned; reports going within nine miles of Eddyville, this side of the river. A portion of Lyon's force is across the river. Captain Flye, commanding gun-boat at this post, has furnished me with two 12-pounder howitzers and men to work them. I am now taking them to the fort, and, when mounted, I am ready for the enemy, if they are disposed to come. Send Captain Bush, Forty-eighth Kentucky, back, with his arms and ammunition, as soon as possible. Received your dispatch sending re-enforcement.

HENRY P. REED,
    Captain, Commanding Post.

SMITHLAND, *December 15, 1864.*

Capt. JAMES GRAHAM,
    Assistant Adjutant-General:

The steamer Naugatuck has just arrived. She reports being fired into this 2 a. m., twelve miles this side of Eddyville, at Kelly's Crossing, by artillery and musketry. One shot passed through her smoke stack and one through the pilot-house. Lyon is reported to have eight pieces of artillery on the river at that place.

H. P. REED,
    Captain, Commanding Post.

[DECEMBER 15, 1864.—For Dodge to Halleck, explaining delay in forwarding troops to Thomas, &c., see Vol. XLI, Part IV, p. 865.]

14 R R—VOL XLV, PT II

SAINT LOUIS, *December 15, 1864—10.20 a. m.*

Maj. Gen. E. UPTON,
   Louisville, Ky.:

A portion of Benteen's brigade that was caught in the ice below here has been taken off of boats, and is moving by rail to Cairo and Smithland; also those on the boat that blew up. All others have gone.

             G. M. DODGE,
                Major-General.

WASHINGTON, D. C., *December 16, 1864.*
          (Sent 11.25 a. m.)

Major-General THOMAS,
   Nashville, Tenn.:

Please accept for yourself, officers, and men the nation's thanks for your good work of yesterday. You made a magnificent beginning. A grand consummation is within your easy reach. Do not let it slip.

              A. LINCOLN.

HEADQUARTERS DEPARTMENT OF THE CUMBERLAND,
  Eight Miles from Nashville, December 16, 1864—6 p. m.
    (Received Washington 5.30 a. m. 17th.)

The PRESIDENT OF THE UNITED STATES,
Hon. E. M. STANTON,
Lieut. Gen. U. S. GRANT, and
Governor ANDREW JOHNSON, *Nashville:*

This army thanks you for your approbation of its conduct yesterday, and to assure you that it is not misplaced. I have the honor to report that the enemy has been pressed at all points to-day on his line of retreat to the Brentwood Hills, and Brigadier-General Hatch, of Wilson's corps of cavalry, on the right, turned the enemy's left, and captured a large number of prisoners, number not yet reported. Major-General Schofield's troops, next on the left of cavalry, carried several heights, captured many prisoners and six pieces of artillery. Brevet Major-General Smith, next on left of Major-General Schofield, carried the salient point of the enemy's line with McMillen's brigade, of McArthur's division, capturing 16 pieces of artillery, 2 brigadier-generals, and about 2,000 prisoners. Brigadier-General Garrard's division, of Smith's command, next on the left of McArthur's division, carried the enemy's intrenchments, capturing all the artillery and troops of the enemy on the line. Brigadier-General Wood's corps, on the Franklin pike, took up the assault, carrying the enemy's intrenchments in his front, captured 8 pieces of artillery, something over 600 prisoners, and drove the enemy within one mile of the Brentwood Pass. Major-General Steedman, commanding detachments of the different armies of the Military Division of the Mississippi, most nobly supported General Wood's left, and bore a most honorable part in the operations of the day. I have ordered the pursuit to be continued in the morning at daylight, although the troops are very much fatigued. The greatest enthusiasm prevails. I must not forget to report the operations of Brigadier-General Johnson, in successfully driving the enemy, with the co-operation of the gun-boats, under Lieutenant-Commander Fitch, from their established batteries on the

Cumberland River below the city of Nashville, and of the services of Brigadier-General Croxton's brigade, in covering and relieving our right and rear, in the operations of yesterday and to-day. Although I have no report of the number of prisoners captured by Johnson's and Croxton's commands, I know they have made a large number. I am glad to be able to state that the number of prisoners captured yesterday greatly exceeds the number reported by me last evening. The woods, fields, and intrenchments are strewn with the enemy's small-arms, abandoned in their retreat. In conclusion, I am happy to state that all this has been effected with but a very small loss to us. Our loss does not probably exceed 3,000;* very few killed.

GEO. H. THOMAS,
Major-General, U. S. Volunteers, Commanding.

[DECEMBER 16, 1864.—For General Thomas' congratulatory orders, see Part I, p. 50.]

CITY POINT, VA., December 16, 1864.

Lieut. Gen. U. S. GRANT,
    Washington, D. C.:

Richmond Dispatch of to-day, after fully confirming the previous reports of the capture of Bristol, states that—

The enemy then advanced up the railroad toward Abingdon, which we presume fell into their hands, though we have no information of the fact. The next we hear of them they had at 9 o'clock yesterday morning pounced down on Glade Spring, a depot on the railroad thirteen miles this side of Abingdon, taking every one there by surprise, and capturing of all the railroad employés, except one, who managed to escape to tell the tale. At last accounts the enemy were pushing up the railroad in the direction of Marion, which is twenty-seven miles on this side of Abingdon. This is a raid in Breckinridge's rear. The raiders, leaving his forces somewhere in the neighborhood of Knoxville, came up the north side of the Holston River, and crossed over to Bristol. It is probable the raiders separated, one party proceeding to Bristol, and the other to Abingdon. If unchecked, it is likely they will come up the railroad even as far as Salem, and thence escape to Kanawha by the route followed by Hunter last summer. It is unknown who is in command of this expedition, but it looks very much like some of Stoneman's galloping work. None of the dispatches received say anything about Saltville. If it is unprotected, it has doubtless been visited by the enemy; if, however, there were any troops there, the Yankees were apt to fight shy of it, and confine their operations to the railroad.

THE BATTLE OF FRANKLIN.

General Hood's official report of the battle of Franklin has at last been received. It will be seen that our reported extraordinary loss of general officers is but too true. The following is General Hood's dispatch:

"HEADQUARTERS ARMY OF TENNESSEE,
"Six Miles from Nashville, Tenn., December 3, 1864. (Via Mobile 9th.)

"Hon. J. A. SEDDON:

"About 4 p. m. November 30 we attacked the enemy at Franklin, and drove them from their center line of temporary works into the inner lines, which they evacuated during the night, leaving their dead and wounded in our possession, and retired to Nashville, closely followed by our cavalry. We captured 7 stand of colors and

---

*As received in the War Department this read 300, and was so repeated in Stanton's dispatches to Dix and others. Corrected in Stanton to Dix, 10 p. m. 17th, p. 228.

about 1,000 prisoners. Our troops fought with great gallantry. We have to lament the loss of many gallant officers and brave men. Major-General Cleburne, Brigadier-Generals John Adams, Gist, Strahl, and Granbury were killed; Maj. Gen. John C. Brown and Brigadier-Generals Carter, Manigault, Quarles, Cockrell, and Scott were wounded; Brigadier-General Gordon was captured.

"J. B. HOOD,
"General."

A subsequent telegram from General Hood says that our loss of officers was excessively large in proportion to the loss of men.

FROM GEORGIA—FORT M'ALLISTER TAKEN BY SHERMAN.

Official intelligence was received yesterday that the enemy on Wednesday carried Fort McAllister by storm. The garrison of the fort consisted of 150 men. Fort McAllister is on the Ogeechee, fifteen miles southwest of Savannah, at the point where the river is crossed by the Savannah, Albany and Gulf Railroad; it is about six miles from the Ossabaw Sound. The capture of this position puts Sherman in communication with the Yankee fleet. Without attempting any military criticism, we cannot withhold the opinion that the exposing of 100 men to the assault of Sherman's whole army was a piece of extravagance that our present military resources do not seem to warrant.

The Examiner has the following:

Fort McAllister commands the entrance to Ogeechee River, and has prevented the enemy heretofore from ascending the river. We believe there are other works farther up the stream which would render the navigation of the stream by the enemy extremely uncomfortable. The fall of Fort McAllister does not, by any means, involve the loss of Savannah, but will necessitate the re-enforcement of the troops defending the city. * * * At Glade Spring the enemy captured an engine and fourteen flats, with some railroad hands. On these a party of men were mounted and sent up the road toward Marion, and a dispatch from the operator at that place on yesterday tells us that they were, at 2 o'clock, within a mile of that place. Their object is easily divined: it is to burn the bridge over the Holston and break the road, to prevent troops from being sent down the line by steam to re-enforce Saltville. To Saltville the main body will undoubtedly go, in all human probability has already gone. There are some fortifications at Saltville and some reserves; what numbers we do not know. If these can check them by any sacrifice, re-enforcements will soon put the place out of danger. At present it is certainly in very great danger.

JNO. A. RAWLINS,
Brigadier-General and Chief of Staff.

CITY POINT, VA., *December 16, 1864.*

Lieut. Gen. U. S. GRANT,
Washington, D. C. :

If you have any further news of General Thomas' success will you please send it, as it inspires the army here with great enthusiasm.

JNO. A. RAWLINS,
Brigadier-General and Chief of Staff.

[DECEMBER 16, 1864.—For Sherman to Grant, referring to Thomas' operations in Tennessee, see Vol. XLIV, p. 728.]

HEADQUARTERS ARMY OF THE POTOMAC,
December 16, 1864—10 a. m.
(Sent 10.15 a. m.)

Brigadier-General RAWLINS:

Your dispatch announcing General Thomas' success has been received with great satisfaction, as the situation of affairs at Nashville was such as to afford cause for anxiety. I had every confidence in the judgment and high soldierly qualities of General Thomas, and am truly rejoiced to hear of his brilliant success.

GEO. G. MEADE,
Major-General.

CLARKSVILLE, TENN., *December 16, 1864—10 a. m.*
(Received 11.10 a. m.)

Hon. GIDEON WELLES, *Secretary of the Navy:*

General Thomas' attack yesterday upon Hood's left resulted in the capture of Chalmers' headquarters train, with papers, 1,000 prisoners, and 16 pieces of artillery, with probable loss to the army not exceeding 500 killed and wounded. Attack will be continued this morning.

S. P. LEE,
Acting Rear-Admiral, Commanding Mississippi Squadron.

NASHVILLE, TENN., *December 16, 1864—2.30 p. m.*

Maj. T. T. ECKERT:

Cipher just received. Hood has fallen back, and is apparently doing his best to get away, while Thomas is pressing him with great vigor, frequently capturing guns and men. Everything so far is perfectly successful, and the prospect very fair to crush Hood's army.

J. C. VAN DUZER.

NASHVILLE, TENN., *December 16, 1864—9 p. m.*

Maj. T. T. ECKERT:

During last night Hood withdrew his right from the river and took a new position, covering Hillsborough, Granny White, and Franklin pikes, which line had been carefully prepared for just this contingency. He was driven from the first line easily, but the second was very stubbornly defended, and at last heavily assaulted three times before succeeding. It was carried, however, and 20 pieces of artillery and 2,000 men, including General Jackson, with the remnant of his division, were taken, the enemy forced back two miles, and his army broken into two parts—one on the [Granny] White pike, and the other on the Franklin, with the range of bluffy hills between them, Steedman and Wood pressing down the latter, and A. J. Smith, Schofield, and the cavalry down the former. Small-arms lay as thick on the completed line as the rebels had stood there. Hood cannot make another such a day's fight, while Thomas is in good condition to press him. Caught more wagons—cannot say number. Everybody, white and black, did splendidly.

J. C. VAN DUZER.

NASHVILLE, *December 16, 1864.*

Captain RAMSEY, *Assistant Adjutant-General:*

CAPTAIN: Our lines are in operation to Louisville and Clarksville. There is some interruption on lines north of Louisville just now.

Very respectfully,

E. C. BOYLE,
Manager Telegraph Office.

HEADQUARTERS DEPARTMENT OF THE CUMBERLAND,
OFFICE CHIEF ENGINEER,
Nashville, Tenn., December 16, 1864.

Maj. JAMES R. WILLETT,
First U. S. Veteran Volunteer Engineers, &c.:

SIR: In accordance with instructions received from the major-general commanding the department, you will move the pontoon train at as early an hour as possible, on the Murfreesborough pike, being prepared to report with it to the commanding general at any point between Brentwood and Columbia. As soon as this is done you will report to him in person for special instructions.

I am, very respectfully, your obedient servant,
H. C. WHARTON,
Lieut. Col. and Chief of Engineers, Dept. of the Cumberland.

HEADQUARTERS DEPARTMENT OF THE CUMBERLAND,
Hale's House, Granny White Pike, December 16, 1864—9.30 p. m.

Brigadier-General WOOD and
Major-General STEEDMAN:

The major-general commanding directs that you move your commands, in your present order, on the Franklin pike, in pursuit of the enemy. Your wagon trains will follow the troops in the order of precedence. Major-General Wilson's command of cavalry will be on the left of and cover your left flank.

I have the honor to be, generals, your obedient servant,
ROBT. H. RAMSEY,
Assistant Adjutant-General.

HEADQUARTERS ARMY OF THE OHIO,
In the Field, December 16, 1864—5.15 a. m.

Major-General THOMAS,
Commanding, &c.:

GENERAL: I am informed by General Couch that the enemy were very busy fortifying to his right and that of General Cox, at 12.10 a. m.

Very respectfully,
J. M. SCHOFIELD,
Major-General.

DECEMBER 16, 1864—11 a. m.

Major-General THOMAS,
Commanding, &c.:

GENERAL: I am at a loss to understand the infantry movement which General Wilson reports,* unless it be troops arriving from a distance. The enemy has not yet made any demonstration on my front. The ground masks his movements from the rear.

Respectfully,
J. M. SCHOFIELD,
Major-General.

---

* See Wilson to Schofield, 10.10 a. m., p. 215.

DECEMBER 16, 1864—1.30 p. m.

Major-General THOMAS, *Commanding, &c.:*

GENERAL: Wilson is trying to push in toward the Granny White pike, about a mile south of my right. My skirmishers on the right are supporting him. The skirmishing is pretty heavy. I have not attempted to advance my main line to-day, and do not think I am strong enough to do so. Will you be on this part of the line soon?

Very respectfully,

J. M. SCHOFIELD,
Major-General.

HEADQUARTERS ARMY OF THE OHIO,
December 16, 1864—7.45 p. m.

Maj. Gen. GEORGE H. THOMAS,
Commanding Department of the Cumberland:

GENERAL: I have the honor to report four pieces of artillery and a considerable number of prisoners captured by General Cox's division this afternoon. General Cox also reported four other pieces and caissons captured in the valley between the hill carried by General McArthur and that taken by General Cox. I learned, however, upon inquiry, that General McArthur's troops claimed, and, I have no doubt, justly, the honor of capturing the last four. My provost-marshal reports seventy-four prisoners captured this p. m. I have conversed with some of the officers captured, and am satisfied Hood's army is more thoroughly beaten than any troops I have ever seen. I congratulate you most heartily upon the result of the two days' operations. My messenger will wait for any orders you may have to send me.

Very respectfully, your obedient servant,

J. M. SCHOFIELD,
Major-General.

HEADQUARTERS DEPARTMENT OF THE CUMBERLAND,
Major-Generals SCHOFIELD and SMITH:

Hale's House, Granny White Pike, December 16, 1864—9.30 [p. m.].

The major-general commanding directs that you move your commands at an early hour in the morning, the head of column starting at 8 o'clock, General Smith in advance, on the Granny White pike, concentrating with the Fourth Corps and the troops of the District of the Etowah at or near Brentwood—the whole army, when united, marching on Franklin. The wagon trains of Generals Schofield's and Smith's commands will follow the troops in order of precedence, on the Granny White pike.

I have the honor to be, generals, your obedient servant,

ROBT. H. RAMSEY,
Assistant Adjutant-General.

HDQRS. CAVALRY CORPS, MIL. DIV. OF THE MISSISSIPPI,
In the Field, December 16, 1864—10.10 a. m.

Major-General SCHOFIELD,
Commanding Twenty-third Army Corps:

GENERAL: The regiment sent to the Granny White pike reports it strongly picketed toward us, with troops moving to our left. This is probably Chalmers' division.   I have heard nothing from Johnson this morning, but, from what General Croxton reports, there is no doubt that Chalmers crossed the Hardin pike, moving toward Brentwood.   The country on the left of the Hillsborough pike, toward the enemy's left, is too difficult for cavalry operations.   It seems to me if I was on the other flank of the army I might do more to annoy the enemy, unless it is intended that I shall push out as directed last night.

Very respectfully,

J. H. WILSON,
Brevet Major-General.

[Indorsement.]

Respectfully forwarded to Major-General Thomas.

J. M. SCHOFIELD,
Major-General.

HEADQUARTERS ARMY OF THE OHIO,
In the Field, December 16, 1864—11.15 a. m.

General WILSON, *Commanding Cavalry:*

I am directed by the major-general commanding to inform you of the receipt of your two dispatches of this a. m., which he will forward to Major-General Thomas.   He desires to know if the enemy reported moving are on the Granny White pike, and, if so, at what point; and he thinks, until you receive other orders from General Thomas, you had better hold your forces in readiness to support the troops here, in case the enemy make a heavy attack.

Very respectfully,

WM. M. WHERRY,
Major and Aide-de-Camp.

HDQRS. COUCH'S DIVISION, TWENTY-THIRD CORPS,
December 16, 1864—12.10 a. m.

CHIEF OF STAFF OF GENERAL SCHOFIELD:

COLONEL: For the information of the general I beg to state that the rebels are very busy fortifying to my right and that of General Cox's. I am fortifying my position.

Respectfully,

D. N. COUCH,
Major-General.

HDQRS. SECOND DIVISION, TWENTY-THIRD ARMY CORPS,
December 16, 1864—12 m.

Major WHERRY, *Chief of Staff:*

The country in direction of Granny White pike is so covered by hills and woods as to prevent me from making the observations as directed.   The rebels have a line of works commencing at the apex of the hill next to the one I took yesterday, running down to the cross-road— cross-road running east and west—and all along that road for at least two miles easterly.   I might take the above hill in front, but am not certain as to my ability to hold it.

Respectfully,

D. N. COUCH,
Major-General.

HDQRS. SECOND DIVISION, TWENTY-THIRD ARMY CORPS,
December 16, 1864—2.30 p. m.

Major WHERRY:

Appearances are that the enemy is in not a heavy force on Smith's front. I have just ordered in a brigade to support McCarthy [McArthur?] in his attempt to carry the hill on my front.

Respectfully,

D. N. COUCH,
Major-General.

HDQRS. COUCH'S DIVISION, TWENTY-THIRD ARMY CORPS,
December 16, 1864—7.45 [a. m.].

Brigadier-General COX:

It is reliably reported that a rebel column has been moving to my right for nearly two hours. You will please read this and send to General Schofield, if you have one of his orderlies with you.

Respectfully,

D. N. COUCH,
Major-General.

HEADQUARTERS DEPARTMENT OF THE CUMBERLAND,
In the Field, December 16, 1864—9.30 a. m.

Maj. Gen. A. J. SMITH,
Comdg. Detach. Army of the Tennessee, in the Field:

GENERAL: The major-general commanding directs that you send a good division to support General Schofield's right against a threatened attack by the enemy. The force you have sent he reports inadequate.

Very respectfully, your obedient servant,

WM. D. WHIPPLE,
Assistant Adjutant-General and Chief of Staff.

HEADQUARTERS DEPARTMENT OF THE CUMBERLAND,
December 16, 1864.

Major-General STEEDMAN,
Commanding District of the Etowah:

What is the position of affairs on your front this morning?

GEO. H. THOMAS,
Major-General, U. S. Volunteers, Commanding.

HEADQUARTERS GENERAL STEEDMAN,
In the Field, December 16, 1864.

Maj. Gen. G. H. THOMAS:

I am out five miles on the Nolensville pike, my right closed up on General Wood's left, pressing the enemy's right and rear; everything he has is on the right of the Nolensville pike.

J. B. STEEDMAN,
Major-General.

GENERAL STEEDMAN'S HEADQUARTERS,
December 16, 1864.

Maj. Gen. G. H. THOMAS:

The enemy have abandoned this part of their line and seem to have moved toward the right. I now occupy Riddle's Hill, and will press forward carefully toward the enemy. Prisoners say their wagon train is on road to Franklin.

Respectfully, your obedient servant,

J. B. STEEDMAN,
Major-General, U. S. Volunteers.

NASHVILLE, *December 16, 1864.*

Maj. Gen. GEORGE H. THOMAS:

GENERAL: On my way out to my command I stopped a moment at General Cruft's quarters to endeavor to communicate with you for orders. I pushed out on the Nolensville pike and joined General Wood at a critical juncture, aiding him to carry the enemy's right. I went without orders, but I hope you are not displeased with my movements. I am on General Wood's left with about 3,000 men, and desire to know your wishes. I went out without anything but ammunition, not expecting to move more than a mile; but feeling that I could best protect the left by keeping well around the flank, I pushed on until I made the junction with General Wood, and went into camp on his left at dark.

With esteem, yours, truly,

JAMES B. STEEDMAN,
Major-General.

HDQRS. CAVALRY CORPS, MIL. DIV. OF THE MISSISSIPPI.
Granny White Pike, Tucker's House, Eight Miles from Nashville,
December 16, 1864—6.30 p. m.

Brigadier-General WHIPPLE,
Chief of Staff:

General Hatch has captured General Rucker, a number of prisoners, and one battle-flag; Rucker is wounded. I will collect my command and cross Harpeth as early as possible. Have already ordered Johnson forward by the Hillsborough pike, with directions to shove into Franklin as rapidly as he can. I will move at daylight, or, if practicable, by 4 a. m. If you wish anything other than the above please send at once.

Very respectfully, your obedient servant,

J. H. WILSON,
Brevet Major-General.

HEADQUARTERS DEPARTMENT OF THE CUMBERLAND,
Hale's House, Granny White Pike, December 16, 1864—9.10 p. m.

Maj. Gen. J. H. WILSON,
Comdg. Cavalry Corps, Military Division of the Mississippi:

The major-general commanding directs that you leave Johnson's division of cavalry on the Hillsborough pike, to observe the enemy and protect our right and rear, and move with the balance of your command over to the Franklin pike, to operate on that road and the road running east of the same. You will express to your entire command the cordial congratulations of the major-general commanding for their success and his hearty thanks for the bravery of the troops.

I have the honor to be, general, very respectfully, your obedient servant,

ROBT. H. RAMSEY,
Assistant Adjutant-General.

HEADQUARTERS FIRST DIVISION CAVALRY,
Hopkinsville, Ky., December 16, 1864—6 p. m.
(Via Russellville 12 m. 18th.)

General J. H. WILSON,
Commanding Cavalry Corps, Nashville, Tenn.:

After marching all last night I struck part of Lyon's command here, routed them, and captured their artillery. Colonel Chenoweth, their commander, is among the prisoners wounded. General Lyon has gone toward Princeton. I will pursue as long as is practicable or profitable. I fear he may scatter his command, although I sent all my transportation back to Bowling Green. From Russellville the roads are so exceedingly bad that it is impossible to move rapidly.

E. M. McCOOK,
Brigadier-General, Commanding.

GENERAL ORDERS, ⎫ HDQRS. SECOND DIV., CAVALRY CORPS,
⎬ MILITARY DIVISION OF THE MISSISSIPPI,
No. 36. ⎭ *Louisville, Ky., December 16, 1864.*

There being a sufficient number of horses to mount the entire division, it is hereby ordered that brigade and regimental commanders get their commands in readiness to march as soon as possible. Brigade and regimental commanders to organize, if they have not already done so, their provost-guards in accordance with existing orders. These guards to be placed under charge of a reliable non-commissioned officer where the scarcity of regimental officers will not admit of a commissioned officer being placed in charge of them. The pioneer corps will be promptly organized, in accordance with orders heretofore issued from these headquarters, a copy of which is herewith inclosed, and the men composing them will be promply furnished with the necessary tools. These parties will also be placed in charge of a good non-commissioned officer where it is impracticable to furnish a commissioned officer. Brigade and regimental commanders will at once provide their men with haversacks and canteens, if they have not already been so provided. As it is impracticable to take an ordnance train from here to Nashville, and not improbable that the command will have fighting to do en route to that place, brigade and regimental commanders will see that their men having guns are provided with 100 rounds of ammunition per man before leaving here and cautioned in reference to taking care of it.

By command of Brig. Gen. Eli Long:

T. W. SCOTT,
Captain and Acting Assistant Adjutant-General.

NEAR BROWN'S HOUSE, ONE MILE SOUTH OF DAVIDSON'S,
December 16, 1864.

[General WILSON:]

GENERAL: We have driven the enemy from this place and following up. At this point the enemy has turned to the left in direction of Hardin pike. I shall follow up, and will again communicate with you when I reach that pike. I commenced operations this morning at 4 o'clock. Please send any news you have. Hatch did nobly; my only regret is that his captures were not made by the Sixth.

Respectfully,

R. W. JOHNSON,
Brigadier-General.

HDQRS. CAVALRY CORPS, MIL. DIV. OF THE MISSISSIPPI,
Hillsborough Pike, Six or Seven Miles from Nashville,
December 16, 1864—9.15 a. m. (Received 3.25 p. m.)

Brig. Gen. R. W. JOHNSON,
Commanding Sixth Division, Cavalry Corps:

GENERAL: All the information we have goes to show that Chalmers has joined the main army with his command. If this is so, and you have no force of the enemy in your front, the general commanding desires you to move your command to this point. He has heard nothing from you to-day.

Very respectfully, your obedient servant,

A. J. ALEXANDER,
Lieutenant-Colonel and Acting Chief of Staff.

HDQRS. CAVALRY CORPS, MIL. DIV. OF THE MISSISSIPPI,
December 16, 1864—10.15 a. m.

Brig. Gen. R. W. JOHNSON,
Commanding Sixth Division, Cavalry Corps:

GENERAL: Your dispatch of this a. m. just received. The general commanding desires you to push the force in your front as rapidly as possible, and should you need assistance send him word. We have no news from the left, where the fighting is. Hatch, Knipe, and Croxton are here, refused on the right of Schofield, the line extending across and perpendicular to the Murfreesborough turnpike.

Respectfully, &c.,

A. J. ALEXANDER,
Lieutenant-Colonel and Acting Chief of Staff.

HARDIN PIKE, *December 16, 1864—10.25 a. m.*

[General WILSON:]

GENERAL: Occupy Hardin pike where it crosses Harpeth. The rebs have all gone toward Franklin by a road which leaves Hardin pike at the brick church (marked on the map). I will push on in pursuit as rapidly as possible. Since leaving pike I have had very bad roads. Have captured a few prisoners and a few wagons without teams.

Respectfully,

R. W. JOHNSON,
Brigadier-General.

TWO MILES WEST OF HILLSBOROUGH PIKE,
December 16, 1864—12.45 p. m.

General WILSON:

GENERAL: The enemy crossed a number of their wagons over the Harpeth at the railroad bridge (Northwestern railroad). Destroyed the railroad bridge, but their troops moved by the road represented on our map as leaving the Hardin pike at the brick church. I am now going into line facing the Hillsborough pike, and will attack as soon as I get my battery up and in position. The enemy pressed a guide to conduct him here, and I have him. He says the rebs had with them twelve pieces of artillery, which they had in use yesterday on the Charlotte and Hardin pikes. Away to my left I can hear small-arms; if our cavalry, and it can press on, they will be in the rear of the guns. The dismounted brigade could not keep up, and I left it on the Hardin pike. All the rebs on my right and rear are beyond the Big Harpeth, and that brigade covers the city. I could not overtake the enemy if I had kept them with me. I hope all is satisfactory. Have not heard from Croxton to-day. Have taken a few more prisoners since my last.

Respectfully,

R. W. JOHNSON,
Brigadier-General.

HILLSBOROUGH PIKE, NEAR TOLL-HOUSE,
December 16, 1864—3.15 p. m.

General WILSON:

GENERAL: Have driven the enemy from his chosen position and now occupy the pike. The enemy left on the pike, and I will push him over the Big Harpeth to-night. Have communicated with General Hammond, immediately in my rear.

Respectfully,

R. W. J[OHNSON].

HDQRS. CAVALRY CORPS, MIL. DIV. OF THE MISSISSIPPI,
Near Compton's House, December 16, 1864—5.30 p. m.

Brig. Gen. R. W. JOHNSON,
Commanding Sixth Division, Cavalry Corps:

GENERAL: Yours received. General Wilson has gone to the front. Hatch, Knipe, and Croxton have gone in and won, capturing some prisoners. I understand the infantry have carried the works and taken a large number of prisoners. Cannot vouch for the truth of the report, but am inclined to believe it. Enemy said to be running at all points. Your movements are satisfactory to General Wilson.

Respectfully, &c.,

A. J. ALEXANDER,
Lieutenant-Colonel, &c.

HDQRS. CAVALRY CORPS, MIL. DIV. OF THE MISSISSIPPI,
Granny White Pike, Eight Miles from Nashville,
December 16, 1864—7 p. m.

General R. W. JOHNSON,
Commanding Sixth Division Cavalry Corps:

I want you to move at the earliest possible moment for Franklin on the Hillsborough pike. Dispatches captured on the person of General

Rucker (now a prisoner) say all their trains were ordered there this morning, and that cavalry of Chalmers must take care of this flank. Go for him with all possible celerity, as Hood says the safety of their army depends upon Chalmers. I will move by the nearest roads to the Harpeth, and connect with you somewhere very early to-morrow near Franklin. The rebels are badly beaten and in full retreat. The day is glorious! Hatch and Knipe have done splendidly. I regret you were not here, but all right to-morrow.

Very respectfully, your obedient servant,

J. H. WILSON,
Brevet Major-General, Commanding.

HDQRS. CAVALRY CORPS, MIL. DIV. OF THE MISSISSIPPI,
Tucker's House, Eight Miles from Nashville,
on Granny White Pike, December 16, 1864.

Brigadier-General JOHNSON,
Comdg. Sixth Division Cavalry Corps:

GENERAL: Your dispatch of 3.15 p. m. is received. Well done. I have sent you orders to keep crowding the enemy and try to get into Franklin. Shove him as closely as possible; give him no peace. A dispatch from General Hood, captured with General Rucker, says the safety of his army depends upon the ability of Chalmers to keep us off; time is all he wants. Don't give him any. I will meet you somewhere on the Harpeth River to-morrow with the whole force. This has been a splendid day. Knipe and Hatch have done splendidly.

By command of Brevet Major-General Wilson:

E. B. BEAUMONT,
Major and Assistant Adjutant-General.

LITTLE HARPETH, *December 16, 1864—7.30 p. m.*

[General WILSON:]

GENERAL: The enemy having fallen back a short distance on the Hillsborough pike, fell back in considerable confusion on roads leading toward Franklin and Brentwood. I am now nine miles from Franklin and the same distance from Nashville. Hammond is not far in my rear. I sent a squadron down the pike to the Big Harpeth, with orders to push in rapidly and return this evening. This force has just returned and reports having met a picket on the pike near Big Harpeth. I do not believe there is any force in that direction, though there may be a small picket. The woods indicate and the citizens all agree that the main rebel cavalry force passed over in the direction of Brentwood or Franklin. I would like to receive instructions to-night. I have ordered my command under arms and ready for work by 4 a. m. Have you any orders in relation to Biddle's dismounted brigade left on the Big Harpeth at the crossing of the Hardin pike? I inclose report of officer sent out to Big Harpeth.

Respectfully,

R. W. JOHNSON,
Brigadier-General.

[Inclosure.]

HEADQUARTERS FIFTH IOWA CAVALRY,
December 16, 1864.

Lieutenant-Colonel BAIRD:

SIR: I have the honor to report that, in accordance with your orders, I advanced on the Hillsborough pike, in the direction of the Big Harpeth River, about two miles and a half. About two miles beyond where we are now camped I discovered a road coming in from the right that appeared to have been traveled to-day by a large column of cavalry and a number of wagons. About a quarter of a mile farther on I found two other roads coming in from the left. These were newly made and well beaten. I would think, from appearances, that artillery had been brought in on one or both of them. A short distance beyond this I came upon a strong picket, so posted that I could not drive it back. After firing several shots, and becoming satisfied that I could not advance any farther without too much risk, I returned.

I have the honor to be, very respectfully, your obedient servant,

W. C. McBEATH,
Captain, Fifth Iowa Cavalry.

HDQRS. CAVALRY CORPS, MIL. DIV. OF THE MISSISSIPPI,
Granny White Pike, Tucker's House, December 16, 1864.
(Received 1.10 a. m. 17th.)

Brigadier-General JOHNSON,
Comdg. Sixth Div., Cav. Corps, Mil. Div. of the Mississippi:

GENERAL: Orders have been sent you by two different messengers; one order by an orderly from your headquarters. Direct Colonel Biddle to join you at the crossing of the Harpeth River by the Hillsborough pike. If possible, let him reach it before you do, and he may pick up some prisoners. A portion of Chalmers' division may still be in front of you. Push him with all your might, and we will attend to him on this line.

By command of Brevet Major-General Wilson:

E. B. BEAUMONT,
Major and Assistant Adjutant-General.

HILLSBOROUGH PIKE, *December 16, 1864.*

Major-General WILSON:

General Knipe not being present, I report from a regiment that I have on the Granny White pike that the pike is very strongly picketed and numerous detachments moving toward our left generally. While I write this I hear scattering fire over there.

Respectfully, your obedient servant,

J. H. HAMMOND,
Brigadier-General.

Major Holahan, Nineteenth Pennsylvania, on Granny White pike, has sent in another courier, saying the enemy's picket-line is strong, and a force in front. I have ordered him to not fall back, unless compelled, and then slowly.

J. H. HAMMOND,
Brigadier-General.

DECEMBER 16, 1864.

General WILSON:

Major Holahan has been obliged to fall back from the Granny White pike. He reports heavy masses of infantry are constantly moving to our left, and have been for nearly an hour. We have ten prisoners—eight from Cheatham's division—all of whom came over from their right last night and this morning; two, also, of General Stewart's escort. Stewart's headquarters on Granny White pike, a mile and a half from here.

  Respectfully,

        J. H. HAMMOND,
         Brigadier-General.

(Copies forwarded by General Wilson to Generals Whipple and Schofield.)

———

    BRICK CHURCH, ON THE HARDIN PIKE,
     December 16, 1864. (Received 10.25 a. m.)

Col. ISRAEL GARRARD,
 Commanding Seventh Ohio Volunteer Cavalry:

COLONEL: I occupy the Hardin pike at this point, and find that the enemy have taken the Franklin road, which branches out at the Hardin pike at this point. General Chalmers passed here at 8 o'clock this morning. Found one abandoned wagon here.

  Yours, obediently,

        R. C. RANKIN,
     Captain, Commanding Detachment.

———

      STEVENSON, *December 16, 1864.*

General MEAGHER:

Telegram from Decherd just received gives the following:

Commanding officer at Duck River reports heaviest cannonading of the campaign now being heard in direction northwestward from there.

        R. S. GRANGER,
         Brigadier-General.

———

      STEVENSON, *December 16, 1864.*

Brigadier-General MEAGHER:

The report of Breckinridge's moving from Manchester to this place has reached us. The artillery firing was heard here, at Larkinsville, and was reported at Duck River as coming from the northwest. Officer at Decherd reports all quiet in that neighborhood. The firing therefore heard by your party must have been that from the vicinity of Nashville or Franklin.

        R. S. GRANGER,
         Brigadier-General.

STEVENSON, *December 16, 1864.*

Brigadier-General MEAGHER,
    Commanding District of the Etowah:

The following telegram has just been received which is the most reliable of anything we have received, and will account for the firing heard
to-day:

DECHERD, *December 16, 1864.*

I have reliable information that Breckinridge, with a force of cavalry, infantry,
and artillery, estimated at 10,000, passed Woodbury, twenty-one miles southeast of
Murfreesborough, going toward Murfreesborough. Heavy artillery firing heard all
day to-day in direction of the latter place.

WILLARD WARNER,
Colonel, Commanding.

R. S. GRANGER,
Brigadier-General.

BRIDGEPORT, *December 16, 1864.*

Capt. HENRY A. FORD,
    Acting Assistant Adjutant-General:

A reliable citizen reports artillery firing distinctly heard on the
mountain thirteen miles from this place on yesterday afternoon, and
this morning in the direction of Decherd Station, and Breckinridge is
reported leaving Manchester with 4,500 men, marching upon Stevenson. The reasonable presumption is that the firing was by his command.

M. C. TAYLOR,
Colonel, Commanding.

PADUCAH, KY., *December 16, 1864.*

Brig. Gen. W. D. WHIPPLE,
    Assistant Adjutant-General, Nashville, Tenn.:

GENERAL: Lyon has captured Princeton, Ky., and Eddyville. He
is conscripting, and taking private property for miles around. The
party of 1,000 men left at Danville crossing have disappeared. The
regiments of infantry which you ordered me to detain for the purpose
of moving against Lyon at Danville are arriving, but without cavalry
it is impossible for me to move against Lyon. Can I detain any of the
cavalry and the infantry and assume the offensive? Please answer.

S. MEREDITH,
Brigadier-General.

LEXINGTON, *December 16, 1864.*

General S. MEREDITH,
    Paducah, Ky.:

No re-enforcements can be spared at present for your district. I
understand a part of General Thomas' cavalry is taking care of Lyon.
Please keep me informed of his movements. The general commanding
expects you will hold Paducah, Columbus, and Smithland, but at present make no offensive movement.

J. BATES DICKSON,
Captain and Assistant Adjutant-General.

SMITHLAND, *December 16, 1864.*

Capt. JAMES GRAHAM,
  Assistant Adjutant-General:

SIR: A reliable scout reports that a small party of rebels entered Dycusburg about noon to-day. Several shots were fired at him, but he escaped. He thinks their object is plunder and conscription.

Very respectfully,

HENRY P. REED,
Captain, Commanding Post.

SPECIAL ORDERS, }   HDQRS. MILITARY DIST. OF KENTUCKY,
  No. 92.   }   *Lexington, Ky., December 16, 1864.*

*   *   *   *   *   *

II. Col. P. W. Stanhope is assigned to the command of the camp of rendezvous, at Covington, Ky., established by Special Orders, No. 26, paragraph V, of date October 5, 1864, from these headquarters, vice G. Clay Smith relieved.

*   *   *   *   *   *   *

By command of Brevet Major-General Burbridge:

J. BATES DICKSON,
Captain and Assistant Adjutant-General.

LEXINGTON, *December 16, 1864.*

Lieut. Col. T. B. FAIRLEIGH,
  Louisville, Ky.:

General Meredith telegraphs that Lyon has captured Princeton and Eddyville, and commands the Cumberland at Kelly's crossing with eight pieces of artillery. What reliable information have you about Lyon?

J. BATES DICKSON,
Captain and Assistant Adjutant-General.

MOUNT STERLING, *December 16, 1864.*

Capt. J. S. BUTLER,
  Assistant Adjutant-General:

A party of thirty rebels has passed down the country between here and Sharpsburg, crossing six miles from this place. They are said to be well mounted. Would it not be well to bring one gun down from fort and post it in the northern end of town, and protect it with a company of infantry?

BARBER,
Captain.
Per JOHN J. SEWELL,
Lieutenant and Post Adjutant.

HEADQUARTERS DISTRICT OF INDIANA,
Indianapolis, December 16, 1864.

Capt. C. H. POTTER,
Assistant Adjutant-General:

I am informed by telegram from Madison, Ind., that Colonel Jessee's men have taken Milton, a small town in Kentucky. They here fired on two steamers, and left in the direction of Bedford, Ky. We must have a small force for the front on the Ohio.

ALVIN P. HOVEY,
Brevet Major-General.

WAR DEPARTMENT,
Washington, December 17, 1864—10 a. m.

Governor SEYMOUR,
Albany:

The great battle between the United States forces under Major-General Thomas and the rebel army under General Hood, before Nashville, resulted yesterday in a great and decisive victory for the Union arms. The rebel army has been broken and routed, a large portion of its artillery and great numbers of prisoners captured. This triumph has been achieved with small loss to our army. General Thomas reports that his loss has been very small, probably not exceeding 300,* and very few killed.

EDWIN M. STANTON,
Secretary of War.

(Same to Governor Andrew, Boston; Governor Smith, Saint Albans, Vt.; Governor Cony, Augusta; Governor Smith, Providence; Governor Curtin, Harrisburg; Governor Brough, Columbus; Governor Morton, Indianapolis; Governor Blair, Jackson, Mich.; Governor Stone, Davenport, Iowa; Governor Yates, Springfield, Ill.; Governor of Wisconsin, Madison; Governor Boreman, Wheeling; Mayor of Pittsburg, Pa.; Mayor of Steubenville, Ohio; Governor Tod, Youngstown, Ohio; Governor of Missouri, Saint Louis; General Meade; General Pope, Milwaukee, Wis.; General Curtis, Fort Leavenworth; General Dodge, Saint Louis; General Cadwalader, Philadelphia; General Lew. Wallace, Baltimore; General Hooker, Cincinnati; and Colonel Sweet, Chicago.)

WAR DEPARTMENT,
Washington, December 17, 1864—8.35 a. m.   (Sent 10.25 a. m.)

Major-General DIX,
New York:

The following official report† of the great victory achieved yesterday by Major-General Thomas and his gallant army over the rebel forces under General Hood, in front of Nashville, was received this morning. One of the most surprising circumstances connected with this great

---

* Three thousand, as reported by Thomas, see p. 210.
† See 6 p. m. of 16th, p. 210.

achievement is the small loss suffered by our troops, evincing, among other things, the admirable skill and caution of General Thomas in his disposition of the battle. In our rejoicings at the defeat of the enemy thanks are due to the Almighty for his protection to our gallant officers and soldiers in the great conflict they have passed through. The report of General Thomas, and also an unofficial report* containing interesting details, are subjoined.

EDWIN M. STANTON,
Secretary of War.

WAR DEPARTMENT,
Washington, D. C., December 17, 1864—10 p. m.

Major-General DIX:

* * * * * * *

Nothing has been heard from General Thomas to-day. Unofficial dispatches state that the provost-marshal at Nashville reports 5,000 prisoners and 49 pieces of artillery as being already secured. It is ascertained that in transmitting General Thomas' report last night a telegraphic mistake was made at Louisville or Nashville in the estimated number of our casualties. The dispatch written by General Thomas stated that his whole loss would not exceed 3,000, and very few were killed.

* * * * * * *

EDWIN M. STANTON,
Secretary of War.

WAR DEPARTMENT,
Washington, December 17, 1864—10 a. m.

Lieutenant-General GRANT,
  Burlington, N. J.:

Thomas victorious yesterday. Hood's army broken; driven back to the Brentwood Hills; many prisoners and cannon taken; pursuit to be renewed to-day. Our loss not over 300.† Sherman took Fort McAllister Wednesday. If you start soon there is yet time for your report to be made as promised. Details will be sent you soon as possible, but the telegraph works badly. Dispatches from Foster are being received, and a messenger with sealed dispatches from Sherman has reached Fortress Monroe on his way up.

EDWIN M. STANTON,
Secretary of War.

HEADQUARTERS DEPARTMENT OF THE CUMBERLAND,
Near Franklin, Tenn., December 17, 1864—8 p. m.

Lieut. Gen. U. S. GRANT:

We have pressed the enemy to-day beyond Franklin, capturing his hospitals, containing over 1,500 wounded, and about 150 of our wounded. In addition to the above, General Knipe, commanding a division of

---

*See Van Duzer to Eckert, 9 p. m. 16th (p. 213), omitting the address and signature.
†Three thousand, as reported by Thomas, see p. 210.

cavalry, drove the enemy's rear guard through Franklin to-day, capturing about 250 prisoners and 5 battle-flags, with very little loss on our side. Citizens of Franklin represent Hood's army as completely demoralized. In addition to the captures of yesterday, reported in my dispatch of last night, I have the honor to report the capture of General Rucker and about 250 prisoners of the enemy's cavalry, in a fight that occurred about 8 o'clock last night between General Rucker and General Hatch, of our cavalry. The enemy has been pressed to-day both in front and on both flanks. Brigadier-General Johnson succeeded in striking him on the flank just beyond Franklin, capturing quite a number of prisoners, number not yet reported. My cavalry is pressing him closely to-night, and I am very much in hopes of getting many more prisoners to-morrow. Luckily, but little damage has been done the railroad, and I expect to have trains close up to the army to-morrow night. I have just heard from General Stoneman, at Kingsport, under date of the 13th instant. He left Knoxville on the 10th, overtook Duke's (formerly Morgan's) command on the 12th, and during the night drove him across the North Fork of Holston River. Next morning crossed the river and attacked, captured and killed nearly the whole command, taking the entire wagon train. Col. R. C. Morgan, a brother of John Morgan, is, with many other officers, a prisoner. Duke's command is considered completely destroyed. The fighting was done by Gillem's command and the Thirtieth Kentucky, of General Burbridge's command. Stoneman in motion for Bristol, where he hopes to intercept Vaughn. A part of the captured train was that lost by Gillem on retreat from Bull's Gap. I now consider the Cumberland perfectly safe from Nashville down, and have directed the chief quartermaster to commence shipping stores up it immediately. As there is also a fair prospect for another rise in the Tennessee River, I have requested Admiral Lee to send some iron-clads and gun-boats up that river, to destroy Hood's pontoon bridge, if possible, and cut off his retreat.

GEO. H. THOMAS,
Major-General, Commanding.

(Same to Major-General Halleck.)

HEADQUARTERS DEPARTMENT OF THE CUMBERLAND,
Near Franklin, Tenn., December 17, 1864.
(Via Pittsburg 5 p. m 18th.)

Major-General HALLECK,
  Washington, D. C.:

Report just received from Major-General Wilson states that at 6 p. m. to-day he attacked and dispersed Stevenson's division of rebel infantry and a brigade of cavalry, capturing three guns. The Fourth U. S. Cavalry and Hatch's division of cavalry, handsomely supported by Knipe's division of cavalry, did the work, making several beautiful charges, breaking the rebel infantry in all directions. Had it only been light the rebel rear guard would have been entirely destroyed; as it is, it has been severely punished. The whole army will continue vigorous pursuit in the morning. This attack was made six miles beyond Franklin.

GEO. H. THOMAS,
Major-General.

LOUISVILLE, KY., *December 17, 1864—10 a. m.*

Lieut. Gen. U. S. GRANT,
    Burlington, N. J.:

Have just arrived. Weather bad; raining since yesterday morning. People here jubilant over Thomas' success. Confidence seemed to be restored. I will remain here to hear from you. All things going right. It would seem best that I return to join my command with Sherman.

JNO. A. LOGAN,
Major-General.

HEADQUARTERS ARMY OF THE POTOMAC,
December 17, 1864—6.30 p. m.   (Sent 6.40 p. m.)

Hon. E. M. STANTON:

I congratulate the President, yourself, and the country on the glorious victory achieved by Major-General Thomas and the troops under his command. I have directed a salute of 100 guns to be fired to-morrow at sunrise in honor of this brilliant triumph.

GEO. G. MEADE,
Major-General, Commanding.

HEADQUARTERS ARMY OF THE SHENANDOAH,
December 17, 1864.   (Received 18th.)

Maj. Gen. G. H. THOMAS:

The Army of the Shenandoah, through me, send their hearty congratulations to yourself and army for the brilliant victory at Nashville on the 15th and 16th instant. We have given you 200 guns and much cheering.

P. H. SHERIDAN,
Major-General, Commanding.

CLARKSVILLE, *December 17, 1864.*

Maj. Gen. G. H. THOMAS:

I have the honor to acknowledge receiving, and to thank you for the early telegraphic copy, of your admirable official report to the President of your great and glorious victory over the enemy of our country and of mankind on the 15th and 16th instant. I am deeply impressed with the belief that our whole country will now or hereafter appreciate the generalship, statesmanship, and patriotism of your campaign, resulting in the signal defeat of General Hood's army, in which centered the strength and hopes of half the rebellion, with little loss, under great difficulties and with probably political consequences and more important than have followed the previous achievements of the war. Permit me on this occasion to express my humble admiration of your distinguished public services, which evince all the high qualities of virtue, patriotism, and ability, characteristic of our first great countryman.

Respectfully and faithfully, yours,

S. P. LEE,
Acting Rear-Admiral, Commanding Mississippi Squadron.

HEADQUARTERS DEPARTMENT OF THE CUMBERLAND,
Near Franklin, December 17, 1864—9.15 p. m.

Admiral S. P. LEE,
Clarksville:

Your dispatch of this day is received, and I sincerely thank you for your very flattering congratulations. I have directed my dispatch of this p. m. to General Halleck to be sent you for your information. If you think it feasible I shall be much obliged if you will permit Lieutenant-Commander Fitch to proceed up the Tennessee River, with one or two iron-clads and a few gun-boats, for the purpose of destroying Hood's pontoon bridge near Florence and at the mouth of Duck River, where it is reported he is now building a bridge.

GEO. H. THOMAS,
Major-General, Commanding.

CLARKSVILLE, *December 17, 1864—6.20 p. m.*

Maj. Gen. G. H. THOMAS:

Convoy arrived at Smithland on the 16th, without encountering opposition. Gun-boats actively patrolling river, but have not seen or heard of rebel force.

S. P. LEE,
Acting Rear-Admiral, Commanding Mississippi Squadron.

HEADQUARTERS DEPARTMENT OF THE CUMBERLAND,
Hale's House, Granny White Pike, December 17, 1864—9 a. m.

Captain MORDECAI,
Chief of Ordnance, Military Division of the Mississippi:

CAPTAIN: The major-general commanding directs that you have collected together all the artillery and small-arms, with other ordnance property, captured from the enemy in the engagements of the 15th and 16th, and a correct inventory of the same forwarded to these headquarters as soon as possible.

I have the honor to be, captain, very respectfully, your obedient servant,

ROBT. H. RAMSEY,
Assistant Adjutant-General.

HEADQUARTERS DEPARTMENT OF THE CUMBERLAND,
Near Franklin, December 17, 1864.

Brig. Gen. J. L. DONALDSON,
Chief Quartermaster, Department of the Cumberland:

GENERAL: The major-general commanding directs me to say that he now considers the Cumberland River perfectly safe, and that he desires you to resume shipments on the river to Nashville from below. The army continues to be successful in taking prisoners. We have to-day taken about 450, and 5 flags. The enemy will be pursued in the morning. All well.

I have the honor to be, general, very respectfully, your obedient servant,

ROBT. H. RAMSEY,
Assistant Adjutant-General.

NASHVILLE, TENN., *December 17, 1864—12 noon.*

Major ECKERT:

No report from the front this morning. From the provost-marshal I get number of prisoners, up to this hour, 5,000, and gather from other sources number of guns 49.

J. C. VAN DUZER.

NASHVILLE, TENN., *December 17, 1864—10 p. m.*

Maj. T. T. ECKERT:

Just in from the front. Enemy made only sufficient resistance to-day to enable him to get his transportation away. General Thomas crowded him as much as possible, and has captured 1,000 prisoners, driving enemy across Harpeth River, but not securing bridges by which he crossed. Cavalry forded and engaged on south bank, when night overtook us. Have captured no guns or wagons so far as I know. Hood is in rapid retreat, and the state of ground is such as to confine pursuit to pike roads, cross-roads and fields impassable for artillery or transportation. Stragglers and rear guard will be picked up daily; not much else.

J. C. VAN DUZER.

CIRCULAR.]   HDQRS. DEPARTMENT OF THE CUMBERLAND,
                Near Franklin, December 17, 1864—9.30 p. m.

The major-general commanding directs that the army will move in pursuit of the enemy, in the present order of the different commands, at as early an hour after daylight as possible to-morrow morning, December 18.

I am, general, very respectfully, your obedient servant,
                                ROBT. H. RAMSEY,
                                Assistant Adjutant-General.

HEADQUARTERS FOURTH ARMY CORPS,
                Near Nashville, December 17, 1864—6 a. m.

Orders of the day for the Fourth Army Corps for to-day, December 17, 1864:

The advance against the enemy will continue this morning, the troops moving upon receipt of this order—General Kimball on the right, General Elliott in the center, General Beatty on the left. Division commanders will deploy one brigade each. The rest of the troops will follow in columns until the enemy is met, when a second brigade will be deployed and the enemy pressed with all vigor possible. Attacks will [not] be made upon his solid works except under special orders.

By order of Brigadier-General Wood:
                                J. S. FULLERTON,
                Lieutenant-Colonel and Assistant Adjutant-General.

HEADQUARTERS FOURTH ARMY CORPS,
Franklin, Tenn., December 17, 1864—8 p. m.

Brigadier-General WHIPPLE,
    Chief of Staff:

Colonel Suman, in charge of building or rather repairing the bridge across the river, reports that it will be impossible to accomplish the work, owing to the rapid rise in the river, the swiftness of the current, and the amount of driftwood coming down the stream. One of the bents that he straightened up has been pushed down again, and he has one bent yet to put in, which he cannot do, as the men cannot work in the river and they have no boats to assist them. I see no other way than to wait for the pontoon train. This should be hurried forward, for I am confident we cannot cross until it comes up. If you will hurry that forward we will put it down and cross immediately.

    Respectfully, your obedient servant,
                TH. J. WOOD,
      Brigadier-General, U. S. Volunteers, Commanding.

HEADQUARTERS FOURTH ARMY CORPS,
Franklin, Tenn., December 17, 1864—8 p. m.

Colonel SUMAN,
    Ninth Indiana:

If the prospects for completing the bridge are no better than when I was there with you. and you are still of the opinion you were when I left you, you may suspend work and go to camp. You had better draw your rations to-night.

    By order of Brigadier-General Wood:
                W. H. SINCLAIR,
      Major and Assistant Adjutant-General.

HEADQUARTERS FOURTH ARMY CORPS,
Near Franklin, Tenn., December 17, 1864—6.30 p. m.

Brigadier-General KIMBALL:

GENERAL: The prospect is that we will not have the bridge finished before a late hour to-night. Let your troops rest as well as they can. We will not move before 3 a. m. Timely notice will be given of the hour.

    By order of Brigadier-General Wood:
                J. S. FULLERTON,
      Lieutenant-Colonel and Assistant Adjutant-General.

(Same to Generals Elliott and Beatty.)

HEADQUARTERS ARMY OF THE OHIO,
In the Field, December 17, 1864.

Maj. Gen. GEORGE H. THOMAS,
    Commanding, &c.:

GENERAL: I have the honor to inform you that citizens on the road in rear of where we fought yesterday report that the universal testimony of rebels, officers and men, is that Forrest was killed certainly at Murfreesborough, where they admit their cavalry was badly whipped.

    Very respectfully, your obedient servant,
                J. M. SCHOFIELD,
                Major-General.

HEADQUARTERS ARMY OF THE OHIO,
December 17, 1864—3.30 p. m.

Major-General THOMAS,
Commanding U. S. Forces:

GENERAL: I have reached the Little Harpeth, on the Granny White pike, or rather the road which is the continuation of it. This is where the road turns off to strike the Franklin pike below Brentwood. General Smith's troops are massed in my front, waiting for the pike to be cleared of trains. It will be hardly possible for me to get further to-night. I will mass my troops here, and try to get up my wagons and issue rations this evening. I am bridging the Little Harpeth where the Granny White road crosses it, so that my infantry may move that way. The road is hardly practicable for artillery.

Very respectfully,

J. M. SCHOFIELD,
Major-General.

HEADQUARTERS ARMY OF THE OHIO,
Near Nashville, Tenn., December 17, 1864.

Maj. Gen. D. N. COUCH,
Commanding Second Division, Twenty-third Army Corps:

GENERAL: The commanding general directs that you march your command on the Granny White pike this morning, directly in the rear of General Smith's column, which starts at 8 o'clock. You will be followed by General Cox. The division ordnance trains and ambulances will move with the troops. All other trains will follow in the rear of General Smith's trains in the order of march of the divisions, one section of the supply train in advance.

I am, general, very respectfully, your obedient servant,

J. A. CAMPBELL,
Assistant Adjutant-General.

HDQRS. THIRD DIVISION, TWENTY-THIRD ARMY CORPS,
On Granny White Pike, December 17, 1864.

Maj. J. A. CAMPBELL,
Assistant Adjutant-General, Army of the Ohio:

MAJOR: I have the honor to claim for my command the capture of eight pieces of the enemy's artillery, in the charge made by the First Brigade last evening. The four pieces captured by the Eighth Tennessee Infantry, as stated by Colonel Doolittle, in the accompanying dispatch, were not put under guard at the moment, and a guard was subsequently put over them and the pieces claimed by McArthur's division, Sixteenth Corps.

J. D. COX,
Brigadier-General, Commanding.

[Inclosure.]

HDQRS. FIRST BRIG., THIRD DIV., 23D ARMY CORPS,
In the Field, December 17, 1864.

Capt. THEODORE COX,
Assistant Adjutant-General:

SIR: I have the honor to report that in the charge on the enemy's work yesterday my brigade captured eight pieces of artillery, light

12's, instead of four, as reported verbally. The four pieces claimed by McArthur's division, Sixteenth Corps, were taken by the Eighth Tennessee, who drove the enemy from them. The Twelfth Kentucky took the other four pieces.

CHS. C. DOOLITTLE,
Colonel Eighteenth Michigan Infantry, Commanding.

[First indorsement.]

HEADQUARTERS ARMY OF THE OHIO,
Franklin, Tenn., December 19, 1864.

Respectfully forwarded to headquarters Department of the Cumberland.

J. M. SCHOFIELD,
Major-General.

[Second indorsement.[

HEADQUARTERS DEPARTMENT OF THE CUMBERLAND,
Duck River, Tenn., December 23, 1864.

Respectfully forwarded to Maj. Gen. H. W. Halleck, Chief of Staff, recommending that Brig. Gen. J. D. Cox be promoted to the grade of major-general.

GEO. H. THOMAS,
Major-General, U. S. Volunteers, Commanding.

HDQRS. THIRD DIVISION, TWENTY-THIRD ARMY CORPS,
December 17, 1864.

Maj. J. A. CAMPBELL,
Assistant Adjutant-General:

SIR: In the condition of the roads I think it certain that the trains will be so late getting up that it will be entirely impracticable to bring rations here from the Franklin pike. I would suggest that the quickest way will be for us to march to the place where the trains are in the morning, and halt there long enough to issue. If this is done, please give me the order of march as early as practicable.

Very respectfully, &c.,

J. D. COX,
Brigadier-General.

HDQRS. FIRST DIVISION, DETACH. ARMY OF THE TENN.,
In the Field, near Nashville, Tenn., December 17, 1864.

ABRAHAM LINCOLN,
President of the United States:

"Smith's guerrillas" again did a noble work yesterday, not the least portion of which is due to the First Division. I respectfully ask, as an act of justice and honor fairly won, that Col. W. L. McMillen, Ninety-fifth Regiment Ohio Infantry Volunteers, Col. L. F. Hubbard, Fifth Regiment Minnesota Infantry Volunteers, commanding the First and Second Brigades, respectively, be appointed brigadier-generals; also Col. S. G. Hill, Thirty-fifth Regiment Iowa Infantry Volunteers, who commanded the Third Brigade, and was killed while gallantly charging the enemy's work, I would recommend to be gazetted a brigadier-general.

J. McARTHUR,
Brigadier-General, U. S. Volunteers.

[First indorsement.]

I heartily concur in the recommendation of General McArthur, and respectfully request the appointments may be made.

A. J. SMITH,
Major-General, Volunteers.

[Second indorsement.]

I witnessed the assault on the enemy's works conducted by the above named officers, and unhesitatingly commend them for their gallant bearing.

GEO. H. THOMAS,
Major-General, U. S. Vols., Comdg. Dept. of the Cumberland.

HEADQUARTERS DETACHMENT ARMY OF THE TENNESSEE,
Granny White Pike, December 17, 1864—7.30 a. m.

Brig. Gen. J. MCARTHUR,
Commanding First Division :

The major-general commanding directs that you move your command out on the Granny White pike at 8 a. m., you taking the advance; the Second and Third Divisions will follow you; and after them, the Twenty-third Corps. Move out the Granny White pike to Brentwood, where you will connect with the Fourth Corps and others, the whole army, when united, to march on Franklin. The wagon trains will follow the troops, in the order of precedence, on the Granny White pike. You will cover the march as far as Brentwood with a strong body of skirmishers, passing over the hills to the east of and bordering the road.

By order of Maj. Gen. A. J. Smith:

J. HOUGH,
Assistant Adjutant-General.

HEADQUARTERS DETACHMENT ARMY OF THE TENNESSEE,
In the Field, December 17, 1864.

Brigadier-General MCARTHUR,
Commanding First Division :

You will march your division at 8 a. m. to-morrow, in rear of the Third Division, Second Division leading. I hope your subsistence train will join you to-night; if so, direct it to follow you.

A. J. SMITH,
Major-General.

HDQRS. FIRST DIVISION, DETACH. ARMY OF THE TENN.,
In the Field, near Nashville, Tenn., December 17, 1864.

Col. L. F. HUBBARD,
Commanding Second Brigade, First Division :

SIR: You will move your command on the Granny White pike at 8 a. m. to Brentwood, following the First Brigade. At Brentwood the division will connect with the Fourth Corps, and when the whole army unites, we move on Franklin. The wagon trains will follow their respective brigades. You will, if necessary, cover the march with a strong body of skirmishers as far as Brentwood, passing over the hills to the east of and bordering the road, moving in conjunction with the skirmishers of the First Brigade.

By command of Brig. Gen. J. McArthur:

W. H. F. RANDALL,
Assistant Adjutant-General.

CHATTANOOGA, TENN., *December 17, 1864.*

COMMANDING OFFICER,
Stevenson, Ala.:

A signal party left here to-day in the 5 p. m. train. Order the party to return.

SOUTHARD HOFFMAN,
Assistant Adjutant-General.

HDQRS. CAVALRY CORPS, MIL. DIV. OF THE MISSISSIPPI,
Granny White Pike, Eight Miles from Nashville,
December 17, 1864—3 a. m.

Brig. Gen. W. D. WHIPPLE,
Chief of Staff:

The order of the major-general commanding, dated 9.10 p. m. yesterday, is received. I shall be compelled, in obedience thereto, to continue on this road as far as Brentwood, and probably farther. It seems to me that I shall be able to do the enemy more damage by crowding him now by the shortest roads, instead of losing any time to get to the other flank. I have already ordered Johnson to move very early by the Hillsborough pike for Franklin, and will do the best I possibly can with the balance of the force. The second copy of your dispatch is just received. I will send Croxton and Knipe direct to the Franklin pike; Hatch will strike it at Brentwood. I sent you word last night that I would try to get into Franklin with the whole force, but your dispatch does not acknowledge the receipt of my communication. I feel obliged to press toward the other flank. General Rucker, who was captured last night, says Hood would have retreated sooner, if he could. A dispatch from Hood to Chalmers says, "Time is all we want." I infer that he expects the arrival of Forrest's forces. The infantry ought, therefore, to crowd the enemy vigorously on the Franklin pike, and, if possible, prevent a junction of Hood and the forces now in the direction of Murfreesborough. I'll have reveille sounded, and move forward at once.

Very respectfully, your obedient servant,

J. H. WILSON,
Brevet Major-General.

HDQRS. CAVALRY CORPS, MIL. DIV. OF THE MISSISSIPPI,
Franklin, Tenn., December 17, 1864—1 p. m.

Brig. Gen. W. D. WHIPPLE,
Chief of Staff, Department of the Cumberland:

GENERAL: The rebels are on a great skedaddle; the last of them, closely pressed by Knipe, passed through this place two hours and a half ago. I have directed Johnson to try and strike them at Spring

Hill.   Knipe is pressing down the Columbia pike; Hatch close on their left; Croxton I shall direct down the Lewisburg pike.   The prisoners report the rebel army in a complete rout, and all the Tennesseeans are deserting.   Colonel Alexander, my chief of staff, is just in from Johnson, who is well down on the Columbia pike, having struck here about the same time that Knipe did.   The rebel rear guard is in position on the hills just south of here.   I have everything in hand except Croxton, and will drive at them without delay.   The Harpeth is rising rapidly; all bridges down.   Shove up the infantry and get up the pontoons.

Very respectfully, your obedient servant,
J. H. WILSON,
Brevet Major-General.

Knipe has 5 battle-flags and 300 prisoners.   The rebel army seems to be down on Hood.

J. H. W.

HDQRS. CAVALRY CORPS, MIL. DIV. OF THE MISSISSIPPI,
Franklin, December 17, 1864—1.30 p. m.
[General WHIPPLE:]

GENERAL: The rebels began passing through here early yesterday morning—cavalry, artillery, and infantry.   One of our surgeons here says he never saw a worse rabble; they are completely demoralized. I'll do what I can for the rear guard.   Can't hear definitely of Forrest, though it is reported he withdrew from Murfreesborough yesterday.

J. H. WILSON,
Brevet Major-General.

HDQRS. CAVALRY CORPS, MIL. DIV. OF THE MISSISSIPPI,
Three Miles North of Thompson's Station, on West Harpeth,
December 17, 1864—6 p. m.
Brig. Gen. W. D. WHIPPLE,
Chief of Staff:

GENERAL: We have " bust up" Stevenson's division of infantry, a brigade of cavalry, and taken three guns.   The Fourth Cavalry and Hatch's division, supported by Knipe, made several beautiful charges, breaking the rebel infantry in all directions.   There has been a great deal of night firing, volleys and cannonading from our guns—the rebels have none.   It is very dark, and our men are considerably scattered, but I'll collect them on this bank of the stream—West Harpeth.   Hatch is a brick!

Very respectfully, your obedient servant,
J. H. WILSON,
Brevet Major-General, Commanding.

HDQRS. CAVALRY CORPS, MIL. DIV. OF THE MISSISSIPPI,
Johnson's House, Six Miles from Franklin,
December 17, 1864—7.10 p. m.
Brigadier-General WHIPPLE,
Assistant Adjutant-General, Dept. of the Cumberland:

GENERAL: Upon further investigation I find that Knipe's division participated most handsomely in the affair of this evening; nothing could have been more brilliant than the behavior of the troops. If it had only been light we would certainly have destroyed their entire rear guard; as it was, they were severely punished. The guns will be sent in as soon as wheels can be fitted to the carriages. My command needs forage badly; this country seems to be entirely stripped. I will assemble everything, except Croxton's brigade, along the line of the West Harpeth to-night. Johnson must be near our right flank. As soon as it is light in the morning, and everything fed, I will push forward.

Respectfully, &c.,

J. H. WILSON,
Brevet Major-General, Commanding.

HEADQUARTERS DEPARTMENT OF THE CUMBERLAND,
December 17, 1864—10.50 [p. m.].
Maj. Gen. J. H. WILSON,
Comdg. Cavalry Corps, Military Division of the Mississippi:

GENERAL: Yours of 6 and 7.10 this eve received. The major-general commanding approves of your suggestion to feed and push on in the morning as early as possible. He also desires to express his high appreciation of the conduct of yourself, officers, and men. He has just learned from General A. J. Smith that he yesterday captured Johnson's entire division, including Johnson himself.

Very respectfully, your obedient servant,

WM. D. WHIPPLE,
Assistant Adjutant-General, &c.

HEADQUARTERS FOURTH ARMY CORPS,
Franklin, Tenn., December 17, 1864—9 p. m.
Brevet Major-General WILSON,
Comdg. Cavalry Corps, Military Division of the Mississippi:

The river rose so rapidly, the driftwood was so heavy, and the current so swift, that I have been unable to make a bridge, and do not expect to get over until the pontoons come. I have notified General Thomas, and asked him to hurry up the pontoons. I tell you of this so you may know how I am situated. If the pontoons get up to-night I hope to get off early in the morning, and will use all possible dispatch in getting up to you. I congratulate you and your command on your distinguished success to-day.

Respectfully,

TH. J. WOOD,
Brigadier-General of Volunteers.

CIRCULAR.]   HDQRS. CAV. CORPS, MIL. DIV. OF THE MISS.,
Granny White Pike, Eight Miles from Nashville,
December 17, 1864—3.30 a. m.

The Cavalry Corps will move at the earliest possible moment after the receipt of this order, by the following lines:

1. Croxton's brigade will march, by the most direct road, to the Franklin pike, pressing the enemy closely by that road and those immediately to the east of it, leaving the pike itself for Knipe's division.

2. Knipe's division will move, by the nearest road, to the Franklin pike, and press the enemy on that road and any that may be found on its immediate right.

3. Hatch's division will follow the enemy, on this road, to Brentwood, and press the enemy closely on the right of the Franklin pike. It may not be necessary to strike Brentwood at all, if roads can be found between the Hillsborough and Franklin pikes. General Hatch will use his discretion.

4. General Johnson will march, in pursuance of instructions last night, by the Hillsborough pike.

5. Cavalry Corps headquarters will be with the Fifth Division. Frequent communications must be sent in by the various columns.

J. H. WILSON,
Brevet Major-General, Commanding.

SPECIAL
FIELD ORDERS,
No. 4.*
}
HEADQUARTERS CAVALRY CORPS,
MILITARY DIVISION OF THE MISSISSIPPI,
Johnson's House, December 17, 1864.

I. Commanding officers will be very active to-night and early to-morrow in obtaining forage, and will see that every horse is well fed.

II. The corps will be assembled in the following order to-morrow: Johnson's division, with one regiment on Carter's Creek, the balance connecting with the Seventh Division, General Knipe, on the West Harpeth River. The Seventh Division will be on the right side of the Columbia pike. The Fifth Division will be on the left of the Columbia pike, its right resting on the left of the Seventh Division. General Croxton's brigade will be on the Lewisburg pike. When this disposition is effected, at 6.30 a. m. to-morrow the command will move forward in that order.

III. Commanders of divisions and detached brigades will detail a suitable officer from their respective commands to report to these headquarters as aides to the general commanding.

IV. Commanding officers will take measures to bring forward supplies of ordnance, and such other supplies as they may need.

By order of Brevet Major-General Wilson:

A. J. ALEXANDER,
Lieutenant-Colonel and Acting Chief of Staff.

MRS. OWEN'S HOUSE,
Wilson Pike, Four Miles and a Half South of Brentwood,
[*December 17*], *1864—9.30 a. m.*

[General WILSON:]

GENERAL: I am at this point, with my advance two miles farther. Have sent scout to Nolensville pike, and will not move farther until I hear from it. Have captured about fifty prisoners. No considerable force moved by this road. Forrest reported to be on my left. Will the infantry follow me on this road? I am two miles and a half from the Franklin pike.

Respectfully, yours,

JOHN T. CROXTON,
Brigadier-General.

---

*Appears as No. 7 in order book.

HEADQUARTERS CAVALRY CORPS,
Seven Miles from Franklin, December 17, 1864.

Brigadier-General CROXTON,
Commanding Brigade:

GENERAL: Generals Hatch and Knipe are in Franklin. Push along as fast as possible by the road you fell back on when Hood advanced on Nashville. Cross the Harpeth River and endeavor to strike the enemy's flank on the Lewisburg pike. Watch well your left. If possible, send a small force through to communicate with the garrison at Murfreesborough, to inform them what has taken place. Keep us well informed of your progress. Orders will be sent you when you reach the Lewisburg pike, or are near it.

By command of Brevet Major-General Wilson:

E. B. BEAUMONT,
Major and Assistant Adjutant-General.

HDQRS. FIRST BRIGADE, FIRST DIVISION, CAVALRY CORPS,
Douglass Church, December 17, 1864—7 p. m.

Major BEAUMONT,
Assistant Adjutant-General:

MAJOR: I am four miles south of Franklin, on the Lewisburg pike. Have sent down three miles farther. Nothing passed on this road save stragglers and about two regiments cavalry. Sent within two miles of Peytonsville and found no force. Have taken to-day 130 prisoners. Had to swim Harpeth. Sent my artillery via Franklin. Rations out to-night. Shall I order up my supply train, or will it be done?

Respectfully, your obedient servant,

JOHN T. CROXTON,
Brigadier-General of Volunteers.

NICHOLS' HOUSE, *December 17, 1864.*

Capt. ROBERT LE ROY,
Asst. Adjt. Gen., First Cav. Div., Dept. of the Cumberland:

CAPTAIN: I have reliable information that Lyon, with a considerable body of men, crossed the Tradewater River at White's old mill about 10 o'clock this morning. He had one piece of artillery, a caisson, and three or four wagons loaded with goods, and burned the bridge immediately after crossing. Several wagons that came from the direction of Princeton after the bridge was burned went up the river to cross at a ford. The river is hardly fordable at White's Mill, but I think we can swim it. My scouts are out. If they bring information I will send it. My impression is that Lyon wishes to spend a few days among his fair friends in Union County. Unless otherwise ordered, I shall march to the mill at daylight, following the train, and try to cross.

Very respectfully,

O. H. LA GRANGE.

HDQRS. SECOND BRIGADE, SECOND DIVISION CAVALRY,
Louisville, Ky., December 17, 1864.

Captain SCOTT,
    Actg. Assistant Adjutant-General, Second Division Cavalry:

SIR: I have to report, for the information of the general command-ing, that a citizen from the Newburg road came in last night and reported that a party of fifteen guerrillas were pillaging the country three miles from here, and had murdered a citizen named Walthers. I immediately sent a lieutenant and twenty-five men of Fourth Michi-gan, with orders to kill. On their return to camp I will report further.
    I am, respectfully, your obedient servant,
                        ROBT. H. G. MINTY.

HDQRS. SECOND BRIGADE, SECOND DIVISION CAVALRY,
Louisville, Ky., December 17, 1864.

Captain SCOTT,
    Actg. Assistant Adjutant-General, Second Division Cavalry:

SIR: The scout which I sent out last night, as reported this a. m., has returned. It went as far as Brumerstown, about twelve miles out. The guerrillas had passed through that place, and had been fired upon by the citizens, and two Kentucky soldiers, whom they held as prison-ers, were shot. The last heard of the guerrillas they were ten miles from Brumerstown.
    I am, respectfully, your obedient servant,
                        ROBT. H. G. MINTY,
                    Colonel, Commanding Brigade.

CAIRO, December 17, 1864.

Major-General WILSON,
    Commanding Cavalry Corps:

Found Winslow's command here—part was ordered to Paducah, by General Meredith; part to Memphis, by General Washburn. Have sent all to Louisville. Telegraph latest orders to Memphis.
                        E. UPTON.

HDQRS. CAVALRY CORPS, MIL. DIV. OF THE MISSISSIPPI,
Near Franklin, December 17, 1864—4 p. m.

General JOHNSON,
    Commanding Sixth Division:

GENERAL: The general commanding desires you to move on the road you are now on until dark; encamp, and communicate with him by a staff officer. Knipe is moving on the Columbia pike, and Hatch parallel to it, on the left.
    Respectfully, &c.,
                    A. J. ALEXANDER,
          Lieutenant-Colonel and Acting Chief of Staff.

DECHERD, *December 17, 1864.*

General WHIPPLE,
    Chief of Staff:

James A. Moore, of General Rousseau's headquarters, and known to Major Polk, assistant adjutant-general, reports to me to-night that Breckinridge passed Woodbury, twenty-one miles southeast of Murfreesborough, on the 13th, with cavalry, artillery, and infantry, estimated at 10,000, going toward Murfreesborough. Heavy firing heard to-day at Duck River, in direction of latter place. All quiet here.

WILLARD WARNER,
Colonel 180th Ohio, Commanding Post.

HEADQUARTERS DEPARTMENT OF THE CUMBERLAND,
Hale's House, Granny White Pike, December 17, 1864—8.30 a. m.

Major-General ROUSSEAU,
    Murfreesborough:

The major-general commanding directs the new regiments recently sent to Murfreesborough, and not a portion of the permanent garrison, be prepared to join the Fourth and Twenty-third Army Corps, according to the assignments made, which will be designated in a future order, when they shall be directed to march. They can now be got ready to obey such order as soon as given by the major-general commanding. In the operations of the 15th and 16th our forces have been signally successful in driving the enemy from every position he has taken, and, very fortunately for us, with but little comparative loss on our side. Our captures for both days' operations sum up as follows: Three brigadier-generals and a large number of prisoners, about 4,000; between 40 and 50 pieces of artillery; and a vast number of small-arms, thrown away by the enemy in his precipitate retreat. The pursuit will be continued this morning, and the enemy will be closely pressed at all points. Orders will be given to the railroad construction parties to repair the Nashville and Chattanooga Railroad in the shortest possible time, and restore our communication by rail to all points on our lines.

I have the honor to be, general, very respectfully, your obedient servant,

ROBT. H. RAMSEY,
Assistant Adjutant-General.

HEADQUARTERS DEPARTMENT OF THE CUMBERLAND,
Near Franklin, December 17, 1864.

Brig. Gen. R. S. GRANGER,
    Stevenson:

The major-general commanding directs that you immediately reoccupy the railroad as far as Decatur, throwing supplies into Decatur by means of steam-boats. The rebel army is in full retreat down the Columbia pike, much demoralized. We have captured Ned Johnson's entire division, including himself, also Bate's division, and broken up Stevenson's division.

WM. D. WHIPPLE,
Assistant Adjutant-General, &c.

HEADQUARTERS DEPARTMENT OF THE CUMBERLAND,
Granny White Pike, December 17, 1864.

Brig. Gen. JOHN F. MILLER,
Commanding Post of Nashville:

GENERAL: The major-general commanding directs that you send a regiment over the field of yesterday to bury the dead, collect the artillery, small-arms, and other material captured from the enemy. Teams sufficient to haul twenty-three pieces of artillery will be required, that being the number captured yesterday.

Very respectfully, your obedient servant,
WM. D. WHIPPLE,
Brigadier-General and Chief of Staff.

CLARKSVILLE, December 17, 1864—5 p. m.

Brigadier-General WHIPPLE,
Assistant Adjutant-General:

I sent a force to prevent Lyon from crossing between this and Donelson this morning. They report Lyon retreating toward Canton.
A. A. SMITH,
Commanding.

LOUISVILLE, KY., December 17, 1864—5.30 p. m.

Maj. THOMAS T. ECKERT:

Following just passed here to General Thomas, dated near Kingsport, Tenn., 13th, via Cumberland Gap 17th:

Left Knoxville 10th; overtook Duke's (formerly Morgan's) command yesterday; drove him across Holston; attacked, captured, and killed nearly the whole command, taking whole wagon train. Colonel Morgan (John's brother) among prisoners. We are now moving to Bristol, where we hope to treat Vaughn in the same manner.

GEO. STONEMAN,
Major-General.

Some of Breckinridge's orders captured, which say orders from Richmond direct all lead and ammunition must be hunted up and sent to Ordnance Department, and guns fired for cleaning must have ball extracted first to save it; also directs utmost economy in forage, it being equally scarce. A reliable report to commander at Decherd, 16th, says Breckinridge passed Woodbury, twenty-one miles east of Murfreesborough, on the 13th, with artillery and infantry, estimated at 10,000, going toward Murfreesborough. Heavy firing heard yesterday in direction of Murfreesborough, from Duck River, by our men.
S. BRUCH,
Captain, Assistant Quartermaster, U. S. Military Telegraph.

KNOXVILLE, December 17, 1864.

Capt. HENRY A. FORD,
Acting Assistant Adjutant-General:

Thank you for your dispatch. Breckinridge was certainly at Strawberry Plains, Tenn., 19th of November, and afterward fell back toward

Virginia. His force cannot have passed through East and Middle Tennessee since that time, or through the mountains of Kentucky. We could not have failed to hear and know of such movement here. Breckinridge himself may be at Murfreesborough, but it seems impossible that it should be with the force he had in East Tennessee.

DAVIS TILLSON,
Brigadier-General of Volunteers.

PADUCAH, KY., <i>December 17, 1864.</i>

Capt. J. BATES DICKSON,
　　Assistant Adjutant-General, Lexington, Ky.:

CAPTAIN: General Thomas has placed at my disposal four regiments of infantry, and ordered me to move against Lyon when he was at Danville crossing. I have telegraphed him for the use of cavalry to enable me to do so. Three regiments have arrived here, and when I assume the offensive I will not withdraw any of the present garrison from the posts in this district. Lyon's headquarters are at Princeton, and his men are scattered all over the country, robbing and conscripting. There is no force of ours after Lyon. General Thomas requests me to move upon him.

S. MEREDITH,
Brigadier-General.

PADUCAH, <i>December 17, 1864.</i>
(Received 12 m.)

Col. E. T. SPRAGUE:

COLONEL: Send on all troops, quick as you can, from Cairo, both cavalry and infantry.

S. MEREDITH,
Brigadier-General.

[Indorsement.]

DECEMBER 17, 1864.

The cavalry is now embarking for Louisville, by order of Major-General Upton, who is here direct from General Thomas. I will forward the infantry as fast as it arrives.

E. T. SPRAGUE,
Colonel, Commanding Post.

SMITHLAND, <i>December 17, 1864.</i>

Capt. JAMES GRAHAM,
　　Assistant Adjutant-General:

All quiet here. A number of citizens from Eddyville and Dycusburg arrived during the night, some of whom escaped after being conscripted. From all the information that I can get Lyon has his force divided in small squads. One squad was near Marion yesterday. The parties that were on this side of the river have recrossed. Captain Flye, with the Lexington, was to open on Eddyville and Dycusburg this a. m. if he sees any of them in these places. The river is now being patrolled with gun-boats from here to Clarksville.

Very respectfully,

HENRY P. REED,
Captain, Commanding Post.

SMITHLAND, *December 17, 1864—8 p. m.*

Capt. JAMES GRAHAM,
    Assistant Adjutant-General:

Six men have just arrived from Princeton this 8 p. m. They were conscripted and furloughed until Monday. General Lyon is there with 400 men and one piece of artillery. He burned the court-house yesterday.

H. P. REED,
Commanding Post.

FRANKFORT, KY., *December 17, 1864.*

Capt. J. S. BUTLER,
    Assistant Adjutant-General:

Nothing from Bridgewater since my last report. His instructions were to follow the guerrillas until they were captured or killed. Information sent Bridgewater through the different stations on the railroad of movements of troops from Lexington and Ohio River, as mentioned in your communication.

D. W. LINDSEY,
Inspector and Adjutant-General.

LEXINGTON, KY., *December 17, 1864.*

COMMANDING OFFICER,
    Burkesville, Ky.:

Take the boats of the pontoon bridge out on north side of river, concealing them as well as possible, and take a plank out of the bottom of each boat and hide the plank by burying some distance from river. After the bridge and boats are rendered useless without the planks, all members of Thirteenth Kentucky Cavalry will go to Camp Nelson to be mustered out. Let no citizen and no more soldiers than possible know where the planks are buried, but make yourself a memorandum, so they can be found when needed, and send it here.

By order of Brig. Gen. N. C. McLean:

J. S. BUTLER,
Assistant Adjutant-General.

PRIVATE.]   HEADQUARTERS NORTHERN DEPARTMENT,
    Cincinnati, Ohio, December 17, 1864.

Hon. HENRY WILSON,
    U. S. Senate:

In my letter of the 8th instant I made no allusion to the case of Major-General Meade. It is one more illustrative of the manner in which promotions are recommended in the army than either of the others I have referred to.

As early as December 1, 1863, the day of the battle of Mine Run, the authorities at Washington had his removal from the command of the Army of the Potomac in serious contemplation, and soon after I was informed reliably that it was the desire of the President and the Secretary of War that I should be restored to that position. I say reliably, for I have letters in my possession to this effect, which would leave no doubt on your mind, could I be allowed to present them to you; besides, I received advices from friends in confirmation of what I state and also in confirmation of the fact that it was freely talked of by those officials. The newspapers also announced it, and I may add that the announcement gave great satisfaction in the Army of the Potomac. The change was not made, and now, after the lapse of a year, he is recommended for a major-generalcy over my head in the regular army. I should add further in regard to General Meade, that it is well known that he has been retained in position for several months by the politicians of Pennsylvania, they making his retention a condition to their support of Mr. Lincoln for re-election; that officer in the meantime having rendered no especial service, and his continuance in position being a serious detriment to the public good. You doubtless are as fully informed of the estimation in which he is held in the Army of the Potomac as I am. You also know of the condition of that army now, and what it has been for some months past. I may also state in this connection that I was made a brigadier-general on the day of the battle of Antietam under circumstances, I believe, without a parallel. It was done on the application of George B. McClellan, then a bitter enemy, stating that it was the desire of the officers of that army that I should be promoted to that position. I think General Meade's date is about the time of the battle of Gettysburg; and who will attempt to institute a comparison of our services since? The Secretary of War will assure you that I saved the Army of the Cumberland last fall, and this spring, in the advance on Atlanta, the losses in killed and wounded in my corps were nearly one-half of those of the armies of which Sherman's force was composed; and they were no unnecessary losses resulting from unskillful maneuvering for battles, or rashness in fighting them. It is enough to say that on that brief campaign I won the hearts of the army I was serving with and the hearts of the West. I dislike to speak of myself in the measure I am doing, and only indulge in it for the reason that I have a greater dislike to being disgraced. For several months the appointment of General Meade to a major-generalcy was kept a profound secret, and when announced by the public prints, it was accompanied with the statement that it had been done at the request of the lieutenant-general. Acts of this character must inspire conscious shame and a desire to avoid the responsibility of them. Would it not be far better to put military commissions in the market, and dispose of them at public auction as any other commodity?

In the face of facts like these one may well tremble with fear in serving an administration which is the representative of the nation in its conflict with treason. In view of all that is passing one may well pause and inquire if it is not a crime to be loyal. You know, Senator—all know—that I have devoted every energy of my soul and body from the beginning of our troubles; that I have been absorbed in the magnitude of our cause morally and politically, and have only prayed that more valor and wisdom might be given me, in order that I could render greater service, and to-day I am compelled by honor and duty to invoke your aid in keeping me from being disgraced.

All officers have been called upon to place on record in the Adjutant-General's Office a statement of the services they have rendered in the rebellion. I forwarded mine, to include the year 1863, and let me advise you before acting on the nominations I have referred to, to request that it be laid before the Military Committee. I have made another effort to appear before the Committee on the Conduct of the War, but the result I have not yet learned. If General Halleck can prevent it, he will. Should I be allowed to go to Washington I shall have no fears of falling a victim to conspiracies which are the offspring of envy and jealousy. It is from these unworthy feelings I am not permitted to go in sight of any army in the field at this time, and, if it can be prevented, I shall not be allowed to the end of the chapter; and yet there is no army that would not welcome my return with enthusiasm such as has not been seen or known in this war. I know the feelings of the armies I have served with, and I know of what I am writing.

I shall request the Senators from the Pacific Coast to watch my interest in the Senate, for they are really the only members of the Senate on whom I feel that I have claims for protection. I have marked my letters private, but this I trust will not prevent your showing them to my friends, should you be disposed to do so. Hurriedly as I have had to write, I should like especially for Mr. Fessenden and Senators Wade and Chandler to read them, if they will do me that favor. I declined the tender of Mr. Fessenden's services while I was master of my sword, but now that I am disarmed, I am constrained to accept.

In reviewing my letter it may be inferred that it was only on one occasion that I was informed that it was the wish of His Excellency the President and of the Secretary of War to relieve General Meade and place me in command of the Army of the Potomac, but almost every month from December to July reports to this effect reached me, and yet it was not done. What power there was behind the throne greater than the throne itself I am not advised. I only know it was not done, and now it is proposed, by the same influence, I suppose, to promote General Meade over my head, and these same authorities appear to have given it their approval. Yesterday General Meade was not fitted for the place he holds, and I was; to-day he was promoted over my head, with no additional service except that of exploding the mine near Petersburg, which matter has been investigated, but the result not made known. Who was at fault?

Excusing myself, as I certainly do, for consuming so much of your time with what relates to myself, and hoping that I may soon have an opportunity to make my acknowledgments to you in person for your many, many kindnesses, I have the honor to remain your friend and servant,

JOSEPH HOOKER,
Major-General, Commanding.

[DECEMBER 18, 1864.—For Grant to Sherman, referring to Thomas' operations, see Vol. XLIV, p. 740.]

WASHINGTON CITY, *December 18, 1864—12.20 p. m.*
Major-General THOMAS,
Nashville, Tenn.:

The armies operating against Richmond have fired 200 guns in honor of your great victory. Sherman has fully established his base on Ossabaw Sound, with Savannah fully invested. I hope to be able to fire a salute to-morrow in honor of the fall of Savannah. In all your operations we hear nothing of Forrest. Great precautions should be taken to prevent him crossing the Cumberland or Tennessee below Eastport. After Hood is driven as far as it is possible to follow him, you want to reoccupy Decatur and all other abandoned points.

U. S. GRANT,
Lieutenant-General.

HEADQUARTERS DEPARTMENT OF THE CUMBERLAND,
In the Field, December 18, 1864—11 p. m.

Lieut. Gen. U. S. GRANT,
Washington:

Yours of 12.20 p. m. to-day received. I have already given orders to have Decatur occupied, and also to throw a strong column on the south side of the Tennessee toward Tuscumbia, for the purpose of capturing Hood's depot there, if possible, and gaining possession of his pontoon bridge. I have also requested Admiral Lee to go up the Tennessee River with a fleet of gun-boats, which he has promised to do, and his vessels are no doubt already on the way. General Wilson informed me to-day that prisoners taken yesterday by him told him that Forrest, Jackson, and another division left Murfreesborough on Thursday for Columbia direct, and that Buford with another division left Murfreesborough the same day and marched continuously until he reached Spring Hill, where he assumed the duties of rear guard to the rebel army. I hope you will be able to fire a salute to-morrow in honor of the capture of Savannah.

GEO. H. THOMAS,
Major-General.

HEADQUARTERS DEPARTMENT OF THE CUMBERLAND,
Near Spring Hill, Tenn., December 18, 1864—7.30 p. m.

Maj. Gen. H. W. HALLECK,
Washington, D. C.:

The enemy have been vigorously pursued to-day, but have studiously avoided any attack by my troops. I have succeeded in taking a few prisoners, some 200 or 300, but our captures are light in comparison with the successes of the past few days. The pursuit will be continued in the morning at as early an hour as the troops can march. The following copies of orders, found in Breckinridge's camp in East Tennessee, are transmitted for your information:

GENERAL ORDERS, } HDQRS. DEPT. OF WEST. VIRGINIA AND EAST TENNESSEE,
No. 27.   }   *Wytheville, Va., December 2, 1864.*

In accordance with orders received from the Ordnance Department at Richmond that it has become of vital importance to husband small-arms ammunition and lead, the order is published that all lead which can be gleaned from battle-fields, or otherwise obtained, will be collected by the brigade ordnance officer, and to be sent to the nearest arsenal or ordnance depot. Whenever guns are to be relieved of their loads the balls should be drawn, if practicable; otherwise, the loads should be discharged into boxes of sand or dirt, so that the lead may be recovered and turned into the ordnance department. The attention of the commanding officers is called to the necessity giving rise to this order, and its rigid enforcement is strictly enjoined.

By command of Major-General Breckinridge:

J. STODDARD JOHNSTON,
Assistant Adjutant-General.

CIRCULAR.]   HDQRS. DEPT. OF WEST. VIRGINIA AND EAST TENNESSEE,
                                Wytheville, Va., December 2, 1864.

The attention of commanding officers is called to the scarcity of forage in this department, and the absolute necessity of ecomony in its consumption. Evidences of its waste have been observed heretofore. The proper officers must, in all cases, superintend the issue of forage, and commanding officers and every company officer must give his strict personal attention.

By command of Major-General Breckinridge:

W. B. MYERS,
Assistant Adjutant-General.

I have found the railroad, thus far, but little disturbed, and my trains will be up by railroad in a day or two at the furthest. The telegraph is up with me now. I find, upon receiving more correct reports of the operations of the 16th instant, that Maj. Gen. Ed. Johnson's entire division, with all the brigade commanders, was captured in the works which were carried by assault, besides destroying a brigade of the enemy's cavalry and capturing its commander, Brigadier-General Rucker. Among the captures made to-day are the rebel Brigadier-General Quarles, wounded, and a number of other rebels, also wounded, lying in the houses by the roadside, unable to get away.

GEO. H. THOMAS,
Major-General, U. S. Volunteers, Commanding.

HEADQUARTERS DEPARTMENT OF THE CUMBERLAND,
Near Franklin, December 18, 1864—9 a. m. (Via Wheeling, Va.)
Maj. Gen. P. H. SHERIDAN,
Headquarters Army of the Shenandoah:

Your telegram of the 17th is just received. Accept my sincere thanks for your very kind congratulations. This army sends greetings to the Army of the Shenandoah. Our operations yesterday were nearly equal to those of the 15th and 16th instant. We captured three pieces of artillery yesterday and a number of prisoners, and had not night settled would have secured almost the entire rear guard of the enemy, consisting of Stevenson's division of infantry and a brigade of cavalry, all of which ran like a flock of sheep. On the 16th we captured the entire division of Maj. Gen. Ed. Johnson, and all his brigade commanders, in their works, which were carried by assault, besides destroying one brigade of cavalry, capturing its commander, Brigadier-General Rucker.

Yours, sincerely,

GEO. H. THOMAS,
Commanding.

WASHINGTON, *December 18, 1864—12.20 p. m.*
Maj. Gen. GEORGE H. THOMAS:

All officers and detachments absent from General Sherman's army, and not on duty with you, will immediately join their respective commands, near Savannah, via New York. The quartermaster at New York will furnish transportation. Officers and detachments belonging to the same army now serving with you will join General Sherman in the same way as relieved. Those who have less than three months to serve will be relieved by you, and be organized provisionally, or be attached to other organizations. Orders will be sent by mail. Please acknowledge receipt of this telegram.

By order of the Secretary of War:

S. F. CHALFIN,
Assistant Adjutant-General.

HEADQUARTERS DEPARTMENT OF THE CUMBERLAND,
In the Field, December 18, 1864.
Maj. S. F. CHALFIN,
Assistant Adjutant-General, Washington:

Your dispatch ordering men of General Sherman's army to join received.

GEO. H. THOMAS,
Major-General.

NASHVILLE, TENN., *December 18, 1864.*
Maj. Gen. M. C. MEIGS,
　　　Quartermaster-General:

We open the Cumberland to-day. Transports here have left under convoy of the gun-boats. We captured yesterday 450 prisoners and 5 flags. We have taken in all over 5,000 prisoners, among whom are Major-General Johnson and Brigadier-Generals Jackson and Smith, and over 250 commissioned officers. Besides, Hood has lost most of his artillery, over 40 pieces already reported, and his army is terribly shattered. He will be fortunate to reach the Tennessee River with half his original force. In his order of battle General Thomas assigned the Quartermaster's Department an important position on interior line of works, and we held the same three days and two nights, thus enabling the general to take a considerably larger force into the field. I withdrew the men yesterday, and now the department is doing all it can to sustain the army in pursuing the enemy, giving up most of the transportation of the department for that purpose.

　　　　　　　J. L. DONALDSON,
　　　　　　　　　Chief Quartermaster.

HEADQUARTERS DEPARTMENT OF THE CUMBERLAND,
　　Near Spring Hill, December 18, 1864—9 p. m.
Brig. Gen. J. L. DONALDSON,
　　Chief Quartermaster, Dept. of the Cumberland, Nashville:

The major-general commanding directs me to inform you that he desires you to send a party to Franklin as soon as possible, to construct a permanent road bridge at the point originally used for such bridge, which has been for some time destroyed.

I have the honor to be, general, your obedient servant,
　　　　　　　ROBT. H. RAMSEY,
　　　　　　　　　Assistant Adjutant-General.

NASHVILLE, *December 18, 1864.*
Capt. R. H. RAMSEY,
　　Assistant Adjutant-General:

Your telegram received. Say to the major-general commanding that the bridge at Franklin has already been provided for. Working party will leave here to-night or early in the morning. Thanks for information as to your movements. Please keep me advised.

　　　　　　　J. L. DONALDSON,
　　　　　　Brigadier-General and Chief Quartermaster.

HEADQUARTERS DEPARTMENT OF THE CUMBERLAND,
　　Near Spring Hill, December 18, 1864—9 p. m.
Col. J. G. PARKHURST,
　　Provost-Marshal-General, Dept. of the Cumberland, Nashville:

The major-general commanding directs me to say that he desires you to repair as soon as possible to Franklin, Tenn., and register the names of the rebel wounded and attendants left at that place by the enemy, and also to make preparations for their speedy removal to the rebel hospital at Nashville. There are also a number of rebel wounded, including the rebel Brigadier-General Quarles, in houses on the road between Franklin and Spring Hill; these are also to be registered and sent to Nashville as rapidly as possible.

I am, colonel, very respectfully, your obedient servant,

ROBT. H. RAMSEY,
Assistant Adjutant-General.

NASHVILLE, TENN., *December 18, 1864.*

Brig. Gen. D. C. McCALLUM,
    Superintendent of Military Railroads:

Everything is working well. Will have the railroad open to-night to Franklin, and we will follow General Thomas as fast as possible. I have parties working on the back end of the break on the Nashville and Chattanooga Railroad, and will have it opened in a few days. There is a very large amount of work blocked out for us ahead.

W. W. WRIGHT,
Chief Engineer.

HEADQUARTERS DEPARTMENT OF THE CUMBERLAND,
December 18, 1864.

Col. W. W. WRIGHT,
    Chief Engineer U. S. Military Railroads,
        Military Division of the Mississippi:

COLONEL: The major-general commanding directs that you immediately proceed to put the railroads of the military division in running order; and to do this you are authorized during the present emergency to appropriate any timber which may be necessary for making ties or bridge timber that may be standing near the lines of roads you are requested to repair. When the emergency is passed and the roads repaired you will procure your ties and timber by contract as heretofore.

Very respectfully, your obedient servant,

WM. D. WHIPPLE,
Brigadier-General and Chief of Staff.

NASHVILLE, TENN., *December 18, 1864.*

Maj. T. T. ECKERT:

General Rousseau commands at Murfreesborough, with 6,000 at least. He reports Forrest killed and 1,500 of his men captured. Colonel Warner, commanding at Decherd, reports that Breckinridge crossed the Chattanooga railroad, ten miles south of Murfreesborough, Friday, 10,000 strong, pushing forward to join Hood. General Thomas knows.

J. C. VAN DUZER.

HEADQUARTERS FOURTH ARMY CORPS,
In the Field, December 18, 1864—9 p. m.

Major-General THOMAS:

GENERAL: My troops are encamped three and a half miles from Rutherford's Creek and about seven miles from Columbia, being about one mile and a half in advance of the cavalry. The troops had a hard march to-day, but the greater part of them were in camp by dark. It is probable that we will have some trouble in crossing Rutherford's Creek, and we may have to build a bridge over it. By all means the pontoon train should be hurried up for the crossing of Duck River. Have you any special orders for me to-morrow?

Very respectfully, your obedient servant,

TH. J. WOOD,
Brigadier-General, Commanding.

HEADQUARTERS DEPARTMENT OF THE CUMBERLAND,
Near Spring Hill, December 18, 1864—12 m.

Brig. Gen. TH. J. WOOD,
Commanding Fourth Army Corps:

GENERAL: I have the honor, by direction of the major-general commanding, to acknowledge the receipt of your report of 9 p. m. this day, and, in reply, to state that the pontoon train has been ordered forward as rapidly as possible, and should be here to-night. There are no further orders than those sent you last evening, viz: to continue the pursuit of the enemy to-morrow morning, marching at about 8 o'clock.

I am, general, very respectfully, your obedient servant,

ROBT. H. RAMSEY,
Assistant Adjutant-General.

HDQRS. CAVALRY CORPS, MIL. DIV. OF THE MISSISSIPPI,
Widow Sayers', December 18, 1864—2 p. m.

Brig. Gen. T. J. WOOD,
Commanding Fourth Army Corps:

GENERAL: I have halted my command at this place, about two miles from Spring Hill, to feed, issue rations, &c. I am informed that the enemy has two pontoon bridges across the Duck River near the old wagon bridge. A little girl, who has just arrived from Tuscumbia, which place she left three days ago, says she saw no troops at that place or this side. Prisoners say that Hood cannot get across the Tennessee River, as our forces at Memphis had repaired the railroad as far as La Grange, and were marching out to attack him in flank.

Very respectfully, your obedient servant,

J. H. WILSON,
Brevet Major-General, Commanding.

HEADQUARTERS FOURTH ARMY CORPS,
Spring Hill, December 18, 1864—3 p. m.

Major-General WILSON:

GENERAL: Your very satisfactory note of 2 p. m. has just been received. The head of my column is now in Spring Hill, and I will push on as far as I can to-night to keep well closed up. On account of the extreme heaviness of the road the men are very much jaded and are straggling some. Captain Stansbury informs me that you will probably leave the turnpike and go to the left; if you do so, please inform me, and certainly try to give me your position to-night, and I will, in return, communicate to you my position.

Very respectfully, your obedient servant,

TH. J. WOOD,
Brigadier-General, Commanding.

HEADQUARTERS FOURTH ARMY CORPS,
Franklin, Tenn., December 18, 1864—7.30 a. m.

Orders of the day for the Fourth Corps:

The bridge that Colonel Suman has been building is just finished, and the corps will start at once—General Kimball's division will lead, followed by General Elliott's, then General Beatty's. Five ammunition wagons, ten ambulances, and one battery will follow each division. Immediately following the troops will follow the Artillery Brigade; then the ammunition trains, in the order in which the divisions march; then artillery ammunition trains; then the hospital trains; then corps head-quarters train, followed by headquarters trains, in the order in which the divisions march; then regimental wagons.

By order of Brigadier-General Wood:

J. S. FULLERTON,
Lieutenant-Colonel and Assistant Adjutant-General.

HEADQUARTERS FOURTH ARMY CORPS,
Three Miles and a Half North of Rutherford's Creek,
December 18, 1864—11.45 p. m.

Orders of the day for the Fourth Corps for to-morrow, December 19, 1864:

The corps will march in pursuit of the enemy, starting at 8 a. m. and moving toward Columbia—the Second Division will lead, followed by the Third, then the First. Division trains will move in the order in which the divisions march, and in the same general order in which they moved to-day. The artillery of the command will also move as to-day.

By order of Brigadier-General Wood:

J. S. FULLERTON,
Lieutenant-Colonel and Assistant Adjutant-General.

HEADQUARTERS DEPARTMENT OF THE CUMBERLAND,
In the Field, December 18, 1864.

Maj. Gen. J. M. SCHOFIELD,
Commanding Army of the Ohio:

GENERAL: The major-general commanding the forces in the field directs that you detail a general officer, to proceed without delay to Murfreesborough, to take command of, and march to join the Twenty-third Army Corps, such regiments as are at that place which have been assigned to it. Major-General Steedman, with his command, is now on his way from Franklin to Murfreesborough, with orders to turn over his transportation, upon his arrival, for the use of the portion of your command above referred to.

I am, general, very respectfully, your obedient servant,

WM. D. WHIPPLE,
Brigadier-General and Chief of Staff.

HEADQUARTERS DEPARTMENT OF THE CUMBERLAND,
Near Spring Hill, December 18, 1864—7.15 p. m.

Maj. Gen. JOHN M. SCHOFIELD,
Commanding Twenty-third Army Corps:

The major-general commanding directs that you move your command, in its present order of march, in the morning of to-morrow (19th), in pursuit of the enemy, at about 8 o'clock.

I have the honor to be, general, very respectfully, your obedient servant,

ROBT. H. RAMSEY,
Assistant Adjutant-General.

Please send me the organization of new regiments assigned to your corps.

R. H. R.

(Same, excepting postscript, to Generals Wood and Smith.)

———

HEADQUARTERS ARMY OF THE OHIO,
Near Brentwood, Tenn., December 18, 1864.

Brig. Gen. J. D. COX,
Commanding Third Division, Twenty-third Army Corps:

GENERAL: The commanding general directs me to inform you that the command will march this morning on the Franklin pike, in the same order as yesterday, but that they will not march until rations are issued, and he desires the troops moved over to the Franklin pike to obtain their rations, or to have the trains taken over to them, which ever will be the easiest or most practicable.

I am, general, very respectfully, your obedient servant,

J. A. CAMPBELL,
Major and Assistant Adjutant-General.

(Same to Major-General Couch.)

———

HEADQUARTERS ARMY OF THE OHIO,
In the Field, Franklin, Tenn., December 18, 1864.

Brigadier-General COX:

GENERAL: The major-general commanding directs that you get your troops over the river, if you can get the bridge before dark, and camp on ground which will be pointed out to you by some officer from these headquarters. If you cannot get the bridge before dark select any convenient ground on the north side and camp, and be ready to move out at daylight to-morrow. He further directs that, in any event, you push all your supply and ammunition trains over to-night, and park them on suitable ground beyond the town. His headquarters will be in the house near the river, on the pike, on the north bank

I am, general, very respectfully, your obedient servant,

CLINTON A. CILLEY,
Assistant Adjutant-General.

HDQRS. CAVALRY CORPS, MIL. DIV. OF THE MISSISSIPPI,
December 18, 1864—8 a. m.

[General WHIPPLE:]

Dispatch received. I have seventy or eighty wounded, scattered along the road, in houses. Please send ambulances for them at once.

J. H. WILSON,
Brevet Major-General

Some of our men captured last night have just come in, and report the enemy's rear guard strongly re-enforced.

J. H. W.

HDQRS. CAVALRY CORPS, MIL. DIV. OF THE MISSISSIPPI,
In sight of Spring Hill, Tenn., December 18, 1864—11 a. m.

Brigadier-General WHIPPLE,
Assistant Adjutant-General, Department of the Cumberland :

GENERAL: A prisoner just taken states that Forrest, with Jackson's division of cavalry and two brigades of infantry, left Murfreesborough day before yesterday for Columbia, where he may be to-day. Buford's division of cavalry left Murfreesborough the same day, and marched continuously until they struck this road, and have since been covering the rear of the infantry. Johnson is now engaging the enemy to the right of Spring Hill, and everything is pressing forward to his assistance. I will push them as rapidly as I can toward Columbia to-night, and then take the route as indicated by the major-general commanding.

Very respectfully, your obedient servant,

J. H. WILSON,
Brevet Major-General, Commanding.

HDQRS. CAVALRY CORPS, MIL. DIV. OF THE MISSISSIPPI,
Eight Miles from Columbia, December 18, 1864—1 p. m.

Brig. Gen. W. D. WHIPPLE,
Chief of Staff, Department of the Cumberland :

GENERAL: All our efforts to bring the rebels to a stand this morning have failed, though their alluring positions have carried us to this place. I have halted to issue rations and ammunition, and will push on to Rally Hill as soon as possible. All indications are that the rebels have no intention of halting this side of Columbia. Lee's and Hood's headquarters were about Spring Hill last night; Cheatham's here. I am not entirely sure that we shall gain time by taking to the left, but we will do the best we can. If you have any further orders, please send them at once.

Very respectfully, your obedient servant,

J. H. WILSON,
Brevet Major-General.

HDQRS. CAVALRY CORPS, MIL. DIV. OF THE MISSISSIPPI,
Three Miles South of Spring Hill, December 18, 1864—2.50 p. m.

Brigadier-General WHIPPLE,
Assistant Adjutant-General, Department of the Cumberland :

GENERAL: After looking at the maps I am satisfied that we shall lose time if we pass to the eastward of the Franklin pike, as previously directed. The rebels will most probably take the route via Mount Pleasant and Lawrenceburg to Florence—this distance is fifty-three miles; to go by Pulaski it is something over sixty miles; and all roads to the eastward are proportionally longer. It seems to me that our march should be by Williamsport, toward Eastport, crowding the enemy on that flank as much as possible. If it is intended to carry the pursuit beyond the Tennessee River, and gun-boats can control it as far as Eastport, we could lay a bridge and cross the whole army there. Please advise me what course I shall pursue.

I have the honor to be, very respectfully, your obedient servant,
J. H. WILSON,
Brevet Major-General, Commanding.

HEADQUARTERS DEPARTMENT OF THE CUMBERLAND,
In the Field, December 18, 1864.
Maj. Gen. J. H. WILSON,
Comdg. Cavalry Corps, Military Division of the Mississippi:

GENERAL: The major-general commanding directs that you press directly after the enemy to-morrow, and await the developments of another day before deciding upon your future route. You are authorized to send to Nashville to be remounted such portions of your command as are now without horses.

Very respectfully, your obedient servant,
WM. D. WHIPPLE,
Brigadier-General and Chief of Staff.

HEADQUARTERS DEPARTMENT OF THE CUMBERLAND,
In the Field, December 18, 1864.
Maj. Gen. J. H. WILSON,
Comdg. Cavalry Corps, Military Division of the Mississippi:

GENERAL: The major-general commanding directs that you concentrate the Fourth Ohio Cavalry, now picketing the river to Carthage, at Nashville, and direct it to there await the arrival of the division to which it belongs. Upon the arrival of the division at Nashville he wishes you to order it to join you as rapidly as possible without making forced marches, as he has important work marked out for it.

Very respectfully, your obedient servant,
WM. D. WHIPPLE,
Brigadier-General and Chief of Staff.

CIRCULAR.]   HDQRS. CAV. CORPS, MIL. DIV. OF THE MISS.,
Mrs. Sayers' House, December 18, 1864—1 p. m.

The Cavalry Corps will halt. Division commanders and commanders of independent brigades will take prompt measures to issue three days' rations and all the ammunition possible to the men, as the command will leave the turnpike this afternoon. Commanders will see that every horse is fed and groomed at once.

By order of Brevet Major-General Wilson:
A. J. ALEXANDER,
Lieutenant-Colonel and Acting Chief of Staff.

SPECIAL   HEADQUARTERS CAVALRY CORPS,
FIELD ORDERS,   MILITARY DIVISION OF THE MISSISSIPPI,
No. 5.*   *December 18, 1864.*

*   *   *   *   *   *   *

II. Commanders of divisions and independent brigades will send to these headquarters, by 10 o'clock this p. m., an approximate report of the effective force and a report of casualties since leaving Nashville.

III. The commanding officer of the Fourth Ohio Cavalry will concentrate his regiment at Nashville, prepare it for the field, and join his division upon its arrival at that place.

IV. The Second Division, Cavalry Corps, Military Division of the Mississippi, Brigadier-General Long commanding, will at once proceed to join the Cavalry Corps in the field. The division will march as rapidly as possible without making forced marches.

By order of Brevet Major-General Wilson:

E. B. BEAUMONT,
Major and Assistant Adjutant-General.

HDQRS. FIRST BRIG., FIRST DIV., CAVALRY CORPS,
MILITARY DIVISION OF THE MISSISSIPPI,
December 18, 1864.

Lieut. Col. A. J. ALEXANDER:

SIR: In obedience to Special Field Orders, No. 5, from headquarters Cavalry Corps, I have the honor to submit the following report of effective strength of this command and regimental casualties since leaving Nashville.

Commissioned officers present, including field and staff of brigade and regiments and regimental line officers, 70; enlisted men, 1,456; total, 1,526.

Casualties: Wounded (slight), 6.

Very respectfully, your obedient servant,

JNO. T. CROXTON,
Brigadier-General, Commanding.

AT THE BRIDGE NEAR WHITE'S MILL,
December 18, 1864—3.30 a. m.

Capt. ROBERT LE ROY,
Assistant Adjutant-General, First Cavalry Division:

CAPTAIN: I will have a foot bridge ready by daylight. The timbers of the bridge are only partially destroyed. My ambulances will come back to you; they cannot cross here. I will follow Lyon as rapidly as possible, and make him a good fight, if I catch him. The turn to Wilson's Bridge is three or four miles from here. Where shall I send my next?

O. H. LA GRANGE,
Colonel.

P. S.—I see no rebel picket near the river. They inquired for Providence.

---

*Appears as No. 8 in order book.

Capt. ROBERT LE ROY,
        Assistant Adjutant-General, First Cavalry Division:

I think I will try to build a foot bridge and swim my horses; it will be quicker and will surprise the rebels; besides, they may have burned the other bridge. I will send you word as soon as I can see the ground in the morning.

Respectfully,

LA GRANGE,
Colonel.

P. S.—Lyon has a strong picket at the burnt bridge.

CROSS-ROADS NEAR PRINCETON, KY.,
December 18, 1864.

Col. O. H. LA GRANGE:

The general commanding directs me to say that he is under the impression that General Lyon will endeavor to get back where he crossed, Petersburg or Gordonsville, and perhaps through Hopkinsville, to the mouth of Yellow Creek. If he takes a different course you have a sufficient force to follow him and defeat him. If he takes the road that I anticipate he will, I can intercept him near Hopkinsville. Communications from you will reach me at that point, or on the road between here and there. If Lyon scatters his command to such an extent that it would be impracticable and unprofitable to pursue him, you will return to Hopkinsville with your command. As to the propriety of this you must be the judge. I send an intelligent guide, Dr. Henry Bell, to you, who is familiar with all that country. The general will expect to hear from you as soon as possible and as often as you deem necessary. If the movement of the enemy renders it necessary to leave Hopkinsville to intercept him, he will leave dispatches for you indicating his route.

I am, colonel, very respectfully, your obedient servant,

ROBERT LE ROY,
Captain and Assistant Adjutant-General.

HEADQUARTERS FOURTH OHIO VOLUNTEER CAVALRY,
Between Nashville and Gallatin, Tenn., December 18, 1864.

Maj. E. B. BEAUMONT,
        Assistant Adjutant-General, Cavalry Corps:

MAJOR: I have the honor to report that we learn from refugees just from the Hermitage that the force of cavalry and artillery stationed there a few days past has gone in the direction of Nashville. The rebel pickets in view on the opposite side of the river have entirely disappeared, and refugees report no rebels above the mouth of Stone's River. Everything quiet in this vicinity.

Very respectfully, your obedient servant,

GEO. W. DOBB,
Major, Commanding Fourth Ohio Volunteer Cavalry.

HEADQUARTERS DEPARTMENT OF THE CUMBERLAND,
In the Field, December 18, 1864.

Maj. Gen. J. B. STEEDMAN,
  Commanding District of the Etowah, in the Field:

GENERAL: The major-general commanding the department directs that you march with your command to Murfreesborough, moving by the most direct road. Upon your arrival at Murfreesborough you will turn in your transportation, for the use of regiments of the Twenty-third Army Corps which are to march from there to join their corps, under command of Brigadier-General Ruger. You will also without delay, after your arrival at Murfreesborough, procure from the south sufficient cars to move your command to Decatur, where you will next proceed, and to which place Brig. Gen. R. S. Granger has been ordered with his command, with directions to throw into that place, by steamboat, an abundance of provisions. General Granger will re-enforce your command with as many troops as he can spare from the garrison of Decatur, retaining only sufficient to hold the place against such small force as the enemy may possibly, but not probably, send against it. You will then, with your increased force, proceed to Tuscumbia and destroy the rebel bridges over the Tennessee at that place. Before moving from Murfreesborough you will order Col. William J. Palmer, commanding Fifteenth Pennsylvania Cavalry, to join you at such place as you may designate, and on your way to Decatur collect with your force such other cavalry as you may find, including that with General Granger. You will also order from Chattanooga the transportation belonging to your command, to move you from Decatur to Tuscumbia.

I am, general, very respectfully, your obedient servant,

WM. D. WHIPPLE,
Brigadier-General and Chief of Staff.

STEVENSON, *December 18, 1864.*

Brigadier-General MEAGHER:
  The following telegram has just been received:

HEADQUARTERS DEPARTMENT OF THE CUMBERLAND,
Near Franklin, Tenn., December 18, 1864—2 a. m.[*]

The major-general commanding directs that you immediately reoccupy Decatur road as far as Decatur, carrying supplies into Decatur by means of steam-boats. The rebel army now in full retreat down the Columbia pike, much demoralized. We have captured Ned Johnson's entire division, including himself, also Bate's division, and broken up Stevenson's division.

WM. D. WHIPPLE,
Brigadier-General.

I have but 1,400 infantry and 500 cavalry to carry out this order, which contemplates garrisoning the road and Decatur. Decatur is garrisoned by Roddey's command—1,000, 1,500, or possibly 2,000 men, with six pieces of artillery. My force, you will see, therefore, is very small to carry out effectually this order. Can you give me any assistance? Six hundred or 800 men, I think, could be made to answer. I cannot have but 1,000 men with which to attack Decatur, without your assistance.

R. S. GRANGER,
Brigadier-General.

---

[*] Recorded in Thomas' "telegrams-sent" book under date of December 17. See p. 243.

STEVENSON, *December 18, 1864—6.30 p. m.*
Major-General THOMAS:

Dispatch of 2 a. m. received. Will immediately set about putting
it in execution. Have for the work 1,400 infantry and 500 cavalry.
Roddey with his command occupy Decatur; has six pieces of artillery.
Does your order mean to attack Decatur? I cannot possibly have more
than 1,000 men to do it, but will try it, if you say so. Roddey will
have quite as many men, and probably twice as many inside.

R. S. GRANGER,
Brigadier-General.

HEADQUARTERS DEPARTMENT OF THE CUMBERLAND,
In the Field, December 18, 1864.
Brig. Gen. R. S. GRANGER,
   Stevenson:

Yours received. Move as far as you can toward Decatur and open
railroad for General Steedman, who is going to same point, and who,
when he joins you, will assume direction of affairs.

WM. D. WHIPPLE,
Brigadier-General and Chief of Staff.

CHATTANOOGA, TENN., *December 18, 1864.*
Brig. Gen. R. S. GRANGER,
   Commanding, Stevenson:

General Meagher has ordered 800 men from Bridgeport to you.
Captain Forrest has been requested, in the name of General Thomas,
to co-operate with you. Transports will be at once sent to Bridgeport,
there to load with rations as ordered by General Thomas. Do you
prefer Caperton's Ferry to Bridgeport? The order is given for Bridgeport, unless you designate the other point.

SOUTHARD HOFFMAN,
Assistant Adjutant-General.

HEADQUARTERS DEPARTMENT OF THE CUMBERLAND,
December 18, 1864.
Brig. Gen. R. S. GRANGER,
   Commanding Department of Northern Alabama:

GENERAL: Major-General Steedman, commanding District of the
Etowah, has been ordered to effect the destruction of the rebel bridges
at Tuscumbia, and the major-general commanding the department
desires that you will co-operate with him in this move by re-enforcing
him with all the troops you can spare from the garrison of Decatur,
and by throwing supplies into Decatur by steam-boat from Chattanooga.
It will probably require but a very small force to defend Decatur
against any force the enemy will be able to send against it.

Very respectfully, your obedient servant,

WM. D. WHIPPLE,
Brigadier-General and Chief of Staff.

HEADQUARTERS DEPARTMENT OF THE CUMBERLAND,
Chattanooga, December 18, 1864.

Col. WILLIAM J. PALMER,
    Commanding Fifteenth Pennsylvania Cavalry, Wauhatchie:

Reported that General Thomas has again defeated Hood, with a loss of 2,000 prisoners and 30 guns. The news comes from Nashville, but not officially.

SOUTHARD HOFFMAN,
Assistant Adjutant-General.

NASHVILLE, TENN., *December 18, 1864.*

Capt. H. M. CIST,
    General Thomas' Headquarters:

In obedience to your telegram to General Miller, I have directed Colonel Matzdorff to proceed with the Seventy-fifth Pennsylvania to Franklin, to occupy its old post there and in block-houses. The One hundred and seventy-fifth Ohio occupied some of the block-houses this side of Columbia.

B. H. POLK,
Major and Assistant Adjutant-General.

NASHVILLE, *December 18, 1864.*

Brigadier-General WHIPPLE:

Captain Laporte, assistant quartermaster at Murfreesborough, is here with twenty wagons loaded with forage. Will it be safe for him to go through to that place with a guard of sixty men?

B. H. POLK,
Major and Assistant Adjutant-General.

HEADQUARTERS DEPARTMENT OF THE CUMBERLAND,
In the Field, December 18, 1864.

Maj. B. H. POLK,
    Assistant Adjutant-General, Nashville:

Yours received. General Steedman leaves Franklin for Murfreesborough with command to-morrow morning. Captain Laporte, with train, can go under his charge.

WM. D. WHIPPLE,
Brigadier-General and Chief of Staff.

CLARKSVILLE, TENN., *December 18, 1864—1 p. m.*
(Received 11.30 p. m.)

Hon. GIDEON WELLES,
    Secretary of the Navy:

The active naval patrol of the Mississippi, preventing the rebel armies west of that river from crossing to join Hood, as required by Jeff. Davis, must have had an influential bearing on the successful result of this campaign. If Lyon's mounted troops have not recrossed the Cumberland during the late thick fog, they will be captured. The country people along this river confidently expected Hood to drive the Union forces out of Tennessee and Kentucky. The great disappointment at General Thomas' victories will probably cause the Kentuckians, Tennesseeans, and North Alabamians to desert and disperse Hood's command. I shall immediately shift sufficient force to destroy Hood's pontoons at Duck River and Florence, and cut off Hood and Lyon's retreat, if stage of water in the Tennessee is sufficient. A full report of successful naval operations on this river will be sent—made as soon as detailed reports are received.

S. P. LEE,
Acting Rear-Admiral, Commanding Mississippi Squadron.

CLARKSVILLE, *December 18, 1864—11 a. m.*

Major-General THOMAS:

Your telegram 9.15 yesterday received at 10.30 to-day, with a copy of your highly interesting telegraphic report to General Halleck of yesterday 8 p. m., for which please accept my thanks, with congratulations on the additional important successes in your department.

S. P. LEE,
Acting Rear-Admiral, Commanding.

CLARKSVILLE, *December 18, 1864—1.15 p. m.*

Major-General THOMAS:

I thank you for informing me that Hood has a pontoon bridge at Florence and is reported building one at mouth of Duck River. I will ascertain, as soon as the existing fog on this river allows us to push a suitable naval force up the Tennessee River, if there be water enough in that river, under Lieutenant Corner, to destroy these bridges and cut off Hood's retreat, and prevent Lyon recrossing Tennessee River, should he now recross the Cumberland under cover of the fog.

S. P. LEE,
Acting Rear-Admiral, Commanding.

HEADQUARTERS DEPARTMENT OF THE CUMBERLAND,
Near Spring Hill, December 18, 1864—7 p. m.

Admiral S. P. LEE,
Clarksville:

Your dispatches of 11 a. m. and 1.15 p. m. are received. I am hopeful that the expedition up the Tennessee River of the iron-clads and gun-boats will be able to reach Florence within six days from the present time, as that will be just about the right time. I shall be much obliged if, in addition to the movement on the Tennessee River mentioned above, you will be as well prepared as possible to convoy either from Johnsonville or Clifton a fleet of transports with troops up the Tennessee River to Florence. I speak of this simply that you might be prepared in case I make the request. Your telegram of 6.20 p. m. [17th] is just received.

GEO. H. THOMAS,
Major-General, U. S. Volunteers, Commanding.

HEADQUARTERS DEPARTMENT OF THE CUMBERLAND,
Chattanooga, December 18, 1864.
Commander FORREST,
Commanding U. S. Naval Forces, Bridgeport:

Major-General Thomas has ordered General Granger to occupy Decatur and the Decatur road. This is to prevent any attempt on the part of Hood to cross at that point. Your fleet will be most effective in preventing any crossing at that point. I therefore, in the name of General Thomas, beg your earnest co-operation with General Granger.

SOUTHARD HOFFMAN,
Assistant Adjutant-General.

HEADQUARTERS DEPARTMENT OF THE CUMBERLAND,
December 18, 1864. (Received 19th.)
Brig. Gen. S. MEREDITH:

Yours of this day received.* The major-general commanding thinks it too late now for you to attempt to prevent Lyon crossing the Cumberland. McCook's division of cavalry is after him, and will be sufficient. Send the infantry up the Cumberland River to Nashville as quickly as possible.

WM. D. WHIPPLE,
Brigadier-General and Assistant Adjutant-General.

LEXINGTON, *December 18, 1864.*
Brig. Gen. S. MEREDITH,
Paducah, Ky.:

When do you move? Please advise me fully.

J. BATES DICKSON,
Captain and Assistant Adjutant-General.

LEXINGTON, KY., *December 18, 1864.*
Brig. Gen. H. EWING,
Louisville, Ky.:

General Meredith telegraphs he is about to assume the offensive against Lyon with troops furnished him by Major-General Thomas. He reports Lyon's headquarters at Princeton, and his men scattered over the country in that vicinity.

J. BATES DICKSON,
Captain and Assistant Adjutant-General.

CITY POINT, VA., *December 19, 1864—3.30 p. m.*
Hon. E. M. STANTON,
Secretary of War, Washington:

On reflection, I think it would have a good effect to allow Sherman's letter to General Halleck,† except such facts as refer to future movements, to be published. It is refreshing to see a commander after a campaign of more than seven months' duration ready for still further operations, and without wanting any outfit or rest.

U. S. GRANT,
Lieutenant-General.

---

* See 16th, p. 225.
† See Vol. XLIV, p. 701.

WAR DEPARTMENT,
Washington City, December 19, 1864—8 p. m.

Lieutenant-General GRANT:

You will see by to-day's papers that Sherman's dispatch, omitting such portions as seemed proper to be left out, has already been published. One or two paragraphs more might have done good, but being doubtful on the point, they were skipped. The weather and rains will probably stop farther pursuit of Hood, but he will have a good time getting to some safe place. What about the major-generalship; has it been won? I have directed a new draft for 300,000 men and will put on 200[,000] more by the 1st of March, if there appears then to be a necessity.

EDWIN M. STANTON,
Secretary of War.

CITY-POINT, VA., *December 19, 1864—4.30 p. m.*

Major-General LOGAN,
Louisville, Ky.:

The news from Thomas so far is in the highest degree gratifying. You need not go farther. Before starting to join Sherman report in Washington.

U. S. GRANT,
Lieutenant-General.

HEADQUARTERS DEPARTMENT OF THE CUMBERLAND,
Near Spring Hill, December 19, 1864—8.30 p. m.

Maj. Gen. H. W. HALLECK,
Washington, D. C.:

The infantry has not been able to march to-day, in consequence of the heavy rain which set in last night and has continued all the day, rendering all the streams impassable. The cavalry, however, was enabled to advance somewhat, driving the enemy whenever they came upon him without much difficulty. We have taken a few prisoners, who, with those taken yesterday, represent Hood's army in a greatly demoralized condition. The day has been profitably employed in concentrating and adjusting the trains of the different commands, issuing rations and ammunition, preparatory to marching early to-morrow morning. The railroad is repaired to the Harpeth bridge, at Franklin, and I hope to have the bridge finished to-morrow in time to have trains loaded with supplies close up to the army to-morrow night. I have a report from Murfreesborough up to noon of the 17th instant. General Rousseau has gallantly held that place against all the attacks of the enemy. I also have reports from other points along the line of the Nashville and Chattanooga Railroad, and find the road has not been disturbed, except between La Vergne and Overall's Creek and for some miles south of Murfreesborough. But, with even three months' supplies in Chattanooga, no serious inconvenience would result to the troops there or along the line until the road shall be repaired. Both the Tennessee and Cumberland Rivers are rising rapidly, and General Donaldson, chief quartermaster, has been ordered to resume shipments up the Cumberland at once.

GEO. H. THOMAS,
Major-General, U. S. Volunteers, Commanding.

WASHINGTON, *December 19, 1864.*

Major-General THOMAS:

I will be in Nashville immediately, to take charge of your prisoners of war.

W. HOFFMAN,
Commissary-General of Prisoners.

———

FRANKLIN, *December 19, 1864.*

Major-General THOMAS:

Three trains just arrived with men and bridge timber to rebuild railroad bridge. General Schofield will have his men and most of his trains over the river to-night.

Very respectfully,

J. P. WILLARD,
Captain and Aide-de-Camp.

———

NASHVILLE, *December 19, 1864.*

Capt. R. H. RAMSEY,
Assistant Adjutant-General:

I have received your dispatch, and will leave for Franklin immediately.

J. G. PARKHURST,
Colonel and Provost-Marshal-General.

———

FRANKLIN, *December 19, 1864.*

General WHIPPLE:

I reported here this evening, and will commence work in the morning.

J. G. PARKHURST,
Provost-Marshal-General.

———

HEADQUARTERS DEPARTMENT OF THE CUMBERLAND,
December 19, 1864.

Col. J. G. PARKHURST,
Provost-Marshal-General, Department of the Cumberland:

COLONEL: The major-general commanding the department desires that you should keep as many scouts as possible around the flanks and in rear of the rebel army, for the purpose of ascertaining its condition, routes of march, and probable intentions. When the scouts have anything of importance to communicate to the major-general commanding, direct them to his headquarters before going to Nashville. General Miller has been directed to keep a line of duty messengers moving by railroad from his headquarters and from the terminus of the road near the army to these headquarters. Couriers will bring dispatches; therefore anything that you have to send out will be brought, if left at General Miller's assistant adjutant-general's office.

Very respectfully,

WM. D. WHIPPLE,
Brigadier-General and Chief of Staff.

NASHVILLE, *December 19, 1864.*

Capt. R. H. RAMSEY,
　Assistant Adjutant-General:

The telegram concerning prisoners is received. Three thousand have already been sent North; 2,000 yet remain. I will hold them until further orders.

　　Very respectfully, your obedient servant,
　　　　　　　　R. M. GOODWIN,
　　　Captain and Assistant Provost-Marshal-General.

NASHVILLE, *December 19, 1864.*

Capt. ROBERT H. RAMSEY,
　Assistant Adjutant-General:

I have sent parties to repair bridge at Franklin and intermediate points. Ten feet on Harpeth Shoals, and rising. The river is now open, and I hope to be in receipt of supplies soon. Fleet started down river yesterday.

　　　　　　　　J. L. DONALDSON,
　　　Chief Quartermaster, Department of the Cumberland.

NASHVILLE, *December 19, 1864.*

Capt. R. H. RAMSEY,
　Assistant Adjutant-General:

General Steedman has taken the Seventeenth Colored Regiment to Murfreesborough, and I understand intended taking it to Tuscumbia. This regiment was given me for my necessary work here, and I would like it ordered back, as I need it.

　　　　　　　　J. L. DONALDSON,
　　　Brigadier-General and Chief Quartermaster

HEADQUARTERS DEPARTMENT OF THE CUMBERLAND,
　　　　　　　　　December 19, 1864.

Brig. Gen. J. L. DONALDSON,
　Chief Quartermaster, Department of the Cumberland:

GENERAL: Your three dispatches of this date are received. I am directed by the major-general commanding to say with regard to the Seventeenth U. S. Colored Regiment that the necessity of its being with Major-General Steedman is so great, and the duty so important, that it cannot be returned to you, until after its services are dispensed with by General Steedman. You will therefore have to do the best you can without the regiment for a short time, and make use of your remaining force to the best advantage.

　　Respectfully, your obedient servant,
　　　　　　　　ROBT. H. RAMSEY,
　　　　　Assistant Adjutant-General.

HEADQUARTERS DEPARTMENT OF THE CUMBERLAND,
　　　　　　　　　December 19, 1864.

Brig. Gen. J. L. DONALDSON,
　Chief Quartermaster, Department of the Cumberland:

GENERAL: The major-general commanding directs that, the Cumberland River being now open, you will push forward supplies to Nashville by the river as rapidly as possible, particularly forage. Confer with the railroad authorities, and be prepared to forward supplies by the North Alabama Railroad whenever required by the army. Colonel Le Duc is acting chief quartermaster, and Captain Beman acting chief commissary for the troops in the field. The major-general commanding desires you to make it your particular business to see that the proper amount of supplies are placed at the different posts and stations immediately, and a regular supply kept up hereafter. General Granger has been ordered to reopen the Memphis and Charleston Railroad as far as Decatur, and you are desired to be prepared to supply all that line. This line will be reopened as the army advances. The Chattanooga and Knoxville line must be resupplied as soon as that road is repaired. The Northwestern Railroad need not be used for the present. Orders will be sent when it is desirable to resume operations on that road.

Very respectfully, your obedient servant,

ROBT. H. RAMSEY,
Assistant Adjutant-General.

NASHVILLE, *December 19, 1864.*

General WHIPPLE,
Chief of Staff:

I have advices this afternoon from Franklin. The bridge is all ready to raise as soon as the water is in condition to work.

W. W. WRIGHT,
Chief Engineer.

NASHVILLE, TENN., *December 19, 1864—1 p. m.*

Major ECKERT:

This forenoon the rains have been so heavy that little progress has been made. Our cavalry skirmished with the enemy a short distance south of Spring Hill, finding Forrest in command. Rivers swelling rapidly.

J. C. VAN DUZER.

HDQRS. CAVALRY CORPS, MIL. DIV. OF THE MISSISSIPPI,
Near Spring Hill, Tenn., December 19, 1864—1 a. m.

Brig. Gen. T. J. WOOD,
Commanding Fourth Army Corps:

GENERAL: I am directed to inform you that General Hatch's division, of this corps, is directed by Major-General Thomas to precede you to-morrow [19th] on the Columbia road. It is ordered to move at 6 a. m. Having no wagons or other baggage it will not delay your column materially.

I have the honor to be, very respectfully, your obedient servant,

A. J. ALEXANDER,
Lieutenant-Colonel and Acting Chief of Staff.

HEADQUARTERS DEPARTMENT OF THE CUMBERLAND,
In the Field, December 19, 1864—8.30 a. m.

Brig. Gen. T. J. WOOD,
 Commanding Fourth Army Corps, near Spring Hill:

GENERAL: On account of the bad state of the weather this morning, the major-general commanding directs that your corps remain in camp to-day, and attend to getting up your trains, if there are any behind, issuing provisions, and making preparations for continuing the pursuit to-morrow. All empty wagons to be sent to Franklin.

 Very respectfully, your obedient servant,
       WM. D. WHIPPLE,
     Brigadier-General and Chief of Staff.

———

HEADQUARTERS FOURTH ARMY CORPS,
Rutherford's Creek, Tenn., December 19, 1864—3.45 p. m.

Brigadier-General WHIPPLE,
 Chief of Staff, Department of the Cumberland:

Pursuant to orders we broke up camp at 8 o'clock this morning and advanced to Rutherford's Creek. There we found a portion of General Hatch's cavalry division had arrived and stopped by the enemy on the other side. The enemy was intrenched on the other side, having slight works thrown up on the hills on both sides of the pike, manned with infantry and a four-gun battery. I ordered up a rifle battery, which, with a battery of the cavalry, succeeded soon in silencing the enemy's guns. The opposite side of the creek being held by his sharpshooters, it was impossible to construct a bridge at the point where the turnpike crosses. For the purpose of driving off these sharpshooters I directed General Elliott to fell trees some distance above across the stream, for the purpose of enabling skirmishers to cross and drive out the sharpshooters, thus making a lodgment on the opposite side; but it was impossible to find any trees that would reach across, though quite a number were cut, and the rapidity of the current would sweep the trees around. General Grose's brigade, of General Kimball's division, is now engaged in trying to construct a bridge below the turnpike crossing, and I trust for success. I have also ordered General Elliott to try and construct a bridge at the turnpike crossing. Your order of 8.30 a. m. not to break up camp was not received until 12.30 p. m., two or three hours after we reached Rutherford's Creek. Rations will be issued as ordered, and the empty wagons will be sent back to Franklin. We will continue operations early to-morrow morning.

 Very respectfully, your obedient servant,
       TH. J. WOOD,
     Brigadier-General, Commanding.

———

HEADQUARTERS DEPARTMENT OF THE CUMBERLAND,
Near Spring Hill, December 19, 1864—9 p. m.

Brig. Gen. TH. J. WOOD,
 Commanding Fourth Army Corps:

The major-general commanding directs that, if at all possible, you will push forward your command across Rutherford's Creek to-morrow morning and move directly against Forrest, who is said to be in camp between Rutherford's Creek and Duck River with about 7,000 cavalry. General Wilson will cross General Hatch's division of cavalry on the ruins of the railroad bridge and strike Forrest on the flank, whilst you attack him in front. Confer with General Wilson and arrange the relative time of starting the two columns. General Smith will co-operate with you by moving from Spring Hill by a road crossing the headwaters of Rutherford's Creek and passing the school-house and church at A. Atkinson's and coming into the Columbia and Raleigh [Rally] Hill road near J. Caldwell's. Take no wagons with you except the necessary ammunition wagons and ambulances. Your supply train can be brought up afterward.

Very respectfully,

ROBT. H. RAMSEY,
Assistant Adjutant-General.

HEADQUARTERS FIRST DIVISION, FOURTH ARMY CORPS,
December 18 [19], 1864.
(Received 10 a. m.)

Lieutenant-Colonel FULLERTON,
Chief of Staff:

COLONEL: General Grose's brigade are at work. They have felled trees, but the trees would not reach across. General Grose is now making a raft and with every prospect of success. He will probably, almost certainly, have his brigade all across before morning. My troops will all be rationed, as you ordered, before morning. I have just come from the creek, and everything is going as well as possible under the circumstances.

Very respectfully,

NATHAN KIMBALL,
Brigadier-General.

The rebels are making their appearance in front of General Grose. They were not there when he first went down.

NATHAN KIMBALL,
Brigadier-General.

HEADQUARTERS FIRST DIVISION, FOURTH ARMY CORPS,
December 18 [19], 1864.
(Received 11.30 p. m.)

Lieut. Col. J. S. FULLERTON,
Chief of Staff, Fourth Army Corps:

COLONEL: General Grose reports that it is impossible for him to get a man across the river on a raft. He has lost two rafts and two men drowned in the attempt, owing to the swiftness of the current. There are no trees he can fell that will reach across. He can only cross the river by bridging it. He has a good engineer (Major Watson) with him.

I am, very respectfully, your obedient servant,

NATHAN KIMBALL,
Brigadier-General.

HEADQUARTERS SECOND DIVISION, FOURTH ARMY CORPS,
Rutherford's Creek, December 19, 1864—2.30 p. m.

Lieut. Col. J. S. FULLERTON,
    Assistant Adjutant-General:

COLONEL: The officer in charge of the bridge-builders reports that he has failed in putting a bridge across the creek, on account of not finding a tree sufficiently large to reach across. The creek is rapidly rising. Enemy's sharpshooters still in our front.

Very respectfully, your obedient servant,

W. L. ELLIOTT,
Brigadier-General of Volunteers.

HEADQUARTERS FOURTH ARMY CORPS,
Near Rutherford's Creek, December 19, 1864—4 p. m.

Brigadier-General ELLIOTT,
    Commanding Second Division:

General Wood directs me to inform you that he has just received information that General Hatch has succeeded in crossing Rutherford's Creek. If this be true, you can learn the fact by pushing your skirmishers, or rather sharpshooters, well down on each side of the pike. If on making the push you find they (the enemy) are gone, commence building a bridge at once, connecting with the pike on each side of creek; tear down houses, use everything to facilitate building the bridge; make it stout enough for artillery and trains. General Wood does not wish Hatch's dismounted men to get ahead of your skirmishers. Please report progress.

I am, your obedient servant,

W. H. SINCLAIR,
Major and Assistant Adjutant-General.

HEADQUARTERS SECOND DIVISION, FOURTH ARMY CORPS,
Rutherford's Creek, December 19, 1864—6.25 p. m.

Col. J. S. FULLERTON,
    Assistant Adjutant-General, Headquarters Fourth Army Corps:

COLONEL: Your communication of 4 p. m. received. My division officer of the day reports that the opposite bank of the creek is free from pickets of the enemy, but that about one regiment of the enemy occupied the hill east of and commanding the pike at the crossing of the stream, compelling the pickets to move their position. The current is very swift and creek still rising. It is not practicable to bridge the stream with the material at hand without the means of raising the logs to the pier, even should the enemy not oppose the working party. The opinion of persons more experienced in bridge-building than myself agree with the above.

Very respectfully, your obedient servant,

W. L. ELLIOTT,
Brigadier-General, U. S. Volunteers, Commanding,

HEADQUARTERS DEPARTMENT OF THE CUMBERLAND,
December 19, 1864—10.30 a. m.

Major-General SCHOFIELD:

The artillery firing is in the direction of Columbia. No report from it yet. Get your troops across Harpeth and attempt to come no farther to-day, but leave the road clear for General Wilson's trains. Send an outpost on Hillsborough road. Be in readiness to march early to-morrow, and report if railroad has been repaired to Franklin or not.

WM. D. WHIPPLE,
Assistant Adjutant-General.

FRANKLIN, December 19, 1864.

Brigadier-General WHIPPLE,
Chief of Staff, Department of the Cumberland:

Harpeth is rising very fast, and I am apprehensive the trestle may be washed away. Where are the pontoons? I think they should be sent down by rail and laid as soon as possible, if they have not already been sent by wagon.

J. M. SCHOFIELD,
Major-General.

HEADQUARTERS DEPARTMENT OF THE CUMBERLAND,
December 19, 1864.

Major-General SCHOFIELD:

The pontoon bridge has been hurried up as much as possible, and should be at Franklin by this time.

WM. D. WHIPPLE,
Assistant Adjutant-General.

HEADQUARTERS,
Franklin, December 19, 1864.

Major-General THOMAS:

The superintendent of repairs is just in. He reports the railroad all right to this point.

J. M. SCHOFIELD,
Major-General.

HEADQUARTERS ARMY OF THE OHIO,
Franklin, December 19, 1864—7.30 p. m.

Major-General THOMAS:

I have my troops and a portion of my trains across the Harpeth. Shall I come forward in the morning?

J. M. SCHOFIELD,
Major-General.

HEADQUARTERS DEPARTMENT OF THE CUMBERLAND,
Near Spring Hill, December 19, 1864.

Maj. Gen. J. M. SCHOFIELD,
Commanding Twenty-third Army Corps:

Your dispatch received. Move forward with your command in the morning at 8 o'clock, giving place, however, to all of General Wilson's supply train. You can go into camp in the neighborhood of Spring Hill.

GEO. H. THOMAS,
Major-General, U. S. Volunteers, Commanding.

HEADQUARTERS ARMY OF THE OHIO,
Franklin, Tenn., December 19, 1864.

Maj. Gen. GEORGE H. THOMAS,
Commanding Department of the Cumberland:

GENERAL: I have the honor to inclose herewith a letter to Major-General Halleck, Chief of Staff, urging the promotion of Brigadier-General Cox, and to urge that it may be forwarded with your indorsement. Unless General Cox can obtain the promotion which he has so often earned he will soon quit the service, which would be an irreparable loss to my command.

I am, general, very respectfully, your obedient servant,
J. M. SCHOFIELD,
Major-General.

[Inclosure.]

HEADQUARTERS ARMY OF THE OHIO,
Franklin, Tenn., December 19, 1864.

Maj. Gen. H. W. HALLECK,
Chief of Staff, U. S. Army, Washington, D. C.:

GENERAL: I desire earnestly to ask your attention, and through you that of the President and Secretary of War, to the claims of Brig. Gen. J. D. Cox to promotion. It is unnecessary to recite in detail the services of so distinguished an officer. He has merited promotion scores of times by skillful and heroic conduct in as many battles. He is one of the very best division commanders I have ever seen, and has often shown himself qualified for a higher command. Permit me to say that in overlooking the merits of such an officer as General Cox, the Government has, unintentionally of course, committed an act of great injustice, and one which must soon deprive the country of his services. An officer cannot exercise for three years a command which he is universally admitted to be eminently qualified for and yet be denied the corresponding rank, while his juniors, notoriously less deserving, are promoted, without feeling such mortification and chagrin as must drive him from the army. Excuse, general, the earnestness with which I refer to this matter. I do not exaggerate the merits of the case; on the contrary, I do not half state it.

I am, general, very respectfully, your obedient servant,
J. M. SCHOFIELD,
Major-General.

[Indorsement.]

HEADQUARTERS DEPARTMENT OF THE CUMBERLAND,
In the Field, Tenn., December 20, 1864.

Respectfully forwarded, earnestly recommending the promotion of Brig. Gen. J. D. Cox to the grade of major-general. His services on the Atlanta campaign entitle him to the promotion asked for, and at the battle of Franklin he was eminently distinguished for personal courage, as well as for the skillful management of his command.

GEO. H. THOMAS,
Major-General, U. S. Volunteers, Commanding.

SPECIAL FIELD ORDERS, {   HDQRS. ARMY OF THE OHIO,
No. 181.   {   *Near Franklin, Tenn., December 19, 1864.*

I. Brig. Gen. Thomas H. Ruger, commanding First Division, Twenty-third Army Corps, will proceed at once to Murfreesborough, Tenn., where he will assume command of the following-named regiments belonging to the Twenty-third Army Corps, and march with them, without delay, by the most practicable route, to Columbia, Tenn., from which place he will move forward and join the Twenty-third Army Corps wherever it may be: One hundred and seventy-fourth Ohio Volunteer Infantry, One hundred and seventy-seventh Ohio Volunteer Infantry, One hundred and seventy-eighth Ohio Volunteer Infantry, One hundred and eightieth Ohio Volunteer Infantry, One hundred and eighty-first Ohio Volunteer Infantry, Eighth Minnesota Volunteer Infantry, and One hundred and fortieth Indiana Volunteer Infantry. General Ruger will draw all the transportation necessary for his command from General J. B. Steedman. The two batteries belonging to the First Division now in Nashville will remain in that place until they can join the command in Columbia.

By command of Major-General Schofield:

J. A. CAMPBELL,
Major and Assistant Adjutant-General.

HEADQUARTERS ARMY OF THE OHIO,
Franklin, Tenn., December 19, 1864.

Maj. Gen. D. N. COUCH,
Comdg. Second Division, Twenty-third Army Corps:

GENERAL: The major-general commanding directs that you have your command in readiness to move at daylight to-morrow, the 20th instant, but not to strike tents until further orders.

Very respectfully, your obedient servant,

WM. M. WHERRY,
Major and Aide-de-Camp.

HEADQUARTERS DEPARTMENT OF THE CUMBERLAND,
December 19, 1864.

Maj. Gen. A. J. SMITH,
Commanding Detachment Army of the Tennessee:

GENERAL: I am directed by the major-general commanding to say to you that General Wood has been ordered to march by the direct road to-morrow morning, if it is possible for his command to cross Rutherford's Creek, and move direct against Forrest, who is said to be in camp between Rutherford's Creek and Columbia with about 7,000 men, while General Wilson moves Hatch's division of cavalry by the ruins of the railroad bridge and attacks Forrest on flank. You will co-operate in this attack by moving your command on General Wood's left, by getting into the road leading from Spring Hill by the school-house and church near A. Atkinson's and striking the Columbia and Raleigh [Rally] Hill road near Caldwell's. This road is indicated to you, but the major-general commanding says if you can find a road near to General Wood's left flank, it will be much better to take that. Take no trains except the necessary ammunition wagons and ambulances, and leave a sufficient guard over your supply train, which can be moved forward after you have cleared the main road. If possible, the major-general commanding desires you to see Generals Wood and Wilson and arrange the relative time for starting the respective commands.

Very respectfully, your obedient servant,

ROBT. H. RAMSEY,
Assistant Adjutant-General.

HDQRS. CAVALRY CORPS, MIL. DIV. OF THE MISSISSIPPI,
Eight Miles North of Columbia, December 19, 1864—6 a. m.

Brigadier-General WHIPPLE,
Chief of Staff, Department of the Cumberland:

GENERAL: With the exception of Hatch's division, my command is entirely without rations and nearly out of ammunition. I confidently expected the trains here last night, but I learn that the troops and trains of Wood's and A. J. Smith's corps so encumbered the road that it was impossible for our supplies to reach us. I started Hatch after the enemy on the Columbia road, but the balance of the command will have to remain here till the train overtakes them. Jackson's division, from Murfreesborough, crossed to Spring Hill night before last.

Very respectfully, your obedient servant,

J. H. WILSON,
Brevet Major-General, Commanding.

HEADQUARTERS DEPARTMENT OF THE CUMBERLAND,
In the Field, December 19, 1864—8 a. m.

Maj. Gen. J. H. WILSON,
Comdg. Cav. Corps, Mil. Div. of the Miss., 3 Miles beyond Spring Hill:

GENERAL: On account of the bad weather of this morning the major-general commanding thinks that you had better not strike your camp to-day, but remain where you are and reconnoiter the country in your neighborhood, get up your ordnance and other trains, issue ammunition and provisions, and make other needed preparations for continuing the pursuit to-morrow.

Very respectfully, your obedient servant,

WM. D. WHIPPLE,
Brigadier-General and Chief of Staff.

P. S.—Also send back ambulances and a medical officer, and collect your wounded left in houses by the roadside and remove them to Franklin. All empty wagons also to be sent to Franklin.

W. D. W.

HDQRS. CAVALRY CORPS, MIL. DIV. OF THE MISS.,
In Camp, Eight Miles North of Columbia,
December 19, 1864—4.30 p. m.

Brigadier-General WHIPPLE,
Chief of Staff:

GENERAL: Hatch succeeded in crossing two regiments dismounted over Rutherford's Creek, and drove the rebel cavalry back upon their main line. Prisoners and one man belonging to our navy just escaped say Lee's corps marched by the Pulaski pike from Columbia this morning, but that Cheatham's and Stewart's were in camp when he left. Forrest, with about 7,000 cavalry, is lying between Rutherford's Creek and Duck River. He could be dislodged quite easily by crossing a division of infantry on the pike and Hatch by the ruins of the railroad bridge.

Very respectfully, your obedient servant,
J. H. WILSON,
Brevet Major-General.

———

HEADQUARTERS DEPARTMENT OF THE CUMBERLAND,
Near Spring Hill, December 19, 1864—9 p. m.

Maj. Gen. J. H. WILSON,
Comdg. Cavalry Corps, Military Division of the Mississippi:

Your dispatch of 4.30 p. m. to-day is received. As I wish the troops to advance in the morning, if possible, I will instruct General Wood to advance by the main road, if he can cross the creek, whilst you move Hatch's division by the ruins of the railroad bridge, as you suggest.
GEO. H. THOMAS,
Major-General, U. S. Volunteers, Commanding.

———

HDQRS. CAVALRY CORPS, MIL. DIV. OF THE MISSISSIPPI,
Near Spring Hill, Tenn., December 19, 1864.

Maj. WILLIAM P. CHAMBLISS,
Special Inspector of Cavalry, Louisville, Ky.:

MAJOR: I have directed two brigades of dismounted men to be sent back to Louisville to be mounted, armed, and equipped. The officers in command are directed to confer with you as to the most expeditious and best means of accomplishing these objects. The winter campaign, as far as these men are concerned, is over, and would prefer some delay rather than they should be hurried forward indifferently armed and mounted. I desire to impress you, and through you the authorities at Washington, with the necessity of arming all these men with the Spencer carbines. The recent active operations of this command have shown that this arm excels all others in use in durability, rapidity of firing, and general effectiveness. It has also been satisfactorily demonstrated that the ammunition was cheaper than any other, from the fact that during the three days and nights of continuous rain in which we have been marching and fighting, these, above all others in use in this corps, have not been affected by moisture, and, from the careful way in which it is prepared, it is not injured by the jostling incident to being carried on horseback. The men of this command have all behaved gallantly, and I think deserve these arms, which they are all so anxious to obtain. By giving this matter your careful attention you will render invaluable service to the cavalry arm of the service. If Brigadier-General Long's command has not marched before this reaches you, I would prefer it should remain until fully armed, mounted, and equipped, as it cannot reach me now until active operations are ended.

Very respectfully, your obedient servant,

J. H. WILSON,
Brevet Major-General, Commanding.

SPECIAL ⎞ HEADQUARTERS CAVALRY CORPS,
FIELD ORDERS, ⎬ MILITARY DIVISION OF THE MISSISSIPPI,
No. 9. ⎠ *Near Spring Hill, Tenn., December 19, 1864.*

I. This command will move forward to-morrow as follows:

The Fifth Division, General Hatch, will pursue the enemy on the direct road to the vicinity of Columbia, commencing the movement at 6 a. m.

II. The remainder of the corps will be held in readiness to move at 7 a. m., but will not move until rations are issued to the men.

III. Brig. Gen. R. W. Johnson, commanding Sixth Division, will proceed to Nashville with his dismounted brigade and the dismounted men of the First Brigade. The latter will be immediately prepared for the field and sent to their respective regiments, under competent officers. General Johnson will confer with Captain Green and Major Chambliss, special inspectors of cavalry, and at Nashville or Louisville, as they may determine, mount, arm, and equip the Second Brigade, and with it rejoin this command in the field as soon as possible.

IV. Brig. Gen. Joseph F. Knipe, commanding Seventh Division, will proceed to Nashville with his dismounted brigade and the dismounted men of his other brigade. The latter will be immediately prepared for the field and sent, under competent officers, to their respective regiments. General Knipe will confer with Captain Green and Major Chambliss, special inspectors of cavalry, and at Nashville or Louisville, as they may determine, mount, arm, and equip the dismounted brigade, and with it rejoin this command in the field as soon as possible. He will also take measures to collect such of his men as may be at Murfreesborough.

By order of Brevet Major-General Wilson:

A. J. ALEXANDER,
Lieutenant-Colonel and Acting Chief of Staff.

HDQRS. SECOND BRIG., FIRST DIV., CAVALRY CORPS,
December 19, 1864.

Capt. ROBERT LE ROY,
Asst. Adjt. Gen., First Division, Cavalry Corps:

CAPTAIN: I would respectfully report that I have reliable information that the rebels are crossing Green River at Ashbysburg, on rafts and by every available means, and I am following closely in the hope of striking them. My main column is within fourteen miles.

Very respectfully, your obedient servant,

O. H. LA GRANGE,
Colonel, Commanding.

HEADQUARTERS FIFTH DIVISION CAVALRY,
Parish House, Three Miles from Duck Creek, December 19, 1864.

Major-General WILSON:

I have succeeded in crossing Rutherford's Creek with dismounted men; not being in force, the enemy drive slowly. I have gone into camp here, with one brigade near Duck River bridge. One of our own men, a prisoner, has just come in. He left Corinth as a Confederate soldier coming to join the army. He left an ammunition train at Lawrenceburg. Two corps, Lee's and Cheatham's, went out of Columbia, on Pulaski pike, early this morning; Stewart's corps has the rear. All their cavalry, except a few companies, passed out of town by 10 p. m. The enemy's wagon train and pontoons not used at Columbia went out on the Lawrenceburg road or Mount Pleasant pike, and he heard orders given by officers which directed stragglers and detachments to report at Lawrenceburg. He saw no artillery go out with the infantry; saw a few pieces in the rear of the enemy. The enemy are already retreating. My men have followed them some distance, and they are probably all in Columbia by this time [*sic*] belonging to their rear guard.

EDWARD HATCH,
Brigadier-General.

NASHVILLE, TENN., *December 19, 1864.*

Capt. HENRY M. CIST,
Major-General Thomas' Headquarters:

The One hundred and seventy-fifth Ohio, about 400 effective, is the only regiment here which was on the Tennessee and Alabama Railroad. I will order it down as soon as I learn our army occupies Columbia. Nearly all the other troops at Columbia, and from there to Athens, before the rebel army came in, were cavalry, mounted and dismounted.

B. H. POLK,
Major and Assistant Adjutant-General.

HEADQUARTERS DEPARTMENT OF THE CUMBERLAND,
December 19, 1864.

Brig. Gen. JOHN F. MILLER,
Commanding Post of Nashville:

GENERAL: The major-general commanding directs that you will have all stragglers belonging to the troops in front whom you may find about the city of Nashville and vicinity arrested, confined in the barracks, and turned out, under guard, every day, to work on the fortifications until further orders, reporting to the major-general commanding the number you have arrested and so employed. You will exercise great vigilance in overlooking the passes of persons permitted to go in and out of Nashville, and all persons who enter Nashville without proper authority should be arrested and put to work on the fortifications, until they can fully satisfy you that they are not enemies of the Government. Travel by railroad and steam-boat to Nashville from Kentucky and the States west of the Ohio River is positively prohibited, except with passes issued from headquarters Military Division of the Mississippi, for good reasons, which must be stated on the pass. This order will be understood as particularly applicable to women desiring to enter Nashville, and none will be admitted unless their loyalty is well established and known, and even loyal women are not to be admitted except upon the best of reasons. You are also directed to make a thorough examination of the country about Nashville for the killed and wounded of the recent battle, and have them provided for, and also collect the arms, &c., found upon the field.

I am, general, your obedient servant,

[ROBT. H. RAMSEY,]
Assistant Adjutant-General.

NASHVILLE, *December 19, 1864.*

General W. D. WHIPPLE,
　　Chief of Staff:

Shall we send forward recruits and loose men belonging to the corps now with you? There are several hundred here. I have arrested many stragglers, and am having them examined, and will put the able-bodied to work on the fortifications. My burial parties are still at work, but are nearly through. We have brought in the wounded. I have strong parties out gathering up arms and other war material. Captain Ramsey's dispatch received this morning, and the orders are being executed. General Cruft has gone. What is to be done with recruits and loose men of General Sherman who come in after this date? Please give me the news. The nation is rejoicing over what has already been done.

I am, general, your obedient servant,

JNO. F. MILLER,
Brigadier-General.

FRANKLIN, *December 19, 1864.*

Capt. H. M. CIST,
　　Assistant Adjutant-General:

In compliance with telegraph dispatch received, dated December 18, fourteen miles Franklin pike, I have the honor to report myself with my mounted command here.

Yours, &c.,

A. V. MATZDORFF,
Lieutenant-Colonel Seventy-fifth Pennsylvania Veteran Volunteers.

FRANKLIN, TENN., *December 19, 1864.*

Capt. H. M. CIST.

Block-house between here and Nashville is occupied. The one between here and Spring Hill will be occupied by to-morrow morning early.

A. V. MATZDORFF,
Lieutenant-Colonel, Commanding.

HEADQUARTERS DEPARTMENT OF THE CUMBERLAND,
　　Spring Hill, December 19, 1864—8.30 p. m.

Col. A. A. SMITH,
　　Clarksville:

The major-general commanding directs that you report from time to time what you learn of the movements of the rebel General Lyon, and also of the movements of General McCook against him.

ROBT. H. RAMSEY,
Assistant Adjutant-General.

NASHVILLE, *December 19, 1864.*

Brigadier-General MEAGHER:

You will order the Fifteenth Pennsylvania Cavalry, Colonel Palmer, the Twenty-ninth Indiana and Eighteenth U. S. Colored Infantry, to report to Colonel Mackay at once, for steam-boat transportation to Decatur. Send all of the men of the Eighteenth [Ohio] and Sixty-eighth Indiana now in Chattanooga. You will relieve the Sixty-eighth New York and order them to march to Stevenson at once, where I will give them orders. You will send by boat 300 boxes of ammunition, caliber .58, and 1,000 rounds of artillery ammunition, one-half shell and one-half canister, for light 12's, to Decatur by boat. Please answer.

JAS. B. STEEDMAN,
Major-General.

HEADQUARTERS DEPARTMENT OF THE CUMBERLAND,
Chattanooga, December 19, 1864.

Col. WILLIAM J. PALMER,
Commanding Fifteenth Pennsylvania Cavalry, Wauhatchie:

The news I telegraphed you yesterday is more than confirmed. Ned Johnson's division, including himself, captured, also Bate's division; Stevenson's division broken up. The enemy completely routed and in full retreat down the Columbia pike.

SOUTHARD HOFFMAN,
Assistant Adjutant-General.

WAUHATCHIE, *December 19, 1864.*

Capt. HENRY A. FORD,
Acting Assistant Adjutant-General:

Please direct the steam-boat to take my regiment on at Kelley's Ferry, three miles from here. It will save half a day's river transportation rounding the Suck from Chattanooga. Can any wagons be taken along? I have twelve days' forage and rations here. Can it be taken along and loaded at Kelley's Ferry? It will take five boats to carry my effective force. Please telegraph when they will be at Kelley's Ferry.

WM. J. PALMER,
Colonel Fifteenth Pennsylvania Cavalry.

WAUHATCHIE, *December 19, 1864.*

Captain FORD,
Acting Assistant Adjutant-General:

Please order up two companies of my regiment left at Dalton, under Capt. William F. Colton. They should start at daylight to-morrow, in order to accompany me on this expedition. Please answer.

WM. J. PALMER,
Colonel Fifteenth Pennsylvania Cavalry.

BRIDGEPORT, *December 19, 1864.*

Capt. HENRY A. FORD,
　　Acting Assistant Adjutant-General:

Your telegram of 10.30 p. m. of the 18th instant was received to-day at 9 a. m., and two trains from Chattanooga reported to me early this morning, after which they proceeded to Stevenson. Exclusive of the battery men and detachments on railroad, there are only 823 enlisted men aggregate at this post for duty; consequently, the post will be unprotected. I have ordered the troops to be in readiness as soon as possible, unless you would prefer to let the 800 troops from Chattanooga en route for this place proceed at once to Stevenson, instead of stopping here.

　　　　　　　　M. C. TAYLOR,
　　　　　　　　　Colonel, Commanding.

———

BRIDGEPORT, *December 19, 1864.*

Capt. HENRY A. FORD,
　　Acting Assistant Adjutant-General:

I have the honor to report that I have furnished the additional 400 men, and have reported the 800 men to General Granger, who is present, and rationed them to go on transports. I would respectfully request permission to-morrow to go to Chattanooga on official business pertaining to my regiment. Please answer.

　　　　　　　　M. C. TAYLOR,
　　　　　　　　　Colonel, Commanding.

———

PADUCAH, *December 19, 1864.*
　　　　　　　　(Received 20th.)

Brigadier-General WHIPPLE,
　　Nashville, Tenn.:

GENERAL: In reply to your telegram of the 18th instant, I have the honor to state that the three regiments of infantry left this place at 4 p. m. this day for Nashville, Tenn., with orders to report to General Thomas. As soon as your dispatch was received I ordered the regiments to leave. They only arrived here on the 17th instant, and I was waiting for a battery from Columbus, which arrived here to-day. The fog was very heavy here these last three nights, and no boat could leave, or I would have left this to meet Lyon last night.

　　　　　　　　S. MEREDITH,
　　　　　　　　　Brigadier-General.

———

PADUCAH, KY., *December 19, 1864.*

Capt. J. B. DICKSON,
　　Assistant Adjutant-General, Lexington, Ky.:

CAPTAIN: I have just received a telegram from General Thomas, at Nashville, not to proceed against Lyon; that it is too late, and that McCook's division of cavalry was taking care of him, and that was sufficient, and I was to send on to Nashville the three regiments of infantry which were waiting here. I have done so, and it therefore is not necessary for me to take the field.

　　　　　　　　S. MEREDITH,
　　　　　　　　　Brigadier-General.

PERSONAL.]   HEADQUARTERS NORTHERN DEPARTMENT,
Cincinnati, Ohio, December 19, 1864.
Hon. E. M. STANTON,
    Secretary of War:

I regret extremely to learn, by letter from George Wilkes of the 13th instant, that you feel "excessively hurt and nettled" at some part of the contents of a letter I had the honor to address you on the 23d ultimo. Of this letter it is alleged, that "after assuming against the Department purposes it never entertained, you impute unworthy motives, and again indicate an intention of throwing up your commission." Fearing that the letter might admit of this interpretation, I have turned to it, and find that it is susceptible of a construction I never intended to have given. I was under the impression that the order making the change of these headquarters to Columbus had been determined on during your illness and without your knowledge, and regarded it as the work of my old adversary, Major-General Halleck. This I meant clearly to have stated, but inadvertently omitted the name of the head of the Cavalry Bureau. It was with this feeling that the whole letter was written, and I desired to make it so prominent as to require no explanation. On reperusal, I am exceedingly sorry to find that it is not, and I hasten to withdraw any part of the letter tending, in your judgment, to give offense to you. After the letter I have received from George Wilkes, communicating your intentions with regard to myself, as well as the many personal assurances I have received of your friendly disposition, I feel that to be insensible of them would evince a want of appreciation, if not of gratitude, toward you. I can only withdraw the offensive part of my letter, and sincerely regret that I should have allowed any words to drop from my pen admitting of a construction directly or indirectly unfavorable to yourself. The letter was written before I received your telegram informing me that the change in question had not been contemplated by the Department. In justice to myself, I may state further, that in addition to the evidences I communicated to you that the headquarters of the department were to be transferred to Columbus, I was informed that Judge Swayne stated on his return from Washington that the order was out making the transfer, and that he had seen it. I may also add that I can find nothing in my letter of the 23d ultimo that will sustain the opinion that I again indicate the intention of throwing up my commission.

    With great respect, I have the honor to be, your friend and servant,
                        JOSEPH HOOKER,
                        Major-General, Commanding.

PRIVATE.]   HEADQUARTERS NORTHERN DEPARTMENT,
Cincinnati, Ohio, December 19, 1864.
Hon. Z. CHANDLER,
    U. S. Senate:

I received your note of the 15th instant, and entirely coincide with its views, as well as those you have expressed in the Senate chamber. I felt it to be my duty to issue the order in question on receiving the news of the action of the provincial authorities of Canada in the case of the Saint Albans raiders, and was only restrained by the conscious weakness of our Government in its foreign policy. To have issued such an order as in my opinion the necessities of the case demanded, I would not have been sustained at headquarters, and the order would have been treated very much as has been that of General Dix. This would have bound me hand and foot for action at the time an opportunity presented itself. Now I am left free to act as I think proper. I assure you, Senator, in case a raid should be attempted from Canada, I intend that somebody shall be hurt, if I have to go into Canada to do it. Then if exception is taken, it can be adjusted by negotiation afterward. I want full swing at the devils once, and I think they will never attempt to disturb our quiet a second time. Cost what it may, the property and persons of our citizens shall be fully protected while I am in the exercise of the command of this department.

I have requested Senator Wade to have me summoned before the Committee on the Conduct of the War, and am daily expecting a reply. It is time that I should be allowed an opportunity to vindicate myself during the time I held command of the Army of the Potomac. Through the ignorance of some and the malice of others much wrong has been done. If Halleck can prevent it, he will, and he exercises as much influence over the Secretary of War as he ever did. There is an infernal conspiracy on foot to promote Sherman, Sheridan, and Meade, my juniors in the Regular Army, over my head, by making them major-generals, the latter having been retained in his present position by the politicians of Pennsylvania for more than six months, they making it a condition to their support of President Lincoln. As for the other two, I am willing that they should be promoted over me, if any of the armies or the people should deem their services, in example or deed, or their qualifications equal to mine.

Sherman insulted me professionally while of his army, from envy, as every officer and soldier of that army will tell you. I hope that you and your colleagues will see that my interests are protected.

Glorious tidings from Thomas.

Have no promotions made, if this injustice is to be perpetrated.

Your friend and servant,

JOSEPH HOOKER,
Major-General, Commanding.

CITY POINT, VA., *December 20, 1864—10.30 a. m.*

Hon. E. M. STANTON,
Washington, D. C.:

I think Thomas has won the major-generalcy, but I would wait a few days before giving it, to see the extent of damages done. Good for the draft ordered. It is to be hoped that we will have no use for more men than we have now, but the number must be kept up. Rebel Congress is now in secret session, and it is believed they are maturing a negro conscript act. These people will all come to us, if they can, but they may be so guarded as to find it difficult to do.

U. S. GRANT,
Lieutenant-General.

HEADQUARTERS DEPARTMENT OF THE CUMBERLAND,
Rutherford's Creek, December 20, 1864—8 p. m.
(Received 10.30 a. m. 21st.)

Maj. Gen. H. W. HALLECK,
Washington, D. C.:

Notwithstanding the rise in Rutherford's Creek, we have succeeded in pushing the enemy's rear guard across Duck River to-day, capturing some guns (verbally reported to me as being 5 in number—the report is not yet officially confirmed) and 50 or 60 prisoners. I hope to get the pontoon train up to-night in time to enable me to throw a bridge across Duck River, and continue the pursuit at an early hour to-morrow morning. I have learned to-day that the head of the enemy's column left Columbia on Sunday morning, but being encumbered with a very large train of wagons and a large pontoon train, which latter he is obliged to take back to the Tennessee River, to enable him to cross at all, I feel almost confident that I will be able to overtake him before he can reach and cross the Tennessee River. On the 17th I requested Admiral Lee, by telegraph, to proceed up the Tennessee River with as many iron-clads as he could secure, in order that he might prevent the enemy throwing a pontoon bridge over the river, or to destroy the bridge, if they had thrown one over. He was to have started the next day. I have also made arrangements to throw a force across the river at Decatur, and move on Tuscumbia, to seize the bridge at Florence, if possible. That force started three days ago, and, if General Granger has acted vigorously, Decatur should be in our possession to-day. If the expedition against Tuscumbia* be successful, I am confident that we shall be able to capture the greater part of Hood's army.

GEO. H. THOMAS,
Major-General, U. S. Volunteers, Commanding.

CITY POINT, VA., *December 20, 1864.*

Hon. EDWIN M. STANTON,
 Secretary of War:

The Richmond Dispatch of to-day has the following:

From Southwestern Virginia.

Telegrams received yesterday from Lynchburg contain the latest intelligence we have from the raiders on the line of the Virginia and East Tennessee Railroad. From the latest of these, it appears that the Yankees on Saturday, having come to Max Meadows, ten miles this side of Wytheville, turned back toward Abingdon, destroying property of all kinds as they went. As they were returning Colonel Witcher struck them at Adkins on Saturday evening about 4 o'clock and fought them till night. Adkins is a point on the railroad seven miles this side of Marion. The result of Colonel Witcher's fight is not given. It is believed that the enemy have succeeded in destroying the machinery at the lead-works, the report that that point was guarded by General Vaughn being untrue. From the celerity of their movements it is doubtful whether the enemy have any artillery, and some think that for the lack of this arm they have not and will not attack the salt-works. The statements of the telegraphs mentioned are based on information telegraphed to Lynchburg by officers of the Virginia and Tennessee Railroad, one of whom escaped from the enemy at Glade Spring, and the other went out from Lynchburg on an engine to make a reconnaissance. These officers also report that the enemy has destroyed every bridge on the railroad between Glade Spring and Max Meadows.

U. S. GRANT,
Lieutenant-General.

FRANKLIN, TENN., *December 20, 1864.*

General W. D. WHIPPLE,
 Chief of Staff:

I have sent out six scouts this morning—three on either flank.

J. G. PARKHURST,
Provost-Marshal-General.

---

* So recorded in Thomas' telegrams-sent book, but as received by Halleck it is Florence.

FRANKLIN, *December 20, 1864—10 a. m.*

Brigadier-General WHIPPLE:

Pontoon train across the creek and started forward.   Bridge will not be done before to-morrow evening.

> WM. G. LE DUC,
> *Lieutenant-Colonel, &c.*

NASHVILLE, *December 20, 1864.*

Major-General THOMAS:

The pontoon train of sixty boats will be ready to-morrow afternoon.

> JAS. R. WILLETT,
> *Major, &c.*

DECEMBER 20, 1864—6 p. m.

Major-General THOMAS:

GENERAL: The pontoon train is now passing through Spring Hill, and will camp near the pike, two miles south of that place, the teams being unable to go on any farther. I will start the train by daylight to-morrow. It will be necessary to take in consideration that forage for the animals of the train (500) will be needed; their forage will be out to-morrow night.

Respectfully,

> JAMES R. WILLETT,
> *Major, &c.*

HEADQUARTERS DEPARTMENT OF THE CUMBERLAND,
December 20, 1864.

Brig. Gen. J. L. DONALDSON,
Nashville:

Send out forage by first train. The construction corps has been ordered to have the road repaired to Spring Hill this p. m.   Portion of army out of forage.

> WM. D. WHIPPLE,
> *Brigadier-General.*

HEADQUARTERS DEPARTMENT OF THE CUMBERLAND,
Rutherford's Creek, December 20, 1864—8.40 p. m.

Brig. Gen. J. L. DONALDSON,
Chief Quartermaster, Dept. of the Cumberland, Nashville:

The major-general commanding directs that you send by railroad as far as Spring Hill three trains of forage and two trains of subsistence stores, at as early an hour to-morrow morning as it is possible.   Please acknowledge receipt.

> ROBT. H. RAMSEY,
> *Assistant Adjutant-General.*

NASHVILLE, *December 20, 1864.*
Capt. R. H. RAMSEY:

We are repairing the railroad to Murfreesborough and turnpike to Franklin as rapidly as possible, and have telegraphed the quartermaster at Chattanooga, via Louisville and Knoxville, to push their repairs from that point to Murfreesborough, and, as soon as open, to send forward subsistence, as they will get their portion open sooner than we will. Trains go to Franklin to-day, and will run to Murfreesborough from Chattanooga to-morrow, as I am informed.

J. L. DONALDSON,
Chief Quartermaster, Department of the Cumberland.

HEADQUARTERS DEPARTMENT OF THE CUMBERLAND,
Rutherford's Creek, December 20, 1864.
Lieutenant HOLLOPETER,
Chief Signal Officer, Dept. of the Cumberland, Chattanooga:

The major-general commanding directs me to say that as soon as you learn that the railroad is in operation to Athens, Ala., you will move your detachment and train by railroad to that place, and join him in the field by wagon road from there, wherever you may know him to be.

ROBT. H. RAMSEY,
Assistant Adjutant-General.

NASHVILLE, TENN., *December 20, 1864—10 p. m.*
Maj. T. T. ECKERT:

Thomas' headquarters moved about 11 a. m. to-day, having been at Spring Hill since Sunday night. Have not heard from his telegraphers at Duck River 'yet; infer that they have gone on to Columbia. It stormed all yesterday, but we pressed enemy hard enough to take in 1,300 of their rear guard. Rousseau's force has joined Thomas, while Steedman takes his darkies to Murfreesborough, and Meagher brings his new troops to Tullahoma. General Granger has started for Decatur, with gun-boats supporting.

J. C. VAN DUZER.

HDQRS. CAVALRY CORPS, MIL. DIV. OF THE MISSISSIPPI,
Eight Miles North of Columbia, December 20, 1864—1 a. m.
Brig. Gen. TH. J. WOOD,
Commanding Fourth Corps:

GENERAL: I have taken the liberty of reading the inclosed instructions,* based upon the first report sent in by Hatch to me this evening. He has subsequently moved back to the north side of Rutherford's Creek, but reports that he thinks Forrest gone. I will direct General Hatch, however, to push out very early in the morning and ascertain in time the true state of affairs to enable you to judge how strongly you ought to push. I don't think it necessary for Smith to leave the pike at all.

Very respectfully, your obedient servant,
J. H. WILSON,
Brevet Major-General, Commanding.

----

* See Thomas to Wood, 9 p. m. 19th, p. 269.

HEADQUARTERS FOURTH ARMY CORPS,
December 20, 1864—3 a. m.

Major-General THOMAS:

GENERAL: Your dispatch dated 9 a. m. [9 p. m. 19th] just received. Every effort will be made to carry out your instructions. Generals Elliott and Kimball have not yet succeeded in crossing any men over the creek. Last night two rafts were swamped and several men, two at any rate, were drowned in the attempt. The water is very deep and runs very swift.

Very respectfully, your obedient servant,

TH. J. WOOD,
Brigadier-General, Commanding.

HEADQUARTERS FOURTH ARMY CORPS,
Near Columbia, Tenn., December 20, 1864—2 p. m.

Brigadier-General WHIPPLE,
Assistant Adjutant-General and Chief of Staff:

GENERAL: This corps is now forming on the north bank of Duck River opposite Columbia, and is only prevented by the want of a pontoon train from crossing the river and continuing the pursuit of the enemy. It is much to be regretted that we have no pontoon train here. The river is quite high and appears to be rising, and it appears to me the only way to cross it will be by a pontoon bridge, as it will take a long time and much trouble to construct any other kind. There is no indication that there is any enemy on the south bank of the river, and every indication and report goes to show that he has retreated. It is reported that his pontoon bridges over Duck River were taken up at daylight this morning. I constructed two passage-ways for infantry, about half a mile apart, over Rutherford's Creek. If the creek does not fall to-day, so as to be fordable, the rear corps should build a bridge for the passage of wagons and artillery, which we had not time to do.

Respectfully, yours,

TH. J. WOOD,
Brigadier-General, Commanding.

HEADQUARTERS DEPARTMENT OF THE CUMBERLAND,
Rutherford's Creek, December 20, 1864—8.30 p. m.

Brig. Gen. TH. J. WOOD,
Commanding Fourth Army Corps:

The major-general commanding directs me to inform you that Major-General Schofield has been instructed to build a trestle bridge over Rutherford's Creek, so that the artillery and trains can cross. Major-General Smith will assist in getting the pontoon train over and hurry it forward to you as rapidly as possible, to enable you to throw bridges over Duck River early in the morning. It is the desire of the major-general commanding that the entire army be over the river before to-morrow night, in which case he is hopeful that the greater part of Hood's army may be captured, as he cannot possibly get his trains and troops across the Tennessee River before we can overtake him.

Very respectfully, your obedient servant,

ROBT. H. RAMSEY,
Assistant Adjutant-General.

Hdqrs. First Division, Fourth Army Corps,
Department of the Cumberland,
Near Rutherford's Creek, December 20, 1864.

Col. J. S. Fullerton,
Chief of Staff, Fourth Army Corps:

Colonel: I have to report that General Grose has a few men across the creek, and that he is crossing his brigade, and will soon have such a bridge as infantry can cross on. The creek has fallen four feet this morning. I am now going to the crossing where General Grose's brigade is at work.

Very respectfully, your obedient servant,
NATHAN KIMBALL,
Brigadier-General.

Spring Hill, *December 20, 1864.*

Brigadier-General Whipple,
Chief of Staff:

General: My troops are in camp at this place. I will await the general's orders here. My pontoon train is now passing, and I have ordered my engineer battalion to report to the officer in charge of the train, to assist in laying the bridges.

Very respectfully,
J. M. SCHOFIELD,
Major-General.

Headquarters Department of the Cumberland,
December 20, 1864.

Maj. Gen. J. M. Schofield,
Commanding Twenty-third Army Corps:

General: The major-general commanding directs me to inquire whether the railroad trains have made their appearance at Spring Hill yet. Please answer by telegraph, stating what they are loaded with, if any have arrived.

Very respectfully, your obedient servant,
ROBT. H. RAMSEY,
Assistant Adjutant-General.

Headquarters Army of the Ohio,
Spring Hill, Tenn., December 20, 1864—10.30 p. m.

Capt. R. H. Ramsey,
Assistant Adjutant-General, Rutherford's Creek:

No railroad train has arrived here. I understand the bridge at Franklin will not be done before to-morrow night. There is no telegraph station here.

Very respectfully, your obedient servant,
J. A. CAMPBELL,
Major and Assistant Adjutant-General.

HEADQUARTERS DEPARTMENT OF THE CUMBERLAND,
In the Field, near Rutherford's Creek, December 20, 1864.
Maj. Gen. J. M. SCHOFIELD,
Commanding Army of the Ohio:

GENERAL: The major-general commanding directs that you move your command to Rutherford's Creek to-morrow, and build a wagon bridge over that stream. Let the force that is detailed for that purpose commence work as early as possible in the morning. It is intended to send the pontoon bridge on direct to Duck River. The Fourth Corps and General Smith's command will cross as soon as the bridge is completed.

Very respectfully, your obedient servant,
WM. D. WHIPPLE,
Brigadier-General and Chief of Staff

SPECIAL FIELD ORDERS, }   HDQRS. ARMY OF THE OHIO,
No. 182.   }   *In the Field, December 20, 1864.*

I. At a general court-martial, which was convened at headquarters Army of the Ohio, December 11, 1864, pursuant to Special Field Orders, No. 176, from these headquarters, dated December 11, 1864, and of which Col. I. N. Stiles, Sixty-third Indiana Infantry, is president, was arraigned and tried

W. C. McReynolds, military telegraph operator.

CHARGE: Disobeying the lawful commands of his superior officers.

Specification I.—In this, that he, the said W. C. McReynolds, was ordered by Major Campbell, assistant adjutant-general, Twenty-third Army Corps, to remain at headquarters of said corps at Columbia, Tenn., and did disobey said order by going to Franklin, Tenn. This at or near Columbia, Tenn., on or about November 27, 1864.

Specification II.—In this, that he, the said W. C. McReynolds, was ordered by Major Wherry, aide-de-camp, General Schofield's staff, from Franklin, Tenn., to Columbia, Tenn., to interpret a dispatch, and that he did disobey said order, and did reply to it in words and figures as follows:

FRANKLIN, *29th—7 a. m.*
Major WHERRY,
Aide-de-Camp:

I have no horse at all; mine was stolen last night. Cipher received by you yesterday repeated and translated, and sent via courier last night. Will return as soon as I get horse. I have escort of fifteen men.

Very respectfully,
McREYNOLDS,
Operator.

All this at or near Columbia, Tenn., on or about November 28, 1864.
To which charge and specifications the accused pleaded as follows:
To the *1st Specification,* "Not guilty."
To the *2d Specification,* "Not guilty."
To the CHARGE, "Not guilty."

FINDING.

The court, having maturely considered the evidence adduced, finds the accused, W. C. McReynolds, military telegraph operator, as follows:
Of the *1st Specification of the charge,* "Guilty."

Of the *2d Specification of the charge*, "Guilty."
Of the Charge, "Guilty."

And the court does therefore sentence him, the said W. C. McReynolds, military telegraph operator, to hard labor for one month on such public works as the general commanding the Department of the Ohio may direct.

Finding and sentence approved. The sentence is remitted, and Mr. W. C. McReynolds will be released from arrest and returned to duty.

The general court-martial of which Col. I. N. Stiles is president is hereby dissolved.

By command of Major-General Schofield:

J. A. CAMPBELL,
Major and Assistant Adjutant-General.

HEADQUARTERS ARMY OF THE OHIO,
Spring Hill, Tenn., December 20, 1864.

Maj. Gen. D. N. Couch,
Commanding Second Division, Twenty-third Army Corps:

GENERAL: The commanding general directs that you march your command to-morrow morning, immediately in rear of General Cox's division to Rutherford's Creek. General Cox's division will march as soon as the road is cleared by the pontoon train now in his front. Your rations will reach you this evening in time to issue before starting in the morning.

I am, general, very respectfully, your obedient servant,

J. A. CAMPBELL,
Major and Assistant Adjutant-General.

HEADQUARTERS ARMY OF THE OHIO,
Spring Hill, Tenn., December 20, 1864.

Brig. Gen. J. D. Cox,
Commanding Third Division, Twenty-third Army Corps:

GENERAL: The commanding general directs that you move your command to-morrow morning, as soon as the road is cleared by the pontoon train, as far as Rutherford's Creek, where you will encamp and detail a force, as large as can be used to advantage, to assist the engineer battalion in building the wagon bridge across the creek. The pontoon train is parked two miles south of town.

I am, general, very respectfully, your obedient servant,

J. A. CAMPBELL,
Major and Assistant Adjutant-General.

HDQRS. CAVALRY CORPS, MIL. DIV. OF THE MISSISSIPPI,
Mrs. Brown's House, Duck River Crossing,
December 20, 1864—12 m.

Brig. Gen. W. D. Whipple,
Chief of Staff:

GENERAL: My advance has been here some time, the last of the enemy—Forrest, Cheatham, and Loring—having left during the night. A few mounted men can be seen on the other side of the river. Mrs.

Brown, a very intelligent woman, who conversed with many of their generals, says they will make no stand this side of the Tennessee River. Duck River is very high, and therefore cannot be passed at any point without the aid of a bridge train; one should be sent forward at once. We shall have no difficulty laying it near the turnpike crossing. Most of the rebels have probably gone by the Pulaski road.

Very respectfully, your obedient servant,

J. H. WILSON,
Brevet Major-General.

HDQRS. CAVALRY CORPS, MIL. DIV. OF THE MISSISSIPPI,
Near Columbia, Tenn., December 20, 1864—3.45 p. m.

Brigadier-General WHIPPLE,
Chief of Staff, Department of the Cumberland:

GENERAL: General Forrest came to the river-bank, under a flag of truce, and requested an exchange of prisoners. I have just sent an officer to inform him that I have no prisoners to exchange.

Very respectfully, your obedient servant,

J. H. WILSON,
Brevet Major-General, Commanding.

HEADQUARTERS DEPARTMENT OF THE CUMBERLAND,
Rutherford's Creek, December 20, 1864—8.30 p. m.

Maj. Gen. J. H. WILSON,
Comdg. Cavalry Corps, Military Division of the Mississippi:

The major-general commanding directs me to say that you did perfectly right in telling Forrest you had no prisoners to exchange with him. Major-General Schofield has been directed to build a trestle bridge across Rutherford's Creek, and the pontoon train will be up with you to-morrow morning early, if the mules are able to haul it. If at all possible the major-general commanding desires the army to be across Duck River before to-morrow night. Hood cannot possibly get all his troops and trains across the Tennessee River before we can overtake him, if we get across Duck River to-morrow.

Very respectfully, your obedient servant,

ROBT. H. RAMSEY,
Assistant Adjutant-General.

HDQRS. DIST. OF WEST FLORIDA AND SOUTH ALABAMA,
Franklin Creek, Jackson County, Miss., December 20, 1864.

Lieutenant-Colonel CHRISTENSEN,
Assistant Adjutant-General, &c.:

COLONEL: Your dispatch of the 15th is this day received.* Upon my representation to General Davidson of my extreme want of cavalry, he kindly gave me the Fourteenth New York, 250 strong, which is now arriving in my camp. My object in requesting General Davidson's cavalry to report to me was to cross it over the Big Dog or Escatawpa

---

* See Vol. XLI, Part IV, p. 863.

River, and then push it up on to the Mobile and Ohio Railroad between the latter river and the Pascagoula, while in the meantime I intended to make a bold demonstration on Mobile. In this manner I felt sure of breaking the trestling and bridges over the headwaters of Pascagoula and Dog Rivers, but the movement of which you advise me is undoubtedly more important just now. With the small force I have will do the best I can. The amount of excellent lumber in our possession will probably be not less than from 3,000,000 to 4,000,000 feet, besides resin, cotton, and steam machinery of value. If the general can possibly spare two or three more regiments of infantry, with the cavalry now here, I think we can hold our position and secure the lumber, besides damaging the rebels not a little. The steamers J. M. Brown, A. G. Brown, Swaim, and Tamaulipas can ascend Dog River to Good's Mill, where the bulk of the lumber is. The rebel papers and prisoners report that Pollard and the Mobile and Montgomery Railroad have " gone up." Please give orders for our transports returning from Lakeport to West Pascagoula for cavalry to bring me such rations, forage, and materials as I may make requisitions for. I need a topographical engineer very much to map the country; our present maps are worthless. The rebels gave us a slight brush day before yesterday, we losing one man; to-day we returned the compliment by bringing down a rebel officer.

I am, colonel, very respectfully,

G. GRANGER,
Major-General, Commanding.

P. S.—I am placing the lumber in cribs, ready for towing or rafting down the river as early as possible.

G. G.

HOPKINSVILLE, *December 20, 1864.*

Col. O. H. LA GRANGE:

I received your dispatch last night, and am much gratified with the vigor of your pursuit. I have sent part of Watkins' command toward the river. I judge from Lyon's attempting to cross at Ashbysburg, he intends taking Morgan's old route, through Elizabethtown and to Eastern Kentucky. I have sent dispatches to Louisville, so that he may be headed off, if he goes that [way]. Let me hear from you if he goes toward Bowling Green, so that I may move down in that direction. I hope, however, that you have struck him before he crossed the river. I will wait here to hear from you.

E. M. McCOOK,
Brigadier-General, Commanding Division.

HEADQUARTERS SECOND BRIGADE,
Ashbysburg, Ky., December 20, 1864.

Capt. ROBERT LE ROY,
Asst. Adjt. Gen., First Cav. Div., Mil. Div. of the Miss.:

CAPTAIN: Lyon crossed Green River at this point, with about 900 men, on the 18th and 19th instant, and destroyed the ferry-boats for ten miles up and down the river. On the evening of the 19th my advance, after marching thirty miles over terrible roads, drove a portion of his rear guard into the river, and compelled him to scatter about 200 of his men on this side of the river, besides abandoning his wagons and releasing a large number of conscripts. One of his men was killed, several were drowned, and several captured. This morning (20th) I sent a detail to Rumsey to bring the steamer D. B. Campbell, which was lying at that point; fortunately, they met a boat. By 12 m. my entire command will be across in good condition, and my advance fifteen miles in pursuit. I feel confident of overtaking and compelling Lyon to fight, unless he breaks his command up into squads, which I fear he will do if hard pressed. I will telegraph you of future movements at Russellville, if possible.

> Very respectfully, your obedient servant,
> > O. H. LA GRANGE,
> > *Colonel, Commanding.*

HDQRS. CAVALRY CORPS, MIL. DIV. OF THE MISSISSIPPI,
Eight Miles from Columbia, December 20, 1864—1 a. m.

Brigadier-General HATCH,
　Commanding Fifth Cavalry Division:

GENERAL: At 6 a. m. push a strong dismounted force across Rutherford's Creek, by the ruins of railroad bridge, and ascertain whether Forrest has actually withdrawn his force. Communicate at once the information obtained to General Wood, commanding Fourth Corps, who is directed to co-operate with you in the attack, if Forrest is still there. I infer from your report of this evening that you are under the impression he has withdrawn. Get all the information you can in regard to position and movements of the enemy's forces.

> Very respectfully,
> > J. H. WILSON,
> > *Brevet Major-General.*

HEADQUARTERS FIFTH DIVISION CAVALRY,
Parish House, December 20, 1864—5.40 a. m.

Major-General WILSON,
　Commanding Cavalry Corps:

GENERAL: Your order to advance at 6 a. m., written 1 a. m., of this date, just received. The railroad bridge was carried out last night. I think I can get within two miles of Columbia, at the mouth of Rutherford's Creek, and will force a crossing there. If the enemy's pontoons are not yet taken up, there is a chance of bringing guns to bear on it. I believe the enemy has left, as my dismounted men pushed him within three miles of Columbia last night.

> Very truly, your obedient servant,
> > EDWARD HATCH,
> > *Brigadier-General.*

ON FRANKLIN AND COLUMBIA PIKE,
December 20, 1864—10.30 a. m.

Brevet Major-General WILSON,
　Comdg. Cavalry Corps, Military Division of the Mississippi:

GENERAL: General Hatch has one brigade across the river, and will cross the other as soon as possible. He crossed at the second railroad bridge, the first one having lodged at the second. Major Forbes, Seventh Illinois, is just this side of Columbia. There is something of a force at that place.

I am, very respectfully, your obedient servant,

G. H. KNEELAND,
Captain and Acting Aide-de-Camp.

HEADQUARTERS FIFTH DIVISION CAVALRY,
Near Columbia, December 20, 1864—7 p. m.

Major-General WILSON, *Commanding Cavalry Corps:*

The officer sent up the river to Huey's Mill reports all fords in that vicinity impassable. Plenty of forage between that point and Columbia for the entire cavalry command.

Very respectfully, your obedient servant,

EDWARD HATCH,
Brigadier-General.

HOPKINSVILLE, KY., *December 20, 1864—9 a. m.*

General H. EWING, or
OFFICER COMMANDING POST AT LOUISVILLE:

Part of Lyon's force was trying to cross the Green River on rafts at Ashbysburg yesterday, one brigade of mine in pursuit, and their advance within four miles. If he gets any of his force across he may try to go through the country between Elizabethtown and Cave City, or along there some place, into Eastern Kentucky. Look out for him.

E. M. McCOOK,
Brigadier-General, Commanding.

MEMPHIS, TENN., *December 20, 1864.*
(Received 22d.)

Major-General WILSON,
Commanding Cavalry Corps, Nashville, Tenn.:

General Dana, under orders from Maj. Gen. H. W. Halleck to use all the available forces of the command to break the Mobile and Ohio Railroad, detains all the cavalry here belonging to the Fourth Division. The expedition leaves to-day, and will be absent about two weeks. Captain Noyes arranged with General C. C. Washburn to leave the Second New Jersey and Seventh Indiana in this department. Telegraph me by name the regiments I am to take to Louisville, so that there may be no misunderstanding.

E. UPTON.
Brevet Major-General, Commanding Fourth Cavalry Division.

CLARKSVILLE, *December 20, 1864—10.30 a. m.*

Capt. R. H. RAMSEY, *Assistant Adjutant-General:*

On Friday last McCook attacked a part of Lyon's force at Hopkinsville, captured one gun, some prisoners, and scattered the rest. A part of my mounted force has been out in that direction two days; will report when they return. Last report of Lyon, near Eddyville.

A. A. SMITH,
Colonel, Commanding.

CHATTANOOGA, *December 20, 1864.*

Major-General STEEDMAN:

The agent will send you 130 cars; all that he has. The 175 cars you took with you to Nashville have not been returned. The last of your forage, rations, and ammunition leave here this morning on board of the Kennesaw. Your cavalry march to Bridgeport to-day. Your train and cavalry cannot be sent to Decatur until two transports up the river return and General Granger releases two of the steamers that have gone with him.

A. J. MACKAY,
Lieutenant-Colonel and Chief Quartermaster.

HEADQUARTERS POST OF NASHVILLE,
Nashville, Tenn., December 20, 1864.

Major BEAUMONT,
Assistant Adjutant-General, Cavalry Corps:

I am informed that between our picket-line and Brentwood Hills there are numerous bands of dismounted cavalry wandering about and committing all manner of depredations. I would respectfully suggest that some step be taken to get these men into camp and under control, that an end may be put to this evil.

I am, major, very respectfully, your obedient servant,

JNO. F. MILLER,
Brigadier-General.

WASHINGTON, *December 21, 1864—12 m.*
(Via Nashville, Tenn.)

Major-General THOMAS:

Permit me, general, to urge the vast importance of a hot pursuit of Hood's army. Every possible sacrifice should be made, and your men for a few days will submit to any hardship and privation to accomplish the great result. If you can capture or destroy Hood's army Sherman can entirely crush out the rebel military force in all the Southern States. He begins a new campaign about the 1st of January, which will have the most important results, if Hood's army can now be used up. A most vigorous pursuit on your part is therefore of vital importance to Sherman's plans. No sacrifice must be spared to attain so important an object.

H. W. HALLECK,
Major-General and Chief of Staff.

HEADQUARTERS DEPARTMENT OF THE CUMBERLAND,
In the Field, December 21, 1864.

Maj. Gen. H. W. HALLECK,
Washington, D. C.:

Your dispatch of 12 m. this day is received. General Hood's army is being pursued as rapidly and as vigorously as it is possible for one army to pursue another. We cannot control the elements, and, you must remember, that to resist Hood's advance into Tennessee I had to reorganize and almost thoroughly equip the force now under my command. I fought the battles of the 15th and 16th instant with the troops but partially equipped, and, notwithstanding the inclemency of the weather and the partial equipment, have been enabled to drive the enemy beyond Duck River, crossing two streams with my troops, and driving the enemy from position to position, without the aid of pontoons, and with but little transportation to bring up supplies of provisions and ammunition. I am doing all in my power to crush Hood's army, and, if it be possible, will destroy it; but pursuing an enemy through an exhausted country, over mud roads, completely sogged with heavy rains, is no child's play, and cannot be accomplished as quickly as thought of. I hope, in urging me to push the enemy, the Department remembers that General Sherman took with him the complete organizations of the Military Division of the Mississippi, well equipped in every respect as regards ammunition, supplies, and transportation, leaving me only two corps, partially stripped of their transportation to accommodate the force taken with him, to oppose the advance into Tennessee of that army which had resisted the advance of the Army of the Military Division of the Mississippi on Atlanta, from the commencement of the campaign until its close, and which is now, in addition, aided by Forrest's cavalry. Although my progress may appear slow, I feel assured that Hood's army can be driven from Tennessee, and eventually driven to the wall, by the force under my command; but too much must not be expected of troops which have to be reorganized, especially when they have the task of destroying a force in a winter campaign which was able to make an obstinate resistance to twice its numbers in spring and summer. In conclusion, I can safely state that this army is willing to submit to any sacrifice to oust Hood's army, or to strike any other blow which would contribute to the destruction of the rebellion.

GEO. H. THOMAS,
Major-General.

HEADQUARTERS DEPARTMENT OF THE CUMBERLAND,
In the Field, December 21, 1864.

Major-General HALLECK,
Washington, D. C.:

I have heard to-day that General McCook attacked a portion of Lyon's force at Hopkinsville on the 17th [16th] and dispersed it, capturing one gun, and that Colonel La Grange attacked another portion at Ashbysburg, on Green River, Ky., scattering his men in all directions, causing him to burn most of his baggage, a considerable number of small-arms and ammunition. La Grange's force drove Lyon's rear guard into the river, killing and drowning a great many. He will continue the pursuit as soon as he can cross the river. The progress of the force under my command is impeded by the high state of water in Harpeth River, Rutherford's Creek, and Duck River; but, with the assistance of pontoons, just up, I hope we shall be able to continue the pursuit in the morning.

GEO. H. THOMAS,
Major-General.

NASHVILLE, *December 21, 1864.*

Capt. R. H. RAMSEY,
  Assistant Adjutant-General:

Telegram received. Forage and subsistence will leave for Spring Hill as soon as possible.

J. L. DONALDSON,
  Chief Quartermaster.

HEADQUARTERS DEPARTMENT OF THE CUMBERLAND,
  In the Field, December 21, 1864.

Brig. Gen. J. L. DONALDSON,
  Nashville:

Yours of yesterday received. The major-general commanding wishes you to push forward the repairs on the Nashville and Chattanooga Railroad as fast as possible, and open communication between those two places at the earliest possible moment, but, by all means, the repairs of the Nashville and North Alabama Railroad must be kept up with the advance of the army, if it is possible.

WM. D. WHIPPLE,
  Brigadier-General.

HEADQUARTERS DEPARTMENT OF THE CUMBERLAND,
  In the Field, December 21, 1864.

Brig. Gen. J. L. DONALDSON,
  Nashville:

When will the steamers leave Nashville for Eastport, according to order of yesterday?

WM. D. WHIPPLE,
  Chief of Staff.

NASHVILLE, *December 21, 1864.*

General W. D. WHIPPLE,
  Chief of Staff:

Your dispatch received, and I send this day by two steamers 10,000 rations to Eastport, as ordered, also model barge to facilitate crossing of artillery. I have asked for 4,000 horses to remount cavalry, and a word from the major-general would be efficacious in hurrying them on. You say nothing of grain for animals in the movement ordered, but I shall send a steamer with grain, also some medical supplies.

J. L. DONALDSON,
  Chief Quartermaster.

FRANKLIN, *December 21, 1864—12 m.*

Brigadier-General WHIPPLE:

There is no probability of the railroad bridge being done to-day. I have put the men sent to build the turnpike bridge on the railroad bridge, to help Mr. Eicholtz. He finds unusual and unexpected difficulties. The wreck of the old bridge is in the bottom of the river, and it is very difficult to get a foundation for the trestles. Everything is being done that can be to hurry it forward. I have ordered forage to be brought up to the bridge. The mud is so deep that wagons can hardly cross. The railroad reported good to Spring Hill; nothing known here farther ahead.

WM. G. LE DUC.

FRANKLIN, December 21, 1864—12 m.

Brigadier-General WHIPPLE:

There are fifteen pontoons here. The water has fallen so much that I do not think they will be needed. They are of the long pattern—long whale-boats—and they report they are unable to move them through the mud across the creek. Do you need them in front? Shall I try to get them over and started on, or send them back to Nashville, or let them remain here subject to further orders? I ordered a hand-car from Nashville this morning, to run out and examine and fix the telegraph line to the front; it has not been sent yet.

WM. G. LE DUC.

FRANKLIN, December 21, 1864—12 m.

Brigadier-General WHIPPLE,
    Assistant Adjutant-General:

Construction train is across the Harpeth. I leave for Spring Hill; others following.

WM. G. LE DUC,
Lieutenant-Colonel, &c.

FRANKLIN, December 21, 1864—5.30 p. m.

Brigadier-General WHIPPLE:

The railroad is reported all right to Duck River, switches and all, by a person who says he has walked over it from Duck River to-day. The bridge will probably be done by to-morrow at 12 m.; I do not think sooner. A company of pioneers should be put to work on the station at Duck River, if necessary, to make a good landing for stores; corduroy will be best.

WM. G. LE DUC,
Lieutenant-Colonel, &c.

HEADQUARTERS DEPARTMENT OF THE CUMBERLAND,
December 21, 1864.

Mr. SYKES WATKINS,
    In Charge of Telegraphic Construction Train:

SIR: The major-general commanding directs that your train follow next after, and keep closed on the supply train of the headquarters of the army, and it will in all respects be considered as a portion of the headquarters train. Should any other train or persons whatsoever attempt to separate your wagons from the other portion of the headquarters train, you will show them this order and insist upon maintaining your place; should they persist in separating your wagons from the rest of the train, you will ascertain their names and report them to these headquarters for disobedience of orders.

    Very respectfully, your obedient servant,

WM. D. WHIPPLE,
Brigadier-General and Chief of Staff.

HEADQUARTERS DEPARTMENT OF THE CUMBERLAND,
Rutherford's Creek, December 21, 1864.
Mr. EICHOLTZ,
    Superintendent of Railroad Repairs, Franklin, Tenn.:

SIR: The major-general commanding was this morning surprised and disappointed to learn that the railroad bridge at Franklin is not yet finished. He says that you must finish it to-day, and have trains as far as Spring Hill this afternoon. The army is suffering for forage, which it was expected the railroad would bring before this.

Very respectfully, your obedient servant,
WM. D. WHIPPLE,
Brigadier-General and Chief of Staff.

U. S. MILITARY RAILROADS,
OFFICE OF ASSISTANT ENGINEER,
Franklin, December 21, 1864.
Brigadier-General WHIPPLE,
    Chief of Staff, &c.:

GENERAL: I regret to say it will be utterly impossible to finish the bridge to-day. We are making but slow progress, on account of the high water and the mass of wreck and iron in the stream, which it is next to impossible to remove. Our ropes freeze and stiffen, and the men are scarcely able to hold themselves on the scaffolding on account of the ice. We cannot possibly cross the bridge before to-morrow noon, unless the water falls and weather moderates. We are doing all that can be done under the circumstances. I have sent for Colonel Wright.

Very respectfully, your obedient servant,
L. H. EICHOLTZ,
Division Engineer.

NASHVILLE, TENN., *December 21, 1864—9 p. m.*
Maj. THOMAS T. ECKERT:

General Thomas' headquarters are two miles north of Duck River to-night. Rebel army south of that stream. Our pontoon train was not up at 5 p. m., but would be during the night. Rain or wet snow has fallen constantly since Saturday. No fighting to-day. River bank full and rising.

J. C. VAN DUZER,
Captain, U. S. Military Telegraph.

HEADQUARTERS FOURTH ARMY CORPS,
Duck River, December 21, 1864—8 a. m.
Major-General THOMAS,
    Commanding Army of the Cumberland:

GENERAL: I respectfully suggest that 15,000 pairs of shoes and 15,000 pairs of socks be brought up, as soon as possible, to the nearest point on the railroad, and then forwarded by wagon train. The men are not barefooted, but traveling on the pike in the wet will, in a very few days, ruin their shoes and disable many of our men.

Respectfully, your obedient servant,
TH. J. WOOD,
Brigadier-General, Commanding.

HEADQUARTERS DEPARTMENT OF THE CUMBERLAND,
December 21, 1864.

Brig. Gen. T. J. WOOD,
 Commanding Fourth Army Corps:

GENERAL: I am directed by the major-general commanding to acknowledge the receipt of your note of this a. m. with the reference to the supply of 15,000 pairs shoes and 15,000 pairs of socks for your troops. In reply I am directed to state that the most certain and expeditious way you can get these things will be for your chief quartermaster to make a requisition for them on the chief quartermaster of the army, when they can be brought up by rail as far as possible, and then by road to the army. Orders will be given, however, to have the articles desired supplied at the earliest possible moment, when requisitions are handed in.

 Very respectfully, your obedient servant,
      ROBT. H. RAMSEY,
      Assistant Adjutant-General.

HEADQUARTERS DEPARTMENT OF THE CUMBERLAND,
Rutherford's Creek, December 21, 1864.

Brig. Gen. THOMAS J. WOOD,
 Commanding Fourth Army Corps:

I have the honor, by direction of the major-general commanding, to say to you that the pontoon train will be up with you as soon as it is possible to get it up. It progresses with a great deal of difficulty, but will be hurried forward as rapidly as possible. The major-general commanding directs me to say, also, that he desires you to have collected for the animals belonging to the pontoon train (about 500 in number) forage sufficient for two days. They have been traveling so constantly that they have been unable to forage for themselves, and are consequently much exhausted. The forage can be collected, so as to be ready for them as soon as the train reaches you.

 I am, general, very respectfully, your obedient servant,
      ROBT. H. RAMSEY,
      Assistant Adjutant-General.

HEADQUARTERS FOURTH ARMY CORPS,
Duck River, December 21, 1864—12 m.

Major-General THOMAS,
 Commanding Army of the Cumberland:

GENERAL: Your letter in reference to hurrying up the pontoon train and collecting forage has just been received. The best that can be done will be done to collect forage for the pontoon train, but I apprehend that very little can be done in that way. The cavalry has pretty effectually scoured the country and cleaned up the forage for some distance around us. I have very few wagons this side of Rutherford's Creek, and if I had ever so many it would be impossible to move off the turnpike—they would be swamped at once. I have no horses to bring up forage. All that can be done will be done.

 Very respectfully, your obedient servant,
      TH. J. WOOD,
      Brigadier-General, Commanding.

HEADQUARTERS FOURTH ARMY CORPS,
Duck River, Tenn., December 21, 1864—1.30 p. m.

Major-General THOMAS,
  Commanding Department of the Cumberland:

Please allow three of my batteries to cross the pontoon bridge as soon as it is laid over Rutherford's Creek, to assist in laying the bridge over Duck River. The enemy has a party of observation on the south bank of the river, defended by strong stone fences. I wish to batter them down.

  Very respectfully, your obedient servant,

  TH. J. WOOD,
  Brigadier-General, Commanding.

HEADQUARTERS FOURTH ARMY CORPS,
Duck River, December 21, 1864—1.30 p. m.

Major GOODSPEED,
  Chief of Artillery, Fourth Army Corps:

See General Thomas and ask him to let you push over three batteries (two rifled and one other) as soon as the pontoon bridge is completed at Rutherford's Creek. Bring them up to the front, to assist in laying the pontoon bridge over Duck River.

  By order of Brigadier-General Wood:

  J. S. FULLERTON,
  Lieutenant-Colonel and Assistant Adjutant-General.

HEADQUARTERS DEPARTMENT OF THE CUMBERLAND,
Rutherford's Creek, December 21, 1864.

Maj. Gen. JOHN M. SCHOFIELD,
  Commanding Twenty-third Army Corps:

The major-general commanding directs that you detail one company from your command, of not less than thirty men and one commissioned officer, for guard duty at the pontoon bridge over Rutherford's Creek. The commanding officer will report to Captain Abdill, now at the bridge, and will relieve Captain Abdill's company, now acting as guards. Trains will cross the bridge in the following order, and the commanding officer of the company on guard will be held responsible that these directions are strictly carried out, and that there be no unnecessary confusion and no damage done the bridge. Order of crossing: First, the pontoon train; second, three batteries belonging to Fourth Army Corps; third, the train of the cavalry command; fourth, the Fourth Corps trains; fifth, the trains of Major-General Smith's command; sixth, the Twenty-third Army Corps trains.

  I am, general, very respectfully, your obedient servant,

  ROBT. H. RAMSEY,
  Assistant Adjutant-General.

HEADQUARTERS DEPARTMENT OF THE CUMBERLAND,
Rutherford's Creek, December 21, 1864—9 p. m.

Maj. Gen. JOHN M. SCHOFIELD,
  Commanding Twenty-third Army Corps:

The major-general commanding directs me to say that, in crossing your command to-morrow morning over Rutherford's Creek, they will follow the command of Major-General Smith, his trains also preceding your troops. In order to save the pontoon bridge the troops will cross on the foot bridge, just above the old permanent bridge.

I am, general, very respectfully, your obedient servant,

ROBT. H. RAMSEY,
Assistant Adjutant-General.

SPECIAL FIELD ORDERS, }   HDQRS. ARMY OF THE OHIO,
    No. 183.   }   *Near Columbia, Tenn., December 21, 1864.*

I. Brig. Gen. N. C. McLean, U. S. Volunteers, is hereby relieved from duty in the District of Kentucky, and will report in person, without delay, to these headquarters, for duty with the army in the field.

*   *   *   *   *   *   *

By command of Major-General Schofield:

J. A. CAMPBELL,
Major and Assistant Adjutant-General.

HEADQUARTERS ARMY OF THE OHIO,
Rutherford's Creek, December 21, 1864—12.10 p. m.

Maj. Gen. D. N. COUCH,
    Comdg. Second Division, Twenty-third Army Corps:

GENERAL: The commanding general directs that you march your command at once to Rutherford's Creek, without waiting for General Cox.

I am, general, very respectfully, your obedient servant,

J. A. CAMPBELL,
Major and Assistant Adjutant-General.

HDQRS. CAVALRY CORPS, MIL. DIV. OF THE MISSISSIPPI,
Near Columbia, December 21, 1864—9.30 p. m.

Brigadier-General WHIPPLE,
    Chief of Staff:

General Hatch has just reported that the Second Iowa Cavalry, sent out this morning toward the Lewisburg pike, has captured 2 cannon, 6 ambulances, 2 wagons. I have sent to inquire from what force they were taken and to direct a thorough scouring of the country in that direction to-morrow.

Very respectfully, your obedient servant,

J. H. WILSON,
Brevet Major-General, Commanding.

SPECIAL   }   HEADQUARTERS CAVALRY CORPS,
FIELD ORDERS, }   MILITARY DIVISION OF THE MISSISSIPPI,
    No. 10.   }   *Brown's House, December 21, 1864.*

I. Lieut. H. W. Barr, Third Tennessee Cavalry, is relieved from duty as aide-de-camp to the brevet major-general commanding, and will report to his regiment, the necessity for having additional staff officers having passed for the present.

II. Capt. J. W. Harper, Ninth Illinois Cavalry, will proceed to Nashville, Tenn., with the enlisted men of his regiment whose terms of service have expired, for the purpose of having them mustered out of the service of the United States.

By order of Brevet Major-General Wilson:

E. B. BEAUMONT,
Major and Assistant Adjutant-General.

CIRCULAR.]   HEADQUARTERS CAVALRY CORPS,
MILITARY DIVISION OF THE MISSISSIPPI,
Mrs. Brown's House, December 21, 1864.

Every exertion must be made to get the forges up, in order that the horses of the command may be shod as rapidly as possible.

By command of Brevet Major-General Wilson:

E. B. BEAUMONT,
Major and Assistant Adjutant-General.

GENERAL ORDERS, ⎰   HDQRS. SECOND DIV., CAV. CORPS,
                          MILITARY DIV. OF THE MISSISSIPPI,
No. 38.   ⎱   *Louisville, Ky., December 21, 1864.*

*   *   *   *   *   *   *

III. The command will move promptly at 7 a. m. on Saturday, the 24th instant. Order of march: First, division headquarters; second, Second Brigade; third, First Brigade. The trains, ambulances, and wagons will march in the rear of their respective brigades, with a rear guard behind them. The division headquarters train will march with and in advance of that of the leading brigade. Brigade commanders will take efficient measures to prevent pillaging of houses and all unnecessary destruction of property on the road. Each brigade will have a field officer of the day, who will have a general superintendence of the guards and prevent straggling, pillaging, and disasters of all kinds on the march. All officers will arrest any soldier galloping his horse, unless he is acting as an orderly or is under orders. Brigade commanders will select a good non-commissioned officer to go on the train to Nashville with what stores they may have to send that way, with three men as a guard for them. This non-commissioned officer will report to Lieut. J. B. Hayden, division acting assistant quartermaster, as soon as practicable, to make arrangements for the transportation of said stores. The brigade commanders will see that each man will have two horseshoes, with nails, to carry along. The pack-mules will be packed and exercised as much as possible between this and the time of starting, and on Friday, as soon after the inspection as possible, the wagons will be loaded and everything got in readiness to move without delay. Saturday morning the command will start with four days' rations.

By command of Brigadier-General Long:

T. W. SCOTT,
Captain and Acting Assistant Adjutant-General.

HEADQUARTERS FIFTH DIVISION CAVALRY,
Left of Columbia Pike, December 21, 1864—9 p. m.

Major-General WILSON,
Commanding Cavalry Corps:

The Second Iowa drove the enemy's cavalry off the Lewisburg pike this evening. Captured 2 guns, 6 ambulances, 2 wagons, a drove of hogs and cattle. The enemy got off in the darkness.

Very truly, your obedient servant,

EDWARD HATCH,
Brigadier-General.

HEADQUARTERS FIFTH DIVISION CAVALRY,
Left of Columbia Pike, December 21, 1864—10.30 p. m.

Major-General WILSON,
Commanding Cavalry Corps:

The Second Iowa is at the junction of the Lewisburg pike and Columbia and Murfreesborough road. The force encountered was the rear guard of French, mostly Texan cavalry, from 200 to 300 strong. This force was cut off from crossing at the pontoon here, and attempted to escape toward the left, and is now scattered, and probably swimming Duck River in small squads. The Second Iowa is about fourteen miles from here, and is force enough to whip anything out there north of Duck River. The entire road is strewn with small-arms.

Very truly, your obedient servant,

E. HATCH,
Brigadier-General.

HEADQUARTERS DISTRICT OF THE TENNESSEE,
Nashville, December 21, 1864—5.20 p. m. (Received 22d.)

Brig. Gen. W. D. WHIPPLE,
Assistant Adjutant-General and Chief of Staff:

I have just arrived from Murfreesborough. As soon as I heard of the result of the battle here, I put construction trains at work on the railroad north and south of Murfreesborough. By working all night night before last, the road was repaired south of Murfreesborough in time for General Steedman's trains to come up from Chattanooga. Ten of them arrived at Murfreesborough last night. He would leave this forenoon for Bridgeport. He asked for four regiments of the troops at Murfreesborough to go on his expedition, and I directed General Milroy, just as I left, to order four of the best to report to him, which I suppose would meet your approbation. Shall I send General Milroy and his command back to Tullahoma? I shall direct the assignment of guards to the road between here and Murfreesborough as fast as it is completed. A wagon train with supplies for the troops at Murfreesborough left here to-day. I sent the train from there two days ago. Everything is in good condition there, and the railroad north of that will be completed in a few days.

LOVELL H. ROUSSEAU,
Major-General.

HEADQUARTERS DEPARTMENT OF THE CUMBERLAND,
December 21, 1864.

Maj. Gen. L. H. ROUSSEAU,
Commanding District of the Tennessee:

GENERAL: The major-general commanding directs that you relieve the detachments of the Tenth Indiana Cavalry now on duty in your command, and direct them to report without delay to the commanding officer of the First Brigade, Seventh Cavalry Division, for duty.

Very respectfully, your obedient servant,

HENRY M. CIST,
Assistant Adjutant-General.

CLARKSVILLE, *December 21, 1864—4 p. m.*

Capt. ROBERT H. RAMSEY,
Assistant Adjutant-General:

My men have returned; they captured a captain. General Lyon left Hopkinsville a week ago to-day with one brigade for Eddyville; he left one brigade at Hopkinsville. On last Friday night Lyon had returned to within fourteen miles of Hopkinsville, and met a portion of his force that McCook had defeated at Hopkinsville. Here he had a fight with McCook's advance, 350 men, and is reported to have driven them back; have not heard from him since. Lyon had but two guns and 1,200 men. McCook took one gun.

A. A. SMITH,
Colonel Eighty-third Illinois, Commanding.

MURFREESBOROUGH, *December 21, 1864.*

General MEAGHER:

Send all the men of the Fourteenth and Forty-fourth Colored Regiments and a sergeant and twenty men of the Eighteenth Ohio Battery to join their commands at Stevenson, and send by train, if you have it, 50,000 rations to Stevenson.

J. B. STEEDMAN,
Major-General.

STEVENSON, *December 21, 1864.*

Brigadier-General MEAGHER:

Two sections with military bridge-builders and track-layers are ordered to Decatur by Major-General Thomas to repair the road. The railroad agent wants a guard. I have sent all the men I could spare as guards to the trains to Murfreesborough. Can I order the Sixty-eighth New York Volunteers from your district as guards?

W. KRZYZANOWSKI,
Colonel, Commanding.

STEVENSON, *December 21, 1864.*

Brigadier-General MEAGHER:

The places occupied by the Sixty-eighth New York Veteran Volunteers will not have to be filled.

W. KRZYZANOWSKI,
Colonel, Commanding.

HEADQUARTERS,
Louisville, Ky., December 21, 1864.

Maj. Gen. G. H. THOMAS,
    Commanding Department of the Cumberland :

The Thirty-ninth Infantry Missouri Volunteers, ordered by General Dodge, commanding Department of the Missouri, to proceed to Nashville, Tenn., has arrived at Louisville, Ky., and 1 deem it proper to report that we have left several cases of small-pox in hospital on our route.

ED. A. KUTZNER,
Lieutenant-Colonel, Comdg. Thirty-ninth Missouri Volunteers.

HEADQUARTERS DISTRICT OF INDIANA,
Indianapolis, December 21, 1864.

Capt. C. H. POTTER,
    Assistant Adjutant-General, Cincinnati, Ohio:

CAPTAIN: There are 300 rebels at Hawesville, Ky., on the Ohio River, conscripting and sending to the rebel army. It is reported that from 100 to 200 are sent south from this point daily. I respectfully ask permission to send a force to the Ohio River and drive them from the border.

Very respectfully, your obedient servant,
ALVIN P. HOVEY,
Brevet Major-General, Commanding.

MEMPHIS, TENN., *December 21, 1864.*
(Received 23d.)

Maj. Gen. H. W. HALLECK,
    Chief of Staff :

In obedience to your orders I have to-day sent all effective cavalry, without a wheel accompanying them, to strike the Mobile and Ohio Railroad above Tupelo, 3,500 strong. Roads in horrible condition, and weather very bad. If successful they will, if possible, destroy the railroad as far as Meridian, and, if considered safe, they will make a dash at Cahawba and attempt a release of our prisoners. General Grierson is in command. Five thousand infantry at the same time make a feint, threatening Corinth.

N. J. T. DANA,
Major-General, Commanding.

MEMPHIS, TENN., *December 21, 1864.*

Maj. Gen. G. H. THOMAS:

I have to-day, general, sent all my effective cavalry, by orders of Maj. Gen. H. W. Halleck, to break the Mobile and Ohio Railroad near Tupelo. I have been compelled to keep an ample force of Winslow's men for that object. Roads and weather very bad and the enemy in some force.

N. J. T. DANA,
Major-General.

[DECEMBER 21, 1864.—For General Orders, No. 6, headquarters Department of Mississippi, publishing complimentary communication from General Canby to General Dana, see Part I, p. 780.]

WAR DEPARTMENT,
Washington, December 22, 1864—9 p. m.

Major-General THOMAS,
        In the Field:

I have seen to-day General Halleck's dispatch of yesterday and your reply. It is proper for me to assure you that this Department has the most unbounded confidence in your skill, vigor, and determination to employ to the best advantage all the means in your power to pursue and destroy the enemy. No Department could be inspired with more profound admiration and thankfulness for the great deeds you have already performed, or more confiding faith that human effort could accomplish no more than will be done by you and the gallant officers and soldiers of your command.

EDWIN M. STANTON,
Secretary of War.

WAR DEPARTMENT,
Washington, December 22, 1864—9 p. m.

Maj. Gen. GEORGE H. THOMAS:

In order that the Department may, as fully as the law will permit, award due promotion to your army, please forward me some time before the 5th of next month a list of such promotions as you desire to recommend. There is no vacancy in the number of major-generals allowed by law, and only two brigadiers; but brevets can be granted, and some vacancies may be created by mustering out useless officers.

EDWIN M. STANTON,
Secretary of War.

CITY POINT, VA., *December 22, 1864.*

Major-General THOMAS,
        Nashville, Tenn.:

You have the congratulations of the public for the energy with which you are pushing Hood. I hope you will succeed in reaching his pontoon bridge at Tuscumbia before he gets there. Should you do it, it looks to me that Hood is cut off. If you succeed in destroying Hood's army, there will be but one army left to the so-called Confederacy capable of doing us harm. I will take care of that and try to draw the sting from it, so that in the spring we shall have easy sailing. You now have a big opportunity, which I know you are availing yourself of. Let us push and do all we can before the enemy can derive benefit either from the raising of negro troops or the concentration of white troops now in the field.

U. S. GRANT,
Lieutenant-General.

HEADQUARTERS DEPARTMENT OF THE CUMBERLAND,
Columbia, Tenn., December 22, 1864.
(Received 2 p. m. 23d.)

Maj. Gen. H. W. HALLECK,
        Chief of Staff:

The Fourth Corps crossed Duck River to-day, and has advanced about two miles beyond town, in the direction of Pulaski. Cavalry will cross by daylight to-morrow and the rest of the infantry during the day. In crossing to-day we captured about 50 prisoners in a rebel hospital, with about 250 rebel wounded and about 50 of our own wounded. Prisoners, on being questioned, stated substantially that Hood's army is greatly demoralized, nearly half of which is unarmed; that the greater portion of the infantry left here two days ago for Pulaski; that five brigades of infantry and Forrest's cavalry now constitute Hood's rear guard, and this force left the vicinity of Columbia this morning upon our approach. I shall push forward rapidly in the morning, and endeavor to overtake him before he reaches the Tennessee River.

> GEO. H. THOMAS,
> *Major-General, Commanding.*

> NASHVILLE, *December 22, 1864.*

Maj. Gen. G. H. THOMAS:

In cases where persons have been conscripted into the rebel ranks since Hood crossed the Tennessee River, and have never been sworn into their service, and have been captured, many of them, in fact, in the act of deserting, would it not be well to release them on satisfactory proof of the facts? General Webster thinks he has no power in the matter, but will act with your approval. I think it would have a good effect to set such persons at liberty. Some of these are cases of hardship. Any assistance or information in examination of these cases will be cheerfully furnished General Webster in making his decisions as to who shall be released.

> ANDREW JOHNSON,
> *Military Governor.*

> NASHVILLE, TENN., *December 22, 1864—7.20 p. m.*

Brevet Major-General MEIGS,
> *Quartermaster-General:*

Will have railroad through to Thomas' rear, at Columbia, to-night, and to Murfreesborough within a day or two. Road from Murfreesborough south all right. Trains running thence to Chattanooga and Huntsville, which we occupied yesterday. Great many cars conveying troops will reach Huntsville from Murfreesborough to-night or early in the morning, and push straight for Decatur. Will have road then, via Huntsville, repaired by Saturday.

> J. L. DONALDSON,
> *Chief Quartermaster.*

> NASHVILLE, *December 22, 1864.*

General W. D. WHIPPLE,
> *Chief of Staff:*

Have already ordered forage forward, as requested in Captain Ramsey's telegram of the 20th; have also sent two steamer-loads to Eastport with subsistence ordered there.

> J. L. DONALDSON,
> *Chief Quartermaster, Department of the Cumberland.*

NASHVILLE, *December 22, 1864.*

General W. D. WHIPPLE,
         Chief of Staff:

Steamers for Eastport left last evening and ought to be at Smithland early to-day. I sent also some medical supplies, quartermaster's stores, and two steamers loaded with grain.

                                 J. L. DONALDSON,
                                      Chief Quartermaster.

FRANKLIN, *December 22, 1864—9 a. m.*

Brigadier-General WHIPPLE,
         Assistant Adjutant-General:

I have ordered three trains of forage to be sent forward to Duck River at once. The bridge will be done within an hour. I will be down on first train.

                                 WM. G. LE DUC,
                                      Lieutenant-Colonel, &c.

SPRING HILL, *December 22, 1864—5.30 o'clock.*

Brigadier-General WHIPPLE:

GENERAL: I have arrived here with train of forage, and others following. The bridge at Carter's Creek being destroyed, cannot go any farther. Supplies are ordered, and will arrive as fast as possible. I have ordered 40,000 pairs of shoes and stockings, also quartermaster's stores, &c. A telegraph operator should be sent here at once. A telegraph station here is absolutely necessary.

Respectfully,

                                 WM. G. LE DUC,
                                      Lieutenant-Colonel, &c.

FRANKLIN, TENN., *December 22, 1864.*

Brig. Gen. W. D. WHIPPLE,
         Assistant Adjutant-General:

We shall establish the subsistence depot at Spring Hill to-night. I have notified the corps by telegraph. I will rejoin headquarters as soon as possible.

                                 EDGAR C. BEMAN,
         Capt. and Actg. Chief Com. of Subsistence, Dept. of the Cumberland.

FRANKLIN, *December 22, 1864—9 a. m.*

General W. D. WHIPPLE:

The bridge will be finished in half an hour. It has been an awful job to complete it.

                                 W. W. WRIGHT,
                                      Chief of Engineers.

HEADQUARTERS DEPARTMENT OF THE CUMBERLAND,
Columbia, December 22, 1864.

Col. W. W. WRIGHT,
    Superintendent of Repairs, U. S. Military Railroads:

COLONEL: The major-general commanding directs me to inform you that he has had the railroad examined to-day up to Duck River, and to give you the following as the result of the examination: The first and second bridges over Carter's Creek are but little damaged; the third is all gone but the debris, which is three-quarters of a mile down the creek; the fourth all down, but wreck there; the fifth all down, and portion of wreck there. Duck River bridge gone, but trestle on south side of the river complete to the bank of the river. Between the third and fourth bridges there is a pile of bridge timber, and there is also a pile of bridge timber between the fourth and fifth bridges. The major-general commanding wishes you to make every effort and push forward the work of repair as rapidly as possible, as it is absolutely necessary that the railroad be opened up in the shortest possible time so as to subsist and forage the army. Please acknowledge receipt.

Very respectfully, your obedient servant,
ROBT. H. RAMSEY,
Assistant Adjutant-General.

CHATTANOOGA, *December 22, 1864.*

Captain RAMSEY,
    Assistant Adjutant-General:

I learn that the railroad is open to Huntsville now. I had better move by rail to Huntsville, and then by wagons to Athens. If so, I can move at once.

J. L. HOLLOPETER,
Acting Chief Signal Officer.

NASHVILLE, TENN., *December 22, 1864—10.30 p. m.*

Maj. T. T. ECKERT:

General Thomas' headquarters broke camp this morning to cross Duck River, and at this hour his telegraph office has not been again opened, so no news from him. Trains will run to Columbia to-morrow, and railroad to Chattanooga will be repaired in a week at the latest.

J. C. VAN DUZER.

CIRCULAR.]   HDQRS. DEPARTMENT OF THE CUMBERLAND,
Duck River, Tenn., December 22, 1864.

The train of the headquarters of the army in the field, including the telegraph construction train, will, while on the road, have the right of way over all other trains whatever, and all troops and trains are ordered to make way for it whenever required by the officer in charge.

By command of Major-General Thomas:
WM. D. WHIPPLE,
Brigadier-General and Chief of Staff.

HEADQUARTERS ARMY OF THE OHIO,
Near Columbia, Tenn., December 22, 1864.

Major-General THOMAS,
Commanding Department of the Cumberland:

GENERAL: I have at Knoxville about 1,000 feet of pontoon bridge, which might be made available for crossing the Tennessee, if you need it. It might be floated down, under convoy of the gun-boats, to the point where you desire to use it.

Very respectfully,

J. M. SCHOFIELD,
Major-General.

HEADQUARTERS ARMY OF THE OHIO,
In the Field, near Columbia, Tenn., December 22, 1864.

Col. E. D. TOWNSEND,
Assistant Adjutant-General, Washington, D. C.:

COLONEL: I desire to ask the attention of the War Department to the necessity of taking some steps to preserve the organization of the Twenty-third Army Corps. The terms of service of nearly all the regiments composing it will expire during the summer and early autumn of 1865. It contains only three veteran regiments and six three-years regiments organized under the call of 1863; the remainder are three-years regiments, whose terms of service are nearly expired, and new one-year regiments. I respectfully request authority to re-enlist all of my regiments and batteries which have served more than two years for one, two, or three years, as they may elect, and to grant them after re-enlistment furloughs for thirty days, according to the rules heretofore observed.

I am, colonel, very respectfully, your obedient servant,

J. M. SCHOFIELD,
Major-General.

NASHVILLE, TENN., *December 22, 1864.*

Maj. J. A. CAMPBELL,
Assistant Adjutant-General, Department of the Ohio:

SIR: I have the honor to state, for the information of the major-general commanding, that the order directing me to proceed to Murfreesborough and take command of and move with certain regiments therein named, from that point to Columbia, Tenn., or to the Twenty-third Army Corps, and which order bore date December 19, was not received by me until the afternoon of the 21st, the orderly who brought it giving as a reason that he could not find my headquarters and the sickness of his horse. I kept the same quarters as when the corps was here, and the order would have duly reached me either by the post headquarters or Captain Stone, of General Thomas' staff. I regret to have to report that I was not able, owing to illness, to go myself to Murfreesborough, as the order required and as I presume was desired by the major-general commanding on account of the regiments having but little experience. I saw Major-General Rousseau on his arrival here on the 21st, who informed me that the regiments were under competent commanders. As soon after receipt of the order as possible I sent orders by my aide-de-camp for the regiments to move at once, under the command of the senior colonel, to Columbia, or wherever the Twenty-third Army

Corps might be, and report to me at Columbia, if I should be there, which I hope to be, or if not, to the commanding officer of the corps. General Rousseau told me that, at the request of General Steedman, he had directed General Milroy to detail four of the best regiments at Murfreesborough to report to and go with General Steedman, and I fear that some of the regiments assigned to the Twenty-third Army Corps may have gone with General Steedman. I directed my aide-de-camp, Mr. Binney, to see General Milroy at once on his arrival and deliver a letter from me, and also show him my order, so that, unless too late, any of the regiments belonging to the Twenty-third Army Corps which might have been ordered to report to General Steedman could be recalled. I made an earnest appeal to General Milroy, in the event of General Steedman having left Murfreesborough, to furnish me transportation, as contemplated by my order for General Steedman to do. There is no transportation to be had here; I cannot get a wagon even for my personal baggage and that of my staff. In relation to the batteries of the First Division, I think that Captain Paddock's battery, the guns of which are to be turned in, and most of the material of which has been inspected and condemned, had better remain here until the order on the inspection is received. Captain Nicholson's battery I have directed to be ready to join the corps by the first opportunity for escort. So soon as I hear from my aide-de-camp at Murfreesborough that matters are attended to there, I shall start for Columbia. I think the regiments will be able to leave Murfreesborough by the 24th. The railroad trains are not running to Murfreesborough, and I was unable to get any escort from here until the 22d.

Very respectfully, your obedient servant,

THOS. H. RUGER,
Brig. Gen. of Vols., Comdg. First Div., Twenty-third Army Corps.

HEADQUARTERS ARMY OF THE OHIO,
Rutherford's Creek, Tenn., December 22, 1864.

Brig. Gen. J. D. COX,
Commanding Third Division, Twenty-third Army Corps:

GENERAL: The commanding general directs that you march your command to this place to-morrow morning.

I am, general, very respectfully, your obedient servant,

J. A. CAMPBELL,
Major and Assistant Adjutant-General.

HDQRS. THIRD DIVISION, TWENTY-THIRD ARMY CORPS,
Spring Hill, Tenn., December 22, 1864.

Maj. J. A. CAMPBELL,
Assistant Adjutant-General, Headquarters Army of the Ohio:

MAJOR: I have the honor to call the attention of the commanding general to the severe suffering of the line officers of the command in inclement weather like the present and under the existing rules with regard to transportation. From the time we left Nashville until last night these gentlemen had no shelter and only such food as they could obtain from the private soldiers—being far worse off than the men, since the latter had their shelter-tents and their rations in haversacks. The officers' rations and their cooking utensils are in the regimental wagons, which are necessarily left behind in movements such as we have lately made, and they must either furnish themselves with knapsacks and haversacks, and carry their cooking utensils upon their own persons or those of their servants, or be utterly destitute. Even if they do this, the wagons of the commissary of subsistence are also at the rear, except upon ordinary days of issue, and it would be necessary to issue to them precisely as is done to the soldiers in the ranks, and so break down the last vestige of distinction in mode of life between them and their commands. As it is, I state what I know from personal observation when I say, that no individuals in any way connected with the army are enduring so much personal suffering and privation upon the present campaign as the officers of the line. As I know the commanding general will be most desirous to make any arrangement which is feasible to reduce the amount of discomfort, I take the liberty of suggesting that during the winter campaign the transportation for each regiment be one wagon for regimental headquarters and for company books and papers, desks, &c., as now, and, in addition, one pack-mule for each company. The pack-mules make little or no obstruction in the road, are easily moved to flank or rear in case of maneuver of troops, and will be up with the command when the regiment goes into camp. Unless some such arrangement is made, I fear many of our officers will break down in health, and many more, becoming disgusted with the hardships of the service, and especially with the difference between themselves and their more fortunate brethren of the staff and staff corps, will seek to leave the army. In many commands some similar arrangements to the one I have suggested have been surreptitiously made, but as I have rigidly enforced the rule turning over to the quartermaster all unauthorized animals, I am the more desirous of obtaining for the gentlemen of the line whom I have the honor to command such authority to regulate their transportation as will save them from the apparently unnecessary hardships they have of late endured, without detracting from the mobility of the division.

Very respectfully, your obedient servant,

J. D. COX,
Brigadier-General, Commanding.

[Indorsement.]

The suggestions of General Cox are approved, and will be carried out as soon as possible. The quartermaster will be ordered to furnish the necessary pack-mules. Until this can be done the baggage wagons will move immediately after their divisions, except in case of absolute necessity.

J. M. S.

CIRCULAR.]   HDQRS. CAVALRY CORPS, MIL. DIV. OF THE MISS.,
Near Columbia, Tenn., December 22, 1864.

Commanders of divisions and detached brigades will take measures immediately to send all horses that are unfit for active service back to Nashville. These horses will be inspected carefully by brigade inspectors, and will then be placed in charge of a detail of men under a competent officer. This detail will be at the rate of one man to every eight horses. Lieutenant Prather, special inspector of the Cavalry Bureau, is charged with this and will organize the detail. The dismounted men will be organized into a train guard, under a sufficient number of officers, and will be under the immediate control of Capt. E. B. Carling, chief quartermaster of the corps.

By command of Brevet Major-General Wilson:

A. J. ALEXANDER,
Lieut. Col., Assistant Adjutant-General and Acting Chief of Staff.

SPECIAL ⎫   HEADQUARTERS CAVALRY CORPS,
FIELD ORDERS, ⎬   MILITARY DIVISION OF THE MISSISSIPPI,
No. 11. ⎭   *Near Columbia, Tenn., December 22, 1864.*

I. Brigadier-General Hatch's division will begin crossing Duck River as soon as the bridge is completed.

II. Brigadier-General Hammond's brigade will follow the Fifth (Hatch's) Division.

III. Brigadier-General Croxton's brigade will follow General Hammond's.

IV. Colonel Harrison's brigade will follow General Croxton's.

V. The Cavalry Corps will go into camp two miles beyond Columbia, upon ground to be designated by the inspector of the Cavalry Corps.

By order of Brevet Major-General Wilson:

E. B. BEAUMONT,
Major and Assistant Adjutant-General.

CIRCULAR.] HDQRS. CAVALRY CORPS, MIL. DIV. OF THE MISS.,
Near Columbia, December 22, 1864.

The order to march to-night is countermanded. The head of General Hatch's column will be at the bridge to cross at 5 to-morrow morning; General Hammond's, at 7 a. m.; General Croxton's, at 8 a. m.; Colonel Harrison's, at 9 a. m.

By command of Brevet Major-General Wilson:

E. B. BEAUMONT,
Major and Assistant Adjutant-General.

HOPKINSVILLE, KY., *December 22, 1864—2 p. m.*
(Received 4.20 p. m. 23d.)

Hon. E. M. STANTON,
Secretary of War:

With Watkins' and La Grange's brigades, of my division, I have defeated General Lyon and captured or scattered the force with which he invaded Kentucky, and captured his artillery.

E. M. McCOOK,
Brigadier-General, Commanding.

HDQRS. CAVALRY CORPS, MIL. DIV. OF THE MISSISSIPPI,
In the Field, Columbia, Tenn., December 22, 1864.

Brig. Gen. E. M. McCOOK,
Commanding First Division, Cavalry Corps:

GENERAL: As soon as you have broken up Lyon's command, proceed with your division to join the Cavalry Corps in the field. General

Wilson leaves it entirely to your discretion as to when you shall abandon the pursuit of Lyon. The troops in Kentucky can take care of the guerrilla bands resulting from the dispersion of Lyon's command.

By command of Brevet Major-General Wilson:

E. B. BEAUMONT,
Major and Assistant Adjutant-General.

HOPKINSVILLE, *December 22, 1864—8.30 a. m.*

Bvt. Brig. Gen. L. D. WATKINS:

The general commanding directs that you send a dispatch to Colonel Welling, directing him to return with his command without delay and to bring the guides he has captured to these headquarters. I am instructed to inform you that the command will not move to-day.

I have the honor to be, very respectfully, your obedient servant,

ROBERT LE ROY,
Captain and Assistant Adjutant-General.

HOPKINSVILLE, *December 22, 1864.*

Bvt. Brig. Gen. L. D. WATKINS:

I am instructed by the general commanding to inform you that Lyon has crossed Green River at Ashbysburg, and La Grange is in pursuit. Your command will move at 7.30 a. m. on the morning of the 23d instant. The general further directs that you inform the battery of the intended movement, and give it a place in your column. The Seventeenth Kentucky Volunteer Cavalry, Major Arneck commanding, with the exception of the company which has not yet been mustered in, and which will proceed to Russellville for that purpose, will remain as a garrison at this place. Major Arneck will receive his instructions from these headquarters.

I am, general, very respectfully, your obedient servant,

ROBERT LE ROY,
Captain and Assistant Adjutant-General.

LONG VIEW, KY., *December 22, 1864—5 a. m.*

Brig. Gen. E. M. McCOOK,
Commanding First Division:

I have followed this force from about ten miles from Hopkinsville on the Butler road. Lyon, with his command, has crossed Green River, and this is a detachment of his command which was cut off. They are estimated between twenty-five and forty-five men. I have captured two of their guides, and both tell the same story. I have not been able to hear of any large force. Shall I follow this force to the river, or return? I will move slowly down the pike till I hear from you.

Respectfully, &c.,

GEO. WELLING,
Lieutenant-Colonel, Commanding Fourth Kentucky Cavalry.

HOPKINSVILLE, *December 22, 1864.*

Major ARNECK,
    Comdg. Seventeenth Regiment Kentucky Volunteer Cavalry:

The Seventeenth Regiment Kentucky Volunteer Cavalry, with the exception of that portion of it which has not yet been mustered in, will remain at Hopkinsville and garrison that place until it receives orders from Lieutenant-Colonel Johnson or other superior authority. The portion not yet mustered will march directly to Russellville. You will give proper receipts for all rations or forage that you may take from citizens for the use of your command. You will not abandon the place without orders, unless attacked by a much superior force.

E. M. McCOOK,
Brigadier-General.

_____

HOPKINSVILLE, *December 22, 1864.*

Col. O. H. LA GRANGE:

I am directed by the general commanding to inform you that the command moves to-morrow to Trenton, and will probably move from there to Nashville. Any dispatches addressed to me at Russellville or Nashville will reach me. If you come back through Hopkinsville you will move directly to Nashville by easy marches, and notify him there of your coming.

I am, colonel, your obedient servant,

ROBERT LE ROY,
Captain and Assistant Adjutant-General.

_____

GENERAL ORDERS,⎞   HDQRS. 2D DIV., CAVALRY CORPS,
                 ⎟   MIL. DIV. OF THE MISSISSIPPI,
    No. 39.   ⎠   *Louisville, Ky., December 22, 1864.*

I. Maj. D. D. Marquis, Ninety-eighth Illinois Volunteers, having been assigned to duty at Saint Louis, Mo., by orders from the War Department, is hereby relieved from duty as assistant inspector-general on the staff of the brigadier-general commanding.

II. Capt. Jesse N. Squire, Third Ohio Cavalry, having reported in obedience with Special Orders, No. 168, from these headquarters, is hereby announced as assistant inspector-general of this division, subject to the approval of the corps commander.

III. Capt. C. C. Starkweather, One hundred and twenty-third Illinois Volunteers, having reported in obedience with Special Orders, No. 168, from these headquarters, is hereby announced as provost-marshal of this division.

By command of Brig. Gen. Eli Long:

T. W. SCOTT,
Captain and Acting Assistant Adjutant-General.

_____

HDQRS. CAVALRY CORPS, MIL. DIV. OF THE MISSISSIPPI,
Columbia, December 22, 1864.

Brigadier-General UPTON,
    Comdg. Fourth Division, Cavalry Corps, Memphis, Tenn.:

Take with you to Louisville the Third and Fourth Iowa, Tenth and Twelfth Missouri, the Sixth Tennessee, and Nineteenth Pennsylvania.

By command of Brevet Major-General Wilson:

E. B. BEAUMONT,
Major and Assistant Adjutant-General.

Hdqrs. First Brig., Seventh Div., Cavalry Corps,
Military Division of the Mississippi,
Near Columbia, December 22, 1864.

Maj. E. B. Beaumont,
Assistant Adjutant-General, Cavalry Corps:

Major: Pursuant to an order to examine the railroad and bridges from my encampment to Duck River, and including Duck River bridge, I sent two officers for that duty. They report the track in good condition; three bridges burned—one of 160 feet length trestle, one 200 feet, and one 250 feet; the last entirely washed away, so that they could not reach Duck River bridge. They are devising measures to reach the river bridge, and will do so in a short time. I will then give a detailed report of the condition of the whole track.

Very respectfully, your obedient servant,
J. H. HAMMOND,
Brevet Brigadier-General.

(Forwarded to Major-General Thomas.)

Christiana, *December 22, 1864.*

Major-General Thomas:

I have just reached this point after being detained forty-two hours at Murfreesborough waiting transportation from the south. The delay was no doubt occasioned by the damage to the road by enemy. The enemy occupied Decatur on night of December 20, by a force estimated at from 2,000 to 4,000, said to be Roddey's. I will cross my force on transports above Decatur, drive him out, and move to Florence as fast as possible.

JAMES B. STEEDMAN,
Major-General.

Christiana, *December 22, 1864.*

General Meagher:

Have you shipped the 50,000 rations to Stevenson for me? Answer.
JAS. B. STEEDMAN,
Major-General, U. S. Volunteers.

Chattanooga, *December 22, 1864.*

Major-General Steedman:

The detachment of the Fourteenth and Forty-fourth Colored Infantry will go forward at daylight to-morrow. No men of the Eighteenth Ohio Battery can be found at the post, as I am informed by Major Church. The rations have been ordered and will go forward by the same train.
THOMAS FRANCIS MEAGHER,
Brigadier-General.

Chattanooga, *December 22, 1864.*

Major-General Steedman:

The detachment of the Eighteenth Ohio Battery has been found, and a sergeant and twenty men ordered to report to you at Stevenson by the first train.

THOS. FRANCIS MEAGHER,
Brigadier-General.

ON BOARD STEAMER STONE RIVER,
Off Whitesburg, December 22, 1864.

Brigadier-General WHIPPLE:

Owing to the unusually severe weather, high winds, snow, and fogs, my miserable fleet of transports could not be gotten to Decatur until 12 m. to-day, where I found the enemy, advised of our approach, had been largely re-enforced, his garrison being now 2,000, and his guns increased to nine, three heavy pieces added to his field battery. My command, from exposure on boats, is reduced to 1,200. I have on this account not believed it practicable to assault the works until I can be re-enforced by General Steedman. My forces have possession of the road to Huntsville. The railroad bridges and roads in running order to that place. Colonel Lyon reported that Roddey was ordered to hold Huntsville at all hazards, and also informed that it was Hood's intention to make Decatur his main position, with his right resting at Huntsville.

R. S. GRANGER,
Brigadier-General.

HEADQUARTERS DEPARTMENT OF THE CUMBERLAND,
Duck River, December 22, 1864.

Brig. Gen. JOHN F. MILLER,
Commanding Post of Nashville:

GENERAL: Your communication of the 26th instant, concerning the disposition to be made of those men of the Army of Savannah, and others, has been received. You will issue the orders from your office sending the men to Savannah, stating in the order that it is pursuant to instructions from the major-general commanding the department. You can commence forwarding the detachments immediately. The major-general commanding thinks it is best that the detachments belonging to the army here who were left behind guarding property be kept together in the camp you have established, until their respective commanders send for them. In the meantime you will exercise control over them. The garrison of Nashville will not be diminished at present, but will be temporarily increased by those Missouri regiments now on their way there, and which you can retain.

Very respectfully, your obedient servant,

WM. D. WHIPPLE,
Brigadier-General and Chief of Staff.

CITY POINT, VA., *December 23, 1864—6 p. m.*

Hon. E. M. STANTON,
Secretary of War:

I think it would be appropriate now to confer on General Thomas the vacant major-generalcy in the Regular Army. He seems to be pushing Hood with energy, and I doubt not but he will completely destroy that army.

U. S. GRANT,
Lieutenant-General.

COLUMBIA, TENN., *December 23,** 1864—8 p. m.*
(Received 1 a. m. 25th.)
Hon. E. M. STANTON,
Secretary of War, Washington, D. C.:

Your two dispatches of 9 p. m. 22d instant are received. I am profoundly thankful for the hearty expression of your confidence in my determination and desire to do all in my power to destroy the enemy and put down the rebellion, and, in the name of this army, I thank you for the complimentary notice you have taken of all connected with it for the deeds of valor they have performed. I will forward the list of meritorious officers to-morrow or next day.

GEO. H. THOMAS,
Major-General, U. S. Volunteers, Commanding.

COLUMBIA, TENN., *December 23, 1864—8 p. m.*
(Received 11.15 p. m.)
Maj. Gen. H. W. HALLECK,
Washington, D. C.:

The troops are still crossing Duck River, and are close up to the enemy's rear guard, on the Pulaski road. I hope to get the whole force across to-morrow and continue the pursuit. The railroad bridges between Spring Hill and this place (five in number) have been destroyed, but the construction corps is hard at work, and I am in hopes they will have the road repaired up to Columbia in the course of four or five days. The railroad between Chattanooga and Murfreesborough is in running order, and I am assured that the road between Nashville and Murfreesborough will be repaired in a few days. General McCook has routed and scattered the rebel General Lyon, who succeeded in crossing the Cumberland River, and, with General Long, will soon join General Wilson, thus increasing my cavalry force sufficiently to enable me to completely destroy Forrest, if I can overtake him, which I shall make every exertion to do.

GEO. H. THOMAS,
Major-General, U. S. Volunteers, Commanding.

HEADQUARTERS DEPARTMENT OF THE CUMBERLAND,
Columbia, December 23, 1864—8 a. m.
Governor ANDREW JOHNSON,
Military Governor of Tennessee, Nashville:

Your telegram of yesterday is received. The major-general commanding directs me to say in reply that in cases where the persons arrested are known to be sincere in their sympathies for the United States, and have really been forced into the rebel service during Hood's last movement, against their will, it will be well enough to release them, as you suggest.

Very respectfully,

ROBT. H. RAMSEY,
Assistant Adjutant-General.

---

* So dated in Thomas' record book, but in Stanton's received it is the 24th.

HEADQUARTERS DEPARTMENT OF THE CUMBERLAND,
Duck River, December 23, 1864.

Brig. Gen. J. L. DONALDSON,
Nashville:

You are authorized to withdraw a portion of the Fifteenth U. S. Colored Troops from Edgefield and Kentucky railroad, for duty in Nashville.

WM. D. WHIPPLE,
Assistant Adjutant-General.

HEADQUARTERS DEPARTMENT OF THE CUMBERLAND,
Duck River, December 23, 1864.

Brig. Gen. J. L. DONALDSON,
Nashville:

Stop the steamers loaded for Eastport at Paducah, unless the gunboats have gone up the Tennessee, when they might as well go along; if stopped, orders will be sent regarding them hereafter, when it is definitely ascertained what is Hood's route.

WM. D. WHIPPLE,
Assistant Adjutant-General.

NASHVILLE, *December 23, 1864.*

Brigadier-General WHIPPLE,
Chief of Staff, Department of the Cumberland:

Telegram received. The steamers for Eastport had orders not to go up the Tennessee River unless convoyed by gun-boats; had written orders to report to commanding officer of gun-boats for that purpose on arriving at Paducah. Will, however, telegraph to Paducah as you directed. Boats last ordered to Eastport with rations, medical supplies, forage, and ordnance stores are still here; were to leave to-night; will hold till further orders.

J. L. DONALDSON,
Chief Quartermaster.

HEADQUARTERS DEPARTMENT OF THE CUMBERLAND,
Columbia, December 23, 1864—8 a. m.

Lieut. J. L. HOLLOPETER,
Actg. Chief Signal Officer, Dept. of the Cumberland, Chattanooga:

Your telegram of yesterday is received. The major-general commanding directs me to say that you had better wait until you learn of the occupation of Huntsville or Athens before you move, so that you will run no risk.

ROBT. H. RAMSEY,
Assistant Adjutant-General.

SPECIAL FIELD ORDERS, } HDQRS. DEPT. OF THE CUMBERLAND,
No. 348.   }   *Duck River, Tenn., December 23, 1864.*

I. Col. W. B. Gaw, Sixteenth U. S. Colored Troops, will proceed with his regiment to Chattanooga, Tenn., and report to Colonel Carlton, commanding post, for engineer duty on fortifications at that place. He will make such returns as Colonel Carlton may require, but will be considered simply on detailed duty. The quartermaster's department will furnish the necessary transportation.

*   *   *   *   *   *   *

V. The Thirty-fourth New Jersey Volunteer Infantry, Colonel Lawrence commanding, is hereby relieved from duty at Paducah, Ky., and will proceed up the Cumberland River, acting as guards to steam-boats, to Nashville, Tenn. Upon its arrival at that place the commanding officer will report without delay to Maj. Gen. A. J. Smith, commanding Detachment Army of the Tennessee.

*   *   *   *   *   *   *

By command of Major-General Thomas:

HENRY M. CIST,
Captain and Assistant Adjutant-General.

HEADQUARTERS FOURTH ARMY CORPS,
Columbia, Tenn., December 23, 1864—1.30 p. m.

Brigadier-General WHIPPLE,
Chief of Staff:

GENERAL: I have the honor to report that I am just starting on the march. I wish to move six or eight miles out on the Pulaski pike, to get out of the way of the cavalry and such other troops as may cross to-night. I do not think the cavalry will all get over the river much before dark. Please allow the remnant of my artillery and trains to cross the pontoons to-night.

Very respectfully, your obedient servant,

TH. J. WOOD,
Brigadier-General, Commanding.

HEADQUARTERS FOURTH ARMY CORPS,
Squire Mack's, Five Miles from Columbia,
December 23, 1864—6.30 p. m.

Brigadier-General WHIPPLE,
Chief of Staff:

GENERAL: I advanced the corps five miles upon the Pulaski pike, and occupy a position about two miles in advance of the cavalry. The position is a gorge between ridges closing down on either side of the road. The gorge was occupied by a force of rebel cavalry, about a brigade, which was readily dispersed by the advance of a skirmish line and a section of artillery. Casualties, so far as known, one rebel captain mortally wounded, who fell into our hands. I will wait to-morrow morning a reasonable time for the cavalry to move out, and if it does not do so I will advance down the pike toward Pulaski.

Very respectfully, your obedient servant,

TH. J. WOOD,
Brigadier-General, Commanding.

HEADQUARTERS FOURTH ARMY CORPS,
Columbia, Tenn., December 23, 1864—7 a. m.

Orders of the day for the Fourth Corps for to-day, December 23, 1864:

This command will make immediate preparations to march, and will move as soon as the cavalry passes by on the Pulaski road, in the following order: First, General Kimball's division; then General Elliott's division; then General Beatty. Each division will be followed by one battery, five ammunition wagons, ten ambulances, four wagons for division headquarters, and three for each brigade. Two wagons and two ambulances for corps headquarters will follow the leading division. If any other wagons than those specified are put in the column, all will be thrown out and be required to march with the baggage train. Artillery Brigade headquarters will follow the batteries, and the batteries, save the three with the divisions, will follow the troops.

By order of Brigadier-General Wood:

J. S. FULLERTON,
Lieutenant-Colonel and Assistant Adjutant-General.

HEADQUARTERS DEPARTMENT OF THE CUMBERLAND,
Duck River, Tenn., December 23, 1864.

Maj. Gen. J. M. SCHOFIELD,
Commanding Twenty-third Army Corps:

GENERAL: The major-general commanding the department directs that you issue five days' rations to 300 sick and wounded, our own and rebel, in hospital at Columbia. All wagons, emptied, can be immediately sent back to Spring Hill to reload.

Very respectfully, your obedient servant,

WM. D. WHIPPLE,
Brigadier-General and Chief of Staff.

SPECIAL FIELD ORDERS, }   HDQRS. ARMY OF THE OHIO,
No. 185.   }   *Near Columbia, Tenn., December 23, 1864.*

I. General Orders, No. 60, current series, headquarters Department of the Ohio, are hereby modified to read as follows: One wagon will be allowed for each regimental headquarters and for carrying company books, papers, &c., and one pack-mule to each company of infantry to carry officers' baggage.

*   *   *   *   *   *   *

IV. The chief quartermaster of the army in the field will furnish the wagons and pack-mules required to carry out the provisions of paragraph I, Special Field Orders, No. 185, current series, from these headquarters, as soon as practicable, and, until the pack-mules are furnished, the baggage wagons will habitually move with the divisions.

By command of Major-General Schofield:

J. A. CAMPBELL,
Major and Assistant Adjutant-General.

HEADQUARTERS ARMY OF THE OHIO,
Rutherford's Creek, Tenn., December 23, 1864.

Maj. Gen. D. N. COUCH,
Commanding Second Division, Twenty-third Army Corps:

GENERAL: The commanding general directs that you send your wagon train at once across Rutherford's Creek and forward toward Columbia; also, that you have your command in readiness to march at any moment. Further orders will be sent you.

I am, general, very respectfully, your obedient servant,

J. A. CAMPBELL,
Major and Assistant Adjutant-General.

HEADQUARTERS DETACHMENT ARMY OF THE TENNESSEE,
Near Columbia, Tenn., December 23, 1864.

Brig. Gen. J. MCARTHUR,
Commanding First Division:

GENERAL: The major-general commanding directs that you have your division in readiness and move forward at 4 a. m. to-morrow morning, December 24, in rear of Second Division, taking with you all your train and all pertaining to your command.

I am, very respectfully, your obedient servant,

J. HOUGH,
Major and Assistant Adjutant-General.

HEADQUARTERS DETACHMENT ARMY OF THE TENNESSEE,
Near Columbia, Tenn., December 23, 1864.

Brig. Gen. K. GARRARD,
Commanding Second Division:

GENERAL: The major-general commanding directs that you have your division in readiness and move to-morrow morning, December 24, at 3 a. m., taking with you your train and all pertaining to your command, and proceed to cross the pontoon. It matters not what is in your road, force your way through. You will take up the line of march promptly, taking the advance.

I am, very respectfully, your obedient servant,

J. HOUGH,
Major and Assistant Adjutant-General.

HEADQUARTERS DETACHMENT ARMY OF THE TENNESSEE,
Near Columbia, Tenn., December 23, 1864.

Col. J. B. MOORE,
Commanding Third Division:

COLONEL: The major-general commanding directs that you have your command in readiness and move to-morrow morning, December 24, at 5 a. m., taking with you all your train and all pertaining to your command, in rear of First Division. You will take up the two regiments of your command on provost duty at Columbia, Tenn.

I am, very respectfully, your obedient servant,

J. HOUGH,
Major and Assistant Adjutant-General.

HEADQUARTERS DEPARTMENT OF THE CUMBERLAND,
Columbia, December 23, 1864.

Brevet Major-General WILSON,
   Comdg. Cavalry Corps, Military Division of the Mississippi:

SIR: Two scouts from these headquarters who crossed the river yesterday and have been some seven miles south of this place have just come in. They report that the entire rebel army has gone on the turnpike from this point to Pulaski; at that place it is reported that they were to divide—the infantry going to Lamb's Ferry, eighteen miles below Florence, while their transportation and artillery go to Decatur. They report that the artillery horses have all given out, and the guns are being hauled by oxen. They report Forrest's cavalry as being in fair condition, but state that the citizens say it does not amount to more than 1,500 mounted, while their dismounted force is some 3,500. The bulk of the latter are very much out of spirits; they are without shoes, and would give themselves up, if pushed. The major-general commanding directs that this information be furnished you for such action as you deem advisable. If the guns are hauled by oxen your cavalry may be able to overtake them, and add them to those we already have.

   Very respectfully, your obedient servant,
                              HENRY M. CIST,
                                 Assistant Adjutant-General.

CAVALRY BUREAU, OFFICE OF SPECIAL INSPECTOR,
   MILITARY DIVISION OF THE MISSISSIPPI,
      Louisville, Ky., December 23, 1864.

Maj. Gen. J. H. WILSON,
   Comdg. Cavalry Corps, Military Division of the Mississippi:

GENERAL: I have the honor to acknowledge the receipt of your communication of the 19th instant, and to state in reply that I have this day written to Major Price on the subject of arming all the cavalry in the Military Division of the Mississippi with the Spencer carbine. I inclose to him your letter, with the urgent request that everything be done possible to carry your wishes into effect. I have asked him to inform me at once what can be done, and how many of that arm I may expect monthly. So soon as his answer is received I will communicate the same to you, so that you can see what to expect. I shall continue to do all in my power, general, not only to meet your wishes, but in all things to try and keep your corps as well mounted and equipped as possible, and that with as little delay [as possible]. If everything has not been done that was desired, you may rest assured it was because the means was not at my command.

   I am, general, very respectfully, your obedient servant,
                              W. P. CHAMBLISS,
   Maj. 4th U. S. Cav. and Special Insp. Cav., Mil. Div. of the Miss.

SPECIAL ⎫   HEADQUARTERS CAVALRY CORPS,
FIELD ORDERS, ⎬   MILITARY DIVISION OF THE MISSISSIPPI,
No. 12. ⎭   *Warfield House, December 23, 1864.*

I. The Cavalry Corps will move to-morrow morning in pursuit of the enemy, in the following order:

First. General Croxton's brigade, on the Pulaski pike, at 5 a. m., followed by General Hammond's brigade at 5.30, by Hatch at 6, and Colonel Harrison at 6.30.

II. The whole command will pass by the front of the infantry, and, when the enemy is encountered, will dispose itself for attack in the following manner: Croxton and Hammond on the right of the road, Hatch on the left, and Harrison ready to act on either flank. It is expected that the infantry under General Wood will be close enough to make all direct attacks, and leave the cavalry to operate on the flanks and rear of the enemy's rear guard.

By command of Brevet Major-General Wilson:

E. B. BEAUMONT,
Major and Assistant Adjutant-General.

TRENTON, *December 23, 1864.*

Maj. Gen. G. H. THOMAS:

I divided my force near Princeton, and sent La Grange toward Green River. He struck Lyon's rear crossing Green River, got his train, some prisoners, and drowned some. Part of his command scattered, and are trying to get through to the Cumberland River in small squads. My men will scour the country to pick them up. Lyon has lost fully half his command, and La Grange is on the other side of Green River in pursuit of the rest. I left a garrison, from Johnson's (Seventeenth Kentucky) regiment, at Hopkinsville, and will move by easy marches from here toward Nashville, unless an order from you directs otherwise. A telegraph sent to Russellville will catch me.

I am, very respectfully, your obedient servant,

E. M. McCOOK,
Brigadier-General, Commanding.

(Same to Brevet Major-General Wilson.)

HEADQUARTERS FIRST BRIGADE, SEVENTH DIVISION,
Near Columbia, December 23, 1864.

Maj. E. B. BEAUMONT,
Assistant Adjutant-General, Cavalry Corps:

MAJOR: I have the honor to report my whole command in camp. Good camp and water, but, arriving after dark, find trouble in getting forage, but will, I think, obtain a feed. The column having passed General Wilson's headquarters too far to turn back, I have placed it on the right of the pike half a mile, say two miles south of headquarters, on Hatch's right.

Very respectfully, your obedient servant,

J. H. HAMMOND,
Brigadier-General.

HEADQUARTERS DEPARTMENT OF THE CUMBERLAND,
Columbia, December 23, 1864.

Maj. Gen. J. B. STEEDMAN,
Stevenson, Ala.:

(To be forwarded.)

Your telegram of yesterday is received. The major-general commanding directs me to say in reply that your proposed movement meets his approbation, and that the reported occupation of Decatur by the enemy is substantially the same as has been learned here. There is a report, and corroborated by prisoners who have been separately examined, that Hood will attempt to cross the Tennessee at Decatur. If this report be found correct, and you are able to detain him until these forces get up, or prevent his crossing altogether, by destroying his bridge, the major-general commanding hopes to capture and destroy the greater portion, if not all, Hood's army.

Respectfully,

ROBT. H. RAMSEY,
Assistant Adjutant-General.

HUNTSVILLE, *December 23, 1864—5 p. m.*

Major-General STEEDMAN,
    Stevenson or Larkinsville:

I have reports which are entitled to some credit that Forrest is advancing on us from the north and will attack early to-morrow morning. I have sent out scouts.

WM. P. LYON,
Colonel, Commanding.

HDQRS. MEMPHIS AND CHARLESTON RAILROAD DEFENSES,
Huntsville, December 23, 1864.

Lieut. SAMUEL M. KNEELAND,
    Acting Assistant Adjutant-General, Whitesburg, Ala.:

I have the honor to acknowledge the receipt of yours of last evening at 5 o'clock this morning. The last we heard of General Steedman's command was that the advanced trains had passed Decherd at about 7 o'clock last evening. The wires are all right, but we get no response from any point east this morning. Three construction trains came over the road yesterday from Chattanooga, and are now here. Steedman's command will be delayed some to get wood and water, but will doubtless commence arriving here in a few hours. We hear nothing of the condition of the railroad toward Decatur, only that it is intact for six miles below, except that a small culvert is burned. All quiet here. We had a second-hand negro report last evening that the enemy were bringing up troops by rail to Indian Creek with the intention of attacking us. A scouting party last evening in that direction failed to see anything of him. Colonel Prosser has gone this morning with the most of his command on a more extended scout in that direction. We scouted yesterday several miles on Fayetteville and Athens roads, but did not find any enemy. We got no news of either Hood or Thomas. The absence of Colonel Prosser's command will account for the small escort I send the general. All is quiet, however, in that direction. I am in the Wheedon House, and shall be happy to entertain general and any of his staff who may accompany him.

Very respectfully, your obedient servant,

WM. P. LYON,
Colonel Thirteenth Wisconsin Vet. Vol. Infantry, Commanding.

HEADQUARTERS DEPARTMENT OF THE CUMBERLAND,
Duck River, December 23, 1864.

Brig. Gen. J. F. MILLER,
  Nashville:

Retain all baggage and detachments in charge of same belonging to this army in one camp at Nashville. Have written you. Forward baggage belonging to General Sherman's army to New York, with detachments in charge.

WM. D. WHIPPLE,
Assistant Adjutant-General.

SPECIAL ORDERS, ⎱ HEADQUARTERS DEFENSES NASHVILLE
                    AND CHATTANOOGA RAILROAD,
  No. 1.   ⎰   *Murfreesborough, Tenn., December 23, 1864.*

I. The following regiments will report to Colonel Thomas, of the Eighth Minnesota Volunteer Infantry, and proceed, under his command, to Columbia, Tenn., in obedience to paragraph I, Special Field Orders, No. 182, from headquarters Army of the Ohio, December 19, 1864, viz: One hundred and seventy-fourth Regiment Ohio Volunteer Infantry, One hundred and seventy-seventh Regiment Ohio Volunteer Infantry, One hundred and seventy-eighth Regiment Ohio Volunteer Infantry, One hundred and eighty-first Ohio Volunteer Infantry, Eighth Minnesota Volunteer Infantry, One hundred and fortieth Indiana Volunteer Infantry.

*   *   *   *   *   *   *

By command of Major-General Milroy:

JNO. O. CRAVENS,
Assistant Adjutant-General.

HEADQUARTERS DISTRICT OF EAST TENNESSEE AND
  FOURTH DIVISION, TWENTY-THIRD ARMY CORPS,
Knoxville, Tenn., December 23, 1864.

Col. C. G. HAWLEY,
  First Ohio Heavy Artillery:

COLONEL: It is my intention to send your regiment some fifteen or twenty miles in front of Strawberry Plains, near the French Broad River, for the purpose of protecting the working party on the opposite side, &c. You had better get your knapsacks, &c., so as to make your men comfortable, as the march will be short, and if rapid movement is required at any time the supplies can be left in camp, as it is not probable that more than two companies will be required at one time. Sixty rounds of cartridges ought to be taken. You will be able to subsist on the country to a great extent, wheat and corn being abundant and good mills convenient. You will please be ready to move as soon as practicable—say Monday or Tuesday. You will take about three days' rations with you of bread. Of coffee, sugar, salt, &c., you had better take at least ten or fifteen days. Beef you can drive along, or perhaps it may be procured in the country, but this is uncertain. I will advise you what to take in time. Please prepare to move, so far as clothing, ammunition, &c., is concerned.

Very respectfully, your most obedient servant,

J. AMMEN,
Brigadier-General.

PADUCAH, *December 23, 1864.*

Brigadier-General WHIPPLE,
        Assistant Adjutant-General:

GENERAL: The Third Illinois Cavalry have been ordered from this place, leaving here a detachment of Kentucky State Guard, whose time expires next week, thus leaving only seventy mounted men in this district. I would respectfully request leave to retain the detachment of Merrill's Horse, numbering 200 men, now at Cairo, Ill.

S. MEREDITH,
Brigadier-General.

HEADQUARTERS MILITARY COMMANDER LOUISVILLE,
        Louisville, Ky., December 23, 1864.

Capt. E. B. HARLAN,
        Assistant Adjutant-General:

CAPTAIN: Three soldiers arrived here to-day from Hartford, Ky., where they, together with the small garrison there, were captured and paroled by the rebel General Lyon on the 20th instant. They inform me that Lyon was there with his whole force and moved them in the direction of Bowling Green. They estimated his forces at 5,000—too much, certainly. The garrison was small, but a detachment from the Fifty-second Kentucky. McCook was reported as crossing Green River in pursuit.

I am, very respectfully,
THOS. B. FAIRLEIGH,
Lieut. Col. Twenty-sixth Kentucky Vols., Military Commander.

HEADQUARTERS NORTHERN DEPARTMENT,
        Cincinnati, Ohio, December 23, 1864.

Bvt. Maj. Gen. A. P. HOVEY,
        Commanding District of Indiana, Indianapolis, Ind.:

GENERAL: I am directed to acknowledge the receipt of your letter dated December 21, 1864, requesting that permission be granted you to send a force from your command across the Ohio River, to drive from the border a rebel force of 100 men reported at Hawesville, Ky., and in reply to state, that your letter has been referred to the commanding officer at Louisville, requesting him to send a force to capture or drive from the [border] the band of rebels referred to. The general commanding feels a delicacy in sending a force into another department. The commanding officer at Louisville was notified that a force would be sent from this department if requested by him.

I am, general, very respectfully, your obedient servant,
C. H. POTTER,
Assistant Adjutant-General.

WAR DEPARTMENT,
Washington City, December 24, 1864—3.18 p. m.
(Via Nashville, Tenn.)

Maj. Gen. GEORGE H. THOMAS,
        Headquarters Department of the Cumberland:

With great pleasure I inform you that for your skill, courage, and conduct in the recent brilliant military operations under your command, the President has directed your nomination to be sent to the Senate as a major-general in the U. S. Army, to fill the only vacancy existing in that grade. No official duty has been performed by me with more satisfaction, and no commander has more justly earned promotion by devoted, disinterested, and valuable service to his country.

EDWIN M. STANTON,
Secretary of War.

COLUMBIA, TENN., December 24, 1864—8 a. m.

Lieut. Gen. U. S. GRANT,
  City Point:

Your telegram of 22d instant is just received. I am now, and shall continue to push Hood as rapidly as the state of the weather and roads will permit. I am really very hopeful that either General Steedman or Admiral Lee will reach the Tennessee in time to destroy Hood's pontoon bridge, in which event I shall certainly be able to capture or destroy almost the entire army now with Hood.

GEO. H. THOMAS,
Major-General, U. S. Volunteers, Commanding.

HDQRS. DEPARTMENT OF THE CUMBERLAND,
McKane's Church, Pulaski Road, Tenn.,
December 24, 1864—11 p. m.
(Received 9 p. m. 25th.)

Maj. Gen. H. W. HALLECK,
  Washington, D. C.:

Have just heard from General Wilson, who was, at 5.30 p. m., six miles from Pulaski. He had been driving Forrest all day, without being able to bring him to an engagement. Late in the evening he made a short stand north of Richland Creek, but Croxton got in on his left and compelled him to retire precipitately to the south side of the creek, where he made a second short stand, but was again driven back. Croxton captured a few prisoners. Forrest has under his command as rear guard Brown's and Walthall's divisions of infantry, and Buford's and Jackson's divisions of cavalry. The infantry encamped last night north of Lynnville, and will probably encamp at Pulaski to-night. A few regiments of Hatch's division, sent to Mount Pleasant and Campbellsville, encountered a force of cavalry at the latter place. The force will be directed to continue the march in the direction of Lawrenceburg and La Fayette. Brigadier-General McCook reports from Trenton, Ky., that he had encountered the rebel General Lyon and scattered his command, except a few that crossed Green River with Lyon, going north, which latter Colonel La Grange encountered near where he crossed Green River, whipping it badly, capturing his train, and driving his rear guard into the river, killing some and causing others to be drowned. It appears, however, from a telegram of the agent of the Louisville and Nashville Railroad to Brigadier-General Donaldson, of this date, that a rebel force, supposed to be Lyon's, had captured Nolin's Station, on that road, burned Nolinsville bridge, and captured a train of cars. As General Long has either left Louisville or will leave to-morrow, I will telegraph him to look after this rebel force as he comes down.

Advices have been received from General Granger to the 22d instant. His forces had possession of the railroad as far as Huntsville, but having learned that the enemy had possession of Decatur with a force of 2,000 men, and his force only numbering 1,250, he deemed it more prudent to await the arrival of General Steedman, daily expected, before moving against Decatur.

GEO. H. THOMAS,
Major-General, U. S. Volunteers, Commanding.

WASHINGTON, *December 24, 1864—3.30 p. m.*
Maj. Gen. G. H. THOMAS,
Commanding Department of the Cumberland:

Applications are made by Governors of States to raise new regiments of volunteers under the recent call for 300,000 men by new regiments. The desire of the Department has been, as far as practicable, to raise recruits for old regiments, and thus keep up their organization. Before any authorization to raise new regiments are given, the Secretary of War desires your views on the subject. Please reply fully by telegraph.

THOS. M. VINCENT,
Assistant Adjutant-General.

NASHVILLE, TENN., *December 24, 1864.*
Brig. Gen. W. D. WHIPPLE,
Chief of Staff, Department of the Cumberland:

Three Missouri regiments have just arrived. Do you want them to go to the front, or shall they return to Missouri?

HENRY STONE,
Assistant Adjutant-General.

NASHVILLE, *December 24, 1864.*
General WILLIAM D. WHIPPLE,
Chief of Staff:

Agent of Louisville road reports rebel General Lyon at Nolin Station, beyond Sonora, having burned Nolin bridge and captured train of cars there yesterday; also burned Glendale Depot and pillaged it generally. Lyon reported at 1,500 strong, and no Union force near him. Up trains from here to-day stopped at Cave City.

J. L. DONALDSON,
Chief Quartermaster.

NASHVILLE, TENN., *December 24, 1864.*
General W. D. WHIPPLE,
Chief of Staff:

In order to sustain and provide for wants of army, I have sent an officer, Capt. F. H. Ruger, assistant quartermaster, to take charge of advance depot of army, to establish himself and stores as far front always as he can, and so follow you up as railroad progresses. Have sent two other officers to report to him to-day. Twenty days' grain on hand and plenty of subsistence.

J. L. DONALDSON,
Chief Quartermaster, Department of the Cumberland.

SPECIAL FIELD ORDERS, } HDQRS. DEPT. OF THE CUMBERLAND,
No. 349.   }   *McKane's Church, Tenn., Dec. 24, 1864.*

I. The Fourth Ohio Volunteer Cavalry will proceed to Nashville, Tenn., and there await the arrival of the Second Cavalry Division, to which it belongs.

*   *   *   *   *   *   *

By command of Major-General Thomas:

HENRY M. CIST,
Captain and Assistant Adjutant-General.

HDQRS. CAVALRY CORPS, MIL. DIV. OF THE MISSISSIPPI,
Three Miles from Lynnville, December 24, 1864—11.40 a. m.

Brig. Gen. T. J. WOOD,
Commanding Fourth Corps:

GENERAL: From the nature of the ground I find it impossible to move off of the turnpike, and as the head of my column is constantly skirmishing with the enemy's rear guard my progress is necessarily slow. I beg, therefore, that you will not become impatient, as I am pushing forward as rapidly as possible.

Very respectfully, your obedient servant,

J. H. WILSON,
Brevet Major-General, Commanding.

HEADQUARTERS FOURTH ARMY CORPS,
Duck River Bridge, December 24, 1864—4 p. m.

General WOOD:

Our trains are just getting in with six days' rations. I saw General Thomas, but he would not give an order for supply train to pass to the exclusion of other trains. The bridge broke many times last night and this a. m., but is working well this p. m. The troops of A. J. Smith are all over, but not his batteries. The cavalry train is passing now, and will get over by dark, if the bridge continues to work well; then Smith's batteries pass over; then comes our turn. I have ordered three days' rations to be got ready, and will cross them first and hurry them forward. General Thomas said we were better off for rations than the rest of the troops, and must wait our turn. If nothing happens to the bridge to-night the rations will get up to-morrow. I would suggest, however, that the men be a little saving of their rations, for fear of some accident. We will do everything we can to get the rations, forward, though. They are just going to work putting down another bridge. Fished out three pieces of artillery from the river this morning.

I am, your obedient servant,

WM. H. SINCLAIR,
Assistant Adjutant-General.

HEADQUARTERS FOURTH ARMY CORPS,
Two Miles and a Half South of Lynnville, December 24, 1864—5 p. m.
Brigadier-General WHIPPLE:

GENERAL: My leading division is just going into camp. We were not able to leave camp before 12 o'clock, on account of being delayed by the cavalry. We have marched sixteen miles and a half to-day. General Wilson is going into camp one mile and a half in advance. The march will be resumed in the morning as soon as the cavalry get out of the road for us. All information goes to show that the enemy is covering his retreat with seven brigades of infantry, commanded by Walthall, and Forrest's cavalry. The enemy's pontoon train camped twelve miles from Columbia Wednesday night, and left there Thursday morning. I hope we will yet be able to strike the enemy before he reaches the Tennessee River, provided we can be supplied with subsistence. I therefore respectfully urge that my wagons be allowed to move up, as we will be out of subsistence to-morrow night.

Very respectfully, &c.,
TH. J. WOOD,
Brigadier-General, Commanding.

———

HEADQUARTERS DEPARTMENT OF THE CUMBERLAND,
McKane's Church, December 24, 1864.
Brig. Gen. T. J. WOOD,
Commanding Fourth Army Corps:

GENERAL: Your dispatch of 5 p. m. this day received. The major-general commanding directs that you continue to push on, and that he will do everything in his power to get up your train and that of the cavalry.

Very respectfully, your obedient servant,
WM. D. WHIPPLE,
Brigadier-General and Assistant Adjutant-General.

———

HEADQUARTERS FOURTH ARMY CORPS,
Five Miles South of Columbia, Tenn., December 24, 1864—7 a. m.

Orders of the day for the Fourth Corps for to-day, December 24:

The corps will move as soon as the cavalry passes—General Elliott will lead; General Beatty will follow; then General Kimball. One battery will accompany each division. The same order for the movement of transportation observed yesterday will be observed to-day, and hereafter until otherwise ordered.

By order of Brigadier-General Wood:
J. S. FULLERTON,
Lieutenant-Colonel and Assistant Adjutant-General.

———

HEADQUARTERS DEPARTMENT OF THE CUMBERLAND,
December 24, 1864.
Maj. Gen. J. M. SCHOFIELD,
Commanding Department of the Ohio:

GENERAL: The major-general commanding directs that you move a brigade of your command into Columbia at once, to act as temporary garrison of the town. Provost guards will be established at once, and the place, as far as possible, protected while our troops are passing through.

Very respectfully, your obedient servant,

ROBT. H. RAMSEY,
Assistant Adjutant-General.

(Forwarded to Brig. Gen. J. D. Cox.)

HEADQUARTERS DEPARTMENT OF THE CUMBERLAND,
McKane's Church, December 24, 1864.

Maj. Gen. J. M. SCHOFIELD,
Commanding Twenty-third Army Corps:

GENERAL: The major-general commanding directs that the trains of the cavalry command and the Fourth Army Corps be permitted to cross the pontoon bridge before all other trains or troops. These commands are now two and a half and four miles beyond Lynnville, and will be out of provisions to-morrow night.

Very respectfully, your obedient servant,

WM. D. WHIPPLE,
Brigadier-General and Chief of Staff.

(Copy to Maj. Gen. A. J. Smith, Detachment Army of the Tennessee.)

HEADQUARTERS ARMY OF THE OHIO,
Near Columbia, Tenn., December 24, 1864.

Maj. Gen. GEORGE H. THOMAS,
Commanding Department of the Cumberland:

GENERAL: I have the honor to request permission to send to Washington an officer, with nine non-commissioned officers and privates of the Twenty-third Corps, to deliver to the War Department nine stand of colors captured from the enemy at Franklin, November 30, 1864. The men I propose to send are those who captured the flags, or the representatives of the captors in cases where the particular soldier is not known.

I am, general, very respectfully, your obedient servant,

J. M. SCHOFIELD,
Major-General.

HEADQUARTERS ARMY OF THE OHIO,
Near Columbia, Tenn., December 24, 1864.

Maj. Gen. GEORGE H. THOMAS,
Commanding Department of the Cumberland:

GENERAL: At the end of the Atlanta campaign I recommended three colonels commanding brigades in the Twenty-third Army Corps for promotion to the rank of brigadier-generals.* These recommendations were approved by Major-General Sherman, and forwarded to Washington with his official report. No one of the three has yet been appointed,

---

* See Vol. XXXIX, Part II, p. 366.

and only one of them, Col. John S. Casement, One hundred and third Ohio Volunteer Infantry, commanding Second Brigade, Third Division, now remains on duty in the field.   In the battle of Franklin, November 30, and in the battles in front of Nashville, December 15 and 16, Colonel Casement has given additional evidences of his gallantry and efficiency as a brigade commander.   I therefore have the honor to renew my recommendation for his promotion, and respectfully request that it may be forwarded with your favorable indorsement to the War Department.

I am, general, very respectfully, your obedient servant,

J. M. SCHOFIELD,
Major-General.

HDQRS. CAVALRY CORPS, MIL. DIV. OF THE MISSISSIPPI,
One Mile South of Lynnville, December 24, 1864—2 p. m.

Brigadier-General WHIPPLE,
Chief of Staff:

GENERAL: I am driving the enemy rapidly, without much fighting.
Very respectfully, your obedient servant,

J. H. WILSON,
Brevet Major-General.

HDQRS. CAVALRY CORPS, MIL. DIV. OF THE MISSISSIPPI,
Richland Creek, Seven Miles from Pulaski,
December 24, 1864—5.30 p. m.

Brigadier-General WHIPPLE,
Chief of Staff:

GENERAL: Our advance is between five and six miles from Pulaski. We have driven Forrest all day without bringing him to an engagement. Late this evening he made a short stand north of Richland Creek, but Croxton got in on their left and compelled them to retire precipitately to the south side of the creek, where they made another short stand, but were again driven back.   Croxton captured a few prisoners, and among them Captain Turk, inspector-general of one of Buford's (Lyon's old) brigades.   The ladies at whose house I have headquarters, relatives of General Buford, say that he received a slight flesh wound in the leg, but is still able to ride.   Forrest has under his command as rear guard Brown's and Walthall's divisions of infantry, Buford's and Jackson's divisions of cavalry.   The infantry camped north of Lynnville last night, and marched from there at about 9 a. m., and I have heard of it all along from citizens, who say it was marching rapidly for Pulaski, where it will probably camp to-night.   The regiment sent by General Hatch toward Mount Pleasant and Campbellsville encountered a force of cavalry at the latter place.   I will direct them to move to-morrow toward Lawrenceburg, and will send a party to-morrow toward La Fayette.   The rebels have burned the railroad bridges as far down as this, but we crowded them so closely that they were unable to destroy the pike bridge across Richland.   Our progress has not been as rapid to-day as I expected, but it was rather from the difficult nature of the country than the resistance of the enemy.   I will push out at an early hour in the morning and try to get in on their flanks if possible.

Very respectfully, your obedient servant,

J. H. WILSON,
Brevet Major-General, Commanding.

HDQRS. CAVALRY CORPS, MIL. DIV. OF THE MISSISSIPPI,
Richland Creek, Tenn., December 24, 1864—6 p. m.

Brigadier-General WHIPPLE,
Chief of Staff:

GENERAL: A deserter from Armstrong's brigade says he heard General Armstrong say this morning that Hood was moving the main force of the rebel army toward Decatur, and that their troops had begun crossing there yesterday. The deserter also says that it is the impression among the troops that the trains were sent to cross at Florence, and it is supposed that Chalmers' division is on the Pleasant Hill and Lawrenceburg road. The stories of the rebels in regard to Sherman's situation are ludicrous. They say he offered to surrender his whole command, provided they were paroled. The Confederates refused to take them on these terms. They say they have "gobbled" him, and that Beauregard is going to re-enforce Hood with the militia 25,000 strong. Croxton captured a battle-flag.

Very respectfully, your obedient servant,
J. H. WILSON,
Brevet Major-General, Commanding.

HEADQUARTERS DEPARTMENT OF THE CUMBERLAND,
McKane's Church, Pulaski Road, December 24, 1864—10.30 p. m.

Maj. Gen. J. H. WILSON,
Comdg. Cav. Corps, Mil. Div. of the Miss., Richland Creek:

Your dispatch of this 5.30 p. m. is received, and the major-general commanding directs me to say that your intention to push on in the morning is approved. It would be well for you to continue a pretty strong force covering your right. Your progress is not considered slow, under the circumstances, but, on the contrary, is quite satisfactory to the major-general commanding. Such orders have been given as is hoped will bring up your train by to-morrow night.

Very respectfully, your obedient servant,
ROBT. H. RAMSEY,
Assistant Adjutant-General.

SPECIAL ⎰ HEADQUARTERS CAVALRY CORPS,
FIELD ORDERS, ⎱ MILITARY DIVISION OF THE MISSISSIPPI,
No. 13. *Richland Creek, Tenn., December 24, 1864.*

The Cavalry Corps will move to-morrow in pursuit of the enemy, in the following order:

I. Harrison's brigade, in advance, at 5 a. m., followed by Hammond's, and then Hatch's division, and then Croxton's brigade.

II. When the country will permit of it the command will move off the road by the flanks of brigades in the following order, from right to left: General Croxton, General Hammond, Colonel Harrison, General Hatch, batteries and ambulances and wagons moving upon the pike.

III. Every effort should be made to push the enemy as rapidly as possible.

By command of Brevet Major-General Wilson:
E. B. BEAUMONT,
Major and Assistant Adjutant-General.

COLUMBIA, *December 24, 1864.*
(Received Allen Smith's house 11 a. m. 25th.)

Brigadier-General McCOOK,
  Commanding First Cavalry Division, Hadensville, Ky.:

Have your horses shod at Nashville, and report in person to General Wilson.

By command of Major-General Thomas:

J. P. WILLARD.

COLUMBIA, TENN , *December 24, 1864.*

Brig. Gen. ELI LONG:

Please keep me advised of your movements.

J. H. WILSON,
  Brevet Major-General.

HDQRS. CAVALRY CORPS, MIL. DIV. OF THE MISSISSIPPI,
  Richland Creek, December 24, 1864—6 p. m.

Brigadier-General HATCH,
  Commanding Fifth Division:

GENERAL: Direct a brigade of your division which is now at Campbellsville to push early to-morrow morning on the road toward Lawrenceburg. Charge the commanding officer specially to investigate and report whether the enemy may not have moved his trains and part of his force in that direction.

By order of Brevet Major-General Wilson:

A. J. ALEXANDER,
  Lieutenant-Colonel and Acting Chief of Staff.

HEADQUARTERS FIRST BRIGADE, SEVENTH DIVISION,
  December 24, 1864.

Maj. E. B. BEAUMONT,
  Assistant Adjutant-General:

MAJOR: I have found a splendid camp; lots of shelter and forage. Am close against General Croxton's right; his men, the Eighth Iowa being his right flank regiment, had gone into camp and was feeding when my staff officer arrived from General Wilson. Striking a due south course, I am two miles and a half from Richland Creek and one mile and a half from the pike. The bearer will bring orders. The people think that Richland Creek is fordable in my front.

Respectfully, your obedient servant,

J. H. HAMMOND,
  Brevet Brigadier-General.

A good many rebel fugitives have gone toward Campbellsville, four miles from here.

HEADQUARTERS DEPARTMENT OF THE CUMBERLAND,
Duck River, December 24, 1864.

Major-General ROUSSEAU,
Commanding District of Tennessee, Nashville:

The Fifteenth Kentucky Infantry is either at Chattanooga or has been mustered out. The major-general commanding directs that you send at once to Columbia sufficient troops to garrison the same and to protect the railroad as fast as it is repaired.

HENRY M. CIST,
Assistant Adjutant-General.

———

NASHVILLE, TENN., *December 24, 1864.*

Capt. H. M. CIST,
Assistant Adjutant-General:

I have ordered the One hundred and seventy-fifth Ohio to Columbia, to garrison that post and the block-houses this side not already occupied by the Seventy-fifth Pennsylvania Volunteers. I will also send the Twenty-first Indiana Battery to Columbia; also to take up old position. If any more troops are needed on that road I do not know where to get them, unless I am allowed to withdraw the Forty-third Wisconsin from Clarksville, which was put there by order of General Thomas. That regiment was formerly at Johnsonville.

LOVELL H. ROUSSEAU,
Major-General.

———

HEADQUARTERS DISTRICT OF TENNESSEE,
Nashville, Tenn., December 24, 1864.

Major MULLENIX,
Commanding 175th Ohio Volunteer Infantry:

MAJOR: The major-general commanding directs that you proceed with your regiment to Columbia, occupying the block-houses or their positions between that place and Franklin not occupied by the Seventy-fifth Pennsylvania Volunteer Infantry. Your regiment should move without unnecessary delay.

I am, major, very respectfully, your obedient servant,

B. H. POLK,
Major and Assistant Adjutant-General.

———

HEADQUARTERS DISTRICT OF TENNESSEE,
Nashville, Tenn., December 24, 1864.

Capt. A. P. ANDREW,
Commanding Twenty-first Indiana Battery:

CAPTAIN: The major-general commanding directs that you take up your old position in the fort at Columbia, with such guns as you have or may be furnished with by the ordnance department. The One hundred and seventy-fifth Ohio, now in camp near Fort Negley, has orders to proceed to Columbia, and if your battery gets ready in time, may move with it.

I am, captain, very respectfully, your obedient servant,

B. H. POLK,
Major and Assistant Adjutant-General.

NASHVILLE, *December 24, 1864.*

Maj. Gen. G. H. THOMAS:

In pursuance to orders from Brigadier-General Meredith, I have the honor to report my arrival here in command of the Forty-fifth, Forty-seventh, and Forty-eighth Regiments Missouri Volunteer Infantry. The men are on board and await orders.

W. H. BLODGETT,
Colonel Forty-eighth Missouri Infantry Volunteers.

HEADQUARTERS POST OF MURFREESBOROUGH,
Murfreesborough, Tenn., December 24, 1864.

Col. THOMAS C. BOONE,
Commanding 115th Ohio Volunteer Infantry:

SIR. The general commanding directs that you send the detachments to those bridges between this place and Nashville that were abandoned during the late siege. The detachments will report at the picket-line on the Nashville pike at 6 o'clock to-morrow morning, and will find transportation by wagon train to their respective places of destination.

Very respectfully, &c.,

H. H. SHEETS,
Acting Assistant Adjutant-General.

CLARKSVILLE, *December 24, 1864.*

Capt. ROBERT H. RAMSEY,
Assistant Adjutant-General:

General McCook reports that he captured Lyon's artillery; part of his men; remainder scattered and leaving country. My scouts have picked up a number.

A. A. SMITH,
Colonel, Commanding.

HEADQUARTERS DEPARTMENT OF THE CUMBERLAND,
In the Field, December 24, 1864.

Brig. Gen. S. MEREDITH,
Paducah:

The major-general commanding directs that Merrill's Horse must come to the front. A regiment has been ordered from General Smith's command to Paducah, which will be temporary relief to you.

WM. D. WHIPPLE,
Brigadier-General.

LOUISVILLE, KY., *December 24, 1864.*

Major ECKERT:

Rebel General Lyon captured Elizabethtown last night with a force estimated at 3,000. He will probably destroy one or two bridges, and play smash with telegraph, which now only works to Colesburg. General McCook is after the enemy, but don't know how close a race.

SAM. BRUCH.

LOUISVILLE, KY., *December 24, 1864—8.30 p. m.*
Maj. T. T. ECKERT:

Enemy still in the vicinity of Elizabethtown, coming toward Muldraugh's Hill, where there are two high trestles, which they want to burn. Re-enforcements have been sent there to defend the place, but have fears will not be enough. Reported that Nolin's bridge and two other small ones have been destroyed near the town.

SAM. BRUCH.

SPECIAL ORDERS, ⎱ HDQRS. MILITARY DISTRICT OF KENTUCKY,
  No. 99.   ⎰   *Lexington, Ky., December 24, 1864.*

I. The One hundred and twenty-second U. S. Colored Infantry is assigned to the Second Division, Military District of Kentucky. The commanding officer will report for orders to Brig. Gen. Hugh Ewing, commanding Second Division.

*   *   *   *   *   *   *

By command of Bvt. Maj. Gen. S. G. Burbridge:

J. BATES DICKSON,
Captain and Assistant Adjutant-General.

MULDRAUGH'S HILL, *December 24, 1864.*
Brig. Gen. HUGH EWING,
    Louisville, Ky.:

Latest intelligence: General Lyon has his headquarters half a mile northeast of Elizabethtown, on the Bardstown turnpike. His force divided—part on Bardstown pike, the other part west of railroad; evidently intends to attack from both front and rear; is waiting for re-enforcements; intends to move soon as they reach; has six pieces 12-pounder brass guns. Probably he intends to be in readiness to open on us by daybreak in the morning.

CHAS. E. BEHLE,
Major, Commanding.

MULDRAUGH'S HILL, *December 24, 1864.*
Brig. Gen. HUGH EWING,
    Louisville, Ky.:

The latest report that I have is that General Lyon's force is this side Elizabethtown. He captured about 200 Federal soldiers at that place and paroled them. His force was estimated at 2,500, with three 12-pounder howitzers, at any rate, and perhaps more artillery. Paroled prisoners state his men were talking confidently of capturing the bridges and forts at Muldraugh's Hill to-day. Lyon's headquarters were a mile this side of Elizabethtown, I judge on the Bardstown turnpike, this morning, after leaving Elizabethtown. I think his entire force is east of the railroad. From the Bardstown turnpike he can strike easily either Forts Sands, Boyle, or Jones. Have made all preparations possible with the small force we have. Think Lyon's force marched and worked all night, and that they have been resting during this forenoon a short distance this side of Elizabethtown.

H. F. POTTER,
Captain, Commanding.

LOUISVILLE, KY., *December 24, 1864.*

Capt. H. F. POTTER,
    Commanding Muldraugh's Hill:

Hold out as long as a man is left.   Re-enforcements are on the way.
The bridges at Salt River, Rolling Fork, and the trestle at the Hill
must be preserved.   Telegraph to the adjoining commands to fight to
the last.

                                        HUGH EWING,
                                            Brigadier-General.

MULDRAUGH'S HILL, *December 24, 1864.*

Brig. Gen. HUGH EWING,
    Louisville, Ky.:

Have just received intelligence that the rebels are marching this way
from Elizabethtown.   Have sent a lieutenant and forty men to Rolling
Fork bridge.

                                        H. F. POTTER,
                                            Captain, &c.

MULDRAUGH'S HILL, *December 24, 1864.*

Brig. Gen. HUGH EWING,
    Louisville, Ky.:

Latest news: From 2,000 to 3,000 rebels in Elizabethtown, with five
or six pieces of artillery; have full possession of the place; captured
and burned hospital train.   Will have things in as good shape as possible to receive attack.

                                        H. F. POTTER,
            Captain, Twelfth U. S. Colored Heavy Artillery, Commanding.

COLESBURG, KY., *December 24, 1864.*

Brig. Gen. H. EWING,
    Louisville, Ky.:

There is a force of rebels, with two pieces of artillery.   They have
taken Elizabethtown and are marching in this direction.

                                        J. F. LAY,
                Lieutenant and Acting Assistant Quartermaster.

COLESBURG, KY., *December 24, 1864.*

Brigadier-General EWING,
    Louisville, Ky.:

Lyon, with 3,000 troops and three batteries, is [at] Elizabethtown.   I
am going to fall back on the fort with my stores.

                                        J. F. LAY,
                Lieutenant and Acting Assistant Quartermaster.

COLESBURG, *December 24, 1864.*

Brig. Gen. HUGH EWING,
 Louisville, Ky.:

Just arrived here with 200 men. Will go into Forts Sands and Boyle and send out to watch his movements. General Lyon's headquarters are a mile north of Elizabethtown. Force estimated at 2,500 to 3,000; four to six pieces artillery. Know nothing of his movements, but will keep you advised.

HERBERT.

LOUISVILLE, KY., *December 24, 1864.*

Captain HERBERT,
 Muldraugh's Hill:

Re-enforcements on the way; protect the trestle to your last squad. If necessary to do so, sally out.

HUGH EWING,
 Brigadier-General.

HEADQUARTERS SECOND BRIGADE, SECOND DIVISION,
 MILITARY DISTRICT OF KENTUCKY,
 Bowling Green, December 24, 1864.

Capt. E. B. HARLAN,
 Assistant Adjutant-General, Second Division, Louisville, Ky.:

CAPTAIN: Four men of the Fifty-second Kentucky Mounted Infantry came in last night from Hartford, Ky., and say they were captured with the small garrison (some forty men) at that place on Tuesday evening and paroled by General Lyon. They state that Lyon's forces left, going in the direction of Litchfield. They heard them say that they expected to form a junction with Forrest at or about Elizabethtown. They thought they must be ignorant of the condition of Hood and his army and was not aware of his defeat. I am of the opinion they are working out an old programme to strike the railroad about Elizabethtown, still expecting Forrest to join him in that neighborhood, not being fully aware of matters as they are.

I am, captain, very respectfully, your obedient servant,

DANL. J. DILL,
 Colonel, Commanding Brigade.

HEADQUARTERS DEPARTMENT OF THE CUMBERLAND,
 Columbia, December 24, 1864—8 a. m.
 (Received 6 p. m.)

Maj. Gen. N. J. T. DANA,
 Memphis, Tenn.:

Your telegram of the 21st instant is received. As soon as your expedition shall have completed the work assigned you, I shall be much obliged if you will return to Nashville the troops belonging to the Military Division of the Mississippi now serving with you.

GEO. H. THOMAS,
 Major-General, U. S. Volunteers, Commanding.

HEADQUARTERS DEPARTMENT OF THE CUMBERLAND,
McKane's Church, Pulaski Road, December 25, 1864—8 a. m.
(Received 6 p. m.)

Hon. EDWIN M. STANTON,
Secretary of War, Washington, D. C.:

I am profoundly sensible of your kind expressions in your telegram of December 24, informing me that the President had directed my name to be sent to the Senate for confirmation as major-general U. S. Army, and I beg to assure the President and yourself that your approbation of my services is of more value to me than the commission itself.

GEO. H. THOMAS,
Major-General, U. S. Volunteers, Commanding.

HDQRS. DEPARTMENT OF THE CUMBERLAND,
Richland Creek, Six Miles from Pulaski,
December 25, 1864—10 p. m.
(Received 3 a. m. 26th.)

Maj. Gen. H. W. HALLECK,
Washington, D. C.:

I forward the following dispatch, received from General Wilson, for your information:

HDQRS. CAVALRY CORPS, MILITARY DIVISION OF THE MISSISSIPPI,
Pulaski, December 25, 1864—9.10 a. m.

My advance, Colonel Harrison commanding, drove the rebels through this place half past 8 on the keen jump. Forrest, with Jackson's and Buford's divisions, is scarcely out of sight. Everything has gone on the road to Lamb's Ferry, the original intention of going to Decatur having been abandoned for fear they would be intercepted. They are trying to reach Florence. I will crowd them ahead as fast as possible. They are literally running away, making no defense whatever. I will open communication with the column in the direction of Huntsville. The rebels have destroyed a large quantity of ammunition, but the bridge across Richland Creek has been saved, thanks to the gallantry of Colonel Baird, commanding Fifth Iowa.
Very respectfully,

J. H. WILSON,
Brevet Major-General.

I learn from the chief engineer that he will soon have the road open as far as Columbia; from thence to Pulaski will be but a small matter. Colonel Lyon telegraphs me from Huntsville, under date of 23d instant, that Colonel Prosser, with 200 men, fought and dispersed 600 men of Roddey's command that morning at Indian Creek, killing several and capturing 60 prisoners and 50 horses. He routed the enemy utterly, and pursued them several miles. Our loss, 1 killed and 3 wounded. Indian Creek heads in Huntsville and empties into Hurricane Creek just above its mouth. Have not yet heard from Admiral Lee, but feel convinced that the water in the Tennessee enables him to get above Eastport, and that he is performing good service. I have my troops well in hand and well provided with provisions and ammunition, and close upon the heels of the enemy, and shall continue to press him as long as there is a chance of doing anything.

GEO. H. THOMAS,
Major-General, U. S. Volunteers, Commanding.

HEADQUARTERS DEPARTMENT OF THE CUMBERLAND,
Richland Creek, December 25, 1864.
Maj. Gen. H. W. HALLECK,
    Chief of Staff, U. S. Army, Washington, D. C.:

GENERAL: Inclosed herewith I have the honor to forward the recommendation of Maj. Gen. J. M. Schofield, commanding Army of the Ohio, for the promotion to the rank of brigadier-general of volunteers of two of his staff officers,* and to concur with him in such recommendation; also the recommendation of Brig. Gen. T. J. Wood, commanding Fourth Army Corps, for the promotion of two deserving colonels† of his command, in which I heartily unite. Letters recommendatory of Colonel Opdycke were forwarded to Headquarters of the Army early in the present month.

I have the honor to recommend the promotion of the following-named officers to the grades named, and for the reasons given in connection with the name of each:

Brig. Gen. T. J. Wood, commanding Fourth Army Corps, to be promoted to the rank of major-general of volunteers, for gallant and meritorious conduct and good generalship displayed in command of the Third Division of the Fourth Corps, and during the present campaign as commander of the Fourth Corps, particularly in the battle of Missionary Ridge, November 25, 1863, throughout the Atlanta campaign, and at the assault upon the enemy's intrenchments at Lovejoy's Station, Ga., where he received a severe wound. Notwithstanding this wound he retained command of his division and participated in the operations against Hood in his movements upon our communications with Atlanta, and later confronted him in his invasion of Tennessee, took a conspicuous part in the battle of Franklin, November 30, 1864, in which seven desperate assaults of the rebels were repulsed, 5,000 of them killed and wounded, and nearly 1,000 of them, with 5 stand of colors, captured. He has also rendered brilliant and important services during the battle of the 15th and 16th instant before Nashville, and since in the campaign which was then inaugurated and is now in progress.

Brig. Gen. J. D. Cox, U. S. Volunteers, for good conduct displayed in the management of his troops on the 15th and 16th instant. Your attention is respectfully invited to the accompanying papers referring to the capture of artillery on the 16th, forwarded by General Schofield and herewith inclosed.‡

Bvt. Maj. Gen. J. H. Wilson, commanding Cavalry Corps, Military Division of the Mississippi, to the rank of full major-general of volunteers, for the excellent management of his corps during the present campaign, in which it has peculiarly distinguished itself, attempting such things as are not expected of cavalry, such as assaulting the enemy in intrenched positions, and always with success, capturing his works, with many guns and prisoners. His corps has also been conspicuous for its energy in the pursuit of the retreating rebel army, which has cost the rebel commander many men, several pieces of artillery, and tended much to the demoralization of his army.

Brig. Gen. Edward Hatch, commanding Fifth Division, Cavalry Corps, to be promoted to major-general of volunteers; recommended by General Wilson for gallant conduct and good generalship displayed in the command of the division from the time of his first confronting the rebel army under Hood during the invasion of Tennessee, November

---

  * Lieut. Col. George W. Schofield and Lieut. Col. William Hartsuff.
  † P. Sidney Post and Emerson Opdycke.
  ‡ See p. 234.

29, until the present time, and particularly at the battle of Brentwood Hills, December 16, 1864, to describe which I quote the language of General Wilson:

In accordance with his instructions General Hatch then crossed the country from Williams' house toward the Hillsborough pike, re-established his connection with the infantry, and, advancing his right flank, struck the enemy's line on the flank and rear, completely enveloping it, drove it rapidly back upon the fortifications constructed upon the Brentwood Hills for its protection. Hastily forming his Second Brigade dismounted, Col. D. E. Coon commanding, he pushed boldly forward and carried the enemy's works, capturing in the first redoubt 4 guns and 65 prisoners, and in the second, a closed work, 6 guns and 175 prisoners.

The same day at night-fall he captured several prisoners, among them Brigadier-General Rucker, commanding a brigade of Chalmers' division rebel cavalry, with Chalmers' division battle-flag.

Bvt. Brig. Gen. J. H. Hammond, commanding Seventh Brigade, Cavalry Corps, for confirmation of his appointment as brevet brigadier-general of volunteers; recommended by General Wilson for general good conduct and skillful management of his brigade during the retreat before the rebel army while it was advancing upon Nashville and during the present campaign, particularly on the 16th and 17th instant, and since during the pursuit of Hood's army, during which he has displayed great activity and energy.

Maj. Gen. A. J. Smith, commanding Detachment Army of the Tennessee, desires to recommend his division commanders, Brigadier-General McArthur and Brig. Gen. K. Garrard, for promotion to the brevet rank of major-general, also Colonels McMillen and Hubbard, commanding brigades, to the rank of brigadier-general; but being unable to hear from him on the subjects, I cannot give specific reasons for the promotion of these officers, or even give their full names and regiments.

In conclusion I would respectfully urge the confirmation by the Senate of Brig. Gen. W. D. Whipple, my chief of staff, for the energy and zeal displayed by him in the discharge of his duties throughout the entire Atlanta campaign as well as during the present one. For additional reasons for this I would invite your attention to my letter recommending his appointment sent from before Atlanta in August last.

I would also request the promotion to the rank of major and assistant adjutant-general of volunteers of Capt. Robert H. Ramsey, assistant adjutant-general of volunteers, a member of my staff, for his intelligence and untiring devotion to duty since he joined me nearly a year ago, particularly during the Atlanta campaign and during the present one.

I have the honor to be, general, very respectfully, your obedient servant,

GEO. H. THOMAS,
Major-General, U. S. Army, Commanding.

HEADQUARTERS DEPARTMENT OF THE CUMBERLAND,
McKane's Church, Pulaski Road, December 25, 1864—8 a. m.

Col. THOMAS M. VINCENT,
Assistant Adjutant-General, Washington, D. C.:

Your telegram of 3.30 p. m. of 24th is received. In reply, I would respectfully state, for the information of the honorable Secretary, that, in my opinion, whilst the raising of new volunteer regiments is an embarrassment to the Government, the filling up of old regiments in the field with recruits keeps the army in an efficient condition at all times. With new regiments, both officers and men are generally ignorant of their duties, are more or less difficult to discipline, and, in consequence of a lack of discipline, are much more liable to disease; while recruits added to old regiments are at once under the hand of discipline, soon learn how to take care of themselves, and by mingling with their comrades who have seen service, readily learn their duties, and in a short time become almost as efficient and reliable as the old troops. Permit me, also, to state, whilst on the subject, that receiving volunteers for one-year's service is also injurious to the efficiency of the army; a soldier who volunteers for one year hardly learns his duty before his time expires. In my opinion, the most efficient way of keeping up an army, after it has once been organized by the acceptance of volunteers, is to perpetuate the old regiments by accepting volunteers for three years, or by drafting for five years.

GEO. H. THOMAS,
Major-General, U. S. Volunteers, Commanding.

NASHVILLE, *December 25, 1864.*
(Received 12.20 p. m.)

Hon. E. M. STANTON:

About 3,000 prisoners of war, including officers, have been forwarded to Northern depots, 1,700 leave to-day, and the remainder, about 700, will leave to-morrow morning, making in all less than 5,500 prisoners. There are about 1,600 wounded prisoners yet to arrive. No captures have been reported from the front since the 21st.

Respectfully,

W. HOFFMAN,
Commissary-General of Prisoners.

HEADQUARTERS DEPARTMENT OF THE CUMBERLAND,
Richland Creek, December 25, 1864—8.30 p. m.
(Via Paducah. To be forwarded.)

Rear-Admiral S. P. LEE:

Our cavalry drove enemy through Pulaski at 9 a. m. to-day. Forrest's cavalry on full run. Rebel army is literally running away, and seems to be making for Lamb's Ferry and Florence. He has been thrown off his intended route to Decatur by fear of being intercepted. I think it best for you to remain as long as possible at Eastport, or, at least, until we ascertain definitely what Hood is trying to do.

GEO. H. THOMAS,
Major-General, Commanding.

HEADQUARTERS DEPARTMENT OF THE CUMBERLAND,
Richland Creek, December 25, 1864.

Col. WILLIAM E. MERRILL,
Chattanooga:

Prepare a pontoon bridge sufficient to span the Tennessee River at Decatur immediately and send it to Bridgeport, subject to orders of Major-General Steedman. Answer.

WM. D. WHIPPLE,
Assistant Adjutant-General.

CHATTANOOGA, *December 25, 1864.*

Brigadier-General WHIPPLE:

Dispatch received. The orders mentioned were given yesterday, and the trains leave here to-morrow morning for Bridgeport.

W. E. MERRILL,
Colonel and Chief Engineer, Department of the Cumberland.

RICHLAND CREEK, *December 25, 1864.*

Col. WILLIAM E. MERRILL,
Chattanooga:

Yours received. O. K. Notify General Steedman.

WM. D. WHIPPLE,
Brigadier-General.

NASHVILLE, *December 25, 1864.*

General W. D. WHIPPLE,
Chief of Staff:

Capt. F. H. Ruger, assistant quartermaster, in charge of advance depot of army, now at Spring Hill, reports great thefts and robberies by troops and others, and says he is without sufficient guards. I have telegraphed him to call on your headquarters for all necessary guards now or hereafter, and respectfully request that his requisitions be honored accordingly. I need scarcely say that it is of the first importance that your advance depot be well regulated and well protected, and supplied with ample details for guards to public property at all times.

J. L. DONALDSON,
Chief Quartermaster.

HEADQUARTERS DEPARTMENT OF THE CUMBERLAND,
Richland Creek, December 25, 1864.

Brig. Gen. J. L. DONALDSON,
Nashville:

Yours of this day received. A regiment has been ordered from Nashville to Spring Hill, as guard to the advanced depot, and with orders to move with it.

WM. D. WHIPPLE,
Assistant Adjutant-General.

COLUMBIA, *December 25, 1864.*

Brigadier-General WHIPPLE:

Railroad repairs progressing well. Bridge over Carter's Creek, No. 7, will be O. K. to-morrow, then builders will go to Duck River bridge. Colonel Wright is at Carter's Creek bridge, and has an operator with him, so you can communicate by telegraph. Line O. K. to Louisville via Chattanooga and Knoxville.

Very respectfully, your obedient servant,

WM. R. PLUM,
Operator, &c.

HEADQUARTERS DEPARTMENT OF THE CUMBERLAND,
Richland Creek, December 25, 1864.

Col. W. W. WRIGHT,
Carter's Creek:

How are you getting along with the rebuilding of the bridges? Can you form any idea when you will get to Columbia? Road from Columbia to Pulaski O. K., except bridge over Richland Creek, which is destroyed. It is of the utmost importance that we get the railroad through as soon as possible.

WM. D. WHIPPLE,
Brigadier-General.

NASHVILLE, TENN., *December 25, 1864—11 a. m.*

Maj. THOMAS T. ECKERT:

Rebels under Lyon hold Louisville railroad near Elizabethtown, Ky., having destroyed a bridge and captured a train. Of course no telegraph at work that way. Just got one wire through over Chattanooga railroad. General Thomas this morning eight miles south of Columbia; will be at Lynnville to-night; is not crowding the rebels; seems to be pushing easy till Steedman gets his forces into position in their rear. Report current that Hood has been superseded by Forrest, whose task it is to get the army out of the scrape into which Hood has fought it.

J. C. VAN DUZER,
Captain, &c.

HEADQUARTERS DEPARTMENT OF THE CUMBERLAND,
Richland Creek, December 25, 1864.

Brig. Gen. T. J. WOOD,
Commanding Fourth Army Corps:

GENERAL: The major-general commanding directs that you place in the haversacks of your men three days' provisions, and move on to the support of Major-General Wilson. The cavalry train, followed by your train, should move immediately in your rear and keep closed. General Wilson has been ordered to continue pressing the rear of the rebel army.

Respectfully, your obedient servant,

WM. D. WHIPPLE,
Brigadier-General and Chief of Staff.

HEADQUARTERS FOURTH ARMY CORPS,
Lamb's Ferry Road, Six Miles South of Pulaski, Tenn.,
December 25, 1864—8.15 p. m.

Brigadier-General WHIPPLE,
Chief of Staff:

GENERAL: I propose to take four batteries with me and leave the rest of my artillery in Pulaski, taking the teams of the guns I leave. This will give me one battery for each division and one reserve battery. I will also take in addition to the five ammunition wagons with each division, thirty additional ones, ten for a division, and each loaded with ten boxes of ammunition. I am obliged to do this on account of the condition of the road from Pulaski to the river. We will issue three days' rations to-morrow morning, with instructions that they must last five days, and will send the empty wagons back to the terminus of the railroad to reload. As soon as the rations are issued the pursuit will be continued as vigorously as possible. At present our information is that the enemy has taken the Lamb's Ferry road, but this we cannot tell certainly until we get to the junction of the Lamb's Ferry and Florence roads. I will promptly advise you of the road which we take. I have a train behind loaded with three days' rations, which I would be glad to have follow me as rapidly as possible.

Very respectfully, &c.,

TH. J. WOOD,
Brigadier-General, Commanding.

HEADQUARTERS FOURTH ARMY CORPS,
Pulaski, Tenn., December 25, 1864—1.30 p. m.

Brevet Major-General WILSON,
Comdg. Cavalry Corps, Military Division of the Mississippi:

I will move my corps south of Richland Creek three or four miles, as I may find the ground suitable for camping, and halt for the night. I will be out of rations to-night, and it will be necessary for me to halt here until our supply train comes up. General Thomas has promised to push it forward as rapidly as possible, but it is uncertain when it will arrive here, though I trust it will arrive some time to-night or to-morrow morning. I will be glad to know your condition in reference to rations, and your intentions in reference to future movements, as I wish to keep the corps up in supporting distance of the cavalry.

Very respectfully, your obedient servant,

TH. J. WOOD,
Brigadier-General, Commanding.

HDQRS. CAVALRY CORPS, MIL. DIV. OF THE MISSISSIPPI,
December 25, 1864.

[General WOOD,
Commanding Fourth Army Corps:]

GENERAL: We are four miles from Pulaski, on the Lamb's Ferry road, and have met a slight check. If you bring up your infantry we may get some prisoners. I am putting General Hatch's division on the skirmish line now, and I think I shall be able to drive Forrest off. Your infantry can materially assist me.

I am, general, very respectfully, your obedient servant,

J. H. WILSON,
Brevet Major-General.

There are eight brigades of infantry in our front, with rail intrenchments. Please hurry up as rapidly as possible.

J. H. W.

HEADQUARTERS FOURTH ARMY CORPS,
Two Miles and a Half South of Lynnville, Tenn.,
December 25, 1864—7 a. m.

Orders of the day for the Fourth Corps for to-day, December 25, 1864:
The corps will march for Pulaski as soon as the cavalry is out of the
way—General Beatty will lead; General Kimball will follow; then
General Elliott. One battery will accompany each division.

By order of Brigadier-General Wood:

J. S. FULLERTON,
Lieutenant-Colonel and Assistant Adjutant-General.

HEADQUARTERS FOURTH ARMY CORPS,
Lamb's Ferry Road, Six Miles South of Pulaski,
December 25, 1864—9 p. m.

Brigadier-General KIMBALL:

GENERAL: You will select ten ammunition wagons from your train,
load each with ten boxes of ammunition and as much forage as they
can carry, and direct the same to follow the reserve battery of the
corps, in the following order: The First Division train leading; then
the Second Division train; then the Third. The ammunition trains
will be in Pulaski to-night.

Three days' rations will be issued to-morrow morning and they must
last five days, as we have been ordered to vigorously pursue the enemy.
Issue your rations as promptly as possible, as we must push ahead to
support the cavalry.

By order of Brigadier-General Wood:

J. S. FULLERTON,
Lieutenant-Colonel and Assistant Adjutant-General.

(Same to Generals Elliott and Beatty.)

HEADQUARTERS ARMY OF THE OHIO,
In the Field, Columbia, December 25, 1864—12 m.

Major-General THOMAS,
Commanding Department of the Cumberland:

GENERAL: The second bridge is nearly completed, and it now seems
possible that General Wood's and General Smith's trains may get over
to-day. The crossing at the upper bridge is extremely slow, but I hope
it will be better at the other. As soon as I can get the bridge I will
cross and move forward at once, unless otherwise directed.

Very respectfully,

J. M. SCHOFIELD,
Major-General.

HEADQUARTERS DEPARTMENT OF THE CUMBERLAND,
Richland Creek, December 25, 1864.

Maj. Gen. J. M. SCHOFIELD,
Commanding Army of the Ohio:

GENERAL: The major-general commanding directs that you move
with your command to Pulaski, with transportation closed up, following
the command of Major-General Smith, which moves with its transpor-

tation closed on it in the same manner.   He also wishes you to direct the commander of the brigade at Columbia to take the three guns which were yesterday hauled out of Duck River, at the bridge, across the river to Columbia, and send them by first train to Nashville, consigned to Capt. A. Mordecai, chief of ordnance, Department of the Cumberland.   There are also three others abandoned by the rebels on the road leading from Columbia to Murfreesborough, which he also wishes secured and sent to Nashville at the same time.

Very respectfully, your obedient servant,
WM. D. WHIPPLE,
Brigadier-General and Chief of Staff.

HEADQUARTERS DEPARTMENT OF THE CUMBERLAND,
Richland Creek, December 25, 1864.
Maj. Gen. J. M. SCHOFIELD,
Columbia:

How soon can a pontoon bridge be spared from Duck River for Elk River? The report now is that Hood is making for Lamb's Ferry and Florence.

WM. D. WHIPPLE,
Brigadier-General and Chief of Staff.

SPECIAL }   HEADQUARTERS ARMY OF THE OHIO,
FIELD ORDERS, }   *In the Field, near Columbia, Tenn.,*
No. 187. }   *December 25, 1864.*

*   *   *   *   *   *   *

VIII. The troops will cross Duck River to-morrow, the 26th, commencing at daylight.   General Cox will use the upper bridge and General Couch the lower one.   The baggage and ammunition trains will follow their respective divisions; other trains will cross at either bridge as soon as practicable, but will give the preference to trains belonging to troops which are in advance.   Each division commander will leave a staff officer at the bridge during the crossing of his artillery and trains, to superintend the crossing.   The greatest care must be taken to prevent accidents and unnecessary delays.   Rations will be issued to the troops this evening.

By command of Major-General Schofield:
J. A. CAMPBELL,
Major and Assistant Adjutant-General.

HEADQUARTERS DEPARTMENT OF THE CUMBERLAND,
December 25, 1864.
Maj. Gen. A. J. SMITH,
Commanding Detachment Army of the Tennessee:

GENERAL: The major-general commanding directs that you move on leisurely with your command to Pulaski, followed by its train, that it may arrive there in good order and be ready for any movement that may be intended for it after arriving at that place.   You will be followed by the Twenty-third Army Corps, with its train.   General Wilson drove the rebels through Pulaski at 9 o'clock this morning on a full run and is still pressing them, supported by the Fourth Corps.   Hood's army is literally running away, and making for Lamb's Ferry.

Very respectfully, your obedient servant,

WM. D. WHIPPLE,
Brigadier-General and Chief of Staff.

HEADQUARTERS DETACHMENT ARMY OF THE TENNESSEE,
Near Columbia, Tenn., December 25, 1864.

Brig. Gen. J. McARTHUR,
Commanding First Division:

GENERAL: The major-general commanding directs that you have your division in readiness and move to-morrow morning, December 26, at 8 o'clock, taking with you your train, and in the advance.

I am, very respectfully, your obedient servant,

J. HOUGH,
Major and Assistant Adjutant-General.

HEADQUARTERS DETACHMENT ARMY OF THE TENNESSEE,
Near Columbia, Tenn., December 25, 1864.

Brig. Gen. K. GARRARD,
Commanding Second Division:

The major-general commanding directs that you have your command in readiness and move to-morrow morning, December 26, at 9 a. m., taking with you your train, Second Division taking the advance.

I am, very respectfully, your obedient servant,

J. HOUGH,
Major and Assistant Adjutant-General.

(Same to Col. J. B. Moore, commanding Third Division.)

HEADQUARTERS CAVALRY CORPS,
Beyond Pulaski, Tenn., December 25, 1864—10.10 a. m.

Brig. Gen. W. D. WHIPPLE,
Chief of Staff:

There seems to be little doubt that the rebels have gone to Bainbridge, eight miles above Florence, fearing a flank movement from Stevenson. Two corps (Stewart's and Lee's) went by this road—the Florence road—to Lexington; Cheatham's went toward Lawrenceburg, striking the old military road, eight miles below Lawrenceburg. The people say the rebels are suffering immensely. Buford's wound is said to be quite severe. A Mr. Carter says the colonel commanding the pontoon train told him he was going to Bainbridge; left here on Thursday morning. Cheatham's ammunition train of fifteen or twenty wagons was abandoned here. The mules were put in to help the pontoons along. General Lee was severely wounded in the foot in the fight at Nashville. His corps is now commanded by Stevenson. The rebels have lost eighteen generals killed, wounded, and captured since they started north. They acknowledge sixty-eight pieces of artillery lost.

J. H. WILSON,
Brevet Major-General.

Headquarters Department of the Cumberland,
Richland Creek, December 25, 1864—4.15 p. m.

Maj. Gen. J. H. Wilson,
    Comdg. Cavalry Corps, Military Division of the Mississippi:

General: Yours of 9.10 a. m. to-day has been received.* The major-general commanding wishes you to continue pressing the rear of the rebel army as you have heretofore done. Your trains and those of the Fourth Corps are well along, yours in advance.

Very respectfully, your obedient servant,
                                    WM. D. WHIPPLE,
                                        Brigadier-General, &c.

———

Hdqrs. Cavalry Corps, Mil. Div. of the Miss.,
    Five Miles Southwest of Pulaski, on Lamb's Ferry Road,
                                    December 25, 1864—6 p. m.

Brig. Gen. W. D. Whipple,
            Chief of Staff:

Harrison's brigade came up with the enemy's infantry, strongly posted in rail breast-works, and after some sharp skirmishing was driven back, losing one gun. The ground was repossessed in ten minutes, but the gun was carried off; forty or fifty prisoners were captured from the enemy, and the position taken. The rebels are now on the march again, and prisoners say they are ordered to go ahead until they get across the river. My advance is two miles beyond here. Two locomotives down below Pulaski were saved from burning by one of Hatch's regiments. The rebel force is eight brigades, of 500 or 600 picked men each. The country is a very broken and poor one. My horses are suffering for forage, and my men are getting short of rations, though I will push on again early in the morning in hopes of getting back the lost gun and one or two besides. Is there any news from Sherman?

Very respectfully, your obedient servant,
                                    J. H. WILSON,
                                        Brevet Major-General.

———

Special   )   Headquarters Cavalry Corps,
Field Orders, >   Military Division of the Mississippi,
No. 14.   )   *Reynolds' House, December 25, 1864.*

The Cavalry Corps will pursue the enemy to-morrow morning, in the following order:

I. Brigadier-General Hammond will take the advance, moving promptly at 5 o'clock; General Hatch will follow; then General Croxton; and then Colonel Harrison.

II. Each command will move promptly, and keep well closed on the rear of the one preceding it.

By order of Brevet Major-General Wilson:
                                    A. J. ALEXANDER,
                                Lieutenant-Colonel and Acting Chief of Staff.

———

* See p. 342.

HEADQUARTERS DEPARTMENT OF THE CUMBERLAND,
In the Field, December 25, 1864.

Brig. Gen. ELI LONG:

Lyon is reported as still roaming through Kentucky. As your troops are the nearest to him, the major-general commanding looks to you to destroy him entirely.

WM. D. WHIPPLE,
Brigadier-General and Chief of Staff.

LOUISVILLE, KY., *December 25, 1864.*

Brevet Major-General WILSON,
Commanding Cavalry Corps:

I sent Third Ohio and Ninety-eighth Illinois to Bardstown this morning. Will leave with remainder of division Wednesday, 28th instant.

E. LONG,
Brigadier-General, U. S. Volunteers, Commanding Division.

HEADQUARTERS DEPARTMENT OF THE CUMBERLAND,
Richland Creek, December 25, 1864. (Via Stevenson.)

Maj. Gen. J. B. STEEDMAN,
Decatur:

The report now is that the enemy is making for Lamb's Ferry and Florence, being thrown off his route to Decatur by fear of being intercepted. Give us such information as you may have received concerning this. The moment you establish a footing on south side of Tennessee River order Colonel Merrill to send you a pontoon bridge from Bridgeport, where he has been ordered to have it ready; establish it at Decatur.

WM. D. WHIPPLE,
Brigadier-General and Chief of Staff.

NASHVILLE, TENN., *December 25, 1864.*

Brig. Gen. W. D. WHIPPLE,
Headquarters Major-General Thomas:

The three Missouri regiments arrived here last night, and will be sent down the line of the Tennessee and Alabama Railroad as soon as I can get them off. One of them is a one-year regiment, and the two others are six-months troops. I have directed General Milroy to occupy the line of the Chattanooga road with the three new Michigan regiments now at Murfreesborough, leaving small garrison at that place and Tullahoma; and to relieve the Sixth Kentucky at Anderson and forward it here for muster out; also to relieve the One hundred and eightieth Ohio at Elk River, Decherd and below, and direct it to join the Twenty-third Corps via Fayetteville. General Milroy's headquarters to be at Tullahoma as before.

L. H. ROUSSEAU,
Major-General.

HEADQUARTERS DEPARTMENT OF THE CUMBERLAND,
In the Field, Richland Creek, December 25, 1864.

Maj. Gen. L. H. ROUSSEAU,
Nashville, Tenn.:

Send one of the Missouri regiments just arrived at Nashville to Spring Hill, as guard to the railroad depot at that place, with orders to follow the advanced depot, to prevent pillaging and robbery and to assist in loading wagons, &c.

WM. D. WHIPPLE,
Assistant Adjutant-General.

NASHVILLE, *December 25, 1864.*

Maj. Gen. R. H. MILROY,
Murfreesborough:

The major-general commanding directs that with the three Michigan regiments now at Murfreesborough you relieve the Sixth Kentucky and One hundred and eightieth Ohio Infantry, and reoccupy the line of railroad in your command, leaving small garrisons at Murfreesborough and Tullahoma. You may furnish transportation to the One hundred and eightieth Ohio, and direct it to join the Twenty-third Corps via Fayetteville, as you propose. The Sixth Kentucky, upon being relieved, will be furnished with transportation by you by rail, and sent to Nashville to be mustered out. You may make your headquarters at Tullahoma as before. Another regiment will be sent you as soon as possible.

B. H. POLK,
Major and Assistant Adjutant-General.

SPECIAL ORDERS, ⎰ HEADQUARTERS DEFENSES NASHVILLE
                              AND CHATTANOOGA RAILROAD,
No. 3.   ⎱   *Murfreesborough, Tenn., December 25, 1864.*

The following regiments now at this post will report to Brig. Gen. H. P. Van Cleve for duty till further orders; all communications and reports will be made through him, viz: Twelfth Indiana Volunteer Cavalry, Sixty-first Illinois Volunteer Infantry, Third Michigan Volunteer Infantry, Fourth Michigan Volunteer Infantry, Twenty-ninth Michigan Volunteer Infantry.

By command of Major-General Milroy:

JNO. O. CRAVENS,
Assistant Adjutant-General.

LEXINGTON, *December 25, 1864.*

Lieut. Col. T. B. FAIRLEIGH,
Louisville, Ky.:

Advise me by telegraph of Lyon's movements. He was reported at Elizabethtown last night.

J. BATES DICKSON,
Captain and Assistant Adjutant-General.

HEADQUARTERS MILITARY COMMANDER,
Louisville, December 25, 1864.

Capt. E. B. HARLAN,
  Assistant Adjutant-General:

CAPTAIN: Captain Scott, Eighty-third Indiana Volunteers, command-ing a detachment of 200 convalescents, en route for New York from Nashville to join General Sherman, was captured by Lyon, at or near Nolin's Bridge, on Friday evening last (December 23), and reported here this morning. The officers and men were paroled by Lyon. Cap-tain Scott arrived at Muldraugh's Hill last evening and proceeded with his command to this place; he reports cannonading heard and our cav-alry in sight when he left. The captain understood that General Mc-Cook and Colonel La Grange had come up with Lyon. The force of the latter is reported by Scott at 2,500 well mounted and equipped men and four pieces of artillery. Scott thinks the rebels divided their force—one brigade destroying the road from Elizabethtown south, the other from that point north. An officer of the Sixth Kentucky Cavalry, which forms a part of Watkins' brigade, of McCook's division, says some thirty of our wounded reached here last night.

I am, very respectfully,

THOS. B. FAIRLEIGH,
Lieut. Col. Twenty-sixth Kentucky Vols., Military Commander.

COLESBURG, KY., *December 25, 1864.*

Capt. E. B. HARLAN, *Louisville, Ky.:*

Reliable information says that Lyon would move to Greensburg and Columbia and cross Cumberland River at Burkesville or higher. Colonel La Grange, of our cavalry, states that Lyon has 1,300 to 1,500 men and one piece of artillery; this is confirmed by several citizens of Litchfield. General McCook in his pursuit. Two reports of artillery were heard this morning at this farm in a southeasterly direction, probably road to Hodgensville. Our scouts were out since 2 a. m. yesterday, and found the above at Elizabethtown.

CHAS. E. BEHLE,
Major.

COLESBURG, *December 25, 1864.*

Capt. E. B. HARLAN, *Louisville, Ky.:*

Lyon's force left Elizabethtown between 12 and 2 p. m., and took the road to Hodgensville. This information is said to be by our scouts of authenticated source. Lyon probably takes his route via Lebanon.

CHAS. E. BEHLE,
Major, Commanding.

HEADQUARTERS DEPARTMENT OF THE CUMBERLAND,
Pulaski, Tenn., December 26, 1864—10 p. m.
(Received 1 p. m. 27th.)

Maj. Gen. H. W. HALLECK,
  Washington, D. C.:

I send the following dispatch, of 10.10 a. m. yesterday, from General Wilson, for your information.*

---

*See p. 351.

A later dispatch, of 6 p. m. 25th instant, states that, in pressing the enemy, Harrison's brigade came upon the enemy's infantry, strongly posted in rail breast-works, and so close did he push up that, in being compelled to fall back, the loss of one gun was involved. The position was, however, taken ten minutes afterward, but the enemy had run the gun off. The rebel force is eight brigades, of 500 to 600 men each. General Wood, commanding the Fourth Corps, is in close support of General Wilson, and both will continue the pursuit zealously. I have heard from General Steedman to-day. He disembarked his troops from cars at Limestone Creek, seven miles from Decatur, and was marching to that place at 7 a. m. to-day.

GEO. H. THOMAS,
Major-General, U. S. Volunteers, Commanding.

HEADQUARTERS DEPARTMENT OF THE CUMBERLAND,
Pulaski, December 26, 1864. (Via Paducah.)

Rear-Admiral S. P. LEE:

General Donaldson has been ordered to send the transports now at Paducah to Eastport, under convoy. Will you please furnish the gunboats, and order them to remain at Eastport until a cavalry force which I am going to send across to that point arrives there and accomplishes the work upon which it is sent.

GEO. H. THOMAS,
Major-General.

[DECEMBER 26, 1864.]

General DONALDSON,
Chief Quartermaster, Nashville:

Has the railroad to Chattanooga been repaired? Answer.

GEO. H. THOMAS,
Major-General, Commanding.

NASHVILLE, *December 26, 1864.*

Maj. Gen. GEORGE H. THOMAS,
Commanding Department of the Cumberland:

Telegram received. Superintendent of railroads reported last night that last bridge on Nashville and Chattanooga Railroad would be done this morning, and some trains, I presume, will pass south at once, but road will not be in thorough operation before Wednesday.

J. L. DONALDSON,
Chief Quartermaster, Department of the Cumberland.

HEADQUARTERS DEPARTMENT OF THE CUMBERLAND,
Pulaski, December 26, 1864—6.30 p. m.

Brig. Gen. J. L. DONALDSON,
Chief Quartermaster, Department of the Cumberland, Nashville:

The major-general commanding directs me to acknowledge the receipt of your telegram of this date, and desires that you notify him when the first train starts south on the Nashville and Chattanooga Railroad and the time of starting.

ROBT. H. RAMSEY,
Assistant Adjutant-General.

NASHVILLE, *December 26, 1864.*

Brigadier-General WHIPPLE,
　　　Chief of Staff:

The superintendent of railroads [reports that, from best information he has, trains will run through to Murfreesborough, and so to Chattanooga, on Wednesday night or Thursday morning.

　　　　　　　J. L. DONALDSON,
　　　Chief Quartermaster, Department of the Ohio.

HEADQUARTERS DEPARTMENT OF THE CUMBERLAND,
　　　Pulaski, December 26, 1864.

Brig. Gen. J. L. DONALDSON,
　　　Nashville:

Please inform us when the Chattanooga road is really open and a train has started south.

　　　　　　　WM. D. WHIPPLE,
　　　　　　　Brigadier-General.

NASHVILLE, *December 26, 1864.*

General W. D. WHIPPLE,
　　　Chief of Staff, Department of the Cumberland:

Naval officer at Paducah reports Admiral Lee gone up the Tennessee with five or six gun-boats some days since. Have you any further orders for me about shipment of supplies to go up Tennessee River? General Allen, Louisville, is asking same question.

　　　　　　　J. L. DONALDSON,
　　　　　　　Chief Quartermaster.

HEADQUARTERS DEPARTMENT OF THE CUMBERLAND,
　　　Pulaski, December 26, 1864.

Brig. Gen. J. L. DONALDSON,
　　　Nashville:

Order the transports loaded with provisions and forage now at Paducah up the Tennessee to Eastport, under convoy. Request Admiral Lee to order the gun-boats to remain at Eastport, to protect the transports until a cavalry force which is to be sent across to that point shall arrive and accomplish the work for which they are sent. Please acknowledge the receipt of this and report when the transports leave Paducah. Hold the steamers loaded for the same point now at Nashville until further orders.

　　　　　　　WM. D. WHIPPLE,
　　　　　　　Brigadier-General.

CARTER'S CREEK, *December 26, 1864.*

Brig. Gen. W. D. WHIPPLE,
　　　Chief of Staff:

Carter's Creek bridge, No. 5, is finished all but laying the track. To-morrow morning at daylight we will commence Rutherford's Creek bridge, No. 1, and will finish it to-morrow night. A force of 300 bridge.

builders have got as far as Spring Hill, and when I can get their train past the block of trains at that point, I will send them to commence work on Duck River bridge.

W. W. WRIGHT,
Chief Engineer.

CARTER'S CREEK, *December 26, 1864.*

Major-General THOMAS:

Mr. Smeed, with the second division of the construction corps, telegraphs me that they will finish the [*sic*] on Wednesday. Shall I send them around to the Decatur end of this road? I think I can have men enough without his force here.

W. W. WRIGHT,
Chief Engineer.

HEADQUARTERS DEPARTMENT OF THE CUMBERLAND,
Richland Creek, December 26, 1864—8.30 p. m.

Col. W. W. WRIGHT,
Carter's Creek:

You may as well send Mr. Smeed to the Decatur road to work in this direction. General Thomas is glad to see your operations begin to assume a good shape. The superintendent of telegraph construction reports the three bridges between here and Columbia down, but they can soon be put up again, not being much damaged.

WM. D. WHIPPLE,
Brigadier-General.

CARTER'S CREEK, *December 26, 1864.*

General W. D. WHIPPLE:

If everything works well, we can get to Columbia in ten days.

W. W. WRIGHT,
Chief Engineer.

NASHVILLE, TENN., *December 26, 1864—9.30 p. m.*

Maj. T. T. ECKERT:

General Thomas' headquarters at Pulaski. Hood destroyed there twenty wagons of ammunition, threw two guns into the river, and burned nearly 10,000 stand of small-arms. His transportation is used up. Citizens report he had 15,000 men only and eight guns when he passed through Pulaski; this exclusive of cavalry. Roads impassable, except pikes. Not known yet what position between Decatur and Florence rebels will go for; but, as Steedman is at Decatur, with gun-boats to cross and depend on, and river very high, looks like taking whole army of Hood's in out of the wet.

J. C. VAN DUZER.

HEADQUARTERS FOURTH ARMY CORPS,
Six Miles from Pulaski, December 26, 1864—4 p. m.

Brigadier-General WHIPPLE,
Chief of Staff:

GENERAL: Owing to the difficulty in getting up our supply train, I have not yet completed the issue of the three days' rations which I mentioned to you last night that I would issue this morning, and consequently have been unable to move. I may yet move one division two miles this evening. The corps will start at 5 a. m. to-morrow, and push forward as vigorously as possible.

Very respectfully, your obedient servant,

TH. J. WOOD,
Brigadier-General, Commanding.

HEADQUARTERS DEPARTMENT OF THE CUMBERLAND,
Pulaski, December 26, 1864.   (Received 10.30 a. m. 27th.)

Brig. Gen. T. J. WOOD,
Commanding Fourth Army Corps:

GENERAL: Yours of 4 p. m. to-day received. The major-general commanding has no orders for you except to push on and support the cavalry as fast as you can and drive the rebels into the Tennessee River. Send word back from time to time with information as to the state of your supplies, and your wagons will be sent forward as fast as possible.

Respectfully,

WM. D. WHIPPLE,
Assistant Adjutant-General.

HEADQUARTERS FOURTH ARMY CORPS,
Six Miles south of Pulaski, Lamb's Ferry Road,
December 26, 1864—7.30 a. m.

Brevet Major-General WILSON,
Commanding Cavalry Corps:

GENERAL: I have received a note from General Thomas, in which he directs that I move on to your support, and that your train follow after my troops and my train after yours. Please give the necessary instructions to have your train so move. Owing to the difficulty of getting rations from Pulaski to camp, it may be noon before we can get them issued; immediately afterward I will march. I suggest that you send a regiment to Elk River for the purpose of cutting trees and filling the stream full, in order that they may float down and destroy the enemy's pontoon bridge over the Tennessee River.

Very respectfully, your obedient servant,

TH. J. WOOD,
Brigadier-General, Commanding.

HDQRS. CAVALRY CORPS, MIL. DIV. OF THE MISS.,
Sugar Creek, Seventeen Miles from Pulaski,
December 26, 1864—1 p. m.   (Received 7 p. m.)

Brig. Gen. T. J. WOOD,
Commanding Fourth Army Corps:

GENERAL: Your dispatch is just received. The enemy made a short stand at this place, but have again retreated. I have stopped a short time to feed my animals. Will you please push forward my supply train as rapidly as possible, as I shall be in need of rations to-morrow. As soon as I cross this stream I will send a brigade to fell trees in the Tennessee River.

Very respectfully, your obedient servant,

J. H. WILSON,
Brevet Major-General, Commanding.

HEADQUARTERS FOURTH ARMY CORPS,
Morris' House, Lamb's Ferry Road, December 26, 1864—8 a. m.

Orders of the day for the Fourth Corps for to-day, December 26, 1864:

The corps will march as soon as rations are issued—General Kimball will lead, followed by General Elliott, then General Beatty. The only wagons that will follow divisions will be the five ammunition wagons and ambulances; all others, including headquarters and baggage wagons, will follow the ammunition of the reserve battery (after the troops). These wagons will move—first, corps headquarters; then division headquarters, in the order in which the divisions march. It will be necessary to make this disposition of trains to facilitate our march for the next two or three days.

By order of Brigadier-General Wood:

J. S. FULLERTON,
Lieutenant-Colonel and Assistant Adjutant-General.

HEADQUARTERS FOURTH ARMY CORPS,
Six Miles South of Pulaski, December 26, 1864—5 p. m.

Orders of the day for the Fourth Corps for to-morrow, December 27, 1864:

The corps will march to-morrow in the same order, in reference to divisions, trains, &c., that it was to have moved to-day. General Kimball will draw out at 5.30 a. m.; General Elliott will draw out at the same hour and follow; and General Beatty will follow General Elliott.

By order of Brigadier-General Wood:

J. S. FULLERTON,
Lieutenant-Colonel and Assistant Adjutant-General.

HEADQUARTERS FOURTH ARMY CORPS,
December 26, 1864—3 p. m.

Brigadier-General ELLIOTT,
Commanding Second Division :

The general commanding directs that no regimental baggage wagons move with the troops. If any have come this side of Pulaski send them back to that place, where they will remain until further orders. In going back do not let them interfere with trains coming this way.

By order of Brigadier-General Wood:

J. S. FULLERTON,
Lieutenant-Colonel and Assistant Adjutant-General.

HEADQUARTERS FOURTH ARMY CORPS,
December 26, 1864—4.45 p. m.

Brigadier-General ELLIOTT,
Commanding Second Division:

If you have not moved out of camp do not do so this evening. Orders will be given for the march to-morrow.

By order of Brigadier-General Wood:

J. S. FULLERTON,
Lieutenant-Colonel and Assistant Adjutant-General.

COLUMBIA, *December 26, 1864.*

General SCHOFIELD:

Lines just got working to Pulaski. Can now reach General Thomas' headquarters.

J. T. JOYCE,
Operator.

COLUMBIA, *December 26, 1864.*

General WHIPPLE:

Your dispatch asking when a pontoon bridge can be spared from Duck River is received. I will try to get my troops and ammunition trains across to-day. If I succeed one bridge might be spared to-night. Up to this time the bridges have been entirely occupied by trains in advance of me. I will inform you during the day what progress is made.

J. M. SCHOFIELD,
Major-General.

COLUMBIA, TENN., *December 26, 1864—12 m.*

Major-General THOMAS:

It is impossible to tell when my trains will be able to cross the river, even with the two bridges; they have not yet commenced, and General Smith still has 200 wagons to cross. The bridges are out of order the greater part of the time. I would advise the construction of trestle bridges over any stream between here and the Tennessee River, rather than to rely upon the pontoons, even if the latter were not in use here. I also think it would be advisable to build a trestle bridge here. I can make a good double-track bridge in two or three days, if my engineer battalion be taken off from the railroad. I think it will take at least ten days yet to get the cars to Columbia; meantime the pontoon bridges will hardly accommodate the trains going to and from Spring Hill. Please direct whether I shall set my engineers to building a bridge here.

J. M. SCHOFIELD,
Major-General.

HEADQUARTERS DEPARTMENT OF THE CUMBERLAND,
Pulaski, December 26, 1864—6 p. m.

Maj. Gen. JOHN M. SCHOFIELD,
    Columbia:

Your telegram of 12 m. to-day is received. You can set your engineers to work building the trestle bridge across Duck River. According to present indications I do not think your troops will be needed about Florence, as per last reports from Wilson and Wood the enemy is doing his best to get out of the way. General Wilson thinks he will try to cross at Bainbridge and Lamb's Ferry. Steedman crossed the Tennessee to-day seven miles above Decatur, and is marching on that place. If Wilson finds the enemy retreating in disorder I shall order him to endeavor to throw a portion of his force across the Tennessee at Eastport and destroy Bear Creek bridge, then put General Smith at Eastport, to form a depot for our operations in the spring, and with the rest of the force cross at Decatur, and, if we can, crowd Hood away from the Tennessee, and then recruit for and organize for an early spring campaign. What do you think of it? Concentrate and reorganize your command either at or near Columbia as soon as possible. It was reported to me at Columbia that the enemy had abandoned three or four guns on the Columbia and Murfreesborough road, north of Duck River and about eight miles from Columbia. Try and find out where they are and have them brought in.

GEO. H. THOMAS,
Major-General, U. S. Volunteers, Commanding.

COLUMBIA, TENN., *December 26, 1864—7.30 p. m.*

Maj. Gen. GEORGE H. THOMAS,
    Pulaski, Tenn.:

Your dispatch of 6 p. m. is just received. The plan you propose seems the best that can be done under the circumstances, if Hood succeeds in getting across the Tennessee. I will reorganize my command as soon as possible. I have not yet heard of the troops from Murfreesborough, and suspect that a portion of them at least went with General Steedman. I have sent a party to find the guns on the Murfreesborough road. I have succeeded in getting one division and most of its trains across the river, and can probably get the other over to-morrow, and will gladly push forward, if you think I can be of any use; if not, it will be better to leave them on the north bank, to save crossing supplies, until the bridge is done.

J. M. SCHOFIELD,
Major-General.

HEADQUARTERS ARMY OF THE OHIO,
Columbia, Tenn., December 26, 1864.

Col. J. S. CASEMENT,
    Commanding Second Brigade, Third Division, 23d Army Corps:

COLONEL: The commanding general directs that you take the three guns which were yesterday hauled out of Duck River, at the bridge, across the river to Columbia, and send them by first train to Nashville, consigned to Captain Mordecai, chief of ordnance, Department of the

Cumberland. There are also three other guns abandoned by the enemy on the road leading from Columbia to Nashville, which he also wishes you to secure and send to Nashville at the same time.

I am, colonel, very respectfully, your obedient servant,

J. A. CAMPBELL,
Major and Assistant Adjutant-General.

HEADQUARTERS DETACHMENT ARMY OF THE TENNESSEE,
Near Lynnville, Tenn., December 26, 1864.

Brig. Gen. K. GARRARD,
Commanding Second Division:

The major-general commanding directs that you have your command in readiness and move to-morrow morning, December 27, at 10 a. m., taking with you your train, Second Division taking the advance.

I am, very respectfully, your obedient servant,

J. HOUGH,
Major and Assistant Adjutant-General.

(Same to Brig. Gen. J. McArthur, commanding First Division.)

HEADQUARTERS DETACHMENT ARMY OF THE TENNESSEE,
Near Lynnville, Tenn., December 26, 1864.

Col. J. B. MOORE,
Commanding Third Division:

The major-general commanding directs that you have your command in readiness and move to-morrow morning, December 27, at 9 a. m., taking the advance, and taking with you your train.

I am, very respectfully, your obedient servant,

J. HOUGH,
Major and AssistantAdjutant-General.

HDQRS. CAVALRY CORPS, MIL. DIV. OF THE MISSISSIPPI,
Dobbin's House, Eighteen Miles from Pulaski,
December 26, 1864—4 p. m.

Brigadier-General WHIPPLE,
Chief of Staff:

GENERAL: The enemy, after another brief stand, have again retreated. I have no doubt Hood's whole army is crossing at Bainbridge.

Very respectfully, your obedient servant,

J. H. WILSON,
Brevet Major-General.

HEADQUARTERS DEPARTMENT OF THE CUMBERLAND,
Pulaski, December 26, 1864—8.30 p. m.

Maj. Gen. J. H. WILSON,
Comdg. Cavalry Corps, Military Division of the Mississippi:

Can you not possibly send a force to Eastport, cross it at that place, and destroy the railroad bridge at Bear Creek? If successful, that would cut off the rebel retreat by Corinth and the Mobile and Ohio

Railroad, and would enable us to change our base to Decatur and operate on Hood's flank and rear as he retreated into Alabama. I will send transports with provisions and forage, under convoy, to Eastport. Bear Creek bridge is from five to eight miles from Eastport, on the south side of the Tennessee. I think General Hatch can do this, and, if successful, it will be a most important service. Answer immediately.

GEO. H. THOMAS,
Major-General, U. S. Volunteers, Commanding.

NASHVILLE, TENN., *December 26, 1864.*

Maj. Gen. G. H. THOMAS:

The following copy of telegram is respectfully furnished for your information:

MUNFORDVILLE, *December 26, 1864.*

Major BEAUMONT,
Assistant Adjutant-General:

Lyon was ten miles from Hodgensville, on the Greensburg road, at daylight yesterday morning, toward Greensburg; reported to have 800 and one piece of artillery. We made a forced march from Ashbysburg to Elizabethtown in forty-eight hours. Arrived in time to save the bridge and drive off a battalion sent to burn the trestle-work. Brigade will move to-day. Horses jaded and want shoes.

O. H. LA GRANGE,
Colonel, Commanding Second Brigade, First Division.

E. B. BEAUMONT,
Major and Assistant Adjutant-General.

HDQRS. CAVALRY CORPS, MIL. DIV. OF THE MISSISSIPPI,
Reynolds' House, December 26, 1864—6 a. m.

Capt. E. B. CARLING,
Chief Quartermaster, Cavalry Corps:

CAPTAIN: The general commanding desires you to push forward your trains as rapidly as possible. The command must have rations to-morrow night. If necessary, call on General Thomas for an infantry guard. We are ordered to pursue the enemy, and must have something to eat.

Very respectfully, your obedient servant,

A. J. ALEXANDER,
Lieutenant-Colonel and Chief of Staff.

HEADQUARTERS DEPARTMENT OF THE CUMBERLAND,
Richland Creek, December 26, 1864.

Brig. Gen. E. M. McCOOK,
Nashville:

Lyon, it seems, is not destroyed or driven out of the country. We hear of him on Louisville and Nashville Railroad. The major-general commanding directs that you keep at work at him until he is finished or driven across the Cumberland.

WM. D. WHIPPLE,
Brigadier-General.

BOWLING GREEN, *December 26, 1864.*
(Received 28th.)
Brigadier-General McCOOK:

Colonel La Grange last heard from at Elizabethtown. Whipped Lyon near there on Saturday evening. Said he would have Lyon and his force.

DANIEL J. DILL,
Colonel Thirtieth Wisconsin Infantry, Commanding Brigade.

HEADQUARTERS DEPARTMENT OF THE CUMBERLAND,
Richland Creek, December 26, 1864.
Brig. Gen. ELI LONG,
En route between Nashville and Louisville:

The major-general commanding directs that you leave the rebel Lyon to General McCook, and join the Cavalry Corps, at the front, as rapidly as possible to arrive in good order.

WM. D. WHIPPLE,
Brigadier-General.

HEADQUARTERS FIFTH CAVALRY DIVISION,
Sugar Creek, December 26, 1864.
Major BEAUMONT,
Assistant Adjutant-General, Cavalry Corps:

MAJOR: My rations are up to-night, and I am low in ammunition. Am doing all I can to-night to get my trains up. I can advance, however, without rations at any time. The regiment sent to Lawrenceburg arrived this evening; say no troops but stragglers have gone through Lawrenceburg, and no trains moved in that direction.

Very truly, your obedient servant,

EDWARD HATCH,
Brigadier-General.

HEADQUARTERS DEPARTMENT OF THE CUMBERLAND,
Richland Creek, December 26, 1864.
Maj. Gen. L. H. ROUSSEAU,
Nashville:

The Twenty-eighth Michigan has been assigned to the Twenty-third Army Corps, and the Third and Fourth Michigan to the Fourth Army Corps. They cannot, therefore, be used to garrison the Nashville and Chattanooga Railroad.

WM. D. WHIPPLE,
Assistant Adjutant-General.

NASHVILLE, *December 26, 1864.*
Brigadier-General WHIPPLE:

I did not know the Third and Fourth Michigan had been assigned, or I should not have ordered General Milroy to use them. I have sent him instructions not to post them on the road. This will leave but two regiments to garrison the road from here to Stevenson, the Twenty-ninth Michigan and One hundred and fifteenth Ohio, 200 men of the latter being prisoners. In addition to Miller's brigade, the One hundred and seventy-third Ohio, Fourth Division, Twentieth Corps, is here doing post duty, but General Miller says he cannot spare it, and that he has your letter assuring him the garrison shall not be diminished. With that regiment and the Forty-third Wisconsin, now at Clarksville by order of the major-general commanding, I could garrison the Chattanooga road. I have heard from General Watkins, at Hadensville, and suppose General McCook will be able to attend to Lyon in Kentucky.

> LOVELL H. ROUSSEAU,
> *Major-General.*

HEADQUARTERS DEPARTMENT OF THE CUMBERLAND,
Pulaski, December 26, 1864.
Maj. Gen. L. H. ROUSSEAU,
  Nashville, Tenn.:

The Forty-fifth, Forty-eighth, and Forty-ninth Missouri Regiments are ordered to report to you. They had better be sent down this road, one to go to Spring Hill and keep the advanced depot. The Forty-third Wisconsin, at Clarksville, is available; also a regiment at Fort Donelson, which was stopped there on its way up the Cumberland—I do not remember the number; this is now available to you. Send the Forty-eighth and Forty-ninth Missouri to this place. The One hundred and eighty-second Ohio can be used to guard the Nashville and Chattanooga road. There are also the Forty-fourth and Forty-fifth Wisconsin, now at Nashville for the purpose of being organized; when organized, they will be available for railroad duty.

> WM. D. WHIPPLE,
> *Assistant Adjutant-General.*

NASHVILLE, TENN., *December 26, 1864.*
Brig. Gen. W. D. WHIPPLE,
  Richland Creek:

I have ordered the Forty-fifth Missouri to Spring Hill, as directed. The following telegram, dated yesterday, received from Colonel Lyon, at Huntsville:

Colonel Prosser, with 200 men of the Twelfth Indiana Cavalry and 120 of the Thirteenth Indiana Cavalry, fought and dispersed 600 of Roddey's command, this a. m., at Indian Creek, killing several and capturing 60 prisoners and 50 horses. He routed the enemy utterly, and pursued him several miles. Our loss, 1 killed and 3 wounded.

> L. H. ROUSSEAU,
> *Major-General.*

NASHVILLE, TENN., *December 26, 1864.*
Brig. Gen. W. D. WHIPPLE,
  Richland Creek:

Please inform me where General Wilson, commanding cavalry, is.

> L. H. ROUSSEAU,
> *Major-General.*

HEADQUARTERS DEPARTMENT OF THE CUMBERLAND,
Pulaski, December 26, 1864.

Maj. Gen. L. H. ROUSSEAU,
Nashville:

General Wilson is still pressing the enemy, and to-night is eight or ten miles from here, on the Lamb's Ferry road.

WM. D. WHIPPLE,
Brigadier-General.

SPECIAL ORDERS, }   HDQRS. DISTRICT OF TENNESSEE,
  No. 297.   }   *Nashville, Tenn., December 26, 1864.*

*   *   *   *   *   *   *

II. The Forty-fifth Missouri Volunteer Infantry will proceed without delay to Spring Hill, by rail, to serve as guard to the railroad depot and stores at that place, to prevent pillaging and robbing, and to assist in loading wagons with supplies and materials for the troops at the front. The regiment will follow the advance depot as the railroad is repaired and other depots are established further south, performing the duty above indicated. The quartermaster's department will furnish the necessary transportation.

*   *   *   *   *   *   *

By command of Major-General Rousseau:

B. H. POLK,
Major and Assistant Adjutant-General.

NASHVILLE, TENN., *December 26, 1864.*

Major-General MILROY,
Murfreesborough:

General Thomas telegraphed that the Third and Fourth Michigan have been assigned to the Fourth Corps, and cannot be used in garrisoning the Nashville and Chattanooga road. As soon as it can be done, other regiments will be sent you.

By command of Major-General Rousseau:

B. H. POLK,
Major and Assistant Adjutant-General.

NASHVILLE, TENN., *December 26, 1864.*

Major-General MILROY,
Murfreesborough:

A dispatch was sent you to-day, directing that the Third and Fourth Michigan be not used in garrisoning the railroad, as they had been assigned to the Fourth Corps. Was it received? General Thomas is beyond Pulaski. Hood has perhaps put his army across the Tennessee.

B. H. POLK,
Major and Assistant Adjutant-General.

HDQRS. DEFENSES NASHVILLE AND CHATTANOOGA R. R.,
Murfreesborough, December 26, 1864.

Col. WILLARD WARNER,
   180th Ohio Volunteer Infantry:

COLONEL: You will take with you the mounted men of the two companies of the Fifth Tennessee Cavalry under Captain Couch, and have them march one day in advance of you, so that they can give you all necessary information. If before arriving at Fayetteville you learn that our troops have not reached Pulaski, you will march to Columbia, instead of Pulaski, as ordered in paragraph II, Special Orders, No. 4; and you will also retain the cavalry with you till you have arrived within safe distance of our forces; but if you find that our troops are at Pulaski, you will send the cavalry back from Fayetteville to Decherd, and will proceed with your command, as directed in paragraph II, Special Orders, No. 4. If you cannot learn the whereabouts of our troops after reaching Fayetteville, you will march to Columbia, as it would be too dangerous for you to march to Pulaski with one regiment, if any part of the enemy is occupying that place.

By command of Major-General Milroy:

JNO. O. CRAVENS,
Assistant Adjutant-General.

NOTE.—If you learn at Fayetteville that the enemy has passed Pulaski, you will march to that point.

By command of Major-General Milroy:

JNO. O. CRAVENS,
Assistant Adjutant-General.

This letter was never transmitted.

JNO. O. CRAVENS,
Assistant Adjutant-General.

HDQRS. DEFENSES NASHVILLE AND CHATTANOOGA R. R.,
Murfreesborough, December 26, 1864.

Col. EDWARD ANDERSON,
   Commanding Second Brigade:

COLONEL: Order one company of the Twelfth Indiana [Cavalry] to start at 6 a. m. to-morrow and march on the Shelbyville pike till they come to the camp of the wagon train which left here this p. m. They will take so much of that train as was designed for the One hundred and eightieth Ohio, and proceed with it to Decherd and deliver it to Colonel Warner. This company will then relieve the detachment of the One hundred and fifteenth Ohio, garrisoned at Block-house No. 16 (first south of Tullahoma), placing an officer and twenty men there. The remainder of the company will take quarters at Tullahoma, and await the arrival of the regiment.

By command of Major-General Milroy:

JNO. O. CRAVENS,
Assistant Adjutant-General.

SPECIAL ORDERS, ⎞   HEADQUARTERS DEFENSES NASHVILLE
            ⎟   AND CHATTANOOGA RAILROAD,
  No. 4.   ⎠   *Murfreesborough, Tenn., December 26, 1864.*

I. The Twenty-ninth Regiment Michigan Volunteer Infantry will proceed to Anderson by rail, without delay, and relieve the Sixth Regiment Kentucky Volunteer Infantry there, and at all other points garrisoned by said regiment. Twenty men and an officer (or an efficient non-commissioned officer) will be placed in each block-house held by the Sixth Kentucky. At Bass Station an officer and thirty men will be garrisoned. The remainder of the regiment will be garrisoned at Anderson, at which place the colonel will establish his headquarters.

II. The Sixth Regiment Kentucky Volunteer Infantry will, as soon as relieved by the Twenty-ninth Regiment Michigan Infantry, proceed by railroad to Nashville and report to Captain Wilson, commissary of musters, for the purpose of being mustered out of the service. The camp and garrison equipage will be taken with the regiment and disposed of as the major-general commanding District of Tennessee may direct.

*   *   *   *   *   *   *

By command of Major-General Milroy:

JNO. O. CRAVENS,
Assistant Adjutant-General.

HUNTSVILLE, *December 26, 1864.*

Major-General THOMAS:

Steedman disembarked his troops at Limestone Creek early this morning, seven miles from Decatur on railroad, and moved on that place. Trestle-work at Lime Creek is burned partly. As far as known, line is O. K. within four miles of Decatur. Will follow advance closely. Will let you know General Steedman's whereabouts this evening. We need three operators at once. General Granger is on river.

GREGG.

HEADQUARTERS DEPARTMENT OF THE CUMBERLAND,
Pulaski, December 27, 1864—8 p. m.

Maj. Gen. H. W. HALLECK,
Washington, D. C.:

The following dispatch, just received, is forwarded for your information:

HDQRS. CAVALRY CORPS, MILITARY DIVISION OF THE MISSISSIPPI,
Twenty Miles Southwest of Pulaski, December 27, 1864—6 a. m.

The enemy made a stand here yesterday, stopping us for a few minutes. My advance pursued him five or six miles beyond here, but the country being entirely desolate I have been compelled to halt here, the body of the command in Sugar Creek Valley, till rations can reach us—say till noon. Our horses are very much fagged, roads very heavy, and no forage to be had. I have sent a detachment to Lamb's Ferry, with directions to ascertain the whereabouts of Steedman. The entire rebel army, with the exception of their rear guard, has already crossed the river at Bainbridge. The rear-guard does not expect to get away. I will send forward at once all the force for whom I can get rations and strong horses, with instructions to reach Bainbridge as soon as possible. I must get out of this region in three or four days, or we shall leave our horses.

J. H. WILSON,
Brevet Major-General.

I have ordered General Wilson to push the enemy as far as possible, or at least across the Tennessee, and then endeavor to cross himself at Eastport, under cover of the gun-boats, which should be there at this time, and destroy the railroad bridge across Bear Creek. Major-General Smith has been ordered to Eastport, to co-operate with and support General Wilson. His command will leave here to-morrow. The roads are in a horrible condition, and the country exhausted of supplies; but I believe we can stand as much hardship as the rebels, and I therefore hope the expedition against Bear Creek bridge will prove successful. General Steedman's operator reported, at 5 p. m. 26th instant, that he was crossing his troops on transports above Decatur, preparatory to marching on that place.

Have you received Major-General Stoneman's telegraphic report of the result of his operations in East Tennessee and Southwestern Virginia, forwarded from Knoxville this date? As the copy I received was addressed to yourself and me, I shall not forward the report, unless you have not received it. The complete success and able management of the expedition reflects great credit upon General Stoneman and upon his entire command, for which I sincerely hope he and his command may receive the thanks of the Department. I have received a report from my ordnance officer to-day, who states that fifty-three pieces of artillery, with carriages complete, and 3,034 small-arms were collected from the battle-fields of the 15th and 16th instant. Two pieces of artillery have since arrived at Nashville from Franklin. Three guns were captured from the enemy, three miles north of Thompson's Station, on the 17th. On the 22d instant two pieces of artillery were reported by General Wilson as captured by Hatch's division of cavalry on the Lewisburg pike. On the same date General Wood reported three pieces abandoned on the Columbia and Murfreesborough road. On the 24th three pieces were taken out of Duck River, and on the 26th two more pieces were taken from Richland Creek, at this place. There is no doubt a number of other pieces, abandoned, buried, and thrown into the streams, which have not yet been discovered. A large amount of ammunition was destroyed at this place, and ammunition wagons and caissons are found, partially and some completely destroyed, lying along roads, as the troops advance. A large number of small-arms were destroyed by fire in the railroad depot at this place, and many more abandoned on the flat on the south side of Richland Creek.

GEO. H. THOMAS,
Major-General, U. S. Volunteers, Commanding.

NASHVILLE, TENN., *December 27, 1864.*
(Received 6.30 p. m.)

Hon. E. M. STANTON,
  Secretary of War:

The railroad is expected to be repaired by Thursday, when the remaining prisoners will be forwarded to Camp Chase.

  Respectfully,

WM. HOFFMAN,
Commissary-General of Prisoners.

FLAG-SHIP FAIRY,
Chickasaw, December 27, 1864.

Hon. G. WELLES,
  Secretary of the Navy:

I have destroyed a new fort at this point and all the enemy's visible means of crossing the Tennessee below Florence, and to-day blew up

two caissons and destroyed two field pieces there, knocking one into
the river and the other into pieces. Several transports with supplies
for General Thomas arrived here to-day. I find from the general's dispatches that my movements have been in good time to meet his movements. Hood's army is reported broken up, and its parts cannot cross
at or below Florence, unless the river falls seriously; it is now falling,
which made it impracticable to-day to reach the crossing which the
enemy is said to be using above Little Mussel Shoals, six miles above
Florence.

S. P. LEE,
Acting Rear-Admiral, Commanding.

(Copy to Lieutenant-General Grant.)

FLAG-SHIP FAIRY,
Tennessee River, Off Chickasaw, Ala., December 27, 1864.
(Via Paducah.)

Major-General THOMAS:

I arrived here on the 24th, and destroyed a new fort and magazine;
no guns. Have been several miles above Florence, and have destroyed
all the enemy's visible means of crossing below Florence. I found the
enemy have field pieces, probably protecting a crossing at foot of
Mussel Shoals, six miles above Florence, which want of water prevented
my reaching. The rebels crossed their prisoners at Garner's Ferry,
twelve miles below Florence, on the 19th instant. I destroyed over a
dozen flats and pontoons there; nothing but one flat at Florence. I
learned that Hood took some pontoons with him, and others got adrift.
Hood has earth-works at Florence, made last spring; saw two on each
side. No guns of on [*sic*] of each looked finished. Hood's troops arriving
near Florence are said to declare that they don't know where his main
army is; that they had orders to scatter and care for themselves; that
no Tennessee troops have come to this river since Hood's defeat; that
100 wagons and a great many troops were grievously disappointed at my
destruction of the ferry-boats at Garner's Ferry, which obliged them to
move thence up river. To-day I destroyed two guns and caissons at
Florence Landing, and found a battery of several field pieces on heights
over left bank at Boone's Ferry. Neither of these places was occupied
yesterday. Enemy is doubtless coming in, seeking crossing. Your
two telegrams of the 21st were received to-night. Your transports
with provisions arrived here to-day, and will remove to Eastport
to-morrow, where they will be well protected. I will immediately dispatch an iron-clad and gun-boats to convoy your troops up from Paducah. If any are there, or expected, shall keep up active patrol of river
above and below.

S. P. LEE,
Acting Rear-Admiral, Commanding.

HEADQUARTERS DEPARTMENT OF THE CUMBERLAND,

Pulaski, December 27, 1864.

Capt. A. MORDECAI,
Nashville:

Put on board steamer, for General Smith's troops, at Eastport, the
following ammunition: 2,000 rounds spherical case, light 12-pounder;

1,000 rounds time-shell, light 12-pounder; 3,000 rounds percussion-shell, Schenkl 3-inch rifle; 1,000 rounds fuse-shell, Hotchkiss 3-inch rifle; 500,000 rounds cartridges, elongated ball, caliber .58. General Donaldson has received orders to take it on board.

WM. D. WHIPPLE,
Brigadier-General.

NASHVILLE, *December 27, 1864.*

Brigadier-General WHIPPLE,
Chief of Staff:
Telegram received. Ammunition will be shipped to-night.

A. MORDECAI,
Captain and Chief of Ordnance.

HEADQUARTERS DEPARTMENT OF THE CUMBERLAND,
Pulaski, December 27, 1864.

Captain MORDECAI,
Nashville:
Report immediately the number of pieces of artillery that has been captured from the enemy during the recent engagements and up to the present time; also the number of small-arms collected on the field.

GEO. H. THOMAS,
Major-General, U. S. Volunteers, Commanding.

NASHVILLE, *December 27, 1864.*

Brig. Gen. W. D. WHIPPLE,
Chief of Staff, Department of the Cumberland:
Fifty-three pieces of artillery, with carriages complete, have been collected, as having been captured on the 15th and 16th instant; two more have arrived from Franklin. Three thousand and thirty-four small-arms have been shipped up from the battle-field of the 15th and 16th instant. A full report is forwarded to-day.

A. MORDECAI,
Captain and Chief of Ordnance, Department of the Cumberland.

HEADQUARTERS DEPARTMENT OF THE CUMBERLAND,
Pulaski, December 27, 1864.

Capt. A. MORDECAI,
Nashville:
Yours of to-day received. More guns, probably six, will be shipped from Columbia as soon as road is open, and we got two out of the creek at this place yesterday. The rebels destroyed much ammunition and about 1,000 muskets here.

WM. D. WHIPPLE,
Brigadier-General.

HEADQUARTERS DEPARTMENT OF THE CUMBERLAND,
Pulaski, December 27, 1864.
Brig. Gen. J. L. DONALDSON,
Nashville:
Send the steamers now at Nashville loaded for Eastport to that place. Take on board a quantity of ammunition, for which I have telegraphed Captain Mordecai, also 1,000 pairs of boots and 4,000 pairs of shoes. Answer.

WM. D. WHIPPLE,
Brigadier-General.

NASHVILLE, December 27, 1864.
Brig. Gen. W. D. WHIPPLE,
Chief of Staff:
Will have steamers off for Eastport with supplies indicated as soon as ordnance officer has his stores ready, either to-night or early in the morning. Have telegraphed Paducah about boats there. Will telegraph you about train to Chattanooga at earliest hour.

J. L. DONALDSON,
Chief Quartermaster.

HEADQUARTERS DEPARTMENT OF THE CUMBERLAND,
Pulaski, December 27, 1864.
Brig. Gen. J. L. DONALDSON,
Nashville:
Yours received. Telegraph us when train actually starts for Chattanooga.

WM. D. WHIPPLE,
Assistant Adjutant-General.

HEADQUARTERS DEPARTMENT OF THE CUMBERLAND,
Pulaski, December 27, 1864.
Brig. Gen. J. L. DONALDSON,
Nashville:
Send sufficient steamers to Clifton to transport thence up the river to Eastport 5,000 men, with provisions enough for two trips and all the forage there is room for for the cavalry horses.

WM. D. WHIPPLE,
Assistant Adjutant-General.

WASHINGTON, December 27, 1864—1 p. m.
Maj. Gen. GEORGE H. THOMAS:
I desire, with your permission, to transfer one division of the construction corps in your department to Savannah, Ga., and have W. W. Wright go there temporarily. During his absence I propose that E. L. Wentz, general superintendent, shall act as chief engineer Division of the Mississippi. The case is urgent; experienced and well trained men are needed, and I know of no other way by which the emergency can be met.

D. C. McCALLUM,
Brevet Brigadier-General.

HEADQUARTERS DEPARTMENT OF THE CUMBERLAND,
                         Pulaski, December 27, 1864.
Col. W. W. WRIGHT,
    Chief Engineer, U. S. Military Railroads, Carter's Creek:
General McCallum wishes you to go with one division construction
corps to Savannah, and nominates Major Wentz to take your place
while you are absent. Major Wentz says he can perform those duties,
in addition to his own, during your absence. Can one division construction corps be spared at this time without injury to the service?
General McCallum says the case is urgent.
                                        WM. D. WHIPPLE,
                                            Brigadier-General.

————

HEADQUARTERS DEPARTMENT OF THE CUMBERLAND,
                         Pulaski, December 27, 1864.
E. L. WENTZ,
    General Superintendent, Nashville:
General McCallum wishes to transfer Col. W. W. Wright and one
division of the construction corps to Georgia temporarily, and proposes
you to take Colonel Wright's place during his absence. Can you perform the duties of chief engineer, in addition to your present duties,
during his absence? Answer immediately.
                                        WM. D. WHIPPLE,
                                            Brigadier-General.

————

NASHVILLE, *December 27, 1864.*
Brigadier-General WHIPPLE:
If the duties of chief engineer are assigned me, as intimated in your
dispatch, I will perform them.
                                        E. L. WENTZ,
    General Supt. of Military Railroads, Mil. Div. of the Mississippi.

————

CIRCULAR.]   HDQRS. DEPARTMENT OF THE CUMBERLAND,
                         Pulaski, Tenn., December 27, 1864.
Corps commanders and the commanding officers of all detachments
of troops in the field will collect together the battle-flags, swords, &c.,
captured by their various commands at the battle of Franklin, and since
entering upon this campaign, and forward them to these headquarters, with a full and complete list of the same, giving a description of
the captured article, the name of the captor, his company, and regiment,
the date and place of capture, and, whenever possible, the incidents
connected therewith. In cases where the name of the captor is not definitely known, and the trophy be held either by the regiment or company making the capture as an organization, it is advisable for such
company or regiment to elect, from among the most brave and deserving
in the command, one who shall be deemed worthy of the honor to be
conferred on him. Wherever the name of the captor is known, even
though he may not have survived the conflict, this fact should also be
stated, and, as in all other cases, be inscribed upon the trophy. It is
the design of the major-general commanding, at the termination of the
present campaign against the enemy, and the completed collection of

the captured articles herein mentioned, to forward the same, in charge of a capable officer, and accompanied by the parties making the capture, to the Department at Washington, recommending that each may receive a medal of honor, or some other fitting acknowledgment of their gallant services. In order that this design may be fully carried out, it is hoped that all commanding officers will cause such prompt and proper efforts to be made as will insure to his command its due proportion of honor.

By command of Major-General Thomas:

ROBT. H. RAMSEY,
Assistant Adjutant-General.

HEADQUARTERS FOURTH ARMY CORPS,
Sugar Creek, Tenn., Pinhook, Twenty Miles from Pulaski,
December 27, 1864—12.30 p. m.

Brigadier-General WHIPPLE,
Chief of Staff:

GENERAL: We have marched fourteen miles to-day and have come up with the cavalry. I have conferred freely with General Wilson—I am writing from his headquarters—and he seems to be of the opinion that the bulk of the rebel army has crossed the Tennessee River; but with a view to determine this certainly he has to-day sent out parties on various roads, from whom he will probably receive reports to-night. He informs me that should the reports of these parties indicate that the enemy has not crossed the Tennessee River he will continue the pursuit, in which case I will follow him up for the purpose of supporting him. On the other hand, should the reports indicate that the enemy has crossed the Tennessee River, he will remain here or in this neighborhood to await further orders from the commanding general; in this case, of course, I will not move from this position until I receive further instructions. The road between this and Pulaski is intolerably bad, and I respectfully suggest that if we move farther south that the commanding general make arrangements to feed us from some other point than Pulaski. If the object in moving farther south is to pursue the enemy (and it appears that he is across the river), that object would seem to have been already fully accomplished. If, however, the commanding general has ulterior objects in view, and desires to place us on the Tennessee River to accomplish them, I would then respectfully suggest that he then indicate some definite point on the Tennessee River for which we may direct our march. I repeat that these suggestions are based upon the hypothesis that the information General Wilson receives this evening should indicate that the enemy has crossed the Tennessee River.

Very respectfully, your obedient servant,

TH. J. WOOD,
Brigadier-General, Commanding.

HEADQUARTERS FOURTH ARMY CORPS,
Lexington Road, Sugar Creek, Tenn., December 27, 1864—7 p. m.

Brigadier-General WHIPPLE,
Chief of Staff:

GENERAL: Our forage was exhausted yesterday. We commenced operations at Nashville provided with ten days', by order, since which time we have not been able to draw any forage from the quartermaster's department. This is the eleventh day since we left Nashville. On account of the limited transportation allowed us, we had but six pounds per day—all that we could draw. To-morrow morning we will be entirely out of forage. We are in a very poor country indeed—sterile soil and limited cultivation, one which promises to yield very little forage. After this has been stripped by the cavalry, which precedes us, I do not believe we will be able to get a pound for our animals, certainly not enough. If any can be gotten for the batteries, and if the movement is to be continued to the Tennessee River on this route, in my judgment it will have to be done without artillery and ambulances. Even if we are able to get there, there is no assurance that we can get forage upon our arrival unless it is sent up the Tennessee River.

Very respectfully, your obedient servant,

TH. J. WOOD,
Brigadier-General, Commanding.

HEADQUARTERS FOURTH ARMY CORPS,
Sugar Creek, December 27, 1864—8.30 p. m.

Brigadier-General WHIPPLE, *Chief of Staff:*

GENERAL: The information received from General Wilson, from his reconnaissance to-day, induces the opinion that the whole of the rebel army is not yet across the Tennessee River. He writes me that he will push on at 5 a. m. in the morning, taking the road to Bainbridge. I will follow him as closely as possible for the purpose of supporting him and making pursuit as vigorously as the condition of the road will allow. I beg again to call attention of the commanding general to our condition and the necessity of pushing forward subsistence and forage as rapidly as possible. I also request full instructions for the guidance of our movements when we reach the Tennessee River, should we get so far.

Very respectfully, your obedient servant,

TH. J. WOOD,
Brigadier-General, Commanding.

HDQRS. CAVALRY CORPS, MIL. DIV. OF THE MISSISSIPPI,
Bull's Mills, December 27 [28?], 1864—4.30 p. m.

Brig. Gen. T. J. WOOD, *Commanding Fourth Army Corps:*

GENERAL: I am directed to inform you that information has been received that the last of the enemy's forces crossed the Tennessee River last evening, and that the bridge was taken up this morning. General Wilson has sent a staff officer to General Thomas with this information and for orders.

Very respectfully, your obedient servant,

A. J. ALEXANDER,
Lieutenant-Colonel and Acting Chief of Staff.

HDQRS. CAVALRY CORPS, MIL. DIV. OF THE MISSISSIPPI,
Pinhook Town, December 27, 1864—6 p. m.

Brig. Gen. T. J. WOOD, *Commanding Fourth Corps:*

I have just received a dispatch from Colonel Spalding, at Lexington, 2 p. m. He says the rebel rear guard left there 10 a. m. A lady from Florence informed him that on the evening of the 25th the rebels had not finished their bridge at Bainbridge. They were fortified to cover the crossing. The gun-boats were shelling Florence this morning. Spalding pushed on at once. I have written to General Thomas that I would press on with all my force early in the morning. The woman's testimony is in some degree corroborated by a rebel prisoner just in. At all events we had better push on as far and as fast as possible. I shall move everything, beginning at 5 a. m., though Hatch has received no rations, and three days of Croxton's were taken by A. J. Smith. The news from Sherman is magnificent. I will send, under a flag of truce, an official copy for the information of General John B. Hood, as our news differs somewhat from that given to his army during his retreat from Nashville.

Very respectfully, your obedient servant,
                                        J. H. WILSON,
                                            Brevet Major-General.

UNOFFICIAL.]   HEADQUARTERS ARMY OF THE OHIO,
                            In the Field, Columbia, December 27, 1864.

Lieut. Gen. U. S. GRANT,
        Commanding U. S. Armies, City Point, Va. :

GENERAL: My corps was sent back to Tennessee by General Sherman instead of remaining with him on his march through Georgia, according to his original design, for two reasons, viz: First, because General Thomas was not regarded strong enough after it became evident that Hood designed to invade Tennessee, and, second, in order that I might fill up my corps from the new troops then arriving in Tennessee. These reasons now no longer exist. By uniting my troops to Stanley's we were able to hold Hood in check at Columbia and Franklin until General Thomas could concentrate at Nashville and also to give Hood his deathblow at Franklin. Subsequent operations have shown how little fight was then left in his army, and have taken that little out of it. He now has not more than 15,000 infantry, about 10,000 of whom only are armed, and they greatly demoralized. With time to reorganize and recruit he could not probably raise his force to more than half the strength he had at Franklin. General Thomas has assigned several new regiments to my command, and I hope soon to make them effective, by distributing them in old brigades. I will have from 15,000 to 18,000 effective men, two-thirds of whom are the veterans of the campaign in East Tennessee and Georgia. A small force, it is true, yet one which would at least be an appreciable addition to your army in Virginia or elsewhere, where decisive work is to be done. It may not be practicable now for me to join General Sherman, but it would not be difficult to transfer my command to Virginia. I am aware that General Thomas contemplates a "spring campaign" into Alabama or Mississippi, with the Tennessee River as a base, and believe he considers my command a necessary part of the operating force. Without reference to the latter point permit me to express the opinion that such a campaign would not be an economical or advantageous use of so many troops. If aggressive operations are to be continued in the Gulf States, it appears to me it would be much better to take Mobile, and operate from that point, thus striking vital points (if there are any such) of rebel territory by much shorter lines. But it appears to me that Lee's army is virtually all that is left of the rebellion. If we can concentrate force enough to destroy that we will destroy with it the rebel Government, and the occupation of the whole South will then be but a matter of a few weeks' time. Excuse, general, the liberty I have taken in expressing my views thus freely and unsolicited. I have no other motive than a desire for the nation's good and a personal wish to serve where my little command can do the most. The change I suggest would, of course, deprive me of my department command; but this would be a small loss to me or to the service. The present arrangement is an unsatisfactory one at best. Nominally, I command both a department and an army in the field; but in fact, I do neither.

I am, general, very respectfully, your obedient servant,

J. M. SCHOFIELD,
Major-General.

HEADQUARTERS DEPARTMENT OF THE CUMBERLAND,
Pulaski, Tenn., December 27, 1864.

Maj. Gen. J. M. SCHOFIELD,
Commanding Twenty-third Army Corps, Columbia:

Your dispatch of last evening is received. I think that inasmuch as the force now in the advance and in pursuit of Hood is sufficient to drive him over the Tennessee River, that it is better you should remain at or near Columbia with your command, concentrating and adjusting it so that you could move to Decatur, if necessary, or any other point, according to circumstances, without delay. In the meantime I wish you to have your engineer brigade construct the trestle bridge over Duck River, as at first suggested by you. The roads down here are almost impassable, and it is a difficult matter to supply the troops and animals that are here now. I will remain in camp at this place to-day.

GEO. H. THOMAS,
Major-General of Volunteers, Commanding.

COLUMBIA, TENN., *December 27, 1864.*

Maj. Gen. GEORGE H. THOMAS,
Pulaski, Tenn.:

I have received your dispatch of this a. m., and will carry out your wishes. My engineers are now at work on the trestle bridge with all the additional force that can be used. If the troops in front are likely to get out of rations I might help them by sending forward as far as Pulaski a section of my supply train. I have one here loaded with about 45,000 rations that I can spare.

J. M. SCHOFIELD,
Major-General.

HEADQUARTERS DEPARTMENT OF THE CUMBERLAND,
Pulaski, December 27, 1864.

Major-General SCHOFIELD,
Columbia:

Yours of this day received. The major-general commanding is much obliged to you for your proffer to send section of your train to this place with rations. Please do so at once, and trains from the front will take the stores beyond this.

WM. D. WHIPPLE,
Brigadier-General, &c.

COLUMBIA, TENN., *December 27, 1864—5.30 p. m.*

General WHIPPLE,
    Chief of Staff:

My supply train has started for Pulaski.

J. M. SCHOFIELD,
Major-General.

HEADQUARTERS DEPARTMENT OF THE CUMBERLAND,
Pulaski, December 27, 1864.

Maj. Gen. J. M. SCHOFIELD,
    Columbia:

Officers and men from all the corps are to be sent to Washington with captured flags. You will get your order to-night, but the major-general commanding wishes you to keep your men until all are ready and send them all together.

WM. D. WHIPPLE,
Assistant Adjutant-General.

HEADQUARTERS ARMY OF THE OHIO,
Columbia, Tenn., December 27, 1864.

Brig. Gen. L. THOMAS,
    Adjutant-General U. S. Army, Washington, D. C.:

GENERAL: I have the honor to forward to the War Department nine stand of colors captured from the enemy by the Twenty-third Army Corps at the battle of Franklin, on the 30th of November, 1864. They are borne by the gallant soldiers who are recognized among their comrades as the actual captors of the flags and as the representatives of the noble regiments to which they belong. The following are the names of the soldiers to whom this special honor is awarded: Capt. John H. Brown,* Company D, Twelfth Kentucky Volunteer Infantry; Capt. George V. Kelley,* Company A, One hundred and fourth Ohio Volunteer Infantry; Corpl. Joseph Davis,* Company C, One hundred and fourth Ohio Volunteer Infantry; Corpl. Newton H. Hall,* Company I, Private John H. Ricksecker,* Company D, Private Abraham Greenwalt,* Company G, Private John C. Gaunt,* Company G, One hundred and fourth Ohio Volunteer Infantry. These flags, with eleven others, were captured by Brig. Gen. J. W. Reilly's brigade (First Brigade, Third Division) along its parapet. They afford, at the same time, evidence of the strength of the enemy's column of attack and of its disastrous repulse.

I am, general, very respectfully, your obedient servant,

J. M. SCHOFIELD,
Major-General.

HEADQUARTERS ARMY OF THE OHIO,
Columbia, Tenn., December 27, 1864.

Maj. Gen. D. N. COUCH,
    Comdg. Second Division, Twenty-third Army Corps:

GENERAL: I am directed by the commanding general to inform you that instructions just received from Major-General Thomas render it unnecessary for you to move any of your command across Duck River.

---

*Awarded a Medal of Honor.

He therefore desires you to put your troops into camp on that side, and make them as comfortable as possible, keeping your trains with you, until further orders.

I have the honor to be, your obedient servant,

WM. M. WHERRY,
Major and Aide-de-Camp.

HEADQUARTERS DETACHMENT ARMY OF THE TENNESSEE,
Pulaski, Tenn., December 27, 1864.

Brig. Gen. J. McARTHUR,
Commanding First Division:

GENERAL: By order of the major-general commanding, I am directed to say we will not move to-morrow. You will forward, by 12 m., a list of all casualties, called for once before, and a report of the late battles in which your command was engaged.

I am, general, very respectfully, your obedient servant,

J. HOUGH,
Major and Assistant Adjutant-General.

HDQRS. CAVALRY CORPS, MIL. DIV. OF THE MISS.,
Pinhook, Twenty Miles Southwest of Pulaski, Tenn.,
December 27, 1864—12.20 p. m.

Brig. Gen. W. D. WHIPPLE,
Chief of Staff:

The communication of the major-general commanding, in regard to the destruction of the Bear Creek bridge, has just been received. In reply, after consulting with General Croxton, who assisted in burning it in April, 1862, I am not confident the operation could be made successful in time to injure the enemy. It is nearly sixty miles from here to Eastport, the roads almost impassable, the country denuded of forage, and my command without rations. General Wood informs me that my train is scattered all the way between here and Pulaski, stuck in the mud, none of it nearer than eight miles. I am now sending details of mounted men to it to get rations for the current use of the men. I hope to get all up by night, but when here they will barely carry us to Eastport. General Croxton thinks it would be very difficult to forage the horses on the trip, says the Bear Creek bridge is ten miles from the river, and, as you know, the railroad is in running order only eighteen miles this side of there. Even if broken, the damage would scarcely be commensurate with the labor necessary to accomplish it. I am willing, however, to undertake it by sending one brigade, or taking the whole effective force, say 5,000 men, if, upon reflection, you think it advisable. Could not an infantry force sent with the gun-boats and supplies accomplish it more certainly and at far less cost than my command? The rebel cavalry trains have been sent to Corinth, and the general belief among the prisoners is that Hood expects to assemble and reorganize his army at that place, but is it not more likely, after the loss of so much material, he will go to Blue Mountain or Columbus? The major-general commanding must determine very soon which way I should march, for I cannot keep my command alive in this region. I have sent all my available force after the enemy, a detachment to Rogersville, and as soon as I hear from them or get rations will move on towards Bainbridge unless otherwise ordered. Whatever may be the ultimate course I shall not be losing time. My impression is that all of the organized rebel force will have crossed by to-night, as it is only twenty-eight miles from here to Bainbridge, and the rear guard left here 3 p. m. yesterday, the infantry at noon. I have heard nothing from the pursuit this morning. At all events, they will scarcely make a stand long enough for Wood's infantry to come to my support, for, in the present condition of the roads, it could not reach Bainbridge in less than two days from to-morrow morning. I shall remain here in person until I hear from you, and in the meantime allow no opportunity for inflicting injury upon the enemy to escape.

Very respectfully, your obedient servant,

J. H. WILSON,
Brevet Major-General.

HDQRS. CAVALRY CORPS, MIL. DIV. OF THE MISSISSIPPI,
Pinhook, December 27, 1864—4 p. m.

Brig. Gen. W. D. WHIPPLE,
Chief of Staff:

GENERAL: Rations for a portion of my command have arrived, but there are none for Hatch's division as yet, and, in the condition of the roads, I fear it will be some time before they reach this place. I have had no news from Colonel Spalding, who went in command of the reconnaissance toward Bainbridge.

Very respectfully, your obedient servant,

J. H. WILSON,
Brevet Major-General, Commanding.

HDQRS. CAVALRY CORPS, MIL. DIV. OF THE MISSISSIPPI,
Pinhook Town, December 27, 1864—6 p. m.

Brig. Gen. W. D. WHIPPLE,
Chief of Staff:

I have just received a dispatch from Colonel Spalding, at Lexington, 2 p. m., to the following effect:

The rebel rear guard, Brigadier-General Jackson commanding, left here at 10 a. m. A lady from Florence reports that on the 25th instant the rebels were trying to pontoon the river at Bainbridge; says they are fortified to protect the crossing; bridge was not completed Sunday evening. Gun-boats were shelling Florence this morning. A rebel prisoner who left Lexington yesterday evening says a courier reported that the bridge was not done yesterday morning.

Colonel Spalding pushed on at once from Lexington. I will follow him in the morning with the entire force, though Hatch's rations have not arrived and Croxton reports three days of his taken by the troops of Smith's command at Rutherford's Creek. It is worse than useless to try to haul any farther than this point. We can live on parched corn long enough to see what can be done at Bainbridge. The news from Sherman is glorious. As General Hood has published different to his command, I will send him an official copy more recent, as well as more reliable, than his.

Very respectfully, your obedient servant,

J. H. WILSON,
Brevet Major-General.

HEADQUARTERS DEPARTMENT OF THE CUMBERLAND,
December 27, 1864—5 p. m.

Maj. Gen. J. H. WILSON,
Commanding Cavalry Corps:

The major-general commanding directs me to forward the above copy of a dispatch* sent last night, inasmuch as he has received no answer thereto as yet. He also directs me to say that he is extremely desirous to have you destroy Bear Creek bridge, if possible. Maj. Gen. A. J. Smith is in Pulaski to-day, and will start with his command early to-morrow morning for the Tennessee River and Eastport, which latter it is hoped he will be able to reach before the enemy.

I have the honor to be, general, very respectfully, your obedient servant,

ROBT. H. RAMSEY,
Assistant Adjutant-General.

———

LOUISVILLE, KY., *December 27, 1864.*

Major-General WILSON,
Cavalry Corps:

General Long will draw horses and equipments for the One hundred and twenty-third Illinois and a portion for use of Seventeenth Indiana to-day; will start for Nashville, via Bardstown, to-morrow, the 28th. Two regiments, Third Ohio Cavalry and Ninety-eighth Illinois, were sent to Bardstown Sunday, 25th, to intercept General Lyon.

WM. P. CHAMBLISS,
Major and Special Inspector, Military Division of the Mississippi.

———

HDQRS. CAVALRY CORPS, MIL. DIV. OF THE MISSISSIPPI,
In the Field, December 27, 1864.

General JOHN B. HOOD,
Comdg. C. S. Army of Tennessee, Bainbridge, Ala.:

GENERAL: I have the honor to forward by flag of truce, for your information, the inclosed official copy† of a dispatch just received from Washington, D. C. This is done that you may furnish the troops of your command more recent, as well as more reliable, intelligence concerning operations in Georgia than that imparted to them during the late campaign in Tennessee.

Very respectfully, your obedient servant,

J. H. WILSON,
Brevet Major-General.

———

CIRCULAR, }   HDQRS. CAVALRY CORPS, MIL. DIV. OF THE MISS.,
No. 2.   }   *Pinhook. Tenn., December 27, 1864.*

Commanding officers will notify their commands that those who have drawn five days' rations must make it last seven, and those who have drawn four must make it last five, as it is not known when we can get more.

By order of Brevet Major-General Wilson:

E. B. BEAUMONT,
Major and Assistant Adjutant-General.

———

* See Thomas to Wilson, 26th, 8.30 p. m., p. 363.
† Not found.

Circular.] Hdqrs. Cavalry Corps, Mil. Div. of the Miss.,
In the Field, December 27, 1864.

Commanders of divisions and detached brigades will immediately send a sufficient detail back to the supply train to bring forward five days' rations for their respective commands. If possible, a portion of these rations should be brought forward in wagons, after they have been lightened by the detail. Arrangements should be made to bring bread in sacks, and boxes should not be carried on horses, except in extreme cases. This will be promptly attended to, and these headquarters will be notified when the rations are issued to the men.

By order of Brevet Major-General Wilson:

A. J. ALEXANDER,
Lieutenant-Colonel and Chief of Staff.

Special   Headquarters Cavalry Corps,
Field Orders,   Military Division of the Mississippi,
No. 15.   *Pinhook Town, December 27, 1864.*

*   *   *   *   *   *   *

II. The Cavalry Corps will move to-morrow morning at 5 o'clock promptly, in the order in which they are now encamped, viz: First, Hammond; second, Hatch; third, Croxton; fourth, Harrison.

By command of Brevet Major-General Wilson:

E. B. BEAUMONT,
Major and Assistant Adjutant-General.

Hdqrs. First Brigade, First Cavalry Division,
Sugar Creek, December 27, 1864.

Lieutenant-Colonel ALEXANDER,
Chief of Staff, Cavalry Corps:

Colonel: The following dispatch has just been received from the officer commanding the scouting party I sent out on the Rogersville road this morning:

ANDERSON'S CREEK, *December 27, 1864.*

Capt. W. A. SUTHERLAND,
Assistant Adjutant-General, First Brigade:

Captain: I have reached Anderson's Creek. Citizens say there were from 200 to 400 rebels passed this road yesterday about 2 o'clock; a great many wounded were along. They were going to cross the river at Lamb's Ferry or Bainbridge.

Respectfully,

J. E. COLVILLE,
Captain, First Tennessee Cavalry.

The orderly who brought the dispatch did not know whether they were cavalry or infantry.

I am, colonel, very respectfully, your obedient servant,

JOHN T. CROXTON,
Brigadier-General, Commanding.

HEADQUARTERS DEPARTMENT OF THE CUMBERLAND,
Pulaski, December 27, 1864.
Capt. E. A. DAVENPORT,
Commissary of Subsistence, Fifth Cavalry Division, Columbia :
Come to this place with your train as rapidly as you can without
breaking down your mules.
WM. D. WHIPPLE,
Brigadier-General.

Captain Davenport has left Columbia with his train.
WM. R. PLUM,
Operator.

LEXINGTON, ALA., *December 27, 1864—2 p. m.*
Major-General WILSON:
The rear guard of Forrest's command passed through here at 10 a. m.,
under command of General Jackson, C. S. Army. A lady from Florence
reports that on the 25th instant the enemy were trying to pontoon the
Tennessee River at Bainbridge; reports that they are fortified at Bainbridge to protect crossing at said place; bridge was not completed Sunday evening. Gun-boats were shelling Florence this morning. You
can find forage for 2,000 horses at second creek, eight miles from Pinhook. I shall push on as rapidly as possible.
Very respectfully, your obedient servant,
GEORGE SPALDING,
Colonel Twelfth Tennessee Cavalry.

DECATUR, *December 27, 1864.*
Maj. Gen. GEORGE H. THOMAS:
GENERAL: I have the honor to report that I arrived at the mouth of
Limestone Creek, five miles above Decatur; found General Granger
there, and the enemy occupying the latter place. Embarked my troops
and forced a landing below the mouth of Flint Creek, driving the enemy
from and occupying this place at 6 p. m. My loss slight.
Very respectfully, your obedient servant,
JAMES B. STEEDMAN,
Major-General, Commanding.

BRIDGEPORT, *December 27, 1864.*
Major-General STEEDMAN:
I have a pontoon train here in the river, consisting of seventy-five
wooden boats, fully equipped. I am directed by the commanding gen-
eral to hold the train subject to your orders.
P. O'CONNELL,
Major, Comdg. Pontoon Train, First U. S. Vet. Vol. Engineers.

HUNTSVILLE, *December 27, 1864.*
Major-General STEEDMAN:
My regiment will reach here in half an hour, at 11 a. m. We have
been compelled, in consequence of the rise of the creek, to come around
its source, crossing the Cumberland Mountain. We have marched

eleven miles this morning, over very bad roads, and can go through to Decatur to-day, if necessary; but, if not imperative, it would be better for the horses to make an ordinary march and reach Decatur at 10 a. m. to-morrow. Please [answer] immediately. I will leave a courier here to bring on dispatch.

WM. J. PALMER,
Colonel, Commanding Fifteenth Penrsylvania Cavalry.

NASHVILLE, *December 27, 1864.*

Brig. Gen. W. D. WHIPPLE:

The Forty-fifth Missouri Volunteers has been sent to Spring Hill, with directions to follow the advance depot, to guard and load stores. The Forty-seventh and Forty-eighth Missouri are here, and have no transportation and can get none from the quartermaster's department. I will send them through to Columbia by rail, and direct the commanding officer there to haul their baggage to Pulaski with the post train. The Forty-ninth Missouri is not here. I have ordered the Forty-second Missouri, at Fort Donelson, and Forty-third Wisconsin, at Clarksville, to this place, and will put them on the Chattanooga railroad. The One hundred and seventy-third Ohio was originally assigned to General Miller's brigade, but by a subsequent order it was taken out, and the One hundred and eighty-second substituted. As soon as General Miller can spare the One hundred and seventy-third I will use it on the railroad.

LOVELL H. ROUSSEAU,
Major-General.

SPECIAL ORDERS, }   HEADQUARTERS DISTRICT OF TENNESSEE,
   No. 298.   }   *Nashville, Tenn., December 27, 1864.*

*   *   *   *   *   *   *

III. The Forty-seventh Missouri Volunteer Infantry will proceed by rail to-morrow to Columbia, Tenn., and from thence by pike to Pulaski, and take post at that place. The quartermaster's department at Columbia will furnish the necessary wagons to haul the baggage of the regiment to Pulaski.

IV. The Forty-eighth Missouri Volunteer Infantry will proceed by rail on Thursday, December 29, 1864, to Columbia, Tenn., and from thence by pike to Pulaski, and take post at that place. The quartermaster's department at Columbia will furnish the necessary wagons to haul the baggage of the regiment to Pulaski.

*   *   *   *   *   *   *

By command of Major-General Rousseau:

B. H. POLK,
Major and Assistant Adjutant-General.

NASHVILLE, TENN., *December 27, 1864.*

Major-General MILROY, *Tullahoma:*

Two regiments are coming up the river, and will be sent you at once upon their arrival. Where do you want them? We are awaiting orders department headquarters in reference to the Third and Fourth Michigan.

B. H. POLK,
Major and Assistant Adjutant-General.

HEADQUARTERS DEPARTMENT OF THE CUMBERLAND,
Pulaski, December 27, 1864.
COMMANDING OFFICER FORTY-FIFTH MISSOURI,
Spring Hill :

Shoot all the stragglers you can catch in the act of plundering trains, and such as you do not shoot send back to General Miller at Nashville.

WM. D. WHIPPLE,
Brigadier-General and Chief of Staff.

HEADQUARTERS DISTRICT OF TENNESSEE,
Nashville, Tenn., December 27, 1864.
COMDG. OFFICER FORTY-SECOND MISSOURI VOL. INFANTRY:

In pursuance of instructions from Major-General Thomas, you will move your regiment, by steam-boat, without delay, to this place, reporting at these headquarters upon your arrival.

By command of Major-General Rousseau:

B. H. POLK,
Major and Assistant Adjutant-General.

(Same to commanding officer Forty-third Wisconsin Infantry.)

SPECIAL ORDERS, ⎫ HEADQUARTERS DEFENSES NASHVILLE
               ⎬   AND CHATTANOOGA RAILROAD,
No. 5.   ⎭   *Murfreesborough, December 27, 1864.*

I. The Twelfth Regiment Indiana Volunteer Cavalry will proceed to Tullahoma by rail immediately. This regiment will relieve all the detachments of the One hundred and fifteenth Ohio Infantry stationed south of Duck River and north of Elk River. The block-houses, Nos. 14 and 15 (first two north of Tullahoma), will be garrisoned as follows: At No. 14, twenty men and an officer; at No. 15, twelve men and an efficient non-commissioned officer. The remainder of the regiment will be stationed at Tullahoma.

II. Col. Edward Anderson will proceed to Tullahoma with the Twelfth Indiana Cavalry, and take command of that post and the troops there.

By command of Major-General Milroy:

JNO. O. CRAVENS,
Assistant Adjutant-General.

HEADQUARTERS DEPARTMENT OF THE CUMBERLAND,
December 27, 1864.
Brig. Gen. J. F. MILLER,
Nashville:

Fire a salute of 100 guns to-morrow, in honor of the capture of Savannah by General Sherman.

WM. D. WHIPPLE,
Assistant Adjutant-General.

NASHVILLE, TENN., *December 27, 1864.*

Col. A. A. SMITH,
        Clarksville:

As soon as transportation can be furnished, send the Forty-third Wisconsin Volunteer Infantry, at Clarksville, and the Forty-second Missouri, at Fort Donelson, to this place.

By command of Major-General Rousseau:

B. H. POLK,
Major and Assistant Adjutant-General.

HEADQUARTERS DEPARTMENT OF THE CUMBERLAND,
        Pulaski, December 27, 1864—10 p. m.

Maj. Gen. GEORGE STONEMAN,
        Knoxville, Tenn.:

I have received the report of this date* of your operations in East Tennessee and Southwestern Virginia, and most cordially congratulate you and the officers and men of your command for your complete and splendid success, and for which you richly deserve, and I have earnestly recommended you receive, the thanks of the War Department. Whilst you were driving Breckinridge from East Tennessee this army gave Hood a very genteel whipping, capturing from him all of sixty-eight pieces of artillery, large numbers of small-arms, and several thousand prisoners. His army is now thoroughly demoralized and retreating as rapidly as the roads will permit across the Tennessee. General Sherman has also made a triumphant march through Georgia to Savannah, which place he captured on the 21st instant, with large quantities of stores, arms, and ammunition, and 150 locomotives. The garrison, under Hardee, made its escape by the Union Causeway toward Charleston.

GEO. H. THOMAS,
Major-General, U. S. Volunteers, Commanding.

LEXINGTON, *December 27, 1864.*

Brig. Gen. S. S. FRY,
        Camp Nelson, Ky.:

Lyon's forces are reported moving out by way of Campbellsville. Send out scouts to watch his motions. It is possible he may be driven toward Camp Nelson. Telegraph any information you can get concerning him.

By order of Brevet Major-General Burbridge:

J. BATES DICKSON,
Captain and Assistant Adjutant-General.

EXECUTIVE MANSION,
        Washington, December 27, 1864.

OFFICER IN COMMAND AT LEXINGTON, KY.:

If within your power send me the particulars of the causes for which Lieutenant-Governor Jacob was arrested and sent away.

A. LINCOLN.

---

*See Part I, p. 807.

CITY POINT, VA., *December 28, 1864—11 a. m.*

Maj. Gen. H. W. HALLECK,
    Washington, D. C.:

General Crocker writes to me that his health is so far improved that he can take the field, and desires to do so. I have never seen but three or four division commanders his equal, and we want his services. Please order him to report to General Thomas.

U. S. GRANT,
Lieutenant-General.

WASHINGTON, D. C., *December 28, 1864—4 p. m.*

Major-General THOMAS,
    Pulaski, Tenn.:

General Stoneman's dispatch is received.* I would respectfully suggest that supplies for the troops pursuing the wrecks of Hood's army be sent to Eastport, or some other point on the Tennessee River; also, that troops not required for this pursuit be sent by water to General Dana, to assist in destroying the railroads and supplies in Mississippi, which may otherwise be used by Hood in his retreat.

H. W. HALLECK,
Major-General and Chief of Staff.

HEADQUARTERS DEPARTMENT OF THE CUMBERLAND,
    Pulaski, Tenn., December 28, 1864—10 p. m.

Maj. Gen. H. W. HALLECK,
    Washington, D. C.:

Your telegram of 4 p. m. this day is received. I have already ordered supplies to be sent to Eastport, and General A. J. Smith's command, with Hatch's division of cavalry, has been ordered to the same place, and I am in hopes will reach there in time to prevent Hood from using the railroad in his retreat. General Steedman reoccupied Decatur yesterday at 5 p. m., as he reports, with but little loss. My previous instructions to him were to move as far in the direction of Tuscumbia as he could, and endeavor to destroy or capture Hood's pontoon, and so prevent him from crossing the Tennessee River, and I feel confident that he will make every exertion to carry out my orders. I telegraphed him again, upon receipt of his reported occupation of Decatur, to the same effect. Generals Wilson and Wood are pressing upon the rear of the enemy, and will, I think, be able definitely to ascertain by to-night whether Hood has crossed the river or not. General Wilson's report of last evening, just received to-day, states that prisoners reported to him that Hood had not succeeded in laying his pontoon bridge at Bainbridge up to the morning of the 26th instant. This report was also confirmed by a lady from Florence, whom he saw, and who also informed him that our gun-boats were shelling Florence. As soon as I can ascertain which route Hood takes, if successful in crossing the Tennessee, I will pursue him, if the roads are at all practicable. Surgeon Cooper, my medical director, informed me this morning that the impression among the wounded rebel prisoners in this place is that Hood will continue his retreat to

---

* See Part I, p. 807.

Meridian. They give as their reason for believing this that, with our large cavalry force to threaten his railroad communications, Hood could not possibly maintain himself at Corinth or any other point north of Meridian, and hope to cover Montgomery and Selma. My belief is that Hood, if he can, will retreat to Talladega, as, with his army at that point, he would more effectually cover Montgomery and Selma than if at Meridian. Brigadier-General Sears, of the rebel army, was found yesterday wounded at a private house on the Elkton pike, and is now a prisoner of war.

GEO. H. THOMAS,
Major-General, U. S. Volunteers, Commanding.

FLAG-SHIP FAIRY,
Off Chickasaw, Ala., December 28, 1864—10 a. m.
Maj. Gen. G. H. THOMAS:

River is falling very rapidly. Enemy can cross anywhere above Waterloo.

S. P. LEE,
Acting Rear-Admiral, Commanding.

NASHVILLE, *December 28, 1864.*
Major-General THOMAS:

Officers are about leaving these headquarters to join General Sherman. Do you wish to send anything?

J. D. WEBSTER,
Brigadier-General.

HEADQUARTERS DEPARTMENT OF THE CUMBERLAND,
Pulaski, Tenn., December 28, 1864.
Brig. Gen. J. D. WEBSTER,
Nashville:

Your dispatch of this date received. Send my most cordial congratulations to General Sherman for his great success, and say to him that the remnant of his army left in Tennessee has been battling manfully. We have whipped Hood, captured 6,000 or 7,000 prisoners, 68 pieces of artillery, large quantities of ammunition and wagons, over 5,000 stand of small-arms, and killed and wounded 16 general officers, and now have Hood jammed up against the Tennessee, trying to lay his pontoon bridges, with the gun-boats shelling them below, and Steedman threatening them from above, and our main force after them direct. Nothing but the impassable condition of the roads will prevent us from capturing his entire army. I ordered to-day a salute of 100 guns fired from the fortifications at Nashville, in honor of his capture of Savannah and glorious termination of his march. Stoneman has been entirely and eminently successful in driving the rebels from East Tennessee and destroying the salt-works at Saltville, Va.

GEO. H. THOMAS,
Major-General, U. S. Volunteers, Commanding.

CHATTANOOGA, *December 28, 1864.*

Captain RAMSEY,
    Assistant Adjutant-General:

Can I move by way of Nashville to join the army, or shall I wait for the Decatur road?

J. L. HOLLOPETER,
    First Lieutenant and Acting Chief Signal Officer.

HEADQUARTERS DEPARTMENT OF THE CUMBERLAND,
    Pulaski, December 28, 1864.

Lieut. J. L. HOLLOPETER,
    Actg. Chief Signal Officer, Dept. of the Cumberland, Chattanooga:

The major-general commanding directs that you wait for the completion of the Decatur railroad before you move, and when it is finished orders will be given you from these headquarters when and where to move.

ROBT. H. RAMSEY,
    Assistant Adjutant-General.

NASHVILLE, *December 28, 1864.*

General WHIPPLE,
    Chief of Staff:

Your telegram about supplies and transportation for Clifton, on Tennessee, received. All available boats here—five boats and some barges—will leave here this afternoon with the supplies ordered, and these, with the boats already gone up the Tennessee and the gun-boats there, will furnish ample transportation for the troops referred to. Have sent a swift dispatch-boat off in advance, to communicate with naval officer at Smithland and Paducah, so as to have convoy ready. Please acknowledge receipt of this.

J. L. DONALDSON,
    Chief Quartermaster, Department of the Cumberland.

NASHVILLE, *December 28, 1864.*

General W. D. WHIPPLE,
    Chief of Staff:

The steamer that had been detained here some days left this morning at daylight for Eastport, with ammunition, commissary stores, &c.

J. L. DONALDSON,
    Chief Quartermaster, Department of the Cumberland.

NASHVILLE, *December 28, 1864.*

General W. D. WHIPPLE,
    Chief of Staff:

The superintendent of the Louisville railroad reports that trains will run regularly again to Louisville, to begin on Friday morning. This is encouraging.

J. L. DONALDSON,
    Chief Quartermaster.

HEADQUARTERS DEPARTMENT OF THE CUMBERLAND,
Pulaski, December 28, 1864.
Brig. Gen. J. L. DONALDSON,
Chief Quartermaster, Dept. of the Cumberland, Nashville:

As soon as the Nashville and Chattanooga Railroad is opened, I wish all deficiencies in supplies at Chattanooga to be made up at once, and hereafter supplies for 40,000 men for four months should be kept on hand constantly at that point.
GEO. H. THOMAS,
Major-General, U. S. Volunteers, Commanding.

NASHVILLE, *December 28, 1864.*
Maj. Gen. GEORGE H. THOMAS:

Telegram received. Will push matter of supplies to Chattanooga as soon as the road is open.
J. L. DONALDSON,
Chief Quartermaster.

NASHVILLE, *December 28, 1864.*
General WHIPPLE,
Chief of Staff:

Superintendent of railroad reports that he can send a train through to Murfreesborough, and so to Chattanooga, by 6 o'clock [this] afternoon, if desired. Regular train will leave at 2 a. m. Friday. Please answer which hour you decide upon, and I will have train ready.
J. L. DONALDSON,
Chief Quartermaster, Department, of the Cumberland.

HEADQUARTERS DEPARTMENT OF THE CUMBERLAND,
Pulaski, December 28, 1864.
Brevet Brigadier-General DONALDSON,
Chief Quartermaster, Department of the Cumberland:

Your dispatch of this date, relative to the sending of rations and supplies up the Tennessee River to Clifton, received. Commence sending trains regularly to Chattanooga on Friday a. m. when you have every preparation made for it.
WM. D. WHIPPLE,
Brigadier-General and Chief of Staff.

NASHVILLE, *December 28, 1864.*
General W. D. WHIPPLE:

Lieutenant-Colonel Le Duc, acting chief quartermaster of the army, telegraphed yesterday that General Thomas directed that no horses be allowed to go by cars to Franklin. Is this order positive and peremptory, or may I use my discretion as to shipping horses by railroad? Regimental officers are daily arriving here with their commands to go to front, and sometimes general and staff officers; and I would respectfully suggest that it is very embarrassing for them to send horses by wagon road, nor is it always safe. We have plenty of cars here to accommodate all such cases, and sometimes it may become necessary to ship even other horses. Please answer immediately.

J. L. DONALDSON,
Chief Quartermaster, Department of the Cumberland.

HEADQUARTERS,
Pulaski, December 28, 1864.

Brig. Gen. J. L. DONALDSON,
    Chief Quartermaster, Dept. of the Cumberland, Nashville:

The major-general commanding directs me to say, in reply to yours of this p. m. relative to the shipment of horses by rail, that that was intended to refer only to artillery and cavalry horses. You can regulate the shipment of all others yourself.

ROBT. H. RAMSEY,
Assistant Adjutant-General.

QUARTERMASTER-GENERAL'S OFFICE,
Washington City, December 28, 1864.

Major-General THOMAS,
    Commanding Department of the Cumberland, Tennessee:

GENERAL: The following is a copy of a telegram sent to your address yesterday:

It is necessary to prepare for railroad operations in Georgia and South Carolina, and as the construction corps in the Department of the Cumberland is larger than now needed, and is well trained and organized, it is proposed to transfer one division (about one-fifth of it) to Savannah. General McCallum has received the necessary instructions. Please give such orders as will facilitate this movement.

M. C. MEIGS,
Quartermaster-General and Brevet Major-General.

Very respectfully, your obedient servant,

CHS. THOMAS,
Asst. Quartermaster-General and Bvt. Brig. Gen., U. S. Army.

RUTHERFORD'S CREEK, *December 28, 1864.*

General W. D. WHIPPLE:

Your dispatch of yesterday is received, also one from General Mc Callum, of same date and same purport, with this addition, that he directs me to confer with General Thomas and get his consent to go and take the men. As the Chattanooga road will be opened to-day, Mr. Smeed's division can be spared for this expedition, and, with General Thomas' consent, I will make arrangements at once for starting. If he wishes, I can send another division of bridge-builders to assist Mr. McDonald on the Decatur end of this road. I have already nearly 1,000 men here; nearly as many as can work to advantage.

W. W. WRIGHT,
Chief Engineer.

RUTHERFORD'S CREEK, *December 28, 1864.*

Brigadier-General WHIPPLE:

Rutherford's bridge, No. 1, is about completed, and we are at work on No. 2; will probably be delayed somewhat by the wreck of the old bridge; this is quite a formidable affair. I have had 200 men on it for two days, and it will take at least till night to get it out of the way. Yesterday I sent a large force to work on the south end of Duck River bridge.

W. W. WRIGHT,
Chief Engineer.

SPECIAL FIELD ORDERS, ⎰ HDQRS. DEPT. OF THE CUMBERLAND,
No. 352.   ⎱   *Pulaski, Tenn., December 28, 1864.*

*   *   *   *   *   *   *

III. Col. W. W. Wright, chief engineer U. S. military railroads, is hereby temporarily relieved from duty in this department, and will, with one division of the construction corps, proceed, via New York City, to Savannah, Ga., reporting en route, by telegraph, to Brig. Gen. D. C. McCallum, at Washington, D. C., and upon his arrival at Savannah, to Maj. Gen. W. T. Sherman, commanding Military Division of the Mississippi. Colonel Wright will take with him such division of the construction corps as will not interfere with or retard the work of repairing the North Alabama Railroad, now in progress. During the absence of Colonel Wright, Mr. E. L. Wentz, in addition to his duties of general superintendent, will perform those of chief engineer of the military railroads of the Military Division of the Mississippi. The quartermaster's department will furnish the necessary transportation.

*   *   *   *   *   *   *

By command of Major-General Thomas:

WM. D. WHIPPLE,
Assistant Adjutant-General.

HEADQUARTERS DEPARTMENT OF THE CUMBERLAND,
Pulaski, December 28, 1864. (Received 12 m. 29th.)

Brig. Gen. T. J. WOOD,
Commanding Fourth Corps:

GENERAL: Your dispatch, dated Pinhook, December 27, 12.30 p. m., is just received. The major-general commanding directs that you order your artillery back to this point to be supplied with forage from the post. He further directs that you hold your infantry where they now are for further orders, ready to move in whatever direction they may be required.

Very respectfully, your obedient servant,

HENRY M. CIST,
Assistant Adjutant-General.

LEXINGTON, *December 29, 1864—1 p. m.*

Bvt. Maj. Gen. J. H. WILSON,
Commanding Cavalry:

GENERAL: I received the above at 12 m.; I regret it did not reach me earlier. I will not start my artillery back till to-morrow morning, as the change of a day's march toward the river may induce General Thomas to change his orders with reference to it. If I hear anything from him this afternoon, I will communicate it to you.

Respectfully, your obedient servant,

TH. J. WOOD,
Brigadier-General of Volunteers, Commanding.

HEADQUARTERS DEPARTMENT OF THE CUMBERLAND,
Pulaski, Tenn., December 28, 1864.
(Received 3.45 p. m. 29th.)

Brig. Gen. T. J. WOOD,
Commanding Fourth Army Corps:

GENERAL: Your two dispatches of 7 and 8.30 p. m. yesterday have been received. The major-general commanding directs me to say that it is not expected that you shall send any portion of your force farther than the Tennessee River, but as General Wilson has gone on with his command it is necessary that there should be an infantry force to support him and keep pushing until the enemy is driven across the river, when the commands will be placed in camps at such places that they can be supplied with forage and preparations made for a spring campaign. We cannot expect to have everything as we would wish it, but bad roads and other difficulties must be looked for. It seems as though, with the railroad terminus at Spring Hill, the chief quartermaster of your corps might have been able to keep the command supplied with a limited quantity of forage by sending back the empty wagons to be reloaded.

Very respectfully, your obedient servant,

WM. D. WHIPPLE,
Assistant Adjutant-General.

HEADQUARTERS FOURTH ARMY CORPS,
Lexington, Tenn., December 28, 1864—9.30 p. m.

Brigadier-General WHIPPLE,
Chief of Staff:

GENERAL: I have received a note this evening from General Wilson, informing me that the last of the enemy crossed the river yesterday evening, and took up the pontoon bridge this morning. This being the case, there is no necessity of going to the Tennessee River as a matter of pursuit. As I have already stated in previous dispatches, the road from Pulaski to the Tennessee River is exceedingly bad, and, in my judgment, utterly impracticable as a route for the supply of troops. My ammunition and hospital trains have not yet reached camp; they are five miles in the rear. I will remain here to await further instructions as to what disposition to make of the corps, but, as my rations will be out in two days, it is of the utmost importance that these orders, or additional supplies, be sent to me at once.

Very respectfully, your obedient servant,

TH. J. WOOD,
Brigadier-General, Commanding.

HEADQUARTERS FOURTH ARMY CORPS,
Sugar Creek, Tenn., December 28, 1864—6.30 a. m.

Order of the day for the Fourth Corps for to-day:

The corps will move for the Tennessee River to-day, following the cavalry—General Elliott will lead; General Beatty will follow; then General Kimball. General Elliott will start at 8 a. m. The trains and artillery will move in the usual order.

By order of Brigadier-General Wood:

J. S. FULLERTON,
Lieutenant-Colonel and Assistant Adjutant-General.

COLUMBIA, TENN., *December 28, 1864.*

Maj. Gen. GEORGE H. THOMAS,
Pulaski, Tenn.:

The trestle bridge will be completed to-morrow, so that the pontoons can be spared, if they are wanted elsewhere.

J. M. SCHOFIELD,
Major-General.

HEADQUARTERS DEPARTMENT OF THE CUMBERLAND,
Pulaski, December 28, 1864—10 p. m.

Maj. Gen. JOHN M. SCHOFIELD,
Commanding Twenty-third Army Corps, Columbia:

Your dispatch of this date is received. The major-general commanding directs that you have the pontoon bridges taken up as soon as the trestle bridge is completed, and instruct the commanding officer in charge of the pontoon train to fully prepare his command to move as soon as he receives orders from these headquarters—that is, to provide himself with rations and forage.

ROBT. H. RAMSEY,
Assistant Adjutant-General.

SPECIAL FIELD ORDERS, }   HDQRS. ARMY OF THE OHIO,
No. 190.   }   *Columbia, Tenn., December 28, 1864.*

* * * * * * *

VI. Lieut. Col. G. W. Schofield, chief of artillery, Department of the Ohio, will proceed to Louisville, Ky., and establish his office in that city until further orders.

* * * * * * *

IX. Capt. Charles E. Morgan, One hundred and third Ohio Infantry, is hereby announced as acting ordnance officer of the Twenty-third Army Corps.

By command of Major-General Schofield:

J. A. CAMPBELL,
Major and Assistant Adjutant-General.

HEADQUARTERS DEPARTMENT OF THE CUMBERLAND,
Pulaski, Tenn., December 28, 1864.
Maj. Gen. A. J. SMITH,
 Commanding Detachment Army of the Tennessee:

GENERAL: The major-general commanding the forces in the field directs that you start to-morrow morning with your command for Eastport, Tenn. [Miss.], marching by way of Lawrence and Waynesborough to Clifton, on the Tennessee River. Steamers have been ordered to Clifton sufficient for the transportation of 5,000 men, with the supposition that upon these boats you will be able to transfer your command to Eastport in two trips, and it was directed that sufficient provisions should be placed upon these boats for the use of your troops during the transit. Upon your arrival at Eastport you will select a good position for the encampment of your troops during the winter, as it is expected they will remain there for two months, and proceed with such reorganization as your command may require, and fit it generally for an early spring campaign. A portion of General Wilson's command has been ordered to Eastport, for the purpose of destroying the railroad bridge over Big Bear Creek, and in this enterprise you will afford him such support as he may require. At Eastport you will find steamers, under convoy of gun-boats, loaded with provisions, forage, ammunition, medical supplies, and clothing. The ammunition and clothing are such as you stated you would require in case you were ordered to that place.

 Very respectfully, your obedient servant,
WM. D. WHIPPLE,
Brigadier-General and Chief of Staff.

HEADQUARTERS DETACHMENT ARMY OF THE TENNESSEE,
Pulaski, Tenn., December 28, 1864.
Brig. Gen. J. McARTHUR,
 Commanding First Division:

The major-general commanding directs that moving to-morrow the divisions take with them the regimental wagons and artillery. The supply trains will follow in the same order of precedence as the troops march. The division in the rear will each day throw out a rear guard and take charge of the supply train. Quartermasters must take the immediate supervision of their trains, and remain with them until they get into camp. The order of march to-morrow will be as follows: First Division at 7 a. m. promptly; Second Division at 8 a. m.; Third Division at 9 a. m. On arriving at Pulaski a guide will be furnished the leading division.

 I am, respectfully, your obedient servant,
J. HOUGH,
Major and Assistant Adjutant-General.

(Same to Brig. Gen. K. Garrard and Col. J. B. Moore.)   •

HEADQUARTERS DEPARTMENT OF THE CUMBERLAND,
Pulaski, Tenn., December 28, 1864—12 m.
Maj. Gen. J. H. WILSON,
 Comdg. Cavalry Corps, Military Division of the Mississippi:

GENERAL: Information has been received at these headquarters of a drove of cattle in a bend of the Elk River near Elkton, guarded by some 200 rebels. The major-general commanding directs that, as soon as you have ascertained that the rebels are across the Tennessee River, you send a sufficient force to look after these cattle and gather them in.

Very respectfully, your obedient servant,

HENRY M. CIST,
Assistant Adjutant-General.

HEADQUARTERS DEPARTMENT OF THE CUMBERLAND,
Pulaski, Tenn., December 28, 1864—12 m.

Maj. Gen. J. H. WILSON,
Comdg. Cavalry Corps, Military Division of the Mississippi:

GENERAL: Your dispatch dated Pinhook, December 27, 12.20 p. m., is just received. The major-general commanding directs that as soon as you have ascertained that the rebel army has crossed the Tennessee River, that you move your command, with the exception of Hatch's division, back to this place, that they may be supplied with forage. He directs that you send Hatch's division, of your command, to Eastport, as he wishes at least enough cavalry on the Tennessee River to operate in conjunction with General Smith's command, which has been ordered to that place. If Hatch's division cannot move from where they now are to Eastport, he directs that they return to this place, to be furnished with supplies and then move, via Lawrenceburg, Waynesborugh, and Clifton, to that point.

Very respectfully, your obedient servant,

HENRY M. CIST,
Assistant Adjutant-General.

HEADQUARTERS DEPARTMENT OF THE CUMBERLAND,
Pulaski, December 28, 1864—1 p. m.

Brevet Major-General WILSON,
Commanding Cavalry Corps:

GENERAL: Your dispatch dated December 27, 6 p. m., just received. The major-general commanding directs that you push on as rapidly as possible. He says that you and General Wood have a glorious chance to do efficient service. Full supplies of rations for your entire command will be in this place this evening, and the general says that he will push them out to you as rapidly as possible.

Very respectfully, your obedient servant,

HENRY M. CIST,
Assistant Adjutant-General.

HDQRS. CAVALRY CORPS, MIL. DIV. OF THE MISSISSIPPI,
Bull's Mills, Blue Water Creek, Ala., December 28, 1864—4 p. m.

Brig. Gen. W. D. WHIPPLE,
Chief of Staff:

I have just received a dispatch from Colonel Spalding, one mile and a half from Bainbridge, saying the rebel rear guard crossed the Tennessee last night and took up the pontoon bridge before daylight this morning. My headquarters are ten miles from Bainbridge, and my

command just arriving at the Blue Water Creek. Shall I return to
Pulaski or go to Waterloo? If you wish my command to occupy a
position on or near the Tennessee, while refitting and reorganizing,
Tuscumbia would probably be the best, as the landing and river could
be used for bringing supplies of forage, rations, horses, &c., and at the
same time we could draw upon the Tennessee Valley as far up as Decatur. It would, however, be imprudent to occupy Tuscumbia with cavalry, unless it is made a base for infantry also. My command is now in
that condition which renders it necessary to have the question of rest,
supplies, and reorganization fully settled as soon as possible. Long
telegraphed me that the last of his division would leave Louisville
to-day. I send Lieutenant Prather, of my staff, with this. He will
explain our condition and the nature of the country. General Wood
marched this morning with me, but [he] cannot be much this side of
Lexington. The roads are intolerable, and I think impassable for
trains.

Very respectfully, your obedient servant,

J. H. WILSON,
Brevet Major-General.

HEADQUARTERS FOURTH ARMY CORPS,
Lexington, Ala., December 28, 1864—8 p. m.

Brevet Major-General WILSON,
Comdg. Cavalry Corps, Military Division of the Mississippi:

Your note of 4.30 p. m. received.* Under the circumstances I will
remain at or near my present position until orders are received from
General Thomas, with whom I will try to communicate at the earliest
moment. If we had any assurance that we would find supplies on the
river, it would be well, in my judgment, to go there, but this is a matter
for which we should await General Thomas' order.

Very respectfully, your obedient servant,

TH. J. WOOD,
Brigadier-General of Volunteers.

HDQRS. CAVALRY CORPS, MIL. DIV. OF THE MISSISSIPPI,
Bull's Mills, Blue Water, December 28, 1864.

Colonel SPALDING:

Please report at once what information you have obtained regarding
the movements of the enemy and his present position; also report
whether you have received dispatches for General Hood, sent to you
this morning by an orderly.

By command of Brevet Major-General Wilson:

E. B. BEAUMONT,
Major and Assistant Adjutant-General.

NASHVILLE, *December 28, 1864—4 p. m.*

Maj. Gen. J. H. WILSON,
Pulaski, Tenn.:

I arrived here to-day with Watkins' brigade and the artillery. They
will need two or three days to shoe horses. Colonel La Grange, at

----

* See Alexander to Wood, 4.30 p. m. 27th [28th?], p. 376.

Elizabethtown, yesterday captured 30 more of Lyon's men, including 1 major and 1 lieutenant on his staff and another field and line officer. The condition of his horses compels a discontinuance of the pursuit. We have had one of the hardest trips I ever made, having marched more than 300 miles, over the worst roads I ever saw. Watkins is in tolerably good condition. La Grange is in need of rest, and will not be here for four or five days. Please send me orders.

E. M. McCOOK,
Brigadier-General, Commanding.

HDQRS. CAVALRY CORPS, MIL. DIV. OF THE MISSISSIPPI,
Bull's Mills, December 28, 1864—3 p. m.

Brigadier-General CROXTON,
    Commanding Brigade:

GENERAL: The brevet major-general commanding desires you to send one battalion of your command to the Tennessee River, via Center Star. The commanding officer will communicate with the detachment sent out by you yesterday; will find out where the enemy have gone, and will tumble logs into the river to-night. He will send all the information he can get in to-night, and will also send word how much forage can be had in that direction.

    Very respectfully, your obedient servant,

A. J. ALEXANDER,
Lieutenant-Colonel and Chief of Staff.

NASHVILLE, *December 28, 1864.*

Major-General WILSON,
    Commanding Cavalry:

GENERAL: The Eighth Michigan, 430 strong, fully mounted, will be here to-night or to-morrow. Had impressed a sufficient number of horses before I received your last instructions on this subject. I suppose he will require a day or so to shoe up. Shall I then send him forward? I sent H[arrison] three days ago 125 men of Fifth Iowa, and will send fifty of Seventh Ohio by day after to-morrow. The Eighth Michigan is armed with pistols and sabers only; no carbines here.

R. W. JOHNSON,
Brigadier-General.

NASHVILLE, *December 28, 1864.*

Brigadier-General WHIPPLE:

The Third and Fourth Michigan are at Murfreesborough awaiting orders. Steam-boats have gone to bring up the Forty-second Missouri and Forty-third Wisconsin. As soon as they arrive I will send them to General Milroy.

LOVELL H. ROUSSEAU,
Major-General.

TULLAHOMA, *December 28, 1864.*

Major-General THOMAS:

The Sixty-eighth Indiana went down to Bridgeport on the 20th instant, and the Eighth Kentucky went yesterday morning.

R. H. MILROY,
Major-General.

HEADQUARTERS DEPARTMENT OF THE CUMBERLAND,
Pulaski, Tenn., December 28, 1864.

Major-General STEEDMAN,
Decatur, Ala.:

Your dispatch of the 27th received. I am very much gratified with your operations against Decatur. The roads from here to Florence are in an almost impassable condition, and the country so completely devastated that we can scarcely get any supplies, but the enemy has been as vigorously pursued as circumstances will admit. It is reported that Hood crossed at Lamb's Ferry and Bainbridge with what force he could get off. He is represented as being in most deplorable condition. I shall try to intercept him at Iuka, if he retreats that way, and I want you to push a strong reconnaissance toward Lamb's Ferry, to see if he has retreated by way of Courtland and Moulton.

GEO. H. THOMAS,
Major-General, U. S. Volunteers, Commanding.

DECATUR, *December 28, 1864.*

Maj. Gen. G. H. THOMAS:

I am preparing and will move in the direction of Courtland this afternoon. I am compelled to go without transportation, my wagons having failed to reach me. I send my wagons and surplus ammunition by transports, convoyed by the gun-boats, to Melton's Bluff. It is rumored that a part of Hood's army has crossed at Lamb's Ferry, but I can get no certain information. We recaptured locomotives and fourteen cars from the enemy. The road will be repaired to this point, I think, to-day.

JAS. B. STEEDMAN,
Major-General.

BRIDGEPORT, *December 28, 1864.*

Major-General STEEDMAN,
Decatur:

Your telegram of the 27th instant is received. I will start for Decatur immediately with the pontoons. Please send me a steamer or gun-boat to convoy and tow me down. There may be some danger in going down without a convoy, and we will travel very slow unless taken in tow by a steamer. It will take thirty-six hours to float down.

P. O'CONNELL,
Major, Commanding Pontoons,

HEADQUARTERS CAVALRY,
Six Miles from Decatur, on Courtland Road,
December 29 [28], 1864—10 p. m.

General STEEDMAN:

GENERAL: I struck the rebel pickets at Boldin's place, four miles and three-quarters from Decatur, and met the main force close behind them, pursuing it to this point, where we captured all the artillery they had, consisting of two 12-pounders, with caissons and horses attached, six prisoners, and a few cavalry horses. My loss is nothing, the advance guard charging so boldly that the rebels fired but a few shots and ran off, leaving their guns in the hands of a sergeant and fifteen men of the Fifteenth Pennsylvania Cavalry. Colonel Windes was in command of the rebels, and told Mr. Boldin (citizen), with whom he took supper, that two regiments of cavalry were coming up to assist him to-night. He received a dispatch at the table, which he said announced this. Mr. Boldin also learned that Hood had crossed at Bainbridge. Two of the prisoners captured state the same thing, and one of them, a hospital steward, is very circumstantial; question him. I see a light in the direction of Lamb's Ferry, or Brown's Ferry, which I take to be the fires of the two cavalry regiments coming to assist Colonel Windes. I would have continued pursuit to Hillsborough, but that my horses would not in that event have been fit for hard work to-morrow.

Yours, respectfully,

WM. J. PALMER.

DECATUR, *December 28, 1864—10.50 p. m.*
(Received 29th.)

Major-General THOMAS:

A part of my command is now garrisoning Decatur, which was abandoned by the enemy without a fight. I understood he commenced evacuating the place as soon as he heard of the crossing of General Steedman's command. General Steedman left this evening in the direction of Courtland. Considerable force of cavalry reported trying to cross at Guntersville. No news from down the river. Cars and locomotives left at Huntsville recaptured. Road is running this evening from Decatur to Stevenson.

R. S. GRANGER,
Brigadier-General.

HUNTSVILLE, *December 28, 1864.*

Lieut. SAM. M. KNEELAND,
Acting Assistant Adjutant-General, Decatur, Ala.:

I have just received the following from the commanding officer at Paint Rock bridge. I do not credit the report:

Colonel LYON:

It is reported to me that a considerable force of rebels is in the vicinity of Claysville now, and that there is a much larger force at or near Guntersville preparing to cross. We got our information from negroes and citizens. All credit I put in it is to keep a sharp lookout for them. All quiet here.

WM. P. LYON,
Col. Thirteenth Wisconsin Veteran Volunteer Infantry, Comdg.

HEADQUARTERS ARMY OF THE OHIO,
Columbia, Tenn., December 28, 1864.

Maj. Gen. GEORGE STONEMAN,
Knoxville, Tenn.:

I have seen your report* to General Thomas of your late operations, and congratulate you most heartily upon your complete success and vindication of your reputation as a general. I may now inform you that, while you were preparing for your late expedition, I was ordered by General Grant and the Secretary of War to relieve you from command, on the ground of your failure in Georgia. The order was revoked upon my earnest protest and assumption of the responsibility for the result. I regret, general, the necessity of calling your attention to the fact that since you started on your expedition you have not thought proper to make any report to me of your operations, although specially requested to do so. I shall be glad of any explanation of the course you appear to have adopted in this respect.

J. M. SCHOFIELD,
Major-General

LEXINGTON, *December 28, 1864.*

ABRAHAM LINCOLN,
President of the United States, Washington, D. C.:

So far as I am informed, Lieutenant-Governor Jacob's offense was making treasonable and seditious speeches, calculated and intended to weaken the power of the Government in its efforts to suppress the rebellion. His arrest was advised by Doctor Breckinridge and other prominent loyal men of Kentucky. General Burbridge will address you fully on the subject upon his return. I have had no communication with him since the 14th instant, and do not know his present location.

Respectfully,

J. BATES DICKSON,
Captain and Assistant Adjutant-General.

HEADQUARTERS DEPARTMENT OF THE CUMBERLAND,
Pulaski, Tenn., December 29, 1864—9 p. m.

Maj. Gen. H. W. HALLECK,
Washington, D. C.:

The following dispatch, received this p. m. from General Wilson, is forwarded for your information.†

I have to-day a dispatch from Admiral Lee, dated Flag-ship Fairy, Tennessee River, off Chickasaw, Ala., December 27, which says he arrived at Chickasaw on the 24th instant, and destroyed a new fort and magazine, as well as all the visible means of the enemy for crossing the river below Florence. He also destroyed a number of flats and pontoons at Garner's Ferry, where the enemy crossed his prisoners on the 19th. The day he dispatched me he destroyed two guns and caissons at Florence Landing. Hood's troops arriving near Florence are said to declare that they do not know where his main army is; that they had orders to scatter and care for themselves; and that no Ten-

---

* See Part I, p. 807.
† See Wilson to Whipple, 4 p. m. 28th (p. 397), omitting that portion beginning "I send Lieutenant Prather," and ending "this side of Lexington."

nessee troops had come to the river since Hood's defeat. One hundred wagons and a great many troops had been grievously disappointed at his destruction of the ferry-boats at Garner's Ferry, which obliged them to move thence up the river. He also states that transports with supplies had arrived at Florence that day, and would go forward to Eastport next morning, where, under the protection of the gun-boats, they would await the arrival of the troops. A dispatch from General Steedman, of the 28th instant, dated at Decatur, says he would start with a portion of his command on the afternoon of that day for Courtland. The railroad is in running order from Stevenson to Decatur. In consequence of the terribly bad weather, almost impassable condition of the roads, and exhausted country, the troops and animals are so much worn down by the fatigues of the last two weeks that it becomes necessary to halt for a short time to reorganize and refit for a renewal of the campaign, if Hood should halt at Corinth. Should he continue his retreat to Meridian, as supposed by many of his officers who have been taken prisoners, I think it would be best for the troops to be allowed till early spring, when the roads will be in a condition to make a campaign into the heart of the enemy's country. I have made diligent inquiries concerning the resources of the country, and believe that an army would find ample supplies on two or three routes south—one in the vicinity of the Mobile and Ohio Railroad; one through the middle of Alabama, from Decatur south; and a third along the west side of the Coosa; all three of which I believe would be practicable in the spring and summer, but are altogether impracticable at this season of the year. If I ascertain, therefore, that Hood has not halted at Corinth, but retreated farther south, I will place the troops at Eastport, Huntsville, and Dalton, where they can be easily supplied, and from which points they can be readily assembled to make a spring campaign.

GEO. H. THOMAS,
Major-General, U. S. Volunteers, Commanding.

HEADQUARTERS DEPARTMENT OF THE CUMBERLAND,
Pulaski, December 29, 1864.
Maj. Gen. H. W. HALLECK,
Washington, D. C.:

In my letter of recommendations for promotion, I forgot to mention the name of Bvt. Maj. Gen. A. J. Smith, whose confirmation I recommend for gallant conduct and good generalship. The names of the two colonels mentioned by him for promotion are Col. W. L. McMillen, Ninety-fifth Ohio Volunteer Infantry, and Col. L. F. Hubbard, Fifth Minnesota, for gallant conduct in the battles of Richland Creek and Brentwood Hills before Nashville, December 15 and 16 instant.

GEO. H. THOMAS,
Major-General, U. S. Volunteers, Commanding.

FLAG-SHIP FAIRY,
Eastport, Miss., December 29, 1864.
Major-General THOMAS.

Enemy are erecting battery on heights above Eastport, in position which we formerly and they subsequently occupied. I am annoying their working party. The river has fallen so low that Hood can cross above without interruption from navy.

S. P. LEE,
Acting Rear-Admiral.

HEADQUARTERS DEPARTMENT OF THE CUMBERLAND,
Pulaski, December 29, 1864—10 p. m.
(Via Paducah.)

Admiral S. P. LEE,
Comdg. Miss. Squadron, Flag-ship Fairy, Chickasaw, Ala.:

Your two telegrams have been received.* We have been pressing the enemy as hard as the condition of the roads would permit, and have succeeded in taking some few prisoners, probably 500 or 600, since the enemy crossed Duck River. From the best information I have at this time, Hood's losses since he invaded the State of Tennessee sum up as follows: 6 general officers killed, 6 wounded, and 1 taken prisoner at Franklin, 13 in all, and about 6,000 men killed, wounded, and taken prisoners at same battle. On the 8th [7th] instant, at Murfreesborough, he had one general officer wounded, about 70 men killed, and 207 taken prisoners, and losing 2 pieces of artillery. In the two battles of the 15th and 16th instant, before Nashville, he had 1 lieutenant-general severely wounded, 1 major-general and 3 brigadier-generals, with 4,462 officers and men, made prisoners, besides losing 53 pieces of artillery and over 3,000 stand of small-arms. During his retreat we have captured 15 more guns and from 1,500 to 2,000 prisoners, and a large number of small-arms have been picked up by the way. Citizens report here that he passed this place with his army completely disorganized, except the rear guard, composed of about 5,000 men. He destroyed a considerable quantity of ammunition at this place, besides abandoning an ammunition train of 15 or 20 wagons about a mile beyond. Your efficient co-operation on the Tennessee River has contributed largely to the demoralization of Hood's army. General A. J. Smith, commanding Detachment Army of the Tennessee, will probably reach Clifton by Sunday next (January 1, 1865), where transports are expected to meet him, to take his command to Eastport. Please afford him every assistance in your power in effecting a secure lodgment at Eastport, and as I consider the Cumberland River now entirely safe, I will be obliged to you if you will have a strong force kept on the Tennessee, to keep open the navigation on that river. In concluding this dispatch, it gives me great pleasure to tender to you, your officers, and men my hearty thanks for your cordial co-operation during the operations of the past thirty days.

GEO. H. THOMAS,
Major-General, U. S. Volunteers, Commanding.

HEADQUARTERS DEPARTMENT OF THE CUMBERLAND,
Pulaski, December 29, 1864.

Maj. Gen. M. C. MEIGS,
Washington:

The necessary orders have been given for Colonel Wright, with one division of construction corps, to go to Savannah.

GEO. H. THOMAS,
Major-General.

(Same to Brig. Gen. D. C. McCallum.)

---

* Probably 27th and 28th, pp. 371, 389.

HEADQUARTERS DEPARTMENT OF THE CUMBERLAND,
Pulaski, December 29, 1864.
Col. J. G. PARKHURST,
Provost-Marshal-General, Nashville:

Can you inform me how many prisoners of war have been sent in up to this date, including those from battle of Franklin and those enrolled in Franklin, Spring Hill, and Columbia hospitals?

WM. D. WHIPPLE,
Assistant Adjutant-General.

NASHVILLE, *December 29, 1864.*
Brigadier-General WHIPPLE,
Chief of Staff:

Whole number of prisoners of war reported to this office to date, including battle of Franklin: Commissioned officers, 557; enlisted men, 7,873; making a total of 8,430 prisoners—this does not include the prisoners captured at Murfreesborough. There are probably 250 prisoners there, but I have no official report relative to them, though I have called for it. I will give you rank of officers in written report. Good many deserters are coming in.

J. G. PARKHURST,
Colonel and Provost-Marshal-General.

NASHVILLE, *December 29, 1864.*
Brigadier-General WHIPPLE,
Chief of Staff:

It is desirable to reopen the Northwestern railroad for some distance at least, for the purpose of securing the wood already contracted and partly paid for on the line of it. The expense, it is reported, will not be great for the length we want reopened, and I respectfully ask permission of the major-general commanding to reopen what I thus find necessary.

J. L. DONALDSON,
Chief Quartermaster, Department of the Cumberland.

HEADQUARTERS DEPARTMENT OF THE CUMBERLAND,
Pulaski, December 29, 1864.
Brig. Gen. J. L. DONALDSON,
Nashville:

You are authorized to reopen the Northwestern railroad, as you propose.

WM. D. WHIPPLE,
Assistant Adjutant-General.

NASHVILLE, *December 29, 1864.*
General W. D. WHIPPLE,
Chief of Staff:

Please say to the major-general commanding I have over a week past been engaged in repairing roads and bridges about Nashville, particularly on the Franklin and Murfreesborough pikes, and will soon have necessary work completed.

J. L. DONALDSON,
Bvt. Brig. Gen. and Chief Quartermaster, Dept. of the Cumberland.

HEADQUARTERS DEPARTMENT OF THE CUMBERLAND,
Pulaski, December 29, 1864.

Brig. Gen. J. L. DONALDSON,
Nashville:

Yours reporting repairs on turnpikes received; also, yours reporting quantity of clothing at Chattanooga. It does not seem necessary to send more to that place, except upon requisitions; so says the general.

WM. D. WHIPPLE,
Assistant Adjutant-General, &c.

NASHVILLE, *December 29, 1864.*

Maj. Gen. G. H. THOMAS:

I estimate that the railroad will be completed in ninety days. There is a large force engaged on the work, and everything is being done that can be done to push forward the work. Mr. Eicholtz is doing his best.

W. W. WRIGHT,
Colonel and Chief Engineer.

HEADQUARTERS DEPARTMENT OF THE CUMBERLAND,
Pulaski, December 29, 1864.

Col. W. W. WRIGHT,
Carter's Creek:

Where will the written order reach you? Do not leave until you have given all necessary instructions for the completion of this part of the railroad.

WM. D. WHIPPLE,
Brigadier-General.

NASHVILLE, *December 29, 1864.*

General W. D. WHIPPLE:

Written orders will reach me here, care of Mr. Wentz. It will take two or three days to put everything in proper shape for the rapid prosecution of the work after I leave.

W. W. WRIGHT,
Chief Engineer.

HEADQUARTERS DEPARTMENT OF THE CUMBERLAND,
Pulaski, Tenn., December 29, 1864.

OFFICER IN CHARGE OF PONTOON BRIDGE AT COLUMBIA:

Take up pontoon bridges at Columbia and take them to Elkton, and there put them down across Elk River. Do this as soon as trestle bridge over Duck River is done. Answer.

WM. D. WHIPPLE,
Chief of Staff.

NASHVILLE, TENN., *December 29, 1864—7 p. m.*

Maj. THOMAS T. ECKERT:

General A. J. Smith marched to-day from Pulaski for Eastport. I am ordered to prepare to build telegraph west from Decatur on Memphis and Charleston Railroad. Rivers getting low very fast. Railroad to Chattanooga and Louisville in order again. Roads drying up, so movements may work.

J. C. VAN DUZER,
Captain, &c.

[DECEMBER 29, 1864.—For General Orders, No. 169, Department of the Cumberland, announcing close of campaign, &c., see Part I, p. 50.]

HEADQUARTERS FOURTH ARMY CORPS,
Lexington, Ala., December 29, 1864—3 p. m.

Brigadier-General WHIPPLE:

GENERAL: Your dispatch of the 28th instant, directing the artillery with me to be sent back and to retain the infantry where it was, was not received until 12 m. to-day. The commanding general was fully advised at 8.30 p. m. December 27 that I would move forward the next morning to support the cavalry, as General Wilson had determined to continue the pursuit farther toward the Tennessee River. As we have advanced one day's march farther south, it occurs to me that the commanding general may not possibly desire the artillery now with me to be sent back to Pulaski. I will, therefore, retain it here until to-morrow morning, by which time, I trust, I will receive an answer to my dispatch of yesterday evening, announcing that the enemy had crossed the river, and asking for orders. If I receive no further orders by to-morrow morning I will send the artillery back to Pulaski and retain the infantry here to await further instructions. In the meantime I will try to get up my supply train from the rear to subsist the infantry.

I repeat that I should be glad to have full instructions from the commanding general for our further movements.

Very respectfully, your obedient servant,

TH. J. WOOD,
Brigadier-General, Commanding.

HEADQUARTERS FOURTH ARMY CORPS,
Lexington, Ala., December 29, 1864—5.30 p. m.

Brigadier-General WHIPPLE,
Chief of Staff:

Your dispatch dated December 28, in reply to my dispatches dated 7 and 8.30 p. m. December 27, has just been received. I desire to state to the commanding general that my note in regard to the forage was by no means intended as a complaint, but was simply designed to communicate a fact and inform him of my situation in regard to forage and other supplies, as I was instructed to do. I have no reason to suppose that the chief quartermaster has been at all remiss in getting up forage from the railroad terminus, for the truth is that it has required the entire capacity of my train to get up subsistence for the men for so long a distance. I did not suppose that it was the general's intention to cross the Tennessee River immediately, but supposing that it would be done at an early day with a view to further operations, it occurred to me that I might facilitate this by our taking post on the river at the earliest possible moment at which subsistence could be obtained there. Hence the reference in my note of 12.30 p. m. of the 27th instant in regard to taking post on the Tennessee River for ulterior objects beyond the present pursuit.

Very respectfully, your obedient servant,

TH. J. WOOD,
Brigadier-General of Volunteers, Commanding.

HEADQUARTERS DEPARTMENT OF THE CUMBERLAND,
Pulaski, Tenn., December 29, 1864.

Brig. Gen. THOMAS J. WOOD, *Commanding Fourth Army Corps:*

GENERAL: The last of the rebel army having been driven across the Tennessee River, the major-general commanding directs that the pursuit cease, and that you march with your corps to Huntsville, Athens, and vicinity, and there go into camp for the winter, and attend to the reorganization of your command and fitting it generally for an early spring campaign. The Cavalry Corps, with the exception of one division, has also been ordered to Huntsville for the winter Should you be unable, from badness of the roads or scarcity of forage, to march directly to Huntsville, you can come back to this point and march from here, or you can march direct and send your wagons by this route, via Elkton. The major-general commanding the forces in the field tenders his thanks to yourself, your officers and men, for the vigor, bravery, and willing endurance of privations and hardships displayed by your command during this long and toilsome pursuit of the retreating rebel army.

Very respectfully, your obedient servant,

WM. D. WHIPPLE,
Brigadier-General and Chief of Staff.

CIRCULAR.]   HEADQUARTERS FOURTH ARMY CORPS,
Lexington, Tenn., December 29, 1864—12.15 p. m.

Division commanders will at once send back their pioneer brigades to the rear, to repair the road or cut out new roads from this point to a point eight miles back toward Pulaski. Each brigade must be under command of a competent and efficient field officer. General Elliott's pioneer brigade will repair the road from this point to a point three miles back; General Kimball's pioneer brigade will repair the road from a point three miles in the rear to a point five miles and a half in the rear; and General Beatty's pioneer brigade will repair the rest of the road to a point eight miles in the rear.

By order of Brigadier-General Wood:

J. S. FULLERTON,
Assistant Adjutant-General.

HEADQUARTERS DEPARTMENT OF THE CUMBERLAND,
Pulaski, December 29, 1864.

Maj. Gen. J. M. SCHOFIELD, *Comdg. Army of the Ohio, Columbia:*

Can you inform me how many flags were captured by Twenty-third Corps, including battle of Franklin and since?

WM. D. WHIPPLE,
Assistant Adjutant-General.

COLUMBIA, *December 29, 1864.*

Brigadier-General WHIPPLE:

The Twenty-third Corps captured twenty-one flags at Franklin, nine of which I now have; none have been captured since. What news from the front ?

J. M. SCHOFIELD,
Major-General.

HEADQUARTERS DEPARTMENT OF THE CUMBERLAND,
Pulaski, December 29, 1864.
Maj. Gen. J. M. SCHOFIELD,
Commanding Army of the Ohio, Columbia:

GENERAL: The rebel army having been entirely driven across the Tennessee River, the major-general commanding the forces in the field has ordered the pursuit to cease, and directs that you march with the Twenty-third Army Corps to Dalton, via this place and Huntsville, or Fayetteville, encamping the corps at Dalton for the winter, and making such reorganization and refitting as is necessary and preparing generally for an early spring campaign. You will load your wagons at Spring Hill with sufficient to take you to Huntsville, where you can replenish.

Very respectfully, your obedient servant,

WM. D. WHIPPLE,
Brigadier-General and Chief of Staff.

HEADQUARTERS ARMY OF THE OHIO,
Columbia, Tenn., December 29, 1864.
COMDG. OFFICER PONTOON TRAIN, ARMY OF THE CUMBERLAND:

SIR: The commanding general directs that you have the pontoon bridges taken up as soon as the trestle bridge is completed, and also that you provide your command with rations and forage, and be prepared to move as soon as you receive orders from Major-General Thomas.

Very respectfully,

J. A. CAMPBELL,
Major and Assistant Adjutant-General.

SPECIAL ⎫ HEADQUARTERS ARMY OF THE OHIO,
FIELD ORDERS, ⎬ *In the Field, Columbia, Tenn.,*
No. 191. ⎭ *December 29, 1864.*
*   *   *   *   *   *   *

VIII. The First Division, Twenty-third Army Corps, is hereby reorganized as follows, under command of Brig. Gen. Thomas H. Ruger, the old First and Second Brigades, broken up by paragraph IX, Special Field Orders, No. 79, current series, from these headquarters, being restored:

First Brigade: One hundred and twentieth Indiana, Captain Barcus; One hundred and twenty-fourth Indiana, Colonel Orr; One hundred and twenty-eighth Indiana, Colonel Packard.

Second Brigade: One hundred and twenty-third Indiana, Colonel McQuiston; One hundred and twenty-ninth Indiana, Colonel Zollinger; One hundred and thirtieth Indiana, Colonel Parrish.

Third Brigade: Eighth Minnesota Volunteer Infantry, One hundred and seventy-fourth Ohio Volunteer Infantry, One hundred and seventy-eighth Ohio Volunteer Infantry.

These brigades will be increased by the addition of new regiments, as soon as the latter shall join the corps. The One hundred and eighty-first Ohio Volunteer Infantry is assigned to the Second Division, Twenty-third Army Corps, Major-General Couch commanding. The One hundred and seventy-seventh Ohio and One hundred and fortieth Indiana Volunteer Infantry are assigned to the Third Division, Twenty-third Army Corps, Brigadier-General Cox commanding. These regiments will be assigned to brigades by the division commanders. This order will take effect immediately. Regimental commanders will accordingly report without delay to the generals commanding divisions to which they are assigned.

*   *   *   *   *   *   *

By command of Major-General Schofield:

J. A. CAMPBELL,
Major and Assistant Adjutant-General.

HEADQUARTERS DETACHMENT ARMY OF THE TENNESSEE,
In Camp, Nine Miles from Pulaski, Tenn., December 29, 1864.

Maj. Gen. G. H. THOMAS,
Commanding Forces in the Field:

The head of my column encamps to-night nine miles from Pulaski, awaiting my supply train. Hereafter, if the roads continue as good as we have found them, we will make from twelve to fifteen miles per day with the supply train. Learning that Hood has gone to Corinth, I will take all necessary precaution until the cavalry arrive, and then feel them. If sufficiently re-enforced, shall I attack? I will be prudent, you may depend.

Very respectfully,

A. J. SMITH,
Major-General.

HEADQUARTERS DETACHMENT ARMY OF THE TENNESSEE,
Camp in the Field, December 29, 1864.

Brig. Gen. J. McARTHUR,
Commanding First Division:

GENERAL: The major-general commanding directs that you have your division in readiness and move to-morrow morning, December 30, at 9 a. m., in rear of Third Division, and taking charge of train.

I am, very respectfully, your obedient servant,

J. HOUGH,
Major and Assistant Adjutant-General.

HEADQUARTERS DETACHMENT ARMY OF THE TENNESSEE,
Camp in the Field, Tenn., December 29, 1864.

Brig. Gen. K. GARRARD, *Commanding Second Division:*

The major-general commanding directs that you have your division in readiness and move to-morrow morning, December 30, at 7 o'clock, the Second Division in front.

I am, very respectfully, your obedient servant,
J. HOUGH,
Major and Assistant Adjutant-General.

(Same to Col. J. B. Moore, commanding Third Division.)

HEADQUARTERS DEPARTMENT OF THE CUMBERLAND,
Pulaski, Tenn., December 29, 1864.

Maj. Gen. J. H. WILSON,
Comdg. Cavalry Corps, Military Division of the Mississippi:

GENERAL: Your communication of 4 p. m. yesterday has been received. The rebel army having been entirely driven across the Tennessee River, the major-general commanding directs that you send one division of your corps to Eastport, to remain during the winter. To this point, Maj. Gen. A. J. Smith, with his command, has also been ordered. You will proceed with the remainder of your force to Huntsville, Ala., put it in camp for the winter, and attend to its reorganization, equipment, remounting, and making general preparation for an early spring campaign. To this point and Athens, the Fourth Army Corps, Maj. Gen. T. J. Wood commanding, has also been ordered. The region of country about Huntsville is very productive, and from it you will be able to draw much forage for your command this winter. Should the division sent to Eastport be unable, from bad roads or scarcity of forage, to march directly across the country, it can be sent back to this place and across, by way of Lawrenceburg and Waynesborough, to Clifton, at the latter of which places forage can be sent it by steamers. This is the road taken by General Smith. Should the main portion of your corps be unable, for similar reasons, to march directly to Huntsville from where you now are, it can also return to this place and march down the roads leading parallel to the railroad, or you can march across the country and send your wagons by this route. The major-general commanding tenders his thanks to yourself, officers, and men for the vigor, skill, bravery, and endurance displayed by your corps in this long and toilsome pursuit of the retreating rebel army.

Very respectfully, your obedient servant,
WM. D. WHIPPLE,
Brigadier-General and Chief of Staff.

HDQRS. CAVALRY CORPS, MIL. DIV. OF THE MISSISSIPPI,
Blue Water Creek, Ala., December 29, 1864—3 p. m.

Brig. Gen. WILLIAM D. WHIPPLE,
Chief of Staff, Department of the Cumberland:

I have the honor to acknowledge the receipt of dispatches from headquarters Department of the Cumberland, December 28, 12 m. and 1 p. m. Croxton's brigade, 1,500 strong, marched from Taylor's Springs this morning, via Gravelly Springs, to Waterloo, with instructions to cross the river at that place, and, if possible, destroy the Bear Creek bridge. No orders to the contrary having been received, Croxton was sent, his command being in better condition to accomplish the work than Hatch's, the latter having not to exceed 3,000 men out of the 4,500 with which he started from Nashville. Without orders to the contrary I will not substitute Hatch, as by so doing one entire day will be lost. Croxton will reach Waterloo to-morrow afternoon. I will send to the bend of Elk River to see about the cattle reported to be there, but I doubt the accuracy of the information. I have had a party on Elk River and all along the Tennessee between there and Bainbridge; they report nothing of the kind. A prisoner who was with the cattle herd of the rebels escaped from them day before yesterday, within six miles of Bainbridge.

In my dispatch to you yesterday from this place I urged the necessity of the major-general commanding designating some point for the concentration of the cavalry, for the purpose of feeding, recuperating, and completing its organization; with a view to this I suggested Waterloo or Tuscumbia. If this meets with the approbation of General Thomas, I can move the whole command to that place, now that I am so near Florence, much more easily than I can return to Pulaski, and if the transports have reached Florence rations can be sooner obtained. I shall, in that case, be ready to co-operate with any movements of General Smith, or any other portion of the army south of the Tennessee, with my whole cavalry force. In this connection I would respectfully suggest that it is too weak to allow of any detachments. I doubt if forage can be obtained at Pulaski, and I am quite sure it cannot be on the road from there here. To get there will therefore require a large detour and take some time. I have sent a staff officer to Florence to open communications with the gun-boats and obtain information of supplies. Having found some corn in this valley I shall remain here until I receive a reply to my dispatch of last night.

All the information I can gather indicates an intention of the enemy to go to Corinth. Should he do so Florence or Eastport, rather than Decatur, it seems to me, will be points in our future lines of operations, and therefore more suitable as halting places for bad weather and the necessary reorganization. Should my impression be correct I would greatly prefer to go to either at once than to trail back on the road to Pulaski, with the ultimate prospect of returning by the same route to make a new campaign against the enemy. The Tennessee River will afford us a safe supply line as long as we want it, one that can't be cut by guerrillas and doesn't preclude the use of the railroad from Nashville via Decatur. Should Smith's movement and the one from Memphis compel the rebels to go to Columbus or Selma, a base below the Mussel Shoals would still be very well situated. From conversations with General Wood, I think these views are concurred in by him. Please let me know the wishes of the major-general commanding as soon as possible; and in the meantime I will endeavor to subsist the command in this country, so that if he decides in favor of Tuscumbia or Eastport no time will be lost in moving in that direction. In doing this I rest easy that no military reasons require the presence of the cavalry in the vicinity of Pulaski, and that therefore I shall not displease General Thomas in delaying to return there.

I have the honor to be, general, very respectfully, your obedient servant,

J. H. WILSON,
Brevet Major-General.

P. S.—It is very doubtful that the trains of rations from Pulaski can reach us here; I have two days' yet on hand.

J. H. W.

HDQRS. CAVALRY CORPS, MIL. DIV. OF THE MISSISSIPPI,
Bull's Mills, December 29, 1864—7 a. m.

Brig. Gen. THOMAS J. WOOD,
Commanding Fourth Corps:

GENERAL: Your note of 8 p. m. 28th was received during the night. I agree with you that, unless General Thomas intends to leave us on the Tennessee, there is no occasion for us to go farther. I have ordered Croxton one day's march on the road to Waterloo, in anticipation of instructions to destroy the Bear Creek bridge, and have sent a staff officer to Florence to communicate with the gun-boats and transports. I shall remain in camp here to-day, where we can obtain forage, and where dispatches may reach us from General Thomas.

Very respectfully, your obedient servant,

J. H. WILSON,
Brevet Major-General.

___

HEADQUARTERS FOURTH ARMY CORPS,
Lexington, December 29, 1864—11 a. m.

Major-General WILSON,
Commanding Cavalry:

GENERAL: I will also remain here to await instructions from General Thomas. Please communicate to me the result of your staff officers' visit to Florence.

TH. J. WOOD,
Brigadier-General, Commanding.

___

HEADQUARTERS FOURTH ARMY CORPS,
Lexington, Ala., December 29, 1864.

Brevet Major-General WILSON,
Commanding:

GENERAL: I have reliable information that there is a party of guerrillas, about 100 in number, near Wise's Mill, on Blue Water, about six miles west of here. This party is splendidly mounted and well armed. It is reported that they have some of the best horses in the country. There are two men who live near the mill who will act as guides to the locality of this band. Mr. Wise, at the mill, will tell where these two men can be found and who they are. I will send an infantry force out to the same place in the morning.

Very respectfully, your obedient servant,

TH. J. WOOD,
Brigadier-General, Commanding.

___

HEADQUARTERS FOURTH ARMY CORPS,
Lexington, Ala., December 29, 1864.

Brevet Major-General WILSON:

GENERAL: I have read your dispatch of this p. m. to General Whipple with great satisfaction, and fully concur in your views. I have suggested similar views to General Thomas, though not so pointedly as you have done in your dispatch. If we are to take post on the Tennessee River at all, it certainly will be a great waste of material and labor to return to Pulaski, and then make the march to the Tennessee River, provided always that arrangements have been made to have subsistence meet us upon our arrival. My instructions from General Thomas, received to-day, are similar to those sent to you. One of his directions is to send back all of the artillery to Pulaski, where it can get forage; but as this direction was given upon the supposition that it would reach me at Pinhook Town, and supposing that a day's march nearer the river might make a change in General Thomas' view in regard to the disposition of the artillery, I have written to him that I will not start it back before to-morrow. I expect in the meantime to receive other instructions from him.

Very respectfully, your obedient servant,

TH. J. WOOD,
Brigadier-General, Commanding.

HDQRS. CAVALRY CORPS, MIL. DIV. OF THE MISSISSIPPI,
Bull's Mills, December 29, 1864.
Brigadier-General CROXTON,
Commanding Brigade:

GENERAL: The brevet major-general directs that you move with your command one day's march on the road to Waterloo, reporting your progress from time to time and any information you can get.

Very respectfully, your obedient servant,

A. J. ALEXANDER,
Lieutenant-Colonel and Acting Chief of Staff.

HDQRS. FIRST BRIGADE, FIRST CAVALRY DIVISION,
December 29, 1864—10 a. m.
Colonel ALEXANDER,
Chief of Staff:

COLONEL: My command is moving; will go, via Huff's Ford, Squire Wilson's, and the Bumpass road, toward Gravelly Springs. Expect to halt to-night on Cypress Creek. Desire to know what shall be done in regard to the squadron at Rogersville; also to say, for the information of the general commanding, that rations ran out night before last, and the detail sent back to obtain more have not been heard from. Will leave a company at Bull's Mills to bring them up.

Respectfully, your obedient servant,

JOHN T. CROXTON,
Brigadier-General of Volunteers.

HDQRS. CAVALRY CORPS, MIL. DIV. OF THE MISSISSIPPI,
Bull's Mills, December 29, 1864.
Brigadier-General HATCH,
Comdg. Fifth Division, Cavalry Corps, Mil. Div. of the Miss.:

GENERAL: You will recall the detachment under Colonel Spalding, leaving a sufficient number of men with Captain Kneeland to enable him to discharge the duties intrusted him by the major-general commanding.

By command of Brevet Major-General Wilson:

E. B. BEAUMONT,
Major and Assistant Adjutant-General.

Special Orders, ⎰ Headquarters Defenses Nashville
       ⎱   and Chattanooga Railroad,
   No. 7.   ⎱   *Tullahoma, December 29, 1864.*

The Twenty-ninth Regiment Michigan Volunteer Infantry is hereby assigned to the Third Brigade of this command, and will make all reports to Col. W. Krzyzanowski, commanding brigade, headquarters at Stevenson.

By command of Major-General Milroy:

JNO. O. CRAVENS,
Assistant Adjutant-General.

Headquarters Post of Murfreesborough,
Murfreesborough, Tenn., December 29, 1864.

Lieutenant-Colonel Blackburn:

I send you a true copy of a dispatch that General Van Cleve has just received from General Milroy:

> One hundred and fifty rebel cavalry crossed the railroad, half a mile north of this place, at 12 o'clock last night. They captured two of the Fifth Tennessee Cavalry, who got away after crossing the railroad, and said there was a rebel general with them who had been cut off from Hood and was trying to go through East Tennessee. Can't you send word to Blackburn to cut them off about McMinnville. The Fifth are all out west.

You will carry out the above instructions.

By command of Brigadier-General Van Cleve:

H. H. SHEETS,
Acting Assistant Adjutant-General.

Headquarters Department of the Cumberland,
Pulaski, December 29, 1864—10 p. m.

Maj. Gen. James B. Steedman,
      Decatur:

(To be forwarded.)

Your dispatch of 28th is received. I wish you to keep me promptly informed of all your movements. The troops will commence moving to-morrow toward Decatur, and will soon be in supporting distance if it should become necessary.

GEO. H. THOMAS,
Major-General, U. S. Volunteers, Commanding.

Headquarters Department of the Cumberland,
Pulaski, December 29, 1864—10.50 p. m. (Received 12 m. 31st.)

Brig. Gen. R. S. Granger,
      Decatur, Ala.:

Your telegram of 10.50 p. m. [28th] this date is received. You will set to work and reorganize your post, and make arrangements to receive and take care of a large amount of stores at Decatur.

GEO. H. THOMAS,
Major-General, U. S. Volunteers, Commanding.

BRIDGEPORT, *December 29, 1864.*

Captain FORD,
    Acting Assistant Adjutant-General:

I have 150 men at work on the fortifications of this place. I am in want of an engineer officer to take charge of the works; can one be ordered?

A. O. MILLINGTON,
Colonel, Commanding Post.

HDQRS. FIRST BRIG., FOURTH DIV., 23D ARMY CORPS,
    Cumberland Gap, December 29, 1864.

Brigadier-General AMMEN,
    Commanding Fourth Division, Twenty-third Army Corps:

GENERAL: I have the honor to acknowledge the receipt of your communication of 21st instant. I have complied with the instructions therein contained, relative to prisoners, by sending to Knoxville under guard all those here. Some of them, Isaac Litteral and Jesse F. McNeal, are notoriously bad characters, having been engaged in deliberate murders, not only of Union soldiers but of women; they certainly do not merit the treatment they are receiving, *i. e.*, that of Confederate prisoners, but death. I had counted largely upon the effect their execution here would have produced; an effect, I feel sure, which would have been most happy. McNeal has always been a most desperate character, and many witnesses to his fiendish acts are now living at this place. Unfortunately the matter of killing them without making prisoners of them is next to impossible, as they have to be tracked to their holes before they can be seen at all. Had I been allowed to have shot them before the command it would have struck a terror to the hearts of such of their fraternity as still are at large as would have compelled them to the pursuance of a different course. I am well satisfied, however, with the fact of having since my arrival at this post captured two and shot one of the Litterals, and of having captured a number of other men of whom the whole of this section of the country stands in awe. I send to-morrow, with the other prisoners, a man, by name William Ball, who has, it seems, been before arrested and on various charges, but who has, through some means or other, been allowed to go at liberty. My reason for arresting him was that an escaped prisoner of ours, while standing near a fire up Virginia Valley, surrounded by Litteral's party, saw Mr. Ball ride up and state that one of our wagon trains was to leave the Gap next day, and advised them to be on the watch so as to capture it. This I got from the man himself who heard the conversation. Mr. Ball has, I think, some claim against the United States, now before the courts in Knoxville, for damages, which claim, if paid, will be so much money out of the pocket of the Government put into that of an arrant rebel. I trust he may be dealt with as the nature of his case merits.

Two men, Franklin Woodward and Cimuel M. Chappell, of Thirty-fourth Kentucky Infantry, who were tried by court-martial, were taken away by Colonel Dillard before their sentences were promulgated. They are sentenced as explained in General Orders, Nos. 27 and 28, November 29 and December 14, from headquarters District of East Tennessee. They are now with their regiments. Another man whom I send, and by name John Stevens, Battery M, First Michigan Light Artillery, is sentenced as explained in General Orders, No. 27, above referred to. I also forward five men, Samuel Brown, Albert Cherry, George Yeager, Henry E. Nugent, and Ephraim A. Hill, sent in here yesterday by Lieutenant Jennings, who states that Captain Hazen delivered them to him as men who had straggled from their commands and allowed themselves to be taken prisoners. They had in their possession an informal document, purporting to be a parole, which they were made to sign; they had torn it, but I have the fragments. These men belong to the Second Ohio Heavy Artillery.

Captain Beebe, of the Second Tennessee Battery, now at this post, sent me the inclosed communication relative to an officer of his battery, who was commissioned at Nashville and sent to him when his battery had its complement of officers. This practice on the part of the authorities at Nashville of mustering officers, independently of any recommendations of the commanding officers of the different Tennessee organizations, is not confined to the case cited, but appears to be of rather frequent occurrence. Meritorious non-commissioned officers and privates are thus prevented receiving the promotion due them for long and faithful service. As applies to this command, the action of authorities generally appears to me to be at least unjust. The command seems to be regarded as an independent affair, capable of self-government and entitled to but little, if any, consideration. Applications of different kinds are noticed, or not, just as the fancy strikes the recipient of them, and thus both officers and men feel justly dispirited and disheartened. For instance, applications for discharge to enable men to accept commissions have been delayed for months, and telegrams on the subject from me receive no more notice than if they had not been sent. If there was any possible way of reminding them that this was a garrison, and an important one, too, I should like to employ it, though I suppose we must bear it as best we may. It is, in my opinion, very necessary that a board for the examination of officers be appointed immediately. The ignorance of many of the officers is truly deplorable, many, yes the majority of them, being apparently ignorant of the fact that there is any such thing as grammar, or that an officer ought to be able to write. In the Second Tennessee Battery, the officers, Captain Beebe tells me, are of no service to him at all, whereas he has a sergeant who is a valuable man, but who cannot be mustered till a vacancy exists. There are many cases, too, which require the action of court-martial; some of the charges are herewith forwarded. The case of Lieutenant Jennings, of my regiment, is one of the most aggravated I know of. I have also a number of men who should be dealt with severely. Cannot a court-martial be ordered to convene here at once?

We are beginning to get forage in again rapidly. Yesterday our train brought in about 1,200 bushels. I want very much to have here a cavalry force which can be used from time to time in scouting about the country.

The permission I received to buy horses has been improved, and now I want saddles and bridles. If I could get about 150 sets of horse equipments I should have a cavalry command ready to throw out at a moment's notice, and I feel sure the result would be advantageous. Will you please order a commissary of musters to be sent here immediately. Many of the officers need to be mustered, and, as pay-day is approaching, the sooner it be done the better. I hope we shall have the pleasure of extending the hospitalities of the Gap before long, and that we can show you some improvements. I obtained permission to send Major Bahney off to Camps Chase and Douglas, and in a few weeks I hope to be able to show at least 700 or 800 men. I telegraphed relative to the issue of arms to citizens. This I, of course, wanted to do by having the loyal men organized into companies for three months—say, to have them regularly mustered and paid by the United States. We could then have a guard in the counties of Hancock, Claiborne, and Lee, which would materially assist in putting down the guerrillas who raise so much trouble about here. I have seen many of these good, loyal men, and they are all anxiously bent upon fighting the rebel bands referred to, asking only for arms, &c. I can learn nothing of the rebel cavalry of which you telegraphed me, though I will look out for them.

I am, general, very respectfully, your obedient servant,

WM. C. BARTLETT,
Lieutenant-Colonel.

SPECIAL ORDERS,)   HDQRS. MILITARY DIST. OF KENTUCKY,
No. 103.   )   *Lexington, Ky., December 29, 1864.*

* * * * * * *

III. Brig. Gen. E. H. Hobson is hereby assigned to the command of the First Division of this military district, vice Brig. Gen. N. C. McLean, relieved by orders from headquarters Army of the Ohio.

* * * * * * *

By command of Brevet Major-General Burbridge:

J. BATES DICKSON,
Captain and Assistant Adjutant-General.

IRONTON, OHIO, *December 29, 1864.*

Capt. J. BATES DICKSON,
Assistant Adjutant-General:

I am on my way to Cincinnati. I telegraphed you from Catlettsburg last night. Expedition a success. Breckinridge defeated and his department broken up. Our loss slight. General and command on way home. Please have rations at Mount Sterling by January 1. All in good spirits. I sent the general's report to Secretary of War, which was my errand from Catlettsburg.

H. P. BARDEN,
Lieutenant and Aide-de-Camp.

HDQRS. MILITARY DIVISION OF WEST MISSISSIPPI,
New Orleans, La., December 29, 1864.

Maj. Gen. H. W. HALLECK,
Chief of Staff, &c., Washington, D. C.:

The operations of Generals Dana and Davidson from the Mississippi, and General Granger from the Gulf, besides the actual damage inflicted upon the enemy, have induced the Governors of Alabama and Mississippi to call out the militia of their States under the belief that Selma and Mobile were both threatened. The operations in which General Dana is now engaged will probably terminate by the end of this month, and General Granger, as soon as he has secured the large amount of naval stores captured by him, will withdraw his troops from Pascagoula. The militia of Alabama will probably return to their homes still more indisposed than they now are to respond to another call. If General Thomas should now be able to carry out the intentions of General Sherman in relation to Selma, I can be of material service by operations from the river and Gulf. I will communicate with General Thomas and be prepared to aid him as far as possible.

E. R. S. CANBY,
Major-General, Commanding.

MEMPHIS, TENN., *December 29, 1864—7 a. m.*

Maj. Gen. H. W. HALLECK,
Chief of Staff:

A few of my colored cavalry who were captured escaped from Corinth on Monday. They report my cavalry as having struck the road, only five miles south of Corinth, on Sunday. Five miles of road had been destroyed, and they were proceeding south, continuing their Yankee repairs to the road.

N. J. T. DANA,
Major-General, Commanding.

MEMPHIS, *December 29, 1864.*

Maj. Gen. GEORGE H. THOMAS:

The Mobile and Ohio road is cut by my cavalry below Corinth. The cavalry is ordered to go to Cahaba, if possible.

N. J. T. DANA.

HEADQUARTERS DEPARTMENT OF THE MISSISSIPPI,
Memphis, Tenn., December 29, 1864.

Lieut. Col. C. T. CHRISTENSEN,
Assistant Adjutant-General, Mil. Div. of West Mississippi:

I have just received a telegram from Collierville, stating that some of my colored cavalry soldiers who had been captured had escaped from Corinth on Monday morning, and they state that my cavalry had struck the Mobile and Ohio road only five miles below Corinth, had destroyed five miles of track, and were still at work. My orders were, in case of a heavy garrison being at Corinth, to give it a wide berth; and from the boldness exhibited by beginning their work so near that place, I infer that we have a gratifying prospect of success.

Respectfully,

N. J. T. DANA,
Major-General.

WASHINGTON, *December 30, 1864—1.30 p. m.*

Lieutenant-General GRANT,
City Point, Va.:

I think, from the tone of General Thomas' telegram of last night, that there is very little hope of his doing much further injury to Hood's army by pursuing it. You will perceive that he is disposed to postpone further operations till spring. This seems to me entirely wrong. In our present financial condition we cannot afford this delay. I therefore respectfully suggest whether Schofield and A. J. Smith, with, say, 20,000 men, should not be sent by water to Pascagoula to assist Canby in taking Mobile, and then using it as a base against Selma and Montgomery. This would prevent any of Hood's force from being sent against Sherman, and the capture of Selma would be almost as disastrous to the enemy as that of Atlanta. Thomas, with the remainder of his forces, could certainly maintain the line of the Tennessee to Chattanooga. If Schofield should be sent, the two departments (Tennessee and Kentucky) should be united under Thomas. If Thomas was as active as Sherman, I would say march directly from Decatur to Talladega, Montgomery, and Selma, living upon the country, and anticipating Hood, should he move by Meridian. But I think Thomas entirely too slow to live on the country. He, however, will make the best possible defense. It is said that the rebels have a very large amount of supplies at Selma and Montgomery. If these can be captured and the railroads destroyed, their Western armies cannot get ammunition and ordnance stores. The reason for not suggesting that Schofield move from Vicksburg by Meridian is that the country is mostly stripped of supplies, and at this season very difficult of passage, while that from Mobile is less swampy, and, moreover, the operating army could be supplied by steamers on the Alabama River.

H. W. HALLECK,
Major-General and Chief of Staff.

CITY POINT, VA., December 30, 1864.

Major-General HALLECK,
    Chief of Staff of the Army:

I have no idea of keeping idle troops in any place, but before taking troops away from Thomas it will be advisable to see whether Hood halts his army at Corinth. I do not think he will, but think he is much more likely to be thrown in front of Sherman; if so, it will be just where we want him to go. Let Thomas collect all troops not essential to hold his communications at Eastport, if he chooses a part of them at Tuscumbia, and be in readiness for their removal where they can be used.

U. S. GRANT,
Lieutenant-General.

HEADQUARTERS DEPARTMENT OF THE CUMBERLAND,
Pulaski, Tenn., December 30, 1864—9 p. m.

Maj. Gen. H. W. HALLECK,
    Washington, D. C.:

I have heard from General Wilson up to 3 p. m. of yesterday, and, as his information leads him to think the enemy will endeavor probably to reach Corinth, I have ordered the cavalry to move to Eastport, to operate against the Mobile and Ohio Railroad, should Hood really halt at Corinth. Croxton, it is expected, would reach Eastport this afternoon, and I hope to hear in a few days that he has succeeded in destroying Bear Creek bridge. I have heard nothing of General Steedman since the morning of the 28th instant. Trains have commenced running on the Nashville and Chattanooga Railroad regularly to-day.

GEO. H. THOMAS,
Major-General, U. S. Volunteers, Commanding.

HEADQUARTERS DEPARTMENT OF THE CUMBERLAND,
Pulaski, December 30, 1864—9 p. m.

Brig. Gen. ANDREW JOHNSON,
Military Governor of Tennessee, Nashville:

As the enemy is now entirely driven out of the State of Tennessee, I would respectfully suggest that immediate measures be taken for the reorganization of the civil government of the State, as it is desirable, if possible, to place as large a force of the army beyond the borders of the State and as close to the enemy as we can, and I should be very happy * to be assured that I could leave the State in the hands of the citizens. All should certainly now feel that the establishment of rebel authority in the State of Tennessee is hopeless, and their own interests should induce them to return to their allegiance to the United States, and restore peace to their State without any further quibbling.

GEO. H. THOMAS,
Major-General, U. S. Volunteers, Commanding.

HEADQUARTERS DEPARTMENT OF THE CUMBERLAND,
Pulaski, December 30, 1864.

Brigadier-General WEBSTER,
Chief of Staff, Nashville:

The major-general commanding directs me to inquire whether you have received his dispatch for Major-General Sherman.

Respectfully,

ROBT. H. RAMSEY,
Assistant Adjutant-General.

HEADQUARTERS DEPARTMENT OF THE CUMBERLAND,
Pulaski, December 30, 1864.

Brig. Gen. J. L. DONALDSON,
Nashville:

Send to Eastport 8,000 pairs of shoes, 16,000 pairs stockings, and a due proportion of other articles of clothing for the use of troops going there.

WM. D. WHIPPLE,
Assistant Adjutant-General.

HEADQUARTERS DEPARTMENT OF THE CUMBERLAND,
Pulaski, December 30, 1864.

Brig. Gen. J. L. DONALDSON,
Nashville:

Send forage to Eastport for the whole of General Wilson's cavalry. There will be no necessity for sending forage to Huntsville, except for the teams of Twenty-third Corps to take en route to Chattanooga and a little to start the Fourth Corps teams.

WM. D. WHIPPLE,
Brigadier-General.

NASHVILLE, *December 30, 1864.*

Major-General THOMAS:

The pontoon train of sixty boats will be ready to-morrow afternoon.

JAS. R. WILLETT,
Major, &c.

HEADQUARTERS DEPARTMENT OF THE CUMBERLAND,
Pulaski, Tenn., December 30, 1864.

Maj. J. R. WILLETT,
Engineers, Nashville:

Yours about the pontoons received. Keep them in Nashville until further orders.

WM. D. WHIPPLE,
Assistant Adjutant-General.

COLUMBIA, *December 30, 1864.*

Brigadier-General WHIPPLE,
Chief of Staff:

Everything is ready for pontoon train to start as soon as trestle bridge is ready.

A. G. TASSIN,
Lieutenant-Colonel, Commanding Pontoon Train.

HEADQUARTERS DEPARTMENT OF THE CUMBERLAND,
Pulaski, Tenn., December 30, 1864.

Lieut. Col. A. G. TASSIN,
Commanding Pontoon Train, Columbia:

Take up one bridge and start it for Elkton, and have party to take up the other as soon as trestle bridge is finished.

WM. D. WHIPPLE,
Chief of Staff.

COLUMBIA, *December 30, 1864.*

General W. D. WHIPPLE,
Chief of Staff:

Started train with one bridge; will reach Pulaski to-morrow night, Elkton next day. I expect stores and material from Nashville to be here to-morrow; trestle bridge will be then completed.

A. G. TASSIN,
Lieutenant-Colonel, Commanding Pontoon Train.

HEADQUARTERS FOURTH ARMY CORPS,
Lexington, Ala., December 30, 1864—2.15 p. m.

Brigadier-General WHIPPLE,
Chief of Staff:

GENERAL: In accordance with instructions just received from Major-General Thomas, we will march from here for Huntsville and Athens to-morrow morning, starting at daylight and taking the most direct routes. I will take all the artillery and wagons that I have with me here along; by doing so I will avoid a long detour by the way of Pulaski, by which route we will have more dirt road and only fifteen miles of turnpike. I will promptly report the disposition I make of my troops in posting them at Huntsville, Athens, and vicinity. I have ordered my chief quartermaster, Colonel Hayes, to bring up, via Athens, all of my trains in the rear, and if any orders are necessary to assist him I would be much obliged to the commanding general if he will give such. It was necessary for me to leave part of my artillery at Pulaski and to use the horses of the same in helping those through now with my command. As soon as we arrive at our destination I will send back my chief of artillery with horses for this artillery.

Very respectfully, your obedient servant,

TH. J. WOOD,
Brigadier-General, Commanding.

HEADQUARTERS FOURTH CORPS,
Lexington, Ala., December 30, 1864.

Brig. Gen. W. D. WHIPPLE,
Assistant Adjutant-General and Chief of Staff:

GENERAL: Every particle of information, however derived, in regard to the condition of Hood's army attests the fact of its complete and perfect demoralization. I have made many inquiries of citizens living on the road we have followed in the pursuit, and have received universally the same answers, namely, that one-half of the retreating troops are unarmed, and that everything like organization is gone. Two escaped prisoners came in yesterday, and their statements fully corroborate the information derived from other sources. One of these prisoners marched, or rather went with Lee's corps (for he says there was nothing like marching among them), to within two miles of the Tennessee River, where he escaped. He says that not more than one-half of the corps was armed; that there was no organization at all in the corps; that he saw nothing like a company, regiment, or brigade, and that the men moved in squads, varying from six or eight to fifteen or twenty, and that these squads moved and halted at their own choice. He further states that from Pulaski to the point at which he escaped the rebels had nothing to eat but parched corn. The other escaped prisoner marched with Cheatham's corps, from Pulaski toward the Tennessee River, by the old military road. He says that out of the whole corps only about a regiment could be got to guard about 140 prisoners, and that the remainder of the corps marched in small squads, these squads moving as they chose. He says that in these squads he saw occasionally a musket or two to shoot cattle, &c., along the line of retreat. Both of these men speak of the destitute condition of the rebels in regard to clothing; they are without blankets, a great number without shoes, and all imperfectly clad. I feel confident that Hood has not taken across the Tennessee River more than half the men he brought across it; that not more than one-half of those taken out are armed; that he lost three-fourths of his artillery; and that, for rout, demoralization, even disintegration, the condition of his command is without a parallel in this war. I am also confident that his command cannot be reorganized for service for some weeks, perhaps not before spring. At present, so far as Hood's command is concerned (and I know of no other force in that event that could oppose us), the whole country from the Tennessee River to Mobile is open to us. Should we not then improve the present opportunity for bringing Alabama—at present the best State for supplies the rebels have—under our control? I firmly believe we can, within the next few weeks, without much opposition, bring the whole State under our control.

The Tennessee River affords us a good line of communication, vastly superior to railroads. Let us establish a depot at or near the head of navigation, and, within the next ten days or two weeks, place in it, by numerous transports, abundant supplies of every kind, as we could, for the troops to be engaged in the expedition. I estimate that 40,000 infantry, 10,000 cavalry, and one battery of artillery to each division of infantry, with a reserve battery to each corps, would be an ample force for the expedition. To raise this force the whole country behind us, if necessary, might be almost entirely stripped of troops, as I am confident our offensive movement would abundantly protect the rear. I am quite sure, after the late experience of Hood in Tennessee, that the rebels would not attempt to check us by a counter invasion. Starting with a force composed as above, and taking with us hard bread, sugar, coffee, and a double allowance of salt for forty days, one day's salt meat in seven, a small supply of forage for exigencies, driving as many cattle with us as could conveniently be done, and trusting to the country to supply the remainder of the meat ration and forage for daily use, I have no hesitation in saying that we could eat our oysters in Mobile in forty days from the date of departure. The distance to be traversed is about 300 miles, and an average of less than ten miles a day would carry us through in the period assigned. I would suggest the route from Tuscumbia, via Tuscaloosa, Selma, giving a side wipe as we passed at Montgomery and destroying the State archives, to Mobile. I have made many inquiries touching the country adjacent to the proposed route, and am sure the roads through it are entirely practicable for military purposes, and that it teems with supplies such as a military force would require. The troops would engage in such an expedition with great ardor, and would cheerfully endure all its hardships and privations. If successful, and of this I have not the shadow of doubt, this movement would deal a blow unequaled in injurious consequences to the hated rebellion.

I respectfully submit these views to the consideration of the commanding general of the forces, and request you will lay this communication before him at your earliest convenience. I do not here touch upon the co-operation we might—in fact, should—receive from our troops on the Mississippi and in the Department of the Gulf, as such co-operation would be matter of arrangement with other commanders; but it seems to me that the arrangements for such co-operation could be made by the time the main force would be ready to move from its base on the Tennessee River.

In conclusion, I would say to the commanding general that the success of the expedition would be greatly facilitated by moving before Hood's command could be reorganized, armed, and equipped, and before a force could be concentrated from other quarters to oppose us.

I am, very respectfully, your obedient servant,

TH. J. WOOD,
Brigadier-General, Commanding.

HEADQUARTERS FOURTH ARMY CORPS,
Lexington, Ala., December 30, 1864—4.30 p. m.

Orders of the day for the Fourth Army Corps for to-morrow, December 31, 1864:

The enemy having been driven over the Tennessee River, by direction of Major-General Thomas, the pursuit will be continued no longer. This corps will move to Huntsville and Athens, Ala., and will start on the march at 7 a. m. to-morrow, the 31st instant—Brigadier-General Beatty's division will lead, followed by General Kimball's division, then General Elliott's. Each division will constitute a column by itself, preceded by all of its pioneers, formed into a brigade, who will repair roads and make crossings over the creeks, and followed by all the trains of the same, with one battery of artillery. One regiment will be detailed from each division to accompany its train and artillery, to assist them in moving. The supply train that arrived to-day will not be sent back to Pulaski, as directed this morning, but will accompany the troops in the march, each division taking its own section. The reserve battery will follow the trains of the rear division of the corps; the artillery ammunition will follow the reserve battery; and the hospital train will follow the artillery ammunition; until otherwise ordered, corps headquarters will follow the ammunition train of the leading division during the march. The leading division of the corps will be conducted by a staff officer from these headquarters.

By order of Brigadier-General Wood:

J. S. FULLERTON,
Assistant Adjutant-General.

HEADQUARTERS FOURTH ARMY CORPS,
Lexington, Ala., December 30, 1864—11.30 a. m.

Brigadier-General KIMBALL:

GENERAL: Three days' rations for your division are just arriving at this point; they must be issued to last five days. As soon as your train is unloaded send it to the rear, and direct the officer having charge of it to report to Surgeon Patterson, One hundred and twenty-fourth Ohio, at Pulaski, for the purpose of transporting sick and wounded from that point to the terminus of the railroad.

By order of Brigadier-General Wood:

J. S. FULLERTON,
Lieut. Col., Assistant Adjutant-General and Chief of Staff.

(Same to Generals Elliott and Beatty.)

HEADQUARTERS FOURTH ARMY CORPS,
Lexington, Ala., December 30, 1864—3 p. m.

Brigadier-General KIMBALL:

The general commanding directs that you send your ordnance officer to Pulaski at once, to turn over the ammunition now in your train at that place, and then to bring forward the empty train to your command, at Huntsville (via Athens) or Athens, whichever place it may be at. The object in turning over the ammunition is to lighten the train; more can be procured via railroad, if it is needed.

Very respectfully, your obedient servant,

J. S. FULLERTON,
Lieutenant-Colonel and Assistant Adjutant-General.

(Same to Generals Elliott and Beatty.)

HEADQUARTERS FOURTH ARMY CORPS,
Lexington, Ala., December 30, 1864—8.30 a. m.

Brigadier-General BEATTY,
Commanding Third Division:

The general commanding directs me to inform you that about six miles west of this place, on the Blue Water, there is a band of guerrillas, about 100 strong. The general is informed that they harbor near a mill owned by a Mr. Wise, who will give information as to the exact place. The party is said to have about 100 of the finest horses in the country. The general commanding also directs me to say that if you will send a regiment to disperse them and capture the horses he will give one horse to each mounted officer and one to each company, to be used as a pack-animal.

I am, general, very respectfully, your obedient servant,
[GEO. SHAFFER,]
Aide-de-Camp.

HEADQUARTERS ARMY OF THE OHIO,
Columbia, Tenn., December 30, 1864.

Brig. Gen. WILLIAM D. WHIPPLE,
Chief of Staff, Dept. of the Cumberland, Pulaski, Tenn.:

GENERAL: I have the honor to acknowledge the receipt of your communication of December 29, conveying the orders of the major-general commanding for me to move the Twenty-third Corps to Dalton, via Pulaski and Huntsville, or Fayetteville. The corps will be ready to move as soon as its trains return from Spring Hill with supplies. I respectfully request the permission of the major-general commanding to visit my department headquarters at Louisville, to attend to department business, while the corps is making the march. I can then join it by rail. Major-General Couch will remain in command of the corps.

I am, general, very respectfully, your obedient servant,
J. M. SCHOFIELD,
Major-General.

COLUMBIA, TENN., *December 30, 1864.*

Maj. Gen. GEORGE H. THOMAS,
Pulaski:

Seven of my new regiments have joined, and I have asked General Rousseau to send the other two which have been assigned. I have to make two consolidations and provide for the muster out of three regiments in a short time. Therefore, I need four more regiments at least to complete my organization. I would be glad if they could be assigned soon, so that I may get my corps in shape as soon as possible.
J. M. SCHOFIELD,
Major-General.

HEADQUARTERS DEPARTMENT OF THE CUMBERLAND,
Pulaski, December 30, 1864—9 p. m.

Maj. Gen. JOHN M. SCHOFIELD,
Commanding Twenty-third Army Corps, Columbia:

Your telegram of to-day making application for four additional regiments is received. So many regiments on duty in the District of Tennessee have been mustered out of service within the last month that I shall be unable to give you any more for the present. Should additional regiments be sent to me, I will assign the four that arrive first to you.

GEO. H. THOMAS,
Major-General, U. S. Volunteers, Commanding.

NASHVILLE, TENN., *December 30, 1864.*

Maj. Gen. J. M. SCHOFIELD,
   Columbia :

The One hundred and eightieth Ohio is at Elk River and Decherd, on the Chattanooga road. A regiment goes down to relieve it to-morrow. It already has orders to join you when relieved. The Twenty-eighth Michigan is here and will be sent as soon as I can get it off.

L. H. ROUSSEAU,
Major-General.

GENERAL ORDERS,   HDQRS. 3D BRIG., 1ST DIV., 23D A. C.,
 No. 1.   *Camp near Columbia, Tenn., December 30, 1864.*

I. The undersigned hereby assumes command of the Third Brigade, First Division, Twenty-third Army Corps.

II. The following officers are hereby designated to act as staff officers on the staff of the brigade commander. They will report for duty as soon as relieved from present duty, and they will be respected and obeyed accordingly: Lieut. and Adjt. George W. Butterfield, Eighth Minnesota Volunteers, acting assistant adjutant-general; Capt. George Atkinson, Eighth Minnesota Volunteer Infantry, acting assistant inspector-general; Lieut. Henry C. Lillibridge, regimental quartermaster One hundred and seventy-eighth Ohio Volunteer Infantry, brigade quartermaster; Lieut. E. E. Hughson, Eighth Minnesota Volunteer Infantry, brigade commissary; Lieut. David M. Howe, One hundred and seventy-fourth Ohio Volunteer Infantry, aide-de-camp; Lieut. Thomas J. Weatherby, One hundred and seventy-fourth Ohio Volunteer Infantry, provost-marshal; F. W. Morrison, surgeon One hundred and seventy-fourth Ohio Volunteer Infantry, acting brigade surgeon.

M. T. THOMAS,
Colonel Eighth Minnesota Volunteer Infantry, Comdg. Brigade.

HEADQUARTERS DETACHMENT ARMY OF THE TENNESSEE,
 Two Miles West of Lawrenceburg, Tenn., December 30, 1864.

Maj. Gen. G. H. THOMAS,
   Commanding U. S. Forces in the Field :

The head of my column is four miles west of Lawrenceburg, and all trains will be closed up to this point to-night. Fourteen miles from here we strike the pike, which the good people of the county call a "dirt pike," no better, probably, than the road we have had to-day. We have been detained two hours to-day in crossing Shoal Creek (twice)— quite a stream. I will get forward as rapidly as possible. Regret the rain of to-day.

  Very respectfully,

A. J. SMITH,
Major-General.

HEADQUARTERS DEPARTMENT OF THE CUMBERLAND,
Pulaski, Tenn., December 30, 1864.

Maj. Gen. A. J. SMITH,
  Commanding Detachment Army of the Tennessee:

GENERAL: Yours from your camp of last night has been received. If you learn that Hood has gone to Corinth, and when re-enforced by the cavalry you think it advisable to attack him, the major-general commanding consents to your doing so.

Very respectfully, your obedient servant,

WM. D. WHIPPLE,
Brigadier-General and Chief of Staff.

HEADQUARTERS DETACHMENT ARMY OF THE TENNESSEE,
Camp in the Field, Tenn., December 30, 1864.

Brig. Gen. J. McARTHUR,
  Commanding First Division,
Brig. Gen. K. GARRARD,
  Commanding Second Division,
Col. J. B. MOORE,
  Commanding Third Division:

The major-general commanding directs that each of you have your divisions in readiness to move to-morrow morning, December 31. The order of march will be as follows: Third Division at 7 a. m.; First Division at 8 a. m.; Second Division at 9 a. m.

I am, very respectfully, your obedient servant,

J. HOUGH,
Major and Assistant Adjutant-General.

HDQRS. CAVALRY CORPS, MIL. DIV. OF THE MISSISSIPPI,
Blue Water Creek, Ala., December 30, 1864—9 a. m.

Brig. Gen. THOMAS J. WOOD,
  Commanding Fourth Corps:

Your dispatch of last night is just received. I have ordered Hammond's brigade up Blue Water, for the purpose of getting him nearer forage, and will tell him to look for the guerrillas. Captain Kneeland, of my staff, returned from Florence last night. The gun-boats had been there on Sunday and captured two batteries, but when the captain arrived they had gone back down the stream. The citizens reported that a party of troops from Memphis had torn up the railroad for fifteen miles, beginning seven miles beyond Tuscumbia and going toward Corinth. Couldn't learn who they were, cavalry or infantry, or where they had gone. The rebels had all disappeared from the opposite side of the river. They had made several strong lines of works at Bainbridge. Captain Kneeland could learn nothing of supplies.

Very respectfully, your obedient servant,

J. H. WILSON,
Brevet Major-General.

HEADQUARTERS FOURTH ARMY CORPS,
Lexington, Ala., December 30, 1864—1 p. m.

Major-General WILSON:

GENERAL: I have just received orders from General Thomas to move my command to Huntsville, Athens, and vicinity, where it will remain, to reorganize and prepare for the spring campaign. We will start at early daylight to-morrow morning and march via Athens, taking the best roads that we can find.

Very respectfully, your obedient servant,
TH. J. WOOD,
Brigadier-General, Commanding.

HDQRS. CAVALRY CORPS, MIL. DIV. OF THE MISSISSIPPI,
Bull's Mills, December 30, 1864.

Brig. Gen. T. J. WOOD,
Commanding Fourth Army Corps:

GENERAL: I am directed to inform you that this command is ordered to move to Huntsville, Ala., and the general commanding desires to know by what means you propose crossing Elk River. He has sent a party to ascertain the condition of the river at Rogersville, and will inform you of the result early to-morrow.

I have the honor to be, very respectfully, your obedient servant,
A. J. ALEXANDER,
Lieutenant-Colonel and Acting Chief of Staff.

HEADQUARTERS FOURTH ARMY CORPS,
Lexington, Ala., December 30, 1864—6.30 p. m.

Major-General WILSON:

GENERAL: In reply to your note of this afternoon, I have the honor to inform you that I expect to cross Elk River at Buck Island Ford; that I expect to construct a bridge, by the use of empty wagons and light trestles, for infantry, provided the stream is not too deep to prevent fording for horses and wagons; if it is, it will be necessary to build a trestle bridge across. I will be glad to hear the result of your reconnaissance to Rogersville as early as you can communicate the same.

Very respectfully, your obedient servant,
TH. J. WOOD,
Brigadier-General, Commanding.

HDQRS. CAVALRY CORPS, MIL. DIV. OF THE MISSISSPPI,
In the Field, December 30, 1864.

Brigadier-General WHIPPLE,
Chief of Staff:

GENERAL: The campaign against the rebels having terminated, probably, in spite of the disorganized condition of troops, particularly of the cavalry, the lateness of the season precluding the idea of further gen-

eral operations south of the Tennessee, I avail myself of this opportunity to present for the consideration of the major-general commanding the following suggestions:

In order that the cavalry forces under his command may render
the service they should in the operations of the next year, it is essential that this Cavalry Corps be concentrated at some point as nearly
as may be on the line of future operations, where full supplies of
forage, arms, equipments, and horses may be furnished with facility,
and where the necessary measures for discipline and reorganization
may be carried into effect. A camp on the north bank of Tennessee,
somewhere near Waterloo or Gravelly Springs or Colbert's Shoals,
would seem to possess all the requisites just enumerated—accessible
at all times by steam-boats, supplies of all kinds could be brought,
at slight expense, from Cairo, Louisville, or Saint Louis; the men could
be kept together, and away from the demoralizing influence of large
towns; ample shelter for men and horses could be erected, without
cost to the Government. At the same time, the position occupied would
serve as a continual menace to the enemy in Northern Alabama, Mississippi, or West Tennessee; enable us to effectually hold the line of the
Tennessee River, covering the railroad communications north of it; and
allow us to forage on all the valley adjacent on both sides of the river.
If necessary, one division might be left at Pulaski or Huntsville.

To perfect the organization already begun and to prepare the Cavalry
Corps for efficient field service, from seventy to ninety days in camp
will be necessary. Without the opportunity this length of time will
afford the cavalry service must continue to be unprofitable, unsatisfactory, and without its proper influence on future military operations.
The same care and attention should be given to the formation of cavalry that is bestowed upon infantry. The men of the command now
scattered on detached duty, at various places from Memphis to Nashville, should be returned to their regiments, every man should be
mounted on a good horse and supplied with the best arm the country
can afford, and all care taken to elevate the standard of the mounted
service. The Spencer carbine is undoubtedly the best fire-arm ever
put into the hands of the soldier, and should be supplied for the entire
command; all other arms are bad by comparison, and we have no
troops poor enough to use any other when the best can be obtained. It
is believed that troops armed with the Spencer carbine, or rifle, consume
less ammunition than any other, and are more effective. A detailed
report will be made on this question as soon as the proper data can be
gathered; in the meantime, enough is known to leave me no hesitation
in making the application for at least 10,000 Spencer carbines—15,000,
if they can be obtained. I shall require also about 10,000 horses, in
addition to those already in the hands of the troops, to complete the
remount; detailed and specific requisitions will be furnished the proper
department as soon as they can be made out. McCook's and Long's
divisions are the only ones completely equipped for field service—in the
aggregate, about 10,000 men for duty; McCook's division will, however, require about 3,000 Spencer carbines. Hatch's division (the Fifth)
will require 1,500 horses and 2,500 Spencer carbines; has at present
2,500 serviceable horses. Johnson's division (Sixth) will require 3,000
horses and 3,000 Spencer carbines; has about 900 serviceable horses.
Knipe's division (Seventh) will require 3,000 horses and about 4,000
Spencer carbines; has at present about 1,000 serviceable horses. The
requirements of Upton's division (the Fourth) are not known, though,
by the time the corps is encamped, they will be fully ascertained. If

the supply departments are active in filling these requisitions, the Cavalry Corps can take the field in the spring with 25,000 men fully armed, mounted, and equipped.

In order that the great destruction of cavalry horses may be hereafter prevented, I have ordered stabling prepared at cavalry depot at Edgefield for the shelter of at least 7,500 horses, and, in conjunction with Capt. John Green, special inspector of cavalry, have taken steps to have sent back all horses broken down by overwork and absence of proper forage before they are completely ruined. I hope, by the time active spring operations begin, to recuperate between 5,000 and 8,000 horses, and I believe that by these means 50 per cent. of the horses, which, under the old system [sic], will be returned to duty and perform better service than fresh horses. It has been the custom heretofore, as soon as a cavalry horse became reduced in flesh, sick, or sore backed, to abandon him or put him out to graze. Those that were abandoned, as well as those that were put out to graze, have generally found their way into the rebel service, or, at least, were entirely lost to ours. Humanity, as well as economy, requires that similar measures be taken, to restore the jaded and broken-down horses, to those adopted for sick and wounded men.

The Quartermaster's Department has complained at various times of the enormous consumption of horses by our cavalry forces, and, in order to reduce the expenses incident thereto, it has been proposed to reduce the number of cavalry regiments. The remedy cannot, however, be applied in that way, without crippling very seriously the military operations. Horses have been killed rather by overwork and injudicious use of cavalry, than by any disposition on the part of the men and officers to neglect them. The cavalry force, instead of being too great, has always been too small to perform the work required of it; it should therefore be increased, rather than diminished. This may be done by completing its organizations, by concentrating it, and by instituting the proper measures for securing its efficiency, and by actually augmenting its numbers. It is utterly impossible to find horses capable of performing continuous labor, and it is just as impossible to find men who can bestow upon their horses every care and attention during campaigns as long as those which characterize the war in this country. The work must be decreased, or the numbers, as well as the capacity of men and horses, required to perform it must be increased; for only in one way or the other can the necessary time be obtained to give the men and horses the rest absolutely required and to enforce the proper rules of discipline. It is a fact, now generally admitted, that our cavalry has hitherto been overworked, generally deprived of the proper opportunity for drill and discipline, and frequently misused entirely; but, fortunately for the good of the public service, its proper use is now well understood, while the necessity for its complete organization in masses is becoming, as the war progresses, a matter of the first importance. With 25,000 men, properly organized, armed, and mounted, I hazard nothing in saying, more may be done by the army in the next campaign than ever before; the rebels can be thrown entirely on the defensive; their cavalry can be broken up, or driven behind their infantry for shelter; their railroads and other lines of communication can be cut; and, finally, their infantry can be attacked and harassed beyond endurance.

The performance of the Cavalry Corps during the recent campaign was such as to leave no doubt of its capacity. With complete organization and armament, which can only be obtained by the means herein indicated, it may be depended upon to perform any service that can justly be required of it.

Trusting that the suggestions may meet with the approval of the major-general commanding, and be carried into effect without delay,

I am, general, very respectfully. your obedient servant,

J. H. WILSON,
Brevet Major-General.

HDQRS. CAVALRY CORPS, MIL. DIV. OF THE MISSISSIPPI,
Blue Water, Ala., December 30, 1864.

Brig. Gen. WILLIAM D. WHIPPLE,
Chief of Staff, Department of the Cumberland:

GENERAL: I send herewith, by Captain Carling, a communication in regard to the cavalry.* It is prepared at the instance of General Thomas, and for his action. I have abstained from going into the details of organization, they being sufficiently indicated by the measures already inaugurated. Captain Carling can explain my views upon any point not sufficiently elucidated in the letter referred to. I wish to say, however, the steps I urge in the final reorganization are not intended to be taken till all operations incidental to the completion of the present campaign are finished; but that you may understand our present condition, I send you the following report of effective strength: 270 officers; 5,561 enlisted men, mounted and effective for line of battle; 70 dismounted; 473 unserviceable horses. Of these, Croxton has 1,500; Hatch, 2,500; the balance nearly equally divided between Harrison and Hammond. Should the general determine to order us to a point on the Tennessee, please authorize Captain Carling to take the necessary measures to furnish supplies at the point indicated. Captain Kneeland, of my staff, returned last night from Florence. The gun-boats had been there, and were reported by the citizens to have captured two batteries. Captain Kneeland was informed by the citizens that a detachment of our troops from Memphis had torn up the railroad for fifteen miles, beginning seven miles beyond Tuscumbia and going toward Bear Creek. He could not learn who they were, whether they were cavalry or infantry, or where they had gone. The gun-boats had gone. The river was falling quite rapidly. The enemy had disappeared from the opposite bank. Colonel Spalding reports that they made several elaborate lines of works covering their bridge at Bainbridge. All the information I can gather still points to an intention, very generally expressed, to go to Corinth and winter there.

Very respectfully, your obedient servant,

J. H. WILSON,
Brevet Major-General.

HDQRS. CAVALRY CORPS, MIL. DIV. OF THE MISSISSIPPI,
Blue Water Creek, Ala., December 30, 1864—6 p. m.

Brig. Gen. W. D. WHIPPLE,
Chief of Staff:

I shall march with my command, via Rogersville, to Huntsville, early to-morrow morning, in pursuance of the orders received this afternoon. Huntsville, in some respects, will be better than Eastport. Major

---
* See next, *ante.*

Beaumont, of my staff, will explain fully all the dispositions I have made in carrying out my orders. If you think Croxton's brigade sufficient force for Eastport, I will order McCook to Huntsville; otherwise, he may proceed to the former place as soon as he refits and rests. His chase after Lyon seems to have been a very hard one, and not very satisfactory. I propose to march via Rogersville, though the command will probably be delayed in crossing Elk River; from all I can learn, it is not now fordable. Where will army headquarters be?

Very respectfully, your obedient servant,

J. H. WILSON,
Brevet Major-General.

HDQRS. CAVALRY CORPS, MIL. DIV. OF THE MISSISSIPPI,
Blue Water Creek, Ala., December 30, 1864—5.30 a. m.

Brig. Gen. J. T. CROXTON,
Commanding First Brigade, First Division:

GENERAL: You will continue your march to the vicinity of Eastport, subsisting your command as you can till supplies arrive there for you. After you arrive there you may organize an expedition for the destruction of the Bear Creek bridge and for obtaining precise information of the ultimate destination of Hood's army. General A. J. Smith's corps is marching for Eastport, also charged with the execution of certain duties, under instructions from General Thomas. You will co-operate with and act under orders of General Smith in any movement he may make to the south of the river. I expect orders for the whole corps to move in that direction to-morrow or next day; but in case I should move in the other direction, detailed instructions will be sent for your future guidance.

J. H. WILSON,
Brevet Major-General.

HDQRS. CAVALRY CORPS, MIL. DIV. OF THE MISSISSIPPI,
Bull's Mills, December 30, 1864—4 p. m.

Brigadier-General CROXTON,
Commanding Brigade:

GENERAL: Upon arriving at Eastport you will select a permanent camp for your brigade, construct stabling for your horses and shelter for your men, and immediately institute measures for putting your brigade in condition for active operations next spring. The balance of your division will probably join you within the next two weeks, and will remain in the neighborhood of Eastport till next spring, unless relieved by some other division of the Cavalry Corps. Until General McCook arrives you will co-operate with General Smith, who is ordered to Eastport, but will take no orders from him except while operating against the enemy in campaigning south of the river. You will make your camp away from the infantry; immediately set to work and gather in all the forage within your reach; make requisition for horses, arms, and equipments necessary for your command. As soon as you have ascertained exactly your wants send a staff officer to the headquarters of the corps, at Huntsville, and authority will be given to him to obtain the necessary supplies and do such other things as may be necessary.

In the meantime, forage and rations will be sent you from Nashville by steamers, your transportation train to join you via Lawrenceburg and Waynesborough. Report to me as often as possible and such information as may be obtained from time to time of the movements and intentions of the enemy.

Very respectfully, you obedient servant,

J. H. WILSON,
Brevet Major-General, Commanding.

P. S.—Your dispatch of this date in relation to Spencer carbines is received. Every effort will be made to obtain them for your entire command. The major-general commanding bears willing testimony to the fact that no portion of the command deserves them more than your gallant brigade.

Respectfully, your obedient servant,

A. J. ALEXANDER,
Lieutenant-Colonel and Acting Chief of Staff.

HDQRS. CAVALRY CORPS, MIL. DIV. OF THE MISSISSIPPI,
Bull's Mills, December 30, 1864.

Brigadier-General HATCH,
Commanding Fifth Division:

GENERAL: The brevet major-general commanding desires you to send an intelligent officer, with ten men, to Rogersville, to ascertain whether the Elk River is fordable or not. Direct him to report before daylight to-morrow morning. He must ascertain all particulars about the river and true, reliable information.

Very respectfully, your obedient servant,

A. J. ALEXANDER,
Lieutenant-Colonel and Acting Chief of Staff.

HDQRS. CAVALRY CORPS, MIL. DIV. OF THE MISSISSIPPI,
Bull's Mills, December 30, 1864.

Brigadier-General HAMMOND,
Commanding Brigade:

GENERAL: The brevet major-general commanding desires you to move your command to the camp spoken of by you yesterday. A band of about 100 guerrillas are reported in the vicinity of Wise's Mill, well armed and equipped. He desires you to look after them. Mr. Wise will give you information concerning their whereabouts.

Very respectfully, your obedient servant,

A. J. ALEXANDER,
Lieutenant-Colonel and Acting Chief of Staff.

HDQRS. FIRST BRIG., SEVENTH DIV., CAVALRY CORPS,
Cowpen Creek, December 30, 1864.

Maj. E. B. BEAUMONT,
Assistant Adjutant-General:

MAJOR: I have a good camp about six miles and a half from you, over a very good road, over which a man can canter the whole way. I have no report from the foragers yet, but as Colonel Coon's command was encamped near here during some time I don't believe I will fare as well as I expected; but I will get enough, no doubt. I am preparing to bake bread at Bough's Mills, four miles from here, and at Cowpen Mills, two miles off. They will forage, grind, and bake corn-cakes, by detail, all night, and as long as the general leaves me here, until I get four days' rations of bread. I am on the Savannah road, sixty miles (good road) to Columbia, thirty-eight to Pulaski, to Eastport forty-two—all good roads. I can travel a country that has not been foraged in, to either Waterloo or Eastport, sixteen miles and a half from Florence. Four miles farther on, along Shoal Creek, I can get more forage, the people say, but General Wilson said about six miles, and I stopped accordingly, and am in reach of both mills. I hear of small guerrilla parties, and will watch for them. The band spoken of by General Wilson is somewhere up near Lexington. One foraging party has returned, and reports abundant forage only one mile and a half distant; also, a band of six in rebel uniform.

Very respectfully, your obedient servant,

J. H. HAMMOND,
Brevet Brigadier-General.

P. S.—I will send you some chickens to-morrow morning.

HDQRS. CAVALRY CORPS, MIL. DIV. OF THE MISSISSIPPI,
Bull's Mills, December 30, 1864.

Brigadier-General HAMMOND,
Commanding Brigade:

GENERAL: The Cavalry Corps has been ordered to Huntsville. Move your command at daylight to-morrow morning, by the most direct route, to Rogersville, and take the Huntsville road.

By command of Brevet Major-General Wilson:

E. B. BEAUMONT,
Major and Assistant Adjutant-General.

NASHVILLE, *December 30, 1864.*

Brigadier-General WHIPPLE:

I greatly desire to be in Kentucky for a few days on business of vital importance to me. Can I go?

LOVELL H. ROUSSEAU,
Major-General.

HEADQUARTERS DEPARTMENT OF THE CUMBERLAND,
Pulaski, December 30, 1864.

Maj. Gen. L. H. ROUSSEAU,
Nashville:

You are authorized to go to Kentucky, as you desire.

WM. D. WHIPPLE,
Assistant Adjutant-General.

COLUMBIA, TENN., *December 30, 1864.*

Major-General ROUSSEAU,
        Nashville, Tenn.:

Will you please order the Twenty-eighth Michigan and One hundred and eightieth Ohio Volunteer Infantry, which have been assigned to my command, to report to me here without delay, and oblige,

J. M. SCHOFIELD,
Major-General.

COLUMBIA, TENN., *December 30, 1864.*

Major-General ROUSSEAU,
        Nashville, Tenn.:

Please detain at Nashville, for the present, the Twenty-eighth Michigan, One hundred and eightieth Ohio, and any other regiments which may be under orders to join my command.

J. M. SCHOFIELD,
Major-General.

NASHVILLE, TENN., *December 30, 1864.*

Brigadier-General WHIPPLE:

General Schofield telegraphs from Columbia to have the Twenty-eighth Michigan sent to him at that place. Shall it be done?

LOVELL H. ROUSSEAU,
Major-General.

HEADQUARTERS DEPARTMENT OF THE CUMBERLAND,
December 30, 1864.

Major-General ROUSSEAU,
        Nashville:

Has the Twenty-eighth Michigan got over the measles? If so, send it to General Schofield.

WM. D. WHIPPLE,
Assistant Adjutant-General.

NASHVILLE, *December 30, 1864.*

Brigadier-General WHIPPLE:

The Forty-seventh and Forty-eighth Missouri have been sent by rail as far as Spring Hill, but can get no farther. They have not a wagon or ambulance, and can get no assistance at Columbia, on account of scarcity of teams there. The quartermaster's department here cannot issue wagons before next Wednesday. The quartermaster and a detachment of each regiment have been detained here, to draw the teams and take them forward ladened with supplies when issued. I would send the regiments forward without teams, if they could supply themselves after reaching Pulaski. The Forty-fifth Missouri is now acting guard to the advance depot.

LOVELL H. ROUSSEAU,
Major-General.

SPECIAL ORDERS, ⎰ HEADQUARTERS DISTRICT OF TENNESSEE,
    No. 301.   ⎱   *Nashville, Tenn., December 30, 1864.*

I. The Forty-third Wisconsin Volunteer Infantry will proceed without delay by rail to Elk River and Decherd, on the Nashville and Chattanooga Railroad—four companies, under the command of the major, to take post at Elk River, and the remainder of the regiment to Decherd. Reports and returns will be made to Maj. Gen. R. H. Milroy, commanding that road.

*   *   *   *   *   *   *

By command of Major-General Rousseau:

B. H. POLK,
Major and Assistant Adjutant-General.

SPECIAL ORDERS, ⎰ HEADQUARTERS DEFENSES NASHVILLE
                              AND CHATTANOOGA RAILROAD,
    No. 7½.   ⎱   *Tullahoma, December 30, 1864.*

I. The Forty-third Regiment Wisconsin Volunteer Infantry will relieve all garrisons held by the One hundred and eightieth Regiment Ohio Volunteer Infantry, beginning at Block-house No. 17 (second south of Tullahoma), and running from thence south on the Nashville and Chattanooga Railroad. At Elk River bridge, the lieutenant-colonel and four companies will be stationed, placing of this force twenty men and an officer in each block-house there; the remainder of the four companies will occupy the fort. The headquarters and the reserve of the regiment will be at Decherd.

II.a As soon as the One hundred and eightieth Regiment Ohio Volunteer Infantry is relieved by the Forty-third Regiment Wisconsin Infantry, Col. Willard Warner will proceed with his regiment to Pulaski, marching via Fayetteville. Colonel Warner will join the Twenty-third Army Corps (to which he has been assigned) at Pulaski, or wherever it may be.

By command of Major-General Milroy:

JNO. O. CRAVENS,
Assistant Adjutant-General.

HDQRS. DEFENSES NASHVILLE AND CHATTANOOGA R. R.,
                              Tullahoma, December 30, 1864.

Col. WILLARD WARNER,
    180th Ohio Volunteer Infantry:

COLONEL: The Forty-third Regiment Wisconsin Volunteer Infantry has been ordered to relieve your regiment at Decherd and all other points. As soon as this has been done you will proceed with your command to Pulaski, marching via Fayetteville. You will take five days' rations, if practicable, carrying three days' in haversacks. When you reach Pulaski you will report to the commanding officer of the Twenty-third Army Corps, to which you have been assigned. If the Twenty-third Corps is not there, you will proceed to join it wherever it may be. You will take the mounted men of the two companies of the Fifth Tennessee Cavalry, under Captain Couch, and order them to march one day in

---

*a*Not promulgated. Regiment received orders from Major-General Schofield.

advance of you, that they may give you all necessary information of the enemy, if there is any in your line of march, and of the whereabouts of the Federal forces. When you get in safe distance of our forces you will order Captain Couch to return to Decherd and report to the commanding officer there for duty.

By command of Major-General Milroy:

JNO. O. CRAVENS,
Assistant Adjutant-General.

DECATUR, *December 30, 1864.*
(Received 31st.)

Major-General THOMAS:

GENERAL: Colonel Polly [?], commanding Thirteenth Indiana Cavalry, reports that he has captured two pieces of artillery and a few prisoners. The prisoners all report that Hood has crossed at Bainbridge, and I am pushing forward as rapidly as possible.

JAS. B. STEEDMAN,
Major-General.

COURTLAND, [*December*] *30, 1864.*
(Received January 1, 1865.)

Major-General THOMAS:

I have the honor to report that the advance of my command arrived at this place last night, 29th instant. I learned that the enemy have reached Tuscumbia en route to Corinth; that General Hood left Tuscumbia Tuesday morning; that Forrest has been at Tuscumbia several days, but is supposed to be moving toward Corinth. I send for orders, hearing a report that the enemy is over the Tennessee River. My whole command is now here, except the cavalry, which advanced to Town Creek. I have captured four commissioned officers and about — men since I left Decatur. Now that General Sherman has taken Savannah, will not Wheeler return toward Chattanooga?

I am, respectfully, your obedient servant.

JAS. B. STEEDMAN,
Major-General.

HEADQUARTERS CAVALRY,
Leighton, Thirteen Miles from Courtland,
December 30, 1864—2 p. m.

General STEEDMAN:

GENERAL: I am here feeding preparatory to a night expedition after Hood's pontoon train, which crossed this road yesterday, and started from La Grange (four miles south of here) this morning at daylight. I can catch it easily before morning, but it is reported here that Jackson's division (Forrest's command) of cavalry has been ordered back here. Please, therefore, have the infantry come on and camp here (at Leighton) to-night, so that I can securely make this expedition. There is forage within three-quarters of a mile from here, and it being the cross-road it is the best position for a camp. The march from your last camp will be only seventeen miles and a half. There are a few hundred cavalry now in my front toward Tuscumbia; I do not know whether this is Jackson's or not. Most of Roddey's men scattered off to the mountains as we came along here. The rear of Hood's army left Tuscumbia at 1 p. m. yesterday. Railroad is in operation to within four miles of Tuscumbia. Reliable report that our cavalry has destroyed the Mobile and Ohio Railroad for twenty miles, from Baldwyn south. Heavy cannonading heard about Eastport yesterday from 2 p. m. till midnight.

Yours,

WM. J. PALMER,
Colonel, Commanding.

HEADQUARTERS DISTRICT OF THE ETOWAH,
Courtland, Ala., December 30, 1864—5.15 p. m.

Col. W. J. PALMER,
Commanding Cavalry :

COLONEL: Your dispatch just received. The infantry, if it should move now, could not reach Leighton before 2 a. m. to-morrow. You will, therefore, have to exercise your own judgment as to whether you can safely make the expedition without support from the infantry. It is fair to suppose that the pontoon train has a guard at least equal to your own force. The service of your command will be needed to scout in the direction of the river and Tuscumbia. I do not wish you to break down your horses, but leave you free to make the expedition, if you think you can do it with perfect safety. Send me a commissioned officer with twenty-five of your men for courier duty. Please inform me whether you pursue the train or not.

By command of Major-General Steedman:

S. B. MOE,
Assistant Adjutant-General.

COLUMBIA, TENN., *December 30, 1864.*

Maj. Gen. GEORGE STONEMAN,
Nashville, Tenn.:

I have received your two dispatches of the 29th, and am more than satisfied with your explanation as well as with the result of your late expedition. The order of the War Department relieving you from the command to which you were assigned has been revoked, and I desire you to return to Louisville and continue a general supervision of the affairs of the department, at least until you can obtain a more desirable command.

J. M. SCHOFIELD,
Major-General.

HEADQUARTERS KENTUCKY VOLUNTEERS,
ADJUTANT-GENERAL'S OFFICE,
Frankfort, December 30, 1864.

Brig. Gen. E. H. HOBSON,
Lexington, Ky.:

GENERAL: I have the honor to report that the forces under my command, operating on the Louisville and Frankfort Railroad, captured, on the 28th instant, near Lockport, in Henry County, two guerrillas, by the names of Smith Johns and ―――― Maddox, both notorious characters. Captain Cockrill reports he sent them to the rear, and they attempted to escape from the guard, were fired upon, and killed. Captain Searcy reports that Jessee has crossed the Kentucky River, and is now in Owen County. I respectfully request that the battalion of colored cavalry now near LaGrange be ordered to Owen County in pursuit of Jessee, as the forces I have along the railroad are sufficient for its protection.

Very respectfully,

D. W. LINDSEY,
Inspector and Adjutant-General.

GENERAL ORDERS, } HEADQUARTERS FIRST DIVISION,
                  MILITARY DISTRICT OF KENTUCKY,
No. 24.   }   *Lexington, Ky., December 30, 1864.*

In obedience to Special Orders, No. 103, headquarters Military District of Kentucky, Lexington, Ky., December 29, 1864, I hereby assume command of First Division, Military District of Kentucky. The following officers are announced as my personal staff: Capt. George G. Lott, additional aide-de-camp; Lieut. W. Lee Osborn, Eleventh Michigan Cavalry, aide-de-camp.

E. H. HOBSON,
Brigadier-General, Commanding.

NEW ORLEANS, *December 30, 1864.*
(Via Cairo, January 7, 1865.)

Maj. Gen. GEORGE H. THOMAS:

If you contemplate any operations in the direction of Selma, I may be of service by demonstrations from some point on the Gulf. I can spare for this purpose from 15,000 to 20,000 men. Let me know in what way I can aid your operations and I will gladly employ all the force that I can gather up. Your successes have given us great gratification.

E. R. S. CANBY,
Major-General, Commanding.

WASHINGTON, *December 31, 1864—10.15 a. m.*

Major-General THOMAS,
       Pulaski, Tenn.:

General A. J. Smith was nominated, confirmed, and commissioned a major-general of volunteers, and accepted his commission the 20th of June. He is full major-general, and not merely brevet. Do you desire any other promotion for him?

E. M. STANTON,
Secretary of War.

HEADQUARTERS DEPARTMENT OF THE CUMBERLAND,
                Pulaski, December 31, 1864—5 p. m.

Hon. E. M. STANTON,
       Secretary of War, Washington, D. C.:

Your dispatch of 10.15 this a. m. received. I respectfully recommend that General A. J. Smith be brevetted one grade in the regular service, for his gallantry and good conduct in battle, before Nashville, on the

15th and 16th instant; also, General T. J. Wood, on the same dates, who was equally conspicuous. I would also recommend Generals Schofield and Stanley be brevetted one grade in the regular service, for gallantry and good conduct at the battle of Franklin, November 30, 1864.

GEO. H. THOMAS,
Major-General, U. S. Volunteers, Commanding.

WASHINGTON, *December 31, 1864—11.30 a. m.*
(Via Nashville, Tenn.)

Major-General THOMAS:

General Grant directs that all of your available forces, not essential to hold your communications, be collected on the Tennessee River, say at Eastport and Tuscumbia, and be made ready for such movements as may be ordered. It is supposed that a portion of the troops in Louisville and other parts of Kentucky and Tennessee can now be availed of for active operations elsewhere. They should be made ready for that purpose. General Dodge wishes you to return to Saint Louis the Thirty-ninth Missouri Infantry, now at Louisville, so that he may complete its organization. Please give us the earliest possible notice of Hood's line of retreat, so that orders may be given for a continuance of the campaign. General Grant does not intend that your army shall go into winter quarters; it must be ready for active operations in the field.

H. W. HALLECK,
Major-General and Chief of Staff.

WASHINGTON, *December 31, 1864—3.30 p. m.*

Major-General THOMAS,
Pulaski, Tenn.:

General Dana telegraphs from Memphis on the 29th that his cavalry struck the railroad on the 26th, five miles south of Corinth, and were destroying it as they went south. It is, therefore, important that your cavalry keep that of Forrest well employed, so that it will not be able to molest that destroying the railroad in Mississippi.

H. W. HALLECK,
Major-General and Chief of Staff.

HEADQUARTERS DEPARTMENT OF THE CUMBERLAND,
Pulaski, Tenn., December 31, 1864—8 p. m.

Maj. Gen. H. W. HALLECK,
Washington, D. C.:

Your telegrams of 11.30 a. m. and 3.30 p. m. this day are received. I am watching Hood closely, to determine his line of retreat, of which I will inform you as soon as ascertained. I have ordered the cavalry to Eastport, and also General A. J. Smith's command. The Fourth Army Corps has been ordered to Huntsville, Ala., as that place will be convenient to furnish the troops with supplies to refit. I had ordered the Twenty-third Army Corps to Dalton, but countermanded the order yesterday, upon a report that Hood was moving toward Corinth. I will now order the Twenty-third Corps to Eastport. I have received a communication from General Wilson to-day, dated the 29th instant, in which he represents his cavalry as very much fagged out and in need of rest, and asks that he may be allowed to assemble it at or near Eastport sufficiently long to reorganize and recuperate, shoe up his horses, and organize his trains. His losses in horses have been very heavy since we left Nashville, owing principally to the intolerably bad weather, the almost impassable condition of the country, caused by constant and heavy rains and snow, and the great scarcity of forage along the route over which we pursued the enemy. The infantry, also, is very much exhausted, having been constantly on campaign duty since early last spring. To continue the campaign without any rest, I fear, will cost us very heavy losses from disease and exhaustion. The troops, however, will be assembled at Eastport and Huntsville as soon as possible, where we will await orders. I must say, however, in justice to all the commands, that they have not yet had sufficient time to get supplied with the transportation which General Sherman had, necessarily, to take from them to supply himself with the requisite amount for his march. I had already taken steps, before receiving your telegram of to-day, to refit the troops under my command as soon as possible, so as to commence the campaign again at the earliest possible moment, and I do believe that it is much the best policy to get well prepared before starting on an important campaign.

GEO. H. THOMAS,
Major-General, U. S. Volunteers, Commanding.

HEADQUARTERS DEPARTMENT OF THE CUMBERLAND,
Pulaski, December 31, 1864—12 m.

Admiral S. P. LEE,
  Flag-ship Fairy, Eastport:

Your dispatch of 29th just received. Do you mean the height at Eastport, or on the river above, and how far above? Is there any indication that the enemy is in force or moving toward Corinth?

GEO. H. THOMAS,
Major-General, U. S. Volunteers.

NASHVILLE, *December 31, 1864.*

Capt. R. H. RAMSEY,
  Assistant Adjutant-General:

I received General Thomas' dispatch for General Sherman. Officers will leave for Savannah to-morrow morning. Please inform me as to the situation of affairs at front.

J. D. WEBSTER,
Brigadier-General.

HEADQUARTERS DEPARTMENT OF THE CUMBERLAND,
Pulaski, December 31, 1864—8 p. m.

Brig. Gen. J. D. WEBSTER,
  Chief of Staff, Nashville, Tenn.:

Your telegram of this date is received. Reports would indicate that Hood will endeavor to halt his retreating army at Corinth, but he cannot do this for any length of time, as General Dana has destroyed the Mobile and Ohio Railroad south from Corinth for some distance. General Thomas' army is being concentrated at Huntsville and Eastport, preparatory to further operations.

Respectfully,

ROBT. H. RAMSEY,
Assistant Adjutant-General.

NASHVILLE, TENN., *December 31, 1864.*

General W. D. WHIPPLE,
　　Chief of Staff and Assistant Adjutant-General:

The quartermaster's gun-boat Newsboy just arrived from Eastport. The commander says Admiral Lee reports that he had effectually cleaned out the rebels at Florence, and that he had destroyed the pontoon bridge across the river at that point; and in verification of Admiral Lee's report the commander of the Newsboy says he met with numerous pieces of a pontoon bridge floating in the Tennessee between Duck River and Eastport. A detailed report to the general by special messenger.

　　　　　　　　　J. L. DONALDSON,
　　Chief Quartermaster, Department of the Cumberland.

NASHVILLE, *December 31, 1864.*

Capt. R. H. RAMSEY,
　　Assistant Adjutant-General:

Please tell me from time to time, as far as may be proper, the situation of our and Hood's army. It may help me in my operations.

　　　　　　　　　J. L. DONALDSON,
　　Chief Quartermaster, Department of the Cumberland.

HEADQUARTERS DEPARTMENT OF THE CUMBERLAND,
　　　　Pulaski, December 31, 1864—8 p. m.

Brig. Gen. J. L. DONALDSON,
　　Chief Quartermaster, Dept. of the Cumberland, Nashville, Tenn.:

Your telegram of this date is received. Reports would indicate that Hood will attempt to halt his retreating army at Corinth, but this can hardly be possible for any length of time, as General Dana has broken the Mobile and Ohio Railroad for some distance below that point. You can be prepared to supply the cavalry command, and also General A. J. Smith's, at Eastport, with, perhaps, the Twenty-third Army Corps. The Fourth Army Corps, General Wood, will, for the present. be posted at Huntsville. Happy New Year.

　　Respectfully.

　　　　　　　　　ROBT. H. RAMSEY,
　　　　　　　　　Assistant Adjutant-General.

SPECIAL ORDERS, ⎫　　HEADQUARTERS OF THE ARMY,
　　　　　　　　⎬　　　　ADJUTANT-GENERAL'S OFFICE,
　　No. 477.　　⎭　　　*Washington, December 31, 1864.*

Brig. Gen. M. M. Crocker, U. S. Volunteers, will report in person, without delay, to the commanding general Army of the Cumberland for assignment to duty.

By command of Lieutenant-General Grant:

　　　　　　　　　E. D. TOWNSEND,
　　　　　　　　　Assistant Adjutant-General.

HDQRS. CAVALRY CORPS, MIL. DIV. OF THE MISSISSIPPI,
On the Road, December 31, 1864.
Brig. Gen. T. J. WOOD,
Commanding Fourth Army Corps:

GENERAL: I am directed to inform you that the Elk River is fordable at the crossing near Rogersville.
Respectfully,

A. J. ALEXANDER,
Lieutenant-Colonel and Acting Chief of Staff.

HEADQUARTERS FOURTH ARMY CORPS,
Lexington, Ala., December 31, 1864—2.15 p. m.
Lieutenant-Colonel HAYES,
Chief Quartermaster, Fourth Army Corps:

The general commanding directs that you send all of the trains and property of the corps, save the artillery, to Athens and Huntsville. The commanding officer at Athens will give you a note stating the particular disposition to be made of the trains. Headquarters will be at Huntsville. You will move directly from Pulaski to Athens.
Very respectfully, your obedient servant,

J. S. FULLERTON,
Lieutenant-Colonel and Assistant Adjutant-General.

COLUMBIA, *December 31, 1864.*
Brigadier-General WHIPPLE,
Chief of Staff:

Is not the route via Lewisburg and Shelbyville better than that via Pulaski and Fayetteville? The road from this place to Shelbyville is all pike, except ten miles.

J. M. SCHOFIELD,
Major-General.

GENERAL THOMAS' HEADQUARTERS,
December 31, 1864.
Major-General SCHOFIELD,
Columbia:

Do not start from Columbia until further orders. Circumstances may render it necessary for the Twenty-third Corps [to move] in another direction.

WM. D. WHIPPLE,
Assistant Adjutant-General.

COLUMBIA, *December 31, 1864.*
Gen. W. D. WHIPPLE:

Your dispatch ordering the movement of Twenty-third Corps to be delayed, and that of General Thomas in relation to the four additional regiments, are received.

J. M. SCHOFIELD,
Major-General.

HEADQUARTERS ARMY OF THE OHIO,
Columbia, Tenn., December 31, 1864.

Lieut. Col. J. H. SIMPSON,
Chief Engineer, Armies of the West, Cincinnati, Ohio:

COLONEL: I have the honor to acknowledge the receipt of your communication of the 13th instant, asking for the names of fifteen officers to be used for the designation of forts in Kentucky. In reply, the major-general commanding the department directs me to furnish you the names of the following officers, belonging to the Army of the Ohio, who have been killed, or died from the effects of wounds received in battle:

Capt. Archibald H. Engle, aide-de-camp on the staff of Major-General Schofield and captain Thirteenth U. S. Infantry, killed in the battle of Resaca, Ga., May 14, 1864. Capt. E. D. Saunders, assistant adjutant-general of volunteers, killed in action in front of Dallas, Ga., June 2, 1864. Lieut. Col. George R. Elstner, Fiftieth Ohio Infantry, killed in action near Utoy Creek, Ga., August 8, 1864. Lieut. Col. Mervin Clark, One hundred and eighty-third Ohio Infantry, killed in the battle of Franklin, Tenn., November 30, 1864. Capt. M. C. Horton, One hundred and fourth Ohio Infantry, killed in action in front of Dallas, Ga., May 28, 1864. Capt. A. J. Southworth, One hundred and fourth Ohio Infantry, killed in action in front of Atlanta, Ga., August 16, 1864. Capt. George W. Hill, Twelfth Kentucky Infantry, killed in action in front of Atlanta, Ga., August 6, 1864. Capt. William Bishop, One hundredth Ohio Infantry, mortally wounded in action in front of Dallas, Ga., May 28, 1864. Capt. J. T. Philpot, One hundred and third Ohio Infantry, killed in the battle of Resaca, Ga., May 14, 1864. Capt. W. W. Hutchinson, One hundred and third Ohio Infantry, killed in the battle of Resaca, Ga., May 14, 1864. Capt. R. J. Showers, Eightieth Indiana Infantry, killed in the battle of Resaca, Ga., May 14, 1864. Capt. Edgar Camp, One hundred and seventh Illinois Infantry, killed in action at Lost Mountain, Ga., June 16, 1864. Capt. G. A. Gallup, Thirteenth Kentucky Infantry, killed in action near Lovejoy's Station, Ga., September 1, 1864. Second Lieut. Julius E. Karnasch, Thirty-fifth Missouri Infantry, topographical engineer on the staff of Major-General Schofield, killed in action near Atlanta, Ga., August 4, 1864. First Lieut. James Coughlan, Twenty-fourth Kentucky Infantry, aide-de-camp on the staff of Major-General Schofield, killed in the battle of Franklin, Tenn., November 30, 1864.

J. A. CAMPBELL,
Major and Assistant Adjutant-General.

———

COLUMBIA, TENN., *December 31, 1864.*

Colonel WHEELER, *Twenty-eighth Michigan, Nashville, Tenn.:*

Remain with your regiment in Nashville until further orders, which will be sent you in a few days.

J. M. SCHOFIELD,
Major-General.

———

COLUMBIA, TENN., *December 31, 1864.*

COMMANDING OFFICER 180TH OHIO VOLUNTEERS,
Decherd, Tenn.:

Remain with your regiment at Decherd until further orders. You will be able to join the Twenty-third Corps near that place.

J. M. SCHOFIELD,
Major-General.

Headquarters Detachment Army of the Tennessee,
In the Field, December 31, 1864.

Brig. Gen. J. McArthur,
    Commanding First Division:

General: The major-general commanding directs that you move forward with your command to-morrow morning, January 1, 1865, at 8 a. m.

I am, very respectfully, your obedient servant,

J. HOUGH,
Major and Assistant Adjutant-General.

Hdqrs. Cavalry Corps, Mil. Div. of the Mississippi,
Bull's Mills, Tenn., December 31, 1864—6 a. m.

Brigadier-General Whipple,
    Chief of Staff:

An intelligent and apparently truthful deserter from Roddey's command says Roddey was driven out of Decatur Tuesday morning, stampeded and scattered from Courtland the next day, and was defeated at a point on the railroad six miles west of Town Creek. The rebels supposed the force after them to be under the command of Granger, and to consist of cavalry and infantry, not less than 15,000. They are badly scared and think they are gone up. Day before yesterday heavy cannonading was heard in the direction of Eastport between 2 p. m. and dark. The deserter reports that the rear guard of Hood's command left Tuscumbia day before yesterday at noon, the advance having left on Tuesday morning. The gun-boats were within a mile of the rebel bridge at Bainbridge, and the people say could have reached it without trouble.

Very respectfully, your obedient servant,

J. H. WILSON,
Brevet Major-General.

Headquarters Department of the Cumberland,
Pulaski, Tenn., December 31, 1864.

Maj. Gen. J. H. Wilson,
    Comdg. Cavalry Corps, Mil. Div. of the Mississippi,
        In the Field, Blue Water, Ala.:

General: I have the honor to acknowledge the receipt of your communications of yesterday, by the hands of Captain Carling. The following is a copy of communication already sent you:

Headquarters Department of the Cumberland,
Pulaski, Tenn., December 30, 1864.

Brevet Major-General Wilson,
    Commanding Cavalry Corps, Military Division of the Mississippi:

Sir: Your dispatch dated Blue Water Creek, Ala., December 29, 3 p. m., just received. The major-general commanding modifies his previous order for your command, and directs that you move with it to Eastport, on the Tennessee River, to reorganize. At this point you will find all the supplies you may need.

Very respectfully, your obedient servant,

HENRY M. CIST,
Assistant Adjutant-General.

The major-general commanding does not particularly desire that you should locate your camp exactly at Eastport, or on the south side of the river, but if you can find a better camp on this side, you are at liberty to locate it there.

Very respectfully, your obedient servant,
WM. D. WHIPPLE,
Brigadier-General and Chief of Staff.

HDQRS. FIRST BRIGADE, FIRST CAVALRY DIVISION,
MILITARY DIVISION OF THE MISSISSIPPI,
Waterloo, Ala., December 31, 1864.
Lieut. Col. A. J. ALEXANDER,
Chief of Staff, Cavalry Corps:

COLONEL: The communications of December 30, 5.30 a. m. and 4 p. m., from the major-general commanding, are just received. I reached this place at dark last night. The transports had been lying here for four days, with ten days' rations and forage for 10,000 cavalry, also medical supplies. Hood's army reached Cherokee last night, and Forrest took the train for Corinth yesterday, at that point, shipping cavalry by rail. I shall immediately begin my winter campaign against this ragged, lawless brigade, and hope to turn it out in good shape in the spring.

Respectfully, your obedient servant,
JOHN T. CROXTON,
Brigadier-General of Volunteers.

ELIZABETHTOWN, KY., *December 31, 1864.*
Bvt. Maj. Gen. J. H. WILSON:

I arrived here with my division to-day.

ELI LONG,
Brigadier-General, U. S. Volunteers, Commanding Division.

HDQRS. CAVALRY CORPS, MIL. DIV. OF THE MISSISSIPPI,
Bull's Mills, December 31, 1864—2 a. m.
Brigadier-General HATCH,
Commanding Division:

GENERAL: The general commanding desires you to move your command, via Rogersville, to Huntsville, by the most direct practicable route. Upon arriving in the vicinity of Huntsville your command will be reported to these headquarters, which will be established in Huntsville. He desires you to move at daylight.

Very respectfully, your obedient servant,
A. J. ALEXANDER,
Lieutenant-Colonel and Acting Chief of Staff.

HDQRS. CAVALRY CORPS, MIL. DIV. OF THE MISSISSIPPI,
Bull's Mills, Tenn., December 31, 1864—2 a. m.
Col. T. J. HARRISON,
Commanding Brigade:

COLONEL: The general commanding desires you to move your command at daylight, via Rogersville, to Huntsville, Ala., by the most direct practicable route. It will be reported, upon arriving at Huntsville, to these headquarters, which will be established in that place. All your transportation, &c., will join you at Huntsville.

I have the honor to be, very respectfully, your obedient servant,

A. J. ALEXANDER,
Lieutenant-Colonel and Acting Chief of Staff.

HEADQUARTERS DEPARTMENT OF THE CUMBERLAND,
Pulaski, December 31, 1864.

Brig. Gen. JOHN F. MILLER,
Nashville:

Send all officers and men who have reported to you since General Steedman left who belong to General Sherman's army to Savannah, without regard to term of service yet remaining. We have not the means of determining when their terms of service expire, and, under existing orders of War Department, cannot muster them out. Send, also, the reserve artillery of Army of the Tennessee to Savannah.

WM. D. WHIPPLE,
Assistant Adjutant-General.

NASHVILLE, *December 31, 1864.*

Brigadier-General WHIPPLE,
Chief of Staff:

Your dispatch relating to officers and men of General Sherman's command just received. There are numbers of men belonging to that army whose term of service has expired. Shall we send such men to the chief mustering officer of the State from whence they came? The detachments of your command, with baggage, here are in camp together, and I am sending forward all men from detachments fit for duty. Will you have the baggage forwarded soon?

JNO. F. MILLER,
Brigadier-General.

HEADQUARTERS DEPARTMENT OF THE CUMBERLAND,
Pulaski, December 31, 1864.

Brig. Gen. J. F. MILLER,
Nashville:

Send all detachments for General Smith's command by steamer to Eastport.

WM. D. WHIPPLE,
Assistant Adjutant-General.

HEADQUARTERS DEPARTMENT OF THE CUMBERLAND,
Pulaski, December 31, 1864.

Brig. Gen. J. F. MILLER,
Nashville:

Hold the 200 of Merrill's Horse at Nashville until the rest of the regiment arrives, then send it overland to Eastport.

WM. D. WHIPPLE,
Brigadier-General.

Special Orders,) Headquarters District of Tennessee,
  No. 302.   )   Nashville, Tenn., December 31, 1864.

I. The Forty-second Missouri Volunteer Infantry will proceed without delay, by rail, as soon as transportation can be furnished, to Tullahoma, the commanding officer reporting, upon his arrival there, to Maj. Gen. R. H. Milroy.

*   *   *   *   *   *   *

By command of Major-General Rousseau:

                                        B. H. POLK,
                          Major and Assistant Adjutant-General.

Hdqrs. Defenses Nashville and Chattanooga R. R.,
                              Tullahoma, December 31, 1864.
Maj. B. H. Polk,
    Assistant Adjutant-General:

Major: While at Murfreesborough I ordered Major Cobb, of the Twelfth Regiment Indiana Volunteer Cavalry, to proceed to Nashville and collect the members of his regiment there and bring them to the regiment at this place. These were men who had been home on furlough, and were stopped on their return at Nashville by the presence of the rebel army. Major Cobb returned to this post to-day, but without the men that he was ordered to bring. He brought a letter addressed to me from Brig. Gen. Joseph F. Knipe, stating that the Twelfth Indiana Cavalry had been assigned to his division, and requesting me to send this regiment to Nashville immediately. I cannot comply with this request from General Knipe, for he has no right to make such a demand upon me. Furthermore, I have no official knowledge whatever that the Twelfth Indiana has been assigned to the Seventh Division, Cavalry Corps, and I cannot obey any order taking this regiment from me, unless it passes through headquarters District of Tennessee. I therefore request that the general commanding order the detachment of the Twelfth Indiana Cavalry now at Nashville to join the regiment here without delay.

                                        R. H. MILROY
                                           Major-General.

Headquarters Post of Murfreesborough,
                      Murfreesborough, Tenn., December 31, 1864.
Maj. J. R. Willett,
    First U. S. Veteran Volunteer Engineers:

The general commanding directs me to say, in answer to your inquiry in regard to rebuilding block-houses, through Lieutenant Conger, that the small detachment of the One hundred and fifteenth Ohio Volunteer Infantry, detailed for the different stations on the railroad, cannot guard the bridges, patrol the road, and at the same time build block-houses. By furnishing all the negroes that could be pressed (about forty) to the officer commanding Block-house No. 6, that was destroyed by Wheeler, it was nearly completed in three months. They should be built by the Engineer Corps. I cannot furnish men to build block-houses.

    I am, major, respectfully, &c.,

                                        H. H. SHEETS,
                             Acting Assistant Adjutant-General.

HEADQUARTERS DEPARTMENT OF THE CUMBERLAND,
Pulaski, December 31, 1864—8 p. m.

Maj. Gen. JAMES B. STEEDMAN,
Decatur:

(To be forwarded.)

Your telegram of the 30th has been received. I would like you to ascertain to a certainty, if possible, what route Hood has taken in his retreat, without incurring too great a risk on your part. Has the pontoon bridge been laid at Decatur? After you are assured of Hood's line of retreat your command can return to Decatur, and thence to Chattanooga.

GEO. H. THOMAS,
Major-General, U. S. Volunteers, Commanding.

COURTLAND, *December 31, 1864—6 p. m.*
(Via Decatur 7 p. m. January 1, 1865.)

Major-General THOMAS:

My cavalry left Leighton, thirteen miles west of this place, at 3 o'clock this a. m., in pursuit of General Hood's pontoon train, which left near La Grange yesterday morning, December 30, in the direction of Russellville. I have 2,500 infantry at Town Creek, nine miles west of this place. There is no enemy at Florence or Tuscumbia. The pontoon train is reported as having been ordered to Columbus, Miss.

JAS. B. STEEDMAN,
Major-General, U. S. Volunteers.

HEADQUARTERS DISTRICT OF NORTHERN ALABAMA,
Huntsville, December 31, 1864.

Major-General STEEDMAN:

GENERAL: The bridge over Paint Rock has been burnt by the enemy's cavalry, 600 strong. I am compelled to order a portion of the garrison of Decatur to that point of the road to protect the bridges of Flint and Hurricane Creeks. I would request that you send 400 men to Decatur to supply their places.

Respectfully, &c.,

R. S. GRANGER,
Brigadier-General.

DALTON, *December 31, 1864.*

[Capt. H. A. FORD,]
Acting Assistant Adjutant-General, District of the Etowah:

One of my scouts from Spring Place informs me that General Runnells, commanding Georgia State troops, has ordered them all to Murray County, with a view of capturing Dalton and Cleveland. General Findley, C. S. Army, commanding in Lumpkin County, is to have immediate command, and is probably at Carter's plantation, on the Coosawattee, the general rendezvous. One regiment, 500 strong, is now encamped at Carter's.

J. B. CULVER,
Colonel Thirteenth Michigan, Commanding.

HEADQUARTERS CAVALRY,
Leighton, December 31, 1864—3 a. m.

Major MOE,
    Assistant Adjutant-General:

MAJOR: I did not receive your reply till after 10 p. m. My men are now saddling up to go after the train. We shall take a trail which will put us on the Russellville road beyond La Grange, so that we shall slip between the two bodies of the enemy in our front—one on the Tuscumbia road and the other on the Mount Hope or La Grange road. The officer and twenty men required by you have been detailed, and will be directed to remain here till daybreak, picketing the roads and keeping up the fires at our camp. They will then return to the other side of Town Creek, and await your arrival. I hope the infantry will make an early start, and be sure to come as far as Leighton before camping, as otherwise I might have difficulty in getting the train back, even if it were captured. I hope to get it uninjured; and in that event I presume the importance of the capture would be greater than otherwise, as it would enable us to lay the bridge at Florence or below, and permit General Thomas' cavalry, or the whole of his forces, to cross. The roads are so bad beyond Tuscumbia that Hood's wagon train will make very slow progress to Corinth, and a large cavalry force on this side of the river might still do them considerable damage. There is no enemy at Bainbridge or Florence, and there was none yesterday p. m. at Tuscumbia. Roddey's train of thirty wagons, with the two 20-pounders, left here yesterday morning at daylight for Cane Creek Station, four miles beyond Tuscumbia, which is the railroad terminus, and where I suppose they will put the heavy cannon on the cars, as Hood sent to Roddey for them. Two regiments of Jackson's division of cavalry (Forrest) went past here, from Bainbridge to Mount Hope, on Wednesday, to feed, &c. I presume this is a portion of the guard for the pontoons. The latter are ordered to Columbus, Miss., and if we find there is no danger of a force being sent from Forrest to intercept us, we shall probably follow till we reach the train. When the infantry reaches here, this p. m., please have one regiment go on to the top of the ridge at La Grange, four miles, so as to prevent Jackson's two regiments from coming in my rear, if they are still out on the Mount Hope road. There is not the slightest probability of any infantry of Hood's being sent back, and I therefore expect and hope that the infantry will march on to-morrow to Tuscumbia, to which point the pontoon train might be brought (a distance of sixteen miles from Russellville). I shall endeavor to ascertain, by scouts across from Russellville, whether or not you are there. Will you please have my wagons and supplies brought from the transports when yours are.

    Yours, respectfully,

WM. J. PALMER,
    Colonel, Commanding.

HUNTSVILLE, ALA., *December 31, 1864.*

Major-General THOMAS:

Your telegram of 10.50 of 29th received at 12 m. Quartermaster immediately set to work to make preparations to receive stores. Fortifications will be repaired as fast as the strength of the limited garrison will permit. Commanding officer at L. telegraphs that the bridge at Paint Rock was burned by 600 rebel cavalry; a portion of the guard at the bridge reports this fact. Am preparing a train, and will move down there myself at once with a force. My force for the defense of the road and Decatur is 1,413 infantry and 200 cavalry, miserably mounted. Colonel Prosser, with all that could be of service in the field, has gone with General Steedman, by your order. All the block-houses this side of Paint Rock have been destroyed, and there are no defenses for the small garrisons. I had eighty men and one piece of artillery at Paint Rock, and yesterday ordered them to be prepared for an attack.

R. S. GRANGER,
Brigadier-General.

HEADQUARTERS DEPARTMENT OF THE CUMBERLAND,
Pulaski, Tenn., December 31, 1864.

Brig. Gen. R. S. GRANGER,
        Decatur, Ala.:

Has Colonel Merrill sent down a pontoon train from Chattanooga and laid a bridge at Decatur yet? What news have you from General Steedman?

GEO. H. THOMAS,
Major-General, U. S. Volunteers, Commanding.

HUNTSVILLE, December 31, 1864.

Major-General THOMAS:

As I expected, the force at Paint Rock was not half of what it was reported to be. Only about ten feet of the bridge was burned. The piece of artillery was not taken. I have taken every means to secure it at once. Sent 150 men from this point down the road. I have heard nothing from General Steedman. The gun-boats went down nearly to the mouth of Elk River, the Wauhatchie passing over the first rapids with Captain Forrest. They saw a few camp-fires and some pickets on the north side of the river. Colonel Merrill, of the pontoon bridge, was reported yesterday coming down river, but had not arrived last evening. I will leave in the morning for Decatur, and superintend everything myself. If the general has them to spare, I would be glad if he would send me some re-enforcements, to guard the road and assist in building up forts and store-houses—1,000 infantry for block-houses and Decatur, and 400 cavalry to look after guerrillas.

R. S. GRANGER,
Brigadier-General.

HEADQUARTERS DISTRICT OF NORTHERN ALABAMA,
Huntsville, Ala., December 31, 1864.

Major-General THOMAS,
        Comdg. Department of the Cumberland, Nashville, Tenn.:

GENERAL: I telegraphed the general commanding to-day that the bridge at Paint Rock had been burned, the party guarding it captured or dispersed, and that this had been done by 600 cavalry. I have since ascertained that the cavalry was commanded by Mead and Johnson. If this be so, they have not half the force reported. They are, however, capable of doing a great deal of damage, as I have not cavalry with which to pursue or hunt him up. General Steedman has taken Colonel Prosser with all his cavalry, except 200 poorly mounted, and which could be of no service in the field, and they are scattered from Larkinsville to Decatur. I would request that the general commanding send 500 or 600 cavalry into the district about Paint Rock and Flint River, to clean out this nest of guerrillas. They will continue to harass us until they are removed. It is a part of the force which, connected with Russell, continued to harass us from Huntsville to Stevenson. I am satisfied that if the officer in command at Paint Rock had conducted himself with any spirit he could have repulsed them. His name is Samuel C. Wagoner, second lieutenant Company G, Thirteenth Wisconsin Volunteer Infantry. I think an example should be made of him.

> Very respectfully, your obedient servant,
> R. S. GRANGER,
> *Brigadier-General.*

HEADQUARTERS DISTRICT OF NORTHERN ALABAMA,
Huntsville, December 31, 1864.

Lieut. Col. A. B. WADE,
Commanding Brownsborough:

COLONEL: The brigadier-general commanding directs me to say that you can use the One hundred and second Ohio, if anything can be done to-night. You will send them forward to Paint Rock, with the train, on a reconnaissance, immediately. The general also directs that you throw up two works, both at Hurricane and Brownsborough, to protect each bridge. They will be twenty feet square, cribbed up with logs, and earth banked up against them. If you cannot use the One hundred and second Ohio to-night, you will send it back with the train, with instructions to report at these headquarters. The cribs above mentioned will be made in conformity with the diagram* below, each flanking the other. You will put two, if possible, one certainly, at each bridge. They should be five feet high. If the enemy has not carried off the piece of artillery at Paint Rock, the banking-up with earth will not be necessary.

> Very respectfully, your obedient servant,
> SAM. M. KNEELAND,
> *First Lieut., Eighteenth Michigan Infantry, Actg. Asst. Adjt. Gen.*

LEXINGTON, *December 31, 1864.*

Maj. GEORGE J. WEST,
Mount Sterling, Ky.:

Keep yourself well informed of the movements of the force which attacked Gerhart at Sharpsburg. If he is attacked again, support him. His orders are to hold his position, if possible; if not, to fall back on Mount Sterling. Telegraph me any further information you may get.

> By order of Brevet Major-General Burbridge:
> J. BATES DICKSON,
> *Captain and Assistant Adjutant-General.*

[DECEMBER 31, 1864.—For Gerhart to Dickson, reporting skirmish at Sharpsburg, Ky., asking instructions, &c., see Part I, p. 876.]

---

* Omitted.

LEXINGTON, *December 31, 1864—3 p. m.*
(Via Mount Sterling.)

Maj. W. R. GERHART,
      Sharpsburg:

Hold your position at Sharpsburg, unless attacked by a much larger force than your own. If compelled to leave, fall back on Mount Sterling. Send to these headquarters any further information you can obtain concerning rebel force, which is probably only guerrillas.

By order of Brevet Major-General Burbridge:

J. BATES DICKSON,
      Captain and Assistant Adjutant-General.

LEXINGTON, *December 31, 1864.*

General S. G. BURBRIDGE,
      Mount Sterling, Ky.:

Yours of last evening just received. I have ordered sent to Mount Sterling, for the command, 10,000 rations of forage and subsistence stores, and 700 blankets, overcoats, and shoes, as Barden tells me many of the men are suffering for want of these things. All well, except Lieutenant Throckmorton, who is laid up by a fall from his horse. General Thomas and staff still here. Barden reached Catlettsburg and got his dispatch off in good time. Your friends here rejoice at your success. By orders from General Schofield, General McLean has been relieved and has gone to Nashville. I have assigned General Hobson to the command of the First Division. Lyon's command crossed the Louisville and Nashville Railroad at Elizabethtown, and was driven out of the State through Campbellsville and Columbia. Trains only interrupted two days on the Louisville and Nashville Railroad. Everett's gang of guerrillas is operating north and east of Mount Sterling. It may be well to leave a detachment at Mount Sterling to look after him. Telegraph me when to expect you.

J. BATES DICKSON,
      Captain and Assistant Adjutant-General.

PADUCAH, *December 31, 1864.*

Col. E. D. TOWNSEND,
      Assistant Adjutant-General:

COLONEL: I respectfully request to know if Columbus, Ky., heretofore composing a portion of the District of Western Kentucky, has been detached and added to the District of Western Tennessee, as the officer commanding District of Western Tennessee so construes General Orders, No. 288, from War Department, and orders commanding officer of said post to report to him. Please answer.

S. MEREDITH,
      Brigadier-General.

MISSISSIPPI SQUADRON,
Flag-ship Fairy, Tennessee River, December 31, 1864.

Brig. Gen. S. MEREDITH,
      Commanding at Paducah, Ky.:

GENERAL: Lieut. Commander J. G. Mitchell, commanding Eighth District, Mississippi Squadron, reports to me, under date of 17th instant, that on that day he met the steamer Poland below Hickman, which reported having been fired on at that place. He landed there and learned that twelve men were pillaging the town, and that they had some citizens "corralled" in a vacant lot. He landed thirty men, and the guerrillas left on their approach; soon after four cavalrymen rode to the top of the hill, were fired on by his picket, and retreated by the Dresden road. A previous report from Lieutenant-Commander Mitchell states that citizens have informed him that a band of bushwhackers are encamped in the swamp below Hickman; the men engaged in pillaging the town probably belonged to this gang. I request that you will take means to prevent the repetition of these raids on Hickman and to break up the guerrilla bands that infest its neighborhood. Naval co-operation will always be cordially extended when required.

I have the honor to be, general, very respectfully, yours,

S. P. LEE,
Acting Rear-Admiral, Commanding Mississippi Squadron.

HEADQUARTERS DEPARTMENT OF THE CUMBERLAND,
Pulaski, December 31, 1864—8 p. m.

Maj. Gen. N. J. T. DANA,
　　Memphis:

Your telegram of 29th instant is received. I will endeavor to attract as much of Forrest's cavalry toward this army as possible, so as to relieve your force now destroying the Mobile and Ohio Railroad south.

GEO. H. THOMAS,
Major-General, U. S. Volunteers, Commanding.

Abstract from return of the Department of the Cumberland, Maj. Gen. George H. Thomas, U. S. Army, commanding, for the month of December, 1864.

Command.	Present for duty.		Aggregate present.	Aggregate present and absent.	Pieces of artillery.	
	Officers.	Men.			Heavy	Field.
General headquarters	26	....	26	28	......	......
Fourth Army Corps (Wood)	613	12,393	15,285	28,684	......	44
District of Tennessee (Rousseau)	557	13,489	17,039	23,015	46	111
District of the Etowah (Steedman)	244	7,575	9,272	12,777	18	99
Artillery Reserve (Smith)	6	439	457	814	......	12
Reserve Brigade (Le Favour)	30	850	1,148	1,818	......	......
Unassigned infantry	30	936	1,234	1,854	......	......
Unassigned artillery	6	202	209	249	4	5
Signal Corps (Hollopeter)	12	56	68	101	......	......
Veteran Reserve Corps (Cahill)	14	364	772	944	......	......
Total	1,538	36,304	45,310	70,284	68	271

Organization of troops in the Department of the Cumberland, commanded by Maj. Gen. George H. Thomas, U. S. Army, December 31, 1864.

FOURTH ARMY CORPS.

Brig. Gen. THOMAS J. WOOD.

FIRST DIVISION.

Brig. Gen. NATHAN KIMBALL.

First Brigade.

Col. ISAAC M. KIRBY.

21st Illinois, Capt. William H. Jamison.
38th Illinois, Capt. Andrew M. Pollard.
31st Indiana, Col. John T. Smith.
81st Indiana, Maj. Edward G. Mathey.
90th Ohio, Lieut. Col. Samuel N. Yeoman.
101st Ohio, Lieut. Col. Bedan B. McDanald.

Second Brigade.

Col. JESSE H. MOORE.

96th Illinois, Maj. George Hicks.
115th Illinois, Lieut. Col. George A. Poteet.
35th Indiana, Lieut. Col. Augustus G. Tassin.
21st Kentucky, Lieut. Col. James C. Evans.
23d Kentucky, Lieut. Col. George W. Northup.
45th Ohio, Lieut. Col. John H. Humphrey.
51st Ohio, Lieut. Col. Charles H. Wood.

Third Brigade.

Brig. Gen. WILLIAM GROSE.

75th Illinois, Col. John E. Bennett.
80th Illinois, Capt. James Cunningham.
84th Illinois, Lieut. Col. Charles H. Morton.
9th Indiana, Col. Isaac C. B. Suman.
30th Indiana (seven companies), Capt. Henry W. Lawton.
36th Indiana (one company), Lieut. John P. Swisher.
84th Indiana, Maj. John C. Taylor.
77th Pennsylvania, Col. Thomas E. Rose.

SECOND DIVISION.

Brig. Gen. WASHINGTON L. ELLIOTT.

First Brigade.

Col. EMERSON OPDYCKE.

36th Illinois, Maj. Levi P. Holden.
44th Illinois, Capt. Alonzo W. Clark.
73d Illinois, Capt. Wilson Burroughs.
74th Illinois, Capt. Thomas J. Bryan.
88th Illinois, Lieut. Col. George W. Smith.
125th Ohio, Maj. Joseph Bruff.
24th Wisconsin, Capt. Charles Hartung.

Second Brigade.

Col. JOHN Q. LANE.

100th Illinois, Lieut. Col. Charles M. Hammond.
40th Indiana, Lieut. Col. Henry Leaming.
57th Indiana, Maj. John S. McGraw.
28th Kentucky, Lieut. Col. J. Rowan Boone.
26th Ohio, Capt. William Clark.
97th Ohio, Capt. Clarkson C. Nichols.

Third Brigade.

Col. JOSEPH CONRAD.

42d Illinois, Lieut. Col. Edgar D. Swain.
51st Illinois Capt. Albert M. Tilton.
79th Illinois,* Col. Allen Buckner.
15th Missouri, Capt. George Ernst.
64th Ohio, Lieut. Col. Robert C. Brown.
65th Ohio, Maj. Orlow Smith.

---

* Veteran detachment 27th Illinois attached.

THIRD DIVISION.

Brig. Gen. SAMUEL BEATTY.

First Brigade.

Col. ABEL D. STREIGHT.

89th Illinois, Lieut. Col. William D. Williams.
51st Indiana, Capt. David W. Hamilton.
8th Kansas, Lieut. Col. John Conover.
15th Ohio, Col. Frank Askew.
49th Ohio, Capt. Joseph R. Bartlett.

Second Brigade.

Col. HENRY K. McCONNELL.

59th Illinois, Lieut. Col. Clayton Hale.
41st Ohio, Lieut. Col. Robert L. Kimberly.
71st Ohio, Capt. John W. Moody.
93d Ohio, Lieut. Col. Daniel Bowman.
124th Ohio, Lieut. Col. James Pickands.

Third Brigade.

Col. FREDERICK KNEFLER.

79th Indiana, Lieut. Col. George W. Parker.
86th Indiana, Col. George F. Dick.
13th Ohio (four companies), Maj. Joseph T. Snider.
19th Ohio, Lieut. Col. Henry G. Stratton.

ARTILLERY BRIGADE.

Maj. WILBUR F. GOODSPEED.

Indiana Light, 25th Battery, Capt. Frederick C. Sturm.
Kentucky Light, 1st Battery, Capt. Theodore S. Thomasson.
1st Michigan Light, Battery E, Capt. Peter De Vries.
1st Ohio Light, Battery G, Capt. Alexander Marshall.
Ohio Light, 6th Battery, Lieut. Aaron P. Baldwin.
Pennsylvania Light, Battery B, Capt. Jacob Ziegler.
4th United States, Battery M, Lieut. Samuel Canby.

DISTRICT OF TENNESSEE.

Maj. Gen. LOVELL H. ROUSSEAU.

FOURTH DIVISION, TWENTIETH ARMY CORPS.

First Brigade.

Col. WILLIAM P. LYON.

73d Indiana, Lieut. Col. Alfred B. Wade.
18th Michigan, Maj. Edwin M. Hulburd.
102d Ohio, Capt. William C. Scott.
13th Wisconsin, Capt. Edgar W. Blake.

Second Brigade.

Col. EDWIN C. MASON.

142d Indiana, Col. John M. Comparet.
45th New York, Lieut. Col. Adolphus Dobke.
176th Ohio, Lieut. Col. William B. Nesbitt.
179th Ohio, Col. Harley H. Sage.
182d Ohio, Col. Lewis Butler.

POST FORCES, NASHVILLE, TENN.

Brig. Gen. John. F. Miller.

28th Michigan, Col. William W. Wheeler.
173d Ohio, Col. John R. Hurd.
78th Pennsylvania, Capt. Henry W. Torbett.
17th U. S. Colored Troops, Col. William R. Shafter.
44th Wisconsin (detachment), } Lieut. Col. Oliver C. Bissell.
45th Wisconsin (detachment), }
Illinois Light Artillery, Bridges' Battery,* Lieut. Lyman A. White.
Indiana Light Artillery, 2d Battery,* Capt. James S. Whicher.
Indiana Light Artillery, 4th Battery,* Capt. Benjamin F. Johnson.
Indiana Light Artillery, 12th Battery,* Capt. James E. White.
Indiana Light Artillery, 21st Battery,* Capt. Abram P. Andrew.
Indiana Light Artillery, 24th Battery,* Lieut. Hiram Allen.
Kansas Light Artillery, 1st Battery,* Capt. Marcus D. Tenney.
1st Michigan Light Artillery, Battery F,* Capt. Byron D. Paddock.
1st Ohio Light Artillery, Battery A,* Capt. Charles W. Scovill.
1st Ohio Light Artillery, Battery E,* Lieut. Frank B. Reckard.
Ohio Light Artillery, 20th Battery,* Capt. William Backus.
1st Tennessee Light Artillery, Battery C,* Lieut Valentine Meyers.
1st Tennessee Light Artillery, Battery D,* Capt. Samuel D. Leinart.
2d U. S. Colored Light Artillery, Battery A,* Lieut. Jerry Lewis.

DECATUR, ALA.

1st Ohio Light Artillery, Battery F, Capt. William H. Pease.

CLARKSVILLE, TENN.

Col. Arthur A. Smith.

83d Illinois (eight companies), Maj. William G. Bond.
2d Illinois Light Artillery, Battery H, Capt. Henry C. Whittemore.

FORT DONELSON, TENN.

Lieut. Col. Elijah C. Brott.

83d Illinois (two companies), Capt. James Moore.
2d Illinois Light Artillery, Battery C, Capt. James P. Flood.

U. S. FORCES ON LOUISVILLE AND NASHVILLE RAILROAD.

Col. James Gilfillan.†

11th Minnesota, Lieut. Col. John Ball.
2d Tennessee Mounted Infantry, Col. John Murphy.
40th U. S. Colored Troops (five companies), Lieut. Col. Arthur F. Reed.
101st U. S. Colored Troops, Company F, Lieut. Stephen H. Eno.
Indiana Light Artillery, 13th Battery, Capt. Benjamin S. Nicklin.

SPRINGFIELD, TENN.

Col. Thomas J. Downey.

15th U. S. Colored Troops, Capt. George T. Armstrong.

BRIDGEPORT, ALA.

Maj. Daniel T. Cockerill.

1st Ohio Light Artillery, Battery B, Capt. Norman A. Baldwin.
Ohio Light Artillery, 9th Battery, Capt. Harrison B. York.

---

* Constituted the garrison artillery under Maj. John J. Ely.
† Also in command of post, Gallatin, Tenn.

TROOPS ON THE NASHVILLE AND NORTHWESTERN RAILROAD.

Col. CHARLES R. THOMPSON.

12th U. S. Colored Troops, Capt. Henry Hegner.
13th U. S. Colored Troops, Col. John A. Hottenstein.
100th U. S. Colored Troops, Maj. Collin Ford.

DEFENSES OF THE NASHVILLE AND CHATTANOOGA RAILROAD.

Maj. Gen. ROBERT H. MILROY.

First Brigade.

Brig. Gen. HORATIO P. VAN CLEVE.

61st Illinois,* Maj. Jerome B. Nulton.
3d Michigan,* Col. Moses B. Houghton.
4th Michigan,* Col. Jairus W. Hall.
115th Ohio, Col. Thomas C. Boone.
1st Michigan Light Artillery, Battery
   D, Capt. Henry B. Corbin.
Ohio Light Artillery, 12th Battery, Capt.
   Frank Jackson.
Wisconsin Light Artillery, 8th Battery,
   Capt. Henry E. Stiles.

Third Brigade.

Col. WLADIMIR KRZYZANOWSKI.

29th Michigan, Col. Thomas Saylor.
58th New York, Maj. Michael Esembaux.
106th Ohio, Lieut. Col. Gustavus Tafel.
180th Ohio, Col. Willard Warner.
1st Ohio Light Artillery, Battery K,
   Capt. Lewis Heckman.

Tullahoma, Tenn.

Col. WILLIAM FORBES.

42d Missouri, Col. William Forbes.
59th Ohio, Capt. Elbert M. Sargent.
New York Light Artillery, 13th Battery, Capt. Henry Bundy.

UNASSIGNED REGIMENTS.

175th Ohio, Capt. Joseph M. Hiestand.
75th Pennsylvania, Lieut. Col. Alvin V. Matzdorff.
43d Wisconsin, Lieut. Col. Byron Paine.

DISTRICT OF THE ETOWAH.

Maj. Gen. JAMES B. STEEDMAN.†

FIRST SEPARATE DIVISION.

Maj. Gen. JAMES B. STEEDMAN.

First Brigade.

Brig. Gen. JOHN H. KING.

15th United States, 2d Battalion, Capt. Thomas H. Norton.
15th United States, 3d Battalion (four companies), Capt. George M. Brayton.
16th United States (ten companies), Capt. Ebenezer Gay.
18th United States, 2d Battalion, Capt. Henry R. Mizner.
19th United States, 1st Battalion, Capt. Thomas Cummings.

Second Brigade.

Col. CALEB H. CARLTON.

29th Indiana, Lieut. Col. Samuel O. Gregory.
32d Indiana (detachment), Capt. Philip Wassem.
44th Indiana, Lieut. Col. James F. Curtis.
68th Indiana, Lieut. Col. Harvey J. Espy.
8th Kentucky (detachment).
18th Ohio, Lieut. Charles Grant.
15th Wisconsin, Lieut. Col. Ole C. Johnson.

---

*Temporarily attached.
† During General Steedman's absence in the field, the troops remaining in the district were commanded by Brig. Gen. Thomas F. Meagher.

Unassigned Infantry.

68th New York, Col. Felix Prince Salm.
14th U. S. Colored Troops, Col. Thomas J. Morgan.
16th U. S. Colored Troops, Col. William B. Gaw.
18th U. S. Colored Troops, Col. Augustus O. Millington.
42d U. S. Colored Troops (seven companies), Lieut. Col. Joseph R. Putnam.
44th U. S. Colored Troops, Col. Lewis Johnson.

Garrison Artillery, Chattanooga.

Lieut. Col. CHARLES S. COTTER.

Indiana Light, 8th Battery, Lieut. Jeremiah Voris.
Indiana Light, 20th Battery, Capt. Milton A. Osborne.
1st Michigan Light, Battery A, Capt. Almerick W. Wilbur.
1st Michigan Light, Battery K, Capt. John C. Schuetz.
1st Minnesota Heavy, Company A, Capt. Clinton N. Sterry.
1st Minnesota Heavy, Company B, Capt. William M. Leyde.
1st Minnesota Heavy, Company C, Capt. George L. Porter.
Minnesota Light, 2d Battery Capt. William A. Hotchkiss.
1st Ohio Light, Battery I, Capt. Hubert Dilger.
1st Wisconsin Heavy, Company C, Capt. John R. Davies.
Wisconsin Light, 3d Battery, Lieut. Joseph W. Wait.

Lookout Mountain, Tenn.

1st Missouri Light Artillery, Battery G, Lieut. Joseph L. Follett.

LIGHT ARTILLERY RESERVE.

Capt. LUTHER R. SMITH.

Indiana Light, 7th Battery, Lieut. Albert S. Bierce.
1st Michigan Light, Battery I, Capt. Luther R. Smith.
1st Ohio Light, Battery M, Lieut. Eben P. Sturges.
Ohio Light, 18th Battery, Capt. Charles C. Aleshire.
5th United States, Battery K, Lieut. David H. Kinzie.

RESERVE BRIGADE.

Col. HEBER LE FAVOUR.

9th Michigan, Lieut. Col. William Wilkinson.
22d Michigan, Lieut. Col. Henry S. Dean.

UNASSIGNED INFANTRY.

1st Battalion Ohio Sharpshooters, Capt. Gersbom M. Barber.
1st U. S. Veteran Volunteer Engineers, Col. William E. Merrill.

UNASSIGNED ARTILLERY.

1st Illinois Light, Battery M, Capt. George W. Spencer.
Indiana Light, 10th Battery, Capt. William A. Naylor.

SIGNAL CORPS.

Lieut. JEHU L. HOLLOPETER.

U. S. VETERAN RESERVE CORPS.

Col. FRANK P. CAHILL.

Abstract from return of the Department of the Ohio, Maj. Gen. John M. Schofield, U. S. Army, commanding, for the month of December, 1864.

[Compiled mainly from subordinate returns.]

Command.	Present for duty.		Aggregate present.	Aggregate present and absent.	Pieces of artillery.		Station.
	Officers.	Men.			Heavy.	Field.	
General headquarters	47	....	47	47	......	......	In the field, Tenn.
Twenty-third Army Corps (Schofield):							
Headquarters*	14	43	57	57	......	......	In the field.
First Division (Ruger).........	208	4,456	5,110	7,840	......	......	Columbia, Tenn.
Second Division (Couch)	239	4,522	5,577	9,488	......	8	Do.
Third Division (Cox)...........	214	5,140	6,225	9,394	......	8	Near Columbia, Tenn.
Fourth Division† (Ammen)	189	5,245	6,854	8,914	4	53	Knoxville, Tenn.
Military District of Kentucky (Burbridge):							
First Division (Hobson)........	205	4,750	5,468	7,268	......	......	Lexington, Ky.
Second Division (Ewing)..	114	3,283	3,914	4,846	......	......	Louisville, Ky.
Engineer Battalion (McClure)......	1	104	141	180	......	......	In the field, Tenn.
1st Ohio Heavy Artillery (Hawley).	36	1,353	1,462	1,893	......	......	Cleveland, Tenn.
Total	1,220	28,896	34,808	49,880	......	......	
District of Western Kentucky (Meredith).	68	1,545	2,084	2,488	......	......	Paducah, Ky.
Grand total	1,343	30,441	36,939	52,415	......	......	
Grand total according to tri-monthly return of the department.	1,419	31,531	39,058	57,394	......	......	

Organization of troops in the Department of the Ohio, commanded by Maj. Gen. John M. Schofield, U. S. Army, December 31, 1864.

TWENTY-THIRD ARMY CORPS.

Maj. Gen. JOHN M. SCHOFIELD.

ENGINEER BATTALION.

Capt. OLIVER S. McCLURE.

SIGNAL CORPS.

Capt. WILLIAM G. McCREARY.

FIRST DIVISION.

Brig. Gen. THOMAS H. RUGER.

First Brigade.

Col. JOHN M. ORR.

120th Indiana, Maj. John M. Barcus.
124th Indiana, Lieut. Col. Henry H. Neff.
128th Indiana, Lieut. Col. Jasper Packard.

Second Brigade.

Col. JOHN C. McQUISTON.

123d Indiana, Maj. Irvin Robbins.
129th Indiana, Col. Charles A. Zollinger.
130th Indiana, Col. Charles S. Parrish.

Third Brigade.

Col. MINOR T. THOMAS.

8th Minnesota, Maj. George A. Camp.
174th Ohio, Col. John S. Jones.
178th Ohio, Col. Joab A. Stafford.

Artillery.

Indiana Light, 22d Battery, Capt. Edward W. Nicholson.
1st Michigan Light, Battery F, Capt. Bryon D. Paddock.

* Includes Signal Corps.
† Also known as District of East Tennessee.

SECOND DIVISION.

Maj. Gen. DARIUS N. COUCH.

First Brigade.

Brig. Gen. JOSEPH A. COOPER.

26th Kentucky, Col. Cicero Maxwell.
25th Michigan, Capt. Samuel L. Demarest.
99th Ohio, Lieut. Col. John E. Cummins.
3d Tennessee, Col. William Cross.
6th Tennessee (seven companies), Maj.
A. Marion Gamble.

Second Brigade.

Col. ORLANDO H. MOORE.

107th Illinois, Capt. John W. Wood.
80th Indiana, Lieut. Col. Alfred D. Owen.
23d Michigan, Col. Oliver L. Spaulding.
111th Ohio, Lieut. Col. Isaac R. Sherwood.
118th Ohio, Maj. Edgar Sowers.

Third Brigade.

Col. JOHN O'DOWD.

91st Indiana, Lieut. Col. Charles H.
Butterfield.
50th Ohio, Lieut. Col. Hamilton S. Gillespie.
181st Ohio, Lieut. Col. John E. Hudson.
183d Ohio, Col. George W. Hoge.

Artillery.

Indiana Light, 15th Battery, Capt. Alonzo
D. Harvey.
Ohio Light, 19th Battery, Capt. Frank
Wilson.

THIRD DIVISION.

Brig. Gen. JACOB D. COX.

First Brigade.

Col. CHARLES C. DOOLITTLE.

12th Kentucky, Capt. John Travis.
16th Kentucky, Capt. Jacob Miller.
100th Ohio, Capt. Frank Rundell.
104th Ohio, Col. Oscar W. Sterl.
8th Tennessee, Capt. James W. Berry.

Second Brigade.

Col. JOHN S. CASEMENT.

65th Illinois, Maj. George H. Kennedy.
65th Indiana, Lieut. Col. John W. Hammond.
103d Ohio, Capt. Henry S. Pickands.
177th Ohio, Col. Arthur T. Wilcox.
5th Tennessee, Lieut. Col. Nathaniel
Witt.

Third Brigade.

Col. ISRAEL N. STILES.

112th Illinois, Capt. Sylvester F. Otman.
63d Indiana, Lieut. Col. Daniel Morris.
140th Indiana, Col. Thomas J. Brady.

Artillery.

Indiana Light, 23d Battery, Lieut. Aaron
A. Wilber.
1st Ohio Light, Battery D, Capt. Giles J.
Cockerill.

FOURTH DIVISION.*

Brig. Gen. JACOB AMMEN.

First Brigade.

Lieut. Col. WILLIAM C. BARTLETT.

2d North Carolina Mounted Infantry (seven companies), Capt. Thomas I. Johnson.
11th Tennessee Cavalry (dismounted), Maj. James H. Johnson.
1st Michigan Light Artillery, Battery M, Capt. Augustus H. Emery.
1st Tennessee Light Artillery, Battery B, Lieut. William G. Bewley.

---

*Also known as District of East Tennessee.

Second Brigade.

Brig. Gen. DAVIS TILLSON.

34th Kentucky, Capt. Joseph B. Watkins.
 3d North Carolina Mounted Infantry (three companies), Lieut. Col. George W. Kirk.
 1st Tennessee, Capt. Thomas J. Rogers.
 2d Tennessee, Capt. William M. Murray.
 4th Tennessee, Lieut. Col. Michael L. Patterson.
12th Kentucky Cavalry, Maj. James B. Harrison.
10th Michigan Cavalry, Lieut. Col. Luther S. Trowbridge.
Illinois Light Artillery, Colvin's Battery, Capt. John H. Colvin.
Illinois Light Artillery, Elgin Battery, Capt. Andrew M. Wood.
Illinois Light Artillery, Henshaw's Battery, Lieut. Azro C. Putnam.
1st Michigan Light Artillery, Battery L, Capt. Carlton Neal.
Ohio Light Artillery, 21st Battery, Capt. James H. Walley.
Ohio Light Artillery, 22d Battery, Lieut. Harvey Burdell.
Indiana Light Artillery, Wilder Battery, Capt. Hubbard T. Thomas.
2d Ohio Heavy Artillery, Col. Horatio G. Gibson.
1st U. S. Colored Heavy Artillery, Col. John A. Shannon.

MILITARY DISTRICT OF KENTUCKY.

Bvt. Maj. Gen. STEPHEN G. BURBRIDGE.

FIRST DIVISION.

Brig. Gen. EDWARD H. HOBSON.

Camp Nelson, Ky.

Brig. Gen. SPEED S. FRY.

43d Indiana, Company F, Capt. James B. Dyer.
 61st Company U. S. Veteran Reserve Corps (2d Battalion), } Capt. George
125th Company U. S. Veteran Reserve Corps (2d Battalion), } Ougheltree.
 1st Kentucky Cavalry, Maj. Alderson T. Keen.
 5th U. S. Colored Cavalry (detachment), Capt. John Anderson.
 6th U. S. Colored Cavalry (four companies), Capt. Joseph T. McKee.

Covington, Ky.

1st Ohio Heavy Artillery (two companies), Capt. William Carroll.

Lexington, Ky.

46th Indiana, Col. Thomas H. Bringhurst.
49th Indiana (six companies), Maj. James Leeper.
1st Kentucky Light Artillery, Battery E, Lieut. Llewyllyn E. P. Bush.
1st Wisconsin Heavy Artillery, Company B, Capt. Charles W. Hyde.

Louisa, Ky.

14th Kentucky, Lieut. Col. Rhys M. Thomas.
24th Kentucky, Col. John S. Hurt.
30th Kentucky (mounted), Col. Francis N. Alexander.
39th Kentucky, Lieut. Col. Stephen M. Ferguson.
79th Company U. S. Veteran Reserve Corps (2d Battalion), Lieut. David G.
    Falconer.

Mount Sterling, Ky.

11th Michigan Cavalry, Col. Simeon B. Brown.
1st Kentucky Light Artillery, Battery C, Lieut. Richard W. McReynolds.

Richmond, Ky.

12th Ohio Cavalry, Lieut. Col. Robert H. Bentley.

SECOND DIVISION.

Brig. Gen. HUGH EWING.

Second Brigade.

Col. DANIEL J. DILL.

47th Illinois (four companies), Lieut. Edward Bonham.
52d Kentucky (mounted—four companies), Maj. John B. Tyler.
 5th U. S. Colored Cavalry, 3d Battalion, Capt. Isaac Gray.
12th U. S. Colored Heavy Artillery (1st Battalion), Maj. Nathaniel H. Foster.
30th Wisconsin, Maj. John Clowney.

Not brigaded.

20th Kentucky, Lieut. Col. Thomas B. Waller.
27th Kentucky, Lieut. Col. John H. Ward.
 2d U. S. Veteran Reserve Corps, Company H, Capt. Adolphus von Dachenhausen.
23d U. S. Veteran Reserve Corps, Company D, Lieut. George W. Kingsbury.
11th Company U. S. Veteran Reserve Corps (2d Battalion), Lieut. Gottlob Hummel.
40th Company U. S. Veteran Reserve Corps (2d Battalion), Capt. Patrick Dwyer.
56th Company U. S. Veteran Reserve Corps (2d Battalion), Lieut. John Stephenson.
67th Company U. S. Veteran Reserve Corps (2d Battalion), ⎰ Lieut. Anthony Ander-
157th Company U. S. Veteran Reserve Corps (2d Battalion), ⎱   son.
68th Company U. S. Veteran Reserve Corps (2d Battalion), Lieut. Usher F. Kelly.
77th Company U. S. Veteran Reserve Corps (2d Battalion), Lieut. James Hart.
83d Company U. S. Veteran Reserve Corps (2d Battalion), ⎰ Lieut. Samuel H. Mor-
84th Company U. S. Veteran Reserve Corps (2d Battalion), ⎱   rison.
141st Company U. S. Veteran Reserve Corps (2d Battalion), Lieut. Noah W. Yoder.

CLEVELAND, TENN.

1st Ohio Heavy Artillery, Col. Chauncey G. Hawley.

DISTRICT OF WESTERN KENTUCKY.

Brig. Gen. SOLOMON MEREDITH.

Paducah, Ky.

Col. JOSHUA J. GUPPEY.

49th Illinois, Lieut. Col. William P. Moore.
 7th Tennessee Cavalry (three companies), Lieut. Col. Isaac R. Hawkins.
 2d Illinois Light Artillery, Battery B, Lieut. Thomas E. Dawson.
 8th U. S. Colored Heavy Artillery, Col. Henry W. Barry.

Smithland, Ky.

Capt. HENRY P. REED.

17th Kentucky Cavalry (one company).
13th U. S. Colored Heavy Artillery (two companies).

Abstract from returns of the Cavalry Corps, Military Division of the Mississippi, Bvt. Maj. Gen. James H. Wilson, U. S. Army, commanding, for the month of December, 1864. *

[Compiled mainly from subordinate returns.]

Command.	Present for duty.		Aggregate present.	Aggregate present and absent.	Pieces of field artillery.	Headquarters.
	Officers.	Men.				
General headquarters...................	9	....	9	9	....	In the field, Tenn.
4th U. S. Cavalry (Hedges)†............	7	265	327	632	....	
First Division (McCook)	160	3,726	4,684	7,749	8	Edgefield, Tenn.
Second Division (Long).................	178	5,195	6,227	8,449	....	Elizabethtown, Ky.
Fifth Division (Hatch).................	149	3,807	4,515	7,710	4	Athens, Ala.
Sixth Division (Johnson)...............	166	3,534	4,258	7,285	....	Edgefield, Tenn.
Seventh Division (Knipe)	130	2,934	4,028	6,955	4	Do.
Total.............................	799	19,461	24,048	38,789	16	
Grand total according to corps return ..	957	22,621	27,554	44,676	24	

Organization of troops in the Cavalry Corps, Military Division of the Mississippi, commanded by Bvt. Maj. Gen. James H. Wilson, U. S. Army, December 31, 1864.

ESCORT.

4th U. S. Cavalry, Lieut. Joseph Hedges.

FIRST DIVISION.

Brig. Gen. EDWARD M. McCOOK.

First Brigade.

Brig. Gen. JOHN T. CROXTON.

8th Iowa, Col. Joseph B. Dorr.
4th Kentucky (mounted infantry), Col. Robert M. Kelly.
2d Michigan, Lieut. Col. Benjamin Smith.
1st Tennessee, Lieut. Col. Calvin M. Dyer.
Illinois Light Artillery, Chicago Board of Trade Battery,‡ Capt. George I. Robinson.

Second Brigade.

Col. OSCAR H. LA GRANGE.

2d Indiana (battalion), Capt. Roswell S. Hill.
4th Indiana, Lieut. Col. Horace P. Lamson.
1st Wisconsin, Maj. Henry Harnden.

Third Brigade.

Bvt. Brig. Gen. LOUIS D. WATKINS.

4th Kentucky, Lieut. Col. George Welling.
6th Kentucky, Maj. William H. Fidler.
7th Kentucky, Col. John K. Faulkner.

Artillery.

Indiana Light, 18th Battery, Capt. Moses M. Beck.

---

*For abstract of the Third Division (Kilpatrick's), see Vol. XLIV, p. 848; for abstract of the Fourth Division (Upton's), see Vol XLI, Part IV, p. 972.
† Serving as escort.
‡ Temporarily attached from Second Division.

SECOND DIVISION.

Brig. Gen. ELI LONG.

First Brigade (mounted infantry).

Col. ABRAM O. MILLER.

98th Illinois, Lieut. Col. Edward Kitchell.
123d Illinois, Lieut. Col. Jonathan Biggs.
17th Indiana, Col. Jacob G. Vail.
72d Indiana, Lieut. Col. Chester G. Thomson.

Second Brigade.

Col. ROBERT H. G. MINTY.

4th Michigan, Capt. Benjamin D. Pritch-ard.
1st Ohio, Col. Beroth B. Eggleston.
3d Ohio, Col. Charles B. Seidel.
4th Ohio, Lieut. Col. George W. Dobb.
7th Pennsylvania, Maj. James F.Andress.

FIFTH DIVISION.

Brig. Gen. EDWARD HATCH.

First Brigade.

Col. ROBERT R. STEWART.

3d Illinois, Lieut. Col. Robert H. Carna-han.
11th Indiana, Lieut. Col. Abram Sharra.
12th Missouri, Lieut. Col. Richard H. Brown.
10th Tennessee, Maj. William P. Story.

Second Brigade.

Col. DATUS E. COON.

6th Illinois, Lieut. Col. John Lynch.
7th Illinois, Maj. John M. Graham.
9th Illinois, Maj. William McManis.
2d Iowa, Maj. Charles C. Horton.
12th Tennessee, Col. George Spalding.

Artillery.

1st Illinois Light, Battery I, Lieut. Joseph A. McCartney.

SIXTH DIVISION.

Brig. Gen. RICHARD W. JOHNSON.

First Brigade.

Col. THOMAS J. HARRISON.

14th Illinois, Maj. Haviland Tompkins.
16th Illinois, Maj. Charles H. Beeres.
8th Michigan, Col. Elisha Mix.
7th Ohio, Col. Israel Garrard.

Second Brigade.

Col. JAMES BIDDLE.

5th Indiana, Maj. Moses D. Leeson.
6th Indiana, Maj. Jacob S. Stevens.
5th Iowa, Lieut. Col. Harlon Baird.
3d Tennessee (three companies), Maj. Benjamin Cunningham.

Tullahoma, Tenn.

5th Tennessee,* Lieut. Col. William J. Clift.

Wauhatchie, Tenn.

15th Pennsylvania Cavalry,* Col. William J. Palmer,

Artillery.

4th United States, Battery I, Lieut. Frank G. Smith.

---

* Constituted, in orders, as the Third Brigade.

SEVENTH DIVISION.

Brig. Gen. JOSEPH F. KNIPE.

First Brigade.	*Second Brigade.*
Bvt. Brig. Gen. JOHN H. HAMMOND.	Col. GILBERT M. L. JOHNSON.
9th Indiana, Col. George W. Jackson.	12th Indiana, Maj. William H. Calkins.
10th Indiana, Maj. Thomas G. Williamson.	13th Indiana, Maj. Ranna S. Moore.
19th Pennsylvania, Maj. Amos J. Holahan.	6th Tennessee, Col. Fielding Hurst.
2d Tennessee, Lieut. Col. William R. Cook.	
4th Tennessee, Maj. Meshack Stephens.	

Artillery.

Ohio Light, 14th Battery, Lieut. William C. Myers.

Abstract from return of the Northern Department, Maj. Gen. Joseph Hooker, U. S. Army, commanding, for the month of December, 1864.

Command.	Present for duty.		Aggregate present.	Aggregate present and absent.	Pieces of artillery.	
	Officers.	Men.			Heavy.	Field.
General headquarters	15		15	15		
Camp Chase, Ohio (Richardson)	23	677	1,033	1,159		
Camp Thomas, Ohio (Caldwell)	2	40	68	84		
Camp Dennison, Ohio (Noyes)	6	39	48	53		
Cincinnati, Ohio (Willich)	24	266	501	582		
Sandusky and Johnson's Island (Hill)	25	1,027	1,676	1,964	7	3
Camp Cleveland, Ohio (Smith)	5	100	112	116		6
Gallipolis, Ohio (Allen)	9	130	201	228		
District of Indiana (Hovey)	71	1,875	2,779	3,289		
District of Illinois (Cook)	136	2,562	4,288	5,851		6
District of Michigan (Hill)	28	424	650	782		
Total	344	7,140	11,371	14,123	7	15

Organization of troops in the Northern Department, commanded by Maj. Gen. Joseph Hooker, U. S. Army, December 31, 1864.

CAMP CHASE, OHIO.

Col. WILLIAM P. RICHARDSON.

37th Iowa (three companies), Lieut. Col. George R. West.
88th Ohio, Col. George W. Neff.

CAMP THOMAS, OHIO.

Maj. JAMES N. CALDWELL.

Permanent Company, 18th United States, Maj. James N. Caldwell.

CAMP DENNISON, OHIO.

Col. EDWARD F. NOYES.

126th Company U. S. Veteran Reserve Corps (2d Battalion), Capt. Joseph O'Neil.

CINCINNATI, OHIO.

Brig. Gen. AUGUST WILLICH.

37th Iowa (five companies), Col. George W. Kincaid.
192d Pennsylvania (one company), Capt. Thomas McLeester.
Detachment of invalids.

SANDUSKY AND JOHNSON'S ISLAND.

Col. CHARLES W. HILL.

128th Ohio, Col. Charles W. Hill.
6th U. S. Veteran Reserve Corps, Col. Moses N. Wisewell.

CAMP CLEVELAND, OHIO.

Col. CHARLES C. SMITH.

GALLIPOLIS, OHIO.

Maj. LYMAN ALLEN.

37th Iowa (two companies), Maj. Lyman Allen.
Trumbull (Ohio) Guards, Capt. Charles W. Smith.
66th Company U. S. Veteran Reserve Corps (2d Battalion), Lieut. Marcus S. Hopkins·

DISTRICT OF INDIANA.

Bvt. Maj. Gen. ALVIN P. HOVEY.

Burnside Barracks.

Col. AMBROSE A. STEVENS.

43d Indiana, Lieut. Col. John C. Major.
 5th U. S. Veteran Reserve Corps, Col. Ambrose A. Stevens.
21st U. S. Veteran Reserve Corps, Company G, Lieut. George Duff.
22d U. S. Veteran Reserve Corps, Company I (detachment), Lieut. Alfred B. Grun-
    well.

Evansville.

25th, 92d, 106th, and 120th Companies U. S. Veteran Reserve Corps (2d Battalion),
    Capt. Edward Tombler.

Indianapolis.

17th U. S. Veteran Reserve Corps, Col. Adoniram J. Warner.
94th Company U. S. Veteran Reserve Corps (2d Battalion), Lieut. Francis Otwell.

Madison.

20th, 91st, 93d, and 103d Companies U. S. Veteran Reserve Corps (2d Battalion), Lieut.
 Germain Dettweiler.

New Albany.

2d U. S. Veteran Reserve Corps, Company I,
45th and 158th Companies U. S. Veteran Reserve Corps (2d } Lieut. John P. Beach.
    Battalion),

DISTRICT OF ILLINOIS.

Brig. Gen. JOHN COOK.

Camp Butler.

Col. CHARLES M. PREVOST.

146th Illinois (detachment), Capt. John M. Lingle.
14th Iowa (detachment), Capt. Orville Burke.
16th U. S. Veteran Reserve Corps (detachment), Col. Charles M. Prevost.
42d Wisconsin (detachment), Lieut. Bartlett M. Low.

Camp Douglas.

Col. BENJAMIN J. SWEET.

8th U. S. Veteran Reserve Corps, Lieut. Col. Lewis C. Skinner.
15th U. S. Veteran Reserve Corps, Maj. James E. Cornelius.
Ohio Light Artillery, 24th Battery, Capt. John L. Hill.

Cairo.

42d Wisconsin (detachment), Col. Ezra T. Sprague.

Quincy.

Col. HENRY H. DEANE.

146th Illinois (detachment), Col. Henry H. Deane.
98th Company U. S. Veteran Reserve Corps (2d Battalion), Lieut. S. F. Cooper.

Rock Island.

Col. ANDREW J. JOHNSON.

108th U. S. Colored Troops, Maj. Andrew J. Krause.
4th U. S. Veteran Reserve Corps,   } Maj. Benjami F. Har-
—— Company U. S. Veteran Reserve Corps (2d Battalion), }   ris.

DISTRICT OF MICHIGAN.

Lieut. Col. BENNETT H. HILL.

19th United States (detachment), Maj. Pinkney Lugenbeel.
2d U. S. Veteran Reserve Corps (six companies), Lieut. Col. Fabian Brydolf.
137th Company U. S. Veteran Reserve Corps (2d Battalion), Capt. Charles J. Hunt.

Draft Rendezvous, Jackson, Mich.

Bvt. Maj. Gen. LYSANDER CUTLER.

PULASKI, TENN., *January 1, 1865—8 p. m.*
(Received 11 p. m.)

Maj. Gen. H. W. HALLECK,
        Washington, D. C.:

A dispatch from Major-General Steedman, dated December 29, received to-day, reports his command at Courtland, Ala., and a small cavalry force with him advanced as far as Town Creek on that day, having made some captures since leaving Decatur, and that prisoners and citizens informed him that Hood had retreated toward Corinth. This information is confirmed by a report from General Wilson, of 6 a. m. yesterday, at Blue Water Creek, Ala. I have ordered all the cavalry to concentrate at Eastport; also, Generals Smith's and Schofield's commands. General Wood has been ordered to Huntsville with his command, where it will be as conveniently located for the resumption of active operations as at Tuscumbia, having a substantial pontoon bridge across the river at Decatur to cross on at any time. All the preliminary orders for getting the troops ready have been issued, and I shall go to Eastport myself, by way of Nashville, starting day after to-morrow (3d instant). I omitted to mention in my dispatch of last night that nearly all the regiments ordered to re-enforce me in November last have been absorbed in replacing regiments whose terms of service have expired, and, therefore, my available force will consist of only the troops which commenced the campaign at Nashville, increased by eight regiments, ordered from Murfreesborough to join General Schofield, Long's division of cavalry, and two brigades of McCook's division of cavalry.

GEO. H. THOMAS,
Major-General, U. S. Volunteers, Commanding.

HEADQUARTERS DEPARTMENT OF THE CUMBERLAND,
Pulaski, January 1, 1865. (Received 8 p. m.)

ADJUTANT-GENERAL,
      Washington, D. C.:

The reserve artillery of the Army of the Tennessee I have ordered to Savannah, to join General Sherman. It is now at Nashville. Do you wish it fully equipped before starting? The batteries require more or less guns, caissons, horses, and harness. Half the batteries have no horses, caissons, or harness.

GEO. H. THOMAS,
Major-General, U. S. Volunteers, Commanding.

[First indorsement.]

ADJUTANT-GENERAL'S OFFICE,
January 1, 1865—9.15 p. m.

Major-General HALLECK,
      Chief of Staff:

GENERAL: Does this require reply to-night; and if so, what answer shall be sent?
      Respectfully,

E. D. TOWNSEND,
Assistant Adjutant-General.

[Second indorsement.]

JANUARY 1, 1865.

This requires no answer to-night. I will answer it in the morning, with other orders. General Sherman does not want any more artillery.

H. W. HALLECK,
Major-General and Chief of Staff.

NASHVILLE, *January 1, 1865.*

Maj. Gen. GEORGE H. THOMAS:

Steps have been taken, and every effort will be made to carry them out, for the reorganization of the State. A convention will assemble here on Monday, the 9th of January. The courts are all being established, and so far are working well. Soon after the meeting of the convention there will be an election held for members of Congress, Legislature, and Senate. The effect of the great victory over Hood's army at Nashville is being seen and felt in every part of the State; its withering influence upon rebels is more decided than anything which has transpired since the beginning of the rebellion. I thank you for the suggestions you have made in regard to placing the State in the hands of the citizens, and the aid you have proposed to give in doing so. I think the work can now be undertaken with greater prospect of success than at any former period, and no effort on my part shall be omitted in trying to accomplish so desirable an end. It is not necessary for me to say that you have a nation's gratitude for what you have done in preserving the Government of the United States, but my prayer is that all your future efforts in the preservation of the Union may be, as the past have been, crowned with success and unfading honor.

ANDREW JOHNSON,
Military Governor of Tennessee.

PULASKI, TENN., *January 1, 1865.*

Brig. Gen. JAMES L. DONALDSON,
Nashville, Tenn.:

On the 30th December I received a dispatch from General Rousseau, notifying me that the Forty-seventh and Forty-eighth Missouri had been sent by rail as far as Spring Hill, but could get no farther for want of wagons, which could not be issued before Wednesday. One of these regiments is intended to garrison Columbia; the other Pulaski. The garrison for these places is much needed. Can they get wagons soon?

WM. D. WHIPPLE,
Brigadier-General.

NASHVILLE, *January 1, 1865.*

Brig. Gen. W. D. WHIPPLE:

Will see that forage for Huntsville and Chattanooga and forage for Eastport get in time. I don't know anything about wagons for garrison at Pulaski, as it is the first I have heard of it. If quartermaster there will inform me of his wants, will see he is promptly supplied. You had better keep me posted as to number of troops and animals at Eastport and what time they will be likely to remain there, so as to make arrangements here accordingly.

J. L. DONALDSON,
Brigadier-General and Chief Quartermaster.

PULASKI, TENN., *January 1, 1865.*

Brig. Gen. JAMES L. DONALDSON,
Nashville, Tenn.:

The Twenty-third Army Corps starts to-morrow morning for Eastport via Clifton. It will reach Clifton by the 7th instant. Please have boats ready to take the corps to Eastport. It is supplied up to 10th instant, and will want, after reaching Clifton, 60,000 pounds forage and 22,000 rations daily. Answer.

> WM. D. WHIPPLE,
> *Brigadier-General.*

PULASKI, TENN., *January 1, 1865.*

Brig. Gen. JAMES L. DONALDSON,
        Nashville, Tenn.:

The whole of Wilson's cavalry is ordered to Eastport; therefore, send forage for it to that place.

> WM. D. WHIPPLE,
> *Brigadier-General.*

PULASKI, *January 1, 1865.*

Brig. Gen. J. L. DONALDSON,
        Nashville, Tenn.:

The Fourth Army Corps is ordered to Huntsville, and will probably require a little forage at first, until they get to foraging for themselves.

> WM. D. WHIPPLE,
> *Brigadier-General.*

HEADQUARTERS DEPARTMENT OF THE CUMBERLAND,
        Pulaski, Tenn., January 1, 1865.

Brig. Gen. T. J. WOOD,
        Commanding Fourth Army Corps:

GENERAL: Your communication of the 30th ultimo, suggesting plan for continued operations this winter, has been received. Probably some such plan will be adopted, as you will see by the inclosed copy of telegram* from General Halleck that the lieutenant-general is not disposed to permit our army to rest long. The major-general commanding directs that Athens be not occupied by your troops, but that the entire corps be concentrated at Huntsville, and all returns made up to date, and full preparations made for continuing the campaign at as early a date as possible.

Very respectfully, your obedient servant,

> WM. D. WHIPPLE,
> *Brigadier-General and Chief of Staff.*

PULASKI, TENN., *January 1, 1865.*

Brig. Gen. T. J. WOOD,
        Athens, Ala.:

Concentrate your whole corps at Huntsville and prepare for an early resumption of the winter campaign. Instructions by letter have been sent you. The Twenty-third Corps goes to Eastport.

> WM. D. WHIPPLE,
> *Brigadier-General and Chief of Staff.*

---

* See 11.30 a. m. December 31, p. 441.

HEADQUARTERS FOURTH ARMY CORPS,
Elk River, January 1, 1865.

Brigadier-General KIMBALL:

GENERAL: The general commanding directs that you send out foraging parties from each brigade of your division, for the purpose of collecting breadstuff and meat only. Household property, animals not fit for meat, &c., must not be taken. Brigade commissaries of subsistence must receipt for all property taken. He also directs that you seize mills in the country and grind for your division.

Very respectfully, your obedient servant,

J. S. FULLERTON,
Assistant Adjutant-General and Chief of Staff.

(Copy to Generals Elliott, Beatty, and Major Goodspeed.)

HEADQUARTERS FOURTH ARMY CORPS,
Elk River, January 1, 1865.

Brigadier-General ELLIOTT,
Second Division:

You will send out fifteen wagons of your supply train, early to-morrow morning, through the country in the vicinity of your camp, for the purpose of collecting flooring for the bridge which is now being constructed at Buck Island Ford. Send at least five men with each wagon, and let them select plank from one inch thick upward. They can take all plank and flooring in all old outbuildings and unoccupied houses they may find. The wagons with the lumber should report to Colonel Suman at the ford by 12 m. to-morrow.

By order of Brigadier-General Wood:

J. S. FULLERTON,
Assistant Adjutant-General and Chief of Staff.

HEADQUARTERS THIRD DIVISION, FOURTH ARMY CORPS,
Near Mount Rozell, Ala., January 1, 1865.

Orders for to-day:

This command will march, following the First Division, to Buck Island Ford, in the following order: Second Brigade, Colonel McConnell; Third Brigade, Colonel Knefler; First Brigade, Colonel Streight; artillery; all wheel vehicles, &c.

By order of Brigadier-General Beatty:

M. P. BESTOW,
Assistant Adjutant-General.

COLUMBIA, TENN., *January 1, 1865.*

Major-General HALLECK,
Chief of Staff, Washington, D. C.:

The Twenty-third Army Corps now contains only a minimum number of regiments, and their terms of service begin to expire very soon. I respectfully request that new regiments may be raised in Ohio, Indiana, Illinois, and any other Western States, for this corps.

J. M. SCHOFIELD,
Major-General.

PULASKI, TENN., *January 1, 1865.*

Maj. Gen. J. M. SCHOFIELD,
　　　　　Columbia:

You are authorized to visit your department; but in view of a continuance of active operations the major-general commanding desires that you will be as expeditious as possible.

　　　　　　　　　　WM. D. WHIPPLE,
　　　　　　　　　　　　Brigadier-General.

COLUMBIA, *January 1, 1865.*

Brigadier-General WHIPPLE,
　　　　　Pulaski:

Your dispatch is received. I do not desire to leave my command in the field, if active operations are to continue. My request was based upon the order of December 29, directing my troops to go into winter camp. If the troops are likely to have three or four weeks' rest, I would like to go to Kentucky. Please inform me what the probabilities are.

　　　　　　　　　　J. M. SCHOFIELD,
　　　　　　　　　　　　Major-General.

HEADQUARTERS DEPARTMENT OF THE CUMBERLAND,
　　　　　　　　Pulaski, January 1, 1865.

Maj. Gen. J. M. SCHOFIELD,
　　　　　Columbia:

After orders had been sent you to go to Dalton the rear-admiral telegraphed that the rebels were fortifying Eastport. This caused a suspension of your order. Since that the lieutenant-general has ordered an immediate prosecution of the campaign, and we are waiting to get information of Hood's line of retreat to issue orders for your corps to move. You will then probably go to Eastport. Dana has cut the Mobile and Ohio Railroad, and is pushing for the Cahawba. Roddey has been thrashed out of Decatur and out of sight by General Granger. Please keep sending the weekly report of effective force, it being necessary to provide provisions; also keep me posted with regard to number of animals in Twenty-third Corps.

　　　　　　　　　　WM. D. WHIPPLE,
　　　　　　　　　　　　Brigadier-General.

HEADQUARTERS DEPARTMENT OF THE CUMBERLAND,
　　　　　　　　Pulaski, January 1, 1865.

Maj. Gen. J. M. SCHOFIELD,
　　　　　Columbia, Tenn.:

The major-general commanding directs that you march the Twenty-third Corps, via Mount Pleasant and Waynesborough, to Clifton, on Tennessee River, and there embark for Eastport. Disembark at latter point, and prepare for an early prosecution of the campaign. Inform me when you will be at Clifton and what you wish sent you by steamer besides provisions and forage.

　　　　　　　　　　WM. D. WHIPPLE,
　　　　　　　　　　　　Brigadier-General.

COLUMBIA, TENN., *January 1, 1865.*

Brigadier-General WHIPPLE,
   Pulaski:

I have received your dispatch ordering the Twenty-third Corps to Eastport via Clifton. I will start to-morrow, and expect to reach Clifton by the 7th. My troops will be supplied up to the 10th. I will want at Clifton 60,000 pounds of forage and 22,000 rations per day.

        J. M. SCHOFIELD,
          Major-General.

HEADQUARTERS ARMY OF THE OHIO,
   Columbia, Tenn., January 1, 1865.

Governor RICHARD J. OGLESBY,
   State of Illinois:

GOVERNOR: I am anxious to have a few new regiments raised in the Western States for the Twenty-third Army Corps, which will soon be much reduced by the muster-out of old regiments. Our noble State is now honorably represented in the corps, though only by two regiments. I have called the attention of the War Department to the matter, and if my proposition meets with approval there, may I not rely on Illinois for at least three or four of the regiments necessary to enable the Twenty-third Corps to maintain its present prestige to the end of the war? Major Wells, who will hand you this, has already received my recommendation for the command of a regiment, for which he is in all respects well qualified.

I am, Governor, very respectfully, your obedient servant,

        J. M. SCHOFIELD,
          Major-General.

SPECIAL ⎫ HEADQUARTERS ARMY OF THE OHIO,
FIELD ORDERS, ⎬ *In the Field, Columbia, Tenn.,*
No. 1. ⎭   *January 1, 1865.*

 *   *   *   *   *   *   *

5. The corps will march to-morrow morning for Clifton, via Mount Pleasant and Waynesborough, in the following order: Third Division; Second Division; First Division. Each division will be followed—first, by its baggage train; second, ammunition train; and third, two sections of supply train (six days' rations of subsistence and forage). The corps train will follow the trains of the last division. The leading division will move habitually at daylight in the morning, and will be followed by the other divisions at convenient marching distance. The divisions may also preserve this distance in encamping, if it be found convenient to do so. The day's march will be from ten to fifteen miles, according to the character of the road.

 *   *   *   *   *   *   *

By command of Major-General Schofield:

        J. A. CAMPBELL,
     Major and Assistant Adjutant-General.

GENERAL ORDERS, }   HEADQUARTERS THIRD DIVISION,
                          TWENTY-THIRD ARMY CORPS,
No. 1.   }   *Columbia, Tenn., January 1, 1865.*

I. During the temporary absence of the general commanding the division, Col. C. C. Doolittle, commanding First Brigade, as senior officer present, will assume command of the division.

II. During the temporary absence of Capt. Theodore Cox, assistant adjutant-general at these headquarters, Lieut. E. E. Tracy, aide-de-camp, will, in addition to his other duties, perform those of assistant adjutant-general of the division. He will be obeyed and respected accordingly.

By command of Brigadier-General Cox:

THEO. COX,
Captain and Assistant Adjutant-General.

GENERAL ORDERS, }   HDQRS. DETACH. ARMY OF THE TENN.,
No. 1.   }   *Camp in Field, January 1, 1865.*

The major-general commanding announces the organization of his staff as follows: Maj. John Hough, U. S. Volunteers, assistant adjutant-general; Maj. J. J. Lyon, Twenty-fourth Missouri Infantry, acting assistant inspector-general; Surg. W. H. Thorne, U. S. Volunteers, medical director; Capt. C. K. Drew, U. S. Volunteers, chief quartermaster; Capt. George W. Baker, U. S. Volunteers, chief commissary; Capt. Ross Wilkinson, Fifth Minnesota Infantry, aide-de-camp and provost-marshal; Capt. George R. Brown, Ninth Indiana Battery, chief of artillery; Lieut. J. B. Pannes, Seventeenth New York Infantry, acting ordnance officer; Lieut. Hunn Hanson, Fourth Missouri Cavalry, aide-de-camp.

A. J. SMITH,
Major-General.

HEADQUARTERS DETACHMENT ARMY OF THE TENNESSEE,
Waynesborough, Tenn., January 1, 1865.

Brig. Gen. K. GARRARD,
  Commanding Second Division:

The major-general commanding directs that you move with your command to-morrow morning, January 2, at 8 a. m., promptly; First Division at 9 a. m., in rear of Second Division; Third Division in rear, taking charge of train. Commanding officers of divisions will be held responsible that there is no straggling in their respective commands. Regimental and company officers will march in the rear of their respective commands.

By order of Maj. Gen. A. J. Smith:

J. HOUGH,
Major and Assistant Adjutant-General.

(Same to Brig. Gen. J. McArthur, commanding First Division; Col. J. B. Moore, commanding Third Division.)

HEADQUARTERS DEPARTMENT OF THE CUMBERLAND,
Pulaski, January 1, 1865—5 p. m.

Maj. Gen. J. H. WILSON,
   Commanding Cavalry Corps, Huntsville:

Upon receipt of your communication expressing a wish to concentrate the cavalry near Eastport, I immediately dispatched you authorizing you to do so, as in your note you said you would remain in your camp until you heard from me. A dispatch received from Washington yesterday directs me to concentrate my forces on the Tennessee, and be prepared to pursue Hood on receipt of orders. I therefore wish you to concentrate your whole force at Eastport, or vicinity, as soon as you can, and make every preparation for a renewal of the campaign.

GEO. H. THOMAS,
Major-General, U. S. Volunteers, Commanding.

HUNTSVILLE, *January 1, 1865—7 p. m.*

Brigadier-General WHIPPLE,
   Chief of Staff:

I arrived here this evening. Find the country eaten out. Must have rations and forage as soon as possible. Please inform me who is to command the town. I would rather be relieved of civil matters.

J. H. WILSON,
Major-General.

HDQRS. CAVALRY CORPS, MIL. DIV. OF THE MISSISSIPPI,
Huntsville, January 1, 1865—8.15 p. m.

Major-General THOMAS:

Your dispatch of 5 p. m. is just received. The suggestions of my communications were based upon [what] I regarded [as] very probable contingencies, but your instructions were so definite that I did not feel at liberty to delay in obeying them. My command is in no condition to make the march you direct; they have for over two weeks ridden over frozen or stony ways, and must have rations and an opportunity to shoe up and refit. Your order, however, is imperative, and I will, therefore, order everything back in the morning, unless authorized to delay. Long and McCook should be directed to march toward Eastport. Please notify Major Beaumont.

J. H. WILSON,
Brevet Major-General.

HUNTSVILLE, *January 1, 1865.*

Brig. Gen. E. M. McCOOK:

As soon as your command is in proper condition march, via Columbia, Mount Pleasant, and Waynesborough, with all your transportation to Eastport.

J. H. WILSON,
Brevet Major-General.

SPECIAL ORDERS, ⎱   HDQRS. SIXTH DIV., CAVALRY CORPS,
                  ⎰   MILITARY DIV. OF THE MISSISSIPPI,
No. 1.   *Edgefield, Tenn., January 1, 1865.*

Col. W. W. Lowe, Fifth Iowa Cavalry, having reported for duty, is hereby assigned to the permanent command of the Second Brigade of this division, and, for the time being, will command all of the dismounted troops of this division heretofore in command of Major Davidson, Fourteenth Illinois Cavalry. Major Davidson, on being relieved, will resume command of his regiment.

By command of Brigadier-General Johnson:

E. T. WELLS,
Assistant Adjutant-General.

HEADQUARTERS SIXTH DIVISION, CAVALRY CORPS,
MILITARY DIVISION OF THE MISSISSIPPI,
Edgefield, Tenn., January 1, 1865.

Col. T. J. HARRISON,
    Commanding Brigade:

COLONEL: General Johnson directs me to acknowledge the receipt of your communication* reporting the operations of your brigade on the 25th ultimo, and to communicate to you his sincere commendations and thanks for the gallantry exhibited by your troops upon that occasion. He expresses the opinion, founded both upon your report and his own previous observations of your command in action, that no troops would have pressed the enemy with more vigor, persistence, or success. He returns to you especially his thanks for this success, the credit of which inures, in a measure, to the whole division, and requests that this may be communicated to your troops.

Very respectfully, your obedient servant,

E. T. WELLS,
Assistant Adjutant-General.

NASHVILLE, TENN., *January 1, 1865.*

Brig. Gen. W. D. WHIPPLE,
        Pulaski:

The Thirty-ninth Missouri Regiment, composed of six and twelve months' troops mustered last fall, came in this morning. What orders have you for the regiment?

L. H. ROUSSEAU,
Major-General.

PULASKI, TENN., *January 1, 1865.*

Maj. Gen. L. H. ROUSSEAU,
    Commanding District of Tennessee, Nashville, Tenn.:

The following order was issued yesterday from these headquarters:

SPECIAL FIELD ORDERS, ⎱   HDQRS. DEPARTMENT OF THE CUMBERLAND,
No. 355.   ⎰   *Pulaski, December 31, 1864.*

IX. In compliance with instructions received from the War Department, the Thirty-ninth Missouri Volunteer Infantry, now at Louisville, Ky., will proceed without

---

* See Part I, p. 603.

delay to Saint Louis, Mo., reporting on arrival at that point to Major-General Dodge, commanding Department of the Missouri, for further orders. The quartermaster's department will furnish the necessary transportation.

By command of Major-General Thomas:

H. M. CIST,
Assistant Adjutant-General.

NASHVILLE, TENN., *January 1, 1865.*

Maj. Gen. J. M. SCHOFIELD:

The One hundred and eightieth Ohio is at Elk River and Decherd, and will be relieved to-day or to-morrow. Where shall it report?

LOVELL H. ROUSSEAU,
Major-General.

COLUMBIA, TENN., *January 1, 1865.*

Major-General ROUSSEAU,
    Nashville:

Your dispatch is received. I will take the One hundred and eightieth Ohio and Twenty-eighth Michigan to join me at Clifton or Eastport on the Tennessee. If [they] can go by boat from Nashville please send them that way; if not let them march via this place and Mount Pleasant.

J. M. SCHOFIELD,
Major-General.

PULASKI, *January 1, 1865.*

Brig. Gen. JOHN. F. MILLER,
    Nashville, Tenn.:

Retain the baggage of this army at Nashville until it is known where the troops will finally stop. In the meantime send men for the Fourth Corps to Huntsville, Twenty-third Corps to Columbia, General Smith's command and the cavalry to Eastport. Will answer soon about the men of General Sherman's army whose terms of service have expired.

WM. D. WHIPPLE,
Brigadier-General.

TULLAHOMA, *January 1, 1865.*

Major-General ROUSSEAU:

The country is full of bushwhackers, stragglers, and deserters from the rebel army. The little Fifth Tennessee Cavalry is wholly inadequate to drive them out and do the scouting required. Can you not send me another cavalry regiment? There are detachments of Companies C, D, and H of the Twelfth Indiana Cavalry, sixty-four men in all, at Brownsborough, all numbered. Can you, at least, order these to join their regiment here? They can march through by Fayetteville.

R. H. MILROY,
Major-General.

PULASKI, *January 1, 1865.*

Brig. Gen. R. S. GRANGER,
    Huntsville or Decatur :

Yours of yesterday received. What force do you refer to as being at Paint Rock? None has been reported to these headquarters. What bridge is that you speak of, and what piece of artillery? Nothing has been said about those before. Did the camp-fires and pickets seen by Wauhatchie belong to rebels or U. S. forces? Report as soon as Colonel Merrill arrives with pontoon bridge at Decatur.

       GEO. H. THOMAS,
    Major-General, U. S. Volunteers, Commanding.

HUNTSVILLE, *January 1, 1865.*

Major-General THOMAS:

GENERAL: The pontoons have arrived, and the bridge will be laid by to-morrow night. I leave for Decatur as soon as a train can be furnished. The bridge over Paint Rock is being repaired and will be finished to-morrow. About one-half of the force stationed there have come in; the lieutenant and other half are probably captured. They were attacked at daylight; undoubtedly surprised. I have an ample force there now, and a competent officer, who will proceed to erect proper defenses.

       R. S. GRANGER,
       Brigadier-General.

PULASKI, *January 1, 1865.*

Brig. Gen. R. S. GRANGER,
    Decatur, Ala.:

Your telegram of this date is received, as also your report of yesterday, relative to the damage to the bridge at Paint Rock. The major-general commanding directs that you inquire more fully into the matter of the attack on the bridge, and make a written report of the same. Measures will be taken to furnish your district with the desired cavalry as soon as the cavalry force can be reorganized.

       ROBT. H. RAMSEY,
      Assistant Adjutant-General.

PULASKI, *January 1, 1865—5 p. m.*

Maj. Gen. JAMES B. STEEDMAN,
    Decatur :
(To be forwarded immediately to Courtland.)

Your telegram of December 30 is just received. As Hood has succeeded in crossing the Tennessee, and is now doubtless well on his way to Corinth, I wish you to return to Chattanooga with your forces, sending back to Nashville Thompson's brigade of colored troops—consisting of the Twelfth, Thirteenth, One hundredth, and part of the Seventeenth Regiments—and all other detachments that belonged in Nashville before the present movement commenced. Answer this by telegraph to me at Nashville upon receipt.

       GEO. H. THOMAS,
    Major-General, U. S. Volunteers, Commanding.

BRIDGEPORT, *January 1, 1865.*

Capt. H. A. FORD, *Acting Assistant Adjutant-General:*

Captain Wemple, Thirteenth Wisconsin Volunteer Infantry, has just reported to me the capture of block-house and an entire company at Paint Rock bridge.

Very respectfully, your obedient servant,

A. O. MILLINGTON,
Colonel, Commanding Post.

BRIDGEPORT, *January 1, 1865.*

Capt. H. A. FORD, *Acting Assistant Adjutant-General:*

I have just learned that Paint Rock bridge has been burned by the rebels.

A. O. MILLINGTON,
Commanding Post.

GENERAL ORDERS, ⎫　　HEADQUARTERS FIRST DIVISION,
　　　　　　　　　⎬　　MILITARY DISTRICT OF KENTUCKY,
No. 1.　　　　　　⎭　　　　*Lexington, Ky., January 1, 1865.*

The brigade organizations in this division are hereby dissolved. The respective regiments heretofore composing the brigade will report direct to these headquarters, except when at Camp Nelson, Lexington, Covington, or Louisa, Ky., in which case they will report to commanding officer U. S. forces or commandant of the post.

By command of Brig. Gen. E. H. Hobson:

J. S. BUTLER,
Assistant Adjutant-General.

CITY POINT, VA., *January 2, 1865—7 p. m.*

Maj. Gen. H. W. HALLECK, *Washington:*

Inform General Thomas that he will require no new outfit of teams; his troops will either operate in a country which will supply them, or the surplus ones will be sent where it is not desirable to transport wagons and mules. There has always been an unnecessary accumulation of teams in the Department of the Cumberland along the railroads, where every supply, but fuel, was brought on the cars. The Department of the Ohio also had a large number of wagons and mules, owing to having attempted to supply themselves through Cumberland Gap.

U. S. GRANT,
Lieutenant-General.

WASHINGTON, D. C., *January 2, 1865—11.30 a. m.*

Major-General THOMAS, *Pulaski:*

The orders of General Grant to concentrate your forces on the Tennessee were not intended to interfere in any manner with your pursuit of Hood, or your cutting off his lines of railroad, &c.; they have reference to what is to be done when your present operations are concluded.

H. W. HALLECK,
Major-General and Chief of Staff.

PULASKI, TENN., *January 2, 1865—8 p. m.*
(Received 10.20 p. m.)

Maj. Gen. H. W. HALLECK,
Washington, D. C.:

Reports received to-day seem to confirm my report that Hood has
gone to Corinth with his army, but I can scarcely believe he will attempt
to halt at Corinth with the railroad broken in his rear; and, besides
this, I have received a telegram from General Steedman, dated Courtland, December 31, in which he states that citizens and deserters inform
him that there is no force of the enemy either at Florence or Tuscumbia;
it being also reported to him that the enemy's pontoon train had left
La Grange on the morning of the 30th for Russellville, with orders to
go to Columbus, Miss., he had sent his cavalry force in pursuit, hoping
to be able to overtake it on the road and destroy it.

GEO. H. THOMAS,
Major-General.

WASHINGTON, *January 2, 1865.*

Major-General THOMAS, *Pulaski, Tenn.:*

No artillery need be sent to General Sherman; we can give him
from here all he may require.

H. W. HALLECK,
Major-General and Chief of Staff.

HEADQUARTERS DEPARTMENT OF THE CUMBERLAND,
Pulaski, January 2, 1865. (Received 1.25 p. m.)

ADJUTANT-GENERAL U. S. ARMY,
Washington:

Many deserters are coming from the enemy, and are, of course, desirous of taking the amnesty oath and being permitted to live at home.
Some bona fide deserters could probably be trusted. What is the policy
of the Administration with regard to these men?

GEO. H. THOMAS,
Major-General, U. S. Volunteers, Commanding.

FLAG-SHIP FAIRY,
Paducah, January 2, 1865.

Major-General THOMAS:

Your two telegrams of the 25th and 26th [ultimo] received to-day.
There are five army transports and two barges here. General Croxton's command came last night. Hood is reported to have crossed at
the foot or over Big Mussel Shoals. This river has fallen nine feet, and
is still falling, preventing continuance of operations above Waterloo.
Pity your cipher operator left me at Clarksville. Of course, Hood,
being near Corinth, which deserters say he is fortifying, attracted by
your transports, will annoy this part of the river. Would like to know
your plans so far as naval co-operation is concerned. How can you
communicate confidentially?

S. P. LEE,
Acting Rear-Admiral.

FLAG-SHIP FAIRY,
Eastport, Miss., January 2, 1865. (Via Paducah.)
Maj. Gen. GEORGE H. THOMAS:

I respectfully suggest that, if consistent with your plans and views, Forrest and his gang be entirely cleaned out of Western Kentucky and Tennessee, and that if Johnsonville is to be reoccupied, a small magazine be built for the use of the naval forces there, and one or more small effective earth-works be constructed on the west side of the river.

S. P. LEE,
Acting Rear-Admiral.

PULASKI, *January 2, 1865.*
Admiral S. P. LEE,
Comdg. Mississippi Squadron, Flag-ship Fairy, Paducah:

Your telegram of this date is received. My troops will concentrate as rapidly as possible at Eastport, on the Tennessee River, preparatory to a continuance of the campaign, and I shall be there myself about the latter part of this week or the beginning of next week, going by water from Nashville. I shall be much obliged if you will make arrangements to convoy transports up the river to Eastport, keeping the river open for them, if possible. I will make an early effort to replace your cipher operator, so that we may again be able to communicate confidentially. Your second dispatch of this date is just received. Your suggestions with reference to the magazine and earth-works at Johnsonville will be carried out as soon as possible.

GEO. H. THOMAS,
Major-General, Commanding.

HEADQUARTERS DEPARTMENT OF THE CUMBERLAND,
Pulaski, January 2, 1865.
Brig. Gen. J. L. DONALDSON,
Nashville:

The Cavalry Corps, Twenty-third Corps, and A. J. Smith's command have been ordered to Eastport. Send a quartermaster there, and make arrangements for getting supplies there. The cavalry force will number 16,000 horses, with due proportion of wagons and teams.

WM. D. WHIPPLE,
Brigadier-General.

HEADQUARTERS DEPARTMENT OF THE CUMBERLAND
Pulaski, January 2, 1865.
Brig. Gen. J. L. DONALDSON,
Nashville:

After all the troops have reached Eastport, the pontoon train can be sent there, when regiments will be designated to receive it and sign receipts.

WM. D. WHIPPLE,
Brigadier-General.

PULASKI, TENN., *January 2, 1865.*

Brig. Gen. J. L. DONALDSON,
Chief Quartermaster, Dept. of the Cumberland, Nashville, Tenn.:

The major-general commanding directs me to say that he desires you to make the necessary arrangements by the 6th instant to move his headquarters, viz, himself and staff, with the present outfit of camp and garrison equipage, three companies of sharpshooters, about forty wagons and ambulances, with their teams, servants, private horses, and all connected therewith, by steamers from Nashville to Eastport, on the Tennessee River. Acknowledge receipt.

ROBT. H. RAMSEY,
Assistant Adjutant-General.

PULASKI, TENN., *January 2, 1865.*

Maj. P. O'CONNELL,
Commanding Pontoon Train, Decatur:

Put down your pontoon bridge across the Tennessee River at Decatur, at the place where the old one was put.

WM. D. WHIPPLE,
Brigadier-General.

SPECIAL FIELD ORDERS, } HDQRS. DEPT. OF THE CUMBERLAND,
No. 2.   }   *Pulaski, Tenn., January 2, 1865.*

I. As soon as the depot of supplies at Spring Hill is broken up, the Forty-fifth Missouri Volunteer Infantry, now at that place, will proceed to Johnsonville, Tenn., via Nashville, for duty at that point.

*   *   *   *   *   *   *

III. The Forty-seventh Missouri Volunteer Infantry will proceed to Pulaski, Tenn., as soon as transportation can be furnished, and relieve the detachment of the Fourth Army Corps, now doing garrison duty at that place, under the command of Lieut. Col. T. Clark. Upon being relieved, Lieutenant-Colonel Clark will proceed without delay to Huntsville, Ala., guarding the wagon train of the Fourth Army Corps to that place.

IV. The Forty-eighth Missouri Volunteer Infantry will proceed without delay to Columbia, Tenn., for the purpose of guarding the railroad between that point and Pulaski, Tenn.

By command of Major-General Thomas:

HENRY M. CIST,
Captain and Assistant Adjutant-General.

HEADQUARTERS DEPARTMENT OF THE CUMBERLAND,
Pulaski, January 2, 1865.

Col. T. CLARK,
Commanding Detachment Fourth Army Corps:

COLONEL: I have the honor to request that you will direct any complete organizations of cavalry that may arrive at Pulaski, such as companies commanded by commissioned officers, battalions, or regiments, to proceed, via Lawrenceburg, by the most direct passable road, to Waterloo, on the Tennessee River, to report to Brevet Major-General Wilson.

Please collect all the mounted stragglers and men reporting themselves as guarding private property belonging to the First, Fifth, Sixth, and Seventh Divisions of the Cavalry Corps, Military Division of the Mississippi, and turn them over to the organizations going to Waterloo. All dismounted men that arrive after our wagon trains have left this place order to report to Col. G. G. Miner, commanding Camp Webster, at Nashville. I have no doubt that there are great numbers of soldiers of the Cavalry Corps prowling around the country, and you will confer a great favor upon General Wilson by collecting them and forwarding to their commands. Some of these stragglers are no doubt engaged in robbing the inhabitants, and any punishment you can devise for them will meet the hearty approval of General Wilson.

I am, colonel, very respectfully, your obedient servant,

E. B. BEAUMONT,
Major and Asst. Adjt. Gen., Cavalry Corps, Mil. Div. of the Miss.

PULASKI, TENN., *January 2, 1865.*

Maj. Gen. JOHN M. SCHOFIELD,
Columbia:

If your pontoon train is not needed in East Tennessee the major-general commanding would like to have it sent to Eastport. It can be floated as far as Bridgeport, and should the river be high all the way to Eastport. Should the river be low they can be loaded upon cars at Bridgeport and sent around via Nashville and the rivers.

WM. D. WHIPPLE,
Brigadier-General.

HEADQUARTERS DEPARTMENT OF THE CUMBERLAND,
Pulaski, Tenn., January 2, 1865.

Maj. Gen. J. M. SCHOFIELD,
Columbia:

Colonel Mackay wishes your wagons now at Chattanooga. I referred a dispatch on this subject to you; if you got it, will you please answer.

WM. D. WHIPPLE,
Brigadier-General.

COLUMBIA, TENN., *January 2, 1865.*

Brigadier-General WHIPPLE,
Pulaski:

I am very unwilling to part with my wagons and mules at Chattanooga. I had to obtain them from Kentucky with no little difficulty. Last spring I had to commence the campaign almost without transportation, because the mules I had collected in Kentucky had been taken without my knowledge for the other armies. I have been all summer and the winter up to this time in collecting the transportation needed for my corps. If I part with it now, the same trouble will exist next spring. I received and answered Colonel Mackay's dispatch on this subject several days ago.

J. M. SCHOFIELD,
Major-General.

HEADQUARTERS ARMY OF THE OHIO,
In the Field, Tenn., January 2, 1865.

Maj. Gen. D. N. COUCH,
Commanding Second Division, Twenty-third Army Corps:

GENERAL: General Cox will start promptly at 6 a. m., and will take the old Waynesborough road, which leaves the pike about three miles from this place, bearing to the right of it; thus the pike will be left clear for your division, from a point three miles ahead to Waynesborough. General Cox thinks he will be out of your way if you start at 7 o'clock. I will probably not go to-morrow beyond the forks of the road; will wait there until I receive reports from you and General Cox concerning the condition of the roads, which are both said to be bad, and decide which road General Ruger shall take. Please send to me to-morrow evening the result of your observation so far as you go, and what you can learn from citizens of the state of the roads beyond. I have ordered the engineer battalion to go in the advance of your column and repair the road as much as possible.

I am, general, very respectfully, your obedient servant,
J. M. SCHOFIELD,
Major-General.

GENERAL ORDERS, } HEADQUARTERS THIRD DIVISION,
TWENTY-THIRD ARMY CORPS,
No. 2. } *Mount Pleasant, Tenn., January 2, 1865.*

I. Paragraphs I and II, General Orders, No. 1, current series, from these headquarters, is hereby rescinded.

By command of Brigadier-General Cox:
THEO. COX,
Captain and Assistant Adjutant-General.

CIRCULAR.] HDQRS. THIRD DIVISION, 23D ARMY CORPS,
Mount Pleasant, Tenn., January 2, 1865.

The command will move forward on the Waynesborough road promptly at 6 o'clock to-morrow morning, in the following order: Second Brigade, Colonel Casement; battery; Third Brigade, Colonel Stiles; battery; First Brigade, Colonel Doolittle.

By command of Brigadier-General Cox:
THEO. COX,
Captain and Assistant Adjutant-General.

CLIFTON, TENN., *January 2, 1865.*
(Received 5th.)

Maj. Gen. GEORGE H. THOMAS:

I arrived here at 4 p. m., and found only five small boats, capable of carrying not over 3,000 men. We have two barges that will carry a battery each, and the horses will be distributed on the boats. I will try and take my transportation by land to Waterloo, as I can never get it there on the steamers furnished. I go up in the morning with the first fleet, and return immediately, and will urge everything forward as rapidly as possible. We found rations and grain, but no hay. I am unable to ascertain the whereabouts of Hood; he went toward Corinth. Some troops have arrived at Waterloo; can't learn who they are. Only 4,000 pairs of shoes and stockings have arrived. We need clothing very much; our estimate was sent in before leaving Pulaski.

Very respectfully,

A. J. SMITH,
Major-General.

HEADQUARTERS SECOND DIVISION,
DETACHMENT ARMY OF THE TENNESSEE,
In the Field, Tenn., January 2, 1865.

Col. E. H. WOLFE,
Commanding Third Brigade:

COLONEL: The First and Third Brigades of this division will embark on transports for Eastport, Miss., to-morrow. The batteries, with battery wagon, and forge, and one six-mule wagon, will go with their brigade, but all other wheels will be left at this point, in charge of brigade quartermasters, until transportation can be furnished. The baggage of officers and men will be taken along, as well as the authorized horses of brigade and regimental officers. The batteries will be placed on the boats, first commencing at 6 a. m., and under the direction of Capt. Lowell, chief of artillery; at 8.30 a. m. the troops will be in readiness to embark, and will be placed on the boats, under the direction of a division staff officer, commencing with the Third Brigade.

By order of Brigadier-General Garrard:

JAMES B. COMSTOCK,
Acting Assistant Adjutant-General.

HDQRS. CAVALRY CORPS, MIL. DIV. OF THE MISSISSIPPI,
Huntsville, Ala., January 2, 1865.

Major-General THOMAS,
Pulaski, Tenn.:

I have made arrangements to have rations issued to my command at Athens. If 2,000 sets of fitted horseshoes and nails could be sent by special train from Nashville, Ala., one from here could connect with it at Paint Rock Creek and deliver them at Athens by to-morrow noon, and in a short time we could march in obedience to your orders. Please answer.

J. H. WILSON,
Brevet Major-General.

PULASKI, *January 2, 1865.*

Maj. Gen. J. H. WILSON,
Huntsville, Ala.:

By direction of the major-general commanding, I have ordered 2,000 fitted horseshoes, with nails complete, to be sent by special train from Nashville, as you request, stating that a train from Athens will connect at Paint Rock Creek. Will inform you when the train starts from Nashville.

ROBT. H. RAMSEY,
Assistant Adjutant-General.

HDQRS. CAVALRY CORPS, MIL. DIV. OF THE MISSISSIPPI,
Huntsville, Ala., January 2, 1865.

Brig. Gen. J. L. DONALDSON,
Chief Quartermaster, Department of the Cumberland :

This command has been ordered to march to Eastport, and the horses are barefooted. Fitted shoes have been shipped to Captain Carling, at Nashville. Will you please send 2,000 of them, with nails, by special train to Athens.

J. H. WILSON,
Brevet Major-General, Commanding.

HDQRS. CAVALRY CORPS, MIL. DIV. OF THE MISSISSIPPI,
Huntsville, January 2, 1865.

Maj. E. B. BEAUMONT,
Assistant Adjutant-General :

Telegram received. Your acts are approved. Go to Nashville and hurry everything forward—horses, arms, horseshoes, clothing, equipments, forage, and transportation. The latter had better go all the way by land, if roads admit. I want 2,000 fitted shoes and nails at Athens before this portion of the corps can go to Eastport. I shall leave here to-morrow morning for Athens, and go thence soon as the command can move. Communicate fully to me by telegraph. I have sent orders to McCook. Find out about Long's, Knipe's, and Upton's troops. Get my horses.

J. H. WILSON,
Brevet Major-General.

HDQRS. CAVALRY CORPS, MIL. DIV. OF THE MISSISSIPPI,
Huntsville, January 2, 1865.

Brig. Gen. A. B. DYER,
Chief of Ordnance, Washington, D. C. :

GENERAL: I have the honor to acknowledge the receipt of your letter requesting a trial of the improved Gallagher carbine, or rifle, and to inform you that the necessary steps have been taken. In this connection, however, permit me to observe that all carbines are bad by comparison with the Spencer, and that the troops of this army will receive no other without protest. There is no doubt that the Spencer carbine is the best fire-arm yet put into the hands of the soldier, both for economy of ammunition and maximum effect, physical and moral. Our best officers estimate one man armed with it equivalent to three with any other arm. I have never seen anything else like the confidence inspired by it in the regiments or brigades which have it. A common belief amongst them is if their flanks are covered they can go anywhere. I have seen a large number of dismounted charges made with them against cavalry, infantry, and breast-works, and never knew one to fail. The experiences of the late campaign from Nashville have been particularly striking in this regard. The confidence in the arm is so widely spread that I have now applications from every regiment in the corps, not already supplied with them, and have most respectfully to request that arrangements may be made to furnish the depot at Nashville with at least 10,000, and, if possible, 15,000, as soon as possible. With such assistance on the part of the Ordnance Department, in a few weeks my corps can take the field with 25,000 men, capable of accomplishing any work that can be assigned them. I have no troops poor enough to use any other than the best arms. I have also to call your attention to the misuse of the surcingle, and the necessity for the breast-strap instead of the crupper. After a close observation for several months, I am able to state that not one trooper out of ten can be induced to put the surcingle around the saddle and belly of his horse, but that in almost every instance the surcingle is used as breast-strap. Would it not be much better to leave the surcingle out altogether, dispense with the crupper, and substitute a very plain breast-strap? I think, upon investigation, you will decide in favor, at least, of providing the breast-strap, even if you do not admit the others. There is certainly a very great necessity for it. In a country where the cavalry fighting is necessarily nearly all dismounted, means should be devised for leaving the sabers with the horses. The Stewart attachment seems to subserve every purpose. I have therefore to request that 20,000 be sent to Nashville depot for issue to my command.

Hoping you will pardon the liberty I have taken,

I am, general, very respectfully, your obedient servent,

J. H. WILSON,
Brevet Major-General.

HDQRS. CAVALRY CORPS, MIL. DIV. OF THE MISSISSIPPI,
Huntsville, Ala., January 2, 1865.

Capt. JOHN GREEN,
Special Inspector Cavalry, High Street, Nashville:

The Corps is ordered to concentrate at Eastport. Do everything in your power to send forward Hatch's, Hammond's, and Harrison's men properly mounted, and to obtain horses for the balance of Johnson's, Knipe's, and Upton's divisions. Horses might be concentrated more easily at Eastport than Nashville; it will take not less than 10,000 to completely mount us; they ought to be got at once. I would like Spencer carbines, without delay, for Hatch and McCook. Please find out from the bureau what can be done. I leave for Eastport to-morrow.

J. H. WILSON,
Brevet Major-General.

PULASKI, *January 2, 1865.*

Captain GRIFFIN,
Acting Assistant Adjutant-General, Cavalry Corps:

Direct General McCook to proceed to Eastport, on the Tennessee River, opposite Waterloo, with all the men of his command, ready for field service. He will be ferried across the Tennessee River at Waterloo. If possible, the wagons will follow the division; if not, they will be sent to Clifton, on Tennessee River, and taken from thence to Eastport by boat. Direct General Long, with his division, to Waterloo and Eastport, and send his teams with General McCook. If the teams can travel with the troops, it will be best. If the condition of the roads prevent carrying loads, the property of the division must be sent by boat from Nashville to Eastport. The wagons will be used to carry light loads of forage, &c.

By command of Brevet Major-General Wilson:

E. B. BEAUMONT,
Major and Assistant Adjutant-General.

NASHVILLE, *January 2, 1865.*

Brevet Major-General WILSON:

Colonel La Grange is expected here on Thursday. Shall McCook move without him, or wait for him?

LEVI T. GRIFFIN,
Captain and Acting Assistant Adjutant-General.

HDQRS. CAVALRY CORPS, MIL., DIV. OF THE MISSISSIPPI,
Huntsville, Ala., January 2, 1865.

Capt. LEVI T. GRIFFIN,
Actg. Asst. Adjt. Gen., Cavalry Corps, High Street, Nashville:

Direct General McCook to march from Nashville when La Grange arrives, and to mount all of the men that are there belonging to Croxton's brigade, and take horses for Croxton's dismounted men. Direct Long to proceed also as soon as he has reset the shoes cast on the march from Louisville. They will march by Columbia and Mount Pleasant. See that forage is deposited at Columbia when they arrive. If the mare has arrived for me send her with the horse by Major Beaumont.

J. H. WILSON,
Brevet Major-General.

HDQRS. CAVALRY CORPS, MIL. DIV. OF THE MISSISSIPPI,
Huntsville, Ala., January 2, 1865.

Capt. LEVI T. GRIFFIN,
Actg. Asst. Adjt. Gen., Cavalry Corps, Nashville, Tenn.:

Direct General Long to march, via Columbia, Mount Pleasant, and Waynesborough, to Eastport, on the Tennessee River.

J. H. WILSON,
Brevet Major-General.

NASHVILLE, *January 2, 1865.*

Brevet Major-General WILSON:

General Long will not reach this point till about Saturday; he did not start as soon as expected. McCook is here with Watkins' brigade, but not La Grange's.

LEVI T. GRIFFIN,
Captain and Acting Assistant Adjutant-General.

NASHVILLE, *January 2, 1865.*

OPERATOR,
Franklin, Ky.:

Has La Grange's cavalry passed Franklin yet on their way here? If so, when?

E. M. McCOOK.

FRANKLIN, KY., *January 2, 1865.*

Brig. Gen. E. M. McCOOK:

La Grange's cavalry are passing through this p. m.

C. P. RECTOR,
Operator.

HDQRS. CAVALRY CORPS, MIL. DIV. OF THE MISSISSIPPI,
Nashville, Tenn., January 2, 1865.

Lieut. Col. G. G. MINER,
Commanding Dismounted Cavalry Camp:

COLONEL: Frequent and bitter complaints are made by the people in the vicinity of Edgefield in regard to depredations that are being made by the cavalry command. General Johnson has applied to these head-quarters to be placed in supreme command of the cavalry force in Edge-field, for the purpose of putting a stop to these practices, at the same time reporting that neither his own nor General Knipe's command are guilty of the acts charged. His application has been returned disapproved. You will therefore take stringent measures to see that your men do not leave camp, without proper passes, that a camp guard is constantly kept on duty, and that Major Moore does likewise. If trouble arises from Major Moore's men, they must be removed to a point under your immediate eye. You will also send out daily such mounted patrols as you can muster and spare in your command, who will scout the country about Edgefield and arrest all stragglers. Should you pick up men belonging to General Knipe's or General Johnson's division, you will turn them over to the division commanders, with a statement in regard to the matter; and do not fail to bring to swift punishment these offenders, who are the cause of so much trouble to peaceful citizens and of so much disgrace to the cavalry command.

By command of Brevet Major-General Wilson:
LEVI T. GRIFFIN,
Captain and Acting Assistant Adjutant-General.

PULASKI, TENN., *January 2, 1865.*

Maj. Gen. L. H. ROUSSEAU,
Nashville, Tenn.:

The three Missouri regiments—Forty-fifth, Forty-seventh, and Forty-eighth—have been assigned to you. The Forty-fifth is ordered to John-sonville. Please designate which shall form the garrison of Columbia and Pulaski, and the order will be issued relieving the temporary garri-son of this place. They have not got their wagons.

WM. D. WHIPPLE,
Brigadier-General.

NASHVILLE, TENN., *January 2, 1865.*

Brig. Gen. W. D. WHIPPLE,
Pulaski:

General Rousseau left here yesterday. I would suggest the Forty-seventh Missouri, being the largest regiment, be posted at Columbia and on the road beyond. A part of the One hundred and seventy-fifth Ohio is now at Columbia, the balance being this side.

B. H. POLK,
Major and Assistant Adjutant-General.

NASHVILLE, TENN., *January 2, 1865.*

Maj. Gen. R. H. MILROY,
        Tullahoma:

The One hundred and eightieth Ohio will join the Twenty-third Corps, upon being relieved, via Columbia and Mount Pleasant.

By command, &c.:

B. H. POLK,
Major and Assistant Adjutant-General.

NASHVILLE, TENN., *January 2, 1865.*

Maj. Gen. R. H. MILROY,
        Tullahoma:

The One hundred and eightieth Ohio can move to Clifton or Eastport, on the Tennessee River, by the shortest route.   The Twenty-third Corps will be found there.

B. H. POLK,
Major and Assistant Adjutant-General.

SPECIAL ORDERS, } HEADQUARTERS DEFENSES NASHVILLE
                        AND CHATTANOOGA RAILROAD,
        No. 1.   }   *Tullahoma, January 2, 1865.*

I. Col. Edward Anderson having been called to Nashville to attend a general court-martial, Maj. W. H. Calkins, Twelfth Regiment Indiana Volunteer Cavalry, is hereby placed in command of this post till further orders.

*   *   *   *   *   *   *

By command of Major-General Milroy:

JNO. O. CRAVENS,
Assistant Adjutant-General.

PULASKI, *January 2, 1865.*

Brig. Gen. JOHN F. MILLER,
        Commanding Post of Nashville:

The major-general commanding directs that no artillery be sent to General Sherman; it must remain in Nashville.   If any has been shipped, and not yet beyond Louisville, you will recall it to Nashville.

ROBT. H. RAMSEY,
Assistant Adjutant-General.

PULASKI, TENN., *January 2, 1865.*

Brig. Gen. JOHN F. MILLER,
        Nashville, Tenn.:

Send all men for Twenty-third Corps by steamer to Eastport.   The corps starts from Columbia for that point this morning.

WM. D. WHIPPLE,
Brigadier-General.

PULASKI, *January 2, 1865.*

Major-General STEEDMAN,
            Decatur:

(To be forwarded by courier immediately to Courtland.)

Your telegram of 6 p. m. December 31 is received. The major-general commanding directs me to say that as soon as your cavalry force returns from the pursuit of the enemy's pontoon train, your command will return to Decatur, and thence proceed to Chattanooga, as previously directed. Send back to Nashville Thompson's brigade of colored troops—consisting of the Twelfth, Thirteenth, One hundredth, and part of the Seventeenth Regiments—with all other detachments belonging in Nashville before the present movement was commenced. Answer by telegraph to Nashville upon receipt.

                    ROBT. H. RAMSEY,
                        Assistant Adjutant-General.

COURTLAND, *January 2, 1865.*
                        (Received 3d.)

Major-General THOMAS:

Your dispatch of 1st instant received. I will commence my return as soon as the cavalry and infantry, now near Tuscumbia, arrives here. I expect them to-day. I will send the Nashville troops, including Colonel Thompson's brigade, back from Stevenson. Will telegraph you again when the cavalry returns here.

            Respectfully,

                    JAS. B. STEEDMAN,
                        Major-General.

DECATUR, *January 2, 1865.*

Major-General THOMAS:

I would request that the general commanding inform something of the amount of stores which are to be sent to this point. There are no buildings here, everything having been burned or torn down. It will therefore be necessary to erect buildings in which to store the supplies. The last building which was intended to be used as a hospital was torn down by Steedman's men in half an hour.

                    R. S. GRANGER.

PULASKI, *January 2, 1865.*

Brig. Gen. R. S. GRANGER,
            Decatur, Ala.:

Your telegrams of December 31, Huntsville, and from Decatur, this day, are received. The major-general commanding directs me to say that it is not his intention to place a large number of troops at Decatur, and you will therefore only construct such buildings for store-houses and hospitals as will accommodate the garrison of Decatur. You will also direct that the pontoon bridge be laid at the same point on the river that it was before Decatur was evacuated, this being the desire of the major-general commanding.

                    ROBT. H. RAMSEY,
                        Assistant Adjutant-General.

DECATUR, *January 2, 1865—11.10 p. m.*
(Received 3d.)

Brigadier-General WHIPPLE,
        Assistant Adjutant-General:

Your telegram of this date [yesterday] received. The bridge referred to is the bridge over Paint Rock. The force guarding the bridge was sixty infantry, twenty cavalry, and a piece of artillery. The force was surprised just at daylight, it is believed, by not exceeding 100 guerrillas, under Mead. The guard was totally routed, and more than half made prisoners, only one man being wounded. The enemy burned one end of the bridge only. The officer in charge, Lieutenant Wagoner, Thirteenth Wisconsin Veteran Volunteer Infantry, was advised by me, through Lyon, to be guarded against an attack of cavalry, which I ascertained was in his neighborhood, to use every minute to strengthen his position, and not to give it up, that he could hold it against any force of cavalry in that district. He neglected these instructions, and allowed himself to be surprised. I will forward a detailed report of the attack on Paint Rock. Mead and Johnson's forces, and other guerrilla forces, Colonel Lyon estimates at 500; I don't believe they exceed half that number, but are very active. Russell was associated with them; has, I think, crossed the river; he has probably 400. A good Union man counted the combined force as it twice passed his house, and says there were in all 600. There may be, in addition, a few scattered bands. With regard to the picket-fires seen by the Wauhatchie, Captain Forrest, who made the report, did not say to whom they belonged. I think he has no means of ascertaining. The pontoon is here, and officer in charge will have it laid to-day. The gun-boat Stone River arrived this morning from Brown's Ferry, and reports General Steedman returning; will probably be here to-day.

                                        R. S. GRANGER,
                                                Brigadier-General.

HDQRS. CAVALRY CORPS, MIL. DIV. OF THE MISSISSIPPI,
                        Huntsville, Ala., January 2, 1865.

Brigadier-General GRANGER,
        Commanding at Decatur:

GENERAL: The Second Tennessee and Tenth, Eleventh, and Thirteenth Indiana Cavalry have been ordered by Major-General Thomas to report. Will you please order the detachments with you to report at once, the dismounted men at Nashville and the mounted men to their regiments in the vicinity of Athens.

                                        J. H. WILSON,
                                Brevet Major-General, Commanding.

                                LEXINGTON, KY., *January 2, 1865.*

Hon. E. M. STANTON,
        Secretary of War:

Major-General Burbridge, with his command, has just returned from a most successful expedition. Five hundred negroes accompanied his command and Gillem. A battalion of the Sixth U. S. Colored Cavalry, 300 strong, attacked and whipped Duke's brigade, of 350—the last remnant of Morgan's force. The rebels were driven half a mile, with a loss on their side of thirty men killed and wounded. They were on the crest of a hill at Marion, and the negroes charged over open ground, and did not fire a gun until within thirty yards of the rebels. This is the first time that any of these men were under fire. Three full regiments of colored troops will leave for the Army of the James about the end of the week. Can I be authorized to send recruiting officers to Cincinnati, where there are a large number of Kentucky negroes, many of whom will, no doubt, enlist? At the request of many influential men of Kentucky, I will attend the convention at Frankfort, the 4th instant. They say my presence there will do much good.

> L. THOMAS,
> *Adjutant-General.*

WASHINGTON, D. C., *January 3, 1865—11 a. m.*

Major-General THOMAS,
        Pulaski, Tenn.:

General Grant directs me to say that you will not require a new outfit of teams for future operations, as no large amount of transportation will be taken with your army. He also says that there has always been an unnecessary accumulation of teams in the interior of Tennessee and Kentucky, and that these, as well as many of the troops, can be brought to the front, if required.

> H. W. HALLECK,
> *Major-General and Chief of Staff.*

CLIFTON, *January 3, 1865—9 p. m.*   (Received 4th.)

Maj. Gen. G. H. THOMAS:

Twenty miles above this, I met General Smith with three [*sic*] of his troops and four [batteries?] of his artillery going up. I brought the five transports and two barges from Eastport, and, with my gun-boats, hope to get half of Smith's artillery and all of his troops, except one division and his transportation, to Eastport to-morrow night. All was quiet there and nothing seen of the enemy, except that he was watching us from the heights over Florence, which, until I used a few shell, he seemed disposed to occupy. I will give the cover of an iron-clad at Johnsonville until it is fortified, if needed. My suggestions respecting driving Forrest and Lyon from West Tennessee to secure safe transportation on this river, should Maj. Gen. E. R. S. Canby call for naval co-operation and the consequent withdrawal of naval force from this river [*sic*].

> S. P. LEE,
> *Acting Rear-Admiral.*

ATHENS, *January 3, 1865—4 p. m.*

Brigadier-General WHIPPLE,
        Chief of Staff:

GENERAL: I have just arrived here with my corps. Was detained two days on Elk River by the necessity of building a bridge for crossing artillery, wagons, &c., the river being impassable otherwise. On my arrival here I received your dispatch of the 1st instant, ordering the concentration of the whole corps at Huntsville and preparations to be made for the immediate resumption of active operations. Orders will be carried out with dispatch. I will report my arrival at Huntsville and the preparations I make there. I would be glad to hear by telegraph from the commanding general whether he has any further orders. I will march from here at daylight in the morning.

TH. J. WOOD,
Brigadier-General, Commanding.

CIRCULAR.] HEADQUARTERS FOURTH ARMY CORPS,
Elk River, January 3, 1865.

Orders of the day for the Fourth Corps for to-day, January 3:

As soon as the bridge is completed, the corps will march, probably by noon to-day—General Kimball's division will lead; then General Beatty's; then General Elliott's. Each division will in itself constitute a separate column, as on the march from Lexington, Ala., to this place, and the divisions will so march with reference to trains, &c., until we arrive at the place of our destination. The pioneers will precede each division, and a good regiment will accompany each train to assist it along. The pioneers of the leading division will repair the roads on the route of march, cut out new roads, &c.

By order of Brigadier-General Wood:

J. S. FULLERTON,
Assistant Adjutant-General and Chief of Staff.

CIRCULAR.] HEADQUARTERS FOURTH ARMY CORPS,
Athens, Ala., January 3, 1865.

Order of the day for the Fourth Corps for to-morrow, January 4:

The corps will march for Huntsville—General Beatty will lead; General Kimball will follow; then General Elliott. General Beatty will start at 6.30 a. m., General Kimball will closely follow, and General Elliott will move out the Huntsville road, following General Kimball, as soon as he reaches Athens.

By order of Brigadier-General Wood:

J. S. FULLERTON,
Assistant Adjutant-General and Chief of Staff.

HEADQUARTERS FOURTH ARMY CORPS,
Athens, Ala., January 3, 1865.

Brigadier-General ELLIOTT,
 Second Division:

The general commanding directs me to say that he is surprised to learn that you have gone into camp seven miles from Athens, and that it is his desire that you hereafter march your division so that it may go into camp with the rest of the corps, unless orders to the contrary are given. He also directs that you make as long a march as you can to-morrow toward Huntsville, and that you go into camp at sundown, unless you come up with the rest of the corps before that time.

Very respectfully, your obedient servant,

J. S. FULLERTON,
Assistant Adjutant-General and Chief of Staff.

HEADQUARTERS ARMY OF THE OHIO,
Mount Pleasant, Tenn., January 3, 1865.

Maj. Gen. GEORGE H. THOMAS,
Nashville, Tenn.:

Please have rations and forage sent to Clifton by the 7th. Some of my trains sent to Spring Hill for forage had to return empty. I will be entirely out of forage on the 7th. We are getting along pretty well, and I think will get through without serious difficulty.

J. M. SCHOFIELD,
Major-General.

HEADQUARTERS ARMY OF THE OHIO,
In the Field, Tenn., January 3, 1865.

Maj. Gen. D. N. COUCH,
Commanding Second Division, Twenty-third Army Corps:

GENERAL: The commanding general desires to know if the two battle-flags captured by your division in front of Nashville on the 15th of December, 1864, are still in possession of your command. If so, he directs me to say that if you will send them to these headquarters with the name, rank, &c., of the captor he will send them to Washington City.

I am, general, your obedient servant,

CLINTON A. CILLEY,
Assistant Adjutant-General.

HEADQUARTERS,
Seven Miles from Mount Pleasant, January 3, 1865.

Captain CILLEY:

So soon as I can find those flags will send them as directed, but am of the opinion that I shall not be successful. Please say to the general that the troops are now on the ridge, with the road very badly cut up, but hope to be able to worry through. Country very poor.

D. N. COUCH,
Major-General.

SPECIAL ORDERS, } HDQRS. SECOND DIV., 23D ARMY CORPS,
                    In the Field, near Henryville, Tenn.,
No. 3.   }   *January 3, 1865.*

I. Capt. A. D. Harvey, Fifteenth Indiana Battery, is hereby announced as chief of artillery of this division. He will be obeyed and respected accordingly.

II. Asst. Surg. N. B. Cole, Fiftieth Regiment Ohio Volunteer Infantry, is hereby detailed for duty as assistant surgeon in charge of the hospital of this division.

By command of Major-General Couch:

S. H. HUBBELL,
Lieutenant and Acting Assistant Adjutant-General.

Hdqrs. Third Division, Twenty-third Army Corps,
January 3, 1865—10.30 a. m.

Major-General Schofield,
Commanding, &c.:

The only hard piece of road I have found is the long hill which we ascend about a mile after leaving the pike. The road is a high ridge road, smooth and good as any country road in a wet season. I am confident it is the best route to Waynesborough. The fork where the road to Laurel Hill Factory and Ashland roads separate is about two miles ahead. The former is reported the best road; it enters the pike eight miles this side of Waynesborough, and that eight miles is reported good road. I have not yet decided which to take, but either of them will be better for General Ruger than following the pike.

Very respectfully, your obedient servant,

J. D. COX,
Brigadier-General, Commanding.

Headquarters Army of the Ohio,
In the Field, Tenn., January 3, 1865.

Brig. Gen. J. D. Cox,
Commanding Third Division, Twenty-third Army Corps:

General: I have just received your dispatch dated 10.30 a. m., and am glad to learn the road is so good. I have not heard from Couch, but fear he is having hard work. Ruger is not yet up. Unless there is very great difference in the Tunnel Hill and Mount Pleasant roads you should take the right hand, so as to leave the pike free for Couch all the way to Waynesborough.

Very respectfully,

J. M. SCHOFIELD,
Major-General.

Hdqrs. Third Division, Twenty-third Army Corps,
Whiteside's, January 3, 1865—6.30 p. m.

Major-General Schofield,
Commanding, &c.:

I have made fifteen miles; have kept the right-hand or Ashland road. My train is not quite up, and rather than work the teams after dark I have ordered them to park and come up at daylight, when I will make an issue to lighten the wagons. Buffalo River is twelve miles ahead. I presume I shall not be able to get farther than that to-morrow, as the train will delay us. I suspect my trains will so cut the road as to make it best for Ruger to go by the Laurel Hill Factory road, which turns off half a mile this side of a deserted house, which is next beyond one where a family named Gilmore live. Nothing is gained in distance by this route; it is a wilderness.

Very respectfully, your obedient servant,

J. D. COX,
Brigadier-General, Commanding.

HDQRS. THIRD DIVISION, TWENTY-THIRD ARMY CORPS,
In the Field, Tenn., January 3, 1865.

The command will continue the movement forward toward Waynes-borough to-morrow morning, at 6.30 a. m., in the following order: Third Brigade, Colonel Stiles; battery; First Brigade, Colonel Doolittle; battery; Second Brigade, Colonel Casement. The rear brigade will furnish one regiment to act as rear guard and to assist the teams of the division in case of need.

By command of Brigadier-General Cox:

THEO. COX,
Captain and Assistant Adjutant-General.

HDQRS. THIRD DIVISION, TWENTY-THIRD ARMY CORPS,
In the Field, Tenn., January 3, 1865.

The command will not move to-morrow morning until rations are issued.

By command of Brigadier-General Cox:

THEO. COX,
Captain and Assistant Adjutant-General.

(To brigade and battery commanders.)

HEADQUARTERS DEPARTMENT OF THE OHIO,
Louisville, Ky., January 3, 1865.

Maj. J. A. CAMPBELL,
Assistant Adjutant-General:

Order section Twenty-fourth Indiana Battery, Lieutenant Allen, to this place. He is in Fort Negley.

G. W. SCHOFIELD,
Lieutenant-Colonel and Chief of Artillery.

HEADQUARTERS TIN-CLAD STEAMER FAIRY,
Tennessee River, January 3, 1865. (Received 4th.)

Maj. Gen. GEORGE H. THOMAS:

In my dispatch of last night I informed you that I had arrived at Clifton, and would accompany the first fleet to Eastport this morning. A few miles below Savannah I met Admiral Lee coming down, with all the transports from Eastport, to assist me in getting up. I will now have boats enough to carry about two-thirds of my command with four batteries and some little transportation. Hood is reported and believed to be at Corinth; if so, my position at Eastport will not be safe, without additional re-enforcements. If we had one more corps (say the Fourth), with sufficient cavalry, we could attack, whip, and drive him from the country. I respectfully request this aid. Can you give it to me? General Croxton is at Waterloo, with about 1,500 cavalry only. Having tied up my fleet until my return, I go with Admiral Lee to Clifton, and will go to Eastport to-morrow, with all the men I can carry, and try to make a landing. There are rebels in the vicinity of Eastport, in what force could not be determined.

Very respectfully,

A. J. SMITH,
Major-General.

HEADQUARTERS DETACHMENT ARMY OF THE TENNESSEE,
Clifton, Tenn., January 3, 1865.

Brig. Gen. J. McARTHUR,
    Commanding First Division:

The major-general commanding directs that you have one brigade of your command in readiness to embark on transports at 8 a. m. to-morrow, and the battery belonging to the brigade sent to the river landing by 6 a. m. to embark. The boats are here and will be assigned by the quartermaster, Captain Drew.

I am, general, very respectfully, your obedient servant,
        J. HOUGH,
    Major and Assistant Adjutant-General.

HEADQUARTERS FIRST DIVISION,
DETACHMENT ARMY OF THE TENNESSEE,
Clifton, Tenn., January 3, 1865.

Col. W. L. McMILLEN,
    Commanding First Brigade:

SIR: By direction of the general commanding, you will embark with your command on board transports to-morrow morning. The battery belonging to your command will be sent to the river by 6 a. m.; the remainder of the command will be in readiness to embark at 8 a. m. Capt. C. K. Drew, assistant quartermaster, will assign the boats.

I am, sir, very respectfully, your obedient servant,
        W. H. F. RANDALL,
    Assistant Adjutant-General.

HDQRS. CAVALRY CORPS, MIL. DIV. OF THE MISSISSIPPI,
Athens, January 3, 1865.

Brigadier-General WHIPPLE,
    Chief of Staff:

The copy of a dispatch from General Halleck to General Thomas has been received. In view of probabilities alluded to therein, I have to request that immediate steps be taken to secure 10,000 horses and all the Spencer carbines to be had. If the Cavalry Bureau cannot furnish the horses at E[astport] in fifteen or twenty days, authority should be obtained from the Secretary of War to impress in Indiana, Ohio, and Illinois. The magnitude of the interests at stake would warrant it. If authority can be obtained, I will send Johnson and Knipe at once north of the Ohio. Please request the general to stir up the Quartermaster-General and the Secretary of War.

        J. H. WILSON,
    Brevet Major-General.

HDQRS. CAVALRY CORPS, MIL. DIV. OF THE MISSISSIPPI,
Athens, Ala., January 3, 1865.

Capt. E. B. CARLING,
    Chief Quartermaster, Cavalry Corps, High Street, Nashville:

Get the corps, division, and brigade flags without delay. Have full supplies of everything sent to Eastport. I will leave here day after to-morrow.

        J. H. WILSON,
    Brevet Major-General.

Hdqrs. Cavalry Corps, Mil. Div. of the Mississippi,
Athens, Ala., January 3, 1865.
Capt. Levi T. Griffin,
Actg. Asst. Adjt. Gen., Cavalry Corps, High Street, Nashville:
Tell General McCook to take 300 extra horses, if he can get them. I will direct Croxton to make out reports as soon as I reach him.

J. H. WILSON,
Brevet Major-General.

Special ⎫   Headquarters Cavalry Corps,
Field Orders, ⎬   Military Division of the Mississippi,
No. 2. ⎭   *Huntsville, Ala., January 3, 1865.*
Lieut. Col. A. J. Alexander, assistant adjutant-general, Seventeenth Army Corps, is relieved from duty with this command, and will report for orders to the headquarters Military Division of the Mississippi, Nashville, Tenn.

By command of Brevet Major-General Wilson:

JOHN N. ANDREWS,
Captain and Aide-de-Camp, Acting Assistant Adjutant-General.

Hdqrs. Cavalry Corps, Mil. Div. of the Mississippi,
Nashville, Tenn., January 3, 1865.
Brig. Gen. E. M. McCook,
Comdg. First Division, Cavalry Corps, Mil. Div. of the Miss.:
General: On Colonel La Grange's arrival you will march with all serviceable men of your command ready for the field to Waterloo, on the Tennessee River; from there you will be ferried across the river to Eastport. If possible, your wagons will follow the command; if not, they will be sent to Clifton, on the Tennessee River, and taken from [there] to Eastport by boat. If the teams can travel with the troops, it will be best; if the condition of roads prevent carrying loads, the property of the division must be sent by boats from Nashville to Eastport, and the wagons used to carry light loads of forage.

By command of Brevet Major-General Wilson:

LEVI T. GRIFFIN,
Captain and Acting Assistant Adjutant-General.

NASHVILLE, TENN., *January 3, 1865.*
Maj. Gen. R. H. Milroy, *Tullahoma:*
General Thomas directs that you permit the Twelfth Indiana Cavalry to come to Nashville, as requested by General Knipe.

B. H. POLK,
Major and Assistant Adjutant-General.

Special Orders, ⎫ Headquarters Defenses Nashville
            ⎬   AND Chattanooga Railroad,
No. 2. ⎭   *Tullahoma, January 3, 1865.*

  *   *   *   *   *   *   *

II. Col. William Forbes, Forty-second Regiment Missouri Volunteer Infantry, is hereby placed in command of this post, and he will enter upon his duties without delay. He will receive of Major Calkins, the former commandant, the records and papers pertaining to the post.

  *   *   *   *   *   *   *

IV. The Forty-second Regiment Missouri Volunteer Infantry will relieve the garrison of the Twelfth Regiment Indiana Volunteer Cavalry at Block-houses Nos. 14 and 15 (first two north of Tullahoma) immediately. These block-houses will be garrisoned as follows: At No. 14, fifteen men and an officer; at No. 15, ten men and a non-commissioned officer; at No. 16, fifteen men and an officer. The detachment will take the first train.

* * * * * * *

By command of Major-General Milroy:

JNO. O. CRAVENS,
Assistant Adjutant-General.

PULASKI, January 3, 1865—9 a. m.

Brigadier-General GRANGER:

Send me by telegraph to Lynnville to-day the most reliable information and facts you have as to the course Hood's army has taken and where it is most likely to halt. I want the best and most reliable information you can give me; if possible, I wish to know to a certainty.

GEO. H. THOMAS,
Major-General.

(Same to Major-General Steedman.)

DECATUR, [January 3, 1865].
(Received 4th.)

Major-General THOMAS:

Your telegram of this date is received. Two negroes who came in day before yesterday from Tuscumbia report that Hood passed through Tuscumbia a week ago last Sunday; that his army was in a deplorable condition, many of his men being without arms; that they saw but eight pieces of artillery—four with Stewart's and four with Stevenson's divisions—they heard that your force had cut the road between Tuscumbia and Corinth, and that Hood was making for some springs in Mississippi—they said Pond Springs. This is all I have been able to gather. Have sent your telegram to General Steedman, and will telegraph immediately soon as hearing from him.

R. S. GRANGER,
Brigadier-General.

DECATUR, January 3, 1865.

Capt. ROBERT H. RAMSEY,
 Assistant Adjutant-General:

The pontoon bridge was completed this afternoon. General Steedman not yet arrived. General Wilson ordered all the cavalry to report to him at Huntsville. I understand he has since left for Eastport. Can I now retain my cavalry when it comes in with General Steedman until more can be sent to this district? It will certainly be in no condition to march to Eastport. They can hardly be said to be mounted, the animals are so poor. They have been constantly in the field since the 26th of November.

R. S. GRANGER,
Brigadier-General.

DECATUR, *January 3, 1865.*

Brig. Gen. W. D. WHIPPLE:

General Steedman and his command will be here to-morrow, and leave immediately on the cars for Chattanooga. His withdrawal from here leaves us uncovered, with only 600 infantry for garrison. The cavalry was all ordered to Huntsville by Major-General Wilson. I feel no immediate apprehension for the safety of the post, but think re-enforcements should be sent here. The fortifications are much out of repair, and could not be held against any considerable force. The work at this post will be considerable if we are to prepare for a large amount of supplies. There is now no cover whatever.

R. S. GRANGER,
Brigadier-General.

WAR DEPARTMENT, ADJUTANT-GENERAL'S OFFICE,
Washington, January 3, 1865.

Brig. Gen. S. MEREDITH, *Commanding, &c., Paducah, Ky.:*

SIR: In reply to your communication of the 31st ultimo, inquiring whether Columbus, Ky., has been transferred to the District of West Tennessee, by direction of General Orders, No. 288, of November 28, 1864, I have the honor to inform you that the order cited does not affect that post, but that it remains under the command of the officer commanding the Military District of the State of Kentucky. All troops east of the Mississippi River, up to the mouth of the Ohio, are subject to the orders of Major-General Canby, commanding Military Division of West Mississippi.

I am, &c.,

E. D. TOWNSEND,
Assistant Adjutant-General.

LEXINGTON, KY., *January 3, 1865.*
(Received 10.30 p. m.)

Hon. E. M. STANTON:

Major-General Burbridge has just returned from a most successful expedition in Southwestern Virginia. I have taken from him several regiments of colored troops which he has raised and sent them to the Army of the James. In this operation he has thrown his whole influence, which is very great in Kentucky. The colored troops are to be formed into a corps with the Army of the James, and I know of no officer who deserves the command of that corps more than General Burbridge. There are a large number of U. S. prisoners at Selma. Give General Burbridge authority to take 5,000 mounted men, and he will quietly move through Cumberland Gap and undoubtedly release these prisoners and restore them to their homes.

L. THOMAS,
Adjutant-General.

HEADQUARTERS MILITARY DISTRICT OF KENTUCKY,
Lexington, Ky., January 3, 1865.

Hon. E. M. STANTON,
Secretary of War, Washington, D. C.:

SIR: I have the honor to transmit for your information copies of letters from George D. Prentice, of Louisville, to Hon. E. M. Bruce, and from J. H. Clemmons, Richmond, Va., to Doctor Marsh, the originals of which were captured during the recent raid of my command in Virginia. Brigadier-General Gillem has in his possession letters of a similar purport, which I will transmit to you so soon as received from him.

Very respectfully, your obedient servent,
S. G. BURBRIDGE,
Brevet Major-General, Commanding.

[Inclosure No. 1.]

JOURNAL OFFICE,
Louisville, Ky., January 24, 1864.

Hon. E. M. BRUCE:

MY DEAR SIR: Yours of the 10th of November, addressed from Madison, Ga., to my son, Major Prentice, of Abingdon, has just been sent to me by your wife. I have just written to her to try to tell her how much I thank you, but perhaps you may one day know the full extent of my gratitude. I have given aid to many Confederate prisoners, and I will give aid to many more, if opportunity affords. If you see Clarence, you can say to him that I omit no chance of serving those who have served with him and love him. I wish he would write to us. Say to him that his silence is almost unkind. May God reward you, Mr. Bruce, for all your goodness.

Forever your friend,
GEORGE D. PRENTICE.

[Inclosure No. 2.]

HOUSE OF REPRESENTATIVES,
Richmond, Va., December 3, 1864.

Doctor MARSH:

There is nothing very new in this town, save the arrival of George D. Prentice, of the Louisville Journal. His excuse for coming is to see his son, who is indicted for murder. He represents that Kentucky is in truly a deplorable condition, and the worst state of despotism reigns there. The Feds have his partner, Shipman, prisoner, bound, and would have done him so but for fear of public sentiment. He says that before he left Bramlette visited him, knowing that he was coming, and that he represents his sentiments when he says there is great dissatisfaction with the Government of the United States existing among the people of the State, and that all the people would rise up if an army could go there. He says to our people that we had all better be buried in one common grave than go back into the Union; that our only hope is to fight on, extermination being preferable to subjugation. He talks more encouragingly than any of our own people, and has imparted new life to some of them. The Feds have sent out Frank Wolford and Lieutenant-Governor Jacob, as Ould, the commissioner of exchange, informed me yesterday. The Louisville Journal of the 25th, however, states that the matter has been reconsidered, and they are permitted to return. He had a private interview with the Secretary of War, and expresses a strong desire to see Davis, but up to this time he has not been invited to see his majesty, as Foote would say. The war news from Georgia is thought to be tolerably good, as the enemy has done nothing there but steal "taters," negroes, &c. I believe Sherman will get to the coast with but little trouble. Hood is up about Columbia, Tenn., and will, I believe, fall back on the enemy at Chattanooga and open the road through East Tennessee to this place. We hear heavy firing below this city, and no doubt they are doing a little work in that direction. I don't think Grant can do anything with Uncle Bob till he gets Sherman to help him, which, I fear, is Sherman's object in going to the coast. If, however, Sherman does, Hood in Kentucky and Price in Missouri, we will be able to do them much damage. The people have got over the panic occasioned by Sherman's move, and are now tolerably hopeful.

I should have remarked, when talking about what Prentice says, that he further remarked that the people of Kentucky were looking with the profoundest interest to Hood's move, and much desire that he shall enter the State. I have not heard a word from home since you left. I am expecting a letter every day. I received yours of the 24th ultimo, and was glad to hear of your gallantry and good luck in escaping unhurt. I again caution you about exposing yourself, as you can never get promotion among the Dukes and Breckinridges. I would do my duty, and nothing more. If you will recollect, no man has ever been noticed for gallantry either by Morgan, Breckinridge, or Duke, who has not come from Lexington or thereabouts. I don't think I will ever have any respect for any such men.

We have been much engaged in Congress discussing in secret sessions a grave question; we will get through it to-day, and then our sessions will be more open and interesting to the public. The negro question I regard as being settled, as there are but few who favor putting them in the army as soldiers. There is a determination upon the part of all officials now to put every man into the field, and a great desire for Hood to go to Kentucky, as it is believed he will get a large army there. Should he go there I shall immediately go home and try and get up a command. I have some arrangements to get up a brigade which I think I can. I have some young men who will assist me who represent that they can raise a company or companies. I am sure I can get up the wind. If we go to Kentucky there will be the greatest time ever known under the sun.

I send this by "C. D. K.," whom you will remember as the "Courier's" correspondent. I will write you again, when an opportunity offers. On yesterday Ould, the commissioner of exchange, proposed (voluntarily) to get Mike exchanged. I hope to get him out by the 1st of January. I have now said all I know.

Yours,

J. H. CLEMMONS.

SPECIAL ORDERS, }   HDQRS. FIRST DIV., MIL. DIST. OF KY.,
    No. 3.   }   *Lexington, Ky., January 3, 1865.*

* * * * * * *

V. Col. T. D. Sedgewick, One hundred and fourteenth U. S. Colored Infantry, with his regiment, will proceed without delay to Virginia, via Parkersburg, W. Va., and report to Maj. Gen. B. F. Butler for duty. Quartermaster's department will furnish transportation.

By command of Brig. Gen. E. H. Hobson:

J. S. BUTLER,
Assistant Adjutant-General.

LEXINGTON, KY., *January 3, 1865.*

Col. R. H. EARNEST,
    115th U. S. Colored Infantry, Paris, Ky.:

Hold your regiment in readiness to move to-morrow by rail. Wait orders by mail from these headquarters.

By order of Brigadier-General Hobson:

J. S. BUTLER,
    Assistant Adjutant-General.

HDQRS. CAVALRY DIVISION, DEPARTMENT OF MISSISSIPPI,
    Mechanicsburg, Miss., January 3, 1865.

Maj. Gen. N. J. T. DANA:

GENERAL: On the morning of the 28th we attacked the enemy at Egypt, on the Mobile and Ohio Railroad, and whipped them, capturing about 500 prisoners, mostly infantry, and a train of cars; thence we swept west and southwest through Houston and Bellefontaine, Miss., to the Mississippi Central Railroad, striking it at Winona. Sent detachment north, to Grenada, and another south, along the railroad. Moved with main column, via Lexington and Benton, toward Vicksburg; will be in Vicksburg on the 5th. Since last dispatch have destroyed ten or twelve miles more of the Mobile and Ohio road, about thirty miles of Mississippi Central road, captured and destroyed three serviceable locomotives and eleven more in process of repair, about fifty cars, large cloth and shoe factory, machine-shops, pile-driver and engine, 700 head of Confederate hogs, and immense amounts of commissary, quartermaster, and ordnance stores. We have with us about 600 prisoners and 800 head of captured stock. Our loss is about 100 killed, wounded, and missing. Will give particulars in my official report.*

Very respectfully, your obedient servant,

B. H. GRIERSON,
    Brigadier-General.

CITY POINT, VA., *January 4, 1865—7.30 p. m.*

Maj. Gen. H. W. HALLECK,
    Washington, D. C.:

I hear nothing, either through rebel papers or direct, from Granger's movement from Pascagoula. I would like to have Canby operate against Mobile this winter, with such force as he can collect from his command, but I will not send any troops to him from Middle Tennessee. If Hood goes south from Corinth, order A. J. Smith and two divisions besides to Baltimore, Md., to be thrown where they may be wanted on arrival.

U. S. GRANT,
    Lieutenant-General.

WASHINGTON, D. C., *January 4, 1865—3.45 p. m.*

Major-General THOMAS,
    Pulaski:

Deserters during a forced retreat can seldom be trusted; they should therefore be held, at least for the present, as prisoners of war.

---

* See Part I, p. 844.

In particular cases, where you are fully satisfied of the character of the parties, they may be permitted to take the amnesty oath; but even then they should be paroled not to leave a particular locality.

H. W. HALLECK,
Major-General and Chief of Staff.

NASHVILLE, TENN., *January 4, 1865—10 p. m.*

Maj. Gen. H. W. HALLECK,
Washington, D. C.:

I send the following dispatch from General Steedman, Courtland, received this evening, for your information:

Colonel Palmer's guide, left by him at Bull's Mountain, reports that Palmer burned the enemy's pontoon train, and had gone toward Pikeville to destroy a train of 600 wagons, intending to return by Danville road. A scouting party from my advance at Leighton found enemy's cavalry in strong force near Russellville. A deserter reports that Hood has been ordered back to Cherokee, and thence to Tuscaloosa.

I have also received a dispatch from General Granger, at Decatur, of this date, in which he says that he learns from two negroes, just come in from Tuscumbia, that Hood's army passed through that place in a deplorable condition on Christmas day, many of the men being without arms. They saw but eight pieces of artillery—four with Stewart's and four with Stevenson's divisions. They say, also, that they understood the railroad had been cut between Tuscumbia and Florence, and that Hood was making for some springs in Mississippi, which they call Pond Springs. I have had reports from General Smith, who will probably reach Eastport this afternoon, and also from General Croxton, who is at Waterloo. General Schofield is now on his way to Eastport. General Smith informs me that the reports he has had are to the effect that Hood is at Corinth. I will start for Eastport immediately upon the arrival of my wagons at this place, probably on Saturday, the 7th instant.

GEO. H. THOMAS,
Major-General, U. S. Volunteers, Commanding.

FLAG-SHIP FAIRY,
Clifton, January 4, 1865.

Major-General THOMAS:

Many and hearty congratulations on the various summary of your successes this campaign in your telegram of 29th, received at Eastport last eve. Foggy weather and a rapidly falling river prevented my reaching and destroying Hood's pontoons at Bainbridge, six miles above Florence. Escaped prisoners say the rebels declared the gun-boats could not get over the shoals to their pontoon bridge. Hood crossed at Florence last fall, using the bridge piers to secure his pontoons. General Jackson's three crossings were, at the military ferry, Carp's Creek, one mile below Florence, or at Melton's Bluff, twelve miles above Big Mussel Shoals and thirty-six miles above Florence, and at Deposit, 120 miles above Florence. Bainbridge was not a regular ferry, and my clever pilot thought the water was too swift there for a crossing. Hood must have been sorely pushed to have resorted to such a place on the shoals. I broke up his ferry at Garner's, Cane Creek, twelve miles below Florence. Hood will probably never venture north of the Tennessee again. My officers and men will be highly gratified, as I am, at your acknowledgment for the cordial co-operation of the navy during the last thirty days.

S. P. LEE,
Rear-Admiral.

HEADQUARTERS FOURTH ARMY CORPS,
Huntsville, Ala., January 4, 1865—8 p. m.

Major-General THOMAS:

The corps arrived in this vicinity this evening, and it will be encamped near this place to-morrow morning, on suitable ground in reference to sanitary and other conditions. Requisitions will be at once made for all supplies necessary to meet your views in reference to coming events, and an officer will be sent to Nashville at once with requisitions for the supplies, and I respectfully request that General Donaldson be directed to fill the requisition as soon as presented and send the supplies to this place without delay. The bridge over Paint Rock being destroyed, I will send a regiment to that place to-morrow, to assist in crossing supplies, &c., over the creek.

TH. J. WOOD,
Brigadier-General, Commanding.

HEADQUARTERS FOURTH ARMY CORPS,
Indian Creek, Ala., January 4, 1865.

Brigadier-General KIMBALL,
   First Division:

GENERAL: The general commanding directs that you march at 6.30 a. m. to-morrow for Huntsville. Your division will lead, General Beatty's will follow. An officer will meet you out of Huntsville, to show you where you will camp.

Very respectfully, your obedient servant,
J. S. FULLERTON,
Assistant Adjutant-General and Chief of Staff.

HEADQUARTERS FOURTH ARMY CORPS,
Indian Creek, Ala., January 4, 1865—3 p. m.

Brigadier-General ELLIOTT,
   Second Division:

The general commanding directs that you march for Huntsville to-morrow at 6.30 a. m. A staff officer will meet you out of Huntsville, to show you where your camp will be. Generals Beatty and Kimball will camp on Indian Creek to-night. General Beatty is now going into camp, and they will start in the morning at 6.30. Corps headquarters will be in Huntsville to-night.

Very respectfully, your obedient servant,
J. S. FULLERTON,
Assistant Adjutant-General and Chief of Staff.

NASHVILLE, TENN., *January 4, 1865—10 p. m.*

Maj. Gen. A. J. SMITH,
  Eastport, Miss.:

Your telegram of 3d instant just received. The major-general commanding directs me to say in reply, that Major-General Schofield's corps is now on its way to Eastport to re-enforce you. His troops will be ready to embark at Clifton on the 6th. The entire cavalry command has also been ordered to concentrate at Eastport, probably on the 7th instant.

         R. H. RAMSEY,
          Assistant Adjutant-General.

SPECIAL ORDERS, } HDQRS. DETACH. ARMY OF THE TENNESSEE,
 No. 3.   }   *Clifton, Tenn., January 4, 1865.*
  *   *   *   *   *   *   *

II. Brig. Gen. Thomas Kilby Smith, U. S. Volunteers, having reported at these headquarters for duty, is hereby assigned to, and will at once assume command of, the Third Division, Detachment Army of the Tennessee. Col. J. B. Moore, now commanding the Third Division, is hereby relieved from such command, and will report to Brig. Gen. T. K. Smith for assignment. In relieving Colonel Moore the major-general commanding desires to express his high appreciation of the able, thorough, and soldierly manner with which he has executed the trust confided to him in this command.

  *   *   *   *   *   *   *

By order of Maj. Gen. A. J. Smith:

         J. HOUGH,
      Major and Assistant Adjutant-General.

HEADQUARTERS FIRST DIVISION,
DETACHMENT ARMY OF THE TENNESSEE,
Clifton, Tenn., January 4, 1865.

Col. W. R. MARSHALL,
  Commanding Third Brigade:

SIR: You will put your command in readiness to embark forthwith. There are two gun-boats that will hold 400 men each without any transportation. You will load these boats with the portion of your command that the boats will contain, and as fast as transportation can be furnished embark the remainder of the command.

By command of Brig. Gen. J. McArthur:

        W. H. F. RANDALL,
       Assistant Adjutant-General.

HDQRS. CAVALRY CORPS, MIL. DIV. OF THE MISSISSIPPI,
      Athens, Ala., January 4, 1865.

Brig. Gen. WILLIAM D. WHIPPLE,
  Chief of Staff, Department of the Cumberland:

Detachments of Fifth Division, in West Tennessee and Kentucky, have not yet been returned to duty with their division, notwithstanding the repeated requests of General Hatch. Men from every regiment are away; one whole company of the Second Iowa Cavalry is kept by General Grierson; clerks in all the departments are retained by General Dana; a large detachment of the Third Illinois is kept by General Meredith at Paducah. Please have General Thomas request a peremptory order from General Grant for the immediate return of these men.

> J. H. WILSON,
> *Brevet Major-General.*

HDQRS. CAVALRY CORPS, MIL. DIV. OF THE MISSISSIPPI,
Athens, Ala., January 4, 1865.

Brig. Gen. WILLIAM D. WHIPPLE,
Chief of Staff, Department of the Cumberland:

A dispatch from General Croxton, just received, dated Waterloo, December 31, says he arrived there the evening before; found supplies of all kinds on transports. Hood's army reached Cherokee the night of the 30th, and Forrest took the train for Corinth the same day at that point, shipping cavalry by rail.

> J. H. WILSON,
> *Brevet Major-General.*

NASHVILLE, TENN., *January 4, 1865.*

Maj. Gen. R. H. MILROY,
Tullahoma:

We have nothing with which to relieve that portion of the One hundred and fifteenth Ohio between here and Mufreesborough.

By command of Major-General Rousseau:

> B. H. POLK,
> *Major and Assistant Adjutant-General.*

NASHVILLE, TENN., *January 4, 1865.*

Major-General MILROY,
Tullahoma:

The Twenty-third Corps is at Eastport, Miss., on the Tennessee River.

> B. H. POLK,
> *Major and Assistant Adjutant-General.*

ATHENS, *January 4, 1865.*

Brigadier-General AMMEN:

The rebels in Madisonville in force; 800 at Jellico Plains last night, twenty-five miles from this place.

> JAS. HOWE,
> *Captain, Commanding Post.*

KNOXVILLE, *January 4, 1865.*

Capt. JAMES HOWE,
Athens:

What number probably at Madisonville, and which way are they moving? Have you any force in that direction or toward Jellico?

> J. AMMEN,
> *Brigadier-General.*

LOUDON, *January 4, 1865.*

General J. AMMEN:

I have no information of rebels at Madisonville, except a band of guerrillas, numbering variously from fifteen to fifty, which has been in and about there for the last two weeks. Have you any suggestion to make? I will be on the lookout and warn my pickets.

FRANK S. CURTISS,
Lieutenant-Colonel, Commanding.

WASHINGTON, D. C., *January 5, 1865—3.05 p. m.*

Major-General THOMAS:

Your letter of recommendation has not reached this department. I have been waiting and holding all nominations back until you were heard from.

EDWIN M. STANTON,
Secretary of War.

NASHVILLE, *January 5, 1865.*
(Received 11.50 a. m. 6th.)

Hon. E. M. STANTON:

Your telegram of 3.05 this day received. My letter of recommendation was forwarded on the 25th of December, 1864, addressed to Maj. Gen. H. W. Halleck, Chief of Staff, or his assistant adjutant-general. For fear it has miscarried, I will have a copy made and sent on immediately. I have received no dispatches from the different commands to-day, but am satisfied all is moving along right.

GEO. H. THOMAS,
Major-General, U. S. Volunteers, Commanding.

QUARTERMASTER GENERAL'S OFFICE,
Washington, D. C., January 5, 1865.

Maj. Gen. GEORGE H. THOMAS,
Commanding Army of the Cumberland, Nashville, Tenn.:

GENERAL: The inclosed copy of a letter from General Sherman gives information in regard to his success in foraging his army and supplying it with horses and mules during his late operations, which, it is believed, will be of interest to you. One of the most difficult tasks of the quartermaster's department is to supply forage for the great number of animals of the armies while resting in advanced positions. Cannot a system of foraging on the border, or in the rebel country, be adopted which will relieve the Government of a large portion of the heavy expense of purchase and transportation of forage? Cannot the cavalry and trains be camped in many cases at some distance from the main body of the army, in a country which will supply them with a large portion of their forage, and yet within call and supporting distance of the infantry, changing the camps from time to time as the forage is exhausted?

I am, very respectfully, your obedient servant,

CHS. THOMAS,
Asst. Quartermaster-General U. S. Army, and Bvt. Brig. Gen.

[Inclosure.]

HEADQUARTERS MILITARY DIVISION OF THE MISSISSIPPI,
In the Field, Savannah, December 25, 1864.

Maj. Gen. M. C. MEIGS,
Quartermaster-General U. S. Army, Washington, D. C.:

GENERAL: In reply to your letter of the 16th [15th] instant, I beg to inform you that I have referred the same to Brig. Gen. L. C. Easton, my chief quartermaster, who will report fully to you in respect to all matters within his department connected with our recent march. As you say, my marches have demonstrated the great truth that armies, even of vast magnitude, are not tied down to bases. In almost any quarter of the South armies of from 30,000 to 50,000 may safely march, sure to find near their route forage of some kind or other for their animals. It is a physical impossibility to supply an army with forage, and you do perfectly right in demanding that each army should provide itself with long forage and a large proportion of its grain. In the interior of Georgia we found an abundance of the best kind of corn and fodder, and even here on the sea-board we find an abundance of rice in the straw, which our animals eat with avidity and seem to like. It will not be long before I shall sally forth again, and I feel no uneasiness whatever on the score of forage. You may use my name in any circular addressed to the quartermasters of the army to the effect that every part of the Southern country will support their animals by a judicious system of foraging. More animals are lost to your department whilst standing idle, hitched to their wagons, than during the long and seemingly hard marches into the interior. I beg to assure you that all my armies have been abundantly supplied by your department, and I am sometimes amazed at the magnitude of its operations. I think I have personally aided your department more than any general officer in the service, by drawing liberally from the enemy, thereby injuring him financially, and to the same extent helping ourselves; and you may always rely upon my cordially co-operating with any system you may establish. General Easton is now endeavoring to reduce to a system of accountability our captures; but so long as we keep our trains and animals well up, and prevent as far as possible the appropriation of public property to private use, I take it for granted you will pardon any mere departure from the established rules of accountability. I want nothing in the way of horses or transportation, and would merely ask from time to time some few artillery horses of a size and weight which cannot be found in this country; at present we need none, as I do not propose to increase my artillery arm; but as I have 400 or 500 miles more to march before spring, it might be prudent to reserve for us 400 or 500 good artillery horses. If my cavalry cannot remount itself in the country it may go afoot.

Thanking you for many expressions of confidence and respect, I am, as ever,

Your friend and servant,

W. T. SHERMAN,
Major-General.

[First indorsement.]

HEADQUARTERS DEPARTMENT OF THE CUMBERLAND,
Eastport, Miss., January 21, 1865.

Respectfully referred to Maj. Gen. J. H. Wilson, commanding Cavalry Corps, Military Division of the Mississippi, for report as to the practicability of obtaining forage for his horses between Pulaski and the Tennessee River while in the recent pursuit of Hood's army; also during his march from Athens to Eastport.

By command of Major-General Thomas:

> HENRY M. CIST,
> *Assistant Adjutant-General.*

[Second indorsement.]

HDQRS. CAVALRY CORPS, MIL. DIV. OF THE MISSISSIPPI,
Gravelly Springs, Ala., February 6, 1865.

Respectfully returned. Attention invited to the letter herewith.

> J. H. WILSON,
> *Brevet Major-General.*

[Inclosure.]

HDQRS. CAVALRY CORPS, MIL. DIV. OF THE MISSISSIPPI,
Gravelly Springs, Ala., February 6, 1865.

Brigadier-General WHIPPLE:

SIR: I have the honor to report for the information of the major-general commanding that during the pursuit of Hood's army and the march from Athens to this place, it was with the greatest difficulty forage could be obtained in sufficient quantities to keep the horses of my command in marching condition. From this scarcity, the percentage of loss was very great, both from actual starvation and diseases partly induced thereby. If the command could have taken time to search for grain during the march, it could have been found, but in that event but little damage would have been inflicted on the enemy. In districts not traveled over by contending armies commands of cavalry marching through them for the first time experience but little difficulty in obtaining forage. But 10,000 or 15,000 horses can consume the surplus of a very rich district in an incredibly short time. No system depending upon the enemy entirely can be devised for keeping and feeding our cavalry force, and therefore depots of grain and hay must be provided when cavalry is to be put upon a basis of thorough sufficiency. Foraging is necessary, proper, and effective during the progress of a campaign, but is always expensive through the fact that it gives license to the men and overwork to the horses. Whenever cavalry is to rest and recuperate, the quartermaster's department should furnish the necessary supplies.

I have the honor to be, very respectfully, your obedient servant,

> J. H. WILSON,
> *Brevet Major-General.*

HEADQUARTERS DEPARTMENT OF THE CUMBERLAND,
Nashville, Tenn., January 5, 1865.

Maj. P. O'CONNELL,
Commanding Pontoon Train, Decatur:

Remain where you are until you receive orders from these headquarters.

> WM. D. WHIPPLE,
> *Brigadier-General.*

WAR DEPARTMENT,
January 5, 1865.

Capt. J. C. VAN DUZER:
(Care of Maj. Gen. George H. Thomas, Nashville, Tenn.)

The following item is taken from the Richmond papers of to-day:

Hood heard from at last. An official dispatch from General Hood, dated Corinth, December 26, was received at the War Department last night. General Hood states that the army has recrossed the Tennessee River, without material loss since the battle in front of Nashville.

THOMAS T. ECKERT.

SPECIAL FIELD ORDERS, } HDQRS. DEPT. OF THE CUMBERLAND,
No. 3.   }   *Nashville, Tenn., January 5, 1865.*

*   *   *   *   *   *   *

II. Col. A. J. Mackay, chief quartermaster, having reported from Chattanooga at these headquarters, Lieut. Col. William G. Le Duc is hereby relieved from duty as acting chief quartermaster of the armies in the field in Middle Tennessee, and will resume his duties under Special Orders, 317, War Department, on Board of Examinations for Quartermasters.

III. Brigadier-General Johnson, commanding Sixth Division, Cavalry Corps, Military Division of the Mississippi, will proceed with his command to Pulaski, Tenn., and take post with his headquarters at that place.

*   *   *   *   *   *   *

VI. Brig. Gen. Edward M. McCook, commanding First Division, Cavalry Corps, Military Division of the Mississippi, will proceed with his command, via Pulaski, Tenn., to Eastport, Miss., reporting to Brevet Major-General Wilson at that place.

By command of Major-General Thomas:

HENRY M. CIST,
Captain and Assistant Adjutant-General.

NASHVILLE, *January 5, 1865.*
(Received 10 p. m.)

Brig. Gen. T. J. WOOD,
Huntsville:

Send a brigade to Decatur to re-enforce the garrison of that place. When the corps moves you can withdraw the brigade.

WM. D. WHIPPLE,
Brigadier-General.

NASHVILLE, *January 5, 1865.*
(Received 10 p. m.)

Brig. Gen. T. J. WOOD,
Huntsville:

The pontoon train at Elkton has been ordered to report to you as soon as the troops and trains of the Fourth Corps have passed. Please have it repaired, refitted, and prepared to accompany your column on next campaign.

WM. D. WHIPPLE,
Brigadier-General.

HEADQUARTERS FOURTH ARMY CORPS,
Huntsville, Ala., January 5, 1865.

Brigadier-General KIMBALL:

The general commanding directs that you send out forage parties, with sufficient guard, for the purpose of procuring forage for the animals of your command, in the direction of New Market and Fayetteville, or in such other directions as your information will lead you to think that forage can be obtained. Nothing must be taken by these foraging parties but forage for animals.

Very respectfully, your obedient servant,

J. S. FULLERTON,
Assistant Adjutant-General and Chief of Staff.

(Same to Generals Elliott and Beatty.)

HEADQUARTERS FOURTH ARMY CORPS,
Huntsville, Ala., January 5, 1865.

Brigadier-General ELLIOTT,
Commanding Second Division, Fourth Army Corps:

GENERAL: The general commanding directs that you send a regiment to Pulaski to-morrow, for the purpose of escorting the artillery and artillery train of this corps, which was left at that place, to Huntsville. Let the regiment report to Major Goodspeed, chief of artillery, Fourth Corps, who will leave here at about daylight to-morrow morning for Pulaski, and who will call for it at your headquarters on his way. The regiment will take five days' rations, and leave behind in camp all barefooted men and those who cannot make the march.

Very respectfully, your obedient servant,

J. S. FULLERTON,
Assistant Adjutant-General.

HEADQUARTERS SECOND DIVISION, FOURTH ARMY CORPS,
Near Huntsville, Ala., January 5, 1865.

Lieut. Col. J. S. FULLERTON,
Chief of Staff, Fourth Army Corps:

COLONEL: I have the honor to submit the following for the information of the general commanding the corps: In compliance with orders of the 3d instant, I made a forced march of twenty-three miles on the 4th; delayed and my division much harassed by the supply trains of the First and Third Divisions, which I was directed to follow. The censure of the general commanding, implied in the communication referred to, if the facts were known by him, would not have been given; and as I am informed by him that the instructions to march my division until sundown were not directed by the general commanding, it is proper that he should know that his instructions to me were exceeded by the assistant adjutant-general of the corps. The staff officer from headquarters of the corps instructed to assign my division to its camp on the 5th did not halt my column until it had passed beyond the ground designated, and then could give me no information as to the facilities for obtaining water for my troops. After examining the country for some distance in the locality designated, I had to encamp my command for the night until I could have time to make further examination.

I am, colonel, very respectfully, your obedient servant,

W. L. ELLIOTT,
Brigadier-General, U. S. Volunteers, Commanding.

SPECIAL ⎞   HEADQUARTERS ARMY OF THE OHIO,
FIELD ORDERS, ⎬   *In the Field, Waynesborough, Tenn.,*
No. 4.   ⎠   *January 5, 1865.*

1. Brig. Gen. N. C. McLean, U. S. Volunteers, will report to Maj. Gen. D. N. Couch, commanding Second Division, Twenty-third Army Corps, for assignment to duty.

By command of Major-General Schofield:

J. A. CAMPBELL,
Major and Assistant Adjutant-General.

HEADQUARTERS ARMY OF THE OHIO,
Waynesborough, Tenn., January 5, 1865.

Maj. Gen. D. N. COUCH,
Commanding Second Division, Twenty-third Army Corps:

GENERAL: I am directed by the commanding general to inform you that it is doubtful whether your supply train will get up to-morrow, and you had better remain in camp until further orders, as it is not desirable that you should move before your supplies arrive, or it is certain that they may be at Clifton. Please inform these headquarters when your trains get up.

Very respectfully, your obedient servant,

WM. M. WHERRY,
Major and Aide-de-Camp.

HDQRS. CAVALRY CORPS, MIL. DIV. OF THE MISSISSIPPI,
Athens, Ala., January 5, 1865.

Maj. WILLIAM R. PRICE,
Chief Inspector Cavalry, War Department:

MAJOR: I inclose for your information a copy of a communication to General Whipple in regard to the continuance of the measures for the cavalry reorganization.* As you will see, it was written under the impression that we should be allowed the privilege of going into winter quarters and completing the work systematically. Since it was written the indications are that this will [not] be allowed, and, therefore, what is done must be done quickly. I have, therefore, suggested to General Thomas the propriety of sending the dismounted brigades north of the Ohio River, with authority from the Secretary of War, if it can be obtained, to impress what horses may be needed; and seems to me the Government can a great deal better afford this measure than to allow us to go into the field without the cavalry or

* See p. 429.

with it poorly mounted. As Johnson's division was organized with a view to its being left for the defense of the country north of the Tennessee, it might be dismounted entirely and its horses turned over to the other troops, provided, however, any troops are necessary north of the Tennessee; but Upton's, Knipe's, and Hatch's divisions should be supplied with as little delay as possible, even if active operations do not begin before spring. The sooner the horses are in the hands of the men the sooner they can be inured to the service. I have written fully to Major Chambliss in regard to this matter, but I would suggest to you that as soon as the corps can be concentrated at Eastport all the horses required should be sent to that point by steam-boat, for in that case I shall be able to concentrate the men of the corps and establish the divisions and brigades. Please inform me, at Eastport, what chance there is of securing the Spencer carbines for the entire command, and how fast, under an extraordinary pressure, the horses can be furnished. The recent campaign has been very severe upon our horses, many of them having been selected from broken-down horses of previous campaigns, and all having been subjected in this to hard work and poor feed. The grease-heel and hoof-rot are again making their appearance. The disease seems to be the same in different forms; attacks officers' horses, as well as those of the men, and no amount of care will prevent it. I have lost three valuable animals myself, notwithstanding the careful treatment they have habitually received. I attribute the disease to overwork, mud roads, and corn, without proper corn or other long forage. You will be glad to know, however, that the services of the cavalry under its organization have been commended in the highest degree by General Thomas, and justly warrant us in hoping that its future career will prove the wisdom of the measures already instituted for its benefit. During the campaign twenty-two guns, eight battle-flags, and nearly 3,000 prisoners were taken by it from breast-works and in open field fights with the enemy.

Very respectfully, your obedient servant,

J. H. WILSON,
Brevet Major-General.

HDQRS. CAVALRY CORPS, MIL. DIV. OF THE MISSISSIPPI,
Athens, Ala., January 5, 1865.

Maj. WILLIAM P. CHAMBLISS,
Special Insp. Cav., Mil. Div. of the Mississippi, Louisville, Ky.:

MAJOR: I inclose for your information a copy of a letter addressed to General Whipple upon the supposition that we should be permitted to go into winter quarters and get ready for spring operations.[*] Since then the indications are that this will not be permitted, and that we may be called upon for active operations at any day. In view of this contingency, I would like to have Upton's division got ready as soon as possible, and after it Knipe's; Johnson's division, having been organized for the defense of the country north of the Tennessee River, may be supplied last. Fearing that operations may be precipitated upon us before the Bureau, in the regular course of business, could supply all the horses necessary, I have suggested to General Thomas the propriety of sending the dismounted men north of the Ohio River, with authority from the Secretary of War to impress horses. During the recent cam-

* See p. 429.

paign the horses of this command have been very hard worked and poorly fed. Grease-heel is again making its appearance and disabling quite a large number. I am, however, trying to save them by sending those infected, as well as those that are sore backed or otherwise disabled, to Nashville. I have directed Captain Wilson and Colonel Miner to push forward the erection of stabling with the greatest possible rapidity, in order that these animals may receive what in humanity as well as in economy they are entitled to—good treatment, shelter, and proper food. By these means, with the proper vigor on the part of the officers charged with the duties, 6,000 or 8,000 horses ought to be got ready by the 1st of April. As soon as the stables are ready I will get every horse that is worth it into them.

I see by the papers that Captain Irvin advertises daily sales of broken-down cavalry horses, and am told that those of the class which are turned into his corrals die almost by hundreds daily. It seems to me that the judicious expenditure of money in securing the proper care for horses which are now down by overwork, ill use, and short feed would save many valuable animals to the service and much expense to the Treasury. The corps will be concentrated at Eastport as soon as it can march there; and in case more horses than enough for Upton's division can be obtained they might be sent directly to that point by steam-boat. Hatch will require 2,000 or 2,500; Knipe, from 3,000 to 4,000; Johnson's wants could be supplied in the usual way. It is my intention, however, to take every man, whether mounted or dismounted, into any campaign which may be inaugurated south of the Tennessee. I also wish to solicit your active co-operation in securing Spencer carbines for the whole command. The reasons are too well known to you to require a recital at my hands. I am sure, too, from the active and most efficient measures which you have adopted in remounting and arming the command, you will do all in your power to assist in the completion of the work. Please write to me, at Eastport, what chance there is of getting the carbines, and how soon, under the pressure of an impending campaign whose completeness depends upon the cavalry, you will probably be able to supply the demand for horses.

Very respectfully, your obedient servant,

J. H. WILSON,
Brevet Major-General, Commanding.

HDQRS. CAVALRY CORPS, MIL. DIV. OF THE MISSISSIPPI,
Athens, Ala., January 5, 1865.

Brig. Gen. ROBERT S. GRANGER,
Commanding District of Northern Alabama:

GENERAL: I have the honor to acknowledge the receipt of your communication of yesterday in regard to the detachments of cavalry serving in your district. Having carefully considered the subject, I cannot consent to the proposition you make in reference to the Second Tennessee, for by so doing it will separate that regiment permanently from the division to which it has been assigned. It and detachments of Indiana regiments ought to be returned to duty with their respective regiments and divisions. The reckless and ill-advised system of scattering the cavalry of this military division in small squads over the country has been productive of more harm than good. It is only by breaking down such a system and concentrating the cavalry into proper brigades and divisions that we can ever hope to regenerate the cavalry service in the West. To this end I have assigned every regiment to a division and am endeavoring to get the divisions together. If successful in this I hope to be able to effectually dispose of the enemy's cavalry, clean out guerrillas, and lend the proper co-operation to the general operations of the infantry. To leave the broken-up and demoralized detachments which are in your district in their present condition would invite rather than repel such operations as you anticipate on the part of Roddey's command; but, in pursuance of the instructions of General Thomas, a division of three brigades, under the command of General Johnson, has been organized for the purpose of looking after the country between Decatur, Chattanooga, and Nashville. If the regiments which belong to it can ever be got together, they will be fully able to accomplish all that may be required of them. The Fifth Tennessee and the Fifteenth Pennsylvania form the Third Brigade of this division, and, when united, ought to make a force of 1,000 good cavalry.

Finally, general, you must allow we cannot overcome the rebels or protect our own lines of communication by remaining on the defensive in block-houses. The only sure way of our disposing of the rebellion is to excel the rebels in the power of offense and in the capacity to use this power. Cavalry, you know as well as I do, properly organized, is essentially the element of mobility in an army, the arm with which to inflict injury on the enemy's communications. The performance of the cavalry in the recent campaign entitles it to a separate existence and organization. It must be got together, or it cannot be organized. I hope you will give me all the assistance in your power, and in return I assure you no effort will be spared to rid the country of guerrillas as well as regularly organized cavalry.

I am, general, very respectfully, your obedient servant,
J. H. WILSON,
Brevet Major-General.

HEADQUARTERS DISTRICT OF NORTHERN ALABAMA,
Decatur, January 5, 1865.

Maj. Gen. J. H. WILSON,
Comdg. Cavalry, Military Division of the Mississippi:

GENERAL: You certainly misunderstand me. I do not desire to retain the detachments of Indiana cavalry, referred to in your note just received, only recently mounted on broken-down horses without instructions and badly disciplined. They can in their present condition be of but little service anywhere. I cheerfully give them up. But the Second Tennessee is not likely to invite a raid from Roddey's cavalry, and could be of excellent service to me, and I regret you do not find it expedient to permit them to remain.

I am, very respectfully, your obedient servant,
R. S. GRANGER,
Brigadier-General.

P. S.—I omitted to state that the cavalry under Lieutenant-Colonel Prosser is still absent with Major-General Steedman. It will be ordered to report to you as soon as it returns.

R. S. G.,
Brigadier-General.

Circular.| Hdqrs. Cav. Corps, Mil. Div. of the Miss.,
                                            Athens, Ala., January 5, 1865.

Commanders of divisions and independent brigades will have their quartermaster's wagons, ambulances, and batteries across the Elk River before to-morrow night (6th), in order to avoid trouble which a rise in the river would cause in crossing the river.

By order of General Wilson:

                                        HENRY E. NOYES,
                    Lieutenant and Acting Assistant Inspector-General.

                                        Nashville, Tenn, *January 5, 1865.*

Major-General Milroy,
            Tullahoma:

If the One hundred and eightieth Ohio has not started send it by cars to this place to join its corps by the way of the Cumberland and Tennessee Rivers.

                                        B. H. POLK,
                            Major and Assistant Adjutant-General.

                                        Tullahoma, *January 5, 1865.*

Col. W. Warner,
            180th Ohio Volunteer Infantry, Decherd:

Get your regiment in readiness to join your corps at Eastport, Miss., via Nashville and Chattanooga Railroad to Nashville, and thence by way of the Cumberland and Tennessee Rivers. Give these headquarters the number of men, so that train can be ordered.

By command of Major-General Milroy:

                                        JNO. O. CRAVENS,
                                Assistant Adjutant-General.

                            Decatur, Ala., *January 5, 1865—7 p. m.*
                                                    (Received 6th.)

Major-General Thomas:

I have just arrived here. Colonel Palmer arrived at Courtland to-day. He captured Hood's pontoon train of 120 wagons and 180 wagons of supplies and 150 prisoners. The trains were burned and the horses and mules were mostly killed. He followed the trains to the Mississippi line. I leave for Chattanooga by steamer to-night; the troops follow by rail in the a. m. Colonel Thompson will proceed to Nashville direct.

                                        JAS. B. STEEDMAN,
                                            Major-General.

            Hdqrs. Cavalry Corps, Mil. Div. of the Mississippi,
                                            Athens, Ala., January 5, 1865.

Maj. E. B. Beaumont,
            24 High Street, Nashville:

Telegram received. Say to General Thomas that I will make arrangements for leaving Johnson in Tennessee with a sufficient force of cavalry for the purpose indicated. Ask him also to stir up the horse department. Hurry Upton's arrangements and Knipe's. Johnson will have to be mounted last. I shall leave here on the morning of the 7th. Send out all the detachments, mounted or dismounted, that belong to Hatch's and Hammond's commands; also the men of the Seventh Ohio and Fifth Iowa, as I shall probably transfer these regiments out of the Sixth Division, and the Fifth Tennessee to it. Let me know how the stables are progressing, and what measures are being taken to collect the broken-down horses in pasture in Tennessee and Kentucky. See that no horses are sold by Captain Irvin that can be recuperated. I have written and telegraphed to everybody for the horses that are needed to remount us. They can be more easily delivered at Eastport than elsewhere. Tell Carling to exert himself to secure good mules, good transportation, and a supply of ambulances.

J. H. WILSON,
Brevet Major-General.

HEADQUARTERS CAVALRY,
Widow King's, near King's Ford of Town Creek, January 5, 1865.
Major MOE,
Assistant Adjutant-General:

MAJOR: I have the honor to report my arrival at this place at 3 o'clock this morning. I destroyed the entire pontoon train of the enemy, consisting of 80 boats and about 200 wagons, near Nauvoo, Ala., and captured all the mules except what the drivers were able to ride off on. The train was a finely appointed one, and I regretted that the presence of two brigades of the enemy's cavalry between my force and our lines prevented me from bringing it off. From Nauvoo I went on to Itawamba County, Miss., and captured and destroyed, on the Guntown road, a supply train of General Hood's of 100 wagons with the mules. On returning I found the enemy's cavalry, under Armstrong, Roddey, and Russell, disposed to prevent my egress. I evaded them by crossing from the vicinity of Bexar to the toll-gate on the military road; thence, via Howell, to Thorn Hill, on the Biler road, and back via Mount Hope. On the top of the mountain, six miles above Mount Hope, I encountered Colonel Russell with the Fourth Alabama Cavalry; attacked and utterly routed him, capturing his four wagons, with all his baggage and headquarters papers, and as many of his men as our tired horses could overtake. I have here about 150 prisoners. My horses are much jaded.

Yours, respectfully,

WM. J. PALMER,
Colonel.

HEADQUARTERS DEPARTMENT OF THE CUMBERLAND,
Nashville, Tenn., January 5, 1865.
Brig. Gen. R. S. GRANGER,
Decatur:

It is not intended to make a depot at Decatur, consequently no great amount of building will be requisite.

WM. D. WHIPPLE,
Brigadier-General.

NASHVILLE, *January 5, 1865.*

Brig. Gen. R. S. GRANGER:

A brigade has been ordered from the Fourth Army Corps to re-enforce you.

WM. D. WHIPPLE,
Brigadier-General.

HDQRS. MEMPHIS AND CHARLESTON RAILROAD DEFENSES,
Huntsville, Ala., January 5, 1865.

Lieut. SAMUEL M. KNEELAND,
Acting Assistant Adjutant-General, Decatur, Ala.:

I have the honor to report that I visited Paint Rock bridge yesterday. The bridge is being rapidly rebuilt, and will, I think, be completed by Saturday night; the master builder says by Friday. This bridge is 100 yards long, forty yards of which will be saved, leaving sixty yards to be rebuilt. I find on further investigation that my report of the loss of the bridge is substantially correct. The Fourth Army Corps has arrived here, and General Wood, who commands it, has sent a regiment there to transfer rations across the river. The corps is encamped outside of town, and thus far its presence here has not affected the administration of affairs at this post.

Very respectfully, your obedient servant,

WM. P. LYON,
Colonel Thirteenth Wisconsin Veteran Vol. Infty., Commanding.

ATHENS, TENN., *January 5, 1865.*

Brig. Gen. J. AMMEN:

We have sixty men in Madisonville. The rebels fell back to Jellico. There are not more than 200, commanded by Captain Lea, of Vaughn's command.

JAS. HOWE,
Captain, Commanding Post.

NASHVILLE, TENN., *January 6, 1865.*
(Received 2.25 p. m. 7th.)

Maj. Gen. H. W. HALLECK,
Washington:

General Wilson, commanding Cavalry Corps, asks that, in view of operations following the concentration at Eastport, immediate steps be taken to furnish him with 10,000 horses and all the Spencer carbines to be had. He says, if the Cavalry Bureau cannot furnish the horses in fifteen or twenty days, authority should be obtained from the Secretary of War to impress horses in Indiana, Ohio, and Illinois. The magnitude of the interests at stake warrants it.

GEO. H. THOMAS,
Major-General.

General Hatch, commanding Fifth Cavalry Division, Military Division of the Mississippi, requests authority for Second, Third, Sixth, Seventh, and Ninth Illinois Cavalry to recruit in their respective States. Will you permit it?

GEO. H. THOMAS,
Major-General.

NASHVILLE, TENN., *January 6, 1865—10 p. m.*
(Received 2.10 p. m. 7th.)

Maj. Gen. H. W. HALLECK,
Washington, D. C.:

The following dispatch, received from General Steedman to-day, is forwarded for your information.*

Have no further reports from any of the commands to-day.

GEO. H. THOMAS,
Major-General.

———

HEADQUARTERS FOURTH ARMY CORPS,
Huntsville, Ala., January 6, 1865.

Brigadier-General WHIPPLE,
Assistant Adjutant-General:

I have not received nor heard anything of the instructions referred to in your dispatch of the 1st instant from Pulaski as having been sent to me, though I have telegraphed to you since my arrival here about them. I should be glad to be furnished with these instructions at once, as without them I am totally ignorant of the commanding general's wishes and instructions.

I am, yours, respectfully,

•   TH. J. WOOD,
Brigadier-General of Volunteers, Commanding.

———

NASHVILLE, *January 6, 1865.*
(Received 11 p. m.)

Brigadier-General WOOD:

A report has been received that the rebel General Lyon crossed the Nashville and Chattanooga Railroad between Decherd and Elk River bridge. He was going in the direction of Larkinsville or Huntsville, with the intention of trying to cross the Tennessee River. The major-general commanding directs that you keep a good lookout for him and capture and destroy his command should the report prove true.

ROBT. H. RAMSEY,
Assistant Adjutant-General.

(Same to Major-General Wilson.)

———

HEADQUARTERS FOURTH ARMY CORPS,
Huntsville, Ala., January 6, 1865.

Brig. Gen. W. L. ELLIOTT,
Commanding Second Division, Fourth Corps:

GENERAL: Please hold a brigade of your division in readiness to go to Decatur, Ala., to re-enforce the garrison at that place. The brigade will be transported by rail, and I will let you know when to move it to the depot.

Respectfully, &c.,

TH. J. WOOD,
Brigadier-General of Volunteers, Commanding.

———

* See Steedman to Thomas, 7 p. m. 5th (p. 520), omitting all after the words "Mississippi line."

HEADQUARTERS FOURTH ARMY CORPS,
Huntsville, Ala., January 6, 1865.

Brig. Gen. W. L. ELLIOTT,
Commanding Second Division, Fourth Army Corps:

GENERAL: Send the brigade to the depot at once. The train is waiting there prepared to take it to Decatur.

Respectfully, your obedient servant,

TH. J. WOOD,
Brigadier-General of Volunteers, Commanding.

[JANUARY 6, 1865.—For General Wood's address to officers and soldiers of the Fourth Army Corps, see Part I, p. 139.]

CIRCULAR.]   HEADQUARTERS ARMY OF THE OHIO,
In the Field, Waynesborough, Tenn., January 6, 1865.

The major-general commanding desires to impress upon the officers and soldiers connected with these headquarters the necessity and propriety of refraining from committing depredations upon the property of citizens, particularly where headquarters are established. Such property as may be required by the troops, and for the use of animals attached to headquarters, will be seized by the proper officers and accounted for, and all unauthorized foraging and plundering will be severely punished. It is hoped the officers and soldiers about headquarters will set an example worthy the emulation of all the other troops, and consider the premises upon which headquarters may be established as under the special protection of the major-general commanding.

By order of Major-General Schofield:

WM. M. WHERRY,
Major and Aide-de-Camp.

HEADQUARTERS ARMY OF THE OHIO,
Waynesborough, Tenn., January 6, 1865.

Maj. Gen. D. N. COUCH,
Commanding Second Division, Twenty-third Army Corps:

GENERAL: Your supply and forage trains will probably reach you some time to-morrow, though not until quite late in the day. After they arrive you may continue your march to Clifton, and General Ruger will follow you. There is no reason for special haste. There are no boats, provisions, nor forage at Clifton, and one division of General Smith's troops is still there awaiting transportation. What forage we have will be equally distributed among the divisions, and we will have to economize as much as practicable. I will go to Clifton to-morrow.

Very respectfully,

J. M. SCHOFIELD,
Major-General.

ATHENS, *January 6, 1865.*

Major BEAUMONT,
Assistant Adjutant-General:

Direct Generals Long and McCook to send in a list of such regiments of their commands as they wish to have filled up. I have requested authority for Upton's regiments. As soon as these lists are in give them to General Thomas, with request that these regiments may be filled up. Tell Green that 271 horses leave here to-morrow for Nashville. I am glad to know he is making such efforts to recuperate broken-down stock. See General Thomas about stabling materials. Exert yourself to get all men on detached duty belonging to Hatch, Long, McCook, Upton, and Knipe, wherever they may be, sent to Eastport without delay. I have telegraphed to General Thomas about this. Tell Carling that he must find mules somewhere, and stir up everybody connected with the mule department; also to send hay, bran, and horse medicines to Eastport; without these we shall lose many horses. Where are my horses? I am almost afoot. You had better remain in Nashville until I reach Eastport.

J. H. WILSON,
Brevet Major-General.

HDQRS. CAVALRY CORPS, MIL. DIV. OF THE MISSISSIPPI,
Nashville, January 6, 1865.

Lieut. Col. G. G. MINER,
Commanding Dismounted Cavalry:

COLONEL: Order all the mounted men of the Fifth Cavalry Division (General Hatch's) to proceed without delay to Eastport, Ala., via Columbia, Tenn., and Waterloo, Ala. Send the dismounted men to Eastport by steamer. The mounted men can accompany the wagons belonging to the Fifth Division that may be sent to Eastport.

By command of Brevet Major General Wilson:

E. B. BEAUMONT,
Major and Assistant Adjutant-General.

SPECIAL ORDERS, }   HEADQUARTERS CAVALRY CORPS,
                {   MILITARY DIVISION OF THE MISSISSIPPI,
No. 4.   }   *Nashville, Tenn., January 6, 1865.*

*   *   *   *   *   *   *

II. Brig. Gen. J. F. Knipe, commanding Seventh Division, Cavalry Corps, Military Division of the Mississippi, will proceed to Huntsville, Decatur, and such other points as he may deem necessary, to collect the detachments of his division and bring them to Nashville for the purpose of equipping and preparing them for the field. The quartermaster's department will furnish the necessary transportation.

*   *   *   *   *   *   *

By command of Brevet Major-General Wilson:

LEVI T. GRIFFIN,
Captain and Acting Assistant Adjutant-General.

SPECIAL) HEADQUARTERS CAVALRY CORPS,
FIELD ORDERS, } MILITARY DIVISION OF THE MISSISSIPPI,
No. 3.)   *Athens, Ala., January 6, 1865.*

I. The Fifth Iowa and Seventh Ohio Cavalry are hereby transferred from the Sixth Division, Cavalry Corps, to the Fourth Division, and will proceed, under command of Colonel Garrard, to Eastport, Ala.

II. Colonel Harrison, with the Sixteenth Illinois Cavalry and the battery attached to his brigade, will proceed by the nearest route to Pulaski, Tenn. On arriving at that point Colonel Harrison will report in person to General Johnson.

III. The Sixth Tennessee Cavalry is hereby transferred from the Fourth Division Cavalry to the Sixth Division Cavalry. Its commanding officer will report without delay to Brigadier-General Johnson.

IV. Brig. Gen. Edward Hatch, being unfit for field service for the present, is authorized to proceed to Nashville, and if not granted a leave of absence will report thence without delay at Eastport.

By command of Brevet Major-General Wilson:

HENRY E. NOYES,
Lieutenant and Acting Assistant Adjutant-General.

———

SPECIAL ORDERS,) HDQRS. SIXTH DIV., CAVALRY CORPS,
} MILITARY DIVISION OF THE MISSISSIPPI,
No. 6.)   *Edgefield, Tenn., January 6, 1865.*

I. Colonel Mix, commanding Eighth Michigan Cavalry, will march with his regiment to-morrow at daylight, crossing the river by the pontoon bridge (or by the railroad bridge, if most convenient). He will divide his command into two nearly equal bodies—one wing moving by the roads to the right of the Nashville and Chattanooga Railroad, via Nolensville and Triune, to Murfreesborough; the other by the turnpike to Beard's Mill, and thence, if parties of the enemy are heard of in that direction, to Lebanon, concentrating afterward with the right wing at Murfreesborough. At Murfreesborough the command will draw rations, and being there divided into two equal detachments as before, will move by such roads as Colonel Mix may think to afford the best opportunities for effecting a thorough patrol of the country to Shelbyville, the two wings concentrating at that point. From Shelbyville the command, dividing into two equal bodies as before, will move to Fayetteville, concentrating at that point, and from there to Pulaski, where the whole division will presently concentrate. The object of the expedition is to pick up the many stragglers from the rebel army who are understood to be lurking in the country, particularly a regiment of Tennessee cavalry under command of Lieutenant-Colonel Withers, which is understood to be scattered through the counties of Davidson, Williamson, Wilson, and Rutherford. The strong probability is that wherever found the enemy will be in inferior force, and they will be, therefore, promptly and vigorously attacked and pressed; but no force of less than one-half the regiment will be detached to operate independently. Colonel Mix will command the left wing, moving by Beard's Mill. The officer commanding the right wing will be furnished with a copy of this order. The wagons of the regiment will be left to follow with the remainder of the division. Special pains will be taken by all officers to preserve the condition of the horses. The general commanding expects that no trooper will become dismounted on this expedition.

When the rations of the command fail provisions will be seized in the country, memorandum receipts being given. Indiscriminate pillage is forbidden. If any complaints of this character reach these headquarters, the general commanding will hold the officer of the regiment responsible.

By command of Brigadier-General Johnson:

E. T. WELLS,
Assistant Adjutant-General.

HEADQUARTERS FIRST BRIGADE, SEVENTH DIVISION,
Camp, near Athens, January 6, 1865.

Lieut. HENRY E. NOYES,
Acting Assistant Inspector-General:

LIEUTENANT: I am nearly through shoeing, and will march as ordered. My sick were conveyed this evening to McDonald's Station, where there is a switch, and whence the hospital train can take them, as the temporary hospital is along side the track. My supply of shoes was totally insufficient, causing me much delay. I will go into town myself in the morning with a detail. Please get some nails for me, that I may finish my shoeing the other side of Elk River; my supply is exhausted.

J. H. HAMMOND,
Brevet Brigadier-General.

TULLAHOMA, *January 6, 1865—12 m.*

Major-General ROUSSEAU:

The rebel leader Lyon, recently from Kentucky, passed through McMinnville yesterday evening with about 800 men, two pieces of artillery, a small wagon and ambulance train. They had a skirmish with Captain Cain, at McMinnville, and captured some of his men. They crossed the railroad between Decherd and Elk River bridge at 2 o'clock this morning, and passed around Winchester, right and left, in two bodies. A portion of the Forty-third Wisconsin were stationed in Winchester. I had no information of them till they passed. They were well mounted and had a large number of led horses, and were going in the direction of Larkinsville or Huntsville, and are going to try to cross the Tennessee River.

R. H. MILROY,
Major-General.

TULLAHOMA, *January 6, 1865.*

Maj. B. H. POLK,
Assistant Adjutant-General:

My regiments are stationed as follows: Fifty-eighth New York at Stevenson; One hundred and sixth Ohio at Block-houses Nos. 29 and 35, inclusive, with reserve at Stevenson; Twenty-ninth Michigan at Cowan, Tunnel, Tantalon, Anderson, Bass, and Block-houses Nos. 20 and 28, inclusive; Forty-third Wisconsin at Block-house No. 17 to Decherd, inclusive; Forty-second Missouri at Block-houses Nos. 14 and 16, inclusive, headquarters at Tullahoma; One hundred and fifteenth Ohio from Block-house No. 1 to Duck River bridge, both inclusive, except those destroyed by the enemy. So many of the One hundred and fifteenth Ohio were captured that two important bridges between Nashville and Murfreesborough are without guards, and I have not the force to take the places of the One hundred and fifteenth Ohio captured.

R. H. MILROY,
Major-General.

HEADQUARTERS POST OF MURFREESBOROUGH,
Murfreesborough, Tenn., January 6, 1865.

Maj. JOHN O. CRAVENS,
Assistant Adjutant-General, Tullahoma, Tenn.:

MAJOR: I have the honor to report that complaints are almost daily brought to me of the conduct of certain men who style themselves "home guards," said to be organized at Shelbyville by one Captain Worthman. These men go about the country and, without warrant, take from the citizens horses and mules and forage, without giving receipts or vouchers; enter houses, order their meals, search trunks and bureau drawers; all, I suppose, in the name of the Government of the United States. I am told that a perfect reign of terror exists at and in the vicinity of Shelbyville. I am further informed that the said Captain Worthman, in less than three days, paroled about 150 rebel deserters, on his own authority and contrary to positive orders from department headquarters. I shall send a party to examine and collect evidence, and, if circumstances warrant, to arrest all the offending parties, when I will make a full report. A few days since Lieutenant Sheets, acting assistant adjutant-general, arrested and sent to Tullahoma a man who represented himself as belonging to the Fifth Tennessee Cavalry, furloughed by his captain and surgeon; unfortunately, the names of the men—the captain and surgeon—were not taken.

H. P. VAN CLEVE,
Brigadier-General, Commanding Post.

NASHVILLE, *January 6, 1865.*

Major-General STEEDMAN:

The major-general commanding directs that you make a report, as soon as possible, of the number and stations of the troops in the District of the Etowah, and also inform him whether you can now dispense with the services of the troops belonging to General Sherman's army, orders having been received to send them at once to Savannah, if they can be spared.

ROBT. H. RAMSEY,
Assistant Adjutant-General.

HUNTSVILLE, *January 6, 1865.*

Major-General STEEDMAN:

One of Morgan's regiments belongs to Nashville; shall it be sent there? Is Colonel Salm's brigade to be distributed to its former place, or go intact to Chattanooga? I cannot cross Paint Rock till 3 p. m. to-morrow, and will reach Chattanooga to-morrow night. All the troops now bivouacked here. Answer at Larkinsville or Stevenson.

CHARLES CRUFT,
Brigadier-General.

NASHVILLE, TENN., *January 6, 1865.*

Col. W. P. LYON,
        Huntsville:

The command of the rebel General Lyon, numbering from 500 to 800 men, passed Winchester this morning and crossed the Nashville and Chattanooga Railroad, going in the direction of Larkinsville, with the intention of crossing the Tennessee River. They are reported to have a large number of led horses. Please report this to General Granger, if you know of his whereabouts. The command is traveling rapidly.

B. H. POLK,
Major and Assistant Adjutant-General.

CAMP NELSON, KY., *January 6, 1865.*

Capt. J. S. BUTLER,
        Assistant Adjutant-General:

Two companies Thirtieth Kentucky are now starting for Lebanon; the remainder will leave to-day for points designated. No more men can be mounted here until I can get supply of horse equipments; there are none here.

S. S. FRY,
Brigadier-General.

SPECIAL ORDERS, }   WAR DEPT., ADJT. GENERAL'S OFFICE,
    No. 10.   }   *Washington, January 7, 1865.*

*   *   *   *   *   *   *

54. As soon as the court for the trial of Brigadier-General Sweeny, of which Brig. Gen. William Vandever, U. S. Volunteers, is a member, has concluded its sessions, Brigadier-General Vandever will report in person to the commanding general Department of the Cumberland for assignment to duty.

*   *   *   *   *   *   *

By order of the Secretary of War:

W. A. NICHOLS,
Assistant Adjutant-General.

CITY POINT, *January 7, 1865—8 p. m.*
            (Received 9.30 a. m. 8th.)

Maj. Gen. H. W. HALLECK,
        Washington, D. C.:

Please order General Thomas, if he is assured of the departure south of Hood from Corinth, to send Schofield here with his corps, with as little delay as possible. I would recommend at the same time the Departments of the Cumberland and the Ohio be united in one department. Schofield's corps might be assembled at Annapolis, Md. Its transportation can be left at Louisville, Ky., until further orders.

U. S. GRANT,
Lieutenant-General.

NASHVILLE, TENN., *January 7, 1865—9 p. m.*
(Received 3.30 a. m. 8th.)

Maj. Gen. H. W. HALLECK,
    Washington, D. C.:

A copy of my letter of recommendations for promotion, sent on the 25th of December, 1864, was mailed to-day, the first copy not having reached the hands of the honorable Secretary of War, as he telegraphs me. Two brigades of McCook's division of cavalry will leave here to-morrow for Eastport. Long's division is en route from Louisville for this place, and will immediately move forward for Eastport upon arrival here. Wood's corps (the Fourth) is concentrated at Huntsville, and is being refitted for a continuation of the campaign. Smith's and Schofield's troops will probably be concentrated at Eastport by the 11th instant. Clothing and other supplies have already been sent to Eastport for them. I hope to be able to get off for Eastport myself to-morrow.

GEO. H. THOMAS,
    Major-General, U. S. Volunteers, Commanding.

MISSISSIPPI SQUADRON, FLAG-SHIP FAIRY,
    Eastport, Miss., January 7, 1865—11 a. m.

Maj. Gen. GEORGE H. THOMAS,
    Pulaski, Tenn.:

Your telegram from Pulaski, 31st of December, was delivered after my dispatch boat had left, on 3d instant, with one telegram from General A. J. Smith and two from me to you. General Smith is now landing about half his force on the cleared heights back of Eastport formerly occupied by the enemy and subsequently by our army. Accounts of Hood and Forrest are conflicting. Military reconnaissance yesterday to Iuka heard that Hood and Forrest were moving south on Mobile and Ohio Railroad. Some deserters and country people say that rebels talk of making a stand at Corinth. General A. J. Smith and myself return with the transports to-day to Clifton for remainder of his artillery and troops, except one brigade, in care of part of transportation, waiting next and third trip from Clifton. I will do my best to cover and assist all army movements in this quarter and to give strong convoys from Paducah to Eastport. The military movements here, present and prospective, may cause some, but I hope not much, delay in giving convoy. I recommend that quartermasters be ordered to send no transports without convoy, so long as enemy are in force along or north of the Memphis and Charleston Railroad. Forrest's men are annoying the Mississippi.

S. P. LEE,
    Acting Rear-Admiral, Commanding Mississippi Squadron.

HEADQUARTERS DEPARTMENT OF THE CUMBERLAND,
    Nashville, January 7, 1865.

WILLIAM J. MELLEN, Esq.,
    Special Supervising Agent, U. S. Treasury Dept., Cincinnati:

SIR: The major-general commanding the department directs me to write that he is willing, and prefers, that permits to trade within the department should be granted by you, when, in your opinion, it would be proper, upon the recommendation of the district commanders, without reference to him, the department commander. It throws into his headquarters a good number of applications, the merit of which he has not the time to investigate, and is satisfied that they should be left to yourself and the district commanders.

Very respectfully,

WM. D. WHIPPLE,
Brigadier-General and Chief of Staff.

SPECIAL FIELD ORDERS, }   HDQRS. DEPT. OF THE CUMBERLAND,
No. 5.   }   *Nashville, Tenn., January 7, 1865.*

*   *   *   *   *   *   *

II. The detachment of the Merrill Horse, composed of 200 men, are hereby detailed for courier duty at these headquarters, and will report to Lieut. M. J. Kelly, chief of couriers, Department of the Cumberland.

*   *   *   *   *   *   *

IV. The reserve artillery of the Army of the Tennessee, now at this place, will report for duty, as a portion of the garrison of Nashville, to Brig. Gen. J. F. Miller, commanding the post. Maj. John Mendenhall, inspector of artillery of the Department of the Cumberland, will give all necessary instructions concerning the armament of the batteries.

*   *   *   *   *   *   *

VI. The One hundred and eightieth Regiment Ohio Volunteer Infantry, en route to join the Twenty-third Army Corps at Eastport, will, upon its arrival at this place, report to Brig. Gen. J. L. Donaldson, chief quartermaster Department of the Cumberland, for the purpose of escorting by land a wagon train to the command of Maj. Gen. A. J. Smith, at Eastport. The commanding officer of the regiment will detail a sufficient number of teamsters for the train.

VII. The Forty-second Missouri Volunteer Infantry is hereby assigned to the Fourth Division, Twentieth Army Corps. The commanding officer will render the required reports and returns to Major-General Rousseau, commanding.

By command of Major-General Thomas:

HENRY M. CIST,
Captain and Assistant Adjutant-General.

HUNTSVILLE, *January 7, 1865.*

General WHIPPLE,
    Assistant Adjutant-General:

Sent a brigade yesterday morning to Decatur. Received last night dispatch in regard to General Lyon. Will try to carry out the commanding general's wishes.

TH. J. WOOD,
Brigadier-General.

HEADQUARTERS FOURTH ARMY CORPS,
Huntsville, Ala., January 7, 1865.

Brigadier-General WHIPPLE,
    Assistant Adjutant-General:

General Cruft is passing through here with several thousand men of Steedman's command, on the way to Chattanooga. He is using all the railroad transportation therefor. I have directed him to leave a force at Paint Rock, Larkinsville, &c., and to scout well thereabouts to find Lyon, and destroy him, if possible.   Please telegraph your approval of this act.   I have also directed General Granger to send part of the brigade I sent him up the river, and for Captain Forrest, of the gun-boat, to patrol down the river from Bridgeport, to prevent the enemy from crossing.

TH. J. WOOD,
Brigadier-General.

NASHVILLE, January 7, 1865.

Brig. Gen. T. J. WOOD:

Your telegram of this date is received and your action as therein taken is approved.   As soon as the forces of General Cruft get through the work assigned by you they will be permitted to go on their way.

GEO. H. THOMAS,
Major-General.

HUNTSVILLE, January 7, 1865.

Brigadier-General WHIPPLE,
          Chief of Staff:

No order has been received assigning the Third and Fourth Michigan to this corps.   Where are these regiments?

TH. J. WOOD,
Brigadier-General.

HEADQUARTERS DEPARTMENT OF THE CUMBERLAND,
Nashville, Tenn., January 7, 1865.

Brig. Gen. T. J. WOOD,
          Huntsville:

The Third and Fourth Michigan were assigned to your corps some time since.   The regiment in charge of the pontoon train still belongs to you, and the train is intended for your corps, and of course you should furnish a regiment to take charge of it.   There are no other regiments which can possibly be assigned to you.

WM. D. WHIPPLE,
Brigadier-General.

HEADQUARTERS DEPARTMENT OF THE CUMBERLAND,
Nashville, Tenn., January 7, 1865.

Brig. Gen. T. J. WOOD,
          Huntsville:

Your men are being sent from hospital to their commands as rapidly as possible.   The War Department has ordered boards of inspectors and special inspectors for the purpose of examining the inmates of hospitals, with a view to sending to the field all fit for duty; and any further attempts to accomplish the same end on the part of the Department of the Cumberland only makes trouble.   If you would call for them individually, and state where they are, the work of collecting them would be somewhat facilitated.

WM. D. WHIPPLE,
Brigadier-General.

NASHVILLE, *January 7, 1865.*

Brig. Gen. T. J. WOOD,
      Huntsville, Ala.:

The instructions sent you were simply to prepare your corps for active operations; those are the orders from the Headquarters of the Army, and beyond that we know nothing. Get your men well clothed, and prepared for three months' campaign; take as little transportation as you can possibly get along with, and have the animals in good condition; make up all returns to date; and when you start take nothing but rations, forage, intrenching tools, a few carpenter tools for repairing, and the necessary blanks and stationery.

WM. D. WHIPPLE,
Brigadier-General.

ATHENS, ALA., *January 7, 1865.*

Brigadier-General WOOD:

Major-General Wilson directs me to telegraph you that he received a dispatch to-day at 12 m., when near Elk River, from Major-General Thomas, dated 1 p. m. 6th, stating that the rebel General Lyon had crossed the railroad between Decherd and Elk River, on his way to Huntsville or Larkinsville, it is supposed, with the intention of crossing the Tennessee River, and that he had orders to pursue him, but the distance being so great and his horses being in such poor condition, he deems it impracticable to do so, thinking the rebel commander might make his escape across the river, even if he had to swim it, before he could be overtaken. He requests that you give him any information you may receive in regard to the movements of General Lyon.

Very respectfully,

W. W. VAN ANTWERP,
Captain and Aide-de-Camp.

HEADQUARTERS FOURTH ARMY CORPS,
Huntsville, Ala., January 7, 1865.

Major-General WILSON:

The latest intelligence received of the movements of the rebel General Lyon indicated that he had crossed the railroad near Larkinsville, apparently on his way to the Tennessee River. General Cruft passed through here to-day with his division, on his way to Chattanooga. I ordered him to detach a portion of his command at Larkinsville and try to capture or destroy Lyon's command. A regiment or two of cavalry would be a great assistance in doing this.

TH. J. WOOD,
Brigadier-General of Volunteers.

HEADQUARTERS FOURTH ARMY CORPS,
Huntsville, Ala., January 7, 1865.

Captain FORREST, U. S. Navy,
      Commanding Gun-boat fleet on Upper Tennessee:

The rebel General Lyon is reported moving southward, toward Guntersville, to cross the river. General Thomas has ordered that, if possible, his force be captured or destroyed. I am sending out to-day to accomplish this. Will you have the river thoroughly patrolled in every quarter where he might attempt a crossing; it will help much to catch him.

TH. J. WOOD,
Brigadier-General of Volunteers, Commanding.

HEADQUARTERS FOURTH ARMY CORPS,
Huntsville, Ala., January 7, 1865.

Col. J. G. MITCHELL,
 Larkinsville, Ala.:

Send out vigorous scouting [parties] at once, and find out in which direction the enemy went; then pursue them at once, and destroy the band, if possible. Send the two companies of negroes to Scottstown.

TH. J. WOOD,
Brigadier-General of Volunteers.

PAINT ROCK, *January 7, 1865.*

Brigadier-General WOOD or GRANGER:

Do you hear anything further of Lyon? Colonel Mitchell's brigade is at Larkinsville; will hear from him soon.

CHAS. CRUFT,
Brigadier-General.

HEADQUARTERS FOURTH ARMY CORPS,
Huntsville, Ala., January 7, 1865.

Brigadier-General CRUFT:

I telegraphed to General Thomas this forenoon the orders I had given to you. I have received this evening a telegram from him approving these orders, and saying that when you had done the work assigned you of cleaning out Lyon's command you could go on your way. I trust you will capture and destroy Lyon's command. Let me hear from you.

TH. J. WOOD,
Brigadier-General of Volunteers, Commanding.

PAINT ROCK STATION, *January 7, 1865.*

Brigadier-General WOOD:

Dispatch received. Will get to Larkinsville soon. Mitchell's brigade is there, and Harrison's with me; not yet heard from him. I learned that General Granger has ordered some of my trains to unload at Brownsborough. Can hear nothing of Lyon's whereabouts thus far.

CHAS. CRUFT,
Brigadier-General.

EASTPORT, MISS., *January 7, 1865.*

Maj. Gen. G. H. THOMAS,
 Nashville, Tenn.:

I have landed about half my command at Eastport, and will return immediately to Clifton for the remainder. It will take yet some time to get up the transportation. My scouts have not yet determined the exact whereabouts of Hood; reports are conflicting. I believe he is yet at Corinth. If General Croxton had furnished me a few cavalry, as I requested, I should have been advised ere this. I have sent to Cairo for coal, hay, and additional subsistence stores.

Very respectfully,

A. J. SMITH,
Major-General.

GENERAL ORDERS, ⎫　HDQRS. SECOND BRIG., FIRST DIV.,
　　　　　　　　　⎬　　DETACH. ARMY OF THE TENNESSEE,
No. 1.　　　　　　⎭　　　　*Clifton, Tenn., January 7, 1865.*

I. The attention of commanding officers of this brigade is called to the fact that their men are in the constant habit of straggling at will from camp, passing beyond the picket-line, and committing the grossest outrages upon citizens of the country. An instance has been brought to the notice of the general commanding of an outrage of the most heinous character committed by men of the Eighth Wisconsin Infantry. A party of scouts in the employ of the military authorities were met by these men beyond the lines, and, by means of personal violence, deprived of their arms and their persons robbed of money and valuables. The general commanding the corps has declared a purpose to visit with the strict rigor of the law all offenders who may be convicted of any violation whatever of existing orders upon the subject of straggling, marauding, and unauthorized foraging.

II. It is necessary, in order to prevent these disgraceful occurrences and preserve the name of the command, that commanding officers of regiments and the battery of this brigade take the most vigorous measures to restrain the propensities of evil-disposed among their men. They must establish regulations that will prevent straggling altogether, either from camp or when upon the march. The men must not be allowed to leave camp, except upon duty or with written permission of regimental or battery commanders, stating the purposes for which such permission is granted.

III. The matter of roll-calls must be more punctually attended to. Commanding officers must know where their men are, and every case of an absentee who is not properly accounted for must be thoroughly investigated, and a proper punishment administered for every violation of orders. Each regiment and the battery of this brigade will have a roll-call at 9 a. m., 12 m., and 3 p. m. each day, in addition to the stated roll-calls at reveille and tattoo.

IV. The indiscriminate discharge of fire-arms in the vicinity of camp or remote therefrom must be stopped. All offenses of this character must receive prompt attention, and each case visited with a sufficient punishment. This order will be observed in all its provisions until it is officially revoked. It will not be considered to expire with the removal of the command from this point, but will be enforced in all its details until otherwise ordered.

By order of Col. L. F. Hubbard:

T. P. GERE,
First Lieutenant and Acting Assistant Adjutant-General.

GENERAL ORDERS, ⎫   HEADQUARTERS CAVALRY CORPS,
                  ⎬ MILITARY DIVISION OF THE MISSISSIPPI,
No. 1.   ⎭   *Nashville, Tenn., January 7, 1865.*

In pursuance of authority from the Cavalry Bureau, Washington, D. C., Capt. John Green is on duty with the Cavalry Corps, Military Division of the Mississippi, and stationed at Nashville, Tenn., as special inspector of cavalry. Orders for the final disposition of unserviceable cavalry horses can be obtained from him. All requisitions for ordnance and ordnance stores and for a new supply of horses must be approved by him before the issues will be made. For the information of the special inspector of cavalry, and to enable him to supply the wants of the cavalry command, the following reports are required: Monthly inspection reports, on blanks furnished, and to be made between the 15th and end of the month. Blanks for these reports will be furnished division and brigade inspectors. The reports must be obtained by personal inspection of brigade inspectors, and not through written reports elicited from regiments for that purpose. The brigade inspector will forward this report to the division inspector, who will immediately forward the reports to Capt. John Green, special inspector of cavalry, Nashville, not later than the 2d of ensuing month. All inspectors will be appointed and relieved by authority from these headquarters. Division inspectors will be held responsible for the execution of this order, and should therefore use all diligence to have the reports made out by the brigade inspectors at the proper time, and in the absence of a brigade inspector should see that another is appointed or attend personally to the inspections and make up the reports. When necessary, the attention of the brigade commander should be called to all carelessness, want of punctuality, and inefficiency on the part of the brigade inspectors, and if the neglect cannot be remedied in this way a special report of the delinquent inspector should be made to these headquarters, that a more energetic and worthy officer may be appointed. All commanding officers of cavalry are urged to cheerfully and earnestly co-operate with the special inspector of cavalry in his efforts to keep the cavalry forces mounted and equipped, as well for the good of the service generally as for the especial credit of this particular command. They are reminded that much of the disorganization of this branch of the service is attributable to their negligence in allowing the necessary reports to be delayed, as, except by the required reports, it is impossible that the wants of the Cavalry Corps can be known to the Cavalry Bureau, upon which it devolves to supply them.

By command of Brevet Major-General Wilson:

E. B. BEAUMONT,
Major and Assistant Adjutant-General.

————

NASHVILLE, *January 7, 1865.*

Maj. Gen. J. H. WILSON:

It is found to be absolutely necessary to keep a division of cavalry in Tennessee; Johnson's division has therefore been ordered to Pulaski. Please give no orders for any portion of this division now here to go to Eastport.

WM. D. WHIPPLE,
Brigadier-General, &c.

Hdqrs. Cavalry Corps, Mil. Div. of the Mississippi,
Crossing of Elk River, on Huntsville Road, January 7, 1865.
Capt. Robert H. Ramsey,
Assistant Adjutant-General, Hdqrs. Dept. of the Cumberland:

Your dispatch of 1 p. m. yesterday in regard to Lyon has just reached me here. I will halt my command and look out for him. Please send me any information that may reach you in regard to his movements.

J. H. WILSON,
Brevet Major-General.

Hdqrs. Cavalry Corps, Mil. Div. of the Mississippi,
Elk River Crossing, January 7, 1865.
Capt. Robert H. Ramsey,
Assistant Adjutant-General to General Thomas:

Since writing my dispatch of 12 m., I have examined the map. It seems to me if Lyon is moving by Larkinsville, he will be able to get across the Tennessee by swimming, if in no other way, before I can possibly intercept him. It is fifty miles from here to Huntsville, and nearly sixty from there to Stevenson, seventy from there to Larkinsville, fifty from Larkinsville to Decherd. To march either of these distances rapidly would dismount the entire command. Please let me know if I shall delay my march to Eastport, and how long. I have directed Colonel Harrison, who goes to Pulaski with one regiment and a battery of his brigade (the balance are transferred and dismounted), to send a reconnaissance toward New Market, and in case the report in regard to Lyon turns out correct, to go after him with all the detachments he can find.

J. H. WILSON,
Brevet Major-General.

Nashville, Tenn., *January 7, 1865—11 p. m.*
Major-General Wilson:

Your two telegrams of to-day are received. Your directions to Colonel Harrison to be on the lookout for General Lyon will, the general commanding says, be sufficient, and your command can proceed on its way to Eastport as soon as they receive rations. General Johnson has also been directed to have a regiment he is sending to Pulaski be on the lookout for Lyon also.

ROBT. H. RAMSEY,
Assistant Adjutant-General.

Hdqrs. Cavalry Corps, Mil. Div. of the Mississippi,
Elk River Crossing, January 7, 1865—12 o'clock.
Col. T. J. Harrison,
Commanding First Brigade, Sixth Division:

I have just received a dispatch from General Thomas saying a report had been received to the effect that the rebel General Lyon had crossed the Chattanooga and Nashville Railroad, between Elk River and Decherd, and was marching toward Larkinsville and Huntsville. I wish you would send a reconnaissance from the Sixteenth Illinois toward La Layette as you go to Pulaski, and see if anything can be learned confirmatory of this report. Should it prove true, gather all the detachments you can find and go after Lyon. I have directed this command to halt till something more definite is heard.

                                        J. H. WILSON,
                                          Brevet Major-General.

CIRCULAR.]   HDQRS. FIRST DIVISION, CAVALRY CORPS,
                    MILITARY DIVISION OF THE MISSISSIPPI,
                              Edgefield, Tenn., January 7, 1865.

On the morning of the 9th of January, 1865, the command will march on the Franklin pike, at 7 o'clock, with transportation and camp equipage, ten days' rations, and all the forage that can be carried. The wagons will be refilled at Columbia. Every effort must be made at that point to carry all the forage possible in wagons, as the country through which the command will pass is exhausted of all supplies.

Order of march: Third Brigade; battery; Second Brigade. The brigades will each day alternate, and, unless otherwise ordered, the rear brigade will each day furnish a good regiment for escort to the wagon train.

By command of Brig. Gen. E. M. McCook:

                                        MART. J. MILLER,
                          Lieutenant and Acting Assistant Adjutant-General.

        HDQRS. CAVALRY CORPS, MIL. DIV. OF THE MISSISSIPPI,
                              Elk River, January 7, 1865—12 m.

The Cavalry Corps will remain wherever this order may find the different brigades and divisions till further notice. A report has been received that Lyon crossed the Chattanooga and Nashville Railroad near Decherd, and is marching toward Huntsville. Any information confirmatory of this will be promptly reported to these headquarters, and the command be in readiness to go in pursuit. Lieutenant Gunther, Fourth Cavalry, has been directed to obtain rations, if possible. The command will be duly notified.

                                        J. H. WILSON,
                                          Brevet Major-General.

                                        PAINT ROCK, *January 7, 1865.*
General STEEDMAN:

My return interrupted by order from General Wood, based on communication from General Thomas to look after rebel General Lyon. Orders have been given to some of the troops on sections following me to disembark at Brownsborough.

                                        CHARLES CRUFT,
                                          Brigadier-General.

                                        HUNTSVILLE, *January 7, 1865.*
Brig. Gen. W. D. WHIPPLE and
Major POLK :

Received telegram this morning 9 a. m., from General Milroy, stating that Colonel Lyon with rebel cavalry had passed Winchester, and will probably attempt to cross Tennessee River at Claysville. As there were no transports at Decatur to move up now with troops, and all the railroad transportation was being used to move General Steedman's command, I came to this place to borrow troops from General Cruft to move up the road after Lyon, but found that General Wood had sent General Cruft to Larkinsville after the enemy. The troops that came up with me belong to Colonels Morgan and Thompson, and I requested to stop at Brownsborough and move to New Market, and have by authority of General Wood so telegraphed to these officers at Brownsborough. No news of the enemy since my arrival here.

R. S. GRANGER,
Brigadier-General.

HEADQUARTERS FOURTH ARMY CORPS,
Huntsville, Ala., January 7, 1865.

General R. S. GRANGER:

It is reliably reported that the rebel General Lyon is making his way south to cross the Tennessee River, probably to cross at Guntersville, Port Deposit, &c. If you have any transports at Decatur, send the brigade I sent to Decatur up the river, to prevent the crossing. I understand the three principal crossings are within ten miles of each other. General Thomas says Lyon's command must be captured or destroyed. Let there be no delay.

TH. J. WOOD,
Brigadier-General of Volunteers.

HUNTSVILLE, *January 7, 1865—1 a. m.*

Captain GIVENS,
Commanding at Larkinsville:

We have been delayed in sending you re-enforcements, but have just started off 500 of General Steedman's men, who will be with you early in the morning. We have every confidence in your ability of holding out, if you should be attacked, until help reaches you.

By command of Col. William P. Lyon:

WM. M. SCOTT,
Lieutenant and Acting Assistant Adjutant-General.

HUNTSVILLE, *January 7, 1865.*

COMMANDING OFFICER,
Paint Rock:

Eight hundred men are just starting out from here, to go to the aid of your post and Larkinsville. Turn out your command, and make every arrangement possible for crossing the force without delay. Three hundred will remain with you, and 500 will go on to Larkinsville.

By command of William P. Lyon, colonel, commanding:

WM. M. SCOTT,
Lieutenant and Acting Assistant Adjutant-General.

KINGSTON, *January 7, 1865.*

Capt. W. P. AMMEN,
    Asst. Adjt. Gen., Fourth Div., Twenty-third Army Corps:

SIR: There is a force of rebels, numbering from 300 to 500, on Tennessee River eight miles below this place.   There is no doubt about the truth of it.   It is supposed they are trying to cross Tennessee River.

I am, respectfully, yours, &c.,

G. W. HOLTSINGER,
    First Lieutenant, Fourth Tennessee Volunteer Infantry.

HEADQUARTERS DEPARTMENT OF THE CUMBERLAND,
    Nashville, January 7, 1865.

Maj. Gen. E. R. S. CANBY,
    New Orleans:

I am assembling the troops on the Tennessee River, ready for any operations I may be ordered to make south, and will let you know in time to enable you to co-operate when I commence the movement.   The last blow we gave Hood was about 2d or 3d of January.   A part of my cavalry destroyed his pontoon train entirely, captured a supply train of nearly 200 wagons and 150 prisoners, between Pikesville, Ala., and Aberdeen, Miss.   I am much obliged for your offer to co-operate, as well as for your kind wishes.

GEO. H. THOMAS,
    Major-General, U. S. Volunteers, Commanding.

WASHINGTON, *January 8, 1865.*

Major-General THOMAS,
    Nashville, Tenn.:

Lieutenant-General Grant directs that, if you are assured of the departure of Hood south from Corinth, you will send General Schofield, with his corps, to Annapolis, Md., with as little delay as possible.   The transportation will be left behind, and trains will be furnished here. The two Departments of the Cumberland and Ohio will be united, under your command, as soon as General Schofield starts.

H. W. HALLECK,
    Major-General and Chief of Staff.

NASHVILLE, TENN., *January 8, 1865.*

Maj. Gen. H. W. HALLECK,
    Washington, D. C.:

The following report of the operations of Col. William J. Palmer, of the Fifteenth Pennsylvania Cavalry, is forwarded for your information:

DECATUR, ALA., *January 7, 1865.*

Brig. Gen. W. D. WHIPPLE,
    Chief of Staff:

As directed, I send by telegraph a full report of the operations of my command since leaving General Steedman's front:

I reached Leighton Station on Friday afternoon, 30th ultimo, having skirmished all day with Roddey's force, most of which drifted southward in squads, toward the mountains, the remainder, with General Roddey, taking the road to Tuscumbia and Florence.   Toward dark a new force appeared in our front in Tuscumbia, believed to be

Armstrong's brigade, which had been sent back by Forrest from Barton Station to re-enforce Roddey and protect Hood's trains at Leighton. I learned that Hood had commenced crossing the river at Bainbridge on Sunday morning, and finished on Tuesday evening, and that they had finished taking up the pontoon on Wednesday morning; also, that the enemy's pontoon train had passed through on Wednesday, and had camped at La Grange, four miles distant, the same night, and that it was bound for Columbus, Miss., with a comparatively small guard. Roddey's so-called cavalry had apparently been relied upon to prevent any advance of our forces until the train could get to a safe distance; but his men had become so demoralized by their successive defeats, from the time my command first advanced from Decatur and captured his artillery, that we could afford to disregard him. I accordingly started from Leighton before daylight on Saturday morning, taking a trail which enabled us to avoid Armstrong's forces and to get to the rear of a portion of Roddey's cavalry at La Grange, where we captured Col. J. M. Warren, of Tenth Alabama Cavalry, and some other prisoners.

About 1 p. m. we passed through Russellville, where we encountered another portion of Roddey's force, which had just arrived from Tuscumbia, and drove it out on the Tuscaloosa road, while we kept on the Cotton-gin road after the train. Some attempt was made to delay us by burning a bridge over Cedar Creek, but we found a ford and caught up with the rear of the pontoon train at dark, ten miles beyond Russellville. We met no resistance, and our advance guard charged through to the front of the train, which extended for five miles, and consisted of 78 pontoon-boats and about 200 wagons, with all the necessary accouterments, material, engineering instruments, &c. All the mules and oxen, except what the pontoniers and guards were able to cut the traces of and ride off, were standing hitched to the wagons. Three boats had been set on fire, but, through carelessness, it had gone out. We captured a few prisoners, and went into camp about the center of the town, fed, and then started the entire command out in either direction to burn the train, which occupied till 3 a. m. I should have been glad to bring the pontoon train, which was an exceedingly well appointed one, back to our lines; but the condition of the mules, the mountainous character of the country, and the presence in our rear of a force of the enemy's cavalry, estimated at three times our strength, prevented. I also learned from a negro servant of Captain Cobb, of the engineers, who commanded the train, that a large supply train of General Hood's, bound from Barton Station to Tuscumbia, was ahead.

Early next morning (Sunday) I pushed on through Nauvoo, taking the Aberdeen road, which I knew would flank the train. I sent a detachment from near Bexar across by a trail to head the train on the Cotton-gin road, and another to follow it, and by 10 p. m. had surprised it in camp, a few miles over the line, in Itawamba County, Miss. It consisted of 110 wagons and over 500 mules. We burned the wagons, shot or sabered the mules we could not lead off or use to mount prisoners, and started back. In one of the wagons was a colonel of Hood's army, badly wounded at Franklin, with whom I left a tent, some stores, and one of the prisoners to take care of him. About twenty of the teamsters were colored soldiers captured by Hood at Dalton. These came back with us. We returned, via Toll-gate and the old military and Hacksburg roads, to within twenty miles south of Russellville, when I found that Roddey's force and the so-called brigades of Biffle and Russell were already stationed at Bear Creek and on the Bexar road to retard us, while Armstrong was reported as being in pursuit.

The country was very difficult and rugged, with very few roads or trails, and scarcely any forage; but, with the aid of Union guides in Marion and Winston Counties, we evaded, by a night's march of twenty-three miles, all the forces except Colonel Russell's, whom we attacked unexpectedly on the Moulton road, twelve miles beyond Thorn Hill, on Wednesday noon, routing him so utterly that he did not delay our march twenty minutes, and this only to pick up prisoners and burn his five wagons, including his headquarters wagon, out of which we got all the brigade and other official papers. We had previously captured a mail bound for Tuscaloosa. We then continued, by way of Mount Hope, toward Leighton, but before getting there learned that all other forces had returned to Decatur, to which place we came on last evening. About seventy-five conscripts that Russell was hustling off to Tuscaloosa were released by our attack; also eight Indiana soldiers captured by Russell near Decatur.

The whole distance marched by the command since we left the infantry at Decatur on Wednesday night, until we saw them again last evening, was about 265 miles.

My entire force was less than 600 men, consisting of the Fifteenth Pennsylvania (Anderson) Cavalry, Lieutenant-Colonel Lamborn commanding, and detachments of the Second Tennessee and Tenth, Twelfth, and Thirteenth Indiana Cavalry, commanded by Colonel Prosser. To these officers, and all those under them, much credit is due for dash, energy, and courage, and all the men behaved gallantly and bore up uncomplainingly with very scanty rations, under the severe weather and loss of sleep.

On this expedition we took about 150 prisoners, including 2 colonels, 2 captains, and 6 lieutenants, and destroyed, in all, between 750 and 1,000 stand of arms, and captured a considerable number of pistols.

Our entire loss was 1 man killed and 2 wounded, all in the charge on Russell's command. The whole of Forrest's cavalry, except Armstrong's, was at Okolona, within one day's march of us, when the supply train was captured.

I do not think General Hood brought across at Bainbridge more than 12,000 or 13,000 infantry.

Very respectfully,

> W. J. PALMER,
> *Colonel Fifteenth Pennsylvania Cavalry, Commanding.*

The report above is another of the very valuable services rendered by Colonel Palmer, and I most heartily recommend him again for appointment as a brigadier-general of volunteers. He certainly deserves the promotion, and I would respectfully urge it. There is no news from the other portions of my command to-day. I leave at daylight in the morning for Eastport.

> GEO. H. THOMAS,
> *Major-General, U. S. Volunteers, Commanding.*

> MISSISSIPPI SQUADRON, FLAG-SHIP FAIRY,
> *Clifton, Tenn., January 8, 1865—10 a. m.*

Maj. Gen. GEORGE H. THOMAS,
> *Pulaski, Tenn.:*

Your telegram of January 2, noon, Pulaski, just received. I have sent Acting Fleet Captain Babcock down to arrange convoys especially for you. Would go myself to meet you, but believe you would prefer me [to] push operations here. Schofield has arrived. I am rejoiced at your coming.

> S. P. LEE,
> *Acting Rear-Admiral, Commanding Mississippi Squadron.*

> HEADQUARTERS DEPARTMENT OF THE CUMBERLAND,
> *Nashville, Tenn., January 8, 1865.*

General J. B. HOOD,
> *Commanding Confederate Forces :*

GENERAL: I have the honor to reciprocate the courtesy shown by you to the guard left by myself at the house of Mrs. A. V. Brown, Melrose, near Nashville, in not making him a prisoner, by returning with this communication to you Private Wright, Thirtieth Alabama, a soldier of your army left at the same place when your forces retreated from the front of Nashville. Incidents of this character are by no means common, and I am free to confess I always heartily appreciate and most willingly acknowledge them when they do occur.

Very respectfully, yours,

> GEO. H. THOMAS,
> *Major-General, U. S. Army, Commanding.*

> HEADQUARTERS FOURTH ARMY CORPS,
> *Huntsville, Ala., January 8, 1865.*

Brigadier-General WHIPPLE,
> *Assistant Adjutant-General and Chief of Staff:*

GENERAL: I have the honor to submit the following special recommendation for the promotion of officers in the Fourth Corps:

First. Brig. Gen. Nathan Kimball to be major-general, for gallant and meritorious conduct in the battle of Franklin, on the 30th November, for the skill, intelligence, and efficiency with which he handled his command in all the conflicts around Nashville, on the 15th and 16th of December, and for the personal gallantry he displayed in those conflicts.

Second. Col. A. D. Streight, Fifty-first Indiana, commanding First Brigade, Third Division, to be brigadier-general, for the skillful manner in which he managed his brigade in the battle of Nashville, for his personal gallantry in the battle, and for his uniform good and soldierly conduct.

Third. Col. P. Sidney Post, Fifty-ninth Illinois Volunteers, commanding Second Brigade, Third Division, to be brigadier-general of volunteers, for gallant and meritorious conduct in the chase after Hood when he attempted to get into our rear and cut our communications, and in the retreat from Pulaski to Nashville, but especially for gallantry in the assault on Montgomery's Hill, on the 15th of December, and in the assault on the Overton Hill, on the 16th of December. Colonel Post's brigade made both of these assaults. In the latter Colonel Post was severely wounded by a grape-shot, the same discharge killing his horse under him.

Fourth. Col. Frederick Knefler, Seventy-ninth Indiana Volunteers, commanding Third Brigade, Third Division, to be brigadier-general of volunteers, for gallantry and meritorious conduct throughout the entire Atlanta campaign, for meritorious conduct in the pursuit of Hood when he attempted to cut our communications, and in the retreat from Pulaski to Nashville, but especially for gallantry and good conduct in the various conflicts around Nashville, on the 15th and 16th of December.

Fifth. Col. Isaac M. Kirby, One hundred and first Ohio Volunteers, to be brigadier-general of volunteers, for gallantry and good conduct through the Atlanta campaign, but especially for distinguished gallantry in the battle of Franklin, on 30th of November and in the various conflicts around Nashville, on the 15th and 16th of December.

Sixth. Col. Emerson Opdycke, One hundred and twenty-fifth Ohio, [to be brigadier-general of volunteers,] for uniform gallantry and good conduct, but more especially for distinguished gallantry and meritorious conduct in the Atlanta campaign, commencing with the assault on Rocky Face Ridge; the battle of Resaca, in which he was severely wounded; the assault of the 27th of June on Kenesaw Mountain, and the battle of Peach Tree Creek; for great skill, judgment, and courage at the battle of Franklin, on the 30th of November, on which occasion, by a bold counter-charge when the enemy had broken our lines, Colonel Opdycke drove him back and recaptured eight pieces of artillery which he had taken from us; for valuable services and aid in the preparations for the battle at Nashville, and for gallant and meritorious conduct in the battle both on the 15th and 16th of December.

I am, general, very respectfully, your obedient servant,
TH. J. WOOD,
Brigadier-General.

HEADQUARTERS FOURTH ARMY CORPS,
Huntsville, January 8, 1865—11.30 p. m.

Major-General THOMAS:

I am informed by General Granger, who is in my quarters, that Colonel Prosser, Second Tennessee, and Colonel Palmer, Fifteenth Pennsylvania, are at Decatur, but that he had ordered them to report to General Wilson, who claimed them on your authority. I wish authority to order (and if you approve, please telegraph me) them to this place to go in pursuit of Lyon's force. Without some cavalry it will be very difficult, if not impossible, to get hold of Lyon. I would not detain Prosser and Palmer longer than absolutely necessary. I telegraphed early to Captain Forrest, at Bridgeport, to patrol the Tennessee River with his flotilla.

TH. J. WOOD,
Brigadier-General of Volunteers, Commanding.

HDQRS. CAVALRY CORPS, MIL. DIV. OF THE MISSISSIPPI,
Near Elk River, January 8, 1865.
(Via Athens. Received 12.30 p. m. 9th.)

Brig. Gen. T. J. Wood,
Huntsville:

Your telegram is received. As Larkinsville is full seventy miles from me, Lyon must either escape or be used up by Cruft long before any of my cavalry, in their present condition, can reach that place. I shall therefore go on to Eastport as soon as I can get rations from Athens.

J. H. WILSON,
Brevet Major-General.

HEADQUARTERS FOURTH ARMY CORPS,
Huntsville, Ala., January 8, 1865.

Brigadier-General CRUFT:

You will disembark the forces that are on the cars immediately, scour the country thoroughly, find out, if possible, where Lyon is, and go in pursuit of him. He must be found, and either destroyed, captured, or driven across the Tennessee River. General Thomas' orders on this subject are emphatic, and he says you must not go on your way till this work is finished. As soon as you have disembarked your men from the cars the trains will be sent immediately to Stevenson to bring up provisions for the troops on this line. The detention of the cars by you has nearly put us out of provisions, and they must not be detained by you while you are hunting Lyon, but must be allowed to go to Stevenson, to bring up provisions.

TH. J. WOOD,
Brigadier-General, Commanding.

LARKINSVILLE, *January 8, 1865.*

Brigadier-General WOOD:

Can get no definite information of any forces of Lyon in vicinity. Think the rumor quite doubtful. Have sent Captain Givens, with 100 mounted men, to ascertain, and will know in three hours if any force is at Maynard's Cove, or Robinson's farm, or any of the points where conflicting stories place it. I wish Colonel Malloy's command, which I left near Huntsville, shipped here.

CHAS. CRUFT,
Brigadier-General.

LARKINSVILLE, *January 8, 1865.*

Brigadier-General WOOD:

Reports from citizens thus far do not support rumor that Lyon is near here. Bushwhacking parties of Russell, Mead, Hayes, and Wilson are in mountain, but changing places constantly, and are usually from fifteen to twenty miles distant, along waters of Paint Rock and in vicinity of New Nashville. Cavalry scout not yet reported; have brigade ready to push out on hearing from it. The best way to clear out parties above with infantry is to start forces from New Market east, and from here and Paint Rock north, say to Robinson's or Duckett's, on Paint Rock. No direct approach will catch them. If I can get information of Lyon's whereabouts will go for him later in the day.

CHAS. CRUFT,
Brigadier-General.

HEADQUARTERS FOURTH ARMY CORPS,
Huntsville, Ala., January 8, 1865—12.30 p. m.

Brigadier-General CRUFT:

Your two dispatches of this date received. Lyon must certainly be in your neighborhood somewhere, either north or south of the railroad, as his course has been traced from Kentucky, by McMinnville and Manchester, to south of Winchester. Order at once the force at Brownsborough to New Market, to move thence east, to co-operate with the force moving north from Larkinsville, without you receive satisfactory intelligence that Lyon is somewhere else, in which case you must go for him strong.

TH. J. WOOD,
Brigadier-General of Volunteers, Commanding.

HEADQUARTERS ARMY OF THE OHIO,
Clifton, Tenn., January 8, 1865.

Maj. Gen. GEORGE H. THOMAS,
Nashville:

My advance reached this place on the 6th, and the whole command will probably arrive to-day. Only a portion of General Smith's troops have yet gone up the river, and I will give him the use of all the transports until his whole command is shipped. I will then move my troops. Transports and supplies arrived last night.

J. M. SCHOFIELD,
Major-General.

SPECIAL ORDERS, ⎰ HDQRS. SECOND DIV., 23D ARMY CORPS,
No. 5. ⎱ *Near Waynesborough, Tenn., January 8, 1865.*

Brig. Gen. N. C. McLean, U. S. Volunteers, having reported to these headquarters pursuant to Special Field Orders, No. 4, headquarters Army of the Ohio, dated Waynesborough, Tenn., January 5, 1865, for assignment to duty, is hereby assigned to the Third Brigade of this division.

*   *   *   *   *   *   *

By command of Major-General Couch:

S. H. HUBBELL,
Lieutenant and Acting Assistant Adjutant-General.

HEADQUARTERS ARMY OF THE OHIO,
Clifton, Tenn., January 8, 1865.

Brig. Gen. J. D.. COX,
     Commanding Third Division, Twenty-third Army Corps:

GENERAL: The commanding general desires you to direct your division quartermaster to receive and issue to the troops now here such quartermaster's stores as are arriving at Clifton.

I am, general, very respectfully, your obedient servant,
J. A. CAMPBELL,
Major and Assistant Adjutant-General.

HEADQUARTERS SECOND DIVISION,
DETACHMENT ARMY OF THE TENNESSEE,
Eastport, Miss., January 8, 1865.

Col. E. H. WOLFE,
     Commanding Third Brigade:

COLONEL: The general commanding directs me to inform you that Colonel Gilbert with his brigade will make a reconnaissance toward Iuka to-morrow; he will leave camp at 6 a. m. He directs that you send out at the same hour strong fatigue parties to work on the rifle-pits, and that all the rest of your command be kept in camp, in readiness for any emergency, until the return of Colonel Gilbert.

Very respectfully, your obedient servant,
JAMES B. COMSTOCK,
Acting Assistant Adjutant-General.

HDQRS. CAVALRY CORPS, MIL. DIV. OF THE MISSISSIPPI,
Near Elk River, on Florence Road, January 8, 1865—12.15 p. m.

Brig. Gen. WILLIAM D. WHIPPLE,
     Chief of Staff, Department of the Cumberland, Nashville:

General Wood telegraphed from Huntsville that Lyon had crossed the railroad near Larkinsville, on the way to the Tennessee River. General Cruft had been directed to debark a portion of his force at that place and go after him. As it is seventy miles from here to Larkinsville, it will be more than useless for me to send any portion of my command in that direction, as Lyon must be safely across the river or disposed of by General Cruft before I can possibly reach him. Your telegram in regard to Johnson's division has been received. I have transferred the Fifth Iowa and Seventh Ohio Cavalry to the Fourth Division, and the Sixth Tennessee to Johnson, leaving him nine regiments, the same number that are in the other divisions, and ample for the defense of the country lying north of the Tennessee River. These transfers are made for the purpose of preparing, as soon as possible, an effective cavalry force for operations north of the main army. No men of Johnson's division, except those belonging to the two regiments just mentioned, have been ordered to Eastport. Colonel Harrison, with the balance of his brigade and battery, have been ordered to Pulaski. When he arrives here he ought to have, with the Eighth Michigan and the other detachments, 1,000 mounted men—enough for any immediate use. Please say to General Thomas that, anticipating the probabilties of an early move, I have directed that the remounts be provided first to the divisions which are intended for the field, and last to Johnson, believing this would meet his approbation. Johnson ought now to have the Fifth Tennessee, Fifteenth Pennsylvania, Sixteenth Illinois, and Eighth Michigan all mounted Unless I have something this evening that renders it more probable than now appears we could pursue Lyon with success, I shall continue the march toward Eastport.

J. H. WILSON,
Brevet Major-General.

GENERAL ORDERS, ⎱ HEADQUARTERS CAVALRY CORPS,
No. 3. ⎰ MILITARY DIVISION OF THE MISSISSIPPI,
Nashville, Tenn., January 8, 1865.

The attention of commanding officers of cavalry is called to the careless and injurious manner of feeding horses. The feeding should be regular. The forage should never be fed on the ground, for, besides being wasted, the horse is liable to injure his digestion by the gravel and sand which he takes up. To remedy this every trooper will carry a nose-bag, in which the grain will be given. Commanding officers of companies, regiments, brigades, and divisions will be held responsible for the execution of this order, and will immediately on its receipt make the necessary requisitions for a sufficient number of nose-bags to supply their commands. Brigade inspectors will be particular in their monthly reports to show the exact number on hand in each regiment. Men losing them carelessly or purposely will immediately be furnished with others, and will be charged with the lost articles on their pay-roll, and otherwise subjected to such punishments as may seem proper to their commanding officers. One commissioned officer at least will attend each stable call, who will require the men to watch the horses until they are done feeding.

By command of Brevet Brigadier-General Wilson:

E. B. BEAUMONT,
Major and Assistant Adjutant-General.

CIRCULAR.] HDQRS. CAVALRY CORPS, MIL. DIV. OF THE MISS.,
Near Elk River, January 8, 1865.

Division and brigade commanders will, with their columns, resume the march toward Eastport to-morrow morning. Should the detachments sent for rations not arrive the march will not be delayed, but a small party as guard will be left until they come up.

By order of General Wilson:

HENRY E. NOYES,
Lieutenant and Acting Assistant Adjutant-General.

EDGEFIELD, TENN., January 8, 1865.

Maj. E. B. BEAUMONT,
    Assistant Adjutant-General, Cavalry Corps:

In reply to your communication I have the honor to designate the following regiments of my division as the ones I desire filled up to their maximum strength: First Wisconsin Cavalry, Second Indiana Cavalry,

Second Michigan Cavalry, Fourth Kentucky Mounted Infantry, Eighth Iowa Cavalry. General Watkins has already made application, which has gone forward, to have the veterans of two Kentucky infantry regiments assigned to the Kentucky regiments of his brigade. I refrain from making any recommendation concerning these regiments until I ascertain what action has been taken upon this application. All the regiments I indicate are veteran organizations, and in every way effective except in point of numbers.

Very respectfully, your obedient servant,

E. M. McCOOK,
Brigadier-General, Commanding Division.

EDGEFIELD, TENN., *January 8, 1865.*

Bvt. Brig. Gen. L. D. WATKINS,
Commanding Third Brigade:

As I will not be with the command on the march, you will take command of your brigade, La Grange's, and the artillery, and march to Eastport, Miss., in accordance with orders received from corps headquarters. Your best route will be through Columbia, Mount Pleasant, and Waynesborough. I will endeavor to have supplies sent to Clifton, on the Tennessee River, seventeen miles from Waynesborough, so that you can again obtain supplies at that point. From Waynesborough you will take the best road to Eastport, and you will only learn this by inquiry. At Columbia you will put all the forage practicable in the wagons and carry it along, as there is little or no forage in the country through which you have to pass. After leaving Columbia it would probably be better to have part of your command march on your flanks, if there are any roads running parallel with your line of march, for the purpose of getting forage, which will be scarce on the main road. Have especial attention paid to the care of your horses, and try to get them through in the best condition possible. They are in good condition now, and though they must necessarily suffer some on a march of this kind, yet additional care on the part of officers and men will save them much. On your arrival at Eastport, or its vicinity, you will report to Major-General Wilson for orders. Eastport is on the other side of the Tennessee; you will strike the river opposite there.

Very respectfully, your obedient servant,

E. M. McCOOK,
Brigadier-General, Commanding Division.

HDQRS. CAVALRY CORPS, MIL. DIV. OF THE MISS.,
Near Elk River Crossing, on Florence Road,
January 8, 1865—12.30 p. m.

Col. T. J. HARRISON,
Commanding First Brigade, Sixth Division:

Several dispatches having been sent you lately, and none having reached, as far as I can hear, I am anxious to get this to you. A dispatch from General Wood says Lyon crossed at Larkinsville day before yesterday, moving toward the Tennessee River. You need not, therefore, send any reconnaissance, but send the Fifth Iowa and

Seventh Ohio, under Colonel Garrard, to Eastport, and go with your battery and the balance of the brigade to Pulaski, whence you will report to General Johnson in person, or if he is not there, by telegraph.

Very respectfully, your obedient servant,

J. H. WILSON,
Brevet Major-General.

HDQRS. DEFENSES NASHVILLE AND CHATTANOOGA R. R.,
Tullahoma, January 8, 1865.

Lieut. Col. W. J. CLIFT,
Commanding Fifth Tennessee Volunteer Cavalry:

COLONEL: Send messengers across the country toward Fayetteville to Major Armstrong, and advise him that Lyon's cavalry has crossed the mountains and gone toward Bellefonte, and that it is unnecessary for him to proceed farther in pursuit, but order him to go on in vicinity of Hazel Green, and then scout the country for bushwhackers east to Winchester, and from there to this place. You will move southeast and strike the road between Salem and Winchester, pass south of the latter place, go through Decherd, take all of Couch's mounted men with you, and go in vicinity of Pelham, and east of or through Hillsborough, and try to intercept Hays, who was at latter place yesterday p. m. These latter instructions are not imperative, and you will act upon the best information you can get, after reaching Pelham, as the course to pursue best calculated to accomplish the interception and destruction of Hays. After reaching the road between Salem and Winchester, if you find Hays has crossed through that country, which is possible, you will give pursuit from that point, of course, instead of following instructions, which are only general.

By command of Major-General Milroy:

JNO. O. CRAVENS,
Assistant Adjutant-General.

CHATTANOOGA, [*January*] *8, 1865.*

Brig. Gen. WILLIAM D. WHIPPLE,
Chief of Staff, Department of the Cumberland:

I am garrisoning the Chattanooga and Knoxville road as far as Loudon, and the Chattanooga and Atlanta road as far as Dalton, and the Chattanooga and Nashville road to Bridgeport. I can send the troops belonging to the Army of the Tennessee, but will require troops to relieve those belonging to the Army of the Cumberland.

JAS. B. STEEDMAN,
Major-General.

NASHVILLE, *January 8, 1865.*

Maj. Gen. JAMES B. STEEDMAN:

Your telegram of this date is received. The major-general commanding directs that you send the troops of the Army of the Tennessee to General Sherman, relieving [retaining] the troops of the Army of the Cumberland until further orders from the major-general commanding.

ROBT. H. RAMSEY,
Assistant Adjutant-General.

HEADQUARTERS DISTRICT OF THE ETOWAH,
Chattanooga, January 8, 1865.

Brigadier-General CRUFT,
        Paint Rock:

Unless your order to stop on the Huntsville road is by direction of Major-General Thomas, you will come forward, as previously directed.

JAMES B. STEEDMAN,
Major-General.

HEADQUARTERS DISTRICT OF THE ETOWAH,
Chattanooga, January 8, 1865.

Brigadier-General CRUFT,
        Paint Rock:

The Seventeenth Colored will proceed to Nashville; the Sixty-eighth New York will stop at Bridgeport. The detachment of the Seventeenth Army Corps can stop at Stevenson, and await orders to proceed to Savannah.

JAMES B. STEEDMAN,
Major-General.

LARKINSVILLE, *January 8, 1865.*

Major-General STEEDMAN:

Here with advance of command. On lookout for Lyon.

CHARLES CRUFT,
Brigadier-General.

LARKINSVILLE, *January 8, 1865.*

Major-General STEEDMAN:

Have intelligence that Lyon crossed the mountains last night and is heading for river near Bellefonte. Can you send a gun-boat or two from Bridgeport, to patrol river from Bellefonte to Gunter's Landing? Harrison is in search of him near Bellefonte, and I will move remainder of the command toward river to-night.

CHARLES CRUFT,
Brigadier-General.

DECATUR, *January 8, 1865.*

Maj. S. B. MOE,
        Assistant Adjutant-General:

Colonel Palmer and Fifteenth Pennsylvania Cavalry have arrived here. They have orders from General Thomas to go to Huntsville and recruit their horses for two weeks.

SAM. M. KNEELAND,
Lieutenant and Acting Assistant Adjutant-General.
(In absence of General Granger.)

HEADQUARTERS DISTRICT OF THE ETOWAH,
Chattanooga, January 8, 1865.

Col. FELIX PR. SALM,
Sixty-eighth New York Volunteers, Bridgeport:

On your arrival at Bridgeport with your regiment you will assume command of the post.

By command of Major-General Steedman:

S. B. MOE,
Assistant Adjutant-General.

NASHVILLE, TENN., *January 8, 1865.*

Brig. Gen. R. S. GRANGER,
Decatur:

Yours to Major Polk received. Colonel Thompson's brigade has been ordered to Johnsonville. Do not give them any orders interfering with his.

WM. D. WHIPPLE,
Brigadier-General.

HUNTSVILLE, *January 8, 1865.*

Major-General STEEDMAN:

Your dispatch received at this place. Colonel Palmer arrived at Decatur on the 6th. Will send my report as soon as possible.

CHAS. R. THOMPSON,
Colonel, &c.

NASHVILLE, *January 8, 1865.*

Col. W. P. LYON,
Huntsville:

General Milroy telegraphs that Lyon's forces crossed the mountain on the road to Bellefonte.

B. H. POLK,
Major and Assistant Adjutant-General.

HDQRS. FIRST REGIMENT OHIO VOL. HEAVY ARTILLERY,
Near Dandridge, Tenn., January 8, 1865.

Capt. W. P. AMMEN,
Assistant Adjutant-General, &c.:

According to the best information I can get, Vaughn is still back as far as vicinity of Greeneville. Some indications point to his moving in this direction. The guerrillas have been very bold in my front, and being remarkably well mounted and many roads, and being without any cavalry, they have the advantage. I sent an expedition by night and took possession of all the fords, and a force in the morning is to follow it up. The fruit was only surprising a squad at Allen's Ford, eleven miles above, killing a Lieutenant Norman, a noted guerrilla, and one of the worst men in this region, and wounding some others. The guerrillas infesting the country amount in aggregate to probably 150, and are well mounted and very bold. They captured one of my posts yesterday, and thirty strong attacked foraging train, but were easily repulsed.

Kirk occupied Newport on morning of the 6th instant; that is the last I have from him. Received communication from Colonel Shannon that on 7th instant he started for Dutch Bottom.

I believe some cavalry could be used here advantageously against the guerrillas; and if I am to stay here any considerable time would respectfully request the assignment of some to my command. I am sorry to report that legitimately and illegitimately the guerrillas have six of my men prisoners, though I hope some of the six have escaped. I have in return only Norman, killed, Hynds, wounded, and four war and three citizen prisoners.

Very respectfully, your obedient servant,

C. G. HAWLEY,
Colonel, Commanding.

[MEMPHIS, *January 8, 1865.*]

[General N. J. T. DANA,
    Memphis, Tenn.:]

On the morning of the 20th sent a brigade from Memphis to make a demonstration toward Bolivar, thence to swing southward and join the main column near Ripley. Owing to the heavy rains on that and several days previous, a crossing of the Wolf River could not be effected, and the command returned to Memphis from Raleigh.

On the morning of the 21st moved the entire command—3,300 men—directly east, threatening Corinth. Sent detachments and destroyed the telegraph from Grand Junction toward Corinth and four bridges and the telegraph on the Mobile and Ohio Railroad between Boonville and Guntown. Moved with main column rapidly on Tupelo; surprised, captured, and dispersed Forrest's camp of dismounted men on the night of the 25th at Verona. Thence moved south along the line of the railroad, destroying it thoroughly to a point between Egypt and Prairie Station; tapped the wires at Okolona, and intercepted dispatches from Lieut. Gen. Dick Taylor, Major-General Gardner, and others, ordering Egypt to be held at all hazards, and indicating that large re-enforcements would be sent from Mobile and other points.

On the morning of the 28th attacked the enemy, about 1,200 strong—cavalry, infantry, and one battery of four guns, on platform cars—at Egypt. Two trains with re-enforcements, under General Gardner, were in sight when the attack was made. Threw a force between them and the garrison at Egypt; captured and destroyed one train of fourteen cars; tore up the track two miles and a half south of Egypt, and captured and dispersed the garrison at Egypt, after an engagement of two hours. Among the rebels killed was Brigadier-General Gholson and several other officers. After securing about 500 prisoners and destroying all captured property, the enemy falling back toward West Point, we swept west and southwest, through Houston and Bellefontaine, to the Mississippi Central Railroad, striking it at Winona. From Houston demonstrations were made southeast toward West Point and north toward Pontotoc. From Bellefontaine made demonstration toward Starkville, threatening again the Mobile and Ohio Railroad;

also sent a detachment to Bankston and destroyed large Government cloth and shoe factories. From Winona sent a detachment to Grenada to destroy the railroad and all Government property on the route and at that point. Sent a brigade south along the line of the railroad to destroy it as far as practicable. This brigade met the enemy at Franklin, four miles west of Goodman Station, and whipped them, killing twenty-five, who were left on the field. Moved the main column, with prisoners, from Winona, via Middleton, Lexington, and Benton, to Vicksburg, arriving at that point with my whole command in good condition, on the 5th of January, with 600 prisoners, about thirty of whom were officers.

The destruction of property is as follows: Forty miles of the Mobile and Ohio Railroad, including twenty-five bridges, large amount of trestle-work, many miles of track, and telegraph, depots, switches, turntables, and water-tanks, thirty miles of the Mississippi Central, including all bridges and the trestle-work and the telegraph. Captured and destroyed 300 army wagons, 5,000 stand of new arms, 4 serviceable locomotives and 10 in process of repair, about 100 cars, a pile-driver and engine, machine-shops, factories which employed 500 hands for the manufacture of clothing, large amount of cloth, wool, cotton, and leather, 700 head of fat hogs, immense amount of corn and wheat, commissary, quartermaster, and ordnance stores.

Our entire loss during the expedition was about 25 killed and 80 wounded, many of the latter slightly.

The command arrived at Vicksburg as well mounted as when it left Memphis, and with about 600 head of extra stock. About 1,000 negroes joined the column on the march and were taken to Vicksburg.

B. H. GRIERSON,
Brigadier-General.

MEMPHIS, *January 8, 1865.*
(Via Cairo. Received 11th.)

Maj. Gen. GEORGE H. THOMAS:

The cavalry expedition which left Memphis on December 21 has arrived at Vicksburg. Fifty miles of Mobile and Ohio Railroad destroyed; thirty miles of Mississippi Central Railroad burnt; immense quantities of stores of all kinds have been destroyed. All Hood's communications are now completely cut.

N. J. T. DANA,
Major-General.

CITY POINT, VA., *January 9, 1865.*

Maj. Gen. H. W. HALLECK,
　　Washington, D. C.:

Were orders sent to General Thomas to send Schofield's corps to Annapolis as soon as Hood was known to have gone south of Corinth? When started, it would be advisable to have the troops transported on boats, if navigation is not closed, to Wheeling and Parkersburg—one-half to come over the Baltimore and Ohio road, the other over the Pennsylvania Central.

U. S. GRANT,
Lieutenant-General.

WASHINGTON, *January 9, 1865—9.20 p. m.*

Lieutenant-General GRANT,
        City Point, Va.:

Your orders about Schofield's corps were immediately transmitted. As soon as an answer is received, transportation by the most expeditious routes will be ordered. I fear the corps is much scattered. You said nothing in your orders about the artillery.

H. W. HALLECK,
Major-General and Chief of Staff.

HEADQUARTERS DEPARTMENT OF THE CUMBERLAND,
        Steamer Tarascon, Cumberland River, January 9, 1865.

Maj. WILLIAM ALLEN,
        Chief Paymaster, Dept. of the Cumberland, Louisville, Ky.:

In reply to your communication of the 23d ultimo, I have the honor to inform you that the Fifteenth, Seventeenth, Fourteenth, and Twentieth Army Corps, with the exception of the Fourth Division, Twentieth Army Corps, together with the following-named artillery, cavalry, and engineer troops, accompanied Major-General Sherman's expedition to Savannah:

Artillery: Battery C, First Illinois Artillery; Fifth Wisconsin Battery; Battery I, Second Illinois Artillery; Nineteenth Indiana Battery; Battery E, Pennsylvania Artillery; Battery C, First Ohio Artillery; Battery I, First New York Artillery; Battery M, First New York Artillery.

Cavalry: Third Indiana Cavalry, Second Kentucky Cavalry, Eighth Indiana Cavalry, Ninety-second Illinois Mounted Infantry, Ninth Ohio Cavalry, First Ohio Squadron, First Alabama Cavalry, Ninth Pennsylvania Cavalry, Tenth Ohio Cavalry, Third Kentucky Cavalry, Fifth Kentucky Cavalry, Ninth Michigan Cavalry, Fifty-eighth [?] Illinois Mounted Infantry, Fifth Ohio Cavalry.

Engineer Troops: First Michigan Engineers and Mechanics, Fifty-eighth Indiana Infantry.

Very respectfully, your obedient servant,

WM. D. WHIPPLE,
Brigadier-General and Chief of Staff.

HEADQUARTERS FOURTH ARMY CORPS,
        Huntsville, Ala., January 9, 1865.

Brigadier-General WHIPPLE,
        Nashville:

Your dispatch in regard to Colonel Thompson's brigade just received. I have telegraphed to General Cruft to send the brigade to Nashville as soon as possible. It is now with him near Larkinsville. Lyon attacked the little garrison at Scottsborough, and was severely repulsed, and is reported this morning flying southeast to Gunter's Ferry. I have telegraphed General Cruft to press him hard against the Tennessee River. I have also telegraphed the commanding officer at Bridgeport to run a force down the river by transports to cut Lyon off, and requested him to communicate the information to Commodore Forrest, with a request to patrol the river in the neighborhood of Gunter's Ferry, Larkin's Landing, &c., with a view to preventing Lyon from crossing. If my directions are vigorously and promptly carried out, I trust we will give Mr. Lyon a hard time.

TH. J. WOOD,
Brigadier-General of Volunteers.

STEVENSON, *January 9, 1865.*

Brigadier-Generals WOOD and GRANGER:

On passing Scottsborough, at 10 a. m. this morning, couriers from Guntersville road, southeast of Scottsborough, reported at 8.30 a. m. Lyon was fleeing on the Guntersville road toward Gunter's Ferry.

E. HATCH,
Brigadier-General.

HEADQUARTERS FOURTH ARMY CORPS,
Huntsville, Ala., January 9, 1865.

COMMANDING OFFICER,
Bridgeport:

Lyon's rebel command was severely repulsed at Scottsborough last night, and is reported this morning flying southeast toward Gunter's Ferry. If you have any transports at Bridgeport, or can get any, by all means move a force down the river and cut him off. We must capture or destroy his force. I will have forces pressed down on his rear. If Commodore Forrest is at Bridgeport, or you can communicate with him, give him this information, and ask him to please patrol all the river in the neighborhood of Gunter's Ferry, Larkin's Landing, &c.

TH. J. WOOD,
Brigadier-General of Volunteers, Commanding.

BRIDGEPORT, *January 9, 1865.*

Brig. Gen. T. J. WOOD:

Your telegram is received. In reply, I have the honor to state that there are no transports at this place. Commodore Forrest is now patrolling the river in the vicinity of Gunter's Ferry and Larkin's Landing.

L. K. BISHOP,
Lieutenant-Colonel, Commanding.

LARKINSVILLE, *January 9, 1865.*

Brigadier-General WOOD,
Fourth Army Corps:

Colonel Morgan's brigade has arrived. Colonel Thompson's will be sent to Nashville as soon as orders can reach it. It is now in pursuit of Lyon.

CHAS. CRUFT,
Brigadier-General.

LARKINSVILLE, *January 9, 1865.*

Major-General THOMAS:

Rebel General Lyon's forces struck railroad at Scottsborough about dark last evening and crossed southward. His crossing was resisted by the small guard at that place. Pursuit was made in direction of Larkinsville, toward which the enemy was apparently retreating, by Colonels Harrison, Malloy, and Mitchell during the night, and is continued this morning. Damage to railroad trifling.

CHAS. CRUFT,
Brigadier-General.

HEADQUARTERS FOURTH ARMY CORPS,
Huntsville, Ala., January 9, 1865.

Brigadier-General CRUFT:

I have just heard that the rebel General Lyon attacked Scottsborough yesterday and captured the garrison. If this is true, it is strange that you have not reported the fact. It is also strange that you did not render assistance to the garrison, especially as artillery was used within four miles of your headquarters. I suppose you are pursuing Lyon, and hope you will destroy him before he can cross the Tennessee River. Has the road been damaged by the enemy?

TH. J. WOOD,
Brigadier-General, Commanding.

LARKINSVILLE, *January 9, 1865.*

Brigadier-General WOOD:

Dispatch received. Lyon crossed railroad at Scottsborough last night. I had Colonel Harrison's brigade at Bellefonte, and Colonel Malloy's brigade reached Scottsborough in time to drive Lyon off and to pursue him all night. I sent Colonel Malloy to Larkin's Ferry in night, and Colonel Thompson right for enemy as soon as he arrived. Every available man I had in the field in pursuit of Lyon, and I have just ridden over from the river to make some dispositions here, and will join the command soon. Mitchell is on enemy's rear closely and Malloy in supporting distance. Pray send me the balance of Malloy's command and Morgan's brigade from New Market as soon as possible. Lyon is retreating rapidly toward Gunter's Landing, and I hope to prevent his crossing. Your information is untrue in regard to Scottsborough affair. I prepared dispatch to you last night, but by some accident was mislaid. If you have a gun-boat at Decatur, please send to Gunter's Landing. I can not hear of those said to be on river near Bellefonte. No damage to railroad by Lyon, except a few rails, and scarce any to garrison.

CHAS. CRUFT,
Brigadier-General.

HEADQUARTERS FOURTH ARMY CORPS,
Huntsville, Ala., January 9, 1865.

Brigadier-General CRUFT:

I have just received a report of the repulse of Lyon at Scottsborough last night, and that this morning he is flying toward Gunter's Ferry.

Press him hard with your forces against the Tennessee River and capture or destroy him. As you will have an ample force of your own proper command for this work, order Colonel Thompson to proceed with his brigade as rapidly as possible to Nashville; General Thomas so directs it.

TH. J. WOOD,
Brigadier-General of Volunteers, Commanding.

LARKINSVILLE, *January 9, 1865.*
(Received 12.10 a. m. 10th.)

Brigadier-General WOOD:

My advance brigade is within eleven miles of Guntersville; at 3 p. m. enemy about four hours ahead, and retreating very fast. Will you send a mounted force from Huntsville at once to Deposit. In case Lyon goes to the mountains, avoiding Gunter's Landing, he may escape me, and cross at Deposit before I can get up to him. A force to delay him crossing at Deposit for six hours will secure him finally, I think.

CHAS. CRUFT,
Brigadier-General.

SPECIAL   HEADQUARTERS ARMY OF THE OHIO,
FIELD ORDERS,   *In the Field, Clifton, Tenn.,*
No. 7.   *January 9, 1865.*

*   *   *   *   *   *   *

6. The troops will move by boat to Eastport in the following order, viz: Second Division; Third Division; First Division. It is expected that one entire division, with its artillery and baggage train, will be able to move at each trip of the transport fleet. If possible, the division ordnance trains will also accompany their divisions. The artillery and ordnance trains will be loaded upon barges and the baggage wagons upon the steamers, with the troops to which they belong. The movement will commence as soon as the transports arrive, which is expected at daylight to-morrow morning, the 10th instant. Division commanders will make ample details of men to load their artillery and wagons, and will see that the boats are loaded as expeditiously as possible. The transport fleet moves under convoy of the gun-boats. The division commanders will. therefore report to Rear-Admiral Lee, U. S. Navy, commanding, as soon as their divisions are embarked, and will move under his orders. On arriving at Eastport, Major-General Couch will disembark his division and take position, in conjunction with Major-General Smith's troops, and will also direct the posting of the other divisions, until the arrival of the major-general commanding.

By command of Major-General Schofield:

J. A. CAMPBELL,
Major and Assistant Adjutant-General.

HEADQUARTERS ARMY OF THE OHIO,
Clifton, Tenn., January 9, 1865.

Brig. Gen. J. D. COX,
Commanding Third Division, Twenty-third Army Corps:

GENERAL: The commanding general directs that you send one piece of artillery at once to the bank of the river, with directions to the officer in charge to stop all boats going up the river. Blank cartridges, or, if necessary, solid shot, will be fired at the boats, if they do not stop when hailed by the officer in charge.

I am, general, very respectfully, your obedient servant,

> J. A. CAMPBELL,
> *Major and Assistant Adjutant-General.*

> WAR DEPARTMENT, CAVALRY BUREAU,
> OFFICE OF INSPECTOR-GENERAL,
> *Washington, D. C., January 9, 1865.*

Col. J. C. KELTON,
> *Assistant Adjutant-General:*

COLONEL: I have the honor to submit the following report for the information of Major-General Halleck, Chief of Staff:

OCTOBER 1 TO DECEMBER 31.

Issued at—	To General Thomas.	To General Burbridge.	Total.
Louisville	17,367	....	17,367
Saint Louis	a 4,044	....	4,044
Lexington	1,500	5,278	6,778
Total	22,911	5,278	28,189

a 3,000 to Nashville.

The following number of horses were issued to the divisions named at Louisville and Saint Louis:

	Issued.	On hand.
First Division, General McCook (Louisville)	3,298	2,282
Second Division, General Long (left Louisville December 27)	7,211	7,000
Fourth Division, General Upton (Saint Louis)	1,090	3,000
Fifth Division, General Hatch (Louisville)	1,700	3,500
Sixth Division, General Johnson (Louisville)	2,631	1,500
Seventh Division, General Knipe	2,396	1,900
Total	18,326	19,182

The balance, nearly 5,000, were shipped to and issued at Nashville.
Estimated strength of cavalry at present in General Thomas' army, 19,182.

Before the recent battles there were about 3,000 horses in General Hatch's command, and 1,900 of Grierson's (now Upton's) command went there mounted. The total number on hand and received to December 31 would be 27,811; estimated present strength, 19,182; broken down and lost in action, 8,629. Of these a large number are at Nashville, and are being cared for there and being returned to Louisville for recuperation. The cavalry of this division have been so actively occupied that I have not been able to get any complete reports. They report the duty as having been uncommonly severe, and it is not thought that the proportion of loss in horses has been much greater than in the operations in the Valley.

I have the honor to be, colonel, very respectfully, your obedient servant,

> WM. REDWOOD PRICE,
> *Major and Assistant Inspector-General Cavalry Bureau.*

SPECIAL ORDERS, ⎰ HEADQUARTERS DEFENSES NASHVILLE
                ⎱   AND CHATTANOOGA RAILROAD,
    No. 8.   ⎰   *Tullahoma, January 9, 1865.*

The Forty-third Regiment Wisconsin Volunteer Infantry is hereby assigned to the Third Brigade of this command, and will make all reports to Col. W. Krzyzanowski, commanding brigade, headquarters at Stevenson, Ala.

By command of Major-General Milroy:

                                    JNO. O. CRAVENS,
                                    Assistant Adjutant-General.

                    HEADQUARTERS DISTRICT OF THE ETOWAH,
                                Chattanooga, January 9, 1865.

Brigadier-General CRUFT,
        Larkinsville:

Unless detained by orders from Major-General Thomas, you will come here with your command at once, leaving Colonel Malloy with troops of the Army of the Tennessee at Stevenson.

                                    JAMES B. STEEDMAN,
                                    Major-General.

                                    LARKINSVILLE, *January 9, 1865.*

Major-General STEEDMAN:

Brigadier-General Wood ordered me, on alleged authority from General Thomas, to stop my command, return, and head off or pursue rebel General Lyon's forces. Lyon crossed railway at Scottsborough last night. Malloy drove him off; Harrison and Malloy, Thompson, Mitchell, and Salm are in pursuit, the latter two close on his rear, near Guntersville. We may possibly catch him. Have just returned from all day and night on road. Will respond to your order promptly as possible. In conflict of orders, it has been difficult to tell what to do, but I have acted on what I supposed to be General Thomas' orders. Can you send the pontoon asked from Bridgeport by transports to Lamb's Ferry or Gunter's Landing to-night? else I must abandon the pursuit, some of the command being wholly out and no means to supply from here.

                                    CHARLES CRUFT,
                                    Brigadier-General.

                        HEADQUARTERS FOURTH ARMY CORPS,
                                Huntsville, Ala., January 9, 1865.

Col. T. J. MORGAN,
        Commanding Brigade:

Join General Cruft with your brigade and Malloy's command as soon as possible.

                                    TH. J. WOOD,
                                    Brigadier-General of Volunteers, Commanding.

COLESBURG, KY., *January 9, 1865.*

Brigadier-General EWING,
     Louisville, Ky.:

Rebels, from 500 to 900 strong, in Elizabethtown. Send re-enforcements for protection of Government property at this station. Have only fifteen men.

A. ANDERSON,
First Lieut., 50th Ohio Vol. Infty., Acting Assistant Quartermaster.

LEXINGTON, *January 9, 1865.*

Brigadier-General FRY,
     Camp Nelson, Ky.:

Send the mounted part of Eleventh Kentucky Cavalry, under good officer, to New Haven, Lebanon road, to operate in region of Raywick, New Haven, and Hodgensville against guerrillas.

By order of Brigadier-General Hobson:

J. S. BUTLER,
Assistant Adjutant-General.

WAR DEPARTMENT,
January 10, 1865—1 p. m.

Lieutenant-General GRANT,
     City Point:

I will at once send Colonel Parsons to the West, to take charge of the transportation of Schofield's corps. No doubt it will be best to move the whole body by boats from Eastport to Parkersburg, if the navigation allows, and thence by Baltimore and Ohio Railroad to Annapolis. When Hooker's force went to Tennessee all were moved over that road with great promptness and success. A capital advantage of that line is that it avoids all large towns. If the Ohio River should be frozen they can be moved by rail from Cairo, Evansville, or Jeffersonville to Parkersburg or Bellaire, according to circumstances. Your order says nothing about artillery; I think that had better be left behind. If the men are needed they can come and find new batteries and horses here.

C. A. DANA,
Assistant Secretary of War.

WASHINGTON, D. C., *January 10, 1865—4 p. m.*

Major-General THOMAS,
     Nashville:

Please answer in regard to Schofield's corps, where and when it will assemble.

H. W. HALLECK,
Major-General and Chief of Staff.

CHIEF QUARTERMASTER'S OFFICE,
DEPARTMENT OF THE CUMBERLAND,
Nashville, Tenn., January 10, 1865.

Maj. Gen. M. C. MEIGS,
 Quartermaster-General, Washington:

DEAR GENERAL: I have your note, and am sorry Mrs. D. will not be able to proceed at once to Savannah. She ought to have it, for I cannot go, and most of our means is involved. She has gone East to make the attempt, and she will have seen you before you receive this. Thomas left yesterday for Eastport, where he is concentrating. I saw him on board, and he opened his heart to me. He feels very sore at the rumored intentions to relieve him, and the major-generalcy does not cicatrize the wound. You know Thomas is morbidly sensitive, and it cut him to the heart to think that it was contemplated to remove him. He does not blame the Secretary, for he said Mr. Stanton was a fair and just man. In bidding him good-by, Thomas took occasion to speak again of the department. He said it was the most thorough and complete thing he had ever seen; that it had done everything he could desire for his army, and that you and myself had reasons to be proud of it. I told him that we had tried to sustain the army; that the breaking of the Chattanooga road after Steedman came up, by which we were cut off from the entire transportation concentrated there, as well as the coming of A. J. Smith's corps without a single wagon, have severely taxed the depot; but we have managed to pull through, and though we could not equip his entire army with transportation, we have given it enough to fight and pursue the enemy to the Tennessee River. Eastport is but a temporary depot till he crosses the Tennessee and moves out, when it will be broken up. Thomas now has the fragments of three armies, and they should be concentrated and consolidated into one. The depot at Johnsonville will be re-established. The railroad is badly damaged, and will not reopen before the 10th or 15th of next month. In the meantime the wrecks there should be removed, as they obstruct both channel and levee.

 Very truly, yours,

J. L. DONALDSON,
Chief Quartermaster.

HEADQUARTERS FOURTH ARMY CORPS,
Huntsville, Ala., January 10, 1865.

Brigadier-General DONALDSON,
 Chief Quartermaster, Department of the Cumberland:

 The country adjacent to this place for many miles has been exhausted of forage; consequently to procure it from the country, if indeed it be possible at all, it will be necessary to send a distance varying from twenty to forty miles. To send so far will keep the transportation of the corps so constantly occupied that it will be impossible to recruit the animals, shoe them up, and repair the wagons. I must hence request that you will ship forage to this place to meet a daily consumption of 60,000 pounds; less will not do us.

 I am, general, very respectfully, your obedient servant,

TH. J. WOOD,
Brigadier-General of Volunteers, Commanding.

HEADQUARTERS FOURTH ARMY CORPS,
Huntsville, Ala., January 10, 1865.

Brigadier-General WHIPPLE:

I have the honor to recommend the following promotions by brevet of officers of the Fourth Corps:

First. Col. John Q. Lane, Ninety-seventh Ohio Volunteers, commanding Second Brigade, Second Division, to be brigadier-general by brevet, for gallant and meritorious services throughout the Atlanta campaign, for gallantry in the battle of Franklin, on the 30th of November, and in the various conflicts around Nashville, on the 15th and 16th of December.

Second. Col. Joseph Conrad, Fifteenth Missouri Volunteers, commanding Third Brigade, Second Division, to be brigadier-general by brevet, for gallant and meritorious conduct throughout the Atlanta campaign, and for gallantry in the battle of Franklin, on the 30th November, and in the several conflicts of the battle of Nashville, fought on the 15th and 16th of December.

Third. Lieut. Col. Robert L. Kimberly, Forty-first Ohio Volunteers, to be colonel by brevet, for uniform gallantry and meritorious conduct in the performance of his duties, but especially for gallantry in the assault on Montgomery's Hill, on the 15th of December, and in the assault on the Overton Hill, on the 16th of December.

Fourth. Lieut. Col. Samuel N. Yeoman, Ninetieth Ohio Volunteers, to be colonel by brevet, for gallant and meritorious conduct in the performance of all his duties, but especially for gallantry in the assault made by his division on the afternoon of the 15th of December, and the other conflicts of the battle of Nashville.

Fifth. Lieut. Col. G. W. Smith, Eighty-eighth Illinois Volunteers, to be colonel by brevet, for soldierly conduct and gallantry in the performance of all his duties, but especially for distinguished gallantry and daring courage at the battle of Franklin, on the 30th of November, when at a most critical moment he aided much by his exertions in saving the day, and for gallantry and good conduct in the various conflicts on the 15th and 16th of December around Nashville.

Sixth. Lieut. Col. J. S. Fullerton, senior assistant adjutant-general on duty with the Fourth Army Corps, to be colonel by brevet, for the zealous, intelligent, faithful, and efficient performance of his duty, and for most valuable services and distinguished personal gallantry on the field, especially displayed in the battle of Franklin, on the 30th of November, and in the several conflicts of the battle fought in the vicinity of Nashville, on the 15th and 16th of December.

Seventh. Lieut. Col. W. H. Greenwood, inspector of the Fourth Army Corps, to be colonel by brevet, for zealous, faithful, and intelligent performance of his duty, and for great personal gallantry and efficiency on the field of battle, particularly exhibited in the battle of Franklin, on the 30th of November, and in the battle of Nashville, on the 15th and 16th of December.

Eighth. Maj. A. R. Z. Dawson, Fifteenth Ohio, chief of outposts and pickets, to be lieutenant-colonel by brevet, for the most faithful, zealous, useful, and intelligent performance of duty, and for the highest personal gallantry displayed in the most distinguished manner in the various conflicts and assaults of the battle of Nashville. In the assault on the Overton Hill, on the 16th of December, Major Dawson was wounded, but did not leave the field. He participated in the grand and successful assault later in the day and in the pursuit, continued more than 100 miles.

TH. J. WOOD,
Brigadier-General of Volunteers, Commanding.

CLAYSVILLE, OPPOSITE GUNTER'S LANDING,
January 10, 1865. (Via Larkinsville 11th.)

Brig. Gen. T. J. WOOD, *Huntsville, Ala.:*

Head of column reached here at 2 p. m.; drove in small party of rebels. The main force left here this morning, breaking into small squads and taking to the woods and mountains. Citizens report General Lyon to have crossed river personally last night by boat, and to have got the piece of artillery over. A few rebels got across during last night at Law's Ferry, and some twenty here. A brigade was pushed to Deposit this afternoon; I have got one at Law's Ferry; and heavy patrol parties through woods in each vicinity seeking for rebel squads. Lyon's command was finely mounted, and could easily keep out of way of infantry. He had with him somewhat over 500 men and one piece of artillery, an ambulance, and a wagon. Citizens report that rebels have abjured the hope of being allowed to cross above Shoals, and are making in that direction in parties, and that not more than 200 left here in an organization. General Lyon had one captain and three men badly wounded in the Scottsborough affair, but brought them off. In case I learn from Colonel Salm, at Deposit, during night that rebels are still running in direction indicated, and keep the start they have, the farther pursuit will probably be abandoned at Paint Rock Creek. The whole country is flooded, and infantry can hardly march. I think Lyon's command will hardly be concentrated this side the river now. The gun-boats have alarmed the rebels much by firing at them during the day.

CHAS. CRUFT,
Brigadier-General.

(Copy to Major-General Steedman.)

HEADQUARTERS ARMY OF THE OHIO,
Clifton, Tenn., January 10, 1865.

Lieut. Col. J. F. BOYD, *Chief Quartermaster, Louisville, Ky.:*

COLONEL: The major-general commanding directs that you move the train of wagons ordered some time since from Kentucky to stop at Louisville and await orders there. He desires you will also procure eight yards blue bunting, six yards white, and four yards red, to repair headquarters flags with, and send them forward by the first opportunity. Lieutenant Washburn is North, and can bring them, if you can see him. I wish him to bring three wall and one hospital tent for these headquarters.

WM. M. WHERRY,
Major and Aide-de-Camp.

HEADQUARTERS DETACHMENT ARMY OF THE TENNESSEE,
Eastport, Miss., January 10, 1865.

Maj. Gen. G. H. THOMAS, *Commanding in the Field:*

I arrived here yesterday with all my command, except twelve companies guarding my transportation to Savannah. I have a good position, and am constructing works rapidly to guard against an attack. I believe I am safe. One brigade of infantry was sent out yesterday to Iuka. Found the enemy had passed that point, and it is generally believed that Hood has left Corinth and gone south to Okolona or Columbus. By to-morrow night my position will be so strong as to defy his whole force. I regret I have no cavalry, or I would be able to send you a more definite report. I occupy all the ground at Eastport; no other corps can possibly land here. Just above Big Bear Creek, at Chickasaw, you will find an excellent camp for one corps, and bridges can easily be constructed to communicate with us. Wilson has not yet arrived. I detain one boat to bring over some cavalry just reported. I send two transports and barges to Clifton to bring up my artillery; the remainder of the fleet go to Savannah to bring up my transportation.

I am, general, very respectfully, your obedient servant,

A. J. SMITH,
Major-General.

HEADQUARTERS DETACHMENT ARMY OF THE TENNESSEE,
On Steamer Norman, January 10, 1865.

Brig. Gen. J. McARTHUR, *Commanding First Division:*

GENERAL: The major-general commanding directs that you debark your troops at once and camp them on the right of the Second Division, in continuation of the same line.

I am, very respectfully, your obedient servant,

J. HOUGH,
Major and Assistant Adjutant-General.

HEADQUARTERS DETACHMENT ARMY OF THE TENNESSEE,
Eastport, Miss., January 10, 1865.

Brig. Gen. T. K. SMITH, *Commanding Third Division:*

GENERAL: The major-general commanding directs that you debark your troops at once and place them in the rear of the First and Second Divisions.

I am, very respectfully, your obedient servant,

J. HOUGH,
Major and Assistant Adjutant-General.

HEADQUARTERS DISTRICT OF THE ETOWAH,
Chattanooga, January 10, 1865.

Brigadier-General WHIPPLE, *Chief of Staff:*

Is it intended that Brigadier-General Meagher, commanding Provisional Division, Army of the Tennessee, will accompany his command to Savannah? He desires to do so.

JAMES B. STEEDMAN,
Major-General.

HEADQUARTERS DISTRICT OF EAST TENNESSEE, AND
FOURTH DIVISION, TWENTY-THIRD ARMY CORPS,
Knoxville, Tenn., January 10, 1865.

Col. C. G. HAWLEY, *First Ohio Heavy Artillery, Dandridge, Tenn.:*

COLONEL: Colonel Shannon, in charge of the party collecting forage, will be on the south side of the river, in Dutch and Irish Bottoms, within a day or two after this reaches you.   I have instructed the commanding officer of the Fourth Tennessee Volunteer Infantry to report to you with his command at Dandridge, to be stationed as you direct. You will please communicate with Colonel Shannon at once, and make such disposition of the force under your command as to protect his operations, and also afford him such assistance as will be necessary to facilitate the work. I suppose Leadvale will be a proper place for a large part of your force, and some troops will be necessary at the fords on the roads from Greeneville and North Carolina. Get the information necessary to place your troops to the best advantage, always keeping in mind that they may have all to act in concert, and keep them in supporting distance. The best information I have fixes General Palmer's force at about 1,000, when all the detachments are together. This force is from Asheville, N. C., toward Paint Creek. General Vaughn is said to be near Jonesborough with about 600, and General Breckinridge in Virginia with some force. You will, of course, keep small parties in advance as scouts, who will give you information, to prevent surprise and disaster, and avail yourself of all means to be advised of the movements of the rebels. We want to get all the forage as soon as practicable, but the safety of the troops must be attended to. You will be on the alert and ready to act as the interests of the service may require.

Inclosed you will find a copy of the instructions* given to the officer commanding Fourth Tennessee Volunteer Infantry.

Very respectfully, your most obedient servant,

J. AMMEN,
Brig. Gen., U. S. Volunteers, Comdg. District and Division.

SPECIAL ORDERS, ⎱   HDQRS. MILITARY DIST. OF KENTUCKY,
No. 9.   ⎰   *Lexington, Ky., January 10, 1865.*

*   *   *   *   *   *   *

VI. The Eleventh Kentucky Cavalry Volunteers will proceed to Louisville, Ky., by railroad, and report to Brig. Gen. H. Ewing, commanding Second Division, for duty.

*   *   *   *   *   *   *

By command of Brevet Major-General Burbridge:

CHAS. M. KEYSER,
Captain and Acting Assistant Adjutant-General.

HDQRS. FIRST DIVISION, MILITARY DIST. OF KENTUCKY,
Lexington, Ky., January 10, 1865.

Lieut. Col. W. B. CRADDOCK,
Thirtieth Kentucky Mounted Infantry Volunteers :

You will proceed to Munfordville or Woodsonville, Ky., where you will await the arrival of Thirtieth Kentucky, which is ordered to move to Taylor, Green, and Barren Counties. You will procure information concerning guerrillas, and operate with such portion of your regiment, properly mounted, in the region above named.

By order of Brigadier-General Hobson:

J. S. BUTLER,
Assistant Adjutant-General.

---

* Not found.

MEMPHIS, *January 10, 1865.*

Hon. E. M. STANTON:

My cavalry force which left Memphis on December 21, after having totally destroyed the Mobile and Ohio Railroad to Egypt, ten miles south of Okolona, has reached Vicksburg in safety and in good condition. General Grierson reports having assaulted and captured the enemy's stockade at Egypt on the 28th. Frank Gardner, with 2,000 infantry, was in sight, on two trains of cars, to re-enforce the garrison, but was prevented, and the place was taken by assault, with 500 prisoners. The enemy having collected south of Egypt in too great force, Grierson then marched west, destroyed all public property at Grenada and thirty miles of the Mississippi Central Railroad, and reached Vicksburg on the 5th instant, having marched 450 miles. Our loss is some 25 killed and 80 wounded. The results of the expedition may be summed up as follows: The enemy lost in killed and wounded 150, including among the former Brigadier-General Gholson, 1 colonel, 1 major. The prisoners brought in are 550, including 2 colonels, 30 other officers. The destruction of 80 miles of railroad, including about 35 bridges; 300 army wagons (mostly captured from Sturgis); 5,000 stand of new arms; 4 serviceable locomotives, and 10 undergoing repairs; 100 cars, and a pile-driver and engine; the new machine-shop at Grenada; the factories for cloth and shoes at Barkston, which employed 500 hands and turned out 1,000 yards per day; large amounts of clothing, wools, cotton, and leather; immense amount of ammunition, commissary stores, new wagons, new pontoons, &c., on the way to Hood; 700 head of fat hogs; heavy stores of corn and wheat. The command arrived at Vicksburg with 1,000 negroes, mostly able-bodied, and 800 head of captured mules and horses. Full particulars of this most brilliant raid will be sent by mail. I am sending Grierson's and Winslow's cavalry to Louisville, in obedience to former orders. Hood and Forrest being now at Corinth, the cavalry not absolutely required in Kentucky or north of the Tennessee River ought to be here.

N. J. T. DANA,
Major-General.

Abstract from return of the Department of the Cumberland, Maj. Gen. George H. Thomas, U. S. Army, commanding, for January 10, 1865.

Command.	Present for duty.		Aggregate present.	Aggregate present and absent.	Pieces of artillery.
	Officers.	Men.			
General headquarters	24		24	26	
Fourth Army Corps (Wood)	641	12,479	15,267	28,686	32
District of Tennessee (Rousseau)	651	14,956	19,473	26,129	153
District of the Etowah (Steedman)	216	7,355	9,197	12,928	137
Artillery Reserve (Aleshire)	13	647	669	784	20
Reserve Brigade (Le Favour)	32	744	1,129	1,805	
Unassigned infantry	24	833	1,159	1,851	
Unassigned artillery	5	243	253	304	9
Signal Corps (Hollopeter)	12	57	69	101	
Veteran Reserve Corps	12	669	749	904	
Total	1,630	37,683	47,989	73,518	351

Abstract from returns of the Department of the Ohio, Maj. Gen. John M. Schofield, U. S. Army, commanding, for January 10, 1865.*

[Compiled mainly from subordinate returns.]

Command.	Present for duty. Officers.	Present for duty. Men.	Aggregate present.	Aggregate present and absent.	Pieces of artillery.	Station.
General headquarters	47		47	47		In the field, Tenn.
Twenty-third Army Corps (Schofield):						
Headquarters†	14	43	57	57		Do.
First Division (Ruger)	171	3,865	4,451	7,672	4	Near Clifton, Tenn.
Second Division (Couch)	237	4,317	5,468	9,518	8	Clifton, Tenn.
Third Division (Cox)	216	4,966	6,007	9,401	8	Near Clifton, Tenn.
Fourth Division (Ammen)	165	4,384	5,762	8,469	749	Knoxville, Tenn.
1st Ohio Heavy Artillery (Hawley)	32	1,297	1,405	1,892		Dandridge, Tenn
Total	882	18,872	23,197	37,056		
District of Western Kentucky (Meredith).	77	1,999	3,186	3,629		
Grand total	959	20,871	26,383	40,685		

Abstract from return of the Cavalry Corps, Military Division of the Mississippi, Bvt. Maj. Gen. James H. Wilson, U. S. Army, commanding, for January 10, 1865.

Command.	Present for duty. Officers.	Present for duty. Men.	Aggregate present.	Aggregate present and absent.	Pieces of artillery.	Station.
General headquarters	9		9	9		In the field.
4th U. S. Cavalry‡ (Hedges)	7	272	336	618		Do.
First Division (Watkins)	157	3,542	4,543	7,566	4	Do.
Second Division (Long)	191	5,264	6,480	8,472	4	Near Nashville, Tenn.
Fifth Division (Hatch)	172	4,449	5,400	8,103	4	In the field.
Sixth Division (Johnson)	95	2,354	2,917	4,759	4	Franklin and Chattanooga, Tenn.
Seventh Division (Knipe)	145	3,041	4,191	7,043	4	Edgefield, Tenn.
Total§	776	18,922	23,876	36,570	20	

PADUCAH, KY., *January 11, 1865—10 a. m.*

Maj. Gen. H. W. HALLECK,
     Washington, D. C.:

I shall start up the Tennessee to-day, and can assemble Schofield's corps by the end of this week, either at Clifton or Eastport. If I receive no further orders from you I will direct Schofield to proceed to Annapolis, Md., as expeditiously as possible. The information I get here confirms the report of Colonel Palmer that Hood has gone to Tuscaloosa and that Forrest is somewhere about Okolona with his main force.

                GEO. H. THOMAS,
                  Major-General, U. S. Volunteers.

---

* Returns of the Military District of Kentucky (Burbridge) not on file.
† Includes Signal Corps.
‡ Serving as escort.
§ Exclusive of the Third and Fourth Divisions, serving in Georgia and Mississippi, respectively.

HEADQUARTERS DEPARTMENT OF THE CUMBERLAND,
Steamer Tarascon, Paducah, Ky., January 11, 1865—11 a. m.

Maj. Gen. H. W. HALLECK, *Washington, D. C.:*

Reports this morning from Generals Wood and Granger inform me that the rebel General Lyon attacked the little garrison at Scottsborough, Ala., where he was handsomely repulsed three times, losing 1 colonel and 16 men killed, with a loss to our forces of 6 wounded and 9 missing. Lyon is retreating in haste toward the Tennessee River, which I have requested the commanding officer of the fleet at Bridgeport to have closely watched and patrolled, to prevent his escape across the river. I am in hopes that the arrangements made will insure his capture.

GEO. H. THOMAS,
Major-General, U. S. Volunteers.

WAR DEPARTMENT,
January 11, 1865—10.55 a. m. (Via Nashville, Tenn.)

Maj. Gen. G. H. THOMAS:

The following is taken from a Richmond paper of the 10th instant:

Latest from the South and Southwest.—The following dispatch has been received at the War Department from Macon, Ga.:

"General Hood reports from Tupelo, January 6, 1865, that Thomas appeared to be moving up the Tennessee River until 9 o'clock a. m. on the 5th. Scouts report six gun-boats and sixty transports had passed Savannah, going toward Eastport, loaded with troops and supplies.

"G. T. BEAUREGARD,
"General."

C. A. DANA,
Assistant Secretary of War.

WAR DEPARTMENT,
Washington City, January 11, 1865—2 p. m.

Maj. Gen. G. H. THOMAS,
Commanding Department of the Cumberland:

Col. L. B. Parsons leaves here to-day, under orders from this Department, to take charge of the transportation of Schofield's corps from the Tennessee to Chesapeake Bay. His headquarters will for the next few days be at Louisville. Please inform him when the troops will probably be ready to start, in order that he may consummate the necessary arrangements, and also communicate with him generally respecting all points essential to the prompt and comfortable accomplishment of this most important movement.

C. A. DANA,
Assistant Secretary of War.

PADUCAH, KY., *January 11, 1865.*

Capt. FORREST,
Comdg. 11th District, Mississippi Squadron, Bridgeport, Ala.:

I shall be much obliged if you will have your gun-boat carry on a lively patrol of the river from Bridgeport to Decatur, to prevent, if possible, the escape of the rebel General Lyon and his command across the river.

GEO. H. THOMAS,
Major-General, U. S. Volunteers, Commanding.

NASHVILLE, TENN., *January 11, 1865—9 p. m.*

Maj. T. T. ECKERT:

Constant rains during past week. River very high; will be very deep. No movement of troops possible. Small guerrilla parties are making some trouble between here and the Tennessee. Delay repairs of telegraph on line of Northwestern Railroad, but will have it working by time General Thomas reaches Eastport.

J. C. VAN DUZER.

SPECIAL ORDERS,)   WAR DEPT., ADJT. GENERAL'S OFFICE,
    No. 17.   \   *Washington, January 11, 1865.*

*   *   *   *   *   *   *

27. The telegraphic order of January 4, 1865, from this Department, directing Maj. Gen. S. G. Burbridge, U. S. Volunteers, to repair to this city without delay and report to the Adjutant-General, is hereby confirmed.

*   *   *   *   *   *   *

By order of the Secretary of War:

W. A. NICHOLS,
Assistant Adjutant-General.

HEADQUARTERS FOURTH ARMY CORPS,
Huntsville, Ala., January 11, 1865.

Brigadier-General DONALDSON,
    Chief Quartermaster, Department of the Cumberland:

Please send forward immediately all of the supplies that have been called for at this post. They are needed for the equipment of the troops, under orders from General Thomas. I have directed that Colonel Hayes, chief quartermaster of the corps, call on you and explain the necessity of everything asked for. Give him all that he requests. You are wrong in supposing that there is plenty of forage in the vicinity of this place. We need 60,000 pounds daily, and you must send us that amount to meet our wants.

TH. J. WOOD,
Brigadier-General of Volunteers, Commanding.

HEADQUARTERS FOURTH ARMY CORPS,
Huntsville, Ala., January 11, 1865.

Maj. Gen. L. H. ROUSSEAU,
    Nashville:

The Third and Fourth Michigan have been assigned to the Fourth Corps. Will you order them to join the corps without delay.

TH. J. WOOD,
Brigadier-General of Volunteers, Commanding.

HEADQUARTERS ARMY OF THE OHIO,
Clifton, Tenn., January 11, 1865.

COMMANDING OFFICERS OF TRANSPORTS:

The officers in charge of transports on which the batteries belonging to the Department and Army of the Tennessee are loaded will proceed without delay with their steamers to Eastport, Miss., in charge of Capt. F. W. Morse, commanding the batteries, and report to Maj. Gen. A. J. Smith.

By command of Major-General Schofield:

WM. M. WHERRY,
Major and Aide-de-Camp.

SPECIAL ⎞ HEADQUARTERS ARMY OF THE OHIO,
FIELD ORDERS, ⎟   *In the Field, Clifton, Tenn.,*
No. 9.   ⎠   *January 11, 1865.*

*   *   *   *   *   *   *

2. Maj. Joshua Healey, One hundred and twenty-eighth Indiana Volunteer Infantry, is hereby detailed as acting assistant inspector-general of the First Division, Twenty-third Army Corps.

*   *   *   *   *   *   *

By command of Major-General Schofield:

J. A. CAMPBELL,
Major and Assistant Adjutant-General.

COLUMBIA, *January 11, 1865.*

Major BEAUMONT,
 Asst. Adjt. Gen., Cavalry Corps, Mil. Div. of the Mississippi:

The First Division of Cavalry is at this place. There is no forage; we are entirely out, and cannot proceed without it. We need seven days' forage for 4,000 animals; please have it sent immediately.

L. D. WATKINS,
Brevet Brigadier-General, Commanding First Cavalry Division.

COLUMBIA, TENN., *January 11, 1865.*

Maj. E. B. BEAUMONT,
 Asst. Adjt. Gen., Cavalry Corps, Mil. Div. of the Miss., Nashville:

The construction corps cannot build a bridge across Duck River, having nothing to do it with. Please send a pontoon to this place immediately; it will be the only way to bridge the river so that my trains can cross. I can then proceed without further delay.

LOUIS D. WATKINS,
Brevet Brigadier-General, Commanding First Cavalry Division.

NASHVILLE, *January 11, 1865.*
(Received 12th.)

Brigadier-General WATKINS,
 Commanding First Division Cavalry:

Forage was sent to you last night. I will order rations, if you will say for how many days and men. I will ascertain without delay what can be done about the bridge.

E. B. BEAUMONT,
Major and Assistant Adjutant-General.

HDQRS. CAVALRY CORPS, MIL. DIV. OF THE MISSISSIPPI,
Nashville, January 11, 1865.

Brig. Gen. ELI LONG,
 Commanding Second Division:

GENERAL: I think you had better delay your movement for a day or so. I have just received the following telegram from General Watkins:

COLUMBIA, TENN., *January 11, 1865.*

 The bridge across Duck River at this place has washed away; half of my command is on this side of the river, and the other half, with all the trains, on the other side. Impossible to cross the river at any place near here at the present stage of water, and there is no forage near here. I shall get my command across as soon as possible, which may be several days, unless I receive different instructions. We shall need forage and rations shipped to this point.

 I am, general, very respectfully, your obedient servant,
E. B. BEAUMONT,
Major and Assistant Adjutant-General.

KNOXVILLE, *January 11, 1865.*

Major-General STEEDMAN,
 Commanding District of the Etowah:

 Arrangements have been made to send the troops at Loudon down to-morrow.
J. AMMEN,
Brigadier-General, Commanding District.

HEADQUARTERS FOURTH ARMY CORPS,
 Huntsville, Ala., January 11, 1865.

Colonel PALMER, *Fifteenth Pennsylvania Cavalry:*

 The general commanding directs that you move your whole available force, as soon as possible, over the Flint River in pursuit of the rebel General Lyon's force. Scour the country well between Flint River and Paint Rock Creek. If you do not find the enemy between these streams, push small scouting parties over Paint Rock and hunt for them. As soon as you find any of Lyon's forces, or discover the direction in which they have gone, pursue them vigorously; overtake and destroy them, if possible. Cross Flint River at the Claysville road crossing. Go without any wagons; take such rations as you can on your horses, and depend on the country for the rest.

 Very respectfully, your obedient servant,
J. S. FULLERTON,
Assistant Adjutant-General and Chief of Staff.

HEADQUARTERS DISTRICT OF THE ETOWAH,
 Chattanooga, January 11, 1865.

Lieutenant-Colonel BISHOP, *Bridgeport:*

 A train will be at Bridgeport to bring your command to this place and Charleston at 4 this p. m. You will be ready to load on its arrival and come at once, bringing all the troops of the Fourteenth Army Corps in your command.

 By command of Major-General Steedman:
S. B. MOE,
Assistant Adjutant-General.

BRIDGEPORT, *January 11, 1865.*

Major MOE, *Assistant Adjutant-General:*

Shall take troops from the block-houses between here and Shell-mound. The Sixty-eighth New York has not arrived here. There are no troops here to relieve them. Please answer.

L. K. BISHOP,
Lieutenant-Colonel, Commanding.

HEADQUARTERS DISTRICT OF THE ETOWAH,
Chattanooga, January 11, 1865.

Lieutenant-Colonel BISHOP, *Bridgeport:*

You have fifty men of the Sixty-eighth New York and fifty men of the Ninth Ohio Light Artillery with which you can relieve the men in block-houses east of Bridgeport. The block-houses at Bridgeport can be garrisoned by Eighteenth U. S. Colored Infantry.

By command of Major-General Steedman:

S. B. MOE,
Assistant Adjutant-General.

HEADQUARTERS DISTRICT OF THE ETOWAH,
Chattanooga, January 11, 1865.

Colonel DILWORTH,
Commanding Post, Cleveland:

COLONEL: As trains cannot run farther than the junction on the Chattanooga and Atlanta road, you will please march the troops of the Fourteenth Army Corps you have at this place along the line of the Chattanooga and Atlanta road, relieving all troops in block-houses south of Chickamauga Station and north of Tunnel Hill. The troops of the Fourteenth Army Corps with wood party you will relieve with an equal number from the Twentieth Corps, and add them to the detachment of the Fourteenth Corps for the above garrison duty. The detachment of the Fourteenth Army Corps now at Tunnel Hill will remain at Tunnel Hill until General Cruft's return, when it will be used to strengthen the garrisons in block-houses this side. Should any be found in the block-houses, they will be ordered to Tunnel Hill to garrison that place until General Cruft's return. You will order the troops relieved to report at once to Brigadier-General Meagher. You will commence the execution of this order at once, and report its completion.

By command of Major-General Steedman:

S. B. MOE,
Assistant Adjutant-General.

HEADQUARTERS DISTRICT OF THE ETOWAH,
Chattanooga, January 11, 1865.

Colonel BOUGHTON, *Cleveland, Tenn.:*

A train will be at Charleston and Cleveland to-morrow morning, January 12, to bring your command to this place. Notify troops at Charleston, and hold yourself in readiness to load on arrival of the train. On your arrival here, you will report to General Meagher.

By command of Major-General Steedman:

S. B. MOE,
Assistant Adjutant-General.

STATE OF INDIANA, EXECUTIVE DEPARTMENT,
Indianapolis, January 11, 1865.

General JOSEPH HOOKER,
 Commanding Department, Cincinnati, Ohio:

DEAR SIR: The region of Kentucky bordering the Ohio River is infested with guerrilla bands, who keep the southern border of this State in constant alarm. They fire on steam-boats, commit robberies, and carry on with disaffected persons on this side of the river a large contraband trade. It is not only desirable, but necessary to the security of our citizens, that these bands should be dispersed and our border protected. The State cannot furnish a force sufficient to guard nearly 400 miles of a line so easily accessible as ours, and I address you for the purpose of securing your co-operation in the work. Either of two modes of operation will be probably effective: to station an adequate force at the more accessible points, or permit the commander of this district, Maj. Gen. A. P. Hovey, to follow the marauding bands into Kentucky, whenever, in his judgment, he may be able to capture or disperse them by such pursuit.

Your early attention to this matter will greatly oblige the people of the State, and
  Yours, very truly,

       O. P. MORTON,
        Governor of Indiana.

CITY POINT, VA., *January 12, 1865—11 a. m.*

Maj. Gen. H. W. HALLECK,
 Washington, D. C.:

You may direct the batteries of Schofield's corps to be left behind. I think, however, it may be advisable for him to bring two companies of artillerists to each division, to be fitted up here, if necessary.
       U. S. GRANT,
        Lieutenant-General.

WASHINGTON, D. C., *January 12, 1865—10.30 a. m.*
    (Via Paducah, Ky. Received 16th.)

Major-General THOMAS:

Colonel Parsons has gone West to superintend the transportation of Schofield's corps. It is thought that river transportation, as far as the ice will permit, will be the most comfortable for the troops. They will be taken from Parkersburg to Annapolis by the Baltimore and Ohio Railroad, if a sufficient number of cars can be obtained; if not, a part will go to Pittsburg. No artillery need be sent without further orders.
       H. W. HALLECK,
      Major-General and Chief of Staff.

WASHINGTON, D. C., *January 12, 1865—1.30 p. m.*
      (Received 16th.)

Major-General THOMAS, *On the Tennessee River:*

General Grant directs that General Schofield bring with him two companies of artillery to each division, which will be supplied with batteries here.
       H. W. HALLECK,
      Major-General and Chief of Staff.

WASHINGTON, *January 12, 1865.*

Brig. Gen. ROBERT ALLEN,
        Louisville:

Col. L. B. Parsons left here last night for Louisville, to take general direction of the transportation of General Schofield's corps from the Tennessee to Chesapeake Bay, just ordered by Lieutenant-General Grant. The movement will be made as far as possible by boats from Eastport. If the state of navigation will allow, the troops will not be debarked till they reach Parkersburg; but if necessary, they will take the rail either at Cairo, Evansville, Jeffersonville, or Cincinnati. Colonel Parsons cannot reach Louisville before Friday night; meanwhile please open any dispatches that may be addressed to him, and make all such arrangements respecting steam-boats as, in your judgment, will expedite and facilitate the movement. The troops only will be moved, leaving their transportation behind.

C. A. DANA,
Assistant Secretary of War.

GENERAL ORDERS,) HEADQUARTERS FOURTH ARMY CORPS,
    No. 1.   }   *Huntsville, Ala., January 12, 1865.*

The system of transportation by the use of pack animals has been so much abused by this command, and has become so great an evil, that it requires an immediate and radical change. During the campaign just closed some of the regiments of this corps collected a number of animals so large that they greatly impeded the march, and consumed large quantities of forage in the country, for the want of which the proper animals of the command suffered. These animals are led by enlisted men, and for each animal a man is lost to the ranks; thus the effective force of many of our regiments is seriously weakened, and opportunity is offered to the skulkers and cowards of the command to lead these animals to the rear in the time of battle and avoid the dangers which their comrades must brave.

To correct these evils, the allowance of pack animals to each regiment of the command will be as follows: Two pack animals for the field and staff officers of a regiment; or where there are not field officers for the headquarters of a regiment. One pack animal for every three line officers of a regiment. Where, in dividing the line officers by three, there is a fraction, one animal will be allowed the fraction. Two pack animals to carry the cooking utensils of a regiment.

In the foregoing enumeration the number of animals that may hereafter be allowed for the pioneers of a regiment, for the purpose of carrying tools only, is not included. All other animals now with the regiments of this command, save those belonging to mounted officers and those used for the transportation of medical panniers, must be at once turned over to the chief quartermaster of the corps to be disposed of.

Enlisted men or officers' servants who have charge of pack animals must carry permits stating by whose authority they so have charge of them, who is responsible for or owns them, and who draws forage for them. These permits must be countersigned and marked "approved" by brigade provost-marshals. On the march all provost-marshals and other staff officers will examine these permits whenever they may see fit to do so, and if any man is found with an animal without such a permit in his possession, he will be arrested and punished and the animal will be at once taken away from him and turned over to the corps quartermaster.

By command of Brig. Gen. Thomas J. Wood:

WM. H. SINCLAIR,
Assistant Adjutant-General.

LOUISVILLE, *January 12, 1865.*
(Received 2 p. m.)

Maj. WILLIAM REDWOOD PRICE,
Assistant Inspector-General:

General Wilson says he wants 6,000 more horses immediately; have written you on the subject.

W. P. CHAMBLISS,
Major, &c.

[Indorsement.]

WAR DEPARTMENT, CAVALRY BUREAU,
OFFICE ASSISTANT INSPECTOR-GENERAL,
January 13, 1865.

Respectfully referred to Major-General Halleck, Chief of Staff, U. S. Army.

Major Chambliss' report, December 31, 1864, shows 502 serviceable horses on hand at that time; a later report gives 1,860 on hand. Receipts at Louisville for the ten days ending December 31 were, 1,141 serviceable horses from regular sources, 1,095 impressed.

WM. REDWOOD PRICE,
Major and Assistant Inspector-General, Cavalry Bureau.

NASHVILLE, *January 12, 1865.*
(Received 13th.)

Brigadier-General WATKINS,
Columbia:

A pontoon bridge has been ordered to Columbia, but the river will probably be fordable before it can be laid. If you require more forage or rations, let me know.

E. B. BEAUMONT,
Major and Assistant Adjutant-General.

NASHVILLE, TENN., *January 12, 1865.*

Colonel BLODGETT,
Columbia:

Brig. Gen. R. W. Johnson has been assigned to the command of the Tennessee and Alabama Railroad from here to the Alabama State line, with headquarters at Pulaski. He left here for that place this morning, and will likely be in Columbia to-day. He will settle all points raised in your letter of the 10th, just received.

By command of Major-General Rousseau:

B. H. POLK,
Major and Assistant Adjutant-General.

HEADQUARTERS DISTRICT OF TENNESSEE,
January 12, 1865.
Brigadier-General VAN CLEVE,
Murfreesborough:

Send the Third and Fourth Michigan Infantry, without delay, by rail, to Huntsville, to report to Brigadier-General Wood, commanding Fourth Army Corps.

By order of Major-General Rousseau:

B. H. POLK,
Major and Assistant Adjutant-General.

LARKINSVILLE, ALA., *January 12, 1865.*
Brigadier-General WHIPPLE:

Abandoned farther pursuit of Lyon near Paint Rock this a. m. The streams were impassable. There are squads of rebels that have crossed to opposite side of Paint Rock and are in woods near the bank of it, and a few squads still higher up, but the whole organization is reported broken up. A citizen says that Major Chenoweth crossed railroad near Woodville with 150. The residue of Lyon's command is beyond Paint Rock, near the mouth. Could not ascertain truth of this. My command captured Lyon's wounded, 1 captain and 3 privates, his ambulances, and destroyed his artillery harness. Colonel Thompson's brigade will be shipped to-night, on reaching Woodville, to Nashville.

CHAS. CRUFT,
Brigadier-General.

(Same to General T. J. Wood.)

LARKINSVILLE, *January 12, 1865.*
Major-General STEEDMAN:

Arrived here 2 p. m.; will ship balance of troops as soon as they strike railroad, and transportation can be had. Abandoned pursuit of enemy near Paint Rock; roads were impassable farther, on account of streams.

CHARLES CRUFT,
Brigadier-General.

LARKINSVILLE, *January 12, 1865.*
Major-General STEEDMAN:

Has Colonel Harrison's command arrived? Hope to ship Colonel Salm and Colonel Mitchell during night. Is there any change in destination since your dispatch on that subject?

CHARLES CRUFT,
Brigadier-General.

HEADQUARTERS NORTHERN DEPARTMENT,
Cincinnati, Ohio, January 12, 1865.
COMMANDING OFFICER,
Louisville, Ky.:

SIR: I have the honor to forward for your information a copy of a letter* I have just received from His Excellency the Governor of Indiana,

---

* See Morton to Hooker, 11th, p. 573.

and a copy of a letter of instructions to Major-General Hovey, command-ing the District of Indiana. I request that you will make use of all the means in your power to assist in breaking up and destroying the bands of guerrillas on the Kentucky side of the river. I have no authority to send a force into your department, nor any force to spare for that service; but sooner than have the feeling of terror and insecurity which now prevails along the border, I shall feel constrained to, if I have to call out every able-bodied man in the department to do it. I know it is possible to put an end to the depredations of these thieves and robbers, and I shall feel it to be a severe reflection on me if it is not done. I beg you will put and keep everything at work on your side of the river. I inclose these letters to your address, as I have just been informed that the depart-ment commander is absent in Washington. If I am in error, please have them forwarded to him.

Very respectfully, your obedient servant,

JOS. HOOKER,
Major-General, Commanding.

[Inclosure.]

HEADQUARTERS NORTHERN DEPARTMENT,
Cincinnati, Ohio, January 12, 1865.

Brevet Major-General HOVEY,
Commanding District of Indiana:

GENERAL: I am directed by the major-general commanding the department to instruct you to dispatch all your available force, if in your judgment it should appear necessary, to exposed points in your district on the Ohio River, for the purpose of protecting our people from the depredations of the gangs of guerrillas infesting the Ken-tucky side of the river. These guerrilla parties are mounted, and prin-cipally live from twelve to thirty miles in the interior, from whence they make excursions to the river in such direction and at such times as suit their convenience and interest. They steal, fire into steamers, and it is alleged are engaged in smuggling, keeping our people in a con-stant state of alarm and excitement. As we have no cavalry, it would be fruitless to send into Kentucky to pursue them. On the Kentucky side we have had a comparatively large cavalry force, and the general will call the immediate attention of the officer in command of that department to the necessity of co-operating with our forces in break-ing up and destroying these bands, as they are the terror and curse of the good people on both sides of the river. With our limited force, the general is decidedly of the opinion that the true course to pursue to insure our citizens the security and protection they have a right to expect from the Government is to make the river our line of defense, and not to cross into Kentucky. If we cannot restore quiet and security by keeping the river between us, we certainly cannot do it by going in pursuit; but be this as it may, good order must and shall be preserved. The major-general commanding directs that you report, without delay, the disposition you make of your forces to accomplish the desired end.

Very respectfully, your obedient servant,

C. H. POTTER,
Assistant Adjutant-General.

HEADQUARTERS DISTRICT OF THE ETOWAH,
Chattanooga, January 12, 1865.

COMMANDING OFFICER, *Loudon, Tenn.:*

As soon as relieved, you will bring your command to this place, taking first train.

JAMES B. STEEDMAN,
Major-General.

SPECIAL ORDERS, } HDQRS. MILITARY DIST. OF KENTUCKY,
  No. 11.   }   *Lexington, Ky., January 12, 1865.*

*   *   *   *   *   *   *

III. The One hundred and twenty-second Regiment U. S. Colored Infantry will proceed without delay by boat to Parkersburg, W. Va., and thence by rail to the Army of the James. Upon its arrival the commanding officer will report for orders to Maj. Gen. B. F. Butler. The quartermaster's department will furnish the transportation.

*   *   *   *   *   *   *

By command of Brevet Major-General Burbridge:

CHAS. M. KEYSER,
Captain and Acting Assistant Adjutant-General.

LEXINGTON, *January 12, 1865.*

Major-General BURBRIDGE:
  (Care of Hon. J. Speed, Washington, D. C.)

I send copy of my dispatch to General Lindsey, at which the Governor has waxed wroth and sent in a special message:

The general commanding desires information as to whether or not the State troops have yet been mustered out of service, in compliance with the orders received from the War Department. If not, he directs that immediate steps be taken to muster out, and that you prevent by order any further recruiting in such organizations, as he understands enlistments are still being made.

From Louisville Journal.

Message from Governor informing the Senate that General D. W. Lindsey had received a telegram from the district headquarters ordering the mustering out of all State troops and the discontinuance of recruiting for the same. The Governor recommended that a committee be appointed by the General Assembly, whose duty it should be to go to Washington and see the President and use efforts to have the order revoked, as the safety of Kentucky's citizens required the same in the absence of Federal protection.

Resolution appointing a committee to visit Washington and lay before the President the grievances of this State. The resolution, after being discussed, was referred to the committee on military affairs.

I send above to you on recommendation of Mr. Eginton. I forward copy of message by mail.

CHAS. M. KEYSER,
Captain and Acting Assistant Adjutant-General.

HEADQUARTERS DEPARTMENT OF THE CUMBERLAND,
Nashville, Tenn., January 13, 1865.

General J. B. HOOD, C. S. Army,
  Commanding C. S. Army of Tennessee:

GENERAL: I take this means of informing you of an act of cold-blooded murder of prisoners of war recently committed by a company of scouts belonging to Forrest's forces and commanded by a Captain Harvey. The circumstances were as follows: On the 20th of December last three officers belonging to the U. S. service were captured by this company of scouts, which numbered thirty-six men, about fourteen miles southeast of Murfreesborough. As soon as captured they were robbed of everything valuable which they had upon their persons, even their clothing. They were kept under guard for three days, with some other prisoners, enlisted men, who had also been captured near Murfreesborough, until they reached a small town named Lewisburg, some eighteen miles south of Duck River. From there the captured officers were sent, under guard of four men, as they were told by the guard, to Forrest's headquarters, and the enlisted men were taken off on a road leading to Columbia. The officers were taken along the turnpike leading from Lewisburg to Mooresville for the distance of about four miles, when they left the road and turned to the right for the purpose, as they were told by the guard, of stopping at a neighboring house for the night. When they had reached a wooded ravine, about half a mile from the turnpike, the leading man of the guard halted, partially turned his horse, and as one of the officers came up drew his revolver and, without uttering word, shot him in the head. The other two officers were then killed by being shot through the head with carbines, and their bodies were next morning decently buried, but not by your troops, upon the premises of a citizen living near. It is supposed that the enlisted men who were taken off on another road met a similar fate to that of the officers. I have the names of these officers in my possession, and the whole that is herein stated is susceptible of proof. It is my desire, as far as lies in my power, to mitigate the horrors of this war as much as possible, but I will not consent that my soldiers shall be thus brutally murdered whenever the fortunes of war place them defenseless within your power. Such acts on the part of the soldiers of your army are of by no means rare occurrence. A case which occurs to my mind now, and of which no mention has heretofore been made to either your predecessor in command or yourself, is that of the murder of ten prisoners of war by a portion of Ross' brigade, of Wheeler's cavalry, at Wood's Gap, between Gordon's Mills and Dalton, early in April last. Should my troops, exasperated by a repetition of such acts, take no prisoners at all in future, I shall in no manner interfere in this exercise of their just vengeance, and you will fully understand their reasons as well as mine; and you will please remember that it is your army, and not mine, who is responsible for the inauguration of the dreadful policy of extermination.

I am, sir, very respectfully, your obedient servant,

GEO. H. THOMAS,
Major-General, U. S. Army, Commanding.

NASHVILLE, TENN., *January 13, 1865—9.30 p. m.*

Maj. T. T. ECKERT:

Message received from headquarters of General Wilson, at Eastport, to-day, dated 11th, says:

Reconnaissance found no rebels in the vicinity there or Corinth, except some sort of partisan bands, merely thieves, which infest whole country not occupied by our forces.

Work of repairing railroads to the Tennessee goes on slowly, if it can be said to go at all. My men have been over the line, but no troops between here and river, except at one point, and people bitterly hostile. Not able to maintain the telegraph yet.

J. C. VAN DUZER.

HUNTSVILLE, *January 13, 1865—10 a. m.*

General WHIPPLE,
    Assistant Adjutant-General:

General Cruft reports having driven Lyon's command to the Tennessee River. Being prevented from crossing by the gun-boats, the rebels broke up into small parties, scattered, and are hiding about, waiting to get over the river individually. General Cruft reports that Lyon and a few men succeeded in evading the gun-boats and crossed the river; but this party, according to the accounts of General Cruft, did not exceed twenty. Further reports that infantry can do nothing more in the pursuit. I have hence authorized him to proceed to his destination with General Steedman's forces. Thirty-six hours since I sent Colonel Palmer, Fifteenth Pennsylvania Cavalry, the regiment being here and unemployed, to scour the country in which Lyon's command had dispersed, to try to capture or destroy all straggling parties. I also ordered Colonel Clift, who was north of this place, with his Tennessee cavalry regiment, to look for Lyon's scattered parties and pitch into whatever he could find.

TH. J. WOOD,
Brigadier-General of Volunteers.

HEADQUARTERS FOURTH ARMY CORPS,
Huntsville, Ala., January 13, 1865.

Brigadier-General CRUFT,
    Larkinsville:

Your dispatch received. If you are satisfied that you have done all that can be done with infantry toward capturing, destroying, or dispersing Lyon's command, you can proceed with General Steedman's forces on your destination. I have sent a cavalry force, more than thirty hours ago, to the country suggested by you.

I thank yourself and command for the vigor displayed in pursuit of Lyon.

TH. J. WOOD,
Brigadier-General of Volunteers, Commanding.

HEADQUARTERS FOURTH ARMY CORPS,
Huntsville, Ala., January 13, 1865—10.30 a. m.

Lieut. Col. TERRENCE CLARK,
    Pulaski:

Move with your battalion of convalescents at once to this place. You should have been here by this time. When you pass Elk River have the pontoon bridge taken up and brought here with you.

TH. J. WOOD,
Brigadier-General of Volunteers, Commanding.

HEADQUARTERS ARMY OF THE OHIO,
Clifton, January 13, 1865.

Major-General THOMAS,
    Commanding Department of the Cumberland:

GENERAL: I have not yet commenced moving my command from this place, General Smith not having finished with the boats. Our commissary supplies are almost entirely exhausted; we can only make what we have here last until the 15th, and I am informed Generals Smith and Wilson will be out on the 16th. You are aware there are no supplies to be had in the country about here. I apprehend that Forrest may have established batteries on the river below here and stopped our boats. The admiral is going down with gun-boats to see about it.

Very respectfully,

J. M. SCHOFIELD,
Major-General.

SPECIAL ORDERS, }   HDQRS. THIRD DIV., 23D ARMY CORPS,
No. 4.   }   *Clifton, Tenn., January 13, 1865.*

*   *   *   *   *   *   *

IV. Col. C. C. Doolittle, Eighteenth Michigan Volunteer Infantry, at his own request, is hereby relieved from the command of the First Brigade, Third Division, Twenty-third Army Corps, to enable him to return to his own command, for the purpose of attending to necessary business connected therewith. He will turn over the command of the brigade to the senior officer present. This order to take effect as soon as transportation can be furnished from this place.

The general commanding takes this opportunity of returning his thanks to Colonel Doolittle for his voluntary services during the late campaign from Nashville, and to express his high admiration for the ability and soldierly qualities shown by him while in command of the brigade.

By command of Brigadier-General Cox:

THEO. COX,
Captain and Assistant Adjutant-General.

HEADQUARTERS DETACHMENT ARMY OF THE TENNESSEE,
Eastport, Miss., January 13, 1865.

Maj. Gen. G. H. THOMAS,
Commanding in the Field:

Hood has, from the best information I get, and I believe it reliable, gone with his whole infantry force to Tupelo, West Point, and Columbus, Miss. Forrest, with what portion of his cavalry he has left, is yet at Corinth. The boats I sent down for my transportation two days since have not yet returned; I do not know what has become of them. Our rations run out on the 16th; please order some up from Clifton, if you have them. I send down one of my commissaries of subsistence to General Schofield for rations.

I am, general, very respectfully, your obedient servant,

A. J. SMITH,
Major-General.

MILITARY DIVISION OF THE MISSISSIPPI,
CAVALRY BUREAU, OFFICE OF SPECIAL INSPECTOR,
Louisville, Ky., January 13, 1865.

Maj. Gen. J. H. WILSON,
Comdg. Cavalry Corps, Military Division of the Mississippi:

GENERAL: I have the honor to acknowledge the receipt of your letter of the 5th instant, inclosing a copy of your letter of the 30th of December ultimo, addressed to Brigadier-General Whipple, assistant adjutant-general, Army of the Cumberland.   Should the future operations of your cavalry assume the shape and direction you now anticipate, and Eastport, on the Tennessee River, become a base of supplies for the army, that point is as accessible by water, or more so, from Louisville as from Nashville, with much greater facilities of transportation at the former place, besides the great saving in time, labor, and expense of shipment to Nashville and reshipment from Nashville to Eastport.   Under these circumstances, is not Louisville the proper point for the accumulation of horses, equipments, and arms for the supply of your command, even should an active campaign be immediately inaugurated ?   The Cavalry Bureau has ample means for the supply of any number of remounts you may require, and the simple question is as to the best mode of getting the horses to the commands requiring them.   Shall the men be sent to Louisville for remounts or shall the horses be shipped to the men ?   I appreciate fully the objections to sending regiments so far to the rear for equipment.   On the other hand, there are practical difficulties in the way of shipment either to Nashville or Eastport.   I have, however, submitted the latter point to General Allen, chief quartermaster Military Division of the Mississippi, and will send you his reply as soon as received.   If transportation can be had, I will send 2,000 horses to Eastport by water for Hatch's division, with as little delay as possible.   You propose sending the dismounted men north of the Ohio River with power to impress horses, provided authority is received for that object.   Would this not consume as much, or more, time as to send them to Louisville ?   The horses can be had here.   The delay heretofore has been caused more by the want of arms and equipments than from any other cause.   I fully concur with you as to the wisdom of the policy you propose for the recuperation of broken-down, diseased, or enfeebled cavalry stock, and had, previous to the reception of your letter, taken measures for the inauguration of a system on that subject.   The following extract from a letter of instructions addressed by me to Captain Wilson, acting assistant quartermaster, cavalry depot at Nashville, will put you in possession of my views on that head:

Stabling for the accommodation of only 4,000 horses, with store-rooms, shops, &c., upon the same scale is the extent to which you are limited at present.   So soon as these are completed I expect you to have on hand constantly about 4,000 horses—2,000 of these will be first-class serviceable cavalry horses, and 2,000 first-class unserviceable.   The first-class, serviceable, to be shipped to you from time to time from this depot.   (The number of first-class unserviceable can be increased if you (General Wilson) should so advise.)   The unserviceable to be kept for recuperation. You will understand that, until otherwise directed by the Cavalry Bureau, the main depot will be at Louisville.   Horses easily recuperated, and which can be put in serviceable condition in a short time, is the only class of unserviceable cavalry stock to be kept at Nashville.   All others (except such as are not worth transporting there, to be sold by you at Nashville) are to be shipped at once to Louisville to Capt. John T. Allen, assistant quartermaster, cavalry depot at that place.   An inspector will inspect all unserviceable cavalry horses received at Nashville and divide them into four classes. First class: Horses but slightly injured, or such as only require rest, good forage, and good grooming for a short time, say thirty days (this time can be increased, if General Wilson thinks it best), to be made fit for reissue, these to be kept at Nashville, and recuperated at your depot.   Second class: All horses unserviceable, but which are capable of being recuperated and made fit for reissue, but not coming under the head of first-class unserviceable, as above defined (this class of stock I would here remark would require from three to four months to recuperate), to be shipped to Captain Allen, assistant quartermaster, depot at Louisville.   Third class: Horses so broken down, injured, or otherwise in condition not capable of recuperation so as to be made fit for reissue, but which would pay for shipment to Louisville for sale, to be sent to Captain Allen, assistant quartermaster, &c., to be sold by him at public auction.   Fourth class: Horses comparatively worthless, and which would not pay for shipment to Louisville, there to be condemned and sold at public auction at Nashville by the quartermaster of the depot.

The depot at Louisville is governed by the same rules, and is expected to be increased so as to accommodate 8,000 horses—5,000 of these to be first-class serviceable, and 3,000 first-class unserviceable. Second class unservicable to be sent to pasture for a time and transferred to first-class unserviceable, as soon as their condition places them under that head. Transfers from the lower to the higher class, and from unserviceable to serviceable, at both depots, will be made as often as the condition of the stock will justify.

I am fully impressed, I assure you, general, with the importance of arming all the cavalry of the Military Division of the Mississippi with the Spencer carbine, and no effort on my part will be spared to attain that end. Immediately on the reception of your former communication on that subject I forwarded the same, with a letter indorsing your views, to the Cavalry Bureau at Washington, with the request to be informed as early as practicable as to what number of that arm I might hope to receive monthly for issue to the cavalry of this military division. Major Price, assistant inspector-general cavalry, replied under date December 29:

I have requested the shipment of 1,200 Spencer carbines from Saint Louis to Louisville. They should reach you in a few days. I am unable to inform you at present of the number that can be forwarded per month, but will be able to notify you in a short time.

With regard to Upton's division, I am ready at any moment to issue to him whatever number of horses, equipments, and arms he may require to put his division in complete order. His requisitions have not yet been received at this office. He has not yet been able to concentrate his command, and at this time has only detachment of a few regiments here—in all, about 1,200 men. I presume he has himself fully advised you of his situation and movements. Knipe's division I shall endeavor to mount and equip at Nashville, but the transportation to be commanded for the shipment of horses is limited and often uncertain. I cannot, therefore, with any degree of certainty, say how long it will require to fit that division out. You may rest assured that all will be done within the compass of the means at my command.

I am, general, very respectfully, your obedient servant,
W. P. CHAMBLISS,
Major Fourth U. S. Cavalry,
Special Inspector of Cavalry, Mil. Div. of the Mississippi.

HEADQUARTERS FIRST DIVISION, CAVALRY CORPS,
MILITARY DIVISION OF THE MISSISSIPPI,
Columbia, Tenn., January 13, 1865.

Maj. E. B. BEAUMONT,
Nashville:

No pontoons have been so far received here. River never low enough in winter for our trains to ford. Rations enough.
L. D. WATKINS,
Brevet Brigadier-General.

CIRCULAR.] HDQRS. CAVALRY CORPS, MIL. DIV. OF THE MISS.,
Waterloo, Ala., January 13, 1865.

The Cavalry Corps will march to-morrow, at 8 a. m., to permanent camps in the neighborhood of Gravelly Springs. Division and brigade commanders will direct their inspectors to precede their commands, and report to the inspector of the corps that the ground for their camps may be assigned. The march will be in the order the command is now encamped.

By command of Brevet Major-General Wilson:

HENRY E. NOYES,
Lieutenant and Acting Assistant Adjutant-General.

SPECIAL ORDERS, }   HDQRS. POST OF MURFREESBOROUGH,
No. 13.   }   *Murfreesborough, Tenn., January 13, 1865.*

*   *   *   *   *   *   *

III. Col. M. B. Houghton, Third Michigan Infantry, is hereby ordered to proceed with his command by rail to Huntsville, Ala., to report to Brigadier-General Wood, commanding Fourth Army Corps. He will report all sick that are unable to travel to the medical director of this post, being careful to provide the surgeon in charge of the hospital with the descriptive roll of each man. He will turn over all surplus ordnance and ordnance stores (serviceable) to Lieut. Ed. S. Wheat, ordnance officer of this post. He will march to the depot at — o'clock, and embark as soon as the train is ready.

IV. Col. J. W. Hall, Fourth Michigan Infantry, is hereby ordered to proceed with his command by rail to Huntsville, Ala., to report to Brigadier-General Wood, commanding Fourth Army Corps. He will report all sick who are unable to travel to the medical director of this post, being careful to provide the surgeon in charge of hospital with a descriptive roll of each man. He will turn over all surplus ordnance and ordnance stores (serviceable) to Lieut. Ed. S. Wheat, ordnance officer of this post. He will march to the depot at — o'clock to-morrow morning, and embark as soon as the train is ready.

By command of Brigadier-General Van Cleve:

H. H. SHEETS,
Acting Assistant Adjutant-General.

HEADQUARTERS DISTRICT OF THE ETOWAH,
Chattanooga, January 13, 1865.
Brigadier-General CRUFT,
Larkinsville :

Send Colonel Mitchell's and Colonel Salm's commands forward at once, and Colonel Malloy's command to Stevenson. Railroad agents must not be permitted to delay your movements.

JAMES B. STEEDMAN,
Major-General.

HEADQUARTERS DISTRICT OF THE ETOWAH,
Chattanooga, January 13, 1865.
COMMANDING OFFICER,
Dalton :

Trains leave here this morning with troops to relieve the troops of the Fifteenth and Seventeenth Army Corps, Army of the Tennessee. Be ready to return with trains without delay.

JAMES B. STEEDMAN,
Major-General.

HEADQUARTERS DISTRICT OF THE ETOWAH,
Chattanooga, January 13, 1865.

Captain MEAD,
    Commanding, Tunnel Hill:

You will move to Dalton to-day, taking only the troops of the Fifteenth and Seventeenth Army Corps, leaving the Fourteenth and Twentieth Army Corps. The troops of your command this side of Tunnel Hill have been relieved, and are now on their way here. Troops in block-houses south of you, if belonging to Army of the Tennessee, you will bring with you, reporting fact to Colonel Mitchell, at Dalton. Answer how you understand this.

By command of Major-General Steedman:

S. B. MOE,
Major and Assistant Adjutant-General.

TUNNEL HILL, *January 13, 1865.*

Maj. S. B. MOE,
    Assistant Adjutant-General:

I understand that I am to take troops of Fifteenth and Seventeenth Corps and proceed to Dalton at once, without reference to relief, taking the troops of same corps at block-houses between here and Dalton.

G. L. PARK,
Captain, Commanding.

CLEVELAND, *January 13, 1865.*

Maj. S. B. MOE,
    Assistant Adjutant-General:

Arrived here at daylight this morning. Now relieving Colonel Boughton's men. Lieutenant-Colonel Bishop has gone to Charleston with 200 men. Arrived there at 9.30 a. m.

C. J. DILWORTH,
Colonel, Commanding.

LEXINGTON, *January 13, 1865.*

Major SLATER,
    Eleventh Kentucky [Cavalry], Lebanon, Ky.:

Move with your detachment to-morrow morning, via Saloma, Pitmansville, Buffalo, and Hodgensville, to Elizabethtown. Scout the country thoroughly on your arrival at Elizabethtown. Report to General Ewing, at Louisville, for orders. Carry rations with you for three days.

By order of Brigadier-General Hobson:

J. S. BUTLER,
Assistant Adjutant-General.

MEMPHIS, *January 13, 1865.*
(Received 16th.)

Major-General THOMAS,
    Eastport:

I have information that Hood's headquarters are at Columbus, Miss. He has furloughed most of his men until the 25th or 30th of January.

Forrest is at Tupelo, and has furloughed his West Tennessee and Mississippi troops, to enable them to trade in cotton and procure supplies. These measures were necessary in order to feed the troops, owing to destruction of their communications.

> N. J. T. DANA,
> *Major-General.*

HEADQUARTERS ARMY OF THE CUMBERLAND,
Clifton, Tenn., January 14, 1865—10.30 a. m.
(Received 12.20 a. m. 16th.)

Maj. Gen. H. W. HALLECK,
Washington, D. C.:

I arrived here this morning, and from all I can learn Hood has gone south of Corinth. Accordingly, General Schofield's corps, in obedience to your orders, has been ordered to Annapolis, and will commence embarking to-morrow.

> GEO. H. THOMAS,
> *Major-General, Commanding.*

LOUISVILLE, KY., *January 14, 1865—2 p. m.*

Hon. C. A. DANA,
Assistant Secretary of War:

Arrived here last night. Nothing here from General Thomas or General Schofield. The telegraph will not be open beyond Nashville till to-morrow. The necessary boats are ordered to rendezvous at Paducah. I go to Paducah to-night. Will be there to-morrow night, and move up Tuesday, unless counter orders come. Is it decided about moving artillery? The horses can be moved so far as the boats go without much difficulty. Rivers are high, and still rising slowly. Present prospects good. Telegraph can reach me at Paducah.

> LEWIS B. PARSONS,
> *Colonel and Chief of Railroad Transportation.*

SPECIAL FIELD ORDERS,⎫ HDQRS. DEPT. OF THE CUMBERLAND,
　　No. 11.　　　　⎬ 　　*Steamer Tarascon, January 14, 1865.*

I. In obedience to telegraphic orders from the lieutenant-general commanding the Armies of the United States, that portion of the Twenty-third Army Corps, Maj. Gen. J. M. Schofield commanding, now serving with him in the field is relieved from duty in the Military Division of the Mississippi, and will proceed with as little delay as possible to Annapolis, Md. The command will move from Clifton, Tenn., to Louisville, Ky., by water, and thence to Annapolis by such route as General Schofield may consider the most practicable. The transportation of the corps will be left behind and new furnished from Washington. The quartermaster's department will furnish the necessary transportation.

*　　　*　　　*　　　*　　　*　　　*　　　*

By command of Major-General Thomas:

> HENRY M. CIST,
> *Assistant Adjutant-General.*

SPECIAL ⎫   HEADQUARTERS ARMY OF THE OHIO,
FIELD ORDERS, ⎬   *In the Field, Clifton, Tenn.,*
No. 12. ⎭   *January 14, 1865.*

1. Special [Field] Orders, No. 7, paragraph 6, of January 9, 1865, directing the troops to move to Eastport, is hereby revoked. The troops will be prepared without delay to move by boat, with five days' rations. All wagons, ambulances, and public animals (except artillery horses, officers' private horses, and those of the escorts and mounted orderlies) will be turned over to an officer to be designated from headquarters Department of the Cumberland, at Clifton. The Third Tennessee Volunteer Infantry will remain at Clifton in charge of quartermaster's property until the same shall be removed or otherwise disposed of, when the regiment will repair to Nashville to be mustered out of service. Major-General Couch will take temporary command of the corps and direct the execution of this order and special instructions furnished him herewith.

*   *   *   *   *   *   *

5. The new forts, constructed and in progress, under the direction of Lieut. Col. J. H. Simpson, Corps of Engineers, U. S. Army, in Kentucky, will be as follows:

Louisville, commencing at the extreme right and extending in the following order to the left of the line: Fort Elstner, after Lieut. Col. George R. Elstner, Fiftieth Ohio Infantry, killed in action near Utoy Creek, Ga., August 8, 1864; Fort Engle, after Capt. Archibald H. Engle, aide-de-camp on the staff of Major-General Schofield, and captain Thirteenth U. S. Infantry, killed in battle of Resaca, Ga., May 14, 1864; Fort Saunders, after Capt. E. D. Saunders, assistant adjutant-general of volunteers, killed in action in front of Dallas, Ga., June 2, 1864; Fort Hill, after Capt. George W. Hill, Twelfth Kentucky Infantry, killed in action in front of Atlanta, Ga., August 6, 1864; Fort Horton, after Capt. M. C. Horton, One hundred and fourth Ohio Infantry, killed in action in front of Dallas, Ga., May 28, 1864; Fort McPherson, after Maj. Gen. James B. McPherson, brigadier-general, U. S. Army, killed in action before Atlanta, Ga., July 22, 1864; Fort Philpot, after Capt. J. T. Philpot, One hundred and third Ohio Infantry, killed in the battle of Resaca, Ga., May 14, 1864; Fort Saint Clair Morton, after Maj. James Saint Clair Morton, Corps of Engineers, U. S. Army, killed in an assault on Petersburg, Va., June 17, 1864; Fort Karnasch, after Second Lieut. Julius E. Karnasch, Thirty-fifth Missouri Infantry, topographical engineer on the staff of Major-General Schofield, killed in action in front of Atlanta, Ga., August 4, 1864; Fort Clark, after Lieut. Col. Mervin Clark, One hundred and eighty-third Ohio Infantry, killed in the battle of Franklin, Tenn., November 30, 1864; Fort Southworth, after Capt. A. J. Southworth, One hundred and fourth Ohio Infantry, killed in action in front of Atlanta, Ga., August 14, 1864.

Lexington: Fort Crittenden, after the late Hon. J. J. Crittenden.

Defenses of Camp Nelson: Battery Studdeford, after First Lieut. Josiah S. Studdeford, adjutant Fourth New Jersey Volunteers, killed in the battle of Crampton's Pass, Md., September 14, 1862.

Louisa: Fort Bishop, after Capt. William Bishop, One hundredth Ohio Infantry, mortally wounded in action in front of Dallas, Ga., May 28, 1864.

*   *   *   *   *   *   *

By command of Major-General Schofield:

J. A. CAMPBELL,
Major and Assistant Adjutant-General.

HEADQUARTERS ARMY OF THE OHIO,
Clifton, Tenn., January 14, 1865.

Col. WILLARD WARNER,
Commanding 180th Ohio Infantry, en route, Clifton:

COLONEL: The major-general commanding directs that if you have not passed Mount Pleasant when this order reaches you, you will return with your command and trains to Nashville, where you will await further orders. If you have passed Mount Pleasant, you will come forward. The lieutenant and escort carrying this order will remain with and receive orders from you.

Very respectfully, your obedient servant,

J. A. CAMPBELL,
Major and Assistant Adjutant-General.

HEADQUARTERS ARMY OF THE OHIO,
Clifton, Tenn., January 14, 1865.

Maj. Gen. D. N. COUCH:

GENERAL: I am about to start for Louisville to make arrangements for the transportation of the corps to Annapolis. You will please take command and move the corps by boat to Louisville, with as little delay as practicable. I will join you at Louisville, or leave further orders for you at department headquarters.

Very respectfully,

J. M. SCHOFIELD,
Major-General, Commanding.

GENERAL ORDERS, }   HDQRS. THIRD DIV., 23D ARMY CORPS,
No. 3.   }   *Clifton, Tenn., January 14, 1865.*

I. During the absence of Capt. Theodore Cox, assistant adjutant-general, Third Division, Twenty-third Army Corps, Capt. Charles D. Rhodes, acting assistant adjutant-general, Second Brigade, Third Division, Twenty-third Army Corps, will perform the duties of assistant adjutant-general of the division.

By command of Brigadier-General Cox:

THEO. COX,
Captain and Assistant Adjutant-General.

GENERAL ORDERS, } HDQRS. DIST. OF EAST TENNESSEE,
           }   AND FOURTH DIV., 23D ARMY CORPS,
No. 2.   }   *Knoxville, Tenn., January 14, 1865.*

My resignation having been accepted by the proper authority, I hereby relinquish the command of the District of East Tennessee, and Fourth Division, Twenty-third Army Corps, to Brig. Gen. Davis Tillson, U. S. Volunteers, he being the ranking officer in the division.

J. AMMEN,
Brigadier-General, U. S. Volunteers.

HEADQUARTERS DEPARTMENT OF THE OHIO,
Louisville, Ky., January 14, 1865.

Colonel WHEELER,
Comdg. Twenty-eighth Michigan Infantry, Nashville, Tenn.:

Should you be ordered from Nashville by any one other than General Schofield, please inform me at once.

G. M. BASCOM,
Lieutenant-Colonel and Assistant Adjutant-General.

SPECIAL FIELD ORDERS, No. 5.

HEADQUARTERS CAVALRY CORPS,
MILITARY DIVISION OF THE MISSISSIPPI,
Gravelly Springs, Ala., January 14, 1865.

I. Division and brigade commanders will, without delay, cause their commands to erect stabling and quarters on the ground assigned for camps. One week will be allowed for this purpose. Too much time must not be consumed in work which may be interrupted by an active campaign.

II. Commanding officers will make requisitions for and see that their troops are supplied with everything necessary for an active campaign. These estimates will be furnished without delay. Brigade and division commanders will report in writing by the 17th instant everything that may be required to render their commands efficient.

III. All duty, till further orders, must be done dismounted. Horses may be ridden to water, and orderlies at division and brigade headquarters on important duty may go mounted. Every effort must be made to recuperate the horses and mules of the command.

IV. The tactics to be used hereafter will be those of 1841, double ranks formation. Instruction in school of the trooper dismounted will be begun as soon as possible.

V. Strong guards will be established by brigade and division commanders about the camps, in order to prevent the men from leaving camp on improper purposes. Marauding and pillaging must be stopped, and for this purpose all officers of the command are authorized to shoot at once those caught in the act of stealing or destroying wantonly the property of unoffending citizens.

VI. Brigade and division commanders will not be permitted to live in the houses of the country, and enlisted men are forbidden to enter farm-houses for any purpose, unless by permission or order of a commissioned officer. Violations of this order will be punished severely.

By command of Brevet Major-General Wilson:

HENRY E. NOYES,
Lieutenant and Acting Assistant Adjutant-General.

NASHVILLE, *January 14, 1865—10.18 a. m.*
(Received 11.15 a. m.)

Brig. Gen. L. D. WATKINS,
Commanding First Division Cavalry:

Inform us whether you have crossed Duck River, and how you are off for forage.

By order, &c.:

LEVI T. GRIFFIN,
Captain and Acting Assistant Adjutant-General.

COLUMBIA, TENN., *January 14, 1865—11.30 a. m.*

Capt. LEVI T. GRIFFIN,
     Nashville:

Part of my command has crossed Duck River. The bridges were carried away, and the pontoon has not been laid, but will be to-day. Plenty of forage on railroad at Duck River.

L. D. WATKINS,
Brevet Brigadier-General, Commanding.

NASHVILLE, *January 14, 1865.*

Brig. Gen. ELI LONG:

Inform us whether you can cross Duck River, and how you are off for forage.

LEVI T. GRIFFIN,
Captain and Acting Assistant Adjutant-General.

GENERAL ORDERS, } FORCES FOR DEFENSE OF TENNESSEE
   No. 1.   }   AND ALABAMA RAILROAD,
               Columbia, Tenn., January 14, 1865.

In accordance with orders from headquarters Department of the Cumberland, the undersigned assumes command of the troops for the defense of the Tennessee and Alabama Railroad, from Nashville to the State line, and announces the following officers as composing his staff: Capt. E. T. Wells, U. S. Volunteers, assistant adjutant-general; First Lieut. L. T. Morris, Nineteenth U. S. Infantry, aide-de-camp; First Lieut. W. R. Lowe, Nineteenth U. S. Infantry, aide-de-camp; Capt. E. D. Baker, U. S. Volunteers, assistant quartermaster; Captain Wilcox, U. S. Volunteers, commissary of subsistence; Capt. T. F. Allen, Seventh Ohio Cavalry, inspector; Capt. J. J. Kessler, Forty-ninth Ohio Infantry, provost-marshal; First Lieut. R. A. McKee, Fifth Iowa Cavalry, ordnance officer. The headquarters of this command will be at Pulaski, Tenn. The post commanders at Franklin and Columbia will forward their returns and reports required by existing orders without delay.

R. W. JOHNSON,
Brigadier-General, U. S. Volunteers.

SPECIAL ORDERS, }   HDQRS. DISTRICT OF THE ETOWAH,
  No. 10.   }   *Chattanooga, January 14, 1865.*

I. In pursuance of orders creating the First Separate Division, Army of the Cumberland, the Eighteenth Ohio Infantry, Twenty-ninth Indiana Infantry, Forty-fourth Indiana Infantry, Sixty-eighth Indiana Infantry, Fifteenth Wisconsin Infantry, Capt. P. Wassem's detachment of the Thirty-second Indiana Infantry, and Lieutenant Puckett's detachment of Eighth Kentucky Infantry, will constitute the Second Brigade of the above division. Lieutenant-Colonel Grosvenor, Eighteenth Ohio Volunteers, and senior officer on duty with the brigade, will assume its command. Returns and reports required by existing orders will be made to these headquarters, also to the post commander for his information, who is authorized to make orders on the brigade commander for such details as may be necessary for the conduct of the business of the post.

*   *   *   *   *   *   *

By command of Major-General Steedman:

S. B. MOE,
Major and Assistant Adjutant-General.

BRIDGEPORT, *January 14, 1865—2.50 p. m.*

Major-General STEEDMAN:

Just returned from below. The fleet has captured in all about 15 prisoners, 30 horses and saddles, and a lot of arms. The rebels thoroughly disorganized, and a very small cavalry force could pick up the whole command. General Cruft has withdrawn his force, and now the rebels can wait their leisure about crossing. I keep my vessels there still, but the people in the neighborhood conceal the rebels.

M. FORREST,
Commanding Eleventh District, Mississippi Squadron.

CLEVELAND, *January 14, 1865.*

Maj. S. B. MOE,
Assistant Adjutant-General:

A reliable citizen reports that about 100 mounted guerrillas crossed the railroad at Varnell's Station this morning at 11 o'clock. They were going toward Chattanooga.

C. J. DILWORTH,
Colonel, Commanding.

BRIDGEPORT, *January 14, 1865.*

Maj. S. B. MOE,
Assistant Adjutant-General:

In compliance with your order of the 8th instant, I assumed command of the post at Bridgeport, Ala., immediately after my arrival, and will report to you in person to-morrow.

FELIX PRINCE SALM,
Colonel, Commanding Post.

TULLAHOMA, *January 14, 1865.*

Major-General STEEDMAN:

Arrived here safe. Colonel Mather's [Malloy's] command passed here 2 p. m. Carried through Stevenson by the conductor in spite of the remonstrances of the lieutenant-colonel commanding. I will have him arrested at Nashville.

T. F. MEAGHER,
Brigadier-General, Commanding.

HEADQUARTERS FORAGING EXPEDITION,
Dutch Bottom, Tenn., January 14, 1865.

Brig. Gen. D. TILLSON,
   Comdg. 2d Brig., 4th Div., 23d Army Corps, Knoxville, Tenn.:

GENERAL: I have the honor to report that the expedition is now at this place gathering the forage in the bottom, and putting it in cribs on the river-bank, in compliance with orders received by Mr. Wild. I would also submit to you the following facts, *i. e.*: The fords on the rivers above us are now passable, and General Vaughn is first on one side of the river and then on the other with from 400 to 500 men, and the independent scouts and guerrillas number about 130 men of the most desperate character, some of whom have been sometimes in sight. There is no force at all above us, and, in fact, none hardly at supporting distance. The First Ohio Heavy Artillery are still at Dandridge, but the French Broad cannot be crossed anywhere between here and there, and then it is eleven miles below us, the nearest route. The Fourth Tennessee Infantry is still at Evans' Island, twenty miles below here. It is only twenty-seven miles to Greeneville, the headquarters of General Vaughn, and eight miles to Newport, where the scouts congregate. In gathering the forage in this valley it is necessary that the force should be scattered sometimes, and as it is every time we do so it exposes us to an attack that might prove disastrous to us. With an addition to the cavalry force I could keep up a more systematic manner of scouting the country, but as it is the forty-five men that I now have are kept so busy that they are injuring their horses. Up the river and on the Pigeon and Crosby there is any quantity of corn and fodder that we cannot touch, owing to the impossibility of hauling it to some accessible place for the boats, and as that is the home of the bushwhackers, and where they keep their stock, and throughout a most damnably secession hole, I would suggest the propriety of sending up quite a cavalry force to live off that country, and either drive out those guerrillas or make the country untenable for any rebel force. There is almost forage enough to fatten all the horses at Knoxville in that section of country, that would have to be left for the benefit of our enemies otherwise. I have not sent Companies D and I of my regiment to Knoxville as yet, because I do not deem the position here as a safe one for so small a force as I would then have. None of the boats have reported yet, and as to our cribbing the corn and leaving it on the banks of the river, the idea is ludicrous, as we would not leave them an hour before they would be burned or destroyed, and I durst not divide my force to guard it. I would respectfully call your attention to the fact that Lieutenant Hall, under my direction, has been acting assistant commissary of subsistence for the expedition. I was obliged to appoint one, as Mr. Wild, the forage agent, received orders not to receipt for any more commissary stores, and we had to live. I have the honor to request that you use your influence in procuring an order appointing him an acting assistant commissary of subsistence, to bear date January 1, 1865. The scouts report that the guerrillas have sent to Asheville for ammunition— their being out of which has kept them quiet; but I have no doubt that when they get a supply we will be bothered with them, as they are remarkably active, almost daily visible, in squads of fifteen to thirty, and always run when fired upon. Their intention seems to be to locate our picket-posts and surprise them. We are equally watchful, and do not intend for them to outwit us in the least; but, in order to prevent surprise, it is necessary to guard the approaches over an extent of three miles on the land side, while we have a guard at the ford on

French Broad, and with a less number of men than we now have it would be utterly impossible to do it. I am impelled, under these circumstances, to earnestly request that two companies of the Tenth Michigan Cavalry be ordered to report to me as soon as practicable.

I am, sir, very respectfully, your obedient servant,

JOHN A. SHANNON,
Colonel, Commanding.

HDQRS. FIRST DIVISION, MILITARY DIST. OF KENTUCKY,
Lexington, Ky., January 14, 1865.

Maj. J. F. HERRICK,
Commanding Twelfth Ohio Volunteer Cavalry:

The general directs that you move with your regiment to Richmond, Ky., to-morrow, and make the headquarters of the regiment at that point. You will send detachments of your command to such points as you deem best in the counties of Madison, Garrard, Lincoln, Casey, Pulaski, Estill, Rockcastle, Laurel, Jackson, and Owsley, and give protection to the counties and citizens by hunting guerrillas and prowling bands of thieves. You will keep your men under good discipline and communicate with them by courier. Any important news will be telegraphed to these headquarters. One company of your regiment will be left at Lexington, Ky., and ordered to report to commandant of post for duty.

Very respectfully, your obedient servant,

J. S. BUTLER,
Assistant Adjutant-General.

EASTPORT, MISS., *January 15, 1865—12 m.*
(Received 5 p. m. 16th.)

Maj. Gen. H. W. HALLECK,
Washington, D. C.:

Arrived at this place this morning. Major-General Smith reports that Hood has gone, with his whole infantry force, to Tupelo, West Point, and Columbus, Miss. Forrest is at and about Okolona with his main force, with small advance parties at Jacinto, Boonville, and Corinth. Forrest's command, as well as Hood's infantry force, is said to be very much broken up and in a disorganized condition. We have had very heavy rains, making the roads almost impracticable. The Tennessee River is also very high, which makes it quite convenient for us to get supplies here, as the largest class of steamers can readily ascend to this point.

GEO. H. THOMAS,
Major-General, Commanding.

EASTPORT, MISS., *January 15, 1865—12 m.*
(Received 6 p. m. 16th.)

Major-General HALLECK,
Washington, D. C.:

The fleet is ready for the troops of Major-General Schofield's corps to embark, which he is now doing. He will proceed to his destination as rapidly as possible.

GEO. H. THOMAS,
Major-General, Commanding.

EASTPORT, MISS., *January 15, 1865—12 m.*
(Received 6 p. m. 16th.)

Maj. Gen. H. W. HALLECK,
       Washington, D. C.:

I would respectfully ask permission from the Department to send to Washington the officers and enlisted men belonging to my army who have captured battle-flags and other trophies from the enemy in the recent battles in Tennessee. I desire to send them with the captured trophies to be delivered at the War Office.

GEO. H. THOMAS,
Major-General, Commanding.

WAR DEPARTMENT,
Washington City, January 15, 1865.

Col. L. B. PARSONS,
       Paducah:

General Thomas telegraphed on the 11th that he would have Schofield's corps assembled at Eastport by yesterday. Of the artillery, the men alone are to be moved.

C. A. DANA,
Assistant Secretary of War.

SPECIAL ORDERS, }   HDQRS. DETACH. ARMY OF THE TENN.,
       No. 12.   }   *Eastport, Miss., January 15, 1865.*

I. The Thirty-fourth New Jersey Infantry Volunteers, Col. William Hudson Lawrence commanding, having reported at these headquarters, is hereby assigned to the Third Brigade, Second Division, and will forthwith report to Col. E. H. Wolfe, commanding Third Brigade, for orders.

*   *   *   *   *   *   *

By order of Maj. Gen. A. J. Smith:

J. HOUGH,
Major and Assistant Adjutant-General.

HEADQUARTERS DEPARTMENT OF THE CUMBERLAND,
Eastport, Miss., January 15, 1865.

Maj. Gen. J. H. WILSON,
       Comdg. Cavalry Corps, Mil. Div. of the Miss., Waterloo, Ala.:

GENERAL: The major-general commanding directs that you detail a party of twenty men to escort a flag of truce to the rebel lines, and that they be crossed to the south bank of the river at this place. It is desirable to send an officer in charge of the flag who is shrewd, observant, and has a good eye for topography. You will detail this officer, and, when ready to start, direct him to report at these headquarters for his communications and instructions. The party should go prepared for a trip of several days' duration, say ten, as it will not be sent by way of Corinth, and might not be halted for several days on any other road upon which it may be sent.

Very respectfully, your obedient servant,

WM. D. WHIPPLE,
Brigadier-General and Chief of Staff.

HEADQUARTERS DEPARTMENT OF THE CUMBERLAND,
Eastport, Miss., January 15, 1865.

Maj. Gen. J. H. WILSON,
Comdg. Cavalry Corps, Mil. Div. of the Miss., Waterloo :

GENERAL: The major-general commanding directs that you place one brigade of cavalry on the south bank of the river, prepared for a reconnaissance to Corinth. When ready have it reported to the major-general commanding, as he desires to accompany it. Let it be crossed below the mouth of Bear Creek, where boats are most convenient.

Very respectfully, your obedient servant,

WM. D. WHIPPLE,
Brigadier-General and Chief of Staff.

HEADQUARTERS SECOND DIVISION CAVALRY,
Near Columbia, Tenn., January 15, 1865.

Capt. LEVI T. GRIFFIN,
Acting Assistant Adjutant-General :

I will not be able to cross the river before the 19th. Have no forage, and there is none in the country. Will want forage for 8,000 animals to include the 19th, four days, and four days' of grain to start from here with in our train on the 19th. Stir up the quartermaster's department. There is no forage here for Minty's brigade to-night, and they promised to send it.

ELI LONG,
Brigadier-General.

CHRISTIANA, *January 15, 1865.*

Major-General STEEDMAN:

Have come up with two battalions of Colonel Malloy's command; the balance gone on. Will send the conductor back to you for punishment. Have ordered troops to follow my train.

T. F. MEAGHER,
Brigadier-General, Commanding.

MURFREESBOROUGH, *January 15, 1865.*

Major-General STEEDMAN:

Just arrived here. A battalion and half of Malloy's command is still ahead. Have telegraphed to the officer in command to halt on his arrival at Nashville depot until I shall come. It was Mr. Bryant, at Stevenson, who ordered our troop trains forward.

THOMAS FRANCIS MEAGHER,
Brigadier-General.

MURFREESBOROUGH, *January 15, 1865.*

Major-General STEEDMAN:

Have reached this place; overtaken all the command; was delayed, owing to an engine running from the track. The command well in hand. Will reach Nashville this evening.

T. F. MEAGHER,
Brigadier-General, Commanding.

MURFREESBOROUGH, *January 15, 1865.*

Major-General STEEDMAN:

The train containing Colonel Malloy's command, which was ahead, has backed down and follows headquarters train, so that the command is in line, headquarters in advance.

THOMAS FRANCIS MEAGHER,
Brigadier-General, Commanding.

HEADQUARTERS DEPARTMENT OF THE CUMBERLAND,
Eastport, Miss., January 16, 1865.

C. A. DANA,
Assistant Secretary of War, Washington, D. C.:

Your telegrams of 10.55 a. m. and 2 p. m. of the 11th instant have been received. I have no additional reliable news from Hood since my last report, but hope to know more of his position in a few days.

GEO. H. THOMAS,
Major-General, U. S. Army, Commanding.

WASHINGTON, D. C., *January 16, 1865—12.30 p. m.*

Lieutenant-General GRANT,
City Point:

There are no accommodations whatever for additional troops at Annapolis, and if General Schofield's corps is to stop there any time they must suffer greatly in this weather. Here and at Alexandria we can give shelter to all without additional expense. I would therefore suggest that they be brought here till transports are ready for them either at Annapolis or Alexandria.

H. W. HALLECK,
Major-General and Chief of Staff.

CITY POINT, VA., *January 16, 1865—3.30 p. m.*

Major-General HALLECK,
Chief of Staff, Washington:

Annapolis was named as the destination of Schofield's corps for the reason that it was most favorable for embarkation, and it was supposed that by the time it reached there present operations would develop the point most important to send it. If you deem it best, however, you may change its destination to Alexandria.

U. S. GRANT,
Lieutenant-General.

HEADQUARTERS DEPARTMENT OF THE CUMBERLAND,
Eastport, Miss., January 16, 1865—9 p. m.
(Received 10 p. m. 18th.)

Maj. Gen. H. W. HALLECK,
Washington, D. C.:

Your telegrams of 10.30 a. m. and 1.30 p. m. 12th instant, also the honorable Assistant Secretary of War's dispatch of 2 p. m. 11th instant, were received to-day. Major-General Schofield commenced embarking his troops yesterday, 15th instant. He consulted with me as to the propriety of taking his troops on boats as far up the Ohio River as possible, which I authorized him to do. I will forward him a copy of your instructions by dispatch boat, and I hope he will be able to communicate with Colonel Parsons by telegraph from Paducah and perfect the arrangements for a comfortable and speedy trip.

GEO. H. THOMAS,
Major-General, U. S. Volunteers.

SPECIAL FIELD ORDERS, ⎱ HDQRS. DEPT. OF THE CUMBERLAND,
          No. 13.   ⎰   *Eastport, Miss., January 16, 1865.*

*   *   *   *   *   *   *

III. Battery A, First Tennessee Artillery, Capt. A. F. Beach commanding, now stationed at Decatur, Ala., will proceed to Pulaski, Tenn., and report to Brigadier-General Johnson, commanding Sixth Cavalry Division, for duty.

IV. The Forty-seventh Regiment Illinois Volunteers, now at Bowling Green, is hereby relieved from duty at that place and will proceed to join its brigade at Eastport, Miss. The quartermaster's department will furnish the necessary transportation.

*   *   *   *   *   *   *

By command of Major-General Thomas:

HENRY M. CIST,
Captain and Assistant Adjutant-General.

HDQRS. FIFTH REGT. MINNESOTA VETERAN VOL. INFANTRY,
Near Eastport, Miss., January 16, 1865.

Maj. J. HOUGH,
          Asst. Adjt. Gen., Detachment Army of the Tennessee:

In reply to a communication from Maj. Gen. A. J. Smith, by Maj. J. Hough, assistant adjutant-general, addressed to Brigadier-General McArthur, commanding First Division, Detachment Army of the Tennessee, referred to me by Col. L. F. Hubbard, commanding Second Brigade, calling for explanation regarding a foraging party captured beyond the lines, I have the honor to submit the following report:

On the 15th instant I ordered a foraging party, consisting of twenty men, in charge of Capt. Orlenzo Morehouse, Company H, with three wagons, to go to the vicinity of a mill about three miles from the camp of the brigade, for the purpose of procuring lumber to build shelters for the line officers of the regiment, and procured the approval of a pass for the party by Colonel Hubbard. Captain Morehouse reports that he proceeded to said mill, and being unable to find lumber there, and being informed by a woman residing near the mill that he could find lumber a mile beyond, at an old camp-meeting ground, he proceeded on the road, sending two mounted men in advance to reconnoiter. After proceeding about three-quarters of a mile, the men he had sent forward being out of sight, he sent another man forward, mounted, to see where the others had gone, who, after going about sixty rods, discovered a body of mounted men approaching on the road, about forty in number, who wore blue overcoats, and whom he supposed to be Federal cavalry; but upon their approach he discovered that some of the force were not dressed in Federal uniform, whereupon he immediately wheeled his horse and hastily returned to inform Captain Morehouse of their approach. They closely pursued him, and just as he was communicating the intelligence to the captain they rushed upon them, firing a volley upon them. At this time, Captain Morehouse states that he was on his horse, in front of the wagons, the guard being in the wagons. He ordered the men to fall in line, but they jumped from the wagons and scattered into the woods, and he was unable to rally them, and the enemy being upon them, he made his escape as best he could, being satisfied that he could make no defense. The guard were in the wagons and wholly unprepared to repel the attack, and Captain Morehouse was directed by me to obtain the lumber this side of the creek near the mill, in going beyond which he exceeded my instructions. The reason of my not sending a larger guard was that like parties had frequently been sent to the same vicinity, both from my own and other regiments, for the purpose of getting lumber, and no danger was apprehended. Of the party sent out, Captain Morehouse and seven men escaped and returned to camp; twelve men are supposed to have been captured, together with three six-mule teams and four horses. With permission of Colonel Hubbard, I took the regiment out to-day to the place where the party were attacked to reconnoiter, and recovered two of the wagons, which I found in the woods about forty rods from the place where they were captured, in a cavalry camp lately occupied, I should judge, by from 200 to 300 men.

I have the honor to be, very respectfully, your obedient servant,

JOHN C. BECHT,
Major, Commanding Regiment.

[First indorsement.]

HEADQUARTERS SECOND BRIGADE, FIRST DIVISION,
DETACHMENT ARMY OF THE TENNESSEE,
Eastport, Miss., January 17, 1865.

Respectfully forwarded.

From the within statement it appears that Captain Morehouse had his men in the wagons at the time he was attacked, a situation certainly very unfavorable in which to make a fight. Had his men been in ranks on the road I believe his twenty muskets would have been sufficient to have repelled the enemy. It also appears that he exceeded his instructions in going so far from camp. My instructions to the command were to allow no foraging parties to venture beyond the creek near Dexter's Mill, about three miles from this point. The practice had been to send from twenty to thirty men with a single wagon, and in no instance but this had more than one wagon been sent out with a single detail; and the pass approved at these headquarters in this case did not authorize the sending of three wagons. Yesterday morning I directed Major Becht to take his regiment to the point where the affair occurred, to reconnoiter and ascertain if any of his men had been killed or wounded. He found no evidence of any casualties of that character, or indications of an enemy further than he mentions. He recovered and returned to camp with two of the captured wagons.

L. F. HUBBARD,
Colonel, Commanding.

[Second indorsement.]

HEADQUARTERS FIRST DIVISION,
DETACHMENT ARMY OF THE TENNESSEE,
Eastport, Miss., January 17, 1865.

Respectfully forwarded.

The instructions for passing pickets, when the First Division came to Eastport, was that the approval of brigade commanders was sufficient, and such has been the rule until the 16th instant, when the instructions were changed.

J. McARTHUR,
Brigadier-General, Commanding.

CIRCULAR.] HDQRS. CAVALRY CORPS, MIL. DIV. OF THE MISS.,
Gravelly Springs, Ala., January 16, 1865.

Division and brigade commanders will send to these headquarters without delay the trophies and reports called for in the official copy of circular from General Thomas' headquarters, and dated Pulaski, Tenn., December 27.

By order of General Wilson:

HENRY E. NOYES,
Lieutenant and Acting Assistant Inspector-General.

HDQRS. CAVALRY CORPS, MIL. DIV. OF THE MISSISSIPPI,
Gravelly Springs, Ala., January 16, 1865.

Brigadier-General CROXTON,
Commanding Brigade:

GENERAL: Immediately on the receipt of this, you will take the effective men of your command and cross the river at the Eastport ferry. After selecting a camp for your brigade, you will report for orders to Major-General Thomas. There is a probability that you may be ordered to remain on the south bank of the river. Commence crossing early to-morrow morning, and be prepared for a reconnaissance toward Corinth.

By order of General Wilson:

HENRY E. NOYES,
Lieutenant and Acting Assistant Inspector-General.

HDQRS. CAVALRY CORPS, MIL. DIV. OF THE MISSISSIPPI,
Gravelly Springs, Ala., January 16, 1865.

Brig. Gen. R. W. JOHNSON,
Commanding Sixth Division, Cavalry Corps:

GENERAL: You will please order Battery I, Fourth U. S. Artillery, to report here at once. General Brannan, chief of artillery, Department of the Cumberland, has ordered another battery to report to you in its place.

By order of General Wilson:

HENRY E. NOYES,
Lieutenant and Acting Assistant Inspector-General.

HDQRS. DEFENSES NASHVILLE AND CHATTANOOGA R. R.,
Tullahoma, January 16, 1865.

Maj. B. H. POLK,
Assistant Adjutant-General, District of Tennessee:

MAJOR: I have the honor to submit the following statement and suggestions regarding the Fifth Regiment Tennessee Volunteer Cavalry for the consideration and action of the major-general commanding the District of Tennessee: When I took command of the defenses of this road, in June, 1864, the Fifth Tennessee Cavalry was stationed at this post. I found it camped outside of the picket-line of the post, men and officers boarding at private houses, inside and out of the lines. I found that officers and men were absent at home and elsewhere without authority. In fact, I found the regiment utterly void of order and discipline. I at once made it a specialty with my then acting assistant inspector-general (Captain Baird) to try and reduce the regiment to some sort of discipline, and to this purpose he worked faithfully, but without any perceptible benefit. I have tried every means known to me to bring about order and efficiency in the regiment, but have not been rewarded with success, even unto this day. In fact, the regiment is as far from being an efficient organization as it was in June. The field officers seem to have no conception of their obligations and duties; have no control over their subordinates or men. Officers and men absent themselves without authority whenever they take the notion to visit their homes. The regiment is about 800 strong, and the largest number that can be paraded in camp at any time will not exceed 200. Most of the 600 absentees are unaccounted for. I have been informed that Colonel Stokes was able to keep the men together, and did hold them under reasonable discipline. I therefore suggest that Colonel Stokes be ordered back to his regiment, because without him the regiment is a rabble and entirely worthless to the service. I further suggest that even if Colonel Stokes is ordered back to his regiment, that it be sent beyond the State of Tennessee—clear beyond the reach of their homes—as a sure means of making them of service to the Government. Many of the officers and men live within one or two days' ride of this place, and so long as they are so situated they will be worthless as soldiers. I respectfully request that this regiment be ordered away from my command, and that a regiment of cavalry from some other State be sent in its stead.

I am, major, very respectfully, your obedient servant,

R. H. MILROY,
Major-General.

NASHVILLE, *January 16, 1865.*

Major-General STEEDMAN,
Commanding District of the Etowah:

GENERAL: Headquarters arrived last night at 7 o'clock. Malloy's and Boughton's commands comfortably camped at Rains' house, one mile outside the artillery. From dispatch received from Stevenson, which reported Colonel Culver there with his brigade at 2.12 p. m. yesterday, I shall have the entire division on board by to-morrow by 2 p. m. at the latest, with the addition of over 200 of the Eighteenth Wisconsin Volunteers, which General Miller desires me to take with me. Shall telegraph to you further particulars a little later. Fully expect to leave this for Louisville to-morrow, Tuesday, morning early.

THOMAS FRANCIS MEAGHER,
Brigadier-General, Commanding Division.

HEADQUARTERS DISTRICT OF TENNESSEE,
Nashville, Tenn., January 16, 1865.

Col. C. R. THOMPSON,
Commanding Brigade U. S. Colored Troops:

COLONEL: The major-general commanding directs that the Twelfth U. S. Colored Infantry proceed without delay and take post on the Northwestern Railroad. They will be so placed as to afford protection to the construction parties on that road, and give aid, as much as possible, toward the rapid completion of it. They will move out with the advance parties of workmen.

I am, colonel, very respectfully, your obedient servant,

B. H. POLK,
Major and Assistant Adjutant-General.

BRIDGEPORT, *January 16, 1865.*

Maj. S. B. MOE,
Assistant Adjutant-General:

On my return here I learned from reliable source that guerrillas infest again the country between here and Shellmound. Some citizens living in the neighborhood are suspected to be in connivance with them. They came as near as a mile from our lines. I have taken the necessary measures to stop the nuisance, and will report again when they are successful.

FELIX PRINCE SALM,
Colonel, Commanding.

HEADQUARTERS DEPARTMENT OF THE CUMBERLAND,
Eastport, January 16, 1865. (Via Paducah.)

Major-General STEEDMAN:

The major-general commanding directs me to say he has to-day received a report from James G. Brown, Dalton, relative to certain movements of the rebels southeast of Dalton, and also to inquire whether you have learned anything of such movements; and if so to make a report of them, with all the information you can gather on the subject. The major-general commanding directs that you send in to these headquarters as soon as possible a full report of your operations from the time you left Chattanooga to take part in the campaign before Nashville up to the time of your return to Chattanooga.

ROBT. H. RAMSEY,
Assistant Adjutant-General.

WASHINGTON, *January 17, 1865—2.30 p. m.*

Lieutenant-General GRANT,
City Point, Va.:

I presumed that your order in regard to Schofield's corps was intended to supersede that in relation to General A. J. Smith's command, and that the latter was to remain with General Thomas. Was I right?

H. W. HALLECK,
Major-General and Chief of Staff.

CITY POINT, *January 17, 1865.*
(Received 6.10 p. m.)

Major-General HALLECK,
            Chief of Staff:

Your understanding of my orders, as expressed in your dispatch of 2.30 to-day, is correct.

U. S. GRANT,
            Lieutenant-General.

WASHINGTON, D. C., *January 17, 1865—10 a. m.*

Major-General THOMAS,
            Eastport, Miss.:

Schofield's corps will come to Washington, instead of Annapolis. Please notify them of the change.

H. W. HALLECK,
            Major-General and Chief of Staff.

WASHINGTON, *January 17, 1865—11.30 a. m.*

Major-General THOMAS,
            Eastport, Miss.:

The Secretary of War authorizes you to send to Washington officers and men who distinguished themselves by the capture of flags, &c., in battle. The number should be limited to the most distinguished. They will be sent with General Schofield's corps, and under a commissioned officer, to be responsible for the discipline and order en route.

H. W. HALLECK,
            Major-General and Chief of Staff.

WASHINGTON, D. C., *January 17, 1865—3 p. m.*

Major-General THOMAS,
            Eastport:

Please telegraph as early as possible about the strength of Schofield's command to come here; also, about the number of batteries of artillery to be supplied here.

H. W. HALLECK,
            Major-General and Chief of Staff.

HEADQUARTERS DEPARTMENT OF THE CUMBERLAND,
            Eastport, Miss., January 17, 1865.

Maj. Gen. H. W. HALLECK,
            Chief of Staff, U. S. Army, Washington, D. C.:

I respectfully recommend and request that the troops now commanded by Maj. Gen. A. J. Smith be organized as an army corps. Major-General Smith's ability as a corps commander is unquestionable, and the soldierly qualities of his troops entitle them to a corps organization.

I have the honor to be, general, very respectfully, your obedient servant,

GEO. H. THOMAS,
            Major-General, U. S. Army, Commanding.

WAR DEPARTMENT,
January 17, 1865.

Col. L. B. PARSONS,
Paducah:

Schofield's corps is to be taken to Alexandria, instead of Annapolis.

C. A. DANA,
Assistant Secretary of War.

HEADQUARTERS DEPARTMENT OF THE CUMBERLAND,
Eastport, Miss., January 17, 1865.

Major WILLETT,
*First Regiment Veteran Volunteer Engineers,
In charge of Engineer Department, Nashville:*

MAJOR: The major-general commanding directs that the pontoon train now at Nashville be sent to this place, and that one-half of the train be turned over to Major-General Smith, commanding Detachment Army of the Tennessee, and that the other half be turned over to Maj. Gen. J. H. Wilson, commanding Cavalry Corps, Military Division of the Mississippi. The land transportation will be sent with it, and the major-general commanding desires that you will also come with it yourself.

Very respectfully, your obedient servant,

WM. D. WHIPPLE,
Brigadier-General and Chief of Staff.

GENERAL ORDERS, }   WAR DEPT., ADJT. GENERAL'S OFFICE,
No. 5.   }   *Washington, January 17, 1865.*

I. By direction of the President, the Department of the Ohio is united to that of the Cumberland, which will embrace such parts of Mississippi, Alabama, and Georgia as may be occupied by troops under the command of Major-General Thomas.

II. Major-General Schofield will turn over to General Thomas all archives, papers, &c., appertaining to the headquarters of the Department of the Ohio.

By order of the Secretary of War:

W. A. NICHOLS,
Assisting Adjutant-General.

SPECIAL FIELD ORDERS, }   HDQRS. DEPT. OF THE CUMBERLAND,
No. 14.   }   *Eastport, Miss., January 17, 1865.*

*   *   *   *   *   *   *

III. The artillery of the Detachment Army of the Tennessee, Maj. Gen. A. J. Smith commanding, will be organized into a brigade, consisting of four batteries of four guns each, two batteries of light 12-pounders, and two of 3-inch Rodmans, all under command of a chief of artillery, who will receive orders from Major-General Smith and the chief of artillery of the Army of the Cumberland. The chief of artillery of Major-General Smith's command will immediately equip his four batteries completely by transferring horses, harness, and other necessary material from the batteries ordered to Johnsonville and Paducah, turning in surplus guns to the ordnance department at Nashville, Tenn. All horses and harness belonging to batteries ordered to Johnsonville and Paducah will, after supplying the batteries of General

Smith's command, be turned in to the quartermaster's department and ordnance department at Nashville. Capt. John W. Lowell, Company G, Second Illinois Light Artillery, is appointed chief of artillery to Major-General Smith's command.

IV. The Ninth Indiana Battery will proceed to Paducah, Ky., to await orders for muster out of service. The quartermaster's department will furnish transportation.

V. The following-named batteries will proceed to Johnsonville, Tenn., and report for duty to the commanding officer of the post; the quartermaster's department will furnish transportation: Battery A, Second Missouri Artillery; Battery I, Second Missouri Artillery; and Cogswell's Independent Illinois Battery.

*   *   *   *   *   *   *

VII. The batteries of the Fourth Corps will be reduced to four four-gun batteries, to be selected by the chief of artillery of that corps. Two of the surplus batteries, to be designated by the corps commanders, will be sent to Decatur, Ala., and one to Bridgeport, Ala., dismounted, the horses and harness sent to Chattanooga and turned in to the quartermaster's department and ordnance department at that post. Battery F, First Ohio Light Artillery, will be retained as the mounted battery at Decatur, Ala.

VIII. The Kansas battery will proceed to Chattanooga, Tenn., and join the light artillery reserve, reporting to Captain Bainbridge, Fifth U. S. Artillery.

IX. The Ninth Ohio Battery, now at Bridgeport, Ala., will be dismounted. The horses and harness will be turned in to the proper departments at Chattanooga, Tenn.

X. Two mounted batteries will be stationed at Nashville as part of the garrison artillery.

By command of Major-General Thomas:

HENRY M. CIST,
Captain and Assistant Adjutant-General.

HEADQUARTERS DEPARTMENT OF THE CUMBERLAND,
Eastport, Miss., January 17, 1865.

Maj. Gen. A. J. SMITH,
Commanding Detachment Army of the Tennessee:

GENERAL: The major-general commanding desires that you will order the commanding officer of the infantry detailed for the reconnaissance to Corinth to report with his command to Brig. Gen. J. T. Croxton, commanding cavalry brigade and reconnaissance, on the Iuka road, at some point beyond and near the picket-line.

I am, general, very respectfully, your obedient servant,

WM. D. WHIPPLE,
Brigadier-General and Chief of Staff.

GENERAL ORDERS, }   HDQRS. DETACH. ARMY OF THE TENN.,
No. 3.   }   *Eastport, Miss., January 17, 1865.*

I. First Lieut. William G. Mead, Seventy-second Illinois Infantry Volunteers, is hereby announced as upon the staff of the major-general commanding as acting assistant adjutant-general, and will be respected and obeyed accordingly.

By order of Maj. Gen. A. J. Smith:

J. HOUGH,
Major and Assistant Adjutant-General.

SPECIAL ORDERS, }   HDQRS. DETACH. ARMY OF THE TENN.,
No. 14.   }   *Eastport, Miss., January 17, 1865.*

*   *   *   *   *   *   *

II. Brig. Gen. Thomas Kilby Smith, U. S. Volunteers, is hereby relieved from the command of the Third Division, Detachment Army of the Tennessee, in order to enable him to comply with telegram from the Secretary of War, to report in person, without delay, to the Adjutant-General of the Army at Washington, D. C. The quartermaster's department will furnish transportation.

III. Col. J. B. Moore, Thirty-third Wisconsin Infantry Volunteers, senior officer, is hereby temporarily assigned to, and will at once assume command of, the Third Division, Detachment Army of the Tennessee.

*   *   *   *   *   *   *

By command of Maj. Gen. A. J. Smith:

J. HOUGH,
Major and Assistant Adjutant-General.

HEADQUARTERS SECOND BRIGADE, FIRST DIVISION,
DETACHMENT ARMY OF THE TENNESSEE,
Eastport, Miss., January 17, 1865.

Maj. J. HOUGH,
Asst. Adjt. Gen., Detachment Army of the Tennessee:

MAJOR: I have the honor to herewith transmit the colors of the Fourth Mississippi Regiment, C. S. Army, captured in the battle before Nashville, on the 16th day of December, 1864. This flag was taken in the works of the enemy, in the position carried by this command, and was captured by, and surrendered to the hands of, First Lieut. and Adjt. Thomas P. Gere, Fifth Minnesota Veteran Infantry, and acting assistant adjutant-general of this brigade.

Respectfully, your obedient servant,

L. F. HUBBARD,
Colonel, Commanding.

HEADQUARTERS DETACHMENT ARMY OF THE TENNESSEE,
Eastport, Miss., January 17, 1865.

Col. J. B. MOORE,
Commanding Third Division:

COLONEL: The major-general commanding directs that you have your command in readiness and move out on the Iuka road just beyond the picket-lines to-morrow morning, January 18, at 8 o'clock, and report to Brig. Gen. J. T. Croxton.

I am, very respectfully, your obedient servant,

J. HOUGH,
Major and Assistant Adjutant-General.

HEADQUARTERS DETACHMENT ARMY OF THE TENNESSEE,
Eastport, Miss., January 17, 1865.

Brig. Gen. T. K. SMITH,
Commanding Third Division:

GENERAL: The major-general commanding directs that you have your command in readiness to move at an early hour to-morrow morning on a reconnaissance. Leaving your camps with the sick and light-duty men, you will take six days' rations—three in haversacks and three in wagons. You will also take your ambulance train, and one wagon to each regiment for cooking utensils. One battery will be sufficient. The cartridge-boxes of the men should be full, and about 30,000 rounds of ammunition taken as a reserve supply. Cavalry will accompany you, and full directions given before the time of starting. You will command the expedition.

I am, very respectfully, your obedient servant,

J. HOUGH,
Major and Assistant Adjutant-General.

HEADQUARTERS DEPARTMENT OF THE CUMBERLAND,
Eastport, Miss., January 17, 1865.

Brig. Gen. JOHN T. CROXTON,
Comdg. First Brigade, First Division, Cavalry Corps:

GENERAL: For the purpose of making the reconnaissance to Corinth there will be a force equal to a division ordered to report to you from the Detachment Army of the Tennessee. Major-general commanding directs that with this force and your own cavalry [you proceed] as far as Corinth, going by way of Iuka and Farmington. Should you find that the enemy still occupies Corinth, and uses the railroad south of that place, you will destroy the railroad bridge over Tuscumbia Creek; or if you can get to it without too much trouble, you had probably better destroy it in any event. Having accomplished this work, ascertaining at the same time all that you can concerning the present position of the enemy and his future intentions, you will return to your camp on the right bank of the river, unless other orders should be given you.

Very respectfully, your obedient servant,

WM. D. WHIPPLE,
Brigadier-General and Chief of Staff.

HUNTSVILLE, *January 17, 1865—11.10 a. m.*

General W. D. WHIPPLE,
Chief of Staff:

On arriving here from Decatur General Wood sent me in pursuit of rebel General Lyon, with directions to go to the mouth of Paint Rock. On reaching that point ascertained that General Lyon, with his artillery and most of the force, had already crossed the Tennessee River. I then got the gun-boats Generals Thomas and Sherman to cross my command, and by night march got in the rear of Lyon's entire force, which was camped near Red Hill, on the road from Warrenton to Tuscaloosa. I descended Sand Mountain at Cold Spring Gap, near Summit, and dividing my command, surprised each of the enemy's three camps a half hour before daylight on Sunday morning, capturing his artillery (one 12-pounder howitzer) and about 100 men, including 3 captains and 3 lieutenants, and also something over 100 good but jaded horses. We also captured General Lyon in his drawers and stockings, but, unfortunately, the sergeant who had charge acceded to the general's request that he should be allowed to get his pants and boots, and went back into the room with him for that purpose, when the general seized a pistol and shot the sergeant dead, and made his escape in the dark, through the back door, on foot. It is possible, however, that he is wounded, as another guard fired six shots at him, and the path by which he escaped was marked with blood. I then returned to Fort Deposit and recrossed the Tennessee River to capture the detachment left on north side, but found they had started toward Woodville in small, scattered bands on Monday night at 10 o'clock, having given up the hope of getting across the Tennessee. Several of Lyon's staff officers were arriving there. Lyon's force has been exaggerated all along. From the best information he entered Kentucky with 800 men and two pieces of artillery, crossed the Memphis and Charleston Railroad at Scottsborough, going south, with 350 men and one piece of artillery, and got across the river with 250 men, of whom we captured about 100. He will not give us much more trouble. My force in this expedition was 180 men. My loss was one sergeant, Arthur P. Lyon, the bravest soldier in my regiment.

W. J. PALMER,
Colonel Fifteenth Pennsylvania Cavalry.

(Copy forwarded by Thomas to Halleck, January 21, 1865.)

HEADQUARTERS DISTRICT OF NORTHERN ALABAMA,
Huntsville, Ala., January 17, 1865.

Maj. B. H. POLK,
Assistant Adjutant-General:

MAJOR: Telegraphic orders from General Thomas directs me to re-occupy Athens, Sulphur Trestle, and the station between Decatur and Elk River. As all the block-houses between these places have been burned, the garrisons must necessarily be much larger, until they can be rebuilt, than they were before the evacuation. I have temporarily provided garrisons for these points from troops furnished by General Wood. There are no troops under my command that are available for this purpose, my own command being barely sufficient to furnish minimum garrisons for the stations on the Decatur and Stevenson road.

The general is probably aware that all the troops of this district except the four regiments of the First Brigade, Fourth Division, Twentieth Army Corps, numbering for duty about 1,430 men on last report; this is not more than a garrison for Decatur alone. There is not a cavalryman in the district, reporting to me.

General Wood informs me that he is directed to remove all the troops belonging to his corps as soon as he is ordered to march. I must therefore urgently request that re-enforcements of infantry and cavalry be sent me with as little delay as practicable. The total number of troops required for this district will be—to garrison the road from Stevenson to Decatur: At Crow Creek, an officer and 30 men; Mud Creek, a company of 50 men; at Bellefonte, an officer and 30 men; at Larkinsville and station at Santa Creek, 100 infantry and 50 cavalry; at Paint Rock and Gurley's Tank, until block-houses are completed, 80 infantry and 20 cavalry; bridge over Hurricane Creek, an officer and 30 men; Brownsborough, 100 infantry and 150 cavalry—this is an important station at all times, and particularly so now, from the fact that the guerrillas under Mead, Johnson, and Whitecotton, some 500 strong, occupy the district included within the headwaters of Paint Rock and Flint Rivers; Huntsville, 350 infantry and 150 cavalry; Branch of Indian Creek, near

Madison Station, an officer and 30 men; Beaver Dam, one company of 50 men; Limestone, a company of 50 men; Piney, a company of 50 men; Decatur, 1,500 infantry and 500 cavalry; four block-houses to Athens, an officer and 30 men each—total, 4 officers and 120 men; Athens, 150 infantry and 150 cavalry; Sulphur Trestle, 150 infantry and 20 cavalry; three block-houses between Sulphur Trestle and Elk River, 3 officers and 90 men; Claysville, 2 officers and 60 men, and 25 cavalry; Whitesburg, 20 infantry and 15 cavalry; Triune, 30 infantry, with an officer. Total infantry effective force, 3,070 enlisted men, and 126 officers; and cavalry, 1,070 enlisted men. The effective force of the brigade, and a small detachment of colored troops will give an effective force of about 1,700 men, which will leave 1,370 effective force for minimum garrison. This furnishes no guards for trains or force to operate in the field; this, at least, should be 1,000 more, giving a total effective force of not less than 4,000 infantry and 1,100 or 1,200 cavalry. I wish the general to understand that this is the effective force absolutely required for this district, and I consider that a less force will constantly invite invasions from the south side of the Tennessee River; and this is a very much smaller force than has been employed to hold this road by any officer who has preceded me.

I earnestly request that the general commanding will give this his immediate attention, and send me the re-enforcements with as little delay as practicable.

Very respectfully, your obedient servant,

R. S. GRANGER,
Brigadier-General, Commanding District.

Since writing the above Colonel Lyon informs me that the officers of the railroad have called upon him for guards to four more stations.

NASHVILLE, TENN., *January 17, 1865.*

Brig. Gen. R. S. GRANGER,
Huntsville:

There is no mounted cavalry whatever here, and there is not a hoof in the district subject to my orders, except the Fifth Tennessee, now with General Milroy. General Thomas is at Eastport.

B. H. POLK,
Major and Assistant Adjutant-General.

NASHVILLE, *January 17, 1865.*

Major-General STEEDMAN:

Last battalion in. Entire command on hand, except some 200 reported at Ringgold and block-houses between Ringgold and Tunnel Hill. Have secured ample water transportation to Pittsburg. Headquarters boat, the Saint Patrick. Command in splendid condition. Encamped a mile from town, near Rains' house.

THOS. F. MEAGHER,
Brigadier-General.

KNOXVILLE, *January 17, 1865.*

Lieut. Col. G. M. BASCOM:

Colonel Kirk, Third North Carolina Mounted Infantry, has come in. Captain Kirk wounded, two men killed, three men wounded. He had several skirmishes, in which he was uniformly successful, killing over 100 of Palmer's men and the guerrillas, and wounding a large number; he captured 32 prisoners and 56 horses. He did not penetrate into North Carolina beyond Warm Springs.

> DAVIS TILLSON,
> *Brigadier-General.*

WASHINGTON, D. C., *January 18, 1865—4.30 p. m.*

Lieutenant-General GRANT,
  City Point:

I learn from General Canby that if General Thomas proposes to move on Selma, or some other point toward the Gulf, he (Canby) can co-operate with a force of from 15,000 to 20,000 men. To do this efficiently he will require remounts for a part of his cavalry. You will remember that since about the 1st of October all cavalry horses purchased in the West and Northwest have been sent to General Thomas, to the entire exclusion of Missouri, Arkansas, Mississippi, and Louisiana. Consequently, these departments must now have a large number of dismounted cavalry. The question now arises whether we shall continue to send all cavalry horses to General Thomas, or whether General Canby's command should receive its due proportion. This must be decided, in a measure, by your plan of ulterior operations in that part of the country. Whatever that may be, it is obviously important that there should be a concert of action between Canby and Thomas, for the former cannot safely reduce his garrisons on the Mississippi River to operate against the interior of Alabama unless the latter assists at the same time by pursuing Hood or keeping him away from Memphis, Vicksburg, Natchez, &c. Canby seems very anxious to make a campaign this winter while the weather is favorable, if a plan can be determined on and he can be certain of the co-operation of Thomas. I feel confident that Selma and Montgomery can be taken this winter, if Thomas' and Canby's forces can either unite or co-operate. General Sherman writes me that abundant supplies will be found in all the interior of Alabama.

> H. W. HALLECK,
> *Major-General and Chief of Staff.*

CITY POINT, VA., *January 18, 1865—9 p. m.*
(Received 11 p. m.)

Maj. Gen. H. W. HALLECK,
  Washington, D. C.:

I now understand that Beauregard has gone west to gather up what can be saved from Hood's army to bring against Sherman. If this be the case Selma and Montgomery will be easily reached. I do not believe, though, that General Thomas will ever get there from the north. He is too ponderous in his preparations and equipments to move through a country rapidly enough to live off of it. West of the Mississippi we do not want to do more than defend what we now hold, but I do want Canby to make a winter campaign, either from Mobile Bay or from Florida. You might order all the cavalry horses now in the West to Canby and direct him to make an independent campaign, looking to the capture of Mobile, first, if the job does not promise too long a one, and Montgomery and Selma, and the destruction of all roads, machine-shops, and stores, the main object. Thomas can do without horses for some time; a portion of his troops could be sent by water to Canby. If Thomas does not* move in co-operation, probably the best route for him to take would be by way of Chattanooga, repairing the road to Rome, and starting from there. These I give as views. What I would order is, that Canby be furnished cavalry horses and be directed to prepare to commence a campaign, and that Thomas be telegraphed to to say what he could do, and when, and get his views upon the choice of routes, looking upon Selma as his objective. Thomas must make a campaign or spare his surplus troops.

U. S. GRANT,
Lieutenant-General.

NASHVILLE, *January 18, 1865.*

Hon. E. M. STANTON:

In order that no injustice may be done I would respectfully request that the report of Maj. Gen. George Stoneman, who commanded the late expedition in Southwestern Virginia, may be examined before any promotions be made for services rendered in that expedition, and I would respectfully call your attention to the services rendered by the Tennessee troops under Brig. Gen. Alvan C. Gillem. I hope the honorable Secretary of War will show this dispatch to His Excellency the President of the United States.

ANDREW JOHNSON,
Military Governor.

WASHINGTON, D. C., *January 18, 1865.*

Major-General THOMAS,
          Eastport:

The proposition of General Wilson to send dismounted cavalry north of the Ohio River to impress horses is entirely disapproved. The places to impress horses are Mississippi, Alabama, and Georgia.

H. W. HALLECK,
Major-General and Chief of Staff.

(Copy to Cavalry Bureau.)

HEADQUARTERS DEPARTMENT OF THE CUMBERLAND,
          Eastport, Miss., January 18, 1865.
Captain VAN ANTWERP:

The major-general commanding directs that you proceed with a flag of truce from this place to Columbus, Miss., the reported headquarters of General J. B. Hood, C. S. Army, where you will turn over to a proper officer, who will deliver the same to General Hood, the several communications addressed to him, placed in your hands with the Con-

---

* So in Grant's record book, but as received by Halleck the word "not" is omitted.

federate soldier Private Wright, Thirtieth Alabama, taking receipts
from the officer to whom you deliver them. This duty performed, you
will return to these headquarters with the command constituting the
flag of truce.

I am, captain, very respectfully, your obedient servant,
                                       HENRY M. CIST,
                          Captain and Assistant Adjutant-General.

———

                HEADQUARTERS FOURTH ARMY CORPS,
                        Huntsville, Ala., January 18, 1865.
Colonel PALMER,
    Fifteenth Pennsylvania Volunteer Cavalry:

I am directed by the general commanding to acknowledge the receipt
of your report* of operations in the pursuit and capture of General
Lyon and a portion of his command, and to express to you and your
gallant little troop of officers and men his thanks for the services you
rendered in giving this party of raiders a finishing touch after they
had succeeded in crossing the Tennessee River and considered themselves safe. The blow you struck him probably used up his command
"as a command," as President Lincoln remarked the other day about
the dog in telling one of his stories to illustrate the situation of the
Confederacy at this time.

I am, colonel, very respectfully, your obedient servant,
                                       WM. H. SINCLAIR,
                                  Assistant Adjutant-General.

———

GENERAL ORDERS, ⎰ HDQRS. DETACH. ARMY OF THE TENN.,
    No. 4.   ⎱   Eastport, Miss., January 18, 1865.

I. Capt. George R. Brown, Ninth Indiana Battery, having been
relieved from further duty as chief of artillery of this command, Capt.
John W. Lowell, Battery G, Second Illinois Light Artillery, is hereby
announced as chief of artillery and as upon the staff of the major-general commanding, and will be respected and obeyed accordingly.
Division commanders will at once direct all the batteries within their
commands to report to the chief of artillery for orders, and will cause
them to be dropped from the rolls of the brigade and divisions.

By order of Maj. Gen. A. J. Smith:
                                       J. HOUGH,
                             Major and Assistant Adjutant-General.

———

SPECIAL   ⎰   HEADQUARTERS CAVALRY CORPS,
FIELD ORDERS, ⎰ MILITARY DIVISION OF THE MISSISSIPPI,
    No. 7.   ⎱   Gravelly Springs, Ala., January 18, 1865.

First Lieut. George B. Rodney, Fourth U. S. Artillery, having
reported for duty at these headquarters, is temporarily assigned to
duty as inspector of artillery for the corps. He will at once make an
inspection of the batteries attached to the command and report their
condition and wants.

By command of Brevet Major-General Wilson:
                                       HENRY E. NOYES,
                      Lieutenant and Acting Assistant Inspector-General.

———

* See Part I, p. 798.

HDQRS. CAVALRY CORPS, MIL. DIV. OF THE MISSISSIPPI,
Gravelly Springs, Ala., January 18, 1865.

Brevet Major-General UPTON,
Comdg. Fourth Division, Cavalry Corps, Louisville, Ky.:

Your telegraph 12th received. You can bring with you what horses and arms, &c., Winslow's command requires and order them here direct; but this is optional with you; use your own discretion in the matter.

J. H. WILSON,
Brevet Major-General.

———

GENERAL ORDERS, }   HDQRS. FIFTH DIV., CAV. CORPS,
                 } MILITARY DIVISION OF THE MISSISSIPPI,
No. 1.   }   *Gravelly Springs, Ala., January 18, 1865.*

I. In compliance with orders from Brevet Major-General Wilson, I hereby assume temporarily the command of the Fifth Division, Cavalry Corps, Military Division of the Mississippi. All returns, reports, and other papers required by regulations and existing orders will be forwarded accordingly.

II. Lieut. Col. Abram Sharra, Eleventh Indiana Cavalry, will assume temporarily the command of the First Brigade, Fifth Division, Cavalry Corps, Military Division of the Mississippi, at once.

By order of Col. R. R. Stewart:

R. B. AVERY,
Lieutenant and Acting Assistant Adjutant-General.

———

SPECIAL ORDERS, }   HDQRS. SIXTH DIV., CAV. CORPS,
                } MILITARY DIVISION OF THE MISSISSIPPI,
No. 9.   }   *Pulaski, Tenn., January 18, 1865.*

*   *   *   *   *   *   *   *

VII. Battery I, Fourth U. S. Artillery, having been transferred from this division, is hereby, in pursuance of orders from Brevet Major-General Wilson, relieved from duty at this post, and will proceed to Gravelly Springs, Ala., where Lieut. F. G. Smith will report to Brevet Major-General Wilson for orders. The detachment of the Ninth Indiana Cavalry now at this place will go as escort to the battery.

By command of Brigadier-General Johnson:

E. T. WELLS,
Assistant Adjutant-General.

———

SPECIAL ORDERS, } HEADQUARTERS DISTRICT OF TENNESSEE,
No. 16.   }   *Nashville, Tenn., January 18, 1865.*

I. The First Kansas Battery will proceed by boat, without delay, to Johnsonville and take post at that place. The quartermaster's department will furnish the necessary transportation.

*   *   *   *   *   *   *

By command of Major-General Rousseau:

B. H. POLK,
Major and Assistant Adjutant-General.

NASHVILLE, *January 18, 1865—2.30 p. m.*

Major-General STEEDMAN:

Boughton's brigade, 2,230 strong, is off in the best condition and highest spirits, the Saint Patrick leading the way. Culver on board Chase, over 2,000 strong, will leave in about an hour. Deficiency in transportation compels us to be slower than we ought or should otherwise be. Malloy, over 2,000, leaves to-morrow. Anything I can do for you let me know. Glorious news from Wilmington; Fort Fisher ours.

T. F. MEAGHER,
Brigadier-General.

BRIDGEPORT, *January 18, 1865.*

Maj. S. B. MOE,
Assistant Adjutant-General:

The detachment of this post garrisoning Shellmound was to be re-enforced, or to be relieved, by a Lieutenant Culbertson, Fourteenth Army Corps, on a verbal order from Colonel O'Brien. This officer had no orders to show assigning him the command, and I therefore most respectfully request you to enlighten me by what authority he was acting, and if the captain of the Eighteenth U. S. Colored Troops in command of Shellmound and of block-houses has to turn over the same or not. Awaiting your answer,

I remain, &c.,

FELIX PRINCE SALM,
Colonel, Commanding Post.

HEADQUARTERS DISTRICT OF THE ETOWAH,
Chattanooga, January 18, 1865.

Col. FELIX PRINCE SALM,
Bridgeport:

All detachments from your command guarding railroad this side of Carpenter's Station, on being relieved by troops from General Cruft's command, will report at once to their respective regiments. Please convey this order to the detachments you have on such duty. The officer sent to relieve them was directed to convey the order.

By command of Major-General Steedman:

S. B. MOE,
Assistant Adjutant-General.

HEADQUARTERS DISTRICT OF THE ETOWAH,
Chattanooga, January 18, 1865.

COMDG. OFFICER DETACH. FORTY-FOURTH INDIANA VOLS.,
Whiteside's:

On being relieved by troops from General Cruft's command, you will return to this place, reporting to your regimental commander.

By command of Major-General Steedman:

S. B. MOE,
Assistant Adjutant-General.

WASHINGTON, D. C., *January 19, 1865.*

Major-General THOMAS,
          Eastport:

If Brigadier-General Tower can be spared from your department direct him to report to the Chief Engineer in Washington.

                               H. W. HALLECK,
                         Major-General and Chief of Staff.

WASHINGTON, D. C., *January 19, 1865—2.30 p. m.*

Major-General THOMAS,
          Eastport:

General Grant has directed that no more cavalry horses be sent to your command till the proposed expeditionary force of General Canby is supplied. General Canby has been ordered to collect all his available force at some point on the Gulf and to move against Selma and Montgomery. It is the wish of General Grant that your army should co-operate by moving upon the same points, if you can be ready in time, or that if this cannot be done, that all your troops not required for defense should be sent to the Gulf to operate with General Canby on that line. It is understood that Beauregard has gone west to bring the remains of Hood's army to South Carolina to oppose Sherman. If so, Canby can easily reach Montgomery, and if not, his movement will hold Hood in check and keep him away from Sherman. You will please communicate your views upon these proposed operations, stating what line you purpose to take, looking at Selma as the objective point, and by what date you will be ready to move; or, if you do not propose a winter campaign from your present base, state how many men you can send to the Gulf. This information is necessary in order that General Grant may give his final instructions for winter operations. If Hood comes to the coast, he will probably leave behind a part of Forrest's cavalry to make raids and demonstrations, but they will not be strong enough to do any serious injury.

                               H. W. HALLECK,
                         Major-General and Chief of Staff.

Memoranda for Cavalry Bureau.

JANUARY 19, 1865.

General Grant directs that no more cavalry horses be sent to General Thomas' command till General Canby's forces, now preparing for the field, are supplied. They will be sent down the Mississippi River to New Orleans, or such other points as General Canby may direct. General Canby will send his requisitions to Saint Louis, and also to Cavalry Bureau. In consideration of these orders, it will not be necessary to establish a new recuperating depot at Nashville; that at Louisville will be sufficient for General Thomas' army. Active measures should be taken to supply General Canby as early as possible.

                               H. W. HALLECK,
                         Major-General and Chief of Staff.

ODIN, ILL., *January 19, 1865—6 p. m.*

C. A. DANA,
    Assistant Secretary of War:

Missed connection here. Will be in Louisville in the morning. Dispatches just received showing about half of the corps had passed Louisville by 3 p. m. to-day, and all the balance in the Ohio at that hour.

PARSONS.

———

HEADQUARTERS FOURTH ARMY CORPS,
    Huntsville, Ala., January 19, 1865.

General KIMBALL:

GENERAL: The recent capture of trains sent on foraging expeditions without proper guards shows that the orders in regard to escorts for forage trains have not been carried out. Hereafter a detail of ten men will be sent with each wagon that goes out foraging, and when the detail for guard exceeds 100 men a field officer will be sent in charge. One-half of the guard will be kept under arms and on the alert, while the remaining half is collecting the forage. A proportional number of officers and non-commissioned officers must always accompany each detail for guard.

By order of Brigadier-General Wood:

WM. H. SINCLAIR,
    Assistant Adjutant-General.

(Copy to Generals Elliott and Beatty, Major Goodspeed, and Captain Laubach.)

———

HEADQUARTERS FOURTH ARMY CORPS,
    Huntsville, Ala., January 19, 1865.

Brigadier-General KIMBALL:

GENERAL: The general commanding directs that you call in all safe-guards you have sent or caused to be sent out from command. This order is rendered necessary from the fact that some of the men have already been captured, and all that are out, especially those at a long distance, are liable to be captured and murdered by guerrillas and bushwhackers any day. If the people cannot keep these villains out of the country we cannot send men out and expose them to capture and the liability of being murdered, while our only object in sending them out is to protect those that in most cases are and have been enemies to the Federal Government. Every means must be taken to bring up the state of discipline in the command to such a standard that the inhabitants will not require guards to protect them from our own troops. Full rations are now issued to the troops, and there is no reasonable excuse for them to forage on the country for anything except feed for animals. Soldiers who take anything else are simply thieves, and must be punished as such. Any officer who permits men of his command to enter dwelling-houses while on foraging expeditions will be arrested and tried.

Very respectfully, your obedient servant,

WM. H. SINCLAIR,
    Assistant Adjutant-General.

(Copy to Generals Elliott and Beatty and Major Goodspeed.)

SPECIAL ORDERS, ⎱   HDQRS. DETACH. ARMY OF THE TENN.,
     No. 16.   ⎰   *Eastport, Miss., January 19, 1865.*

I. Company A, Seventh Minnesota Volunteer Infantry, is hereby detailed for detached service as provost-guard, and will forthwith report to Capt. Ross Wilkinson, provost-marshal at these headquarters, for duty.

*   *   *   *   *   *   *

V. Company G, Eighth Wisconsin Volunteer Infantry, is hereby relieved from further duty as guard at these headquarters, and will forthwith rejoin their regiment for duty.

By command of Maj. Gen. A. J. Smith:

J. HOUGH,
Major and Assistant Adjutant-General.

ATHENS, *January 19, 1865.*
Major-General STEEDMAN:

We have a report that some 400 to 800 rebels, supposed to be from Hood's command, are at John Gallagher's, on the north side of the Tennessee River, and have torn down a warehouse and are building boats to cross the river below Kingston. I will start a scout in a few minutes.

JOHN McGAUGHEY,
Major, Commanding.

P. S.—A scout in states that they are crossing now.

MOUNT STERLING, KY., *January 19, 1865.*
Capt. J. S. BUTLER,
     Assistant Adjutant-General:

Information received, deemed here reliable, that Peter Everett, with 200 or 300 men, contemplates attacking the railroad trains near Paris, for the purpose of taking the paymaster who they are informed is to pay the troops at Mount Sterling. They are reported to go down Licking and cross by Millersburg. We are in a bad fix now, seven rounds of cartridges to a man; not horses enough to mount ten besides the pickets. I sent 100 dismounted men to Flat Rock on the 17th instant. They discovered nothing in that vicinity. Can five or ten boxes of Spencer cartridges be forwarded to me from Lexington, to supply me until I obtain a supply on my requisition? The attack is to be made this afternoon or to-morrow.

Yours, very respectfully,

S. B. BROWN,
Colonel, Commanding Eleventh Michigan Cavalry.

MOUNT STERLING, KY., *January 19, 1865.*
Capt. J. S. BUTLER,
     Assistant Adjutant-General:

The rebels, over 300, returned from the direction of Paris about an hour and half since. They crossed the pike about six miles north of here in direction of Owingsville. They traveled through the fields mostly, and were armed with revolvers, no guns or carbines; so say the Union citizens whom they arrested and took with them, and after crossing the pike released them.

S. B. BROWN,
Colonel Eleventh Michigan Cavalry.

PARIS, KY., *January 19, 1865.*

Brigadier-General HOBSON:

Sixty rebels passed within six miles of Paris, going toward Jackson and Sharpsburg. We have not sufficient horses to follow. Colonel Jessee supposed to be with them. They are robbing citizens. Another squad reported by an escaped prisoner are coming up.

JOHN W. THROCKMORTON,
Lieutenant and Aide-de-Camp.

HEADQUARTERS NORTHERN DEPARTMENT,
Cincinnati, Ohio, January 19, 1865.

Maj. Gen. A. P. HOVEY,
Commanding District of Indiana:

GENERAL: I have the honor to acknowledge your communication of the 17th instant, and am instructed by the major-general commanding the department to state in reply that His Excellency the Governor of Indiana complains to him of the depredations committed on the citizens of Southern Indiana by guerrillas from Kentucky, and requests that proper steps may be taken by the military authorities to prevent it. The general is satisfied that the complaint is just and the request reasonable, and he believes that the available force in your district, in conjunction with the Union forces in Kentucky, is sufficient to remove all cause of complaint on this score. The character of the people engaged in these marauding parties is not such as to render them formidable in any respect. They are mostly horse-thieves and that class of wretches who prefer to make a living by stealing rather than honest labor and are not inclined to expose their persons to danger in the accomplishment of their infamous purposes. They will starve sooner than fight, except to save their necks from the halter. It is this class of persons who are infesting the country south of Ohio and who must be kept from crossing into Indiana to threaten and plunder our people, and the general is determined that an end shall be put to it if he has to go there himself. In his opinion no considerable force will be required at any one point. An efficient corporal's guard at any one point will suffice for the protection of persons and property. Indeed the citizens themselves, if requested to put their rifles, double-barrel shotguns, and pistols in order and to place them where they can conveniently lay their hands on them, would in most instances answer the purpose. It is quite as necessary to have the persons and property of our people protected as Government property, where you state you have troops stationed. In your letter you say that the only mode of driving the guerrillas from the border is to send a mounted force across the river, when you know that repeated applications made from this office for horses have been uniformly refused by the Government, as the general believes, for good and sufficient reasons. So long as this is the case the general believes it is our duty to make use of the means given us in our own department, instead of making application for a force we have not, to regulate the department of others.

If in your judgment it should be necessary to employ the Forty-third [Indiana] Regiment to insure perfect security and protection in that part of your district bordering on the Ohio River, he directs that you make use of it irrespective of the indications to which you refer. We must put an end to these complaints. It is our duty and if we can't do that we had better go to bed. As these complaints have been communicated through His Excellency the Governor of Indiana, the major-general commanding requests that you will confer with that officer and, if possible, make such arrangements for the preservation of good order and the security of the southern portion of the State as will be satisfactory to both of you.

Very respectfully, your obedient servant,
C. H. POTTER,
Assistant Adjutant-General.

WAR DEPARTMENT, ORDNANCE OFFICE,
Washington, D. C., January 20, 1865.
ASST. ADJT. GEN., DEPARTMENT OF THE CUMBERLAND,
Chattanooga, Tenn.:

SIR: In order that an accurate list may be prepared in this office of all the forts, permanent batteries, and field works in the possession of the United States on the 1st day of January, 1865, you are requested to furnish this office, as soon as practicable, with a complete list of all such works in your department at that time. Every detached work of any description which is armed with field, siege, or garrison guns in position, not accounted for to the office on a light battery return of ordnance stores, should be included. The name or number of the work, its geographical position, the number and kind of guns mounted, the name of the commanding officer and post-office address, should all be given. Printed forms showing the particulars required, and on which the statement is to be made, are sent herewith.

Respectfully, your obedient servant,
WM. MAYNADIER,
Colonel and Acting Chief of Ordnance.

HEADQUARTERS DEPARTMENT OF THE CUMBERLAND,
Eastport, Miss., January 20, 1865.
Brig. Gen. J. L. DONALDSON,
Chief Quartermaster, Dept. of the Cumberland, Nashville, Tenn.:

GENERAL: Yours of January 12 has been received. I am about to return to Nashville and remove the headquarters from Chattanooga to that place. For that reason, and that the general commanding may himself return at any time to Nashville, would render it inconvenient for you to occupy any of the buildings set apart as headquarters of the department. There was considerable room in the house situated upon the corner of Union and Cherry streets, which you could make use of.

Very respectfully, your obedient servant,
WM. D. WHIPPLE,
Brigadier-General and Assistant Adjutant-General.

Special Orders, }　War Dept., Adjt. General's Office,
　　No. 31.　　}　　　　　*Washington, January 20, 1865.*

*　　　*　　　*　　　*　　　*　　　*　　　*

35. Maj. Gen. Joseph Hooker, U. S. Volunteers, commanding Northern Department, will repair to this city, and report in person as a witness to the chairman of the Committee on the Conduct of the War, as soon as his duties will permit. As soon as his services can be dispensed with by the Committee he will immediately return to his proper station.

*　　　*　　　*　　　*　　　*　　　*　　　*

By order of the Secretary of War:

　　　　　　　　　　　E. D. TOWNSEND,
　　　　　　　　　　　Assistant Adjutant-General.

Hdqrs. Cavalry Corps, Mil. Div of the Mississippi,
　　　　　　　Gravelly Springs, Ala., January 20, 1865.
Capt. John Green,
　　Special Inspector, Cav. Corps, Mil. Div. of the Mississippi:

Captain: I am doing everything in my power to get the men together and ready for the field, and have sent back from time to time such instructions as I thought necessary, also such general information as I could gather for your guidance. Before leaving Athens I sent an order directing all dismounted men to be sent to this place, and wrote to Chambliss and Price requesting that remnants be sent to this place from Cairo, Saint Louis, and Louisville by water, giving general data upon which to base estimates. General Thomas yesterday telegraphed General Halleck requesting him to do the same thing, or to issue the necessary orders. You cannot fail to see the advantage of having everything concentrated here, and of everybody doing his utmost to push forward the equipment and organization. I want Hatch's division fixed up as soon as Upton's is complete, and then Knipe's. Johnson having to remain north of the Tennessee, or at all events not to start until everything else has moved, may be left to the last to receive his horses and new outfit. The question of arms is a very grave one. I hope when you arrive here nothing will remain to be done in the matter. I have written, I believe, more than once to everybody in the United States approximately or remotely concerned in horses and Spencer carbines. Colonel Miner's letter in regard to the depot at Edgefield is very satisfactory. As soon as they are done, find horses somewhere to put in them. There are plenty that will amply repay you for the expense and trouble. In regard to the workmen, say to Colonel Miner that I will not allow details for a permanent party, but will send him all the scalawags, convicts, and shirks I can get for hard-labor men. If this don't supply the demand the quartermaster's department must employ others. In regard to Knipe's dismounted brigade, I think it had better come here at once, so that it will be ready to go mounted, if possible, but dismounted, if necessary. Our camps here are fine. Everybody is hard at work, and the command is doing well. I send you a report of horse stock. The class called second are receiving extra care and attention. I wrote to Beaumont to have you come down here. You can render me valuable assistance in every way. If you have matters back which require your care, leave an officer with proper instructions to carry out your wishes.

　　Yours, very respectfully,

　　　　　　　　　　　J. H. WILSON,
　　　　　　　　　　　Brevet Major-General.

GENERAL ORDERS,   HDQRS. DIST. OF EAST TENNESSEE,
                   AND FOURTH DIV., 23D ARMY CORPS,
    No. 3.   *Knoxville, Tenn., January 20, 1865.*

Pursuant to telegraphic instructions from headquarters Department of the Ohio, Brig. Gen. S. P. Carter having been relieved from duty as provost-marshal-general of East Tennessee, Lieut. Col. L. S. Trowbridge, Tenth Michigan Cavalry Volunteers, is hereby appointed provost-marshal-general of the District of East Tennessee. He will be respected and obeyed accordingly.

By command of Brigadier-General Tillson:

N. A. REED, JR.,
Aide-de-Camp and Acting Assistant Adjutant-General.

EASTPORT, MISS., *January 21, 1865.*
(Received 12.20 a. m. 24th.)

Maj. Gen. H. W. HALLECK,
    Washington, D. C.:

Your dispatch of the 17th instant just received. Strength of Twenty-third Corps about 20,000. I do not know the number of companies of artillery to be supplied with batteries.

GEO. H. THOMAS,
Major-General, U. S. Volunteers.

EASTPORT, MISS., *January 21, 1865.*

Maj. Gen. H. W. HALLECK,
    Washington:

Your telegram of the 17th instant, 10 a. m., is received, instructing me to notify General Schofield to move his corps to Washington, instead of Annapolis. General Schofield, who left Clifton several days ago with his corps, is now too far away for me to communicate with him. Your dispatch of 11.30 a. m. 17th instant also received. The soldiers carrying the flags to Washington will be organized as you direct.

GEO. H. THOMAS,
Major-General, U. S. Army.

EASTPORT, MISS., *January 21, 1865—noon.*
(Received 12.10 a. m. 24th.)

Maj. Gen. H. W. HALLECK,
    Washington:

A reconnaissance sent by me to Corinth on the 19th instant has returned to Iuka, the cavalry portion only having reached Corinth. The commanding officer reports only straggling parties of the rebels at Corinth, which ran away at his approach. I also have reports from scouts sent out in the direction of Columbus, Miss., that Hood's headquarters are at that place, and that Forrest's headquarters are at Tupelo, and also that they have furloughed most of their Mississippi, Alabama, and Tennessee troops until the 25th of this month, and that they were forced to resort to this measure on account of the destruction of their railroad communication. The above report of Hood's and Forrest's situation is confirmed by General Dana in a dispatch from Memphis.

The commanding officer of the expedition to Corinth, as well as the scouts sent out, reports the roads in an impassable condition for wagons and artillery, and that it would be impossible to make a move of any magnitude until the weather becomes more favorable. Awaiting a more favorable change in the weather, I am doing everything possible to organize General Smith's command for a long march, and also equipping and mounting the cavalry as thoroughly as possible, which I am confident I shall be able to accomplish by the time the roads become passable, and shall then have a force which will be sufficient to overcome any resistance which the enemy may be able to bring against me. In this connection I respectfully request that you will order all horses required for the remount of the cavalry to be sent by steamers to this point, rather than to Louisville or Nashville. General Wilson has a fine location for thoroughly organizing and disciplining his command, which he can accomplish in a few weeks. He will then have a force which the enemy will be utterly unable to resist; and I earnestly recommend that I may be permitted to put my command in thorough shape before being again ordered to take the field. You may be assured I will not delay matters, but will be fully prepared before the roads are practicable, if sufficient horses can be furnished to remount the cavalry.

GEO. H. THOMAS,
Major-General, U. S. Army.

HEADQUARTERS MILITARY DIVISION OF THE MISSISSIPPI,
In the Field, Savannah, Ga., January 21, 1865.

Maj. Gen. GEORGE H. THOMAS,
Commanding Army in the Field, North Alabama, via Nashville:

GENERAL: Before I again dive into the interior and disappear from view, I must give you, in general terms, such instructions as fall within my province as commander of the division. I take it for granted that you now reoccupy in strength the line of the Tennessee from Chattanooga to Eastport. I suppose Hood to be down about Tuscaloosa and Selma, and that Forrest is again scattered to get horses and men and to divert attention. You should have a small cavalry force of, say, 2,000 men to operate from Knoxville through the mountain pass along the French Broad into North Carolina, to keep up the belief that it is to be followed by a considerable force of infantry. Stoneman could do this, whilst Gillem merely watches up the Holston. At Chattanooga should be held a good reserve of provisions and forage, and in addition to its garrison a small force that could at short notice relay the railroad to Resaca, prepared to throw provisions down to Rome, on the Coosa. You remember I left the railroad track from Resaca to Kingston and Rome with such a view. Then with an army of 25,000 infantry and all the cavalry you can get, under Wilson, you should move from Decatur and Eastport to some point of concentration about Columbus, Miss., and thence march to Tuscaloosa and Selma, destroying former, gathering horses, mules (wagons to be burned), and doing all the damage possible; burning up Selma, that is the navy-yard, the railroad back toward the Tombigbee, and all iron foundries, mills, and factories. If no considerable army opposes you, you might reach Montgomery and deal with it in like manner, and then at leisure work back along the Selma and Rome road, via Talladega and Blue Mountain, to the Valley of Chattooga, to Rome or La Fayette. I believe such a raid perfectly practicable and easy, and that it will have an excellent effect. It is nonsense to suppose that the people of the South are enraged or united by such movements. They reason very differently. They see in them the sure and inevitable destruction of all their property. They realize that the Confederate armies cannot protect them, and they see in the repetition of such raids the inevitable result of starvation and misery. You should not go south of Selma and Montgomery, because south of that line the country is barren and unproductive. I would like to have Forrest hunted down and killed, but doubt if we can do that yet. Whilst you are thus employed I expect to pass through the center of South and North Carolina, and I suppose Canby will also keep all his forces active and busy. I have already secured Pocotaligo and Grahamville, from which I have firm roads into the interior. We are all well.

Yours, truly,

W. T. SHERMAN,
Major-General, Commanding.

EASTPORT, MISS., *January 21, 1865.*

Hon. C. A. DANA,
Assistant Secretary of War, Washington, D. C.:

Your telegram of 10.40 a. m. 17th instant, announcing the capture of Fort Fisher, was received to-day. The good news will be published to the troops of this army at this place. A deputation of citizens of Northern Alabama waited on me yesterday to consult with me as to the best mode of bringing their section back into the Union. I advised them to call a convention of the people living north of the Tennessee River, and adopt the necessary measures in convention for re-establishing civil law in their district, and then to make a petition to the President to be admitted into the Union as a section of Alabama, prepared in all respects to perform their duties as loyal citizens of the Government of the United States, acknowledging the practical abolition of slavery, and expressing a desire that the institution may never be restored; then to send a delegation to Washington with a copy of the proceedings of their convention and their petition to lay before the President. I think these people are sincere, and hope that they may be encouraged to reorganize civil authority in their district, believing it will greatly facilitate any future efforts that may be made to re-establish civil authority in the State of Alabama, and its restoration to the Union.

GEO. H. THOMAS,
Major-General, U. S. Army, Commanding.

HEADQUARTERS DEPARTMENT OF THE CUMBERLAND,
Eastport, Miss., January 21, 1865—12 m.

Brig. Gen. J. L. DONALDSON,
Chief Quartermaster, Dept. of the Cumberland, Nashville:

The major-general commanding directs that measures be at once taken to prevent all steamers coming to Eastport, or to any point on the Tennessee River above Paducah, carrying any citizens or other persons, except those who have passes from the proper military authority at Nashville, Louisville, and Paducah, up the river on military business.

ROBT. H. RAMSEY,
Assistant Adjutant-General.

SPECIAL ORDERS, } WAR DEPT., ADJT. GENERAL'S OFFICE,
No. 33.   }   *Washington, January 21, 1865.*

*   *   *   *   *   *   *

26. The court-martial of which he was a member having adjourned, Brig. Gen. George S. Greene, U. S. Volunteers, will immediately repair to Nashville, Tenn., and report to Major-General Thomas, U. S. Army, for duty.

*   *   *   *   *   *   *

By order of the Secretary of War:

E. D. TOWNSEND,
Assistant Adjutant-General.

SPECIAL FIELD ORDERS, } HDQRS. DEPT. OF THE CUMBERLAND,
No. 18.   }   *Eastport, Miss., January 21, 1865.*

*   *   *   *   *   *   *

II. The Second Tennessee Mounted Infantry is hereby relieved from duty at Gallatin, Tenn., and will, without unnecessary delay, march to Clifton, Tenn., where it will take post.

*   *   *   *   *   *   *

V. Brig. Gen. Ferdinand Van Derveer, U. S. Volunteers, having reported to these headquarters in obedience to the orders of Maj. Gen. W. T. Sherman, commanding Military Division of the Mississippi, will proceed to Huntsville, Ala., and report to Brig. Gen. T. J. Wood, commanding Fourth Army Corps, for assignment. The quartermaster's department will furnish the transportation.

*   *   *   *   *   *   *

By command of Major-General Thomas:

HENRY M. CIST,
Captain and Assistant Adjutant-General.

HEADQUARTERS DEPARTMENT OF THE CUMBERLAND,
Eastport, Miss., January 21, 1865.

Brig. Gen. T. J. WOOD,
Commanding Fourth Army Corps, Huntsville, Ala.:

GENERAL: Brig. Gen. Ferdinand Van Derveer has this day been ordered to report to you for assignment. The major-general commanding desires that he be assigned to the command of the brigade from which Colonel Blake was relieved, if he (Colonel Blake) was relieved from it because he was the ranking colonel. I do not see, however, how sending Colonel Blake to Nashville makes any change in commanders, as, unless I am mistaken, General Grose commands the brigade to which Colonel Blake's regiment belongs This desire of the major-general commanding is, however, expressed under the supposition that you desired to get a commander for that brigade other than Colonel Blake. Should you think it advisable, you are at liberty to assign General Van Derveer to some other brigade. Colonel Blake has been relieved from duty at Nashville and ordered to join his regiment.

Very respectfully, your obedient servant,

WM. D. WHIPPLE,
Brigadier-General and Chief of Staff.

EASTPORT, *January 21, 1865.*

Brig. Gen. T. J. WOOD,
        Commanding Fourth Army Corps:

Your telegram of 10 a. m. 13th is received. The major-general commanding directs me to say to you that your directions to Brigadier-General Cruft to proceed to Chattanooga is approved; as also your directions to Colonel Palmer, Fifteenth Pennsylvania Cavalry, to pursue the scattered forces of the rebel general Lyon. Your telegram respecting Bridges' battery has been also received, and it will receive attention from General Brannan, chief of artillery.

ROBT. H. RAMSEY,
Assistant Adjutant-General.

HEADQUARTERS SIXTH DIVISION, CAVALRY CORPS,
MILITARY DIVISION OF THE MISSISSIPPI,
Pulaski, Tenn., January 21, 1865.

Col. E. MIX,
        Commanding Eighth Michigan Cavalry:

COLONEL: By direction of the general commanding you will detail one company from your regiment, well mounted and in command of an energetic and intelligent officer, to proceed to Columbia, Tenn., starting about noon to-morrow, so as to arrive there at night. They will go very light; rations and forage can be procured at the post of Columbia, so that none need be taken. Upon arriving at Columbia the officer commanding will report to Colonel Blodgett, commanding that post. It is expected that Colonel Blodgett will have guides and scouts ready to go with them, so that on their arrival there, after resting and feeding their horses, they can at once proceed to the duty intended for them, which is the capture or annihilation of a gang of bushwhackers now in that neighborhood. Colonel Blodgett will be telegraphed to expect them late to-morrow night and to have guides ready. They must go light, and march slowly and steadily, in order not to fatigue the horses. Only men who are well mounted should be of the party. The officer in command will report at these headquarters before starting from town. He will be furnished a copy of this letter.

Very respectfully, your obedient servant,

E. T. WELLS,
Assistant Adjutant-General.

HEADQUARTERS SIXTH DIVISION, CAVALRY CORPS,
MILITARY DIVISION OF THE MISSISSIPPI,
Pulaski, Tenn., January 21, 1865.

Colonel BLODGETT,
        Commanding Post:

COLONEL: General Johnson directs me to say, in answer to your communication of this date, that the man (Gamer) ought not to be captured, but should have been killed on the spot. He directs me further to say that a company of cavalry will be sent to report to you probably to-morrow, starting late, so as to arrive in the night-time. You will be telegraphed when to expect them, but the general suggests the propriety of keeping their arrival a secret, and that you have scouts or guides ready to send out with them as soon as they get off there, so that Gamer's people may not in the meantime get wind of their coming and make off.

Very respectfully, your obedient servant,

E. T. WELLS,
Assistant Adjutant-General.

SPECIAL ORDERS, }   HDQRS. DISTRICT OF THE TENNESSEE,
No. 19. }   *Nashville, Tenn., January 21, 1865.*

*   *   *   *   *   *   *

VII. Col. Charles R. Thompson, Twelfth U. S. Colored Infantry, is assigned to the command of the troops and defenses on the Nashville and Northwestern Railroad. Commanders of regiments on that road will forward all reports, returns, and current papers through Colonel Thompson.

VIII. The detachments of the One hundred and sixth, One hundred and tenth, and One hundred and eleventh Regiments U. S. Colored Infantry are assigned to duty on the Nashville and Northwestern Railroad. The commanding officers of those detachments will report to Col. C. R. Thompson for orders.

*   *   *   *   *   *   *

By command of Major-General Rousseau:

B. H. POLK,
Major and Assistant Adjutant-General.

HEADQUARTERS DISTRICT OF THE ETOWAH,
Chattanooga, January 21, 1865.

Brig. Gen. W. D. WHIPPLE,
Chief of Staff:

I do not believe there is any considerable force of the enemy in this country. The number and strength of guerrilla squads have been increased during the campaign. I consider James G. Brown a very unreliable individual. Will forward my report as soon as I can get reports from brigade commanders. Have sent Gowin's Sixth Tennessee Mounted toward Summerville, via La Fayette. Will advise you of any change in situation.

JAMES B. STEEDMAN,
Major-General of Volunteers.

SPECIAL ORDERS, }   HDQRS. MILITARY DISTRICT OF KENTUCKY,
No. 20. }   *Lexington, January 21, 1865.*

*   *   *   *   *   *   *

IV. Col. N. S. Andrews, Twelfth U. S. Colored Artillery (heavy), is hereby relieved from duty with his regiment and announced on the staff of the general commanding as chief of artillery for the Military District of Kentucky, with headquarters at Lexington, Ky. He will be obeyed and respected accordingly. This order to date from July 25, 1864.

*   *   *   *   *   *   *

By command of Brevet Major-General Burbridge:

CHAS. M. KEYSER,
Captain and Acting Assistant Adjutant-General.

40 R R—VOL XLV, PT II

HEADQUARTERS DEPARTMENT OF THE CUMBERLAND,
Eastport, January 21, 1865—12 m.

Maj. Gen. N. J. T. DANA,
Commanding Department of the Mississippi, Memphis, Tenn.:

Your telegram of the 13th instant is received. All that I am able to learn tends to confirm the information you send me, and in addition I am in receipt of reports that Hood is assembling his troops at Columbus, Miss., but has orders to proceed to Georgia with them. I will let you know from time to time the reports I get of his movements and will be obliged to you if you will communicate any information you receive.

GEO. H. THOMAS,
Major-General, U. S. Army.

HEADQUARTERS DEPARTMENT OF THE CUMBERLAND,
Eastport, Miss., January 22, 1865.

Brig. Gen. R. W. JOHNSON,
Pulaski, Tenn.:

The major-general commanding directs me to say that he is constantly in receipt of rumors that there are great numbers of guerrillas in the country west of Pulaski, and between the Tennessee River and Duck River. You are directed to have the country thoroughly patrolled and scouted, and all such persons destroyed, and you are also instructed to frequently explore and examine the country north of Huntsville, and about New Market, Fredericksburg, and Salem, which is also reported infested by guerrillas. Immediately upon receipt of this the major-general commanding desires you to make him a report by telegraph as to how you are getting along at Pulaski and also what is the condition of the country.

ROBT. H. RAMSEY,
Assistant Adjutant-General.

HEADQUARTERS DEPARTMENT OF THE CUMBERLAND,
Eastport, Miss., January 22, 1865.

Col. C. R. THOMPSON,
Commanding Post of Johnsonville:

COLONEL: The major-general commanding directs me to say that you will return with your command to Johnsonville and occupy the Northwestern Railroad as before the recent demonstrations of the rebel army in front of Nashville. There is now a white regiment at Johnsonville, to which will be added two or three batteries of artillery, to man the fortifications at that place, which will be constructed in accordance with the plans laid out by Maj. J. R. Willett, of the Engineer Department, Nashville. The troops referred to above will remain at Johnsonville, and form part of the garrison of the place. The major-general commanding directs also that you will use every means to permanently and thoroughly clear the country of the guerrillas now infesting it, and for this purpose you are authorized to mount from 200 to 500 of the men of your command upon horses taken from rebel sympathizers along the line of the railroad and the surrounding country.

I have the honor to be, colonel, very respectfully, your obedient servant,

HENRY M. CIST,
Captain and Assistant Adjutant-General.

WASHINGTON, D. C., *January 23, 1865.*

Major-General THOMAS,
         Eastport:

More troops are asked for to guard prisoners of war at Chicago.
None available except from your command. Can you not send a small
regiment for that purpose?

                              H. W. HALLECK,
                    Major-General and Chief of Staff.

SPECIAL ORDERS, ⎱ HDQRS. CAV. CORPS, MIL. DIV. OF THE MISS.,
     No. 13.   ⎰   *Gravelly Springs, Ala., January 23, 1865.*

      *   *   *   *   *   *   *

IV. Brevet Brigadier-General Watkins is hereby relieved from the
command of the Third Brigade, First Division, Cavalry Corps, Military
Division of the Mississippi, and will report to Brig. Gen. R. W. Johnson for assignment to the command of a brigade in the Sixth Division,
Cavalry Corps, Military Division of the Mississippi. The quartermaster's department will furnish transportation for General Watkins' horses.

V. The Third Brigade, First Division, Cavalry Corps, Military Division of the Mississippi, will be broken up upon the receipt of this order,
and Brigadier-General Croxton will assign the regiments comprising it
to the remaining brigades of the division.

      *   *   *   *   *   *   *

By command of Brevet Major-General Wilson:

                              E. B. BEAUMONT,
                    Major and Assistant Adjutant-General.

         HEADQUARTERS DISTRICT OF THE ETOWAH,
                    Chattanooga, January 23, 1865.

Colonel PALMER,
         Fifteenth Pennsylvania Cavalry, Huntsville:

Unless ordered by Major-General Thomas to remain at Huntsville,
you will march with your command for Chattanooga at once.

                              JAMES B. STEEDMAN,
                    Major-General, U. S. Volunteers.

         HEADQUARTERS DEPARTMENT OF THE CUMBERLAND,
                    Eastport, Miss., January 24, 1865.

Maj. Gen. H. W. HALLECK,
         Washington, D. C.:

Your dispatch of 2.30 p. m. 19th instant is received this day. In my
dispatch of 12 m. 21st instant I reported the condition of the roads in
this region of the country, and since writing that dispatch an officer
sent by me on flag of truce toward Columbus has returned. He succeeded in getting ten miles beyond Fulton, and reports that both the
road he went out on and the one he returned by are at this time impracticable for artillery and wagon trains. I have also received the same
reports, from reliable scouts and from refugees, of the condition of the
roads leading from Tuscumbia, via Russellville, to Tuscaloosa and

Columbus. I therefore think that it will be impossible to move from the Tennessee River upon Montgomery and Selma with a large force during this winter. It was my purpose, after having driven Hood out of Tennessee, to have assembled my available force at or near Huntsville, Ala., for the winter, and, as soon as the roads became practicable in the spring, to cross the Tennessee River at Whitesburg and Decatur, move by Somerville and Blountsville, through Brown's and Murphree's Valleys, via Elyton, Cedar Grove, Montevallo, and Summerville [Summerfield?], upon Selma, this country having been represented by various persons as being perfectly practicable and abounding in supplies. That country, however, is in the same condition as the country between this point and Columbus, Miss., at this season of the year, and I do not believe I could make a winter campaign, with any reasonable chance of complete success, starting from either this point or Decatur. Should Lieutenant-General Grant determine upon a winter campaign from some point on the Gulf I could send General Canby Maj. Gen. A. J. Smith's command and all of the cavalry now here, except two divisions, feeling able to securely hold the line of the Tennessee and all the territory now held in East Tennessee with the Fourth Army Corps, the troops in East Tennessee, and two divisions of cavalry. General Smith's command, if all present for duty, would number about 18,000 men. He reports present for duty about 12,000. The cavalry force I could send would also number about 12,000 men.

GEO. H. THOMAS,
Major-General, U. S. Army, Commanding.

CONFEDERATE CORRESPONDENCE, ETC.

MONTGOMERY, ALA., *December 1, 1864.*
(Via Tallahassee. Received 3d.)

General S. COOPER,
Adjutant and Inspector General, Richmond, Va.:

Four 10-inch banded guns have been shipped from Selma to Wilmington. General Maury needs them. As they cannot reach Wilmington, can General Maury have them?

G. T. BEAUREGARD.

GENERAL FIELD ORDERS, }   HDQRS. ARMY OF TENNESSEE,
       No. 38.   }   *Near Franklin, December 1, 1864.*

The commanding general congratulates the army upon the success achieved yesterday over our enemy by their heroic and determined courage. The enemy have been sent in disorder and confusion to Nashville, and while we lament the fall of many gallant officers and brave men, we have shown to our countrymen that we can carry any position occupied by our enemy.

By command of General Hood:

A. P. MASON,
Colonel and Assistant Adjutant-General.

To be read at the head of each regiment.

Circular.]   Headquarters,
                                                    December 1, 1864.

Corps commanders will have details sent on the field to gather up
and stack the arms found there.   Send also officers in all directions to
gather up their men.
     By order of General Hood:

                                                  A. P. MASON,
                                Colonel and Assistant Adjutant-General.

Circular.]   Headquarters Army of Tennessee,
                              Near Franklin, December 1, 1864.

Corps commanders will send in at once a list of the division, brigade,
and regimental commanders, by name and rank, who were killed or
wounded so as to be unfit for service in the engagement of yesterday
evening.
     By command of General Hood:

                                                  A. P. MASON,
                                Colonel and Assistant Adjutant-General.

Division commanders will hold their commands in readiness to move
at 3 o'clock this evening.

                                                    Headquarters,
                                 December 1, 1864—11.30 a. m.

Lieutenant-General Stewart,
               Commanding:

   General: General Hood directs that you get over the river this
evening above the town and cook rations.   You will have some two or
three days' breadstuffs given you, which he desires you to cook up.
Cheatham will cross at the town.
     Yours, respectfully,

                                                  A. P. MASON,
                                Colonel and Assistant Adjutant-General.

                                                    Headquarters,
                            Franklin, December 1, 1864—1.30 p. m.

[General Stewart:]

   General: General Hood directs that you will go into bivouac in the
first good place you can find beyond the river, taking your artillery and
trains with you.   Make yourself as familiar as you can with the roads
leading both to the Franklin pike and to the Nolensville pike from your
point of bivouac.   Army headquarters will be on the Franklin pike, a
short distance over the river, in the direction of Nashville.   As soon as
you are in bivouac send some of your couriers to find army headquarters, that General Hood may communicate further with you.
     Yours, respectfully,

                                                  A. P. MASON,
                                Colonel and Assistant Adjutant-General.

HEADQUARTERS,
December 1, 1864—6 p. m.

Lieutenant-General STEWART:

GENERAL: General Hood directs that you move at daylight in the morning and follow General Lee on the pike toward Nashville. General Forrest reports the enemy in full retreat from Brentwood, and he pressing them.

Yours, respectfully,

A. P. MASON,
Colonel and Assistant Adjutant-General.

CIRCULAR.]   HEADQUARTERS LEE'S CORPS,
December 1, 1864.

General Lee directs that you have your command in readiness to move at 12 m. to-day. He also directs that you send your empty wagons back to Columbia for ammunition.

Respectfully,

J. W. RATCHFORD,
Assistant Adjutant-General.

MONTGOMERY, ALA., *December 1, 1864.*

General P. D. RODDEY,
Corinth, Miss.:

General Beauregard wishes to know if Athens and Huntsville have been evacuated by the enemy?

GEORGE WM. BRENT,
Colonel and Assistant Adjutant-General.

MOBILE, *December 1, 1864.*

Col. GEORGE W. BRENT,
Assistant Adjutant-General, Montgomery, Ala.:

Enemy left Tangipahoa this morning for Mobile. Two brigades cavalry, under General Davidson, eight guns, eighty-seven wagons, eight wagons bearing pontoon trains. Urge Clanton's brigade to Meridian, to report to General Gardner.

D. H. MAURY,
Major-General, Commanding.

MOBILE, *December 1, 1864.*

Governor WATTS,
Montgomery, Ala.:

Enemy advancing from Tangipahoa on Mobile. Please send all the State troops you can to Pollard.

D. H. MAURY,
Major-General, Commanding.

MOBILE, *December 1, 1864.*

Brig. Gen. D. W. ADAMS,
   Montgomery:

Enemy left Tangipahoa this morning, under Davidson, 4,000 cavalry, destination Mobile. Send all the men you can to Pollard, so that I can use Armistead to oppose them.

        D. H. MAURY,
       Major-General, Commanding.

MOBILE, *December 1, 1864.*

Brigadier-General LIDDELL,
   Blakely, Ala.:

Enemy, with strong cavalry force, left Tangipahoa for Mobile this morning. I have ordered General Adams to send additional force to Pollard. Draw to vicinity of Blakely either Colonel Maury's cavalry force or that recently arrived under Armistead, whichever is nearest, so that I may be quickly re-enforced when necessary.

        D. H. MAURY,
       Major-General, Commanding.

MOBILE, *December 1, 1864.*

Lieut. Col. A. H. CHALMERS:
   (To be forwarded from East Pascagoula.)

Enemy in strong force; cavalry moved from Tangipahoa this morning for Mobile. Push forward toward Columbia; oppose his advance. Send information by quickest means.

        D. H. MAURY,
       Major-General, Commanding.

MOBILE, *December 1, 1864.*

General F. GARDNER,
   Jackson, Miss.:

Clanton's brigade is being hurried on to Meridian. Do you want Abbay's battery now, or anything else that I can help you in?

        D. H. MAURY,
       Major-General, Commanding.

MOBILE, *December 1, 1864.*

General F. GARDNER,
   Jackson, Miss.:

If enemy is moving against Mobile and Ohio Railroad he will probably strike it between Bucatunna and Shubuta. Have some militia infantry sent to that vicinity. I will have McCulloch and some other cavalry in readiness. Do you wish Abbay's [battery] sent to Meridian, or stopped at some point this side?

        D. H. MAURY,
       Major-General, Commanding.

HEADQUARTERS CAVALRY FORCES,
Mossy Creek, December 1, 1864.

Major-General BRECKINRIDGE,
Comdg. Dept. of Western Virginia and East Tennessee:

GENERAL : The above is all the information I have at this time.* I will fall back on the Warrensburg road on a line with Morristown, and will closely watch the movements of the enemy and try and protect myself. You had better have everything ready for this advance. I will communicate with you in regard to the movements of the enemy as fast as I learn them.

J. C. VAUGHN,
Brigadier-General.

MOSSY CREEK, *December 1, 1864.*
(Via Jonesborough 2d.)

Major-General BRECKINRIDGE:

A force of the enemy from Cumberland Gap—said to be Burbridge with five regiments, two white and three negro—have advanced to Clinch River, on the Morristown road, and repairing the road and fords. I will have more reliable information this evening. The Cincinnati Commercial of the 26th reports Burbridge at the Gap.

J. C. VAUGHN,
Brigadier-General.

Abstract from return of the Department of Alabama, Mississippi, and East Louisiana, Maj. Gen. D. H. Maury, C. S. Army, commanding, for December 1, 1864.

Command.	Present for duty.		Effective total present.	Aggregate present.	Aggregate present and absent.
	Officers.	Men.			
General staff	17			17	17
District of the Gulf: *a*					
General staff	13			13	13
Liddell's command	141	1,449	1,449	2,462	5,310
Thomas' command	17	160	160	330	858
Burnet's command	54	671	671	935	1,643
Taylor's command	47	367	367	635	1,200
Fuller's command	38	342	342	471	1,329
Total	310	2,989	2,989	4,846	10,353
McCulloch's brigade *b* (cavalry)		565	565	915	1,942
Detachment 7th Mississippi Cavalry		139	139	234	525
Total		704	704	1,149	2,467
District of North Alabama *a* (Roddey)	199	1,784	1,784	2,468	4,579
District of Central Alabama *c* (D. W. Adams)	252	1,657	1,657	2,188	3,881
Total	451	3,441	3,441	4,656	8,460
District of Mississippi and East Louisiana *d* (Gardner)	603	3,325	3,325	4,924	10,851
Grand total	1,381	10,459	10,459	15,592	32,148

a November 20.
b McCulloch's brigade, 1,942 men, transferred to west side of the bay from General Liddell's command. This cavalry being in motion in Florida, no reports were received.
c No report from this district since last return, October 31. Armistead's brigade, then detached, not reported.
d No report since last return, November 15.

----

* See Day to Vaughn, Part I, p. 1262.

Organization of the Army of Department of Alabama, Mississippi, and East Louisiana, commanded by Maj. Gen. Dabney H. Maury, December 1, 1864.*

DISTRICT OF THE GULF.

Maj. Gen. DABNEY H. MAURY.

LIDDELL'S DIVISION.

Brig. Gen. ST. JOHN R. LIDDELL.

Baker's Brigade.

Brig. Gen. ALPHEUS BAKER.

37th Alabama ⎫
40th Alabama ⎬ Col. John H. Higley.
42d Alabama ⎭
54th Alabama, Capt. Charles C. McCall.
3rd Battalion, Alabama Reserves, ⎫
4th Battalion, Alabama Reserves, ⎬ Lieut. Col. E. M. Underhill.
22d Louisiana, ⎭

Artillery.

Col. ISAAC W. PATTON.

Culpeper's (South Carolina) battery, Lieut. J. L. Moses.
Owens' (Arkansas) battery, Lieut. W. C. Howell.
Water batteries, Col. Marshall J. Smith.

Cavalry.

15th Confederate, Col. Henry Maury.

THOMAS' COMMAND.

Brig. Gen. BRYAN M. THOMAS.

1st Alabama Reserves, Col. Daniel E. Huger.

TAYLOR'S COMMAND.

Col. THOMAS H. TAYLOR.

4th Alabama Reserves, Col. William M. Stone.
21st Alabama (detachment), Capt. B. Frank Dade.
Alabama Cadets, Capt. H. E. Witherspoon.
City Battery (1st Mobile Volunteers), Lieut. Col. Stewart W. Cayce.

FULLER'S COMMAND.

Col. CHARLES A. FULLER.

2d Alabama Reserves, Col. Olin F. Rice.
1st Louisiana Artillery.
Alabama State Artillery, Companies C and D.
Coffin's (Virginia) battery, Company D, 12th Louisiana Battalion Artillery.

M'CULLOCH'S CAVALRY BRIGADE.

Col. ROBERT McCULLOCH.

7th Mississippi (detachment), Capt. Thomas Ford.
8th Mississippi.
18th Mississippi Battalion, Lieut. Col. Alexander H. Chalmers.
2d Missouri.

SEMPLE'S BATTALION ARTILLERY.

Maj. HENRY C. SEMPLE.

Abbay's (Mississippi) battery, Capt. George F. Abbay.
Charpentier's (Alabama) battery, Capt. Stephen Charpentier.
Winston's (Tennessee) battery, Capt. William C. Winston.
Third Missouri Battery, Lieut. Thomas B. Catron.

* See foot-notes to table, next, *ante.*

BURNET'S COMMAND.

Col. William E. Burnet.

1st Mississippi Artillery, Capt. Marquis L. Cole.
Battery Buchanan, Lieut. F. S. Barrett, C. S. Navy.
Battery Gladden, } Lieut. Col. Paul J. Quattlebaum.
Battery McIntosch, }
Battery Missouri, Capt. Samuel Barnes.

DISTRICT OF NORTH ALABAMA.

Brig. Gen. Philip D. Roddey.

4th Alabama Cavalry, Lieut. Col. F. M. Windes.
5th Alabama Cavalry, Lieut. Col. James M. Warren.
10th Alabama Cavalry, Col. Richard O. Pickett.
Burtwell's (Alabama) cavalry, Col. John R. B. Burtwell.
Moreland's (Alabama) cavalry, Lieut. Col. M. D. Moreland.
Stuart's (Alabama) battalion cavalry, Maj. James H. Stuart.
Ferrell's (Georgia) battery, Capt. Coleman B. Ferrell.

DISTRICT OF CENTRAL ALABAMA.

(Includes also posts of Demopolis, Montgomery, Selma, Cahaba, Opelika, Talladega, and Tuscaloosa.)

Brig. Gen. Daniel W. Adams.

Armistead's Cavalry Brigade.

Col. Charles G. Armistead.

8th Alabama, Col. Charles P. Ball.
16th Confederate [12th Mississippi], Col. Charles G. Armistead.
Barbiere's (Alabama Reserves) battalion, Maj. Joseph Barbiere.
Hardie's (Alabama Reserves) battalion, Maj. Joseph Hardie.
Lewis' (Alabama) battalion, Maj. William V. Harrell.

Clanton's Brigade.

Brig. Gen. James H. Clanton.

6th Alabama Cavalry, Col. Charles H. Colvin.
8th Alabama Cavalry, Lieut. Col. Henry J. Livingston.
Escort to district commander, Capt. T. B. Shockley.
State Reserves, at Selma, Lieut. Col. Young L. Royston.
Company H, 3d Confederate Reserves, at Demopolis, Capt. W. B. Ragan.
Company Reserves (firemen), at Montgomery, Maj. Walter Jones.
Light-duty men, detailed at Talladega, Maj. W. T. Walthall.
Light-duty men, detailed at Tuscaloosa, Capt. A. B. Hardcastle.
Dismounted cavalry, at Coosa Bridge, Lieut. Col. Nathaniel Wickliffe.
Six companies 3d Regiment Reserves, at Cahaba, Lieut. Col. Samuel Jones.

Artillery.

Clanton's (Alabama) battery, Capt. N. H. Clanton.
Merrin's (Mississippi) battery, Capt. F. W. Merrin.

DISTRICT OF MISSISSIPPI AND EAST LOUISIANA.

Maj. Gen. Franklin Gardner.

NORTHERN SUB-DISTRICT.

Brig. Gen. Wirt Adams.

Escort Company.

Company F, Wood's Mississippi Cavalry.

Denis' Brigade.

Col. Jules C. Denis.

1st Regiment Mississippi Reserve Cavalry }
2d Battalion Mississippi Reserve Cavalry } Col. Jules C. Denis.
3d Battalion Mississippi Reserve Cavalry }
Moorman's (Mississippi) battalion cavalry, Lieut. Col. George Moorman.

Mabry's Brigade.

Brig. Gen. HINCHIE P. MABRY.

14th Confederate Cavalry, Maj. Pinkney C. Harrington.
4th Mississippi Cavalry, Col. C. C. Wilbourn.
5th Mississippi Cavalry, Maj. W. G. Henderson.
6th Mississippi Cavalry, Lieut. Col. Thos. C. Lipscomb.
38th Mississippi Infantry (mounted), Col. Preston Brent.

CENTRAL SUB-DISTRICT.

Col. ROBERT C. WOOD, Jr.

Blackburn's (Kentucky) cavalry squadron, Capt. Joseph C. S. Blackburn.
Wood's (Mississippi) cavalry, Capt. William S. Yerger.
Stubbs' battalion (Mississippi) State troops, Maj. George W. Stubbs.
Peyton's battalion (Mississippi) State troops, Maj. E. A. Peyton.

DISTRICT OF SOUTHWEST MISSISSIPPI AND EAST LOUISIANA.

Brig. Gen. GEO. B. HODGE.

1st Louisiana Cavalry, Col. John S. Scott.
3d Louisiana Cavalry.
Ogden's (Louisiana) battalion cavalry, Lieut. Col. Frederick N. Ogden.
Powers' (Louisiana and Mississippi) cavalry, Col. Frank P. Powers.
Gober's mounted infantry, Col. Daniel Gober.
Battalion Louisiana State Guard.
Lay's (Mississippi) cavalry, Col. Benjamin D. Lay.
Unattached company cavalry, Capt. H. R. Doyal.

ARTILLERY.

Bradford's (Mississippi) battery, Capt. J. L. Bradford.
Ratliff's (Mississippi) battery, Capt. William T. Ratliff.
Rice's (Tennessee) battery, Capt. T. W. Rice.
Thrall's (Arkansas) battery, Capt. James C. Thrall.

POSTS.

Demopolis, Lieut. Col. John T. Plattsmier.
Meridian, Lieut. Col. Geo. W. Law.
Corinth, Col. John C. Reid.
Columbus, Lieut. Col. Levi McCullom.
Macon, Maj. Bell G. Bidwell.
Lauderdale, Col. Joseph P. Nuckols, jr.
Enterprise, Maj. Matthew S. Ward.
Jackson, Lieut. Col. Archibald Macfarlane.
Canton, Capt. John N. Archer.
Grenada, Capt. S. S. Angevine.
Oxford, Capt. Wm. M. Vosburg.
Goodman, Lieut. Peter James.
Panola, Capt. Richard C. Walsh.
Brandon, Capt. Wm. R. Spears.
Okolona, Maj. E. G. Wheeler.
Clinton, La., Lieut. Col. Wm. E. Pinkney.
Selma, Col. Young L. Royston.
Cahaba, Lieut. Col. Samuel Jones.
Coosa Bridge, Lieut. Col. Nathaniel Wickliffe.
Montgomery, Maj. Walter Jones.
Talladega, Maj. William T. Walthall.
Tuscaloosa, Capt. A. B. Hardcastle.
Opelika, Lieut. Col. John W. Buford.

MONTGOMERY, ALA., *December 2, 1864.*
(Via Tallahassee, Fla. Received 3d.)

President JEFFERSON DAVIS,
Richmond, Va.:

Generals Steele and A. J. Smith are reported to be re-enforcing General Thomas at Nashville. Cannot I send General E. Kirby Smith to re-enforce General Hood in Middle Tennessee, or take offensive in Missouri? His assistance is absolutely necessary at this time.

G. T. BEAUREGARD,
General.

[Indorsement.]

DECEMBER 4, 1864.

SECRETARY OF WAR:

If General Smith can now act as suggested it would be well that he should do so. There is no objection to his being called on, but he has failed heretofore to respond to like necessities, and no plans should be based on his compliance.

J. D.

MONTGOMERY, ALA., *December 2, 1864.*
(Via Savannah. Received 4th.)

General COOPER,
Adjutant and Inspector General, Richmond, Va.:

Telegram of 30th ultimo received here on my way to Mobile.* I shall repair forthwith to Atlantic coast.

G. T. BEAUREGARD.

MONTGOMERY, ALA., *December 2, 1864—9.15 p. m.*
(Via Savannah 6th. Received 6th.)

General S. COOPER,
Adjutant and Inspector General, Richmond, Va.:

General Roddey reports from Decatur that Athens and Huntsville are evacuated. Lieutenant-Colonel Windes captured two locomotives with tenders, twenty-eight cars, and pontoon bridge across river, mostly in good condition.

G. T. BEAUREGARD,
General.

MONTGOMERY, ALA., *December 2, 1864—9.30 p. m.*
(Via Savannah 6th. Received 6th.)

General S. COOPER,
Adjutant and Inspector General, Richmond, Va.:

Scouts report that General Steele, with 15,000 men, landed at Memphis on 24th, and went up river on 26th; it is supposed to re-enforce Thomas at Nashville. General Hood has been informed of the fact.

G. T. BEAUREGARD,
General.

----

* See Vol. XLIV, p. 911.

HEADQUARTERS MILITARY DIVISION OF THE WEST,
Montgomery, Ala., December 2, 1864.

General S. COOPER,
Adjutant and Inspector General, Richmond, Va.:

GENERAL: I have been informed that Maj. L. Mims, chief quartermaster of the State of Mississippi, has been authorized by the honorable Secretary of War to superintend the exchange of Government cotton for army supplies. No official communication of such authority has ever been received by me, nor has any information reached Major Mims or myself as to the extent of his powers, nor any instructions given as to the extent of his powers, nor any instructions given as to the mode and manner of carrying out this power. The subject is a delicate one and of grave importance. Our armies in this military division are sadly in need of every description of military supplies—horses and mules for artillery and other transportation, blankets, clothing, bacon, &c., are needed. This section has been drained of these supplies. Any further drafts on its resources will materially impair, if not destroy, the productive powers of its laboring population. Even if the supplies were at hand, they cannot be obtained for want of funds. Money is needed, not only for the purchase of quartermaster and commissary stores, but it is also required for the payment of the troops. A portion of the Army of Tennessee has not been paid since the 31st of December last, *i. e.*, Stewart's corps; Cheatham's and Lee's corps, since the 30th of April last; and the cavalry, since the 29th of February last. Funds have been recently sent to pay off these arrearages in part. To meet the immediate and pressing wants of the army the subject of cotton exchange becomes of serious import. Government cotton is here, badly put up, exposed to weather, to depredation, and at times liable to capture and destruction by the enemy. This, I believe, with proper management and under proper regulation, can be used to procure from the enemy's lines all needful army supplies. The interruption of communication with the seat of Government precludes us of all hope at present of looking to that quarter as a source of supply, and another must be sought. The one above suggested presents itself as the most feasible. Lieutenant-General Taylor, who was authorized to act in this matter, has, under instructions from the Government at Richmond, ceased to exercise any further authority over this subject. It is, therefore, important that some one should be intrusted with this authority, whose powers should be ample, and whose instructions should be full and clear. As it is now probably our sole source of supply I respectfully request and urge the department to take such steps as will enable us to exchange the cotton now lying useless here for such supplies and material of war as we may need. I herewith inclose a communication of Major Willis, my chief quartermaster, to the honorable Secretary of the Treasury, in connection with this subject. It meets with my approval. I have no desire myself to have any connection with the supervision of contracts for exchange, but will cheerfully afford all such facilities and aid in my power to the agent selected by the Government to effect this object. My present solicitude is that some one shall be designated for that purpose, full and ample powers conferred upon him, and such clear and definite instructions given me as will best carry out the intentions of the Government, protect it against fraud and peculation, and supply the great and pressing wants of our army in the field.

I have the honor to be, general, respectfully, your obedient servant,

G. T. BEAUREGARD,
General.

[First indorsement.]

ADJUTANT AND INSPECTOR GENERAL'S OFFICE,
December 16, 1864.

Respectfully submitted to the Secretary of War.

H. L. CLAY,
Assistant Adjutant-General.

[Second indorsement.]

DECEMBER 18, 1864.

ASSISTANT SECRETARY:

What would you advise in this matter? Can you explain the impression entertained that a quartermaster had been commissioned to make purchases, and the statement that General Taylor had received instructions excluding any control or action by him? I am not aware of any instructions which would warrant such statements.

J. A. S.,
Secretary.

[Third indorsement.]

Hon. SECRETARY OF WAR:

In March last a letter was addressed to each of the department commanders on the subject of the act concerning trade. A limited and special control was given to the department commanders to allow contracts to be made, under the supervision of trustworthy officers, and requiring the permission to be countersigned by the commander himself. Permissions were granted by General Polk to a liberal extent and by subordinate officers in his command, leading to abuse and augmenting a mischievous traffic. This was made known to the Department through inspection reports. A letter was addressed to General Taylor, 27th of September last, communicating the fact of these abuses, referring him to the act and orders, and informing him that Mr. Clapp had been appointed by the Treasury, and referring him to Mr. C. for information of the cases in which such trade could be licensed. He was also informed that but few contracts had been made; that those had not been productive, and had expired by limitation. General Taylor's circular is prior in date to this letter, and therefore his action was not affected by it. Three letters have since been addressed to General Taylor by you, in which a concurrence in his circular is expressed and his supervision of the trade recognized to be legitimate. I know of no communication from this Department to any quartermaster that would justify the making of contracts for supplies through the use of cotton.

J. A. CAMPBELL,
Assistant Secretary of War.

[Fourth indorsement.]

FEBRUARY 4, 1865.

ADJUTANT-GENERAL:

The whole matter has been now arranged by the appointment (in concert with the honorable Secretary of the Treasury) of an officer or agent to make and superintend the execution of all contracts for supplies in the Mississippi Department.

J. A. S.,
Secretary.

[Inclosure.]

OFFICE CHIEF QUARTERMASTER,
GENERAL BEAUREGARD'S COMMAND,
Montgomery, Ala., December 1, 1864.

Hon. G. A. TRENHOLM,
Secretary of the Treasury, Richmond, Va.:

As chief quartermaster of this military division, I respectfully request that 5,000 bales of cotton from that now in the hands of the tithe agent, or agent of the produce loan, or any other cotton in the State of Mississippi, be turned over to Maj. L. Mims, chief quartermaster of the State of Mississippi, who has been ordered by the honorable Secretary of War to superintend the exchange of Government cotton for army supplies. There is now the most pressing necessity for blankets, shoes, axes, stationery, medicines, hardware, leather, horses and mules, bacon and salt, to meet the immediate wants of the army. I have ascertained that prompt payment in cotton will readily secure adequate supplies, and in this manner a considerable quantity of cotton—badly put up, now exposed to the weather, and liable to be destroyed by the enemy—might be utilized before it becomes utterly worthless. No draft would then have to be made upon the supplies accumulating at Richmond, which could be devoted exclusively to General Lee's army. Large expense in transportation would be saved, both from and to the seaboard, and to that extent the overburdened railroad facilities relieved. The late and frequent interruptions of railroad communications has caused much suffering in the army, and as this may continue some time, it is suggested that some other source of supply must be sought. Arrangements can be made to meet this end fully, on a basis of 40 cents per pound for cotton in Federal currency, and invoice cost for goods, governed by prices current of the date, at the place of purchase, allowing $33\frac{1}{3}$ per cent. on the prime cost to cover all expenses to the agreed point of delivery, and the supplies made deliverable within reach of the army. Believing this proposition will be beneficial, both pecuniarily and as a means of supplying our wants, I trust that it will meet your approval. Should it do so, I will cheerfully undertake any labor to secure its full results, and enforce entire obedience to such instructions as you may think proper to give.

I am, with the greatest respect.

E. WILLIS,
Chief Quartermaster, Military Division of the West.

HEADQUARTERS MILITARY DIVISION OF THE WEST,
Montgomery, Ala., December 2, 1864.

General E. KIRBY SMITH,
Commanding Trans-Mississippi Department:

GENERAL: You are probably aware that the Army of Tennessee, under General J. B. Hood, has penetrated into Middle Tennessee as far as Columbia, and that the enemy is concentrating all his available forces, under General Thomas, to oppose him. It is even reliably reported that the forces under Generals A. J. Smith, in Missouri, and Steele, in Arkansas, have been sent to re-enforce Thomas. It becomes, then, absolutely necessary, to insure the success of Hood, either that you should send him two or more divisions, or that you should at once threaten Missouri, in order to compel the enemy to recall the re-enforcements he is sending to General Thomas. I beg to urge upon you prompt and decisive action. The fate of the country may depend upon the result of Hood's campaign in Tennessee. Sherman's army has lately abandoned Atlanta on a venturesome march across Georgia to the Atlantic coast about Savannah. His object is, besides the destruction of public and private property, probably to re-enforce Grant and compel Lee to abandon Richmond. It is hoped that Sherman may be prevented from effecting his object, but, should it be otherwise, the success of Hood in Tennessee and Kentucky would counterbalance the moral effect of the loss of Richmond. Hence the urgent necessity of either re-enforcing Hood or making a diversion in Missouri in his favor.

Hoping that you may give us the desired assistance, I remain, your obedient servant,

G. T. BEAUREGARD,
General.

MONTGOMERY, ALA., *December 2, 1864.*
Governor JOSEPH E. BROWN,
Macon, Ga.:

It is important to put in running order the railroad from West Point, via Atlanta, to Augusta. Cannot you impress or otherwise obtain 900 negroes, to report to Major Hottle, assistant quartermaster, who has charge of the work? Prompt action is necessary.

G. T. BEAUREGARD.

MONTGOMERY, ALA., *December 2, 1864—3 p. m.*
Maj. Gen. HOWELL COBB,
Macon, Ga.:

I will leave in the morning for Savannah.

*   *   *   *   *   *   *

G. T. BEAUREGARD.

MONTGOMERY, ALA., *December 2, 1864.*
(Via Corinth and Tuscumbia.)
General J. B. HOOD,
Commanding Army of Tennessee:

Scouts from vicinity of Memphis report Steele passing up river on 24th with 15,000 men. They are doubtless intended to re-enforce Thomas. Endeavor to defeat either before a junction. Keep me advised of your movements.

G. T. BEAUREGARD.

CONFIDENTIAL CIRCULAR.]   HDQRS. ARMY OF TENNESSEE,
Near Nashville, December 2, 1864.

General Lee will form his corps with his center upon the Franklin pike; General Stewart will form on General Lee's left; and General Cheatham on General Lee's right.

The entire line of the army will curve forward from General Lee's center so that General Cheatham's right may come as near the Cumberland as possible above Nashville, and General Stewart's left as near the Cumberland as possible below Nashville. Each position will be strengthened as soon as taken, and extended as fast as strengthened. Artillery will be placed in all favorable positions. All engineer officers will be constantly engaged in examining the position of the enemy and looking to all his weak points. Corps commanders will give all necessary assistance. Not a cartridge of any kind will be burned until further orders, unless the enemy should advance on us.

By command of General Hood:

A. P. MASON,
Colonel and Assistant Adjutant-General.

[DECEMBER 2, 1864.—For Mason to Cheatham and Mason to Bate, relative to operations against railroad from Murfreesborough to Nashville, &c., see Part I, p. 744.]

GENERAL FIELD ORDERS, {   HDQRS. FORREST'S CAVALRY,
No. 1.   }   *In the Field, December 2, 1864.*

I. There are four regularly organized and recognized companies of scouts for this command, viz: Capt. T. Henderson's company, Captain Harvey's company, Captain Kizer's company, and Captain Cobb's company. None others will be recognized, and all men acting as scouts on the independent order or under instructions otherwise than from these headquarters will be ordered to report at once to their respective commands.

II. All quartermasters and C. S. army sergeants, non-commissioned officers of the staff and line, and privates who do not have a gun, by the 1st day of January, 1865, will be dismounted and placed in infantry.

By command of Major-General Forrest:

J. P. STRANGE,
Assistant Adjutant-General.

MONTGOMERY, ALA., *December 2, 1864.*
Maj. Gen. D. H. MAURY,
Mobile, Ala.:

I intended visiting Mobile in a few days, but have to leave immediately for the Atlantic coast. My headquarters will remain here. Meanwhile direct all matters in your department.

G. T. BEAUREGARD.

MONTGOMERY, ALA., *December 2, 1864.*
Maj. Gen. D. H. MAURY,
Mobile, Ala.:

Action in case of General Smith approved. Is General Leadbetter in Mobile, and can he be spared? Your communication in regard to Halligan has been forwarded, but General Beauregard desires you will confer with Commodore Farrand, and act as you shall decide on.

GEORGE WM. BRENT,
Colonel and Assistant Adjutant-General.

MOBILE, *December 2, 1864.*

Col. GEORGE W. BRENT,
   Assistant Adjutant-General, Montgomery, Ala.:

Enemy reported in Franklinton, La., yesterday, moving east. Fewer ships in lower bay than usual. Hartford gone. Salute of thirteen guns fired yesterday, probably for Granger.

D. H. MAURY,
Major-General, Commanding.

GENERAL ORDERS, } HDQRS. DEPT. OF ALA., MISS., AND E. LA.,
   No. 145.   }   *Mobile, Ala., December 2, 1864.*

I. All officers and men serving in this department, who are absent on leaves of absence, or furloughs, and able to perform duty, will immediately rejoin their respective commands, and their leaves of absence and furloughs are hereby revoked, as every man able to render service is needed immediately. It is expected that this order will be promptly complied with, and as soon as the existing emergency has passed a renewal of the leaves and furloughs thus revoked will be granted.

II. Until further orders, no leaves of absence or furloughs will be approved at these headquarters, except in extraordinary cases.

III. It is enjoined upon all officers to use their utmost exertion toward effecting the immediate return to their commands of all absentees.

By command of Major-General Maury:

WILLIAM M. LEVY,
Lieutenant-Colonel and Assistant Adjutant and Inspector General.

MOBILE, *December 2, 1864.*

Brig. Gen. DAN. W. ADAMS,
         Talladega:

Please send Dawson's and Brown's companies to Pollard; they are Confederate cavalry. Will you be able to send any forces to me?

D. H. MAURY,
Major-General, Commanding.

MOBILE, *December 2, 1864.*

General F. GARDNER,
      Jackson, Miss.:

Abbay will go to Meridian this evening. Jenifer went to Montgomery. I telegraphed Brent your wish. Davidson will probably move toward Winchester or to Pascagoula. I hope you will be able to assemble sufficient force on Mobile and Ohio Railroad at such points as will best protect it. Governor Clark will be able, I think, to place militia near Winchester or Shubuta in time.

D. H. MAURY,
Major-General, Commanding.

MOBILE, *December 2, 1864.*

Col. Y. L. ROYSTON,
 Commanding Post of Selma:

Has Clanton's brigade passed Selma; if so, how soon can it reach Meridian?

WM. M. LEVY,
Assistant Adjutant and Inspector General.

MOBILE, *December 2, 1864.*

Maj. J. D. SAYERS,
 Assistant Adjutant-General, Meridian:

Where is Clanton's brigade? has it reached Selma yet? when will it reach Meridian? Find out all about it, and hurry it forward to Meridian.

W. M. LEVY,
Assistant Adjutant and Inspector General.

MORRISTOWN, *December 2, 1864.*
(Via Jonesborough 3d.)

Maj. J. S. JOHNSTON,
 Assistant Adjutant-General:

Enemy encamped last night four miles beyond Bean's Station, estimated at 1,500 or 2,000 men. Perhaps a movement on Bristol. They are from Cumberland Gap. General Vaughn negotiating terms [for] exchange of political and other prisoners, but assumes command this morning. Vaughn's brigade now holding six miles northwest of this point on Chucky River road. My own brigade, wagons, section artillery, &c., at this point awaiting further developments of the enemy's plans.

B. W. DUKE,
Brigadier-General.

[DECEMBER 3, 1864.—For Thompson to Benjamin, relating to affairs on the northern frontier of the United States, &c., see Vol. XLIII, Part II, p. 930.]

HEADQUARTERS ARMY OF TENNESSEE,
Six Miles from Nashville, on the Franklin Pike, December 3, 1864.
(Received 14th.)

Hon. J. A. SEDDON:

About 4 p. m. November 30 we attacked the enemy at Franklin and drove them from their center lines of temporary works into their inner lines, which they evacuated during the night, leaving their dead and wounded in our possession, and retired to Nashville, closely pursued by our cavalry. We captured several stand of colors and about 1,000 prisoners. Our troops fought with great gallantry. We have to lament the loss of many gallant officers and brave men. Major-General Cleburne, Brig. Gens. John Adams, Gist, Strahl, and Granbury were killed; Maj. Gen. John C. Brown, Brigadier-Generals Carter, Manigault, Quarles, Cockrell, and Scott were wounded; Brigadier-General Gordon was captured.

J. B. HOOD,
General.

(Same to Beauregard, December 3.)

HEADQUARTERS,
Overton's House, December 3, 1864—2.30 p. m.

Lieutenant-General STEWART,
   Commanding:

GENERAL: General Hood desires to see you here this evening. He does not desire your wet guns to be fired for the present.
   Yours, respectfully,

A. P. MASON,
Colonel and Assistant Adjutant-General.

MONTGOMERY, ALA., *December 3, 1864.*

Maj. Gen. H. COBB,
   Macon, Ga.:

General Beauregard directs that during present emergency, while separated from Army of Tennessee, you will assume control and direct administration of District of Georgia, without reference to army headquarters. All communications may be forwarded for the present to these headquarters.

GEORGE WM. BRENT,
Colonel and Assistant Adjutant-General.

MOBILE, *December 3, 1864.*

Col. G. W. BRENT,
   Assistant Adjutant-General, Montgomery, Ala.:

Where is Clanton's brigade? Steele reported to have landed at Memphis on Wednesday and passed up river on Thursday with 15,000 men.

D. H. MAURY,
Major-General, Commanding.

MONTGOMERY, ALA., *December 3, 1864.*

Maj. Gen. D. H. MAURY,
   Mobile, Ala.:

Clanton's brigade, about 350 effectives, leaves this evening by boat for Selma.

GEORGE WM. BRENT,
Colonel and Assistant Adjutant-General.

MOBILE, *December 3, 1864.*

General G. T. BEAUREGARD,
   Montgomery, Ala.:

Last accounts report enemy passed through Franklinton, La., on the 2d, marching very slowly eastward. Governor Clark is actively turning out militia. In Alabama little has been done. A good re-enforcement of State troops for guard of eastern lines of communication with Mobile will enable me to act more efficiently for defense of Mobile and Ohio Railroad.

D. H. MAURY,
Major-General, Commanding.

MONTGOMERY, ALA., *December 3, 1864.*

Maj. Gen. D. H. MAURY,
Mobile:

Governor Watts has been requested to place under your command such of the militia of Alabama as you may call for.

GEORGE WM. BRENT,
Colonel and Assistant Adjutant-General.

MONTGOMERY, ALA., *December 3, 1864.*

Maj. Gen. F. GARDNER,
Meridian, Miss.:

General Beauregard desires a detailed report of General Hodge's surprise below Centerville. He is informed pickets in Mississippi and East Louisiana levy blackmail on cotton sent in enemy's lines.

GEORGE WM. BRENT,
Colonel and Assistant Adjutant-General.

MOBILE, *December 3, 1864.*

Major-General GARDNER,
Jackson, Miss.:

I will go to Meridian to-morrow. Clanton left Montgomery this evening for Selma and Meridian. Berry's and Crews' battalions left here this morning for Corinth. You had better stop them at Meridian, if you will need them. Concentrate all you can in time to defend the Mobile and Ohio road.

D. H. MAURY,
Major-General, Commanding.

MOBILE, *December 3, 1864.*

General F. GARDNER,
Jackson, Miss.:

Abbay's battery has seventy men more than are necessary to work his guns; armed with rifles, they will be very useful. Inform General Kirby Smith of all important movements, as Davidson's and Steele's, asking him to help you by sending troops over or by creating diversion. General Beauregard is in Montgomery, but going eastward again at once. When will you and Governor Clark be in Meridian? Twelve field guns left here this morning, with party in charge, destined for Corinth. How are militia turning out? Mobile and Ohio Railroad between Enterprise and Bucatunna should be well guarded, also telegraph line. Have you good officer and militia, or other force, to place there?

D. H. MAURY,
Major-General, Commanding.

MONTGOMERY, ALA., *December 3, 1864.*

Capt. W. A. REID,
    Assistant Adjutant-General, Corinth, Miss.:

Mabry's constitutes garrison at Corinth. Patterson is under orders of General Roddey. If pickets and details are needed from Patterson, call on General Roddey for them.

GEORGE WM. BRENT,
Colonel and Assistant Adjutant-General.

HEADQUARTERS CAVALRY, &C.,
Midway, December 3, 1864—10 p. m.

Maj. J. STODDARD JOHNSTON,
    Assistant Adjutant-General:

MAJOR: The enemy under General Irvin [?] moved from Bean's Station above Mooresburg yesterday, but returned in the evening. This force came from Kentucky. Scouts from the rear of the enemy, in the direction of Cumberland Gap, report their strength to be from 2,000 to 3,000. Information derived from Union sources represents the forces under Irvin [?] to have come to Bean's Station for the purpose of protecting a wagon train moving in the direction of Strawberry Plains. A force came up to Russellville this evening, driving in my pickets. I did not ascertain their strength. I suppose it to be the same force that was at Mooresburg, having crossed at Noah's Ferry, north of Morristown. No enemy have made their appearance this side of Strawberry Plains. A portion of Gillem's command is moving up the south side of the French Broad River. In view of the enemy's re-enforcement, I have fallen back this side of Lick Creek. I would suggest the propriety of the country west of Saltville, in the direction of Cumberland Gap, being watched, for fear the major portion of Burbridge's force moving in that direction. I shall guard, as far as possible, all approaches in the direction of the railroad. I have Major Day's battalion on the Rogersville road. My trains are at Evans' Cross-Roads, east of Warrensburg.

I am, very respectfully, your obedient servant,

JOHN C. VAUGHN,
Brigadier-General, Commanding.

P. S.—Major Day will scout in the direction of Cumberland Gap. General Duke is with me as yet.

Semi-weekly return of French's division, December 3, 1864.

Command.	Effective total.	Total.	Aggregate.
General staff		10	15
Cockrell's brigade	247	403	438
Sears' brigade	810	964	1,046
Total	1,057	1,377	1,499

RICHMOND, *December 4, 1864.*

General G. T. BEAUREGARD:

Your telegram of the 2d instant is referred to me for answer. If General E. K. Smith can now act as you suggest it would be well he should do so. You are authorized so to inform him, and to request his prompt attention. He has, however, failed heretofore to respond to like emergencies, and no plans should be based on his compliance.

JAMES A. SEDDON,
Secretary of War.

NEAR MACON, *December 4, 1864.*
(Received 6th.)

General S. COOPER:

General Hood reports, from near Columbia, Tenn., 28th ultimo, enemy's force has evacuated Columbia, retreating to Nashville. He anticipates no difficulty about supplies.

G. T. BEAUREGARD,
General.

HEADQUARTERS,
December 4, 1864—8.35 p. m.

Lieutenant-General STEWART,
Commanding:

GENERAL: I inclose a note from Chalmers. General Hood directs you to place a brigade on the Hillsborough pike and send a couple of Parrott guns to Chalmers. The brigade should be properly posted, and should connect with the other portion of your skirmish line to guard against any misfortune.

Yours, respectfully,

A. P. MASON,
Colonel and Assistant Adjutant-General.

[Inclosure.]

HEADQUARTERS CHALMERS' DIVISION,
December 4, 1864.

Col. A. P. MASON,
Assistant Adjutant-General:

COLONEL: It would be of great assistance to me in my operations on the river if a brigade of infantry can be sent to occupy this (Hillsborough) pike, so as to relieve Colonel Rucker's brigade and enable me to move him down to the river. I think the infantry would be of more service to me if used in that way than in any other. I would be glad to have the section of Parrott guns belonging to General Stewart's corps ordered to report to me for duty on the river. I have now a good supply of ammunition for my two Parrott guns, but have almost none for my other two guns (James' rifles). At the last account there were six gun-boats and one monitor in the river, and two guns are scarcely sufficient to attack them successfully. I am informed (unofficially) that a considerable body of cavalry was heard moving down on the opposite side of the river last night, but have heard nothing of them since.

Respectfully, your obedient servant,

JAS. R. CHALMERS,
Brigadier-General.

HEADQUARTERS ENGINEER CORPS, ARMY OF TENNESSEE,
December 4, 1864—9 p. m.

Lieut. Gen. A. P. STEWART,
Commanding Army Corps:

GENERAL: General Hood directs me to request that you will, before daylight to-morrow morning, withdraw one division from your front and post it on the hill to your left and rear, leaving two divisions to occupy the present line. He thinks the troops are too much crowded on the "burnt house hill," and liable to suffer from the enemy's artillery fire.

I have the honor to be, general, very respectfully, your obedient servant,

S. W. PRESSTMAN,
Lieut. Col. and Acting Chief Engineer, Army of Tennessee.

HEADQUARTERS SKIRMISH LINE, FRENCH'S DIVISION,
December 4, 1864.

Major SANDERS,
Assistant Adjutant-General, French's Division.

MAJOR: The cavalry do not connect with the pickets of General Sears' brigade. I am unable to find or hear anything of them. I have extended the pickets of General Sears' brigade far enough to the left to protect our flank during the day.

Very respectfully,

SAML. D. HARRIS,
Commanding Division Pickets.

HEADQUARTERS,
December 4, 1864—3 p. m.

Brigadier-General CHALMERS,
Commanding:

GENERAL: General Hood directed Rucker this morning to advance his pickets that the infantry might extend their left, but he now desires you to inform Rucker that this need not be done, as this extension will not take place at present, but you will continue to stop all the transports you can, and if an infantry brigade will assist it can be ordered to you from General Stewart.

Yours, respectfully,

A. P. MASON,
Colonel and Assistant Adjutant-General.

HEADQUARTERS CHALMERS' DIVISION CAVALRY,
At Mr. Compton's, on Hillsborough Pike, December 4, 1864.

Capt. W. D. GALE,
Assistant Adjutant-General:

CAPTAIN: I am directed by Brigadier-General Chalmers to say that he would like to have the guns report at his headquarters at 8 a. m. to-morrow, and to have Colonel Rucker's pickets relieved by that time. He has no horses which he can send for the artillery, as you suggest.

Respectfully, your obedient servant,

W. A. GOODMAN,
Captain and Assistant Adjutant-General.

MOBILE, *December 4, 1864.*
(Received 7.20 10th.)
Hon. J. A. SEDDON:

Farragut has gone to the North. The Hartford and other heavy vessels have disappeared from down bay. Steele, with 15,000 men, reported to have gone from Memphis up river last week. Governor Harris reports all of Tennessee south of Duck River in our possession. People of Tennessee and army in high spirits. A column of cavalry, under Davidson, 4,000 strong, reported moving from East Louisiana for Mobile and Ohio Railroad. Halligan, recently appointed lieutenant, has not yet used his torpedo boat; I do not believe he ever will. His boat is reported a most valuable invention. Many officers, army and navy, are urgent for command of her. May not Commodore Farrand or myself place proper officer in command, to attack enemy at once?

D. H. MAURY,
Major-General, Commanding.

———

MIDWAY, *December 4, 1864.*
(Via Jonesborough.)
General BRECKINRIDGE:

Below you will find dispatch from Major Day, north of Holston River. Enemy near Bull's Gap last night advancing.

WARRENSBURG, TENN.
General VAUGHN:

My scouts from Rocky Springs have returned. I do not think there is any doubt about General Burbridge being in the vicinity of Bean's Station with his Saltville crew force; but I do not think that he will advance on Bristol by this route, but rather think that he will go to the railroad by the way of Noah's or Long's Ford. Make your arrangements to meet heavy re-enforcements in East Tennessee; they are here. Will return to a point three miles above Warrensburg to-night. Dispatch to me by Collier's Ford. The enemy blockaded Flat Gap yesterday. There is no danger by Sneedsville. Let me hear from you.

J. C. VAUGHN,
Brigadier-General, Commanding.

———

MONTGOMERY, ALA., *December 5, 1864.*
General G. T. BEAUREGARD,
(Care of General Cobb, Macon, Ga. :)

General Gardner reports to-day from Meridian that he has information considered reliable that the troops lately landed at Memphis have gone up river. He will go to Corinth soon as he can be spared.

GEORGE WM. BRENT,
Colonel and Assistant Adjutant-General.

———

MONTGOMERY, ALA., *December 5, 1864.*
General G. T. BEAUREGARD:
(Care of General Cobb, Macon, Ga.)

Dispatch from Grand Junction, December 3, reports General A. J. Smith and forces coming down river to Memphis; Washburn and forces moving up river; also troops from direction Vicksburg moving up river without stopping at Memphis.

GEORGE WM. BRENT,
Colonel and Assistant Adjutant-General.

SPECIAL ORDERS, }   HDQRS. MILITARY DIV. OF THE WEST,
     No. 22.   }   *December 5, 1864.*

I. Maj. Gen. William T. Martin, with his personal staff, will report to Maj. Gen. F. Gardner for duty.

*   *   *   *   *   *   *

By command of General Beauregard:

GEORGE WM. BRENT,
Colonel and Assistant Adjutant-General.

HEADQUARTERS,
Six Miles from Nashville, on Franklin Pike, December 5, 1864.

Hon. JAMES A. SEDDON,
     Secretary of War, Richmond:

Our loss of officers in the battle of Franklin, on the 30th, was excessively large in proportion to the loss of men. The medical director reports a very large proportion of slightly wounded men.

J. B. HOOD,
General.

(Copy to General Beauregard.)

HEADQUARTERS,
Six Miles from Nashville, on Franklin Pike, December 5, 1864.

General G. T. BEAUREGARD,
     Macon, Ga.:

Your telegrams of the 26th received.* There is no major-general in this army who could now be spared for the duty specified. Brigadier-General Armstrong is the best person I could recommend from this army, provided he could be promoted to the proper rank.

J. B. HOOD,
General.

HEADQUARTERS,
Six Miles from Nashville, on Franklin Pike, December 5, 1864.

Capt. W. A. REID,
     Assistant Inspector-General, Corinth, Miss.:

Send forward at once all men belonging to this army in proper detachments, with officers to preserve discipline and prevent straggling on the march.

J. B. HOOD,
General.

HEADQUARTERS,
Six Miles from Nashville, on Franklin Pike, December 5, 1864.

Capt. S. S. SEMMES,
     Staff Paymaster, Army of Tennessee, Mobile, Ala.:

Rejoin the army without delay. Trains with escorts are constantly coming to the army from Cherokee Station.

By order of General Hood:

A. P. MASON,
Colonel and Assistant Adjutant-General.

---

* See Vol. XLIV, pp. 898, 899.

SPECIAL FIELD ORDERS, ⎰   HDQRS. ARMY OF TENNESSEE,
        No. 161.   ⎱   *In the Field, December 5, 1864.*

*   *   *   *   *   *   *

II. Col. James T. Wheeler, First [Sixth] Tennessee Cavalry, and Maj. J. H. Akin, Ninth Battalion Tennessee Cavalry, will report with their commands to Major-General Forrest, commanding cavalry, for temporary duty.

*   *   *   *   ·   *   *   *

By command of General Hood:

JAS. COOPER,
Captain and Acting Assistant Adjutant-General.

CIRCULAR.]   HEADQUARTERS ARMY OF TENNESSEE,
        Near Nashville, Tenn., December 5, 1864.

General Hood desires me to inform you that Major-General Forrest captured, this morning, the block-house and fort at La Vergne, with some commissary stores, 100 prisoners, two pieces of artillery, 100 small-arms and ammunition, with about 20 wagons and some teams. General Bate has burned three block-houses. General Hood desires that this news be furnished to the troops.

Very respectfully, your obedient servant,

A. P. MASON,
Colonel and Assistant Adjutant-General.

Consolidated return of the effective, total, and aggregate present of infantry and cavalry in Stewart's corps, from morning reports of December 5, 1864.

Commands.	Effective.	Total.	Aggregate present.
Loring's division:			
Infantry	2,463	3,652	3,977
Artillery	261	304	319
French's division:			
Infantry	1,551	2,261	2,492
Artillery	221	244	259
Walthall's division:			
Infantry	1,292	2,335	2,528
Artillery	258	319	321
Grand total	6,046	9,115	9,896

Effective strength of Lee's Army Corps, near Nashville, Tenn., December 5, 1864.

Command.	Effective present.	Total present.	Aggregate present.
Stevenson's division	2,706	3,713	4,075
Clayton's division	1,944	2,635	2,959
Johnson's division:			
Deas' brigade	628	898	981
Manigault's brigade	838	1,115	1,202
Sharp's brigade	532	777	822
Brantly's brigade	363	586	617
Total	2,361	3,376	3,622
Total infantry	7,011	9,724	10,656
Artillery	635	798	835
Grand total	7,646	10,522	11,491

The Fifty-eighth North Carolina Regiment at Columbia, and had at last report—effective, 246; total, 311; aggregate, 338.

HEADQUARTERS,
Near Nashville, on Franklin Pike, December 5, 1864.

Major-General BATE,
  Commanding, &c.:

Your dispatch of 7 a. m. this morning just received. Two good brigades, with a battery each, have just been sent to the vicinity of Murfreesborough. General Hood directs that you will report to Major-General Forrest, and that the defeat of that portion of the enemy at Murfreesborough is of the first importance.

A. P. MASON,
Colonel and Assistant Adjutant-General.

SPRING HILL, *December 5, 1864.*

Dr. J. B. COWAN,
  Chief Surgeon, Forrest's Cavalry:

SIR: In accordance with your order I began the removal of wounded from Franklin to Columbia, but arriving at this place with six wounded men I learned that no hospital had been established at Columbia for our men, and that those who were there were suffering very much for comfortable lodging and medical attention. I therefore deemed it best to acquaint you with these facts before I proceed further. Those men I brought to Spring Hill have comfortable places, and I have placed them under the charge of Dr. Fitz Gerald, assistant surgeon Seventh Tennessee, who was left in charge of the wounded at Spring Hill. Those men at Franklin are doing well. The citizens have plenty and are anxious for them to remain. I will return to Franklin to attend those wounded and to await your decision.

Very respectfully, your obedient servant,

D. C. McCAMPBELL,
Surgeon in Charge Chalmers' Division Hospital.

HEADQUARTERS,
Near Nashville, on Franklin Pike, December 5, 1864.

Brigadier-General RODDEY,
  Commanding Cavalry, &c., Northern Alabama:

General Hood directs that you not only destroy the railroad from Huntsville to Stevenson, but also from Stevenson to Murfreesborough. Communicate with General Hood in order that he may send you further orders.

A. P. MASON,
Colonel and Assistant Adjutant-General.

HEADQUARTERS,
Near Greeneville, December 5, 1864. (Via Jonesborough.)

General BRECKINRIDGE:

Major Day dispatches me, 3 p. m. yesterday, from the north side of the Holston, that Burbridge with seven regiments was at Bean's Station on the 3d instant. Scouts report no enemy in the vicinity of Bull's

Gap and Russellville; that they have fallen back in the direction of Morristown. Do not think that the enemy will advance any farther in this direction.

J. C. VAUGHN,
Brigadier-General, Commanding.

[DECEMBER 6, 1864.—For Beauregard to Davis, relating to Sherman's operations and Hood's campaign into Tennessee, &c., see Vol. XLIV, p. 931.]

MONTGOMERY, ALA., *December 6, 1864.*

General G. T. BEAUREGARD:
(Care of General Cobb, Macon, Ga.)

General Wirt Adams telegraphs from Panola, 6th:

Scouts report 10,000 to 12,000 troops having landed at Memphis during last few days.

GEORGE WM. BRENT,
Colonel and Assistant Adjutant-General.

HEADQUARTERS,
Near Nashville, Six Miles on Franklin Pike, December 6, 1864.
(Received 14th.)

Hon. JAMES A. SEDDON,
Secretary of War, Richmond, Va.:

I respectfully recommend that Major-General Breckinridge, with his forces, either be ordered into Kentucky or to join this army.

J. B. HOOD,
General.

HEADQUARTERS ARMY OF TENNESSEE,
Six Miles from Nashville, Tenn., December 6, 1864.

General G. T. BEAUREGARD,
Macon, Ga.:

Please have the railroad repaired to Decatur as soon as possible. Orders should be given for the impressment of the labor and material necessary at once. The Alabama and Tennessee Railroad is now in good order from here to Pulaski, and can soon be run to Decatur. Have now on it two good engines and three cars. Will have more cars in a day or two. It is important that the garrisons from Corinth to Decatur, including both places, should be garrisoned by troops other than from this army; perhaps the reserves in Alabama and Mississippi could be used for the purpose.

J. B. HOOD,
General.

GENERAL FIELD ORDERS, ⎱ HDQRS. ARMY OF TENNESSEE,
No. 39. ⎰ *Near Nashville, Tenn., December 6, 1864.*

I. The general commanding desires to call the attention of the officers and men to the fact that success and safety in battle consists in piercing the enemy's lines as quickly as possible after coming under his fire. No halts should be made, except those temporary ones necessary for partial rectification of the alignment.

II. Commanding officers will forward, with as little delay as possible, the names of those officers and soldiers who passed over the enemy's interior line of works at Franklin, on the evening of the 30th of November, that they may be forwarded to the War Department and placed upon the roll of honor.

By command of General Hood:

A. P. MASON,
Colonel and Assistant Adjutant-General.

HEADQUARTERS LORING'S DIVISION,
In Field, December 6, 1864.

Captain GALE,
Assistant Adjutant-General:

CAPTAIN: I have the honor to report that the men detailed to work on batteries finished works for eight guns, and, if necessary, they may be put into position to-night. For want of tools the men were not able to finish the work for the remaining four guns, but will do so to-night. The line, as run out by the engineers on the right of my division, seems to be too much on the side of the ridge, so much so that the view in front is shut out by the summit, forty or fifty yards in front; therefore, to establish a battery on this part of the line, it would be necessary to establish it fifty yards in front of the main line. I fear some error has been made, and would like to have the engineer to look over this part of the line that it may be rectified if necessary. The engineer did not report last night as expected, but I believe the works have been very well laid out. In case you wish to put artillery in position to-night be kind enough to let us know before dark, that everything may be put in readiness beforehand. There seems to be no change in my front.

Respectfully,

W. W. LORING,
Major-General.

HEADQUARTERS FRENCH'S DIVISION,
December 6, 1864.

Major HAMPTON,
Officer of the Day:

MAJOR: If it can be done I wish a work thrown up behind the house where we have the pickets. The house can then at some time be burnt. Also let our skirmishers advance to the stone wall that separates them from the enemy as soon as it is dusk.

S. G. FRENCH,
Major-General.

ON THE LINE, *December 6, 1864.*

Maj. Gen. S. G. FRENCH:

GENERAL: I deem it entirely unnecessary to advance skirmishers to the stone wall, as our pits can be strengthened without it and such a position is very much exposed.

Very respectfully, your obedient servant,

E. H. HAMPTON,
Major, Twenty-ninth North Carolina.

Increase the party at the house.

S. G. F.

HEADQUARTERS LEE'S CORPS,
Near Nashville, Tenn., December 6, 1864.

Maj. Gen. C. L. STEVENSON,
Commanding Division:

GENERAL: General Lee directs that where you have good abatis in your front you will withdraw your troops as far as possible, in complete organization, and bivouac them at some safe place in rear and convenient to the line, leaving a single rank in the trenches.

Very respectfully, your obedient servant,

J. W. RATCHFORD,
Assistant Adjutant-General.

HEADQUARTERS,
Six Miles from Nashville, on Franklin Pike, December 6, 1864.

Brigadier-General RODDEY,
Commanding Cavalry:

General Hood directs that you will join the army here, with your command, as soon as possible, leaving a garrison, however, at Decatur; and any wagons you can spare for the purpose of hauling material for building a bridge over the river at Decatur. As you march to join the army destroy as much as you can of the railroad between Huntsville and Stevenson and between Stevenson and Murfreesborough.

A. P. MASON,
Colonel and Assistant Adjutant-General.

MOBILE, ALA., *December 6, 1864.*

Col. GEORGE WILLIAM BRENT,
Assistant Adjutant-General, Montgomery, Ala.:

COLONEL: The following is respectfully submitted for the information of General Beauregard, and gives an account of engineering operations bearing upon the safety of the communications of the Army of Tennessee: At Corinth, Fort Williams, the stronghold of the place, is repaired, made self-sustaining, and needs but its garrison (200 men) and its armament (six field pieces, viz, two Parrotts, two Napoleons, and two howitzers) to make it hold out against a large force until starved into surrender. By the present date it is expected that the remaining points around the town are finished and also ready to be manned; wells and bombproofs will then be prepared in all. A good position for batteries to defend the passage of the river against gunboats is reported four miles below Savannah, the western being the concave side and its banks being sufficiently elevated to command the ground opposite; good roads lead to and from this crossing. The battery at Chickasaw Creek is being rapidly completed. Buoys for torpedoes, constructed in accordance with General Beauregard's plan, are commenced, and the torpedoes first sent have arrived. The reserve pontoon boats to be collected at Corinth will reach about as follows:

At Corinth or en route:	Pontoon-boats.
December 5	32
December 12	10
December 19	20
December 26	20
December 31	18
Making the number ordered	100

Decking for above boats already at Corinth. Fair progress, considering the scarcity of trains, is being made on the Memphis and Charleston Railroad. The Mobile and Ohio Railroad is reported in fair running condition. Attention is respectfully called to the necessity of furnishing clothing for the negroes impressed by the Government. At least 3,000 suits should, if possible, be placed subject to my orders, together with same number of pairs of shoes.

I am, respectfully, your obedient servant,

M. L. SMITH,
Major-General and Chief Engineer, Military Div. of the West.

[Indorsement.]

HEADQUARTERS MILITARY DIVISION OF THE WEST,
Montgomery, December 10, 1864.

Respectfully referred to Lieutenant-General Taylor for his information.

By command of General Beauregard:

GEORGE WM. BRENT.

HEADQUARTERS,
Six Miles from Nashville, on Franklin Pike, December 6, 1864.

Maj. Gen. D. H. MAURY,
Comdg. Dept. of Ala., Miss., and East La., Mobile, Ala.:

I respectfully request that you will have the railroad to Decatur, Ala., repaired as soon as possible. Orders should at once be given to impress the labor and material necessary, and the work placed in the hands of some energetic man. I am running the Tennessee and Alabama Railroad from here to Pulaski, and will run to Decatur in a day or two.

J. B. HOOD,
General.

HEADQUARTERS ARMY OF TENNESSEE,
Near Nashville, Tenn., on Franklin Pike, December 6, 1864.

General D. H. MAURY,
Commanding Department of Mississippi and East Louisiana:

GENERAL: I earnestly request that you have the railroad repaired as quickly as possible to Decatur, Ala., and that orders may at once be issued for the impressment of the necessary labor and material, the whole to be placed under the control of some good railroad officer, who will push the matter through. There are certain supplies necessary to this army which cannot be obtained from the surrounding country, and which, therefore, must be brought from the rear. Wagon transportation, at all times slow and limited, will become in the bad weather, which must soon set in, a matter of impossibility. The Tennessee and Alabama Railroad is now in running order from this point to Pulaski, and will be to Decatur in a few days. There are now upon it two fine engines and three cars; additional cars are now being moved from the Chattanooga and Nashville Railroad across the country to be placed upon it. There is also a train and engine at Decatur in good order, so that rolling stock will be abundant. I telegraphed to-day both to General Beauregard and yourself urging the rebuilding of the Memphis and Charleston Railroad to Decatur. The permanent occupation of this country absolutely requires that this road be repaired. At this distance it is not possible for me to give the matter personal attention, and I must rely upon your kindness to help me.

Very respectfully, your obedient servant,

J. B. HOOD,
General.

[Indorsement.]

HEADQUARTERS DISTRICT OF THE GULF,
Mobile, December 19, 1864.

Respectfully forwarded to lieutenant-general commanding.

DABNEY H. MAURY,
Major-General.

JONESBOROUGH, *December 6, 1864.*

General BRECKINRIDGE:

No advance of the enemy above Russellville as yet.

J. C. VAUGHN,
Brigadier-General.

JONESBOROUGH, *December 6, 1864.*

General BRECKINRIDGE:

My command goes to Rogersville to-morrow. May I remain there?

B. W. DUKE,
Brigadier-General.

NARROWS, VA., *December 6, 1864.*

Maj. J. S. JOHNSTON:

Your telegram received. Will march via Dublin. Send any letters for the command to that place.

G. B. COSBY,
Brigadier-General.

[DECEMBER 7, 1864.—For Seddon to Hardee, transmitting dispatch to E. Kirby Smith, relative to crossing of troops to aid Hood, &c., see Vol. XLI, Part I, p. 123.]

MONTGOMERY, ALA., *December 7, 1864.*

General G. T. BEAUREGARD:
  (Care of General Cobb, Macon, Ga.)

General Maury reports:

Repeated rumors and reports of preparations at Pensacola to attack Mobile. Only one heavy ship in lower bay. Transports unusually active. Raiders crossed Pearl River; moved on morning 5th toward Mobile and Ohio Railroad. General Gardner will send some troops to defend road. Governor Clark will have militia sent for same purpose. Does General Beauregard desire the construction of 100 pontoons to continue? The work absorbs all my mechanics. The present condition Army of Tennessee may render them unnecessary.

General Taylor has reached here. Have directed pontoons to be continued, which will be done in a few days.

GEORGE WM. BRENT,
Colonel and Assistant Adjutant-General.

GENERAL ORDERS, } HDQRS. MILITARY DIVISION OF THE WEST,
No. 6.   }   *Montgomery, Ala., December 7, 1864.*

I. General Beauregard has seen, with pain and mortification, that large numbers of the Confederate cavalry are absent from their colors without leave, avoiding all duty, shirking from contact with the enemy, roaming over the country engaged in the pillage and robbery of defenseless women and loyal citizens, and devastating a fair and fruitful country, on the productions of which our country depends. He has determined that a rigid scrutiny shall be had in regard to all such acts, and will bring to punishment offenders. He enjoins on all commanders to institute immediate inquiry, arrest offenders, and bring them to trial. Existing orders and regulations on the subject of transferring dismounted cavalrymen—those guilty of improper conduct in face of the enemy and of violence to citizens—must be strictly executed.

II. To this end depots will be established at Macon, Opelika, and Okolona, under command of officers of rank and discretion, to which commanders of cavalry will all immediately send all cavalrymen who are dismounted, or who do not keep themselves prepared with serviceable horses, or shall misbehave before the enemy, or shall be guilty of illegally wasting, spoliating, or appropriating to their own use any private property, or doing violence to any citizen. Brigade or regimental commanders of cavalry will, at the same time, detail a suitable officer to proceed with such officers and men to the nearest camp, and will forward duplicate descriptive lists of all such as may be sent—one to the army headquarters and the other to the commandant of the camp.

III. All cavalry soldiers found absent from their commands without proper authority will be arrested and sent with a written statement of the facts concerning their arrest to the nearest camp, and duplicate to his commander. Their horses and equipments will be turned over to the nearest post quartermaster, who will receipt for the same, and immediately notify the chief quartermaster of the army of the fact.

IV. The commanding officers of the camps will forward weekly to army headquarters [lists] of all officers and men sent to their camp, with such other statements and remarks as will enable the army commander to make the necessary order of transfer to infantry commands. Those returns will be promptly revised by the army commander, who will, with as little delay as practicable, make transfer in all cases deemed by him proper, and forward to these headquarters copies of his orders, with his reasons for the transfer.

V. Commanding officers of these camps will be held responsible for the drill and discipline of the men under his command. He will organize them into companies and assign them suitable officers. Guard duty will be strictly performed, and the roll called, and other duties prescribed in army regulations, and general orders will be duly observed.

VI. The necessary officers of the different staff departments will be assigned by army commanders, and until this shall be done officers will be detailed to act as such.

VII. The following officers are assigned as commandants of said camps, and will report accordingly: Selma, Brig. Gen. R. C. Tyler, Provisional Army, C. S.; Opelika, Lieut. Col. J. W. Buford; Okolona, Col. J. W. Colquitt, First Arkansas Volunteers.

By command of General Beauregard:

GEORGE WM. BRENT,
Colonel and Assistant Adjutant-General.

HEADQUARTERS ARMY OF TENNESSEE,
Six Miles from Nashville, on Franklin Pike, December 7, 1864.
(Received 10.10 18th.)

Hon. J. A. SEDDON:

I withdraw my recommendation in favor of the promotion of Major-General Cheatham, for reasons which I will write more fully.

J. B. HOOD.

HEADQUARTERS,
Six Miles from Nashville, on Franklin Pike, December 7, 1864.
General G. T. BEAUREGARD,
Macon, Ga.:

Captain Reid, commanding at Corinth, Miss., reports that "scouts from vicinity of Memphis report that Steele with 15,000 men landed at that point on last Thursday and passed up the river Saturday." I respectfully request that all men belonging to this army and any re-enforcements that can be spared be sent forward as soon as possible.

J. B. HOOD,
General.

HEADQUARTERS,
Six Miles from Nashville, on Franklin Pike, December 7, 1864.
General G. T. BEAUREGARD,
Macon, Ga.:

Whenever you can I will be pleased if you could visit this army.

J. B. HOOD,
General.

CIRCULAR.]   HEADQUARTERS ARMY OF TENNESSEE,
Near Nashville, Tenn., December 7, 1864.

Corps commanders will make a report to these headquarters stating the number of flags that were captured by the enemy in the engagements of November 29 and 30, designating the regiments which lost them.

By command of General Hood:

A. P. MASON,
Colonel and Assistant Adjutant-General.

HEADQUARTERS,
Six Miles from Nashville, on Franklin Pike,
December 7, 1864—8 a. m.

Major-General FORREST,
          Commanding, &c.:

General Hood directs me to say that he has received your suggestion, through Lieutenant-Colonel Henry, of falling back a little to give the enemy a chance of going toward Lebanon if they will. General Hood thinks the idea a good one, and to strike them while they are moving.

A. P. MASON,
Colonel and Assistant Adjutant-General.

HEADQUARTERS,
Six Miles from Nashville, on Franklin Pike, December 7, 1864.

Major-General FORREST,
          Commanding, &c.:

General Hood directs that Col. B. J. Hill, with his command, be sent to Bedford, Giles, and Marshall Counties to break up and destroy the home guards in those counties, to collect animals for the army, and to conscribe men liable to military duty. The home guards are reported to be doing great damage to the country and especially to the mills, which are of great use to us. Colonel Hill should place them all in running order as soon as possible. Among the principal mills are Lillard's, Joyce's, Widow Robinson's, Morrison's, White's, and all in the neighborhood of Shelbyville.

A. P. MASON,
Colonel and Assistant Adjutant-General.

MOBILE, *December 7, 1864.*

Governor CHARLES CLARK,
          Macon, Miss.:

Push your militia to Shubuta and Bucatunna as rapidly as possible.

D. H. MAURY,
Major-General, Commanding.

MOBILE, *December 7, 1864.*

Lieutenant-General TAYLOR,
          Montgomery:

Hear from my scouts and Gardner that enemy, 4,000, crossed Pearl River on the 4th. Seems approaching railroad about Shubuta. Gardner has sent about 500 men, Clanton's brigade, and gone to Corinth to-day. If not threatened here I can send McCulloch and Maury, who are ready to move as soon as route of enemy ascertained. I have ordered the prisoners to be moved from Meridian at once; stores to be ready to move when necessary. Have sent General Thomas to Meridian to take command of all militia and other forces at Meridian, Shubuta, and Bucatunna. Gardner reports to-night he can send no forces from above Meridian. I have telegraphed him if Corinth not threatened to send all available. Last report of enemy is approaching Ellisville, west of Bucatunna.

D. H. MAURY,
Major-General, Commanding.

MOBILE, *December 7, 1864.*

Lieut. Gen. R. TAYLOR,
    Montgomery, Ala.:

Reports indicate the enemy as marching on Shubuta, Mobile and Ohio Railroad. Clanton's brigade reaches Shubuta to-day. Governor Clark promised to have all the militia whom he could send at Shubuta during the week. General Gardner has been directed to send all the supernumerary and dismounted men in camp at Crawfordsville to Shubuta; intends putting 1,000 men at Shubuta and same number at Bucatunna. Have directed prisoners at Meridian to be moved to Cahaba and stores to be ready to move to Demopolis. I hold such cavalry as I can spare here in readiness to move against the column reported to be advancing by lower road on Mobile and Ohio Railroad or its vicinity. Still receive reports of preparations at Pascagoula to move against Mobile. No movements yet commenced from Pensacola. Believe Farragut has gone North.

D. H. MAURY,
Major-General, Commanding.

HDQRS. DEPARTMENT OF ALA., MISS., AND EAST LA.,
    Mobile, December 7, 1864.

Brigadier-General THOMAS,
    Mobile, Ala.:

GENERAL: The major-general commanding directs that you will proceed to Meridian and direct the movements of the troops against the enemy, who is moving from Pearl River toward the Mobile and Ohio Railroad. General Gardner has gone to Corinth, but a telegram has been sent recalling him to Meridian. Put yourself in communication with him as quickly as possible. The dismounted men of Clanton's brigade, about 350, leave Meridian for Shubuta this evening. The governor of Mississippi will send militia as rapidly as possible to aid in the protection of the railroad. There is a company of cavalry of the Eighteenth Mississippi Regiment marching from Enterprise, which I have ordered to be stopped at Shubuta to report to Colonel Colvin, to scout, &c. I will hold as much of the cavalry in the District of the Gulf as can be spared to aid in operations against the enemy. When it becomes necessary to remove the stores from Meridian or elsewhere on the road they will be sent to Demopolis. You will report to General Gardner and act under his orders. In default of your ability to communicate with him rely on your own judgment and the above instructions.

Very respectfully, your obedient servant,

WM. M. LEVY,
Lieut. Col. and Assistant Adjutant and Inspector General.

HDQRS. DEPARTMENT OF ALA., MISS., AND EAST LA.,
    Mobile, December 7, 1864—10.45 p. m.

Col. R. McCULLOCH,
    Dog River Factory:

I am directed by the major-general commanding to say that you will move at daydawn to-morrow with all your available force (leaving only the necessary pickets) to Leakesville, Miss., where telegraphic orders will be sent you from Citronelle. Please throw out scouts in the direction of Augusta and Ellisville, and in any other direction likely to be taken by the enemy. Colonel Maury, with 250 cavalry and Tobin's light battery, will reach here to-night from Blakely. He will be ordered to report to you, and to move on the Leakesville road at daylight or as soon thereafter as practicable. If you take with you Tobin's battery, it is deemed expedient to leave behind the section of Winston's guns which you have with you. Your quartermaster has been instructed to place six days' forage of corn at Citronelle. At Bucatunna you will find a supply of forage for your animals and rations for your men. Colonel Colvin, with 350 men and a battery, arrived at Shubuta or Bucatunna to-night. Put yourself in communication with him in the defense of the Mobile and Ohio Railroad. Colvin will probably have with him the company of sixty-six men of the Eighteenth Mississippi which left Enterprise yesterday morning. The general commanding places great reliance upon your known vigor and promptness, and hopes, with the co-operating force of Colvin and others which are expected, that you will be able to thwart the designs of the enemy.

Very respectfully, your obedient servant,

D. W. FLOWERREE,
Assistant Adjutant-General.

MOBILE, *December 7, 1864.*

General GARDNER:

If there is no movement against Corinth send at once every man you can spare to Meridian and to points on the railroad below Meridian which may be threatened. I have sent General Thomas to Meridian, and ordered him to take command of all troops there and below as far as Bucatunna and oppose the enemy. I hold the available cavalry and light artillery here ready to move to meet the column reported advancing in this direction. Did Hood order the troops away from Crawfordsville? I ordered them to be sent to Bucatanna before I left Meridian. General Martin is ordered to you by General Beauregard, also Captain Jenifer. Thomas is sent to Meridian for this emergency. I have ordered the prisoners away at once to Cahaba, and stores when necessary. Urge Governor Clark to urge out the militia.

D. H. MAURY,
Major-General, Commanding.

MOBILE, *December 7, 1864.*

Maj. Gen. F. GARDNER,
Meridian, Miss.:

A company of McCulloch's brigade, sixty-six strong, marched yesterday morning from Enterprise toward Mobile. Orders will find it at Shubuta or Bucatunna. Use it if you find it necessary, informing me where you send it. Send King's company down to Bucatunna at once, giving them small-arms. Send their cannon with them if they have any. How soon can you have troops at Bucatunna, and what force?

D. H. MAURY,
Major-General, Commanding.

MOBILE, *December 7, 1864.*

Maj. J. D. SAYERS,
    Assistant Adjutant-General, Meridian, Miss.:

A company of cavalry, sixty-six strong, marched from Enterprise to Shubuta this morning. Order the commanding officer to halt at Shubuta. Send out pickets and scouts toward the enemy, and report to Colonel Colvin, commanding Clanton's brigade, who will reach Shubuta to-night.

                                W. M. LEVY,
            Assistant Adjutant and Inspector General.

MOBILE, *December 7, 1864.*

Maj. J. D. SAYERS,
    Assistant Adjutant-General, Meridian, Miss.:

Orders were sent this morning to move the prisoners to Cahaba and the stores to Demopolis when necessary.

                                D. H. MAURY,
                Major-General, Commanding.

MOBILE, *December 7, 1864.*

Brig. Gen. B. M. THOMAS,
        Shubuta, Miss.:

Assume command of all troops at Meridian and between Meridian and Bucatunna, and endeavor to attack the enemy before he reaches the railroad. Establish yourself where you think best. Call on Governor Clark, at Macon, to hasten the militia to you.

                                D. H. MAURY,
                Major-General, Commanding.

MOBILE, *December 7, 1864.*

Col. C. H. COLVIN,
        Shubuta, Miss.:

Stop at Shubuta or Bucatunna, as you find best, in order to defeat the enemy in his attempt to strike the railroad. A company of cavalry left Enterprise this morning sixty-six strong, on its way to join McCulloch here; stop it, and use as scouts or otherwise. General Thomas is on the up train of cars to Meridian, to command in absence of General Gardner. Keep me informed of all that transpires.

                                D. H. MAURY,
                Major-General, Commanding.

HEADQUARTERS CAVALRY FORCE,
    December 7, 1864. (Via Jonesborough 8th.)

Major-General BRECKINRIDGE:

Burbridge was still at Noah's Ferry and Bean's Station yesterday evening.

                                J. C. VAUGHN,
                Brigadier-General, Commanding.

GREENEVILLE, TENN., *December 7, 1864—7 p. m.*

Major-General BRECKINRIDGE:

Yours of the 6th instant has just reached me. In regard to sending General Duke's command north of the Holston River as soon as I can spare them, that time will not come as long as the forces remain in East Tennessee that were in our front when you left us, and now there is a force that came from Cumberland Gap of from 2,000 to 4,000 men, so all my scouts and citizens report. But it is my intention to send General Duke's command to Hawkins County to-morrow or next day, if everything is quiet. My scouts were at Noah's Ferry, or Ford, yesterday p. m., and the enemy were still encamped in the vicinity of Bean's Station, with pickets at all the fords on the Holston near there. This county is full of parties from the Federal Army bushwhacking. General Duke's men were attacked to-day, while foraging, within four or five miles of Greeneville, and two of his men captured. The forces of Colonel Palmer do us no good. The enemy have foraged none above the Strawberry Plains since you left south of the Holston River. General Carter and I agreed to exchange all citizen prisoners, except a few who are indicted for treason. I have sent a copy of the agreement to the Secretary of War. Whether they will agree to it or not is to be seen. I did what I thought was best for our friends. The railroad is repaired only about half way to Greeneville at this time. To send Cosby's and Giltner's brigades into Hawkins or Hancock Counties, in Tennessee, or Lee County, Va., would threaten Cumberland Gap and cause the force at Bean's Station to fall back. There is plenty of supplies of all kinds in either of those counties.

Very respectfully, your obedient servant,

JOHN C. VAUGHN,
Brigadier-General.

———

GREENEVILLE, *December 7, 1864.*
(Via Jonesborough.)

Major-General BRECKINRIDGE:

Burbridge's forces still at Bean's Station, Tenn., yesterday. I think he is awaiting the result of Hood's campaign in Middle Tennessee.

J. C. VAUGHN,
Brigadier-General.

———

MONTGOMERY, ALA., *December 8, 1864.*
(Received 14th.)

General G. T. BEAUREGARD:
(Care of General Cobb, Macon, Ga.)

P. Ellis, assistant adjutant-general, reports following from Jackson, Miss., 7th:

Fourteen boats loaded with troops reported went up river from Memphis on 3d instant.

GEORGE WM. BRENT,
Colonel and Assistant Adjutant-General.

(Copy to General S. Cooper, Adjutant and Inspector General, Richmond, Va.)

MONTGOMERY, ALA., *December 8, 1864.*

General G. T. BEAUREGARD:

(Care of General Cobb, Macon, Ga.)

The following received.*

Strange dispatch. It would be well to recommend to Department that General Bragg be sent at once to relieve Smith, and organize and administer trans-Mississippi, and General R. Taylor to command troops. This would be a strong concentration and secure prompt action. Otherwise, we shall not be able to open spring campaign.

GEORGE WM. BRENT,
Colonel and Assistant Adjutant-General.

HEADQUARTERS ARMY OF TENNESSEE,
Six Miles from Nashville, December 8, 1864.
(Received 10.20 17th.)

Hon. J. A. SEDDON:

A good lieutenant-general should be sent here at once, to command the corps now commanded by Major-General Cheatham. I have no one to recommend for the position.

J. B. HOOD.

HEADQUARTERS ARMY OF TENNESSEE,
Six Miles from Nashville, December 8, 1864.
(Received 10.20 17th.)

Hon. J. A. SEDDON:

Major-General Cheatham made a failure on the 30th of November, which will be a lesson to him. I think it best he should remain in his position for the present. I withdraw my telegrams of yesterday and to-day on this subject.

J. B. HOOD.

CIRCULAR.]   HEADQUARTERS ARMY OF TENNESSEE,
Near Nashville, Tenn., December 8, 1864.

The commanding general directs that regular and frequent roll-calls be made in the respective commands of the army as a preventive of straggling, it having been reported that straggling soldiers are depredating upon the property of citizens of this neighborhood. The attention of corps and all other commanding officers is called to the importance of a strict enforcement of this order.

By command of General Hood:

A. P. MASON,
Colonel and Assistant Adjutant-General.

CIRCULAR.]   HEADQUARTERS ARMY OF TENNESSEE,
Near Nashville, Tenn., December 8, 1864.

General Hood directs that you will have your entire line examined late each evening and very early each morning, to observe the enemy closely, to ascertain if any change should take place.

By order of General Hood:

A. P. MASON,
Colonel and Assistant Adjutant-General.

---

* See Seddon to Beauregard, 4th, p. 647.

HEADQUARTERS,
Six Miles from Nashville, on Franklin Pike,
December 8, 1864—2 p. m.

Major General FORREST,
    Commanding Cavalry, Army of Tennessee:

General Hood directs me to say that he sent Lieutenant Wade, aide-de-camp, this morning to tell you to drive the enemy back; he does not wish that you shall so construe this order as to mean to attack the enemy's works at Murfreesborough, but you will endeavor to drive them back to Murfreesborough, and then give them an opportunity to go out from there either toward Lebanon or any other direction they may choose. General Hood is fully satisfied that you have done all that could be done in the case, and desires that you will continue to act upon your best judgment of the case.

A. P. MASON,
Colonel and Assistant Adjutant-General.

HEADQUARTERS,
Six Miles from Nashville, on Franklin Pike,
December 8, 1864—6.30 p. m.

Major-General FORREST,
    Commanding Cavalry:

General Hood directs that you will send Major-General Bate's division and Sears' brigade back to the army, keeping the other two brigades of infantry and whatever artillery you deem necessary. As soon as Bate's division arrives here General Hood will send you another division of infantry, one of the best in the army. Keep your scouts out well in the direction of Lebanon.

A. P. MASON,
Colonel and Assistant Adjutant-General.

MOBILE, *December 8, 1864.*

Governor CLARK,
    Macon, Miss.:

I have sent General Thomas to Meridian to command the troops. McCulloch's brigade, with Maury, go toward Bucatunna. Gardner has ordered down Mabry and others, sufficient, I believe, to check him, and if your State troops get out promptly he will be ruined. Urge everything out to report to General Thomas at Meridian, those about Bucatunna to Colonel Colvin.

D. H. MAURY,
Major-General, Commanding.

MOBILE, *December 8, 1864—2.30 a. m.*

Lieutenant-General TAYLOR:

Have just heard from Gardner and Governor Clark. Enough troops are in motion to defeat enemy. Think they will concentrate in time, probably near Bucatunna. Nothing will be moved from Meridian, unless road is cut below and near. Prisoners will be sent off at once.

I hear reports of intended attack here, and you know my force, but I do not hesitate to detach cavalry to defeat this raid.   Have placed supplies at Shubuta, Bucatunna, and Citronelle.

D. H. MAURY,
Major-General, Commanding.

MOBILE, *December 8, 1864.*

Lieutenant-General TAYLOR,
Montgomery:

Nothing further from raiding party.   Please use all of your influence with the Governor and Legislature to get militia and State troops into service at once.   Have received dispatches this morning from Colonel Armistead that boats are being prepared in Choctawhatchie Bay to send marauding party up the Chattahoochee after cotton and other plunder.

D. H. MAURY,
Major-General, Commanding.

MOBILE, *December 8, 1864—10 p. m.*

General R. TAYLOR,
Montgomery:

Nothing of enemy's whereabouts yet.   Have sent your orders to Gardner.   Thomas reports this morning "enemy seems marching slowly," afterward, that he could hear nothing from him.   Thomas is at Bucatunna.   Send any force to Pollard you can rake up.

D. H. MAURY,
Major-General, Commanding.

MOBILE, *December 8, 1864.*

General THOMAS,
Bucatunna:

The company of Eighteenth Mississippi Battalion of Cavalry was ordered to march from Enterprise toward Mobile on the morning of 6th.   Telegraph in my name to Enterprise and Shubuta any orders you may desire to give.

D. H. MAURY,
Major-General, Commanding.

MOBILE, *December 8, 1864.*

General THOMAS,
Meridian:

Have sent McCulloch and Maury to Leakesville.   They will probably be at or near Bucatunna to-morrow.   Colvin can communicate and co-operate with them.   Gardner and Governor Clark are sending troops.   Endeavor to concentrate and attack enemy before he can cut the road.   Have telegraph line carefully watched.   I think he will strike for Bucatunna.   Colvin ought to be moved there.

D. H. MAURY,
Major-General, Commanding.

MOBILE, *December 8, 1864.*

Major SAYERS,
        Assistant Adjutant-General, Meridian, Miss.:

If small-arms were not issued to any men of Abbay's battery, send them, with accouterments, ammunition, &c., about forty rifles. Tell Major Young King's battery (dismounted) has been ordered down from Verona. He and chief of ordnance must ascertain what horses and harness, &c., it requires, and equip it soon as possible; meantime they will use small-arms. Do not be precipitate in moving stores from Meridian. I have ordered McCulloch's brigade and Maury to Leakesville, thence toward Bucatunna, if enemy moves that way. Give orders for prompt issue of supplies, which may be needed.

D. H. MAURY,
Major-General, Commanding.

MOBILE, *December 8, 1864.*

Colonel COLVIN,
        At Shubuta or Meridian:

Your best position will be at or near Bucatunna. I think McCulloch's brigade will be at Leakesville to-night, probably near Bucatunna to-morrow night. Communicate and co-operate with him. Take every means you can to guard telegraph line. There are some negro dogs in your vicinity, use them to trail who ever may cut it, and deal summarily.

D. H. MAURY,
Major-General, Commanding.

MOBILE, *December 8, 1864—10 p. m.*

Col. R. McCULLOCH,
        Commanding Cavalry, Leakesville:
(To be forwarded by courier from Citronelle.)

Colonel Maury's regiment left town about 9 a. m.; it is not far behind you. Tobin's battery left about sunset; is in camp a few miles out. Send orders where it can find you. Send me frequent information of enemy's movements to Citronelle, or by other shorter means. Keep some of your forces always between me and enemy.

D. H. MAURY,
Major-General, Commanding.

MOBILE, *December 8, 1864.*

General HODGE:

Send every man you can after enemy. Direct Scott to join nearest troops to him on Mobile and Ohio Railroad and co-operate against enemy. He will find supplies at Shubuta, Bucatunna, and Citronelle.

D. H. MAURY,
Major-General, Commanding.

ROGERSVILLE, *December 8, 1864.*
(Via Bristol 10th.)

General BRECKINRIDGE:

General Burbridge's command retreated from Mooresburg to Bean's Station yesterday. The force is estimated 3.500. He takes all horses, cattle, and hogs. My scouts annoy his pickets. I send the same to Vaughn.

GEO. W. DAY,
Major, Commanding at Rogersville.

DUBLIN, *December 8, 1864.*

Maj. J. STODDARD JOHNSTON,
Assistant Adjutant-General:

General Cosby's brigade left this morning.

R. D. GARDNER,
Lieutenant-Colonel, Commanding Post.

HEADQUARTERS,
Six Miles from Nashville, on Franklin Pike, December 9, 1864.

General G. T. BEAUREGARD,
Montgomery, Ala.:

It is very important that the two Kentucky brigades, of Lewis and Williams, should be sent to this army as soon as the interests of the public service will allow.

J. B. HOOD,
General.

HEADQUARTERS,
Six Miles from Nashville, on Franklin Pike,
December 9, 1864—2.20 p. m.

Lieutenant-General STEWART,
Commanding Corps, Army of Tennessee:

General Hood directs that you will push forward, with all possible haste, the work of fortifying the hills in rear of your left upon which you are now working, that you may be in readiness, whenever called upon, to move with two of your divisions and one other division from another corps, with a battery to each of these divisions, to prevent the enemy from re-enforcing Murfreesborough, or to capture the force now at Murfreesborough should it attempt to move off.

A. P. MASON,
Colonel and Assistant Adjutant-General.

HEADQUARTERS,
Overton's House, December 9, 1864—10.30 a. m.

Lieutenant-General STEWART,
Commanding:

GENERAL: General Hood desires that you will ride over to see him, and bring with you the commanding officer of the Missouri brigade.

Yours, respectfully,

A. P. MASON,
Colonel and Assistant Adjutant-General.

HEADQUARTERS,
Six Miles from Nashville, on Franklin Pike,
December 9, 1864—8 a. m.

Major-General FORREST,
    Commanding Cavalry:

I wrote you yesterday that General Hood directed you should send up Bate's division and Sears' brigade, and that he would send you another division of infantry. He now desires me to inform you that you will send up Bate and Sears, as heretofore directed, but that he will not send you another division of infantry. The two brigades of infantry which you will retain you will make intrench themselves strongly on Stewart's Creek, or at La Vergne, as you may deem best, to constitute a force in observation of the enemy. Keep a battery with these two brigades, or two, if you think one will not be enough. General Hood directs also that you have a brigade of cavalry in the neighborhood of Lebanon, to picket from there to the "Hermitage," and hold the remainder of your cavalry in observation of the enemy at Murfreesborough, keeping your headquarters on or near the main Nashville and Murfreesborough road.

A. P. MASON,
Colonel and Assistant Adjutant-General.

HEADQUARTERS,
Six Miles from Nashville, on Franklin Pike,
December 9, 1864—2.20 p. m.

Major-General FORREST,
    Commanding, &c.:

General Hood is making such dispositions as to endeavor to prevent the enemy from re-enforcing Murfreesborough, and also to defeat the force at Murfreesborough should they attempt to leave there.

A. P. MASON,
Colonel and Assistant Adjutant-General.

SPECIAL ORDERS, }   HEADQUARTERS FORREST'S CAVALRY,
    No. 171.   }   *In the Field, December 9, 1864.*

*   *   *   *   *   *   *

V. Capt. C. S. Hill is announced on the staff of the major-general commanding as chief of ordnance, and will be obeyed and respected accordingly.

*   *   *   *   *   *   *

By command of Major-General Forrest:

J. P. STRANGE,
Assistant Adjutant-General.

MOBILE, *December 9, 1864.*

Lieutenant-General TAYLOR,
    Montgomery:

Following dispatch just received, dated Shubuta, December 9, 1864:

No very reliable information of enemy's movements. Scout, arrived here this morning, who has been forty miles south, reports having seen Colonel Scott's cavalry, who said enemy crossed Leaf River, at Enon, Wednesday night, with 8,000 infantry and 2,000 cavalry, moving in direction of Winchester or State line, and says he obtained this information from a major in Colonel Scott's command. A citizen arrived at Waynesborough last night; states he traveled from Woodville on a line parallel to enemy twelve miles distant; saw Scott's men, who said enemy were 5,000 cavalry, two negro and one white regiment of infantry, with wagons and pontoons. All statements agree that they are moving slowly. Rained slowly all night and now very hard, which must raise streams.

Enon is on Leaf River, twelve miles west of Augusta, about fifty miles due west of Mobile and Ohio Railroad, and on the lower road to Mobile. All previous accounts represent the enemy's force as exclusively cavalry, with seventeen pieces of artillery.

D. H. MAURY,
Major-General, Commanding.

MOBILE, *December 9, 1864—7 p. m.*

Major-General GARDNER,
    Meridian, Miss.:

Reports from Mr. Fleming, at Shubuta, this morning, say enemy crossed Leaf River on Wednesday night, at Enon. Please push troops down to Bucatunna, and have preparations made to move them still lower. Thomas reports that he can learn nothing of any enemy above Shubuta.

D. H. MAURY,
Major-General, Commanding.

MOBILE, *December 9, 1864—7 p. m.*

General THOMAS,
    Enterprise:

If you cannot hear of other position of enemy act on the report of his having crossed Leaf River on Wednesday. Draw more troops to Bucatunna, and be prepared to move them promptly down from there. Let me hear from you fully and often.

D. H. MAURY,
Major-General, Commanding.

[DECEMBER 9, 1864.—For abstract from field return of Stewart's corps, see Part I, p. 679.]

HEADQUARTERS CAVALRY FORCES, EAST TENNESSEE,
Greeneville, December 9, 1864.

Major-General BRECKINRIDGE:

DEAR SIR: Captain Messick, who was captured a week ago by Burbridge's forces, made his escape from Bean's Station on the night of the 7th. Below you will find a copy of his letter:

RUSSELLVILLE, *December 8, 1864.*

General VAUGHN or DUKE:

While a prisoner among the Yankees at Bean's Station, I learned that General Burbridge had with him three brigades—the First, commanded by Colonel Brown; the Second, by Colonel Buckley; the Third, by Colonel Wade, of the Sixth U. S. (colored) Regulars—nine regiments: Eleventh Kentucky (Colonel Boyle), Twelfth, Thirtieth,

Fifty-fourth, Thirty-ninth (or Fifty-ninth) Kentucky Regiments, Twelfth Ohio (Lieutenant-Colonel Bentley), Eleventh Michigan, two negro regiments, five pieces of artillery that I saw (eight in all, I think), one 12 the others 6 pounders. His couriers represented three regiments of infantry on Clinch Mountain on the 6th, on their way to the station. He has between 5,000 and 6,000 cavalry and mounted infantry.

Respectfully, yours,

W. R. MESSICK.

Burbridge's forces have remained stationary at the station for one week; they certainly are waiting the movements of Hood's army. If Hood should be defeated, I think he will make a move up the country, but I think it quite likely that he is protecting the evacuation of East Tennessee by way of Big Creek and Cumberland Gaps. I have pickets and scouts, about 100 strong, at Russellville, and shall watch them closely and keep you posted.

I am, general, with great respect, your obedient servant,

JOHN C. VAUGHN,
Brigadier-General, Commanding.

CIRCULAR.]   HEADQUARTERS ARMY OF TENNESSEE,
Near Nashville, Tenn., December 10, 1864.

I. General Hood deems it highly probable that we will fight a battle before the close of the present year, and it is necessary, therefore, that our troops should be kept well in hand at all times. Should it occur in front of Nashville, he directs that, when it appears imminent to corps commanders, they will send all their wagons, except the artillery, ordnance, and ambulances, to the vicinity of Brentwood to go into park.

II. Lieutenant-General Stewart will at once select all good points in rear of his left flank, and have them fortified with self-supporting detached works to secure it against any attempt the enemy might make to turn it. Major-General Cheatham will do the same on his right flank.

III. Lieutenant-General Lee will select all good points in rear of his right and left flank, and fortify them with strong self-supporting detached works, so that should it become necessary to withdraw either of the corps now upon his flanks that the flank thus becoming the right or left flank of the army may be in condition to be easily defended.

IV. General Hood desires that corps commanders will superintend in person as much as possible these works, not leaving them either to subordinate commanders or engineer officers. Let them urge upon all officers and men the importance of pressing forward these works that we may be fully prepared to meet any movement of the enemy.

By command of General Hood:

A. P. MASON,
Colonel and Assistant Adjutant-General.

HEADQUARTERS STEWART'S CORPS,
December 10, 1864.

General WALTHALL:

GENERAL: I am directed by General Stewart to say to you that he considers it of the greatest importance to hold the hill at the burnt house, and for this purpose he desires you to leave one of your guns in position to protect it. He considers the risk of losing the gun as more than counterbalanced by the additional security afforded.

I am, general, respectfully,

W. D. GALE,
Assistant Adjutant-General.

[Indorsement.]

HEADQUARTERS WALTHALL'S DIVISION,
December 10, 1864.

Major Trueheart will leave one gun in position at the burnt house, pursuant to the within order.

By order of Major-General Walthall:

A. F. SMITH,
Lieutenant and Acting Assistant Adjutant-General.

HEADQUARTERS,
Six Miles from Nashville, on Franklin Pike,
December 10, 1864—2 p. m.

Major-General FORREST, *Comdg. Cavalry, Army of Tennessee:*

General Hood directs me to say that there are still reports coming in of the talk among the enemy of their cavalry (which is now concentrated at Edgefield) fitting up for a raid, although their newspapers say Thomas is much crippled for the want of cavalry. Should they cross up the river, General Hood thinks it would be best for you to meet them and drive them back with your main force of cavalry, leaving some with the infantry on Stewart's Creek to observe the enemy at Murfreesborough, sending your trains back to La Vergne.

A. P. MASON,
Colonel and Assistant Adjutant-General.

HEADQUARTERS,
Overton's House, December 10, 1864—11.40.

Brigadier-General CHALMERS, *Commanding Cavalry:*

GENERAL: General Hood directs that you will send Biffle's command to the right flank of the army. Give him one piece of artillery, or a section if you think you can spare it. Order Biffle to ride forward here and report in person to General Hood for instructions.

Yours, respectfully,

A. P. MASON,
Colonel and Assistant Adjutant-General.

HEADQUARTERS,
Six Miles from Nashville, on Franklin Pike, December 10, 1864.

Maj. Gen. D. H. MAURY, *Mobile, Ala.:*

Copy of General Beauregard's letter to you of 22d of November received.* Please send forward all men belonging to this army. The States of Alabama and Mississippi ought to furnish the local garrisons from Corinth to Huntsville, inclusive. Please urge this upon the governors of those States.

J. B. HOOD,
General.

---

* See Brent to Maury, Part I, p. 1238.

MOBILE, *December 10, 1864.*

Governor T. H. WATTS,
            Montgomery:

A large force of the enemy is approaching Mobile from the west. If you can get together any State troops or volunteers please send them to Pollard with utmost dispatch.

D. H. MAURY,
Major-General, Commanding.

MOBILE, *December 10, 1864—10 a. m.*

Lieut. Gen. R. TAYLOR,
            Selma, Ala.:

Following from Shubuta last night: Six of Scott's scouts arrived this evening, who say they have been following enemy; that enemy crossed Leaf River at Enon on Wednesday night, 8,000 cavalry and mounted infantry. They are inquiring roads for State line and Winchester; said their object was to destroy Bucatunna bridge and trestle on their way to Mobile. Same scouts say enemy started with twenty-one days' rations, thirteen of which have passed, and were driving cattle and moving very slowly.

Dispatch just received from Jackson reports enemy at Augusta on 7th.

D. H. MAURY,
Major-General, Commanding.

MOBILE, *December 10, 1864.*

Lieut. Gen. R. TAYLOR,
            Selma:

From the best information the enemy's strength near Augusta, 8th, is about 4,000 cavalry and eight pieces artillery. General Thomas, in command at Bucatunna and vicinity, has 1,500 dismounted men and one battery light artillery. Troops are en route to join him; will make his force equal, if not superior, to enemy. Colonel McCulloch, with 1,200 mounted men and battery horse artillery, in front of and near the enemy, will co-operate with General Thomas. The enemy's fleet in the lower bay is reported increased. Letter from General Gordon Granger, at Fort Morgan, dated 7th, was received this morning, relative to sending the cotton to purchase supplies for our prisoners.

D. H. MAURY,
Major-General, Commanding.

If General Taylor has left Selma for Meridian repeat to him at Meridian.

MOBILE, *December 10, 1864.*

Brig. Gen. B. M. THOMAS,
            Bucatunna, Miss.:

Latest information places enemy at Salem on 8th; part of his force between Leaf and Chickasawha Rivers; whole force about 4,000, including 500 foot pioneers, 7 or 8 pieces of artillery, near 100 wagons,

McCulloch was near Leakesville, probably, last night. Have ordered trains to be ready to move your force at Bucatunna lower down should you find it necessary. Communicate with McCulloch. Endeavor to unite with him at proper time to attack enemy. Let me hear from you often as to your present force, re-enforcements coming down to you, and reported position of enemy. You are in command of all forces operating against enemy. Notify McCulloch of this, as I shall endeavor to do. Do not permit your command to be prevented from coming to Mobile when necessary.

D. H. MAURY,
Major-General, Commanding.

MOBILE, *December 10, 1864—4 p. m.*
Brigadier-General THOMAS:

McCulloch at Leakesville this morning; believe enemy will cross Pascagoula at Farley's Ferry. Unless better information control you, move your main force to Citronelle. Leave guard at Bucatunna. Communicate McCulloch by telegraph to Citronelle; couriers are there. Keep General Gardner informed of yours and enemy's movements. Keep enemy constantly harassed by your cavalry. Keep as close to him as you can. Attack him with all your force together. Do you need wagons or supplies? Answer.

D. H. MAURY,
Major-General, Commanding.

MOBILE, *December 10, 1864—9 p. m.*
Maj. Gen. FRANK. GARDNER,
Meridian, Miss.:

The dispatch which you supposed was intended for Thomas was a copy for your information. Enemy captured four of McCulloch's men last night at Robert's Ferry, on Chickasawha, short distance above Farley's Ferry. McCulloch is near the enemy, who seems marching upon Mobile. Please continue to organize and send down troops. General Taylor will probably be here to-morrow. Is the militia turning out well?

D. H. MAURY,
Major-General, Commanding.

MOBILE, *December 10, 1864.*
Maj. J. D. SAYERS,
Assistant Adjutant-General, Meridian:

Following dispatch received:

JACKSON, TENN., *December 5, 1864.*

I require at once a commissary and quartermaster and supporting force. I think I can raise a considerable force here.

MARCUS J. WRIGHT,
Brigadier-General.

Submit it to chief quartermaster and chief commissary for action relative to quartermaster and commissary, and to General Gardner relative to supporting force.

W. M. LEVY,
Assistant Adjutant and Inspector General.

MOBILE, *December 10, 1864.*

Col. R. McCulloch:
    (To be forwarded by courier from Citronelle.)

Your dispatch of 6 a. m. received. Keep close to the enemy; dispute the passage of the fords and ferries. Communicate with and co-operate with General Thomas at Bucatunna, whom I have ordered to take command of all the troops operating against the enemy. Your scouts from the Pearl report force of enemy, 3,500 cavalry, 7 pieces of artillery, and 500 pioneers, and 100 wagons.

D. H. MAURY,
Major-General, Commanding.

[DECEMBER 10, 1864.—For statements of the strength of the Army of Tennessee, see Part I, pp. 663, 678.]

MONTGOMERY, ALA., *December 11, 1864.*

General G. T. BEAUREGARD:
    (Care of General Cobb, Macon, Ga.)

Henderson's scouts report:

Osband with his entire command left Vicksburg for Memphis on 7th instant. Three companies Marine Brigade gone to Skipwith's Landing.

GEORGE WM. BRENT,
Colonel and Assistant Adjutant-General.

HEADQUARTERS,
Overton's House, December 11, 1864—7 p. m.

Lieutenant-General STEWART,
    Commanding:

GENERAL: General Hood directs that, as Biffle's brigade is to be withdrawn from Chalmers to-morrow, you will send a regiment on picket to John Williams' house, on the Hardin pike, to support our cavalry.

Yours, respectfully,

A. P. MASON,
Colonel and Assistant Adjutant-General.

HEADQUARTERS,
Overton's House, December 11, 1864—11 p. m.

Lieutenant-General STEWART,
    Commanding:

GENERAL: General Hood directs me to inclose you this note* of General Lee, for your information, and to say that, should the enemy attack Lee upon the front line, he desires you will support Lee. One of the main objects in taking the second line is that you may have a better left flank.

Yours, respectfully,

A. P. MASON,
Colonel and Assistant Adjutant-General.

* Not found.

HEADQUARTERS,
Overton's House, December 11, 1864—8 a. m.

Brigadier-General CHALMERS,
        Commanding:

GENERAL: General Hood directs that you send Biffle's command to the right of the army, as ordered yesterday.

        Very respectfully,

A. P. MASON,
Colonel and Assistant Adjutant-General.

HEADQUARTERS,
Six Miles from Nashville, on Franklin Pike, December 11, 1864.

Col. BEN. J. HILL,
        Commanding Cavalry, Near Shelbyville, Tenn.:

Capt. Jordan Hays, commanding battalion cavalry, has been ordered to report to you with his command without delay. His battalion will constitute a portion of your command.

        By command of General Hood:

JAS. COOPER,
Captain and Acting Assistant Adjutant-General.

HEADQUARTERS,
Six Miles from Nashville, on Franklin Pike, December 11, 1864.

Capt. JORDAN HAYS,
        Near Winchester, Tenn.:

You will report with your battalion to Col. B. J. Hill, near Shelbyville, Tenn., without delay.

        By command of General Hood:

JAS. COOPER,
Captain and Acting Assistant Adjutant-General.

MOBILE, *December 11, 1864.*

General DAN. W. ADAMS:

Send every man to Pollard you can, and report what and when you send them. Troops must concentrate here immediately. Enemy was across Pascagoula yesterday, advancing on Mobile road.

D. H. MAURY,
Major-General, Commanding.

MONTGOMERY, ALA., *December 11, 1864.*

Maj. Gen. D. H. MAURY,
        Mobile, Ala.:

Have forwarded dispatch to General Adams. Directed, also, 200 troops from Carthage to Mobile. McGuirk's regiment will be here to-morrow en route for Mobile. Shall I send these to Pollard? Please keep me advised.

GEORGE WM. BRENT,
Colonel and Assistant Adjutant-General.

MOBILE, *December 11, 1864.*

Governor WATTS,
     Montgomery, Ala.:

The column from Baton Rouge is approaching Mobile by way of Augusta, Salem, Farley's Ferry. McCulloch repulsed one part of enemy's force near Leakesville yesterday. Send every man you can to Pollard, and notify me of what you will be able to send.

> D. H. MAURY,
> *Major-General, Commanding.*

ENGINEER OFFICE, DISTRICT OF THE GULF,
        Mobile, December 11, 1864.

Weekly report of operations for the defense of Mobile, Ala., during the week ending December 10, 1864:

FIRST DIVISION.

I. A small force has been engaged in assisting the carpenters on bomb-proof.

N. Work continued on N on the middle traverse and on the scarp on southwest face, also upon the curtain between I and K.

Repairs were being made at D until yesterday, when the hands were withdrawn.

On the 6th instant the hands were distributed to place the redans in fighting condition, and were placed on those between G and H, H and I, K and L, L and M, and M and N, which have been sufficiently completed for the present; and to-day hands have been sent to redan between G and F, and F and E. A force will commence on redan between I and K, which will be ready in a few days.

SECOND DIVISION.

Gladden: Repairs on bomb-proof and traverses.
McIntosh: Repairs on traverses.
Tilghman: Sand has been put on this battery and repairs made.

THIRD DIVISION.

Blakely: Hands have been employed on redoubt in rear of brickyard and in transporting earth and sod to Huger and Tracy.
Huger: Thickening magazine.
Spanish Fort: Troops have been engaged in making changes on Redoubt No. 2. Piles prepared for obstruction.

FOURTH DIVISION.

The manufacture of torpedoes has been delayed by the want of powder and the shipping of stores to Corinth.

FIFTH DIVISION.

Eight pontoons were made and shipped during the week. A planing-mill has been added to the workshops.

In the absence of Lieutenant-Colonel Sheliha I have the honor to submit the above report.

> W. P. GAZZAM,
> *Acting Adjutant.*

MOBILE, *December 11, 1864—3 a. m.*

Maj. Gen. FRANK. GARDNER,
        Meridian, Miss.:

Enemy advancing for Mobile. Push down troops as rapidly as possible.

                    D. H. MAURY,
                Major-General, Commanding.

MOBILE, *December 11, 1864—8 a. m.*

General GARDNER:

Enemy is certainly coming here. Fleet increased in down bay and on the sound. McCulloch checked enemy's column near Leakesville yesterday evening. Have ordered Thomas down to Mobile with his infantry. Please push re-enforcements to me as fast as you can. Send Scott and other cavalry down west of railroad to join McCulloch, guarding road and telegraph.

                    D. H. MAURY,
                Major-General, Commanding.

MOBILE, *December 11, 1864.*

General GARDNER:

Latest reports show enemy crossing Pascagoula River, below confluence of Leaf and Chickasawha, and advancing this way.

                    D. H. MAURY,
                Major-General, Commanding.

MOBILE, *December 11, 1864.*

Major-General GARDNER,
        Meridian, Miss.:

Send any re-enforcements you may have to Mobile, which seems to be the objective point of the enemy. Please let Scott unite with McCulloch. Thomas, with his brigade, arrived here.

                    D. H. MAURY,
                Major-General, Commanding.

MOBILE, *December 11, 1864.*

Major-General GARDNER,
        Meridian:

Please not approve any dispatches for press or other parties, giving information of enemy's movements. This is only way by which co-operating force can obtain information.

                    D. H. MAURY,
                Major-General, Commanding.

MOBILE, *December 11, 1864.*

General GARDNER,
      Meridian, Miss.:

Send supplies to Bucatunna for any re-enforcements which may come down for the guards or troops there and for co-operating force.

D. H. MAURY,
Major-General, Commanding.

MOBILE, *December 11, 1864—3 a. m.*

Brigadier-General THOMAS:

Bring your command to Mobile at once. Enemy advancing on the road to city.

D. H. MAURY,
Major-General, Commanding.

MOBILE, *December 11, 1864—11 a. m.*

Col. R. McCULLOCH:

If enemy turns and goes toward Pascagoula, pursue, attack, and harass him all you can. Maury has been so instructed. Scott is believed to be as far down as Shubuta, with a considerable force of cavalry, to co-operate with you. Thomas arrived here this morning with his command. Cover well the railroad. Supplies for both man and horse are at Citronelle and Chunchula.

D. H. MAURY,
Major-General, Commanding.

MOBILE, *December 11, 1864.*

Col. J. S. SCOTT,
      Shubuta :

I am gratified by your soldierly action in following the enemy as you have. Endeavor to unite your command with Colonel McCulloch's brigade, last night guarding Mason's Ferry and Ward's bridge on Big Dog or Escatawpa River.

D. H. MAURY,
Major-General, Commanding.

HEADQUARTERS ARMY OF TENNESSEE,
Six miles from Nashville, on Franklin Pike, December 12, 1864.

Hon. J. A. SEDDON,
      Secretary of War:

When Sherman completes his raid I think it important that all available cavalry should be sent to this army.

J. B. HOOD,
General.

CORINTH, MISS., *December 12, 1864.*

Col. E. J. HARVIE,
Inspector-General, Army of Tennessee:

COLONEL: On the night of the 10th I received the following telegram, dated December 5:

Send forward at once all men belonging to this army in proper detachments, with officers, to preserve discipline and prevent straggling on the march.

J. B. HOOD,
General.

I designed sending a detachment of about 300 officers and men this morning, and orders were given for them to be in readiness to leave by the train, but were late in reporting, and some other delay occasioned the departure to be postponed. There is no transportation that can be had to transport rations for the men from Barton Station to the army. It is necessary to issue three days' rations here to the men, and have at least five days' hauled. For the detachment of 300 men and 17 officers, which will leave in the morning in command of Major Raxsdale, I have found it necessary to impress two wagons and eight mules from a Captain Calhoun, under orders of Major Dillard, to proceed to the Army of Tennessee to collect hides. He applied to me to be allowed to go to Barton, and there wait until a train should leave for the army with an escort. He represented that his wagons would go up well nigh empty, only having personal baggage and perhaps a little salt, some two or three sacks. I proposed that he should go with his three wagons, and at the same time transport the necessary rations for the detachment. This he objected to for various reasons, none of which could be considered good in view of the necessity of having the transportation for the detachment. He desired to remain a few days to look after some business matters, and will proceed to the army with the remaining wagon left him. Please arrange it so that some quartermaster shall take charge of the two wagons and mules and hold them subject to Captain Calhoun's orders. Captain Calhoun acknowledged to me that my taking this transportation from him did not interfere with the execution of his orders. I shall also send a detachment of 150 men, with complement of 7 officers, to-morrow morning to report to the ordnance officer at Barton, for the purpose of guarding the ordnance train to start from Barton on the 14th. This detachment goes under the command of Capt. R. W. Atkinson. The men of both detachments go armed, but with no accouterments. There are none of the latter on hand, and none expected here from below. Ten rounds of cartridges will be issued. I showed General Hood's order about sending all the men of the Army of Tennessee to the front to Colonel Reid, commandant of the post. He telegraphed a copy of it to Colonel Brent, and called his attention to the following order:

HEADQUARTERS MILITARY DIVISION OF THE WEST,
November 18, 1864.

I am directed by General Beauregard * * * . You will retain of the troops returning to the Army of Tennessee for the defense of the post, 1,000 infantry, including a complement of field and company officers. * * *

A. R. CHISOLM,
Aide-de-Camp.

The following is a reply to Colonel Reid's dispatch:

MONTGOMERY, *December 11, 1864.*

Col. J. C. REID:
Retain enough men to garrison Corinth. Send rest as ordered by General Hood.

GEORGE WM. BRENT,
Colonel and Assistant Adjutant-General.

The commandant of the post, Colonel Reid, consulted Major Wintter, the engineer officer, as to what garrison should be kept here. They both determined on the necessity of having 1,000 men as a garrison. I can therefore only send the excess of that number. I will send forward the men as rapidly as possible. All of Colonel Patterson's brigade has left here, except one regiment doing picket duty. All of Colonel Mabry's command of cavalry has also left. The Mobile and Ohio Railroad was recently threatened near Shubuta, below Meridian. A call for 500 infantry, from General Gardner, to go there and protect the bridge was responded to as requested, this place not being threatened and not then having orders to send any immediately to the army. The danger to the road seems now to have passed, and probably in a day or two the force will return. At all events this force goes to make up the 1,000 to be retained here, and also a detachment of 100 at Chickasaw Battery, on the Tennessee River.

I am, colonel, very respectfully, your obedient servant,

WM. A. REID,
Captain and Assistant Inspector-General.

PROVOST-MARSHAL'S OFFICE,
December 12, 1864.

Captain WATKINS,
Provost-Marshal, Jackson's Division:

CAPTAIN: The orders are to arrest and send forward all men liable to military duty from seventeen to fifty. All questions of exemption are settled at army headquarters. Look after all men that are straggling, both infantry and cavalry, and send them forward. The section of country in which you operate is left to your own discretion.

Respectfully, your obedient servant,

JOHN GOODWIN,
Captain and Chief Provost-Marshal, Forrest's Corps.

HEADQUARTERS BRIGADE,
December 12, 1864—11 p. m.

[General JACKSON:]

GENERAL: A train of fifteen box-cars with troops ran out of Murfreesborough at dark, and scouts at Christiana report that they passed there and went on down toward Stevenson. I had some of the track torn up behind them, and will destroy more of it in the morning and try to capture the train if it returns. It was possibly only going to the block-house below Christiana, and may attempt to return to-night

Very respectfully, your obedient servant,

L. S. ROSS,
Brigadier-General.

MONTGOMERY, ALA., *December 12, 1864.*

Lieut. Gen. R. TAYLOR,
Mobile, Ala.:

General Hood has ordered Colonel Reid, Corinth, to send him all his men detained there. If Mabry's brigade has been ordered to Mobile,

Corinth will not have a sufficient garrison. It is now an important post, and I have ordered Colonel Reid to retain men enough to garrison it until you can provide for its defense.

GEORGE WM. BRENT,
Colonel and Assistant Adjutant-General.

MOBILE, *December 12, 1864.*

Col. GEORGE W. BRENT,
    Montgomery:

Ample arrangements have been made against the enemy's raiding party. Mabry's brigade ordered to Mobile. Garrison at Corinth will be attended to.

R. TAYLOR,
Lieutenant-General, Commanding.

HDQRS. DEPARTMENT OF ALA., MISS., AND EAST LA.,
Mobile, Ala., December 12, 1864.

His Excellency THOMAS H. WATTS,
    Governor of Alabama:

SIR: I desire to call your attention to the condition of the military defenses of the State of Alabama, and to urge the necessity of such action on the part of its Legislature as will strengthen the Confederate authorities in their efforts to secure the State from invasion. The events of the war have removed the enemy from your eastern frontier, the Army of Tennessee protects your northern boundary, and on your western confines the State troops and militia of Mississippi afford protection against any invading or raiding parties. From the Gulf and the southwestern portion of the State alone are any apprehensions of attack to be entertained. The occupation of the lower bay by the enemy's fleet renders the city of Mobile liable to an attack at any moment. While the fortifications and other defenses of the city are in good condition, they can only be held by the requisite number of troops. The force of this department now in Mobile, or who in any emergency can be thrown into it, are inadequate to its successful defense if a serious and determined attack should be made. The only source from which the garrison can be increased is the militia of your State, and in view of the importance of the matter I sincerely hope that such legislation will be had as will enable you to send an adequate number to serve during the winter and spring, until the probability of an attack on Mobile ceases to exist. While Alabama is free from danger of invasion in every other quarter, this vulnerable point should surely not be neglected. The serious results which would follow the fall of Mobile, the penetration by the enemy into the very heart of the State, and the devastation and ruin which would be inflicted upon the people, cannot be portrayed in too strong language, and I therefore beg to urge upon you the necessity of such action by your State Legislature as will strengthen the military authorities and avert the danger of a disaster.

I am, sir, very respectfully, your obedient servant,

R. TAYLOR,
Lieutenant-General, Commanding.

MOBILE, *December 12, 1864.*

Major-General GARDNER,
        Meridian:

Lieutenant-General Taylor has assumed command of this department.

W. M. LEVY,
        Assistant Adjutant and Inspector General.

MOBILE, *December 12, 1864.*

Col. R. McCULLOCH:

The instructions to pursue enemy yesterday were based on report from Colonel Maury that enemy were moving down west bank of Pascagoula. He reports at 10 p. m. yesterday, and enemy is advancing and crossing Pascagoula. Of course, you will get quicker and better information than any I can send you, and must act accordingly. Try and communicate with Colonel Scott, now moving from direction of Shubuta; get him to re-enforce you.

D. H. MAURY,
        Major-General, Commanding.

MOBILE, *December 12, 1864.*

COMMANDING OFFICER,
        Bucatunna, Miss.:

Send here as soon as possible King's battery and the dismounted men of Bucatunna.

D. H. MAURY,
        Major-General, Commanding.

MONTGOMERY, ALA., *December 13, 1864.*

General G. T. BEAUREGARD:
        (Care of General Cobb, Macon, Ga.)

General Adams reports that all troops arriving at Memphis are forwarded up Cumberland River to Thomas. No indication of move against Corinth.

GEORGE WM. BRENT,
        Colonel and Assistant Adjutant-General.

MONTGOMERY, ALA., *December 13, 1864.*

General G. T. BEAUREGARD:
        (Care General Cobb, Macon, Ga.)

General Taylor reports enemy's raiding party retreating rapidly to Mississippi City. All quiet at Mobile. All General Hood's men will be sent immediately to Corinth.

GEORGE WM. BRENT,
        Colonel and Assistant Adjutant-General.

HEADQUARTERS,
Six Miles from Nashville, on Franklin Pike, December 13, 1864.
General G. T. BEAUREGARD,
Montgomery, Ala.:

Major Ayer, chief quartermaster, informs me that Major Bridewell, at Augusta, has fifty bales of blankets belonging to this army. Please have them sent forward at once in charge of some officer who will push them through. The weather is severe, the ground covered with snow, and the men stand much in need of them. If possible, order Major Bridewell also to send forward 10,000 suits of clothing and all the blankets that can be spared to this army.

J. B. HOOD,
General.

HEADQUARTERS,
Six Miles from Nashville, on Franklin Pike, December 13, 1864.
General G. T. BEAUREGARD,
Montgomery, Ala.:

Major Whitfield, the quartermaster charged with rebuilding the railroad from Cherokee toward Decatur, still complains of not being able to obtain the necessary labor and material. Please give him the authority to impress at once all that is necessary.

J. B. HOOD,
General.

HEADQUARTERS,
Six Miles from Nashville, on Franklin Pike, December 13, 1864.
General G. T. BEAUREGARD,
Montgomery, Ala.:

Can Baker's brigade, of this army, now at Mobile, be returned? All the troops we can get are needed here. I would be glad to know the news of Sherman. Can hear nothing here.

J. B. HOOD,
General.

HEADQUARTERS ARMY OF TENNESSEE,
PROVOST-MARSHAL-GENERAL'S DEPARTMENT,
In the Field, December 13, 1864.
Col. E. J. HARVIE,
Inspector-General, Army of Tennessee:

COLONEL: I respectfully submit the following as my report of the number of recruits received at this office since the army entered the State of Tennessee: Cheatham's corps, 85; Stewart's corps, 36; Lee's corps, 31; post duty, 7; cavalry, 4; artillery, 1; total, 164. Johnson's division has had assigned to it 296 dismounted cavalry, of whom all have deserted except 42.

Very respectfully,

WM. F. MILLER,
Captain and Assistant Provost-Marshal-General.

HEADQUARTERS,
Overton's House, December 13, 1864—3 p. m.
Lieutenant-General STEWART,
Commanding:

GENERAL: General Hood directs me to say that information has been received that the enemy was crossing his cavalry all day yesterday from Edgefield to Nashville. He thinks therefore that you had better put a brigade of infantry on the Hardin pike, instead of a regiment. Should the enemy commence operating with their cavalry on Chalmers' side, you must give Chalmers such assistance as you think necessary, keeping in communication with Chalmers. The brigade you send should cover the Hardin pike.

Yours, respectfully,

A. P. MASON,
Colonel and Assistant Adjutant-General.

P. S.—General Hood deems this information reliable. He desires to see you this evening.

A. P. M.

OVERTON HOUSE, *December 13, 1864—3 p. m.*
Brigadier-General CHALMERS,
Commanding:

GENERAL: I am directed by General Hood to inform you that information has been received that the enemy was crossing their cavalry all day yesterday from Edgefield to Nashville, so you must be on the alert. General Stewart is ordered to place a brigade on the Hardin pike. Communicate with General Stewart if the enemy moves out on you, and he will give you all the assistance he can.

Yours, respectfully,

A. P. MASON,
Colonel and Assistant Adjutant-General.

MOBILE, *December 13, 1864.*
Col. G. W. BRENT,
Assistant Adjutant-General, Montgomery:

Enemy's raiding party retreating rapidly to Mississippi City. All quiet here. All of General Hood's men will be sent immediately to Corinth.

R. TAYLOR,
Lieutenant-General, Commanding.

MOBILE, *December 13, 1864.*
Maj. Gen. FRANK. GARDNER,
Meridian:

King's battery will be retained here for the present, and fully equipped and returned to North Mississippi when required by General Jackson.

W. M. LEVY,
Assistant Adjutant and Inspector General.

[DECEMBER 13, 1864.—For abstract from field return of Cheatham's corps, see Part I, p. 680.]

BRISTOL, *December 13, 1864.*

General J. C. BRECKINRIDGE:

Following just received:

GREENEVILLE, *December 13, 1864.*

The enemy is advancing north the Holston; was at Rogersville yesterday at 12 o'clock. General Duke is on that road, and I will keep you posted, but you had better ask General Breckinridge for instructions.

J. C. VAUGHN.

JNO. F. TERRY,
Lieutenant-Colonel, Commanding Post.

MONTGOMERY, ALA., *December 14, 1864.*

General G. T. BEAUREGARD:
(Care General Cobb, Macon, Ga.)

General Taylor this day telegraphs that General Hood has drawn off all the force of Roddey in the direction of Huntsville. I have telegraphed General Taylor to maintain a sufficient garrison at Corinth and let Roddey execute the orders of General Hood.

GEORGE WM. BRENT,
Colonel and Assistant Adjutant-General.

HEADQUARTERS,
Near Nashville, on Franklin Pike, December 14, 1864.

Brig. Gen. P. D. RODDEY,
Commanding, &c.:

General Hood directs that, unless the line between Corinth and Tuscumbia, which you are now protecting, is threatened by the enemy, you will join the main army with your command as soon as possible, leaving the regiment at Decatur, as heretofore directed.

A. P. MASON,
Colonel and Assistant Adjutant-General.

HEADQUARTERS,
Near Nashville, on Franklin Pike, December 14, 1864.

Col. B. J. HILL,
Commanding, &c..

Your dispatches of yesterday have been received. General Hood directs me to inform you that, on the 11th instant, Captain Jordan Hays, commanding battalion of scouts, was ordered to report to you with his command, without delay. Please inform me whether the order has been complied with.

A. P. MASON,
Colonel and Assistant Adjutant-General.

OFFICE CHIEF QUARTERMASTER, CHALMERS' DIV., &C.,
December 14, 1864.

Maj. W. O. KEY,
Quartermaster, Rucker's Brigade:

MAJOR: In foraging for the brigade you must use regimental wagons, and not those belonging to the ordnance and supply trains.

By order of Brigadier-General Chalmers:

WM. BARNEWALL, JR.,
Major and Chief Quartermaster, Chalmers' Division, &c.

MONTGOMERY, ALA., *December 14, 1864.*

Lieut. Gen. R. TAYLOR,
        Meridian:

General Clanton reports enemy advancing in heavy force this side Pine Barren. Maintain sufficient garrison at Corinth. If you can do this without Roddey let him execute the orders of General Hood.

GEORGE WM. BRENT,
        Colonel and Assistant Adjutant-General.

HDQRS. DEPARTMENT OF ALA., MISS., AND EAST LA.,
        Meridian, December 14, 1864.

Col. GEORGE WILLIAM BRENT,
        Assistant Adjutant-General, Montgomery, Ala.:

COLONEL: I arrived here this morning and had an interview with his excellency, Governor Charles Clark. He informs me that only 1,000 of the militia of Mississippi have responded to his call, and does not speak hopefully of any material increase of that number. I also found Major-General Gardner at this place, who will leave to-morrow for the northern portion of his district. Major-General Maury has been directed to send forward to Corinth immediately all the men now in the District of the Gulf who belong to General Hood's army, and these troops will be hastened to their appropriate commands. Such dismounted men as can be made available for that purpose, including those of Gholson's brigade, will be sent to Corinth for post duty. The mounted pickets and scouts between Corinth and Memphis will be given timely notice of any movement from the direction of the Mississippi River, and Roddey's command will render the same service to the east, while a small mounted force will suffice for observation in the front along the Tennessee River. The scarcity of forage in the vicinity of Corinth, and the distance which it has to be transported, render it important to keep only such cavalry as are absolutely necessary in that locality. Much confusion and conflict arise relative to the post at Corinth, as to the command to which it properly belongs. Orders are issued by General Hood relative to its conduct, and, whilst it is within the limits of my department, military control is exercised over it by General Hood. If any instructions have been given from division headquarters on this subject, I respectfully ask that a copy may be communicated to me so that I may be guided thereby. A portion of Roddey's command has been ordered to Corinth and its vicinity by General Hood, and while operating at and near that place it holds itself independent of the post and district commander, and takes no orders nor instructions from those officers. In obedience to the instructions of General Beauregard, I directed General Roddey, with his command, to report to General Hood, commanding Army of Tennessee, but unless orders to that effect have issued from General Beauregard's headquarters, I do not conceive that Roddey's command can operate within my department independent of me and my local subordinates. Be pleased to advise me of any orders issued by you on this subject also. The confusion existing in the hospital at Columbus, and perhaps at other points in this department, cannot, under existing arrangements, be well rectified by me. The hospitals of General Hood, under the control of his own medical director, have been removed to localities within my department, but they are not placed within my control or that of my medical director. Several camps of dismounted men belonging to the Army of Tennessee have been established in this department by General Hood, without any consultation with or notification to me. Complaints are made by the governors of the States of Alabama and Mississippi, and citizens, of lawless conduct and frequent depredations upon private property committed by these bands of men. Unless specific instructions from division headquarters require me to allow these camps to remain, I shall take steps to remove them, and order all such men to rejoin the Army of Tennessee.

Citizens residing in the northern counties of Mississippi and Alabama represent that officers, acting under the orders of General Hood, are seizing their good mules, substituting in their places worthless and broken-down animals. The right thus to impress or seize property within my department by an officer commanding another army or department will not be recognized by me, unless I am ordered to do so. Major Ewing, chief of field transportation for a district comprised within my department, is impressing mules and transportation generally for the use of General Hood's army, and this without my authority or consent. I shall interpose to prevent such action, unless he is acting under orders from division headquarters. Be pleased to inform me whether the action of the officers herein referred to is based upon instructions from your headquarters; and, if so, I respectfully ask to be furnished with copies of the same. Be pleased to inform me what orders have been issued from division headquarters relative to Gholson's brigade; I understood that it had been ordered to report to Major-General Gardner. I would be glad if you would inform me of the locality of General Gholson himself.

I am, colonel, very respectfully, your obedient servant,

                R. TAYLOR,
                Lieutenant-General.

                ABINGDON, *December 14, 1864.*

Maj. J. S. JOHNSTON:

I am informed by numbers of straggling cavalry that Bristol was captured by the enemy at 4 a. m. I can but credit their reports.

                J. G. MARTIN,
                Captain, Commanding Post.

                ABINGDON, *December 14, 1864.*

Major JOHNSTON,
    Assistant Adjutant-General:

General Duke sends dispatch by courier that the enemy, at 4 a. m., were moving in heavy column, in the direction of this place, on Reedy Creek road.

                J. G. MARTIN,
                Captain, Commanding Post.

                HEADQUARTERS,
Near Nashville, on the Franklin Pike, December 14, 1864.

Brig. Gen. GIDEON J. PILLOW, Provisional Army, C. S.:

In sending you the inclosed,* I am directed by General Hood to say that the prompt organization of these forces is of great importance to us,

---

            * Not found.

and knowing no one who can perform this duty as well as yourself, he hopes that you will enter upon it at once. Brig. Gen. M. J. Wright has been similarly assigned by General Beauregard in West Tennessee; the two portions of the State being in different military departments, renders separate assignments necessary for the present. Please communicate your news freely on the subject, and General Hood will cheerfully extend to you all the aid which the limited means now under his control permit.

A. P. MASON,
Colonel and Assistant Adjutant-General.

HEADQUARTERS,
Near Nashville, on Franklin Pike, December 15, 1864.

Hon. J. A. SEDDON,
Secretary of War, Richmond, Va.:

The enemy claim that we lost thirty colors in the fight at Franklin. We lost thirteen, capturing nearly the same number. The men who bore ours were killed on and within the enemy's interior line of works.

J. B. HOOD,
General.

HEADQUARTERS,
Near Nashville, on Franklin Pike, December 15, 1864.

General G. T. BEAUREGARD,
Montgomery, Ala.:

Please order Captain Hazlehurst, now on duty with Major-General Smith, to report to Lieutenant-Colonel Presstman. His services are needed on the railroad from Pulaski to Decatur.

J. B. HOOD,
General.

HEADQUARTERS,
Near Nashville, on Franklin Pike, December 15, 1864.

Capt. W. A. REID,
Assistant Adjutant and Inspector General, Corinth, Miss.:

The officers of the military courts must come forward at once, bringing their personal baggage on their horses, or in any other way they can, taking advantage of loaded wagons that may be coming forward, but no wagons can be allowed exclusively for them and their effects. The public service requires that all wagons coming to the army now should bring either ordnance, commissary, or quartermaster stores. When the courts reach the army I will give them such transportation as I can. Order them up at once, in my name.

J. B. HOOD,
General.

CIRCULAR.] HEADQUARTERS ARMY OF TENNESSEE,
Near Nashville, Tenn., December 15, 1864.

The inclosed works which are now being built on the flanks of the army will be so pierced for artillery that it may fire in any direction from them. The artillery placed in each of these works will be supported by 75 or 100 men, in proportion to the size of the work. The party for each work will be selected at once, and as far as practicable camped near the work which they are to defend, and positive orders must be given to the officers and men that they are to hold the work at all hazard, and not to surrender under any circumstances.

By command of General Hood:

A. P. MASON,
Colonel and Assistant Adjutant-General.

HEADQUARTERS ARMY OF TENNESSEE,
Near Nashville, on Franklin Pike, December 15, 1864.

Lieutenant-General STEWART,
Commanding Corps, Army of Tennessee:

I am directed by General Hood to inclose to you the order granting leave of absence to Major-General French, and to say that you will make such temporary disposition of the brigades composing his division as you may deem best.

A. P. MASON,
Colonel and Assistant Adjutant-General.

HEADQUARTERS LEE'S CORPS,
December 15, 1864—10.10 a. m.

General STEWART,
Commanding Corps:

GENERAL: I am in receipt of your note of this date. I feel secure in my line; have made the same dispositions you mention for your lines. Am engaged to-day in throwing up redoubts on my flanks. I think you may look out for a demonstration on your left to-day from present indications. Please keep me posted. Will send a staff officer to stay with you in case I hear much firing.

Yours respectfully,

S. D. LEE,
Lieutenant-General.

SPECIAL ORDERS, }   HEADQUARTERS STEWART'S CORPS,
No. —.   }   *Near Nashville, Tenn., December 15, 1864.*

Sears' and Ector's brigades and all the staff officers of Major-General French will report at once for duty to Major-General Walthall.

By command of Lieutenant-General Stewart:

W. D. GALE,
Assistant Adjutant-General.

DECEMBER 15, 1864—10.45 a. m.

Lieutenant General STEWART,
Commanding Corps:

GENERAL: The enemy are advancing in two lines of battle, with a strong line of skirmishers in front of General Sears' left, and are now engaging our skirmishers at the brick house to the left of the Hillsborough road and in front of the fort on the left of the Hillsborough road. They have no artillery.

I am general, very respectfully, &c.,

J. M. WILLIAMS.

[DECEMBER 15, 1864.]

Major-General LORING:

GENERAL: There seems to be a movement of some magnitude on our left. They are now pressing Sears' skirmishers. General Sears, however, thinks that the movement is in his front and to his left.

ROBT. LOWRY,
Colonel, &c.

DECEMBER 15, 1864.

Major SANDERS,
Assistant Adjutant-General:

MAJOR: The enemy's line of battle, say one brigade, is still stationary in front of Sears' pickets, with a strong line of skirmishers in front; three lines of battle are formed in front of the cavalry pickets, which are on our left. A heavy column of infantry is moving to our left.

W. E. ESTES,
Major, Commanding Division Line Skirmishers.

[Indorsement.]

10 A. M.

Respectfully referred to Lieutenant-General Stewart.

C. W. SEARS,
Brigadier-General, Commanding Division.

HEADQUARTERS FRENCH'S DIVISION,
December 15, 1864—10 a. m.

Col. W. D. GALE,
Assistant Adjutant-General:

COLONEL: Brigadier-General Sears requests me to inform you that the demonstration of the enemy on the left is increasing.

I am, colonel, very respectfully, your obedient servant,

D. W. SANDERS,
Assistant Adjutant-General.

HEADQUARTERS STEWART'S CORPS,
December 15, 1864.

Lieutenant-General STEWART:

GENERAL: A staff officer of General Loring has just come in and says the officer of the day reports the enemy to have moved out in front of Adams' brigade, General Loring's left, in line of battle, and to have laid down on the ground.

I am, general, respectfully,

W. D. GALE,
Assistant Adjutant-General.

On the Field, [*December 15, 1864*]—*3.30 p. m.*
General WALTHALL:

General Johnson's brigades have fallen back on your left. Watch your left and right and hold as long as you can. Cheatham is coming with two divisions.

Respectfully,

ALEX. P. STEWART,
Lieutenant-General.

HEADQUARTERS FORREST'S CAVALRY CORPS,
December 15, 1864—9 p. m.
Brigadier-General JACKSON,
Commanding Division:

GENERAL: The major-general commanding directs that you withdraw all your forces at daylight in the morning, and concentrate on the Wilkinson pike at or near George Smith's. He has directed the infantry wagon train and the artillery wagons, three or four miles from the Nashville pike, up Stewart's Creek in the direction of Nolensville pike, and wishes your train placed there also to-morrow morning. The enemy attacked our lines in several places to-day around Nashville, and at 2 o'clock were attempting to turn our left flank; hence his desire to concentrate all his force as rapidly as possible, and place it between the garrison at Murfreesborough and Nashville. Bell will be at or near mouth of Overall's Creek, on Stone's River, and the infantry brigades on the pike near the block-house.

I am, general, very respectfully, &c.,

CHAS. W. ANDERSON,
Assistant Inspector-General.

P. S.—Generals Ross and Armstrong will read and act upon this order in the event General Jackson is not present, forwarding this to him.

By order of Major-General Forrest:

CHAS. W. ANDERSON,
Assistant Inspector-General.

MONTGOMERY, ALA., *December 15, 1864.*
Lieut. Gen. R. TAYLOR,
Meridian:

Operator at Pollard left this morning and reported enemy in two miles. Will organize and send all troops that can be raised down to Pollard.

GEORGE WM. BRENT,
Colonel and Assistant Adjutant-General.

(Same to Maj. Gen. D. H. Maury, Mobile.)

HDQRS. DEPARTMENT OF ALA., MISS., AND EAST LA.,
Meridian, December 15, 1864.
Col. GEORGE WILLIAM BRENT,
Asst. Adjt. Gen., Hdqrs. Mil. Div. of the West, Montgomery, Ala.:

COLONEL: I am informed by the chief purchasing commissaries of Mississippi and Alabama that the chief commissary of subsistence of the Army of Tennessee has applied to them to have 1,000,000 of rations placed at Corinth, to be held at that point subject alone to the order, and intended solely for the use, of the Army of Tennessee. I would respectfully present for the consideration of the general commanding the Military Division of the West the following suggestions: With such an accumulation of rations, a constituent portion of which would be meal, at least four-fifths of it would spoil before it was ready for use. If General Hood should be able to maintain his occupation of Tennessee, I understand that his chief commissary states that he can abundantly support his army in the country which he occupies. If he is forced to retire from that country, his retrograde movement would surely not be practicable via Corinth, or by any route whence it would be practicable to draw his supplies from Corinth, as the enemy, having control of the Tennessee River, would effectually prevent his keeping up communication with that place, and in all probability render Mussel Shoals the most available point for crossing the river. If I am correct in the views which I have advanced, I think the proposed accumulation of these supplies at Corinth by no means advisable, and respectfully submit the matter to the general commanding for his consideration and action.

I am, colonel, very respectfully, your obedient servant,

R. TAYLOR,
Lieutenant-General.

HDQRS. DISTRICT OF MISSISSIPPI AND EAST LOUISIANA,
Meridian, December 15, 1864.

Maj. J. D. SAYERS,
Assistant Adjutant-General, Department Headquarters:

MAJOR: I have the honor to report that I have just been informed that all the troops sent by me to Bucatunna were not sent to Mobile, as first reported, but that militia and a few other troops were retained at Bucatunna. I respectfully request that orders may be given for the return of these troops, as well as those that have gone to Mobile from this district, if such be the determination of the lieutenant-general commanding.

I am, major, very respectfully, your obedient servant,

FRANK. GARDNER,
Major-General.

HDQRS. DEPARTMENT OF ALA., MISS., AND EAST LA.,
Meridian, December 15, 1864.

Brig. Gen. D. W. ADAMS,
Comdg. District of Central Alabama, Talladega, Ala.:

GENERAL: I am instructed by the lieutenant-general commanding to state to you as follows:

Col. J. C. Reid has been relieved from command of the post at Corinth, Miss., and ordered to report to you. There are several companies belonging to Colonel Reid's command in Walker and adjoining counties, and quite a considerable number of his men scattered about your district. You will direct Colonel Reid to collect his command, and, as soon as this is done, relieve the men of Clanton's, Armistead's, and other commands on duty in the field who are at posts, and on other light duty, in your district, replacing them with Reid's and other new men, and, if necessary, with militia and State troops, whom Governor Watts will, he assures me, at once furnish on your application to him. The men of Clanton's, Armistead's, and others who are on duty at Opelika, Tuscaloosa, Talladega, Selma, Cahaba, Coosa bridge, and other posts and garrisons, should be sent forward to their respective commands as rapidly as possible; and as it is important that this should be done speedily, the lieutenant-general commanding desires that you will adopt prompt and energetic measures to cause Reid's and the other troops referred to to be collected and stationed as indicated above.

I am, general, very respectfully, your obedient servant,

WILL. M. LEVY,
Assistant Adjutant and Inspector General.

GLADE SPRINGS, *December 15, 1864.*

Maj. J. S. JOHNSTON:

Enemy at Abingdon and moving in this direction. Am moving to Saltville with the forces I have. Push forward all the troops carefully, and let them stop at Seven-Mile Ford and march over to Saltville. See that they have arms and ammunition as they pass. Direct Witcher to move with all possible haste to Saltville. Send horses to Seven-Mile Ford to be sent across to Saltville.

JOHN C. BRECKINRIDGE,
Major-General.

SALTVILLE, VA., *December 15, 1864—2 p. m.*

Maj. J. STODDARD JOHNSTON,
Assistant Adjutant-General, Wytheville:

The enemy were at Glade Springs this morning, and have moved up the railroad toward Marion. Keep a bright lookout for them. Let everything coming this way move cautiously.

JOHN C. BRECKINRIDGE.

MONTGOMERY, ALA., *December 16, 1864.*
(Received Richmond 18th.)

General S. COOPER,
Richmond, Va.:

Enemy, about 800 strong, occupied Pollard at 7 this a. m. Brigadier-General Tyler, with 800 strong, left this afternoon for that point. Two brigades are moving against this force from Tensas and Blakely. Brigadier-General Clanton held the enemy with a small force in check for many hours.

GEORGE WM. BRENT,
Colonel and Assistant Adjutant-General.

(Same to General G. T. Beauregard, care of General Cobb, Macon.)

MONTGOMERY, ALA., *December 16, 1864.*

General G. T. BEAUREGARD,
                Savannah:
(Care General Cobb, Macon, Ga.)

General Hood, six miles from Nashville, on the 9th, telegraphs that it is very important that Lewis' and Williams' brigades should be sent to the Army of Tennessee as soon as the interest of the public service will allow. Enemy's cavalry, supposed to be 700 strong, appeared opposite Pollard at 9 a. m. yesterday. Communication with Pollard stopped. Clanton's brigade moving up from Tensas, and another brigade cavalry operating from Blakely. Will be able to send 600 men from this place this a. m.

GEORGE WM. BRENT,
Colonel and Assistant Adjutant-General.

HEADQUARTERS,
Near Lea's House, December 16, 1864—8 a. m.

Lieutenant-General STEWART:

GENERAL: Should any disaster happen to us to-day, General Hood directs that you will retire by the Franklin pike, and Lee is directed to hold it in front of this large ridge, that you may pass to his rear. After passing Brentwood you would again form your corps in the best position you can find, and let the whole army pass through you. There are some narrow gorges beyond Brentwood toward Franklin. At all times the road must be left open for artillery and wagons, the men marching through the fields and woods.

A. P. MASON,
Colonel and Assistant Adjutant-General.

Cheatham would move by the Granny White pike.

A. P. M.

HEADQUARTERS WALTHALL'S DIVISION,
December 16, 1864.

Pursuant to orders from General Hood, General Reynolds will withdraw his brigade for the purpose of cutting off a small Federal force on our left and rear. He will move his command up the trenches toward the left to the rear of the hill occupied by General Bate, where special instructions will be given him. Colonel Shotwell and General Shelley will fill the gap occasioned by his withdrawal. Brigade commanders will see that all their men are notified of the object of this movement before it commences, and will take all steps necessary to prevent confusion.

E. C. WALTHALL,
Major-General.

IN THE FIELD, [*December 16, 1864*]—*2 p. m.*

General WALTHALL:

Should Bate fall back, keep your left connected with him, falling back from your left toward right and forming a new flank line extending to hills in rear.

Respectfully,

A. P. STEWART,
Lieutenant-General.

[DECEMBER 16, 1864.]

General WALTHALL:

If it be possible, under cover of the mist, get Reynolds out. It is important to check the force operating against left flank.

Respectfully,

ALEX. P. STEWART,
Lieutenant-General.

———

HEADQUARTERS STEWART'S CORPS,
Granny White's Gap, December 16, 1864.

Major-General WALTHALL:

GENERAL: You will have everything in readiness to retire to-night, in accordance with circular order of to-day. Further particulars will be furnished.

By order of Lieutenant-General Stewart:

W. D. GALE,
Assistant Adjutant-General.

———

HEADQUARTERS,
In the Field, December 16, 1864—3.15 p. m.

Brigadier-General CHALMERS:

GENERAL: Your dispatch, saying you were fighting the enemy with one regiment on the Granny White pike, received. General Hood says you must hold that pike; put in your escort and every available man you can find.

Yours, respectfully,

A. P. MASON,
Colonel and Assistant Adjutant-General.

———

MONTGOMERY, ALA., *December 16, 1864.*

Lieut. Gen. R. TAYLOR,
Meridian:

Seven hundred Yankee cavalry struck Mobile and Great Northern Railroad at Escambia at 8 o'clock yesterday morning, and were opposite Pollard at 9 a. m. This I learn by special messenger sent yesterday after the wires ceased. Will hasten in that direction all troops in reach. I have difficulty about arms and ammunition.

GEORGE WM. BRENT,
Colonel and Assistant Adjutant-General.

(Same to Maj. Gen. D. H. Maury, Mobile.)

———

MONTGOMERY, ALA., *December 16, 1864—11 a. m.*

Lieut. Gen. R. TAYLOR,
Meridian:

Eight hundred enemy's cavalry and artillery two miles from Pollard at 2 o'clock this morning. Burned Big Escambia bridge. General Clanton has held them in check twenty-four hours. Our loss so far, twenty killed, wounded, and missing.

GEORGE WM. BRENT,
Colonel and Assistant Adjutant-General.

(Same to Maj. Gen. D. H. Maury, Mobile.)

SIX MILES EAST OF MARION,
December 16, 1864—6 a. m.

Major-General BRECKINRIDGE:

GENERAL: The enemy attacked me as I was moving a portion of Vaughn's brigade from Marion, General Vaughn having taken the larger portion in the direction of the lead-mines after the raiders. My force is falling back in some confusion on Wytheville. Artillery safe, but horses give out.

Respectfully,

JAS. W. GILLESPIE,
Colonel, Commanding.

HEADQUARTERS DETACHMENT,
Near Mount Airy, December [16], 1864.

Major JOHNSTON,
Assistant Adjutant-General:

MAJOR: The enemy is pressing me closely in large force. I shall avoid an engagement, if possible. My troops are too much exhausted to do the work as it should be. Please inform General Vaughn, if possible.

Respectfully,

JAS. W. GILLESPIE,
Colonel, Commanding.

TUSCUMBIA, ALA., *December 16, 1864.*

Lieutenant-General TAYLOR,
Commanding Department:

GENERAL : I have received orders from General Hood to join the army near Nashville as soon as possible, but to destroy the railroad from Huntsville to Stevenson and from Stevenson to Murfreesborough on the march, and am now making every disposition in my power to obey the order promptly. I will leave one regiment to garrison Decatur and protect the battery. A company of engineers from General Hood's army has arrived at Decatur to replace the pontoon bridge and to assist in getting the captured engines on this side when needed. I shall continue to send reports to you and keep you advised of everything of interest. No other force will be left except the regiment indicated, one or two companies of which will be kept on detached duty in the more disloyal neighborhood.

Very respectfully,

P. D. RODDEY,
Brigadier-General.

MONTGOMERY, ALA., *December 16, 1864.*

General CLANTON, or
Major WILLIS,
Evergreen, Ala.:

General Maury telegraphs, 15th instant, that your brigade, dismounted, will go up toward Pollard by rail from Tensas. A brigade of cavalry is also operating from Blakely. Get into communication with them.

GEORGE WM. BRENT,
Colonel and Assistant Adjutant-General.

HEADQUARTERS,
Spring Hill, Tenn., December 17, 1864.

Hon. JAMES A. SEDDON,
Secretary of War, Richmond, Va.:

In front of Nashville on the morning of the 15th the enemy attacked both of our flanks about the same time. On our right they were repulsed with heavy loss, but towards evening they succeeded in driving in our infantry outposts upon our left flank. Dispositions were made during the night to meet any renewed attack. Early on the 16th they made a general attack on our entire line, and all their assaults were handsomely repulsed, with heavy loss, till 3.30 p. m., when a portion of our line to the left of the center suddenly gave way, causing, in a few minutes, our line to give way at all points, our troops retreating rapidly down the Franklin pike. We lost in the two days' engagements fifty pieces of artillery, with several ordnance wagons. Our loss in killed and wounded is very small. Maj. Gen. Ed. Johnson, Brig. Gens. T. B. Smith and H. R. Jackson, are among the prisoners. Our loss in prisoners is not yet fully ascertained, but I think it comparatively small. I still have artillery enough with the army, and am moving to the south of Duck River.

J. B. HOOD,
General.

(Same to General Beauregard.)

MONTGOMERY, ALA., *December 17, 1864.*

General S. COOPER,
Richmond, Va.:

General Clanton reports that the enemy, after burning the Government and railroad buildings and a portion of the town, retired from Pollard, going the same direction they came.

GEORGE WM. BRENT,
Colonel and Assistant Adjutant-General.

(Same to General G. T. Beauregard, care General Cobb, Macon, and Lieut. Gen. R. Taylor, Meridian.)

SPRING HILL, *December 17, 1864—10 v. m.*

Lieutenant-General STEWART,
Commanding:

GENERAL: Don't burn the railroad; there is a train here still to go down.
Yours, respectfully,

A. P. MASON,
Colonel and Assistant Adjutant-General.

CIRCULAR.]   HEADQUARTERS STEWART'S CORPS,
Near Springfield [Spring Hill], Tenn., December 17, 1864.

The troops of this corps will resume the march to-morrow morning at daylight, the division of General Walthall in front, that of General Loring following. All the wagons and ambulances of the corps will be sent forward at once to Columbia. The ambulances, brigade ordnance wagons, and tool wagons will be stopped on this side of the river, and all other wagons will cross over the river and be parked at a place to be indicated by Major McGuire.   Major McGuire, quartermaster of Loring's division, is charged with taking care of this train, and will be obeyed accordingly.

By command of Lieutenant-General Stewart:

> W. D. GALE,
> *Assistant Adjutant-General.*

> HEADQUARTERS STEWART'S CORPS,
> *December 17, 1864.*

General WALTHALL:

GENERAL: I am directed by General Stewart to inform you that a battery from Storrs' battalion has been ordered back to Spring Hill at an early hour to-morrow morning, to report to General Cheatham.

Respectfully,

> W. D. GALE,
> *Assistant Adjutant-General.*

> HEADQUARTERS,
> *Spring Hill, December 17, 1864—2.07 p. m.*

Brigadier-General CHALMERS:
(Through Lieutenant-General Lee.)

GENERAL: General Hood directs that you will report to Lieutenant-General Lee until General Forrest comes up.

Yours, respectfully,

> A. P. MASON,
> *Colonel and Assistant Adjutant-General.*

> HEADQUARTERS,
> *Spring Hill, Tenn., December 17, 1864.*

COMMANDING OFFICER,
    Corinth, Miss.:

Direct Major Wintter, engineer officer, to forward to Barton Station all the pontoon boats (with rope and flooring) that he has on hand. You will also collect and send to the same point sufficient transportation to forward the boats, &c., to any point on the river that may be designated.

> J. B. HOOD,
> *General.*

> MONTGOMERY, ALA., *December 17, 1864.*

Lieut. Gen. R. TAYLOR,
    Meridian:

General Hood telegraphs, near Nashville on the 10th, urging that all troops belonging to his army be hastened forward, and Mississippi and Alabama should furnish garrisons from Corinth to Huntsville inclusive. He requests that this be urged on the governors.   Please comply with his request.

> GEORGE WM. BRENT,
> *Colonel and Assistant Adjutant-General.*

MONTGOMERY, ALA., *December 17, 1864.*

Lieut. Gen. R. TAYLOR,
    Meridian:

About 500 enlisted foreigners, under Colonel O'Neal, of Hood's command, leave per first boat unarmed. If needed, they might be used between Corinth and Huntsville. Clanton reports he just started in pursuit of enemy toward Pensacola.

GEORGE WM. BRENT,
Colonel and Assistant Adjutant-General.

HEADQUARTERS MILITARY DIVISION OF THE WEST,
Montgomery, Ala., December 17, 1864.

Lieut. Gen. R. TAYLOR,
    Commanding, &c., Meridian, Miss.:

GENERAL: I have the honor to acknowledge the receipt this day of your communication of the 14th instant, in regard to the movements and distribution of troops, and the confusion and conflict existing at Corinth, growing out of orders in your department issued by General Hood. In the absence of General Beauregard, I hasten to advise you of all orders emanating from these headquarters touching the several inquiries contained in your letter.

First. There is no order detaching General Roddey from your command at these headquarters. On October 23, 1864, these headquarters were advised by you, among other things, that General Roddey was directed to co-operate in every possible manner with General Hood to divert enemy's attention, threaten his communication, or attack Huntsville, as may be best, and to obey promptly any orders from General Hood. In your communication of the 27th of October is the following:

At the railroad crossing of Bear Creek, General Roddey had better make the necessary defenses, and he being accessible to General Hood, proper orders may be given him directly by General Hood.

What interpretation and effect were given to these instructions by Generals Beauregard or Hood I am unable to say, except that on the 8th day of November, in a communication of the former to the latter, the following passage occurs:

Brigadier-General Roddey's command is now the only one available, scouting in the direction of Memphis, which he was told by me to do when I last saw him. It might be well for you to repeat the order, as he is now subject to your orders.

This is all the information of record at these headquarters.

Second. On the subject of hospital arrangements and accommodations, I can find no order. An officer has been ordered to inspect the difficulties which may exist growing out of this anomalous condition of affairs, and all necessary orders and instructions given to rectify them.

Third. No instructions have issued from these headquarters authorizing the establishment of camps of dismounted cavalrymen in the limits of your department without notification or consultation with you. The lawless conduct of these men, and depredations committed upon the persons and rights of the citizens, are clearly within your reach and power, and steps should be at once taken to have them arrested, collected, and forwarded to their appropriate commands in the Army of Tennessee.

Fourth. The only powers conferred on General Hood, allowing him to exercise authority within the limits of your department, are embraced in the following communications: One from General Beauregard to General Hood, of date November 15, 1864; the following is an extract:

General Taylor and myself will always be anxious to aid you in your present campaign with all the means at our control, but these being limited, ample previous notice of what may be required should be given, to enable us to make all necessary preparations. It will also give me pleasure to confer on you such powers as you may deem necessary to secure your communications, repair roads, and hasten supplies to your army whilst operating in the department of Lieutenant-General Taylor.

On the 17th of November, whilst General Beauregard was en route for Georgia and yourself absent, I addressed a communication to General Hood, advising him that General Beauregard desired that he would immediately take the offensive, and conferred on him the following authority:

To relieve you from any embarrassment whilst operating in North Alabama and Middle Tennessee, General Beauregard authorizes you to issue all such orders in General Taylor's department [as] you may deem necessary to secure the efficient and successful administration and operation of your army, sending to Lieutenant-General Taylor, or whoever may be in command, copies of all such orders.

The subject of this authority was to carry out the promise embodied in letter of the 15th of November. No powers have been conferred from these headquarters on Major Ewing, inspector of field transportation, to impress horses and mules, generally for the transportation of General Hood's army. Major Ewing's authority to impress is conferred by General Orders, No. 142, Adjutant and Inspector-General's Office, series 1863. No authority beyond this has been given to him from this source. On the 23d of November, Major Ewing authorized Capt. J. F. Cummings, acting quartermaster, an officer reporting, to proceed to certain enumerated counties to obtain horses and mules for the transportation of the armies, upon which the following indorsement was made:

Horses are needed for transportation. Every facility will be given by officers, and citizens are requested to aid Captain Cummings in the discharge of his duty.

No power was given or intended to be conferred by this indorsement, but simply to verify the official character of Captain Cummings, and to secure for him all proper official aid in the discharge of his duties. On the same day Major Ewing addressed another application regarding impressments in this department, and requesting orders. This whole subject was referred to Major-General Maury, on the 25th, for his consideration and report.

Fifth. On the 2d instant Brigadier-General Gholson was ordered to proceed to Okolona, to collect there the debris of his brigade. McGuirk was then at Macon. At your request I ordered the latter to report with his command at Mobile. I then advised you that as soon as General Gholson had gathered his command General Beauregard had directed that he should report to Major-General Gardner. Whilst you were here it was, I think, understood between us that you would order the command then collecting at Okolona to Corinth. Orders to him at Okolona will reach him.

I shall be happy, general, to co-operate with you in any way to secure concert of action, harmony, and success.

I have the honor to be, respectfully, your obedient servant,

GEORGE WM. BRENT,
Colonel and Assistant Adjutant-General.

Hdqrs. Department of Ala., Miss., and East La.,
Meridian, December 17, 1864.

Maj. Gen. D. H. Maury,
        Commanding District of the Gulf, Mobile:

General: I am instructed by the lieutenant-general commanding to state to you as follows:

Unless the most reliable information which he can gather is at fault any investment or serious attack of Mobile at this time is improbable. The movements of the enemy from Baton Rouge and Pensacola are evidently raids, and intended to occupy the attention of the troops in and about Mobile and prevent their use in other important localities. The best information indicates that Davidson's force hardly exceeded 3,000 men, while the raiding party now operating against Pollard does not exceed 1,000 or 1,500. With the troops at your disposal the party now at Pollard ought not to be allowed to escape to Pensacola. The impunity with which they have made previous expeditions to that point has emboldened the enemy, and vigorous measures, with rapid concentration on your part, should enable you to crush them. The reports relative to the force at Pascagoula are extremely confused and conflicting, and steps should be taken to prevent officers on outpost duty from forwarding loose and inaccurate statements and reports which they surely take no means to verify, and which serve only to excite the public mind, while they tend to demoralize our troops by the frequency of false alarms. If, as it occurs to the lieutenant-general commanding, the troops on the west side of the bay can be rapidly thrown against the enemy at or near Pollard, it should be done speedily and the raiding party destroyed, captured, or driven into Pensacola. Any lodgement made by the enemy at East Pascagoula should, if possible, be broken up. A rapid movement to that point in force might be effected so as to surprise them; or if any force of, say, from 4,000 to 6,000 (which is the extent of the number which can concentrate at any point south of Vicksburg) should come out toward Mobile it should be met at once. It is of the greatest importance that the troops belonging to General Hood's army should be sent forward to him without delay as soon as they can possibly be spared, and this necessity operates in favor of vigorous and speedy steps toward ridding your district of the threatening presence of these parties of the enemy. The summary punishment of officers sending false reports, or those which they have not duly verified and authenticated by proper vigilance and caution, would doubtless have a salutary effect in checking the wild and vague information which they so often forward. I advised you by telegraph of the disposition made by Colonel Brent from Montgomery of troops sent toward Pollard. Concert of action between the officers commanding above and below Pollard is of great moment, and if communication has not been already opened it should at once be done.

I am, general, very respectfully, your obedient servant,

WILLIAM M. LEVY,
Lieutenant-Colonel and Assistant Adjutant and Inspector General.

Near Fort Chiswell, *December 17, 1864—12 m.*

Maj. J. Stoddard Johnston,
        Assistant Adjutant-General, Dublin:

Major: I have met here a scouting party just from Wytheville. They report the enemy to have evacuated the place at 2 o'clock this morning, returning as they came, having burned the ordnance and medical purveyor's depots; also Wytheville and Max Meadows depots and intermediate bridges. They report that it was the combined force of Stoneman, Burbridge, and Gillem. Enemy reported that Saltville had been taken at 12 o'clock yesterday, but not credited. Nothing heard from General Breckinridge; Vaughn reported near Wytheville.

J. F. KENT.

The enemy were within two miles and a half of Wytheville when our scout left.

D. S. HOUNSHELL.

CENTRAL [DEPOT], December 17, 1864.

Maj. J. STODDARD JOHNSTON:

Just arrived with my forces from Lynchburg. Have assumed command. Keep me informed of the movements of the enemy.

M. S. LANGHORNE,
Colonel, Commanding.

HEADQUARTERS MILITARY DIVISION OF THE WEST,
Montgomery, December 18, 1864.

[General G. T. BEAUREGARD:]

GENERAL: I was informed about 1 o'clock that you had ordered Major Willis hence, and I avail myself of the occasion to forward you a copy of a journal kept of our proceedings from the 9th instant to this date. I have advised daily by telegraph of all movements and events of a general nature which have taken place.

   *   *   *   *   *   *

You will perceive by the journal that two days since I was considerably embarrassed when the raid on Pollard was threatened. We succeeded in organizing enough troops to resist and defeat the enemy, but we could not obtain guns nor ammunition. Columbus, Ga., and Selma were both called on, and the replies of Colonels Wright and Moore were that they had no guns and ammunition. This is an important matter and deserves attention. Arms and ammunition are becoming a desideratum. The arsenal at Columbus is closed; the one here is idle. Should our communications continue to be interrupted, serious difficulties might occur for want of arms and ammunition here. In my judgment a small depot for arms, &c., should be established at this place.

   *   *   *   *   *   *

There is another difficulty existing which requires attention; it is the total want of quartermasters' funds. Owing to this, all the branches of the service are at a standstill, transportation is embarrassed, supplies slowly and with difficulty obtained, and impressments also totally impossible. Certificates of indebtedness will not be received by the people, and the indebtedness of the different departments has become so great as to become a source not only of embarrassment to public officers in the discharge of their duties, but also one of suffering and discontent to the citizens.

   *   *   *   *   *   *   *

Major Mobley is now absent in Northern Mississippi to see about means of supply. When the present stock on hand and that to be obtained from the tax in kind has been exhausted, it is difficult to ascertain from what source supplies will be obtained. Whilst the army is in Tennessee every effort should be made to add to our stock. But one difficulty stares us right in the face—the want of money.

*   *   *   *   *   *   *

All proper orders have been issued for the speedy completion of the railroads destroyed by the enemy, and confusion was likely to grow out of the fact that Colonel Meriwether and Major Hottle were acting in regard to the same subject under different orders. Colonel Meriwether a few days ago asked that the rails on the Columbus and Girard railroad might be taken, in order to complete the West Point and Atlanta railroad and save the Gainesville Branch for the removal, of which he had authority from the Secretary of War. I did not feel warranted in issuing this order. Major Willis informs me that this whole subject has been placed in his charge by you, and I have no doubt his energy will insure the prompt completion of the roads.

*   *   *   *   *   *   *

I am, very truly, your friend,

GEORGE WM. BRENT,
Colonel and Assistant Adjutant-General.

[First indorsement.]

HEADQUARTERS MILITARY DIVISION OF THE WEST,
Charleston, S. C., December 27, 1864.

Respectfully forwarded to the War Department for its information and attention.

G. T. BEAUREGARD,
General.

[Second indorsement.]

ADJUTANT AND INSPECTOR GENERAL'S OFFICE,
January 4, 1865.

Respectfully referred to the Quartermaster-General, who will please make his response to so much of this communication as pertains to his department, and afterward refer the paper to the Chief of Ordnance for the like object.

By command of the Adjutant and Inspector General:

H. L. CLAY,
Assistant Adjutant-General.

[Third indorsement.]

QUARTERMASTER-GENERAL'S OFFICE,
January 7, 1865.

Respectfully returned.

I cannot too earnestly join in the opinion that our army is paralyzed by want of funds in the Quartermaster's Department, on which it entirely depends for every prompt movement.

A. R. LAWTON,
Quartermaster-General.

[Fourth indorsement.]
ADJUTANT AND INSPECTOR GENERAL'S OFFICE,
January 12, 1865.

Respectfully submitted to the Secretary of War.

H. L. CLAY,
Assistant Adjutant-General.

[Fifth indorsement.]

JANUARY 15, 1865.

Mr. S[HEPHERD]:

Send to the honorable Secretary of the Treasury the remarks relative to the want of funds and General Lawton's indorsement, and invite his attention.

J. A. S.,
Secretary.

[Sixth indorsement.]

Respectfully returned to the Adjutant and Inspector General.

On the 17th of December, one of the "two days" referred to within, there were 320 rifles in store at Columbus, Ga., and 831 muskets, caliber .69, at Mobile, with over 1,600,000 rounds of small-arm ammunition at the latter place.

J. GORGAS,
Chief of Ordnance.

CIRCULAR.]   HEADQUARTERS ARMY OF TENNESSEE,
In the Field, December 18, 1864.

All horses and mules taken from artillery and wagons lost in the recent engagements or on the retreat will be at once turned over to Major Landis, inspector of field transportation.

By command of General Hood:

JAS. COOPER,
Acting Assistant Adjutant-General.

HEADQUARTERS,
Near Columbia, on the Pulaski Pike, December 18, 1864—1.10 p. m.
Lieutenant-General STEWART, *Commanding:*

GENERAL: General Hood desires you will let your wagons move out on the Pulaski pike, camping within a mile or two miles of the town.

Yours, respectfully,

A. P. MASON,
Colonel and Assistant Adjutant-General.

GENERAL ORDERS, }   HEADQUARTERS LEE'S CORPS,
No 67.   }   *In the Field, December 18, 1864.*

Before taking temporary leave of this corps, I desire to express to the officers and men of my command my high appreciation of the good conduct and gallantry displayed by them at Nashville in the engagement of the 16th instant, and to assure them that they can be held in no manner responsible for the disaster of that day. I extend to them all my thanks for the manner in which they preserved their organization in the midst of temporary panic, rallying to their colors and presenting a determined front to the enemy, thus protecting the retreat of the army. I would also respectfully thank the officers and men of Holtzclaw's and Gibson's brigades, of Clayton's division, and of Pettus' brigade, of Stevenson's division, for the gallantry and courage with which they met and repulsed repeated charges of the enemy upon their line, killing and wounding large numbers of the assailants and causing them to retreat in confusion. I desire also to tender my heartfelt thanks to Major-General Stevenson and the officers and men of Pettus' and Cumming's brigades, of his division, for their skillful, brave, and determined conduct while protecting the retreat of the army from Franklin yesterday; constantly attacked in front and on either flank, these brave troops maintained an unshaken line, repulsed incessant attacks, and inflicted heavy loss upon the enemy.

In conclusion, my brave comrades, I beg to assure you that I am not only satisfied with your conduct in the recent campaign, but that I shall repose unalterable confidence in you in the future—a future which, despite the clouds which seem to lower around us, will yet be rendered bright by the patriotic deeds of our gallant army, in which none will gain prouder laurels or do more gallant deeds than the veterans whom I have the honor to command.

S. D. LEE,
Lieutenant-General.

Hdqrs. Strahl's Brigade, Cheatham's Division,
Army of Tennessee,
In the Field, December 18, 1864.

Maj. A. P. Mason,
Assistant Adjutant-General, Army of Tennessee:

Sir: It is a duty I owe myself, brigade, division, to the commanding general, and to the country to state facts in regard to the panic of the army on the afternoon of the 16th. The lines were broken about 3 p. m. on a high hill west of the Granny [White] pike about half a mile, which hill was occupied by Tyler's brigade, Bate's division, and given up to the enemy without a struggle. My command was on Tyler's left, and the right of Cheatham's division. This hill, occupied by the enemy, overlooked the right of the army, and the troops seeing it in the hands of the enemy, and seeing the left wing of the army running without making a stand, fled also. It was not by fighting, nor the force of arms, nor even numbers, which drove us from the field. As far as I can now learn, I did not lose more than thirty men and about thirty-five small-arms, already replaced. For the first time in this war we lost our cannon. Give us the first chance and we will retake them.

Respectfully, your obedient servant,

ANDREW J. KELLAR,
Colonel, Commanding.

Engineer Office,
Mobile, December 18, 1864.

Weekly report of operations for the defense of Mobile during the week ending December 17, 1864:

FIRST DIVISION.

I have the honor to state that the past week has been occupied in placing the redans along the line in fighting condition. All but the one between I and K are in condition for a fight, but are not complete.

The merlons are all in but one. No revetment has yet been put to the merlons. At redan between I and K a large force is employed in strengthening the parapets and connecting the curtains.

Buchanan has been repaired.

SECOND DIVISION.

Gladden: Finishing bomb-proof and repairing traverses; making new wharf northeast of battery.

McIntosh: Making parapet on east side and raising gun; making gallery in rear of bomb-proof, and transporting sand for bomb-proof.

Round battery: Sodding and finishing battery.

THIRD DIVISION.

Blakely: Battery in rear of brickyard completed. Battery near saw-mill completed except platforms and embrasures. Clearing extended to road leading to Spanish Fort. Loading barges, getting wood, &c.

Spanish Fort: In No. 2 six embrasures have been made. A short line of abatis made in front of batteries. Constructing traverses in No. 1. Repairing damages by rains and improving drainage. Driving piles in channel.

Huger: Excavation for new magazine completed. Parapet around gun on magazine nearly completed.

Tracy: Repairing interior slope with sod.

FOURTH DIVISION.

Torpedoes: Seven Singer's torpedoes in a line across Bay Minette, 2,500 yards south of Spanish Fort and beginning at the lower point of island separating Blakely River from Bay Minette. Seven Rains' torpedoes in a line 50 feet north of those above described; all anchored in from 9 to 10½ feet water, half flood tide. Preparing material.

Respectfully submitted.

V. SHELIHA,
Lieutenant-Colonel and Chief of Engineers, District of the Gulf.

MONTGOMERY, ALA., *December 18, 1864.*

Brig. Gen. J. H. CLANTON, or
Brig. Gen. R. C. TYLER,
        Pollard :

Retain men enough to protect Pollard against a raid, and forward all troops, infantry and dismounted men, to Mobile to General Maury. He apprehends an attack.

GEORGE WM. BRENT,
Colonel and Assistant Adjutant-General.

DECEMBER 18, 1864.

Major JOHNSTON:

Colonel Kent requested me to bring you this dispatch, and to tell you that Brigadier-General Vaughn had retreated toward Hillsville. My horse gave out. I will come down in the morning.

Very respectfully,

W. T. BALDWIN,

HEADQUARTERS CENTRAL DEPOT,
December 18, 1864.

Maj. J. S. JOHNSTON,
  Dublin:

MAJOR: Yours of to-day was handed me by Captain Stanton. If Gillespie's men can be found they will be sent out on the lead-mines road (east side) to scout as far as the mines. If no enemy is found they will join their command. As General Breckinridge came out to attack the enemy he will either defeat them or be defeated himself before we could render him any aid, and if defeated will either make his way back to Saltville or come to our relief. I therefore think it unsafe to leave New River bridge uncovered. Moreover, these men under my command are mostly convalescent men, and would not be able to make a march. Captain Stanton is anxious to take the troops under Lieutenant Peyton up to Wytheville. With the forces you have west of this place I consider it hazardous; but, as he thinks you have information and instruction from General Breckinridge that will justify such a move, I consent to it. But, major, every caution should be taken to prevent their being cut off. My opinion is that it would be much safer to blockade the roads, as directed by General B[reckinridge], with the Thurmond command and the forces you have with you.

Very respectfully, major, your obedient servant,
M. S. LANGHORNE,
Colonel, Commanding.

MONTGOMERY, ALA., *December 19, 1864.*

General G. T. BEAUREGARD,
  Charleston, S. C.:

General Hood, on the 12th, says when Sherman completes his raid he deems it important that all available cavalry should be sent to him. Wants Baker's brigade at Mobile, and all troops that can be spared.
GEORGE WM. BRENT,
Colonel and Assistant Adjutant-General.

MONTGOMERY, *December 19, 1864.*

General G. T. BEAUREGARD,
  Charleston, S. C.:

General Clanton telegraphs the following from Pollard, 18th instant:

We pursued the enemy thirty miles, capturing a portion of his transportation, baggage, and supplies. The road for miles is strewn with his dead, principally negro troops. General Liddell, our commander, acted with great spirit and energy, as did his entire command. Our men and horses were completely exhausted, which rendered farther pursuit impossible.

GEORGE WM. BRENT,
Colonel and Assistant Adjutant-General.

(Same to General S. Cooper, Adjutant and Inspector General, Richmond, Va.)

MONTGOMERY, ALA., *December 19, 1864.*
(Via Corinth.)

General J. B. HOOD,
　　Near Nashville:

Baker's brigade is essential to Mobile.   All available troops will be forwarded, if possible.   Sherman has destroyed the bridge over the Ogeechee, on the Gulf and Savannah Railroad, and is threatening Savannah.

GEORGE WM. BRENT,
Colonel and Assistant Adjutant-General.

CIRCULAR.]
HEADQUARTERS,
December 19, 1864.

Corps commanders will send at once to Pulaski all transportation not actually necessary with the troops.   Brigade ordnance wagons will be sufficient to retain.   Reserve ordnance wagons will be sent to Pulaski.

By order of General Hood:

A. P. MASON,
Colonel and Assistant Adjutant-General.

HEADQUARTERS,
December 19, 1864—8.25.

Lieutenant-General STEWART:

GENERAL: General Hood directs me to inform you that Cheatham is ordered to this side, following Stevenson.   The cavalry will cross late this evening.

Yours, respectfully,

A. P. MASON,
Colonel and Assistant Adjutant-General.

HEADQUARTERS,
December 19, 1864—7 p. m.

Lieutenant-General STEWART,
　　Commanding:

GENERAL: I have just written to General Cheatham to come to this side of the river as soon as he can, and also to Forrest to follow Cheatham as soon as he safely can.   General Hood directs that you will cross your command as soon as the cavalry is over, or at the earliest moment thereafter you deem safe, going into camp on the Pulaski pike.

Yours, respectfully,

A. P. MASON,
Colonel and Assistant Adjutant-General.

DECEMBER 19, 1864.

General WALTHALL:

GENERAL: General Stewart desires me to say to you that as the night bids fair to be so bad, that he thinks you had better move your artillery with your first brigade.

I am, general, respectfully,

W. D. GALE,
Assistant Adjutant-General.

DECEMBER 19, 1864—10 a. m.

Col. W. H. TAYLOR,
    Assistant Adjutant-General, Army of Northern Virginia:

Enemy burned furnace at lead-mines on evening of 17th and retired toward Marion. My last dispatch from General Breckinridge was 6 p. m. 16th, at Saltville. Indications are that he is beleaguered. His force is 1,600 cavalry and a few reserves. Enemy's force at least 4,500. Should disaster befall him the force at New River—700 reserves of loose organization—cannot hold the line of New River, and the country will be open to Lynchburg. There is no cavalry in this department except with General Breckinridge, Vaughn's brigade being scattered and disorganized. Will re-establish telegraphic communication with Wytheville in a few hours, and will keep you advised of latest information.

                    J. STODDARD JOHNSTON,
                        Assistant Adjutant-General.

RICHMOND, *December 19, 1864.*

Maj. J. S. JOHNSTON:

Telegram received. Order troops down from New River as you suggest. General Early has been directed to send a brigade or more by rail to New River. Communicate with him if the troops are not needed, so that they may be stopped. Who is in command of troops now at New River?

                    W. H. TAYLOR,
                        Assistant Adjutant-General.

[DECEMBER 19, 1864.]

Col. W. H. TAYLOR,
    Assistant Adjutant-General:

General Breckinridge, leaving garrison of 500 men at salt-works, met enemy and fought him yesterday near Marion. Result indecisive, though he repulsed him frequently with slight loss to himself. My judgment is that, leaving bridge guard at New River, the troops here should be sent to Wytheville, where, should he fall back, he would reasonably expect to find them. In absence of his orders my position does not authorize me to order a movement so important. I apprise you of status here in order that general commanding may instruct me as exigency requires.

                    J. STODDARD JOHNSTON,
                        Assistant Adjutant-General.

HEADQUARTERS,
December 19, 1864.

Maj. J. S. JOHNSTON:

Collect all the reserves and organize them under good officers. Erect works at New River, and hold the line of communication with Breckinridge, that, if necessary, he can fall back to that line.

                    R. E. LEE.

DUBLIN, *December 19, 1864.*

Major-General BRECKINRIDGE:

I am here. In absence of your orders, General Lee has directed me to hold troops at New River, that you may fall back to that line if necessary. They are ready to go forward whenever you order. I await your instructions.

J. STODDARD JOHNSTON,
Assistant Adjutant-General.

LYNCHBURG, *December 19, 1864.*

Major JOHNSTON:

Is it certain that the enemy are finally retreating? What news from the salt-works? Will any more re-enforcements be needed?

R. E. COLSTON,
Brigadier-General.

CENTRAL [DEPOT], *December 19, 1864.*

Maj. J. S. JOHNSTON,
Assistant Adjutant-General, Dublin:

MAJOR: Your several favors of yesterday and to-day have been received. I am satisfied that it is not your wish or intention to assume improperly to rank me by the virtue of your position as assistant adjutant-general of General Breckinridge's department. On my arrival at this place, on the 17th, I telegraphed you that I had assumed command of the forces at this place, of course including those at the bridge. Until communication is opened with General B[reckinridge], it will afford me much pleasure, major, to co-operate with you and the forces with you for the defense of this place and any other point that may be necessary and proper. Please keep me advised of the movements of the enemy and anything that may be proper or useful for me to know.

I am, major, very respectfully, your obedient servant,

M. S. LANGHORNE,
Colonel, Commanding.

CENTRAL [DEPOT], *December 19, 1864.*

Major JOHNSTON:

Please have the following dispatch forwarded to General Breckinridge. If you think it safe to state the number of troops here, you can let him know that I have about 400 convalescent and detailed men and a battery of four pieces:

Major-General BRECKINRIDGE:

Shall I leave New River bridge with the forces I have to join you?

M. S. LANGHORNE,
Colonel, Commanding.

WYTHEVILLE, *December 19, 1864—8 o'clock.*

Maj. Gen. J. C. BRECKINRIDGE:

GENERAL: Inclosed you will find a dispatch from Major Johnston, and you will understand by it that the troops at New River bridge cannot move without your order. If you wish them here send rapid courier to me, and I will telegraph in your name. If all are brought they will number 1,200. They are well armed and supplied with ammunition. Major Johnston and I have been trying to get them here for three days. In a dispatch to me Major Johnston says:

> I cannot order Langhorne on my own responsibility. Orders direct from Richmond to keep open communication with General Breckinridge and hold troops at New River bridge for him to fall back upon if necessary.

Of course, the troops are subject to your order. Do you wish telegraph line extended to Mount Airy? If so, inform me at once, and I will send Mr. Bowyer forward.

Respectfully, your obedient servant,

H. T. STANTON,
Assistant Adjutant-General.

WYTHEVILLE, *December 19, 1864.*

Maj. J. STODDARD JOHNSTON:

To avoid delay consequent upon sending couriers to General Breckinridge, do you not think it would be the better policy to telegraph full statement of affairs to General Lee, showing the utter impossibility of the enemy's cavalry coming to New River bridge after their almost unprecedented marches? If the troops can be pushed to Saltville they will save the works. Enemy will never undertake to come back this way. Numbers of their stragglers are being picked up through the country. They are nearly broken down, and with so much fighting their ammunition must be almost exhausted. I make free to suggest this, because my position here enables me to understand affairs better than you can at Dublin.

H. T. STANTON,
Assistant Adjutant-General.

WYTHEVILLE, *December 19, 1864.*

Maj. J. S. JOHNSTON:

Duke, Cosby, Giltner, and Witcher all with General Breckinridge· Vaughn's brigade scattered to the four winds. If Langhorne will not send troops, telegraph General Lee. Do anything to get them here. Trains can come three miles west of Max Meadows, but ammunition must be taken off at Max Meadows. Have sent General B[reckinridge] 6,000 rounds ammunition found at this place. Have had verbal dispatches from him. Thurmond arrived; came in office.

H. T. STANTON,
Assistant Adjutant-General.

WYTHEVILLE, *December 19, 1864.*

Maj. J. STODDARD JOHNSTON:

General Breckinridge fought enemy two miles east [of] Marion all day yesterday. Drove them at every charge. Loss small. Courier says enemy had column on each flank of our forces. General Breckinridge says he is out of ammunition and will come to Mount Airy to-night.

Send ammunition to Max Meadows at once. Wagons will go from here to bring it. Five hundred troops left at Saltville. All troops should come up without delay.

> H. T. STANTON,
> *Assistant Adjutant-General.*

WYTHEVILLE, *December 19, 1864.*

Maj. J. S. JOHNSTON:

No orders of any kind from General B[reckinridge] with regard to forwarding troops. Will send your message to him. Sent him long account of affairs at the bridge this morning by his own courier. Expect reply in morning.

> H. T. STANTON,
> *Assistant Adjutant-General.*

HEADQUARTERS,
December 20, 1864—8.40.

Lieutenant-General STEWART,
        Commanding:

GENERAL: General Hood directs you will have your men to cook rations this morning, and march at 11 or 12 o'clock to-day. He desires you to make a march of not less than fifteen miles. Walthall, with such troops as will be indicated, will form a rear guard, and will not move with the remainder.

> Yours, respectfully,

> A. P. MASON,
> *Colonel and Assistant Adjutant-General.*

P. S.—Your march will be toward Pulaski.

> A. P. M.

SPECIAL ORDERS, }   HEADQUARTERS STEWART'S CORPS,
    No. 10.   }   *Near Columbia, Tenn., December 20, 1864.*

I. The brigades of Generals Featherston, Reynolds, Ector, and Quarles, with their brigade ordnance wagons, ambulances, tool and cook wagons, will report for duty to Major-General Walthall, at his headquarters on the Pulaski pike.

By order of Lieutenant-General Stewart:

> W. D. GALE,
> *Assistant Adjutant-General.*

HEADQUARTERS FORREST'S CAVALRY CORPS,
At Mr. Warfield's House, December 20, 1864—5 p. m.

Maj. Gen. E. C. WALTHALL:

GENERAL: The major-general directs that you send 200 men to picket from the old mill on Duck River, to extend down to the fort. The mill is about half a mile above where our pontoon bridges were stationed. You will keep a picket there until further orders, and will order up the artillery, if you think it necessary. The artillery is camped between these headquarters and Columbia on this (Pulaski) pike.

Respectfully,
                              J. P. STRANGE,
                                   Assistant Adjutant-General.

HEADQUARTERS FOREST'S CAVALRY CORPS,
At Mr. Warfield's House, December 20, 1864—5.20 p. m.

Maj. Gen. E. C. WALTHALL:

GENERAL: The major-general directs me to say that your dispatch is received; that you will make provision return for the number of men you may have on Maj. G. V. Rambaut, chief commissary of subsistence, to-morrow morning; and he also desires that you send to these headquarters a field return of your command in the morning.

Respectfully,
                              J. P. STRANGE,
                                   Assistant Adjutant-General.

Major Rambaut will be at these headquarters.

GENERAL ORDERS, }   HEADQUARTERS INFANTRY FORCES
                          IN REAR OF ARMY OF TENNESSEE,
No. 1.   }   *Columbia, Tenn., December 20, 1864.*

The brigades of this command will be temporarily united, as follows: Featherston's and Quarles', under command of Brigadier-General Featherston; Ector's and Reynolds', under command of Brigadier-General Reynolds; then Strahl's and Maney's, under command of Colonel Feild; Smith's and Palmer's, under command of Colonel Palmer. This command will stand in line in the following order: Featherston's brigade on the right, Feild's, Palmer's, and Reynolds', in the order they are named.

By command of Major-General Walthall:
                              D. W. SANDERS,
                                   Assistant Adjutant-General.

CIRCULAR.]   HEADQUARTERS INFANTRY FORCES
                        IN REAR OF ARMY OF TENNESSEE,
                              December 20, 1864.

The number of arms-bearing men in this command will at once be reported to these headquarters.*
The name and rank of each regimental and battalion commander will, with the least delay, be returned to these headquarters.

[By command of Major-General Walthall:
                              D. W. SANDERS,
                                   Assistant Adjutant-General.]

---

*For the returns furnished in compliance with this order, see Part I, pp. 728-730.

CIRCULAR.]   HEADQUARTERS INFANTRY FORCES
                        IN REAR OF ARMY OF TENNESSEE,
                                December 20, 1864.

These headquarters are established between the Pulaski and Bigby-ville Pike, one mile and a half from Columbia.

By command of Major-General Walthall:

D. W. SANDERS,
Assistant Adjutant-General.

———

CIRCULAR.]   HEADQUARTERS INFANTRY FORCES
                        IN REAR OF ARMY OF TENNESSEE,
                                December 20, 1864.

Commanders will at all times hold their troops well in hand, so as to move promptly whenever ordered.

By command of Major-General Walthall:

D. W. SANDERS,
Assistant Adjutant-General.

———

DUBLIN, *December 20, 1864.*
(Received 12 o'clock.)

Major-General BRECKINRIDGE:

Dispatch received. Am sending forward everything, as instructed. General Lee telegraphs that General Early has been ordered to send brigade of infantry, and to countermand order if not needed. Have not done so, and shall not, unless you order.

J. STODDARD JOHNSTON,
Assistant Adjutant-General.

———

ENGINEER OFFICE,
Mobile, Ala., December 20, 1864.

Maj. JAMES H. ALEXANDER,
Assistant Adjutant-General, Engineer Bureau, Richmond, Va.:

MAJOR: I have the honor to submit the following report of operations for the month of November, 1864, in the Department of Alabama, Mississippi, and East Louisiana. I beg leave to state that this report has been delayed on account of my not receiving the report of Major Wintter, which he was unable to furnish from being constantly engaged in the field. During the month I visited, with Major-General Smith, the Army of Tennessee, at Tuscumbia and Florence, Ala., with a view of making arrangements for rendering such assistance to that army as this department could furnish, to facilitate its operations beyond the Tennessee River. Maj. D. Wintter was put in charge of all operations tending to this result and stationed at Corinth, Miss. The following is his report for these and other operations in the District of Mississippi and East Louisiana:

The pontoon bridge at Columbus, Miss., was taken up and forwarded by Maj. Gen. Frank Gardner's command to South Mississippi; pontoon bridge at Vinton, Miss., moved to Columbus, Miss.; fortifications repaired at Corinth, Miss.; reconnaissances made on the Tennessee River from Pride's Ferry, Ala., to six miles below

Savannah, Tenn.; batteries thrown up at Chickasaw Bluffs, on the Tennessee River; ferry established at Cheatham's and Garner's Ferries, on the Tennessee River, and the supply-train for General Hood's army forwarded. The Memphis and Charleston Railroad from Corinth, Miss., to Barton Station, Ala., repaired.

Twenty pontoon boats were turned over to Lieutenant-Colonel Presstman, chief engineer Army of Tennessee, to complete his train. In accordance with instructions from General Beauregard, I directed 100 pontoon boats to be made as a reserve train for the Army of Tennessee—one-half to be constructed at Demopolis, Ala., and the remainder at Mobile. At Mobile the facilities for getting seasoned timber being greater than at Demopolis, the work of constructing the boats was commenced about the 15th of November, and about two boats made per day as soon as the work was well under way. Twenty boats were completed at this point. At Demopolis the lumber had to be gotten out and kiln-dried, and the operation of putting the boats together did not commence until about the 1st of December. The frame-work for fifty boats were gotten out, and the boats will soon be completed. Arrangements were made with the quartermaster's department at Meridian, Miss., to saw and send to Corinth, Miss., the necessary number of balks, chess, and other bridge timber; but from some cause unknown to me the timber though gotten out in good season, or at least part of it, was not shipped to Corinth before the Mobile and Ohio Railroad was cut by a raid of the enemy, which rendered such shipment impossible. The pontoon boats at Columbus, Miss., ordered by Major-General Gardner to Panola, were stopped at Meridian and sent to Corinth. The fortifications at Corinth were repaired and rendered tenable for a garrison of 1,000 men against a large force, by taking the salient points of the enemy's works, making inclosed works of them, and repairing the detached works already existing. Reconnaissances were made along the Tennessee River from Florence to Savannah, with a view of making a thorough map of the country, determining the best crossings and best positions for obstructing navigation. The battery made at Chickasaw Bluffs, on the river, was for four Parrott guns. The ferries established at Cheatham's and Garner's Ferries were kept in operation by the engineer troops. The repairs on the railroad were made by engineer troops and engineer negro force.

In the District of Central Alabama, Capt. P. Robinson in charge, the work on the detached redoubts around the city of Montgomery was continued, repairs made on works at Opelika, and a force employed in finishing works already in progress, and in making arrangements for free communication between the works. At Coosa and Yellow Leaf bridges, on the Alabama and Tennessee River Railroad, laborers were engaged on the road between the two points and in finishing redoubt at the latter place.

In the District of the Gulf, Lieut. Col. V. Sheliha, chief engineer, repairs were made on works around the line of city intrenchments, rendered necessary by rains. Work was continued on N and other unfinished redoubts, and Battery Gladden repaired and put in fine condition. Repairs were made on Battery McIntosh and additional galleries commenced for bomb-proofs. The round battery was placed between Gladden and McIntosh by order of the major-general commanding, and secured in position and work of refitting it commenced. Sandbags having been taken up were replaced by sods on Camel battery, and a heavy gun has been mounted on the left flank of this battery; its magazine is in good condition. Pile obstructions have been placed in Conway's Creek, and a pass made through the lower obstructions by removing piling has been again closed by crucial obstructions. At Battery Huger the magazines and bomb-proofs have been very much strengthened, and the parapet has been raised one foot on the old glacis; the service magazines have been made stronger, superior and exterior slopes sodded, and the covered way strengthened. The manufacture of torpedoes has been delayed from want of powder. A large quantity of torpedo stores has been shipped to Major Wintter at Corinth, Miss. In the workshops at this point machinists have been engaged in putting up machinery, carpenters in framing magazines, making pontoons, &c., and blacksmiths in making and repairing tools, carts, and other engineer materials. During the month I also visited and inspected the works at Demopolis, Selma, and Montgomery, Ala.

I have the honor to be, major, very respectfully, your obedient servant,
SAML. H. LOCKETT,
Colonel and Chief Engineer, Dept. of Ala., Miss., and East La.

HDQRS. DEPARTMENT OF ALA., MISS., AND EAST LA.,
Meridian, December 20, 1864.

Lieutenant-General TAYLOR,
Commanding Department:

GENERAL: I have the honor to report that, in obedience to orders, I visited the District of the Gulf for the purpose of inspecting the hospitals therein. After visiting the Nott hospital, which I found cleanly, well administered, and well appointed in all respects, I learned that Surgeon Brodie, medical director of the Western Division, had just completed an inspection, which I concluded would obviate the necessity of any official action on my part for the present. I have the honor to furnish you the accompanying list of hospitals in the district, their capacity, names of officers in charge, and number of patients now under treatment. I have the honor also to state that Surgeon Heustis, medical director of hospitals of this department, informed [me] that the capacity of the hospital in Mobile could be largely increased, sufficiently so to meet any emergency that may occur.

I have the honor to remain, most respectfully, &c.,
P. B. McKELVEY,
Surgeon and Assistant Inspector of Hospitals,
Department of Alabama, Mississippi, and East Louisiana.

List of hospitals in the Gulf District.

Hospitals.	Capacity.	Station.	Surgeon in charge.
	Beds.		
Ross	250	Mobile, Ala	S. L. Nidelet.
Cantey	150	....do	William Henderson.
Moore	123	....do	W. C. Cavenagh.
Le Vert	30	....do	R. H. Redwood.
Nott	51	....do	G. A. Nott.
Nidelet	120	....do	S. L. Paine.
Heustis	90	....do	J. M. Heard.
Miller	170	Greenville, Ala	G. Owen.
General hospital	150	....do	R. B. Maury.

Total sick in hospital, 712.

Circular.]   HEADQUARTERS ARMY OF TENNESSEE,
Pulaski, Tenn., December 21, 1864.

General Hood desires to call the attention of corps commanders to the importance of preserving the artillery and transportation of the army on its present march. To do this with hope of success, it is necessary that strong fatigue details, under energetic officers, should be placed with all trains, and in cases of necessity animals will be taken from the wagons to draw the artillery, and the loads of any wagons will be partially or entirely thrown out to preserve the wagons and teams. Every possible exertion will be made to collect forage at this point, that teams may leave here with a supply, which will be used as sparingly as possible. Battery commanders will have grass pulled for their animals wherever it can be found.

By command of General Hood:

A. P. MASON,
Colonel and Assistant Adjutant-General.

HEADQUARTERS ARMY OF TENNESSEE,
Pulaski, Tenn., December [21?], 1864.

Major-General STEVENSON,
Commanding Corps:

Unless otherwise ordered, General Hood directs that you will move forward with your two divisions at early dawn to-morrow morning, marching in rear of the pontoon train, and making as good a day's march as possible without pushing the troops too much. Push forward all the wagons with you.

A. P. MASON,
Colonel and Assistant Adjutant-General.

Circular.]   HEADQUARTERS INFANTRY FORCES
IN REAR OF ARMY OF TENNESSEE,
December 21, 1864.

Brigade commanders will at once order all the tool wagons of their respective commands to be unloaded, and the wagons sent down the Pulaski pike, three or four miles, to gather up forage. The wagons will turn off to the left of the pike three or four miles from here and search diligently for forage, and return with the least delay.

By command of Major-General Walthall:

D. W. SANDERS,
Assistant Adjutant-General.

[DECEMBER 21, 1864.—For abstract from inspection report of the artillery, Army of Tennessee, see Part I, p. 682.]

COLUMBIA, TENN., *December 21, 1864.*

Maj. D. W. SANDERS,
Assistant Adjutant-General, Walthall's Division:

MAJOR: Citizens report that the enemy are trying to effect a crossing at Johnson's Knob, about two miles above this place. Johnson's

Knob is on the opposite bank of the river and commands a large extent of country on this side.   Reports say that the enemy are digging down the bank at that point.

Very respectfully,

H. R. FEILD,
Colonel, Commanding Maney's and Strahl's Brigades.

HDQRS. DISTRICT OF MISSISSIPPI AND EAST LOUISIANA,
Jackson, Miss., December 21, 1864.

Lieut. Col. WILLIAM M. LEVY,
Assistant Adjutant and Inspector General, Meridian, Miss.:

COLONEL. I have the honor to report that I have ordered back a train of impressed wagons that was transporting arms to the Trans-Mississippi Department, under Lieutenant-Colonel Crow, because the movements of the enemy left the train without proper support and under the risk of being captured.   The wagons have been ordered to be returned to their owners, and the arms are at Brandon.

I deem it my duty to report that the transportation of arms in large numbers across the Mississippi River is impracticable.   The only way in which arms or other supplies can be crossed with anything like safety is to send a small number at a time.   Large trains attract attention, and the enemy is sure to be informed of the movement, while small ones move with more rapidity, are less liable to capture, and the supplies carried can be gotten out of the way with much more ease and facility.

I am, colonel, very respectfully, your obedient servant,

FRANK. GARDNER,
Major-General.

MONTGOMERY, ALA., *December 22, 1864.*

General G. T. BEAUREGARD,
Charleston, S. C.:

General Taylor reports that naval force at Mobile is substantially a part of the local defenses, and that all should be under one head.   A conflict exists between land and naval commanders in regard to a torpedo boat—the former ordering it into active service, the latter refusing to obey.   What must be done?

GEORGE WM. BRENT,
Colonel and Assistant Adjutant-General.

SPECIAL ORDERS, }   ADJT. AND INSP. GENERAL'S OFFICE,
No. 305.   }   *Richmond, December 22, 1864.*

*   *   *   *   *   *

III. The following-named assistant adjutants-general are assigned to duty with the undermentioned commands in the Department of Alabama, Mississippi, and East Louisiana, in accordance with paragraph VI, General Orders, No. 44, current series.   They will report immediately, and will not change their assignments except on orders from this office: Cavalry Division, Brig. Gen. J. R. Chalmers commanding, Capt. W. A. Goodman, Capt. R. M. Hooe.

*   *   *   *   *   *   *

By command of Secretary of War:

ED. A. PALFREY,
Assistant Adjutant-General.

CIRCULAR.]   HEADQUARTERS,
                                   Pulaski, December 22, 1864—7 a. m.

Corps commanders will at once send all their pioneer parties, under charge of an engineer officer, to work the road from Richland Creek out to the ridge, some five miles, corduroying well all bad places. The senior engineer officer present will direct the whole.

By order of General Hood:

                                             A. P. MASON,
                               Colonel and Assistant Adjutant-General.

                                                  HEADQUARTERS,
                                       December 22, 1864—8 a. m.

Lieutenant-General STEWART, *Commanding:*

GENERAL: General Hood directs that you will move your command at once while the ground is frozen, marching some eight or ten miles out on the Lamb's Ferry road. Get all your wagons out to that point, and artillery; gather forage there, and collect your rations at that point. General Hood desires to see you at once.

                                             A. P. MASON,
                               Colonel and Assistant Adjutant-General.

                                                  HEADQUARTERS,
                                Pulaski, December 22, 1864—Sunset.

Lieutenant-General STEWART, *Commanding:*

GENERAL: I inclose you two notes.* General Hood says you must judge for yourself when you arrive at this point, six miles and a half, as to which will be the best road for you to move by. Push forward as far as you can to-morrow, and after crossing Sugar Creek send your best teams back to get the ordnance trains over that creek.

Yours, respectfully,

                                             A. P. MASON,
                               Colonel and Assistant Adjutant-General.

[Inclosure.]

                           SIX MILES AND A HALF FROM PULASKI,
                                          LAMB'S FERRY ROAD,
                                      December 22, 1864—1 p. m.

General J. B. HOOD, *Commanding Army of Tennessee:*

GENERAL: At this point I take the right-hand or Powell road; it intersects the Florence road four miles this side of Lexington and is five miles shorter; has not been traveled, and is the best route, with a good ford over Sugar Creek. I have sent an officer to examine the lower ford, and, if not fordable, will send boats sufficient to bridge it, and to remain till ordered to be taken up by you. Will camp to-night sixteen miles from Pulaski. Have already passed the worst portion of the road, and will make better speed to-morrow.

I have the honor to be, general, very respectfully, your obedient servant,

                                             S. W. PRESSTMAN,
                    Lieutenant-Colonel and Actg. Chief Engineer, Army of Tenn.

---

*Only one found as an inclosure.

HEADQUARTERS FORREST'S CAVALRY CORPS,
At Warfield's House, December 22, 1864—9 a. m.

Major-General WALTHALL,
        Commanding :

GENERAL: The major-general has just received information that the Yankees have placed a pontoon between one and two miles above town. Lieutenant-Colonel Taylor is now fighting them. About 200 have crossed on this side. The major-general is not here at this time. I have, however, sent him the information, and presume he will call and see you.

Respectfully,

J. P. STRANGE,
Assistant Adjutant-General.

HEADQUARTERS ARMY OF TENNESSEE,
Pulaski, Tenn., December 22, 1864.

Lieutenant-Colonel WITHERS,
Commanding Carter's Regiment of Scouts :

General Hood directs that you continue to gather stock, as heretofore directed, but that you at the same time scout the country in the direction of Shelbyville and Fayetteville, and between those points and this place, keeping in communication with General Forrest, to whom you will report any movements of the enemy. General Forrest is now near Columbia. You will report with your command when he retires to Tennessee River. General Forrest will notify you when to join his command.

JAS. COOPER,
Captain and Acting Assistant Adjutant-General.

MONTGOMERY, ALA., *December 22, 1864.*

Lieut. Gen. R. TAYLOR,
        Meridian :

No portion of Tyler's command was ordered back to Montgomery. He left his force at Pollard, except 175 Georgia militia, who have gone back to Georgia. General Adams left this morning for Pollard. He has some reserves at Selma waiting orders. If you wish, I can get for you from conscript officer 250 men, but you must arm and equip them. Answer, and direct where they shall report.

GEORGE WM. BRENT,
Colonel and Assistant Adjutant-General.

HDQRS. DEPARTMENT OF ALA., MISS., AND EAST LA.,
Meridian, Miss., December 22, 1864.

Col. GEORGE WILLIAM BRENT,
        Assistant Adjutant-General :

COLONEL: I have the honor to acknowledge the receipt of your communication of 17th instant. The communication of Brigadier-General Roddey, with indorsements thereon, forwarded to you on yesterday, will explain the matters of which I wrote to you on the 14th, and remove the confusion which previously existed in my mind. I wrote you for the purpose of obtaining a clear understanding on the subjects therein referred to, to enable me to act advisedly, and render more substantial co-operation, because it would then be clearer. Regarding the lines of communication with Mobile and the safety of that city as of vital importance, not only to this department, but to the maintenance of General Hood in Tennessee, and as those lines are threatened by the enemy, I have ordered General Gardner to send all his forces from Southern and Central Mississippi and East Louisiana to a point on the Mobile and Ohio Railroad, whence they can co-operate with Major-General Maury either in an attack on the enemy or in resisting and driving back any attempt to strike the road. While this leaves the Mississippi Valley unprotected, I am led to the adoption of this course by the following reasons: The concentration of the forces under General Granger near East Pascagoula indicates that the enemy must have reduced all its garrisons on the Mississippi River; and the cavalry, under Davidson, being still near West Pascagoula, the enemy cannot at present send any considerable force into the interior. Even should re-enforcements be sent to Canby to enable him to send raiding parties into East Louisiana and Mississippi, they could only temporarily occupy the country and plunder the people, while the interruption of the line of communication above referred to, for any considerable length of time, would cause the loss of Mobile and probably entail disaster upon the Army of Tennessee. My arrangements have placed every disposable man within my department in position to co-operate in the defense of Mobile and its communications. Mabry's and Gholson's commands and the Mississippi reserves will garrison Corinth, and as the pickets extend to within a short distance of Memphis, timely notice would be given of any movement from that place. Hood's army protects Corinth from the front and east, and no other arrangements can be made to provide against the enemy sending a force up the Tennessee River on boats and landing their troops within a day or two's march of that place.

I am, colonel, very respectfully, your obedient servant,

R. TAYLOR,
Lieutenant-General.

MONTGOMERY, ALA., *December 22, 1864.*

Brig. Gen. D. W. ADAMS,
Pollard:

All your troops at Selma are needed at Mobile. I have given the order, but please repeat it.

GEORGE WM. BRENT,
Colonel and Assistant Adjutant-General.

HDQRS. DEPARTMENT OF ALA., MISS., AND EAST LA.,
Meridian, December 22, 1864.

Governor CHARLES CLARK,
Macon, Miss.:

GOVERNOR: The enemy have landed at East Pascagoula between 6,000 and 8,000 men (a large proportion being infantry), under command of Maj. Gen. Gordon Granger, who now threaten Mobile and its communications. The greater portion of Davidson's (Federal) cavalry, which made the recent raid through East Louisiana and Southern Mississippi, is still near West Pascagoula. The threatening attitude assumed by the enemy renders it necessary that all the troops which can possibly be concentrated should be placed in position to enable them to co-operate with the forces in Mobile and protect the lines of communication with that city, on which depends not only the safety of Mobile, but the maintenance of General Hood's army in Tennessee. I have therefore been compelled to withdraw the forces from Southern and Central Mississippi and East Louisiana, and the section of your State bordering on the Mississippi River will, for the present, be left with no adequate protection against raiding parties which the enemy may send into that section. The meager forces at my disposal render this unavoidable; and while the concentration made by the enemy near Mobile renders it improbable that he can do more than plunder certain localities, the evil thus inflicted must be submitted to rather than incur the greater risk of interruption of the above-mentioned communications and loss of Mobile. I communicate this information to Your Excellency, who is aware of the small disposable force at my command, of which I am obliged to leave an adequate garrison at Corinth and a sufficient force to picket toward Memphis. Your own judgment and discretion will enable you to decide upon the propriety or expediency of calling out the local militia in the exposed section of your State after the holiday season has passed.

I am, Governor, very respectfully, your obedient servant,

R. TAYLOR,
Lieutenant-General.

HDQRS. DEPARTMENT OF ALA., MISS., AND EAST LA.,
Meridian, December 22, 1864.

Maj. Gen. D. H. MAURY,
Commanding District of the Gulf, Mobile:

GENERAL: The lieutenant-general commanding instructs me to state to you as follows:

O'Neal's regiment, 450 strong, leaves here this evening for Mobile to report to you. Major-General Gardner has to-day been ordered to send all the forces in Central and Southern Mississippi and East Louisiana to a point on the Mobile and Ohio Railroad between this place and Mobile, where they can co-operate with the forces under your command. This will leave General Gardner only sufficient troops to garrison Corinth and picket toward Memphis. The force displayed by the enemy, or which he can probably collect at this time against Mobile, will not be sufficient for him to invest the city, but he will doubtless occupy them in attempts against your communications. The utmost vigilance should be exercised, and at every favorable opportunity he should be attacked. By confining him to his selected position, and attacking him on every occasion which promises success, he will be seriously annoyed, and the offensive operations on our part will afford the best protection to the line of communications which it is so essential to preserve intact. As the enemy indicates the western shore as the theater of his operations, you should make similar dispositions of all your available forces, leaving on the eastern shore only sufficient garrisons for your works, and throwing mounted pickets as near as possible to Pensacola, so as to give you timely notice of any movement from that quarter to enable you to meet and defeat it. It would seem from the telegraphic communications which reached these headquarters that your cavalry on picket and outpost duty failed to communicate to you the recent movement of the enemy from Pensacola on Pollard, as the first information on the subject appears to have been given by General Clanton, who, being en route to Mobile, discovered the enemy to be within a few miles of Pollard. If the officer or officers on outpost and picket duty failed to give you prompt and timely notice, the causes should be investigated, and if there was neglect of duty, the guilty party should be brought to punishment.

I am, general, very respectfully, your obedient servant,

WILL. M. LEVY,

Lieutenant-Colonel and Assistant Adjutant and Inspector General.

HDQRS. DEPARTMENT OF ALA., MISS., AND EAST LA.,
Meridian, December 22, 1864.

Maj. Gen. FRANK. GARDNER,

Comdg. District of Mississippi and East Louisiana, Jackson:

GENERAL: The lieutenant-general commanding directs me to state to you as follows:

In the present condition of affairs the only important points which should engage the attention of the forces in this department are the defense of Mobile and keeping open the line of communication therewith, and the rendering all practicable assistance and co-operation in the movements of General Hood's army. The latest information from Mobile shows that Major-General Granger with a considerable force (say from 6,000 to 8,000), a large proportion of which is infantry, is east of East Pascagoula. Davidson's cavalry is still at or near West Pascagoula. It is very clear that the concentration of these troops under Granger has reduced greatly the garrison on the Mississippi, and no movement of importance can be undertaken by the enemy from that quarter. At any rate, it is of paramount importance that the line of communication with Mobile should be kept open, as upon it depends not only the safety of Mobile itself, but that of Hood's army, which is dependent upon its remaining unbroken for maintenance in its present position or ulterior operations. You will, therefore, move all the forces which can be collected from Southern and Central Mississippi and East Louisiana, and march them, with as little delay as possible, to some point on the Mobile and Ohio Railroad between Meridian and Mobile, whence, in conjunction with the other cavalry, now outside of Mobile, they can operate against the enemy as opportunity presents itself or can be made, and defend the railroad against any attempt of the enemy to strike it. These troops should be placed under the command of an active cavalry officer, who from his rank may control all the cavalry outside of Mobile in the event of a siege of that city. Gholson's, Mabry's, and the Mississippi reserves will constitute the forces in the Northern District of Mississippi, garrisoning Corinth and watching the enemy toward Memphis. The officer whom you assign to the command of the troops whom you send to the Mobile and Ohio Railroad will report in person to the lieutenant-general commanding at department headquarters.

I am, general, very respectfully, your obedient servant,

WILL. M. LEVY,

Lieutenant-Colonel and Assistant Adjutant and Inspector General.

CHARLESTON, *December 23, 1864.*
(Received January 3, 1865.)

General J. B. HOOD:

I regret to inform you that no re-enforcements can possibly be sent you from any quarter. General Taylor has no troops to spare, and every available man in Georgia and South Carolina is required to oppose Sherman, who is not on a raid, but an important campaign. Should you be unable to gain any material advantage in Tennessee with your present means you must retire at once behind the Tennessee River, and come with or send to Augusta, by best and quickest routes, all forces not absolutely required to hold defensive line referred to.

G. T. BEAUREGARD,
General.

———

HEADQUARTERS,
Eighteen Miles from Pulaski, December 23, 1864.

Lieutenant-General STEWART,
Commanding:

GENERAL: General Hood directs that you will send back in the morning early 200 men, under energetic officers, to bring forward those broken pontoons we passed to-day. Let this force be divided into details for each boat.

Yours, respectfully,

A. P. MASON,
Colonel and Assistant Adjutant-General.

[Indorsement.]

HEADQUARTERS STEWART'S CORPS,
December 23, 1864.

General Loring will furnish 100 men and General Shelley also 100 men, in compliance with the within order.

By order of Lieutenant-General Stewart:

W. D. GALE,
Assistant Adjutant-General.

———

HEADQUARTERS,
Waldrop's, Three Miles North of Lynnville,
December 23, 1864—7.05 a. m.

Brigadier-General CHALMERS,
Commanding Division:

GENERAL: The major-general directs me to say that as our forces and trains have not all left Pulaski, it is important that we hold the enemy in check as long as possible, and therefore the major-general directs that you move back at once toward Columbia until you meet the enemy, and demonstrate strongly upon him, as if you intended to reoccupy the town. Generals Buford and Jackson have been ordered to advance on this pike. The major-general will not leave here to-day unless forced back.

Respectfully,

J. P. STRANGE,
Assistant Adjutant-General.

The major-general will go in person to the front this morning.

J. P. S.

MONTGOMERY, ALA, *December 23, 1864.*

Lieut. Gen. R. TAYLOR,
        Meridian:

Captain Reid, assistant adjutant-general, at Corinth, says scouts report no indication of raid from Memphis. Large number of transports passed, supposed to take troops up river. Force in Memphis estimated 25,000, new recruits, 2,000 cavalry, besides two regiments mounted negroes. Scouts also report from near Collierville heavy column enemy's infantry passed Forrest Hill, at 12 o'clock on 21st, on State Line road. Brigade infantry camped White's Station night of 21st, where cars are running. Enemy are preparing to run Memphis and Charleston Railroad.

GEORGE WM. BRENT,
Colonel and Assistant Adjutant-General.

HDQRS. DEPARTMENT OF ALA., MISS., AND EAST LA.,
        Meridian, December 23, 1864.

Governor CHARLES CLARK,
        Macon, Miss.:

GOVERNOR: Dispatches have just been received by me to the effect that the enemy in considerable force is moving out from Memphis on the line of the Memphis and Charleston Railroad. The object, doubtless, is to attack Corinth or interrupt the line of communication with Hood's army. If successful in this, it is by no means improbable that they would penetrate and desolate the rich interior prairie country of Mississippi. With these threatening forces near Corinth and Mobile, you can readily perceive that, with the small force at my disposal, my hands are full. In Northwestern Mississippi, Major-General Martin, with his little force, and in Northeastern Mississippi, Col. W. R. Miles, have the only troops which are at present available to resist any serious advance of the enemy in the northern portion of Mississippi. In our last interview we discussed the matter of an invasion of your State and the immediate danger thereof. I therefore hasten to communicate to you the latest information which I have on the subject, in order that you may decide in your mind upon the propriety and practicability of calling out the militia or organizing State troops to assist in repelling the invasion. I need not renew to you, Governor, the assurance that in the event of your calling out the militia, or adopting any other measures which will render assistance at this juncture, I shall use all the means in my power toward placing such troops on the most efficient footing and supplying, to the extent of my ability, their wants. I would be glad to have your views on the subject-matter of this communication.

I am, Governor, very respectfully, your obedient servant,
R. TAYLOR,
Lieutenant-General.

HDQRS. DEPARTMENT OF ALA., MISS., AND EAST LA.,
        Meridian, December 23, 1864.

Maj. Gen. D. H. MAURY,
        Commanding District of the Gulf:

GENERAL: I am instructed by the lieutenant-general commanding to state to you as follows:

Dispatches just received indicate a movement of the enemy in considerable force from Memphis on the line of the Memphis and Charleston Railroad. Every available man in the department has been ordered to the Mobile and Ohio Railroad between Meridian and Mobile, leaving the western portion of Mississippi entirely without troops. The garrison at Corinth is an exceedingly small one, and the forces operating between that place and Memphis are insufficient to repel any advance from that direction. By this time your strength at Mobile must have been materially increased by troops sent via this place and Montgomery and those whom Governor Watts has sent you. The lieutenant-general commanding desires you to keep him fully advised of all the accessions which have been made to your strength, indicating not only the number, but the character—*i. e.*, arm of service. This, together with the prompt communication of accurate information as to the movements of the enemy, is most important, as it is essential that the troops of General Hood's army should be sent to Corinth at the first moment when they are not absolutely necessary for the defense of Mobile.

I am, general, very respectfully, your obedient servant,

WILL. M. LEVY,
Assistant Adjutant and Inspector General.

HDQRS. DEPARTMENT OF ALA., MISS., AND EAST LA.,
Meridian, December 23, 1864.

Brig. Gen. D. W. ADAMS,
Montgomery, Ala.:

GENERAL: I am instructed by the lieutenant-general commanding to state to you as follows:

Inclosed is a copy of letter written to you on the 15th instant,* which may have failed to reach you. He desires you to take prompt steps toward carrying out the instructions therein contained. It is of great importance that every man who can possibly be spared should be sent to the command in the field to which he belongs. It is also desirable that measures should be adopted now, while North Alabama is free from the enemy, toward breaking up the bands of jayhawkers and arresting the stragglers and deserters who infest that section. Colonel Reid's command can be used, perhaps, advantageously for that purpose, and the laws of Alabama and the disposition of the Governor will enable the local county militia to be used for the purpose of arresting these deserters, &c. You were ordered to Pollard for the purpose of concentrating and commanding the troops which could be collected against the enemy's recent raiding expedition to that point. Your return to Montgomery after the enemy had gone back was proper. The lieutenant-general commanding desires you to use all the means in your power toward sending the men referred to in the inclosed letter to the front.

I am, general, very respectfully, your obedient servant,

WILL. M. LEVY,
Assistant Adjutant and Inspector General.

HEADQUARTERS ARMY OF NORTHERN VIRGINIA,
December 24, 1864. (Received 3.15 p. m.)

Hon. J. A. SEDDON,
Secretary of War:

General Breckinridge reports that the enemy, after having been roughly handled in the engagements of Saturday and Sunday near

---

* See p. 694.

Marion, many having been killed and wounded, gained possession of Saltville during the night of the 20th. The garrison retreated up Rice Valley. His advance arrived at daylight on the 21st, and the enemy retired that night and the morning of 22d toward Huyter's Gap. They are being pursued, our troops bearing the fatigue and exposure with great cheerfulness. The damage to the works can soon be repaired. Many bridges and depots on railroad have been burned.

R. E. LEE.

MONTGOMERY, ALA., December 24, 1864.

General G. T. BEAUREGARD,
   Charleston, S. C.:

General Taylor reports enemy left Memphis on 21st, moving on State Line road. His advance reached La Fayette Depot 11 a. m. 20th. Force—two brigades negroes, one of white cavalry. Object of movement not developed. Have nothing official from Hood.

GEORGE WM. BRENT,
Colonel and Assistant Adjutant-General.

HEADQUARTERS,
December 24, 1864.

Lieutenant-General STEWART,
   Commanding:

GENERAL: General Hood directs you send forward before daylight all your pioneer parties, to report to Colonel Presstman at the river, at Bainbridge. Have all your empty wagons filled with plank for decking, gathering it from buildings on the road, and let them go to Presstman also.

Yours, respectfully,

A. P. MASON,
Colonel and Assistant Adjutant-General.

HEADQUARTERS,
December 24, 1864—4.10 p. m.

Lieutenant-General STEWART:

GENERAL: Headquarters will be for the night at Joiner's house, on Blue Creek; we are now at that point. General Hood directs that to-morrow you will move on and get your command over Shoal Creek, sending back and bringing over all your wheels. As soon as you cross the creek select a line for the protection and defense of the ford, and fortify it as well as possible, having special reference to a good abatis.

Yours, respectfully,

A. P. MASON,
Colonel and Assistant Adjutant-General.

HEADQUARTERS,
December 24, 1864—6.20 p. m.

Lieutenant-General STEWART,
   Commanding:

GENERAL: General Hood directs that to-morrow you keep an officer at the rear of your column, and if Major Green, of the engineers, catches up to you give him the road and let him pass with his train of decking, &c. He expected to be in Lexington this evening with the rear of his train.

Yours, respectfully,

A. P. MASON,
Colonel and Assistant Adjutant-General.

HEADQUARTERS,
December 24, 1864—6.40.

Lieutenant-General STEWART,
Commanding:

GENERAL: General Hood directs you will move your command to-morrow and get it over Shoal Creek, sending back for all your wheels. As soon as you get over get the best line you can find for the protection of the ford and fortify it as well as you can. Major Green, of the engineers, expected to be with his train this evening at Lexington. If he catches you to-morrow, give him the road and let him pass.

Yours, respectfully,

A. P. MASON,
Colonel and Assistant Adjutant-General.

HEADQUARTERS,
Two Miles and a Half South of Lynnville,
December 24, 1864—2.30 p. m.

Major-General WALTHALL,
Commanding Infantry:

GENERAL: The major-general commanding directs me to say that the enemy is now pressing his rear heavily, and directs that you get into position and [occupy*] your works with all possible haste, [and*] directs that you halt all cavalry stragglers, with guns, going to the rear, and form them with your line and make them fight.

Respectfully,

J. P. STRANGE,
Assistant Adjutant-General.

HEADQUARTERS, &C.,
December 24, 1864—10.15 p. m.

Maj. J. P. STRANGE:

MAJOR: In your note dated 6 o'clock this evening I am directed to move from my old position at 3 o'clock in the morning. As my position was changed before your note was received, please advise me when I am expected to move from my present position. Armstrong's, and not Ross', cavalry is behind me.

Respectfully, your obedient servant,

E. C. WALTHALL,
Major-General.

---

* Original torn.

MONTGOMERY, ALA., *December 24, 1864.*

Lieut. Gen. S. D. LEE,
  Okolona and Columbus:

I have no report of events from Tennessee since 15th instant.

GEORGE WM. BRENT,
  Colonel and Assistant Adjutant-General.

MONTGOMERY, ALA., *December 24, 1864.*

Lieut. Gen. R. TAYLOR,
  Meridian:

Be good enough to see to pontoons for General Hood's army.   They ought to be at Corinth by this time.

GEORGE WM. BRENT,
  Colonel and Assistant Adjutant-General.

MONTGOMERY, ALA., *December 24, 1864.*

Lieut. Gen. R. TAYLOR,
  Meridian:

Have heard nothing from General Hood.

GEORGE WM. BRENT,
  Colonel and Assistant Adjutant-General.

MONTGOMERY, ALA., *December 25, 1864.*

General G. T. BEAUREGARD,
  Charleston:

General S. D. Lee reports from Florence he will be at Okolona in a few days; states he would be glad to have General Beauregard's views in regard to recent events in Tennessee.   There are no advices whatever from that quarter, and do not understand General Lee's telegraph. Am apprehensive that some reverse may have occurred.

GEORGE WM. BRENT,
  Colonel and Assistant Adjutant-General.

HEADQUARTERS,
  Bainbridge, December 25, 1864.
  (Via Corinth January 3, 1865.)

Hon. J. A. SEDDON,
  Secretary of War:

I am laying a pontoon here to cross the Tennessee River.

J. B. HOOD,
  General.

HEADQUARTERS,
  Bainbridge, December 25, 1864.

General G. T. BEAUREGARD,
  Montgomery, Ala.:

I am laying a pontoon here to cross the Tennessee River.   Please come to Tuscumbia or Bainbridge.

J. B. HOOD,
  General.

TUSCUMBIA, ALA., *December 25, 1864.*

His Excellency JEFFERSON DAVIS:

SIR: I arrived here last night, leaving the army some fifteen miles beyond the Tennessee River, on the Bainbridge route. Our stay in Tennessee was so short and engagements so constant and pressing that we did not recruit to any considerable extent. If we could have remained there a few weeks longer we could and would have recruited to a great extent. The men are there, and thousands were making their arrangements to join the army, but the unfortunate result of the battle at Nashville and immediate retreat of the army was very discouraging to our people; I hope, however, to be able to get a great many of those men out, notwithstanding we have left the State. I have been with General Hood from the beginning of this campaign, and beg to say, disastrous as it has ended, I am not able to see anything that General Hood has done that he should not, or neglected anything that he should have done which it was possible to do; indeed, the more that I have seen and known of him and his policy the more I have been pleased with him; and regret to say that if all had performed their parts as well as he, the results would have been very different. But I will not detain Colonel Johnson except to say, or rather to suggest, that if General Hood is to command this army he should, by all means, be permitted to organize the army according to his own views of the necessities of the case.

Very respectfully,

ISHAM G. HARRIS.

HEADQUARTERS,
On the River-bank at Bainbridge, December 25, 1864—11 a. m.

Lieutenant-General STEWART:

GENERAL: General Hood directs that, for the present, you keep your command beyond Shoal Creek, to hold the roads over on that side. Take the best line you can find for the purpose. Keep one battery with you, but push forward all your other wheels to this side the creek. Don't let this work stop, night or day, till you get everything to this side of Shoal Creek. You can strengthen the position on the other side as much as you think necessary for the protection of the roads. General Hood will send you orders when to withdraw to this side of Shoal Creek, and when you do come over you can carry out the previous orders about fortifying on this side the creek.

Yours, respectfully,

A. P. MASON,
Colonel and Assistant Adjutant-General.

[Indorsement.]

Colonel SEVIER:

Keep a battery, and find a place for troops to bivouac. Preserve this order. Keep the tool wagons with the troops.

ALEX. P. STEWART,
Lieutenant-General.

HEADQUARTERS ARMY OF TENNESSEE,
At the River, December 25, 1864—3.30 p. m.

Lieutenant-General STEWART,
Commanding Corps:

GENERAL: General Hood directs me to say that two fords on Shoal Creek above the one over which the army is now crossing have been reported to him—one a mile above, and the other three miles above; the latter is called Huff's, and the road on the other side may be partially blocked. Have them both examined at once, and if in your judgment you can save time by it cross your wheels at either or both of them. Captain Smith, of General Hood's staff, reports the one a mile above a good ford, without obstruction and not deep. Let us know when your wheels are over Shoal Creek.

Yours, respectfully,

A. P. MASON,
Colonel and Assistant Adjutant-General.

[HEADQUARTERS,
December 25, 1864.]

Lieutenant-General STEWART:

GENERAL: General Hood directs that as soon as all of your wheels are over Shoal Creek you will cross your command and carry out the order written you yesterday, to take position on this side of that creek, with reference to holding it.

Yours, respectfully,

A. P. MASON,
Colonel and Assistant Adjutant-General.

MONTGOMERY, ALA., *December 25, 1864.*

Lieut. Gen. R. TAYLOR,
Meridian:

Captain Reid telegraphs from Corinth that Lieutenant Vernon, engineer troops, reports enemy landed at Chickasaw yesterday morning. Saw their boats; whether transports or gun-boats unknown.

GEORGE WM. BRENT,
Colonel and Assistant Adjutant-General.

HDQRS. DEPARTMENT OF ALA., MISS., AND EAST LA.,
Meridian, Miss., December 25, 1864.

Maj. Gen. F. GARDNER,
Commanding District of Miss. and East La., Jackson, Miss.:

Rumors from above, and the official reports of the enemy, seem to establish the fact that General Hood has sustained a serious reverse. The lieutenant-general desires you, in consequence, to be governed by your own information as to how far the troops under General Adams shall be sent on to the support of Martin and Mabry, whom it is presumed will be able to meet the force coming out under Grierson. Should General Hood cross the Tennessee the enemy may push him some fifty miles south of it, or as far as the condition of the roads will allow, and will then doubtless deflect that portion of his army furnished by Canby, some 20,000 men, for a serious attack on Mobile. In this event General Hood will have ample cavalry for his purpose, while all of yours will be needed near Mobile and along the Mobile and Ohio railroad to harass the enemy and protect our line of communication. I am directed to add that the telegram sent you to-day with regard to Colonel Scott's command was forwarded with the view of authorizing you to give him such instructions as you might propose. To repeat, push forward General Adams only in case he can arrive in time to be available and in the event that General Hood does not cross the Tennessee.

Very respectfully, general, your obedient servant,

A. J. WATT,
Assistant Adjutant-General.

Hdqrs. Department of Ala., Miss., and East La.,
Meridian, December 25, 1864.

Maj. Gen. D. H. Maury,
Commanding District of the Gulf:

General: I am directed by the lieutenant-general commanding to state to you that, from the rumors which reach him from our own army and from the official reports of the enemy, he is satisfied that General Hood has suffered a severe reverse. He now feels convinced, for the first time, that Mobile will be seriously threatened, not immediately, but so soon as the enemy, having pressed his pursuit of our army as far south of the Tennessee as the condition of the roads will permit, shall be in a position to return the force, some 20,000 men, which he obtained from Canby. The lieutenant-general commanding desires you, therefore, to make steady and energetic preparations for the anticipated movement, weighing well your dispositions to meet it and studying carefully every means by which the enemy can be annoyed and harassed by our cavalry. Your defensive works should be pushed forward with all possible vigor, and, if necessary, you should employ your soldiers to complete them. The lieutenant-general commanding will place at your command all the assistance he can himself control and all that he can obtain from Governor Watts and General Withers.

I have the honor to be, general, very respectfully, your obedient servant,

A. J. WATT,
Assistant Adjutant-General.

Engineer Office,
Mobile, December 25, 1864.

Weekly report of operations for the defense of Mobile, Ala., during week ending December 24, 1864:

FIRST DIVISION.

Redans: During the week the force was kept on the redans, the larger part being upon the one between I and K, which is rapidly approaching completion.

I: Completing magazine and galleries. Steam engine burst on Friday, killing two negroes and scalding and wounding five or six others. The engineer was badly scalded. The machine is a complete wreck.

SECOND DIVISION.

Gladden: The wharf is nearly completed, and pile-driver still engaged in driving obstructions on the front, to prevent boat attacks. All the repairs have been finished.

Tilghman: There remains to be done only the leveling of the platforms for the two guns, with a few trifling repairs.

McIntosh: Repairing traverses and raising the parapet on the left flank. Owing to the fact of there being only one steam-boat to do the work of this and the Third Division, the operations on the Bay batteries have been retarded fully one-third. The hands get to work late every day, and work frequently stops for want of transportation of material.

THIRD DIVISION.

Blakely: Three batteries completed on fronts, with the exception of platforms and embrasures; the fourth will be in a similar state of completion by noon to-day. Platforms laid in two batteries. Clearing continued around entire line. Fifty yards of rifle-pits completed.

Spanish Fort: Work progressing very slowly, in consequence of the small number of hands engaged.

FOURTH DIVISION.

Torpedoes: Ten Singer's torpedoes anchored about 2,000 yards below the point designated in last report, in from 12 to 20 feet of water, the line marked by a stake on the eastern bank Bay Minette and a small towhead on western side. Four Rains' torpedoes continuing the line above described.

The week has been devoted to work on the electric battery.

Respectfully submitted.

> V. SHELIHA,
> *Lieutenant-Colonel and Chief Engineer, District of the Gulf.*

CHARLESTON, *December 26, 1864.*

General S. COOPER,
    Adjutant and Inspector General:

General Taylor reports that naval force at Mobile is substantially a part of the local defenses, and that all should be under one head. A conflict exists between land and naval commanders as to a torpedo boat— the former ordering it into active service, the latter refusing to obey. What must be done?

> G. T. BEAUREGARD,
> *General.*

[First indorsement.]

DECEMBER 27, 1864.

Respectfully referred to the honorable Secretary of the Navy.

Cannot harmony between the two branches of the service be secured in respect to this boat. If the navy objects to using it, and volunteers from the army are anxious to test it, may not the liberty be allowed, with a caution to the officers of the previous sad experience with similar boats.

> J. A. SEDDON,
> *Secretary of War.*

[Second indorsement.]

DECEMBER 29, 1864.

Respectfully returned to honorable Secretary of War.

I know nothing of the boat referred to, and have heard nothing of the want of harmony to which General Beauregard refers, and had no reason to believe from the information before me that any existed. I will refer the subject of the boat, with appropriate suggestions looking to the public interest, to Captain Farrand.

S. R. MALLORY,
Secretary of the Navy.

HEADQUARTERS,
River-bank, December 26, 1864—10.30 a. m.

Col. E. J. HARVIE,
Inspector-General:

COLONEL: Reid's dispatch forwarded by yourself just received. General Hood directs that such forces as can be spared from Corinth be sent at once to drive the enemy off the railroad. Reid must endeavor to judge of how much Corinth is now threatened and what force can be spared from there. Communicate with General Maury at once, and ask his assistance. Forces from this army will reach Barton to-morrow night, unless we should have some unforeseen accident.

Yours, respectfully,

A. P. MASON,
Colonel and Assistant Adjutant-General.

HEADQUARTERS,
December 26, 1864—11 a. m.

Col. E. J. HARVIE,
Inspector-General:

COLONEL: General Hood directs that you take immediate steps to repair the damage which the enemy have done our railroad. This work should be pushed forward at once and with great energy. Keep this river well watched by good scouts from Florence to, or below, Chickasaw.

Yours, respectfully,

A. P. MASON,
Colonel and Assistant Adjutant-General.

MONTGOMERY, ALA., *December 26, 1864.*

Lieut. Gen. R. TAYLOR,
Meridian:

General Beauregard approves of your views in relation to the large accumulation of stores at Corinth. He thinks they should be distributed and held within reach of the Memphis and Charleston Railroad. You can, therefore, have them distributed at such localities and in such quantities as you may deem proper. When necessary, such orders will be given from these headquarters to carry out your views. General

Hood has been directed that should he be unable to gain any material advantage in Tennessee, to recross the river and send to Augusta by quickest route all forces not absolutely needed for that defensive line.

GEORGE WM. BRENT,
Colonel and Assistant Adjutant-General.

Subsistence stores in Mississippi and East Louisiana, December 15, 1864.

Depot.	Beeves.	Hogs.	Sheep.	Calves.	Pigs.	Bacon.	Lard.	Hard bread.	Flour.
Grenada and vicinity	1,677	2,678				5,194	250	8,020	27,015
Columbus	368	27				2,262	1,246		118,496
West Point	164					4,682	1,488	11,136	38,461
Okolona	424	90				1,059			11,215
Aberdeen and Crawford	454	50				7,096			4,266
Canton and Carthage	48	754	3			1,059	279		639
Jackson and Brandon	47	26				4,085	79	5,025	7,143
Goodman	37					147			
Macon and Brookville	22					1,162	198	449	4,274
Shuqualak and Lauderdale	111			1		1,258	516		33,243
Newton, Forest, and Hillsborough.	44	128				798			544
Conenatta	27	4							4,232
Enterprise	75	12				24	107		4,934
Shubuta	38					210			215
Mississippi City	13								
Brookhaven	75	3						73	1,005
Hazlehurst	274	382	68			144			20
Mount Carmel	50	269				35			233
Clinton, Woodville, and Meadville.	188	282							142
Meridian	58					12,792		10,717	11,238
Cuba, Ala	10	106	483	4	26		32,865		63,910
Gainesville, Ala	5,614	167		137	136				
Corinth, Miss								240,689	
Nashville			1,436						
Total	9,818	4,978	1,990	142	162	42,007	37,028	276,109	331,225

Depot.	Meal.	Beans.	Peas.	Rice.	Wheat.	Corn.	Rye.	Coffee.	Tea.
Grenada and vicinity	2,529		93	2,750	2,622	2,628	120	8	
Columbus	100,431			4,661	11,777	238	926		
West Point	27,080	349		1,180	168	1	223	52	
Okolona	26,641				94		77	104	
Aberdeen and Crawford	2,226				146	1,902	234		
Canton and Carthage	222			460	334	60			
Jackson and Brandon	13,420			140	65		18		
Goodman	259	4			348	302	44		
Macon and Brookville	61,650			1,638	1,445	8,928			
Shuqualak and Lauderdale	4,847		2	480	5,320	300	164	65	
Newton, Forest, and Hillsborough.	203			5	318	110	15		
Conehatta					16				
Enterprise	14,322		69	769			4		
Shubuta	432			22	54		16		
Mississippi City						56			
Brookhaven	960		24	614		67	40		
Hazlehurst	63				129				
Mount Carmel			99	9,801		646	20		
Clinton, Woodville, and Meadville.			20	62		301			
Meridian	24,644		47	1,290	141	211	9	1,689	47
Cuba, Ala			35	9,139					
Gainesville, Ala									
Corinth, Miss	596,090			2,925					
Nashville									
Total	876,019	353	389	35,936	22,848	15,879	1,910	1,918	47

Subsistence stores in Mississippi and East Louisiana, December 15, 1864—Continued.

Depot.	Sugar.	Mo-lasses.	Whisky.	Can-dles.	Soap.	Salt.	To-bacco.	Wool.	Salt pork.
Grenada and vicinity......	12,772	......	......	......	......	10,775	2,519	......	......
Columbus..................	7,336	144	......	128	3,073	33,162	1,664	......	4,704
West Point	8,827	99	......	......	460	9,246	......	......	12,053
Okolona..................	578	......	......	167	3,194	5,325	1,847	......	......
Aberdeen and Crawford...	108	......	......	......	74	2,624	6	......	......
Canton and Carthage	986	......	......	......	41	1,119	720	......	......
Jackson and Brandon	673	150	......	......	1,143	3,157	895	......	......
Goodman..................	1,062	......	......	......	......	205	120	......	......
Macon and Brookville.....	7,540	......	41	81	964	29,110	3,178	......	......
Shuqualak and Lauderdale	6,136	73	......	......	1,952	3,133	197	......	......
Newton, Forest, and Hills-borough.	......	......	......	......	69	1,540	22	......	......
Conehatta................	......	......	......	......	......	......	......	......	......
Enterprise	......	......	......	10	1,080	1,896	1,470	......	......
Shubuta..................	......	......	......	......	94	140	15	......	......
Mississippi City.........	......	......	......	......	......	......	......	......	......
Brookhaven...............	60	......	......	14	......	2,589	835	......	......
Hazlehurst...............	......	......	......	......	......	433	......	......	......
Mount Carmel.............	3,907	......	......	......	......	80	......	......	......
Clinton, Woodville, and Meadville.	......	......	......	......	......	1,817	......	......	......
Meridian.................	7,442	766	464	30	3,260	7,697	9,394	......	......
Cuba, Ala...............	......	......	......	......	......	131,813	......	124	197,732
Gainesville, Ala.........	......	......	......	......	......	......	......	......	......
Corinth, Miss	......	......	......	......	100	......	......	......	......
Nashville................	......	......	......	......	......	......	......	861	......
Total................	57,427	1,232	505	430	15,504	245,861	22,882	985	214,489

W. H. DAMERON,
*Major and Chief Commissary of Subsistence for
Mississippi and East Louisiana.*

MERIDIAN, MISS., *December 26, 1864.*

CHARLESTON, *December 27, 1864.*

General S. COOPER,
Adjutant and Inspector General:

General Lee telegraphs from Florence that he will be at Okolona in a few days, and wishes my views relative to recent events in Tennessee. I have no advices whatever from that quarter, and do not understand General Lee's telegram. I am apprehensive some reverse may have occurred. I will leave here as soon as practicable, unless otherwise instructed.

G. T. BEAUREGARD,
General.

CHARLESTON, *December 27, 1864.*

General S. COOPER,
Adjutant and Inspector General:

General Taylor reports enemy left Memphis on 20th [21st] moving on State Line road. His advance reached La Fayette Depot on 20th. His force consists of two brigades negroes, and one of white cavalry. Object of movement not yet developed.

G. T. BEAUREGARD,
General.

[DECEMBER 27, 1864.—For Beauregard to Cooper, relative to a visit to Army of Tennessee, and change of base of operations, &c. (two dispatches), see Vol. XLIV, p. 993.]

MONTGOMERY, ALA., *December 27, 1864.*

General G. T. BEAUREGARD,
            Charleston:

General Taylor telegraphs that enemy's cavalry has struck Mobile and Ohio Railroad at Verona, while a large force is advancing from Memphis. Have directed General D. W. Adams to establish a line of couriers to communicate with General Hood, and to ascertain the practicability of sending a supply train for his army by Blue Mountain route, which I suppose would be, under the circumstances, the best route for communication and supplies. Am endeavoring to communicate with General Hood by different lines.

GEORGE WM. BRENT,
Colonel and Assistant Adjutant-General.

MONTGOMERY, ALA., *December 27, 1864.*

General G. T. BEAUREGARD,
            Charleston:

If you can be spared from your present duties, I think it important that you should come here as soon as practicable.

GEORGE WM. BRENT,
Colonel and Assistant Adjutant-General.

MONTGOMERY, ALA., *December 27, 1864.*

General G. T. BEAUREGARD,
            Charleston :

No intelligence yet from General Hood.

GEORGE WM. BRENT,
Colonel and Assistant Adjutant-General.

MONTGOMERY, ALA., *December 27, 1864.*

Brig. Gen. W. W. MACKALL,
            Macon :

Have no advices from General Hood since 15th instant; am fearful of bad news. Enemy struck railroad at Verona, and are moving on Corinth.

GEORGE WM. BRENT,
Colonel and Assistant Adjutant-General.

HEADQUARTERS MILITARY DIVISION OF THE WEST,
Montgomery, Ala., December 27, 1864.

General J. B. HOOD,
      Commanding Army of Tennessee, &c.:

GENERAL: In accordance with instructions from General Beauregard, I telegraphed you on yesterday as follows:

General Beauregard instructs me to say that no re-enforcements can possibly be sent you from any quarter. General Taylor has no troops to spare, and every available man in Georgia and South Carolina is required to oppose Sherman, who is not on a raid but on an important campaign. Should you be unable to gain any material advantage in Tennessee with your present force you will retire at once across Tennessee River, and come with or send to Augusta, by best and quickest route, all forces not absolutely required to hold that defensive line. We have no advices, since telegram of the morning of the 15th instant, about Captain Hazlehurst.

Since then I have been informed that the enemy's cavalry has cut the Mobile and Ohio Railroad, and a large force is now moving on Corinth. This movement may possibly cut you off from your retrograde march via Corinth, and force you to adopt another route, possibly higher up the river, basing yourself on the Blue Mountain road. Be good enough to let us know your plans, so that we may provide for you accordingly. General D. W. Adams, at Talladega, Ala., has been directed to establish a line of couriers to communicate with you.

I am, general, respectfully, your obedient servant,

GEORGE WM. BRENT,
Colonel and Assistant Adjutant-General.

MONTGOMERY, ALA., *December 27, 1864.*
(Via Corinth, Miss.)

General J. B. HOOD:

Telegraphed you on yesterday as follows:*

Since that have been informed that Corinth may be taken and your march may be another line to recross the river. Let us know by courier, via both Columbus and Talladega, of your plans, so that supplies may be furnished.

GEORGE WM. BRENT,
Colonel and Assistant Adjutant-General.

HEADQUARTERS,
Tuscumbia, Ala., December 27, 1864—3 p. m.

Lieutenant-General STEWART,
Commanding:

GENERAL: General Hood directs me to inform you that Major-General Bate has batteries in position on this side of the river, which will protect the pontoon, and you can therefore withdraw the batteries on your side.

Yours, respectfully,

A. P. MASON,
Colonel and Assistant Adjutant-General.

HEADQUARTERS STEWART'S CORPS,
Bainbridge, December 27, 1864.

Major-General WALTHALL,
Commanding Division:

GENERAL: General Stewart directs that you will move your command back and occupy the line which Major Foster will indicate to you, leaving a brigade to watch the ford of Shoal Creek and the roads in your front. When in the new position you will dispose of your force as

---

* Same as embodied in next, *ante.*

directed by Major Foster. You will relieve a picket of twenty or twenty-five men of the Missouri Brigade, now at the junction of the Florence road and a road leading from this down the valley. Place a picket also at the junction of the Florence and Shoal Creek road. Put out skirmishers in your front. Major Foster will meet you on the road to the new line.

I am, general, respectfully, your obedient servant,

W. D. GALE,
Assistant Adjutant-General.

You will send at once 200 men with their officers to report to the officer in charge of the pontoon bridge, to relieve General Loring's men at that point.

W. D. GALE,
Assistant Adjutant-General.

MONTGOMERY, ALA., *December 27, 1864.*

Brig. Gen. D. W. ADAMS,
Talladega:

Enemy has cut the line of Mobile and Ohio Railroad. Establish as early as possible a line of couriers, to open a rapid communication with General Hood via Decatur or Tuscumbia. Report whether a supply train for that command is practicable by same route.

GEORGE WM. BRENT,
Colonel and Assistant Adjutant-General.

HDQRS. DEPARTMENT OF ALA., MISS., AND EAST LA.,
Meridian, December 27, 1864.

Brig. Gen. D. W. ADAMS,
Commanding District of Central Alabama:

GENERAL: Information from Federal sources, and confirmatory intelligence on our own part, satisfies me that General Hood has met a serious reverse and is retreating from Tennessee. The interruption by the enemy of the Mobile and Ohio Railroad near Verona, and movements of the enemy from Memphis on Corinth and via the Tennessee River, will, in all probability, cut him off from the reception of supplies at Corinth. You will, therefore, open communication immediately by line of couriers with General Hood via Tuscumbia, and communicate to me, with utmost promptness, all news which you may receive as to the movements of our army. It may be that supplies will have to be forwarded to our army from Blue Mountain, and of this your communication, via Tuscumbia, will convince you as to the necessity. You will, therefore, make all necessary preparatory arrangements to organize a supply train from Blue Mountain, and impress for such temporary use as will be thus required wagons and teams to organize the train, and have everything in readiness to start the train as soon as the intelligence which reaches you may render it necessary, adopting such route as General Hood may point out, or, in default of intelligence directly from him, your own discretion indicates as proper and the most available, without waiting for further instructions from me. Use the utmost diligence, and exhaust all means within your power to establish speedy communication with General Hood, and keep me promptly advised of all information which you may acquire. Cattle upon the hoof will be forwarded to General Hood's army, and corn and breadstuffs are the only articles which your supply train need forward to sustain the army in its march over the barren country between Tennessee River and the Blue Mountain country. Communicate also to Col. G. W. Brent, assistant adjutant-general, Military Division of the West, Montgomery, all important information which reaches you. This communication is forwarded by the hands of Capt. J. McCloskey, one of my aides-de-camp, who will explain to you fully my views on the subject-matters of this letter.

I am, general, very respectfully, your obedient servant,

R. TAYLOR,
Lieutenant-General.

MONTGOMERY, ALA., *December 27, 1864.*

Lieut. Gen. R. TAYLOR,
Meridian:

Have telegraphed General Adams, but communication in this way with him I have found unreliable. General Beauregard has taken away all the staff, and I have no one to send toward Blue Mountain. Can you send a staff officer to investigate the practicability of furnishing supply train by that route?

GEORGE WM. BRENT,
Colonel and Assistant Adjutant-General.

MONTGOMERY, ALA., *December 27, 1864.*

Lieut. Gen. R. TAYLOR,
Meridian:

Can obtain, I think, ample transportation to send to Blue Mountain when it becomes necessary. Be good enough to ascertain of Major Dameron, commissary of subsistence, his amount of supplies which may be made available. General Hood is short of ammunition. What number of Enfield cartridges can you spare him?

GEORGE WM. BRENT,
Colonel and Assistant Adjutant-General.

HDQRS. DISTRICT OF MISSISSIPPI AND EAST LOUISIANA,
Jackson, Miss., December 27, 1864.

Brig. Gen. WIRT ADAMS,
Commanding Central District of Mississippi:

GENERAL: I am instructed by the major-general commanding to inform you that the enemy's cavalry, under Grierson, struck the Mobile and Ohio Railroad late evening before last. He thinks that they will move down the road, destroying it as much as possible, until forced off by troops from below, when they will most probably strike out to the west or southwest, possibly passing through Jackson or Canton. He directs, therefore, that you place all your forces in such a position as to be able to strike them, should this supposition prove correct. In order to keep advised you will send scouts some forty or fifty miles out, in a northeast direction, with courier lines to connect them with your headquarters. He wishes you to reach the enemy and punish him as much as possible should he pass within striking distance.

I am, general, respectfully, your obedient servant,

P. ELLIS, JR.,
Assistant Adjutant-General.

[Indorsement.]

HDQRS. DISTRICT OF MISSISSIPPI AND EAST LOUISIANA,
Jackson, Miss., January 12, 1865.

Respectfully forwarded, accompanying report of Major-General Gardner.*

These instructions were directed before leaving Jackson, and the information embodied is obtained from telegrams.

F. GARDNER,
Major-General.

HDQRS. DEPARTMENT OF ALA., MISS., AND EAST LA.,
Meridian, December 27, 1864.

Maj. Gen. D. H. MAURY,
Commanding District of the Gulf:

GENERAL: I have the honor to acknowledge the receipt of your communication of the 25th instant, which has been submitted to the lieutenant-general commanding, who directs me to state to you as follows: The lieutenant-general commanding did not think that the enemy contemplated in his present movements the siege of Mobile. Your dispatch of the 21st instant represented that—

Captain Moore reports that he saw an infantry force landing at Grand Bay yesterday morning. Four thousand infantry, five guns, and a squadron of cavalry were added to the force now on Franklin Creek. The whole infantry amounts to 7,000, according to least estimate. I went to General Thomas' command yesterday. His whole force, 1,450.

In view of this, and apprehending that the enemy intended to attack the railroad communication with Mobile, General Gardner's forces were ordered toward the road for the purpose of protecting it, and, if feasible, attack the enemy whenever it could be done with advantage. On the 20th you telegraphed as follows:

Forces now here can defend Mobile against any known force of enemy. Enemy on Franklin Creek cannot be attacked unless he leaves that position. Please arrest movement of troops to this place required elsewhere, &c.

About this time, also, the movement on the Mobile and Ohio Railroad from Memphis developed itself, and General Gardner's troops were arrested in their march toward the lower line of the railroad and ordered above. The lieutenant-general commanding has written you since the date of your letter, explaining his views fully relative to the probable designs of the enemy in this department looking to ulterior movements against Mobile. It is important that whenever the reports which reach you of strength and movements of enemy in your district or vicinity are contradicted or disproved you will immediately inform him of such contradiction.

I am, general, very respectfully, your obedient servant,
WILL. M. LEVY,
Lieutenant-Colonel and Assistant Adjutant and Inspector General.

[DECEMBER 28, 1864.—For Beauregard to Cooper, requesting recall of order extending limits of his command to Atlantic coast, &c., see Vol. XLIV, p. 996.]

---

* See Part I, p. 865.

HEADQUARTERS,
Tuscumbia, Ala., December 28, 1864—10.15 a. m.
Lieutenant-General STEWART:

GENERAL: General Hood directs that you will order General Forrest to hurry Patterson and Burtwell to Roddey as rapidly as possible. The enemy took possession of Decatur last night at dark. As soon as your command is over the river let them move to the vicinity of this place and go into camp. Get them over as soon as you can.

Yours, respectfully,

A. P. MASON,
Colonel and Assistant Adjutant-General.

CIRCULAR.]   HEADQUARTERS STEWART'S CORPS,
Tuscumbia, Ala., December 28, 1864.

The march will be resumed to-morrow morning at sunrise, left in front, passing through Tuscumbia and going toward Iuka. The division of General Walthall will move in front, that of General Loring following. General Loring will place two regiments in his rear as a rear guard. The trains will move in advance of the troops.

By command of Lieutenant-General Stewart:

W. D. GALE,
Assistant Adjutant-General.

CIRCULAR.]   HDQRS. INFTY. FORCES OF THE REAR GUARD,
December 28, 1864—3 a. m.

Featherston's brigade will move promptly (without further orders) at daybreak across the bridge, to be followed by Feild and then Palmer. General Reynolds will withdraw his command from Shoal Creek in time to reach the main line by daybreak, and leave a skirmish line behind for a half hour; he will follow Palmer. Ector's brigade will cover the road until the whole command has passed, then will follow, leaving a line of skirmishers behind until the rear of the brigade has passed on to the bridge. It is important that the movement be conducted with promptness and in good order.

By command of Major-General Walthall:

E. D. CLARK,
Acting Assistant Adjutant-General.

HEADQUARTERS GILTNER'S CAVALRY BRIGADE,
Near Glade Springs, Va., December 28, 1864.
Major JOHNSTON,
Assistant Adjutant-General:

SIR: Having been left temporarily in command of this brigade by the absence of Colonel Giltner, who has gone ahead to see his family in Russell (having applied to the major-general commanding to do so), I have the honor to report my location, &c., for the information of the general commanding, and ask for instructions, orders, &c., as directed by Colonel Giltner. The men are generally well collected in camp here, or en route to the rendezvous at Hanson's, in Russell County, where it was expected they would meet the brigade. All of our wagons, by direction of Colonel Giltner, have gone from Liberty Hill, via Lebanon, to Hanson's, except three, which were sent to the brigade to assist in hauling the ordnance and commissary stores. These arrived here this evening. I started one of these this morning at daylight to Wytheville for the purpose of procuring horse-shoes and nails, of which we are very much in need. Lieutenant Carrington, the brigade ordnance officer, went ahead yesterday to see to procuring them if possible. I understand from him that he has now with the brigade here some ninety rounds of ammunition to the man, making two good wagon loads. I have two commissary wagons also, intended to haul a supply of salt and meal. The horses have improved very much in the few days rest, and everything is ready to move, subject to your written orders and instructions. By making easy marches the wagons to Wytheville after horse-shoes, &c., would be able to overtake us very soon, and the barefooted horses shod at the country shops on the line of march. I understood from Colonel Giltner that I was to await the arrival of the wagons, &c., and inform you of my readiness to move and await your order. I have the honor now to do so. We have pretty well fed out the surplus grain, &c., in this neighborhood, and when compelled to move on account of forage I shall move west, in the line I presume the brigade will pursue when ordered. The members of the brigade who were left with disabled horses have, many of them, assembled under Lieutenant Garrard, of Fourth Kentucky, at Charles Smith's, in Russell. I sent an officer this morning to collect them and all other absentees together, and take them, by Lebanon, to Little Moccasin Gap, at Hanson's. I understand from the wagoners who returned to-day that none of our wagons, teams, or loads were lost—that is, none belonging to Giltner's brigade.

Hoping to hear from you by return of courier, I have the honor to be, most respectfully, your obedient servant,

A. L. PRIDEMORE,
Colonel, Commanding Giltner's Cavalry Brigade.

P. S.—Please send all mail coming to this brigade; some of it may be directed to Cosby's brigade.

MONTGOMERY, ALA., December 29, 1864.

General G. T. BEAUREGARD,
Charleston, S. C.:

General Taylor reports that enemy was reported to be five miles from Okolona on the 27th. He supposed the force small. We have 1,000 men there, and 500 more expected that day under General Gardner. Private dispatch of same date, from Columbus, states that Okolona was occupied by enemy. Courier line established from Talladega to Tennessee River.

GEORGE WM. BRENT,
Colonel and Assistant Adjutant-General.

MONTGOMERY, ALA., December 29, 1864.

General G. T. BEAUREGARD,
Charleston:

No tidings yet from General Hood. General Taylor telegraphs to-night that communication with Corinth not reopened, and fears enemy is between Corinth and Tuscumbia, and Corinth gone.

GEORGE WM. BRENT,
Colonel and Assistant Adjutant-General.

MONTGOMERY, ALA., *December 29, 1864.*

Lieut. Gen. R. TAYLOR,
    Meridian:

General Adams has opened line of couriers to the Tennessee and has sent dispatches to General Hood. If communication with Corinth has not been re-established, would it not be well for you to send by courier from Columbus orders to send pontoons and supplies from Corinth to Tuscumbia?

GEORGE WM. BRENT,
Colonel and Assistant Adjutant-General.

MONTGOMERY, ALA., *December 29, 1864.*
(Via Talladega.)

Colonel MILES,
    Corinth:

If General Hood has not recrossed the Tennessee all stores at Corinth should be moved toward Tuscumbia to supply his army—pontoons, ammunition, and provisions.

GEORGE WM. BRENT,
Colonel and Assistant Adjutant-General.

HEADQUARTERS ENGINEERS,
Mobile, Ala., December 29, 1864.

Col. S. H. LOCKETT,
    Chief Engineer Department of Ala., Miss., and East La.:

COLONEL: On your arrival I wish you to turn your attention particularly to the following, while urging all the works forward: Prepare positions for light artillery around the works at Spanish Fort, particularly at No. 3, for guns to fire in front of No. 2 and on the approaches to it. These guns will require to be traversed or placed just to the right and near the terminus of the main work and countersunk. No. 3, I think, can be defended best from No. 4, or from points between Nos. 3 and 4. A safe communication between No. 2 and some fresh water for the use of troops is also needed, as also a direct communication between Nos. 2 and 3. A communication to the rear from No. 3 also seems necessary, as well as from the heavy battery to No. 2. Push forward the abatis, both at Blakely and Spanish Fort, until it becomes impassable under fire. The track across the marsh to Battery Huger ought to be commenced at the earliest possible moment; small piles driven in the marsh by hand, with light cross pieces joining them together, will probably give sufficient strength for the plank roadway and any weight that may pass over it. The heavy gun at No. 2 ought also to be mounted, and the covering at the magazine finished. Keep the troops at work on the abatis. I have directed more piles to be cut, in order to fill up the gap just left in the obstructions near Spanish Fort, and if there is time will drive piles across the channel leading over the bar of the Apalachee and Blakely Rivers. I wish you to study No. 2, and see if you cannot still strengthen it without great expenditure of time and labor, as it may very well have a fire from the fleet as well as land batteries.

Very respectfully, your obedient servant,

M. L. SMITH,
Major-General and Chief Engineer, Mil. Div. of the West.

[Indorsement.]

The above instructions will be strictly carried out, and with as little delay as possible.

SAML. H. LOCKETT,
Colonel and Chief Engineer, Dept. of Ala., Miss., and East La.

SPECIAL ORDERS, }   ADJT. AND INSP. GENERAL'S OFFICE,
No. 308.   }   *Richmond, December 29, 1864.*

*   *   *   *   *   *   *

XVI. Maj. J. P. Horbach, quartermaster, is assigned to duty as quartermaster of General Chalmers' division, Army of Tennessee, to relieve Maj. William Barnewall, jr., quartermaster.

By command of the Secretary of War:

H. L. CLAY,
Assistant Adjutant-General.

[DECEMBER 30, 1864.—For Davis to Beauregard, directing the latter to resume command of the district west of Augusta, see Vol. XLIV, p. 1010.]

MONTGOMERY, ALA., *December 30, 1864.*
(Received January 1, 1865.)

General G. T. BEAUREGARD
Charleston, S. C.:

General Hood, under date 27th, headquarters in the field, dispatches General Taylor that some spare troops from Corinth have been ordered down the Mobile road to drive enemy away, and requests that he co-operate from below with sufficiently large force to accomplish this purpose. Colonel Miles, at Corinth, says enemy's gun-boats have all gone down river, and that railroad is but slightly damaged this side of Tupelo, which will be repaired in a few days. Enemy's cavalry, at last accounts, said to be at Ellisville. General Taylor says communication will be open with Corinth soon as possible. Following just received:

MERIDIAN, *December 30, 1864.*

Enemy moved yesterday evening in direction of Houston, leaving their wounded, 40 in number, and ours, 5 or 6. General Gholson badly wounded. No damage to railroad above Tupelo.

WM. M. LEVY,
Assistant Inspector-General.

General Gardner reports from West Point that enemy last night were moving on two roads to Grenada and Jackson, and that he had ordered cavalry to meet them from the west.

GEORGE WM. BRENT,
Colonel and Assistant Adjutant-General.

(Copy to S. Cooper, adjutant and inspector-general, Richmond, Va., and Maj. Gen. H. Cobb, Macon, Ga.)

HEADQUARTERS FORREST'S CAVALRY CORPS,
Iuka, December 30, 1864.

[General W. H. JACKSON:]

GENERAL: You will leave Brigadier-General Ross at this place (Iuka) with his brigade, leaving one regiment at Bear Creek bridge, and send one regiment to Eastport to picket the Tennessee River from the mouth of Bear Creek to the mouth of Yellow Creek. You will bring General Ross' train to Burnsville, except commissary, with a sufficient [*sic*] to procure forage from the country for the present. The regiment sent to the river must forage from the citizens until the road is opened. General Ross will report to me at Burnsville, for the present, any movements of the enemy. You will stop General Armstrong's train and General Ross', if you think best, up Bear Creek for the present. General Armstrong, with a portion of his brigade, has been ordered back to Tuscumbia, General Roddey being hard pressed by the enemy from Decatur. I desire you to take charge of Bell's brigade and Rucker's brigade, and proceed to Jackson, Tenn. You can make your arrangements accordingly. Bell's and Rucker's brigades have been ordered to Burnsville, where you meet them, and you can report to me in person at Burnsville. Harvey's scouts have been ordered on Tennessee River, in the vicinity of Eastport, and will scout and act in conjunction with the regiment that you may send over to Eastport.

Yours, respectfully,

N. B. FORREST,
Major-General.

The major-general thinks probably you had better stop General Ross, and General Armstrong's wagon train up Bear Creek, where they can procure forage.

Respectfully,

J. P. S[TRANGE],
Assistant Adjutant-General.

HEADQUARTERS MILITARY DIVISION OF THE WEST,
Montgomery, Ala., December 30, 1864.

Lieut. Gen. R. TAYLOR,
Commanding, &c., Meridian, Miss.:

GENERAL: I have the honor to acknowledge the receipt this day of your communication of the 25th instant, inclosing copy of your instructions to Major-General Maury for the defense of Mobile, and asking that Governor Watts and General Withers be requested to send to that point every available man under their control. In accordance with your wishes, I have this day written to them to impress upon them the danger which threatens Mobile, and to urge them to send forward every man they can raise for its defense.

I am, general, very respectfully, your obedient servant,
GEORGE WM. BRENT,
Colonel and Assistant Adjutant-General.

WEST POINT, *December 30, 1864.*

[General FRANK. GARDNER:]

The enemy's cavalry reported near Collierville on the 22d instant; artillery and infantry near there. Notice of above received on the 23d.

I at once telegraphed Commander Mabry's brigade, at Macon, to move up at once, via Okolona and Ellistown. Same dispatch sent to Wade's regiment. Telegraphed Brigadier-General Gholson and Lieut. Col. W. G. Henderson to move up with all their cavalry and King's battery, and send up all dismounted men on railroad to Corinth; also dispatched for all men to be sent up from Lauderdale Springs, Macon, and Okolona. On 24th instant I received notice that the enemy's cavalry had crossed Mississippi Central Railroad, and were marching rapidly through Lamar on road to Salem. I at once dispatched Henderson at Verona, Gholson at Okolona, Wade at Columbus, Colonel Lipscomb at Macon, to concentrate in front of Tupelo or Okolona to resist raid from Memphis; made known to them the approach of the enemy. The enemy moved without halting but once to the Mobile and Ohio Railroad, striking it at Booneville and between Baldwyn and Guntown, doing but little damage to the track at Booneville and partially destroying one bridge below Baldwyn. The two columns above named went west, and joined main forces near Ellistown. The whole force then moved down and struck the road at Tupelo and Verona, destroying most of the bridges and burning depots, but doing but little damage to the track elsewhere.

Very respectfully, your obedient servant,

H. P. MABRY,
Colonel, &c.

CHARLESTON, S. C., *December 31, 1864.*

President JEFFERSON DAVIS,
Richmond, Va.:

On reaching the Army of the Tennessee, am I authorized to appoint General Taylor to its command, should I find its condition such as to require a change of commander? Please answer at Montgomery.

G. T. BEAUREGARD,
General.

MONTGOMERY, ALA., *December 31, 1864.*

General G. T. BEAUREGARD,
Charleston:

General Taylor reports this evening, on authority of an officer from General Hood's army, that he crossed the river at Bainbridge Ferry, a short distance from Florence, on the 26th and 27th instant.

GEORGE WM. BRENT,
Colonel and Assistant Adjutant-General.

(Copy to General S. Cooper, Richmond, and Brig. Gen. D. W. Adams, Talladega.)

SPECIAL ORDERS, }   HEADQUARTERS,
No. —.   }   *Burnsville, Miss., December 31, 1864.*

I. Lieutenant-General Stewart will take post with his command at this point, and repair at once the dirt road from here to Corinth.

II. Major-General Stevenson will take post with his command at Rienzi, first repairing a piece of swamp between here and Rienzi, and then repairing the dirt road from Rienzi to Tupelo.

III. Major-General Cheatham, with his command, will take post at Corinth, repairing at once the dirt road from Corinth to Rienzi and also the works at Corinth.

By order of General Hood:

A. P. MASON,
Colonel and Assistant Adjutant-General.

HEADQUARTERS,
Burnsville, December 31, 1864—11.30 a. m.

Lieutenant-General STEWART,
Commanding:

GENERAL: General Hood directs that you will halt your command for the present at Iuka and send your wagons up on Bear Creek to find forage. There is said to be some on the upper part of Bear Creek. While you are halting at Iuka you must work the road from Iuka to this place. Keep your pickets out toward the Tennessee. You will not probably be at Iuka more than two or three days, but General Hood desires you will gather all the forage you can, as the road is cut below us.

Yours, respectfully,

A. P. MASON,
Colonel and Assistant Adjutant-General.

HDQRS. DEPARTMENT OF ALA., MISS., AND EAST LA.,
Meridian, Miss., December 31, 1864.

AGENT OF THE SOUTHERN RAILROAD,
Meridian, Miss.:

SIR: The last dispatch from General Gardner reports the enemy, at 3 p. m. yesterday, going south on road from Sparta to "Wilboro." This is supposed to mean "Hillsborough," eight miles north of Forest, on your road, and though General Taylor thinks it doubtful that the enemy will make for that point, he directs that you be informed of the report so that you can make your preparations accordingly.

Very respectfully, your obedient servant,

A. J. WATT,
Assistant Adjutant-General.

WYTHEVILLE, *December 31, 1864.*

[General BRECKINRIDGE:]

GENERAL: Colonel Tucker writes me that the brigade is still unable to move from the region of its present encampment on account of the condition of the horses and their want of shoeing. He tells me that forage can easily be procured and that the horses are rapidly improving. Many men are badly in need of clothing, and all are clamorous for their pay. Guns, saddles, and cartridge-boxes are also needed. I trust that these wants may in a great measure be supplied, but aware of the difficulties under which you have labored and still experience I am prepared to wait with patience until your quartermaster and ordnance officer can furnish the articles required. I, however, hope that pay funds will soon be provided, as nothing will more tend to satisfy the men than the receipt of their pay. If you will conclude to station my brigade in the front and vicinity of Abingdon, as seemed your intention when I conversed with you upon the subject, I will beg that you give me early notice so that I may endeavor to provide comfortable quarters for the men and make arrangements to secure forage.

I am, general, your obedient servant,

B. W. DUKE,
Brigadier-General.

MONTGOMERY, ALA., *January 1, 1865.*

General G. T. BEAUREGARD,
Charleston, S. C.:

Dispatch of 26th ultimo asks if General Hardee has reported, &c. I suppose you mean Hood. He reported by telegraph December 3, and forwarded to you on the 8th, the day of its receipt; also by letter received the 29th ultimo and forwarded you the 30th by mail; copies forwarded to War Office.

The following just received from Lieutenant-General Taylor:

Federal raiders all going westward. Mobile and Ohio Railroad clear. Couriers are stationed across the gap from Egypt to Tupelo, and telegraph communication thus established with Corinth and Hood's army.

GEORGE WM. BRENT,
Colonel and Assistant Adjutant-General.

MONTGOMERY, *January 1, 1865.*
(Received 3d.)

General J. B. HOOD:

General Beauregard desires a report of your operations since your report of 11th of December. Advise by telegraph as far as practicable. Write fully the condition of the army and what is necessary to give it effective means for operations. We have no dispatches since yours of the 15th of December.

GEORGE WM. BRENT,
Colonel and Assistant Adjutant-General.

HEADQUARTERS FORREST'S CAVALRY CORPS,
Corinth, January 1, 1865.

Brig. Gen. J. R. CHALMERS,
Commanding, &c.:

GENERAL: The major-general commanding directs that on your arrival at Rienzi you will consolidate, temporarily, Holman's, Biffle's, Wheeler's, Ninth Tennessee Battalion, First Confederate, and that portion of the Seventh Alabama Regiment that have horses, into four regiments, which will compose one brigade, placing the senior officer in command of the consolidated companies and regiments. The dismounted men of the Seventh Alabama Regiment you will furlough for twenty days, and send them in charge of an officer to their homes, to collect absentees, procure clothing for those left behind, and mount themselves, and report at Rienzi or wherever your headquarters may be. You will furlough the Fifth Mississippi Regiment for fifteen days, to assemble at the expiration of that time as directed. You will furlough the Tennessee brigade until the 20th instant, to assemble at the point designated above, and instruct them that all men, on their return, that will bring with them a deserter or a recruit well mounted will be entitled to a furlough of twenty days in the next twelve months. Colonel Kelley will proceed in charge of the Tennessee brigade, at or near Brownsville, Tenn., and will at all times have 200 men in camp. Colonel Kelley will report with his brigade at Rienzi, or wherever it may be, by the 20th instant. Your battery will be left at this place, and you will endeavor to procure corn and send to this place for the horses. As soon as one regiment is organized with from 400 to 500 men, you will order the commanding officer to report to these headquarters at this place. You will endeavor to collect all the Middle Tennessee companies and parts of companies, and organize them into one of the regiments, temporarily, which you are instructed to organize. You will send forward details from the Fifth Mississippi Regiment, with orders to collect all men absent from McCulloch's and other commands, and report with them at Rienzi. You will make requisitions for all clothing, cooking utensils, and other quartermaster supplies you may need, and endeavor to have that portion of your command in camp ready to move at a moment's notice. Holman's regiment is yet behind, but as soon as he comes up will be ordered to report to you.

Respectfully,

J. P. STRANGE,
Assistant Adjutant-General.

MOBILE, *January 1, 1865.*

General S. COOPER:

Col. T. H. Taylor, commanding Mobile, reports $35,000 four per cent. bonds, counterfeit, were received through the post-office here. The postmark of the letter containing the bonds was counterfeit; also post-office way bill. Many other counterfeit bonds reported to be in circulation in Montgomery and other points. Please send out proper detectives and orders.

D. H. MAURY,
Major-General.

[First indorsement.]

Secretary of Treasury will confer with Secretary of War and adopt proper measures.

J. D.

[Second indorsement.]

JANUARY 4, 1865.

Respectfully returned to His Excellency the President. The detective of this department, Mr. McGibbon, who is in Montgomery, has been ordered by telegraph to proceed immediately to Mobile and take all necessary steps to detect the offenders and bring them to trial.

G. A. TRENHOLM,
Secretary of Treasury.

MONTGOMERY, ALA., *January 1, 1865.*

Maj. Gen. H. COBB,
  Macon:

General Beauregard directs that the railroad from Atlanta to Chattanooga be thoroughly destroyed.

GEO. WM. BRENT,
Colonel and Assistant Adjutant-General.

MONTGOMERY, ALA., *January 1, 1865.*

Lieut. Gen. R. TAYLOR,
  Meridian:

General Beauregard leaves Charleston to-day for this place.

GEO. WM. BRENT,
Colonel and Assistant Adjutant-General.

RICHMOND, VA., *January 2, 1865.*

General G. T. BEAUREGARD,
  Montgomery, Ala.:

Yours of 31st of December received. If you find it necessary to make the change suggested, you are authorized to employ General Taylor as proposed.

JEFF'N DAVIS.

CHARLESTON, *January 2, 1865.*
(Received 12 o'clock.)

General COOPER:

The Federal raiders are reported to have retired from the Mobile and Ohio Railroad, going westward; they left forty wounded. General Gholson badly wounded. The damage to the road will be repaired in about ten days. No report from General Hood since December 3. I leave to-day for the West.

G. T. BEAUREGARD,
General.

[JANUARY 2, 1865.—For Hardee to Cooper, in relation to line of division between the commands of Generals Beauregard and Hardee, see Vol. XLVII.]

CONFIDENTIAL.] CORINTH, *January 2, 1865.*

Lieutenant-General STEWART:

As soon as you can cook three days' bread rations continue the march of your troops to Tupelo, but send all your wheels that can be spared from your troops, including those of your artillery, direct to Columbus, Miss. Let a staff officer move with them, and report to Major-General Elzey upon arriving at Columbus. When you get to Tupelo you will probably move to West Point.

J. B. HOOD,
General.

CORINTH, *January 2, 1865.*

Lieutenant-General STEWART:

Send all your artillery to Columbus, and take most direct route for your troops to Tupelo. Let your barefooted men move with your troops to Tupelo; if necessary, organize them together under good officers. You need not make hard marches.

J. B. HOOD,
General.

CORINTH, *January 2, 1865.*

Lieutenant-General STEWART:

Wednesday will be time enough for you to start; ambulances and wagons for your cooking utensils will be sufficient to have with the troops.

J. B. HOOD,
General.

CIRCULAR.]   HEADQUARTERS STEWART'S CORPS,
Burnsville, Miss., January 2, 1865.

I am directed by Lieutenant-General Stewart to instruct you to collect all the barefooted men of your command, to place them under charge of suitable officers, with three days' cooked rations, and to send them to Tupelo. They will start in the morning at daylight; will go as far as Jacinto to-morrow.

Respectfully, your obedient servant,

W. D. GALE,
Assistant Adjutant-General.

CIRCULAR.]   HEADQUARTERS STEWART'S CORPS,
Burnsville, Miss., January 2, 1865.

All of the wagons of the corps, except cook wagons, ambulances, and enough of those of the supply train to transport what remains of the subsistence stores—four days' rations—now on hand, after issuing three days' rations, will proceed to Columbus, Miss., following the artillery on the road to Fulton. A quartermaster from each division will be placed in charge of the train of each division, and will report to Lieutenant-Colonel Williams, commanding artillery. Three days' cooked rations of bread, from 4th to 6th inclusive, will be prepared during the day to-morrow and issued to the troops. Three days' cooked rations will be prepared as soon as possible and issued to the barefooted men, who will then be sent, under suitable officers, to Tupelo, starting in time to reach Jacinto to-morrow night. Lieutenant-Colonel Williams will take charge of the train and report to Major-General Elzey, at Columbus, Miss.

By command of Lieutenant-General Stewart:

W. D. GALE,
Assistant Adjutant-General.

[Indorsement.]

11.30 P. M.

Brigade headquarters wagons are excluded from the operation of this order. They can remain with the troops.

By order of Major-General Walthall:

E. D. CLARK,
Acting Assistant Adjutant-General.

HEADQUARTERS,
Corinth, Miss., January 2, 1865.

Maj. Gen. C. L. STEVENSON,
Commanding Lee's Corps:

General Hood directs that you will continue your march to Tupelo, sending all your wheels that can possibly be spared from the troops at once to Columbus, Miss. The troops can obtain rations from the railroad, but the men that go with the wheels must take bread at least to last them to Columbus. When you reach Tupelo you will receive there orders to move to West Point or Columbus. Send the carriages of your artillery, and those of General Cheatham's also, to Columbus, and not to Tupelo, as directed in my note on the cars, written this morning. The officer in charge of your wheels will report to Major-General Elzey on arriving at Columbus.

A. P. MASON,
Colonel and Assistant Adjutant-General.

(Copy to General Stewart, dated January 3.)

CIRCULAR.]   HEADQUARTERS LEE'S CORPS,
In the Field, January 2, 1865.

The corps will be in readiness to continue its march in the direction of Booneville at 9 a. m. to-morrow, in the following order: Deas, Clayton, Pettus. One-half of the brigade ordnance wagons, such ambulances as have serviceable animals, the cook wagon, such of the supply train as will be designated by the chief of subsistence of the corps, the headquarters wagons, with such baggage only as may be indispensably necessary on the march, one tool wagon, with select tools, one forge to a division, and the medical wagon, lightly loaded, of divisions, will accompany the troops, moving habitually in front of and assisted forward by their respective divisions; all other wheels, including the artillery of this corps, and such of Cheatham's as may be at this point (the guns being left in charge of an officer of each corps), and a suitable guard at the depot (to be shipped by rail), will be collected by the chief of the departments of divisions and battalions to which they respectively belong, not later than 9.30 a. m. to-morrow, near the depot; there to be organized into a train, under the charge of an officer who will be ordered from these headquarters. One regiment from each division, commanded by an officer below the grade of lieutenant-colonel, will be selected by the division commander, to report to the commander of the train at the depot at 8.30 a. m. to-morrow, as guard to the train; an engineer officer, and one company of pioneers, to be selected by the chief engineer officer, will accompany the train. The pioneer companies of the corps will at once be increased temporarily, until further orders, to thirty-five men. No one not assigned to any of the regiments or battalions with the train will be permitted to accompany it, without special permission from the officer in charge. The troops with the trains will be furnished with not less than eight days of breadstuff and a fair proportion of the cooking utensils, the latter from the commands to which they belong.

By command of Maj. Gen. C. L. Stevenson:

J. W. RATCHFORD,
Assistant Adjutant-General.

MONTGOMERY, ALA., *January 2, 1865.*

Lieut. Gen. R. TAYLOR,
  Meridian:

General Beauregard left Charleston to-day at 11 o'clock. Have no doubt he desires to see you. When he leaves Macon will advise you so that you may meet him here.

GEORGE WM. BRENT,
Colonel and Assistant Adjutant-General.

HEADQUARTERS FORREST'S CAVALRY CORPS,
Corinth, Miss., January 2, 1865.

Lieut. Gen. R. TAYLOR,
  Commanding Department:

GENERAL: I have the honor to state that I have just had an interview with General Hood, and am informed by him that the Army of Tennessee is ordered to Augusta, and that I will be left to defend as well as can be done this section of the country. I regret to say that the means at my disposal are not adequate to the task devolving upon me. My command is greatly reduced in numbers and efficiency by losses in battle and in the worn-down and unserviceable condition of animals. The Army of Tennessee was badly defeated and is greatly demoralized, and to save it during the retreat from Nashville I was compelled almost to sacrifice my command. Aside from the killed, wounded, and captured of my command, many were sent to the rear with barefooted, lame, and unserviceable horses, who have taken advantage of all the confusion and disorder attending the hasty retreat of a beaten army, and are now scattered through the country or have gone to their homes. The enemy have about 10,000 cavalry, finely equipped and recently mounted on the best of horses, and I ask that you will send McCulloch's brigade to me at once, with any other cavalry you can possibly spare. I am also greatly in need of artillery horses. I have four batteries of four guns each, but have not a sufficiency of serviceable horses to haul two of them. I desire to state further that my horses are suffering badly for forage, and are only getting one-third of a ration of corn per day (say four pounds to the horse), and if they remain much longer upon that allowance they will be worthless; in fact, from the hard service performed and want of forage, it will require at least six weeks to put them in condition for active service in the field. I shall remain in General Hood's rear until he moves off from here, and if the railroad can not supply me with forage in a short time will be compelled to leave a small force here and follow him down to the prairies and save my stock, if possible to do so. Our mules are also worn down and many of them unfit for service, and unless recruited will prove a total loss.

I assure you, general, that any assistance you may have it in your power to give me in fitting up my transportation and artillery will be appreciated, and, if in your power to do so, would be glad to see you up here, or have the privilege of visiting you myself, as I am anxious to see you personally in regard to changes, &c., in the cavalry of my command. Many regiments are greatly reduced, and it is absolutely necessary to reorganize it. As soon as the Army of Tennessee gets away, I will forward you full reports, giving the effective strength, &c., of my command. So much am I impressed with the necessity of reorganizing the cavalry, and never having visited Richmond, I would like much to visit the capital and urge upon the Department the adoption of such measures as will increase its efficiency and bring it under proper control and discipline. I am confident the trip would prove beneficial to the service and a recreation to myself, and the latter is much needed, as I have had no rest or relief from duty since I came into this department, and, whenever circumstances will allow it, I respectfully ask that Major-General Gardner or some other competent officer be placed in command of my troops and permission given me to make the visit proposed. There is a column of the enemy at Courtland and a large force of cavalry on the north bank of the river, with six gun-boats and seven transports in the Tennessee River between Eastport and Florence. My scouts also report thirty transports below Savannah, and I fear they will cross the river and follow up General Hood's army, or with their heavy force of cavalry cross at Decatur or Bainbridge and move on Selma. Should they move on us here, I shall (after the departure of General Hood's army) be compelled to fall back before them, as my force is not sufficient to meet and defeat them.

I am, general, very respectfully, your obedient servant,

N. B. FORREST,
Major-General.

CORINTH, MISS., *January 3, 1865.*

His Excellency PRESIDENT DAVIS,
Richmond, Va.:

I respectfully ask for authority to furlough the Trans-Mississippi troops of this army. Their effective strength at present does not much exceed 2,000, which could, I think, by this means be much increased; I think it of vital importance. Please answer. Lieut. Col. J. P. Johnson will explain to you the campaign in Tennessee, in addition to my dispatch to the Secretary of War from Spring Hill, Tenn., and from the Bainbridge crossing of the Tennessee.

J. B. HOOD,
General.

CORINTH, MISS., *January 3, 1865.*

Hon. J. A. SEDDON,
Secretary of War, Richmond, Va.:

The army has recrossed the Tennessee River, without material loss since the battle in front of Nashville.* It will be assembled in a few days in the vicinity of Tupelo, to be supplied with shoes and clothing, and to obtain forage for the animals.

J. B. HOOD,
General.

(Same to General Beauregard.)

CORINTH, MISS., *January 3, 1865.*

General G. T. BEAUREGARD,
Montgomery, Ala.:

Your telegrams of 26th, 27th, and 29th [December], from Charleston and Montgomery, respectively, received. Steps are being taken to execute your orders therein contained, but a certain time is absolutely

---

* See dispatch as repeated by Beauregard, p. 768.

necessary, that the army may have some rest and obtain a supply of shoes and clothing. I am assembling the army at Tupelo for these purposes. It is important that you should visit this army before the projected move, if you can leave your present position.

J. B. HOOD,
General.

CORINTH, MISS., January 3, 1865.

General G. T. BEAUREGARD,
Montgomery, Ala. :

Your dispatch of January 1 received. My dispatch from Spring Hill, Tenn., informed you of the result of the battle of Nashville, after which I thought it best to withdraw the army from Tennessee, which was done, crossing the river at Bainbridge. To make the army effective for operations, some rest is absolutely necessary, and a good supply of clothing and shoes. I think it of vital importance that the Trans-Mississippi troops should be furloughed by organizations for 100 days, and will so telegraph the President. It would be well if you could visit this army.

J. B. HOOD,
General.

UNOFFICIAL.]   HDQRS. CHALMERS' DIV., FORREST'S CAV.,
Rienzi, Miss., January 3, 1865.

Maj. Gen. N. B. FORREST,
Commanding Cavalry Corps, Corinth, Miss.:

GENERAL: To "learn wisdom from your enemy" is one of the wisest maxims of history. At Nashville our enemy had a large force of cavalry, but instead of wasting its strength in the front, he kept it quietly in the rear of his infantry, resting and recruiting, until the time for action came, and then he moved it out fresh and vigorous with telling effect. We have now a good force of cavalry, and there is a rich country in our rear where we can rest and recruit it; here we cannot procure forage except by taking the bread from the mouths of a people who have already suffered greatly in this war, and even this can supply us but a day or two longer. You will remember that General Bragg's cavalry were starved at Corinth when he had three railroads at his command, and that this railroad frequently failed last summer to supply Buford's and my divisions with full rations when they had all their rolling-stock complete; but now since the late heavy destruction of corn by the enemy, and with the large increase of horses and mules of this army, it will not be able when finished to supply more than quarter rations, and until it is finished our stock must suffer greatly. We can not expect to hold Corinth if the enemy crosses at Eastport, for when he reaches Iuka he will be south of Corinth, with many roads leading to our rear; he will be nearer Aberdeen and Columbus than we are, and will have a good road without any troublesome streams in his way, while we will have three or four streams behind us that are almost impassable in winter; and if the enemy crosses at Eastport we may expect his cavalry certainly to move down on the east side of the Tombigbee and make an attack either upon our rear or the Alabama railroad, and from here we cannot intercept him. Under these circumstances, if we keep the main body of our cavalry here, we whip ourselves faster than the enemy could possibly do it, for every day that we remain here without forage we will be losing strength faster than if engaged in battle. As the horses become emaciated the men become disheartened, and I appeal to you to save your cavalry, if possible, from a position in which they must, in my judgment, certainly meet with ruin and disgrace. If we had time to reorganize, recruit, and fit up the command in a place where forage could be procured, we can whip the enemy's cavalry, and every man in your command is anxious that you should have a fair trial of strength with Major-General Wilson. You will pardon me for the plainness of this letter, but there are times when every man should think, and should not hesitate to express his thoughts.

I remain, general, very truly, yours,

J. R. CHALMERS,
Brigadier-General.

MERIDIAN, *January 3, 1865.*

General J. B. HOOD,
Corinth, Miss.:

I will leave for Okolona on Thursday morning, 5th, if you can meet me there; if you cannot, I will endeavor to meet you at Tupelo, as requested. A raid from Decatur reported forty miles from Columbus, Miss. Let me know if you know anything of it, and advise me whether you can come to Okolona.

R. TAYLOR,
Lieutenant-General.

MERIDIAN, *January 3, 1865.*

Governor CHARLES CLARK,
Macon, Miss.:

General Hood's army crossed Tennessee River at Bainbridge on 26th and 27th ultimo. General Hood telegraphs me from Corinth to-day. Don't believe a word of presence of enemy at Smithville. In any event, Columbus will be defended.

R. TAYLOR,
Lieutenant-General.

MERIDIAN, *January 3, 1865.*

Colonel MILES,
Commanding Post, Corinth, Miss.:

Raid of enemy reported coming south from Decatur. Send me immediately any information you have on subject.

By order of Lieutenant-General Taylor:

W. F. BULLOCK, JR.,
Assistant Adjutant-General.

HEADQUARTERS DISTRICT OF NORTHEAST MISSISSIPPI,
Corinth, January 3, 1865.

Capt. P. ELLIS, Jr.,
Assistant Adjutant-General:

Yours of the 28th ultimo by courier just received. The dispatch for General Hood has just been repeated to him at Burnsville, the original kept to be delivered to him to-night or to-morrow. The enemy struck the railroad at Booneville on the morning of the 25th [December], and tore it up at intervals from there to Tupelo. From the latter place to Okolona the road was badly damaged; but large working parties are engaged repairing it, and the cars will be running by Thursday or Friday. On the 26th I sent an engine down the road to ascertain the extent of damage. On the 27th I sent down a construction train and another train with 500 men, under Colonel Cole, as a guard. The road was repaired as far as Tupelo, and both trains reached there that night. At that point Colonel Cole telegraphed me he could gain no reliable information and asked further instructions. In reply, i sent him telegrams Nos. 1 and 2. From Tupelo Colonel Cole moved forward to Okolona, from which point he telegraphed me on the 29th that a fight had occurred at Egypt, resulting in the loss of 500 prisoners by us, and that they were being sent back to Memphis under a guard 800 strong. Colonel Cole also announced his intention to intercept the guard and liberate the prisoners. Since then I have not heard from him, and suppose he is in pursuit. I sent scouts as far as Grand Junction, who bring me word that no infantry or artillery is advancing; on the contrary, the force that had come as far as Moscow had returned to Memphis. General Hood's army is all this side of the Tennessee River, and I understand one corps is to be stationed here. Should this prove true, I shall move my headquarters to some point nearer the center of the district. I have just seen Major-General Forrest, a small portion of whose command is here and will move on to Rienzi to-night. He promises to push on after the enemy to-morrow, if his whereabouts can be ascertained, though his horses and men are too much jaded for efficient service.

I am, captain, very respectfully, your obedient servant,

W. R. MILES,
Colonel, Commanding.

[Inclosure No. 1.]

CORINTH, *December 27, 1864.*

Colonel COLE, *Tupelo:*

Stay where you are, unless forced back, until you can get reliable information from your own scouts. Send them out at once, with orders to bring you positive information, and let me know early in the morning. Is Colonel Mabry with you yet?

W. R. MILES.

[Inclosure No. 2.]

CORINTH, *December 27, 1864.*

Your mission is to protect the road, if practicable, but you must not let the enemy get between you and this place. Keeping this in view, use your best discretion in your movements, and I will send you rations in the morning.

W. R. MILES.

MERIDIAN, *January 3, 1865.*

Brig. Gen. DAN. W. ADAMS, *Talladega:*

Enemy's raid reported coming from Decatur and at Smithville on yesterday. Do you know anything of it? Answer immediately.

By order of Lieutenant-General Taylor:

W. F. BULLOCK, JR.,
Assistant Adjutant-General.

HDQRS. DEPARTMENT OF ALA., MISS., AND EAST LA.,
Meridian, January 3, 1865.

JOHN ARMSTRONG, Esq.,
Editor, &c., Meridian:

DEAR SIR: The lieutenant-general commanding desires me to say that he thinks your information relative to the enemy having been to Grenada, &c. (as published in your paper of this morning), is erroneous. Brigadier-General Adams reports a fight with the enemy on yesterday, between Big Black and Yazoo Rivers, and says he has seen citizens who positively state the enemy has not been to Grenada. Nothing has been received here to justify the belief that the trains referred to in your paragraph have been captured; indeed, all the information we have induces the belief that the trains have not been captured, nor the enemy visited Grenada. From the fact that your paper is published so near headquarters of department, it has occurred to the general that more importance will be attached to your assertions than if they appeared in sheets published elsewhere. He therefore requests that you will hereafter, on receipt of such information as that referred to, give him the opportunity of either verifying or contradicting the same, as the publication of such rumors must cause much unnecessary alarm and uneasiness to those persons having friends or other interests at or near designated points. I am further instructed to assure you the lieutenant-general commanding will at any time take pleasure in furnishing you for publication all information received at headquarters which can be properly be made public.

I am, very respectfully, your obedient servant,
W. F. BULLOCK, JR.,
Assistant Adjutant-General.

SPECIAL ORDERS, }   HDQRS. FORREST'S CAVALRY CORPS,
No. 2.   }   *Corinth, January 4, 1865.*

*   *   *   *   *   *   *

IV. Brig. Gen. James R. Chalmers, commanding, will relieve Capt. H. A. Gartrell's company, now commanded by Lieut. C. W. Hooper, and order him, with his company, to report to these headquarters.

*   *   *   *   *   *   *

VI. Brig. Gen. James R. Chalmers, commanding, will relieve all detachments which properly belong to regiments now in Georgia, to report to Colonel Harvie, inspector-general of the Army of Tennessee, at once; those of the Ninth and Tenth Tennessee Regiments, and should a majority of the Ninth Battalion Tennessee Cavalry, Major Akin, be in your command, it will be retained or not, as Major Akin may think best, and all unattached and unorganized companies from Middle Tennessee are excepted, which will remain with your command; all others will be relieved, and ordered to report as directed.

By order of Major-General Forrest:
J. P. STRANGE,
Assistant Adjutant-General.

HEADQUARTERS FORREST'S CAVALRY CORPS,
Corinth, January 4, 1865—9 p. m.

Brigadier-General CHALMERS:

GENERAL: The major-general commanding directs that you will collect all the effective cavalry you can find, and also send for the Ken-

tucky cavalry under Colonel Shacklett, which went in the neighborhood of Booneville, and have them in readiness to move to-morrow evening, with five days' cooked rations and sixty rounds of ammunition to the man.   If any should be without arms they can be supplied by Captain Hill, ordnance officer, who will take 100 stand of arms down in the morning.   You will also send for Captain Cobb's company of scouts; they were ordered down to Blackland to be shod up.   You will also send men down as far as Tupelo to collect all cavalry they may find, and order them across to Ripley and Holly Springs.   You will also order some men immediately to proceed to Coldwater, and order them to destroy all the boats on Coldwater between Panola and Hernando, with instructions to report to the major-general either at Cockrum's Cross-Roads or in the vicinity of Holly Springs.   You will order Cobb's scouts to proceed immediately to Coldwater, to assist in destroying the boats; and if the enemy should attempt to cross he will cross on the north side, and endeavor to prevent it.   The major-general commanding directs me to say that Grierson has burned Grenada and is quietly wandering about destroying the country, and his object is to get between him and Memphis, and it will require all the troops he can raise to capture him; and you will use every effort to collect all the force you can, and instruct the men you may send down the railroad, and also those they may find that cannot return to Rienzi to-morrow evening, that they meet the major-general at Ripley with those they may collect on the evening of the 6th, or at Holly Springs on the evening of the 7th instant.   The major-general will be at Rienzi to-morrow morning and move with you.
 Respectfully,

        J. P. STRANGE,
       Assistant Adjutant-General.

 P. S.—The major-general directs me to say that he will not take any wheels with him.

        IUKA, *January 4, 1865—8 p. m.*
Brigadier-General JACKSON,
   Corinth:
 Dispatch directing move to Rienzi received.   If command is to go on any expedition please have the serviceable cavalry with Colonel Montgomery to join me; also 111 men sent off yesterday, under Lieutenant-Colonel Whitfield, with wagon train, to Verona, most of whose horses, though in bad condition, can still be used.   I will be at Rienzi to-morrow evening.
 Respectfully, &c.,

        L. S. ROSS,
       Brigadier-General.

General JACKSON:
 The major-general directs that you will order General Ross to send after his men himself.
 Respectfully,

        J. P. STRANGE,
       Assistant Adjutant-General.

MERIDIAN, *January 4, 1865.*

Brig. Gen. D. W. ADAMS,
  Talladega, Ala.:

Enemy's cavalry raid reported coming through Pikeville, Ala.

By order of Lieutenant-General Taylor:

  W. F. BULLOCK, JR.,
    Assistant Adjutant-General.

Abstract from field return of Duke's brigade, January 4, 1865.a

Battalion.	Aggregate effective.	Aggregate present.
1st Kentucky Battalion, Lieut. Col. Robert A. Alston	90	97
2d Kentucky Battalion,———	29	32
3d Kentucky Battalion, Col. Joseph T. Tucker	93	100
4th Kentucky Battalion, Maj. Thomas B. Webber	91	101
Total	303	330

a At Lutheran Church near Seven-Mile Ford.

HEADQUARTERS ARMSTRONG'S BRIGADE,
  Fulton, January 5, 1865.

Maj. J. P. STRANGE,
  Assistant Adjutant-General:

MAJOR: In obedience to orders from General Jackson, I have the honor to report my position at this place. The raid reported moving in direction of Columbus has gone toward Moulton, Ala.; Roddey and Holman in front of them. There is no forage in this vicinity; I can't feed my horses here. The nearest corn is at Smithville, seventeen miles south, on Aberdeen road. I hope I will be permitted to leave here very soon.

  Respectfully,

    F. C. ARMSTRONG,
      Brigadier-General.

HEADQUARTERS ARMSTRONG'S BRIGADE,
  Fulton, Miss., January 5, 1865.

Major STRANGE,
  Assistant Adjutant-General:

MAJOR: I hope the general will keep his promise and furlough my men as soon as possible. They are nearly all now within a few days' ride of home. I hope he will grant about thirty days, in order to give them time to recruit their horses, many of which are broken down and need rest, but are good.

  Respectfully,

    F. C. ARMSTRONG,
      Brigadier General.

Giltner's Cavalry Brigade.*

Col. A. L. PRIDEMORE.

4th Kentucky Cavalry, Capt. John G. Scott.
10th Kentucky Mounted Rifles, Col. Benjamin E. Caudill.
10th Kentucky Cavalry, Lieut. Col. George R. Diamond.
64th Virginia Cavalry, Maj. James B. Richmond.
Jenkins' (Kentucky) Cavalry Company, Capt. Barton W. Jenkins.

TUPELO, MISS., *January 6, 1865.*

Hon. J. A. SEDDON,
      Secretary of War, Richmond, Va.:

Thomas appears to be moving up the Tennessee River. Up to 9 a. m. on the 5th scouts report six gun-boats and sixty transports had passed Savannah, going toward Eastport, loaded with troops and supplies.

J. B. HOOD,
General.

(Copy to General Beauregard.)

RIENZI, *January 6, 1865.*

Major-General FORREST,
      Corinth:

Wheeler and the detachments belonging in Georgia were ordered off yesterday. I have sent Nixon at once to Jacinto. Biffle went out last night seven miles for forage; he will be in to-night, and move at once. Cobb's scouts went to Coldwater under your first order, and cannot be overtaken before they reach there.

JAS. R. CHALMERS,
Brigadier-General.

HEADQUARTERS TRANS-MISSISSIPPI DEPARTMENT,
Shreveport, January 6, 1865.

General S. COOPER,
      Adjutant and Inspector General, C. S. Army, Richmond, Va.:

GENERAL: I have the honor to acknowledge a dispatch from the honorable Secretary of War, received at these headquarters on the 29th ultimo,† directing, if practicable, the crossing of troops in aid of General Hood, or a diversion in his favor by a movement into Missouri.

The heavy rains which have fallen, unusual even at this season, with the exhausted condition of the country and our limited transportation, make it impossible, before early summer, either to attempt crossing troops or to renew operations against the enemy.

I have delayed my reply to this dispatch until the views of Lieutenant-General Buckner could be obtained, the matter being then under consideration, a letter previously received from General Beauregard on the same subject having been submitted to him.

I inclose copies of Lieutenant-General Buckner's letter; also of General Beauregard's communication, with my reply thereto.

I am, general, very respectfully, your obedient servant,

E. KIRBY SMITH,
General.

---

* Glade Springs Depot, Va., January 5, 1865, as shown by inspection reports.
† See December 7, 1864, Vol. XLI, Part I, p. 123.

[Inclosure No. 1.]

HEADQUARTERS TRANS-MISSISSIPPI DEPARTMENT,
Shreveport, January 3, 1865.

Lieutenant-General BUCKNER,
Commanding District of West Louisiana:

GENERAL: Inclosed are dispatches from the honorable Secretary of War dated December 7, from General Beauregard and Colonel Brent December 2* and 3, and from Maj. Gen. Frank. Gardner December 2 and 8,† all of which relate to the operations of the enemy, urge the movement of troops from this department for the relief of our forces east of the Mississippi, or suggest the means by which this object may be accomplished. As you command the district from which the troops must be chiefly drawn, and from which the crossing to the east of the Mississippi must be made, if possible, the commanding general directs that you report upon the practicability of effecting the transfer of a force to the other bank of the Mississippi and of carrying out the suggestions of General Beauregard.

I am, general, very respectfully, your obedient servant,

J. F. BELTON,
Assistant Adjutant-General.

[Inclosure No. 2.]

HEADQUARTERS DEPARTMENT OF WEST LOUISIANA,
Shreveport, January 5, 1865.

Col. J. F. BELTON,
Assistant Adjutant-General:

COLONEL: Your letter of the 3d instant relating to the crossing of troops to the east bank of the Mississippi River, and inclosing copies of correspondence on that subject, has been received. In reply I have the honor to state that, in my opinion, it is impracticable at this season of the year to cross any considerable body of men. The following are some of the reasons upon which this opinion is based. When the attempt was made last summer, under the direction of Lieutenant-General Taylor, the roads leading to the Mississippi River were practicable for all arms of the service, and the country through which the movement was made abounded in forage and provisions. A concentration of troops, with a view of forcing or surprising a passage of the river, induced a corresponding concentration of the enemy's gun-boats. After making renewed attempts to effect a crossing General Taylor abandoned the enterprise as hopeless, expressing the opinion that it was impracticable. The vigilance of the enemy and their means of visiting the crossing were so great that Major-General Wharton, commanding the cavalry, after a careful reconnaissance, made use of the illustration "that a bird, if dressed in Confederate gray, would find it difficult to fly across the river." The only feasible plan to have crossed at that time would have been to have crossed the army in small squads at various points, leaving it virtually without organization and making it equivalent in the disaffected condition of the troops at that time, to a disorganization and dispersion of two-thirds of the army.

If it were impracticable when Lieutenant-General Taylor so justly pronounced it so, the difficulties are greatly increased at this time. The country is exhausted of its provisions and forage. The swamps

---

*See p. 641.   † Neither found.

are utterly impracticable for an army. The country would not support the troops, and provisions cannot be carried with them. The Washita River being now high, any troops occupying the country east of it would be isolated between the rivers, and must be ultimately lost, for I have no artillery of sufficient caliber to prevent the occupation of the Washita by the enemy's iron-clad vessels. It would be impossible to place in the river the system of torpedoes suggested by General Beauregard, because the preliminary preparations would necessarily be known to the enemy, and a concentration of their gun-boats would prevent the placing of even one of the frames suggested. In my opinion the only means of crossing a force, at any time, would be to occupy two points on the bank with artillery of sufficiently heavy caliber to control the river, and to support the batteries thus established with a force sufficiently strong to prevent their capture by a land force. But there is not a gun in my command which would make an impression on a heavy iron-clad, and experience at Port Hudson and Vicksburg shows that even with numerous heavy batteries the Mississippi cannot be blockaded. These reasons induce me to think that it is entirely impracticable to cross an army over the Mississippi River at this time. The utmost that can be done is to pass men in small squads, with the disorganization and demoralization attendant upon such a proceeding.

I am, sir, respectfully, your obedient servant,

S. B. BUCKNER,
Lieutenant-General.

[Inclosure No. 3.]

HEADQUARTERS TRANS-MISSISSIPPI DEPARTMENT,
Shreveport, La., January 6, 1865.

General G. T. BEAUREGARD,
Commanding Military Division of the West:

GENERAL: Your letter of December 2, from Montgomery, Ala., together with a communication from Colonel Brent, assistant adjutant-general, of the 3d of the same month, were delivered by your aide, Captain Toutant, on the 20th ultimo. Feeling convinced of the utter impracticability of operating during the winter season, I delayed answering your letter until Lieutenant-General Buckner, commanding District of West Louisiana, to whom it had been submitted, could be consulted. I inclose you a copy of his reply.* The swamps on the Mississippi are at this season impassable for conveyances, the bayous and streams all high and navigable for the enemy's gun-boats. The country has been so devastated by the contending armies and is so exhausted that the troops would require transportation for supplies for near 300 miles from the interior to the Mississippi.

Appreciating our necessities in your department and ardently desiring the transfer of this army to your aid, I am powerless to assist you either by crossing troops or by operating in North Arkansas and Missouri. The country north of Red River is bare of supplies and is at this season utterly impracticable for the operations of armies and the movement of troops. More than 200 miles of destitution intervenes between our supplies and the enemy's works on the Arkansas, near 500 of desert separate our base on Red River from the productive region of Missouri.

* See p. 765.

Trusting you appreciate the difficulties under which I labor and believe in an honest desire on my part to assist you, I remain your friend and obedient servant,

E. KIRBY SMITH,
General.

[Indorsement on copy received by General Beauregard.]

HEADQUARTERS MILITARY DIVISION OF THE WEST,
Columbia, S. C., February 13, 1865.

Respectfully forwarded for the information of the War Department. Notwithstanding the opinions of General Smith and Lieutenant-General Buckner, I am still of the opinion that troops can be crossed to this side of the Mississippi River, even if it be in canoes constructed by the troops near the points selected for them to cross. No reference is made as to why a movement cannot be made against New Orleans, that troops may be drawn off from the armies of the United States now operating on this side of the Mississippi.

G. T. BEAUREGARD,
General.

HDQRS. DISTRICT OF MISSISSIPPI AND EAST LOUISIANA,
Jackson, Miss., January 6, 1865.

Lieut. Col. E. SURGET,
Assistant Adjutant-General:

COLONEL: I have the honor to inclose herewith special orders* in reference to Colonel Scott's command. I deem these orders necessary, because of the great number of stragglers in that country, whom Colonel Scott assures me, by his presence (with the assistance of the few men marching in this direction), he can immediately get back and reorganize. It is also necessary, on account of the threatening aspect of affairs at Baton Rouge, as Scott's command can arrive at Summit on its present march as soon as it could reach this place, and the prospect of getting the whole command together, to be immediately ready for service, is important. Colonel McGuirk's regiment has already been ordered to Brandon, which will more than replace the men Scott moves south. I had also ordered Mabry with all the cavalry, except Wade's (which I leave under his command to be organized), to march to Canton as soon as relieved from the present raid of the enemy toward Columbus. But it seems that General Forrest has assumed command of that cavalry, by what authority I am not informed. I inclose a copy of a telegram this morning to Colonel Mabry.

I am, colonel, very respectfully, your obedient servant,

FRANK. GARDNER,
Major-General.

[Inclosure.]

JACKSON, MISS., *January 6, 1865.*

Col. H. P. MABRY,
West Point, Miss.:

Inform Major-General Forrest that you are moving your troops under my orders. If he has instructions to take command of any of my troops he must communicate them to me.

FRANK. GARDNER,
Major-General.

---

* Not found.

HDQRS. SEVENTH CONFEDERATE BATTALION CAVALRY,
Stony Creek, January 6, 1865.

Major-General BRECKINRIDGE,
Commanding Department:

SIR: I have very reliable information of the enemy being in the lower end of this county and Lee, committing depredations of all characters. A scout from this battalion, just returned, state that they found a party of home guards encamped on Looney's Creek, in Wise County. They have robbed citizens of everything they could conveniently carry away, and are still making their appearance. I would most respectfully ask that you would send by the courier some ammunition. In the condition of the battalion now we could do nothing, and if furnished with the necessary amount of ammunition they can be driven away. Captain Jones, commanding the scout, engaged the enemy near the Stone Gap of Stone Mountain, killing eight and driving the enemy entirely away; his loss, none. Stone Gap is about twelve miles from my camp.

Very respectfully, your obedient servant,

GEO. D. FRENCH,
Captain, Commanding Battalion.

RICHMOND, VA., *January 7, 1865.*

General G. T. BEAUREGARD,
Montgomery, Ala.:

Hardee needs aid. If Hood has not complied with your suggestion, please give the matter prompt attention.

JEFF'N DAVIS.

MACON, *January 7, 1865—11 a. m.*

General S. COOPER,
Richmond:

General Hood reports from Spring Hill, December 27 [17], 1864, that on morning of 15th instant, in front of Nashville, the enemy attacked both flanks of his army. They were repulsed on the right with heavy loss, but toward evening they drove in his infantry outposts on the left flank. Early on 16th the enemy made a general attack on his entire line. All their assaults were handsomely repulsed with heavy loss, until 3.30 p. m., when a portion of our line to left of center suddenly gave way, causing our lines to give way at all points, our troops retreating rapidly. Fifty pieces of artillery and several ordnance wagons were lost by us on that day. Our loss in killed and wounded very small; in prisoners, not ascertained. Maj. Gen. Ed. Johnson, Brig. Gens. T. B. Smith and H. R. Jackson are captured.

G. T. BEAUREGARD.

MACON, *January 7, 1865.*
(Received 4 o'clock.)

General S. COOPER:

General Hood reports from Corinth, Miss., January 3, 1865, that the army recrossed Tennessee River at Bainbridge, without material loss since battle of Franklin,* and that will be assembled in few days in

---

* See dispatch as sent by Hood, p. 757.

vicinity of Tupelo, to be supplied with shoes and clothing and forage, which are necessary to render it efficient for military operations, and that it absolutely requires rest. He deems it of vital importance that the Trans-Mississippi troops should be furloughed by organization for 100 days.

G. T. BEAUREGARD,
General.

MACON, *January 7, 1865.*
(Received 4 o'clock.)

General S. COOPER:

General Hood reports from Tupelo, January 6, 1865, that Thomas appeared to be moving up Tennessee River until 9 a. m. on the 5th. Scouts report six gun-boats and sixty transports had passed Savannah, going toward Eastport, loaded with troops and supplies.

G. T. BEAUREGARD,
General.

MACON, GA., *January 7, 1865—9 a. m.*

Col. GEORGE WM. BRENT,
 Assistant Adjutant-General, Montgomery, Ala.:

I leave this evening. Order General Hood, in writing, to make report of his operations from Tuscumbia to Nashville, and back to Tupelo. I have telegraphed him to same effect.

G. T. BEAUREGARD,
General.

MERIDIAN, *January 7, 1865.*

General R. TAYLOR,
 Tupelo:

Your two dispatches of yesterday received. General Brandon informs me that he has called on General Gardner to order Colonel Denis, with First Brigade of Reserves, to report to him, to enable him to execute orders of War Department. As it received orders from General B[randon], he has the right to recall them now, unless you object, when the law requires the matter be referred to War Department. Have informed him that the brigade can possibly be spared to report to him in a few days.

E. SURGET,
Assistant Adjutant-General.

MERIDIAN, *January 7, 1865.*

Lieutenant-General TAYLOR,
 Tupelo, Miss.:

Brig. Gen. D. W. Adams telegraphs he needs more troops; says he has communication and scouts extending near Decatur, but he has no report of any raid.

W. F. BULLOCK, JR.,
Assistant Adjutant-General.

WAR DEPARTMENT, C. S. A.,
Richmond, Va., January 8, 1864.

General BEAUREGARD, Selma:

Repress by all means the proposition to furlough the Trans-Mississippi troops; the suggestion merely is dangerous; compliance would probably be fatal; extinguish, if possible, the idea.

J. A. SEDDON,
Secretary of War.

WAR DEPARTMENT,
Richmond, Va., January 8, 1865.

General J. B. HOOD, Tupelo, Miss.:

The proposition to furlough the Trans-Mississippi troops cannot be entertained; the suggestion is regarded as dangerous; compliance would probably be fatal; extinguish the thought in the troops, if practicable.

J. A. SEDDON,
Secretary of War.

JACINTO, January 8, 1865.
(Via Rienzi.)

Major-General FORREST:

Some of my horses have not had a grain of corn for two days and nights, and none more than six each. Some of my men are deserting, and great many horses giving out.

JAS. R. CHALMERS,
Brigadier-General.

SALTILLO, January 8, 1865.

Brig. Gen. W. H. JACKSON, Corinth:

Major Paul is ordered with train by General Forrest to Shannon. Shall he take the escort and provost-guard with him?

J. R. HULL.

MONTGOMERY, ALA., January 8, 1865.

Lieut. Gen. R. TAYLOR, Tupelo, Miss.:

General Beauregard will leave to-morrow for Tupelo. If circumstances will permit he desires you will await him there.

GEORGE WM. BRENT,
Colonel and Assistant Adjutant-General.

MONTGOMERY, January 9, 1865.

President JEFFERSON DAVIS:

I will leave as soon as practicable for Hood's army, and will send to Hardee's assistance all troops which can be spared. Condition of common roads and breaks in railroads will, however, delay their arrival. Should circumstances permit I will return with them.

G. T. BEAUREGARD,
General.

MONTGOMERY, ALA., *January 9, 1865.*
(Received 2 p. m.)

Hon. J. A. SEDDON,
Secretary of War, Richmond, Va. :

Your views on the application of General Hood, relative to his Trans-Mississippi troops, coincide fully with my own. Your instructions shall be followed at once.

G. T. BEAUREGARD.

Resolved, That a joint committee of five on the part of the Senate and nine on the part of the House of Delegates be appointed to proceed forthwith to take into consideration the state of the country and devise and report to the general assembly such means as they may think adapted to the present emergency, and that such committee have leave to sit during the session of the general assembly and to confer with such persons as they deem expedient in order to advance the objects of this resolution.

Adopted January 9, 1865.

WM. F. GORDON, JR.,
Clerk House of Delegates and Keeper of Records of Virginia.

In joint committee, January 9, 1865,

Resolved, That the chairman of the committee communicate to the President of the Confederate States a copy of the joint resolution under which the committee have been appointed, and to request respectfully on behalf of the joint committee an interview upon the subject thereof at his earliest convenience.

CONCURRENT RESOLUTION.

Resolved (the House of Representatives concurring), That if the President will appoint General J. E. Johnston to the command of the Army of Tennessee, it will, in the opinion of the Congress of the Confederate States, be hailed with joy by the army and will receive the approval of the country.

[Indorsements.]

A concurrent resolution relative to the assignment of General Joseph E. Johnston.

SENATE,
January 16, 1865.

Passed the Senate.

JAMES H. NASH,
Secretary.

HOUSE OF REPRESENTATIVES,
January 18, 1865.

Considered and passed.

OFFICE OF THE SECRETARY OF THE SENATE, C. S. A.,
January 21, 1865.

I do hereby certify that this resolution originated in the Senate; and that the within is a true copy of the same as finally passed by the two houses of Congress.

JAMES H. NASH,
Secretary.

MONTGOMERY, ALA., *January 9, 1865.*

General J. B. HOOD,
    Tupelo, Miss. :

Secretary of War disapproves application relative to your Trans-Mississippi troops. He considers that to grant it would be dangerous, and might be fatal. I agree with him. Discountenance it in full.

G. T. BEAUREGARD,
General.

MONTGOMERY, ALA., *January 9, 1865.*

General J. B. HOOD,
    Commanding Army of Tennessee, Tupelo, Miss. :

President orders that whatever troops you can spare be sent forthwith to General Hardee's assistance. Consult General Taylor, if with you, and prepare accordingly. I will be at Tupelo as soon as practicable.

G. T. BEAUREGARD,
General.

MERIDIAN, *January 9, 1865.*

General J. B. HOOD,
    Tupelo, Miss. :

Following received from Colonel Wade, commanding at Columbus, dated to-day:

Scouts sent out report a body of Federals, 1,200 strong, at Pikeville last night, but have returned to the valley in the direction of Russellville.

R. TAYLOR,
Lieutenant-General.

MERIDIAN, *January 9, 1865.*

His Excellency President DAVIS:

I have just returned from a visit to General Hood and his army. The army needs rest, consolidation, and reorganization. Not a day should be lost in effecting these latter. If moved in its present condition, it will prove utterly worthless; this applies to both infantry and cavalry. Full powers should be immediately given to the commander. For prudential reasons I use one of the former key-words instead of the last.

R. TAYLOR,
Lieutenant-General.

HDQRS. DEPARTMENT OF ALA., MISS., AND EAST LA.,
Meridian, January 9, 1865.

Hon. JAMES A. SEDDON,
    Secretary of War, Richmond :

SIR: I have the honor to acknowledge the receipt of your communication of the 22d ultimo, relative to the exchange of cotton for army supplies. Your order on the subject and the plan you propose of placing the entire business in the hands of one general agent, under orders from your office, accord fully with my own views, and when Mr. Wallis' arrives, I shall take pleasure in rendering every facility to enable him to carry out to best advantage the wishes and interests of the Department. With regard to my circular, referred to in your letter, I have the honor to state that it ceased to be in operation sometime since, and that no contracts under it ever existed.

I am, sir, very respectfully, your obedient servant,

R. TAYLOR,
Lieutenant-General.

[First indorsement.]

JANUARY 27, 1865.

Colonel BAYNE:

For his information.

J. A. SEDDON,
Secretary of War.

[Second indorsement.]

JANUARY 28, 1865.

Respectfully returned to the honorable Secretary of War, with thanks.

THOS. L. BAYNE,
Lieutenant-Colonel.

BURNSVILLE, *January 9, 1865.*

Captain SYKES,
Assistant Adjutant-General, Corinth:

General Smith is at Eastport—part on this side, and part on the opposite side of the river. Enemy's pickets out three miles from the river. There is no enemy or boats above Chickasaw Landing. By reference to dispatch sent last night to Major Strange from Lieutenant Tison, you will see full particulars, which dispatch I asked to be sent to General Jackson. Please ask General Ross to relieve me with another regiment by to-morrow morning.

J. S. BOGGESS,
Lieutenant-Colonel, Commanding Third Texas Cavalry.

MONTGOMERY, *January 10, 1865.*
(Received 11th.)

General J. B. HOOD:

Should Thomas' forces move toward Atlanta Jackson's division of cavalry must be sent forthwith to hold them in check until you can send other troops.

G. T. BEAUREGARD,
General.

TUPELO, MISS., *January 10, 1865.*

General G. T. BEAUREGARD,
Montgomery, Ala.:

I am preparing to obey the orders contained in your cipher telegram of the 9th. Have had a full consultation with Lieutenant-General Taylor, but will be able to make no shipment before your arrival here, which will, I hope, be very soon.

J. B. HOOD,
General.

MONTGOMERY, ALA., *January 10, 1865.*

Lieut. Gen. R. TAYLOR,
   Meridian, Miss.:

General Beauregard will leave this evening for Meridian.

GEORGE WM. BRENT,
   Colonel and Assistant Adjutant-General.

HEADQUARTERS WALTHALL'S DIVISION,
   Near Tupelo, Miss., January 10, 1865.

General FRENCH:

DEAR GENERAL: This has been the first opportunity since I reached the Tennessee River I have had to write to anyone, and take advantage of this chance to say a few words about your division and things in general. After the first day's fight at Nashville your division and staff were ordered to report to General Walthall, and this arrangement still continues. Major Sanders has been sick and unable for duty since the 24th of December; he leaves us to-morrow for home on a thirty days' sick leave. Storrs has gone to Columbus, Miss., with his artillery; he was the only one in the corps who saved his artillery. Walthall lost every piece, and his chief of artillery, Loring, most of his. The second day's fight was a perfect rout and defeat. The line broke first at the salient point—that is, the large hill in rear of Stewart's headquarters. The line toward the right was more or less parallel to the Franklin pike, the left retiring and following the range of hills, you may remember, which runs toward the Franklin pike. The salient, which was held the day before by Ector's brigade, was strongly intrenched that night and held by Bate's division; he gave way about 4 p. m., which broke the whole line; not a man was in reserve to meet the enemy as he came up. A few minutes after every man took his own counsel and made the best of his way to Franklin; an effort was made to rally the men at Brentwood, but did not succeed well. I think, from all the information I can gather, we lost four or five general officers and 6,000 or 7,000 prisoners and most of the artillery. Walthall had command of the infantry forces which composed the rear guard. Not many wagons were lost after leaving Columbia, but the enemy's cavalry captured the remains of our pontoon train on this side of the river, near Tuscumbia, and 400 or 500 wagons which had been started to Tuscaloosa without a guard. It is reported that the enemy had only 250 men. We expect to go into winter quarters somewhere near here in a few days. Lee's and Stewart's corps are here; Cheatham at Corinth until the place can be evacuated. Hood seems undecided whether to winter here or at West Point. Cockrell's brigade joined us at the Tennessee River. Ector's brigade expects to be furloughed as a brigade in a short time; at least, Hood approves it, but says he will have to get the permission of the Secretary of War. Sears' brigade is now commanded by Major Nelson. General Sears was near me when he was wounded; a solid shot passed through his horse and struck him just below the knee; the lower part of his leg was amputated. It was found impracticable to bring him out, so he was left a short distance this side of Pulaski. Captain Henderson and Lieutenant Harper were both very badly wounded and left in enemy's hands. Cockrell, I think, was brought out, but Colonel Gates left; his arm was amputated. I was slightly wounded in the foot by a shell, which prevented me from walking a few days only. Your division is still under command of Walthall, which is not very pleasant; all are looking for you back anxiously. I think your division numbers more than any other at this time. If you will return soon you will be able to save it, but if not, I much fear it will be broken up. I have nothing scarcely to do, and my present position is anything but agreeable. The whole army cannot muster 5,000 effective men. Great numbers are going home every day, many never more to return, I fear. Nine-tenths of the men and line officers are barefooted and naked. I hope, general, you will have sufficiently recoved to return and take command; it will make you more popular than ever; we all feel like outsiders in this present arrangement, and are treated more or less so accordingly. I do not know where Shingleur is; I have heard he was at Corinth.

You will please excuse this letter, as I have to sit by the fire to keep warm, while at the same time it is snowing. When I see you, which I hope will be soon, I will then be able to give you a better understanding about matters during the past month. It is reported, general, here, that you are married; if such is the case, I am pleased to congratulate you on your good fortune. I would be pleased to hear from you.

Truly, your friend,

E. T. FREEMAN.*

CHARLESTON, *January 10, 1865.*

Lieut. Gen. W. J. HARDEE:

On the 3d day of October last I was put in arrest by order of General Bragg and ordered to report to General Hood in Georgia for trial. This order is herewith inclosed, marked "A." I went to Georgia in obedience to this order, but found General Hood gone to Tennessee. I followed and overtook him near Columbia, when he informed me that he had no charges or even a complaint against me. He could not then and there give me the investigation asked, and therefore ordered me to report to General Beauregard, to whom he wrote a note asking him (Beauregard) to cause an investigation of my case as soon as possible. This letter is filed herewith, marked "B." General Beauregard by written indorsement upon said letter referred the case to you. It is thus that, without any charges against me, I have been dragged across the country for more than 2,000 miles as a public prisoner, greatly to the damage of my military reputation. I do not desire to have this case dismissed without an investigation. If I have been guilty of an offense against the laws of my country, I should be punished for it; if I have been improperly arrested, the officer making the arrest should be rebuked for his conduct. I hope, therefore, you will take such steps as will procure me justice in the premises.†

I have the honor to be, your obedient servant,

JOHN S. WILLIAMS,
Brigadier-General.

[Inclosure A.]

RICHMOND, *October 3, 1864.*

General BRECKINRIDGE:
(Forwarded from Dublin.)

Arrest Brig. Gen. J. S. Williams, commanding detachment of Wheeler's cavalry, and order him to report in person immediately to General Hood in Georgia for trial.

B. BRAGG,
General.

---

* Acting Assistant Inspector-General on staff of General French.
† See also Lee to Breckinridge and Bragg to Hood, Vol. XXXIX, Part III, pp. 786, 801.

[Indorsement.]

HDQRS. DEPARTMENT OF WESTERN VA. AND EAST TENN.,
Abingdon, October 4, 1864.

Brig. Gen. J. S. WILLIAMS,
          Commanding, &c.:

GENERAL: The major-general commanding directs me to say in pursuance of above dispatch, of which I send copy, that you consider yourself under arrest, and report in person to General Hood in Georgia, immediately. You will turn over your command at once to your next ranking officer.

I am, general, very respectfully, &c.,

W. B. MYERS,
Asssistant Adjutant-General.

[Inclosure B.]

HEADQUARTERS ARMY OF TENNESSEE,
Near Waynesborough, November 23, 1864.

General G. T. BEAUREGARD,
          Commanding, &c.:

GENERAL: Brigadier-General Williams having reported to me in arrest, in obedience to orders of General Bragg, for his conduct during the expedition which Major-General Wheeler made into Tennessee in August and September last, and it not being possible for me to have the case investigated now, as General Wheeler is not within my reach, I have ordered General Williams to report to you, and respectfully request that you will have the case investigated as soon as possible.

Very respectfully, your obedient servant,

J. B. HOOD.
General.

[First indorsement.]

GEORGIA RAILROAD,
January 4, 1865.

Respectfully referred to Lieutenant-General Hardee for investigation, and, if necessary, a report to be forwarded to the War Department.

By command of General Beauregard:

J. B. EUSTIS,
Assistant Adjutant-General.

[Second indorsement.]

CHARLESTON, *January 10, 1865.*

Respectfully referred to the Adjutant-General, who is requested to give this officer a speedy trial. I have no charges against him, and know nothing of the facts which caused him to be arrested.

W. J. HARDEE,
Lieutenant-General.

[Third indorsement.]

ADJUTANT AND INSPECTOR GENERAL'S OFFICE,
February 2, 1865.

Respectfully submitted to the Secretary of War.

Brig. Gen. John S. Williams was arrested at Abingdon, Va., on an order by telegraph of General Bragg, of the 3d of October, 1864, and directed to report in person immediately to General Hood in Georgia for trial. General Hood having moved from Georgia into Tennessee,

Brigadier-General Williams followed and reported to him in Columbia. No charges having been filed against him and an investigation being impracticable in that army, he was directed to report to General Beauregard. In General Hood's letter to General Beauregard the cause of his arrest is stated to be his conduct during the expedition which Major-General Wheeler made into Tennessee in August and September last. The case was referred by General Beauregard to General Hardee, who states that he has no charges against General Williams, knows nothing of the facts which caused him to be arrested, and refers the matter to this office, with the request that a speedy trial be ordered. General Williams desires that the matter may not be dismissed without investigation, that he may be punished if guilty of any offense, and that if improperly arrested, the officer ordering his arrest may be rebuked. It is ascertained, from inquiry at General Bragg's office, that the order for Brigadier-General Williams' arrest was made upon the written, though unofficial, report of an officer of Major-General Wheeler's staff to General Bragg that General Williams had separated himself from General Wheeler in Tennessee without orders, and had thereby seriously interfered with the success of the movement. Lieutenant-General Hardee was telegraphed to ascertain from General Wheeler whether charges had been preferred against General Williams, and their nature, and replies that General Wheeler states that charges for conduct to the prejudice of good order and military discipline had been forwarded to General Hood. The course pursued toward General Williams, if not a persecution, seems to have been harsh and unusual. The arrest of an officer of high rank, at the head of his troops, and the order to report several hundreds of miles off for trial, upon the report of a subordinate staff officer, without informing him of the accusation or allowing him to be heard, is not in accordance with military usage, and meets with my grave disapprobation; and the failure to follow up the case seems to indicate, at least, that the offense, if any, was trivial in its nature. Just before his arrest General Williams had rendered valuable service in the defeat of the enemy's movement on Southwestern Virginia, for which he has received the thanks of Congress. It does not appear to me that an investigation in this case would be for the good of the service or required for the ends of justice.

I recommend that General Williams be released from arrest and restored to his command, with an expression of the Department of its disapprobation of the course pursued to him.

S. COOPER,
Adjutant and Inspector General.

Returned to Major Barton. It is not necessary to take action on this case at this time.   S. C.

———

MERIDIAN, January 11, 1865.
(Received 2 o'clock 14th.)

Hon. J. A. SEDDON:

Cannot authority be granted to people of North Mississippi and North Alabama to exchange cotton in limited quantity for provisions? Unless something is done for relief, many in these sections must starve. Cotton is constantly going out surreptitiously, benefiting speculators only.

Respectfully,

R. TAYLOR,
Lieutenant-General.

TUPELO, MISS., *January 11, 1865.*

General G. T. BEAUREGARD,
    Montgomery, Ala.:

Your telegram in relation to Jackson's division received. When shall I expect you here? It will require four days to remove the sick and wounded and stores from this place. When these are removed will be ready to carry out the orders of the President.

                                    J. B. HOOD,
                                            General.

TUPELO, MISS., *January 11, 1865.*

General G. T. BEAUREGARD,
    Montgomery, Ala.:

I am very anxious to see you here in reference to the Trans-Mississippi troops, and also as to some system of furlough for other troops, and on other important matters.

                                    J. B. HOOD,
                                            General.

DEMOPOLIS, *January 12, 1865.*

General J. B. HOOD:

Roads are in such bad condition don't await my arrival before commencing movement of troops already ordered.

                                    G. T. BEAUREGARD,
                                            General.

HEADQUARTERS,
    Tupelo, Miss., January 12, 1865.

Lieutenant-General STEWART,
    Commanding:

GENERAL: I have just received your note of this morning about your present camp. General Hood says you can move near Verona whenever you think best, but give timely information, that supplies can be placed there for you; also get all the information you can of the roads leading toward West Point and Columbus. No furloughs will be granted till the railroad is cleared of sick, wounded, and stores, and a general system commenced for the whole army.

    Yours, respectfully,

                                    A. P. MASON,
                Lieutenant-Colonel and Assistant Adjutant-General.

RICHMOND, VA., *January 12, 1865.*

General R. TAYLOR,
    Meridian, Miss.:

Yours of 9th received. General Beauregard went to Army of Tennessee with large discretionary power. Your name was referred to, and it would be well for you to see him. Sherman's campaign has produced bad effect on our people. Success against his future operations is needful to reanimate public confidence. Hardee requires more aid than Lee can give him, and Hood's army is the only source to which we can now look. If you can hold Thomas in check with the addition to your present force of Polk's old corps, restored to your department, and the cavalry of Hood's army, which cannot be profitably sent to the East, then, as fast as it can be done consistently with the efficiency of the troops, the rest of Hood's army should, I think, be sent to look after Sherman. The presence of those veterans will no doubt greatly increase the auxiliary force now with Hardee. You may show this to General Beauregard.

JEFF'N DAVIS.

HEADQUARTERS MILITARY DIVISION OF THE WEST,
Montgomery, January 12, 1865.
Lieut. Gen. RICHARD TAYLOR,
Commanding, &c.:
GENERAL: General Beauregard instructs me to ask whether the block-houses and small field-works for the protection of the bridges and trestles on the Mobile and Ohio Railroad have been constructed?
I am, general, respectfully, your obedient servant,
GEORGE WM. BRENT,
Colonel and Assistant Adjutant-General.

[First indorsement.]

HDQRS. DEPT. OF ALABAMA, MISSISSIPPI, &C.,
ENGINEER OFFICE,
Meridian, January 21, 1865.
Respectfully referred to Maj. D. Wintter, engineer in charge, District Mississippi and East Louisiana.
WALTER J. MORRIS,
Capt. and Actg. Chief Engineer, Dept. of Ala., Miss., and East La.

[Second indorsement.]

ENGINEER OFFICE,
Meridian, Miss., January 21, 1865.
Respectfully returned, with the information that no block-houses or small field-works have been erected on the Mobile and Ohio Railroad.
D. WINTTER,
Major, Engineers.

ENGINEER OFFICE,
Mobile, January 12, 1865.
Col. A. L. RIVES,
Assistant Chief Engineer, Richmond, Va.:
COLONEL: Inclosed I have the honor to forward your letter of the 15th ultimo to Lieut. Col. V. Sheliha, chief engineer, District of the Gulf, with the accompanying indorsement of the major-general commanding. I beg leave to submit the following statements in addition: I think the arrangements already made for commanding Garrow's Bend sufficient to prevent any fleet of the enemy lying in that bay to bombard the city. Maj. Gen. M. L. Smith and myself have of late given particular attention to the works on the eastern shore and care-

fully studied them, especially No. 2, with the view of making this important part of our defenses as secure as possible. No. 2 has been greatly strengthened by putting the field guns in embrasures, protecting them by traverses, or countersinking them where the position was an exposed one. A heavy gun (7-inch Brooke) has been mounted on the right flank of this work for distant fire on D'Olives Bay and the bar of Blakely River. A very strong abatis has been made encircling this work, and the work generally put in good condition. I consider it safe against assault, and in its present condition will compel a siege, and is as well able to stand one as if twice the work was expended on it that it has already received—that is, its present condition will force the enemy to sapping and mining operations, which will not in the least be retarded by any additional labor in thickening and raising the parapet or deepening the ditch. A safe communication with a stream of water behind the hill that No. 2 occupies is being prepared. The store-houses will also be under this hill and protected by it. A safe magazine for ammunition is nearly finished in the center of the work. I have had no bomb-proofs for the garrison made, as I think past experience in this district indicates very plainly that such temptations to the garrison to leave its post on the parapet are extremely dangerous, or, at least, of doubtful propriety. The other accessory works to Spanish Fort have been also strengthened by traverses, embrasures, abatis, &c. In regard to the location of Huger and Tracy you will find by consulting the map that they are at the farther point from the hills on the eastern shore, which was the prevailing reason, I am informed, that influenced the selection of their present site. They are also at the junction of Blakely and Appachee Rivers, and are mutual supports to each other. I agree with you in thinking that these works would have been better located near Blakely, but there has been too much labor expended on the works as they now stand to admit of any change. I have scrupulously avoided making any material alterations in the works at this point, as this policy has already been pursued almost to a ruinous extent, resulting in great increase of expense and retardation of operations that long since should have been completed. The floating battery was placed between Gladden and McIntosh by order of the major-general commanding. Colonel Sheliha and myself united in desiring to have it placed to the east of McIntosh. To do this it would have been necessary to open a gap in the obstructions, which the major-general commanding did not think advisable at the time.

I have the honor to be, colonel, very respectfully, your obedient servant,

SAML. H. LOCKETT,
Colonel and Chief Engineer, Dept. of Alabama, Mississippi, &c.

MERIDIAN, MISS., *January 13, 1865.*

President DAVIS,
Richmond, Va. :

I regret to inform you that, from General Taylor's report of the disorganization and demoralization of the Army of Tennessee, and from the bad condition of the common roads and railroads hence to Augusta, no re-enforcements can be sent in time to General Hardee from that army, which does not now number 15,000 infantry.

G. T. BEAUREGARD.

MERIDIAN, MISS., *January 13, 1865—10 a. m.*
(Received 13th.)

General J. B. HOOD,
Commanding Army of Tennessee, Tupelo:

I will leave here to-morrow morning. Meanwhile suspend movement of troops ordered until my arrival at Tupelo.

G. T. BEAUREGARD,
General.

HEADQUARTERS,
Tupelo, Miss., January 13, 1865.

Hon. J. A. SEDDON,
Secretary of War, Richmond:

I respectfully request to be relieved from the command of this army.

J. B. HOOD,
General.

MOBILE, *January 13, 1865.*

President DAVIS:

Halligan, with torpedo and boat, will not attack enemy; has been transferred by Commodore Farrand. Please have him and boat placed under my orders, with authority to me to place an officer of the army or navy in command, that the enemy may be attacked at once. The boat is said to be the best of the kind. Halligan and five or six men have now been for months exempt from service on account of her. There has never been so good an opportunity for a torpedo boat to operate as is afforded by the fleet off Mobile.

DABNEY H. MAURY,
Major-General.

[Indorsement.]

JANUARY 18, 1865.

Secretary of Navy does not know that his Department has any control over the boat, but has directed Captain Farrand, if under his control, to turn it over to you.

J. D.

MOBILE, *January 13, 1865.*
(Received 4.30 o'clock 16th.)

Hon. J. A. SEDDON:

Have this day delivered to Captain Noyes, U. S. Army, the officer designated to receive the 1,000 bales of cotton to be disposed of for benefit of C. S. prisoners. The elements and inclemency of the weather have occasioned the delay. A boat of the lighest draught was selected, and even then a portion of the cotton had to be lightered over the obstructions. The receipt will be forwarded as soon as the cotton is transferred to a U. S. vessel lying some distance down the bay.

D. H. MAURY,
Major-General, Commanding.

Proclamation.

HDQRS. DEPARTMENT OF WESTERN VA. AND EAST TENN.,
Wytheville, Va., January 13, 1865.

A proclamation dated November 7, 1864, having been issued from these headquarters offering pardon to all citizens of East Tennessee who, having joined the U. S. Army, should, prior to January 1, in good faith abandon the service and return to their homes for the pursuit of their lawful avocations, notice is hereby given that the limit therein fixed is extended to the 1st of March, 1865. Deserters from the Confederate Army and persons who have been guilty of high crimes are alone excluded from the benefit of these terms. All others who embrace the terms of the proclamation shall be held free from molestation of any kind, subject only to the conditions that they shall conduct themselves as peaceable citizens and refrain from all acts in violation of civil laws or military orders.

JOHN C. BRECKINRIDGE,
Major-General.

TUPELO, *January 14, 1865.*
(Received 4 o'clock 16th.)

Hon. J. A. SEDDON:

General Beauregard will arrive here to-morrow. I will then communicate more fully in regard to my request contained in cipher telegram of yesterday morning. I have only [the] interest of my country at stake.

J. B. HOOD,
General.

HEADQUARTERS ARMY OF TENNESSEE,
Tupelo, Miss., January 14, 1865.

Colonel FLEMING,
Chief Engineer and Superintendent
Mobile and Ohio Railroad, West Point, Miss.:

We are rapidly running out of breadstuffs at Tupelo and Okolona. General Hood requests that you will push your trains forward with all possible speed. We are almost out of provisions.

E. J. HARVIE,
Colonel and Inspector-General.

CIRCULAR.]   HEADQUARTERS ARMY OF TENNESSEE,
Tupelo, Miss., January 14, 1865.

I. Corps commanders will cause a thorough inspection to be made to-morrow at 10 a. m. of their entire commands.

II. Regular drills of all troops not on guard or fatigue duty will be commenced on Monday, the 16th instant, and continued daily, whenever the weather will permit, until further orders. Companies and battalions will be properly sized for drill without reference to their real organization.

By command of General Hood:

A. P. MASON,
Lieutenant-Colonel and Assistant Adjutant-General.

Circular.]　　　　　　HEADQUARTERS ARMY OF TENNESSEE,
Tupelo, Miss., January 14, 1865.

The general commanding desires to call the attention of all commanding officers to depredations daily committed in the vicinity of the army by soldiers with arms in their hands. To endeavor in some measure to prevent this, arms will be kept constantly stacked on the color lines, and company rolls called frequently during the day, to ascertain absentees from camp.

By command of General Hood:

A. P. MASON,
Lieutenant-Colonel and Assistant Adjutant-General.

HEADQUARTERS,
Tupelo, Miss., January 14, 1865.

Lieutenant-General STEWART,
Commanding Corps:

General Hood directs that you keep a guard at Verona, to get all your men who come up on the trains; they now come here, and have to march back to camp.

A. P. MASON,
Lieutenant-Colonel and Assistant Adjutant-General.

HEADQUARTERS ARMY OF TENNESSEE,
Tupelo, Miss., January 14, 1865.

Lieutenant-General STEWART,
Commanding Corps:

General Hood directs that you will keep all commanding officers on the lookout for deserters, and should men desert have them promptly reported to these headquarters, and at the same time take every measure to find out the route they have taken and endeavor to capture them. If the first few parties who desert can be caught and promptly punished it will perhaps deter others. Depredations of all kinds are daily increasing in the vicinity of the army, and commanding officers should use every means to keep their men constantly employed in camp, and patrols, under good officers, should be sent out to arrest and bring to punishment men who are caught depredating.

Very respectfully, &c.,

A. P. MASON,
Lieutenant-Colonel and Assistant Adjutant-General.

(Same to Generals Cheatham and Stevenson.)

HEADQUARTERS,
Tupelo, Miss., January 14, 1865.

Maj. Gen. N. B. FORREST,
Commanding Cavalry:

General Hood directs that you will keep some picked bodies of cavalry near at hand that they may be ready to pursue and capture any men that may desert from the army. If the first party of deserters can be caught and promptly punished, it will perhaps deter others from doing the same.

A. P. MASON,
Lieutenant-Colonel and Assistant Adjutant-General.

MONTGOMERY, *January 14, 1865.*

Hon. JEFF. DAVIS:

DEAR SIR: Although I am aware of the great press of official business daily presenting itself, and, above all, your constant thought for the welfare of our country, yet I thought I would write a line, though done with some pain, owing to a slight injury to my right hand, and speak of the condition of things in this section. Though not as favorable as they have been, yet they may be a great deal worse; but come what may, there is yet a determination on the part of [the] majority of our people to continue firm and to use all our resources to conquer or die. I regret to say, however, that since Sherman's raid through Georgia and the possession of Savannah, together with the falling back of Hood's army, some are disposed to despair of our cause. It is true the present is not encouraging as the past, but we must expect reverses. Our resources are yet sufficient, if properly applied, to gain our independence, and without it we must not stop. Reconstruction is subjugation. Many now think that you were right in recommending the placing in the service the able-bodied negroes in the field. Better to drill them to fight for us than to fight against us, which they will be made to do if taken by the enemy. The removal of Johnston whilst at Atlanta was not well received at first, but our people, having such confidence in you, complained but little; but now that Hood has been tried, and by many believed incompetent in so important a position and somehow exerts but little moral influence on his men, the opinion and feeling among our people and with those now returning from Tennessee is that it would produce a happy influence if General Johnston could be returned to the command of the army. Whilst none question your ability to decide or your self-sacrificing spirit for the good of our country, I will candidly state that the return of Johnston at this time would have a better influence than anything that could be done. I hope it may be done.

The complaint yet exists, and not without cause, that too many hearty young men occupy places in this section that could be filled by others not able to perform the duty of a soldier. If General Bragg, or some other competent officer, could take hold of this matter, it would be of great service. I know you will bear with me in what I have suggested, as I have no object but the good of my country.

Very respectfully, yours,

EDMD. HARRISON.

[Indorsement.]

Respectfully referred, by direction of the President, to the honorable Secretary of War.

BURTON N. HARRISON,
Private Secretary.

———

WAR DEPARTMENT, C. S. A.,
Richmond, Va., January 15, 1865.

General G. T. BEAUREGARD,
Meridian:

(To be forwarded.)

By telegraph of yesterday [13th], General Hood requests to be relieved from command of Army of Tennessee. His request is granted, and you will place Lieutenant-General Taylor in command, he retaining command of his department as heretofore; and you, with such troops as may be spared, will return to Georgia and South Carolina.

J. A. SEDDON,
Secretary of War.

TUPELO, *January 15, 1865.*
(Received 11.45 o'clock 16th.)

General S. COOPER,
    Adjutant and Inspector General:

I arrived here to-day. I will examine at once the condition of the army and report result.

G. T. BEAUREGARD,
General.

RICHMOND, *January 15, 1865.*
(Received 17th.)

General J. B. HOOD:

Your request is complied with. General Beauregard is instructed to relieve you. On being relieved, you will report to the War Department in Richmond.

J. A. SEDDON,
Secretary of War.

MERIDIAN, MISS., *January 15, 1865.*

His Excellency President DAVIS:

My telegram of the 9th expressed the conviction that an attempt to move Hood's army at this time would complete its destruction. Hood failed to hold Thomas in check with Forrest, Roddey, and his own cavalry, and 30,000 troops to assist them. To represent those 30,000, I have barely 3,000 inefficient cavalry outside of the inadequate garrison of Mobile. I think it would be beneficial to the cause for me to see you.

R. TAYLOR,
Lieutenant-General.

GENERAL ORDERS, }   HDQRS. DIST. OF MISS. AND EAST LA.,
   No. 2.   }   *Jackson, Miss., January 15, 1865.*

I. In obedience to Special Orders, No. 11, of January 11, 1865, from department headquarters, Maj. Gen. Frank. Gardner relinquishes the command of this district to Maj. Gen. Will. T. Martin.

*   *   *   *   *   *   *

By order of Maj. Gen. Frank. Gardner:

P. ELLIS, JR.,
Assistant Adjutant-General.

TUPELO, *January 16, 1865.*
(Received 6.30 o'clock 17th.)

General SAM. COOPER:

To prevent disorder and desertion in Army of Tennessee, I have approved a judicious system of furlough. Copy of order will be forwarded for information of War Department.

G. T. BEAUREGARD.

MONTGOMERY, ALA., *January 16, 1865.*

General G. T. BEAUREGARD,
    Tupelo, Miss.:

General Cobb has been ordered by War Department to change head quarters to Augusta. The West Point railroad will be repaired in two days.

GEORGE WM. BRENT,
Colonel and Assistant Adjutant-General.

TUPELO, *January 16, 1865.*

His Excellency President DAVIS:

If I am allowed to remain in command of this army, I hope you will grant me authority to reorganize it and relieve all incompetent officers. If thought best to relieve me, I am ready to command a corps or division, or do anything that may be considered best for my country.

J. B. HOOD,
General.

WEST POINT, *January 16, 1865.*

Col. E. J. HARVIE:

Captain Goodman, General Chalmers' adjutant-general, informs me that General Forrest ordered General Chalmers to furlough all West Tennesseeans for thirty days, dismounted Mississippians for fifteen days, and dismounted Alabamians for twenty days. I am having all such arrested, and Colonel Forrest, who is now here, is doing likewise.

POLLOK B. LEE,
Assistant Inspector-General, Army of Tennessee.

MERIDIAN, MISS., *January 16, 1865.*

Col. E. J. HARVIE,
    Inspector-General:

SIR: Colonel Henry called on me yesterday and requested a written statement of the capacity of the railroads and their ability to move troops, as well as the condition of the roads. I gave him the report, and added a few suggestions. Probably he has forwarded the report to you. In case he has not, a few lines from me will do no harm. If the ordnance should be sent to Columbus, it can be sent from there on boats direct to Montgomery without being unloaded. This would save a great deal in the way of transportation, and would save several handlings, and would get it through faster than it could be sent by railroad. I would also advise that the boats be ordered to Columbus for it at once. I learn there is now a fine stage of water in the Bigbee River for boats, and if the boats were ordered now there would be no danger of the river getting too low before the boats could get up to Columbus. The hospitals at Columbus can be sent by boats also to Montgomery. I reported to Colonel Henry that I thought at least one-third of the men should be sent via Selma. If you think as I do, please order the transportation given accordingly, and then when the men arrive here I will know exactly what men are to go on to Mobile and what men are to go via Selma. I think we should be able to move from 2,500 to 3,000 men per day, easy. Lieutenant Harvey has not yet arrived; will tell him when he comes to telegraph to Tupelo to you, and await your reply before he goes on.

Yours, respectfully,

GEORGE WHITFIELD,
Major and Quartermaster.

HEADQUARTERS ARMY OF TENNESSEE,
Tupelo, January 16, 1865.

Maj. W. CLARE,
Assistant Inspector-General, Okolona, Miss.:

MAJOR: I have received your telegram of yesterday's date and submitted it for the consideration of the medical director. He promises to send a surgeon and vaccine matter at once to Okolona. General Hood desires these Yankee prisoners to be marched to Meridian. Railroad transportation cannot be furnished. He desires you to look into this matter and start them off at once if it be practicable to do so. Of course, small-pox cases and those pronounced unfit for marching by the medical department will have to be retained at Okolona. These are the general's wishes. Comply with them or not as you deem them practicable. I would like further to know your views as to retaining a post at Okolona. What business is there necessary to be transacted that cannot be done elsewhere? What number of men should be kept there? I would much prefer bringing every one to the army, if proper to do so. Give me your views.

Very respectfully, your obedient servant,

E. J. HARVIE,
Colonel and Inspector-General.

MERIDIAN, *January 16, 1865.*

Col. E. J. HARVIE,
Inspector-General:

Trains from Montgomery and Selma come in nightly crowded with soldiers returning to the army. Should they not be stopped at Selma? I send you a communication by train this morning.

G. A. HENRY, JR.,
Lieutenant-Colonel and Assistant Inspector-General.

SPECIAL ORDERS, }
No. 12. }

ADJT. AND INSP. GENERAL'S OFFICE,
Richmond, January 16, 1865.

* * * * * * *

XXVI. The Sixteenth Georgia Battalion Cavalry, Lieut. Col. S. J. Winn, having been increased to ten companies by the addition of three companies of non-conscripts, raised under authority of the War Department, will constitute the Thirteenth Regiment Georgia Cavalry, the organization to take effect from May 2, 1864.

*   *   *   *   *   *   *

By command of the Secretary of War:

> JNO. WITHERS,
> *Assistant Adjutant-General.*

HEADQUARTERS ARMY OF TENNESSEE,
Tupelo, Miss., January 16, 1865.

Lieutenant-General STEWART,
Commanding Corps:

GENERAL: If you have any troops in your command who live sufficiently near the present position of the army to justify, in your opinion, the granting them ten days' furlough, the same will be done and proper application made at once, provided the men go by organization, under officers, and pledge themselves to return at the expiration of the time. All obtaining such furloughs will be debarred the benefit of General Orders, No. 1, from army headquarters.

By command of General Hood:

> A. P. MASON,
> *Lieutenant-Colonel and Assistant Adjutant-General.*

(Same to Generals Cheatham and Stevenson.)

TUPELO, MISS., *January 16, 1865.*

Lieut. Gen. R. TAYLOR,
Meridian, Miss.:

Soon as your public duties will permit come here for one day to confer with me relative to matters in your department.

> G. T. BEAUREGARD.

GENERAL ORDERS, }   HDQRS. DIST. OF MISS. AND EAST LA.,
No. 3.   }   *Jackson, Miss., January 16, 1865.*

I. In obedience to orders from department headquarters, I hereby assume command of the District of Mississippi and East Louisiana.

II. The district staff will remain unchanged.

III. Lieuts. G. P. Yoe and J. H. Martin, aides-de-camp, are announced as the personal staff, and will be obeyed and respected accordingly.

> WILL. T. MARTIN,
> *Major-General.*

HDQRS. DISTRICT OF MISSISSIPPI AND EAST LOUISIANA,
Jackson, Miss., January 16, 1865.

Lieut. Col. E. SURGET,
Assistant Adjutant-General, Meridian, Miss.:

COLONEL: I have the honor to report that I have this day assumed command of the District of Mississippi and East Louisiana, in obedience to Special Orders, No. 11, of the 11st instant, from department headquarters.

Very respectfully, your obedient servant,

> WILL. T. MARTIN,
> *Major-General.*

TUPELO, MISS., *January 17, 1865.*

President JEFFERSON DAVIS,
    Richmond, Va.:

I am fully satisfied the Army of Tennessee requires immediate reorganization and consolidation, removing at same time all inefficient and supernumerary officers. Generals Hood, Taylor, Forrest, and corps commanders agree fully with me in that opinion. Cannot necessary authority be granted me, at once, to that effect? The army cannot otherwise be made reliable for active operations.

G. T. BEAUREGARD,
General.

TUPELO, MISS., *January 17, 1865.*

President JEFFERSON DAVIS,
    Richmond, Va.:

To divide this small army at this juncture to re-enforce General Hardee would expose to capture Mobile, Demopolis, Selma, Montgomery, and all the rich valley of the Alabama River. Shall that risk be now incurred?

G. T. BEAUREGARD,
General.

TUPELO, MISS., *January 17, 1865.*

Hon. WILLIAM PORCHER MILES, M. C.,
    Richmond, Va.:

I beg yourself and friends in Congress to support actively the plan I have to-day recommended by telegraph to the President relative to this army. Generals Hood, Taylor, Forrest, and corps commanders agree fully with me in the absolute necessity of the measure.

G. T. BEAUREGARD,
General.

TUPELO, *January 17, 1865.*
(Received 3 o'clock 24th.)

Hon. J. A. SEDDON,
    Secretary of War:

Telegram of the 15th instant received. I will leave for Georgia and South Carolina soon as practicable after having placed General Taylor in command of the Army of Tennessee, and take, after conference with him, as many troops as can be spared from here.

G. T. BEAUREGARD.

TUPELO, *January 17, 1865.*
(Received 18th.)

General S. COOPER,
    Adjutant and Inspector General:

Roddey's brigade is useless as at present located by War Department. I desire authority to dispose of it to best advantage, according to circumstances.

G. T. BEAUREGARD,
General.

[First indorsement.]

Respectfully submitted to honorable Secretary of War.

JOHN W. RIELY,
Major and Assistant Adjutant-General.

[Second indorsement.]

SECRETARY OF WAR:

On each occasion when this officer has been sent with his command to distant service, serious calamity to Alabama has followed. It is desirable to know what disposition General Beauregard proposes to make of this force.

J. D.

[Third indorsement.]

JANUARY 18, 1865.

ADJUTANT-GENERAL:

Inquire of General B. the purpose for which General Roddey's brigade is wanted. Twice his removal has been followed by unfortunate results, and hence some hesitation is felt in authorizing change of locality.

J. A. S.,
Secretary.

[Fourth Indorsement.]

File with original. See telegram to General Beauregard, January 19, 1865.

J. W. R.,
Assistant Adjutant-General.

TUPELO, MISS., *January 17, 1865.*

Col. GEORGE WILLIAM BRENT,
Chief of Staff, Montgomery, Ala.:

Order General Smith to inspect works at Choctaw and Oven Bluffs, and give such orders as may be necessary for defense of river at those points. Obstructions and torpedoes recommended for Tennessee River must be used there.

G. T. BEAUREGARD,
General.

MERIDIAN, MISS., *January 17, 1865.*

Col. E. J. HARVIE,
Inspector-General:

SIR: I think I can send from 2,000 to 2,500 men per day via Selma. It would be safe policy only to have the transportation given to this point, and then all the men I cannot send via Selma can send on via Mobile. Will do everything possible to forward the men rapidly, and have the troops forwarded without delay.

Yours, respectfully,

GEORGE WHITFIELD,
Major and Quartermaster.

[Indorsement.]

Major AYER:

There is conflict about this transportation. If you will let Major Beecher send every telegram affecting this business everything can be satisfactorily arranged.

Respectfully,

E. J. H.

SPECIAL ORDERS, }   ADJT. AND INSP. GENERAL'S OFFICE,
No. 13.   }   *Richmond, Va., January 17, 1865.*

*   *   *   *   *   *   *

XXIX. The nine companies composing the organization known as Inge's Twelfth Mississippi Battalion Cavalry, with Company C of the Fifty-sixth Alabama Regiment, a Mississippi company, which is hereby transferred, will constitute the Tenth Regiment Mississippi Cavalry.

*   *   *   *   *   *   *

By order of the Secretary of War:

JNO. WITHERS,
Assistant Adjutant-General.

RICHMOND, VA., *January 17, 1865.*

General R. TAYLOR,
          Meridian, Miss.:

Yours of 15th received. I would be most happy to confer with you in person, but do not see how you can be spared to come here, and I cannot now go to you. To hold Thomas in check I proposed that you should have, in addition to your present force, the cavalry of Hood's army and Polk's old corps. To this I hoped you would be able to add many reserves and militia, and did not see how more force could be given, unless troops are sent from the Trans-Mississippi, the call for which has been reiterated.

JEFF'N DAVIS.

TUPELO, MISS., *January 17, 1865—8 p. m.*

Lieut. Gen. R. TAYLOR,
          Meridian, Miss.:

General Hood having applied to be relieved, the Secretary of War orders me to place you in command of this army. You will retain, also, command of your present department. Operator at Meridian will deliver this dispatch to General Taylor to-morrow morning on the cars from Mobile.

G. T. BEAUREGARD.

TUPELO, MISS., *January 18, 1865.*

Col. GEORGE WILLIAM BRENT,
          Chief of Staff, Montgomery, Ala.:

Order rapid reconnaissance and field maps or sketches made forthwith of country embraced within lines from Corinth to Meridian, thence to West Point, Guntersville, and Corinth, commencing near as practicable to enemy's lines along Tennessee River. Those roads which cannot be examined must be located from best information obtained.

G. T. BEAUREGARD,
General.

TUPELO, MISS., *January 18, 1865.*
Capt. R. T. BEAUREGARD,
    Columbus, Miss.:
I propose leaving here to-morrow for Montgomery, via Mobile.

G. T. BEAUREGARD,
General.

TUPELO, MISS., *January 18, 1865.*
His Excellency JEFFERSON DAVIS:
General Taylor will arrive to-morrow, and I will leave soon after for Richmond. Please consider the propriety of my going west of the Mississippi River. I would like it; I think I can be of more service there than east of the river.

J. B. HOOD,
General.

HEADQUARTERS MILITARY DIVISION OF THE WEST,
Tupelo, Miss., January 18, 1865.
General J. B. HOOD,
    Commanding Army of Tennessee:
GENERAL: General Beauregard directs that you will hold Lee's corps in readiness to move as soon as necessary preparations can be made for its transportation, and that you will cause it to be thoroughly equipped for the field as soon as practicable.

He also directs that you will cause a battalion of three light batteries of Napoleons, composed, if practicable, of South Carolina and Georgia companies, thoroughly equipped for the field, to proceed to Macon, Ga. (under a good field officer), as soon as they can be equipped, and there await further orders.

They will take steamer at Columbus for Montgomery, Ala. The field transportation of the above-named troops shall accompany them.

Respectfully, your obedient servant,

HENRY BRYAN,
Major and Assistant Adjutant-General.

HEADQUARTERS MILITARY DIVISION OF THE WEST,
Tupelo, Miss., January 18, 1865.
General J. B. HOOD,
    Commanding Army of Tennessee:
GENERAL: Understanding that the transportation of Lee's corps will be ready in the morning I desire the movement of Lee's corps from here to Augusta, via Montgomery, Macon, and Milledgeville, should commence as soon as practicable. The troops should leave here

with at least twenty rounds of ammunition in their cartridge-boxes, with three days' cooked rations, which should be renewed at Meridian and Montgomery, and four days at Macon. The troops sent via Mobile will renew their rations at that point, instead of Meridian. The artillery moving from Columbus, Miss., will be supplied with rations and forage sufficient to last to Montgomery, where they will renew their supplies, as well as at Macon. Your chief quartermaster and commissary will make the necessary arrangements for the rapid transportation of these troops to their destination.

Respectfully, your obedient servant,

G. T. BEAUREGARD,
General.

HEADQUARTERS ARMY OF TENNESSEE,
Tupelo, Miss., January 18, 1865.

Col. L. J. FLEMING,
West Point, Miss.:

The first shipment of about 8,000 troops commences to-morrow morning. They will go by both routes—Mobile and Selma—and as rapidly as transportation can be furnished.

E. J. HARVIE,
Colonel and Inspector-General.

MERIDIAN, *January 18, 1865.*

Col. E. J. HARVIE:

Major Ayer telegraphs Major Whitfield to arrange for the shipping of troops immediately, and you to suspend for the time; both same date. Answer.

G. A. HENRY, JR.,
Assistant Inspector-General.

HEADQUARTERS ARMY OF TENNESSEE,
Tupelo, Miss., January 18, 1865.

Lieut. Col. G. A. HENRY,
Assistant Inspector-General, Meridian, Miss.:

Troops are ordered to leave here. Let Major Whitfield comply with Major Ayer's telegram.

E. J. HARVIE,
Colonel and Inspector-General.

HEADQUARTERS ARMY OF TENNESSEE,
Tupelo, Miss., January 18, 1865.

Lieut. Col. G. A. HENRY,
Assistant Inspector-General, Meridian, Miss.:

All men belonging to Lee's corps must be held in readiness and ordered to rejoin their commands as they pass on the cars.

E. J. HARVIE,
Colonel and Inspector-General.

(Same to Maj. P. B. Lee and Maj. W. Clare.)

SPECIAL ORDERS, }   HEADQUARTERS ARMY OF TENNESSEE,
    No. 18.   }   *Tupelo, Miss., January 18, 1865.*

*   *   *   *   *   *   *

IV. Gibson's brigade is relieved from duty with Bate's division. Brigadier-General Gibson with his brigade will march to Verona, Miss., and report to Lieutenant-General Stewart, commanding corps.

*   *   *   *   *   *   *

By command of Lieutenant-General Taylor:

JAS. COOPER,
Acting Assistant Adjutant-General.

[Indorsement.]

Captain GALE:

When General Gibson reports give him an order to report temporarily to General Loring.

A. P. S.

———

TUPELO, MISS., *January 18, 1865.*

Maj. Gen. N. B. FORREST,
    Verona, Miss.:

If General Taylor comes here in train to-night I desire to confer with him and yourself at 11 a. m. to-morrow.

G. T. BEAUREGARD.

———

VERONA, *January 18, 1865.*

Brigadier-General CHALMERS:

Take command of Colonel Wheeler's and all other cavalry at Pikeville, or that may be ordered there, and officers refusing to obey your orders you will arrest.

N. B. FORREST,
Major-General.

———

RICHMOND, VA., *January 18, 1865.*

Governor CHARLES CLARK,
    Columbus, Miss.:

Can you furnish General Taylor any additional force; if so, how many and how soon? You will appreciate the necessity of our position, and I need not urge you to extraordinary exertion.

JEFF'N DAVIS.

———

TUPELO, MISS., *January 18, 1865.*

Maj. Gen. D. H. MAURY,
    Mobile, Ala.:

I expect to visit Mobile 21st or 22d instant.

G. T. BEAUREGARD,
General.

GENERAL ORDERS,)   HDQRS. DIST. OF MISS. AND EAST LA.,
    No. 4.   )   *Jackson, Miss., January 18, 1865.*

I. The two sub-districts heretofore known as the Sub-district of Northwest Mississippi and the Sub-district of Central Mississippi, are hereby consolidated into one, which will be known as the Sub-district of West Mississippi.

II. Brig. Gen. Wirt Adams, commanding at present the Sub-district of Central Mississippi, is assigned to the command of the Sub-district of West Mississippi.

By order of Maj. Gen. Will. T. Martin:

P. ELLIS, JR.,
Assistant Adjutant-General.

TUPELO, MISS., *January 19, 1865—9 a. m.*
(Received 20th.)

General S. COOPER,
    Adjutant and Inspector General, Richmond, Va.:

Lee's corps, about 5,000 strong, has commenced moving to-day. It will be pushed forward as rapidly as possible. General Taylor arrived here last night. I will probably leave this evening via Mobile and Montgomery.

G. T. BEAUREGARD,
General.

RICHMOND, *January 19, 1865.*

General G. T. BEAUREGARD,
    Tupelo, Miss.:

For what purpose do you desire General Roddey's brigade? His removal from his present locality has been twice followed by unfortunate results, and hence some hesitation is felt in authorizing a change.

S. COOPER,
Adjutant and Inspector General.

HEADQUARTERS MILITARY DIVISION OF THE WEST,
Tupelo, Miss., January 19, 1865.

Lieut. Col. A. P. MASON,
    Assistant Adjutant-General, Hdqrs. Army of Tennessee:

COLONEL: General Beauregard desires that General Hood will send with the troops going to Georgia 100 rounds of small-arms ammunition per man, including what they have in their cartridge-boxes, and 100 rounds of ammunition per gun for the light batteries. He desires, also, that the ordnance wagons, ambulances, and a due proportion of the supply train belonging to them, should also be sent.

Very respectfully, your obedient servant,

HENRY BRYAN,
Major and Assistant Adjutant-General.

HEADQUARTERS MILITARY DIVISION OF THE WEST,
Tupelo, Miss., January 19, 1865.

General J. B. HOOD,
    Commanding Army of Tennessee:

GENERAL: General Beauregard directs that you hold Cheatham's corps (except Gibson's brigade, ordered to Mobile) in readiness to move at any time an order may be issued to that effect from these head-quarters. He also directs that you hold in readiness to move, upon the receipt of similar orders, another battalion of three light batteries at Columbus, Miss.

Very respectfully, your obedient servant,

HENRY BRYAN,
Major and Assistant Adjutant-General.

GENERAL ORDERS, }   HDQRS. CHALMERS' DIVISION,
                         FORREST'S CAVALRY CORPS,
No. 1.   }   *Near Buena Vista, January 19, 1865.*

I. In obedience to orders from Major-General Forrest, the following organizations will be made:

The Ninth and Tenth Tennessee consolidated, under command of the senior officer; the Fourth and Seventh Alabama consolidated, under command of the senior officer; the Fourth and Eleventh Tennessee consolidated, under command of Colonel Holman.

By order of Brigadier-General Chalmers:

L. T. LINDSEY,
Acting Assistant Adjutant-General.

HEADQUARTERS ARMY OF TENNESSEE,
Tupelo, Miss., January 19, 1865.

Colonel WHEELER,
Commanding Cavalry, near Okolona:

COLONEL: The general commanding directs that you collect as far as possible all the scattered remnants of General Wheeler's command, and proceed immediately with your whole command to Columbus, Miss., from which place you will escort the wagon train of General Lee's corps to Milledgeville, Ga. You will go as a guard for this train, and be responsible for its safety. It is not expected, however, that you will interfere with the officer having charge of it. He will regulate its marches and select camps. Please acknowledge the receipt of this, and comply with the order as soon as it reaches you.

Very respectfully, your obedient servant,

E. J. HARVIE,
Colonel and Inspector-General.

TUPELO, *January 19, 1865.*

Lieutenant-Colonel SURGET,
Assistant Adjutant-General, Meridian:

General [Taylor] desires you to direct Major-General Martin to now make such disposition of his troops as will enable him to concentrate rapidly in front of and fight and harass enemy effectively in the event of his attempting cavalry raid from Mississippi River toward railroad.

W. F. BULLOCK, JR.,
Assistant Adjutant-General.

TUPELO, *January 19, 1865.*

Lieutenant-Colonel SURGET,
    Assistant Adjutant-General, Meridian:

The general desires you to obtain from Major-General Martin, as soon as practicable, full information of enemy's movements in Mississippi. Direct him to get full reports from scouts as to forces going down the river; while they report comparatively few passing down, a large force is reported below organizing for expedition.

W. F. BULLOCK, JR.,
    Assistant Adjutant-General.

TUPELO, MISS., *January 19, 1865.*

Brig. Gen. D. W. ADAMS,
    Talladega:

Ascertain and report as soon as practicable what force and time will be required to obstruct main roads leading from Tennessee River to iron and coal region of Alabama and erect ordinary and field works thereon to defend obstructions.

By order of Lieutenant-General Taylor:

W. F. BULLOCK, JR.,
    Assistant Adjutant-General.

MOBILE, ALA., *January 19, 1865.*

Hon. JAS. A. SEDDON,
    Secretary of War:

Canby's army reported returning from Tennessee toward New Orleans, and preparations making to attack Mobile. My present effective force of infantry and artillery about 4,500.

D. H. MAURY,
    Major-General.

HEADQUARTERS GILTNER'S BRIGADE,
Rye Cove, Scott County, Va., January 19, 1865.

Maj. J. STODDARD JOHNSTON,
    Assistant Adjutant-General:

MAJOR: Inclosed I send a petition of a number of citizens of Russell County representing the disorderly character of Colonel Prentice's command, and asking for protection from it; also, a letter from a Mr. John Burton upon the same subject. The whole country is filled with complaints of this command, and I have many applications from the citizens to inform how to proceed to rid themselves of the presence of these marauders, for they have degenerated into a band of thieves and plunderers and are a plague to the country they pretend to be defending. It is but just, though, to say that I hear of no complaints from the company commanded by Captain Carter. He, I believe, is a good officer, and controls his men; he is camped separate from his battalion and keeps his men in camp, and is generally in good repute through this county in which he is now located. Upon the application of the citizens of Russell I sent Captain Barrett with fifty men to Castlewoods, with instructions to arrest all soldiers improperly absent from our army that be found in that county; to treat the marauders of Prentice's command with the utmost severity, and to burn all the houses occupied by public women. Captain Barrett will remain there as long as his detachment can be foraged and subsisted.

I am, major, most respectfully, your obedient servant,

H. L. GILTNER,
Colonel, Commanding Brigade.

[Indorsement.]

Referred to General Echols for attention. If necessary, this command will have to be broken up.

J. C. B[RECKINRIDGE].

[Inclosure No. 1.]

Colonel GILTNER:

DEAR SIR: You will see from the statements of the within petition that a bad state of things is getting up up in our county, and unless some steps are taken to put a stop to it I fear something severe will grow out of it. What is done should be done quickly to be in time. I have had nothing to do with the matter, but it is among my neighbors, and at their request I came as far as Mr. Shoemaker's to see you, and would have come on only that my family are unwell. The petition, from the best information I have, states the truth, and you may rely upon the statements of Mr. Vaughan and Mr. Monk, who will hand you this paper. I trust you will adopt some means to have those men removed from the neighborhood.

Most respectfully,

W. B. ASTON.

[Sub-inclosure.]

Col. H. GILTNER,
Commanding, &c.:

The undersigned citizens of Russell County, protesting that they are good, loyal, and peaceable citizens of the Confederacy, would most respectfully represent that a few men professing to belong to the command of Col. C. J. Prentice have congregated together in the lower end of Castlewoods, in Russell County, a number of bad women, where they stay together for unlawful purposes and keep a most disorderly house or houses; that they have gone through the neighborhood of Copper Ridge and other places and wantonly robbed various good and lawful citizens of their provisions, clothing, bed-clothing, stock, &c., and carried them to those women for their support. To such an extent has this thing been carried on that the whole neighborhood was in continual dread and alarm for their lives and property, as some of the same company have, or are believed to have, committed sundry murders in the country. In view of this state of things, and to try to put a stop to its continuance, a few of the citizens a few nights ago assembled together and went for the purpose of trying to break up the bad houses above named and to secure back some of the stolen property in their possession, and they burned up one of the houses in which they were congregated and recovered back some of the stolen property, and in the encounter a man by the name of Fletcher, a ringleader of the band, was killed by a soldier that had gone along with the citizens. Your petitioners now understand that, instead of desisting from their unlawful practices, the said party are now making arrangements to take revenge upon the citizens by killing, and burning their houses—ten for one, as they allege.   Your petitioners do not wish to engage in anything unlawful or without proper authority, or having the semblance of disloyalty. They therefore pray that such steps may be taken by the military authorities as will effectually put a stop to such unlawful proceedings or to further bloodshed; and, as in duty bound, they will ever pray, &c.

JOHN P. CARTY.
R. P. VICARY.
JAMES HARTSOCK.
JAMES BAKER.
L. D. VAUGHAN.
JAMES B. MONK.
[And 67 others.]

[Inclosure No. 2.]

WISE COUNTY, VA., *January —, 1865.*

Col. B. E. CAUDILL:

DEAR SIR: I drop you a line, informing you that my house has been pillaged and my family abused by Lieut. A. J. Ciphers, James C. Talbert, William D. Horn, and S. P. Porter, of Prentice's command. They, in open daylight, came to my house, there being no person but my wife at the house; endeavored to take some of my bed clothes; my wife caught hold of them; they jerked her down and around, abusing her person, and in spite of her succeeded in taking off some few articles of my own manufacture. I therefore pray you that such men may be apprehended and held accountable for their conduct. This is the second time some of the same party have pillaged my house. You will please, if in your power, have something done with the party, or forward for me to the proper authorities. If we can get no protection from some source, we will be ruined by those thieves of Prentice's.

Yours, truly,

JOHN BURTON.

Abstract from return of Stevenson's division, Lee's corps, Brig. Gen. Edmund W. Pettus, C. S. Army, commanding, for January 19, 1865.

Command.	Effective total.	Total present.	Aggregate present.
General headquarters			5
Pettus' brigade (Dedman):			
Headquarters			3
20th Alabama	241	305	334
23d Alabama	155	202	220
30th Alabama	186	256	275
31st Alabama	132	180	200
46th Alabama	116	174	190
Cumming's brigade (Henderson):			
Headquarters			2
34th Georgia	171	219	238
36th and 56th Georgia	171	232	253
39th Georgia	134	177	197
Palmer's brigade (Palmer):			
Headquarters			4
58th North Carolina	263	310	334
60th North Carolina and 63d Virginia	275	340	379
3d, 18th, 23d, 26th, 32d, and 45th Tennessee	306	471	571
54th Virginia	181	212	235
Total	2,331	3,078	3,440

TUPELO, MISS., *January 20, 1865.*

Col. GEORGE WILLIAM BRENT,
  Assistant Adjutant-General, Montgomery, Ala.:

Lee's and Cheatham's corps, about 15,000 strong, with six batteries, have been ordered to Augusta. Transportation and supplies on the way have been ordered. Thirty days' supplies must be collected for them in Augusta and at Thomson and Berzelia, on Georgia Railroad.

G. T. BEAUREGARD.

TUPELO, *January 20, 1865.*
(Received 3 o'clock 24th.)

Hon. J. A. SEDDON:

By direction of General Beauregard, Lee's and Cheatham's corps are moving to Georgia; Stewart's remains here. What disposition will be made of the officers of the general staff regularly assigned to duty at army headquarters by orders from the War Department?

J. B. HOOD,
General.

SPECIAL ORDERS, }   ADJT. AND INSP. GENERAL'S OFFICE,
  No. 16.   }   *Richmond, Va., January 20, 1865.*

*   *   *   *   *   *   *

XXVII. Brig. Gen. W. T. Wofford, Provisional Army, C. S., is hereby assigned to the command of the Reserve Forces of Northern Georgia, and will report to Maj. Gen. Howell Cobb, commanding, &c., Macon, Ga.

*   *   *   *   *   *   *

By command of the Secretary of War:

JNO. WITHERS,
Assistant Adjutant-General.

VERONA, *January 20, 1865.*

Brigadier-General CHALMERS:

You will retain Holman's, DeMoss', Biffle's, and Russell's regiments, and send Wheeler's and the Fourth Tennessee Regiment and all other parts of regiments and detachments whose command may be in Georgia.

N. B. FORREST,
Major-General.

HDQRS. DISTRICT OF MISSISSIPPI AND EAST LOUISIANA,
  Jackson, January 20, 1865.

Lieut. Col. E. SURGET,
  Assistant Adjutant-General, Meridian, Miss.:

COLONEL: Your dispatch of last evening is received. There is no doubt that a large force of the enemy is below from Natchez to New Orleans. It seems probable from the indications reported that a column of cavalry, at least, will attempt to march from the Mississippi River eastwardly. An expedition to Red River is much spoken of along the river. I had already ordered Griffith to move with his regiment to General Hodge's assistance.   Colonel Wood's regiment is en route for south-western Copiah County.   Mabry's brigade and McGuirk's regiment are marching to concentrate at or near Canton.   These latter commands are pretty well marched down.   All the force that is available will be used to harass and impede any column that attempts to cross this district.   I had hoped to retain Henderson's scouts in this district; they are almost the only reliable scouts I have, knowing the whole country in front and the people along the river, and having established channels of communication which cannot be easily re-established.

Very respectfully,

WILL. T. MARTIN,
Major-General.

WEST POINT, *January 20, 1865.*

Major-General MAURY,
Mobile:

Holtzclaw's brigade has been ordered to Mobile to relieve Baker's brigade.   Have Baker's brigade in readiness to move to Montgomery on arrival of former.

W. F. BULLOCK, JR.,
Assistant Adjutant-General.

[JANUARY 20, 1865.—For abstract from inspection report of the Army of Tennessee, see Part I, p. 664.]

Organization of troops of Stevenson's division, Lee's corps, commanded by Brig. Gen. Edmund W. Pettus, C. S. Army, for January 20, 1865.

Pettus' Brigade.

Col. JAMES M. DEDMAN.

20th Alabama, Lieut. Col. John W. Davis.
23d Alabama, Maj. James T. Hester.
30th Alabama, Lieut. Col. James K. Elliott.
31st Alabama, Lieut. Col. Thomas M. Arrington.
46th Alabama, Capt. George E. Brewer.

Cumming's Brigade.

Col. ROBERT J. HENDERSON.

34th Georgia, Capt. Russell A. Jones.
36th Georgia, Capt. Thomas Williams.
56th Georgia, Capt. Benjamin T. Spearman.
39th Georgia, Capt. William P. Milton.

Palmer's Brigade.

Brig. Gen. JOSEPH B. PALMER.

58th North Carolina, Lieut. Col. Samuel M. Silver.
60th North Carolina, Maj. James T. Huff.
3d and 18th Tennessee, Lieut. Col. William R. Butler.
32d Tennessee, Col. John P. McGuire.
23d, 26th, and 45th Tennessee, Col. Anderson Searcy.
54th Virginia, Capt. William G. Anderson.
63d Virginia, Lieut. Col. Connally H. Lynch.

MERIDIAN, *January 21, 1865.*
(Received 9.20 o'clock 24th.)

General S. COOPER:

General Beauregard's suggestions about Roddey were made at my request, and did not contemplate leaving North Alabama unprotected, but simply to delocalize the troops for the good of the service.

Respectfully,

R. TAYLOR,
Lieutenant-General.

MERIDIAN, *January 21, 1865.*

Col. GEORGE W. BRENT,
Assistant Adjutant-General, Montgomery, Ala.:

About 2,500 white and 6,000 negro troops reported to be at New Orleans on 4th. On 5th an army corps, said to be from Thomas' army, went down Mississippi on fourteen transports; destination believed to be Mobile.

R. TAYLOR,.
Lieutenant-General.

HDQRS. DEPARTMENT OF ALA., MISS., AND EAST LA.,
Meridian, January 21, 1865.

Mr. WINTER,
Agent State of Louisiana:

DEAR SIR: I have represented to the honorable Secretary of War the necessities and sufferings of the people of those sections of Alabama, Mississippi, and Louisiana which have been the theater of active military operations for so long a time and thereby rendered destitute of provisions, but have failed in my efforts to induce the Department to authorize the exchanges of limited quantities of private or State cotton for necessary family supplies. General Beauregard has however told me that he would, in the absence of any prohibitory instructions from the War Department to him on the subject, grant the necessary authorizations for such exchanges upon the application of the Governors of the respective States. I therefore lose no time in notifying you of the fact, in order that no unnecessary delay may occur in forwarding to General Beauregard the required application and obtaining from him the authority to relieve the above referred to citizens of Louisiana.

I am, sir, very respectfully, yours, &c.,

R. TAYLOR,
Lieutenant-General.

(Similar letters to Governors Charles Clark and T. H. Watts, of Mississippi and Alabama.)

MERIDIAN, *January 21, 1865.*

Captain HUMPHREYS,
Army of Tennessee, Depot Ordnance Officer, Columbus, Miss.:

Lee's and Cheatham's corps are moving to South Carolina. General Beauregard directed orders to you, from Tupelo, to ship to Montgomery fair proportions for these two corps of your entire supply of ordnance, naming exact amount; balance to Demopolis, to be subject to my orders. If those orders have miscarried, telegraph General Hood at Tupelo immediately for their repetition.

R. TAYLOR,
Lieutenant-General.

ENGINEER OFFICE,
Mobile, January 21, 1865.

Col. I. W. PATTON,
Commanding, &c., Spanish Fort:

COLONEL : I have ordered Lieutenant Elmore, of the Engineers, to send all the hands from Spanish Fort to this place to-day. This is to carry out instructions from General Maury to put up a new work on this side at once. I hope your lines are now secure, or, at least, in such condition that the troops can finish the necessary work. I directed Lieutenant Elmore to leave you a supply of tools. I am sorry I could not have Spanish Fort sodded, but the storm of two weeks ago interfered greatly with my plans by driving three of my flats high and dry on the marsh. General Maury is anxious to have the sub-terra shells placed in front of No. 2—Lieutenant Elmore can help you in that; also to have additional obstructions. I recommend a fraise in rear of the abatis, thus,* and pits in front of it. I would like to furnish you with wire, but hardly think it possible. I suppose by this time that your magazine is finished, slopes revetted with logs, traverses and embrasures all made, as indicated on my last visit. Please direct Lieutenant Elmore to have fascines made to replace the sand-bags, as they will not last long in this wet weather; also to have head-logs made and placed on the infantry parapets. The sand-bags when removed from the embrasures can be used to make loop-holes for infantry. Your men all understand these processes. I would have been over last week, and went as far as Blakely, but was brought back by General Taylor, who concluded to go no farther. Will have to go up to Choctaw Bluff in a day or so, and will visit you on my return.

Very respectfully and truly, yours,

S. H. LOCKETT,
Colonel, &c.

SPECIAL ORDERS, }   HDQRS. CHALMERS' DIVISION,
                          FORREST'S CAVALRY CORPS,
No. —.   }   *Near Buena Vista, January 21, 1865.*

I. Lieut. James Dinkins, Provisional Army, C. S., is relieved from duty on the staff of the brigadier-general commanding, and will report to Capt. C. T. Smith, commanding escort, for duty with his company.

*   *   *   *   *   *   *

By order of Brigadier-General Chalmers:

L. T. LINDSEY,
Acting Assistant Adjutant-General.

---

* Diagram omitted.

MOBILE, *January 22, 1865*.
(Received 5 o'clock 24th.)

General S. COOPER:

General Taylor reports from Meridian yesterday that 2,500 white and 6,000 black troops were in New Orleans on 5th instant, and that one of Thomas' army corps is reported to have gone down the Mississippi; destination supposed to be Mobile. General Maury reports about 6,000 of enemy at Pascagoula.

G. T. BEAUREGARD.

MOBILE, *January 22, 1865*.
(Received 5 o'clock 24th.)

General S. COOPER:

General Hood reports loss of all his pontoon train—83 boats, 150 wagons, and 400 mules—due to inability of General Roddey to bring his troops from their homes. I wish to substitute another brigade in its place, and put all the cavalry of this department under one commanding general—Forrest.

G. T. BEAUREGARD.

MOBILE, *January 23, 1865*.
(Received 5 o'clock 24th.)

General S. COOPER:

City land defenses next the lower bay, where enemy will probably attack, are still unfinished. System of barbette guns adopted for land batteries worst possible; their fire will be silenced by enemy's sharpshooters as soon as they get within range.

G. T. BEAUREGARD,
General.

MOBILE, *January 23, 1865*.
(Received 5 o'clock 24th.)

General S. COOPER:

I find my presence here necessary one or two days longer.

G. T. BEAUREGARD,
General.

TUPELO, *January 23, 1865*.

His Excellency the PRESIDENT:

I wish to cross the Mississippi River to bring to your aid 25,000 troops. I know this can be accomplished, and earnestly desire this chance to do you so much good service. Will explain my plan on arrival. I leave to-day for Richmond.

J. B. HOOD,
General.

Special Orders, ⟩   Adjt. and Insp. General's Office,
No. 18.   ⟨   *Richmond, January 23, 1865.*

*   *   *   *   *   *   *

XXXVI. Paragraph XXVII, Special Orders, No. 16, Adjutant and Inspector General's Office, current series, is hereby revoked, and Brig. Gen. W. T. Wofford, Provisional Army, C. S., will proceed to Northern Georgia, with full power to collect such stragglers and deserters and to dissolve such illegal organizations as may be found in that section. He will place them in temporary organizations for immediate duty until they can be sent to their proper commands. He will also enroll all men liable to conscription who have thus far evaded the service. To accomplish these ends and to disperse such bands of deserters as may infest the country, he is authorized to obtain from Maj. Gen. Howell Cobb, commanding, &c., such force as may be necessary.

*   *   *   *   *   *   *

By command of the Secretary of War:

JNO. WITHERS,
Assistant Adjutant-General.

———

Special Field Orders, ⟩   Hdqrs. Mil. Div. of the West,
No. —.   ⟨   *January 23, 1865.*

I. General J. B. Hood is relieved, at his own request, by the War Department from the command of the Army of Tennessee. He will report for orders to the War Department, at Richmond, Va.

II. Lieut. Gen. R. Taylor, commanding Department of Alabama, Mississippi, and East Louisiana, will assume command of the Army of Tennessee until further orders.

G. T. BEAUREGARD,
General.

———

Headquarters Army of Tennessee,
Tupelo, Miss., January 23, 1865.

Soldiers: At my request I have this day been relieved from the command of this army. In taking leave of you accept my thanks for the patience with which you have endured your many hardships during the recent campaign. I am alone responsible for its conception, and strived hard to do my duty in its execution. I urge upon you the importance of giving your entire support to the distinguished soldier who now assumes command, and I shall look with deep interest upon all your future operations and rejoice at your successes.

J. B. HOOD,
General.

———

Headquarters Army of Tennessee,
Tupelo, January 23, 1865.

Lieutenant-General Stewart,
Commanding Corps:

General: Lieutenant-General Taylor arrived last night, and desires to see you this morning.

Very respectfully, your obedient servant,

A. P. MASON,
Lieutenant-Colonel and Assistant Adjutant-General.

SPECIAL ORDERS, }   HDQRS. CHALMERS' DIVISION,
                         FORREST'S CAVALRY CORPS,
No. —. }   *Near Buena Vista, January 23, 1865.*
*   *   *   *   *   *   *

II. Lieut. Col. W. G. Henderson, commanding Fifth Mississippi Cavalry, will assume command of all detachments and scattered remnants of McCulloch's brigade in this neighborhood. He will send in a report of his command daily, showing its strength and designating the commands to which they belong.

III. Captain Owen, commanding company, Carter's regiment, will, in pursuance of orders from General Hood, report with his command to Colonel Wheeler, at Columbus, Miss., for the purpose of rejoining his command in Georgia.

IV. Captain Cochran, assistant quartermaster Forrest's cavalry regiment, will report to Major Key at these headquarters at once.

V. Colonel Biffle, commanding brigade, will, in the absence of countermanding orders, move with his command on the 26th through Houston, thence by the nearest route to Verona, leaving Prairie Mound to the right, crossing Chewappa at Garman's Mills. He will report to General Forrest for further orders on his arrival at Verona. The wagon train of the brigade will move with them.

By order of Brigadier-General Chalmers:

L. T. LINDSEY,
Acting Assistant Adjutant-General.

ALTERNATE DESIGNATIONS

OF

ORGANIZATIONS MENTIONED IN THIS VOLUME.*

Abbay's (George F.) **Artillery.** See *Mississippi Troops, Confederate, 1st Regiment, Battery K.*

Abdill's (William J.) **Infantry.** See *Union Troops, Colored, 16th Regiment.*

Adams' (Wirt) **Cavalry.** See *Mississippi Troops, Confederate.*

Akin's (James H.) **Cavalry.** See *Tennessee Troops, Confederate, 9th Battalion.*

Aleshire's (Charles C.) **Artillery.** See *Ohio Troops, 18th Battery.*

Alexander's (Francis N.) **Infantry.** See *Kentucky Troops, Union, 30th Regiment.*

Allen's (Hiram) **Artillery.** See *Indiana Troops, 24th Battery.*

Allen's (Lyman) **Infantry.** See *Iowa Troops, 37th Regiment.*

Alston's (Robert A.) **Cavalry.** See *Kentucky Troops, Confederate, 1st Battalion, Special.*

Anderson Cavalry. See *Pennsylvania Troops, 15th Regiment.*

Anderson's (Anthony) **Infantry.** See *Union Troops, Veteran Reserve Corps, 2d Battalion, 67th and 157th Companies.*

Anderson's (Edward) **Cavalry.** See *Indiana Troops, 12th Regiment.*

Anderson's (John) **Cavalry.** See *Union Troops, Colored, 5th Regiment.*

Anderson's (William G.) **Infantry.** See *Virginia Troops, Confederate, 54th Regiment.*

Andress' (James F.) **Cavalry.** See *Pennsylvania Troops, 7th Regiment.*

Andrew's (Abram P.) **Artillery.** See *Indiana Troops, 21st Battery.*

Armistead's (Charles G.) **Cavalry.** See *Mississippi Troops, Confederate, 12th Regiment.*

Armstrong's (George T.) **Cavalry.** See *Union Troops, Colored, 15th Regiment.*

Arneck's Cavalry. See *Kentucky Troops, Union, 17th Regiment.*

Arrington's (Thomas M.) **Infantry.** See *Alabama Troops, Confederate, 31st Regiment.*

Askew's (Frank) **Infantry.** See *Ohio Troops, 15th Regiment.*

Backus' (William) **Artillery.** See *Ohio Troops, 20th Battery.*

Baird's (Harlon) **Cavalry.** See *Iowa Troops, 5th Regiment.*

Baldwin's (Aaron P.) **Artillery.** See *Ohio Troops, 6th Battery.*

Baldwin's (Norman A.) **Artillery.** See *Ohio Troops, 1st Regiment, Battery B.*

Ball's (Charles P.) **Cavalry.** See *Alabama Troops, Confederate, 8th Regiment.*

Ball's (John) **Infantry.** See *Minnesota Troops, 11th Regiment.*

Barber's (Gershom M.) **Sharpshooters.** See *Ohio Troops, 1st Battalion.*

Barbiere's (Joseph) **Cavalry.** See *Alabama Troops, Confederate.*

Barcus' (John M.) **Infantry.** See *Indiana Troops, 120th Regiment.*

Barry's (Henry W.) **Heavy Artillery.** See *Union Troops, Colored, 8th Regiment.*

Bartlett's (Joseph R.) **Infantry.** See *Ohio Troops, 49th Regiment.*

Beach's (Albert F.) **Artillery.** See *Tennessee Troops, Union, 1st Battalion, Battery A.*

Beach's (John P.) **Infantry.** See *Union Troops, Veteran Reserve Corps, 2d Regiment; also 2d Battalion, 45th and 158th Companies.*

Becht's (John C.) **Infantry.** See *Minnesota Troops, 5th Regiment.*

Beck's (Moses M.) **Artillery.** See *Indiana Troops, 18th Battery.*

---

* References, unless otherwise indicated, are to index following.

Beebe's (William O.) **Artillery.**   See *Tennessee Troops, Union, 1st Battalion, Battery B.*

Beeres' (Charles H.) **Cavalry.**   See *Illinois Troops, 16th Regiment.*

Bennett's (John E.) **Infantry.**   See *Illinois Troops, 75th Regiment.*

Bentley's (Robert H.) **Cavalry.**   See *Ohio Troops, 12th Regiment.*

Berry's Cavalry.   (Official designation not of record.)   See ――― *Berry.*

Berry's (James W.) **Infantry.**   See *Tennessee Troops, Union, 8th Regiment.*

Bewley's (William G.) **Artillery.**   See *Tennessee Troops, Union, 1st Battalion, Battery B.*

Biddle's (James) **Cavalry.**   See *Indiana Troops, 6th Regiment.*

Bierce's (Albert S.) **Artillery.**   See *Indiana Troops, 7th Battery.*

Biffle's (Jacob B.) **Cavalry.**   See *Tennessee Troops, Confederate.*

Biggs' (Jonathan) **Infantry.**   See *Illinois Troops, 123d Regiment.*

Bissell's (Oliver C.) **Infantry.**   See *Wisconsin Troops, 44th and 45th Regiments.*

Blackburn's (Joseph C. S.) **Cavalry.**   (Official designation not of record.)   See *Joseph C. S. Blackburn.*

Blake's (Edgar W.) **Infantry.**   See *Wisconsin Troops, 13th Regiment.*

Blake's (John W.) **Infantry.**   See *Indiana Troops, 40th Regiment.*

Bond's (William G.) **Infantry.**   See *Illinois Troops, 83d Regiment.*

Bonham's (Edward) **Infantry.**   See *Illinois Troops, 47th Regiment.*

Bonnaffon's (Augustus B.) **Infantry.**   See *Pennsylvania Troops, 78th Regiment.*

Boone's (J. Rowan) **Infantry.**   See *Kentucky Troops, Union, 28th Regiment.*

Boone's (Thomas C.) **Infantry.**   See *Ohio Troops, 115th Regiment.*

Bowman's (Daniel) **Infantry.**   See *Ohio Troops, 93d Regiment.*

Boyle's (William O.) **Cavalry.**   See *Kentucky Troops, Union, 11th Regiment.*

Bradford's (J. L.) **Artillery.**   See *Mississippi Troops, Confederate, 1st Regiment, Battery F.*

Brady's (Thomas J.) **Infantry.**   See *Indiana Troops, 140th Regiment.*

Brayton's (George M.) **Infantry.**   See *Union Troops, Regulars, 15th Regiment, 3d Battalion.*

Brent's (Preston) **Infantry.**   See *Mississippi Troops, Confederate, 38th Regiment.*

Brewer's (George E.) **Infantry.**   See *Alabama Troops, Confederate, 46th Regiment.*

Bridges' (Lyman) **Artillery.**   See *Illinois Troops.*

Bringhurst's (Thomas H.) **Infantry.**   See *Indiana Troops, 46th Regiment.*

Brown's Cavalry.   (Official designation not of record.)   See ――― *Brown.*

Brown's (Richard H.) **Cavalry.**   See *Missouri Troops, Union, 12th Regiment.*

Brown's (Robert C.) **Infantry.**   See *Ohio Troops, 64th Regiment.*

Brown's (Simeon B.) **Cavalry.**   See *Michigan Troops, 11th Regiment.*

Bruff's (Joseph) **Infantry.**   See *Ohio Troops, 125th Regiment.*

Bryan's (Thomas J.) **Infantry.**   See *Illinois Troops, 74th Regiment.*

Brydolf's (Fabian) **Infantry.**   See *Union Troops, Veteran Reserve Corps, 2d Regiment.*

Buckner's (Allen) **Infantry.**   See *Illinois Troops, 79th Regiment.*

Bundy's (Henry) **Artillery.**   See *New York Troops, 13th Battery.*

Burdell's (Harvey) **Artillery.**   See *Ohio Troops, 22d Battery.*

Burke's (Orville) **Infantry.**   See *Iowa Troops, 14th Regiment.*

Burroughs' (Wilson) **Infantry.**   See *Illinois Troops, 73d Regiment.*

Burtwell's (John R. B.) **Cavalry.**   See *Alabama Troops, Confederate, 11th Regiment.*

Bush's (Llewyllyn E. P.) **Artillery.**   See *Kentucky Troops, Union, Battery E.*

Butler's (J. R.) **Cavalry.**   See *Kentucky Troops, Confederate, 3d Regiment.*

Butler's (Lewis) **Infantry.**   See *Ohio Troops, 182d Regiment.*

Butler's (William R.) **Infantry.**   See *Tennessee Troops, Confederate, 3d (Volunteers) and 18th Regiments.*

Butterfield's (Charles H.) **Infantry.**   See *Indiana Troops, 91st Regiment.*

Caldwell's (James N.) **Infantry.**   See *Union Troops, Regulars, 18th Regiment.*

Calkins' (William H.) **Cavalry.**   See *Indiana Troops, 12th Regiment.*

Camp's (George A.) **Infantry.**   See *Minnesota Troops, 8th Regiment.*

Canby's (Samuel) **Artillery.** See *Union Troops, Regulars, 4th Regiment, Battery M.*

Carnahan's (Robert H.) **Cavalry.** See *Illinois Troops, 3d Regiment.*

Carroll's (William) **Heavy Artillery.** See *Ohio Troops, 1st Regiment.*

Carter's (Nathan W.) **Cavalry.** See *Tennessee Troops, Confederate.*

Catron's (Thomas B.) **Artillery.** See *Saint Louis Artillery, post.*

Caudill's (Benjamin E.) **Mounted Rifles.** See *Kentucky Troops, Confederate, 11th Regiment, Infantry, Mounted.*

Cayce's (Stewart W.) **Infantry.** See *Mobile Infantry, post.*

Chalmers' (Alexander H.) **Cavalry.** See *Mississippi Troops, Confederate, 18th Battalion.*

Charpentier's (Stephen) **Artillery.** See *Alabama Troops, Confederate.*

Chicago Board of Trade Artillery. See *Illinois Troops.*

Civic Guard (Chattanooga). See *Tennessee Troops, Union.*

Clanton's (N. H.) **Artillery.** See *Alabama Troops, Confederate.*

Clark Artillery. See *Missouri Troops, Confederate.*

Clark's (Alonzo W.) **Infantry.** See *Illinois Troops, 44th Regiment.*

Clark's (William) **Infantry.** See *Ohio Troops, 26th Regiment.*

Clift's (William J.) **Cavalry.** See *Tennessee Troops, Union, 5th Regiment.*

Clowney's (John) **Infantry.** See *Wisconsin Troops, 30th Regiment.*

Cobb's (Joseph T.) **Scouts, Cavalry.** See *Texas Troops.*

Cobb's (Josiah B.) **Cavalry.** See *Indiana Troops, 12th Regiment.*

Cockerill's (Giles J.) **Artillery.** See *Ohio Troops, 1st Regiment, Battery D.*

Cockrill's (Simon) **Infantry.** See *Kentucky Troops, Union, 47th Regiment.*

Coffin's (W. Norris) **Heavy Artillery.** See *Louisiana Troops, Confederate, 12th Battalion, Battery D.*

Cogswell's (William) **Artillery.** See *Illinois Troops.*

Cole's (Marquis L.) **Artillery.** See *Mississippi Troops, Confederate, 1st Regiment.*

Colvin's (Charles H.) **Cavalry.** See *Alabama Troops, Confederate, 6th Regiment.*

Colvin's (John H.) **Artillery.** See *Illinois Troops.*

Comparet's (John M.) **Infantry.** See *Indiana Troops, 142d Regiment.*

Conover's (John) **Infantry.** See *Kansas Troops, 8th Regiment.*

Cook's (William R.) **Cavalry.** See *Tennessee Troops, Union, 2d Regiment.*

Cooper's (Stearns F.) **Infantry.** See *Union Troops, Veteran Reserve Corps, 2d Battalion, 98th Company.*

Corbin's (Henry B.) **Artillery.** See *Michigan Troops, 1st Regiment, Battery D.*

Cornelius' (James E.) **Infantry.** See *Union Troops, Veteran Reserve Corps, 15th Regiment.*

Couch's (Reuben C.) **Cavalry.** See *Tennessee Troops, Union, 5th Regiment.*

Cox's (Nicholas N.) **Cavalry.** See *Tennessee Troops, Confederate.*

Craddock's (William B.) **Infantry.** See *Kentucky Troops, Union, 30th Regiment.*

Crews' Cavalry. (Official designation not of record.) See ——— *Crews.*

Cross' (William) **Infantry.** See *Tennessee Troops, Union, 3d Regiment.*

Culpeper's (James F.) **Artillery.** See *Palmetto Battalion, Artillery, post, Battery C.*

Cummings' (Thomas) **Infantry.** See *Union Troops, Regulars, 19th Regiment, 1st Battalion.*

Cummins' (John E.) **Infantry.** See *Ohio Troops, 99th Regiment.*

Cunningham's (Benjamin) **Cavalry.** See *Tennessee Troops, Union, 3d Regiment.*

Cunningham's (James) **Infantry.** See *Illinois Troops, 80th Regiment.*

Curtis' (James F.) **Infantry.** See *Indiana Troops, 44th Regiment.*

Dachenhausen's (Adolphus von) **Infantry.** See *Union Troops, Veteran Reserve Corps, 2d Regiment.*

Dade's (B. Frank) **Infantry.** See *Alabama Troops, Confederate, 21st Regiment.*

Davies' (John R.) **Heavy Artillery.** See *Wisconsin Troops, 1st Regiment, Battery C.*

Davis' (John W.) **Infantry.** See *Alabama Troops, Confederate, 20th Regiment.*

Dawkins' (Richard C.) **Infantry.** See *Kentucky Troops, Union, 6th Regiment.*

Dawson's Cavalry. (Official designation not of record.) See ——— *Dawson.*

Dawson's (Thomas E.) **Artillery.** See *Illinois Troops, 2d Regiment, Battery B.*

Day's (George W.) **Cavalry.** See *Tennessee Troops, Confederate, 12th Battalion.*

Dean's (Henry S.) **Infantry.** See *Michigan Troops, 22d Regiment.*

Deane's (Henry H.) **Infantry.** See *Illinois Troops, 146th Regiment.*

Demarest's (Samuel L.) **Infantry.** See *Michigan Troops, 25th Regiment.*

De Moss' (William E.) **Cavalry.** See *Nicholas N. Cox's Cavalry, ante.*

Dettweiler's (Germain) **Infantry.** See *Union Troops, Veteran Reserve Corps, 2d Battalion, 20th, 91st, 93d, and 103d Companies.*

De Vries' (Peter) **Artillery.** See *Michigan Troops, 1st Regiment, Battery E.*

Diamond's (George R.) **Cavalry.** See *Kentucky Troops, Confederate, 10th Regiment (May's).*

Dick's (George F.) **Infantry.** See *Indiana Troops, 86th Regiment.*

Dilger's (Hubert) **Artillery.** See *Ohio Troops, 1st Regiment, Battery I.*

Dobb's (George W.) **Cavalry.** See *Ohio Troops, 4th Regiment.*

Dobke's (Adolphus) **Infantry.** See *New York Troops, 45th Regiment.*

Dorr's (Joseph B.) **Cavalry.** See *Iowa Troops, 8th Regiment.*

Doyal's (H. R.) **Cavalry.** (Official designation not of record.) See *H. R. Doyal.*

Duff's (George) **Infantry.** See *Union Troops, Veteran Reserve Corps, 21st Regiment.*

Dwyer's (Patrick) **Infantry.** See *Union Troops, Veteran Reserve Corps, 2d Battalion, 40th Company.*

Dyer's (Calvin M.) **Cavalry.** See *Tennessee Troops, Union, 1st Regiment.*

Dyer's (James B.) **Infantry.** See *Indiana Troops, 43d Regiment.*

Earnest's (Robert H.) **Infantry.** See *Union Troops, Colored, 115th Regiment.*

Eggleston's (Beroth B.) **Cavalry.** See *Ohio Troops, 1st Regiment.*

Elgin Artillery. See *Illinois Troops.*

Elliott's (James K.) **Infantry.** See *Alabama Troops, Confederate, 30th Regiment.*

Emery's (Augustus H.) **Artillery.** See *Michigan Troops, 1st Regiment, Battery M.*

Eno's (Stephen H.) **Infantry.** See *Union Troops, Colored, 101st Regiment.*

Ernst's (George) **Infantry.** See *Missouri Troops, Union, 15th Regiment.*

Esembaux's (Michael) **Infantry.** See *New York Troops, 58th Regiment.*

Espy's (Harvey J.) **Infantry.** See *Indiana Troops, 68th Regiment.*

Evans' (James C.) **Infantry.** See *Kentucky Troops, Union, 21st Regiment.*

Everett's (Peter M.) **Cavalry.** See *Kentucky Troops, Confederate, 1st Battalion, Rifles.*

Falconer's (David G.) **Infantry.** See *Union Troops, Veteran Reserve Corps, 2d Battalion, 79th Company.*

Faulkner's (John K.) **Cavalry.** See *Kentucky Troops, Union, 7th Regiment.*

Ferguson's (Stephen M.) **Infantry.** See *Kentucky Troops, Union, 39th Regiment.*

Ferrell's (Coleman B.) **Artillery.** See *Georgia Troops.*

Fidler's (William H.) **Cavalry.** See *Kentucky Troops, Union, 6th Regiment.*

Flood's (James P.) **Artillery.** See *Illinois Troops, 2d Regiment, Battery C.*

Follett's (Joseph L.) **Artillery.** See *Missouri Troops, Union, 1st Regiment, Battery G.*

Forbes' (William) **Infantry.** See *Missouri Troops, Union, 42d Regiment.*

Ford's (Collin) **Infantry.** See *Union Troops, Colored, 100th Regiment.*

Ford's (Thomas) **Cavalry.** See *Mississippi Troops, Confederate, 7th Regiment.*

Foster's (Nathaniel H.) **Heavy Artillery.** See *Union Troops, Colored, 12th Regiment, 1st Battalion.*

French's (George D.) **Cavalry.** See *Confederate Troops, Regulars, 7th Battalion.*

Gamble's (A. Marion) **Infantry.** See *Tennessee Troops, Union, 6th Regiment.*

Garrard's (Israel) **Cavalry.** See *Ohio Troops, 7th Regiment.*

Gartrell's (H. A.) **Cavalry.** See *Georgia Troops.*

Gaw's (William B.) **Infantry.** See *Union Troops, Colored, 16th Regiment.*

Gay's (Ebenezer) **Infantry.** See *Union Troops, Regulars, 16th Regiment.*

Gibson's (Horatio G.) **Heavy Artillery.** See *Ohio Troops, 2d Regiment.*

Gillespie's (Hamilton S.) **Infantry.** See *Ohio Troops, 50th Regiment.*

Gober's (Daniel) **Mounted Infantry.** See *Louisiana Troops, Confederate.*

Gowin's (George A.) **Infantry.** See *Tennessee Troops, Union, 6th Regiment, Mounted.*

Graham's (John M.) **Cavalry.** See *Illinois Troops, 7th Regiment.*

Grant's (Charles) **Infantry.** See *Ohio Troops, 18th Regiment.*

Gray's (Isaac) **Cavalry.** See *Union Troops, Colored, 5th Regiment.*

Gregory's (Samuel O.) **Infantry.** See *Indiana Troops, 29th Regiment.*

Griffith's (John) **Infantry.** See *Arkansas Troops, Confederate, 11th and 17th Regiments.*

Grunwell's (Alfred B.) **Infantry.** See *Union Troops, Veteran Reserve Corps, 22d Regiment.*

Hale's (Clayton) **Infantry.** See *Illinois Troops, 59th Regiment.*

Hall's (Jairus W.) **Infantry.** See *Michigan Troops, 4th Regiment.*

Hamilton's (David W.) **Infantry.** See *Indiana Troops, 51st Regiment.*

Hammond's (Charles M.) **Infantry.** See *Illinois Troops, 100th Regiment.*

Hammond's (John W.) **Infantry.** See *Indiana Troops, 65th Regiment.*

Hardie's (Joseph) **Cavalry.** See *Alabama Troops, Confederate.*

Harnden's (Henry) **Cavalry.** See *Wisconsin Troops, 1st Regiment.*

Harper's (Joseph W.) **Cavalry.** See *Illinois Troops, 9th Regiment.*

Harrell's (William V.) **Cavalry.** See *Thomas H. Lewis' Cavalry, post.*

Harrington's (Pinkney C.) **Cavalry.** See *Confederate Troops, Regulars, 14th Regiment.*

Harris' (Benjamin F.) **Infantry.** See *Union Troops, Veteran Reserve Corps, 4th Regiment.*

Harrison's (James B.) **Cavalry.** See *Kentucky Troops, Union, 12th Regiment.*

Hart's (James) **Infantry.** See *Union Troops, Veteran Reserve Corps, 2d Battalion, 77th Company.*

Hartung's (Charles) **Infantry.** See *Wisconsin Troops, 24th Regiment.*

Harvey's (Addison) **Scouts.** (Official designation not of record.) See *Addison Harvey.*

Harvey's (Alonzo D.) **Artillery.** See *Indiana Troops, 15th Battery.*

Hawkins' (Isaac R.) **Cavalry.** See *Tennessee Troops, Union, 7th Regiment.*

Hawley's (Chauncey G.) **Heavy Artillery.** See *Ohio Troops, 1st Regiment.*

Hays' (Jordan) **Cavalry.** (Official designation not of record.) See *Jordan Hays.*

Heckman's (Lewis) **Artillery.** See *Ohio Troops, 1st Regiment, Battery K.*

Hedges' (Joseph) **Cavalry.** See *Union Troops, Regulars, 4th Regiment.*

Hegner's (Henry) **Infantry.** See *Union Troops, Colored, 12th Regiment.*

Henderson's (Samuel) **Cavalry.** See *Mississippi Troops, Confederate.*

Henderson's (Thomas) **Scouts.** See *Mississippi Troops, Confederate.*

Henderson's (W. G.) **Cavalry.** See *Mississippi Troops, Confederate, 5th Regiment.*

Henshaw's (Edward C.) **Artillery.** See *Illinois Troops.*

Herrick's (John F.) **Cavalry.** See *Ohio Troops, 12th Regiment.*

Hester's (James T.) **Infantry.** See *Alabama Troops, Confederate, 23d Regiment.*

Hicks' (George) **Infantry.** See *Illinois Troops, 96th Regiment.*

Hiestand's (Joseph M.) **Infantry.** See *Ohio Troops, 175th Regiment.*

Higley's (John H.) **Infantry.** See *Alabama Troops, Confederate, 37th, 40th, and 42d Regiments.*

Hill's (Charles W.) **Infantry.** See *Ohio Troops, 128th Regiment.*

Hill's (John L.) **Artillery.** See *Ohio Troops, 24th Battery.*

Hill's (Roswell S.) **Cavalry.** See *Indiana Troops, 2d Regiment.*

Hoge's (George W.) **Infantry.** See *Ohio Troops, 183d Regiment.*

Holahan's (Amos J.) **Cavalry.** See *Pennsylvania Troops, 19th Regiment.*

Holden's (Levi P.) **Infantry.** See *Illinois Troops, 36th Regiment.*

Holman's (Daniel W.) **Cavalry.** See *Tennessee Troops, Confederate.*

Hooper's (C. W.) **Cavalry.** See *H. A. Gartrell's Cavalry ante.*

Hopkins' (Marcus S.) **Infantry.** See *Union Troops, Veteran Reserve Corps, 2d Battalion, 66th Company.*

Horton's (Charles C.) **Cavalry.** See *Iowa Troops, 2d Regiment.*

Hotchkiss' (William A.) **Artillery.** See *Minnesota Troops, 2d Battery.*

Hottenstein's (John A.) **Infantry.** See *Union Troops, Colored, 13th Regiment.*

Houghton's (Moses B.) **Infantry.** See *Michigan Troops, 3d Regiment.*

Howell's (W. C.) **Artillery.** See *James A. Owens' Artillery, post.*

Hudson's (John E.) **Infantry.** See *Ohio Troops, 181st Regiment.*

Huff's (James T.) **Infantry.** See *North Carolina Troops, Confederate, 60th Regiment.*

Huger's (Daniel E.) **Infantry.** See *Alabama Troops, Confederate, 1st Regiment, Reserves.*

Hulburd's (Edwin M.) **Infantry.** See *Michigan Troops, 18th Regiment.*

Hummel's (Gottlob) **Infantry.** See *Union Troops, Veteran Reserve Corps, 2d Battalion, 11th Company.*

Humphrey's (John H.) **Infantry.** See *Ohio Troops, 45th Regiment.*

Hunt's (Charles J.) **Infantry.** See *Union Troops, Veteran Reserve Corps, 2d Battalion, 137th Company.*

Hurd's (John R.) **Infantry.** See *Ohio Troops, 173d Regiment.*

Hurst's (Fielding) **Cavalry.** See *Tennessee Troops, Union, 6th Regiment.*

Hurt's (John S.) **Infantry.** See *Kentucky Troops, Union, 24th Regiment.*

Hyde's (Charles W.) **Heavy Artillery.** See *Wisconsin Troops, 1st Regiment, Battery B.*

Inge's (William M.) **Cavalry.** See *Mississippi Troops, Confederate, 10th Regiment.*

Jackson's (Frank) **Artillery.** See *Ohio Troops, 12th Battery.*

Jackson's (George W.) **Cavalry.** See *Indiana Troops, 9th Regiment.*

Jamison's (William H.) **Infantry.** See *Illinois Troops, 21st Regiment.*

Jenkins' (Barton W.) **Cavalry.** See *Kentucky Troops, Confederate.*

Jessee's (George M.) **Cavalry.** See *Confederate Troops, Regulars, 6th Battalion.*

Johnson's (Benjamin F.) **Artillery.** See *Indiana Troops, 4th Battery.*

Johnson's (James H.) **Cavalry.** See *Tennessee Troops, Union, 11th Regiment.*

Johnson's (Lewis) **Infantry.** See *Union Troops, Colored, 44th Regiment.*

Johnson's (Ole C.) **Infantry.** See *Wisconsin Troops, 15th Regiment.*

Johnson's (Samuel F.) **Cavalry.** See *Kentucky Troops, Union, 17th Regiment.*

Johnson's (Thomas I.) **Infantry.** See *North Carolina Troops, Union, 2d Regiment, Mounted.*

Jones' (John S.) **Infantry.** See *Ohio Troops, 174th Regiment.*

Jones' (Russell A.) **Infantry.** See *Georgia Troops, 34th Regiment.*

Jones' (Samuel) **Infantry.** * See *Alabama Troops, Confederate, 3d Regiment, Reserves.*

Keen's (Alderson T.) **Cavalry.** See *Kentucky Troops, Union, 1st Regiment.*

Kelly's (Robert M.) **Infantry.** See *Kentucky Troops, Union, 4th Regiment.*

Kelly's (Usher F.) **Infantry.** See *Union Troops, Veteran Reserve Corps, 2d Battalion, 68th Company.*

Kennedy's (George H.) **Infantry.** See *Illinois Troops, 65th Regiment.*

Kimberly's (Robert L.) **Infantry.** See *Ohio Troops, 41st Regiment.*

Kincaid's (George W.) **Infantry.** See *Iowa Troops, 37th Regiment.*

King's (Houston) **Artillery.** See *Clark Artillery, ante.*

Kingsbury's (George W.) **Infantry.** See *Union Troops, Veteran Reserve Corps, 23d Regiment.*

Kinzie's (David H.) **Artillery.** See *Union Troops, Regulars, 5th Regiment, Battery K.*

Kirk's (George W.) **Infantry.** See *North Carolina Troops, Union, 3d Regiment, Mounted.*

Kitchell's (Edward) **Infantry.** See *Illinois Troops, 98th Regiment.*

Kizer's (Thomas N.) **Cavalry.** (Official designation not of record.) See *Thomas N. Kizer.*

---

* Temporarily commanding.

Krause's (Andrew J.) Infantry.   See *Union Troops, Colored, 108th Regiment.*
Kutzner's (Edward A.) Infantry.   See *Missouri Troops, Union, 39th Regiment.*
Lamborn's (Charles B.) Cavalry.   See *Pennsylvania Troops, 15th Regiment.*
Lamson's (Horace P.) Cavalry.   See *Indiana Troops, 4th Regiment.*
Lawrence's (William H.) Infantry.   See *New Jersey Troops, 34th Regiment.*
Lawton's (Henry W.) Infantry.   See *Indiana Troops, 30th Regiment.*
Lay's (Benjamin D.) Cavalry.   See *Mississippi Troops, Confederate.*
Leaming's (Henry) Infantry.   See *Indiana Troops, 40th Regiment.*
Leeper's (James) Infantry.   See *Indiana Troops, 49th Regiment.*
Leeson's (Moses D.) Cavalry.   See *Indiana Troops, 5th Regiment.*
Leinart's (Samuel D.) Artillery.   See *Tennessee Troops, Union, 1st Battalion, Battery D.*
Lewis' (Jerry) Artillery.   See *Union Troops, Colored, 2d Regiment, Battery A.*
Lewis' (Thomas H.) Cavalry.   See *Alabama Troops, Confederate.*
Leyde's (William M.) Heavy Artillery.   See *Minnesota Troops, 1st Regiment, Battery B.*
Lingle's (John M.) Infantry.   See *Illinois Troops, 146th Regiment.*
Lipscomb's (Thomas C.) Cavalry.   See *Mississippi Troops, Confederate, 6th Regiment.*
Livingston's (Henry J.) Cavalry.   See *Alabama Troops, Confederate, 8th Regiment.*
Low's (Bartlett M.) Infantry.   See *Wisconsin Troops, 42d Regiment.*
Lugenbeel's (Pinkney) Infantry.   See *Union Troops, Regulars, 19th Regiment.*
Lynch's (Connally H.) Infantry.   See *Virginia Troops, Confederate, 63d Regiment.*
Lynch's (John) Cavalry.   See *Illinois Troops, 6th Regiment.*
McCall's (Charles C.) Infantry.   See *Alabama Troops, Confederate, 54th Regiment.*
McCartney's (Joseph A.) Artillery.   See *Illinois Troops, 1st Regiment, Battery I.*
McCoy's (Daniel) Infantry.   See *Ohio Troops, 175th Regiment.*
McDanald's (Bedan B.) Infantry.   See *Ohio Troops, 101st Regiment.*
McGraw's (John S.) Infantry.   See *Indiana Troops, 57th Regiment.*
McGuire's (John P.) Infantry.   See *Tennessee Troops, Confederate, 32d Regiment.*
McGuirk's (John) Cavalry.   See *Mississippi Troops, Confederate, 3d Regiment.*
McKee's (Joseph T.) Cavalry.   See *Union Troops, Colored, 6th Regiment.*
McLeester's (Thomas) Infantry.   See *Pennsylvania Troops, 192d Regiment.*
McLemore's (William S.) Cavalry.   See *Tennessee Troops, Confederate.*
McManis' (William) Cavalry.   See *Illinois Troops, 9th Regiment.*
McQuiston's (John C.) Infantry.   See *Indiana Troops, 123d Regiment.*
McReynolds' (Richard W.) Artillery.   See *Kentucky Troops, Union, Battery C.*
Major's (John C.) Infantry.   See *Indiana Troops, 43d Regiment.*
Marshall's (Alexander) Artillery.   See *Ohio Troops, 1st Regiment, Battery G.*
Mathey's (Edward G.) Infantry.   See *Indiana Troops, 81st Regiment.*
Matzdorff's (Alvin V.) Infantry.   See *Pennsylvania Troops, 75th Regiment.*
Maury's (Henry) Cavalry.   See *Confederate Troops, Regulars, 15th Regiment.*
Maxwell's (Cicero) Infantry.   See *Kentucky Troops, Union, 26th Regiment.*
Merrill's Horse, Cavalry.   See *Missouri Troops, Union, 2d Regiment.*
Merrill's (William E.) Engineers.   See *Union Troops, Volunteers, 1st Regiment, Veteran.*
Merrin's (F. W.) Artillery.   See *Mississippi Troops, Confederate, 14th Battalion, Battery C.*
Meyers' (Valentine) Artillery.   See *Tennessee Troops, Union, 1st Battalion, Battery C.*
Miller's (Jacob) Infantry.   See *Kentucky Troops, Union, 16th Regiment.*
Millington's (Augustus O.) Infantry.   See *Union Troops, Colored, 18th Regiment.*
Milton's (William P.) Infantry.   See *Georgia Troops, 39th Regiment.*
Mississippi Marine Brigade, Infantry.   See *Missouri Troops, Union.*
Mix's (Elisha) Cavalry.   See *Michigan Troops, 8th Regiment.*
Mizner's (Henry R.) Infantry.   See *Union Troops, Regulars, 18th Regiment, 2d Battalion.*

Mobile Infantry. See *Alabama Troops, Confederate.*
Moody's (John W.) **Infantry.** See *Ohio Troops, 71st Regiment.*
Moore's (James) **Infantry.** See *Illinois Troops, 83d Regiment.*
Moore's (Ranna S.) **Cavalry.** See *Indiana Troops, 13th Regiment.*
Moore's (William P.) **Infantry.** See *Illinois Troops, 49th Regiment.*
Moorman's (George) **Cavalry.** See *Mississippi Troops, Confederate.*
Moreland's (M. D.) **Cavalry.** See *Alabama Troops, Confederate.*
Morgan's (Thomas J.) **Infantry.** See *Union Troops, Colored, 14th Regiment.*
Morris' (Daniel) **Infantry.** See *Indiana Troops, 63d Regiment.*
Morrison's (Samuel H.) **Infantry.** See *Union Troops, Veteran Reserve Corps, 2d Battalion, 83d and 84th Companies.*
Morton's (Charles H.) **Infantry.** See *Illinois Troops, 84th Regiment.*
Moses' (J. L.) **Artillery.** See *Palmetto Battalion, Artillery, post, Battery C.*
Mullenix's (Edward E.) **Infantry.** See *Ohio Troops, 175th Regiment.*
Murphy's (John) **Infantry.** See *Tennessee Troops, Union, 2d Regiment, Mounted*
Murray's (William M.) **Infantry.** See *Tennessee Troops, Union, 2d Regiment.*
Myers' (William C.) **Artillery.** See *Ohio Troops, 14th Battery.*
Naylor's (William A.) **Artillery.** See *Indiana Troops, 10th Battery.*
Neal's (Carlton) **Artillery.** See *Michigan Troops, 1st Regiment, Battery L.*
Neff's (George W.) **Infantry.** See *Ohio Troops, 88th Regiment.*
Neff's (Henry H.) **Infantry.** See *Indiana Troops, 124th Regiment.*
Nesbitt's (William B.) **Infantry.** See *Ohio Troops, 176th Regiment.*
Nichols' (Clarkson C.) **Infantry.** See *Ohio Troops, 97th Regiment.*
Nicholson's (Edward W.) **Artillery.** See *Indiana Troops, 22d Battery.*
Nicklin's (Benjamin S.) **Artillery.** See *Indiana Troops, 13th Battery.*
Northup's (George W.) **Infantry.** See *Kentucky Troops, Union, 23d Regiment.*
Norton's (Thomas H.) **Infantry.** See *Union Troops, Regulars, 15th Regiment, 2d Battalion.*
Nulton's (Jerome B.) **Infantry.** See *Illinois Troops, 61st Regiment.*
Ogden's (Frederick N.) **Cavalry.** See *Louisiana Troops, Confederate.*
O'Neal's Regiment. (Official designation not of record.) See *Colonel O'Neal.*
O'Neil's (Joseph) **Infantry.** See *Union Troops, Veteran Reserve Corps, 2d Battalion, 126th Company.*
Orr's (John M.) **Infantry.** See *Indiana Troops, 124th Regiment.*
Osborne's (Milton A.) **Artillery.** See *Indiana Troops, 20th Battery.*
Otman's (Sylvester F.) **Infantry.** See *Illinois Troops, 112th Regiment.*
Otwell's (Francis) **Infantry.** See *Union Troops, Veteran Reserve Corps, 2d Battalion, 94th Company.*
Ougheltree's (George) **Infantry.** See *Union Troops, Veteran Reserve Corps, 2d Battalion, 61st and 125th Companies.*
Owen's Cavalry. See *Nathan W. Carter's Cavalry, ante.*
Owen's (Alfred D.) **Infantry.** See *Indiana Troops, 80th Regiment.*
Owens' (James A.) **Artillery.** See *Arkansas Troops, Confederate.*
Packard's (Jasper) **Infantry.** See *Indiana Troops, 128th Regiment.*
Paddock's (Byron D.) **Artillery.** See *Michigan Troops, 1st Regiment, Battery F*
Paine's (Byron) **Infantry.** See *Wisconsin Troops, 43d Regiment.*
Palmer's (William J.) **Cavalry.** See *Pennsylvania Troops, 15th Regiment.*
Palmetto Battalion, Artillery. See *South Carolina Troops.*
Parker's (George W.) **Infantry.** See *Indiana Troops, 79th Regiment.*
Parrish's (Charles S.) **Infantry.** See *Indiana Troops, 130th Regiment.*
Patterson's (Michael L.) **Infantry.** See *Tennessee Troops, Union, 4th Regiment.*
Pease's (William H.) **Artillery.** See *Ohio Troops, 1st Regiment, Battery F.*
Pelham Cadets, Infantry. See *Alabama Troops, Confederate.*
Peyton's (E. A.) **Cavalry.** See *Mississippi Troops, Confederate.*
Pickands' (Henry S.) **Infantry.** See *Ohio Troops, 103d Regiment.*

Pickands' (James) **Infantry.** See *Ohio Troops, 124th Regiment.*

Pickett's (Richard O.) **Cavalry.** See *Alabama Troops, Confederate, 10th Regiment.*

Pollard's (Andrew M.) **Infantry.** See *Illinois Troops, 38th Regiment.*

Porter's (George L.) **Heavy Artillery.** See *Minnesota Troops, 1st Regiment, Battery C.*

Poteet's (George A.) **Infantry.** See *Illinois Troops, 115th Regiment.*

Powers' (Frank P.) **Cavalry.** See *Louisiana Troops, Confederate.*

Prentice's (Clarence J.) **Cavalry.** See *Confederate Troops, Regulars, 7th Battalion.*

Prevost's (Charles M.) **Infantry.** See *Union Troops, Veteran Reserve Corps, 16th Regiment.*

Pritchard's (Benjamin D.) **Cavalry.** See *Michigan Troops, 4th Regiment.*

Puckett's (John M.) **Infantry.** See *Kentucky Troops, Union, 8th Regiment.*

Putnam's (Azro C.) **Artillery.** See *Edward C. Henshaw's Artillery, ante.*

Putnam's (Joseph R.) **Infantry.** See *Union Troops, Colored, 42d Regiment.*

Ragan's (W. B.) **Infantry.** See *Confederate Troops, Regulars, 3d Regiment, Reserves* [?].

Ratliff's (William T.) **Artillery.** See *Mississippi Troops, Confederate, 1st Regiment, Battery A.*

Reckard's (Frank B.) **Artillery.** See *Ohio Troops, 1st Regiment, Battery E.*

Reed's (Arthur F.) **Infantry.** See *Union Troops, Colored, 40th Regiment.*

Rice's (Olin F.) **Infantry.** See *Alabama Troops, Confederate, 2d Regiment, Reserves.*

Rice's (T. W.) **Heavy Artillery.** See *Tennessee Troops, Confederate.*

Richmond's (James B.) **Infantry.** See *Virginia Troops, Confederate, 64th Regiment.*

Robbins' (Irvin) **Infantry.** See *Indiana Troops, 123d Regiment.*

Robinson's (George I.) **Artillery.** See *Chicago Board of Trade Artillery, ante.*

Rogers' (Thomas J.) **Infantry.** See *Tennessee Troops, Union, 1st Regiment.*

Rose's (Thomas E.) **Infantry.** See *Pennsylvania Troops, 77th Regiment.*

Rundell's (Frank) **Infantry.** See *Ohio Troops, 100th Regiment.*

Russell's (Alfred A.) **Cavalry.** See *Alabama Troops, Confederate, 4th Regiment.*

Russell's (Robert M.) **Cavalry.** See *Tennessee Troops, Confederate.*

Sage's (Harley H.) **Infantry.** See *Ohio Troops, 179th Regiment.*

Saint Louis Artillery. See *Missouri Troops, Confederate.*

Salm's (Felix Prince) **Infantry.** See *New York Troops, 68th Regiment.*

Sargent's (Elbert M.) **Infantry.** See *Ohio Troops, 59th Regiment.*

Saylor's (Thomas) **Infantry.** See *Michigan Troops, 29th Regiment.*

Schuetz's (John C.) **Artillery.** See *Michigan Troops, 1st Regiment, Battery K.*

Scott's (John G.) **Cavalry.** See *Kentucky Troops, Confederate, 4th Regiment.*

Scott's (John S.) **Cavalry.** See *Louisiana Troops, Confederate, 1st Regiment.*

Scott's (William C.) **Infantry.** See *Ohio Troops, 102d Regiment.*

Scovill's (Charles W.) **Artillery.** See *Ohio Troops, 1st Regiment, Battery A.*

Searcy's (Anderson) **Infantry.** See *Tennessee Troops, Confederate, 23d, 26th, and 45th Regiments.*

Sedgewick's (Thomas D.) **Infantry.** See *Union Troops, Colored, 114th Regiment.*

Seidel's (Charles B.) **Cavalry.** See *Ohio Troops, 3d Regiment.*

Sellon's (William R.) **Infantry.** See *Union Troops, Colored, 12th Regiment.*

Shafter's (William R.) **Infantry.** See *Union Troops, Colored, 17th Regiment.*

Shannon's (John A.) **Heavy Artillery.** See *Union Troops, Colored, 1st Regiment.*

Sharra's (Abram) **Cavalry.** See *Indiana Troops, 11th Regiment.*

Sherwood's (Isaac R.) **Infantry.** See *Ohio Troops, 111th Regiment.*

Silver's (Samuel M.) **Infantry.** See *North Carolina Troops, Confederate, 58th Regiment.*

Skinner's (Lewis C.) **Infantry.** See *Union Troops, Veteran Reserve Corps, 8th Regiment.*

Slater's (Frederick) **Cavalry.** See *Kentucky Troops, Union, 11th Regiment.*

Smith's (Benjamin) **Cavalry.** See *Michigan Troops, 2d Regiment.*

Smith's (Charles W.) **Infantry.** See *Trumbull Guards, Infantry, post.*

Smith's (Frank G.) **Artillery.** See *Union Troops, Regulars, 4th Regiment, Battery I.*
Smith's (George W.) **Infantry.** See *Illinois Troops, 88th Regiment.*
Smith's (John T.) **Infantry.** See *Indiana Troops, 31st Regiment.*
Smith's (Luther R.) **Artillery.** See *Michigan Troops, 1st Regiment, Battery 1.*
Smith's (Orlow) **Infantry.** See *Ohio Troops, 65th Regiment.*
Snider's (Joseph T.) **Infantry.** See *Ohio Troops, 13th Regiment.*
Sowers' (Edgar) **Infantry.** See *Ohio Troops, 118th Regiment.*
Spalding's (George) **Cavalry.** See *Tennessee Troops, Union, 12th Regiment.*
Spaulding's (Oliver L.) **Infantry.** See *Michigan Troops, 23d Regiment.*
Spearman's (Benjamin T.) **Infantry.** See *Georgia Troops, 56th Regiment.*
Spencer's (George W.) **Artillery.** See *Illinois Troops, 1st Regiment, Battery M.*
Sprague's (Ezra T.) **Infantry.** See *Wisconsin Troops, 42d Regiment.*
Stafford's (Joab A.) **Infantry.** See *Ohio Troops, 178th Regiment.*
Stephens' (Meshack) **Cavalry.** See *Tennessee Troops, Union, 4th Regiment.*
Stephenson's (John) **Infantry.** See *Union Troops, Veteran Reserve Corps, 2d Battalion, 56th Company.*
Sterl's (Oscar W.) **Infantry.** See *Ohio Troops, 104th Regiment.*
Sterry's (Clinton N.) **Heavy Artillery.** See *Minnesota Troops, 1st Regiment, Battery A.*
Stevens' (Ambrose A.) **Infantry.** See *Union Troops, Veteran Reserve Corps, 5th Regiment.*
Stevens' (Jacob S.) **Cavalry.** See *Indiana Troops, 6th Regiment.*
Stiles' (Henry E.) **Artillery.** See *Wisconsin Troops, 8th Battery.*
Stokes' (William B.) **Cavalry.** See *Tennessee Troops, Union, 5th Regiment.*
Stone's (William M.) **Infantry.** See *Alabama Troops, Confederate, 4th Regiment, Reserves.*
Story's (William P.) **Cavalry.** See *Tennessee Troops, Union, 10th Regiment.*
Stratton's (Henry G.) **Infantry.** See *Ohio Troops, 19th Regiment.*
Stuart's (James H.) **Cavalry.** See *Alabama Troops, Confederate.*
Stubbs' (George W.) **Cavalry.** See *Mississippi Troops, Confederate.*
Sturges' (Eben P.) **Artillery.** See *Ohio Troops, 1st Regiment, Battery M.*
Sturm's (Frederick C.) **Artillery.** See *Indiana Troops, 25th Battery.*
Suman's (Isaac C. B.) **Infantry.** See *Indiana Troops, 9th Regiment.*
Swain's (Edgar D.) **Infantry.** See *Illinois Troops, 42d Regiment.*
Swisher's (John P.) **Infantry.** See *Indiana Troops, 36th Regiment.*
Tafel's (Gustavus) **Infantry.** See *Ohio Troops, 106th Regiment.*
Tassin's (Augustus G.) **Infantry.** See *Indiana Troops, 35th Regiment.*
Taylor's (John C.) **Infantry.** See *Indiana Troops, 84th Regiment.*
Tennessee (Confederate) **First [Sixth] Cavalry.** See *James T. Wheeler's Cavalry, post.*
Tennessee (Confederate) **Fourth Cavalry.** See *William S. McLemore's Cavalry, ante.*
Tennessee (Confederate) **Ninth [Nineteenth] Cavalry.** See *Jacob B. Biffle's Cavalry, ante.*
Tennessee (Confederate) **Tenth Cavalry.** See *Nicholas N. Cox's Cavalry, ante.*
Tennessee (Confederate) **Eleventh Cavalry.** See *Daniel W. Holman's Cavalry, ante.*
Tenney's (Marcus D.) **Artillery.** See *Kansas Troops, 1st Battery.*
Thomas' (Hubbard T.) **Artillery.** See *Wilder Artillery, post.*
Thomas' (Rhys M.) **Infantry.** See *Kentucky Troops, Union, 14th Regiment.*
Thomasson's (Theodore S.) **Artillery.** See *Kentucky Troops, Union, Battery A.*
Thomson's (Chester G.) **Infantry.** See *Indiana Troops, 72d Regiment.*
Thrall's (James C.) **Artillery.** See *Arkansas Troops, Confederate.*
Thurmond's (William D.) **Partisans.** See *Virginia Troops, Confederate.*
Tilton's (Albert M.) **Infantry.** See *Illinois Troops, 51st Regiment.*
Tobin's (Thomas F.) **Artillery.** See *Tennessee Troops, Confederate.*

Tombler's (Edward) **Infantry.** See *Union Troops, Veteran Reserve Corps, 2d Battalion, 25th, 92d, 106th, and 120th Companies.*

Tompkins' (Haviland) **Cavalry.** See *Illinois Troops, 14th Regiment.*

Torbett's (Henry W.) **Infantry.** See *Pennsylvania Troops, 78th Regiment.*

Travis' (John) **Infantry.** See *Kentucky Troops, Union, 12th Regiment.*

Trowbridge's (Luther S.) **Cavalry.** See *Michigan Troops, 10th Regiment.*

Trumbull Guards, Infantry. See *Ohio Troops.*

Tucker's (Joseph T.) **Cavalry.** See *Kentucky Troops, Confederate, 3d Battalion, Special.*

Tyler's (John B.) **Infantry.** See *Kentucky Troops, Union, 52d Regiment.*

Underhill's (E. M.) **Infantry.** See *Alabama Troops, Confederate, 3d and 4th Battalions, Reserves ;* also *Louisiana Troops, Confederate, 22d Regiment.*

Vail's (Jacob G.) **Infantry.** See *Indiana Troops, 17th Regiment.*

Voris' (Jeremiah) **Artillery.** See *Indiana Troops, 8th Battery.*

Wade's Cavalry. (Official designation not of record.) See *Colonel Wade.*

Wade's (Alfred B.) **Infantry.** See *Indiana Troops, 73d Regiment.*

Wait's (Joseph W.) **Artillery.** See *Wisconsin Troops, 3d Battery.*

Waller's (Thomas B.) **Infantry.** See *Kentucky Troops, Union, 20th Regiment.*

Walley's (James H.) **Artillery.** See *Ohio Troops, 21st Battery.*

Ward's (John H.) **Infantry.** See *Kentucky Troops, Union, 27th Regiment.*

Warner's (Adoniram J.) **Infantry.** See *Union Troops, Veteran Reserve Corps, 17th Regiment.*

Warner's (Willard) **Infantry.** See *Ohio Troops, 180th Regiment.*

Warren's (James M.) **Cavalry.** See *Alabama Troops, Confederate, 5th Regiment.*

Wassem's (Philip) **Infantry.** See *Indiana Troops, 32d Regiment.*

Watkins' (Joseph B.) **Infantry.** See *Kentucky Troops, Union, 34th Regiment.*

Weatherford's (James W.) **Cavalry.** See *Kentucky Troops, Union, 13th Regiment.*

Webber's (Thomas B.) **Cavalry.** See *Kentucky Troops, Confederate, 4th Battalion, Special.*

Welling's (George) **Cavalry.** See *Kentucky Troops, Union, 4th Regiment.*

West's (George R.) **Infantry.** See *Iowa Troops, 37th Regiment.*

Wheeler's (James T.) **Cavalry.** See *Tennessee Troops, Confederate.*

Wheeler's (William W.) **Infantry.** See *Michigan Troops, 28th Regiment.*

Whicher's (James S.) **Artillery.** See *Indiana Troops, 2d Battery.*

White's (James E.) **Artillery.** See *Indiana Troops, 12th Battery.*

White's (Lyman A.) **Artillery.** See *Lyman Bridges' Artillery, ante.*

Whittemore's (Henry C.) **Artillery.** See *Illinois Troops, 2d Regiment, Battery H.*

Wilber's (Aaron A.) **Artillery.** See *Indiana Troops, 23d Battery.*

Wilbourn's (Christopher C.) **Cavalry.** See *Mississippi Troops, Confederate, 4th Regiment.*

Wilbur's (Almerick W.) **Artillery.** See *Michigan Troops, 1st Regiment, Battery A.*

Wilcox's (Arthur T.) **Infantry.** See *Ohio Troops, 177th Regiment.*

Wilder Artillery. See *Indiana Troops.*

Wilkinson's (William) **Infantry.** See *Michigan Troops, 9th Regiment.*

Williams' (Thomas) **Infantry.** See *Georgia Troops, 36th Regiment.*

Williams' (William D.) **Infantry.** See *Illinois Troops, 89th Regiment.*

Williamson's (Thomas G.) **Cavalry.** See *Indiana Troops, 10th Regiment.*

Wilson's (Frank) **Artillery.** See *Ohio Troops, 19th Battery.*

Windes' (F. M.) **Cavalry.** See *Alabama Troops, Confederate, 4th Regiment (Roddey's).*

Winn's (Samuel J.) **Cavalry.** See *Georgia Troops, 16th Battalion.*

Winston's (William C.) **Artillery.** See *Tennessee Troops, Confederate.*

Wisewell's (Moses N.) **Infantry.** See *Union Troops, Veteran Reserve Corps, 6th Regiment.*

Withers' (Robert) **Cavalry.** See *Nathan W. Carter's Cavalry, ante.*

Witherspoon's (H. E.) **Infantry.** See *Pelham Cadets, Infantry, ante.*

Witt's (Nathaniel) **Infantry.** See *Tennessee Troops, Union, 5th Regiment.*

Wood's (Andrew M.) **Artillery.** See *Elgin Artillery, ante.*

Wood's (Charles H.) **Infantry.** See *Ohio Troops, 51st Regiment.*

Wood's (John W.) **Infantry.** See *Illinois Troops, 107th Regiment.*

Wood's (Robert C., jr.) **Cavalry.** See *Wirt Adams' Cavalry, ante.*

Worthman's Home Guards. (Official designation not of record.) See *Captain Worthman.*

Yeoman's (Samuel N.) **Infantry.** See *Ohio Troops, 90th Regiment.*

Yerger's (William S.) **Cavalry.** See *Wirt Adams' Cavalry, ante.*

Yoder's (Noah W.) **Infantry.** See *Union Troops, Veteran Reserve Corps, 2d Battalion, 141st Company.*

York's (Harrison B.) **Artillery.** See *Ohio Troops, 9th Battery.*

Young's (J. Morris) **Cavalry.** See *Iowa Troops, 5th Regiment.*

Ziegler's (Jacob) **Artillery.** See *Pennsylvania Troops, Battery B.*

Zollinger's (Charles A.) **Infantry.** See *Indiana Troops, 129th Regiment.*

INDEX.

Brigades, Divisions, Corps, Armies, and improvised organizations are "Mentioned" under name of commanding officer; State and other organizations under their official designation. (See Alternate Designations, pp. 807–818.)

*Also called 10th Mounted Rifles; finally, 13th Cavalry.

*Also called 3d Battery.

---

*Sometimes called 1st Squadron.